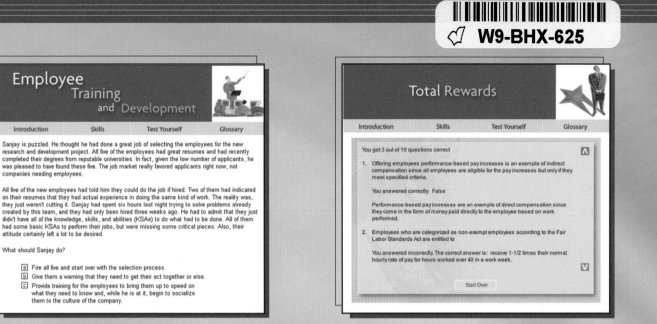

Employee Training and Development

| Introduction | Skills | Test Yourself | Glossary |

Sanjay is puzzled. He thought he had done a great job of selecting the employees for the new research and development project. All five of the employees had great resumes and had recently completed their degrees from reputable universities. In fact, given the low number of applicants, he was pleased to have found these five. The job market really favored applicants right now, not companies needing employees.

All five of the new employees had told him they could do the job if hired. Two of them had indicated on their resumes that they had actual experience in doing the same kind of work. The reality was, they just weren't cutting it. Sanjay had spent six hours last night trying to solve problems already created by this team, and they had only been hired three weeks ago. He had to admit that they just didn't have all of the knowledge, skills, and abilities (KSAs) to do what had to be done. All of them had some basic KSAs to perform their jobs, but were missing some critical pieces. Also, their attitude certainly left a lot to be desired.

What should Sanjay do?

- a Fire all five and start over with the selection process.
- b Give them a warning that they need to get their act together or else.
- c Provide training for the employees to bring them up to speed on what they need to know and, while he is at it, begin to socialize them to the culture of the company.

Total Rewards

| Introduction | Skills | Test Yourself | Glossary |

You got 3 out of 10 questions correct

1. Offering employees performance-based pay increases is an example of indirect compensation since all employees are eligible for the pay increases but only if they meet specified criteria.

 You answered correctly: False

 Performance-based pay increases are an example of direct compensation since they come in the form of money paid directly to the employee based on work performed.

2. Employees who are categorized as non-exempt employees according to the Fair Labor Standards Act are entitled to

 You answered incorrectly. The correct answer is: receive 1-1/2 times their normal hourly rate of pay for hours worked over 40 in a work week.

Start Over

Each module contains an introduction, a skills section that allows the student to apply his or her knowledge through interactive exercises, and finally a quiz that tests students on the material covered in the module. Also included on this CD-ROM is the HR Skills Video Series.

Job Analysis

| Introduction | Skills | Test Yourself | Glossary |

The first decision that you have to make involves deciding how to go about preparing these job descriptions. Put the following steps in the order in which they should occur:

Review the information with job incumbents and supervisors	1	
Identify the purpose for doing the job analysis	2	
Collect the data Prepare the job description Review relevant background information Select the positions to analyze	3	
	4	
Please select step 1.	5	
	6	

Videos

Choose from the segments below:

1. A Case of Sexual Harrassment
2. Interviewing Job Candidates
3. Appraising Performance
4. Establishing Pay Plans
5. Labor Relations
6. Managing Human Resources In an International Business

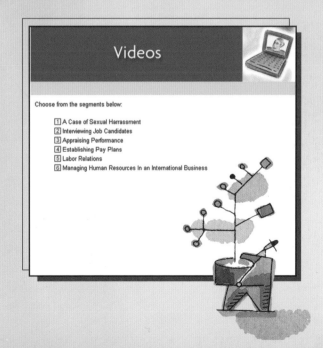

HUMAN RESOURCE MANAGEMENT

HUMAN RESOURCE MANAGEMENT

Ninth Edition

Gary Dessler
Florida International University

Prentice
Hall

Upper Saddle River, New Jersey 07458

Library of Congress Cataloging-in-Publication Data
Dessler, Gary
    Human resource management / Gary Dessler.—9th ed.
      p.cm.
    Includes bibliographical references and index.
    ISBN 0-13-066492-8
     1. Personnel management.   I. Title.

HF5549.D4379 2002
658.3—dc21   2001051376

Acquisitions Editor: Melissa Steffens
Editor-in-Chief: Jeff Shelstad
Managing Editor (Editorial): Jennifer Glennon
Assistant Editor: Melanie Olsen
Editorial Assistant: Kevin Glynn
Media Project Manager: Michele Faranda
Senior Marketing Manager: Shannon Moore
Marketing Assistant: Christine Genneken
Managing Editor (Production): Judy Leale
Production Assistant: Dianne Falcone
Permissions Coordinator: Suzanne Grappi
Associate Director, Manufacturing: Vincent Scelta
Production Manager: Arnold Vila
Design Manager: Patricia Smythe
Art Director: Janet Slowik
Interior Design: Craig Ramsdell
Cover Design: Janet Slowik
Cover Illustration: Robin Jareaux/Artville Stock Images
Illustrator (Interior): ElectraGraphics, Inc.
Associate Director, Multimedia Production: Karen Goldsmith
Manager, Print Production: Christy Mahon
Composition: UG/GGS Information Services, Inc.
Full-Service Project Management: Terri O'Prey/UG/GGS Information Services, Inc.
Printer/Binder: R. R. Donnelly/Willard

Credits and acknowledgments borrowed from other sources and reproduced, with permission, in this textbook appear on appropriate page within text. Photo credits appear on page 536.

Pearson Education Ltd.
Pearson Education Australia PTY, Limited
Pearson Education Singapore, Pte. Ltd.
Pearson Education North Asia Ltd.
Pearson Education, Canada, Ltd.
Pearson Educación de Mexico, S.A. de C.V.
Pearson Education–Japan
Pearson Education Malaysia, Pte. Ltd.

10 9 8 7 6 5 4 3 2 1
ISBN 0-13-066492-8

Dedicated to my son, Derek

Brief Contents

Contents

HUMAN RESOURCE MANAGEMENT

NINTH EDITION

It's 3 AM, and the Delta mechanic, fresh off his shift, comes home and throws off his coat. He turns on his computer, and spends the next two hours taking a required FAA course, over the net.

She walks through the door of Kinko's in downtown Miami. Ten minutes later, she's having her job interview — by net-based video conference—with a Cisco interviewer in San Diego.

It's December, and a handful of Pitney Bowes HR specialists are using their new benefits portal. They're helping thousands of their employees change their benefits plans, before the year-end deadline.

GARY DESSLER

www.prenhall.com/dessler

We all do business today in a networked world. Gary Dessler has always aimed *Human Resource Management* at providing students and practicing managers with a complete and applied review of essential HR concepts and techniques in a highly readable and understandable form. That certainly hasn't changed in this edition. It's still packed with the practical applications and high readability that make this book a best-seller. And, since all managers perform personnel-related tasks, it's still aimed at all managers, not just HR managers. But, one thing that has changed is the book's new emphasis on *connectivity*. It shows vividly, with dozens of new examples, how managers use the Internet to improve their HR operations' functionality and efficiency.

Connectivity doesn't just mean the Internet. Managers today can't just pay lip service to thinking strategically. Your whole effort must be coherent, and integrated. The only way you can compete is by making sure you've linked your firm's HR and other activities with the firm's strategies. This book contains the most complete and specific coverage of strategy and HR in the market. All chapters start with a strategic overview focused on a real firm. It shows the firm facing a strategic challenge. And, it suggests how management might use HR to advance the firm's strategy. Strategy & HR features in the chapters then show what HR actually did. The net result—a student better prepared for success as a manager.

Key Features of The Ninth Edition

Text Features

New! Strategy and HR Coverage Chapter 1 contains a brief outline of strategic management and its relevance to HR. All chapters begin with a **Strategic Overview** focused on a real firm. It shows the firm facing a strategic challenge and suggests HR's possible role; a **Strategic HR** feature in the chapter then shows what the firm actually did. Some of these firms are large, well-known companies; others are small to medium-size operations. Features for each chapter include: Dell Computer and cost cutting (Chapter 1); Sutter Health's IT shortage (Chapter 4); Longo Toyota's diversity program (Chapter 2); UK's Channel 4's world class training effort (Chapter 7); Crystal Gateway Marriott, winning employee commitment (Chapter 10); Con Edison and safety first (Chapter 15); Siemens, becoming a global company (Chapter 16).

STRATEGIC HR

Dell

From its start in Michael Dell's college dorm room, Dell Computer's competitive strategy was always to be the PC industry's low-cost leader. While others like Apple competed based on differentiating features like multimedia software, Dell stripped away the retailers' profit and drove its costs down by selling direct and relentlessly slashing costs. That's why it was, and is, the industry's low-cost leader. But recently, with PC sales falling, it was aggressively slashing prices, and the executives of its various divisions had to make sure that their own strategies were in sync with the firmwide strategy to further cut costs.

As at many firms in the same situation, Dell HR's first task was to manage Dell's downsizing. In the first half of 2001, 4,000 Dell workers were let go. HR had to manage the system for choosing those who would leave the firm, and then handle the thousands of details involved in the dismissals. Terminated workers got their yearly bonuses early, severance packages including two months' salary and health benefits, and job counseling, among other benefits.[69]

Dell's HR managers have found a variety of other, ongoing ways to help Dell's top management execute the firm's low-cost leader strategy. For one thing—and as you might imag-

New! HR.*NET* features show how managers use the Web to improve HR functions. Some HR.*NET* topics include: Using the Internet to Boost Diversity; Recruiting Online; GE's Technology-Based Training; Telecommuting; Doing an Internet-Based Salary Survey; Managing 401(k) Plans Online; Global HR Information Systems.

The HR Portal

HR portals, usually hosted on a company's intranet, provide employees with a single access point or "gateway" to all HR information.[61] They let the firm's employees, managers, and executives interactively (and selectively) access and modify HR information. They thereby streamline the HR process and enable HR managers to focus more on strategic issues.

www.prenhall.com/dessler

New! The New Workplace: Diversity Management and Global HR This feature highlights issues in diversity and global HR management. There is expanded coverage of diversity management in Chapter 2, and about half the New Workplace boxes provide examples and tips for managing diversity. About half illustrate global HR applications, such as training employees going abroad,

formulating salary plans for expatriates, dealing with labor unions in other countries, and other important topics. There is also a revised and expanded chapter on international HR practices (Chapter 16). It provides in-depth coverage of the international aspects of HR selection, training, compensation management, intercountry differences in personnel laws and requirements, and more.

THE NEW WORKPLACE

Enforcing the 1991 Civil Rights Act Abroad

Federal legislation generally applies only within U.S. territorial borders unless specifically stated otherwise.[46] With the passage of CRA 1991, EEO coverage was greatly expanded. The law amended the definition of the term employee in Title VII to include U.S. citizens employed in a foreign country by a U.S.-owned or U.S.-controlled company.[47] At least theoretically, U.S. citizens working overseas for U.S. companies now enjoy the same equal employment opportunity protection as those working within U.S. borders.[48]

Two factors limit the application of CRA 1991 to U.S. employees abroad. First, there are numerous exclusions to the civil rights protections. For example, an employer need not comply with Title VII if doing so would cause the employer to violate the law of the host country. (Some foreign countries, for instance, have statutes prohibiting the employment of women in management positions.)

A more vexing problem is the practical difficulty of enforcement. For example, the EEOC investigator's first duty is to analyze the finances and organizational structure of the overseas employer. But in practice, few investigators are trained for this duty and no standards exist for such investigations.[49] And one expert argues that U.S. courts "will be little help in overseas investigations, because few foreign nations cooperate with the intrusive enforcement of U.S. civil law."[50] Here, therefore, CRA 1991's bark will be worse than its bite.[51]

Entrepreneurs + HR Managers in small and mid-sized businesses face unique challenges in managing human resources. The 9th edition continues our use of a special feature that illustrates how that chapter's material can be and is applied in a small-business context. This feature is found in about half of the chapters and includes topics such as Expanding the Management Team (Chapter 4); Empowering Employees: Lois Melbourne of Time Vision (Chapter 8); Incentive Plans in a Small Business (Chapter 12); Dot-coms and Unions (Chapter 14).

Research Insight As in the eighth edition, these special text sections illustrate recent research findings in areas like interviewing and appraisal, helping to provide a lively, real-life "picture" of that topic. You'll find one or two per chapter.

New! High-Performance Insights These text sections illustrate how firms use modern HR practices to build better, faster, and more competitive organizations. For instance, Chapter 4's shows how GE and Cisco Systems are responding faster and more competitively by using Internet HR techniques to recruit high-tech workers; Chapter 13's illustrates how Weirton Steel Corp. drives down costs with its workers' compensation methods; and Chapter 15's feature shows how Dayton Parts Corp. reduced expenses and boosted performance with a new safety management program.

New! WEBNOTES This feature uses actual screen shots to illustrate the many ways in which HR managers can use the Internet to carry out basic HR functions. WEBNOTES appear in each chapter of the text.

Margin Glossary

Key terms appear in boldface within the text, and with their definitions in the margin.

authority
The right to make decisions, direct others' work, and give orders.

line manager
A manager who is authorized to direct the work of subordinates and responsible for accomplishing the organization's goals.

staff manager
A manager who assists and advises line managers.

▲ **WEBNOTE**
The U.S. Department of Labor now has a Web site for working women from its Women's Bureau.
www.dol.gov

End-of-Chapter Features

Chapter Summaries

Each chapter contains a point-by-point chapter summary students can use to quickly refresh their memories and get an overview of what they've read in that chapter.

New! Tying It All Together

Each chapter also ends with a brief description of what precedes and what follows that chapter so that the topics covered in each chapter are related to one another.

Exercises and Assignments

Reviewers wanted more resources to aid and encourage experiential learning, and we've responded by strengthening the end-of-chapter exercises. In each chapter you'll find:

Discussion Questions

Each chapter has a set of discussion questions that can be used as the basis for class discussion or homework assignments.

---

1. Working individually or in groups, develop lists showing how trends like workforce diversity, technological innovation, globalization, and changes in the nature of work have affected the college or university you are attending now. Present in class.
2. Working individually or in groups, contact the HR manager of a local bank. Ask the HR manager how he or she is working as a strategic partner to manage human resources, given the bank's strategic goals and objectives. Back in class, discuss the responses of the different HR managers.

Individual and Group Activities

Individual and Group Activities A set of 3 to 4 individual and group activities can be used in class or in study groups outside of class. Notes for each activity are in the instructor's manual.

Experiential Exercises These exercises help students apply their knowledge in an interactive group situation. Notes for these exercises are in the instructor's manual.

Cases Each chapter contains two types of cases: Application cases are longer, more in-depth, and provide the basis for class discussion or for written assignments. A new! Continuing case, LearnInMotion.com, appears at the end of each chapter and gives students an opportunity to solve the problems faced by a dot-com startup.

EXPERIENTIAL EXERCISE *HRM As a Strategic Partner*

Purpose: The purpose of this exercise is to provide practice in identifying trends important to HR today, and in understanding their impact on an organization's HR practices.

Required Understanding: Be thoroughly familiar with the material in this chapter.

How to Set Up the Exercise/Instructions:
1. Divide the class into teams of three to four students.
2. Read this:
   You are a strategic planning task force at your university. You must identify trends and how they will affect the university and its human resource needs. The team has already identified a partial list of trends (see following table).

3. Expand the list of "Critical Issues" and complete the other two columns in the table.
4. Present your team's conclusions to the class.
5. When the teams have had time to discuss their responses, consider the following questions:
   A. Which environmental trend would have the greatest impact on the human resource needs of the university?
   B. What environmental change will be the most difficult for your HR group to manage?
   C. Overall, how will this combination of trends affect your organization?

Causing Issues	Effect on Existing Employees	Potential HR Role(s)
(Example)	*(Example)*	*(Example)*
1. Distance learning technology	Need for better computer skills	Provide greater technical training
2. Government reductions in funding to higher education		
3. Greater workforce diversity		
4. More international students		
5. High percentage of faculty to retire		

CONTINUING CASE: LEARNINMOTION.COM *Introduction*

The main theme of this book is that HR management—activities like recruiting, selecting, training, and rewarding employees—is not just the job of some central HR group, but rather one in which every manager must engage. Perhaps nowhere is this more apparent than in the typical small service business. Here the owner-manager usually has no personnel staff to rely on. However, the success of his or her enterprise (not to mention his or her family's peace of mind) often depends largely on the effectiveness with which workers are recruited, hired, trained, evaluated, and rewarded.

The idea the two came up with was LearnInMotion. The basic idea of the Web site was to list a vast array of web-based, CD-ROM-based, or textbook-based business-related continuing-education-type courses for "free agent learn-ers"—in other words, for working people who wanted to take a course in business from the comfort of their own homes. The idea was that users could come to the Web site to find and then take a course in one of several ways. Some courses could be completed interactively on the Web via the site; others were in a form that was downloadable directly to

APPLICATION CASE *Jack Nelson's Problem*

As a new member of the board of directors for a local bank, Jack Nelson was being introduced to all the employees in the home office. When he was introduced to Ruth Johnson, he was curious about her work and asked her what her machine did. Johnson replied that she really did not know what the machine was called or what it did. She explained that she had only been working there for two months. She did, however, know precisely how to operate the machine.

According to her supervisor, she was an excellent employee.

At one of the branch offices, the supervisor in charge spoke to Nelson confidentially, telling him that "something was wrong," but she didn't know what. For one thing, she explained, employee turnover was too high, and no sooner had one employee been put on the job than another one resigned. With customers to see and loans to be made, she

Teaching and Learning Package

Online support

In addition to the dozens of new technology-based text examples, such as how to recruit employees and conduct salary surveys on the Internet, we've achieved this expansion in technology in several ways:

New! This edition offers a fully developed online course for HRM in the following formats:

Companion Web Site
(www.prenhall.com/dessler).

The 9th edition's Web site represents a tremendous leap forward, offering the most robust, content-rich Web support available with any HRM text. This site provides professors with a customized course Web site, including communication tools, one-click navigation of chapter content, resources such as current events and Internet exercises, as well as the Video Guide for the On Location Video Series. For students, there is an interactive study guide (multiple-choice, true/false, and essays), an Internet Resource section that provides Web links for all of the companies and Web resources listed in the Dessler text, additional HR forms and figures, appendices to the 9th edition (Establishing HR Systems, Managing Your Career, and Quantitative Job Evaluation Methods), self-assessment exercises, a video tutorial, and an HRCI Certification Exam Guide.

A powerful new point-and-click syllabus creation tool

that faculty can use for each course and section they teach. Additionally, faculty can annotate and link each resource on the Web site to their syllabi. **Faculty can even upload their own personal resources to our site** and have these resources available to their students via their personalized syllabus.

Check it out: www.prenhall.com/dessler

New! On Location! Video.

In these part-ending video segments, students will watch a panel of real-life HR executives from companies like BMG and hotjobs discuss current Human Resource issues like sexual harassment and discrimination, recruiting, the complexities of restructuring, incentives and benefits, labor relations, and the successes and failures of expatriate employees.

New! Human Resource Management Skills CD-ROM.

Developed by Mary Gowan, of University of Central Florida, this student CD-ROM focuses on essential HR skills such as Strategic Planning and Recruitment, Job Analysis, and Total Rewards. Each module contains an introduction, a skills section that allows the student to apply his or her knowledge through interactive exercises, and finally a quiz that tests students on the material covered in the module. Also included on this CD-ROM is the HR Skills Video Series.

Multimedia PowerPoint Presentation.

Available on the Instructor's Resource CD-ROM, and prepared by George A. Wynn, of University of South Florida, this comprehensive set of PowerPoints contains over 800 color slides, allowing professors the flexibility to create a presentation that will best suit their classroom needs. In addition to key chapter material, as well as text figures and tables, this presentation includes original content not found in the new edition, slide notes to aid instructors, and multimedia components such as video clips, audio, additional Web links and resources, and animated graphics.

Instructor's Resource CD-ROM.

On a single CD, professors can find the Instructor's Manual, PowerPoint presentation, and the Win/PH Test Manager. Containing all of the questions in the printed Test Item File, Test Manager is a comprehensive suite of tools for testing and assessment and allows educators to easily create and distribute tests for their courses.

Instructor's Resource Manual.

In the new edition of the Instructor's Resource Manual, instructors will find chapter summaries, annotated lecture outlines with PowerPoint references, key terms, and answers to all end-of-chapter and case material. Also included is a Video Guide that provides video cases and teaching notes.

Test Item File.

Over 100 questions per chapter including multiple-choice, true/false, short-answer and essays.

www.prenhall.com/dessler

Acknowledgments

While I am of course solely responsible for the content in *Human Resource Management*, I want to thank several people for their professional assistance. This includes first, the faculty who reviewed this edition: Fred A. Ware, Valdosta State University; Larry Zachrich, Northwest State Community College; Lewis Lash, Barry University; and Mitchell A. Sherr, Purdue University. Thanks also to my colleagues Herman Dorsett and Ronnie Silverblatt at Florida International University.

At Prentice Hall, I am grateful for the support and dedicated assistance of several people. Senior editor Melissa Steffens worked with me to develop, rework, and rework again the new themes and design of this book and deserves much of the credit for the book's improvements, which I believe are considerable. The intelligence, editorial skills, and good humor of development editor Jeanine Ciliotta make this a far better book than it might have been. I am again very grateful to Judy Leale, managing editor, production, for working with me and for supervising with great skill all the intricacies involved in bringing a book like this to market. Thanks to Janet Slowik and her design team for their skill and patience in working with me on the design of this book. Even after nine editions, a book like this would likely just gather dust on someone's shelf without the dedicated efforts of all the professionals in the Prentice Hall sales force who have enthusiastically promoted this and the previous editions of this book. I want to thank Amy Wang, Jorge Thames, and the other Pearson International professionals for their efforts in managing the internationalization of this book: Because of them, it is now available and used in Chinese, Russian, Indonesian, Spanish, and Lithuanian and in numerous other international versions around the world. Thanks to Kevin Glynn at Prentice Hall for ably assisting with the book's review process and numerous other details.

I was particularly careful in this ninth edition to go back and review the book's very first edition to make sure the ninth was faithful to that first book's mission—"to provide a complete, comprehensive review of essential personnel management concepts and techniques in a highly readable and understandable form." When we published edition one, my executive editor, Frederick K. Easter, said that this book would "go on and on." To the extent that this book is now in its ninth edition and is a best-seller throughout the world, I owe much to Fred, a great editor, for all his advice, support and assistance.

At home, I again want to acknowledge the support and patience of my wife, Claudia. My son Derek, certainly the best people manager I know and a source of enormous pride, was always in my thoughts as I worked on these pages. My mother Laura was always a great source of support and encouragement.

Gary Dessler

HUMAN RESOURCE MANAGEMENT

Chapter 1

The Strategic Role of Human Resource Management

After studying this chapter, you should be able to:

- Explain what human resource management (HR) is and how it relates to the management process.
- Give at least eight examples of how managers can use HR concepts and techniques.
- Illustrate the HR management responsibilities of line and staff (HR) managers.
- Illustrate HR's role in formulating and executing company strategy.
- Outline the plan of this book.

STRATEGIC OVERVIEW   The headline said it all: "Despite plummeting profit margins, Dell Computer Corp. has no intention of backing off from an aggressive PC pricing strategy initiated earlier this year." The first few years of the 21st century had thrown the (PC) industry for a loop. To maintain its new position as the world's number one personal computer maker, Dell's average price per computer fell to about $2,000 in the first quarter of 2001, from about $2,300 the year before. Its profit margin fell from 21% to 18%. The only way it could keep that 18% margin intact while cutting prices was to find new ways to slash costs.[1] For a company that had always pursued a low-cost leader strategy, doing so wouldn't be easy. How could Dell cut costs from an already lean operation? The firm's HR managers had to decide what they could do to support Dell's new cost-cutting efforts.

The purpose of this chapter is to explain what human resource management is and the plan of this book. We'll see that HR management—activities like recruiting, hiring, training, compensation, appraising, and developing employees—is part of every manager's job. And we'll see that it is also a separate "staff" function, and that the HR manager assists all managers in many important ways. The main topics we'll cover are the manager's human resource management jobs, strategic planning and important strategic trends, and HR's strategic role in formulating and executing the company's strategy. The following chapter completes

the introductory part of the book and provides you with the knowledge you'll need to deal effectively with equal employment opportunity questions on the job. ▨

THE MANAGER'S HUMAN RESOURCE MANAGEMENT JOBS

Most writers agree that there are certain basic functions all managers perform. These are planning, organizing, staffing, leading, and controlling. In total, they represent what managers call the **management process**. Some of the specific activities involved in each function include:

management process
The five basic functions of planning, organizing, staffing, leading, and controlling.

Planning. Establishing goals and standards; developing rules and procedures; developing plans and forecasting.

Organizing. Giving each subordinate a specific task; establishing departments; delegating authority to subordinates; establishing channels of authority and communication; coordinating the work of subordinates.

Staffing. Determining what type of people should be hired; recruiting prospective employees; selecting employees; setting performance standards; compensating employees; evaluating performance; counseling employees; training and developing employees.

Leading. Getting others to get the job done; maintaining morale; motivating subordinates.

Controlling. Setting standards such as sales quotas, quality standards, or production levels; checking to see how actual performance compares with these standards; taking corrective action as needed.

human resource management (HRM)
The policies and practices involved in carrying out the "people" or human resource aspects of a management position, including recruiting, screening, training, rewarding, and appraising.

We are going to focus on one of these functions in this book—the staffing, personnel management, or (as it's usually called today) the **human resource management (HRM)** function. Human resource management is the process of acquiring, training, appraising, and compensating employees, and attending to their labor relations, health and safety, and fairness concerns. The topics we'll discuss should therefore provide you with the concepts and techniques you need to carry out the "people" or personnel aspects of your management job. These include:

▨ Conducting job analyses (determining the nature of each employee's job)
▨ Planning labor needs and recruiting job candidates
▨ Selecting job candidates
▨ Orienting and training new employees
▨ Managing wages and salaries (compensating employees)
▨ Providing incentives and benefits
▨ Appraising performance
▨ Communicating (interviewing, counseling, disciplining)
▨ Training and developing managers
▨ Building employee commitment

And what a manager should know about:

▨ Equal opportunity and affirmative action
▨ Employee health and safety
▨ Handling grievances and labor relations

Why Is HR Management Important to All Managers?

Why are these concepts and techniques important to all managers? Perhaps it's easier to answer this by listing some of the personnel mistakes you *don't* want to make while managing. For example, you don't want to:

- Hire the wrong person for the job
- Experience high turnover
- Find your people not doing their best
- Waste time with useless interviews
- Have your company taken to court because of discriminatory actions
- Have your company cited under federal occupational safety laws for unsafe practices
- Have some employees think their salaries are unfair and inequitable relative to others in the organization
- Allow a lack of training to undermine your department's effectiveness
- Commit any unfair labor practices

Carefully studying this book will help you avoid mistakes like these. And, more important, it can help ensure that you get the right results. Remember, you can do everything else right as a manager—lay brilliant plans, draw clear organization charts, set up modern assembly lines, and use sophisticated accounting controls—but still fail as a manager by hiring the wrong people or by not motivating subordinates, for instance. On the other hand, many managers—presidents, generals, governors, supervisors—have been successful even with inadequate plans, organization, or controls. They were successful because they had the knack of hiring the right people for the right jobs and motivating, appraising, and developing them. Remember as you read this book that *getting results* is the bottom line of managing, and that, as a manager, you will have to get those results through people. As one company president summed up:

> For many years it has been said that capital is the bottleneck for a developing industry. I don't think this any longer holds true. I think it's the work force and the company's inability to recruit and maintain a good work force that does constitute the bottleneck for production. I don't know of any major project backed by good ideas, vigor, and enthusiasm that has been stopped by a shortage of cash. I do know of industries whose growth has been partly stopped or hampered because they can't maintain an efficient and enthusiastic labor force, and I think this will hold true even more in the future. . . .[2]

Line and Staff Aspects of HRM

All managers are, in a sense, HR managers, since they all get involved in activities like recruiting, interviewing, selecting, and training. Yet most firms also have a human resource department with its own top manager. How do the duties of this HR manager and his or her staff relate to "line" managers' human resource duties? Let's answer this question, starting with a short definition of line versus staff authority.

Line Versus Staff Authority Authority is the right to make decisions, to direct the work of others, and to give orders. In management, we usually distinguish between line authority and staff authority.

Line managers are authorized to direct the work of subordinates—they're always someone's boss. In addition, line managers are in charge of accomplishing the organization's basic goals. (Hotel managers and the managers for production and sales are generally line managers, for example.) **Staff managers**, on the other hand, are authorized to assist and advise line managers in accomplishing these basic goals. HR managers are generally staff managers. They are responsible for assisting and advising line managers in areas like recruiting, hiring, and compensation.

authority
The right to make decisions, direct others' work, and give orders.

line manager
A manager who is authorized to direct the work of subordinates and responsible for accomplishing the organization's goals.

staff manager
A manager who assists and advises line managers.

Line Managers' HRM Responsibilities According to one expert, "The direct handling of people is, and always has been, an integral part of every line manager's responsibility, from president down to the lowest-level supervisor."[3]

For example, one major company outlines its line supervisors' responsibilities for effective human resource management under the following general headings:

1. Placing the right person on the right job
2. Starting new employees in the organization (orientation)
3. Training employees for jobs that are new to them
4. Improving the job performance of each person
5. Gaining creative cooperation and developing smooth working relationships
6. Interpreting the company's policies and procedures
7. Controlling labor costs
8. Developing the abilities of each person
9. Creating and maintaining department morale
10. Protecting employees' health and physical condition

In small organizations, line managers may carry out all these personnel duties unassisted. But as the organization grows, they need the assistance, specialized knowledge, and advice of a separate human resource staff.[4] The human resource department provides this specialized assistance. In doing so, the HR manager carries out three distinct functions:

1. A line function. The HR manager directs the activities of the people in his or her own department and in related service areas (like the plant cafeteria). In other words, he or she exerts **line authority** within the HR department.[5] While they generally can't wield line authority outside HR, they are likely to exert **implied authority**. This is because line managers know HR has top management's ear in areas like testing and affirmative action. As a result, HR managers' "suggestions" are often seen as "orders from top-side." And, as you might imagine, this carries even more weight with supervisors troubled by staffing problems.

2. A coordinative function. HR managers also coordinate personnel activities, a duty often referred to as **functional control**. Here the HR manager and department act as the "right arm of the top executive" to ensure that line managers are implementing the firm's HR objectives, policies, and procedures (for example, adhering to its sexual harassment policies).

3. Staff (service) functions. Assisting and advising line managers is the "bread and butter" of the HR manager's job. For example, HR *assists* in the hiring, training, evaluating, rewarding, counseling, promoting, and firing of employees. It also administers the various benefit programs (health and accident insurance, retirement, vacation, and so on). It helps line managers comply with equal employment and occupational safety laws, and plays an important role in handling grievances and labor relations. It carries out an *innovator* role, by providing "up-to-date information on current trends and new methods of solving problems"—such as today's interest in instituting six-sigma quality programs and creating "learning organizations." And it plays an **employee advocacy** role: It helps define how management should be treating employees, makes sure employees can contest unfair practices, and represents the employees' interests within the framework of its main obligation to senior management.[6] In most firms today, HR also plays a *strategic* role, by helping the CEO craft and implement the firm's strategy. We'll return to this in a moment.

Figure 1-1 shows the traditional HR positions you might find in a large organization. They include compensation manager, recruitment and placement super-

line authority
The authority exerted by an HR manager by directing the activities of the people in his or her own department and in service areas (like the plant cafeteria).

implied authority
The authority exerted by an HR manager by virtue of others' knowledge that he or she has access to top management (in areas like testing and affirmative action).

functional control
The authority exerted by an HR manager as coordinator of personnel activities.

employee advocacy
HR must take responsibility for clearly defining how management should be treating employees, make sure employees have the mechanisms required to contest unfair practices, and represent the interests of employees within the framework of its primary obligation to senior management.

▼ **FIGURE 1-1   HR Department Organizational Chart (Large Southern Hospital)**

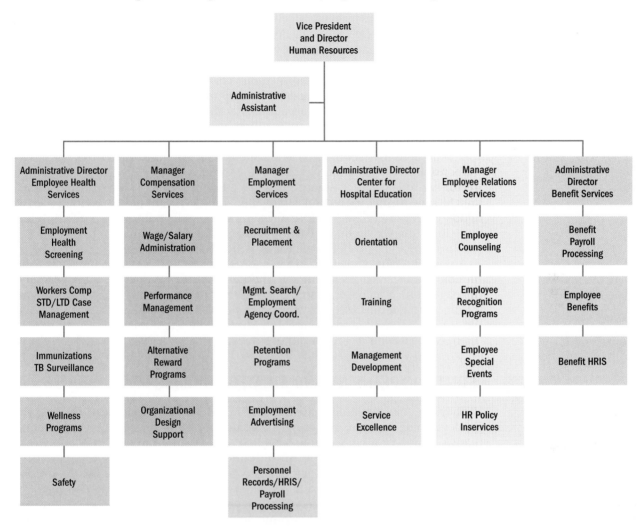

Source: Adapted from *BNA Bulletin to Management,* June 29, 2000.

visor, training specialist, employee relations manager, and safety supervisor. Examples of HR job duties include:

Recruiters. Search for qualified job applicants.

Equal employment opportunity (EEO) coordinators. Investigate and resolve EEO grievances, examine organizational practices for potential violations, and compile and submit EEO reports.

Job analysts. Collect and examine information about jobs to prepare job descriptions.

Compensation managers. Develop compensation plans and handle the employee benefits program.

Training specialists. Plan, organize, and direct training activities.

Labor relations specialists. Advise management on all aspects of union–management relations.[7]

Cooperative Line and Staff HR Management: An Example

Exactly which HR management activities are carried out by line managers and by staff managers? There's no single division of responsibilities we could apply across the board in all organizations, but we can make some generalizations.[8]

For example, in recruiting and hiring, it's generally the line manager's responsibility to specify the qualifications employees need to fill specific positions. Then the HR staff takes over. They develop sources of qualified applicants and conduct initial screening interviews. They administer the appropriate tests. Then they refer the best applicants to the supervisor (line manager), who interviews and selects the ones he or she wants.

Some activities tend to be HR's alone. For example, 83% of firms assign responsibility for pre-employment testing exclusively to HR, 75% assign college recruiting to HR, 86% insurance benefits administration, 84% exit interviewers, and 88% personnel/HR recordkeeping. But employers split most activities, such as employment interviews, performance appraisal, skills training, job descriptions, and disciplinary procedures, between HR and line departments.[9]

In summary, you should see that HR management (as discussed in this book) is an integral part of every manager's job. Whether you're a first-line supervisor, middle manager, or president; or whether you're a production manager, sales manager, office manager, hospital administrator, county manager (or HR manager!), getting results through committed people is the name of the game. And to do this, you'll need a good working knowledge of the human resource management concepts and techniques in this book.

STRATEGIC PLANNING AND STRATEGIC TRENDS

strategy
The company's long-term plan for how it will balance its internal strengths and weaknesses with its external opportunities and threats to maintain a competitive advantage.

Perhaps the most striking change in HR's role today is its increased involvement in developing and implementing the company's strategy. **Strategy**—the company's long-term plan for how it will balance its internal strengths and weaknesses with its external opportunities and threats to maintain a competitive advantage—was traditionally a job mostly for the firm's top operating (line) managers. Thus, the president and his or her staff might decide to enter new markets, drop product lines, or embark on a five-year cost-cutting plan. Then he or she would more or less leave the personnel implications of that plan (hiring or firing new workers, hiring outplacement firms for those fired, and so on) for HR management to carry out. Today, HR usually plays a more central role.

The Basics of Strategic Planning

Managers engage in three levels of strategic planning for their firms. Many firms, such as AOL/Time Warner, consist of several businesses: AOL, Warner Music, Warner Pictures, and Turner Networks. They therefore need a *corporate-level strategy*. A company's corporate-level strategy identifies the portfolio of businesses that comprise the organization, and the ways in which these businesses relate to one another. The AOL/Time Warner business portfolio consists of media-related businesses. Firms like GE are more widely diversified, with a portfolio that spans jet engines and lightbulbs.

At the next level down, each of these businesses (such as Warner Music) needs a *business-level competitive strategy*. This strategy identifies how its managers will build and strengthen that business's long-term competitive position in the marketplace.[10] It identifies, for instance, how Warner Music will compete with Sony, or how Wal-Mart will compete with Kmart. Thus, Volvo differentiates itself based on safety, Rolex on quality, AOL on usability, and Wal-Mart on price. Every business also has (or should have) a *competitive advantage* that supports its competitive strategy and sets it apart from those it competes with. As with many firms today, AOL's usability, Rolex's quality, and Saturn's low-cost, high-quality cars all reflect their decisions to build their competitive advantages around the quality of their employees.

Finally, each business—AOL, Warner Music, GE Jet Engines—is itself comprised of departments, such as sales, manufacturing, and human resource management. *Functional strategies* identify the basic courses of action that each of the departments will pursue in order to help the business attain its competitive goals. These functional strategies have to make sense in terms of the business's competitive strategy: For example, it would be foolish for Wal-Mart's construction division to build stunningly expensive stores, or for Rolex HR to hire any but the finest craftspeople. We'll see that HR takes on added significance in firms that build their competitive advantage around their people.

The Strategic Planning Process

There is nothing particularly mysterious about the strategic planning process. The heart of strategic planning entails *SWOT analysis*, which stands for strengths, weaknesses, opportunities, and threats. The best strategic plans endeavor to balance the firm's capabilities—its strengths and weaknesses—with the opportunities and threats the firm faces. Thus, faced with the threat posed by Microsoft's Internet Explorer, AOL bought Netscape, which happened to be for sale. When AOL bought Time Warner to form a huge multimedia company, Seagram decided to sell its Universal Music and other media properties to the French Internet and telecom company Vivendi, which was seeking media properties. Managers are forever scanning the environment for opportunities and threats.

What may be an important opportunity or threat to one firm may be meaningless to another. For example, it probably doesn't matter to General Motors that Time Warner and AOL merged (although that merger was a big event for Seagram). However, there are several basic trends that have been important across the board in determining the strategic direction of most firms today. Let's look at these.

Basic Strategic Trends

Globalization **Globalization** refers to the tendency of firms to extend their sales, ownership, and/or manufacturing to new markets abroad. The rate of globalization in the past decade has been striking. For example, the total value of U.S. imports and exports almost tripled, from $907 billion in 1991 to $2.5 trillion in 2000.[11]

Globalization of markets is perhaps the most obvious: Sony, Calvin Klein, The Gap, Nike, and Mercedes-Benz are some of the firms that market all over the world. Firms are globalizing their production, too, by putting facilities where they'll be most advantageous. Toyota produces its Camry in Georgetown, Kentucky, with almost 80% U.S.-made parts, for instance. And with globalized markets and production, globalized ownership increasingly makes more sense. Four out of five "American" textbook publishers, for example—Prentice Hall, Harcourt, Houghton Mifflin, and Wiley—are owned by firms outside America (Britain's Pearson owns Prentice Hall).

Globalization has strategic implications. Firms that once competed only with local firms—from airlines to automakers to banks—now face foreign competitors. As one expert puts it, "The bottom line is that the growing integration of the world economy into a single, huge marketplace is increasing the intensity of

globalization
The tendency of firms to extend their sales, ownership, and/or manufacturing to new markets abroad.

▲ *Technology not only changes the nature of work but also creates brand new kinds of jobs. Katie Carmichael, content specialist for a company called SurfControl in Scott's Valley, California, performs tasks that would have been unheard of a few years ago. She surfs the Web every day to find Web sites that employees (or parents) might want to restrict, and she maintains and updates lists of those where SurfControl's clients feel their employees might spend unproductive time while on the job. Carmichael finds job satisfaction in the feeling of being "in touch with humanity" that the Internet affords her.*

competition in a wide range of manufacturing and service industries."[12] Thus, Ford and GM are pressuring Fiat in Europe, while Germany's Deutsche Bank pressures Citicorp in New York. *Deregulation* has reinforced this trend, as nations eliminate the legal barriers that protected industries like banking and aviation from unbridled competition.

More globalization means more competition, and more competition means more pressure to improve—to lower costs, to make employees more productive, and to find new ways to do things better and less expensively. Some firms are therefore transferring operations abroad, not just to seek cheaper labor, but to tap what *Fortune* magazine calls "a vast new supply of skilled labor around the world."[13] Levi Strauss—once a leading "made in the USA" advocate—closed most of its remaining U.S. plants in 1991, shifting more production overseas. Others, like Saturn, depend on highly motivated self-managing teams to ensure continuous improvements in operations. It's in programs like these that HR (hiring the right people and training them, for instance) understandably plays a more strategic role.

Technological Advances Similarly, the Internet and information technology have been forcing—and enabling—firms to become more competitive. For example, Carrier Corporation—at $10 billion in yearly sales and 40,000 employees, the world's largest manufacturer of air conditioners—saves an estimated $100 million per year with the Internet. In Brazil, for instance, Carrier handles all its transactions with its channel partners (its 550 dealers, retailers, and installers) over the Web. More than 80% of its revenues there now passes through Carrier's Web-enabled partners. "The time required to get an order entered and confirmed by our channel partners has gone from six days to six minutes."[14] Around the world, Carrier's gain is some competitor's loss: Firms that can't match its Web technology simply can't compete.

The Nature of Work Technology is doing more than reducing costs and opening up new ways to compete: It's also changing the nature of work.

This does not apply just to new jobs at dot-com firms like Amazon; even factory jobs are becoming more technologically demanding. For one thing, "knowledge-intensive high-tech manufacturing jobs in such industries as aerospace, computers, telecommunications, home electronics, pharmaceuticals, and medical instruments"[15] are replacing factory jobs in steel, auto, rubber, and textiles. Even heavy manufacturing jobs are becoming more high tech. At Alcoa Aluminum's Davenport, Iowa, plant, a computer stands at each work post to help each employee control his or her machines. As *Fortune* magazine says, today "practically every package delivery, bank teller, retail clerk, telephone operator, and bill collector in America works with a computer."[16]

Technology is not the only trend driving this change from "brawn to brains." There is also a continuing shift from manufacturing jobs to service jobs in North America and Western Europe. Today, over two-thirds of the U.S. work-force is employed in producing and delivering services, not products. It's esti-mated that between 1998 and 2008, the number of jobs in goods-producing industries will stay almost unchanged, at about 25.5 million, while the number of jobs in service-producing industries will climb from 99 million to 118.8 mil-lion.[17] These service jobs will in turn require new types of "knowledge" workers, new HR management methods to manage them, and a new focus on human capital.[18] **Human capital** refers to the knowledge, education, training, skills, and expertise of a firm's workers, and you can see it's more important than it has ever been before.[19]

What does this mean for managing companies? For one thing, "the center of gravity in employment is moving fast from manual and clerical workers to knowledge workers, who resist the command and control model that business took from the military 100 years ago."[20] Firms need new, world-class HR sys-tems to select, train, and motivate these employees, and to win their commit-ment to the technologies and continuous improvement programs firms today depend on.[21]

The Workforce   Workforce demographics are changing as well. Most notably, the workforce is becoming more diverse as women, minority-group members, and older workers enter the workforce. Diversity has been defined as "any attribute that humans are likely to use to tell themselves, 'that person is different from me,'" and thus includes such factors as race, sex, age, values, and cultural norms.[22]

For example, between 1992 and 2005, people classified as Asian and other (including Native Americans) in the workforce will have jumped by just over 81%. The number of Hispanics in the workforce will have jumped by almost 64%, so that Hispanics will represent 11% of the civilian labor force in 2005, up from 8% in 1992.[23] Women represented 46% of the workforce in 1994, and will represent an estimated 47.8% by 2005.[24] About two-thirds of all single mothers (separated, divorced, widowed, or never married) are in the labor force today, as are almost 45% of mothers with children under three years old (see Webnote).

The labor force is also getting older. The median age of the labor force, 37.8 years in 1995, is projected to rise to 40.5 years in 2005.[25] (This is due mostly to the aging of the baby-boom generation, those born between 1946 and 1964, since baby boomers now comprise just over half the U.S. labor force.[26]) Employees will also likely remain in the work-force past the age at which their parents retired, due to Social Security and Medicare changes and the termina-tion of traditional benefit plans by many employers.[27]

Creating unanimity from a diverse workforce may turn out to be a considerable challenge for HR. As sev-eral experts have said, there are "two fundamental and inconsistent realities operating today with regard to diversity. One is that organizations claim they seek to maximize diversity in the work place, and maximize the capabilities of such a diverse workforce. The other is that traditional human resources systems will not allow diversity, only similarity."[28] What they mean is that employers traditionally hire, appraise, and promote people who fit their image of what their firm's employ-ees should believe and act like, and there's a tendency to screen out those who don't "fit."[29] Establishing HR pro-grams that don't just pay lip service to diversity may thus be a challenge for many employers.[30]

human capital
The knowledge, education, training, skills, and expertise of a firm's workers.

▲ **WEBNOTE**
The U.S. Department of Labor now has a Web site for working women from its Women's Bureau.
www.dol.gov

Managerial Consequences of the Basic Trends

Managers have to craft strategies that balance opportunities and threats like those above with their firm's strengths and weaknesses, and this has produced the strategies and organizational changes with which you're already probably familiar. A strategy of *global expansion* has been perhaps the most obvious response to these trends: Firms ranging from giants like GE to smaller ones like Carrier to even the smallest entrepreneurial enterprises have a growing international presence.

Improved competitiveness is another popular strategy, one aimed at buttressing the firm's strengths and reducing its weaknesses. This strategy manifests itself in many ways: in downsizing, to boost productivity; in mergers, to achieve increased size while stripping redundant costs; in programs aimed at continuously improving operations; and in using the Web (as does Carrier) to "integrate channels." This lets firms and their suppliers and customers interact directly and thus further strip costs from operations.

Global expansion and improved competitiveness are in turn driving other, *organizational* changes. Rather than pyramidal chains with 9 or 10 levels, firms are flat; self-directed teams of empowered employees, close to the customers, now make decisions that once had to be shifted up for managerial review. *Boundaryless decision making* means employees interact freely across departmental and level boundaries to get the information and decisions they need quickly. *Knowledge management* initiatives mean systems are in place to ensure that employees across the company can share their special expertise.

The bases of power are also therefore changing. In the new workplace, says one expert, position, title, and authority are no longer adequate tools for managers to rely on to get their jobs done.[31] Instead, "success depends increasingly on tapping into sources of good ideas, on figuring out whose collaboration is needed to act on those ideas, and on working with both to produce results. In short, the new managerial work implies very different ways of obtaining and using power."[32]

▲ *The increasing diversity of the U.S. workforce brings employees many benefits, such as the opportunity to draw on different points of view, a wide range of skills and talents, and various kinds of work and life experience. One of the many challenges that accompanies increasing diversity is the widening range of employee needs, which employers are meeting with such benefits as flextime, job-sharing, telecommuting, and child and elder care programs. At Evolution Film & Tape, a television production company in California, the 10 full-time and 70 freelance workers create their own hours, dress as they like, and bring their children to work.*

HR'S STRATEGIC ROLE

Of course (since this is an HR book), the question is, "What does this all mean for human resource management?" The answer, in brief, is that firms today are instituting HR practices aimed at gaining competitive advantage from their employees. For example, GE's former Chairman Jack Welch has said, "The only way I see to get more productivity is by getting people involved and excited about their jobs. You can't afford to have anyone walk through a gate of a factory or into an office who is not giving 120%."[33] A survey of 377 CEOs from the world's 2,000 largest companies shows that GE's emphasis isn't unique. About half the CEOs said they spend a "great deal" of time "reshaping corporate culture and employee behavior," even more time than they spend monitoring corporate financial information. Another study found that 70% of companies with above-average financial performance considered employee training and development a critical factor in corporate success. These companies help build competitive advantage by developing their human capital.[34]

HR's Evolving Role

Today, it's the firm's workforce—its knowledge, commitment, skills, and training—that provides the competitive advantage for world-class companies like Microsoft, Sony, AOL, and GE.[35] And it's HR's job to build that competitive advantage.

That means an upgrading of HR's traditional role. In the early 1900s, personnel people first took over hiring and firing from supervisors, ran the payroll department, and administered benefit plans. The job consisted largely of ensuring that procedures were followed. As new technology in areas like testing and interviewing began to emerge, the personnel department began to play an expanded role in employee selection, training, and promotion.[36]

The emergence of union legislation in the 1930s led to a new HR emphasis on protecting the firm in its interaction with unions. The discrimination legislation of the 1960s and 1970s meant the potential for more lawsuits, and effective personnel practices became even more important. However, the emphasis was still on what HR could do to protect the organization rather than the positive contribution it made to the firm's effectiveness.

Today, HR's role is shifting from protector and screener to strategic partner and change agent. The metamorphosis of "personnel" into "human resource management" reflects that. In today's flattened, downsized, and high-performing organizations, trained and committed employees—not machines—are the firm's competitive key.

Strategic Human Resource Management

If a firm's competitiveness depends on its employees, then the business function responsible for acquiring, training, appraising, and compensating those employees has to play a bigger role in the firm's success. The notion of employees as competitive advantage has therefore led to a new field of study known as **strategic human resource management**, "the linking of HRM with strategic goals and objectives in order to improve business performance and develop organizational cultures that foster innovation and flexibility."[37] Ideally, HR and top management together craft the company's business strategy. That strategy then provides the framework that guides the design of specific HR activities such as recruiting and training. This should produce the employee competencies and behaviors that in turn should help the business implement its business strategy and realize its goals.[38]

HR strategies are the courses of action HR uses to help the company achieve its strategic aims. One of FedEx's strategic aims is to achieve superior levels of customer service and high profitability through committed employees. Its basic HR objective is thus to build a committed workforce, preferably in a nonunion environment.[39] FedEx pursues specific HR strategies to accomplish that strategic aim. It uses mechanisms (such as special grievance procedures) to build healthy two-way communication; it screens out potential managers whose values are not people oriented; it provides highly competitive salaries and pay-for-performance incentives; it provides for fair treatment and employee security for all employees; and it uses promotion from within and developmental activities to give employees every opportunity to use their skills and gifts at work. Let's take a closer look at HR's strategic partner role.

strategic human resource management
The linking of HRM with strategic goals and objectives in order to improve business performance and develop organizational cultures that foster innovation and flexibility.

HR's Role As a Strategic Partner

Unfortunately, HR's long history as a staff or advisory function has left it with a somewhat impoverished reputation—some still tend to view it as less than it is. For example, one view is that HR is strictly operational and that HR activities are not strategic at all.[40] According to this line of reasoning, HR activities "involve putting out small fires—ensuring that people are paid on the right day; the job advertisement meets the newspaper deadline; and a suitable supervisor is recruited for the night shift by the time it goes ahead. . . ."[41]

A second, more expansive, view is that HR's role is to fit or adapt to the company's strategy. Here HR's strategic role is to adapt individual HR practices (recruiting, rewarding, and so on) to fit specific corporate and competitive strategies. Top management crafts a corporate strategy—such as AOL's decision to merge with Time Warner—and then HR creates the HR programs required to execute that corporate strategy. As two strategic planning experts have argued, "the human resources management system must be tailored to the demands of business strategy."[42] The idea here is that "for any particular organizational strategy, there is purportedly a matching human resource strategy."[43]

A third view of HR management is that it is an equal partner in the strategic planning process. Here, HR's role is not just to adapt its activities to the firm's business strategy, nor, certainly, just to carry out operational day-to-day tasks like paying employees. Instead, the need to forge the firm's workforce into a competitive advantage means that HR management must be an equal partner in both the formulation and the implementation of the company's strategies. Here, for instance, HR participates in and influences decisions like AOL's decision to merge with Time Warner.[44]

Is this third view realistic? One study of top HR managers in New Zealand is probably typical and suggests the answer is "yes and no."[45] By their own descriptions, most of these managers were "more intimately involved with the implementation of strategic change and with the recruitment and development of key staff, notably managers" than with actually formulating the firm's strategic plans.[46] Yet even in this sample, there was a tendency for HR executives to increasingly take a broader view of the business as a whole and its wider environment.[47] A study by PricewaterhouseCoopers found that about 27% of the responding companies included HR's perspective when starting their strategic planning cycles.[48] HR managers therefore both traditionally and today seem to have their greatest strategic impact on executing a company's plans; however, the opportunity and need exists for their involvement in strategy formulation as well.

HR's Role in Executing Strategy Execution has traditionally been the heart of HR's strategic role, and that makes sense. A firm's functional strategies should support its competitive strategies. For example, FedEx's competitive strategy is to differentiate itself from its competitors by offering superior customer service and guaranteed on-time deliveries. This requires highly committed employees—ones who'll "go the extra mile" to do their best. Since the same basic technologies are available to UPS, DHL, and FedEx's other competitors, it is FedEx's workforce—its human resource—that provides FedEx with its competitive advantage. This means FedEx, as discussed earlier, must design its HR processes to create a committed, competent, and customer-oriented workforce. A different firm with a different competitive strategy might well have a very different approach to HR.[49]

HR supports strategy implementation in other ways. For example, HR handles the execution of most firms' downsizing and restructuring strategies—by outplacing employees, instituting pay-for-performance plans, reducing health care costs, and retraining employees. When Wells Fargo acquired First Interstate Bancorp, HR played a strategic role in merging two "wildly divergent" cultures. It helped deal with the uncertainty and initial shock that rippled through both organizations when management announced the merger.[50]

HR and Value Chain Analysis Strategy execution usually involves identifying and reducing costs, and therefore **value chain analysis**. A company's value chain "identifies the primary activities that create value for customers and the related support activities."[51] As in Figure 1-2, every business consists of a chain of activities, each of which contributes to designing, producing, marketing, and delivering a product or service. Each activity gives rise to costs. Managers use the value chain for visualizing their firm's strategic activities, and as a tool for isolating and analyzing the company's strategic costs. Value chain analysis prompts questions such as: "How do our costs for this activity compare with our competitors'?" "Is there some way we can gain a competitive advantage with this activity?" "Is there a more efficient way for us to deliver these services?" "And do we have to perform these services in house?"

By applying value chain analysis, HR managers are finding ingenious ways to deliver their own services more cost effectively. IBM's HR group, faced with drastic cost cutting in the 1990s, first slimmed down from 3,400 to 2,000 employees. Told to cut costs by another 40% to 50%, the HR team consolidated all its service functions into a centralized human resource service center based in Raleigh, North Carolina. This technology-rich call center helps more than 700,000 IBM "customers" (employees and their families), handling over 7 million transactions a year. It reportedly saved IBM over $180 million in its first six or so years.[52]

Outsourcing—letting outside vendors provide services—is another option. In one survey, about 71% of respondents said they were outsourcing one or more HR activities such as temporary staffing, recruiting, benefits administration, payroll, and training. Cost reduction was the most commonly cited explanation.[53]

HR's Role in Formulating Strategy Formulating a strategic plan requires identifying, analyzing, and balancing the company's external opportunities and threats, and its internal strengths and weaknesses. HR plays a role here, too.

For example, HR management can help with what strategic planners call environmental scanning, identifying and analyzing external opportunities and threats that may be crucial to the company's success. Thus, American Airlines considered and then rejected the opportunity to acquire USAir, a smaller and relatively weak airline. While American had several reasons for rejecting a bid, HR considerations loomed large. American had doubts about its ability to successfully negotiate new labor agreements with USAir's employees, and felt the problems of assimilating them might be too great.

value chain analysis
Identifying the primary activities that create value for customers and the related support activities.

outsourcing
Letting outside vendors provide services.

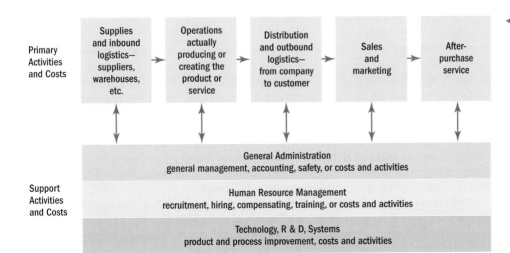

◀ **FIGURE 1-2**
The Value Chain Approach to Analyzing a Company's Activities and Costs

Formulating plans requires competitive intelligence, and HR management can supply useful information. Details regarding new competitors' incentive plans, and information about pending legislation like labor laws or mandatory health insurance are some examples. Furthermore:

> *From public information and legitimate recruiting and interview activities, you ought to be able to construct organization charts, staffing levels and group missions for the various organizational components of each of your major competitors. Your knowledge of how brands are sorted among sales divisions and who reports to whom can give important clues as to a competitor's strategic priorities. You may even know the track record and characteristic behavior of the executives.*[54]

HR also supplies information regarding the company's internal strengths and weaknesses. For example, AOL's decision to buy Netscape was probably prompted in part by AOL's assessment that its own human resources were inadequate for the task of creating a browser that could compete with Internet Explorer, or at least doing so quickly enough.

Some firms even build their strategies around an HR-based competitive advantage. For example, in the process of automating its factories, farm equipment manufacturer John Deere developed a workforce that was exceptionally talented and expert in factory automation. This in turn prompted the firm to establish a New-Technology division to offer automation services to other companies.[55] As another example, the firm Arthur Andersen developed unique human resource capabilities in training. The firm's Illinois training facility is so technologically advanced that it provides the firm with a competitive advantage, enabling it to provide fast, uniform training in house and "react quickly to the changing demands of its clients."[56]

HR and Technology

Indeed, technology can be an engine of strategic change. At IBM, for instance, creating a centralized HR call center did more than save the company $180 million. Studies (like one conducted at pharmaceuticals company Warner-Lambert) show that as much as 70% of HR employees' time is devoted to transactional tasks like checking leave balances, maintaining address records, and monitoring employee benefits distributions.[57] Consolidating and digitizing transactional services like these therefore meant IBM could redeploy HR assets to more value-added services—like helping divisional managers develop their employees and create their strategic plans. Doing so helped turn IBM HR into a truly strategic partner. We'll look at how technology is changing HR in this section.

Basic HR Systems HR can be an enormously paper-intensive process. For example, just recruiting and hiring an employee might require a Notice of Available Position, a help wanted advertising listing, an employment application, an interviewing checklist, and a telephone reference checklist. You then need an employment agreement, a confidentiality and noncompete agreement, and a hiring authorization form and employee background verification. To keep track of the employee once he or she is on board, you'd need—just to start—an employee change form, personnel data sheet, and daily or weekly time records. Then come the performance appraisal forms, notice of probation, and dozens of other, similar forms—and this list doesn't even scratch the surface.

Where do forms and systems like these come from? For a start-up business, office supply stores such as Office Depot and OfficeMax sell paper-and-pencil forms. For example, Office Depot sells packages of individual personnel forms, including an employment application, performance evaluation, and weekly expense report. But as your company grows, it becomes increasingly unwieldy and inefficient to rely on manual HR systems. Conducting performance appraisals for a few employees and tracking the results may not be much of a problem for a small store, but for a company with 40 or 50 employees, the management time devoted to conducting appraisals can multiply into weeks. It is at about this stage that most small- to medium-sized firms begin computerizing individual HR tasks.

There are many sources of help available. For example, the Web site for the international association for human resource information management www.ihrim.org/marketplace/buyers_guide/buyers_guide_cat.html contains a buyer's guide listing software vendors by functional category. These vendors provide software solutions for virtually all HR tasks, including compensation management, payroll, and time and attendance systems. HR supply firms such as G. Neil Companies and HR Direct sell off-the-shelf software packages for controlling attendance, employee record keeping, writing job descriptions, and conducting computerized employee appraisals.

Human Resource Information Systems (HRIS)   As companies grow, they integrate their separate HR systems into *human resource information systems (HRIS)*. An HRIS is "interrelated components working together to collect, process, store, and disseminate information to support decision-making, coordination, control, analysis, and visualization of an organization's human resource management activities."[58]

Integrating separate HR systems can be highly cost effective. For example, W. H. Brady Company, a Milwaukee-based manufacturer of identification products such as labels, reportedly cut several hundred thousand dollars a year from its HR budget through the use of HRIS.[59] The cost effectiveness derives from three factors: streamlined transactions processing (for instance, computerizing more of the firm's HR processes, such as appraisal); improved reporting capability (for instance, letting the CEO quickly access reports on things like health care cost per employee, and cost per hire); and making it easier for the firm to put its HR systems online. We'll turn to online HR next.

HR and the Internet   The Internet triggered a revolution in what HR departments do and how they do it. First, the Internet enabled any HR department to shift some activities to specialized online HR service providers. For example, Swales Aerospace recruits many engineers, and uses hire.com for its recruiting. Hire.com does not just post job openings. When a client position becomes available, hire.com sifts through its active and passive files to identify likely candidates. According to Swales's HR director, "hire.com was able to meet all our needs for building a pool of people that only we had access to, that we knew were interested in our company, and that had the skills we were looking for."

Yet, while turning to specific online services like these is beneficial, it's the movement to *HR portals* that prompted the most striking changes in what HR does and how it does it. As the head of the technology group for the Society for Human Resource Management has said, "the number one trend from a technology perspective is the evolution of intranets into full-fledged portals."[60]

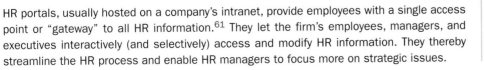

The HR Portal

HR portals, usually hosted on a company's intranet, provide employees with a single access point or "gateway" to all HR information.[61] They let the firm's employees, managers, and executives interactively (and selectively) access and modify HR information. They thereby streamline the HR process and enable HR managers to focus more on strategic issues.

Sometimes the firm's gateway HR portal supports just a few HR specialists. Anheuser-Busch used this approach when the time came for annual benefits package enrollments. HR knew there would be a large number of employee inquiries. It therefore replaced its manual inquiry process with Authoria HR, an HR portal from Authoria, Inc. (www.authoria.com). Doing so let HR digitize and aggregate through a single source (the new portal) all the former paper benefits reports, electronic spreadsheets, and benefit summaries that the firm's benefits counselors had been using. That made it much easier for specialists in Anheuser-Busch's HR call center to answer employees' questions as they came in. The aim is to eventually allow employees to research and answer their own HR questions through a browser-based interface.[62]

Wells Fargo used an HR portal when it merged with Norwest Corporation. The merger meant moving 90,000 employees to a new benefits plan, which of course triggered numerous employee inquiries. As at Anheuser-Busch, Wells Fargo armed its HR call center counselors with a specialized portal; this helped them research and answer employees' inquiries.

NCR also installed an HR portal. It is called HR eXpress, and is organized into three information areas: benefits and compensation, training and career growth, and NCR values and HR policies.[63] NCR also added a Forms Center to the site's title bar. HR eXpress gives NCR employees a shortcut to all the information they need to manage HR tasks, such as those relating to company benefits and updating their personal information. The Forms Center gives them quick access to any forms they need.

Again, putting HR services online doesn't just cut costs by letting employees research their own inquiries or by letting HR call center counselors do their jobs more easily (although it certainly does both). It also enables HR to redeploy its assets and focus on more strategic issues. As one manager put it: "We weren't looking for cost savings but to transform the work HR was doing from reactionary—dealing with paper and manual tasks—to proactive, being on the cutting edge, making people better employees."[64]

HR and Employee Performance and Commitment

It is one thing to argue that HR can help create competitive advantage; the real question is: "Can HR have a measurable impact on a company's bottom line?" There is evidence that the answer is yes. The U.S. government, for instance, found that using personnel screening tests to select high-potential computer programmers saved millions of dollars per year. For many firms, instituting tough headcount controls is the first line of attack in lowering labor costs. HR generally plays a major role in planning and implementing corporate downsizings, and then in maintaining the morale of the remaining employees.

A study by HR consulting firm Watson Wyatt Worldwide of Bethesda, Maryland, found that significant improvements in key HR management practices correlated with significant increases in market value in the 405 publicly traded firms studied. We can't draw any conclusions regarding cause and effect. However, significantly improving recruiting practices was linked to a 10% increase in market value, while establishing clear rewards and accountability was associated with a 9.2% market value rise.[65]

Employee behavior (and therefore HR) is especially important in service firms like banks and retail stores. If your customer is confronted by a salesperson who is tactless, unprepared to discuss the different products, or (even worse) discourteous, all your other efforts—advertising campaigns and redecorated stores, for instance—will have been wasted. That makes service firms especially dependent on employees' attitudes and motivation—and on HR management. One study of service firms found that HR practices (such as facilitating employees' career progress and providing orientation or socialization programs) improved customer service from the customers' point of view.[66] FedEx built its competitive advantage on this idea. Fred Smith, its chairman and founder, calls this "People-Service-Profits": Use HR to build employee commitment; employees will then provide excellent customer service, which in turn will generate profits.

FedEx is not alone in using HR to help build employee **commitment**—an employee's identification with and agreement to pursue the company's or the unit's mission. Many firms today know they need employees to work "as if they own the company." At Toyota Motor Manufacturing in Georgetown, Kentucky, employee commitment helps explain the firm's superior performance and product quality. Toyota instituted an HR system that cultivates commitment. For example, Toyota has programs that guarantee fair treatment of employees' grievances and disciplinary concerns. It also has programs that help ensure employees can use all their skills and gifts at work, such as career-oriented performance appraisal procedures and extensive training and development opportunities.[67]

▲ *A 2000 survey by a Washington consulting firm found that 43% of large companies allowed employees to work from home at least some of the time that year. Lisa Grau, a vice president at public relations firm Brodeur Worldwide, was one such employee. Grau telecommuted to the company's Phoenix office from her home in San Diego beginning with her hire two years ago and was promoted twice during that time. HR departments play a large part in making such innovative arrangements work, allowing employees to build their commitment to the firm.*

commitment
An employee's identification with and agreement to pursue the company's or the unit's mission.

HR practices also enable companies to respond faster to product and technological innovations and competitors' moves. For example, downsizing, empowering employees, and organizing around teams—all HR jobs—aim to improve communications and make it easier for employees to make decisions. At Levi Strauss, HR helped create the firm's team-based manufacturing system. This system ties employees' incentives to team goals and, along with Levi's new flexible-hours program, helps inject more flexibility into the firm's production process.[68] The photo above illustrates how HR can affect a company's bottom line.

STRATEGIC HR   Dell

From its start in Michael Dell's college dorm room, Dell Computer's competitive strategy was always to be the PC industry's low-cost leader. While others like Apple competed based on differentiating features like multimedia software, Dell stripped away the retailers' profit and drove its costs down by selling direct and relentlessly slashing costs. That's why it was, and is, the industry's low-cost leader. But recently, with PC sales falling, it was aggressively slashing prices, and the executives of its various divisions had to make sure their own strategies were in sync with the firmwide strategy to further cut costs.

As at many firms in the same situation, Dell HR's first task was to manage Dell's downsizing. In the first half of 2001, 4,000 Dell workers were let go. HR had to manage the system for choosing those who would leave the firm, and then handle the thousands of details involved in the dismissals. Terminated workers got their yearly bonuses early, severance packages including two months' salary and health benefits, and job counseling, among other benefits.[69]

Dell's HR managers have found a variety of other, ongoing ways to help Dell's top management execute the firm's low-cost leader strategy. For one thing—and as you might imagine—Dell now delivers most of its HR services via the Web. A Manager Tools section on the firm's intranet contains about 30 automated Web applications (including executive search reports, hiring tools, and automated employee referrals) allowing managers to perform HR tasks that previously required costly participation by HR department personnel. The intranet also lets Dell employees administer their own 401(k) plans, check job postings, and monitor their total compensation statements. This dramatically reduces the number of HR people required to administer these activities, and thus the cost of doing so.[70]

Dell also reorganized its delivery of HR services.[71] Rather than a traditional organization with HR heads for areas such as employment services, compensation, and employee health, Dell distinguishes between HR "operations" and HR "management." Operations staff deal directly with employees and coordinate transactional functions such as benefits, compensation, and employee relations through a central call center. Operations staff members rarely have contact with managers of Dell's business units. In contrast, HR management includes the company's education and training function (Dell University), as well as functions like recruitment and selection. HR management staff report to both the vice president of a business unit (such as Laptop Computers) and the vice president of HR. They attend their business unit's staff meetings as consultants, develop HR strategies for that particular line of business, and assist with matters such as identifying personnel needs, training employees, and contributing HR's perspective to the business unit's strategic plan.[72]

This division of work lets Dell's central HR operations staff efficiently address routine matters, while each business unit's relatively small HR management staff can efficiently provide specialized HR support in areas like personnel testing and strategic planning. That—along with Dell's use of Web-based self-serve HR services—illustrates how Dell HR helps Dell Computer remain the PC industry's low-cost leader.

Is There a "One Best HR Way"?

Assuming HR can affect the bottom line, is there a set of HR "best practices" (such as a particular way to appraise or compensate employees) that is applicable to all or most companies and strategies? Or do we have to adjust the HR practice to fit each situation? This question has been the subject of much debate, and we can draw some conclusions.

First, studies do suggest that some HR approaches are applicable to all or most companies. For example, profit sharing, results-oriented appraisals, and employment security all had strong relationships with measures of organizational performance in a range of situations.[73] Similarly, several HR practices seem "universal" for firms that do business globally: fostering informal relationships between employees with the aim of promoting worldwide communication; developing global executives through international assignments; having people with international experience in key global HR management positions; and having a global HR person on the initial business strategy team when entering new markets.[74]

On the other hand, there appears to be no "best practices" magic bullet, except to organize a firm's HR practices to fit its strategy and to "support the firm's operating and strategic initiatives."[75] In other words, dropping an HR practice into your firm just because it worked well in another is risky.

◆ **RESEARCH INSIGHT** Two studies illustrate this. In a study of banks, researchers measured performance on two financial measures: return on average assets, and return on equity.[76] They found that "the results of these analyses show that differences in HR practices are associated with rather large differences (approximately 30%) in financial performance."[77] However, whether the banks benefited from the specific types of HR practices (such as employee participation, results-oriented appraisals, and internal career opportunities) depended on the type of bank, and on what it was trying to achieve strategically (cut costs, boost quality, expand geographically, or something else).[78] A study of 97 manufacturing plants in the metalworking industry similarly concluded that HR practices did affect plant performance. However, how you design the HR practice has to fit the company's strategy and what the company wants to achieve.[79]

For current and future managers, the best advice seems to be to learn as much as possible about the HR practices we'll discuss in the following chapters, and then design a practice that's consistent with what your company wants to achieve. The corollary is that flexibility is advisable: You may have to modify an HR practice (such as a compensation plan) as competitive conditions cause you to modify your firm's business strategy.

THE PLAN OF THIS BOOK

Before moving on to Chapters 2 through 16, let's step back and get an overview of where we are heading. What should you keep in mind as you read this book? Two things. First, *HR management is the responsibility of every manager*—not just those in the HR department. Throughout this book, you'll therefore find an emphasis on practical material that you as a manager will need to carry out your day-to-day management responsibilities.

Second (as we've seen in this chapter), *HR practices today must address several basic issues*, including improving competitiveness, globalizing the firm's operations, implementing technological and Internet-based advances, and contributing to the firm's strategic success. In each chapter, you'll therefore find specific aids or features aimed at highlighting HR's role. For example, "High-Performance Insights" illustrate how HR helps make firms better, faster, and more competitive, and "HR.*NET*" features show how managers use the Web to improve HR. Strategy, because of its importance, deserves a special word: All chapters start with a "Strategic Overview" focused on a real firm. It shows the firm facing a strategic challenge, and suggests HR's possible role; a "Strategic HR" feature later in the chapter then shows what HR actually did.

Here is a brief overview of the chapters to come:

Chapter 2: Equal Opportunity and the Law. What you'll need to know about equal opportunity laws as they relate to human resource management activities such as interviewing, selecting employees, and evaluating performance.

Part II: Recruitment and Placement

Chapter 3: Job Analysis. How to analyze a job; how to determine the human resource requirements of the job, as well as its specific duties and responsibilities.

Chapter 4: HR Planning and Recruiting. Determining what sorts of people need to be hired; recruiting them.

Chapter 5: Employee Testing and Selection. Techniques you can use to ensure that you're hiring the right people.

Chapter 6: Interviewing Candidates. How to interview candidates to help ensure that you hire the right person for the right job.

Part III: Training and Development

Chapter 7: Training and Developing Employees. Providing the training necessary to ensure that your employees have the knowledge and skills needed to accomplish their tasks; concepts and techniques for developing more capable employees, managers, and organizations.

Chapter 8: Managing Strategic Organizational Renewal. HR techniques such as quality improvement programs and team building that firms use to help them manage quality and productivity.

Chapter 9: Appraising and Managing Performance. Techniques for appraising performance.

Chapter 10: Managing Careers and Fair Treatment. Techniques such as career planning and promotion from within that firms use to help ensure employees can achieve their potential and be treated fairly.

Part IV: Compensation

Chapter 11: Establishing Strategic Pay Plans. How to develop equitable pay plans for your employees.

Chapter 12: Pay-for-Performance and Financial Incentives. Pay-for-performance plans such as financial incentives, merit pay, and incentives that help tie performance to pay.

Chapter 13: Benefits and Services. Providing benefits that make it clear the firm views its employees as long-term investments and is concerned with their welfare.

Part V: Employee Security and Safety

Chapter 14: Labor Relations and Collective Bargaining. Concepts and techniques concerning the relations between unions and management, including the union organizing campaign; negotiating and agreeing upon a collective bargaining agreement between unions and management; and managing the agreement via the grievance process.

Chapter 15: Employee Safety and Health. The causes of accidents, how to make the workplace safe, and laws governing your responsibilities for employee safety and health.

Part VI: International HRM

Chapter 16: Managing Global Human Resources. The growing importance of international business, and HR's role in managing the personnel side of multinational operations.

We invite you to visit **www.prenhall.com/dessler** on the Prentice Hall Web site for our online study guide, Internet exercises, current events, links to related Web sites, and more.

Summary

1. All managers perform certain basic functions—planning, organizing, staffing, leading, and controlling. These represent the management process.

2. Staffing, personnel management, or human resource management includes activities like recruiting, selecting, training, compensating, appraising, and developing employees.

3. HR management is a part of every manager's responsibilities. These line responsibilities include placing the right person in the right job, and then orienting, training, and compensating to improve his or her job performance.

4. The HR manager and HR department carry out three main functions. First, the manager exerts line authority in his or her unit and implied authority elsewhere in the organization. He or she ensures that the organization's HR objectives and policies are coordinated and implemented. And he or she provides various staff services to line management, such as assisting in the hiring, training, evaluating, rewarding, promoting, and disciplining of employees at all levels.

5. Trends such as globalization, technological advances, and deregulation mean that companies must be better, faster, and more competitive to survive and thrive today. Other important trends include growing workforce diversity and changes in the nature of work, such as the movement toward a service society and a growing emphasis on human capital.

6. Trends like globalization and technological innovation are changing the way firms are managed. For example, the traditional pyramid-shaped organization is flattening; employees are being empowered to make more decisions; work is increasingly organized around teams and processes; the bases of power are changing; and managers today must build commitment. Changes like these mean that organizations must depend more on self-disciplined and committed employees. HR activities can have measurable effects on a company's bottom line, and on making a company better, faster, and more competitive.

7. HR management is often involved in both the formulation and the implementation of a company's strategies, given the need for the firm to galvanize employees to promote the firm's competitive advantage.

8. We defined strategic human resource management as "the linking of HRM with strategic goals and objectives in order to improve business performance and develop organizational cultures that foster innovation and flexibility." HR is a strategic partner in that HRM works with other top managers to formulate the company's strategy as well as to execute it.

Tying It All Together

It's convenient to think of human resource management activities as a logical series of steps: Jobs need to be designed; employees then need to be recruited, selected, trained, appraised, and compensated; and their safety and security concerns attended to. We've seen in this chapter that you can't design activities like these in a vacuum. For one thing, how you recruit and select employees, and the amount of effort you put into training them, needs to be consistent with what your company wants to achieve. In other words, they need to be consistent with the company's strategy. Dell's low-cost strategy approach to screening candidates may make less sense for a firm like Arthur Andersen, which recruits mostly professionals. Similarly, there's virtually no HR decision that's not influenced in one way or another by equal employment opportunity laws and legislation. We'll turn to this topic in Chapter 2, before moving on to personnel planning and recruiting—the first of the basic HR activities.

Discussion Questions

1. Explain what HR management is and how it relates to the management process.
2. Give examples of how HR management concepts and techniques can be of use to all managers.
3. Illustrate the HR management responsibilities of line and staff managers.
4. Why is it important for companies today to make their human resources into a competitive advantage? Explain how HR can contribute to doing this.
5. Discuss and illustrate HR's role in the strategic planning process.

Individual and Group Activities

1. Working individually or in groups, develop lists showing how trends like workforce diversity, technological innovation, globalization, and changes in the nature of work have affected the college or university you are attending now. Present in class.
2. Working individually or in groups, contact the HR manager of a local bank. Ask the HR manager how he or she is working as a strategic partner to manage human resources, given the bank's strategic goals and objectives. Back in class, discuss the responses of the different HR managers.

3. Working individually or in groups, interview an HR manager; based on that interview, write a short presentation regarding HR's role today in building more competitive organizations.

4. Working individually or in groups, bring several business publications such as *Business Week* and the *Wall Street Journal* to class. Based on their contents, compile a list entitled "What HR managers and departments do today."

EXPERIENTIAL EXERCISE *HRM As a Strategic Partner*

Purpose: The purpose of this exercise is to provide practice in identifying trends important to HR today, and in understanding their impact on an organization's HR practices.

Required Understanding: Be thoroughly familiar with the material in this chapter.

How to Set Up the Exercise/Instructions:

1. Divide the class into teams of three to four students.

2. Read this:

You are a strategic planning task force at your university. You must identify trends and how they will affect the university and its human resource needs. The team has already identified a partial list of trends (see following table).

3. Expand the list of "Critical Issues" and complete the other two columns in the table.

4. Present your team's conclusions to the class.

5. When the teams have had time to discuss their responses, consider the following questions:

   a. Which environmental trend would have the greatest impact on the human resource needs of the university?

   b. What environmental change will be the most difficult for your HR group to manage?

   c. Overall, how will this combination of trends affect your university?

Critical Issues	Effect on Existing Employees	Potential HR Role(s)
(Example)	*(Example)*	*(Example)*
1. Distance learning technology	Need for better computer skills	Provide greater technical training
2. Government reductions in funding to higher education		
3. Greater workforce diversity		
4. More international students		
5. High percentage of faculty to retire over next decade		
6. A local large business is developing its own corporate university		
7. Continuing education and nontraditional degree programs are increasing in popularity		

APPLICATION CASE *Jack Nelson's Problem*

As a new member of the board of directors for a local bank, Jack Nelson was being introduced to all the employees in the home office. When he was introduced to Ruth Johnson, he was curious about her work and asked her what her machine did. Johnson replied that she really did not know what the machine was called or what it did. She explained that she had only been working there for two months. She did, however, know precisely how to operate the machine. According to her supervisor, she was an excellent employee.

At one of the branch offices, the supervisor in charge spoke to Nelson confidentially, telling him that "something was wrong," but she didn't know what. For one thing, she explained, employee turnover was too high, and no sooner had one employee been put on the job than another one resigned. With customers to see and loans to be made, she continued, she had little time to work with the new employees as they came and went.

All branch supervisors hired their own employees without communication with the home office or other branches. When an opening developed, the supervisor tried to find a suitable employee to replace the worker who had quit.

After touring the 22 branches and finding similar problems in many of them, Nelson wondered what the home office should do or what action he should take. The banking firm was generally regarded as a well-run institution that had grown from 27 to 191 employees during the past eight years. The more he thought about the matter, the more puz-

zled Nelson became. He couldn't quite put his finger on the problem, and he didn't know whether to report his findings to the president.

Questions

1. What do you think is causing some of the problems in the bank home office and branches?

2. Do you think setting up an HR unit in the main office would help?

3. What specific functions should an HR unit carry out? What HR functions would then be carried out by supervisors and other line managers? What role should the Internet play in the new HR organization?

Source: From *Supervision in Action*, 4th ed., by Claude S. George, 1985. Adapted by permission of Prentice Hall, Inc., Upper Saddle River, NJ.

CONTINUING CASE: LearnInMotion.com *Introduction*

The main theme of this book is that HR management—activities like recruiting, selecting, training, and rewarding employees—is not just the job of some central HR group, but rather one in which every manager must engage. Perhaps nowhere is this more apparent than in the typical small service business. Here the owner-manager usually has no personnel staff to rely on. However, the success of his or her enterprise (not to mention his or her family's peace of mind) often depends largely on the effectiveness with which workers are recruited, hired, trained, evaluated, and rewarded.

To help illustrate and emphasize the front-line manager's HR role, throughout this book we will use a continuing ("running") case, based on an actual small business in the northeastern United States. Each segment will illustrate how the case's main players—owner-managers Jennifer Mendez and Mel Hudson—confront and solve personnel problems each day by applying the concepts and techniques presented in that particular chapter. The names of the company and principals have been changed, as have a few of the details, but the company, people, dates, and HR and other problems are otherwise real. Here's some background information you'll need to answer questions that arise in subsequent chapters.

LearnInMotion.com: A Profile Jennifer and Mel graduated from State University as business majors in June 1999, and got the idea for LearnInMotion.com as a result of a project they worked on together their last semester in their entrepreneurship class. The professor had divided the students into two- or three-person teams, and given them

the assignment "create a business plan for a dot-com company."

The idea the two came up with was LearnInMotion.com. The basic idea of the Web site was to list a vast array of Web-based, CD-ROM-based, or textbook-based business-related continuing-education-type courses for "free agent learners"—in other words, for working people who wanted to take a course in business from the comfort of their own homes. The idea was that users could come to the Web site to find and then take a course in one of several ways. Some courses could be completed interactively on the Web via the site; others were in a form that was downloadable directly to the user's computer; others (which were either textbook or CD-ROM based) could be ordered and delivered (in several major metropolitan areas) by independent contractor deliverypeople using bicycles or motorized scooters. Their business mission was "to provide work-related learning when, where, and how you need it."

Based on their research, they knew the market for work-related learning like this was booming. The $63-billion U.S. corporate training market was (and is) growing at 10% annually, for instance, with no firm controlling more than 2%. In 1999, when they created their plan, 76 million adult U.S. learners participated in at least one education activity. Over 100,000 U.S. training and consulting firms offered seminars, courses, and other forms of training. They estimated that worldwide markets were at least two or three times the U.S. market.

At the same time, professional development activities like these were increasingly Internet based. Thirteen percent of training was delivered via the Internet when they did their class project in 1999, and projections were for the e-learning/distance learning market to grow over 90% annually for the following three years. Tens of thousands of on- and offline training firms, universities, associations, and other content providers were trying to reach their target customers via the Internet. Jennifer and Mel understandably thought they were in the right place at the right time. And perhaps they were.

Their business plan contained about 25 pages, including financial projection tables, and covered the usual array of topics: company summary; management; market trends and opportunities; competition; marketing plan; financial plan; and appendices. The one-page executive summary contained a synopsis of the plan and covered "the business," "the market," "strategies," "competition," "value proposition," "the revenue drivers," "the management," and "financials and funding." Most of this is self-descriptive. *Revenue drivers* referred to how the company would generate revenues (in this case, online banner ads and sponsorships, content providers' listing fees, and fees for courses actually taken). *Financials and funding* included basic financial projections as well as likely "exit strategies," which in this case included the possibility of a public offering, a merger with related sites, or sale of the site, perhaps to one of the super-portals that were aggregating specialized sites as part of their strategies. They got an A for the business plan, an A for the course, and a standing ovation from the businesspeople the professor had invited to help evaluate the presentations.

When the two graduated in June 1999, it looked like the Internet boom would go on forever. It was not unusual for entrepreneurs still in their teens to create and sell Web sites. Some were selling their Web sites for literally hundreds of millions of dollars. Jennifer's father had some unused loft space in the SoHo area of New York, so with about $45,000 of accumulated savings, Jennifer and Mel incorporated and were in business. They retained the services of an independent contractor programmer and hired two people—a Web designer to create the graphics for the site (which would then be programmed by the programmer), and a content manager whose job was basically to keypunch information onto the site as it came in from content providers. By the end of 1999, they also completed upgrad-

ing their business plan into a form they could show to prospective venture capitalists. They sent the first version to three New York area venture capitalists. Then they waited.

And then they waited some more. They never heard back from the first three venture capitalists, so they sent their plan to five more. By now it was March 2000, and a dramatic event occurred: The values of a wide range of Internet and Internet-related sites dropped precipitously on the stock market. In some cases, entrepreneurs who had been worth $1 billion in February 1999 were worth $20 million or less by April. "Well, $20 million isn't bad," Mel said, so they pressed on. By day they called customers to get people to place ads on their site, to get content providers to list their available courses, and to get someone—anyone—to deliver textbook- and CD-ROM-based courses, as needed, in the New York area.

By May 2000, they had about 300 content providers offering courses and content through LearnInMotion.com. In the summer, they got their first serious nibble from a venture capital firm. They negotiated with this company through much of the summer, came to terms in the early fall, and closed the deal—getting just over $1 million in venture funding—in November 2000.

After a stunning total of $75,000 in legal fees (they had to pay both their firm's and the venture capital firm's lawyers to navigate the voluminous disclosure documents and agreements), they had just over $900,000 to spend. The funding, according to the business plan, was to go toward accomplishing five main goals: redesigning and expanding the Web site; hiring about seven more employees; moving to larger office space; designing and implementing a personal information manager (PIM)/calendar (users and content providers could use the calendar to interactively keep track of their personal and business schedules); and, last but not least, driving up sales. LearnInMotion was off and running.

Questions and Assignments

1. Would a company like this with just a few employees and independent contractors have any HR tasks to address? What do you think those might be?

2. Based on your review of the online catalogs of firms such as Office Max, Staples, and HRNext.com, what basic HR systems would you recommend to Jennifer and Mel?

Chapter 2

Equal Opportunity and the Law

After studying this chapter, you should be able to:

- Avoid employment discrimination problems.
- Cite the main features of at least five employment discrimination laws.
- Define *adverse impact* and explain how it is proved and what its significance is.
- Cite specific discriminatory personnel management practices in recruitment, selection, promotion, transfer, layoffs, and benefits.
- Explain and illustrate two defenses you can use in the event of discriminatory practice allegations.
- Define and discuss *diversity management*.

STRATEGIC OVERVIEW Some experts argue that diverse workforces produce conflicts and rising costs.[1] But that argument is lost on the owners of Longo Toyota in El Monte, California.[2] Longo's strategy is to cater to its increasingly diverse customer base by hiring and developing salespeople who speak everything from Spanish and Korean to Mandarin and Tagalog. And by following that strategy, Longo may now be one of America's top-grossing auto dealers.

Chapter 1 laid out the plan of this book, and explained that we'll focus on basic HR practices like recruiting and selecting employees, and on training, appraising, and compensating them. But as a practical matter, no manager can handle tasks like these without facing discrimination-related issues.

Every time you advertise a job opening, recruit, interview, test, or select a candidate or appraise an employee, it's necessary to take equal rights laws into account. The main purpose of this chapter is to provide you with the knowledge you'll need to deal effectively with equal employment opportunity questions on the job. The main topics we'll cover are equal opportunity laws from 1964 to 1991, the laws from 1991 to the present, defenses against discrimination allegations, illustrative discriminatory employment practices, the EEOC enforcement process, and diversity management and affirmative action programs. In the following chapter, Job Analysis, we'll discuss, among other things, how laws like these apply to writing job descriptions and specifying the sorts of people required for those jobs.

EQUAL EMPLOYMENT OPPORTUNITY 1964–1991

Legislation barring discrimination against members of minority groups in the United States is certainly nothing new. For example, the Fifth Amendment to the U.S. Constitution (ratified in 1791) states, "no person shall be deprived of life, liberty, or property, without due process of the law." The 13th Amendment (ratified in 1865) outlawed slavery, and courts have held it bars racial discrimination. The 14th Amendment (ratified in 1868) makes it illegal for any state to "make or enforce any law which shall abridge the privileges and immunities of citizens of the United States," and the courts have generally viewed this law as barring discrimination based on sex, national origin, or race. Section 1981 of Title 42 of the U.S. Code, passed over 100 years ago as the Civil Rights Act of 1866, gives all persons the same right to make and enforce contracts and to benefit from the laws of the land.[3] Other laws as well as various court decisions made discrimination against minorities illegal as early as the turn of the 20th century—at least in theory.[4]

But as a practical matter, Congress and various presidents were reluctant to take dramatic action on equal employment issues until the early 1960s. At that point, "they were finally prompted to act primarily as a result of civil unrest among the minorities and women" who were eventually protected by the new equal rights legislation we discuss in this chapter.[5]

Title VII of the 1964 Civil Rights Act

Title VII of the 1964 Civil Rights Act
The section of the act that says an employer cannot discriminate on the basis of race, color, religion, sex, or national origin with respect to employment.

Title VII of the 1964 Civil Rights Act was one of the first of these 1960s-era laws. Title VII (as amended by the 1972 Equal Employment Opportunity Act) states that an employer cannot discriminate based on race, color, religion, sex, or national origin. Specifically, it states that it shall be an unlawful employment practice for an employer:

(1) To fail or refuse to hire or to discharge an individual or otherwise to discriminate against any individual with respect to his/her compensation, terms, conditions, or privileges of employment, because of such individual's race, color, religion, sex, or national origin.
(2) To limit, segregate, or classify his/her employees or applicants for employment in any way that would deprive or tend to deprive any individual of employment opportunities or otherwise adversely affect his/her status as an employee, because of such individual's race, color, religion, sex, or national origin.[6]

Who Does Title VII Cover? Title VII bars discrimination on the part of most employers, including all public or private employers of 15 or more persons. In addition, it covers all private and public educational institutions, the federal government, and state and local governments. It bars public and private employment agencies from failing or refusing to refer for employment any individual because of race, color, religion, sex, or national origin. And it bars labor unions with 15 or more members from excluding, expelling, or classifying their membership because of race, color, religion, sex, or national origin. Joint labor–management committees established for selecting workers for apprenticeships and training similarly cannot discriminate against individuals.

The EEOC Title VII established the **EEOC**, which stands for **Equal Employment Opportunity Commission**. The EEOC consists of five members appointed by the president with the advice and consent of the Senate. Each member serves a five-year term.

The EEOC receives and investigates job discrimination complaints from aggrieved individuals. When it finds reasonable cause that the charges are justified, it attempts (through conciliation) to reach an agreement eliminating all aspects of the discrimination. If this conciliation fails, it has the power to go to court to enforce the law. Under the Equal Employment Opportunity Act of 1972, the EEOC may file discrimination charges on behalf of aggrieved individuals, or the individuals may file themselves. We'll discuss this procedure later in this chapter.

Executive Orders

Various U.S. presidents have issued executive orders expanding equal employment in federal agencies. For example, Executive Orders 11246 and 11375, issued by the Johnson administration (1963–1969), don't just ban discrimination; they require that contractors take **affirmative action** to ensure equal employment opportunity (we will explain affirmative action below). All federal contractors with contracts over $50,000 and 50 or more employees must develop and implement such programs.

These orders also established the **Office of Federal Contract Compliance Programs (OFCCP)**. It implements the orders and ensures compliance. For example, it reached a settlement with aviation contractor Triad International Management Company, which paid over $240,000 to settle claims that women and blacks were subjected to a "perversely hostile work environment," including racial slurs.[7]

Equal Pay Act of 1963

The **Equal Pay Act of 1963** (amended in 1972) made it unlawful to discriminate in pay on the basis of sex when jobs involve equal work; require equivalent skills, effort, and responsibility; and are performed under similar working conditions. Differences based on a seniority system, a merit system, a system that measures earnings by quantity or quality of production, or based on any factor other than sex do not violate the act.

Age Discrimination in Employment Act of 1967

The **Age Discrimination in Employment Act of 1967 (ADEA)** made it unlawful to discriminate against employees or applicants for employment who are between 40 and 65 years of age. Subsequent amendments eliminated the age cap, effectively ending most mandatory retirement at age 65. A 1973 Supreme Court ruling held that most states and local agencies, when acting in the role of employer, must also adhere to provisions of the act that protect workers from age discrimination.

How young is young? In *O'Connor v. Consolidated Coin Caterers Corp.*, the Supreme Court held that an employee who is over 40 may sue for discrimination if he or she is replaced by a "significantly younger" employee, even if the replacement is also over 40. The Court didn't specify what "significantly younger" meant, but did seem to suggest that just three or four years would be insignificant. O'Connor had been replaced by someone 16 years younger.

Equal Employment Opportunity Commission (EEOC)
The commission, created by Title VII, is empowered to investigate job discrimination complaints and sue on behalf of complainants.

---

affirmative action
Steps that are taken for the purpose of eliminating the present effects of past discrimination.

Office of Federal Contract Compliance Programs (OFCCP)
This office is responsible for implementing the executive orders and ensuring compliance of federal contractors.

Equal Pay Act of 1963
The act requiring equal pay for equal work, regardless of sex.

Age Discrimination in Employment Act of 1967
The act prohibiting arbitrary age discrimination and specifically protecting individuals over 40 years old.

One-fifth of court actions filed by the EEOC recently were ADEA cases. (Another 30% were sex discrimination cases.) This act is a "favored statute" among employees and lawyers, since it allows jury trials and double damages to those proving "willful" discrimination.[8]

Vocational Rehabilitation Act of 1973

The **Vocational Rehabilitation Act of 1973** requires employers with federal contracts over $2,500 to take affirmative action in employing handicapped persons. It does not require hiring an unqualified person. It does require an employer to take steps to accommodate a handicapped worker unless doing so imposes an undue hardship on the employer.[9] A federal district court held that compensatory damages (a payment for "future pecuniary losses, emotional pain, suffering, inconvenience, mental anguish, loss of enjoyment of life, and other nonpecuniary losses") are available under the 1973 Rehabilitation Act.[10]

Vietnam Era Veterans' Readjustment Assistance Act of 1974

The provisions of the **Vietnam Era Veterans' Readjustment Assistance Act of 1974** require that employers with government contracts of $10,000 or more take affirmative action to employ and advance disabled veterans and qualified veterans of the Vietnam era. OFCCP administers the act.[11]

Pregnancy Discrimination Act of 1978

Congress passed the **Pregnancy Discrimination Act (PDA)** in 1978 as an amendment to Title VII. It prohibits using pregnancy, childbirth, or related medical conditions to discriminate in hiring, promotion, suspension, or discharge, or any term or condition of employment.[12] Also, if an employer offers its employees disability coverage, then it must treat pregnancy and childbirth like any other disability, and include it in the plan as a covered condition.[13] The U.S. Supreme Court ruled in *California Federal Savings and Loan Association v. Guerra* that if an employer offers no disability leave to any of its employees, it can (but need not) grant pregnancy leave to a woman disabled for pregnancy, childbirth, or a related medical condition.[14]

Federal Agency Guidelines

The federal agencies charged with ensuring compliance with these laws and executive orders issue their own guidelines. These spell out recommended procedures to follow in complying with the law.

The EEOC, Civil Service Commission, Department of Labor, and Department of Justice together have **uniform guidelines** for employers to use. They set forth "highly recommended" procedures regarding matters like employee selection, record keeping, preemployment inquiries, and affirmative action programs. As an example, they specify that employers must validate any employment selection devices (including but not limited to written tests) that screen out disproportionate numbers of women or minorities. They also explain how to validate a selection device. (We explain this procedure in Chapter 5.) The OFCCP has its own guidelines.[15] The EEOC and other agencies also periodically issue updated guidelines clarifying and revising their positions on matters such as national origin discrimination and sexual harassment.[16]

The American Psychological Association has its own Standards for Educational and Psychological Testing. Many experts expect that this document, which represents a consensus among testing authorities, to "help judges resolve disagreements about the quality of . . . validity studies that arise during litigation."[17]

Sexual Harassment

EEOC guidelines say employers have an affirmative duty to maintain a workplace free of **sexual harassment** and intimidation.[18] Harassment based on sex violates Title VII, when such conduct has the purpose or effect of substantially interfering with a person's work performance or creating an intimidating, hostile, or offensive work environment. The Civil Rights Act of 1991 (discussed below) added teeth to this. It permits victims to have jury trials and to collect compensatory damages for pain and suffering and punitive damages where the employer acted with "malice or reckless indifference" to the individual's rights.[19]

EEOC guidelines define sexual harassment as "unwelcome sexual advances, requests for sexual favors, and other verbal or physical conduct of a sexual nature that takes place under any of the following conditions":

> *(1) Submission to such conduct is made either explicitly or implicitly a term or condition of an individual's employment.*
> *(2) Submission to or rejection of such conduct by an individual is used as the basis for employment decisions affecting such individual.*
> *(3) Such conduct has the purpose or effect of unreasonably interfering with an individual's work performance or creating an intimidating, hostile, or offensive work environment.[20]*

Employees can also file discrimination suits claiming sexual harassment by people of their own gender.[21] In one case, a worker on an offshore oil rig claimed his male supervisors restrained him while another worker harassed him, and that he ultimately had to quit for fear of being raped.

An employee can prove sexual harassment in three main ways.

Quid Pro Quo Prove that rejecting a supervisor's advances adversely affected tangible benefits, like raises or promotions. In one case, the employee was able to show that continued job success, advancement, and positive performance evaluations were dependent on her agreeing to the sexual demands of her supervisors.[22]

Hostile Environment Created by Supervisors Showing tangible consequences is not always necessary. In one case, the court found that a male supervisor's sexually harassing behavior affected a female employee's emotional and psychological ability to the point she felt she had to quit her job. Although there were no direct threats or promises in exchange for sexual advances, the fact that the advances interfered with performance and created an offensive work environment was enough to prove that sexual harassment existed.

Hostile Environment Created by Co-Workers or Nonemployees The advances do not have to come from the person's supervisor. EEOC guidelines state that an employer is liable for the sexually harassing acts of its nonsupervisory employees if the employer knew or should have known of the harassing conduct.

Court Decisions The U.S. Supreme Court's first decision on sexual harassment was **Meritor Savings Bank, FSB v. Vinson**, decided in June 1986. In this case, there were three issues before the Court:

> *(1) Whether a hostile work environment (due to the victim's sex) in which the victim does not suffer any economic injury violates Title VII,*
> *(2) Whether an employee's voluntary participation in sexual acts with a manager constitutes a valid defense for an employer to a Title VII complaint, and*
> *(3) Whether an employer is liable for the conduct of supervisors or co-workers when the employer is unaware of that conduct.[23]*

sexual harassment
Harassment on the basis of sex that has the purpose or effect of substantially interfering with a person's work performance or creating an intimidating, hostile, or offensive work environment.

Meritor Savings Bank, FSB v. Vinson
The U.S. Supreme Court's first decision on sexual harassment, holding that the existence of a hostile environment even without economic hardship is sufficient to prove harassment, even if participation was voluntary.

The Court's ruling endorsed the EEOC guidelines (issues 1 and 2). The clear message was that employers should establish accessible and meaningful complaint procedures for employee claims of sexual harassment. (The majority, in a 5 to 4 split, declined to issue a definitive ruling on employers' automatic liability, issue 3.) However, the gist of more recent decisions is that employers *are* responsible if the employers' managers knew or reasonably should have known about the harassing behavior.

In one, *Burlington Industries v. Ellerth*, the employee accused her supervisor of "quid pro quo" harassment. She said her boss propositioned her and threatened her with demotion if she did not respond. He did not carry out the threats, and the employer did promote her. In a second case, *Faragher v. City of Boca Raton*, the employee accused the city of condoning a hostile work environment; she said she quit her lifeguard job after repeated taunts from other lifeguards. The Court ruled in favor of the employees in both cases. These decisions will make some harassment lawsuits against employers easier to win, but will limit the exposure of employers who have antiharassment policies in place.

What the Employer Should Do Employers (1) should take steps to ensure harassment does not take place, and (2) should take immediate corrective action, even if the offending party is a nonemployee, once it knows (or should know) of harassing conduct.[24] Liability is another matter.

Experts say the EEOC and the courts will ask two basic questions when determining whether a company is liable for sexual harassment:

1. Did the company know or should it have known that harassment was taking place?
2. Did the company take any action to stop the harassment?[25]

Employers can take steps to prevent such claims from arising and to minimize liability if someone files a sexual harassment claim:

1. Take all complaints about harassment seriously. As one sexual harassment manual for managers and supervisors advises, "When confronted with sexual harassment complaints or when sexual conduct is observed in the workplace, the best reaction is to address the complaint or stop the conduct."[26] One study concludes: If complaints are not taken seriously, or it's risky to complain, or perpetrators are unlikely to be punished, the firm's employees are likely to experience considerably higher levels of harassment.[27]
2. Issue a strong policy statement condemning such behavior. This should include a definition of sexual harassment, spell out possible actions against those who harass others, and make it clear that the employer will not tolerate retaliatory action against an employee who makes charges. An example in Figure 2-1 states that "such behavior may result in . . . dismissal."
3. Inform all employees about the policy and of their rights under the policy.
4. Install a complaint procedure.

▶ **FIGURE 2-1**
Sample Sexual
Harassment Policy

The company's position is that sexual harassment is a form of misconduct that undermines the integrity of the employment relationship. No employee—either male or female—should be subject to unsolicited and unwelcome sexual overtures or conduct, either verbal or physical. Sexual harassment does not refer to occasional compliments of a socially accepted nature. It refers to behavior that is not welcome, that is personally offensive, that debilitates morale, and that, therefore, interferes with work effectiveness. Such behavior may result in disciplinary action up to and including dismissal.

Source: Adapted from *Sexual Harassment Manual for Managers and Supervisors*, Commerce Clearing House, Inc., October 1991, p. 46.

5. Establish a management response system that includes an immediate reaction and investigation by senior management. There is less likelihood of employer liability when the employer's response is "adequate" and "reasonably calculated to prevent future harassment."[28]
6. Train supervisors and managers to increase their awareness of the issues.
7. Discipline managers and employees involved in sexual harassment.
8. Keep thorough records of complaints, investigations, and actions taken.
9. Conduct exit interviews that uncover any complaints and that acknowledge by signature the reasons for leaving.
10. Republish the sexual harassment policy periodically.
11. Encourage upward communication through periodic written attitude surveys, hot lines, suggestion boxes, and other feedback procedures to discover any evidence of sexual harassment.[29]

What the Employee Can Do Employees should recognize sexual harassment when they see it. Quid pro quo is relatively obvious. "Hostile environment" sexual harassment generally means discriminatory intimidation and ridicule permeated the workplace, and that the insult was sufficiently severe or pervasive to alter the conditions of employment. (Courts look at whether the questionable conduct is frequent or severe; whether it is physically threatening or humiliating, or a mere offensive utterance; and whether it unreasonably interferes with an employee's work performance.[30]) *Did* the person perceive the work environment as abusive? Courts will look at things such as whether she or he welcomed the conduct or immediately made it clear that the conduct was unwelcome, undesirable, or offensive.[31]

Steps an employee can take include:

1. File a verbal contemporaneous complaint or protest with the harasser and the harasser's boss stating that the unwanted overtures should cease because the conduct is unwelcome; follow up in writing if necessary.
2. If the unwelcome conduct does not cease, file a report regarding the unwelcome conduct and unsuccessful efforts to get it to stop with the harasser's manager and/or with the human resource director verbally and in writing.
3. If the letters and appeals to the employer do not suffice, turn to the local office of the EEOC.[32]
4. The employee can also consult an attorney about suing the harasser for assault and battery, intentional infliction of emotional distress, and injunctive relief, and to recover compensatory and punitive damages if the harassment is serious.

The **Federal Violence Against Women Act of 1994** provides another avenue through which women can seek relief for violent sexual harassment. It provides that a person "who commits a crime of violence motivated by gender and thus deprives another" of her rights shall be liable to the party injured.

Early Court Decisions Regarding Equal Employment Opportunity

Several court decisions between 1964 and 1991 helped create the interpretive foundation for EEO laws such as Title VII.

Griggs v. Duke Power Company *Griggs* was a landmark case, since the Supreme Court used it to define unfair discrimination. Lawyers sued the Duke Power Company on behalf of Willie Griggs, an applicant for a job as a coal handler. The company required its coal handlers to be high school graduates. Griggs claimed this requirement was illegally discriminatory because it wasn't related to success on the job and because it resulted in more blacks than whites being rejected for

Federal Violence Against Women Act of 1994
Provides that a person who commits a crime of violence motivated by gender shall be liable to the party injured.

Griggs v. Duke Power Company
A case heard by the Supreme Court in which the plaintiff argued that his employer's requirement that coal handlers be high school graduates was unfairly discriminatory. In finding for the plaintiff, the Court ruled that discrimination need not be overt to be illegal, that employment practices must be related to job performance, and that the burden of proof is on the employer to show that hiring standards are job related.

these jobs. *Griggs* won the case. The decision of the Court was unanimous, and in his written opinion, Chief Justice Burger laid out three crucial guidelines affecting equal employment legislation.

First, the Court ruled *discrimination by the employer need not be overt*. In other words, the employer does not have to be shown to have intentionally discriminated against the employee or applicant; it need only be shown that discrimination did take place. Second, the Court held that an employment practice (in this case requiring the high school degree) *must be job related* if it has an unequal impact on members of a **protected class**. (For example, if verbal ability is not required to perform the job's main functions, one should not test for it.) Third, Chief Justice Burger's opinion placed the *burden of proof on the employer* to show that the hiring practice is job related. Thus, the employer must show that the employment practice (in this case, requiring a high school degree) is necessary for satisfactory job performance if the practice discriminates against members of a protected class. In the words of Justice Burger,

> *The act proscribes not only overt discrimination, but also practices that are fair in form, but discriminatory in operation. The touchstone is business necessity. If an employment practice which operates to exclude Negroes cannot be shown to be related to job performance, the practice is prohibited.*[33]

Griggs established the following principles:

1. A test or other selection practice must be job related, and the burden of proof is on the employer.
2. An employer's intent not to discriminate is irrelevant.[34]
3. If a practice is "fair in form but discriminatory in operation," the courts will not uphold it.
4. *Business necessity* is the defense for any existing program that has adverse impact. The court did not define business necessity.
5. Title VII does not forbid testing. However, the test must be job related or valid, in that performance on the test must be related to performance on the job.

protected class
Persons such as minorities and women protected by equal opportunity laws, including Title VII.

Albemarle Paper Company v. Moody The *Albemarle* case is important because here the Court provided more details regarding how an employer should validate its screening tools. It helped clarify how employers could prove that the test or other screening tools are related to or predict performance on the job.[35] The Court said that if an employer is to use a test to screen candidates for a job, then the nature of that job—its specific duties and responsibilities—must first be carefully analyzed and documented. Furthermore, the performance standards for employees on the job in question should be clear and unambiguous, so the employer can identify which employees are performing better than others. The Court's ruling also had the effect of establishing the EEOC (now federal) guidelines on validation as the procedures for validating employment practices.[36]

Albemarle Paper Company v. Moody
The Supreme Court case in which it was ruled that the validity of job tests must be documented and that employee performance standards must be unambiguous.

Equal Employment Opportunity 1989–1991: A Shifting Supreme Court

After more or less championing the cause of minorities and women in the workplace for three decades, in a series of decisions in 1989 the Supreme Court signaled a shift toward a narrower scope for civil rights protection. Various factors, including the addition of several conservative justices to the Court, caused the change. But whatever the factors, the results were quite dramatic.

In one case, *Price Waterhouse v. Hopkins*, the plaintiff, a woman, was a candidate for partnership in the Price Waterhouse accounting firm, but her promotion was held for further consideration.[37] She responded by resigning and bringing suit under Title VII.

At the trial, the Court found that both lawful and unlawful factors contributed to her being passed over. She showed that her sex had been an unlawful factor in her denial of promotion, while the employer showed that "abrasiveness" had been a lawful factor. She won her case and won on appeal, but the U.S. Supreme Court eventually (on May 1, 1989) reversed the U.S. Court of Appeals. The Supreme Court found she would have been passed over anyway due to her "abrasiveness,"[38] and so found the firm's actions were not illegally discriminatory.

In *Wards Cove Packing Company v. Atonio*, the Supreme Court acted in a case of alleged racial discrimination in Alaskan salmon canneries.[39] Nonwhite Alaskans filled most unskilled jobs in the canneries. White employees filled most higher-paid noncannery jobs (carpenters, accountants, and so forth); they also got more desirable, better-insulated bunkhouses. The racial minorities sued, claiming that the employment practices had the effect of blocking them from getting the higher-paying jobs. Lower courts' decisions were mixed; the U.S. Supreme Court's ruling favored the employer.

The result was dramatic. It put the burden of proof on the employee. In *Griggs*, the Supreme Court had placed the burden of proof on the employer to show that the hiring practice in question is job related when it adversely affects members of a protected class.[40] After the *Griggs* case, proving that you were illegally discriminated against often meant just showing statistically, for example, that one classification of jobs was primarily held by whites while a second, less attractive classification was held mostly by nonwhites. With this statistical case made, the burden of proof shifted *to the employer* to prove that its employment practices served a necessary business purpose. This defense became known as the **business necessity** defense. Mounting a defense in such a case was often so expensive that many employers didn't try.

Wards Cove changed that. After *Wards Cove*, the *employee* had the burden of proving that the statistical imbalance was caused by an employment policy or practice of the employer.[41]

EQUAL EMPLOYMENT OPPORTUNITY 1991–PRESENT

Supreme Court rulings such as *Wards Cove* and *Price Waterhouse* had the effect of limiting women and minority groups' protection under equal employment laws, and this prompted Congress to act. The **Civil Rights Act of 1991 (CRA 1991)** became law in November 1991.

The Civil Rights Act of 1991

CRA 1991's basic effect was to reverse several U.S. Supreme Court decisions, including *Wards Cove* and others. But CRA 1991 didn't just roll back the clock: The effect was to make it even more important for employers and their managers to adhere to both the letter and spirit of EEO law. We can summarize the act's main provisions as follows.

Burden of Proof (*Wards Cove*) Here the Civil Rights Act of 1991 basically turns the EEO clock back to where it was prior to *Wards Cove*. With the passage of CRA 1991, the burden today is once again on employers to show that the practice (such as a test) is required as a business necessity.

Money Damages CRA 1991 provides that an employee who is claiming intentional discrimination (disparate treatment) can ask for (1) compensatory damages and (2) punitive damages. To do so, the employer must have engaged in discrimination "with malice or reckless indifference to the federally protected rights of an aggrieved individual."[42] (Before CRA 1991, victims of intentional discrimination

---

Wards Cove v. Atonio
The U.S. Supreme Court decision that makes it difficult to prove a case of unlawful discrimination against an employer.

business necessity
Justification for an otherwise discriminatory employment practice, provided there is an overriding legitimate business purpose.

Civil Rights Act of 1991 (CRA 1991)
It places burden of proof back on employers and permits compensatory and punitive damages.

who had not suffered financial loss and who sued under Title VII could not then sue for compensatory or punitive damages. They could only expect to have their jobs reinstated or to be awarded a particular job. They were also eligible for back pay, attorney fees, and court costs.)

Mixed Motives (*Price Waterhouse*) Under CRA 1991, an employer can no longer avoid liability by proving it would have taken the same action even without the discriminatory motive.[43] CRA 1991 states:

> *An unlawful employment practice is established when the complaining party demonstrates that race, color, religion, sex, or national origin was a motivating factor for any employment practice, even though other factors also motivated the practice.*[44]

Proof of Discrimination CRA 1991 could actually make it a bit more difficult for minorities to prove discrimination. One section says that test scores cannot be "adjusted" to "alter the results of employment related tests on the basis of race, color, religion, sex, or national origin." Up to 1991 some employers might have allowed the hiring of minority applicants who scored, say, 80, on a test, while nonminority applicants had to score 90. CRA 1991 does not permit such adjustments.[45]

THE *NEW* WORKPLACE

Enforcing the 1991 Civil Rights Act Abroad

Federal legislation generally applies only within U.S. territorial borders unless specifically stated otherwise.[46] With the passage of CRA 1991, EEO coverage was greatly expanded. The law amended the definition of the term *employee* in Title VII to include U.S. citizens employed in a foreign country by a U.S.-owned or U.S.-controlled company.[47] At least theoretically, U.S. citizens working overseas for U.S. companies now enjoy the same equal employment opportunity protection as those working within U.S. borders.[48]

Two factors limit the application of CRA 1991 to U.S. employees abroad. First, there are numerous exclusions to the civil rights protections. For example, an employer need not comply with Title VII if doing so would cause the employer to violate the law of the host country. (Some foreign countries, for instance, have statutes prohibiting the employment of women in management positions.)

A more vexing problem is the practical difficulty of enforcement. For example, the EEOC investigator's first duty is to analyze the finances and organizational structure of the overseas employer. But in practice, few investigators are trained for this duty and no standards exist for such investigations.[49] And one expert argues that U.S. courts "will be little help in overseas investigations, because few foreign nations cooperate with the intrusive enforcement of U.S. civil law."[50] Here, therefore, CRA 1991's bark will be worse than its bite.[51]

The Americans with Disabilities Act

Americans with Disabilities Act (ADA)
The act requiring employers to make reasonable accommodations for disabled employees; it prohibits discrimination against disabled persons.

The **Americans with Disabilities Act (ADA)** of 1990 prohibits employment discrimination against qualified disabled individuals.[52] Employers with 15 or more workers are prohibited from discriminating against qualified individuals with disabilities with regard to applications, hiring, discharge, compensation, advancement, training, or other terms, conditions, or privileges of employment.[53] It also says employers must make "reasonable accommodations" for physical or mental limitations unless doing so imposes an "undue hardship" on the business.

ADA does not list specific disabilities. Instead, the EEOC's guidelines say an individual is disabled when he or she has a physical or mental impairment that substantially limits one or more major life activities. Impairments include any physiological disorder or condition, cosmetic disfigurement, or anatomical loss affecting one or more of several body systems, or any mental or psychological disorder.[54] The act does specify certain conditions that are not to be regarded as disabilities, including homosexuality, bisexuality, voyeurism, compulsive gambling, pyromania, and certain disorders resulting from the current illegal use of drugs.[55]

The EEOC's position is that the ADA prohibits discriminating against people with AIDS, and numerous state laws also protect people with AIDS from discrimination. Similarly, the Labor Department's Office of Federal Contract Compliance Programs requires treating AIDS-type diseases under the Vocational Rehabilitation Act.[56] The bottom line for most employers is that discriminating against people with AIDS is generally unlawful.[57]

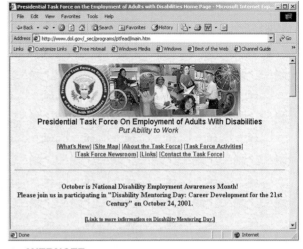

▲ **WEBNOTE**

Presidential Task Force on the Employment of Adults with Disabilities home page, which says: "Our mission is to create a coordinated and aggressive national policy to bring adults with disabilities into gainful employment at a rate . . . as close as possible to that of the general adult population."

www2.dol.gov

Qualified Individual Simply being disabled doesn't qualify someone for a job, of course. Instead, the act prohibits discrimination against **qualified individuals**—those who, with (or without) a reasonable accommodation, can carry out the *essential functions* of the job. The individual must have the requisite skills, educational background, and experience to do the job. A job function is essential when, for instance, it is the reason the position exists, or it is so highly specialized the person is hired for his or her expertise or ability to perform that particular function.

qualified individuals
Under the ADA, those who can carry out the essential functions of the job.

Reasonable Accommodation If the individual can't perform the job as currently structured, the employer must make a "reasonable accommodation" unless doing so would present an "undue hardship." Reasonable accommodation might include redesigning the job, modifying work schedules, or modifying or acquiring equipment or other devices to assist the person. Undue hardship is the rule, though: An employee with a bad back who worked as a Wal-Mart store door greeter asked Wal-Mart if she could sit on a stool while on duty, and the store rejected her request. She sued. The federal district court agreed with Wal-Mart that door greeters must act in an "aggressively hospitable manner," which can't be done sitting on a stool.[58] Standing was an essential job function.

Attorneys, employers, and the courts are still working through the question of what "reasonable accommodation" means. One expert noted, "three federal appeals courts have held that for it to be a reasonable accommodation, the employee must show that the costs of the accommodation do not outweigh the benefit."[59]

Many employers have successfully defended themselves. In one case, a social worker threatened to throw her co-worker out a window and to "kick her [butt]," and continued her tirade after returning from a 10-day suspension. After transfer to another job, she was diagnosed as paranoid; after telling her supervisor several times she was "ready to kill her," she was fired. She sued under ADA. The court dismissed her case because, although she had a debilitating mental illness, ADA does not require retention of employees who make threats.[60] In another case, the Court held that the employer did not discriminate against a blind bartender by requiring her to transfer to another job because she was unable to spot underage or intoxicated customers.[61] On the other hand, one U.S. circuit court held that punctuality was not an essential job function of a laboratory assistant who was habitually late. The court decided he could perform 7 1/2 hours of data entry even if he arrived late.[62]

Mental Impairments and the ADA The types of disabilities alleged in ADA charges have been somewhat surprising. They haven't been common conditions associated with disability, like vision, hearing, or mobility impairments. Mental disabilities now account for the greatest number of claims brought under the ADA.[63]

Under EEOC guidelines, "mental impairment" includes "any mental or psychological disorder, such as. . . . emotional or mental illness." Examples include major depression, anxiety disorders, panic disorders, obsessive-compulsive disorder, and personality disorders. The guidelines basically say employers should be alert to the possibility that traits normally regarded as undesirable (such as chronic lateness, hostility to co-workers, or poor judgment) may be linked to mental impairments covered by the ADA. Reasonable accommodation, says the EEOC, might then include providing room dividers, partitions, or other barriers between work spaces to accommodate individuals who have disability-related limitations.

Employer Obligations The ADA imposes certain legal obligations on employers:[64]

1. An employer must not deny a job to a disabled individual if the person is qualified and able to perform the essential functions of the job. If the person is otherwise qualified but unable to perform an essential function, the employer must make a reasonable accommodation unless doing so would result in undue hardship.[65]
2. Employers are not required to lower existing performance standards or stop using tests for a job. However, those standards or test must be job related and uniformly applied to all employees and job candidates.
3. Employers may not make preemployment inquiries about a person's disability, but they may ask questions about the person's ability to perform specific essential job functions. Preemployment medical exams or medical histories may not be required, but employers may condition job offers on the results of a postoffer medical exam. Under EEOC guidelines, "disability-related" questions cannot be asked at the initial interview stage. For example, the EEOC says it is illegal to ask: "Do you have AIDS?" "Have you ever filed for workers' compensation?" "What prescription drugs are you currently taking?" "Have you been treated for mental health problems?" "How much alcohol do you drink each week?"

    On the other hand, an employer can legally ask questions such as, "Can you perform the functions of this job with or without reasonable accommodation? Please describe or demonstrate how you would perform these functions." "Can you meet the attendance requirements of the job?" "Do you have the required licenses to perform these jobs?"[66]
4. Much the same limitations apply to medical exams for *current* employees. In one case, superiors ordered a Chicago police officer to take a blood test to determine if the level of Prozac his physician said he was taking would seriously impair his ability to do his job. At the time, the officer had not engaged in any behavior that suggested any performance problems. The court said the blood test was therefore not job related and violated the ADA's prohibition against inquiries into the nature or severity of an individual's disability.[67]
5. Employers should review job application forms, interview procedures, and job descriptions for illegal questions and statements. For example, check for questions about health, disabilities, medical histories, or previous workers' compensation claims.[68]

6. The ADA does not require employers to have job descriptions, but it's probably advisable to have them. As one expert writes, "In virtually any ADA legal action, a critical question will be, what are the essential functions of the position involved? . . . If, for example, a disabled employee is terminated because he or she cannot perform a particular function, in the absence of a job description that includes such function it will be difficult to convince a court that the function truly was an essential part of the job."[69]

The ADA in Practice ADA complaints are flooding the EEOC and the courts. However, the chances of prevailing in ADA cases are against the plaintiff: Employers prevailed in almost 96% of federal circuit court decisions in one recent year.[70]

Employees are failing to show that they are disabled and/or qualified to do the job.[71] One expert says that just because an employee has a disability does not mean he or she is protected under the ADA. Instead, many things determine if he or she is protected. Employers should ask questions such as, "Does the employee have a disability that substantially limits a major life activity?" "Is the employee qualified to do the job?" "Can the employee perform the essential functions of the job?" "Can any reasonable accommodation be provided without creating an undue hardship on the employer?" "Is the impairment permanent or of significant duration to be qualified as an ADA disability?"

▲ *New tools for the disabled include speaking Web browsers and Braille readers that sit under a computer's keyboard. James Gashel, who is blind, uses both these tools in his work as director of governmental affairs for the National Federation of the Blind, an advocacy group in Baltimore. Gashel and others hope to make the Internet more accessible to those with visual handicaps.*

However, don't assume employers always prevail. Wal-Mart recently had to reinstate hearing-impaired workers and pay a $750,000 fine for discrimination under the ADA.[72]

State and Local Equal Employment Opportunity Laws

In addition to the federal laws, all states and many local governments prohibit employment discrimination.

The effect of the state and local laws is usually to further restrict employers' treatment of job applicants and employees. Many state laws cover employers (like those with fewer than 15 employees) not covered by federal legislation.[73] Some extend the protection of age discrimination laws to young people, barring discrimination against not only those over 40, but those under 17; here, for instance, it would be illegal to advertise for "mature" applicants, because that might discourage some teenagers from applying.

The point is that many actions that might be legal under federal laws are illegal under state and local laws.[74] In Arizona, for instance, the legislature amended the Arizona Civil Rights Act so that plaintiffs can bring sexual harassment claims against employers with as few as one employee. Massachusetts's Fair Employment Practice Act requires employers to adopt policies against sexual harassment, and encourages employers to conduct sexual harassment employee training. In both New York and New Jersey, genetic testing is now generally barred, as is discrimination based on genetic information.[75]

State and local equal employment opportunity agencies (often called Human Resources Commissions, Commissions on Human Relations, or Fair Employment Commissions) play a role in the equal employment compliance process. When the EEOC receives a discrimination charge, it usually defers it for a limited time to the state and local agencies that have comparable jurisdiction. If that doesn't achieve satisfactory remedies, the charges go back to the EEOC for resolution.

Table 2-1 summarizes selected equal employment opportunity laws, actions, executive orders, and agency guidelines.

▼   **TABLE 2-1 Summary of Important Equal Employment Opportunity Actions**

Action	What It Does
Title VII of 1964 Civil Rights Act, as amended	Bars discrimination because of race, color, religion, sex, or national origin; instituted EEOC
Executive orders	Prohibit employment discrimination by employers with federal contracts of more than $10,000 (and their subcontractors); establish office of federal compliance; require affirmative action programs
Federal agency guidelines	Indicate policy covering discrimination based on sex, national origin, and religion, as well as employee selection procedures; for example, require validation of tests
Supreme Court decisions: *Griggs v. Duke Power Co.*, *Albemarle v. Moody*	Rule that job requirements must be related to job success; that discrimination need not be overt to be proved; that the burden of proof is on the employer to prove the qualification is valid
Equal Pay Act of 1963	Requires equal pay for men and women for performing similar work
Age Discrimination in Employment Act of 1967	Prohibits discriminating against a person 40 or over in any area of employment because of age
State and local laws	Often cover organizations too small to be covered by federal laws
Vocational Rehabilitation Act of 1973	Requires affirmative action to employ and promote qualified handicapped persons and prohibits discrimination against handicapped persons
Pregnancy Discrimination Act of 1978	Prohibits discrimination in employment against pregnant women, or related conditions
Vietnam Era Veterans' Readjustment Assistance Act of 1974	Requires affirmative action in employment for veterans of the Vietnam war era
Ward Cove v. Atonio	Made it more difficult to prove a case of unlawful discrimination against an employer
Price Waterhouse v. Hopkins	Unlawful actions may not be discriminatory if lawful actions would have resulted in the same personnel decision
Americans with Disabilities Act of 1990	Strengthens the need for most employers to make reasonable accommodations for disabled employees at work; prohibits discrimination
Civil Rights Act of 1991	Reverses *Wards Cove, Price Waterhouse*, and other decisions; places burden of proof back on employer and permits compensatory and punitive money damages for discrimination

Note: The actual laws (and others) can be accessed at: http://www.legal.gsa.gov/legal(#1)fed.htm.

DEFENSES AGAINST DISCRIMINATION ALLEGATIONS

Discrimination law distinguishes between disparate *treatment* and disparate *impact. Disparate treatment* "requires no more than a finding that women (or protected minority group members) were intentionally treated differently because of their gender."

Disparate impact "means that an employer engages in an employment practice or policy that has a greater adverse impact (effect) on the members of a protected group under Title VII than on other employees, regardless of intent."[76] Requiring a college degree for a job would have an adverse impact on some minority groups, for instance. Disparate impact claims do not require proof of discriminatory intent. Instead, the plaintiff must show a significant disparity between the proportion of (say) women in the available labor pool and the proportion hired, and an apparently neutral employment practice (such as word-of-mouth advertising) that is causing the disparity.[77] He or she must show there's been an *adverse impact*.

Adverse Impact

Showing **adverse impact** therefore plays a central role in discriminatory practice allegations. Under Title VII and the Civil Rights Act of 1991, a person who believes he or she was unintentionally discriminated against as a result of an employer's practices need only establish a *prima facie* case of discrimination. This means showing that the employer's selection procedures (like requiring a college degree for the job) did have an adverse impact on a protected minority group. Adverse impact "refers to the total employment process that results in a substantially different rate of hiring, promotions, or other employment decisions which works to the disadvantage of members of a minority or other protected group."[78]

adverse impact
The overall impact of employer practices that result in significantly higher percentages of members of minorities and other protected groups being rejected for employment, placement, or promotion.

What does this mean? If a protected group applicant feels he or she was a victim of discrimination, the person need only show that the employer's selection process resulted in an adverse impact on his or her group. (For example, if 80% of the white applicants passed the test, but only 20% of the black applicants passed, a black applicant has a *prima facie* case proving adverse impact.) Then, once the employee had proved his or her point, the burden of proof shifts to the employer: It becomes the employer's task to prove that its test, application blank, interview, or the like is a valid predictor of performance on the job (and that it was applied fairly and equitably to both minorities and nonminorities).

How Can Someone Show Adverse Impact? It is actually not too difficult for an applicant to show that one of an employer's procedures (such as a selection test) has an adverse impact on a protected group. There are four basic approaches:

1. **Disparate rejection rates.** This means comparing the rejection rates for a minority group and another group (usually the remaining nonminority applicants). For example, ask, "Is there a disparity between the percentage of blacks among those *applying* for a particular position and the percentage of blacks among those *hired* for the position?" Or, "Do proportionately more blacks than whites fail the written examination we give to all applicants?" If the answer to either question is yes, your firm could be faced with a lawsuit.

disparate rejection rates
A test for adverse impact in which it can be demonstrated that there is a discrepancy between rates of rejection of members of a protected group and of others.

Federal agencies have a formula to determine disparate rejection rates: "a selection rate for any racial, ethnic or sex group which is less than 4/5 or 80% of the rate for the group with the highest rate will generally be regarded as evidence of adverse impact, while a greater than 4/5 rate will generally not be regarded as evidence of adverse impact." For example, suppose 90% of male applicants are hired, but only 60% of female applicants. Since 60% is less than four-fifths of 90%, adverse impact exists as far as these federal agencies are concerned.[79]

2. Restricted policy. The **restricted policy** approach means demonstrating that the employer's policy intentionally or unintentionally excluded members of a protected group. Here the problem is usually obvious—such as policies against hiring bartenders under six feet tall. Evidence of restricted policies such as these is enough to prove adverse impact and to expose an employer to litigation.

3. Population comparisons. This approach compares (1) the percentage of Hispanic (or black or other minority/protected group) and white workers in the organization with (2) the percentage of the corresponding groups in the labor market, where labor market is usually defined as the U.S. Census data for that Standard Metropolitan Statistical Area.

For some jobs, such as laborer or secretary, it makes sense to compare the percentage of minority employees with the percentage of minorities in the surrounding community, since these employees will come from that community. However, for other jobs, such as engineers, the surrounding community may not be the relevant labor market, since recruiting may be nationwide or even global. Determining whether an employer has enough black engineers might thus involve determining the number of black engineers available nationwide rather than just in the surrounding community. Defining the relevant labor market is therefore crucial.

4. McDonnell-Douglas test. In this approach (which grew out of a case at the former McDonnell-Douglas Corporation), the applicant was qualified but the employer rejected the person and continued seeking applicants. This test is for (intentional) disparate treatment situations, rather than (unintentional) adverse impact ones (lawyers use approaches 1 through 3 for the latter).

The U.S. Supreme Court set the following conditions for applying the McDonnell-Douglas approach: (a) that the person belongs to a protected class; (b) that he or she applied and was qualified for a job for which the employer was seeking applicants; (c) that, despite this qualification, he or she was rejected; and (d) that, after his or her rejection, the position remained open and the employer continued seeking applications from persons with the complainant's qualifications. If the plaintiff meets all these conditions, then a *prima facie* case of disparate treatment is established. At that point, the employer must articulate a legitimate nondiscriminatory reason for its action and produce evidence but not prove that it acted on the basis of such a reason. If it meets this relatively easy standard, the plaintiff then has the burden of proving that the employer's articulated reason is merely a pretext for engaging in unlawful discrimination.

Adverse Impact: Example   Assume you turn down a member of a protected group for a job with your firm. You do this based on a test score (although it could have been interview questions, application-blank responses, or something else). Further assume that this person feels he or she was discriminated against due to being in a protected class, and decides to sue your company.

Basically, all he or she must do is show that your HR procedure (such as the selection test) had an adverse impact on members of his or her minority group. There are four approaches that he or she can apply here: disparate rejection rates, restricted policy, population comparisons, and the McDonnell-Douglas test. Once the person shows the existence of adverse impact to the court's satisfaction, the burden of proof shifts to you to defend against the discrimination charges.

Note that there is nothing in the law that says that because one of your procedures has an adverse impact on a protected group, you cannot use the procedure. In fact, it could (and does) happen that some tests screen out disproportionately higher numbers of, say, blacks than whites. What the law does say is that once your applicant has made his or her case (showing adverse impact), the burden of proof shifts to you. Now you (or your company) must defend use of the procedure.

There are then basically two defenses employers use to justify an employment practice that has an adverse impact on members of a minority group:[80] the bona fide occupational qualification (BFOQ) defense and the business necessity defense.

Bona Fide Occupational Qualification

An employer can claim that the employment practice is a **bona fide occupational qualification (BFOQ)** for performing the job. Title VII provides that "it should not be an unlawful employment practice for an employer to hire an employee . . . on the basis of religion, sex, or national origin *in those certain instances where religion, sex, or national origin is a bona fide occupational qualification* reasonably necessary to the normal operation of that particular business or enterprise."

Courts usually interpret the BFOQ exception narrowly. It is essentially a defense to a disparate treatment case based upon direct evidence of *intentional* discrimination, and not to disparate impact (unintentional) discrimination. As a practical matter, employers use it mostly as a defense against charges of intentional discrimination based on age.

Age As a BFOQ The Age Discrimination in Employment Act (ADEA) permits disparate treatment in those instances when age is a BFOQ. For example, age is a BFOQ when federal requirements impose a compulsory age limit, such as when the Federal Aviation Agency sets a ceiling of age 60 for pilots.[81] In March 2001—over objections by the FAA and the two major commercial pilots unions—Congress passed new legislation allowing commercial airline pilots to fly up to age 65, if in good health—a five-year increase.[82] Actors required for youthful or elderly roles or persons used to advertise or promote the sales of products designed for youthful or elderly consumers suggest other instances when age may be a BFOQ. A court said a bus line's maximum-age hiring policy for bus drivers was a BFOQ. The court said the essence of the business was safe transportation of passengers, and given that, the employer could strive to employ the most qualified persons available.[83]

Employer defenses against such claims usually fall into one of two categories: BFOQ or FOA (factors other than age). Employers using the BFOQ defense admit they based their personnel decisions on age, but seek to justify them by showing that the decisions were reasonably necessary to normal business operations (for instance, a bus line arguing its maximum-age driver requirement is necessary for safely transporting passengers). An employer who raises the FOA defense generally argues that its actions were "reasonable" based on some factor other than age, such as the terminated person's poor performance.

Religion As a BFOQ Religion may be a BFOQ in the case of religious organizations or societies that require employees to share their particular religion. For example, religion may be a BFOQ when hiring persons to teach in a denominational school. Similarly, practices such as requiring Saturday work that adversely affect certain religious groups are justifiable if the employer "is unable to reasonably accommodate . . . without undue hardship."[84] However, remember courts construe the BFOQ defense very narrowly.

Gender As a BFOQ Gender may be a BFOQ for positions requiring specific physical characteristics necessarily possessed by one sex. These include positions like actor, model, and rest room attendant. However, for most jobs today, it's difficult to

bona fide occupational qualification (BFOQ)
Requirement that an employee be of a certain religion, sex, or national origin where that is reasonably necessary to the organization's normal operation. Specified by the 1964 Civil Rights Act.

▲ *Legal and social pressures against gender discrimination may soon increase worldwide, but in Japan at least, change has been slow to arrive. Despite stronger legislation against discrimination and a huge labor shortage, Yoko Hayakawa (left) and Yukayo Hirano, top graduates of one of Japan's best universities, found themselves being directed away from the high-tech jobs they sought and into clerical and secretarial tracks. Both have since found professional-level positions.*

claim that gender is a BFOQ. For example, gender is not a BFOQ for parole and probation officers.[85] It is not a BFOQ for positions just because the positions require overtime or the lifting of heavy objects.

National Origin As a BFOQ A person's country of national origin may be a BFOQ. For example, an employer who is running the Chinese pavilion at a fair might claim that Chinese heritage is a BFOQ for persons to deal with the public.

Business Necessity

"Business necessity" is a defense created by the courts. It requires showing that there is an overriding business purpose for the discriminatory practice and that the practice is therefore acceptable.

It's not easy proving business necessity.[86] The Supreme Court has made it clear that business necessity does not encompass such matters as avoiding an inconvenience, annoyance, or expense to the employer. For example, an employer can't generally discharge employees whose wages have been garnished merely because garnishment (requiring the employer to divert part of the person's wages to pay his or her debts) creates an inconvenience. The Second Circuit Court of Appeals held that business necessity means an "irresistible demand," and that to be used the practice "must not only directly foster safety and efficiency" but also be essential to these goals.[87] Furthermore, ". . . the business purpose must be sufficiently compelling to override any racial impact; and the challenged practice must effectively carry out the business purpose it is alleged to serve."[88]

However, many employers have used the business necessity defense successfully. In *Spurlock v. United Airlines*, a minority candidate sued United Airlines, stating that its requirements that pilot candidates have 500 flight hours and college degrees were unfairly discriminatory. The court agreed that the requirements did have an adverse impact on members of the person's minority group. But it held that in light of the cost of the training program and the tremendous human and economic risks involved in hiring unqualified candidates, the selection standards were a business necessity and were job related.[89]

In general, when a job requires a small amount of skill and training, the courts scrutinize closely any preemployment standards or criteria that discriminate against minorities. The employer in such instances has a heavy burden to demonstrate the practices are job related. There is a correspondingly lighter burden when the job requires a high degree of skill, and when the economic and human risks of hiring an unqualified applicant are great.[90]

Attempts by employers to show that their selection tests or other employment practices are valid are an example of the business necessity defense. Here the employer is required to show that the test or other practice is job related—in other words, that it is a valid predictor of performance on the job. Where the employer can establish such validity, the courts have generally supported the use of the test or other employment practice as a business necessity. In this context, *validity* means the degree to which the test or other employment practice is related to or predicts performance on the job; Chapter 5 explains validation.

Other Considerations in Discriminatory Practice Defenses

There are three other points to remember about discrimination charges. First, good intentions are no excuse. As the Supreme Court held in the *Griggs* case,

> *Good intent or absence of discriminatory intent does not redeem procedures or testing mechanisms that operate as built-in headwinds for minority groups and are unrelated to measuring job capability.*[91]

Second, do not count on hiding behind collective bargaining agreements (for instance, by claiming that the discriminatory practice is required by a union agreement). Courts have often held that equal employment opportunity laws take precedence over the rights embodied in a labor contract.[92]

Finally, remember that although a defense is often the most sensible response to charges of discrimination, it is not the only response. When confronted with the fact that one or more of your personnel practices is discriminatory, you can react by agreeing to eliminate the illegal practice and (when required) by compensating the people you discriminated against.

SOME DISCRIMINATORY EMPLOYMENT PRACTICES

Before proceeding, let's review what federal fair employment laws allow (and do not allow) you to say and do.

Federal laws like Title VII usually don't expressly ban preemployment questions about an applicant's race, color, religion, sex, or national origin. In other words, "with the exception of personnel policies calling for outright discrimination against the members of some protected group," it's not the questions but their impact.[93] For example, it is not illegal to ask a job candidate about her marital status (although at first glance such a question might seem discriminatory). You can ask such a question as long as you can show either that you do not discriminate or that you can defend the practice as a BFOQ or business necessity.

But, in practice, there are two good reasons why most employers avoid such questions. First, although federal law may not bar asking such questions, many state and local laws do. Second, the EEOC has said that it will disapprove of such practices, so just asking the questions may draw its attention.

Inquiries and practices like those on the next few pages are thus usually not illegal per se. They are "problem questions" because they tend to identify an applicant as a member of a protected group or to adversely affect members of a protected group. They become illegal if a complainant can show they are used to screen out a greater proportion of his or her protected group's applicants, and the employer can't prove the practice is required as a business necessity or BFOQ.

The EEOC approves the use of "testers"—individuals who pose as applicants to test a firm's equal employment procedures. This makes it even more important to be careful in devising selection procedures and training recruiters.[94] Let's look now at some of the potentially discriminatory HR practices you should avoid.[95]

Discriminatory Recruitment Practices

Word of Mouth You cannot rely upon word-of-mouth dissemination of information about job opportunities when your workforce is all (or substantially all) white or all members of some other class such as all female, all Hispanic, and so on. Doing so reduces the likelihood that others will become aware of the jobs and thus apply for them.

Misleading Information It is unlawful to give false or misleading information to members of any group or to fail or refuse to advise them of work opportunities and the procedures for obtaining them.

Help Wanted Ads "Help wanted—male" and "help wanted—female" advertising classifications are violations unless gender is a bona fide occupational qualification for the job.[96] The same applies to ads that suggest you discriminate based on age. For example, you cannot advertise for a "young" man or woman.

Discriminatory Selection Standards

Educational Requirements Courts have found educational qualifications to be illegal when (1) minority groups are less likely to possess the educational qualifications (such as a high school degree) and (2) such qualifications are also not job related.

Tests Courts deem tests unlawful if they disproportionately screen out minorities or women and are not job related. According to former Chief Justice Burger,

> *Nothing in the [Title VII] act precludes the use of testing or measuring procedures; obviously they are useful. What Congress has forbidden is giving these devices and mechanisms controlling force unless they are demonstrating a reasonable measure of job performance.*

Preference to Relatives You cannot give preference to relatives of current employees with respect to employment opportunities if your current employees are substantially nonminority.

Height, Weight, and Physical Characteristics Requirements for physical characteristics (such as height and weight) are unlawful unless the employer can show they're job related. For example, the court held that a company's requirement that a person weigh a minimum of 150 pounds for positions on its assembly lines discriminated unfairly against women. Maximum-weight rules generally don't trigger adverse legal rulings. However, some minority groups have a higher incidence of obesity, so employers must be sure their weight rules don't adversely impact these groups. To qualify for reasonable accommodation, obese applicants must demonstrate they are 100% above their ideal weight or there is a physiological cause for their disability. In practice, employers sometimes treat overweight female applicants and employees to their disadvantage, and this is a potential problem.

Arrest Records Unless security clearance is necessary, you cannot ask an applicant whether he or she has ever been arrested or spent time in jail, or use an arrest record to disqualify a person for a position automatically. There is always a presumption of innocence until proven guilty. In addition, (1) arrest records in general are not valid for predicting job performance, and (2) police have arrested a higher proportion of minorities than whites. Thus, disqualifying applicants based on arrest records automatically has an adverse impact on minorities. However, you can ask about conviction records, and then determine on a case-by-case basis whether the facts justify refusal to employ an applicant in a particular position.

Application Forms Employment applications generally shouldn't contain questions about applicants' disabilities, workers' compensation history, age, arrest record, or U.S. citizenship. Personal information required for legitimate tax or benefit reasons (such as who to contact in case of emergency) is best collected after you hire the person.[97]

Discharge Due to Garnishment A disproportionately higher number of minorities are subjected to garnishment procedures (in which creditors make a claim to a portion of the person's wages). Therefore, firing a minority member whose salary is garnished is illegal, unless you can show some overriding business necessity.

Sample Discriminatory Promotion, Transfer, and Layoff Practices

Fair employment laws protect not just job applicants but also current employees.[98] Any employment practices regarding pay, promotion, termination, discipline, or benefits that (1) are applied differently to different classes of persons; (2) adversely impact members of a protected group; and (3) cannot be shown to be required as a BFOQ or business necessity may be held to be illegally discriminatory. For example, the Equal Pay Act requires that equal wages be paid for substantially similar work performed by both men and women.

Personal Appearance Regulations and Title VII Employees have filed suits against employers' dress and appearance codes under Title VII, usually claiming sex discrimination but sometimes claiming racial discrimination. A sampling of what courts have ruled to be acceptable or unacceptable follows:[99]

- *Dress.* In general, employers do not violate Title VII's ban on sex bias by requiring all employees to dress conservatively. For example, a supervisor's suggestion that a female attorney tone down her attire was permissible when the firm consistently sought to maintain a conservative dress style and it also counseled men on dressing conservatively.
- *Hair.* Here again, the courts usually rule in favor of the employers. For example, employer rules against facial hair do not constitute sex discrimination because they discriminate only between clean-shaven and bearded men, a type of discrimination not qualified as sex bias under Title VII. In many cases, courts also rejected arguments that grooming regulations (such as prohibitions against cornrow hairstyles) are racially biased and infringe on black employees' expression of cultural identification. In one case involving American Airlines, the court decided (in favor of American) that a braided hairstyle is a characteristic easily changed and not worn exclusively or even predominantly by black people.
- *Uniforms.* When it comes to discriminatory uniforms and suggestive attire, however, courts have frequently sided with the employee. For example, a bank's dress policy requiring female employees to wear prescribed uniforms consisting of five basic color-coordinated items but requiring male employees only to wear "appropriate business attire" is an example of a discriminatory policy. And requiring female employees (such as waitresses) to wear sexually suggestive attire as a condition of employment has also been ruled as violating Title VII in many cases.[100]

THE EEOC ENFORCEMENT PROCESS

People file about 80,000 charges of alleged discrimination annually with the EEOC.[101] Even the most prudent employer may encounter an employment discrimination claim, so it is helpful to be familiar with the EEOC enforcement process.

Processing a Charge

Under CRA 1991, the charge itself is to be filed within two years after the alleged incident took place. It must be filed in writing and under oath, by (or on behalf of) either the aggrieved person or by a member of the EEOC who has reasonable cause to believe that a violation occurred. The EEOC's common practice is to accept a charge and orally refer it to the state or local agency on behalf of the charging party. If the agency waives jurisdiction or cannot obtain a satisfactory solution, the EEOC processes it upon the expiration of the deferral period without requiring the filing of a new charge.[102]

After a charge is filed (or the state or local deferral period has ended), the EEOC has 10 days to serve notice on the employer. The EEOC then investigates the charge to determine whether there is reasonable cause to believe it is true; it is to make this determination within 120 days. If no reasonable cause is found, the EEOC must dismiss the charge, and must issue the charging party a Notice of Right to Sue. The person then has 90 days to file a suit on his or her own behalf.

If the EEOC does find reasonable cause for the charge, it must attempt a conciliation. If this conciliation is not satisfactory, it may bring a civil suit in a federal district court, or issue a Notice of Right to Sue to the person who filed the charge. Figure 2-2 summarizes important questions an employer should ask after receiving a bias complaint from the EEOC. They include, for example, "To what protected group does the worker belong?" and "Is the employee protected by more than one statute?"[103]

Conciliation Proceedings

The EEOC has 30 days to work out a conciliation agreement between the parties before bringing suit. The EEOC conciliator meets with the employee to determine what remedy would be satisfactory and then tries to persuade the employer to accept it. If both parties accept the remedy, they sign and submit a conciliation agreement to the EEOC for approval. If the EEOC can't obtain an acceptable conciliation agreement, it may sue the employer in a federal district court. The EEOC is also experimenting with using outside mediators to settle claims in selected cities.[104]

The EEOC seems to be getting more efficient. In one recent year its backlog of pending cases dropped from about 81,000 to about 65,000. And in 2000, the EEOC won a record $307.3 million in benefits for discrimination victims.[105] It obtains much of this money without suing, during the preliminary, administrative, and conciliation processes. In one year, the EEOC obtained about $178 million for plaintiffs that way—which underscores the need to understand how to respond to a discrimination charge and deal with the EEOC.[106]

▶ **FIGURE 2-2**
Questions to Ask When an Employer Receives Notice That a Bias Complaint Has Been Filed

1. To what protected group does the worker belong? Is the employee protected by more than one statute?
2. Would the action complained of have been taken if the worker were not a member of a protected group? Is the action having an adverse impact on other members of a protected group?
3. Is the employee's charge of discrimination subject to attack because it was not filed on time, according to the applicable law?
4. In the case of a sexual harassment claim, are there offensive posters or calendars on display in the workplace?
5. Do the employee's personnel records demonstrate discriminatory treatment in the form of unjustified warnings and reprimands?
6. In reviewing the nature of the action complained of, can it be characterized as disparate impact or disparate treatment? Can it be characterized as an individual complaint or a class action?
7. What are the company's probable defenses and rebuttal?
8. Who are the decision makers involved in the employment action, and what would be their effectiveness as potential witnesses?
9. What are the prospects for a settlement of the case that would be satisfactory to all involved?

Source: Gail J. Wright, assistant counsel for the NAACP's Legal Defense and Education Fund, quoted in Bureau of National Affairs, *Fair Employment Practices*, January 7, 1988, p. 3.

How to Respond to Employment Discrimination Charges

Here are some key things to keep in mind when confronted by a charge of illegal employment discrimination.[107]

The EEOC Investigation   First, remember that EEOC investigators are not judges and aren't empowered to act as courts; they cannot make findings of discrimination on their own but can merely make recommendations. If the EEOC eventually determines that an employer may be in violation of a law, its only recourse is to file a suit or issue a Notice of Right to Sue to the person who filed the charge.

Some experts advise meeting with the employee who made the complaint to clarify all the relevant issues. For example, ask: What happened? Who was involved? When did the incident take place? Did it affect the employee's ability to work? Were there any witnesses? Then prepare a written statement summarizing the complaints, facts, dates, and issues involved and request that the employee sign and date it.[108]

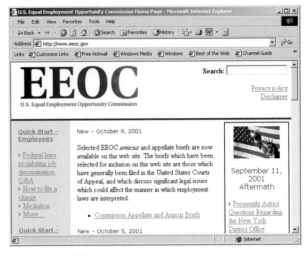

▲ **WEBNOTE**

The EEOC Web site provides a wealth of information for both employees and employers that includes guidelines for how to file a charge, as well as information on mediation.

www.eeoc.gov

With respect to providing documents to the EEOC, it is often in the employer's best interests to cooperate (or to appear cooperative). However, remember that the EEOC can only ask employers to submit documents and ask for the testimony of witnesses under oath.[109] It cannot compel employers to comply. If an employer refuses to cooperate, the commission's only recourse is to obtain a court subpoena. The "High-Performance Insight" on page 49 shows how one firm controls its EEOC document processing costs.

It may also be in the employer's best interest to give the EEOC a position statement based on its own investigation of the matter. One congressional investigation found that (at least in the EEOC's Chicago office) EEOC investigators were using the employer's position statement to write up cases because the EEOC was under pressure to resolve cases quickly. According to one management attorney, employers' position statements should contain words to the effect that "We understand that a charge of discrimination has been filed against this establishment and this statement is to inform the agency that the company has a policy against discrimination and would not discriminate in the manner charged in the complaint." Support the statement with some statistical analysis of the workforce, copies of any documents that support the employer's position, and/or an explanation of any legitimate business justification for the decision that is the subject of the complaint.[110]

If a settlement isn't reached, the EEOC will do a thorough investigation. Here there are three major principles an employer should follow. First, ensure there is information in the EEOC's file demonstrating lack of merit of the charge. Often the best way to do that is not by answering the EEOC's questionnaire, but by providing a detailed statement describing the firm's defense in its best and most persuasive light.

Second, limit the information supplied to only those issues raised in the charge itself. For example, do not respond to an EEOC request for a breakdown of employees by age and sex if the charge only alleges sex discrimination. Releasing too much information may just invite more probing by the EEOC.[111] Third, get as much information as possible about the charging party's claim, in order to ensure you understand the claim and its ramifications.

The Fact-Finding Conference The EEOC says these conferences are informal meetings held early in the investigation, aimed at defining issues and determining if there is basis for negotiation. According to one expert, however, the EEOC's emphasis is on settlement. Its investigators use the conferences to find weak spots in each party's respective position that they can use as leverage to push for a settlement.

If an employer wants a settlement, the fact-finding conference can be a good place to negotiate, but there are four things to look out for. First, the only official record is the notes taken by the EEOC investigator, and the parties cannot have access to them to rectify mistakes or clarify facts. Second, the employer can bring an attorney, but the EEOC often "seems to go out of its way to tell employers that an attorney's presence is unnecessary."[112] Third, these conferences often occur soon after a charge is filed, before the employer is fully informed of the charges and facts of the case.

Fourth, the parties may use witnesses' statements as admissions against the employer's interests. Therefore, before appearing, witnesses (especially supervisors) need to be aware of the legal significance of the facts they will present and of the possible claims the charging party and other witnesses may make.

EEOC Determination and Attempted Conciliation If the fact-finding conference does not solve the matter, the EEOC's investigator will determine whether there is reason to believe ("cause") or not too believe ("no cause") that discrimination may have taken place. There are several things to keep in mind here.

First, the investigator's recommendation is often the determining factor in whether the EEOC finds cause, so it is usually best to be courteous and cooperative (within limits). Second, if there is a finding of cause, you should review the finding very carefully; make sure to point out inaccuracies in writing to the EEOC. Use this letter to again try to convince the EEOC, the charging party, and the charging party's attorney that the charge is without merit. Finally, keep in mind that even with a no-cause finding, the charging party will still get a Notice of Right to Sue letter from the EEOC, and have 90 days from receipt to bring his or her own lawsuit.

If the EEOC issues a cause finding, it has (as noted above) 30 days to work out a conciliation agreement between the parties. Some experts argue against conciliating. First, the EEOC often views conciliation not as a compromise but as complete relief to the charging party. Second, "if you have properly investigated and evaluated the case previously, there may be no real advantage in settling at this stage. It is more than likely (based on the statistics) that no suit will be filed by the EEOC."[113] Even if the EEOC or the charging party later files a suit, the employer can consider settling after receiving the complaint.

Voluntary Mediation Today, the EEOC refers about 10% of its charges to a voluntary mediation mechanism. It says this is "an informal process in which a neutral third party assists the opposing parties to reach a voluntary, negotiated resolution of a charge of discrimination" (www.eeoc.gov/mediate/facts). If the plaintiff agrees to mediation, the EEOC asks the employer to participate. A mediation session usually lasts up to four hours. If no agreement is reached or one of the parties rejects participation, the charge is then processed through the EEOC's usual mechanisms.[114] The program seems to be successful. Since its implementation, about 11,600 private sector charges have been resolved; charging parties have obtained more than $150 million. Nine out of 10 participants say they would participate again.[115]

Faced with an offer to mediate, three responses are generally possible: agree to mediate the charge; make a settlement offer without mediation; or prepare a "position statement" for the EEOC. If the employer does not mediate or make an offer, the position statement is required. It should include information relating to the company's business and the charging party's position; a description of any rules or policies and procedures that are applicable; and the chronology of the offense that led to the adverse action.[116]

Mandatory Arbitration of Discrimination Claims

Conciliation, mediation, and litigation are not the only options when it comes to resolving claims: Arbitration is another. The U.S. Supreme Court's decisions (in *Gilmer v. Interstate/Johnson Lane Corp.* and similar cases) make it clear that "employment discrimination plaintiffs [employees] may be compelled to arbitrate their claims under some circumstances."[117] (In *Gilmer*, the Supreme Court held that an agreement, entered into for mandatory arbitration of all employment-related disputes, can require the employee to arbitrate claims arising under the Age Discrimination in Employment Act.) Since many courts may come to view compulsory arbitration as an acceptable alternative to litigation, the following suggestions are in order:[118]

- Employers should review all employment discrimination suits filed against them in state and federal courts immediately to determine whether they involve an employee subject to some type of agreement to arbitrate. They should then decide whether to move to compel arbitration of the claim.[119]
- Employers "may wish to consider inserting a mandatory arbitration clause in their employment applications or employee handbooks."[120]
- To protect such a process against appeal, the employer should institute steps to protect against arbitrator bias; allow the arbitrator to afford a claimant broad relief (including reinstatement); and allow for a reasonable amount of prehearing discovery (fact finding).

For example, after a long and expensive equal employment lawsuit, Rockwell International implemented a grievance procedure that provides for binding arbitration as the last step. Initially, Rockwell's 970 executives had to sign a mutual agreement to arbitrate employment disputes as a condition of participation in an executive stock plan. Rockwell later extended the program (called, as is traditional, an **alternative dispute resolution or ADR program**) to cover all nonunion employees at some locations. New hires at Rockwell must sign the agreement as a condition of employment, and current employees must sign it prior to promotion or transfer.[121] ADR plans are becoming more popular, although the EEOC reasserted its opposition to such plans for handling workplace bias claims.[122]

alternative dispute resolution or ADR program
Grievance procedure that provides for binding arbitration as the last step.

◆ **HIGH-PERFORMANCE INSIGHT** With or without ADR, handling EEOC claims can be expensive, and the documentation accounts for much of the expense. Typical complaints include complex files with hundreds or thousands of pages. The data are private and sensitive. Case files must be available for review at various levels in a company, and forwarded to the EEOC hearings. Many complaints could be in process at any given time. Labor and resources for handling these tasks must be diverted from other activities and can undermine a firm's competitiveness.

In response, Rock Island Arsenal (RIA) set up a new computer system (the "Paperless EEO Complaint System") to automate the processing of EEO complaints. The firm previously created documents manually, stored them in cabinets, and transferred them by mail. Postage and copying costs were high, and security was a problem. Case files were sometimes lost or misfiled.

To safeguard and reduce the time and cost of handling EEO case files, RIA purchased a computerized system that electronically creates, maintains, and transfers the files. RBP Associates of Landover, Maryland, designed the system for approximately $25,000. It runs on a Pentium-based PC, has a 40-page-per-minute scanner, and provides secure transmission over the Internet and encryption on CD-ROMs. The Paperless EEO System eliminates reproduction costs and misfiled or misplaced documents. It provides increased accessibility, greater security, and lower overall processing costs. The new system reduced overall processing costs by nearly 70%.[123]

DIVERSITY MANAGEMENT AND AFFIRMATIVE ACTION PROGRAMS

To some extent, the goals of equitable and fair treatment driving equal employment legislation are being overtaken by demographic changes and globalization. Today, white males no longer dominate the labor force, and women and minorities represent the lion's share of labor force growth over the foreseeable future. Furthermore, globalization increasingly requires employers to hire minority members with the cultural and language skills global companies need.

As a result, companies today are increasingly striving for racial, ethnic, and sexual workforce balance, "not because of legal imperatives, but as a matter of enlightened economic self-interest."[124] Increasingly, in other words, employers realize they have to actively recruit and maintain a diverse workforce in order to tap the changing demographics in this country and abroad. At least one study suggests that cultural diversity contributes to improved productivity, return on equity, and marker performance.[125]

While there's no unanimity about what diversity means, there's considerable agreement about its components. In one study, most respondents listed race, gender, culture, national origin, handicap, age, and religion. In other words, these comprised the demographic building blocks that represent diversity at work, and that people often think of when they ask what diversity means to employers.[126]

Managing Diversity

Managing diversity means taking steps to maximize diversity's potential advantages while minimizing the potential barriers—such as prejudice and bias—that can undermine the functioning of a diverse workforce.

In practice, diversity management involves both compulsory and voluntary management actions. First, there are (as we've just seen) laws requiring that employers minimize discrimination at work. But while such compulsory actions can reduce the more blatant diversity barriers, blending a diverse workforce into a close-knit and thriving community also requires voluntary steps. Based on his review of research studies, one diversity expert concludes that five sets of voluntary organizational activities are at the heart of any diversity management program. These are:

1. Provide strong leadership. Chief executives who champion diversity—such as David Kearns, the former Xerox chairman—typically have companies with exemplary reputations in managing diversity. Leadership in this case means, for instance, taking a strong personal stand on the need for change and becoming a role model for the behaviors required for the change. Some firms are more proactive than others. AOL Time Warner recently appointed Patricia Fili-Krushel, a former WebMD executive, to head efforts to improve opportunities for women and minorities in the company's workforce.[127]

2. Assess the situation. The company must assess the current state of affairs with respect to diversity management. This might entail administering surveys to measure current attitudes and perceptions toward different cultural groups within the company. Tools for measuring diversity include equal employment hiring and retention metrics, employee attitude surveys, management and employee evaluations, and focus groups.[128]

3. Provide diversity training and education. One expert says that "the most commonly utilized starting point for . . . managing diversity is some type of employee education program."[129]

4. Change culture and management systems. For example, change the performance appraisal criteria to measure supervisors based partly on their success in reducing intergroup conflicts.

5. Evaluate the managing diversity program. For example, do the employee attitude surveys now indicate any improvement in attitudes toward diversity?

STRATEGIC HR

Longo Toyota's Competitive Advantage

Evidence suggests most firms don't address diversity beyond what the EEOC requires, and that "many organizations have interpreted diversity as a human resource cost to be managed instead of a human resource asset to be fostered." However, taking that view may be a mistake.[130]

Workforce diversity actually makes strategic sense. For one thing, different opinions provided by culturally diverse groups may produce better decisions: In one study, ideas produced by ethnically diverse groups were judged to be of higher quality than those produced by homogeneous groups. Employers that overcome resistance to diversity may also be in a better position to handle other types of change. Companies pursuing growth strategies may need employees who are flexible in their thinking, and diversity may foster such flexibility. And, "as firms reach out to a broader customer base, they need employees who understand particular customer preferences and requirements."[131]

Longo Toyota built its competitive strategy on that last advantage. With a 60-person sales force that speaks more than 20 languages, Longo's staff provides it with a powerful competitive advantage for catering to an increasingly diverse customer base. The HR department has thus contributed to Longo's success. While other dealerships lose half their salespeople every year, Longo retains 90% of its staff, in part by emphasizing a promotion-from-within policy that's made more than two-thirds of its managers minorities. It's also taken steps to attract more women—for instance by adding a sales management staff to spend time providing the training inexperienced salespeople usually need. In a business in which competitors can easily imitate products, showrooms, and most services, Longo has built a competitive advantage based on employee diversity.

Boosting Workforce Diversity

As we'll see throughout this book, employers use various means to boost workforce diversity. For example, Baxter Healthcare's diversity program starts with a written philosophy ("Baxter International believes that a multi-cultural employee population is essential to the company's leadership in healthcare around the world").

Next, Baxter takes tangible steps to foster workplace diversity. The company evaluates its diversity program efforts, recruits minority members to the board of directors, and interacts with representative minority groups and networks. Diversity training at Baxter aims to sensitize all employees to the need to value

▲ *As vice president of global workforce diversity for IBM Corp., Ted Childs is responsible for the company's workforce diversity programs and policies, which include compliance with applicable laws. Says Childs, "My effort to diversify the workforce has moved from being a moral imperative to being a strategic imperative—shifting the conversation away from affirmative action and toward the marketplace . . . Ultimately, promoting diversity is good for business."*

differences, build self-esteem, and generally create a more smoothly functioning and hospitable environment for the firm's diverse workforce.

Some employers manage diversity through voluntary affirmative action programs. *Affirmative action* means employers make an extra effort to hire and promote those in protected (female or minority) groups. The aim is to voluntarily enhance employment opportunities for women and minorities (in contrast to the involuntary affirmative action programs courts imposed on some employers since enactment of the 1964 Civil Rights Act).

Read literally, CRA 1991 may bar employers from giving consideration to an individual's status as a racial or ethnic minority or as a woman when making an employment decision.[132] Employers therefore need to emphasize the external recruitment and internal development of better-qualified minority and female employees, "while basing employment decisions on legitimate criteria."[133] Furthermore, nonbeneficiaries may react negatively when they feel such programs result in them being treated unfairly.[134] Even beneficiaries may react badly. In one study, subjects who felt they'd benefited from affirmative-action-based preferential selection gave themselves unfavorable self-evaluations.[135] Yet, in spite of this, voluntary programs are often advisable. And sometimes, the court orders them.

Equal Employment Opportunity Versus Affirmative Action

Equal employment opportunity aims to ensure that anyone, regardless of race, color, sex, religion, national origin, or age, has an equal chance for a job based on his or her qualifications.

Affirmative action goes beyond equal employment opportunity by requiring the employer to make an extra effort to hire and promote those in the protected group. Affirmative action thus includes specific actions (in recruitment, hiring, promotions, and compensation) to eliminate the present effects of past discrimination. According to the EEOC, results are the most important measure of an affirmative action program. It should result in "measurable, yearly improvements in hiring, training, and promotion of minorities and females" in all parts of the organization.

Affirmative Action: Two Basic Strategies

When designing an affirmative action plan, employers can use two basic strategies—the **good faith effort strategy** or the **quota strategy**. Each has its own risks.[136] The first emphasizes identifying and eliminating the obstacles to hiring and promoting women and minorities on the assumption that this will result in increased utilization of women and minorities. The quota strategy mandates bottom-line results through hiring and promotion restrictions.

The good faith effort strategy aims to change the practices that contributed to minority groups' or females' exclusion or underutilization. Specific actions here might include placing advertisements where they can reach target groups, supporting day care services and flexible working hours for women with small children, and establishing a training program to enable minority-group members to better compete for entry-level jobs. The assumption is that if the firm identifies and eliminates obstacles, the desired results (improved utilization of minority members and women) will follow. The risk is that if the program is compulsory and the desired results are not achieved, the employer must convince the EEOC that (1) a reasonable effort to hire or promote more protected individuals has

good faith effort strategy
Employment strategy aimed at changing practices that have contributed in the past to excluding or underutilizing protected groups.

quota strategy
Employment strategy aimed at mandating the same results as the good faith effort strategy through specific hiring and promotion restrictions.

been made and (2) that failure to do so resulted from factors outside the employer's control.

Whereas the good faith strategy tries to get results by eliminating obstacles, the quota strategy aims at getting results through hiring and promotion restrictions. With the quota strategy, "desirable" hiring goals are treated as required employment quotas.

The courts have been grappling with the use of quotas in hiring, and particularly with claims by white males of **reverse discrimination**. Many cases addressed these issues, but no consistent answer has emerged. For example, in *Bakke v. Regents of the University of California* (1978), the University of California at Davis Medical School denied admission to white student Allen Bakke, allegedly because of the school's affirmative action quota system, which required that a specific number of openings go to minority applicants. In a 5 to 4 vote, the Court struck down the policy that made race the only factor in considering applications for a certain number of class openings and thus allowed Bakke's admission.

In *Wygant v. Jackson Board of Education* (1986), the Court struck down a mechanism in a collective bargaining agreement that gave preferential treatment to minority teachers in the event of a layoff.[137] In *International Association of Firefighters v. City of Cleveland* (1986), the Court upheld a consent decree that reserved a specific number of promotions for minority firefighters and established percentage goals for minority promotions.[138] In *U.S. v. Paradise* (1987), the Court ruled that the lower courts can impose racial quotas to address the most serious cases of racial discrimination.[139] In *Johnson v. Transportation Agency, Santa Clara County* (1987), the Court held that public and private employers may voluntarily adopt hiring and promotion goals to benefit minorities and women. This ruling limited claims of reverse discrimination by white males.[140] And in June 2001, the U.S. Supreme Court refused to hear Texas's challenge to a ruling that its law school affirmative action program, which gives special consideration to black and Mexican American student applicants, discriminated against whites.

The legal uncertainties suggest that the good faith strategy is often preferable to the quota strategy.[141] An employer might reasonably ask, therefore, "What specific actions should I take to be able to show that I have in fact made a good faith effort?"

One study helps answer this question. Researchers sent questionnaires to EEOC compliance officers. It asked them to rate the importance of about 30 possible actions for evaluating the compliance effort of a hypothetical company. The questionnaire described the company as having determined that it had underutilized minorities in several blue-collar and white-collar jobs. They had to indicate which of the 30 possible actions they thought the employer could take in order to show it had an acceptable good faith effort affirmative action program. The results showed the compliance officers preferred six areas for action:

1. Increasing the minority or female applicant flow.
2. Demonstrating top-management support for the equal employment policy—for instance, by appointing a high-ranking EEO administrator.
3. Demonstrating equal employment commitment to the local community—for instance, by providing in-house remedial training.
4. Keeping employees informed about the specifics of the affirmative action program.
5. Broadening the work skills of incumbent employees.
6. Institutionalizing the equal employment policy to encourage supervisors' support of it—for instance, by making it part of their performance appraisals.

reverse discrimination
Claim that due to affirmative action quota systems, white males are discriminated against.

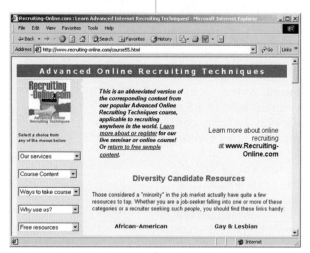

▲ **WEBNOTE**

Recruiting-Online is a good source of information and resources for recruiting minority candidates: its Web site contains links to African-American; Hispanic, Latino, and Native American; Gay & Lesbian; and Asian sites.

www.recruiting-online.com

Talking about hiring more minorities is one thing; actually doing it is another. In practice, many minorities are less likely to be using the Internet, for instance, and less likely to hear about good jobs from their friends. As Keith Fulton, director of technology programs and policy at the National Urban League, puts it, "it's one thing to be trained, but if [companies] don't know where to find the pools of ready and willing workers, you may miss qualified people by default."[142]

One option is to direct recruiting ads to one or more of the online minority-oriented job markets. For example, recruiting-online lists dozens of online diversity candidate resources (www.recruiting-online.com/course55.html). As the Webnote shows, diversity candidate Web sites with job banks include the African American Network, National Action Council of Minorities in Engineering, National Urban League, Hispanic Online, Latino Web, Society of Hispanic Engineers, Gay.com, Association for Women in Science, and Minorities Job Bank.

The National Urban League's Web site is a good example (www.nul.org/). Clicking on its Career Center tab brings you to a page with five options: Job Search; Post A Job; Resume Center; Job Agents; and Career Resources. The job agents section lets job seekers create their own job profiles. It then searches for employers' listings that may match, and sends a message to the job seeker when it finds a match.

We invite you to visit **www.prenhall.com/dessler** on the Prentice Hall Web site for our online study guide, Internet exercises, current events, links to related Web sites, and more.

Summary

1. Legislation barring discrimination is nothing new. For example, the Fifth Amendment to the U.S. Constitution (ratified in 1791) states that no person shall be deprived of life, liberty, or property without due process of law.

2. Legislation barring employment discrimination includes Title VII of the 1964 Civil Rights Act (as amended), which bars discrimination because of race, color, religion, sex, or national origin; various executive orders; federal guidelines (covering procedures for validating employee selection tools, and more); the Equal Pay Act of 1963; and the Age Discrimination in Employment Act of 1967. In addition, various court decisions (such as *Griggs v. Duke Power Company*) and state and local laws bar discrimination.

3. Title VII of the Civil Rights Act created the EEOC. It is empowered to try conciliating discrimination complaints, but if this fails, the EEOC has the power to go to court to enforce the law.

4. The Civil Rights Act of 1991 had the effect of reversing several Supreme Court equal employment decisions. It placed the burden of proof back on employers, said postem-

ployment decisions were covered by the 1866 Civil Rights Act, held that a nondiscriminatory reason was insufficient to let an employer avoid liability for an action that also had a discriminatory motive, and said that Title VII applied to U.S. employees of U.S. firms overseas. It also now permits compensatory and punitive damages, as well as jury trials.

5. The Americans with Disabilities Act prohibits employment discrimination against the disabled. Specifically, qualified persons cannot be discriminated against if the firm can make reasonable accommodations without undue hardship on the business.

6. A person who feels he or she was discriminated against by a personnel procedure or decision must prove either that he or she was subjected to unlawful disparate treatment (intentional discrimination) or that the procedure in question has a disparate impact (unintentional discrimination) upon members of his or her protected class. Once a *prima facie* case of disparate treatment is established, an employer must produce evidence that its decision was based upon legitimate nondiscriminatory reasons. Once a *prima facie* case of disparate impact has been established, the employer must produce evidence that the allegedly discriminatory practice or procedure is job related and is based upon a substantial business reason.

7. There are various specific discriminatory human resource management practices that an employer should avoid in recruitment and in selection. For example, employers generally cannot advertise for "man only."

8. In practice, the EEOC often first refers a charge to a local agency. When it does proceed (and if it finds reasonable cause to believe that discrimination occurred), the EEOC has 30 days to try to work out a conciliation. Important points for the employer to remember include: (a) EEOC investigators can only make recommendations; (b) you cannot be compelled to submit documents without a court order; and (c) you may limit the information you do submit. Also, make sure to clearly document your position (as the employer).

9. An employer can use two basic defenses in the event of a discriminatory practice allegation—business necessity, and bona fide occupational qualification. An employer's "good intentions" and/or a collective bargaining agreement are not defenses. (A third defense is that the decision was made on the basis of legitimate nondiscriminatory reasons—such as poor performance—having nothing to do with the prohibited discrimination alleged.)

Tying It All Together

This chapter completes the first part of the book, which presents the book's overall plan (Chapter 1) and the basic legal information (Chapter 2) you need to address the rest of the manager's HR management jobs. Knowing what the job entails is a prerequisite to preparing properly validated screening procedures and to defending against discrimination claims. In the following chapter, Job Analysis, we'll focus on the tools managers use to analyze the specific duties of jobs.

Discussion Questions

1. Explain the main features of Title VII, Equal Pay Act, Pregnancy Discrimination Act, Americans with Disabilities Act, Civil Rights Act of 1991.
2. What important precedents were set by the *Griggs v. Duke Power Company* case? The *Albemarle v. Moody* case?
3. What is adverse impact? How can it be proved?
4. What is sexual harassment? How can an employee prove sexual harassment?
5. What are the two main defenses you can use in the event of a discriminatory practice allegation, and what exactly do they involve?

Individual and Group Activities

1. Working individually or in groups, respond to these three scenarios based on what you learned in Chapter 2. Under what conditions (if any) do you think the following constitute sexual harassment? (a) A female manager fires a male employee because he refuses her requests for sexual favors. (b) A male manager refers to female employees as "sweetie" or "baby." (c) Two male employees are overheard by a third female employee exchanging sexually oriented jokes.

2. Working individually or in groups, discuss how you would set up an affirmative action program.

3. Compare and contrast the issues presented in *Bakke* with new court rulings on affirmative action. Working individually or in groups, discuss the current direction of affirmative action as a policy in light of the *Johnson* ruling.

4. Working individually or in groups, write a paper entitled "how the EEOC handles a person's discrimination charge."

5. Explain the difference between affirmative action and equal employment opportunity.

6. Explain how the Civil Rights Act of 1991 "turned back the clock" on equal employment Supreme Court cases decided from 1989 to 1991.

7. Assume you are a supervisor on an assembly line; you are responsible for hiring subordinates, supervising them, and recommending them for promotion. Working individually or in groups, compile a list of potentially discriminatory management practices you should avoid.

EXPERIENTIAL EXERCISE *Too Informal?*

Dan Jones had run his textile plant in a midsized southern town for many years without a whiff of trouble with the EEOC. He did not take formal steps to avoid making EEO-type mistakes; just the opposite. In fact, a professor from a local college had once told him to be more careful about how applicants were recruited and screened and employees were treated. However, Jones's philosophy was, "If it ain't broke, don't fix it," and because he'd never had any complaints, he assumed that his screening process wasn't "broke."

For many years, if Jones needed a new employee, he simply asked his current employees (most of whom were Hispanic) if they had any friends who were looking for jobs. Sometimes he would also ask the local state employment office to list the open jobs and send over some candidates. He then had his sewing supervisor and plant manager (both also Hispanic) interview the applicants. No tests or other background checks were carried out, in part, said Jones, because "most of these applicants are friends and relatives of my current employees, and they wouldn't send me any lemons."

Now Jones is being served with a formal notice from the county's Equal Rights Commission. It seems that of the 20 or so non-Hispanic applicants sent to Jones's firm last year from the state employment office, none had received a job offer. In fact, Jones's supervisor had not even returned the follow-up card to the employment office to verify that each applicant had shown up and been interviewed. Jones was starting to wonder if his HR process was too informal.

Purpose: The purpose of this exercise is to provide practice in analyzing and applying knowledge of equal opportunity legislation to a realistic problem.

Required Understanding: Be thoroughly familiar with the material presented in this chapter. In addition, read the "Too Informal?" case on which this experiential exercise is based.

How to Set Up the Exercise/Instructions:

1. Divide the class into groups of four or five students.
2. Each group should develop answers to the following questions:
   a. How could the EEOC prove adverse impact?
   b. Cite specific discriminatory personnel practices at Dan Jones's company.
   c. How could Jones's company defend itself against the allegations of discriminatory practice?
   d. Did Dan Jones rely on a discriminatory recruitment practice to hire individuals? If so, what discriminatory recruitment practice did he use, and why is it discriminatory?
3. If time permits, a spokesperson from each group can present his or her group's findings. Would it make sense for this company to try to defend itself against the discrimination allegations?

APPLICATION CASE *A Case of Racial Discrimination?*

John Peters (not his real name) was a 44-year-old cardiologist on the staff of a teaching hospital in a large city in the southeastern United States. Happily married with two teenage children, he had served with distinction for many years at this same hospital, and in fact served his residency there after graduating from Columbia University's medical school.

Alana Anderson (not her real name) was an attractive African American registered nurse on the staff at the same hospital with Peters. Unmarried and without children, she lived in a hospital-owned apartment on the hospital grounds and devoted almost all her time to her work at the hospital or to taking additional coursework to further improve her already excellent nursing skills.

The hospital's chief administrator, Gary Chapman, took enormous pride in what he called the extraordinary professionalism of the doctors, nurses, and other staff members at his hospital. Although he took a number of rudimentary steps to guard against blatant violations of equal employment opportunity laws, he believed that most of the professionals on his staff were so highly trained and committed to the highest professional standards that "they would always do the right thing," as he put it.

Chapman was therefore upset to receive a phone call from Peters, informing him that Anderson had (in Peters's eyes) "developed an unwholesome personal attraction" to him and was bombarding the doctor with Valentine's Day cards, affectionate personal notes, and phone calls—often to the doctor's home. Concerned about hospital decorum and the possibility that Peters was being sexually harassed, Chapman met privately with Anderson. He explained that Peters was very uncomfortable with the personal attention she was showing to him, and asked that she please not continue to exhibit her show of affection for the doctor.

Chapman assumed that the matter was over. Several weeks later, when Anderson resigned her position at the hospital, Chapman didn't think much of it. He was therefore shocked and dismayed to receive a registered letter from a local attorney, informing him that both the hospital and Peters and Chapman personally were being sued by Anderson for racial discrimination: Her claim was that Chapman, in their private meeting, had told her, "We don't think it's right for people of different races to pursue each other romantically at this hospital." According to the lawyer, his preliminary research had unearthed several other alleged incidents at the hospital that apparently supported the idea that racial discrimination at the hospital was widespread.

Questions

1. What do you think of the way Chapman handled the accusations from Peters and his conversation with Anderson? How would you have handled them?
2. Do you think Peters had the basis for a sexual harassment claim against Anderson? Why or why not?
3. What would you do now if you were Chapman to avoid further incidents of this type?

CONTINUING CASE: LearnInMotion.com *A Question of Discrimination*

One of the problems LearnInMotion's Jennifer and Mel faced concerned the inadequacies of the firm's current personnel management practices and procedures. The previous year had been a swirl of activity—creating and testing the business model, launching the site, writing and rewriting the business plan, and finally getting venture funding. And, it would be accurate to say that in all that time, they put absolutely no time into employee manuals, personnel policies, or HR-related matters. Even the 25-page business plan was of no help in this regard. The plan provided considerable detail regarding budgetary projections, competition, market growth, and business strategy. However, it was silent when it came to HR, except for containing short bios of the current employees, and projections of the types of positions that would have to be staffed in the first two years.

Almost from the beginning, it was apparent to both of them that they were "out of our depth" (as Mel put it) when it came to the letter and spirit of equal employment opportunity laws. Having both been through business school, they were familiar with the general requirements, such as not asking applicants their ages. However, those general guidelines weren't always easy to translate into practice during the actual applicant interviews. Two incidents particularly concerned them. One of the applicants for a sales position was in his 50s, which made him about twice as old as any other applicant. While Mel didn't mean to be discriminatory, he found himself asking this candidate questions such as "Do you think you'll be able to get up to speed selling an Internet product?" and "You know, we'll be working very long hours here; are you up to that?"—questions that he did not ask of other, younger candidates. There was also a problem with a candidate for the other, content manager, position. This person had been incarcerated for a substance abuse problem several years before. Mel asked him several questions about this, as well as whether he was now "clean" or "under any sort of treatment." Jennifer thought questions like these were probably okay, but she wasn't sure.

There was also a disturbing incident in the office. There were already two content management employees, Ruth and Dan, whose job was to actually place the courses and other educational content on the Web site. Dan, along with Alex the Web surfer, occasionally used vulgarity—for instance, when referring to the problems the firm was having getting the computer supplier to come to the office and repair a chronic problem with the firm's server. Mel's attitude was that "boys will be boys." However, Jennifer saw Ruth cringe several times when "the boys" were having one of these exchanges, and felt strongly that this behavior had to stop. However, she was not sure language like this constituted "a hostile environment" under the law, although she did feel that at a minimum it was uncivil. The two owners decided it

was time to institute and implement some HR policies that would ensure their company and its employees adhere to the letter and the spirit of the equal employment opportunity laws. Now they want you, their management consultants, to help them actually do it. Here's what they want you to do for them:

Questions and Assignments

1. Our company is in New York City. Given the fact that we now have only about five employees, and are only planning on hiring about three or four more, is our company in fact even covered by equal rights legislation? (Hint: Does the government's Web site provide any clues?)

2. Were we within our legal rights to ask the possibly age-related and substance-abuse-related questions? Why or why not?

3. Did Dan and Alex create a hostile environment for Ruth? Why or why not? How should we have handled this matter?

4. What have we been doing wrong up to now with respect to EEO-related matters, and how do you suggest we rectify the situation in the future?

Chapter 3

Job Analysis

After studying this chapter, you should be able to:

- Discuss the nature of job analysis, including what it is and how it's used.
- Use at least three methods of collecting job analysis information, including interviews, questionnaires, and observation.
- Write job descriptions, including summaries and job functions, using the Internet and traditional methods.
- Write job specifications using the Internet as well as your judgment.
- Explain job analysis in a "jobless" world, including what it means and how it's done in practice.

STRATEGIC OVERVIEW   Todd Berkley, U.S. Bank's new manager for sales support and customer retention, plays a strategic role at that bank. Concerned about the number of big customers who were closing their accounts and moving to competitors, U.S. Bank recently refocused its competitive strategy. It's now emphasizing identifying—and quickly eliminating—the customer service problems that are causing its customers to leave. But Todd has discovered that doing so has affected every aspect of the bank's HR policies and procedures. To make sure they emphasize customer service and deal with angry customers at once, HR had to write new job descriptions for employees ranging from teller to guard to vice president, to include their new service-related duties. And then, of course, the bank had to train these employees, and institute new hiring standards to recruit and hire service-oriented people to fill the new positions. All the firm's HR efforts had to support U.S. Bank's new customer service strategy if that strategy was to succeed.[1] And at U.S. Bank, that had to start with job analysis.

The EEOC issues we addressed in Chapter 2 usually first come into play when the firm turns to analyzing its jobs and writing its job descriptions. The main purpose of this chapter is to show you how to analyze a job and write job descriptions. We'll see that analyzing jobs involves determining in detail what the job entails and what kind of people the firm should hire for the job. We discuss several

techniques for analyzing jobs, and how to use the Internet and more traditional methods to draft job descriptions and job specifications. Then, in the following chapter, HR Planning and Recruiting, we'll turn to the methods managers use to actually find the employees they need. ■

THE NATURE OF JOB ANALYSIS

job analysis
The procedure for determining the duties and skill requirements of a job and the kind of person who should be hired for it.

job description
A list of a job's duties, responsibilities, reporting relationships, working conditions, and supervisory responsibilities—one product of a job analysis.

job specification
A list of a job's "human requirements," that is, the requisite education, skills, personality, and so on—another product of a job analysis.

Organizations consist of positions that have to be staffed. **Job analysis** is the procedure through which you determine the duties of these positions and the characteristics of the people to hire for them.[2] Job analysis produces information used for writing **job descriptions** (a list of what the job entails) and **job specifications** (what kind of people to hire for the job).

The supervisor or HR specialist normally collects one or more of the following types of information via the job analysis:[3]

- *Work activities*. First, he or she collects information about the job's actual work activities, such as cleaning, selling, teaching, or painting. This list may also include how, why, and when the worker performs each activity.
- *Human behaviors*. The specialist may also collect information about human behaviors like sensing, communicating, deciding, and writing. Included here would be information regarding job demands such as lifting weights or walking long distances.
- *Machines, tools, equipment, and work aids*. This category includes information regarding tools used, materials processed, knowledge dealt with or applied (such as finance or law), and services rendered (such as counseling or repairing).
- *Performance standards*. The employer may also want information about the job's performance standards (in terms of quantity or quality levels for each job duty, for instance). Management will use these standards to appraise employees.
- *Job context*. Included here is information about such matters as physical working conditions, work schedule, and the organizational and social context—for instance, the number of people with whom the employee would normally interact. Information regarding incentives might also be included here.
- *Human requirements*. This includes information regarding the job's human requirements, such as job-related knowledge or skills (education, training, work experience) and required personal attributes (aptitudes, physical characteristics, personality, interests).

Uses of Job Analysis Information

As summarized in Figure 3-1, job analysis information is the basis for several interrelated HR management activities.

Recruitment and Selection Job analysis provides information about what the job entails and what human characteristics are required to perform these activities. This information, in the form of job descriptions and specifications, helps management decide what sort of people to recruit and hire.

Compensation Job analysis information is crucial for estimating the value of each job and its appropriate compensation. Compensation (such as salary and bonus) usually depends on the job's required skill and education level, safety hazards, degree of responsibility, and so on—all factors you can assess through job analy-

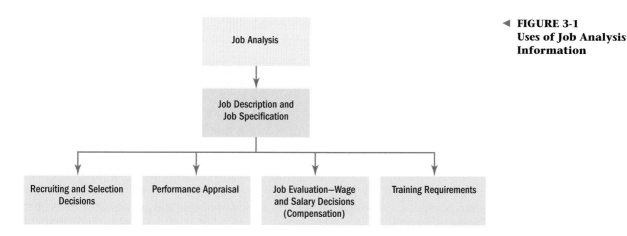

sis. Furthermore, many employers group jobs into classes (say, secretary III and IV). Job analysis provides the information to determine the relative worth of each job—and thus its appropriate class.

Performance Appraisal A performance appraisal compares each employee's actual performance with his or her performance standards. Managers use job analysis to determine the job's specific activities and performance standards.

Training The job description should show the activities and skills—and therefore the training—that the job requires.

Discovering Unassigned Duties Job analysis can also help reveal unassigned duties. For example, your company's production manager says she's responsible for a dozen or so duties, such as production scheduling and raw material purchasing. Missing, however, is any reference to managing raw material inventories. On further study, you learn that none of the other manufacturing people are responsible for inventory management, either. You know from your review of other jobs like these that someone should be managing inventories. You've uncovered an essential unassigned duty, thanks to job analysis.

EEO Compliance Job analysis also plays a big role in EEO compliance. U.S. Federal Agencies' Uniform Guidelines on Employee Selection stipulate that job analysis is a crucial step in validating all major personnel activities.[4] For example, employers must be able to show that their selection criteria and job performance are actually related. Doing this, of course, requires knowing what the job entails—which in turn requires a job analysis.

Steps in Job Analysis

There are six steps in doing a job analysis. Let's look at each of them.

Step 1 Decide how you'll use the information, since this will determine the data you collect and how you collect them. Some data collection techniques—like interviewing the employee and asking what the job entails—are good for writing job descriptions and selecting employees for the job. Other techniques, like the position analysis questionnaire described later, do not provide qualitative information for job descriptions. Instead, they provide numerical ratings for each job; these can be used to compare jobs for compensation purposes.

Step 2 Review relevant background information such as organization charts, process charts, and job descriptions.[5] **Organization charts** show the organizationwide division of work, how the job in question relates to other jobs, and where the job fits in the overall organization. The chart should show the title of each position and, by means of interconnecting lines, who reports to whom and with whom the job incumbent communicates.

A **process chart** provides a more detailed picture of the work flow. In its simplest form a process chart (like that in Figure 3-2) shows the flow of inputs to and outputs from the job you're analyzing. (In Figure 3-2 the inventory control clerk is expected to receive inventory from suppliers, take requests for inventory from the two plant managers, provide requested inventory to these managers, and give information to these managers on the status of in-stock inventories.) Finally, the existing job description, if there is one, usually provides a starting point for building the revised job description.

Step 3 Select representative positions. Why? Because there may be too many similar jobs to analyze. For example, it is usually unnecessary to analyze the jobs of 200 assembly workers when a sample of 10 jobs will do.

Step 4 Actually analyze the job—by collecting data on job activities, required employee behaviors, working conditions, and human traits and abilities needed to perform the job. For this step, use one or more of the job analysis methods explained later in this chapter.

Step 5 Verify the job analysis information with the worker performing the job and with his or her immediate supervisor. This will help confirm that the information is factually correct and complete. This review can also help gain the employee's acceptance of the job analysis data and conclusions, by giving that person a chance to review and modify your description of the job activities.

Step 6 Develop a job description and job specification. These are two tangible products of the job analysis. The *job description* (to repeat) is a written statement that describes the activities and responsibilities of the job, as well as its important features, such as working conditions and safety hazards. The *job specification* summarizes the personal qualities, traits, skills, and background required for getting the job done. It may be in a separate document or in the same document as the job description.

organization chart
A chart that shows the organizationwide distribution of work, with titles of each position and interconnecting lines that show who reports to and communicates with whom.

process chart
A work flow chart that shows the flow of inputs to and outputs from a particular job.

▶ **FIGURE 3-2**
Process Chart for Analyzing a Job's Work Flow

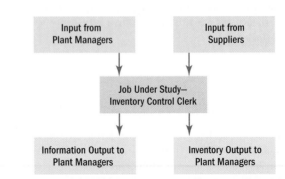

Source: Richard J. Henderson, *Compensation Management: Rewarding Performance*, 2nd ed., 1985, p. 158. Reprinted by permission of Prentice Hall, Upper Saddle River, N.J.

METHODS OF COLLECTING JOB ANALYSIS INFORMATION

There are various ways to collect information on the duties, responsibilities, and activities of a job, and we'll discuss the most important ones in this section. In practice, you could use any one of them, or you could combine the techniques that best fit your purpose. Thus, an interview might be appropriate for creating a job description, whereas the position analysis questionnaire may be more appropriate for quantifying the worth of a job for compensation purposes.

Conducting the job analysis usually involves a joint effort by an HR specialist, the worker, and the worker's supervisor. The HR specialist (perhaps an HR manager, job analyst, or consultant) might observe and analyze the job and then develop a job description and specification. The supervisor and worker may fill out questionnaires listing the subordinate's activities. The supervisor and worker may then review and verify the job analyst's conclusions regarding the job's activities and duties.

In practice, firms usually collect job analysis data from multiple "subject matter experts" (mostly job incumbents) using questionnaires and interviews. They then average data from several employees from different departments to determine how much time a typical employee spends on each of several specific tasks. The problem is that employees who have the same job title but work in different departments may experience very different pressures. Therefore, simply adding up and averaging the amount of time that, say, HR assistants need to devote to "interviewing candidates" could end in misleading results. The point is that you must understand the job's departmental context: The way someone with a particular job title spends his or her time is not necessarily the same from department to department.

Interviews, questionnaires, observations, and diary/logs are the most popular methods for gathering job analysis data. They all provide realistic information about what job incumbents actually do. Managers use them for developing job descriptions and job specifications.

The Interview

Managers use three types of interviews to collect job analysis data—individual interviews with each employee, group interviews with groups of employees who have the same job, and supervisor interviews with one or more supervisors who know the job. They use group interviews when a large number of employees are performing similar or identical work, since it can be a quick and inexpensive way to gather information. As a rule, the workers' immediate supervisor attends the group session; if not, you can interview the supervisor separately to get that person's perspective on the job's duties and responsibilities.

Whichever kind of interview you use, you need to be sure the interviewee fully understands the reason for the interview, since there's a tendency for such interviews to be viewed, rightly or wrongly, as "efficiency evaluations." If so, interviewees may hesitate to describe their jobs accurately.

Pros and Cons The interview is probably the most widely used method for identifying a job's duties and responsibilities, and its wide use reflects its advantages. It's a relatively simple and quick way to collect information, including information that might never appear on a written form. A skilled interviewer can unearth important activities that occur only occasionally, or informal contacts that wouldn't be obvious from the organization chart. The interview also provides an opportunity to explain the need for and functions of the job analysis. And the employee can vent frustrations that might otherwise go unnoticed by management.

▲ *The job analysis process begins when the analyst collects information from the worker and supervisor about the nature of the work and the specific tasks the worker does.*

Distortion of information is the main problem—whether due to outright falsification or honest misunderstanding.[6] Job analysis is often a prelude to changing a job's pay rate. Employees therefore may legitimately view the interview as an efficiency evaluation that may affect their pay. They may then tend to exaggerate certain responsibilities while minimizing others. Obtaining valid information can thus be a slow process, and prudent analysts get multiple inputs.

Typical Questions Despite their drawbacks, interviews are widely used. Some typical interview questions include:

What is the job being performed?

What are the major duties of your position? What exactly do you do?

What physical locations do you work in?

What are the education, experience, skill, and [where applicable] certification and licensing requirements?

In what activities do you participate?

What are the job's responsibilities and duties?

What are the basic accountabilities or performance standards that typify your work?

What are your responsibilities? What are the environmental and working conditions involved?

What are the job's physical demands? The emotional and mental demands?

What are the health and safety conditions?

Are you exposed to any hazards or unusual working conditions?

The best interviews follow structured or checklist formats. Figure 3-3 presents one example—a job analysis questionnaire. It includes a series of detailed questions regarding matters like the general purpose of the job; supervisory responsibilities; job duties; and education, experience, and skills required. Of course, structured lists are not just for interviewers: Job analysts who collect information by personally observing the work or by using questionnaires—two methods explained below—can also use lists like these.[7]

Interview Guidelines Keep several things in mind when conducting a job analysis interview. First, the job analyst and supervisor should work together to identify the workers who know the job best—and preferably those who'll be most objective in describing their duties and responsibilities.

Second, quickly establish rapport with the interviewee. Know the person's name, speak in easily understood language, briefly review the interview's purpose, and explain how the person was chosen for the interview.

Third, follow a structured guide or checklist, one that lists questions and provides space for answers. This ensures you'll identify crucial questions ahead of time and that all interviewers (if there's more than one) cover all the required questions. (However, also make sure to give the worker some leeway in answering questions, and provide some open-ended questions like, "Was there anything we didn't cover with our questions?")

Fourth, when duties are not performed in a regular manner—for instance, when the worker doesn't perform the same job over and over again many times a day—ask the worker to list his or her duties in order of importance and frequency of occurrence. This will ensure that you don't overlook crucial but infrequently performed activities—like a nurse's occasional emergency room duties.

Finally, after completing the interview, review and verify the data. Specifically, review the information with the worker's immediate supervisor and with the interviewee.

Job Analysis Information Sheet

Job Title_____ Date _____

Job Code_____ Dept. _____

Superior's Title _____

Hours worked _____ AM to _____ PM

Job Analyst's Name _____

1. **What is the job's overall purpose?**
_____

2. **If the incumbent supervises others,** list them by job title; if there is more than one employee with the same title, put the number in parentheses following.
_____

3. **Check those activities** that are part of the incumbent's supervisory duties.
☐ Training
☐ Performance Appraisal
☐ Inspecting work
☐ Budgeting
☐ Coaching and/or counseling
☐ Others (please specify) _____

4. **Describe the type and extent of supervision** received by the incumbent.
_____

5. **JOB DUTIES:** Describe briefly WHAT the incumbent does and, if possible, HOW he/she does it. Include duties in the following categories:

   a. daily duties (those performed on a regular basis every day or almost every day)
   _____

   b. periodic duties (those performed weekly, monthly, quarterly, or at other regular intervals)
   _____

   c. duties performed at irregular intervals
   _____

6. Is the incumbent performing duties he/she considers unnecessary? If so, describe.
_____

7. Is the incumbent performing duties not presently included in the job description? If so, describe.
_____

8. EDUCATION: Check the box that indicates the educational requirements for the job (not the educational background of the incumbent).

   ☐ No formal education required   ☐ Eighth grade education

   ☐ High school diploma (or equivalent)   ☐ 2-year college degree (or equivalent)

   ☐ 4-year college degree (or equivalent)   ☐ Graduate work or advanced degree
   (specify)

   ☐ Professional license (specify)

Source: www.hrnext.com, accessed July 28, 2001.   *(Continued)*

► **FIGURE 3-3**
Job Analysis Questionnaire for Developing Job Descriptions

Use a questionnaire like this to interview job incumbents, or have them fill it out.

► **FIGURE 3-3**
(Continued)

9. **EXPERIENCE:** Check the amount of experience needed to perform the job.

    ☐ None   ☐ Less than one month

    ☐ One to six months   ☐ Six months to one year

    ☐ One to three years   ☐ Three to five years

    ☐ Five to ten years   ☐ More than ten years

10. **LOCATION:** Check location of job and, if necessary or appropriate, describe briefly.

    ☐ Outdoor   ☐ Indoor

    ☐ Underground   ☐ Pit

    ☐ Scaffold   ☐ Other (specify)

11. **ENVIRONMENTAL CONDITIONS:** Check any objectionable conditions found on the job and note afterward how frequently each is encountered (rarely, occasionally, constantly, etc.)

    ☐ Dirt   ☐ Dust

    ☐ Heat   ☐ Cold

    ☐ Noise   ☐ Fumes

    ☐ Odors   ☐ Wetness/humidity

    ☐ Vibration   ☐ Sudden temperature changes

    ☐ Darkness or poor lighting   ☐ Other (specify)

12. **HEALTH AND SAFETY:** Check any undesirable health and safety conditions under which the incumbent must perform and note how often they are encountered.

    ☐ Elevated workplace   ☐ Mechanical hazards

    ☐ Explosives   ☐ Electrical hazards

    ☐ Fire hazards   ☐ Radiation

    ☐ Other (specify)

13. **MACHINES, TOOLS, EQUIPMENT, AND WORK AIDS:** Describe briefly what machines, tools, equipment, or work aids the incumbent works with on a regular basis:

_____

14. Have concrete work standards been established (errors allowed, time taken for a particular task, etc.)? If so, what are they?

_____

15. Are there any personal attributes (special aptitudes, physical characteristics, personality traits, etc.) required by the job?

_____

16. Are there any exceptional problems the incumbent might be expected to encounter in performing the job under normal conditions? If so, describe.

_____

17. Describe the successful completion and/or end results of the job.

_____

18. What is the seriousness of error on this job? Who or what is affected by errors the incumbent makes?

_____

19. To what job would a successful incumbent expect to be promoted?

[**Note:** this form is obviously slanted toward a manufacturing environment, but it can be adapted quite easily to fit a number of different types of jobs.]

Questionnaires

Having employees fill out questionnaires to describe their job-related duties and responsibilities is another good way to obtain job analysis information.

You have to decide how structured the questionnaire should be and what questions to include. Some questionnaires are very structured checklists. Each employee gets an inventory of perhaps hundreds of specific duties or tasks (such as "change and splice wire"). He or she is asked to indicate whether or not he or she performs each task and, if so, how much time is normally spent on each. At the other extreme the questionnaire can be open-ended and simply ask the employee to "describe the major duties of your job." In practice, the best questionnaire often falls between these two extremes. As illustrated in Figure 3-3, a typical job analysis questionnaire might have several open-ended questions (such as "state your main job duties") as well as structured questions (concerning, for instance, previous experience required).

Whether structured or unstructured, questionnaires have both pros and cons. A questionnaire is a quick and efficient way to obtain information from a large number of employees; it's less costly than interviewing hundreds of workers, for instance. However, developing the questionnaire and testing it (perhaps by making sure the workers understand the questions) can be expensive and time consuming.

Observation

Direct observation is especially useful when jobs consist mainly of observable physical activities—assembly-line worker and accounting clerk are examples. On the other hand, observation is usually not appropriate when the job entails a lot of mental activity (lawyer, design engineer). Nor is it useful if the employee only occasionally engages in important activities, such as a nurse who handles emergencies. And *reactivity*—the worker's changing what he or she normally does because you are watching—can also be a problem.

Managers often use direct observation and interviewing together. One approach is to observe the worker on the job during a complete work cycle. (The *cycle* is the time it takes to complete the job; it could be a minute for an assembly-line worker or an hour, a day, or longer for complex jobs.) Here you take notes of all the job activities. Then, after accumulating as much information as possible, you interview the worker. Ask the person to clarify points not understood and to explain what other activities he or she performs that you didn't observe. You can also observe and interview simultaneously, asking questions while the worker performs his or her job.

Participant Diary/Logs

Another approach is to ask workers to keep a **diary/log** of what they do during the day. For every activity he or she engages in, the employee records the activity (along with the time) in a log. This can produce a very complete picture of the job, especially when supplemented with subsequent interviews with the worker and the supervisor. The employee, of course, might try to exaggerate some activities and underplay others. However, the detailed, chronological nature of the log tends to mediate against this.

Some firms take a high-tech approach to diary/logs. They give employees pocket dictating machines and pagers. Then at random times during the day, they page the workers, who dictate what they are doing at that time. This approach can avoid one pitfall of the traditional diary/log method: relying on workers to remember what they did hours earlier when they complete their logs at the end of the day.

diary/logs
Daily listings made by workers of every activity in which they engage along with the time each activity takes.

Quantitative Job Analysis Techniques

Qualitative approaches like interviews and questionnaires are not always suitable. For example, if your aim is to compare jobs for pay purposes, you may want to be able to assign quantitative values to each job. The position analysis questionnaire, the Department of Labor approach, and functional job analysis are three popular quantitative methods.

position analysis questionnaire (PAQ)
A questionnaire used to collect quantifiable data concerning the duties and responsibilities of various jobs.

Position Analysis Questionnaire The **position analysis questionnaire (PAQ)** is a very structured job analysis questionnaire.[8] The PAQ contains 194 items, each of which (such as "written materials") represents a basic element that may or may not play an important role in the job. The job analyst decides if each item plays a role and, if so, to what extent. In Figure 3-4, for example, "written materials" received a rating of 4, indicating that written materials (like books, reports, and office notes) play a considerable role in this job. The analyst can do this online; see www.paq.com.

The advantage of the PAQ is that it provides a quantitative score or profile of any job in terms of how that job rates on five basic activities: (1) having decision-making/communication/social responsibilities, (2) performing skilled activities, (3) being physically active, (4) operating vehicles/equipment, and (5) processing information. The PAQ's real strength is thus in classifying jobs. In other words, it lets you assign a quantitative score to each job based on its decision-making, skilled activity, physical activity, vehicle/equipment operation, and information-processing characteristics. You can therefore use the PAQ results to quantitatively compare jobs to one another,[9] and then assign pay levels for each job.[10]

Department of Labor job analysis procedure
Standardized method for rating, classifying, and comparing virtually every kind of job based on data, people, and things.

Department of Labor (DOL) Procedure The **U.S. Department of Labor (DOL) job analysis procedure** also provides a standardized method by which different jobs can be quantitatively rated, classified, and compared. The heart of this analysis is a data, people, and things rating for each job.

Here's how the procedure works. As Table 3-1 (on page 70) shows, a set of basic activities called *worker functions* describes what a worker can do with respect to data, people, and things. With respect to data, for instance, the basic functions include synthesizing, coordinating, and copying. With respect to people, they include mentoring, negotiating, and supervising. With respect to things, the basic functions include manipulating, tending, and handling.

Note also that each worker function gets an importance level. Thus, "coordinating" is 1, whereas "copying" is 5. If you were analyzing the job of a receptionist/clerk, for example, you might label the job 5, 6, 7, which would represent copying data, speaking—signaling people, and handling things. On the other hand, you might code a psychiatric aide in a hospital 1, 7, 5 in relation to data, people, and things. In practice, you would analyze each task that the worker performed in terms of data, people, and things. Then the highest combination (say 4, 6, 5) would be used to identify the job, since this is the highest level that a job incumbent would be expected to attain.

As illustrated in Figure 3-5 (on page 70) the schedule produced from the DOL procedure contains several types of information. The job title, in this case dough mixer in a bakery, is listed first. Also listed are the industry in which this job is found and the industry's standard industrial classification code. There is a one- or two-sentence summary of the job, and the worker function ratings for data, people, and things—in this case 5, 6, 2. These numbers mean that in terms of difficulty, a dough mixer copies data, speaks/signals with people, and operates/controls with respect to things. Finally, the schedule specifies the

INFORMATION INPUT

1 INFORMATION INPUT

	Extent of Use (U)
NA	Does not apply
1	Nominal/very infrequent
2	Occasional
3	Moderate
4	Considerable
5	Very substantial

1.1 Sources of Job Information

Rate each of the following items in terms of the extent to which it is used by the worker as a source of information in performing his job.

1.1.1 Visual Sources of Job Information

1 | 4 Written materials (books, reports, office notes, articles, job instructions, signs, etc.)

2 | 2 Quantitative materials (materials which deal with quantities or amounts, such as graphs, accounts, specifications, tables of numbers, etc.)

3 | 1 Pictorial materials (pictures or picturelike materials used as *sources* of information, for example, drawings, blueprints, diagrams, maps, tracings, photographic films, x-ray films, TV pictures, etc.)

4 | 1 Patterns/related devices (templates, stencils, patterns, etc., used as *sources* of information when *observed* during use; do *not* include here materials described in item 3 above)

5 | 2 Visual displays (dials, gauges, signal lights, radarscopes, speedometers, clocks, etc.)

6 | 5 Measuring devices (rulers, calipers, tire pressure gauges, scales, thickness gauges, pipettes, thermometers, protractors, etc., used to obtain visual information about physical measurements; do *not* include here devices described in item 5 above)

7 | 4 Mechanical devices (tools, equipment, machinery, and other mechanical devices which are *sources* of information when *observed* during use or operation)

8 | 3 Materials in process (parts, materials, objects, etc., which are *sources* of information when being modified, worked on, or otherwise processed, such as bread dough being mixed, workpiece being turned in a lathe, fabric being cut, shoe being resoled, etc.)

9 | 4 Materials *not* in process (parts, materials, objects, etc., not in the process of being changed or modified, which are *sources* of information when being inspected, handled, packaged, distributed, or selected, etc., such as items or materials in inventory, storage, or distribution channels, items being inspected, etc.)

10 | 3 Features of nature (landscapes, fields, geological samples, vegetation, cloud formations, and other features of nature which are observed or inspected to provide information)

11 | 2 Man-made features of environment (structures, buildings, dams, highways, bridges, docks, railroads, and other "man-made" or altered aspects of the indoor or outdoor environment which are *observed* or *inspected* to provide job information; do not consider equipment, machines, etc., that an individual uses in his work, as covered by item 7)

◀ **FIGURE 3-4**
Portions of a Completed Page from the Position Analysis Questionnaire

Note: The 194 PAQ elements are grouped into six dimensions. This exhibits 11 of the "information input" questions or elements. Other PAQ pages contain questions regarding mental processes, work output, relationships with others, job context, and other job characteristics.

Source: E. J. McCormick, P. R. Jeanneret, and R. D. Mecham, *Position Analysis Questionnaire*. Copyright 1989 by Purdue Research Foundation, West Lafayette, IN. Reprinted with permission.

▶ **TABLE 3-1**
Basic Department of
Labor Worker
Functions

	Data	People	Things
Basic Activities	0 Synthesizing	0 Mentoring	0 Setting up
	1 Coordinating	1 Negotiating	1 Precision working
	2 Analyzing	2 Instructing	2 Operating/controlling
	3 Compiling	3 Supervising	
	4 Computing	4 Diverting	3 Driving/operating
	5 Copying	5 Persuading	4 Manipulating
	6 Comparing	6 Speaking/signaling	5 Tending
		7 Serving	6 Feeding/offbearing
		8 Taking instructions/helping	7 Handling

Note: Determine employee's job "score" on data, people, and things by observing his or her job and determining, for each of the three categories, which of the basic functions illustrates the person's job. "0" is high; "6," "8," and "7" are lows in each column.

human requirements of the job, for instance, in terms of training time required, aptitudes, temperaments. As you can see, each job ends up with a numerical score (such as 5, 6, 2). You can thus group together (and assign the same pay to) all jobs with similar scores, even for very different jobs like job dough mixer and mechanic's helper.

▶ **FIGURE 3-5**
Sample Report Based
on Department of
Labor Job Analysis
Technique

JOB ANALYSIS SCHEDULE

1. Established Job Title _____ DOUGH MIXER _____

2. Ind. Assign _____ (bake prod.) _____

3. SIC Code(s) and Title(s) _____ 2051 Bread and other bakery products _____

4. JOB SUMMARY:

Operates mixing machine to mix ingredients for straight and sponge (yeast) doughs according to established formulas, directs other workers in fermentation of dough, and curls dough into pieces with hand cutter.

5. WORK PERFORMED RATINGS:

	D	P	(T)
Worker Functions	Data	People	Things
	5	6	2

Work Field _____ Cooking, Food Preparing _____

6. WORKER TRAITS RATING: (To be filled in by analyst)

Training time required

Aptitudes

Temperaments

Interests

Physical Demands

Environment Conditions

Functional Job Analysis **Functional job analysis** is similar to the DOL method, but differs in two ways.[11] First, functional job analysis rates the job not just on data, people, and things, but also on four more dimensions: the extent to which specific instructions are necessary to perform the task; the extent to which reasoning and judgment are required to perform the task; the mathematical ability required to perform the task; and the verbal and language facilities required to perform the task. Second, functional job analysis also identifies performance standards and training requirements. It therefore lets you answer the question, "To do this task and meet these standards, what training does the worker require?"

You may find both the DOL and functional job analyses methods in use. However, analysts increasingly use other methods instead, including the U.S. government's online initiatives, which we'll discuss below.

> **functional job analysis**
> A method for classifying jobs similar to the DOL method, but additionally taking into account the extent to which instructions, reasoning, judgment, and mathematical and verbal ability are necessary for performing job tasks.

Using Multiple Sources of Information

There are obviously many ways to obtain job analysis information. You can get it from individual workers, groups, or supervisors; or from the observations of job analysts, for instance. You can use interviews, observations, or questionnaires. Some firms use just one basic approach, like having the job analyst do interviews with current job incumbents. Yet a recent study suggests that using just one source may not be wise.[12]

The problem is the potential inaccuracies in people's judgments. For example, in a group interview, some group members may feel forced to go along with the consensus of the group; or an employee may be careless about how he or she completes a questionnaire. What this means is that collecting job analysis data from just interviews, or just observations, may lead to inaccurate conclusions. It's better to try to avoid such inaccuracies by using several sources.[13] For example, where possible, collect job analysis data from several types of respondents—groups, individuals, observers, supervisors, and analysts; make sure the questions and surveys are clear and understandable to the respondents. And if possible, observe and question respondents early enough in the job analysis process to catch any problems while there's still time to correct them.

WRITING JOB DESCRIPTIONS

A job description is a written statement of what the worker actually does, how he or she does it, and what the job's working conditions are. You use this information to write a job specification; this lists the knowledge, abilities, and skills required to perform the job satisfactorily.

There is no standard format for writing a job description. However, most descriptions contain sections that cover:

1. Job identification
2. Job summary
3. Responsibilities and duties
4. Authority of incumbent
5. Standards of performance
6. Working conditions
7. Job specifications

Figures 3-6 and 3-7 present two sample forms of job descriptions.

OLEC CORP.
Job Description

Job Title: Marketing Manager
Department: Marketing
Reports To: President
FLSA Status: Non Exempt
Prepared By: Michael George
Prepared Date: April 1, 2002
Approved By: Ian Alexander
Approved Date: April 15, 2002

SUMMARY

Plans, directs, and coordinates the marketing of the organization's products and/or services by performing the following duties personally or through subordinate supervisors.

ESSENTIAL DUTIES AND RESPONSIBILITIES include the following. Other duties may be assigned.

Establishes marketing goals to ensure share of market and profitability of products and/or services.

Develops and executes marketing plans and programs, both short and long range, to ensure the profit growth and expansion of company products and/or services.

Researches, analyzes, and monitors financial, technological, and demographic factors so that market opportunities may be capitalized on and the effects of competitive activity may be minimized.

Plans and oversees the organization's advertising and promotion activities including print, electronic, and direct mail outlets.

Communicates with outside advertising agencies on ongoing campaigns.

Works with writers and artists and oversees copywriting, design, layout, pasteup, and production of promotional materials.

Develops and recommends pricing strategy for the organization which will result in the greatest share of the market over the long run.

Achieves satisfactory profit/loss ratio and share of market performance in relation to pre-set standards and to general and specific trends within the industry and the economy.

Ensures effective control of marketing results and that corrective action takes place to be certain that the achievement of marketing objectives are within designated budgets.

Evaluates market reactions to advertising programs, merchandising policy, and product packaging and formulation to ensure the timely adjustment of marketing strategy and plans to meet changing market and competitive conditions.

Recommends changes in basic structure and organization of marketing group to ensure the effective fulfillment of objectives assigned to it and provide the flexibility to move swiftly in relation to marketing problems and opportunities.

Conducts marketing surveys on current and new product concepts.

Prepares marketing activity reports.

SUPERVISORY RESPONSIBILITIES

Manages three subordinate supervisors who supervise a total of five employees in the Marketing Department. Is responsible for the overall direction, coordination, and evaluation of this unit. Also directly supervises two non-supervisory employees. Carries out supervisory responsibilities in accordance with the organization's policies and applicable laws. Responsibilities include interviewing, hiring, and training employees; planning, assigning, and directing work; appraising performance; rewarding and disciplining employees; addressing complaints and resolving problems.

QUALIFICATIONS

To perform this job successfully, an individual must be able to perform each essential duty satisfactorily. The requirements listed below are representative of the knowledge, skill, and/or ability required. Reasonable accommodations may be made to enable individuals with disabilities to perform the essential functions.

EDUCATION and/or EXPERIENCE

Master's degree (M.A.) or equivalent; or four to ten years related experience and/or training; or equivalent combination of education and experience.

LANGUAGE SKILLS

Ability to read, analyze, and interpret common scientific and technical journals, financial reports, and legal documents. Ability to respond to common inquiries or complaints from customers, regulatory agencies, or members of the business community. Ability to write speeches and articles for publication that conform to prescribed style and format. Ability to effectively present information to top management, public groups, and/or boards of directors.

MATHEMATICAL SKILLS

Ability to apply advanced mathematical concepts such as exponents, logarithms, quadratic equations, and permutations. Ability to apply mathematical operations to such tasks as frequency distribution, determination of test reliability and validity, analysis of variance, correlation techniques, sampling theory, and factor analysis.

REASONING ABILITY

Ability to define problems, collect data, establish facts, and draw valid conclusions. Ability to interpret an extensive variety of technical instructions in mathematical or diagram form.

◄ **FIGURE 3-7**
"Personnel Manager"
Description from
Dictionary of
Occupational Titles

> **166.117–018   MANAGER, PERSONNEL (profess. & kin.) alternate titles:**
>   **manager, human resources**
>
> Plans and carries out policies relating to all phases of personnel activity: Recruits, interviews, and selects employees to fill vacant positions. Plans and conducts new employee orientation to foster positive attitude toward company goals. Keeps record of insurance coverage, pension plan, and personnel transactions, such as hires, promotions, transfers, and terminations. Investigates accidents and prepares reports for insurance carrier. Conducts wage survey within labor market to determine competitive wage rate. Prepares budget of personnel operations. Meets with shop stewards and supervisors to resolve grievances. Writes separation notices for employees separating with cause and conducts exit interviews to determine reasons behind separations. Prepares reports and recommends procedures to reduce absenteeism and turnover. Represents company at personnel-related hearings and investigations. Contracts with outside suppliers to provide employee services, such as canteen, transportation, or relocation service. May prepare budget of personnel operations, using computer terminal. May administer manual and dexterity tests to applicants. May supervise clerical workers. May keep records of hired employee characteristics for governmental reporting purposes. May negotiate collective bargaining agreement with BUSINESS REPRESENTATIVE, LABOR UNION (profess. & kin.) *187.167–018. GOE: 11.05.02 STRENGTH: S GED: R5 M5 L5 SVP: 8 DLU: 88*

Source: Dictionary of Occupational Titles, 4th ed. (Washington, DC: U.S. Department of Labor, Employment Training Administration, U.S. Employment Service, 1991).

Job Identification

As in Figure 3-6 , the job identification section contains several types of information.[14] The *job title* specifies the name of the job, such as supervisor of data processing operations, marketing manager, or inventory control clerk. The *FLSA status* section permits quick identification of the job as exempt or nonexempt. (Under the Fair Labor Standards Act, certain positions, primarily administrative and professional, are exempt from the act's overtime and minimum wage provisions.) *Date* is the date the job description was actually written, and *prepared by* indicates who wrote it.

There is also space to indicate who approved the description and perhaps a space that shows the location of the job in terms of its plant/division and department/section. This section might also include the immediate supervisor's title and information regarding salary and/or pay scale. There might also be space for the grade/level of the job, if there is such a category. For example, a firm may classify programmers as programmer II, programmer III, and so on.

Job Summary

The job summary should describe the general nature of the job, and includes only its major functions or activities. Thus (in Figure 3-6), the marketing manager "Plans, directs, and coordinates the marketing of the organizations products and/or services." For the job of materials manager, the summary might state that the "materials manager purchases economically, regulates deliveries of, stores, and distributes all material necessary on the production line." For the job of mailroom supervisor, "the mailroom supervisor receives, sorts, and delivers all incoming mail properly, and he or she handles all outgoing mail including the accurate and timely posting of such mail."[15]

Include general statements like "performs other assignments as required" with care. Such statements can give supervisors more flexibility in assigning duties. Some experts, however, state unequivocally that "one item frequently found that should never be included in a job description is a 'cop-out clause' like 'other duties, as assigned,' "[16] since this leaves open the nature of the job—and the people needed to staff it.

Relationships

There is occasionally a relationships statement (not in the example), which shows the jobholder's relationships with others inside and outside the organization. For a human resource manager, such a statement might look like this:[17]

Reports to: Vice president of employee relations.

Supervises: Human resource clerk, test administrator, labor relations director, and one secretary.

Works with: All department managers and executive management.

Outside the company: Employment agencies, executive recruiting firms, union representatives, state and federal employment offices, and various vendors.[18]

Responsibilities and Duties

This section presents a list of the job's major responsibilities and duties. As in Figure 3-6, list each of the job's major duties separately, and describe it in a few sentences. In the figure, for instance, the duties include "establishes marketing goals to ensure share of market," "develops and executes marketing plans and programs," "communicates with outside advertising agencies," and "develops and recommends pricing strategy." Typical duties for other jobs might include maintaining balanced and controlled inventories, making accurate postings to accounts payable, maintaining favorable purchase price variances, and repairing production-line tools and equipment.

You can use the Department of Labor's *Dictionary of Occupational Titles* here for itemizing the job's duties and responsibilities. Take the HR manager's duties, as shown in Figure 3-7. These duties include "plans and carries out policies relating to all phases of personnel activity"; "recruits, interviews, and selects employees to fill vacant positions"; and "conducts wage surveys within labor markets to determine competitive wage rate."

This section should also define the limits of the jobholder's authority, including his or her decision-making authority, direct supervision of other personnel, and budgetary limitations. For example, the jobholder might have authority to approve purchase requests up to $5,000, grant time off or leaves of absence, discipline department personnel, recommend salary increases, and interview and hire new employees.[19] You also need to comply with ADA regulations: See the New Workplace feature following.

▲ *Job analysis can help clarify the responsibilities and duties of newly created job positions, such as the job of Jules Polonetsky, chief privacy officer of the Internet firm DoubleClick. Some privacy experts suggest this position should include such duties as setting up a privacy committee, assessing privacy risks of all the firm's operations that utilize personal data, and developing a corporate privacy code. Here Mr. Polonetsky participates in a roundtable on privacy issues.*

THE NEW WORKPLACE

Congress enacted the Americans with Disabilities Act (ADA) to reduce or eliminate serious problems of discrimination against disabled individuals. Under the ADA, the individual must have the requisite skills, educational background, and experience to perform the job's essential functions. A job function is essential when it is the reason the position exists or when the function is so specialized that the firm hired the person doing the job for his or her expertise or ability to perform that particular function. If the disabled individual can't perform the job as currently structured, the employer is required to make a "reasonable accommodation," unless doing so would present an "undue hardship."

As we said earlier, the ADA does not require job descriptions, but it's probably advisable to have them. Virtually all ADA legal actions will revolve around the question, "What are the essential functions of the job?" Without a job description that lists such functions, it will be hard to convince a court that the functions were essential to the job. The corollary is that you should clearly identify the essential functions: don't just list them along with other duties on the description.

Essential job functions are the job duties that employees must be able to perform, with or without reasonable accommodation.[20] Is a function essential? Questions to ask include:

1. Does the position exist to perform that function?[21]
2. Are employees in the position actually required to perform the function?[22]
3. Is there a limited number of other employees available to perform the function?
4. What is the degree of expertise or skill required to perform the function?
5. What is the actual work experience of present or past employees in the job?
6. What is the amount of time an individual actually spends performing the function?
7. What are the consequences of not requiring the performance of the function?

Writing Job Descriptions That Comply with the ADA

Standards of Performance and Working Conditions

Some job descriptions contain a standards of performance section. This lists the standards the employee is expected to achieve under each of the job description's main duties and responsibilities.

Setting standards is never an easy matter. However, most managers soon learn that just telling subordinates to "do their best" doesn't provide enough guidance. One straightforward way of setting standards is to finish the statement: "I will be completely satisfied with your work when . . ." This sentence, if completed for each duty listed in the job description, should result in a usable set of performance standards.[23] Here are some examples:

Duty: Accurately Posting Accounts Payable

1. Post all invoices received within the same working day.
2. Route all invoices to proper department managers for approval no later than the day following receipt.
3. An average of no more than three posting errors per month.

Duty: Meeting Daily Production Schedule

1. Work group produces no less than 426 units per working day.
2. Next work station rejects no more than an average of 2% of units.
3. Weekly overtime does not exceed an average of 5%.

The job description may also list the working conditions involved on the job. These might include things like noise level, hazardous conditions, or heat.

Using the Internet for Writing Job Descriptions

Most employers probably still write their own job descriptions, but more are turning to the Internet. One site, www.jobdescription.com, illustrates why. The process is simple. Search by alphabetical title, keyword, category, or industry to find the desired job title. This leads you to a generic job description for that title—say, "Computers & EDP systems sales representative." You can then use the wizard to customize the generic description for this position. For example, you can add specific information about your organization, such as job title, job codes, department, and preparation date. And you can indicate whether the job has supervisory abilities, and choose from a number of possible desirable competencies and experience levels.

▲ **WEBNOTE**

Many employers are turning to Web sites that create customized job descriptions in a few simple clicks.

www.jobdescription.com

The U.S. Department of Labor's occupational information network, called O*NET, is another useful Web tool (you'll find it at www.doleta.gov/programs/onet). It's replacing the *Dictionary of Occupational Titles* as a source of occupational information. O*NET contains data adapted from preexisting sources, including the *Dictionary of Occupational Titles*. However, it is growing fast and adding new data about jobs in today's increasingly information-based economy. Built-in software allows users to see the most important characteristics of occupations, as well as the experience, education, and knowledge required to do each job well. Both the *Dictionary of Occupational Titles* and O*NET include the specific tasks associated with many occupations. O*NET also provides skills, including basic skills such as reading and writing, process skills such as critical thinking, and transferable skills such as persuasion and negotiation.

O*NET improves on the *Dictionary of Occupational Titles* in other ways. For example, an O*NET listing also includes information on worker requirements (required knowledge, for instance), occupation requirements (based on work activities such as compiling, coding, and categorizing data), and experience requirements (including education and job training). You can also check the job's labor market characteristics (such as employment projections and earnings data).[24] The Entrepreneurs + HR feature on page 79 shows you how to use O*NET.

WRITING JOB SPECIFICATIONS

The job specification takes the job description and answers the question, "What human traits and experience are required to do this job well?" It shows what kind of person to recruit and for what qualities that person should be tested. The job specification may be a section of the job description or a separate document entirely. Often—as in Figure 3-6—the employer presents it as part of the job description.[25]

Specifications for Trained Versus Untrained Personnel

Writing job specifications for trained employees is relatively straightforward. For example, suppose you want to fill a position for a bookkeeper (or counselor or programmer). In cases like these, your job specifications might focus mostly on traits like length of previous service, quality of relevant training, and previous job performance. Thus, it's usually not too difficult to determine the human requirements for placing already trained people on a job.

The problems are more complex when you're filling jobs with untrained people (with the intention of training them on the job). Here you must specify qualities such as physical traits, personality, interests, or sensory skills that imply some potential for performing or for being trained to do the job.

For example, suppose the job requires detailed manipulation in a circuit board assembly line. Here you might want to ensure that the person scores high on a test of finger dexterity. Your goal, in other words, is to identify those personal traits—those human requirements—that validly predict which candidates would do well on the job and which would not. Employers identify these human requirements through a subjective, judgmental approach or through statistical analysis. Let's examine both approaches in detail.

Specifications Based on Judgment

Most job specifications come from the educated guesses of people like supervisors and human resource managers. The basic procedure here is to ask, "What does it take in terms of education, intelligence, training, and the like to do this job well?"

There are several ways to get educated guesses or judgments. You could simply create them yourself, or you could choose them from the competencies listed in Web-based job descriptions like those at www.jobdescription.com. The typical job description there lists competencies like "Generates creative solutions" and "Manages difficult or emotional customer situations." O*NET online is another good option. Job listings there include complete descriptions of educational and other experience and skills required.

The *Dictionary of Occupational Titles* can also still be useful. For each job in the dictionary, job analysts and vocational counselors have made judgments regarding its human requirements. The dictionary assigns ratings and letters to human requirements or traits as follows: G (intelligence), V (verbal), N (numerical), S (spatial), P (perception), Q (clerical perception), K (motor coordination), F (finger dexterity), M (manual dexterity), E (eye-hand-foot coordination), and C (color discrimination). The ratings reflect the amount of each trait or ability possessed by people with different performance levels currently working on the job, based on the experts' judgments.

Use common sense when compiling a list of the job's human requirements. Certainly job-specific human traits like those unearthed through job analysis—manual dexterity, say, or educational level—are important. However, don't ignore the fact that some work behaviors may apply to almost any job (although they might not normally surface through a job analysis).

▲ *The job specifications for already trained candidates, such as the customer service operator shown here, should clearly indicate which skills, like computer literacy, are job requirements.*

◆ **RESEARCH INSIGHT** One researcher, for example, obtained supervisor ratings and other information from 18,000 employees in 42 different hourly entry-level jobs in predominantly retail settings.[26] Regardless of the job, here are the work behaviors (with examples) that he found to be "generic"—in other words, that seem to be important to all jobs:

Job-Related Behavior	Some Examples
Industriousness	Keeps working even when other employees are standing around talking; takes the initiative to find another task when finished with regular work.
Thoroughness	Cleans equipment thoroughly, creating a more attractive display; notices merchandise out of place and returns it to the proper area.
Schedule flexibility	Accepts schedule changes when necessary; offers to stay late when the store is extremely busy.
Attendance	Arrives at work on time; maintains good attendance.
Off-task behavior (reverse)	Uses store phones to make personal unauthorized calls; conducts personal business during work time; lets joking friends be a distraction and interruption to work.
Unruliness (reverse)	Threatens to bully another employee; refuses to take routine orders from supervisors; does not cooperate with other employees.
Theft (reverse)	(As a cashier) Underrings the price of merchandise for a friend; cheats on reporting time worked; allows nonemployees in unauthorized areas.
Drug misuse (reverse)	Drinks alcohol or takes drugs on company property; comes to work under the influence of alcohol or drugs.

Perhaps the bigger challenge is to make sure that in doing the job analysis, you don't miss the forest for the trees. Consider a recent study of 50 testing engineers at a Volvo plant in Sweden. When asked what determined job competence for a testing engineer, most of the engineers focused on traditional criteria such as "to make the engine perform according to specifications." But the most effective testing engineers defined the job's main task differently: "to make sure the engine provides a customer with a good driving experience." As a result, these engineers went about their jobs testing and tuning the engines "not as engineers trying to hit a number, but as ordinary drivers—imagining themselves as seniors, students, commuters, or vacationers." This subgroup of the testing engineers worked hard to develop their knowledge of customers' driving needs, even when it meant reaching out to people outside their own group, such as designers or marketers.

The point, says the researcher, is that "if people don't recognize or value the attributes that really determine success, how easy will it be for them to acquire those attributes?" Employers should therefore "shift the focus of their recruitment and training programs from flawed attribute checklists toward identifying and, if necessary, changing people's understanding of what jobs entail." In other words, in developing the job description and job specification, make sure you really understand the reason for the job and therefore the skills a person actually needs to be competent at it.[27]

Specifications Based on Statistical Analysis

Basing job specifications on statistical analysis is the more defensible approach, but it's also more difficult. The aim here is to determine statistically the relationship between (1) some predictor or human trait, such as height, intelligence, or finger dexterity, and (2) some indicator or criterion of job effectiveness, such as performance as rated by the supervisor. The procedure has five steps: (1) analyze the job and decide how to measure job performance; (2) select personal traits like finger dexterity that you believe should predict successful performance; (3) test candidates for these traits; (4) measure these candidates' subsequent job performance; and (5) statistically analyze the relationship between the human trait (finger dexterity) and job performance. Your objective is to determine whether the former predicts the latter.

This method is more defensible than the judgmental approach because equal rights legislation forbids using traits that you can't prove distinguish between high and low job performers. Hiring standards that discriminate based on sex, race, religion, national origin, or age may have to be shown to predict job performance. Ideally, this is done with a statistical validation study.

ENTREPRENEURS HR

A Practical Job Analysis Approach

Without their own job analysts or (in many cases) HR managers, many small-business owners face two hurdles when doing job analyses and job descriptions. First, they often need a more streamlined approach than those provided by questionnaires like the one shown in Figure 3-3. Second, there is always the reasonable fear that in writing their job descriptions, they will overlook duties that subordinates should be assigned, or assign duties not usually associated with such positions. What they need is an encyclopedia listing all the possible positions they might encounter, including a detailed listing of the duties normally assigned to these positions.

Help is at hand: The small-business owner has at least three options. The *Dictionary of Occupational Titles*, mentioned earlier, provides detailed descriptions of thousands of jobs and their human requirements. Web sites like www.jobdescription.com provide customizable descriptions by title and industry. And the Department of Labor's O*NET is a third alternative. We'll focus on using O*NET in this feature.

Step 1. Decide on a Plan

Start by developing at least the broad outline of a corporate plan. What do you expect your sales revenue to be next year, and in the next few years? What products do you intend to emphasize? What areas or departments in your company do you think will have to be expanded, reduced, or consolidated, given where you plan to go with your firm over the next few years? What kinds of new positions do you think you'll need in order to accomplish your strategic plans?

Step 2. Develop an Organization Chart

Next, develop an organization chart for the firm. Show who reports to the president and to each of his or her subordinates. Complete the chart by showing who reports to each of the other managers and supervisors in the firm. Start by drawing up the organization chart as it is now. Then, depending upon how far in advance you're planning, produce a chart showing how you'd like your chart to look in the immediate future (say, in two months) and perhaps two or three other charts showing how you'd like your organization to evolve over the next two or three years.

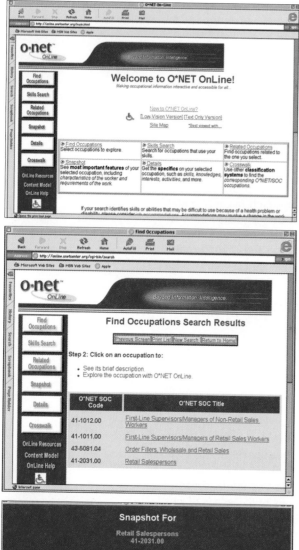

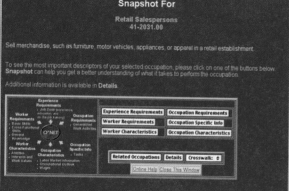

▲ **WEBNOTE**

Shown in the three screen captures above, O*NET easily allows the user to develop job descriptions.

online.onetcenter.org

You can use several tools here. For example, MS Word includes an organization charting function: On the insert menu, click *Object*, then *Create New*. In the *Object* type box, click *MS Organization Chart*, and then *OK*. Software packages such as OrgPublisher for Intranet 3.0 from TimeVision of Irving, Texas, are another option.[28]

Step 3. Use a Job Analysis/Description Questionnaire

Next, use a job analysis questionnaire to determine what the job entails. You can use one of the more comprehensive questionnaires (see Figure 3-3); however, the job description questionnaire in Figure 3-8, is a simpler and often satisfactory alternative. Fill in the required information, then ask the supervisors and/or employees to list the job's duties (on the bottom of the page), breaking them into daily duties, periodic duties, and duties performed at irregular intervals. You can distribute a sample of one of these duties (Figure 3-9) to supervisors and/or employees to facilitate the process.

Step 4: Obtain Lists of Job Duties from O*NET

The list of job duties you uncovered in the previous step may or may not be complete. We'll therefore use O*NET to compile a more comprehensive list. (Refer to the Webnote for a visual example as you read along.) Start by going to http://online.onet center.org (top). Here, click on *Find Occupations*. Assume you want to create job descriptions for retail salespeople. Type in *Retail Sales* for the occupational titles, and *Sales and Related* from the job families drop-down box. Click *Find Occupations* to continue, which brings you to the *Find Occupations Search Result* (middle). Clicking on *Retail Salespersons*—snapshots—produces the job summary and specific occupational duties for retail salespersons (bottom). For a small operation, you might want to combine the duties of the retail salesperson with those of first-line supervisors/managers of retail sales workers.

Step 5: Compile the Job's Human Requirements from O*NET

Next, return to the *Snapshot for Retail Salesperson* (bottom). Here, instead of choosing occupation-specific information, choose, for example, *Worker Experiences*, *Occupational Requirements*, and *Worker Characteristics*. You can use this information to develop a job specification for recruiting, selecting, and training the employees.

STEP 6: Complete Your Job Description

Finally, using Figure 3-8, write an appropriate job summary for the job. Then use the information obtained in Steps 4 and 5 to create a complete listing of the tasks, duties, and human requirements of each of the jobs you will need to fill.

Background Data for Job Description

Job Title _____   Department _____

Job Number _____   Written by _____

Today's Date _____   Applicable DOT Codes _____

I. Applicable DOT Definition(s):

II. Job Summary:
(List the more important or regularly performed tasks)

III. Reports To:

IV. Supervises: _____

V. Job Duties: _____
(Briefly describe, for each duty, what employee does and, if possible, how employee does it. Show in parentheses at end of each duty the approximate percentage of time devoted to duty.)

A. Daily Duties:

B. Periodic Duties:
   (Indicate whether weekly, monthly, quarterly, etc.)

C. Duties Performed at Irregular Intervals:

Example of Job Title: Customer Service Clerk

Example of Job Summary: Answers inquiries and gives directions to customers, authorizes cashing of customers' checks, records and returns lost charge cards, sorts and reviews new credit applications, works at customer-service desk in department store.

Example of One Job Duty: Authorizes cashing of checks: authorizes cashing of personal or payroll checks (up to a specified amount) by customers desiring to make payment by check. Requests identification, such as driver's license, from customers, and examines check to verify date, amount, signature, and endorsement. Initials check and sends customer to cashier.

JOB ANALYSIS IN A "JOBLESS" WORLD

Job is generally defined as "a set of closely related activities carried out for pay," but over the past few years the concept of a job has been changing quite dramatically. As one observer put it:

> The modern world is on the verge of another huge leap in creativity and productivity, but the job is not going to be part of tomorrow's economic reality. There still is and will always be enormous amounts of work to do, but it is not going to be contained in the familiar envelopes we call jobs. In fact, many organizations are today well along the path toward being "de-jobbed."[29]

From Specialized to Enlarged Jobs

The term *job* as we know it today is largely an outgrowth of the industrial revolution's emphasis on efficiency. During this time, experts like Adam Smith and Frederick Taylor wrote glowingly of the positive correlation between specialization and efficiency.[30] Jobs and job descriptions, until quite recently, tended to follow their prescriptions and to be fairly detailed and specific.

By the mid-1900s other writers were reacting to what they viewed as the "dehumanizing" aspects of pigeonholing workers into highly repetitive and specialized jobs; many proposed solutions like job enlargement, job rotation, and job enrichment. **Job enlargement** means assigning workers additional same-level activities, thus increasing the number of activities they perform. Thus, the worker who previously only bolted the seat to the legs might attach the back as well. **Job rotation** means systematically moving workers from one job to another.

Psychologist Frederick Herzberg argued that the best way to motivate workers is to build opportunities for challenge and achievement into their jobs via job enrichment. **Job enrichment** means redesigning jobs in a way that increases the opportunities for the worker to experience feelings of responsibility, achievement, growth, and recognition—for instance, by letting the worker plan and control his or her own work instead of having it controlled by outsiders.[31]

job enlargement
Assigning workers additional same-level activities, thus increasing the number of activities they perform.

job rotation
Systematically moving workers from one job to another.

job enrichment
Redesigning jobs in a way that increases the opportunities for the worker to experience feelings of responsibility, achievement, growth, and recognition.

Why Managers Are Dejobbing Their Companies

Whether specialized, enlarged, or enriched, however, workers still generally have had specific jobs to do, and these jobs have required job descriptions. In many firms today, however, jobs are becoming more amorphous and more difficult to define. In other words, the trend is toward dejobbing.

Dejobbing—broadening the responsibilities of the company's jobs, and encouraging employees not to limit themselves to what's on their job descriptions—is a result of the changes taking place in business today. Organizations need to grapple with trends like rapid product and technological change, global competition, deregulation, political instability, demographic changes, and a shift to a service economy. This has increased the need for firms to be responsive, flexible, and generally more competitive. In turn, the organizational methods managers use to accomplish this have helped weaken the meaning of *job* as a well-defined and clearly delineated set of responsibilities. Here is a sampling of methods that have contributed to this weakening.

dejobbing
Broadening the responsibilities of the company's jobs, and encouraging employees not to limit themselves to what's on their job descriptions.

Flatter Organizations   Instead of traditional pyramid-shaped organizations with seven or more management layers, flat organizations with just three or four levels are becoming more prevalent. Most firms (including AT&T, ABB, and General

Electric) have already cut their management layers from a dozen to six or fewer. Because the remaining managers have more people reporting to them, they can supervise them less, so the jobs of subordinates end up bigger in terms of both breadth and depth of responsibilities.

Work Teams Managers increasingly organize tasks around teams and processes rather than around specialized functions. For example, at Chesebrough-Ponds USA, a subsidiary of Unilever, managers replaced a traditional pyramidal organization with multiskilled, cross-functional, and self-directed teams; the latter now run the plant's four product areas. Hourly employees make employee assignments, schedule overtime, establish production times and changeovers, and even handle cost control, requisitions, and work orders. They also are solely responsible for quality control under the plant's continuous quality improvement program.[32] In an organization like this, employees' jobs change daily; there is thus an intentional effort to avoid having employees view their jobs as a specific set of responsibilities.

The Boundaryless Organization In a **boundaryless organization** the widespread use of teams and similar structural mechanisms reduces and makes more permeable the boundaries that typically separate departments (like sales and production) and hierarchical levels.[33] Boundaryless organizations foster responsiveness by encouraging employees to rid themselves of the "it's-not-my-job" attitudes that typically create walls between one employee's area and another's. Instead the focus is on defining the project or task at hand in terms of the overall best interests of the organization, thereby further reducing the idea of a job as a clearly defined set of duties.

boundaryless organization
Organization marked by the widespread use of teams and similar structural mechanisms that reduce and make more permeable the boundaries that typically separate departments.

Reengineering **Reengineering** is "the fundamental rethinking and radical redesign of business processes to achieve dramatic improvements in critical contemporary measures of performance, such as cost, quality, service, and speed."[34] In their book *Reengineering the Corporation*, Michael Hammer and James Champy argue that the principles that shaped the structure and management of business for hundreds of years—like highly specialized divisions of work—should be retired. Instead, the firm should emphasize combining tasks into integrated, unspecialized processes (such as customer service) assigned to teams of employees.

reengineering
The fundamental rethinking and radical redesign of business processes to achieve dramatic improvements in critical, contemporary measures of performance, such as cost, quality, service, and speed.

You can reengineer jobs in many ways. For example, you can combine several specialized jobs into a few relatively enlarged and enriched ones.[35] Typically, in reengineered situations workers tend to become collectively responsible for overall results rather than being individually responsible for just their own tasks: "They share joint responsibility with their team members for performing the whole process, not just a small piece of it. They not only use a broader range of skills from day to day, they have to be thinking of a far greater picture."[36] Most important, "while not every member of the team will be doing exactly the same work . . . the lines between [the workers' jobs] blur."

The Future of Job Descriptions Most firms today continue to use job descriptions and to rely on jobs as traditionally defined. However, it's clear that more firms are moving toward new organizational configurations built around jobs that are broad and that may change every day. As one writer said, "In such a situation people no longer take their cues from a job description or a supervisor's instructions. Signals come from the changing demands of the project. Workers learn to focus their individual efforts and collective resources on the work that needs doing, changing as that changes. Managers lose their 'jobs,' too. . . ."[37] Yet some feel that "job descriptions, although they include the ubiquitous phrase, 'and all other duties as assigned,' are still relatively rigid and limiting."[38]

Some employers are moving from traditional to more performance-based job descriptions. For example, Acxiom Corporation in Little Rock, Arkansas, recently moved from more traditional job descriptions to a new system. Instead of listing specific language skills (such as Java) for a software developer's job description, it now emphasizes behavioral competencies, such as self-directed learning. This is because Acxiom has decided that it's this self-directed learning that's really important for keeping software developers up to date. The typical job description at Acxiom now includes just a few statements describing overall responsibilities. Supervisors then set specific expectations by defining the skills (such as "learn two new software languages") the employee needs at that time. The job description thus becomes more of a flexible, living, performance-based document.[39]

Dejobbing also triggers broader HR issues. For example, "you must find people who can work well without the cue system of job descriptions."[40] This puts a premium on hiring people with the skills and values to handle empowered jobs:

> For multi-dimensional and changing jobs, companies don't need people to fill a slot, because the slot will be only roughly defined. Companies need people who can figure out what the job takes and do it, people who can create the slot that fits them. Moreover, the slot will keep changing.[41]

There's also a shift from training to education, from teaching employees the "how" of a job to enhancing their insight and understanding regarding its "why." This is because in a fast-changing global environment, jobs change so quickly that it's impossible to hire people "who already know everything they're ever going to need to know."[42]

◆ **HIGH-PERFORMANCE INSIGHT** Modern job analysis/job design techniques can help companies implement high-performance strategies. In one firm—British Petroleum's exploration division—the need for more efficient, faster-acting, flatter organizations and empowered employees inspired management to replace job descriptions with matrices listing skills and skill levels.[43] Senior managers wanted to shift employees' attention from a job description/"that's-not-my-job" mentality to one that would motivate them to obtain the new skills they needed to accomplish their broader responsibilities.

The solution was a skills matrix like that in Figure 3-10. They created skills matrices for various jobs within two groups of employees, those on a management track and those whose aims lay elsewhere (such as to stay in engineering). HR prepared a matrix for each job or job family (such as drilling manager). As in Figure 3-10, the matrix listed (1) the basic skills needed for that job (such as technical expertise) and (2) the minimum level of each skill required for that job or job family. The emphasis is no longer on specific job duties. Instead, the focus is on developing the new skills needed for the employees' broader, empowered, and often relatively undefined responsibilities.

The skills matrix approach triggered other HR changes in this division. For example, the matrices gave employees a constant reminder of what skills they must improve. The firm instituted a new skill-based pay plan that awards raises based on skills improvement. Performance appraisals now focus more on skills acquisitions. And training emphasizes developing broad skills like leadership and planning—skills applicable across a wide range of responsibilities and jobs. The result was a new firm-wide emphasis on performance.

▼ **FIGURE 3-10   The Skills Matrix for One Job at BP**
The light blue boxes indicate the minimum level of skill required for the job.

H	H	H	H	H	H	H
G	G	G	G	G	G	G
F	F	F	F	F	F	F
E	E	E	E	E	E	E
D	D	D	D	D	D	D
C	C	C	C	C	C	C
B	B	B	B	B	B	B
A	A	A	A	A	A	A
Technical Expertise	Business Awareness	Communication and Interpersonal	Decision Making and Initiative	Leadership and Guidance	Planning and Organizational Ability	Problem Solving

STRATEGIC HR

Implementing the New Strategy at U.S. Bank

U.S. Bank's new customer service and retention manager, Todd Berkley, discovered that focusing the bank's competitive strategy on customer service affected every aspect of the bank. Employees must now perform a multitude of new tasks. When they meet with customers closing their accounts, service reps now have to try to understand the customer's reason for leaving, and keep detailed records of frequent complaints. The bank is installing complaint identification initiatives to identify, track, and solve complaints in all branches, call centers, and Web sites. Salespeople must gather more information about customer preferences when they open new accounts. Employees across the bank have had to learn how to use the bank's new complaint-monitoring software. The bank designed new jobs to place care calls when customers complain. The bank is developing a new customer assurance unit, which will swing into action when high-value accounts are in danger of leaving.

All of which means Todd and his colleagues had to reanalyze all of the bank's jobs, from teller to guard to vice president; add duties like those above to current lists of job functions; and create several new jobs (such as customer assurance manager). Todd and his colleagues found, in other words, that they couldn't implement the bank's new strategy without a keen understanding of job analysis.[44]

We invite you to visit **www.prenhall.com/dessler** on the Prentice Hall Web site for our online study guide, Internet exercises, current events, links to related Web sites, and more.

Summary

1. Developing an organization structure results in jobs that have to be staffed. Job analysis is the procedure through which you find out (1) what the job entails and (2) what kinds of people you should hire for the job. It involves six steps: (1) determine the use of the job analysis information, (2) collect background information, (3) select the positions to be analyzed, (4) collect job analysis data, (5) review information with participants, and (6) develop a job description and job specification.

2. You can use four basic techniques to gather job analysis data: interviews, direct observation, questionnaires, and participant diary logs. These are good for developing job descriptions and specifications. The Department of Labor, functional job analysis, and PAQ approaches result in quantitative ratings of each job and are usually useful for classifying jobs for pay purposes.

3. The job description should portray the work of the position so well that the duties are clear without reference to other job descriptions. Always ask, "Will the new employee understand the job if he or she reads the job description?"

4. The job specification takes the job description and uses it to answer the question, "What human traits and experience are necessary to do this job well?" It tells what kind of person to recruit and for what qualities that person should be tested. Job specifications are usually based on the educated guesses of managers; a more accurate statistical approach to developing job specifications can also be used, however.

5. Use the *Dictionary of Occupational Titles* to help you write job descriptions. Find and reproduce the DOT descriptions that relate to the job you're describing. Then use those DOT descriptions to "anchor" your own description and particularly to suggest duties to be included. You can also use Internet sources like jobdescription.com.

6. Firms increasingly use O*NET to create job descriptions. To use this tool, start at http://online.onetcenter.org.

7. Dejobbing is ultimately a product of the rapid changes taking place in business today. As firms try to speed decision making by taking steps such as reengineering, individual jobs are becoming broader and much less specialized. Increasingly, firms don't want employees to feel limited by a specific set of responsibilities like those listed in a job description. As a result, more employers are substituting brief job summaries, perhaps combined with summaries of the skills required for the position.

Tying It All Together

In the previous chapter we discussed the EEOC and the legal factors managers should consider when recruiting and hiring employees. The purpose of the current chapter, Job Analysis, was to explain how managers determine what jobs need to be done, what these jobs' specific duties are, and the characteristics of the employees who will fill these jobs. The chapter covered such topics as methods for collecting job analysis information and how to use the Internet, as well as traditional methods of writing job descriptions and job specifications. In the following chapter, HR Planning and Recruiting, we'll turn to the methods managers use to find the employees they need to fill their positions.

Discussion Questions

1. What items are typically included in the job description? What items are not shown?
2. What is job analysis? How can you make use of the information it provides?
3. We discussed several methods for collecting job analysis data—questionnaires, the position analysis questionnaire, and so on. Compare and contrast these methods, explaining what each is useful for and listing the pros and cons of each.
4. Describe the types of information typically found in a job specification.
5. Explain how you would conduct a job analysis.
6. Do you think companies can really do without detailed job descriptions? Why or why not?

7. In a company with only 25 employees, is there less need for job descriptions for the employees of the company? Why or why not?

1. Working individually or in groups, obtain copies of job descriptions for clerical positions at the college or university where you study, or the firm where you work. What types of information do they contain? Do they give you enough information to explain what the job involves and how to do it? How would you improve on the description?
2. Working individually or in groups, use O*NET to develop a job description for your professor in this class. Based on that, use your judgment to develop a job specification. Compare your conclusions with those of other students or groups. Were there any significant differences? What do you think accounted for the differences?
3. Working individually or in groups, obtain a copy of the DOT from your library. Choose any two positions and compare the jobs' data-people-things ratings. (These are the fourth, fifth, and sixth digits of the job's DOT number; ratings are explained at the end of the DOT.) Do the ratings make sense based on what you know about the jobs? Why or why not?

EXPERIENTIAL EXERCISE

Purpose: The purpose of this exercise is to give you experience in developing a job description, by developing one for your instructor.

Required Understanding: You should understand the mechanics of job analysis and be thoroughly familiar with the job analysis questionnaires. (See Figure 3-3 and the job description questionnaire, Figure 3-8.)

How to Set Up the Exercise/Instructions: Set up groups of four to six students for this exercise. As in all exercises in this book, the groups should be separated and should not converse with each other. Half the groups in the class will develop the job description using the job analysis questionnaire (3.3), and the other half of the groups will develop it using the job description questionnaire (3.8). Each student should review his or her questionnaire (as appropriate) before joining his or her group.

1. Each group should do a job analysis of the instructor's job; half the groups (to repeat) will use the job analysis questionnaire for this purpose, and half will use the job description questionnaire.
2. Based on this information, each group will develop its own job description and job specification for the instructor.
3. Next, each group should choose a partner group, one that developed the job description and job specification using the alternate method. (A group that used the job analysis questionnaire should be paired with a group that used the job description questionnaire.)
4. Finally, within each of these new combined groups, compare and critique each of the two sets of job descriptions and job specifications. Did each job analysis method provide different types of information? Which seems superior? Does one seem more advantageous for some types of jobs than others?

APPLICATION CASE *Tropical Storm Allison*

In June 2001 tropical storm Allison hit North Carolina and the Optima Air Filter Company. Many employees' homes were devastated, and the firm found that it had to hire almost three completely new crews, one for each of its shifts. The problem was that the "old-timers" had known their jobs so well that no one had ever bothered to draw up job descriptions for them. When about 30 new employees began taking their places, there was general confusion about what they should do and how they should do it.

The storm quickly became old news to the firm's out-of-state customers, who wanted filters, not excuses. Phil Mann, the firm's president, was at his wit's end. He had about 30 new employees, 10 old-timers, and his original factory supervisor, Maybelline. He decided to meet with Linda Lowe, a consultant from the local university's business school. She immediately had the old-timers fill out a job questionnaire that listed all their duties. Arguments ensued almost at once: Both Phil and Maybelline thought the old-timers were exaggerating to make themselves look more important, and the old-timers insisted that the lists faithfully reflected their duties. Meanwhile, the customers clamored for their filters.

Questions

1. Should Phil and Linda ignore the old-timers' protests and write up the job descriptions as they see fit? Why? Why not? How would you go about resolving the differences?
2. How would you have conducted the job analysis?

CONTINUING CASE: LearnInMotion.com *Who Do We Have to Hire?*

As the excitement surrounding the move into their new offices wound down, the two principal owners of LearnInMotion.com, Mel and Jennifer, turned to the task of hiring new employees. In their business plan they'd specified several basic aims for the venture capital funds they'd just received, and hiring a team topped the list. They knew their other goals—boosting sales and expanding the Web site, for instance—would be unreachable without the right team.

They were just about to place their ads when Mel asked a question that brought them to a stop: "What kind of people do we want to hire?" It seemed they hadn't really considered this. They knew the answer in general terms, of course. For example, they knew they needed at least two salespeople, plus a programmer, a Web designer, and several content management people to transform the incoming material into content they could post on their site. But it was obvious that job titles alone really didn't provide enough guidance. For example, if they couldn't specify the exact duties of these positions, how could they decide whether they needed experienced employees? How could they decide exactly what sorts of experiences and skills they had to look for in their candidates if they didn't know exactly what these candidates would have to do? They wouldn't even know what questions to ask.

And that wasn't all. For example, there were obviously other tasks to do, and these weren't necessarily included in the sorts of things that salespeople, programmers, Web designers, or content management people typically do. Who was going to answer the phones? (Jennifer and Mel had originally assumed they'd put in one of those fancy automated call directory and voice-mail systems—until they found out it would cost close to $10,000.) As a practical matter, they knew they had to have someone answering the phones and directing callers to the proper extension. Who was going to keep track of the monthly expenses and compile them for the

accountants, who'd then produce monthly reports for the venture capitalist? Would the salespeople generate their own leads? Or would LearnInMotion.com have to hire Web surfers to search and find the names of people for the sales staff to call or e-mail? What would happen when the company had to purchase supplies, such as fax paper or computer disks? Would the owners have to do this themselves, or should they have someone in house do it for them? The list, it seemed, went on and on.

It was obvious, in other words, that the owners had to get their managerial act together and draw up the sorts of documents they'd read about as business majors—job descriptions, job specifications, and so forth. The trouble is, it all seemed a lot easier when they read the textbook. Now they want you, their management consultants, to help them actually do it. Here's what they want you to do for them.

Questions and Assignments

1. Draw up a set of job descriptions for each of the positions in the case: salesperson, Web designer, programmer, content manager. You may use whatever sources you want, but preferably search the Internet and relevant Web sites, since you want job descriptions and lists of duties that apply specifically to dot-com firms.
2. Next, using sources similar to those in Question 1—and whatever other sources you can think of—draw up specifications for each of these jobs, including things such as desirable work habits, skills, education, and experiences.
3. Next, keeping in mind that this company is on a tight budget, write a short proposal explaining how it should accomplish the other activities it needs done, such as answering the phones, compiling sales leads, producing monthly reports, and purchasing supplies.

Chapter 4

HR Planning and Recruiting

STRATEGIC OVERVIEW Faced with an information technology employee shortage of monumental proportions, Sutter Health, a nonprofit health care network in Sacramento, California, knew its expansion strategy would be stifled if it couldn't fill its 10,000 job openings. The company's future depended on attracting many more recruits—but how should it do so? Sutter Health decided to move its job opening postings online, only to find that this was not the solution. Project manager Keith Vencel had to help Sutter devise a new answer.[1]

In the previous chapter, we discussed job analysis and the methods managers use to create job descriptions and job specifications. The main purpose of this chapter is to improve your effectiveness in recruiting job candidates. The main topics we'll discuss include personnel planning and forecasting, recruiting job candidates, and developing and using application forms. In the following chapter, Employee Testing and Selection, we'll turn to the methods managers use to select the best employees.

Personnel planning is the first step in the recruiting and selecting process. We can conveniently view this process as a series of hurdles, as shown in Figure 4-1:

1. Decide what positions you'll have to fill, by engaging in personnel planning and forecasting.

2. Build a pool of candidates for these jobs by recruiting internal or external candidates.

▶ **FIGURE 4-1**
Steps in Recruitment
and Selection Process

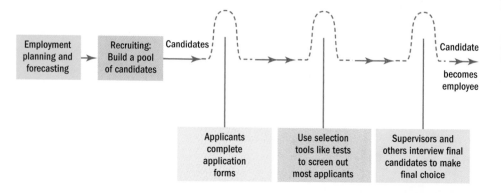

The recruitment and selection process is a series of hurdles aimed at selecting the best candidate for the job.

3. Have applicants complete application forms and perhaps undergo an initial screening interview.

4. Use selection techniques like tests, background investigations, and physical exams to identify viable candidates.

5. Finally, decide who to make an offer to, by having the supervisor and (perhaps) others on the team interview the final candidates.

We'll cover recruitment and selection in this and the next two chapters. This chapter focuses on employment planning and forecasting (in other words, on how to determine what positions are to be filled) and on recruiting techniques. Chapter 5 addresses selection techniques, including tests, background checks, and physical exams. Chapter 6 focuses on interviewing—by far the most widely used selection technique. ■

EMPLOYMENT PLANNING AND FORECASTING

employment or personnel planning
The process of deciding what positions the firm will have to fill, and how to fill them.

Employment or personnel planning is the process of deciding what positions the firm will have to fill, and how to fill them. Personnel planning covers all the firm's future positions, from maintenance clerk to CEO. However, most firms use *succession planning* to refer to the process of deciding how to fill the company's most important executive jobs.

Employment planning is an integral part of a firm's strategic and HR planning processes. As with Sutter Health's plan to expand, plans to enter new businesses, build new plants, or reduce costs all influence the types of positions the firm will need to fill. Thus, when JDS Uniphase, which designs, develops, and manufactures and markets products for the fiber optics market, decided to expand its Melbourne, Florida, operations, it expanded its employment there from 140 people to almost 750. One big question is whether to fill projected openings from within or from outside the firm. In other words, should you plan to fill them with current employees or by recruiting from outside?

Each option produces its own set of HR plans. Current employees may require training, development, and coaching before they're ready to fill new jobs. Going outside requires deciding what recruiting sources to use, among other things.

Like all good plans, management builds employment plans on premises—basic assumptions about the future. Forecasting generates these premises. If you're planning for employment requirements, you'll usually need to forecast three things: personnel needs; the supply of inside candidates; and the supply of out-side candidates. We'll start with personnel needs.

How to Forecast Personnel Needs

The expected demand for your product or service is paramount when forecasting personnel needs.[2] The usual process is therefore to forecast revenues first. Then estimate the size of the staff required to achieve this volume. In addition to expected demand, staffing plans may reflect:

1. Projected turnover (as a result of resignations or terminations)
2. Quality and skills of your employees (in relation to what you see as the changing needs of your organization)
3. Strategic decisions to upgrade the quality of products or services or enter into new markets
4. Technological and other changes resulting in increased productivity
5. The financial resources available to your department

Following are several methods to predict employment needs.

Trend Analysis **Trend analysis** means studying variations in your firm's employment levels over the last few years to predict future needs. Thus, you might compute the number of employees in your firm at the end of each of the last five years, or perhaps the number in each subgroup (like sales, production, secretarial, and administrative people) at the end of each of those years. The purpose is to identify trends that might continue into the future. Trend analysis can provide an initial estimate, but employment levels rarely depend just on the passage of time. Other factors (like changes in sales volume and productivity) also affect staffing needs.

trend analysis
Study of a firm's past employment needs over a period of years to predict future needs.

Ratio Analysis Another approach, **ratio analysis**, means making forecasts based on the ratio between (1) some causal factor (like sales volume) and (2) the number of employees required (for instance, number of salespeople). For example, suppose a salesperson traditionally generates $500,000 in sales. If the sales revenue to salespeople ratio remains the same, you would require six new salespeople next year (each of whom produces an extra $500,000) to produce a hoped-for extra $3 million in sales.

Like trend analysis, ratio analysis assumes that productivity remains about the same—for instance, that each salesperson can't be motivated to produce much more than $500,000 in sales. If sales productivity were to increase or decrease, the ratio of sales to salespeople would change. A forecast based on historical ratios would then no longer be accurate.

ratio analysis
A forecasting technique for determining future staff needs by using ratios between, for example, sales volume and number of employees needed.

The Scatter Plot A **scatter plot** shows graphically how two variables—such as a measure of business activity and your firm's staffing levels—are related. If they are, then if you can forecast the level of business activity, you should also be able to estimate your personnel requirements.

For example, assume a 500-bed hospital expects to expand to 1,200 beds over the next 5 years. The director of nursing and the human resource director want to forecast the requirement for registered nurses. The human resource director decides to determine the relationship between size of hospital (in terms of number of beds) and number of nurses required. She calls five hospitals of various sizes and gets the following figures:

scatter plot
A graphical method used to help identify the relationship between two variables.

Size of Hospital (Number of Beds)	Number of Registered Nurses
200	240
300	260
400	470
500	500
600	620
700	660
800	820
900	860

Figure 4-2 shows hospital size on the horizontal axis. Number of nurses is shown on the vertical axis. If the two factors are related, then the points will tend to fall along a straight line, as they do here. If you carefully draw in a line to minimize the distances between the line and each one of the plotted points, you will be able to estimate the number of nurses needed for each given hospital size. Thus, for a 1,200-bed hospital, the human resource director would assume she needs about 1,210 nurses.[3]

Using Computers to Forecast Personnel Requirements Employers also use software programs to forecast personnel requirements.[4] Typical data needed include direct labor hours required to produce one unit of product (a measure of productivity), and three sales projections—minimum, maximum, and probable—for the product line in question. Based on such data, a typical program generates figures on average staff levels required to meet product demands, as well as separate **computerized forecasts** for direct labor (such as assembly workers), indirect staff (such as secretaries), and exempt staff (such as executives). With programs like these, employers can quickly translate projected productivity and sales levels into forecasts of personnel needs, and estimate the effects of various productivity and sales level assumptions on personnel requirements.[5]

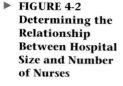

computerized forecast
Determination of future staff needs by projecting sales, volume of production, and personnel required to maintain this volume of output, using software packages.

▶ **FIGURE 4-2**
Determining the Relationship Between Hospital Size and Number of Nurses

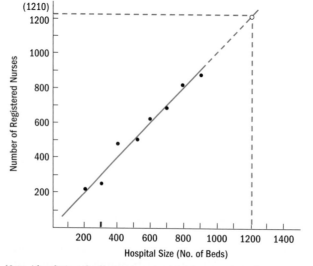

Note: After fitting the line, you can extrapolate—project—how many employees you'll need, given your projected volume.

Many firms use such automated employee forecasting systems. In retailing, for instance, automated labor scheduling systems help retailers estimate their required staffing needs based on sales forecasts and estimated store traffic.[6]

Managerial Judgment Whichever forecasting method you use, managerial judgment will play a big role. It's rare that any historical trend, ratio, or relationship will simply continue unchanged into the future. You'll therefore have to modify the forecast based on factors—such as projected turnover or a desire to enter new markets—you believe will be important.

In practice, making personnel forecasts usually isn't mechanical, even for major firms. For example, in 1999, Bank of America laid off many brokers when it merged with NationsBank. About a year later, its rival First Union Corporation hired 700 new investment brokers. In response, BOA's investments division, Banc of America Investment Services, beefed up its 600-person brokerage staff by hiring 200 licensed brokers and training another 1,000 employees to sell investment products like mutual funds.[7]

It's sometimes difficult to take a long-term perspective, particularly when market conditions change dramatically. For example, after reducing its workforce by about 9%, AmericaTrade Holding Corporation soon announced an additional 7% cut, due to "increasingly adverse market conditions."[8]

Forecasting the Supply of Inside Candidates

Knowing your staffing needs only satisfies half the staffing equation. Next, you have to estimate the likely supply of both inside and outside candidates. Most firms start with the inside candidates.

Here, the main task is determining which current employees might be qualified for the projected openings. For this you need to know your current employees' skills sets—their current qualifications. Sometimes it's obvious how you have to proceed. For example, when Bill Gates needed someone to lead Microsoft's new user interface project, his first question was, "Where's Kai-Fu?" His firm's voice recognition expert, Kai-Fu Lee, was in China at the time establishing a new research lab for the firm.[9] Sometimes it's not so obvious, and managers turn to **qualifications inventories**. These contain data on things like performance records, educational backgrounds, and promotability. They help managers determine which current employees are available for promotion or transfer. Such inventories may be manual or computerized.

Manual Systems and Replacement Charts Managers use several simple manual devices to track employees' qualifications. A personnel inventory and development record like that in Figure 4-3 compiles qualifications information on each employee. The information includes education, company-sponsored courses taken, career and development interests, languages, and skills.

Personnel replacement charts (Figure 4-4) are another option, particularly for the firm's top positions. They show the present performance and promotability for each position's potential replacement. As an alternative, you can develop a **position replacement card**. Here you create a card for each position, showing possible replacements as well as their present performance, promotion potential, and training.

Computerized Information Systems Companies don't generally track the qualifications of hundreds or thousands of employees manually. Most firms computerize this information, using various packaged software systems.[10]

In many of these systems, the employees and the HR department enter information about the employees' backgrounds, experience, and skills, often using the company intranet. When a manager needs a person for a position, he or she

qualifications inventories
Manual or computerized records listing employees' education, career and development interests, languages, special skills, and so on, to be used in selecting inside candidates for promotion.

personnel replacement charts
Company records showing present performance and promotability of inside candidates for the most important positions.

position replacement card
A card prepared for each position in a company to show possible replacement candidates and their qualifications.

▼ **FIGURE 4-3   Personnel Inventory Form Appropriate for Manual Storage and Retrieval**

PERSONNEL INVENTORY AND DEVELOPMENT RECORD | Date: month, year

| Department | Area or sub-department | Branch or section | Location |

| Company service date (month, day, year) | Birthdate (month, day, year) | Marital status | Job title |

Education | Degree, year obtained, college, and major field of study

Grade school 6   7   8 | High school 9 10 11 12 13

College 1   2   3   4   5

Courses (company sponsored)

Type of course	Subject or course	Year	Type of course	Subject or course	Year

Career and development interests

| Are you interested in an alternative type of work?   Yes ☐   No ☐ | Would you accept transfer to another division?   Yes ☐   No ☐ | Would you accept lateral moves for further development?   Yes ☐   No ☐ | Photo |

| If yes, specifically what type? | Comment on any qualifying circumstances | |

What type of training do you believe you require to: | A) Improve your skills and performance in your present position. | |

| B) Improve your experience and abilities for advancement. | Last name |

| | First name |

What other assignments do you believe you are qualified to perform now?

Languages	Written	Spoken	Middle name
	☐ ☐	☐ ☐	SS Number
	☐ ☐	☐ ☐	

Societies and organizations | Memberships in community organizations, etc., within last five years, indicate name of association and office held, if any

Skills

Type of skill	Certification, if any	Type of skill	Certification, if any

Other significant work experience, and/or military service. (Omit repetitive experiences)

	Location	From yr.	To yr.	

Comments: Other significant experience, recreational activities, hobbies, interests, or personal data.

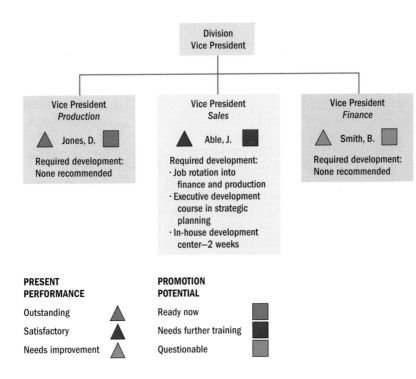

◀ **FIGURE 4-4**
Management
Replacement
Chart Showing
Development Needs
of Future Divisional
Vice President

describes the position (for instance, in terms of education and skills). After scanning its database of possible candidates, the system produces a list of qualified candidates.

Such a computerized skills inventory might include:

Work experience codes. A list of work experience titles, or codes describing the person's jobs within the company.

Product knowledge. The employee's level of familiarity with the employer's product lines or services.

Industry experience. The person's industry experiences, since for some positions work in related industries is very useful.

Formal education. Each postsecondary educational institution attended, field of study, degree granted, and year granted.

Training courses. Those taken or conducted by the employee, including courses taught by outside firms like the American Management Association.

Foreign language skills. Which languages; degree of proficiency, spoken and written.

Relocation limitations. The employee's willingness to relocate and the locales he or she would prefer.

Career interests. Work experience codes to indicate what the employee would like to be doing for the employer in the future.

Performance appraisals. Updated periodically, along with a summary of the employee's strengths and deficiencies.[11]

Skills. Skills such as "design graphic interface" (number of times performed, date last performed, time spent), as well as skill level, perhaps ranging from level 1 (can lead or instruct others) to level 3 (has some experience: can assist experienced workers).[12]

In practice, the data elements could number 100 or more. For example, one vendor of a package reportedly used by over 2,000 companies suggests 140 elements, ranging from home address to driver's license number, weight, salary, sick leave used, skills, and veteran status.[13]

The Matter of Privacy Several things make it increasingly important to secure the data in the firm's personnel data banks. First, as you can see, there is a lot of employee information in most such data banks. Second, Internet/intranet access and other changes mean it's often easier for more people to access these data.[14] Third, legislation, such as the Federal Privacy Act of 1974 and the New York Personal Privacy Act of 1985, gives some employees legal rights regarding who has access to information about their work history and job performance.

Balancing the employer's legitimate right to make this information available to those in the firm who need it with the employees' right to privacy isn't easy. One approach is to use the access matrices incorporated in many database management systems. These matrices define the rights of users (specified by name, rank, or functional identification) to various kinds of access (such as "read only" or "write only") to each database element. So the system might authorize employees in accounting to read information such as the employee's address, phone number, Social Security number, and pension status. The HR director, on the other hand, could both read and write all items.

Forecasting the Supply of Outside Candidates

If you won't have enough inside candidates to fill the anticipated openings (or you want to go outside for another reason), you need to focus on trying to anticipate the availability of outside candidates. This may involve several activities. For example, you may want to consider general economic conditions and the expected unemployment rate. Usually, the lower the rate of unemployment, the more difficult it will be to recruit personnel.

Information like this is easy to find: For example, *Business Week* presents a weekly snapshot of the economy on its Outlook page, as well as a yearly forecast in December. *Fortune* magazine has a monthly forecast for the coming year. Similar information is readily available in the *Economist* and *Wall Street Journal* newspapers, as well as on the Internet (see www.infoplease.com). The U.S. Council of Economic Advisors prepares economic indicators each month showing the trend to date of various indicators. The regional Federal Reserve banks also publish monthly economic reports. Some recruiting firms also make projections. For example, the temporary employment services firm Manpower, Inc., conducts employer surveys and then projects demand for workers in cities across the country.[15] Local labor market conditions are important too. For example, the buildup of computer and semiconductor companies in California's Silicon Valley resulted in relatively low unemployment there a few years ago, quite aside from general economic conditions around the country.

Your plans may also require that you forecast the availability of potential job candidates in specific occupations such as nurses, computer programmers, or teachers. Recently, for instance, there has been an undersupply of computer specialists and nurses. The Bureau of Labor Statistics of the U.S. Department of Labor publishes annual occupational projections in the *Monthly Labor Review* and, often, in *Occupational Outlook Quarterly*. O*NET (discussed in Chapter 3) includes online projections for most occupations. The National Science Foundation regularly forecasts labor market conditions in the science and technology fields. Other federal agencies providing occupational forecasts include the U.S. Public Health Service, the U.S. Employment Service, and the U.S. Office of Education.

Some occupations are so in demand that they seem to remain in demand even when the economy slows. For example, when the economy slowed in 2001 (and many dot-coms went out of business), the head of IT human resources for the Hartford Insurance Company reported seeing a "slight uptick" in the number of candidates available. However, it had not shifted "to the point where it's a buyer's market now."[16]

Recent shortages of registered nurses across the country have been a particular problem. In some fast-growing areas, such as San Antonio, Texas, hospital administrators describe the shortage as possibly having "life-threatening implications."[17]

The jobs in high demand aren't necessarily always high tech. For example, life insurance firms have recently found it difficult to recruit high-producing agents, in part because of increased competition from financial services firms such as banks and stock brokerages.[18]

EFFECTIVE RECRUITING

Assuming the company authorizes you to fill a position, the next step is to develop an applicant pool, using one or more of the recruitment sources described below. It's hard to overemphasize the importance of effective recruiting. The more applicants you have, the more selective you can be in your hiring. If only two candidates apply for two openings, you may have little choice but to hire them. But if 10 or 20 applicants appear, you can use techniques like interviews and tests to screen out all but the best.

Effective recruiting is increasingly important today, for several reasons. First, the ease of recruiting tends to ebb and flow with economic and unemployment levels. The U.S. unemployment rate declined each year for 10 years through mid-2001; this led some experts to refer to the recruiting situation up to that time as one of "evaporated employee sources."[19] High average turnover rates for some occupations are another problem; the average annual turnover rate for high-tech employees was recently 14.5%, according to one study.[20] The increased emphasis on technology and therefore on skilled human capital also demands more selective hiring—and thus a bigger applicant pool.

Finding the right inducements for attracting and hiring employees can be a problem.[21] A few years ago, for example, about 47,000 computer animator jobs opened up worldwide, but only 14,000 animators graduated from art school. With a little experience, these people could therefore earn $100,000 a year.[22] Similarly, $10,000 to $20,000 signing bonuses were often common for MBA students in the late 1990s.[23]

Aggressive recruiting is therefore often the name of the game. "Poaching workers is fair game," reads one HR newsletter headline. Some recruiters even have their own jargon. They call luring workers away from other high-tech firms "nerd rustling."[24] As explained in Chapter 3, all recruiting must conform to EEO antidiscrimination laws.[25]

The Recruiting Yield Pyramid

Some employers use a **recruiting yield pyramid** to calculate the number of applicants they must generate to hire the required number of new employees. In Figure 4-5, the company knows it needs 50 new entry-level accountants next year. From experience, the firm also knows the ratio of offers made to actual new hires is 2 to 1; about half the people to whom it makes offers accept them. Similarly, the firm knows that the ratio of candidates interviewed to offers made is 3 to 2, while the ratio of candidates invited for interviews to candidates actually interviewed is about 4 to 3. Finally, the firm knows that of six leads that come in from all its recruiting efforts, only one applicant typically gets an interview—a 6 to 1 ratio.

recruiting yield pyramid
The historical arithmetic relationships between recruitment leads and invitees, invitees and interviews, interviews and offers made, and offers made and offers accepted.

► **FIGURE 4-5**
Recruiting Yield
Pyramid

50	New hires
100	Offers made (2 : 1)
150	Candidates interviewed (3 : 2)
200	Candidates invited (4 : 3)
1,200	Leads generated (6 : 1)

Given these ratios, the firm knows it must generate 1,200 leads to be able to invite 200 viable candidates to its offices for interviews. The firm will then get to interview about 150 of those invited, and from these it will make 100 offers. Of those 100 offers, about 50 will accept.

◆ **RESEARCH INSIGHT** Of course, it's not recruiting but effective recruiting that's important. Consider this study of college recruiter effectiveness. The subjects were 41 graduating students from four colleges (arts and sciences, engineering, industrial relations, and business) of a northeastern university. Researchers questioned the students twice during the spring semester, once just after they'd had their first round of employer interviews and once after their second round.

The quality of a firm's recruiting had a big impact on candidates' opinions of the firm. When asked after the initial job interview why they thought a particular company might be a good fit, all 41 students mentioned the nature of the job. However, 12 also mentioned the impression made by the recruiters themselves, and 9 said the comments of friends and acquaintances affected their impressions. Unfortunately, the reverse was also true. When asked why they judged some firms as bad fits, 39 mentioned the nature of the job, but 23 said they'd been turned off by recruiters: Some were dressed "sloppily"; others were "barely literate"; some were rude; and some made offensive, sexist comments. Not exactly the kind of recruiters you want representing your firm.[26]

Line and Staff Cooperation The HR manager who recruits for a vacant job is seldom the one responsible for supervising its performance. He or she must therefore know exactly what the job entails, and this means speaking with the supervisor involved. For example, the recruiter might want to know about the supervisor's leadership style and about the work group—is it a tough group to get along with, for instance? He or she might also want to visit the work site, to review the job description with the supervisor to ensure that the job hasn't changed, and to obtain any additional insight into the skills and talents the new worker will need. Line and staff coordination is therefore essential. Now let's look at the main sources of job candidates, both internal and external.

INTERNAL SOURCES OF CANDIDATES

Recruiting may bring to mind employment agencies and classified ads, but current employees are often the best source of candidates.

Filling open positions with inside candidates has many benefits. First, there's really no substitute for knowing a candidate's strengths and weaknesses. It is often therefore safer to promote employees from within, since you're likely to have a more accurate view of the person's skills than you would an outsider's. Inside candidates may also be more committed to the company. Morale may rise, to the extent that employees see promotions as rewards for loyalty and competence. Inside candidates may also require less orientation and training than outsiders.

However, hiring from within can also backfire. Employees who apply for jobs and don't get them may become discontented; telling unsuccessful applicants why they were rejected and what remedial actions they might take to be more successful in the future is thus crucial.[27] Similarly, many employers require managers to post job openings and interview all inside candidates. Yet the manager often knows ahead of time exactly whom he or she wants to hire. Requiring the person to interview a stream of unsuspecting inside candidates can be a waste of time for all concerned. Groups are sometimes not as satisfied when their new boss is appointed from within their own ranks as when he or she is a newcomer: it may be difficult for the insider to shake off the reputation of being "one of the gang."[28]

Inbreeding is another potential drawback. When all managers come up through the ranks, they may have a tendency to maintain the status quo, when a new direction is what's required. Many "promote from within" firms like J.C. Penney, IBM, and Delta Airlines went outside for CEOs in the 1990s when their boards decided they needed new vision and leadership. Balancing the benefits to morale and loyalty with the possible inbreeding problem can be a challenge.

Finding Internal Candidates

To be effective, promotion from within requires using job posting, personnel records, and skills banks.[29] **Job posting** means publicizing the open job to employees (often by literally posting it on bulletin boards or intranets) and listing the job's attributes, like qualifications, supervisor, work schedule, and pay rate. Some union contracts require job posting to ensure union members get first choice of new and better positions. Yet job posting can be a good practice even in nonunion firms, if it facilitates the transfer and promotion of qualified inside candidates. (However, firms often don't post supervisory jobs; management often prefers to select supervisory candidates based on things like supervisors' recommendations, and appraisal and testing results.[30])

Personnel records are also important. An examination of personnel records (including application forms) may reveal employees who are working in jobs below their educational or skill levels. It may also reveal persons who have potential for further training or who already have the right background for the open job. Computerized records systems (like those discussed above) can help ensure you consider qualified inside candidates for the opening. Some firms also develop "skillsbanks" that list current employees with specific skills. For example, if you need an aerospace engineer in unit A, and the skillsbank shows a person with those skills in unit B, that person may be approached about transferring.

job posting
Publicizing an open job to employees (often by literally posting it on bulletin boards) and listing its attributes, like qualifications, supervisor, working schedule, and pay rate.

Hiring Employees—the Second Time Around

Until recently, many managers considered it unwise to rehire former employees, such as those who'd left voluntarily for better jobs. Quitting was often seen as a form of betrayal. Managers often assumed that those they'd dismissed might exhibit disloyalty or a bad attitude if hired back.[31]

Today—thanks partly to high turnover in some high-tech occupations—rehiring former employees is back in style. For example, with many former employees finding that the life of a start-up entrepreneur is not all they'd hoped it would be, EDS executive Troy Todd in Plano, Texas, says his company rehired over 500 "boomerang" employees just between January and July 2000. And with more dotcom firms facing tough times recently, employers are reportedly "sniffing around" these beleaguered firms to find employees who want back into the "bricks-and-mortar" world.[32]

AT&T now routinely reemploys former workers, and in one recent year rehired more than 130 employees it had previously let go.[33] Will McPherson, who leads a sales team for Phoenix, Arizona–based Brill Pharmaceutical Corporation, recently faced such a situation. A salesperson who had left about a year earlier to pursue a start-up venture returned when it didn't work out. McPherson decided to rehire him. "I felt a little used—and I told him that—but when you've got someone who you know will do well asking for a job, it's hard to turn him down. You can't just not hire somebody [out of] principle."[34]

Rehiring former employees has its pros and cons. On the plus side, former employees are known quantities (more or less), and are already familiar with the company's culture, style, and ways of doing things. On the other hand, employees who were let go may return with less-than-positive attitudes. And hiring former employees who left for greener pastures back into better positions may signal your current employees that the best way to get ahead is to leave the firm.

In any event, there are several ways to reduce the chance of adverse reactions.[35] For example, once rehired employees have been back on the job for a certain period, credit them with the years of service they had accumulated before they left. This may have a positive impact on benefits such as vacation time, and thereby on morale. In addition, inquire (before rehiring them) about what they did during the layoff and how they feel about returning to the firm: "You don't want someone coming back who feels they've been mistreated," said one manager.[36]

Succession Planning

succession planning
The process of ensuring a suitable supply of successors for current and future senior or key jobs.

Forecasting the availability of inside executive candidates is particularly important in **succession planning**—"the process of ensuring a suitable supply of successors for current and future senior or key jobs." Succession planning often involves a complicated series of steps. For example, potential successors for top management might be routed through the top jobs at several key divisions as well as overseas, and then through Harvard's Advanced Management Program. Jeffrey Immelt, the new CEO of GE, moved through these positions from 1989 through 2001: vice president, consumer services, GE appliances; vice president, worldwide marketing and product management; vice president and general manager—GE Plastics America commercial division; president and CEO, GE medical systems; president and chairman, GE.

Succession planning typically includes activities like these:

Determining the projected need for managers and professionals by company level, function, and skill

Auditing current executive talent to project the likely future supply from internal sources

Planning individual career paths based on objective estimates of future needs and assessments of potential

Career counseling in the context of the future needs of the firm, as well as those of the individual

Accelerated promotions, with development targeted against the future needs of the business

Performance-related training and development to prepare individuals for future roles as well as current responsibilities

Planned strategic recruitment to fill short-term needs and to provide people to meet future needs

Actually filling the positions—via recruiters, promotion from within, and so on[37]

OUTSIDE SOURCES OF CANDIDATES

Firms can't always get all the employees they need from their current staff, and sometimes they just don't want to. For example, when Delta Airlines's board decided it needed to inject a new perspective into running the airline, it turned to an outsider, Leo Mullin, to be the new CEO. We'll look at the sources firms use to find outside candidates next.

Advertising

Everyone is familiar with employment ads, and most of us have probably responded to one or more. To use help wanted ads successfully, employers have to address two issues: the advertising media and the ad's construction.[38]

The Media   The selection of the best medium—be it the local paper, the *Wall Street Journal*, TV, or the Internet—depends on the positions for which you're recruiting. For example, the local newspaper is usually the best source for blue-collar help, clerical employees, and lower-level administrative employees. On the other hand, if you're recruiting for blue-collar workers with special skills—such as maintaining textile-weaving looms—you'd probably want to advertise in the heart of the textile industry, the Carolinas or Georgia, even if your plant is in Tennessee. The point is to target your ads where they'll do the most good. Most employers, as we'll see, are also tapping the Internet.

For specialized employees, you can advertise in trade and professional journals like *American Psychologist, Sales Management, Chemical Engineering, Electronics News, Travel Trade,* and *Women's Wear Daily,* or in publications like *American Banker, Hospital Administration,* and *The Chronicle of Higher Education.* Similarly, help wanted ads in papers like the *Wall Street Journal* and *International Herald Tribune* can be good sources of middle- or senior-management personnel. The *Wall Street Journal,* for instance, has several regional editions, so the entire country or the appropriate geographic area can be targeted.

One drawback to this type of trade paper advertising is the long lead time that's usually required. There may be a month or more between insertion of the ad and publication of the journal or specialized paper (although more are supplementing their hard-copy publications with online Web sites).

Constructing the Ad   Construction of the ad is important. Experienced advertisers use a four-point guide called AIDA (attention, interest, desire, action) to construct ads. You must, of course, attract attention to the ad, or readers may just miss or ignore it. Figure 4-6 shows an ad from one paper's classified section. Why does this ad attract attention? Ads like this with wide borders or heavy backgrounds stand out. For this reason, employers usually advertise key positions in separate display ads.

Develop interest in the job. You can create interest by the nature of the job itself, with lines such as "you'll thrive on challenging work." You can also use other aspects of the job, such as its location, to create interest.

Create desire by spotlighting the job's interest factors with words such as *travel* or *challenge,* for instance. Keep your target audience in mind. For example, having a graduate school nearby may appeal to engineers and professional people.

▲ *Jerry Holder's ongoing recruiting efforts for the workers he needs in the two Allegra Print and Imaging locations he manages in Tulsa begin with help wanted advertising. Holder places "friendly" newspaper ads, written in warm, welcoming language, to attract candidates for sales, production, and quality-control positions. The ads' message is, "Let's see if it fits. Come in and see the place." Holder then offers each prospect a shop tour and introductions to key employees.*

▶ **FIGURE 4-6**
Help Wanted Ad

Source: *New York Times*, September 23, 2001, p. BU16. Used with permission.

Finally, make sure the ad prompts action with a statement like "call today," or "write today for more information."

After over 30 years of living with EEO laws, we might imagine that by now most employers are familiar with the sorts of things they usually can't put in ads (such as "man wanted," or "young woman preferred"). Yet the results of one recent study on illegal recruitment advertisement suggests that questionable or illegal ads still do slip into recruitment advertising, so this is apparently still an area that requires caution.[39]

Being Creative Employers today are making their ads more creative: "Today, recruitment ads sell the company's image, promote its benefits, and often bear more resemblance to ads for products than ads for jobs." Firms are pushing their family friendliness (the consulting firm Booz, Allen & Hamilton has a diaper pin in one ad, for instance). They're also having advertising firms develop professional-looking ads. And they're being more careful about placement: One sporting goods store now places help wanted ads in the newspaper's sports section—not on the help wanted pages—on the assumption "that's where the avid sports fans go daily, and they are the people an employer would like to hire."[40]

Employment Agencies

There are three types of employment agencies: (1) public agencies operated by federal, state, or local governments; (2) agencies associated with nonprofit organizations; and (3) privately owned agencies.[41]

Public and Nonprofit Agencies   Every state has a public, state-run employment service agency. The U.S. Department of Labor supports these agencies, in part through grants, and in part through other assistance such as a nationwide computerized job bank. The National Job Bank enables agency counselors in one state to advise applicants about available jobs not just in their local area, but in other areas as well.

These agencies are an important source of blue-collar and white-collar workers, but some employers have had mixed experiences with them. For one thing, applicants for unemployment insurance are required to register and to make themselves available for job interviews. A fraction of these people are not interested in getting back to work, so employers can end up with applicants who have little or no real desire for immediate employment. And fairly or not, employers probably view some of these local agencies as somewhat lethargic in their efforts to fill area employers' jobs.

Yet these agencies' usefulness is actually on the rise. Beyond just filling jobs, for instance, counselors will visit an employer's work site, review the employer's job requirements, and even assist the employer in writing job descriptions. Some states, like Illinois and Wisconsin, are turning their local state employment service agencies into "one-stop" shops. The 1998 Workforce Investment Act required states to give any citizen access to one-stop-shop neighborhood training/employment/educational services centers. One user says of the Queens New York One Stop Career Center in Jamaica, "I love it: I've made this place like a second home."[42] Services available to employers include recruitment services, tax credit information, training programs and access to local and national labor market information.[43]

Other employment agencies are tied to nonprofit organizations. Most professional and technical societies, such as the Institute for Electrical and Electronic Engineers (IEEE), have units that help members find jobs. Many public welfare agencies try to place people who are in special categories, such as those who are physically disabled or are war veterans.

Private Agencies   Private employment agencies are important sources of clerical, white-collar, and managerial personnel. They charge fees (set by state law and posted in their offices) for each applicant they place. Market conditions generally determine whether candidate or employer pays the fee. The trend is toward fee-paid jobs, in which the employer pays the fee. Employers correctly assume this is the best way to attract qualified, currently employed applicants who might not be so willing to switch jobs if they had to pay the fees.

Why turn to an agency? Reasons include:

1. Your firm doesn't have its own HR department and is not geared to doing recruiting and screening.
2. Your firm has found it difficult in the past to generate a pool of qualified applicants.
3. You must fill a particular opening quickly.
4. There is a perceived need to attract a greater number of minority or female applicants.
5. You want to reach currently employed individuals, who might feel more comfortable dealing with agencies than with competing companies.
6. You want to cut down on the time you're devoting to interviewing.[44]

Yet employment agencies are no panacea. For example, the employment agency's screening may let poor applicants bypass the preliminary stages of your own selection process.[45] Unqualified applicants may thus go directly to the supervisors responsible for hiring, who may in turn naively hire them. Such errors show up in high turnover and absenteeism rates, morale problems, and low quality and productivity. Conversely, improper testing and screening at the employment agency could block potentially successful applicants from entering your applicant pool.

To help avoid such problems, experts suggest the following:

1. Give the agency an accurate and complete job description. The better it understands the job you want filled, the greater the likelihood it will produce a reasonable pool of applicants.
2. Tests, application blanks, and interviews should be a part of the agency's selection process. At the very least, you should know which devices the agency uses and consider their relevance to the selection process. Any subjective decision-making procedures should be of particular concern.
3. Periodically review data on candidates accepted or rejected by your firm, and by the agency. Check on the effectiveness and fairness of the agency's screening process.
4. If feasible, develop a long-term relationship with one or two agencies. It may also make sense to designate one person to serve as the liaison between employer and agency.
5. Screen the agency. Check with other managers or HR people to find out which agencies have been the most effective at filling the sorts of positions you need filled. Review the Internet and a few back issues of the Sunday classified ads to discover the agencies that handle the positions you want. Then question them: What is the background of the agency's staff? What are their education and experience levels? Do they have the qualifications to understand the sorts of jobs for which you are recruiting? What is their reputation in the community and with the Better Business Bureau?

Temp Agencies and Alternative Staffing

Employers often supplement their permanent workforce by hiring contingent or temporary workers, often through temporary help employment agencies. Also known as *part-time* or *just-in-time workers*, the contingent workforce is big and growing. It recently accounted for about 20% of all new jobs created in the United States. Such workers are broadly defined as workers who don't have permanent jobs.[46]

Today's contingent workforce isn't limited to clerical or maintenance staff. In one year, almost 100,000 people found temporary work in engineering, science, or management support occupations, for instance.[47] And growing numbers of firms use temporary workers as short-term chief financial officers, or even chief executive officers. It's estimated that 60% of the total U.S. temporary payroll is nonclerical and includes "CEOs, human resources directors, computer systems analysts, accountants, doctors, and nurses."[48] Over 84% of employers now reportedly use temp agencies, and their use is on the rise.[49]

Some firms today employ so many temporary workers that they hire temporary agencies to help manage them. New York–based MasterCard, for instance, has a temporary workforce of 200 to 400 workers on any given day, and retained Manpower, Inc., a large temporary staffing agency, to coordinate the hiring, training, and paperwork of new temporary workers. The temporary employment agency may even assign on-site supervisors to help manage duties like these.[50] Some temp agencies are even opening in shopping malls. Olsten Staffing Services opened centers in six locations to assist mall tenants in areas such as job postings, temporary employment, candidate screening and interviewing, background checks, reliability and integrity testing, and training.[51]

Benefits and Costs Contingent staffing is on the rise for several reasons. Historically, of course, employers have always used "temps" to fill in for permanent employees who were out sick or on vacation. But today's desire for ever-higher productivity also contributes to temp workers' growing popularity. As one expert puts it, "Productivity is measured in terms of output per hour paid for," and "if employees are paid only when they're working, as contingent workers are, overall productivity increases."[52] Employers also find that by tapping temporary help agencies, they can save the time and expense of personally recruiting and training new workers, as well as the expenses involved in personnel documentation (such as filing payroll taxes and maintaining absence records).[53] Corporate downsizings are another factor: For example, while DuPont cut its workforce by about 47,000 in recent years, it also says that only 70% of those people actually stopped working for the company.

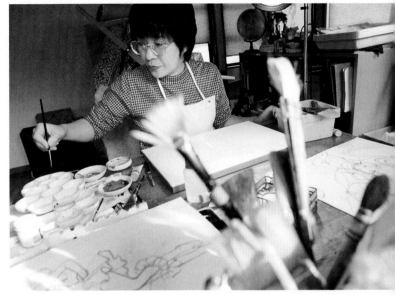

▲ *Temporary and freelance employees are increasing in number both within and outside the United States. Alemi Takada is a noted Japanese freelance animator who manages her workload and enhances her reputation abroad by working with an agency instead of for one of her many long-term clients. The agency, Creek & River company, represents about 15,000 people in media and publishing careers and has organized exhibitions of Takada's work in the United States and Taiwan.*

The remaining 30%—about 14,000 workers—returned in some temporary capacity, or as vendors or contractors.[54] Temp firms can be especially useful for seasonal hires. The HR director for one Long Beach, California, restaurant chain says: "Most of the time, it is a better quality labor force: Candidates arrive already pretested and trained."[55]

The benefits of contingent staffers don't come without a price. They may be more productive and less expensive to recruit and train, but contingent workers from temporary agencies generally cost employers 20% to 50% more than comparable permanent workers (per hour or per week), since the agency gets a fee. Furthermore, "people have a psychological reference point to their place of employment. Once you put them in the contingent category, you're saying they're expendable."[56] One would also assume that such expendable workers are less likely to exhibit the loyalty many employers expect from their permanent workers. The fact that a lot of these workers take temp jobs hoping "to get a full-time job" (although "additional income" is the top stated reason) may intensify this problem, to the extent that a temp finds his or her hopes dashed.[57] Periods of low unemployment may also lead some temporary agencies to become less selective in choosing the people they send out to employers.[58]

Guidelines for Success In order to make such employment relationships as fruitful as possible, anyone recruiting temps should understand these employees' main concerns. In one survey, six key concerns emerged. Temporary workers said they were:

1. Treated by employers in a dehumanizing, impersonal, and ultimately discouraging way.
2. Insecure about their employment and pessimistic about the future.

3. Worried about their lack of insurance and pension benefits.
4. Misled about their job assignments and in particular about whether temporary assignments were likely to become full-time positions.
5. "Underemployed" (particularly those trying to return to the full-time labor market).
6. In general angry toward the corporate world and its values; participants repeatedly expressed feelings of alienation and disenchantment.[59]

Given such concerns, what can employers do to boost the probability that relationships with temporary workers will be mutually beneficial? Here are some guidelines:[60]

1. Provide honest information to both temporary agencies and temporary workers about the length of the job assignment.
2. Implement personnel policies that ensure fair, nondiscriminatory treatment of temporary workers, as you do for permanent ones.
3. Use independent contractors (people who—like consultants—work for themselves rather than for the company) and permanent part-time employees to complement the conventional temporary agency workforce. These people are likely to be more familiar with your firm's procedures and more committed to its goals than are temporary workers.
4. Before hiring temporary workers, consider their potential impact on regular full-time employees. For example, any apparent exploitation or mistreatment of contingent workers may have a corrosive effect on permanent workers' morale.
5. Provide the necessary training and orientation. One survey's comments included, "[Organizations] need to be more specific in their instructions to temps. Give them the [correct] tools and materials to do their jobs."
6. Don't use a classification such as "independent contractor" to avoid paying the taxes to which temp (or regular) employees are actually entitled.[61]

Working with temporary agencies also requires special care. Ensure basic policies and procedures are in place, including:

Invoicing. Get a sample copy of the agency's invoice. Make sure it fits your company's needs.

Time sheets. With temps, the time sheet is not just a verification of hours worked. Once the worker's supervisor signs it, it's usually an agreement to pay the agency's fees.

Temp-to-perm policy. What is the policy if the client wants to hire one of the agency's temps as a permanent employee?

Recruitment of and benefits for temp employees. Find out how the agency plans to recruit employees and what sorts of benefits it pays.

Dress code. Specify the appropriate attire at each of your offices or plants.

Equal employment opportunity statement. Get a document from the agency stating that it is not discriminating when filling temp orders.

Job description information. Have a procedure whereby you can ensure the agency understands the job to be filled and the sort of person, in terms of skills and so forth, you want to fill it.[62]

alternative staffing
The use of nontraditional recruitment sources.

Alternative Staffing Temporary employees are examples of what HR professionals call **alternative staffing**—basically, the use of nontraditional recruitment sources. The use of alternative staffing sources is widespread and growing; one survey found that about 1 of 10 U.S. employees is employed in some type of alternative work arrangement.[63] Other alternative staffing arrangements include "in-house temporary employees" (people employed directly by the company, but on an explicit short-term basis), and "contract technical employees" (highly skilled workers like engineers, who are supplied for long-term projects under contract from an outside technical services firm).

Executive Recruiters

Executive recruiters (also called headhunters) are special employment agencies retained by employers to seek out top-management talent for their clients. They fill jobs in the $60,000-and-up category, although $80,000 is often the lower limit. The percentage of your firm's positions filled by these services might be small. However, these jobs would include crucial executive and technical positions. For executive positions, headhunters may be your only source of candidates. The employer always pays their fees.

Two trends—technology and specialization—are changing the executive search business. Top firms used to take up to seven months to complete a big search. Much of that time was spent shuffling chores between headhunters and researchers who dig up the initial "long list" of candidates.[64] This time frame is too long in today's fast-moving environment. Most recruiting firms are therefore establishing Internet-linked computerized databases the aim of which, according to one senior recruiter, is "to create a long list by pushing a button."[65] Korn/Ferry launched a new Internet service called Futurestep to draw more managerial applicants into its files; in turn, it has teamed up with the *Wall Street Journal*, which runs a career Web site of its own.[66]

Executive recruiters are also becoming more specialized, and the large ones are creating new businesses aimed specifically at specialized functions or industries. For example, LAI Ward Howell recently launched a new business specializing in financial executives, with bases in London and New York.[67]

Recruiters can be useful. They have many contacts and are especially adept at contacting qualified, currently employed candidates who aren't actively looking to change jobs. They can also keep your firm's name confidential until late into the search process. The recruiter can save top management's time by advertising for the position and screening what could turn out to be hundreds of applicants. The recruiter's fee might actually turn out to be insignificant compared with the cost of the executive time saved.

But there are pitfalls. As an employer, it is essential for you to explain completely what sort of candidate is required—and why. Some recruiters are also more salespeople than professionals. They may be more interested in persuading you to hire a candidate than in finding one who will really do the job. Recruiters also claim that what their clients say they want is often not really accurate. Therefore, be prepared for some in-depth dissecting of your request.

In choosing a recruiter, guidelines include:[68]

1. Make sure the firm is capable of conducting a thorough search. Under the code of the Association of Executive Recruiting Consultants, a recruiter can't approach the executive talent of a former client for a vacancy with a new client for a period of two years after completing a search for the former client. Since former clients are off limits for two years, the recruiter must search from a constantly diminishing pool. Particularly for the largest executive recruiting firms, it could turn out to be very difficult to deliver a top-notch candidate, since the best potential candidates may already be working for the recruiter's former clients.

2. Meet the individual who will actually handle your assignment. If this person hasn't the ability to seek out top candidates and sell them on your firm, it's unlikely you'll get to see the best candidates. In wooing you as a new client, the search firm may send someone with a record of successfully signing new clients. This may not be the person who will do the actual search.

3. Ask how much the search firm charges. There are several things to keep in mind here. Search firm fees range from 25% to 35% of the guaranteed annual income of the position. They are often payable one-third as a retainer at the outset, one-third at the end of 30 days, and one-third after 60 days. Often a fee is on a "retained" rather than on a contingency basis—it's payable whether or not the search is terminated for any reason. The out-of-pocket expenses are extra and could run to 10% to 20% of the fee itself, and sometimes more. Get the agreement in writing.[69]

4. Choose a recruiter you can trust with privileged information. This person will find not only your firm's strengths, but also its weaknesses.

5. Talk to some of the firm's clients. Get the names of two or three companies for whom the firm has recently completed assignments. Ask such questions as: "Was the recruiter's appraisal of the candidate accurate?" "Was the placement a success? Did the firm conduct a search, or just fill the job from its files?" "And did the recruiter accurately craft the job specifications?"[70]

ENTREPRENEURS HR

Expanding the Management Team

There comes a time in the life of most small businesses when it dawns on the owner that his or her managers are incapable of taking the company to the next level. If the company is to expand, the entrepreneur must decide what kinds of people to hire from outside, and how to hire them. Should the owner recruit this person? Or is an outside expert required?

While most large firms don't think twice about hiring executive search firms, small-firm owners will understandably hesitate before committing to a fee that could reach $20,000 to $30,000 (with expenses) for a $60,000 to $70,000 marketing manager. As an entrepreneur, however, you should keep in mind that such thinking can be shortsighted.

Engaging in a search like this by yourself is not at all like looking for secretaries, supervisors, or data entry clerks. When you are looking to hire a key executive to help you run your firm, chances are you are not going to find your candidate by placing ads or using most of the other traditional approaches. For one thing, the person you seek is probably employed and not reading the want ads. If he or she does happen to glance at the ads, chances are the person is happy enough not to make the effort to embark on a job search with you.

In other words, what you'll end up with is a drawer of résumés of people who are, for one reason or another, out of work, unhappy with their work, or unsuited for your job. It is then going to fall on you to try to find several gems in this group by devoting the time to interview and assess these applicants.

Doing so is harder than it sounds. First, as a nonexpert, you may not even know where to begin. You won't know where to place or how to write the ads; you won't know where to search, who to contact, or how to do the sort of job that needs to be done to screen out the laggards and misfits who may well appear on the surface to be viable candidates. You also won't know enough to really do the kind of background checking that a position at this level requires. Second, this process is going to be extremely time consuming and will divert your attention from other duties. Many business owners find that when they consider the opportunity costs (of not making sales calls, for instance), they are not saving any money at all.

Some owners do have success doing their own executive recruiting. Before retaining a recruiter, they make a list of five or ten competitors in their area, and contact individuals there who might be logical prospects. Sometimes the approach is direct, and sometimes it's not: The manager might describe the position and say something like "is there anyone in your network who you could recommend?"[71]

If you do decide to do the job yourself, consider retaining the services of an industrial psychologist to spend four or five hours assessing the problem-solving ability, personality, interests, and energy level of the two or three candidates in which you are most interested. Although you certainly don't want the psychologist to make the decision for you, the input can provide a valuable perspective on the candidates.

Exercise special care when recruiting applicants from competing companies. Always check to see if applicants are bound by noncompete or nondisclosure agreements, for instance. And (especially when recruiting other firms' higher-level employees) you may want to check with an attorney before asking certain questions—regarding patents or potential antitrust issues, for instance.[72]

College Recruiting

Sending an employer's representatives to college campuses to prescreen applicants and create an applicant pool from that college's graduating class is an important source of management trainees, promotable candidates, and professional and technical employees. One study concluded, for instance, that new college grads filled about 38% of all externally filled jobs requiring a college degree; the percentage just for entry-level jobs requiring a college degree would probably be much higher. [73]

There are two main problems with on-campus recruiting. First, it is expensive and time consuming. Schedules must be set well in advance, company brochures printed, records of interviews kept, and much time spent on campus. Second, as mentioned earlier, recruiters themselves are sometimes ineffective, or worse. Some recruiters are unprepared, show little interest in the candidate, and act superior. Many recruiters also don't effectively screen their student candidates. Such findings underscore the need to train recruiters in how to interview candidates, in what the company has to offer, and in how to put candidates at ease.[74]

Like other recruiting sources, college recruiting seems to fall off as economic conditions wind down. For example, as the economy slowed in 2001, BellSouth Telecommunications cut its recruiting from graduating classes by about 50% compared with the previous year.[75]

College Recruiting Goals The campus recruiter has two main goals. The main one is determining whether a candidate is worthy of further consideration. Exactly which traits to look for will depend on your company's specific needs. However, the report in Figure 4-7 is typical. Traits to assess include communication skills, education, experience, and interpersonal skills.[76]

The other aim is to attract good candidates. A sincere and informal attitude, respect for the applicant as an individual, and prompt follow-up letters can help sell the employer to the interviewee. Employers therefore have to choose recruiters and schools carefully. Employers naturally look among their employees for those who can do the best job of identifying top applicants and filling vacancies. Factors in selecting schools in which to recruit include the school's reputation and the performance of previous hires from that source.[77]

On-Site Visits Employers generally invite good candidates to the employer's office or plant for an on-site visit, and there are several ways to make this visit fruitful.[78] The invitation letter should be warm and friendly but businesslike, and should give the person a choice of dates to visit the company. Assign someone to meet the applicant, preferably at the airport or at his or her hotel, and to act as host. A package describing the applicant's schedule as well as other information regarding the company—such as annual reports and employee benefits—should be waiting

▼ **FIGURE 4-7 Campus Applicant Interview Report**

NORTH DAKOTA STATE COLLEGE OF SCIENCE
INTERVIEW REPORT

This is an official document. Complete in pen. Please limit your evaluation comments strictly to objective statements, which may be supported as reflecting the actual requirements of the position. Non-job related factors should not be part of the selection process.

Name of person interviewed _____

Applying for position of _____

Department _____

1. Qualifications (job related)	Excellent	Satisfactory	Unsatisfactory
A. Communication			
B. Education			
C. Related Experience			
D. Interpersonal Skills			
E. Ability to Analyze & Solve Problems			
F. Adaptability to Change			

2. Remarks (related to overall qualifications necessary for the position as stated in the position description). This section must be completed.

A. Strengths_____
_____
_____

B. Weaknesses _____
_____
_____

3. Other Comments_____
_____

Reason for selection/nonselection: _____
      (circle one)
_____

Completed by_____   _____
      Signature of Interviewer   Date

"NDSCS is an Equal Opportunity/Affirmative Action Employer"

5/97

NDSCS Home Page	Table of Contents	HR Home Page

Source: North Dakota State College of Science. Used with permission.

for the applicant at the hotel. Carefully plan the interviews and adhere to the schedule. Interruptions should be avoided; give the candidate the undivided attention of each person with whom he or she interviews. Luncheon should be hosted by one or more other recently hired graduates with whom the applicant may feel more at ease. Make an offer, if any, as soon as possible, preferably at the time of the visit. If this is not possible, tell the candidate when to expect a decision. If an offer is made, keep in mind that the applicant may have other offers, too. Frequent follow-ups to "find out how the decision process is going" or to "ask if there are any other questions" may help to tilt the applicant in your favor.

Internships Many college students get their jobs through college internships, a recruiting approach that has grown dramatically in recent years. It's estimated that almost three-quarters of all recent college students took part in an internship before they graduated, for instance.[79]

Internships can be win–win situations for both students and employers. For students, it may mean being able to hone business skills, check out potential employers, and learn more about their likes (and dislikes) when it comes to choosing careers. And employers, of course, can use the interns to make useful contributions while evaluating them as possible full-time employees.

Referrals and Walk-Ins

"Employee referrals" campaigns are another option. The firm posts announcements of openings and requests for referrals in its bulletin and on its wallboards and intranet; prizes or cash rewards are offered for referrals that culminate in hirings. Employee referrals have been the source of almost half of all hires at AmeriCredit since the firm kicked off its "you've got friends, we want to meet them" employee referrals program. Employees making a referral receive $1000 awards, with the payments spread over a year. As the head of recruiting says, "Quality people know quality people. If you give employees the opportunity to make referrals, they automatically suggest high caliber people because they are stakeholders. . . ."[80]

Employee referral programs have pros and cons. Current employees can and usually will provide accurate information about the job applicants they are referring, especially since they're putting their own reputations on the line.[81] The new employees may also come with a more realistic picture of what working in the firm is like after speaking with friends there. But the success for the campaign depends a lot on employee morale.[82] And the campaign can backfire if an employee's referral is rejected and the employee becomes dissatisfied. Using referrals exclusively may also be discriminatory if most current employees (and their referrals) are male or white.

Employee referral programs are increasingly popular. Of the firms responding to one survey, 40% said they use an employee referral system and hire about 15% of their employees that way. A cash award for referring hired candidates is the most common incentive. Large firms reportedly spent about $34,000 annually on their referral programs (including cash payments for candidates), medium companies spent about $17,000, and small ones with fewer than 500 employees spent about $3,600. The cost per hire, however, is usually low; average per-hire expenses were only $388, far below the cost of an employment service.[83] However some employee referrals programs pay more. For example, the learning Web site Docent™ (www.docent.com) pays $5,000 for each technical person hired.[84]

Recruiting high-tech employees (remember nerd rustling?) is especially amenable to referral programs. Sources like the Internet are widely used for recruiting high-tech workers, but some experts contend that the most effective recruiting method is to encourage existing employees to refer qualified friends and colleagues. Awards for referrals can go as high as $5,000 for a new hire.[85] Even fast-moving Internet firms like Double-click, Inc., rely heavily on employee referral programs. For example, the company's internal referrals were up 43% in the first quarter of 2000.[86]

Referrals can also facilitate hiring a diverse workforce. One survey found 70% of minority/ethnic candidates search for jobs on corporate Web sites; 67% use general job listing sites, 53% classified ads, 52% referrals, and 35% headhunter/agencies. However only 6% listed "corporate Web site" as one of the top five ways they actually found jobs; 25% listed referrals.[87]

Particularly for hourly workers, walk-ins—direct applications made at your office—are a major source of applicants; employers encourage this by posting HIRING signs on the property. Treat walk-ins courteously and diplomatically, for the sake of both the employer's community reputation and the applicant's self-esteem. Many employers give every walk-in a brief interview with someone in the HR office, even if it is only to get information on the applicant "in case a position should be open in the future." Good business practice also requires answering all letters of inquiry from applicants promptly and courteously.

Don't underestimate the importance of employee referrals or in-house job postings. One review of recruitment sources concluded, for instance, that "referrals by current personnel, in-house job postings, and the rehiring of former employees are the most effective sources. Walk-ins have been slightly less effective, and the least effective sources are newspaper ads, school placement services, and employment agencies (government/private)."[88]

▲ *Jose Martin is head of human resources at Electronic Arts, maker of some of the world's most popular computer games. EA has assembled a pool of 34,000 potential job candidates using an interactive Web-based application called e-Recruiter. If the candidate's interests and talents match a current opening in the firm, the system notifies both the candidate and a hiring manager, but if there is no current match, EA takes one more step—instead of ending the interaction, the program offers the option of receiving future e-mails about new products and new job openings. Well over half those currently registered have said "yes."*

Recruiting on the Internet

A large and fast-growing proportion of employers use the Internet as a recruiting tool. The percentage of Fortune 500 companies recruiting via the Internet jumped from 10% in 1997 to 75% in 2000.

Not surprisingly, computer-related positions were the jobs most commonly filled through Internet postings (accounting for 59% of the workers hired).[89] Most résumés still arrive through traditional routes, however. In one recent survey, 42% of résumés came through regular mail, 30% came via fax, 6% were hand-delivered, 17% came via e-mail, and 5% came through firms' Web sites.[90]

Employers are using Internet recruiting in numerous ways. A Boston-based recruiting firm posts job descriptions on its Web page.[91] NEC Electronics, Inc., Unisys Corporation, and LSI Logicorp have all posted Internet-based "cyber fairs" to recruit for applicants.[92] Cisco Systems, Inc., has a Web site with a Careers at Cisco page. This offers links to such things as hot jobs (job descriptions for hard-to-fill positions); Cisco culture (a look at Cisco work life); Cisco College (internships and mentoring program information); and jobs (job listings).[93]

Using a corporate Web site to attract surfers requires making it easy to use the site. Thus, 71% of The Standard & Poors 500 place employment information just one click away from their home pages.[94] Job seekers can submit their résumés online at 90% of the Fortune 500 Web sites; however, only about 25% give job seekers the option of completing online applications, although it is the method many applicants prefer, according to one expert.[95]

Employers list several advantages of Internet recruiting. First, it is cost effective: Newspapers can charge from $50 to $100 to several thousand dollars for print ads; job listings on the Internet may cost as little as $10 each. The newspaper ad might also have a life span of perhaps 10 days, whereas the Internet ad may keep attracting applications for 30 days or more.[96] Internet recruiting can also be more timely. Responses to electronic job listings may come the day the ad is posted, whereas responses to newspaper ads can take a week just to reach an employer (although including a fax-response number can provide quick responses, too). Employers can use Internet support tools such as Recruiter Toolbox to develop online ads that include prescreening tests which further automate the recruiting process.[97] They can use a variety of job search sites, such as dice.com (see Webnote) and monster.com. A list of Web sites is presented in Table 4-1.[98]

Some firms have been phenomenally successful using Internet recruiting. For example, when Boeing Company had to hire 13,000 employees fast, it opened its recruiting Web site. Only 200 résumés were received the first month, but within three months 19,000 résumés had arrived, and in six months, 50,000.[99]

Some employers cite just such a flood of responses as a downside of Internet recruiting. The problem is that the relative ease of responding to Internet ads encourages unqualified job seekers to apply; furthermore, applications may arrive from geographic areas that are unrealistically far away. On the whole, though, more applicants are usually better than fewer, and more companies are using their computers to scan, digitize, and process applicant résumés automatically.[100]

▲ **WEBNOTE**

Job search Web sites such as dice.com also give employers access to large pools of candidates.

www.dice.com

HR NET

Recruiting Online

Online recruiting Web sites like monster.com actually represent just the tip of the iceberg for employers seeking good résumés. For example, one online recruiter pointed out that "while monster and its competitors have about 5 million unique resumes in their databases, you can find double or triple that number on the open Internet." These résumés are hidden away at the Web sites of virtual communities such as GeoCities and Tripod, and at the Web sites of archived newsgroup postings and listserve messages.

Suppose, for example, you want to find résumés of programmers in Florida who are comfortable on the UNIX platform. On GeoCities, go to www.geocities.com and in the text field under Explore Our Neighborhoods, type: resume *and* programmer *and* UNIX *and* Florida. Then click *Search* and start reviewing résumés.

You can get even better results on sites like Angelfire or Tripod. These allow you to use Boolean operators (such as *and*, *or*, *not*, and *near*), and even to focus on specific telephone area codes for your search. So, for your programmer search on Angelfire, type: resume *and* programmer *and* UNIX *and* (Florida *near* 305 or 954). Then click the *Go Get It* button for personal Web sites and résumés—possible candidates.

You can also adjust your search to see through walled-off areas of Web sites or to unearth hard-to-find links. For example, on Alta Vista's advanced search function, type in Cisco.com *and* business development. You'll find about 80 pages, including the firm's promotion announcements and executive news. Would you like an applicant who graduated from Wharton and has experience at McKinsey & Co.? Type in Wharton.penn.edu *and* McKinsey.

Sources: Glenn Gutmacher, "Secrets of Online Recruiters Exposed!" *Workforce,* October 2000, pp. 44–50. Anna Muoio, "The Great Talent Caper," *Fast Company,* September 2000, pp. 44–46.

▶ **TABLE 4-1**
Sample List of
Recruiting Web Sites

America's Job Bank www.ajb.dni.us
On this site candidates can search for jobs by occupation, location, education and experience levels, and salary. Those with a military background can search for civilian jobs that match their areas of expertise. Employers can cull a pool of nearly 2 million job seekers.

CareerBuilder www.careerbuilder.com
CareerBuilder offers information about career advancement and workplace trends, including tips and news for students and recent grads. Users can search more than 50 leading job sites that are part of the CareerBuilder network, with access to more than 3 million job postings.

CareerMosaic www.careermosaic.com
CareerMosaic offers insider profiles on such companies as Microsoft and Canon. Job seekers can search for openings by geographic area, job description, or company name. CareerMosaic has links to more than a dozen countries in North America, Europe, and the Pacific Rim.

CareerShop.com www.careershop.com
In addition to providing easy searches for job seekers and a pool of nearly 300,000 résumés for employers, CareerShop offers a marketplace for freelancers and employers, guidance for employers on human resource issues, and a variety of counseling services.

ComputerJobs.com www.computerjobs.com
ComputerJobs.com is the leading information technology employment site, with job opportunities organized by specific skills and regional markets. As part of its virtual recruiting service for employers, ComputerJobs.com will do online behavioral testing and credit checks of candidates.

Dice.com www.dice.com
This is the first place to look for many IT professionals. This site lists over 150,000 job openings, both permanent and contractual.

Employment911.com www.employment911.com
This meta-site can speed your search by quickly scanning its own listings and those of 35 other sites.

JobOptions www.joboptions.com
Contemplating a move? On the JobOptions site, users can compute comparable salaries for different cities based on housing and other factors, and they can search by job classification, location, and qualifications. Employers can search more than 250,000 résumés.

Jobs.com www.jobs.com
Get the inside scoop on working for major companies with jobs.com's Testify section. Jobs.com offers free software that simplifies the process of writing and delivering a résumé via the Internet. The site features interactive career fairs (with chat and video Web casts) with employers.

JobTrak.com www.jobtrak.com
JobTrak.com is the largest site for college students and alumni. It has partnerships with more than 1,000 university career centers, MBA programs, and alumni associations. Students can receive advice from college counselors, contact alumni, and learn to negotiate a salary package.

Monster.com www.monster.com
The big daddy of job boards with 3 million resumes, Monster.com has "communities" for students, techies, and the self-employed. Users can create a career management account where they can store up to five résumés, track applications, and receive news tailored to their interests.

Applicant Tracking Indeed, more firms are also installing applicant tracking systems to support their on- and offline recruiting efforts. Well-known tracking systems (such as recruitsoft.com, and Itrack-IT solutions) help employers monitor applicants.[101] They provide employers with several services, including requisitions management (for monitoring open jobs), applicant data collection (for scanning applicants' data into the system), and reporting (to create various recruiting-related reports such as cost per hire and hire by source).[102] See the Strategic HR box for how Sutter Health used these services.

STRATEGIC HR

With 10,000 job openings per year, Sutter Health had to generate a lot more recruits to continue its fast-growth strategy. However, moving its job postings online not only didn't help, but actually complicated the process.[103]

Moving the postings online did generate many more applications—300,000 a year, to be exact—but it didn't speed up the hiring process. Sutter Health was hit by so many résumés coming in by e-mail and through its Web site that the applications ended up in a huge pile, waiting for Sutter affiliates' HR departments to get to them. It was obvious that if the company wanted to grow and to provide the value-added services to its affiliates it had built its reputation on, it needed a new recruiting approach.

Sutter Health's solution was to sign on with a company called Recruitsoft, Inc., of San Francisco. Recruitsoft is an e-recruiting applications service provider (ASP), and it now does all the work of hosting Sutter Health's job site (see Webnote). As an applications service provider, Recruitsoft doesn't just post Sutter Health job openings and collect its résumés. Recruitsoft also gives Sutter Health "an automated way to evaluate, rank and match IT and other job candidates with specific openings." For example, Recruitsoft's system automatically screens incoming résumés, compares them with Sutter's job requirements, and flags high-priority applicants. And this, says Keith Vencel, the project manager who came up with this solution, helped Sutter cut its recruiting process from weeks to days—and thereby helped ensure that Sutter's expansion strategy stays on track.

▲ **WEBNOTE**

E-recruiting applications service providers like recruitsoft.com host company job sites and speed the recruiting process by screening candidates.

www.recruitsoft.com

◆**HIGH-PERFORMANCE INSIGHT** When it comes to effective recruiting, the rubber really hits the road, as they say, when it comes to recruiting high-tech workers. Turnover among these in-demand elites is reportedly around 17%. And according to the Information Technology Association of America, about 1 out of 10 information technology jobs in the United States is unfilled.[104]

The recruiting methods used by one industry leader—GE Medical—illustrate how employers apply best practices to the job of recruiting high-tech workers. GE Medical's competitive strategy of staying on the cutting edge of equipment design makes hiring large numbers of top-flight tech workers essential. In fact, the company hires about 500 technical workers a year to invent and make sophisticated medical devices such as CT scanners and magnetic resonance imagers. Since GE Medical must compete for talent with the likes of Intel, Microsoft, and Cisco Systems, it's interesting that it recently managed to cut its cost of hiring by 17%, reduced time to fill the positions by 20% to 30%, and cut in half the percentage of new hires who don't work out.[105]

GE Medical accomplished this by applying the sorts of best practices management techniques that made its parent, General Electric Corporation, a profit powerhouse. According to one of its managers, the firm decided to "benchmark off procurement and supplier management initiatives in other areas of the business. We know everything about acquiring wires and screws and boards and computers."[106] What GE Medical did was apply the same techniques to the job of high-tech recruiting.

For example, GE Medical draws up a "multigenerational staffing plan" to go with each of its product's multiyear product plan. That way, management can predict two or three years ahead the sorts of specific needs (such as for "absolute algorithm" experts) for which it's going to have to hire and train.

GE Medical has also applied some of its purchasing techniques to its dealings with recruiters. For example, it called a meeting several years ago and told 20 recruiters that it would work with only the 10 best of them. To measure "best," the company created measurements inspired by manufacturing techniques, such as the percentage of résumés that result in interviews and the percentage of interviews that lead to offers.

Applying a more benchmarks-oriented approach also worked with college recruiting. For example, GE Medical's chief recruiter analyzed the recruiting system and found that former summer interns were twice as likely to accept the job offer as other candidates. GE Medical then tripled the size of the internship program. And to make sure they don't spend their time photocopying files, interns are given challenging group and team projects.

Similarly, GE's corporatewide quality control program enabled GE Medical to discover that current employees are very effective as references for new high-tech employees. Overall, for instance, GE Medical calls for interviews just 1% of applicants whose résumés it receives, while 10% of employee referrals result not just in interviews, but also in actual hires.

As a result, GE Medical took steps that doubled the number of employee referrals. For example, it simplified the referral forms, eliminated bureaucratic submission procedures, and added a small reward like a Sears gift certificate for referring a qualified candidate. And it upped the ante—$2,000 if someone referred is hired, and $3,000 if he or she is a software engineer.

RECRUITING A MORE DIVERSE WORKFORCE

Recruiting a diverse workforce isn't just socially responsible: It's a necessity, given the rapid increase in minority, older worker, and women candidates. Doing so means taking special steps to recruit these people.

Recruiting Single Parents

About two-thirds of all single parents are in the workforce today, and this group is an important source of candidates.

Attracting single parents begins with understanding the problems they encounter in balancing work and family life.[107] In one survey, working single parents (the majority single mothers) said their work responsibilities interfered significantly with their family life. They described the challenge of having to do a good job at work and being a good parent; many expressed disappointment at feeling like failures in both endeavors. To quote from the survey's report:

> Many described falling into bed exhausted at midnight without even minimal time for themselves. They reported rushing through every activity and constantly feeling pressured to keep on going and do more. Vacations, which can be a time to rejuvenate, were often used for children's appointments or to handle unexpected emergencies. They often needed personal sick time or excused days off to care for sick children. As one mother noted, "I don't have enough sick days to get sick."[108]

The respondents viewed themselves as having "less support, less personal time, more stress and greater difficulty balancing job and home life" than other working parents.[109] However, most were hesitant to dwell on their single-parent status at work; they feared that doing so would affect their jobs and careers adversely. Thirty-five percent of the single mothers reported feeling that it was more difficult for them to achieve a proper work–family balance compared with 10% of the dual-earner mothers.[110] Some single mothers said the firms treated them differently than their male colleagues at work. For example, "When a single mother asks if she can go to her child's school play, she is seen as not committed to her job and often not allowed to go, while a male single parent is more often told 'Sure. It's just great that you are so interested in your children.'"[111]

Given such concerns, the first step in attracting (and keeping) single mothers is to make the workplace as user friendly for them as is practical. Many firms aim at being more family friendly, but their programs may not be extensive enough, particularly for single parents. For example, many employers already give employees some schedule flexibility (such as one-hour windows at the beginning or end of the day). The problem is that "for some single mothers, this flexibility can help but it may not be sufficient to really make a difference in their ability to juggle work and family schedules."[112] In addition to flexibility, employers can and should train their supervisors to have an increased awareness of and sensitivity to the sorts of challenges single parents face. As two researchers concluded: "Very often, the single mother's relationships with her supervisor and coworkers is a significant factor influencing whether she perceives the work environment to be supportive."[113] Ongoing support groups and other forums at which single parents can share their concerns can also help.

Older Workers As a Source of Candidates

Employers are increasingly looking to older workers as a source of recruits, for several reasons. Supply is one thing: Because of buyouts and early retirements, many workers retired early and are ready and willing to reenter the job market.[114] Furthermore, the number of annual retirees will soon double to approximately 4 million, and "there will be, I guarantee it, many millions of boomers who will have to work beyond age 65 because they simply haven't saved enough money to retire," says a demographer.[115] Demand is another: Fewer 18- to 25-year-olds are available to enter the workforce.[116]

Is it practical in terms of productivity to keep older workers on? The answer seems unequivocally to be yes. Age-related changes in physical ability, cognitive performance, and personality have little effect on workers' output except in the most physically demanding tasks.[117] Similarly, creative and intellectual achievements don't decline with age, but absenteeism drops. Older workers also usually display more company loyalty than younger workers, tend to be more satisfied with their jobs and supervision, and can be trained or retrained as effectively as anyone.

Recruiting older workers involves any or all the sources described earlier (advertising, employment agencies, and so forth), but with one big difference: It also requires a comprehensive HR effort to make the company an attractive place for older workers.[118] For example, limiting benefits for part-time workers, promoting early retirement, or not offering flexible benefits or flexible schedules can impede older worker recruitment and/or retention. At Wrigley Company, workers over 65 can progressively shorten their work schedules; another company uses "mini shifts" to accommodate those interested in working less than full time.[119] At Xerox, unionized hourly workers over 55 with 15 years of service and those over 50 with 20 years of service can bid on jobs at lower stress and lower pay levels if they so desire.

THE NEW WORKPLACE

Recruiting and hiring older employees is one thing; supervising them—especially when you're 20 or 30 years younger than they are—can be a challenge.

Gregg Levin's experiences provide an example. Levin, 31, is chief executive of Perfect Curve, a company in Sudbury, Massachusetts, that makes racks for baseball caps and related products. His father—one of his employees—doesn't use a computer, but instead "takes out his legal pad and spends an hour on something that takes me 4½ minutes on a computer," says Gregg. Sometimes, he says, "I feel I'm just playing. A president is in his 50s or 60s, not 31." Maintaining authority is one of the challenges in a situation like this. Gregg Levin does this in part by dressing up: "I'm always in a suit and tie," he says. "If I'm going to represent my company, I've got to do it in a mature manner."

Mary Rodas is in a similar situation. At 24, she's vice president of kardz.com, a New York company that delivers inexpensive gifts matched with greeting cards. Her five subordinates are much older than she is. "When people meet me, their first reaction is: 'Who's this little kid?' Or else they say, 'Can I speak to your boss?' And I point to myself and say, 'That's her.'" She says she earns respect through hard work and getting to know her workers. "I know my business, and with time people realize that I'm talking to them as an individual and an equal. I've been in this industry for 11 years [she created a balloon ball at age 11 that brought in $70 million in sales for a toy company in New York]. I know what I'm doing."[120]

Recruiting Minorities and Women

The same prescriptions that apply to recruiting older workers apply to recruiting minorities and women. In other words, you should formulate comprehensive plans for attracting and retaining these groups, plans that may include reevaluating personnel policies, developing flexible work options, redesigning jobs, and offering flexible benefit plans. For example, to the extent that many minority applicants may not meet the educational or experience standards for a job, many companies (including Aetna Life & Casualty) offer remedial training in basic arithmetic and writing.[121] Diversity data banks or minority-focused recruiting publications are another option. For example, Hispan Data provides recruiters at companies like McDonald's access to a computerized data bank; it costs a candidate $5 to be included.[122] Checking with your own minority employees can be very useful. About 32% of job seekers of Hispanic origin cited "check with friends or relatives" as a strategy when looking for jobs.[123] Specialized job search Web sites are another option, as explained earlier, on page 54.

Welfare-to-Work

The Federal Personal Responsibility and Welfare Reconciliation Act of 1996 prompted many employers to implement "welfare-to-work" programs for attracting and assimilating former welfare recipients. The act required 25% of people receiving welfare assistance to be either working or involved in a work training program by September 30, 1997, with the percentage rising each year to 50% by September 30, 2002.[124] In that time welfare caseloads seem to have dropped, from about 5 million families in 1994 to 2.2 million in June 2000.[125]

Some companies report difficulty hiring and assimilating people previously on welfare. Applicants sometimes lack basic work skills such as reporting for work on time, working in teams, and "taking orders without losing their temper."[126] The key to a welfare-to-work program's success seems to be the employer's "pretraining" program, during which participants get counseling and basic skills training over several weeks.[127] For example, Marriott International hired 600 welfare recipients under its Pathways to Independence program. The heart of the program is six weeks of preemployment training focused on work and life skills, and designed to rebuild self-esteem and instill positive attitudes about work.[128]

The Global Talent Search

Recruiting internationally is important for several reasons. Sometimes the employer has virtually no choice. For example, many U.S. companies are looking in the United Kingdom, Germany, and Western Europe for high-tech employees to fill jobs that are going begging in the U.S.[129] Desperate for qualified nurses, many hospitals—such as Sinai and Northwest hospitals in the Baltimore, Maryland, area—are recruiting in countries like the Philippines, India, and China.[130]

Technology can make global searches easier. For example, a series of high-tech recruitment expos in San Jose, California, used videoconferencing to put American employers in contact with candidates in Bombay, London, Tel Aviv, and several other U.S. and foreign cities.[131] The Internet and fax are useful, too, for placing ads more easily and expediting the transfer of documents.[132] Ads placed in the *International Herald Tribune* also appear in the paper's online edition.

Global firms recruit internationally as a normal part of satisfying their worldwide recruiting needs.[133] For example, Gillette International has an international graduate training program aimed at identifying and developing foreign nationals. Gillette subsidiaries abroad hire outstanding business students from top local universities. They then train these foreign nationals for 6 months at Gillette facilities in their home countries. Some then spend 18 months in training at the firm's Boston headquarters in areas like finance and marketing. Some of these trainees get offers of entry-level management positions at Gillette facilities in their home countries. In addition to recruiting students abroad, Coca-Cola looks for foreign students studying in well-known international business programs like those at UCLA and the American Graduate School of International Management in Arizona.

Seeking "global" employees doesn't have to just mean hiring employees to work in a different country.[134] With business increasingly multinational, "every employee needs to have a certain level of global awareness. . . ."[135] Many employers therefore have their recruiters look for evidence of global awareness in their interviews. For example, at the U.S. headquarters of Tetra PAK, Inc., the personnel manager looks for expatriate potential every time she makes a hire: "We don't often go out and search for someone to go abroad next year . . . but when we recruit, we always look for candidates who have global potential. We're interested in people who eventually could relocate internationally and handle that adjustment well."[136] International experience (including internships and considerable travel abroad) as well as language proficiency are two of the things for which employers look.

DEVELOPING AND USING APPLICATION FORMS

Purpose of Application Forms

Once you have a pool of applicants, the selection process can begin, and the **application form** is usually the first step in this process. (Some firms first require a brief, prescreening interview.)

A filled-in form provides four types of information. First, you can make judgments on substantive matters, such as whether the applicant has the education and experience to do the job. Second, you can draw conclusions about the applicant's previous progress and growth, a trait that is especially important for management candidates. Third, you can draw tentative conclusions regarding the

application form
The form that provides information on education, prior work record, and skills.

applicant's stability based on previous work record. (Here, however, be careful not to assume that an unusual number of job changes necessarily reflects on the applicant's stability; for example, the person's last two employers may have had to lay off employees.) Fourth, you may be able to use the data in the application to predict which candidates will succeed on the job and which will not.

In practice, most organizations need several application forms. For technical and managerial personnel, for example, the form may require detailed answers to questions concerning the applicant's education and training. The form for hourly factory workers might focus on the tools and equipment the applicant has used.

Equal Opportunity and Application Forms

Employers should carefully review their application forms to ensure they comply with equal employment laws. Questions concerning race, religion, age, sex, or national origin are generally not illegal per se under federal laws, but they are illegal under certain state laws. However, the EEOC views them with disfavor, and the burden is always on the employer to prove that the potentially discriminatory items are both related to success or failure on the job and not unfairly discriminatory. For example, you generally can request photographs prior to employment and even ask such potentially discriminatory questions as, "Have you ever been arrested?" The problem is that an unsuccessful applicant might establish a case of discrimination by demonstrating that the item produces an adverse impact. The burden of proof would then shift to you to show that the item is a valid predictor of job performance and that you apply it fairly to all applicants—that, for instance, you check the arrest records of all applicants, not just of minority applicants.

Unfortunately, many application forms are still highly questionable. Questions to beware of include:

Education. A question on the dates of attendance and graduation from various schools—academic, vocational, or professional—is one potential violation. This question may be illegal insofar as it may reflect the applicant's age.

Arrest record. The courts have usually held that employers violate Title VII by disqualifying applicants from employment because of an arrest record. This item has an adverse impact on minorities, and employers usually can't show it's required by business necessity.

Notify in case of emergency. It is generally legal to require the name, address, and phone number of a person to notify in case of emergency. However, asking the relationship of this person to the applicant could indicate the applicant's marital status or lineage.

Membership in organizations. Many forms ask the applicant to list memberships in clubs, organizations, or societies along with offices held. Employers should add instructions not to include organizations that would reveal race, religion, physical handicaps, marital status, or ancestry.

Physical handicaps. It is usually illegal to require the listing of an applicant's physical handicaps, defects, or past illnesses unless the application blank specifically asks only for those that "may interfere with your job performance." Similarly, it is generally illegal to ask whether the applicant has ever received workers' compensation for a previous injury or illness.

Marital status. In general, the application should not ask whether an applicant is single, married, divorced, separated, or living with anyone, or the names, occupations, and ages of the applicants' spouse or children.

Housing. Asking whether an applicant owns, rents, or leases a house may also be discriminatory. It can adversely affect minority groups and is difficult to justify on grounds of business necessity.

Figure 4-8 presents one employer's approach to collecting application form information—the employment application for the FBI.

▼ **FIGURE 4-8   Employment Application**

		FIELD OFFICE USE ONLY Right Thumb Print

FEDERAL BUREAU OF INVESTIGATION

**Preliminary Application for
Special Agent Position
(Please Type or Print in Black Ink)**

Date: _____

Div: _____   Program: _____

I. PERSONAL HISTORY

Name in Full   (Last, First, Middle) | List College Degree(s) Already Received or Pursuing, Major, School, and Month/Year:

Marital Status: ☐ Single   ☐ Engaged   ☐ Married   ☐ Separated   ☐ Legally Separated   ☐ Widowed   ☐ Divorced

Birth Date (Month, Day, Year)
Birth Place: | Social Security Number: (Optional) | Do you understand FBI employment requires availability for assignment anywhere in the U.S.?

Current Address

Street _____   Apt. No. _____   Home Phone _____

City _____   State _____   Zip Code _____   Work Phone _____

Area Code _____   Number _____

Area Code _____   Number _____

Are you: CPA ☐ Yes ☐ No   Licensed Driver ☐ Yes ☐ No   U. S. Citizen ☐ Yes ☐ No

Have you served on active duty in the U. S. Military? ☐ Yes ☐ No   If yes, indicate branch of service and dates (month/year) of active duty. Include military school attendance (month/year):

How did you learn or become interested in FBI employment as a Special Agent? | Have you previously applied for FBI employment? ☐ Yes ☐ No
If yes, location and date:

Do you have a foreign language background? ☐ Yes ☐ No   List proficiency for each language on reverse side.

Have you ever been arrested for any crime (include major traffic violations such as Driving Under the Influence or While Intoxicated, etc.)?
☐ Yes ☐ No If so, list all such matters on a continuation sheet, even if not formally charged, or no court appearance or found not guilty, or matter settled by payment of fine or forfeiture of collateral. Include date, place, charge, disposition, details, and police agency on reverse side.

II. EMPLOYMENT HISTORY

Identify your most recent three years FULL-TIME work experience, after high school (excluding summer, part-time and temporary employment).

From Month/Year	To Month/Year	Title of Position and Description of Work	# of hrs. Per week	Name/Location of Employer

III. PERSONAL DECLARATIONS

Persons with a disability who require an accommodation to complete the application process are required to notify the FBI of their need for the accommodation.

Have you used marijuana during the last three years or more than 15 times? ☐ Yes ☐ No

Have you used any illegal drug(s) or combination of illegal drugs, other than marijuana, more than 5 times or during the last 10 years? ☐ Yes ☐ No

All Information provided by applicants concerning their drug history will be subject to verification by a preemployment polygraph examination.

Do you understand all prospective FBI employees will be required to submit to an urinalysis for drug abuse prior to employment? ☐ Yes ☐ No

Please do not write below this line.

I am aware that willfully withholding information or making false statements on this application constitutes a violation of Section 1001. Title 18, U.S. Code and if appointed, will be the basis for dismissal from the Federal Bureau of Investigation. I agree to these conditions and I hereby certify that all statements made by me on this application are true and complete, to the best of my knowledge.

_____
Signature of applicant as usually written (**Do Not Use Nickname**)

Employers need to keep several practical guidelines in mind. The "Employment History" section should request detailed information on each prior employer, including the name of the supervisor and his or her telephone number—all essential for following up on the reference. Also, in signing the application, the applicant should certify his or her understanding of several things: that falsified statements may be cause for dismissal; that investigation of credit and employment and driving record is authorized; that a medical examination may be required; that drug screening tests may be required; and that employment is for no definite period of time.

Alternative Dispute Resolution

While the EEOC is generally opposed to the idea, more employers are requiring applicants to sign mandatory alternative dispute resolution forms as part of the application process. This typically requires applicants to agree to arbitrate certain legal disputes related to their employment with or dismissal from the company (including, for instance, those relating to the Age Discrimination in Employment Act).[137]

While mandatory arbitration is on the rise, it is also under attack.[138] Several years ago, a Maryland federal court ruled that Circuit City, Inc., could not force its arbitration program on a job applicant in a case there. A recent U.S. Supreme Court decision allows workers with employment disputes to go to court even though they signed prehire arbitration agreements.[139] Many firms that supply arbitrators are refusing to do so unless the employers have dispute resolution policies that are fair to the aggrieved employees—for instance, in terms of giving them an equal right to representation and factual investigation.[140]

Using Application Forms to Predict Job Performance

Some firms use application forms to predict which candidates will be successful and which will not, in much the same way that employers use tests for screening. They do this by conducting statistical studies to find the relationship between (1) biodata responses on the application form and (2) measures of success on the job.

Here it is important to choose the biodata items (such as "does not own automobile" or "not living at home") with two things in mind. First, of course, equal employment law will obviously limit the sorts of items you'll want to use. You may also want to avoid using items that are invasive. In one study, items such as "dollar sales achieved," "received cash bonus for good job," and "grade point average in math" were perceived by subjects as not too invasive. Others such as "frequently attends religious services," "birth order," and "frequent dates as senior in high school" were more invasive. Basically, items that were seen as more verifiable, more transparent in purpose, and more impersonal were seen as less invasive.[141]

We invite you to visit **www.prenhall.com/dessler** on the Prentice Hall Web site for our online study guide, Internet exercises, current events, links to related Web sites, and more.

Summary

1. Developing personnel plans requires three forecasts: one for personnel requirements, one for the supply of outside candidates, and one for the supply of inside candidates. To predict the need for personnel, first project the demand for the product or service. Next, project the volume of production required to meet these estimates; finally, relate personnel needs to these production estimates.

2. With personnel needs projected, the next step is to build a pool of qualified applicants. There are several sources of candidates, both internal (promotion from within) and external (advertising, employment agencies, executive recruiters, college recruiting, the Internet, and referrals and walk-ins). Remember that it is unlawful to discriminate against any individual with respect to employment because of race, color, religion, sex, national origin, or age (unless religion, sex, or origin are bona fide occupational qualifications).

3. The initial selection screening in most organizations begins with an application form. Most managers use these just to obtain background data. However, you can use application form data to make predictions about the applicant's future performance. For example, employers use application forms to predict job tenure, job success, and employee theft.

Tying It All Together

In Chapter 3, we discussed job analysis and the methods managers use to create job descriptions and job specifications. The main purpose of the current chapter was to explain the methods managers use to build a pool of candidates so they can recruit the best employees. The more qualified applicants you have, the higher your selection standards can be. Selection usually begins with effective testing and interviewing, to which we turn in the next chapter.

Discussion Questions

1. What are the pros and cons of five sources of job candidates?
2. What are the four main types of information application forms provide?
3. How, specifically, do equal employment laws apply to personnel planning and recruiting activities?
4. What are some Internet sites employers can use to find job candidates?
5. What are the main things you would do to recruit and retain a more diverse workforce?

Individual and Group Activities

1. Working individually or in groups, bring to class several classified and display ads from the Sunday's help wanted ads. Analyze the effectiveness of these ads using the guidelines discussed in this chapter.
2. Working individually or in groups, obtain a recent copy of the *Monthly Labor Review* or *Occupational Outlook Quarterly*, both published by the U.S. Bureau of Labor Statistics. Based on information in either of these publications, develop a forecast for the next five years of occupational market conditions for five occupations such as accountant, nurse, and engineer.
3. Working individually or in groups, visit the local office of your state employment agency. Come back to class prepared to discuss the following questions: What types of jobs seemed to be available through this agency, predominantly? To what extent do you think this particular agency would be a good source of professional, technical, and/or managerial applicants? What sorts of paperwork are applicants to the state agency required to complete before their applications are processed by the agency? What other services did the office provide? What other opinions did you form about the state agency?
4. Working individually or in groups, find at least five employment ads either on the Internet or in a local newspaper that suggest that the company is family-friendly and should appeal to women, minorities, older workers, and single parents. Discuss what they're doing to be family-friendly.
5. Working individually or in groups, interview a manager between the ages of 25 and 35 at a local business who manages employees 40 or older. Ask the manager to describe three or four of his or her most challenging experiences managing older employees.

EXPERIENTIAL EXERCISE *Creating a Recruitment Ad*

Purpose: The purpose of this exercise is to give you experience creating a recruitment ad for the job of marketing manager.

Required Understanding: You should be thoroughly familiar with the material on creating recruitment ads in Chapter 4. Come to class with a copy of the job description in Figure 3-6 (page 72) and, if possible, with several recruitment ads for marketing managers from your local newspaper, the *Wall Street Journal*, and/or from Internet job search Web sites.

How to Set Up the Exercise/Instructions: Set up groups of four to six students for this exercise. The groups should work separately and should not converse with each other during their deliberations.

1. Assume you have enough budget to create a 2-column by 5-inch display ad for the marketing manager's job in Figure 3-6 (page 72). Create such an ad for the company in which one of the group members works. If time permits, modify the ad on the assumption you will be placing it on a job search Web site such as monster.com.

2. Present each group's ad in class and discuss the similarities, differences, pros, and cons.

APPLICATION CASE *Finding People Who Are Passionate About What They Do*

Trilogy Software, Inc., of Austin, Texas, is one of the fastest-growing software companies in the industry, with current earnings in the $100-million to $200-million range. It prides itself on its unique and unorthodox culture. Many of its approaches to business practice are unusual, but in Trilogy's fast-changing and highly competitive environment they seem to work.

There is no dress code and employees make their own hours, often very long. They tend to socialize together (the average age is 26), both in the office's well-stocked kitchen and on company-sponsored events and trips to places like local dance clubs and retreats in Las Vegas and Hawaii. An in-house jargon has developed, and the shared history of the eight-year-old firm has taken on the status of legend. Responsibility is heavy and comes early, with a "just do it now" attitude that dispenses with long apprenticeships. New recruits are given a few weeks of intensive training, known as Trilogy University and described by participants as "more like boot camp than business school." Information is delivered as if with "a fire hose," and new employees are expected to commit their expertise and vitality to everything they do. Jeff Daniel, director of college recruiting and only 28 himself, admits the intense and unconventional firm is not the employer for everybody. "But it's definitely an environment where people who are passionate about what they do can thrive."

The firm employs about 700 such passionate people. Trilogy's managers know the rapid growth they seek depends on having a staff of the best people they can find, quickly trained and given broad responsibility and freedom as soon as possible. Founder and CEO Joe Liemandt says, "At a software company, people are everything. You can't build the next great software company, which is what we're trying to do here, unless you're totally committed to that. Of course, the leaders at every company say, 'People are everything.' But they don't act on it."

Trilogy makes finding the right people a companywide mission. Recruiters actively pursue the freshest if least experienced people in the job market, scouring college career fairs and computer science departments for talented overachievers with ambition and entrepreneurial instincts. Top managers conduct the first rounds of interviews, letting prospects know they will be pushed to achieve but will be well rewarded. Employees take top recruits and their significant others out on the town when they fly into Austin for the standard three-day preliminary visit. A typical day might begin with grueling interviews but ends with mountain biking, Roller Blading, or laser tag. Liemandt has been known to fly out to meet and woo hot prospects who couldn't make the trip.

In one recent year, Trilogy reviewed 15,000 résumés, conducted 4,000 on-campus interviews, flew 850 prospects in for interviews, and hired 262 college graduates, who account for over a third of its current employees. The cost per hire was $13,000; Jeff Daniel believes it was worth every penny.

Questions

1. Identify some of the established recruiting techniques that underlie Trilogy's unconventional approach to attracting talent.

2. What particular elements of Trilogy's culture most likely appeal to the kind of employees it seeks? How does it convey those elements to job prospects?

3. Would Trilogy be an appealing employer for you? Why or why not? If not, what would it take for you to accept a job offer from Trilogy?

4. What suggestions would you make to Trilogy for improving their recruiting processes?

Source: Chuck Salter, "Insanity, Inc.," *Fast Company*, January 1999, pp. 101–108.

CONTINUING CASE: LearnInMotion.com *Getting Better Applicants*

If you were to ask Jennifer and Mel what the main problem was in running their business, their answer would be quick and short: hiring good people. They were simply astonished at how hard it was to attract and hire good candidates.

After much debate, they decided to post openings for seven positions: two salespeople, a Web designer, two content management people, an office manager, and a Web surfer. Their first approach was to design and place a large display ad in two local newspapers. The display ad listed all the positions available; Jennifer and Mel assumed that by placing a large ad with the name of the company prominently displayed and a bold border around the ad, it would draw attention and therefore generate applicants. For two consecutive weekends, the ad cost the fledgling company close to $1,000. It produced a handful of applicants. After speaking with them by phone, Jennifer and Mel rejected three outright; two said they weren't interested; and two scheduled interviews but never showed up.

The owners therefore decided to change their approach. They used different recruiting methods for each position. In the paper, they placed ads for the salespeople under "Sales" and for the office manager under "Administrative." They advertised for a Web designer by placing an ad on monster.com. And for the content managers and Web surfer, they placed neatly typed help wanted ads in the career placement offices of a technical college and a community college about 10 minutes away from their offices. They also used this job posting approach to find independent contractors they could use to deliver courses physically to users' homes or offices.

The results were disappointing. Over a typical weekend, literally dozens of want ads for experienced salespeople appear, as well as almost as many for office managers. The ad for salespeople generated about three calls, one of whom Jennifer and Mel felt might be a viable candidate, although the person wanted a much higher salary than they had planned to pay. One possible candidate emerged for the office manager position.

They decided to replace the sales ad, but this time to change its positioning in the newspaper. The ad had previously run under "Salespersons Wanted." This time (since the job involved entirely inside phone sales) they decided to place the ad under "Phone Sales," which is a separate category. They were surprised to find, however, that while the newspaper would extend them credit and bill them for all their previous help wanted ads, the ads for "Phone Sales" had to be paid up front, via credit card. While they thought that was strange, they went ahead and placed the ad, but soon found out what the problem was. A number of firms that place these ads are nomadic sales operations. Many of the calls they got (not all of them, but many) were from salespeople who were used to working in what some people called "boiler-room" operations. In other words, they sit at the phone all day making cold calls from lists provided by their employers, selling anything from burglar alarms to homeowners, to investments to doctors, all under very high-pressure conditions. They weren't interested in LearnInMotion, nor was LearnInMotion interested in them.

They fared a little better with the Web designer ad, which produced four possible applicants. They got no phone calls from the local college job postings; when they called to ask the placement offices why, they were told that their posted salary of $7 per hour was "way too low." They went back and replaced the job postings with $10 hourly rates.

"I just don't understand it" is the way Jennifer put it. Especially for the sales job, Jennifer and Mel felt that they were offering perfectly acceptable compensation packages, so the lack of applicants surprised them. "Maybe a lot of people just don't want to work for dot-coms anymore," said Mel, thinking out loud. "Since the bottom fell out of the dot-com market in March 2000, a lot of good people have gotten burned by working for a series of two or three failed dot-coms, so maybe they've just had enough of the wired world."

In any case, they want you, their management consultants, to help them out. Here's what they want you to do for them.

Questions and Assignments

1. Tell us what we're doing wrong.
2. Provide a detailed list of recommendations concerning how we should go about increasing our pool of acceptable job applicants, so we no longer have to hire almost anyone who walks in the door. (Your recommendations regarding the latter should include completely worded advertisements and recommendations regarding any other recruiting strategies you would suggest we use.)

5 Chapter

Employee Testing and Selection

After studying this chapter, you should be able to:

- Describe the overall selection process.
- Explain what is meant by reliability and validity.
- Give examples of some of the ethical and legal considerations in testing.
- Explain how you would go about validating a test.
- List eight tests you could use for employee selection, and how you would use them.
- Cite and illustrate our testing guidelines.
- More effectively select employees.
- Explain the key points to remember in conducting background investigations.

STRATEGIC OVERVIEW   City Garage, a 200-employee chain of 25 auto service and repair shops in Dallas–Fort Worth, had expanded rapidly since its founding in 1993. Its growth strategy was hampered by the problems it was having hiring and keeping good managers and employees.[1] "Because we grew so quickly, there were certain aspects we didn't concentrate on as much as we did others. One was hiring," said training director Rusty Reinoehl. One thing it discovered was that not all its managers had the same level of interviewing and hiring skills. The result was more turnover, and too few managers to staff new stores. For a firm planning to expand to 50 or 60 shops throughout Texas in the next few years, City Garage knew its growth strategy would be hampered without a new approach to employee testing and selection.

The previous chapter focused on the methods managers use to build an applicant pool. The purpose of this chapter, Employee Testing and Selection, is to show you how to use various tools and techniques to select the best candidates for the job. The main topics we'll cover include the selection process, basic testing techniques, background and reference checks, ethical and legal questions in testing, types of tests, and work samples and simulations. In the following chapter, Interviewing Candidates, we turn to the techniques you can use to improve your skills with what is probably the most important screening tool, the selection interview.

WHY CAREFUL SELECTION IS IMPORTANT

With a pool of applicants, the next step is to select the best candidates for the job. This usually means whittling down the applicant pool by using the screening tools explained in this chapter: tests, assessment centers, and background and reference checks. Then the prospective supervisor can interview likely candidates and decide who to hire.[2]

Selecting the right employees is important for three main reasons. First, your own performance always depends in part on your subordinates. Employees with the right skills and attributes will do a better job for you and the company. Employees without these skills or who are abrasive or obstructionist won't perform effectively, and your own performance and the firm's will suffer. The time to screen out undesirables is before they are in the door, not after.

Second, it is important because it's costly to recruit and hire employees. Hiring and training even a clerk can cost $5,000 or more in fees and supervisory time. The total cost of hiring a manager could easily be 10 times as high once you add search fees, interviewing time, reference checking, and travel and moving expenses.

Third, it's important because of the legal implications of incompetent hiring. For one thing (as we saw in Chapter 2), EEO laws and court decisions require nondiscriminatory selection procedures for protected groups. Furthermore, courts will find employers liable when employees with criminal records or other problems take advantage of access to customers' homes (or similar opportunities) to commit crimes. Lawyers call hiring workers with such backgrounds, without proper safeguards **negligent hiring**.[3] In one case, *Ponticas v. K.M.S. Investments*, an apartment manager with a passkey entered a woman's apartment and assaulted her. The court found the apartment complex's owner and operator negligent in not properly checking the manager's background before hiring him.

Negligent hiring underscores the need to think through what the job's human requirements really are.[4] For example, 'non-rapist' isn't likely to appear as a required knowledge, skill, or ability in a job analysis of a repair person. But it is that type of requirement that has been the focus of many negligent hiring suits.[5]

Employers protect against negligent hiring claims by:

- Carefully scrutinizing all information supplied by the applicant on his or her employment application. For example, look for unexplained gaps in employment.
- Getting the applicant's written authorization for reference checks, and carefully checking references.
- Saving all records and information you obtain about the applicant.
- Rejecting applicants who make false statements of material facts or who have conviction records for offenses directly related and important to the job in question.
- Keeping in mind the need to balance the applicant's privacy rights with others' "need to know," especially when you discover damaging information.
- Taking immediate disciplinary action if problems develop.[6]

▲ *When the 3,000-room Bellagio Hotel opened in Las Vegas it urgently needed to hire nearly 10,000 workers in a mere 24 weeks. Arte Nathan, then vice president of human resources, devised a highly automated "battle plan" he likened to Operation Desert Storm to get the job done. In one of many early screening processes, the job candidates met with staff members who checked their applications for completeness, but more important, they assessed applicants' communication skills and overall demeanor. This screening process eliminated about 20 percent of the more than 80,000 people who applied for jobs.*

negligent hiring
Hiring workers with questionable backgrounds without proper safeguards.

BASIC TESTING CONCEPTS

Effective selection is therefore important and depends, to a large degree, on the basic testing concepts of validity and reliability.

Validity

A test is a sample of a person's behavior, but some tests are more clearly representative of the behavior being sampled than others. A typing test, for example, clearly corresponds to an on-the-job behavior. At the other extreme, there may be no apparent relationship between the items on the test and the behavior. This is the case with projective personality tests. Thus, in the Thematic Apperception Test illustrated in Figure 5-1, the psychologist asks the person to explain how he or she interprets an ambiguous picture. The psychologist uses that interpretation to draw conclusions about the person's personality and behavior. In such tests, it is more difficult to prove that the tests are measuring what they are said to measure—that they're valid.

Test validity answers the question, "Does this test measure what it's supposed to measure?"[7] With respect to employee selection tests, *validity* often refers to evidence that the test is job related—in other words, that performance on the test is a valid predictor of subsequent performance on the job. A selection test must be valid since, without proof of validity, there is no logical or legally permissible reason to continue using it to screen job applicants. In employment testing, there are two main ways to demonstrate a test's validity: **criterion validity** and **content validity**. A third, construct validity, is used less often.[8]

Criterion Validity Demonstrating criterion validity means demonstrating that those who do well on the test also do well on the job, and that those who do poorly on the test do poorly on the job.[9] Thus, the test has validity to the extent that the people with higher test scores perform better on the job. In psychological measurement, a *predictor* is the measurement (in this case, the test score) that you are trying to relate to a *criterion*, like performance on the job. The term *criterion validity* reflects that terminology.

Content Validity Employers demonstrate the content validity of a test by showing that the test constitutes a fair sample of the content of the job.[10] The basic procedure here is to identify job tasks and behaviors that are critical to performance, and then randomly select a sample of those tasks and behaviors to be tested. A data entry test used to hire a data entry clerk is an example. If the content you choose for the data entry test is a representative sample of what the person needs to know for the job, then the test is probably content valid.

---

test validity
The accuracy with which a test, interview, and so on measures what it purports to measure or fulfills the function it was designed to fill.

---

crtierion validity
A type of validity based on showing that scores on the test (predictors) are related to job performance (criterion).

---

content validity
A test that is content valid is one that contains a fair sample of the tasks and skills actually needed for the job in question.

▶ **FIGURE 5-1**
Sample Picture from Thematic Apperception Test

How do you interpret this picture?

Harvard University Press. Used with permission.

Demonstrating content validity sounds easier than it is in practice. Demonstrating that (1) the tasks the person performs on the test are really a comprehensive and random sample of the tasks performed on the job, and (2) the conditions under which the person takes the test resemble the work situation, is not always easy. For many jobs, employers must demonstrate other evidence of a test's validity—such as its criterion validity.

Reliability

Reliability is a test's second important characteristic and refers to its consistency. It is "the consistency of scores obtained by the same person when retested with the identical tests or with an equivalent form of a test."[11] A test's reliability is very important; if a person scored 90 on an intelligence test on a Monday and 130 when retested on Tuesday, you probably wouldn't have much faith in the test.

There are several ways to estimate consistency or reliability. You could administer the same test to the same people at two different points in time, comparing their test scores at time 2 with their scores at time 1; this would be a *retest estimate*. Or you could administer a test and then administer what experts believe to be an equivalent test later; this would be an *equivalent form estimate*. The Scholastic Assessment Test (SAT) is an example.

A test's *internal consistency* is another measure of its reliability. For example, suppose you have 10 items on a test of vocational interests; you believe these measure, in various ways, the person's interest in working outdoors. You administer the test and then statistically analyze the degree to which responses to these 10 items vary together. This would provide a measure of the internal reliability of the test. Psychologists refer to this as an *internal comparison estimate*. Internal consistency is one reason you find apparently repetitive questions on some test questionnaires.

What could cause a test to be unreliable? A number of things. For example, the questions may do a poor job of sampling the material; test 1 focuses more on Chapters 1, 3, 5, and 7, while test 2 focuses more on Chapters 2, 4, 5, and 8. Or there might be errors due to changes in the testing conditions; for instance, the room the test is in next month may be noisy. (You'll find more on reliability and validity in this chapter's Internet appendix.)

How to Validate a Test

What makes a test like the Graduate Record Examination useful for college admissions directors? What makes a mechanical comprehension test useful for a manager trying to hire a machinist?

The answer to both questions is usually that people's scores on these tests predict how they perform. Thus, other things being equal, students who score high on the graduate admissions tests also do better in graduate school. Applicants who score high on the mechanical comprehension test perform better as engineers.

In order for any selection test to be useful, you should be fairly sure test scores relate in a predictable way to performance on the job. In other words, you should validate the test before using it by ensuring that scores on the test are a good predictor of some *criterion* like job performance. (In other words, you must demonstrate the test's *criterion validity*.) This validation process is usually done by an industrial psychologist. The HR department coordinates the effort. Line management's role is to describe the job and its requirements so that the human requirements of the job and its performance standards are clear to the psychologist.

The validation process consists of five steps: analyze the job, choose your tests, administer the tests, relate the test scores and the criteria, and cross-validate and revalidate.

reliability
The consistency of scores obtained by the same person when retested with the identical or equivalent tests.

Step 1. Analyze the Job The first step is to analyze the job and write job descriptions and job specifications. Here, you need to specify the human traits and skills you believe are required for adequate job performance. For example, must an applicant be verbal, a good talker? Is programming required? Must the person assemble small, detailed components? These requirements become the *predictors*. These are the human traits and skills you believe predict success on the job. In this first step, you also must define what you mean by "success on the job," since it's this success for which you want predictors. The standards of success are *criteria*. You could focus on production-related criteria (quantity, quality, and so on), personnel data (absenteeism, length of service, and so on), or judgments of worker performance (by persons like supervisors). For an assembler's job, your predictors might include manual dexterity and patience. Criteria that you would hope to predict with your test might include quantity produced per hour and number of rejects produced per hour.

Some employers make the mistake of carefully choosing predictors (such as manual dexterity) while virtually ignoring the question of which criteria best predict performance. Doing so can be a mistake. An illustrative study involved 212 gas utility company employees. In this study, the researchers found a significant relationship between the test battery that was used as a predictor and two performance criteria—supervisor ratings of performance and objective productivity indices. However, there was virtually no relationship between the same test battery and an objective quality index or employee self-ratings.[12]

Step 2. Choose the Tests Next, choose tests that you think measure the attributes (predictors) important for job success. Employers usually base this choice on experience, previous research, and "best guesses." They usually don't start with just one test. Instead, they choose several tests and combine them into a *test battery*. The test battery aims to measure an array of possible predictors, such as aggressiveness, extroversion, and numerical ability.

What tests are available and where do you get them? Given the EEO and ethical issues involved, the best advice is probably to use a professional, such as a licensed industrial psychologist. However, many firms publish tests. Psychological Assessment Resources, Inc., in Odessa, Florida, is typical. It publishes and distributes many tests; some are available to virtually any purchaser, but many are available only to qualified buyers (such as those with degrees in psychology or counseling).

Some companies publish employment tests that are generally available to anyone. For example, Wonderlic Personnel Test, Inc., publishes a well-known intellectual capacity test, and also other tests, including technical skills tests, aptitude test batteries, interest inventories, and reliability inventories. G. Neil Companies of Sunrise, Florida, offers employment testing materials including, for example, a clerical skills test, telemarketing ability test, service ability test, management ability test, team skills test, and sales abilities test. Again, though, don't let the widespread availability of personnel tests blind you to this important fact: You should use the tests in a manner consistent with equal employment laws, and in a manner that is ethical and protects the test taker's privacy. We'll return to this point in a moment.

Step 3. Administer the Test Next administer the selected test(s) to employees. You have two choices here. One option is to administer the tests to employees presently on the job. You then compare their test scores with their current performance; this is *concurrent validation*. Its main advantage is that data on performance are readily available. The disadvantage is that current employees may not be representative of new applicants (who of course are really the ones for whom you are interested in developing a screening test). Current employees have already had on-the-job training and been screened by your existing selection techniques.[13]

Predictive validation is the second and more dependable way to validate a test. Here you administer the test to applicants before they are hired. Then hire these applicants using only existing selection techniques, not the results of the new tests you are developing. After they have been on the job for some time, measure their performance and compare it to their earlier test scores. You can then determine whether you could have used their performance to predict their subsequent job performance. In the case of an assembler's job, the ideal situation would be to administer, say, the Test of Mechanical Comprehension (see page 137) to all applicants. Then ignore the test results and hire assemblers as you usually do. Perhaps six months later, measure your new assemblers' performance (quantity produced per hour, number of rejects per hour) and compare this performance to their Mechanical Comprehension test scores (as in step 4).

Step 4. Relate Your Test Scores and Criteria The next step is to determine if there is a significant relationship between scores (the predictor) and performance (the criterion). The usual way to do this is to determine the statistical relationship between (1) scores on the test and (2) job performance through *correlation analysis*, which shows the degree of statistical relationship.

If there's a correlation between test and job performance, you can develop an **expectancy chart**. This presents the relationship between test scores and job performance graphically. To do this, split the employees into, say, five groups according to test scores, with those scoring the highest fifth on the test, the second highest fifth, and so on. Then compute the percentage of high job performers in each of these five test score groups and present the data in an expectancy chart like that in Figure 5-2. This shows the likelihood that employees who score in each of these five test score groups will be high performers. In this case, someone scoring in the top fifth of the test has a 97% chance of being rated a high performer, while one scoring in the lowest fifth has only a 29% chance of being rated a high performer.[14]

expectancy chart
A graph showing the relationship between test scores and job performance for a group of people.

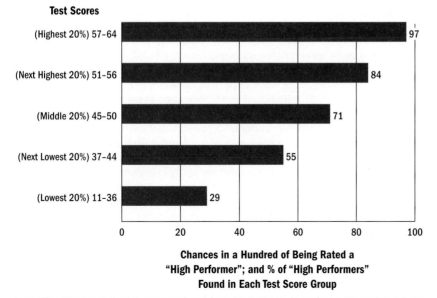

◀ **FIGURE 5-2**
Expectancy Chart

Test Scores

(Highest 20%) 57–64	97
(Next Highest 20%) 51–56	84
(Middle 20%) 45–50	71
(Next Lowest 20%) 37–44	55
(Lowest 20%) 11–36	29

0   20   40   60   80   100

**Chances in a Hundred of Being Rated a
"High Performer"; and % of "High Performers"
Found in Each Test Score Group**

Note: This expectancy chart shows the relation between scores made on the Minnesota Paper Form Board and rated success of junior draftspersons. Example: Those who score between 37 and 44 have a 55% chance of being rated above average and those scoring between 57 and 64 have a 97% chance.

Step 5. Cross-Validate and Revalidate Before putting the test into use, you may want to check it by cross-validating, by again performing steps 3 and 4 on a new sample of employees. At a minimum, an expert should revalidate the test periodically.

The procedure you would use to demonstrate *content validity* differs from that used to demonstrate criterion validity (as described in steps 1 through 5). Content validity tends to emphasize judgment. Here, you first do a careful job analysis to identify the work behaviors required. Then combine several samples of those behaviors into a test. A typing and computer skills test for a clerk would be an example. The fact that the test is a comprehensive sample of actual, observable, on-the-job behaviors is what lends the test its content validity. Criterion validity is determined through the five-step procedure previously described. Table 5-1 summarizes important testing guidelines such as "use tests as supplements."

Equal Employment Opportunity Aspects of Testing

Various federal, state, and local laws bar discrimination with respect to race, color, age, religion, sex, disability, and national origin. With respect to testing, the laws boil down to this: You must be able to prove (1) that your tests are related to success or failure on the job (validity), and (2) that your tests don't

▶ **TABLE 5-1**
Testing Program
Guidelines

1. *Use tests as supplements.* Don't make tests your only selection tool; use them to supplement other tools like interviews and background checks.
2. *Validate the tests.* It's best to validate them in your own organization. However, the fact that the same tests have proven valid in similar organizations—called validity generalization—is usually adequate.
3. *Monitor your testing/selection program.* Ask questions such as, "What proportions of minority and nonminority applicants are rejected at each stage of the hiring process?" and "Why am I using this test—what does it mean in terms of actual behavior on the job?"
4. *Keep accurate records.* Record why you rejected each applicant. A general note such as "not sufficiently well qualified" is not enough. Your reasons for rejecting the person may be subject to validation at a later date.
5. *Use a certified psychologist.* Developing, validating, and using selection standards (including tests) generally require a qualified psychologist. Most states require persons who offer psychological services to the public be certified or licensed. A Ph.D. degree (the bachelor's degree is never sufficient) is usually one qualification. Potential consultants should provide evidence of similar work and experience in test validation, and demonstrate familiarity with federal and state equal rights laws and regulations.
6. *Manage test conditions.* Administer tests in areas that are reasonably private, quiet, well lighted, and ventilated, and make sure all applicants take the tests under the same test conditions. Once completed, keep test results confidential. Give them only to individuals with a legitimate need for the information and the ability to understand and interpret the scores (including the applicant). Train your supervisors regarding test result confidentiality.
7. *Revalidate periodically.* Employer's needs and applicant's aptitudes change over time. You should have your testing program revalidated periodically.

Source: See Floyd L. Ruch, "The Impact on Employment Procedures of the Supreme Court Decisions in the Duke Power Case," *Personnel Journal*, vol. 50, no. 4 (October 1971), pp. 777–783; Hubert Field, Gerald Bagley, and Susan Bagley, "Employment Test Validation for Minority and Non-minority Production Workers," *Personnel Psychology*, vol. 30, no. 1 (spring 1977), pp. 37–46; Ledvinka, Federal Regulations, p. 110; Dale Beach, *Personnel* (New York: Macmillan, 1970); M. K. Distefano, Jr., Margaret Pryer, and Stella Craig, "Predictive Validity of General Ability Tests with Black and White Psychiatric Attendants," *Personnel Psychology*, vol. 29, no. 2 (summer 1976). Schultz and Schultz, *Psychology and Work Today*, pp. 101–109. "The Use (and Misuse) of Psychological Testing in Employment Litigation," *Employee Relations Law Journal*, vol. 23, no. 1 (summer 1997), pp. 35–53.

unfairly discriminate against minority or nonminority subgroups. Faced with a charge, the employer must demonstrate the validity and selection fairness of the allegedly discriminatory item.

Employers can't avoid EEO laws just by avoiding tests: EEO guidelines and laws apply to all selection devices, including interviews, applications, and references. You could have to prove the validity, fairness, and job relatedness of any screening or selection tool that has an adverse impact on a protected group.[15] (You'll find additional aspects of test unfairness in the Internet appendix to this chapter, on the book's Web site.)

Alternatives Let's review where we are at this point. Assume that you've used a test and that a rejected minority candidate has demonstrated adverse impact to the satisfaction of a court. How might the person have done this? One is to show that the selection rate (for, say, the applicant's racial group) was less than four-fifths that for the group with the highest selection rate. Thus, if 90% of white applicants passed the test but only 60% of blacks passed, then (since 60% is less than four-fifths of 90%) adverse impact exists.

The employer would then have three alternatives with respect to its testing program. One is to institute another valid selection procedure that does not have an adverse impact.[16] The second is to show that the test is valid—in other words, that it is a valid predictor of performance on the job. Ideally, you would do this by conducting your own validation study.[17] In any event, the plaintiff would then have to prove that your explanation for using the test is inadequate.

A third alternative—in this case aimed at avoiding adverse impact rather than responding to it—is to monitor the selection test to see if it has disparate impact. If not, it's generally permissible to use the device, even if it's not valid—but why would you want to?

Test Takers' Individual Rights and Test Security

Test takers have rights to privacy and information under the American Psychological Association's standard for educational and psychological tests.[18] They have the right to the confidentiality of test results and the right to informed consent regarding use of these results. They have the right to expect that only people qualified to interpret the scores will have access to them, or that sufficient information will accompany the scores to ensure their appropriate interpretation. And they have the right to expect the test is fair to all. For example, no one taking it should have prior access to the questions or answers.[19]

◆ **RESEARCH INSIGHT** What else determines perceived fairness?[20] Following good test practices—a quiet test-taking environment, privacy, and so on—is important.[21] Another factor is the obviousness of the link between (1) the selection procedure and (2) performing the job (in other words, the selection procedure's "face validity"). In one study, 259 college students from France and the United States rated the "favorability" of 10 selection procedures, and then specified what prompted them to rate some procedures as more favorable than others.[22]

The "perceived face validity of the selection procedure was the strongest correlate of favorability reactions among both samples."[23] Students' reactions were highly favorable toward interviews and work sample tests, both of which had obvious links to the job itself. They were moderately favorable toward biographical information and written ability tests. Favorability reactions were neutral toward personality and honesty tests, and negative toward graphology. In general, they were more favorable when they felt the employer had the right to obtain information with a particular technique, and when the procedure was widely used in industry.

The Issue of Privacy

In addition to the APA's test privacy and security standard, some privacy protections are embedded in U.S. law. At the federal level, the Constitution does not expressly provide for the right to privacy, but certain U.S. Supreme Court decisions do protect individuals from intrusive governmental action in a variety of contexts.[24] For example, if you are a federal employee or (in many jurisdictions) a state or local government employee, there are limits on disclosure of personnel information to individuals within or outside the agency.[25] The Federal Privacy Act gives federal employees the right to inspect personnel files, and limits the disclosure of personnel information without the employee's consent, among other things.[26]

The common law of torts also provides some protection against disclosing information about employees to people outside the company. The best-known application here involves defamation (either libel or slander). If your employer or former employer discloses information that is false and defamatory and that causes you serious injury, you may be able to sue for defamation of character.[27] In general, though, this is easier said than done. Employers providing a recommendation generally can't be sued for defamation unless the employee can show "malice"—that is, ill will, culpable recklessness, or disregard of the employee's rights. But this is usually hard to prove.[28] Someone may also sue an employer for interference with business or prospective business relations if the employer willfully provides information to another with the aim of harming a former employee. In addition, an employer may not disclose to another company that a former employee had filed a discrimination charge or a lawsuit alleging discrimination or other labor law violation; doing so may constitute unlawful retaliation.

Some states recognize common law as it applies to invasion of privacy. Such cases usually revolve around "public disclosure of private facts." Employees can sue employers for disclosing to a large number of people true but embarrassing private facts about the employee. (For example, your personnel file may contain private information regarding your health, test results, or job performance that you may not want disclosed outside the firm.) In invasion-of-privacy suits, truth is no defense.

One case involved a supervisor in a shouting match with an employee. The supervisor yelled out that the employee's wife had been having sexual relations with certain people. The employee and his wife sued the employer for invasion of privacy. The jury found the employer liable for invasion of the couple's privacy. It awarded damages to both of them, as well as damages for the couple's additional claim that the supervisor's conduct amounted to an intentional infliction of emotional distress.[29] Since many people sue these days, more discretion is required than some employers have shown in the past.

Guidelines to follow here include:

1. Train your supervisors regarding the importance of employee confidentiality.[30]
2. Adopt a "need to know" policy. For example, if an employee has been rehabilitated after a period of drug use and that information is not relevant to his or her functioning in the workplace, then a new supervisor may not "need to know."
3. Disclose procedures. If you know your firm can't keep information—such as test results—confidential, you may limit your liability by disclosing that fact before testing. For example, if employees who test positive on drug tests will have to use the firm's employee assistance program, explain that before giving the tests.

Using Tests at Work

Tests are widely used by employers today. For example, about 45% of 1,085 companies the American Management Association surveyed tested applicants for basic skills (defined as the ability to read instructions, write reports, and do arithmetic adequate to perform common workplace tasks).[31] However, testing has actually fallen off a bit in the past few years. For example, 47% of the respondents in one survey required employees to take drug tests in 2000, down from 70% in 1996. About one-third of the respondents required some form of psychological measurement in 2000, about the same as in 1999, but down from 51% in 1998.[32] If you want to see what such tests are like, try the short test in Figure 5-3 to see how prone you might be to on-the-job accidents.

Tests are not just for lower-level workers. For example, consultants McKinsey & Co. recently flew 54 MIT MBA students to Miami for two days of multiple-choice business knowledge tests, case-oriented case studies, and interviews. Barclays Capital gives graduate and undergraduate job candidates aptitude tests instead of first-round interviews.[33]

Employers don't use tests just to find good employees, but also to screen out bad ones. This can be important. By some estimates, 75% of employees have stolen from their employers at least once; 33% to 75% have engaged in behaviors such as theft, vandalism, and voluntary absenteeism; almost 25% say they've had knowledge of illicit drug use among co-workers; and 7% of a sample of employees reported being victims of physical threats.[34] Occupational fraud and abuse reportedly cost U.S. employers about $400 billion annually, or about nine dollars per day per employee or 6% of annual revenues.[35] No wonder prudent employers test their applicants.

Tests come from test publishers, who provide various services to facilitate the testing process. One service is automated scoring and test interpretation. Some tests, such as the 16PF personality profile, must be professionally scored and interpreted. The 16PF is a 187-item personality profile psychologists use to measure management characteristics including creativity, independence, leadership, and self-control. Wonderlic, Inc., lets an employer administer the 16PF. The employer then faxes or mails the answer sheet to Wonderlic, which scores the candidate's profile and mails or faxes back the interpretive report in one day. Today, psychol-

◀ **FIGURE 5-3**
Sample Test

CHECK YES OR NO   YES   NO

1. You like a lot of excitement in your life.

_____

2. An employee who takes it easy at work
   is cheating on the employer.

_____

3. You are a cautious person.

_____

4. In the past three years you have found yourself
   in a shouting match at school or work.

_____

5. You like to drive fast just for fun.

_____

Analysis: According to John Kamp, an industrial psychologist, applicants who answered no, yes, yes, no, no to questions 1, 2, 3, 4, and 5 are statistically likely to be absent less often, to have fewer on-the-job injuries, and, if the job involves driving, to have fewer on-the-job driving accidents. Actual scores on the test are based on answers to 130 questions.

Source: Courtesy of NYT Permissions.

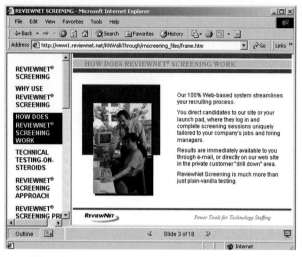

▲ **WEBNOTE**

Steve Linton is in charge of recruiting at On!contact, a maker of customer-relationship management software. He often needs to hire people with high technical competence, and one way to test for such competence is through Web-based skills testing programs such as ReviewNet, a sample page of which is shown here.

www.reviewnet.net

ogists also easily score many psychological tests, including the MMPI personality test, using interpretive Windows-based software.

Computer-Interactive Testing

Computerized testing today is increasingly replacing conventional paper-and-pencil and manual tests. In a large manufacturing company, researchers developed a computerized testing procedure for the selection of clerical personnel.[36] They constructed eight test components to represent actual work performed by secretarial personnel, such as maintaining and developing databases and spreadsheets, answering the telephone, filing, and handling travel arrangements. For the word processing test, applicants had three minutes (monitored by the computer) to type as much of a letter as possible; the computer recorded and corrected the manuscript. For the travel expense form completion task, applicants had to access the database file, use some of the information in it to compute quarterly expenses, and transfer this information to the travel expense form. Some other computerized tests include numerical ability tests, reading comprehension tests, and a clerical comparing and checking test.[37] Many firms such as Kinko's have applicants take online or offline computerized tests—sometimes by phone, using the touch-tone keypad—to quickly prescreen applicants prior to more in-depth interviews and background checks.[38]

TYPES OF TESTS

We can conveniently classify tests according to whether they measure cognitive (mental) abilities, motor and physical abilities, personality and interests, or achievement.[39]

Tests of Cognitive Abilities

Cognitive tests include tests of general reasoning ability (intelligence) and tests of specific mental abilities like memory and inductive reasoning.

Intelligence Tests Intelligence (IQ) tests are tests of general intellectual abilities. They measure not a single trait but rather a range of abilities, including memory, vocabulary, verbal fluency, and numerical ability.

Originally, IQ (intelligence quotient) was literally a quotient. The procedure was to divide a child's mental age (as measured by the intelligence test) by his or her chronological age, and then multiply the results by 100. If an 8-year-old child answered questions as a 10-year-old might, his or her IQ would be 10 divided by 8, times 100, or 125.

For adults, of course, the notion of mental age divided by chronological age wouldn't make sense. Therefore, an adult's IQ score is actually a derived score. It reflects the extent to which the person is above or below the "average" adult's intelligence score.

Intelligence is often measured with individually administered tests like the Stanford-Binet Test or the Wechsler Test. Employers can administer other IQ tests such as the Wonderlic to groups of people. Other intelligence tests include the

Kaufman Adolescent and Adult Intelligence Test, the Slosson Intelligence Test, the Wide Range Intelligence Test, and the Comprehensive Test of Nonverbal Intelligence.

Specific Cognitive Abilities There are measures of specific mental abilities, such as inductive and deductive reasoning, verbal comprehension, memory, and numerical ability.

Psychologists often call such tests *aptitude tests*, since they purport to measure aptitude for the job in question. Consider the Test of Mechanical Comprehension in Figure 5-4, which tests the applicant's understanding of basic mechanical principles. It may reflect a person's aptitude for jobs—like that of machinist or engineer—that require mechanical comprehension. Other tests of mechanical aptitude include the Mechanical Reasoning Test and the SRA Test of Mechanical Aptitude.

Tests of Motor and Physical Abilities

You might also want to measure motor abilities, such as finger dexterity, manual dexterity, and reaction time. The Crawford Small Parts Dexterity Test is an example. It measures the speed and accuracy of simple judgment as well as the speed of finger, hand, and arm movements. Other tests include the Stromberg Dexterity Test, the Minnesota Rate of Manipulation Test, and the Purdue Peg Board. The Roeder Manipulative Aptitude Test screens individuals for jobs where dexterity is a main requirement. The revised Minnesota Paper Form Board Test consists of 64 two-dimensional diagrams cut into separate pieces. It provides insights into an applicant's mechanical spatial ability; you'd use it for screening applicants for jobs such as designers, draftspeople, or engineers.

◀ **FIGURE 5-4**
Two Problems from the Test of Mechanical Comprehension

Look at Sample X on this page. It shows two men carrying a weighted object on a plank, and it asks, "Which man carries more weight?" Because the object is closer to man "B" than to man "A," man "B" is shouldering more weight; so blacken the circle under "B" on your answer sheet. Now look at Sample Y and answer it yourself. Fill in the circle under the correct answer on your answer sheet.

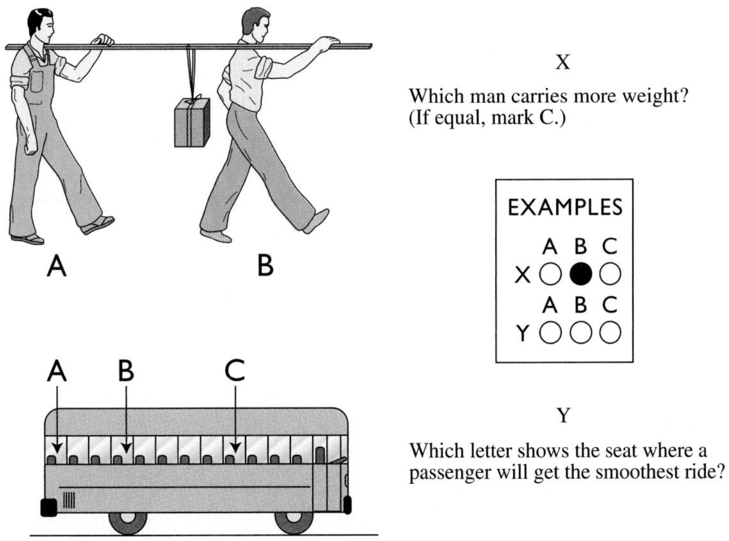

X

Which man carries more weight? (If equal, mark C.)

Y

Which letter shows the seat where a passenger will get the smoothest ride?

Source: Reproduced by permission. Copyright 1967, 1969 by The Psychological Corporation, New York, NY. All rights reserved. Author's note: 1969 is latest copyright on this test, which is still the main one used for this purpose.

Tests of physical abilities may also be required.[40] These include static strength (such as lifting weights), dynamic strength (like pull-ups), body coordination (as in jumping rope), and stamina.[41] Lifeguards, for example, must show they can swim a course before they're hired.

Measuring Personality and Interests

A person's cognitive and physical abilities alone seldom explain his or her job performance. Other factors, like motivation and interpersonal skills, are very important. As a consultant recently put it, most people are hired based on qualifications, but most are fired for nonperformance. And nonperformance (or performance) "is usually the result of personal characteristics, such as attitude, motivation, and especially, temperament."[42]

Employers use personality and interests inventories to measure and predict such intangibles. Firms including Dell Computer, Motorola, and GE increasingly use personality tests to help screen even top-level candidates. For example, as part of its selection process for CEO candidates, Hewlett-Packard put its eventual choice Carly Fiorina and other finalists through a two-hour 900-question personality test. Candidates had to indicate whether statements like "When I bump into a piece of furniture, I usually get angry" were true or false.[43] Small business owners also need to test. The Entrepreneurs + HR feature describes some available resources.

ENTREPRENEURS + HR

Testing

Just because a company is small doesn't mean it shouldn't engage in testing. Quite the opposite: One or two mistakes may not be a big problem for a very large firm, but could cause chaos in a small operation.

Some tests are so easy to use they are particularly good for smaller firms. One is the Wonderlic Personnel Test, which measures general mental ability. It takes less than 15 minutes to administer the four-page booklet. The tester reads the instructions, and then keeps time as the candidate works through the 50 problems on the two inside sheets. The tester then scores the test by totaling the number of correct answers. Comparing the person's score with the minimum scores recommended for various occupations shows whether the person achieved the minimally acceptable score for the type of job in question.

The Predictive Index is another example of a test. It measures work-related personality traits, drives, and behaviors—in particular dominance, extroversion, patience, and blame avoidance—on a two-sided sheet. A template makes scoring simple.

Each candidate will probably have a unique pattern of responses. To help employers analyze the results, the Predictive Index program includes 15 standard patterns. For example, there is the "social interest" pattern, for a person who is generally unselfish, congenial, persuasive, patient, and unassuming. This person would be good with people and a good personnel interviewer, for instance.

Computerized testing programs like those described earlier in this chapter are especially useful for small employers. For example, when hiring office help, smaller employers usually depend on informal typing and filing tests. A better approach is to use a program like the Minnesota Clerical Assessment Battery published by Assessment Systems Corporation, which runs on a personal computer. It includes a typing test, proofreading test, filing test, business vocabulary test, business math test, and clerical knowledge test. Because it is computerized, administration and scoring are simple, and it is easy to adapt each test to the particular position being applied for.[44]

Personality tests measure basic aspects of an applicant's personality, such as introversion, stability, and motivation. Many of these tests are *projective*. The psychologist presents an ambiguous stimulus (like an ink blot or clouded picture) to the person. The psychologist then asks the person to interpret or react to it. Since the pictures are ambiguous, the person's interpretation must come from within— he or she supposedly projects into the picture his or her own emotional attitudes about life. A security-oriented person might describe the woman in Figure 5-1 (page 128) as "my mother worrying about what I'll do if I lose my job."

Other projective techniques include Make a Picture Story (MAPS), House-Tree-Person (H-T-P), and the Forer Structured Sentence Completion Test. Other examples of personality tests (more properly called personality inventories) include the Thematic Apperception Test, the Guilford-Zimmerman Temperament Survey, and the Minnesota Multiphasic Personality Inventory. The Guilford-Zimmerman survey measures personality traits like emotional stability versus moodiness and friendliness versus criticalness. The Minnesota Multiphasic Personality Inventory taps traits like hypochondria and paranoia. The Interpersonal Style Inventory is a self-report inventory composed of 300 true/false items covering scales such as sociable, sensitive, deliberate, stable, conscientious, trusting, and directive. The Meyer-Kendall Assessment Survey contains 105 yes/no items and assesses personal functioning on 12 scales, including dominance, attention to detail, stability, people concern, anxiety, and extroversion.

Wonderlic's Personal Characteristics Inventory is another example. It measures five personality dimensions and links these dimensions to job performance. The manager administers this test, and faxes it to Wonderlic, which scores it and returns the report the same day. The Leadership Ability Evaluation measures leadership abilities and behavior, and identifies the test taker's decision-making styles. The Supervisory Practices Inventory presents a series of typical job situations followed by three ways a supervisor might handle them. The Sales Achievement Predictor creates a report showing the individual's percentile ranked on scales such as "sales disposition" and "sales closing" and rates the test taker as highly recommended, recommended, or not recommended for sales. The Personal Style Inventory produces a profile of the approaches someone typically uses to meet personal and professional challenges. You'll find sample personality tests online at www.psychtests.com.

Employers sometimes need personality inventories they can use worldwide. An international team of psychologists recently developed the Global Personality Inventory, based on data from 11 countries and 10 languages for use worldwide. The inventory's five main factors (with sample subscales) are agreeableness (consideration, empathy, openness, trust); conscientiousness (attention to detail, dutifulness, responsibility); extroversion (adaptability, competitiveness, desire for achievement, energy level, influence, taking charge); neuroticism (emotional control, optimism, stress tolerance); and openness to experience (innovativeness, creativity, social astuteness, independence).[45]

Personality tests—particularly the projective type— are the most difficult tests to evaluate and use. An expert must analyze the test taker's interpretations and reactions and infer from them his or her personality. The usefulness of such tests for selection rests on the

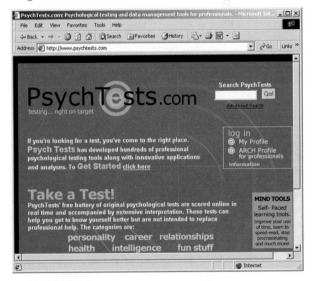

▲ **WEBNOTE**

www.psychtests.com *illustrates some of the many employment tests available, and lets you take a sample test online—such as the Classic Intelligence Test—and scores it for you while you wait.*

www.psychtests.com

assumption that you can find a relationship between a measurable personality trait (like introversion) and success on the job.[46]

Effectiveness The difficulties notwithstanding, personality tests can help organizations do a better job of screening. Researchers recently administered an aggression questionnaire to high school hockey players prior to the season; preseason aggressiveness as measured by the questionnaire predicted how many minutes they spent in the penalty box for offenses like fighting, slashing, and tripping.[47] Researchers used the responsibility, socialization, and self-control scales of the California Psychological Inventory to successfully predict dysfunctional job behaviors among law enforcement officers.[48] At a multinational company, emotional stability, extroversion, and agreeableness predicted whether expatriates would leave their assignments early.[49] At another firm, employee testing predicted employee theft.[50]

Industrial psychologists often emphasize the "big five" personality dimensions as they apply to personnel testing: extroversion, emotional stability, agreeableness, conscientiousness, and openness to experience.[51] One study focused on the extent to which these five personality dimensions predicted performance (for instance, in terms of job and training proficiency) for professionals, police officers, managers, sales workers, and skilled/semiskilled workers. Conscientiousness showed a consistent relationship with all job performance criteria for all the occupations. Extroversion was a valid predictor of performance for managers and sales employees—the two occupations involving the most social interaction. Both openness to experience and extroversion predicted training proficiency for all occupations.[52] Another study, with 89 university employees, concluded that (1) absenteeism and (2) extroversion and conscientiousness were inversely related.[53]

◆ **RESEARCH INSIGHT** An interesting question is whether it's personality or intelligence (or both) that drives career success. It would seem the answer is both. Researchers in one study defined career success in terms of intrinsic success (job satisfaction) and extrinsic success (income and occupational status). Their studies suggest that hard work certainly seems to pay off: Conscientiousness positively predicted both intrinsic and extrinsic career success. Neuroticism negatively predicted extrinsic success. General mental ability positively predicted extrinsic career success.[54]

Employers should use personality tests cautiously, particularly if the focus is on aberrant behavior. One report concluded that personality tests can help determine whether an employee's erratic behavior will pose a threat to workplace safety. However, they can also create legal problems for employers—for instance, if rejected candidates claim the results are false, or that they violate the Americans with Disabilities Act or employees' privacy.[55]

interest inventory
A personal development and selection device that compares the person's current interests with those of others now in various occupations so as to determine the preferred occupation for the individual.

Interest Inventories **Interest inventories** compare your interests with those of people in various occupations. Thus, a person who takes the Strong-Campbell Inventory would receive a report comparing his or her interests to those of people already in occupations like accounting, engineering, management, or medical technology. These inventories have many uses. One example is career planning, since a person will likely do better in jobs that involve activities in which he or she is interested. These tests can also be useful as selection tools. Clearly, if you can select people whose interests are roughly the same as those of successful incumbents in the jobs for which you are recruiting, it is more likely that the applicants will be successful.[56]

Achievement Tests

Achievement tests measure what a person has learned. Most of the tests you take in school are achievement tests. They measure your "job knowledge" in areas like economics, marketing, or personnel. Achievement tests are also popular at work.

For example, the Purdue Test for Machinists and Machine Operators tests the job knowledge of experienced machinists with questions like, "What is meant by 'tolerance'?" Other tests are available for other occupations. In addition to job knowledge, achievement tests measure the applicant's abilities; a typing test is one example. The use of the Internet in testing is illustrated in the following HR.*NET* box.

HR.*NET*

Firms are increasingly using the Web for testing and screening applicants. For example, in the late 1990s, the financial firm Capital One was using three paper-and-pencil tests for pre-employment screening: a cognitive skills test, a math test, and a "bio test data" job history test (which the firm used to predict job stability).[57] The process was reportedly time consuming and inefficient: "In Tampa, we were having to process several thousand people a month just to hire 100," says a company officer. The company's new online system eliminates the paper-and-pencil process. Call center applicants working online complete the application and the upgraded math and biodata tests. They also take an online role-playing call simulation. They put on a headset, and the CD-ROM program plays seven different customer situations. Applicants (playing the role of operators) answer multiple-choice questions online as to how they would respond. The company is in the process of expanding its online preemployment testing program to the United Kingdom and France.

Using the Web for Testing and Screening

WORK SAMPLES AND SIMULATIONS

Experts consider **work samples** and simulations (such as the assessment centers in this section) tests. However, they differ from most tests we've discussed, because they measure job performance directly. With video-based situational tests, for example, you present examinees with situations representative of the job for which they're applying, and evaluate their responses to these hypothetical situations.[58]

work samples
Actual job tasks used in testing applicants' performance.

Work Sampling for Employee Selection

The **work sampling technique** measures how a candidate actually performs some of the job's basic tasks.[59] This has several advantages. It measures actual on-the-job tasks, so it's harder for applicants to fake answers. Work samples more clearly relate to the job you are testing for, so in terms of fairness and fair employment, you may be on safer ground. The work sample's content—the actual tasks the person must perform—is not as likely to be unfair to minorities as a personnel test that might emphasize middle-class concepts and values.[60] Work sampling does not delve into the applicant's personality or psyche. So there's almost no chance of it being viewed as an invasion of privacy. Designed properly, work sampling tests also exhibit better validity than do other tests designed to predict performance.

    The basic procedure is to choose several tasks crucial to performing the job and to test applicants on samples of each.[61] An observer monitors performance on each task, and indicates on a checklist how well the applicant performs. Here is an example. In developing a work sampling test for maintenance mechanics, experts first listed all possible job tasks (like "install pulleys and belts" and "install and align a motor"). Four crucial tasks were installing pulleys and belts, disassembling and installing a gearbox, installing and aligning a motor, and pressing a bushing into a sprocket.

work sampling technique
A testing method based on measuring performance on actual basic job tasks.

CHECKS KEY BEFORE INSTALLING AGAINST:		
_____ shaft	score	3
_____ pulley	score	3
_____ neither	score	1

This is one step in installing pulleys and belts.

They then broke down these four tasks into the steps required to complete them. Mechanics could perform each step in a slightly different way, of course. Since some approaches were better than others, the experts gave a different weight to different approaches.

Figure 5-5 shows one of the steps required for installing pulleys and belts—"checks key before installing." As the figure shows, possible approaches here include checking the key against (1) the shaft, (2) the pulley, or (3) neither. The right of the figure lists the weights reflecting the worth of each method. The applicant performs the task, and the observer checks off the approach used.

Management Assessment Centers

management assessment center
A simulation in which management candidates are asked to perform realistic tasks in hypothetical situations and are scored on their performance. It usually also involves testing and the use of management games.

A **management assessment center** is a two- to three-day simulation in which 10 to 12 candidates perform realistic management tasks (like making presentations) under the observation of experts who appraise each candidate's leadership potential. The center itself may be a plain conference room, but it is often a special room with a one-way mirror to facilitate observation. Typical simulated exercises include:

- *The in basket.* These exercises confront the candidate with an accumulation of reports, memos, notes of incoming phone calls, letters, and other materials collected in the actual or computerized in basket of the simulated job he or she is about to start. The candidate must take appropriate action on each item. Trained evaluators then review the candidate's efforts.
- *Leaderless group discussion.* Trainers give a leaderless group a discussion question and tell members to arrive at a group decision. They then evaluate each group member's interpersonal skills, acceptance by the group, leadership ability, and individual influence.
- *Management games.* Participants solve realistic problems as members of simulated companies competing in a marketplace. They may have to decide, for instance, how to advertise and manufacture, and how much inventory to stock.
- *Individual presentations.* Trainers evaluate each participant's communication skills and persuasiveness by having each make an assigned oral presentation.
- *Objective tests.* A center typically includes tests of personality, mental ability, interests, and achievements.
- *The interview.* Most require an interview between at least one trainer and each participant, to assess the latter's interests, past performance, and motivation.

In practice, employers use assessment centers for selection, promotion, and development. Supervisor recommendations usually play a big role in choosing center participants. Line managers usually act as assessors and typically arrive at their ratings through a consensus process.[62]

Assessment centers can be effective.[63] However, whether they do their job less expensively than other selection techniques is not clear. One study suggests that the approach is financially efficient.[64] Another concludes that a review of the participants' personnel files did as good a job of predicting which participants would succeed as did their assessment center evaluations.[65] Perhaps the best approach is to combine the two. In one study, a combination of the assessment center and an evaluation of the candidate's records was a relatively good predictor.

Video-Based Situational Testing

Video-based tests are also *situational tests* (which present examinees with situations representative of the job); others include work sampling, discussed above, and situational interviews, discussed in Chapter 6.[66] The typical video-based test presents the candidate with several scenarios, each followed by a multiple-choice question. A scenario might depict an employee handling a situation on the job. At a critical moment, the scenario ends and the video asks the candidate to choose from among several courses of action. An example of a typical video-based scenario/judgment question, about one minute long, follows:

(*A manager is upset about the condition of the department and takes it out on one of the department's employees*).

> Manager: Well, I'm glad you're here.
>
> Associate: Oh? Why is that?
>
> Manager: Look at this place, that's why! I take a day off and come back to find the department in a mess. You should know better.
>
> Associate: But I didn't work late last night.
>
> Manager: Maybe not. But there have been plenty of times before when you've left this department in a mess.

(*The scenario stops here.*)
   If you were this associate, what would you do?

   a. Let the other associates responsible for the mess know that you had to take the heat.
   b. Straighten up the department, and try to reason with the manager later.
   c. Suggest to the manager that he talk to the other associates who made the mess.
   d. Take it up with the manager's boss.[67]

While the evidence is somewhat mixed, the results suggest that video-based situational tests can be useful for selecting employees.[68]

The Miniature Job Training and Evaluation Approach

The idea here is to train candidates to perform a sample of the job's tasks, and then to evaluate their performance. The approach assumes that a person who demonstrates that he or she can learn and perform the sample of tasks will be able to learn and perform the job itself.

An example illustrates this selection method's usefulness. The study focused on navy recruits who'd been deemed unacceptable candidates for various naval schools based on their performance on traditional tests. The recruits participated in several miniature job training and evaluation situations. In one, trainers showed them how to read a simplified plot diagram of the positions of two ships, their headings, and speed, and how to extrapolate the new position of each ship and evaluate the danger of collision. Recruits who normally would have been barred from moving on to such training based on their initial test scores were found to be competent to pursue it, because of their performance in the mini training session.

The approach has pros and cons. It tests applicants with actual samples of the job rather than just with paper-and-pencil tests, so it's "content relevant." It may thus be more acceptable (and fair) to disadvantaged applicants than most paper-and-pencil tests. However, it emphasizes individual instruction during training, and so is a relatively expensive screening approach.[69]

OTHER SELECTION TECHNIQUES

Testing is usually just part of an employer's selection process. Other tools may include background investigations and reference checks, preemployment information services, honesty testing, graphology, and substance abuse screening.

Background Investigations and Reference Checks

Most employers try to check and verify the job applicant's background information and references. Some estimate that about 95% of U.S. corporations now employ such background checks,[70] with the vast majority probably using telephone inquiries. The remainder use background sources, like traditional or Internet-based commercial credit checking agencies and reference letters.

Background checks can be quite comprehensive. As *Fortune* magazine noted, applicants may be in for a rude surprise:

> *Chances are, your new employer will delve into your driving record, check for criminal charges or convictions, survey your creditworthiness, examine whether you've been sued or have run afoul of the IRS, and sometimes even query co-workers and neighbors about your reputation. Your educational history, past employment, and references listed on your resume are in for fierce scrutiny.[71]*

While that description may overstate the situation, it does appear that employers use background and reference checks more extensively today. Commonly verified data include legal eligibility for employment (in compliance with immigration laws), dates of prior employment, military service (including discharge status), education, and identification (including date of birth and address to confirm identity).[72]

There are two main reasons to conduct preemployment background investigations and/or reference checks—to verify factual information previously provided by the applicant and to uncover damaging information such as criminal records and suspended driver's licenses.[73] Lying on one's application is not unusual. For example, BellSouth's security director estimates that 15% to 20% of applicants conceal a dark secret. As he says, "It's not uncommon to find someone who applies and looks good, and then you do a little digging and you start to see all sorts of criminal history."[74] The omissions are often subtle. One well-known executive reportedly claimed he worked for Sterling Pulp and Paper from 1967–1975, and for American Can 1975–1982. Missing from his résumé were two firms that fired him, one in 1973, and one in 1976. Neither of the two headhunting firms that subsequently placed him found the omissions.[75]

Even relatively sophisticated companies fall prey to criminal employees, in part because they haven't conducted proper background and reference checks. In Chicago, a major pharmaceutical firm discovered it had hired gang members in mail delivery and computer repair. The crooks were stealing close to a million dollars a year in computer parts, and then using the mail department to ship them to a nearby computer store they owned.[76] Thorough background checks might have prevented the losses.

The actual background investigation/reference check can take many forms. Most employers at least try to verify an applicant's current (or former) position and salary with his or her current (or former) employer by phone (assuming doing so was cleared with the candidate). Others call the applicant's current and previous supervisors to try to discover more about the person's motivation, technical competence, and ability to work with others (although many employers have policies against providing such information). Some employers get background reports from commercial credit rating companies. The latter can provide information about credit standing, indebtedness, reputation, character, and lifestyle. Some employers ask for written references. Figure 5-6 shows a form used for this purpose (although you could use it for phone references too).

Effectiveness The background check can be useful. It's an inexpensive and straightforward way to verify factual information about the applicant, such as current and previous job titles, current salary range, dates of employment, and educational background.

However, reference checking can backfire. Laws (like the Fair Credit Reporting Act of 1970) increase the likelihood that rejected applicants will have access to the

◀ **FIGURE 5-6**
Employee Reference
Check Form

EMPLOYMENT REFERENCE CHECK FORM

Applicant: 1. Please print out this Reference Check Form.
2. Fill out the top section of the form.
3. Send it to a former employer to complete and return to:

Human Resources Department
Winter Sports, Inc./Big mountain Ski & Summer Resort
PO Box 1400, Whitefish, MT 59937\or Fax to: 406-862-2955

REFERENCE CHECK FORM   Please Type or Print Legibly

To Be Completed by Applicant _____

Applicant's Name _____

Name of Reference _____

Business Name _____

I have applied for a position with Winter Sports, Inc. at Big mountain Ski and Summer Resort. In order to be considered for employment, they have requested information from my previous employers. I would appreciate your cooperation in providing the answers to the following questions. I have been advised this information will be held in confidence by the Winter Sports, Inc. Human Resource Department.

_____   _____
     Applicant's Signature   Date

To be Completed by Employer:

Employed From_____ To_____

Position(s) Held

Reason for Separation: ____ Quit ____Laid-off ____Discharged
                            Other _____

Comments: _____
_____
_____

As an employee, was this person:

Responsible? ____YES ____NO

Able to work well with others? ____YES ____NO

Trustworthy? ____YES ____NO

Dependable (Attendance)? ____YES ____NO

Eligible for rehire? ____YES ____NO

A positive customer service representative? (if applies) ____YES ____NO

Please comment briefly on "NO" responses: _____
_____

Additional comments from supervisor, if possible _____
_____

Signature of person filling out form: _____

Title: _____ Date: _____

Source: Winter Sports Inc./Big Mountain, Whitefish, Montana. Used with permission.

background information; they may then sue both the source of that information and the recruiting employer. In practice, it's not always easy to prove that the person deserved the bad reference. The rejected applicant has various legal remedies, including suing the source of the reference for defamation of character.[77] In one case, a court awarded a man $56,000 after he was turned down for a job because, among other things, the former employer called him a "character." This happens often enough to cause former employers to limit their comments.

It is not just the fear of legal reprisal that can undermine a reference. Many supervisors don't want to damage a former employee's chances for a job; others might prefer giving an incompetent employee good reviews if it will get rid of him or her. Even when checking references via phone, therefore, you have to be careful to ask the right questions. You must also try to judge whether the reference's answers are evasive and, if so, why.

HR managers don't seem to view reference letters as very useful. In one study, only 12% replied that reference letters were "highly valuable," 43% called them "somewhat valuable," and 30% viewed them as having "little value," or (6%) "no value." Asked whether they preferred written or telephone references, 72% favored the telephone reference, because it allows a more candid assessment and provides a more personal exchange. Not having a written record is also an appealing feature. In fact, reference letters ranked lowest—seventh out of seven—as selection tools. Ranked from top to bottom, the tools were interview, application form, academic record, oral referral, aptitude and achievement tests, psychological tests, and reference letters.[78]

Giving References: Know the Law Federal laws that affect references include the Privacy Act of 1974, the Fair Credit Reporting Act of 1970, the Family Education Rights and Privacy Act of 1974 (and Buckley Amendment of 1974), and the Freedom of Information Act of 1966. These laws give individuals in general and students (the Buckley Amendment) the right to know the nature and substance of information in their credit files and files with government agencies, and (under the Privacy Act) to review records pertaining to them from any private business that contracts with a federal agency. It is therefore quite possible that the person you're describing may be shown your comments.

Common law (and in particular the tort of defamation) applies to any information you supply. Communication is defamatory if it is false and tends to harm the reputation of another by lowering the person in the estimation of the community or by deterring other persons from associating or dealing with him or her. There are companies that, for a small fee, will call former employers on behalf of employees who believe they're getting bad references from the former employers. One supervisor, describing a former city employee, reportedly "used swear words, said he was incompetent and said he almost brought the city down on its knees."[79]

Companies fielding requests for references need policies regarding this. They should ensure that only authorized managers provide information. Other suggested guidelines for defensible references include "Don't volunteer information," "Avoid vague statements," and "Do not answer trap questions such as, 'Would you rehire this person?'" In practice, many firms have a policy of not providing any information about former employees except for their dates of employment, last salary, and position titles.[80]

Defamation is an increasing concern. In one case, an employer fired four employees for "gross insubordination" after they disobeyed a supervisor's request to review allegedly fabricated expense account reports. The jury found that the expense reports were actually honest. The employees then argued that although their employer didn't publicize the expense account matter to others, the employer should have known that the employees would have to admit the reason for their firing when explaining and defending themselves to future employers. The court agreed and upheld jury awards to these employees totaling more than a million dollars. In another case, a manager who claimed he was wrongly accused of stealing from his former employer won $1.25 million in a slander suit.[81] Perhaps this explains why in one survey only 11% of respondents said the information they get about a candidate's violent or "bizarre" behavior is adequate. Fifty-four percent of the respondents specifically said that they get inadequate information in this area. Of 11 types of information sought in background checks, only 3 were ranked by a majority of respondents as ones for which they received adequate information: dates of employment (96%), eligibility for rehire (65%), and job qualifications (56%). With regard to salary history, reasons for leaving a previous job, work habits, personality traits, human relations skills, special skills or knowledge, and employability, "fewer than half of HR managers responding to the survey said they were able to obtain adequate information."[82]

Not disclosing relevant information can be dangerous, too. In one Florida case, an employee was fired for allegedly bringing a handgun to work. After his subsequent employer fired him (for absenteeism), he returned to the second company and shot a supervisor as well as the HR director and three other people before taking his own life. The injured parties and the relatives of the murdered employees sued the original employer, who had provided the employee with a clean letter of recommendation. The letter stated his departure was not related to job performance, allegedly because that first employer didn't want to anger the employee over his firing.

Making Background Checks More Useful So what is the prospective employer to do? Is there any way to obtain better information?

Yes. First, include on the application form a statement for applicants to sign explicitly authorizing a background check. For example, include a statement such as:

> *I hereby certify that the facts set forth in the above employment application are true and complete to the best of my knowledge. I understand that falsified statements or misrepresentation of information on this application or omission of any information sought may be cause for dismissal, if employed, or may lead to refusal to make an offer and/or to withdrawal of an offer. I also authorize investigation of credit, employment record, driving record, and, once a job offer is made or during employment, workers' compensation background if required.*

Second (since telephone references apparently produce more candid assessments), it's probably best to rely on telephone references than on written ones. Similarly, remember that you can probably count on getting more accurate information regarding dates of employment, eligibility for rehire, and job qualifications than other background information (such as reasons for leaving a previous job).

Persistence and a sensitivity to potential red flags can also improve results. For example, if the former employer hesitates or seems to qualify his or her answer when you ask, "Would you rehire?" don't just go on to the next question. Instead, try to unearth what the applicant did to make the former employer pause.

Another suggestion is to use the references offered by the applicant as a source for other references. You might ask each of the applicant's references, "Could you please give me the name of another person who might be familiar with the applicant's performance?" In that way, you begin getting information from references who may be more objective, because they weren't referred directly by the applicant. Ask open-ended questions, such as, "How much structure does the applicant need in his/her work?" in order to get the references to talk more about the candidate.[83]

PREEMPLOYMENT INFORMATION SERVICES

There was a time when the only source of background information was what a candidate provided on the application form and what the employer could obtain through private investigators. Today, preemployment information services use databases to accumulate information about matters such as workers' compensation and credit histories, and conviction and driving records. For example, a South Florida firm advertises that for under $50 it will do a criminal history report, motor vehicle/driver's record report, and (after the person is hired) a workers' compensation claims report history, plus confirm identity, name, and Social Security number. Employers are increasingly turning to information services in order to make the right selection decision.

There are two reasons to use caution when delving into an applicant's criminal, credit, and workers' compensation histories.[84] First (as discussed in Chapter 2), various equal employment laws discourage or prohibit the use of such information in employee screening. For example, the 1990 Americans with Disabilities Act (ADA) prohibits employers from making preemployment inquiries into the existence, nature, or severity of a disability. Therefore, asking about a candidate's previous workers' compensation claims (before offering the person a job) is usually unlawful. Courts might also view making employment decisions based on someone's arrest record as unfairly discriminatory. (Use of conviction information for particular jobs—for instance, where security is involved—would be less of a problem.) The EEOC says a poor credit history should not by itself preclude someone from getting a job.

Second, other non-EEO laws regulate such information. For example, in New York State, "It is unlawful for an employer to inquire into or act on information about an arrest not resulting in conviction unless such use is permitted by law. It is unlawful to discriminate against an applicant for licensing or employment because the person has been convicted of one or more criminal offenses or because of a finding of a lack of 'good moral character' based on the conviction."[85] New York also requires employers to notify an applicant before requesting a consumer report. Under the Federal Fair Credit Reporting Act, employers that take adverse actions based on a consumer report must advise the employee or candidate that they turned the person down based on the consumer report. They must also supply him or her with the name and address of the consumer reporting agency. And the employer may not obtain a consumer report from a reporting agency under false pretenses.[86]

To bring the problem into perspective, consider the debate about a national antitheft database named Theftnet, tested by retailers including Home Depot and J. C. Penney. The database contains the names of workers across the country who have been prosecuted for theft or who have signed admissions statements with former employers.[87]

Using a database like Theftnet would seem straightforward. Yet in practice, it raises serious issues. For example, one attorney says supplying information to the database could make an employer liable for defamation and retaliation claims unless it has "clear proof of an employee's guilt."[88] Employees who have signed admissions statements may in fact be guilty; however, they may also have signed for unrelated reasons, such as coercion or promises by the employer. One attorney contends that a database like this could pose an incalculable risk of harm to employees.[89] Employers tapping into such a database should therefore balance the pros and cons; consider the legal issues involved; ensure they have "clear proof" of an employee's guilt; and use the information as just one part of the background check. Table 5-2 summarizes suggestions for collecting background information, such as "check all applicable laws."

Some suggestions for collecting background information include the following:

1. Check all applicable state laws.
2. Review the impact of federal equal employment laws.
3. Remember the Federal Fair Credit Reporting Act.
4. Do not obtain information that you're not going to use.
5. Remember that using arrest information will be highly suspect.
6. Avoid blanket policies (such as "we hire no one with a record of workers' compensation claims").
7. Use information that is specific and job related.
8. Keep information confidential and up to date.
9. Never authorize an unreasonable investigation.

Source: Jeffrey M. Hahn, "Pre-Employment Services: Employers Beware?" *Employee Relations Law Journal* 17, no. 1 (summer 1991), pp. 45–69.

The Polygraph and Honesty Testing

Some firms still use the polygraph (or lie detector) for honesty testing, even though current law severely restricts its use. The polygraph is a device that measures physiological changes like increased perspiration. The assumption is that such changes reflect changes in emotional state that accompany lying.

The usual procedure is to attach a person to the machine with painless electronic probes. The polygraph expert then asks the person a series of neutral questions (such as, "Is your name John Smith?" and "Do you currently reside in New York?"). Once the expert ascertains the person's reaction to neutral questions, he or she starts asking questions like "Have you ever taken anything without paying for it?" or "Have you ever committed a crime?" In theory, at least, the expert can then determine with some accuracy whether or not the applicant is lying.

Complaints about offensiveness plus grave doubts about the polygraph's accuracy culminated in the Employee Polygraph Protection Act of 1988. With a few exceptions, the law prohibits employers from conducting polygraph examinations of all job applicants and most employees. (Also prohibited under this law are other mechanical or electrical devices that attempt to measure honesty or dishonesty, including psychological stress evaluators and voice stress analyzers. Federal laws don't prohibit paper-and-pencil tests and chemical testing [as for drugs].)[90] Local, state, and federal government employers (including the FBI) can continue to use polygraph exams, but many local and state government employers are further restricted under state laws.

Other employers permitted to use polygraph tests include: industries with national defense or security contracts; certain businesses with nuclear-power-related contracts with the Department of Energy; businesses and consultants with access to highly classified information; those with counterintelligence-related contracts with the FBI or Department of Justice; and private businesses that are (1) hiring private security personnel, (2) hiring persons with access to drugs, or (3) doing ongoing investigations involving economic loss or injury to an employer's business, such as a theft.

Even in the case of ongoing investigations of theft, the employer's rights are limited. To administer such a test during an ongoing investigation, an employer must meet four standards. First, the employer must show that it suffered an economic loss or injury. Second, it must show that the employee in question had access to the property. Third, it must have a reasonable suspicion before asking the employee to take the polygraph. Fourth, the employee must be told the details of the investigation before the test, as well as the questions to be asked on the polygraph test itself.

A sample case underscores the importance of adhering to the four standards.[91] A doctor reported $200 missing from his hospital locker. The hospital questioned workers who had access to the locker room and searched their lockers. Each employee was told there might be a lie detector test, and only one expressed reluctance. The hospital fired that employee based on its "strong suspicion" that he was the culprit. The employee then successfully sued the hospital under the Employee Polygraph Protection Act. He showed that the employer hadn't, as required, proved that there was a loss to the business, since the theft from the doctor's locker didn't affect the "business of patient care." He also showed the hospital had failed to follow several procedures under the act.

Paper-and-Pencil Tests The virtual elimination of the polygraph as a screening device has triggered a burgeoning market for other types of honesty testing devices. Paper-and-pencil honesty tests are psychological tests designed to predict job applicants' proneness to dishonesty and other forms of counterproductivity.[92] Most of these tests measure attitudes regarding things like tolerance of others who steal, acceptance of rationalizations for theft, and admission of theft-related activities. Tests include the Phase II profile, owned by Wackenhut Corporation of Coral Gables, Florida, which provides security services to employers. London House, Inc., and Stanton Corporation publish similar tests.[93]

◆ **RESEARCH INSIGHT** Psychologists initially raised concerns about the proliferation of paper-and-pencil honesty tests, but recent studies support the validity of these selection tools.[94] One study focused on 111 employees hired by a major retail convenience store chain to work at store or gas station counters.[95] The firm estimated that "Shrinkage" equaled 3% of sales, and internal theft was believed to account for much of this. The researchers found that scores on an honesty test successfully predicted theft in this study, as measured by termination for theft. One large-scale review of the use of such tests for measuring honesty, integrity, conscientiousness, dependability, trustworthiness, and reliability recently concluded that the "pattern of findings" regarding the usefulness of such tests "continues to be consistently positive."[96]

Paper-and-pencil honesty testing may also help companies predict white-collar crime.[97] Subjects in one study included 329 federal prison inmates incarcerated for white-collar crime and 344 individuals from several midwestern firms employed in white-collar positions. Researchers administered three instruments, including the California Psychological Inventory (a personality inventory), the Employment Inventory (a second personality inventory), and a biodata scale. They concluded that "there are large and measurable psychological differences between white-collar offenders and nonoffenders. . . ." and that it was possible to use a personality-based integrity test to differentiate between the two.[98]

What Employers Can Do In practice, detecting dishonest candidates involves not just tests, but a comprehensive antitheft screening procedure. One expert suggests the following steps:

■ *Ask blunt questions.*[99] Ask direct questions in the face-to-face interview. For example, says this expert, there is nothing wrong with asking the applicant, "Have you ever stolen anything from an employer?" Other questions to ask include, "Have you recently held jobs other than those listed on your application?" "Have you ever been fired or asked to leave a job?" "What reasons would past supervisors give if they were asked why they let you go?" "Have past employers ever disciplined you or warned you about absences or lateness?" "Is any information on your application misrepresented or falsified?"

- *Listen, rather than talk.* Allow the applicant to do the talking so you can learn as much as possible about the person.
- *Do a credit check.* Include a clause in your application form that gives you the right to conduct background checks including credit checks and motor vehicle reports.
- *Check all employment and personal references.*
- *Use paper-and-pencil honesty tests and psychological tests.*
- *Test for drugs.* Devise a drug-testing program and give each applicant a copy of the policy.
- *Establish a search-and-seizure policy and conduct searches.* Give each applicant a copy of the policy and require each to return a signed copy. The policy should state that all lockers, desks, and similar property remain the property of the company and may be inspected routinely.

The Adolf Coors Company uses a three-step honesty-screening program. First, it uses an outside lab to conduct a urinalysis test. Next, applicants take a Stanton Corporation paper-and-pencil survey on attitudes toward honesty and theft. Stanton provides a written report categorizing applicants by levels of risk. (For example, low-risk individuals are those who have never been involved in any extensive thefts, while marginal-risk applicants might be tempted to steal if they feel they won't be caught.) Finally, Equifax Services performs applicant references and background checks. These involve contacting previous employers and educational institutions.[100]

Honesty testing still requires some caution. Having just taken and "failed" what is fairly obviously an "honesty test," the candidate may leave the premises feeling his or her treatment was less than proper. Some "honesty" questions also pose invasion-of-privacy issues. And there are state laws to consider: For instance, Massachusetts and Rhode Island limit the use of paper-and-pencil honesty tests.

Graphology

The use of graphology (handwriting analysis) assumes that handwriting reflects basic personality traits.[101] Handwriting analysis thus has some resemblance to projective personality tests, although graphology's validity is highly suspect.

In graphology, the handwriting analyst studies an applicant's handwriting and signature to discover the person's needs, desires, and psychological makeup. According to the graphologist, the writing in Figure 5-7 exemplifies "uneven pressure, poor rhythm, and uneven baselines." The variation of light and dark lines shows a "lack of control" and is "one strong indicator of the writer's inner disturbance."

Graphology's place in screening sometimes seems schizophrenic. Studies suggest it is generally not valid, or that when graphologists do accurately size up candidates, it's because they are also privy to other background information. Yet

◄ **FIGURE 5-7**
Handwriting Exhibit
Used by Graphologist

Source: Reproduced with permission from Kathryn Sackhein, *Handwriting Analysis and the Employee Selection Process* (New York: Quorum Books, 1990), p. 45.

some firms continue to use graphology—indeed, to swear by it. It tends to be bigger in Europe, where "countries like France or Germany have one central graphology institute, which serves as the certifying body."[102] Fike Corporation in Blue Springs, Missouri, a 325-employee maker of valves and other industrial products, uses profiles based on handwriting samples to design follow-up interviews. Sharon Stockham, senior HR vice president for Exchange Bank in Santa Rosa, California, says her company "lives and dies" by handwriting analysis, using it as one element for screening officer candidates.[103]

Physical Examination

Once the person is hired, a medical exam is often the next step in the selection process (although it may also take place after the new employee starts work).

There are several reasons for preemployment medical exams. One is to verify that the applicant meets the physical requirements of the position, and discover any medical limitations you should take into account in placing the applicant. The exam will also establish a record and baseline of the applicant's health for future insurance or compensation claims. By identifying health problems, the examination can also reduce absenteeism and accidents and, of course, detect communicable diseases that may be unknown to the applicant.

In the largest firms, the employer's medical department performs the exam. Smaller employers retain the services of consulting physicians. But remember that under the Americans with Disabilities Act, a person with a disability can't be rejected for the job if he or she is otherwise qualified and can perform the essential job functions with reasonable accommodation. The ADA permits a medical exam during the period between the job offer and commencement of work if such exams are standard practice for all applicants for that job category.[104]

Substance Abuse Screening

Many employers conduct drug screenings. The most common practice is to test candidates just before they're formally hired. Many also test current employees when there is reason to believe the person has been using drugs—after a work accident, or in the presence of obvious behavioral symptoms, chronic lateness, or high absenteeism. Some firms routinely administer drug tests on a random or periodic basis, while others require drug tests when they transfer or promote employees to new positions.[105]

No drug test is foolproof. Although 96% of employers who test use urine sampling,[106] some of these tests can't distinguish between legal and illegal substances—for example, Advil and Nuprin can produce positive results for marijuana. Dr. David Feinstein, a medical review officer with Connecticut health care provider Industrial Health Care, says "anyone" can go online and purchase drug-free samples to try to beat the tests.[107]

Other employers find such tests too personal, and use hair follicle testing. The method, radio-immunoassay of hair (RIAH), requires a small sample of hair, which the lab analyzes to detect prior ingestion of illicit drugs.[108] Classified ads advertise chemicals that can be added to specimens or rubbed on the scalp to fool the test.

Drug testing also raises ethical issues.[109] Unlike the roadside breathalyzer tests given to inebriated drivers, urine and blood tests for drugs indicate only whether drug residues are present; they can't measure impairment or, for that matter, habituation or addiction.[110] Without strong evidence linking blood or urine drug levels to impairment, some argue that testing is not justifiable on the grounds of boosting workplace safety.[111] Many feel the testing procedures themselves are degrading and intrusive. Others argue that use of drugs during leisure hours might have little or no relevance to the job itself.[112]

Drug testing raises legal issues, too.[113] As one attorney writes, "It is not uncommon for employees to claim that drug tests violate their rights to privacy under common law or, in some states, a state statutory or constitutional provision."[114] Hair follicle testing is less intrusive than urinalysis but can actually produce more personal information: A three-inch hair segment will record six months of drug use.

Several federal laws affect workplace drug testing. Under the Americans with Disabilities Act, a court would probably consider a former drug user (who no longer uses illegal drugs and has successfully completed or is participating in a rehabilitation program) a qualified applicant with a disability.[115] Under the Drug Free Workplace Act of 1988, federal contractors must maintain a workplace free from illegal drugs. While this doesn't require contractors to conduct drug testing or rehabilitate affected employees, many do. Under the U.S. Department of Transportation workplace regulations, firms with over 50 eligible employees in transportation industries must conduct alcohol testing on workers with sensitive or safety-related jobs. These include mass transit workers, air traffic controllers, train crews, and school bus drivers.[116] Other laws, including the Federal Rehabilitation Act of 1973 and various state laws, protect rehabilitating drug users or those who have a physical or mental addiction.[117]

What should an employer do when a job candidate tests positive? Most companies will not hire such candidates, and a few will immediately fire current employees who test positive.[118] For example, 120 of the 123 companies responding to the question, "If test results are positive, what action do you take?" indicated that applicants testing positive are not hired. Current employees have more legal recourse; employers must tell them the reason for dismissal if the reason is a positive drug test.[119]

However, particularly where sensitive jobs are concerned, courts appear to side with employers. In one case, the U.S. Court of Appeals for the First Circuit (which includes Maine, Massachusetts, New Hampshire, Rhode Island, and Puerto Rico) ruled that Exxon acted properly in firing a truck driver who failed a drug test. Exxon's drug-free workplace program included random testing of employees in safety-sensitive jobs. The employee drove a tractor-trailer carrying 12,000 gallons of flammable motor fuel and tested positive for cocaine. The union representing the employee challenged the firing, an arbitrator reduced the penalty to a two-month suspension, and the appeals court reversed the arbitrator's decision. It ruled that the employer acted properly in firing the truck driver, given the circumstances.[120]

◆ **HIGH-PERFORMANCE INSIGHT** Franciscan Health System of Dayton operates two skilled nursing care facilities and one acute care facility in Dayton, Ohio.[121] It faced several problems, including turnover of 146% per year. This was adversely affecting the firm's productivity and quality of care.

Working with a consultant, the company devised a nursing assistant test battery consisting of three tests: (1) an employment inventory aimed at identifying people who show conscientious work behaviors; (2) a personality survey aimed at identifying candidates who are more people oriented and more likely to interact positively with others; and (3) a job preferences inventory that looks for a match between actual job conditions and people's preferences for those job conditions.

The testing program was very successful. Turnover rates dropped to 71% annually one year after instituting the test battery, and to 51% within two years of its implementation. The company also reports saving more than $300,000 annually due to reduced turnover and higher overall productivity among nursing assistants.[122] Other studies similarly suggest testing can boost performance.[123]

STRATEGIC HR

City Garage's New
Hiring Process

City Garage's top managers knew they'd never be able to implement their growth strategy without a dramatic change in how they tested and hired employees.[124] Their hiring process consisted of a paper-and-pencil application and one interview, immediately followed by a hire/don't hire decision. While that might work for a slow-growth operation, it was unsatisfactory for a fast-growing operation like City Garage. For one thing, local shop managers didn't have the time to evaluate every applicant, so "if they had been shorthanded too long, we would hire pretty much anybody who had experience," said training director Rusty Reinoehl. There was also inconsistency: Some managers had better interviewing and hiring skills than others. Complicating the problem was that City Garage's competitive strategy didn't rely just on finding talented mechanics with toolboxes. City Garage competitively differentiates itself with an "open garage" arrangement, where customers interact directly with technicians. Therefore, finding mechanics who not only tolerate but react positively to customer inquiries is essential.

City Garage's solution was to purchase the Personality Profile Analysis online test from Dallas-based Thomas International USA. Doing so added a third step to the application and interview process. After a quick application and background check, likely candidates take the 10-minute, 24-question PPA. City Garage staff then enter the answers into the PPA Software system, and test results are available in less than two minutes. These show whether the applicant is high or low in four personality characteristics; it also produces follow-up questions about areas that might cause problems. For example, applicants might be asked how they've handled possible weaknesses such as lack of patience. If candidates answer those questions satisfactorily, they're asked back for extensive, all-day interviews, after which hiring decisions are made.

It's too early to tell for sure if the new testing process will significantly improve City Garage's performance, but early results are promising. With the cost of replacing a manager at $40,000, and replacing technicians at $7,000 to $10,000, "at a minimum, we feel like we'll be able to put $500,000 on the bottom line each year, if it does what we expect it to in terms of retention and right hiring," says Reinoehl. And perhaps more important, the new hiring process should make it more likely the firm will be able to implement its growth strategy.

Complying with Immigration Law

Under the Immigration Reform and Control Act of 1986, employees hired in the United States must prove they are eligible to work in the United States. A person does not have to be a U.S. citizen to be employable. However, employers should ask a person they're about to hire whether he or she is a U.S. citizen or an alien lawfully authorized to work in the United States. To comply with this law, employers should follow these procedures:

1. Hire only citizens and aliens lawfully authorized to work in the United States.
2. Advise all new job applicants of your policy.
3. Require all new employees to complete and sign the verification form (the "I-9 form") designated by the Immigration and Naturalization Service (INS) to certify that they are eligible for employment.
4. Examine documentation presented by new employees, record information about the documents on the verification form, and sign the form.
5. Retain the form for three years or for one year past the employment of the individual, whichever is longer.
6. If requested, present the form for inspection by INS or Department of Labor officers. No reporting is required.[125]

Prospective employees can prove their eligibility for employment in two ways. One is to show a document such as a U.S. passport or alien registration card with photograph that proves both the person's identity and employment eligibility. Many prospective employees won't have either of these documents. The other way to verify employment eligibility is to see a document that proves the person's identity, along with a document showing the person's employment eligibility, such as a work permit.

The documents some applicants submit may be fakes. For example, INS agents recently seized over 2 million counterfeit documents ranging from green cards and Social Security cards to driver's licenses, from nine different states.

Employers protect themselves in several ways. Systematic background checks are the most obvious. Preemployment screening should include employment verification, criminal record checks, drug screens, and reference checks. You can verify Social Security cards by calling the Social Security Administration. Employers can avoid accusations of discrimination by verifying the documents of all applicants, not just those they may think suspicious.[126]

Employers should not use the so-called I-9 Employment Eligibility Verification form to discriminate based on race or country of national origin. The requirement to verify eligibility does not provide any basis to reject an applicant just because he or she is a foreigner, or not a U.S. citizen, or an alien residing in the United States, as long as that person can prove his or her identity and employment eligibility.

Congress tried to clarify and simplify the worker verification process by passing the Illegal Immigration Reform and Immigrant Responsibility Act of 1996. The act mandated simplifying the verification process and reducing the number of documents allowed for employment verification from 29 to 6.[127] However, as of recently, the Immigration and Naturalization Service has not issued firm guidelines on how to implement the act. For the time being, employers should therefore keep using the existing I-9 form.[128]

We invite you to visit **www.prenhall.com/dessler** on the Prentice Hall Web site for our online study guide, Internet exercises, current links to related Web sites, and more.

---

1. In this chapter, we discussed several techniques for screening and selecting job candidates; the first was testing.
2. Test validity answers the question, "What does this test measure?" We discussed criterion validity and content validity. Criterion validity means demonstrating that those who do well on the test do well on the job; content validity is demonstrated by showing that the test constitutes a fair sample of the content of the job.
3. As used by psychologists, the term *reliability* always means "consistency." One way to measure reliability is to administer the same (or equivalent) tests to the same people at two different points in time. Or you could focus on internal consistency, comparing the responses to roughly equivalent items on the same test.
4. There are many types of personnel tests in use, including intelligence tests, tests of physical skills, tests of achievement, aptitude tests, interest inventories, and personality tests.
5. For a selection test to be useful, scores should be predictably related to performance on the job; you must validate the test. This requires five steps: (1) analyze the job, (2) choose your tests, (3) administer the test, (4) relate test scores and criteria, and (5) cross-validate and validate the test.

Summary

6. Under equal rights legislation, an employer may have to be able to prove that its tests are predictive of success or failure on the job. This usually requires a predictive validation study, although other means of validation are often acceptable.

7. Some basic testing guidelines include (a) use tests as supplements, (b) validate the tests for appropriate jobs, (c) analyze all current hiring and promotion standards, (d) beware of certain tests, (e) use a certified psychologist, and (f) maintain good test conditions.

8. The work sampling selection technique is based on "the assumption that the best indicator of future performance is past performance." Here you use the applicant's actual performance on the same (or very similar) job to predict his or her future job performance. The steps are: (a) analyze the applicant's previous work experience, (b) have experts list component tasks for the open job, (c) select crucial tasks as work sample measures, (d) break down these tasks into steps, (e) test the applicant, and (f) relate the applicant's work sample score to his or her performance on the job.

9. Management assessment centers are another screening device and expose applicants to a series of real-life exercises. Performance is observed and assessed by experts, who then check their assessments by observing the participants when they are back at their jobs. Examples of "real-life" exercises include a simulated business game, an in-basket exercise, and group discussions.

10. Even though most people prefer not to give bad references, most companies still carry out some sort of reference check on their candidates. These can be useful in raising red flags, and questionnaires (page 145) can improve the usefulness of the responses you receive.

11. Other selection tools include the polygraph, honesty tests, and graphology. While graphology appears to have little predictive value, honesty tests have been used with success although they (and polygraphs) must be used with an eye toward the legal and ethical issues involved.

Tying It All Together

We've seen that the employee selection process can conveniently be thought of as a series of hurdles: You determine the jobs that have to be filled and, through job analysis, the specific duties of these jobs and the skills and characteristics of the people you want to fill them. You use techniques including employment agencies, advertising, and the Internet to create a pool of viable candidates. Of course, the pool of applicants is only part (although a very important part) of the selection process: You also need to bring to bear the best possible tools and techniques to select the best candidates. Chapter 5 focused on the selection process, and on many of the selection techniques (including testing and reference checks) that managers use (or should use) every day. Virtually every manager uses one selection tool every time he or she hires a new employee: the selection interview. We'll turn to this important technique in the following chapter.

Discussion Questions

1. Explain reliability and validity. What is the difference between them? In what respects are they similar?

2. Explain how you would go about validating a test. How can this information be useful to a manager?

3. Explain why you think a certified psychologist who is specifically trained in test construction should (or should not) always be used by a company developing a personnel test battery.

4. Explain how you would validate an employment selection test.

5. Give some examples of how to use interest inventories to improve employee selection. In doing so, suggest several examples of occupational interests that you believe might predict success in various occupations, including college professor, accountant, and computer programmer.

6. Why is it important to conduct preemployment background investigations? How would you go about doing so?

7. Explain how you would get around the problem of former employers being unwilling to give bad references on their former employees.
8. How can employers protect themselves against negligent hiring claims?

1. Write a short essay discussing some of the ethical and legal considerations in testing.
2. Working individually or in groups, develop a list of selection techniques that you would suggest your dean use to hire the next HR professor at your school. Also, explain why you chose each selection technique.
3. Working individually or in groups, contact the publisher of a standardized test such as the Scholastic Assessment Test and obtain from it written information regarding the test's validity and reliability. Present a short report in class discussing what the test is supposed to measure and the degree to which you think the test does what it is supposed to do, based on the reported validity and reliability scores.

EXPERIENTIAL EXERCISE *A Test for a Reservation Clerk*

Purpose: The purpose of this exercise is to give you practice in developing a test to measure *one specific ability* for the job of airline reservation clerk for a major airline. If time permits, you'll be able to combine your tests into a test battery.

Required Understanding: You should be fully acquainted with the procedure for developing a personnel test and should read the following description of an airline reservation clerk's duties:

> Customers contact our airline reservation clerks to obtain flight schedules, prices, and itineraries. The reservation clerks look up the requested information on our airline's online flight schedule systems, which are updated continuously. The reservation clerk must deal courteously and expeditiously with the customer, and be able to quickly find alternative flight arrangements in order to provide the customer with the itinerary that fits his or her needs. Alternative flights and prices must be found quickly, so that the customer is not kept waiting, and so that our reservations operations group maintains its efficiency standards. It is often necessary to look under various routings, since there may be a dozen or more alternative routes between the customer's starting point and destination.

You may assume that we will hire about one-third of the applicants you see as airline reservation clerks. Your objective is to create a test that is useful in selecting a third of those available.

How to Set Up the Exercise/Instructions: Divide class into teams of five or six students.

The ideal candidate will obviously have to have a number of skills and abilities to perform this job well. Your job is to select a single ability and to develop a test to measure that ability. Only use the materials available in the room, please. The test should permit quantitative scoring and may be an individual or a group test.

Please go to your assigned groups and, as per our discussion of test development in this chapter, each group should make a list of the abilities that seem relevant to success on the airline reservation clerk's job. Each group should then rate the importance of these abilities on a five-point scale. Then, develop a test to measure what you believe to be the top ranked ability. If time permits, the groups should combine the various tests from each group into a test battery. If possible, leave time for a group of students to take the test battery.

APPLICATION CASE *Honesty Testing at Carter Cleaning Company*

Donna Carter, president of the Carter Cleaning Centers, and her father have what the latter describes as an easy but hard job when it comes to screening job applicants. It is easy because for two important jobs—the people who actually do the pressing and those who do the cleaning-spotting—the applicants are easily screened with about 20 minutes of on-the-job testing. As with typists, as Donna points out, "applicants either know how to press clothes fast enough or how to use cleaning chemicals and machines, or they don't and we find out very quickly by just trying them out on the job."

On the other hand, applicant screening for the stores can also be frustratingly hard because of the nature of the qualities that Donna would like to screen for. Two of the most critical problems facing her company are employee turnover and employee honesty. Donna and her father sorely need to implement practices that will reduce the rate of employee turnover. If there is a way to do this through employee testing and screening techniques, Donna would like to know about it because of the management time and money that are now being wasted by the never-ending need to recruit and hire new employees. Of even greater concern to Donna and her father is the need to institute new practices to screen out those employees who may be predisposed to steal from the company.

Employee theft is an enormous problem for the Carter Cleaning Centers, and one that is not just limited to employees who handle the cash. For example, the cleaner-spotter and/or the presser often open the store themselves without a manager present to get the day's work started, and it is not unusual to have one or more of these people steal supplies or "run a route." Running a route means that an employee canvasses his or her neighborhood to pick up people's clothes for cleaning and then secretly cleans and presses them in the Carter store, using the company's supplies, gas, and power. It would also not be unusual for an unsupervised person (or his or her supervisor, for that matter) to accept a one-hour rush order for cleaning or laundering, quickly clean and press the item, and return it to the customer for payment without making out a proper ticket for the item posting the sale. The money, of course, goes into the person's pocket instead of into the cash register.

The more serious problem concerns the store manager and the counter workers who actually have to handle the cash. According to Jack Carter, "you would not believe the creativity employees use to get around the management controls we set up to cut down on employee theft." As one extreme example of this felonious creativity, Jack tells the following story: "To cut down on the amount of money my employees were stealing, i had a small sign painted and placed in front of all our cash registers. The sign said: YOUR ENTIRE ORDER FREE IF WE DON'T GIVE YOU A CASH REGISTER RECEIPT WHEN YOU PAY. CALL 555-5555. It was my intention with this sign to force all our cash-handling employees to place their receipts into the cash register where they would be recorded for my accountants. After all, if all the cash that comes in is recorded in the cash register, then we should have a much better handle on stealing in our stores, right? Well, one of our managers found a diabolical way around this. I came into the store one night and noticed that the cash register that this particular manager was using just didn't look right, although the sign was dutifully placed in front of it. It turned out that every afternoon at about 5 P.M. when the other employees left, this character would pull his own cash register out of a box that he hid underneath our supplies. Customers coming in would notice the sign and of course the fact that he was meticulous in ringing up every sale. But unknown to them and us, for about five months the sales that came in for about an hour every day went into his cash register, not mine. It took us that long to figure out where our cash for that store was going."

Questions

1. What would be the advantages and disadvantages to Donna's company of routinely administering honesty tests to all its employees?
2. Specifically, what other screening techniques could the company use to screen out theft-prone and turnover-prone employees, and how exactly could these be used?
3. How should her company terminate employees caught stealing, and what kind of procedure should be set up for handling reference calls about these employees when they go to other companies looking for jobs?

CONTINUING CASE: LearnInMotion.com *Do You Have Sales Potential?*

Of all the positions LearnInMotion had to fill, none were more pressing—or problematic—than those of the company's salespeople. The job was pressing because the clock was already ticking on the uses of the company's funds. The firm was already paying over $5,000 a month in rent and had signed obligations for a wide range of other expenses, including monthly computer payments to Compaq ($2,000 a month), a phone system ($800 a month), a burglar alarm ($200 a month), advertising (required by their venture capital fund, and equal to $4,000 a month), their own salaries ($10,000 a month), high-speed DSL lines ($600 a month), phones ($400 a month), and the services of a consulting programmer ($4,000 a month). As a result, even "doing nothing" they were burning through almost $40,000 per month. They had to have a sales force.

However, hiring good salespeople was becoming increasingly difficult. Hiring people like this should have been fairly straightforward: LearnInMotion's salespeople have to sell to basically two types of customers. They have to try to get potential customers to purchase banner space or button space on LearnInMotion's various Web site pages. To make this easier, Jennifer and Mel had prepared an online media kit. It describes the Web site metrics—for instance, in terms of monthly page views, and in terms of typical user metrics such as reported age and income level. In addition to selling banner ads, salespeople also have to try to get the companies that actually produce and make available educational CD-ROMs and courses to make those courses and programs available through LearnInMotion.com. None of these are "big-ticket" sales: Because the site is new and small, they can't really charge advertisers based on the number of users who click on their ads, so they simply charge a quarterly fee of $1,500 to list courses, or place ads. Content providers also have to agree to split any sales 50-50 with LearnInMotion. The Web surfer and office manager spend part of their time scouring the Web to identify specific people as potential customers. The salespeople then contact these people, "take them through" the Web site to show its advantages and functions, and answer the potential customer's questions.

This sales job, in other words, was fairly typical, so shouldn't have been so difficult to fill, but difficult it was. Perhaps it was because it was a dot-com, or perhaps they just weren't offering enough compensation; whatever it was, the two owners were finding it extremely difficult to hire one, let alone two good salespeople.

Perhaps the biggest problem here was deciding which of the personable candidates who showed up actually had sales potential. Jennifer and Mel did learn a couple of interesting things about interviewing sales candidates. For example, when they asked the first what his average monthly sales had been in the past six months at his former employer, he answered, "Oh, I got the award for highest sales last month." That seemed great to Mel, until, later, Jennifer pointed out to him that that answer really didn't answer their question. Things got even "weirder"—to use Mel's term—when five out of six of the next sales candidates gave more or less the same answer: "I was the top producer"; "I was one of the top three producers"; "they sent me to Las Vegas for being the top sales producer"; and so on. Getting applicants to actually divulge, specifically, what their average monthly sales had been in the past six months was, as they say, like pulling teeth.

Given that fact, and the relatively few sales candidates they have had, it has become increasingly obvious to the owners that basing their hiring decision solely on the person's experience is not going to work. In other words, they have to have some way to ascertain whether the candidate had sales potential, and whether he or she has the cognitive aptitude to discuss LearnInMotion's services with what were, in fact, quite sophisticated customers. They want you, their management consultants, to help them. Here's what they want you to do for them:

Questions and Assignments

1. What would be the advantages and disadvantages to our company of routinely administering a "sales potential" test to salesperson candidates? Which would you suggest?

2. Specifically, what other screening techniques should our company use to select high-potential sales candidates?

3. Tell us: What have we been doing wrong, and what should we do now?

6 Chapter

Interviewing Candidates

After studying this chapter, you should be able to:

- List the main types of selection interviews.
- Explain and illustrate at least six factors that affect the usefulness of interviews.
- Explain and illustrate each guideline for being a more effective interviewer.
- Effectively interview a job candidate.

STRATEGIC OVERVIEW   Brian Light, chief information officer for Staples, Inc., of Framingham, Massachusetts, faces some interesting challenges when it comes to spotting and hiring technology talent. Finding candidates with the experience and technical mastery to do these jobs is never easy. At Staples, the firm's strategy complicates the task. Staples is a rapid-growth, fast-paced entrepreneurial company, so the candidates it interviews and hires have to reflect the sort of confidence and assertiveness that fit with Staples's entrepreneurial style. But how do you get that sort of personality information from an interview?[1]

The previous chapter, Employee Testing and Selection, focused on important methods managers use to select employees. The purpose of the current chapter, Interviewing Candidates, is to improve your effectiveness at using what is perhaps the most important screening tool, the selection interview. The main topics we'll cover include types of interviews, the factors that can undermine an interview's usefulness, and designing and conducting an effective interview. In the following chapter, Training and Developing Employees, we'll turn to the techniques you can use to make sure the new employees you hire have the knowledge and skills they need to perform their jobs.

BASIC FEATURES OF INTERVIEWS

An *interview* is a procedure designed to obtain information from a person through oral responses to oral inquiries; a *selection interview*, which we'll focus on in this chapter, is "a selection procedure designed to predict future job performance on the basis of applicants' oral responses to oral inquiries."[2]

Since the interview is only one of several selection tools, you could reasonably ask, "Why devote a whole chapter to this one tool?" The answer is that the interview is by far the most widely used personnel selection procedure; one study of 852 employers found that 99% used interviews for employee selection, for instance.[3] The point is that while not all companies use tests, assessment centers, or even reference checks, it would be highly unusual for a manager not to interview a prospective employee. Interviewing is thus an indispensable management tool.

As we'll see below, experts have criticized the interview for its low validity.[4] However recent reviews have been more favorable, and an interview—at least one done properly—can be "a much better predictor of performance than previously thought and is comparable with many other selection techniques."[5]

Types of Interviews

Managers use interviews for several purposes. For example, there are selection, appraisal, and exit interviews. An *appraisal interview* is a discussion, following a performance appraisal, in which supervisor and employee discuss the employee's rating and possible remedial actions. When an employee leaves a firm for any reason, HR often conducts an *exit interview*. This interview aims at eliciting information about the job or related matters that might give the employer some insight into what's right or wrong about the firm. Many techniques covered in this chapter apply equally to appraisal and exit interviews. However, we'll postpone a complete explanation of these types of interviews until Chapters 9 and 10, respectively, so we can focus here on *selection interviews*. We can classify selection interviews according to (1) how structured they are, (2) their "content"—the types of questions they contain—and (3) how the firm administers the interviews. Let's look at these.

Structured Versus Unstructured Interviews In **unstructured or nondirective interviews**, there is generally no set format to follow, so the interview can take various directions. The lack of structure allows the interviewer to ask follow-up questions and pursue points of interest as they develop. Interviewees for the same job may or may not get the same or similar questions. A few questions might be specified in advance, but they're usually not, and there is seldom a formal guide for scoring answers. This type of interview "could even be described as little more than a general conversation."[6]

On the other hand, in **structured or directive interviews**, the questions and acceptable responses are specified in advance and the responses are rated for appropriateness of content.[7] McMurray's patterned interview was one early example. The interviewer followed a printed form to ask a series of questions, such as "How was the person's present job obtained?" Comments printed beneath the questions (such as "Has he/she shown self-reliance in getting his/her jobs?") then guide the interviewer in evaluating the answers.

In practice, not all structured interviews go so far as to specify acceptable answers. Figure 6-1 shows a relatively structured interview guide that stops short of specifying the answers to watch for. Indeed (as we'll explain in more detail on pages 174 and 175), there are different ways to structure an interview, many of which have nothing to do with using structured guides like the one in Figure 6-1.

unstructured or nondirective interview
An unstructured conversational-style interview in which the interviewer pursues points of interest as they come up in response to questions.

structured or directive interview
An interview following a set sequence of questions.

▶ **FIGURE 6-1**
Structured
Interview Guide

APPLICANT INTERVIEW GUIDE

To the interviewer: This Applicant Interview Guide is intended to assist in employee selection and placement. If it is used for all applicants for a position, it will help you to compare them, and it will provide more objective information than you will obtain from unstructured interviews.

Because this is a general guide, all of the items may not apply in every instance. Skip those that are not applicable and add questions appropriate to the specific position. Space for additional questions will be found at the end of the form.

Federal law prohibits discrimination in employment on the basis of sex, race, color, national origin, religion, disability, and in most instances, age. The law of most states also ban some or all of the above types of discrimination in employment as well as discrimination based on marital status or ancestry. Interviewers should take care to avoid any questions that suggest that an employment decision will be made on the basis of any such factors.

Job Interest

Name _____ Position applied for _____

What do you think the job (position) involves? _____

Why do you want the job (position)? _____

Why are you qualified for it? _____

What would your salary requirements be? _____

What do you know about our company? _____

Why do you want to work for us? _____

Current Work Status

Are you now employed? _____ Yes _____ No. If not, how long have you been unemployed? _____

Why are you unemployed? _____

If you are working, why are you applying for this position? _____

When would you be available to start work with us? _____

Work Experience

(Start with the applicant's current or last position and work back. All periods of time should be accounted for. Go back at least 12 years, depending upon the applicant's age. Military service should be treated as a job.)

Current or last
employer _____ Address _____

Dates of employment: from _____ to _____

Current or last job title _____

What are (were) your duties? _____

Have you held the same job throughout your employment with that company? _____ Yes _____ No. If not,

describe the various jobs you have had with that employer, how long you held each of them, and the main

duties of each. _____

What was your starting salary? _____ What are you earning now? _____ Comments _____

_____

Name of your last or current supervisor _____

What did you like most about that job? _____

What did you like least about it? _____

Why are you thinking of leaving? _____

Why are you leaving right now? _____

Interviewer's comments or observations _____

_____

(continued)

Source: Copyright 1992 The Dartnell Corporation, Chicago, IL. Adopted with permission.

What did you do before you took your last job? _____

   Where were you employed? _____

   Location _____ Job title _____

   Duties _____

   Did you hold the same job throughout your employment with that company? _____ Yes _____ No. If not,

   describe the jobs you held, when you held them and the duties of each. _____

   _____

   What was your starting salary? _____ What was your final salary? _____

   Name of your last supervisor _____

   May we contact that company? _____ Yes _____ No

   What did you like most about that job? _____

   What did you like least about that job? _____

   Why did you leave that job? _____

   Would you consider working there again? _____

   Interviewer: If there is any gap between the various periods of employment, the applicant should be asked

   about them. _____

   Interviewer's comments or observations _____

What did you do prior to the job with that company? _____

What other jobs or experience have you had? Describe them briefly and explain the general duties of each.

_____

Have you been unemployed at any time in the last five years? _____ Yes _____ No. What efforts did you make

to find work? _____

What other experience or training do you have that would help qualify you for the job applied for? Explain how

and where you obtained this experience or training. _____

_____

Educational Background

What education or training do you have that would help you in the job for which you have applied? _____

_____

Describe any formal education you have had. (Interviewer may substitute technical training, if relevant.) _____

_____

Off-Job Activities

What do you do in your off-hours? ___ Part-time job ___ Athletics ___ Spectator sports ___ Clubs ___ Other

Please explain. _____

Interviewer's Specific Questions

Interviewer: Add any questions to the particular job for which you are interviewing, leaving space for brief answers.

(Be careful to avoid questions which may be viewed as discriminatory.)

_____

_____

_____

Personal

Would you be willing to relocate? _____ Yes _____ No

Are you willing to travel? _____ Yes _____ No

(continued)

► **FIGURE 6-1**
(Continued)

What is the maximum amount of time you would consider traveling? _____

_____

Are you able to work overtime? _____

What about working on weekends? _____

Self-Assessment

What do you feel are your strong points? _____

_____

What do you feel are your weak points? _____

_____

Interviewer: Compare the applicant's responses with the information furnished on the application for employment.

Clear up any discrepancies. _____

_____

Before the applicant leaves, the interviewer should provide basic information about the organization and the job opening, if this has not already been done. The applicant should be given information on the work location, work hours, the wage or salary, type of remuneration (salary or salary plus bonus, etc.), and other factors that may affect the applicant's interest in the job.

Interviewer's Impressions

Rate each characteristic from 1 to 4, with 1 being the highest rating and 4 being the lowest.

Personal Characteristics	1	2	3	4	Comments
Personal appearance					
Poise, manner					
Speech					
Cooperation with interviewer					
Job-related Characteristics					
Experience for this job					
Knowledge of job					
Interpersonal relationships					
Effectiveness					

Overall rating for job

1	2	3	4	5
___ Superior	___ Above Average	___ Average	___ Marginal	___ Unsatisfactory
	(well qualified)	(qualified)	(barely qualified)	

Comments or remarks _____

_____

_____

Interviewer _____ Date _____

Structured and nonstructured interviews each have pros and cons. In structured interviews, all interviewers generally ask all applicants the same questions; partly because of this, these interviews tend to be more reliable and valid. Structured interviews can also help those who may be less comfortable doing interviews to conduct better interviews. Standardizing the administration of the interview also increases consistency across candidates, enhances job relatedness, reduces overall subjectivity (and thus the potential for bias), and may "enhance the ability to withstand legal challenge."[8] On the other hand, structured interviews don't always provide the opportunity to pursue points of interest as they develop.

Interview Content: Types of Questions We can also classify interviews based on the "content" or focus of their questions. For example, in a **situational interview**, you ask the candidate what his or her behavior would be in a given situation.[9] For example, you might ask a supervisory candidate how he or she would respond to a subordinate coming to work late three days in a row. Interviews can be both structured and situational; here you use predetermined situational questions and answers. In such a *structured situational interview*, you might evaluate the applicant on, say, his or her choice between letting the subordinate off with a warning versus suspending the subordinate for a week.

Whereas situational interviews ask interviewees to describe how they would react to a hypothetical situation today or tomorrow, **behavioral interviews** ask interviewees to describe how they reacted to actual situations in the past.[10] For example, when Citizen's Banking Corporation in Flint, Michigan, found that 31 of the 50 people in its call center quit in one year, Cynthia Wilson, the center's head, switched to behavioral interviews. Many of those who left did so because they didn't enjoy fielding questions from occasionally irate clients. So Wilson no longer tries to predict how candidates will act based on asking them if they want to work with angry clients. Instead, she asks behavioral questions like, "Tell me about a time you were speaking with an irate person, and how you turned the situation around." Wilson says this makes it much harder to fool the interviewer, and, indeed, only four people left her center in the following year.[11]

Interviews like these can produce a lot of tension. "It's pretty intense," said one applicant for a consultant's job with Accenture, the consulting firm, "You can pretty much fake one or two answers, but the third time they come back to it you pretty much can't. You're pulling from real life, and you're nervous. [The interviewer] asked how I would prepare for something important. He came back to that again and again to make sure what I said was true. The whole time they are writing constantly."[12]

In a **job-related interview**, the interviewer tries to deduce what the applicant's on-the-job performance will be based on his or her answers to questions about past behaviors. The questions here don't revolve around hypothetical situations or scenarios. Instead, the interviewer asks job-related questions (such as, "Which courses did you like best in business school?") in order to draw conclusions about, say, the candidate's ability to handle the financial aspects of the job to be filled.

In a **stress interview**, the interviewer seeks to make the applicant uncomfortable with occasionally rude questions. The aim is supposedly to spot sensitive applicants and those with low or high stress tolerance. The interviewer might first probe for weaknesses in the applicant's background, such as a job that the applicant left under questionable circumstances. The interviewer then zeroes in on these weaknesses, hoping to get the candidate to lose his or her composure. Thus, a candidate for customer relations manager who obligingly mentions having had four jobs in the past two years might be told that frequent job changes reflect irresponsible and immature behavior. If the applicant then responds with a reasonable explanation of why the job changes were necessary, the interviewer might pursue another topic. On the other hand, if the formerly tranquil applicant reacts explosively with anger and disbelief, the interviewer might deduce that the person has a low tolerance for stress.

Stress interviews may help unearth hypersensitive applicants who might overreact to mild criticism with anger and abuse. However, the stress interview's invasive and ethically questionable nature demands that the interviewer be both

situational interview
A series of job-related questions that focus on how the candidate would behave in a given situation.

behavioral interviews
A series of job-related questions that focus on how they reacted to actual situations in the past.

job-related interview
A series of job-related questions that focus on relevant past job-related behaviors.

stress interview
An interview in which the applicant is made uncomfortable by a series of often rude questions. This technique helps identify hypersensitive applicants and those with low or high stress tolerance.

skilled in its use and sure the job really calls for a thick skin and an ability to handle stress. This is definitely not an approach for amateur interrogators or for those without the skills to keep the interview under control.

Puzzle questions are popular today. Recruiters for technical, finance, and occasionally other types of jobs like to use them to see how candidates think under pressure. For example, an interviewer at Microsoft asked a tech service applicant this: "Mike and Todd have $21 between them. Mike has $20 more than Todd. How much money has Mike, and how much money has Todd?"[13] (You'll find the answer at the end of the first paragraph in the Personal Interviews section.)

STRATEGIC HR

Staples's IT Employees

At Staples, Inc., it's not enough for the firm's IT employees to be technically competent, although that's important. Staples's strategy entails growing fast and emphasizing an entrepreneurial spirit, and that means IT employees can't just be "order takers" who look to the other divisions to prioritize their projects. Instead, says Brian Light, the firm's chief information officer, the firm has to look for "confident and assertive people who can be proactive in identifying opportunities, who can work with ambiguity, and have a strong desire to achieve and work well in teams."[14] Once at work, for instance, Staples encourages its IT employees to develop expertise in business topics such as warehouse operations and store operations, so they're able to talk knowledgeably about the business, and propose more innovative IT solutions to the company's operating divisions.

One way the IT division identifies employees like these is by using carefully crafted behavioral interviews. In looking for IT employees, for instance, behaviorally based questions aim to identify strong achievers, as well as those who are able to lead change and to position others for success. Junior people, in the questions they answer, "must demonstrate confidence and be self-starters." That way, the firm can be more confident that the people it hires are already well on their way to supporting the Staples strategy of rapid growth and entrepreneurship.

Administering the Interview

Interviews can also be administered in various ways: one on one or by a panel of interviewers; sequentially or all at once; and computerized or personally.

Personal Interviews Most interviews are *one-on-one*: Two people meet alone, and one interviews the other by seeking oral responses to oral inquiries. Most interview processes are also sequential. In a *sequential interview*, several persons interview the applicant, in sequence, before a decision is made. In an **unstructured sequential interview**, each interviewer may ask different questions and form an independent opinion. In a **structured sequential interview**, each interviewer rates the candidates on a standard evaluation form. The hiring manager then reviews and compares the evaluations before deciding who to hire.[15] (Answer: Mike had $20.50, Todd $.50).

In a **panel interview**, a group (or panel) of interviewers questions the candidate. This has several advantages. In sequential interviews, candidates may cover the same ground over and over again with each interviewer. The panel format lets interviewers ask follow-up questions based on the candidate's answers, much as reporters do in press conferences. This may elicit more meaningful responses than are normally produced by a series of one-on-one interviews.

unstructured sequential interview
An interview in which each interviewer forms an independent opinion after asking different questions.

structured sequential interview
An interview in which the applicant is interviewed sequentially by several persons; each rates the applicant on a standard form.

panel interview
An interview in which a group of interviewers questions the applicant.

On the other hand, some candidates find panel interviews more stressful, so they may actually inhibit responses. An even more stressful variant is the **mass interview**. Here a panel interviews several candidates simultaneously. The panel poses a problem and then sits back and watches to see which candidate takes the lead in formulating an answer.

Some interviews are done entirely by telephone. These can actually be more accurate than face-to-face interviews for judging an applicant's conscientiousness, intelligence, and interpersonal skills. Since neither side has to worry about things like clothing and handshakes, both parties can focus on substantive answers. Or perhaps candidates—somewhat surprised by an unexpected call from the recruiter—just give more spontaneous answers.[16]

mass interview
A panel interviews several candidates simultaneously.

Computerized Interviews Today, it's often computers, not people, that administer the interview. A *computerized selection interview* is one in which a job candidate's oral and/or computerized responses are obtained in response to computerized oral, visual, or written questions and/or situations. Most present the applicant with a series of specific questions regarding his or her background, experience, education, skills, knowledge, and work attitudes that relate to the job for which the person has applied.[17] Other, video-based, computerized interviews may also confront candidates with realistic scenarios (such as irate customers) to which they must respond.

Typical computerized interviews present questions in a multiple-choice format, one at a time; the applicant is expected to respond to the questions on the screen by pressing a key. For example, a sample interview question for a person applying for a job as a retail store clerk might be:

How would your supervisor rate your customer service skills?

a. Outstanding
b. Above average
c. Average
d. Below average
e. Poor[18]

Questions on a computerized interview come in rapid sequence and require the applicant to concentrate.[19] The typical computerized interview program measures the response time to each question. A delay in answering certain questions—such as "Can you be trusted?"—can flag a potential problem.

Computer-aided interviews are generally used to reject unacceptable candidates and to select those who will move on to face-to-face interviews. For example, Pic'n Pay stores, a chain of 915 self-service shoe stores headquartered in North Carolina, gives job applicants an 800 number to dial for the computerized interview, which they can take on any touch-tone phone. The interview contains 100 questions and lasts about 10 minutes. Applicants press 1 for *yes* and 0 for *no*. Every Pic'n Pay applicant then gets a follow-up live telephone interview, from one of the firm's six dedicated interviewers.

Computer-aided interviews can be advantageous. Systems like those at Pic'n Pay and Great Western Bank of California reduce the amount of time managers devote to interviewing what often turn out to be unacceptable candidates.[20] Applicants are reportedly more honest with computers than they would be with people, presumably because computers aren't judgmental.[21] The computer can also be sneaky; if an applicant takes longer than average to answer certain questions, he or she may be summarily screened out or at least questioned more deeply in that area

▲ *Panel interviews can be useful in allowing each interviewer to follow up on the candidate's answers.*

by a human interviewer. Several of the interpersonal interview problems we'll discuss later in this chapter (such as making a snap judgment about the interviewee based on appearance) are also obviously avoided with this approach.[22] On the other hand, the mechanical nature of computer-aided interviews can leave applicants feeling that the employer is rather impersonal.

◆ **HIGH-PERFORMANCE INSIGHT** When Bonnie Dunn, 20 years old, tried out for a teller's job at Great Western Bank in Chatsworth, California, she faced a lineup of tough customers.[23] One young woman sputtered contradictory instructions about depositing a check and then blew her top when the transaction wasn't handled fast enough. Another customer had an even shorter fuse: "You people are unbelievably slow," he said.

Both tough customers appeared on a computer screen, as part of a 20-minute automated job interview. Ms. Dunn was seated in front of a personal computer, responding via a color touch screen and a microphone. She was tested on making change and on sales skills, as well as keeping cool in tense situations.

When applicants sit down facing the computer at Great Western's bank branches, they hear it say, "Welcome to the interactive assessment aid." The computer doesn't understand what applicants say at that point, although it records their comments to be evaluated later. To begin the interview, applicants touch a label on the screen, eliciting an ominous foreword: "We'll be keeping track of how long it takes you and how many mistakes you make. Accuracy is more important than speed."

First, the computer tests the applicant on money skills, asking him or her to cash a check for $192.18, including at least three $5 bills and two dollars in quarters. Then, when an angry customer appears on the screen, the system expects candidates to grab the microphone and mollify him. Later, a bank official who listens to the recorded interviews give applicants 5 points for maintaining a friendly tone of voice, plus up to 15 points for apologizing, promising to solve the customer's problem, and, taking a cue from the screen, suggesting that in the future he use the bank's deposit-only line.

The touchy young woman on the screen is tougher. Speaking fast, she says she wants to cash a $150 check, get $40 in cash, and put $65 in savings and the rest in checking. As an applicant struggles to sort that out, she quickly adds, "No, it has to be $50 in checking because I just wrote a check this morning." If the applicant then touches a label on the screen that says "?" the woman fumes, "How many times do I have to tell you?"

Great Western reports success with its new system. It dramatically reduced useless interviewing of unacceptable candidates, and, partly because the candidates see what the job's really like, those hired are reportedly 26% less likely to quit or be fired within 90 days of hiring.

HR.NET

Online Interviews

It's expensive conducting face-to-face interviews, and Cisco Systems, Inc., is doing something about that: It's equipping every Cisco HR recruiter with PC-based video cameras, so they can conduct at least preliminary interviews via online Web casts. The basic idea is this: Cisco will ask the applicant to go to a local Kinko's or similar business. There, at the appointed time, he or she will link to Cisco via Web video for the interview. Cisco doesn't plan to eliminate face-to-face interviews. However, it hopes its new approach will reduce travel and recruiting expenses, and make things easier for candidates. And for a company that hires about 1,000 employees a month (and interviews about 20,000 candidates per year), the savings can be substantial.[24]

Cisco isn't the first to be using live or recorded online video to streamline the interviewing process. For example, Jobs.com conducts frequent live interactive online career fairs. Job seekers go to the jobs.com interactive career fair Web site and select a city and job category. They can then participate in a live, interactive career fair event. The U.S. Army also now does online recruiting (see Webnote).

Are Interviews Useful?

While used by virtually all managers, interviews received low marks for reliability and validity in early studies. However, today (as noted previously), studies confirm that the "validity of the interview is greater than previously believed,"[25] and that the interview is "generally a much better predictor of performance than previously thought and is comparable with many other selection techniques."[26]

But there are two caveats. First, you should structure the interviews.[27] The research generally suggests that structured interviews (particularly structured situational interviews) have validities about twice those of unstructured interviews.[28] Situational interviews yield a higher mean validity than do job-related (or behavioral) interviews, which in turn yield a higher mean validity than do psychological interviews.[29] However, structured interviews, regardless of content, are more valid than unstructured interviews.[30]

The second caveat is this: Be careful what sorts of traits you try to assess. A recent study illustrates why. Interviewers were able to size up the interviewee's extraversion and agreeableness. What they could *not* assess accurately were the traits that often matter most on jobs—like conscientiousness and emotional stability.[31] The implication seems to be: Don't try to focus (as many do) on hard-to-assess traits like conscientiousness. Limit yourself mostly to situational and job knowledge questions that help you assess how the candidate will actually respond to typical situations on that job. We'll explain how to do this later in the chapter.

▲ **WEBNOTE**
The U.S. Army's RecruiterChat site allows possible candidates to interact in real time with Army and Army Reserve representatives; it can also function as a screening device.
www.goarmy.com

WHAT CAN UNDERMINE AN INTERVIEW'S USEFULNESS?

Hiring the right people is one of your most important management jobs, and you can't do that job well if you don't know how to interview. Several things can undermine an interview's usefulness. Let's look at them next.

First Impressions

One of the most consistent findings is that interviewers tend to jump to conclusions—make snap judgments—about candidates during the first few minutes of the interview (or even before the interview starts, based on test scores or résumé data). One researcher estimates that in 85% of the cases, interviewers had made up their minds before the interview began, based on first impressions gleaned from candidates' application forms and personal appearance. In one study, giving interviewers candidates' test scores biased their ultimate assessment of the candidates.[32] For example, interview results related to hiring decisions only when the candidates had low passing scores on a previous selection test. For candidates with high test scores, the interview results were not related to the interviewers' decisions.[33]

First impressions are thus especially damaging when the information about the candidate is negative. In another study, interviewers who previously received unfavorable reference letters about applicants gave those applicants less credit for past successes and held them more personally responsible for past failures after the interview. And their final decisions (to accept or reject applicants) were always tied to what they expected of the applicants based on the references, quite aside from the applicants' interview performance.[34]

In other words, interviewers seem to have a consistent negative bias. They are more influenced by unfavorable than favorable information about the candidate. And their impressions are much more likely to change from favorable to unfavorable than from unfavorable to favorable. Indeed, a common interviewing mistake is to turn the interview into a search for negative information. In a sense, therefore, most interviews are probably loaded against the applicant. An applicant who starts well could easily end up with a low rating, because unfavorable information tends to carry more weight in the interview. An interviewee who starts out poorly will find it hard to overcome that first bad impression.[35]

One London-based psychologist who recently interviewed the chief executives of 80 top companies came to the same conclusions about snap judgments in selection interviews: "Really, to make a good impression, you don't even get time to open your mouth . . . An interviewer's response to you will generally be pre-verbal—how you walk through the door, what your posture is like, whether you smile, whether you have a captivating aura, whether you have a firm, confident handshake. You've got about half a minute to make an impact and after that all you are doing is building on a good or bad first impression . . . It's a very emotional response."[36]

Misunderstanding the Job

It's also important to know what you're looking for in an ideal candidate. Interviewers who don't know precisely what the job entails and what sort of candidate is best suited for it usually make their decisions based on incorrect stereotypes of what a good applicant is. They then erroneously match interviewees with their incorrect stereotypes.

One study involved 30 professional interviewers.[37] Half got just a brief description of the jobs for which they were recruiting: They were told the "eight applicants here represented by their application blanks are applying for the position of secretary." The other 15 interviewers got much more explicit job information, in terms of typing speed and bilingual ability, for instance.

More job knowledge translated into better interviews. The 15 interviewers who had more job information generally agreed among themselves about each candidate's potential, while those without complete job information did not. The latter also did not discriminate as well among applicants—they tended to give them all high ratings.

candidate-order error
An error of judgment on the part of the interviewer due to interviewing one or more very good or very bad candidates just before the interview in question.

Candidate-Order (Contrast) Error and Pressure to Hire

Candidate-order (or contrast) error means that the order in which you see applicants affects how you rate them. In one study, managers had to evaluate a candidate who was "just average" after first evaluating several "unfavorable" candidates. They scored the average candidate more favorably than they might otherwise have done since, in contrast to the unfavorable candidates, the average one looked better than he actually was. This contrast effect can be huge: In some studies, evaluators based only a small part of the applicant's rating on his or her actual potential.[38]

Pressure to hire accentuates problems like this. Researchers told one group of managers to assume they were behind in their recruiting quota. They told a second group they were ahead of their quota. Those "behind" evaluated the same recruits much more highly than did those "ahead."[39]

Nonverbal Behavior and Impression Management

The applicant's nonverbal behavior can also have a surprisingly large impact on his or her rating. In one study, 52 HR specialists watched videotaped job interviews in which the applicants' verbal content was identical, but their nonverbal behavior differed markedly. Researchers told those in one group to exhibit minimal eye contact, a low energy level, and low voice modulation. Those in a second group demonstrated the opposite behavior. Of the 26 personnel specialists who saw the high-eye-contact, high-energy-level candidate, 23 would have invited him or her for a second interview. None who saw the low-eye-contact, low-energy-level candidate would have recommended a second interview.[40] It certainly seems to pay for interviewees to "look alive."

In another study, interviewers listened to audio interviews and watched video interviews. Vocal cues (such as the interviewee's pitch, speech rates, and pauses) and visual cues (such as physical attractiveness, smile, and body orientation) correlated with the evaluator's judgments of whether or not the interviewees could be liked and trusted, and were credible.[41]

Why are the candidates' nonverbal behaviors so important? Perhaps because, accurately or not, interviewers infer the interviewee's personality from the way he or she acts in the interview. In one study, 99 graduating college seniors completed questionnaires both before and after their job interviews; the questionnaires included measures of personality, among other things.[42] They then reported their success in generating follow-up job interviews and job offers. The interviewee's personality, particularly his or her level of extroversion, had a pronounced influence on whether or not he or she received follow-up interviews and job offers. In part, this seems to be because "interviewers draw inferences about the applicant's personality based on the applicant's behavior during the interview."[43]

Of course, clever interviewees take advantage of this, by managing the impression they present. One study found some used ingratiation to persuade interviewers to like them, for instance by praising them or appearing to agree with their opinions. Others used self-promotion tactics, for instance by making complimentary comments about their own accomplishments.[44]

Effect of Personal Characteristics: Attractiveness, Gender, Race

Interviewers also have to guard against letting an applicant's attractiveness and gender play a role.[45] In general, individuals ascribe more favorable traits and more successful life outcomes to attractive people.[46] In one study, subjects had to evaluate candidates for promotion based on photographs. They perceived men as being more suitable for hire and more likely to advance to a next executive level than they did equally qualified women; they preferred more attractive candidates, especially men, over less attractive ones:[47] "Even when female managers exhibited the same career-advancing behaviors as male managers, they still earned less money and were offered fewer career-progressing transfer opportunities."[48]

Race can also play a role, depending on how you conduct the interview. In one study, the interviewees appeared before three panels whose racial composition was either primarily black (75% black, 25% white), racially balanced (50% black, 50% white), or primarily white (75% white, 25% black).[49] On the primarily black panels, black and white raters judged black and white candidates similarly. In the primarily white and in the racially balanced panels, white interviewers rated white candidates higher, while black interviewers rated black candidates higher. However, in all cases, structured interviews produce less of a difference between minority and white interviewees on average than do unstructured interviews.[50] The following box shows why caution here is especially prudent today.

THE *NEW* WORKPLACE

Employment Discrimination Testers

Employment discrimination is always abhorrent, but the use of "testers" makes nondiscriminatory interviewing even more important today. As defined by the EEOC, testers are "individuals who apply for employment which they do not intend to accept, for the sole purpose of uncovering unlawful discriminatory hiring practices."[51] Although they're not really seeking employment, testers have legal standing, with the courts[52] and with the EEOC.[53]

A case illustrates the usual approach. A private, nonprofit civil rights advocacy group sent four university students—two white, two black—to an employment agency supposedly in pursuit of a job. The testers were given backgrounds and training to make them appear almost indistinguishable from each other in terms of qualifications; however, the white applicants and black applicants were allegedly treated differently. For example, the white tester/applicants got interviews and job offers, while the black tester/applicants got neither interviews nor offers.[54] A study by the Urban Institute suggests that such unequal treatment is "entrenched and widespread."[55]

An employer's best strategy is to be actively nondiscriminatory. However, a prudent employer will also take steps in planning the interview process and conducting the actual interviews to ensure that its interviewers avoid tester claims. For example:

1. Caution interviewers that testers may be posing as applicants.
2. Train interviewers to make careful notes during and after the interview. Substantiate differences among applicants, and record responses to questions and other items of interest not on the applicant's résumé or application.
3. Have applicants execute a statement acknowledging that they are applying for the job out of a sincere interest in the job and for no other purpose. Signing that and later returning with a claim as a "tester" could constitute evidence of deceit if there's a lawsuit.
4. Remember that testers often enter the employment process with phony résumés and fabricated qualifications, so carefully checking references is important.[56]

Interviewer Behavior

The interviewer's behavior also has an effect. For example, some interviewers inadvertently *telegraph* the expected answers,[57] as in: "This job calls for handling a lot of stress. You can do that, can't you?" Telegraphing isn't always so obvious. For example, subtle cues (like a smile or nod) can telegraph the desired answer.[58] Some interviewers talk so much applicants have no time to answer questions. At the other extreme, some interviewers let the applicant dominate the interview, and so don't ask all their questions.[59] Neither is a good situation.

Other interviewers play district attorney or psychologist. It's smart to be alert for inconsistencies, but uncivil to play "gotcha" by gleefully pouncing on them. Some interviewers play amateur psychologist, unprofessionally probing for hidden meanings in everything the applicants say.[60]

DESIGNING AND CONDUCTING THE EFFECTIVE INTERVIEW

There are two basic ways to avoid these interview problems. One is obvious: Keep them in mind and avoid them (don't play psychologist or make snap decisions, for instance). The second is not quite so obvious: Be careful how you design and structure the interview. Let's look next at structuring the interview, and at some guidelines for an effective interview.

The Structured Situational Interview

There is little doubt that the structured situational interview—a series of hypothetical job-oriented questions with predetermined answers that interviewers ask of all applicants for the job—produces superior results.[61] For these interviews, people familiar with the job develop situational ("What would you do if . . .") and job knowledge questions based on the actual job duties. They then reach consensus on what are and are not acceptable answers. The procedure is as follows.[62]

Step 1. Job Analysis Write a job description with a list of job duties, required knowledge, skills, abilities, and other worker qualifications.

Step 2. Rate the Job's Duties Identify the job's main duties. To do so, rate each job duty, based on its importance to job success and on the time required to perform it compared to other tasks.

Step 3. Create Interview Questions Create interview questions that are based on actual job duties, with more questions for the important duties.

Structured situational interviews may actually contain three types of questions. *Situational questions* pose a hypothetical job situation, such as "What would you do if the machine suddenly began heating up?" *Job knowledge questions* assess knowledge essential to job performance. These often deal with technical aspects of a job (such as "What is HTML?"). *Willingness questions* gauge the applicant's willingness and motivation to meet the job's requirements—to do repetitive physical work or to travel, for instance.

The people who create the questions usually write them in terms of critical incidents. For example, for a supervisory candidate, the interviewer might ask:

Your spouse and two teenage children are sick in bed with colds. There are no relatives or friends available to look in on them. Your shift starts in three hours. What would you do in this situation?

Step 4. Create Benchmark Answers Next, develop answers and a five-point rating scale for each, with ideal answers for good (a 5 rating), marginal (a 3 rating), and poor (a 1 rating). Consider the preceding situational question, where the spouse and children are sick. Each member of

▲ *Former chairman Dick Mueller (left) and CEO Ed Ossie, of MTW Corp, a Kansas Web-based software and consulting services firm, credits careful hiring with its enviably high retention rate, which is over 93% compared with the industry average of 70%. Part of the hiring process is a thorough interview process that includes phone interviews with company recruiters and technologists, followed by on-site interviews with about five staff members, two of whom are senior managers. "We want [candidates] to get a sense of the long-term potential of the job," says Ossie, "and the only way they can get that is by speaking one-on-one with someone from senior management."*

the committee writes good, marginal, and poor answers based on things they have actually heard in an interview from people who then turned out to be good, marginal, or poor (as the case may be) on the job. After a group discussion, they reach consensus on the answers to use as benchmarks for each scenario. Three benchmarks for the example question might be "I'd stay home—my spouse and family come first" (1); "I'd phone my supervisor and explain my situation" (3); and "Since they only have colds, I'd come to work" (5).

Step 5. Appoint the Interview Panel and Conduct Interviews Companies generally conduct structured situational interviews using a panel, rather than sequentially. The panel usually consists of three to six members, preferably the same employees who wrote the questions and answers. It may also include the job's supervisor and/or incumbent, and an HR representative. The same panel interviews all candidates for the job.[63]

The panel members generally review the job description, questions, and benchmark answers before the interview. One panel member usually introduces the applicant, and asks all questions of all applicants in this and succeeding interviews (to ensure consistency). However, all panel members record and rate the applicant's answers on the rating scale sheet; they do this by indicating where the candidate's answer to each question falls relative to the ideal poor, marginal, or good answers. At the end of the interview, someone explains the follow-up procedure and answers any questions the applicant has.[64]

How to Conduct an Interview

You may not have the time or inclination to create structured situational interviews. However, there is still a lot you can do to make your interviews more effective. (The Entrepreneurs + HR feature summarizes another shortcut approach.) Suggestions include:

Structure Your Interview There are several things you can do to increase the standardization of the interview or otherwise assist the interviewer to ask more consistent and job-relevant questions.[65] They include:[66]

1. Base questions on actual job duties. This will minimize irrelevant questions based on beliefs about the job's requirements. It may also reduce the likelihood of bias, because there's less opportunity to "read" things into the answer.
2. Use job knowledge, situational, or behaviorally oriented questions and objective criteria to evaluate the interviewee's responses. Questions that simply ask for opinions and attitudes, goals and aspirations, and self-descriptions and self-evaluations allow candidates to present themselves in an overly favorable manner or avoid revealing weaknesses. Structured interview questions can reduce subjectivity and therefore the chance for inaccurate conclusions, and bias.[67] Examples of structured questions include: (1) situational questions like "Suppose you were giving a sales presentation and a difficult technical question arose that you could not answer. What would you do?"; (2) past behavior questions like "Can you provide an example of a specific instance where you developed a sales presentation that was highly effective?"; (3) background questions like "What work experiences, training, or other qualifications do you have for working in a teamwork environment?"; (4) job knowledge questions like "What factors should you consider when developing a TV advertising campaign?"
3. Train interviewers. For example, review EEO laws with prospective interviewers and train them to avoid irrelevant or potentially discriminatory questions and to avoid stereotyping minority candidates. Also train them to base their questions on job-related information.

4. Use the same questions with all candidates. When it comes to asking questions, the prescription seems to be "the more standardized, the better." Using the same questions with all candidates can also reduce bias "because of the obvious fairness of giving all the candidates the exact same opportunity."

5. Use rating scales to rate answers. For each question, provide a range of possible ideal answers and a quantitative score for each. Then you can rate each candidate's answers against this scale. This ensures that all interviewers are using the same standards.

6. Use multiple interviewers or panel interviews. Doing so can reduce bias, by diminishing the importance of one interviewers' idiosyncratic opinions, and by bringing in more points of view.

7. If possible, use a structured interview form. Interviews based on structured guides like the one in Figure 6-1 (pages 162–164), usually result in the best interviews.[68] At the very least, list your questions before the interview.

8. Control the interview. Limiting the interviewers' follow-up questions (to ensure all interviewees get the same questions), using a larger number of questions, and prohibiting questions from candidates until after the interview are other "structuring" techniques.[69]

Prepare for the Interview The interview should take place in a private room where telephone calls are not accepted and you can minimize interruptions. Prior to the interview, review the candidate's application and résumé, and note any areas that are vague or that may indicate strengths or weaknesses. In one recent study, about 39% of the 191 respondents said interviewers were unprepared or unfocused.[70]

Remember, it's essential that you know the duties of the job, and the specific skills and traits you should be looking for. Most interviews probably fail to unearth the best candidate because the interviewer is unprepared, or overconfident, or just plain lazy. General questions like "What are your main strengths?" or "Why did you leave your last job?" may not be totally useless. But what you really want to do is go into the interview with a set of specific questions that focus like a laser on the skills and experiences the ideal candidate for that job needs. At a minimum, review the job specification. Start the interview with an accurate picture of the traits of an ideal candidate, know what you're going to ask—and keep an open mind about the candidate! Remember that interviewers often make snap judgments based on first impressions. Keep a record of the answers, and review them after the interview. Make your decision then.[71]

Establish Rapport The main reason for the interview is to find out about the applicant. To do this, you need to put the person at ease. Greet all applicants—even drop-ins—courteously and start the interview with a noncontroversial question—perhaps about the weather.

Be aware of the applicant's status. For example, if the person is unemployed, or is coming back to the workforce after many years, he or

▲ Colleen Aylward (left) is the founder of Devon James Associates Inc., a growing recruiting firm based in Seattle. Shown here with client Kathleen Controy of employeesavings.com, Aylward believes she has heard just about every interview question ever asked. Among those she believes elicit useful information are "Describe the way you work under tight deadlines," "Persuade me to move to your city," and "In the past three years, what part of your professional skill set have you improved the most?"

she may be exceptionally nervous, and you may want to take additional steps to relax the person.[72]

Ask Questions Follow your list of questions. (Figure 6-2 presents additional questions.) Some do's and don'ts for actually asking questions include: Don't ask questions that can be answered yes or no; don't put words in the applicant's mouth or telegraph the desired answer; don't interrogate the applicant as if the person is a criminal, and don't be patronizing, sarcastic, or inattentive; don't monopolize the interview or let the applicant dominate the interview; do ask open-ended questions; do listen to the candidate to encourage him or her to express thoughts fully; and do draw out the applicant's opinions and feelings by repeating the person's last comment as a question (such as "You didn't like your last job?").

Finally, when you ask for general statements of a candidate's accomplishments, ask for examples.[73] If the candidate lists specific strengths or weaknesses, follow up with "What are specific examples that demonstrate each of your strengths?"

One way to get more candid answers is to mention you're going to conduct reference checks. Ask, "If I were to arrange for an interview with your boss, and if the boss were very candid with me, what's your best guess as to what he or she would say as your strengths, weaker points, and overall performance?"[74]

Close the Interview Leave time to answer any questions the candidate may have and, if appropriate, to advocate your firm to the candidate.

Try to end the interview on a positive note. Tell the applicant whether there is any interest and, if so, what the next step will be. Make rejections diplomatically: for instance, "Although your background is impressive, there are other candidates whose experience is closer to our requirements." If the applicant is still being considered but you can't reach a decision now, say so. If your policy is to inform candidates of their status in writing, do so within a few days of the interview.

Review the Interview Once the candidate leaves, and while the interview is fresh in your mind, review your notes and fill in the structured interview guide (if you used one and if you did not fill it in during the interview). Whether note taking during the interview is a good idea seems to depend on the interviewer's personal preferences. In one study, whether the interviewers took notes didn't have too much effect on the interview's validity. However, when note taking was voluntary, the note takers did tend to make somewhat more valid ratings than did the

▶ **FIGURE 6-2**
Some Questions to Ask Interviewees

- Why do you want to change jobs or why did you leave your last job?
- What do you identify as your most significant accomplishment in your last job?
- What did you like and dislike about your last job?
- What best qualifies you for the available position?
- What interests you most about the available position?
- Have you kept up in your field? How?
- What do you do in your spare time?
- What are your career goals for the next five years?
- What are your greatest strengths and weaknesses?
- What steps are you taking to help achieve your goals?
- What professional associations do you belong to?
- What motivates you to work?
- What do you think of the current economic and political situation?
- Why should we hire you?

Source: H. Lee Rust, *Job Search, The Complete Manual for Job Seekers* (New York: AMACOM, 1991), pp. 232–233.

non–note takers.[75] For those who prefer to take notes, the main caution is to do so in a way that doesn't interfere with the interview's flow.[76]

Reviewing the interview shortly after the candidate leaves can also help minimize snap judgments and negative emphasis. Some interviewers find videotaping interviews helps them review the top candidates.[77]

ENTREPRENEURS HR

A Streamlined Effective Interview

Prescriptions like "know the job," "know the skills and experiences you're looking for," and "ask questions that focus on the skills an ideal candidate needs" are easier said than done. Many firms (especially small, fast-moving entrepreneurial ones) often don't have the time or inclination to create structured situational interviews. What follows is a streamlined procedure for crafting job-relevant questions and interviews.[78]

Preparing for the Interview

Even a busy entrepreneur can spell out the kind of person who would be best for the job. One quick way to do so is to focus on four basic factors—knowledge and experience, motivation, intellectual capacity, and personality—and to ask the following questions:

- What must the candidate know to perform the job? What experience is absolutely necessary to perform the job? (Knowledge and Experience)
- What should the person like doing to enjoy this job? Is there anything the person should not dislike? Are there any essential goals or aspirations the person should have? Are there any unusual energy demands on the job? (Motivation)
- Are there any specific intellectual aptitudes required (mathematical, mechanical, and so on)? How complex are the problems the person must solve? What must a person be able to demonstrate he or she can do intellectually? How should the person solve problems (cautiously, deductively, and so on)? (Intellectual)
- What are the critical personality qualities needed for success on the job (ability to withstand boredom, decisiveness, stability, and so on)? How must the job incumbent handle stress, pressure, and criticism? What kind of interpersonal behavior is required in the job up the line, at peer level, down the line, and outside the firm with customers? (Personality)

Specific Factors to Probe in the Interview

Next, use a combination of situational questions, plus open-ended questions like those in Figure 6-2, to probe the candidate's suitability for the job. For example:

- *Intellectual factor.* Here, assess such things as complexity of tasks the person has performed, grades in school, test results (including scholastic aptitude tests, and so on), and how the person organizes his or her thoughts and communicates.
- *Motivation factor.* Probe such areas as: the person's likes and dislikes (for each thing done, what he or she liked or disliked about it); aspirations (including the validity of each goal in terms of the person's reasoning about why he or she chose it); and energy level, perhaps by asking what he or she does on, say, a "typical Tuesday."
- *Personality factor.* Probe by looking for self-defeating behaviors (aggressiveness, compulsive fidgeting, and so on) and by exploring the person's past interpersonal relationships. Ask questions about the person's past interactions (working in a group at school, working with fraternity brothers or sorority sisters, leading the work team on the last job, and so on). Also, try to judge the person's behavior in the interview itself—is the candidate personable? Shy? Outgoing?

■ *Knowledge and experience factor*. Probe with situational questions such as "How would you organize such a sales effort?" "How would you design that kind of Web site?"

Conducting the Interview

Have a plan and follow it. You should also devise and use a plan to guide the interview. According to John Drake, significant areas to cover include the candidate's:

■ College experiences
■ Work experiences—summer, part time
■ Work experience—full time (one by one)
■ Goals and ambitions
■ Reactions to the job you are interviewing for
■ Self-assessments (by the candidate of his or her strengths and weaknesses)
■ Military experiences
■ Present outside activities[79]

Follow your plan. Perhaps start with an open-ended question for each topic, such as "Could you tell me about what you did when you were in high school?" Keep in mind that you are trying to elicit information about four main traits—intelligence, motivation, personality, and knowledge and experience. You can then accumulate the information as the person answers. You can follow up on particular areas that you want to pursue by asking questions like "Could you elaborate on that, please?"

Match the Candidate to the Job

After following the interview plan and probing for the four factors, you should be able to summarize the candidate's general strengths and limitations and to draw conclusions about the person's intellectual capacity, knowledge and experience, motivation, and personality. You should then compare your conclusions to both the job description and the list of behavioral specifications developed earlier. This should provide a rational basis for matching the candidate to the job—one based on an analysis of the traits and aptitudes actually required.

◆ **HIGH-PERFORMANCE INSIGHT** Progressive companies like Toyota and FedEx put enormous effort into combining interviews and other screening procedures like those covered in the last few chapters into *total selection programs* designed to find the best people.[80]

Toyota's hiring process takes about 20 hours and six phases, spread over five or six days. The Kentucky Department of Employment Services conducts the initial prescreening, where applicants fill out application forms summarizing their work experience and skills and view a video describing Toyota's work environment and selection system. This gives applicants a realistic preview of work at Toyota and of the hiring process's extensive scope. Many applicants simply drop out at this stage.

Phase II aims to assess the applicant's technical knowledge and potential and is also conducted by the Kentucky Department of Employment Services. Here, applicants take the U.S. Employment Services' General Aptitude Test Battery (GATB), which helps identify problem-solving skills and learning potential, as well as occupational preferences. Skilled trades applicants (experienced mechanics, for example) also take a six-hour tool and die or general maintenance test. Kentucky Employment Services scores all tests and submits the files to Toyota.

In Phase III, Toyota takes over the screening. The aim here is to assess interpersonal and decision-making skills. All applicants participate in four hours of group and individual problem-solving and discussion activities in the firm's assessment center. This is a separate location where applicants engage in exercises under the observation of Toyota screening experts. The individual problem-solving exercises are aimed at assessing each applicant's problem-solving ability in terms of facets such as insight, flexibility, and creativity.

Production-line assembly candidates participate in a five-hour production assembly simulation. In one of these, candidates play the roles of the management and workforce of a firm that makes electrical circuits. During a series of planning and manufacturing periods, the team must decide which circuits should be manufactured and how to assign people, materials, and money to produce them.

A one-hour group interview constitutes Phase IV. Here groups of candidates discuss their accomplishments with Toyota interviewers. This phase helps give the Toyota assessors a more complete picture of what drives each candidate. Phase IV also gives Toyota another opportunity to watch candidates interact in groups. Those who successfully complete Phase IV (and are tentatively tapped as Toyota employees) then undergo physical and drug/alcohol tests at area hospitals (Phase V). Toyota also closely monitors, observes, and coaches the new employees on the job to assess their job performance and to develop their skills during their first six months at work.

Toyota's total selection process illustrates how selection can translate into improved performance. The process is geared to hiring people who fit the firm's needs and values. For example, the whole thrust of Toyota's production process is to improve job processes through team-based worker commitment to top quality. Toyota is therefore looking first for interpersonal skills. This focus on having the workers improve the system helps explain Toyota's emphasis on reasoning and problem-solving skills and on hiring intelligent, educated employees.

Toyota's production system is based on consensus decision making, job rotation, and flexible career paths. These require open-minded, flexible team players. Quality is a central value of Toyota, and so the firm also seeks a history of quality commitment in the people it hires. This is one reason for the group interview that probes "one's proudest accomplishments."

The important thing is to know exactly what you're hiring for. At the highly successful Southwest Airlines, for instance, "it is the people; it has always had to do with their selection," one expert says, "They are selected primarily for attitude, and most people primarily select for skills. They have a particular view for people who will fit into a team oriented organization and the airline industry is team oriented. If you have people pointing fingers, you have problems."[81]

We invite you to visit **www.prenhall.com/dessler** on the Prentice Hall Web site for our online study guide, Internet exercises, current events, links to related Web sites, and more.

Summary

1. There are several basic types of interviews—situational, nondirective, structured, sequential, panel, stress, and appraisal interviews. We can classify interviews according to content, structure, and method of administration.
2. Several factors and problems can undermine the usefulness of an interview. These are making premature decisions, letting unfavorable information predominate, not knowing the requirements of the job, being under pressure to hire, the candidate-order effect, and sending visual cues to telegraph enthusiasm.

3. The five steps in the interview are: Plan, establish rapport, question the candidate, close the interview, and review the data.

4. Guidelines for interviewers include: Use a structured guide, know the requirements of the job, focus on traits you can more accurately evaluate (like motivation), let the interviewee do most of the talking, delay your decision until after the interview, and remember the EEOC requirements.

5. The steps in a structured or situational interview are: Analyze the job, evaluate the job duty information, develop interview questions with critical incidents, develop benchmark answers, appoint an interview committee, and implement.

6. As an interviewee, keep in mind that interviewers tend to make premature decisions and let unfavorable information predominate; your appearance and enthusiasm are important; you should get the interviewer to talk; it is important to prepare before walking in—get to know the job and the problems the interviewer wants solved; and you should stress your enthusiasm and motivation to work, and how your accomplishments match your interviewer's needs. (See the Appendix to Chapter 6, Guidelines for Interviewees, on the book's Web site.)

7. A quick procedure for conducting an interview is to develop behavioral specifications; determine the basic intellectual, motivational, personality, and experience factors to probe for; use an interview plan; and then match the individual to the job. The procedure is especially useful in small firms without HR groups, but can be used in large firms as well.

8. Value-based hiring can contribute to building employee commitment. It assumes that management has clarified the values it cherishes (such as quality at Toyota), spends adequate time in the selection process, and provides for realistic previews.

Tying It All Together

As we saw in the last two chapters, we can conveniently view the employee selection process as a series of hurdles. You determine the jobs that you have to fill and the specific duties of those jobs, and then use techniques including employment agencies and the Internet to create a pool of candidates. You then use techniques like those discussed in Chapter 5, including testing and reference checking, to whittle down the pool of applicants. In the current chapter, we turned to a detailed explanation of the one screening tool that virtually every manager uses before hiring an employee—namely, the selection interview. We talked about different types of interviews, the problems that can undermine an interview, and in particular the need to understand the job's human requirements before writing your questions and holding the interview. Once you decide who to hire, the employee needs to be brought on board, signed on, and oriented and trained. We turn to these topics in Chapter 7, Training and Developing Employees.

Discussion Questions

1. Explain and illustrate the basic ways in which you can classify selection interviews.
2. Briefly describe each of the following possible types of interviews: unstructured panel interviews; structured sequential interviews; job-related structured interviews.
3. For what sorts of jobs do you think computerized interviews are most appropriate? Why?
4. Why do you think "situational interviews yield a higher mean validity than do job-related or behavioral interviews, which in turn yield a higher mean validity than do psychological interviews"?
5. Similarly, how do you explain the fact that structured interviews, regardless of content, are more valid than unstructured interviews for predicting job performance?
6. Briefly discuss and give examples of at least five common interviewing mistakes. What recommendations would you give for avoiding these interviewing mistakes?

7. Explain why you think that it is (or is not) important to select candidates based on their values, as well as on usual selection criteria such as skills and experience.
8. Briefly discuss how an interviewer can improve his or her performance.

1. Prepare and give a short presentation titled, "How to Be Effective As an Interviewer."
2. Use the Internet to find employers who now do preliminary selection interviews with the aid of the Web. Print out and bring examples to class. Do you think these interviews are useful? Why or why not?
3. In groups, discuss and compile examples of "the worst interview I ever had." What was it about these interviews that made them so bad? If time permits, discuss as a class.
4. In groups, prepare an interview (including a sequence of at least 20 questions) you'll use to interview candidates for the job of teaching a course in Human Resources Management. Each group should present their interviews in class.
5. Some firms swear by unorthodox interview methods. For example, Tech Planet, of Menlo Park, CA, uses weekly lunches and "wacky follow-up sessions" as substitutes for first-round job interviews. During the informal meals, potential staffers are expected to mingle, and they're then reviewed by the Tech Planet employees they meet at the luncheons. One Tech Planet employee asks candidates to ride a unicycle in her office to see if "they'll bond with the corporate culture or not." Toward the end of the screening process, the surviving group of interviewees has to solve brainteasers, and then openly evaluate their fellow candidates' strengths and weaknesses. What do you think of a screening process like this? Specifically, what do you think are its pros, and cons? Would you recommend a procedure like this? If so, what changes, if any, would you recommend?[82]

EXPERIENTIAL EXERCISE

Purpose: The purpose of this exercise is to give you practice using some of the interview techniques you learned from the chapter.

Required Understanding: You should be familiar with the information presented in this chapter.

How to Set Up the Exercise/Instructions:

1. Set up groups of five or six students. Two students will be the interviewees, while the other students in the group will serve as panel interviewers. The interviewees will develop an interviewer assessment form, and the panel interviewers will develop a structured situational interview for a marketing manager position (see job description, Figure 3-6, page 72).
2. Instructions for the interviewees: The interviewees should leave the room for about 20 minutes. While out of the room, the interviewees should develop an "interviewer assessment form" based on the information presented in the chapter regarding factors that can undermine the usefulness of an interview. During the panel interview, the interviewees should be taking notes on a copy of the interviewer assessment form. After the panel interviewers have conducted the interview, the interviewees should leave the room to discuss their notes. Did the interviewers exhibit any of the factors that can undermine the usefulness of an interview? If so, which ones? What suggestions would you (the interviewees) make to the interviewers on how to improve the usefulness of the interview?

3. Instructions for the interviewers: While the interviewees are out of the room, the panel interviewers will have 20 minutes to develop a structured situational interview form for a marketing manager position, as in Figure 6-1 (page 162). The panel interview team will interview two candidates for the position. The interviewers will assume that the interviewees have similar credentials. During the panel interview, each interviewer should be taking notes on a copy of the structured situational interview form. After the panel interview, the panel interviewers should discuss their notes. What were your first impressions of each interviewee? Were your impressions similar? Which candidate would you all select for the position and why?

APPLICATION CASE *The Out-of-Control Interview*

Maria Fernandez is a bright, popular, and well-informed mechanical engineer who graduated with an engineering degree from State University in June 2001. During the spring preceding her graduation, she went out on many job interviews, most of which she thought were conducted courteously and reasonably useful in giving both her and the prospective employer a good impression of where each of them stood on matters of importance to both of them. It was, therefore, with great anticipation that she looked forward to an interview with the one firm in which she most wanted to work, Apex Environmental. She had always had a strong interest in cleaning up the environment and firmly believed that the best use of her training and skills lay in working for a firm like Apex, where she thought she could have a successful career while making the world a better place.

The interview, however, was a disaster. Maria walked into a room in which five men—the president of the company, two vice presidents, the marketing director, and another engineer—began throwing questions at her that she felt were aimed primarily at tripping her up rather than finding out what she could offer through her engineering skills. The questions ranged from unnecessarily discourteous ("Why would you take a job as a waitress in college if you're such an intelligent person?") to irrelevant and sexist ("Are you planning on settling down and starting a family anytime soon?") Then, after the interview, she met with two of the gentlemen individually (including the president), and the discussions focused almost exclusively on her technical expertise. She thought that these later discussions went fairly well. However, given the apparent aimlessness and even mean-spiritedness of the panel interview, she was astonished when several days later she got a job offer from the firm.

The offer forced her to consider several matters. From her point of view, the job itself was perfect—she liked what she would be doing, the industry, and the firm's location. And in fact, the president had been quite courteous in subsequent discussions, as had been the other members of the management team. She was left wondering whether the panel interview had been intentionally tense to see how she'd stand up under pressure, and, if so, why they would do such a thing.

Questions

1. How would you explain the nature of the panel interview Maria had to endure? Specifically, do you think it reflected a well-thought-out interviewing strategy on the part of the firm or carelessness on the part of the firm's management? If it was carelessness, what would you do to improve the interview process at Apex Environmental?

2. Would you take the job offer if you were Maria? If you're not sure, is there any additional information that would help you make your decision, and if so, what is it?

3. The job of applications engineer for which Maria was applying requires: (a) excellent technical skills with respect to mechanical engineering; (b) a commitment to working in the area of pollution control; (c) the ability to deal well and confidently with customers who have engineering problems; (d) a willingness to travel worldwide; and (e) a very intelligent and well-balanced personality. What questions would you ask when interviewing applicants for the job?

CONTINUING CASE: LearnInMotion.com *The Better Interview*

Like virtually all the other personnel-management-related activities at LearnInMotion.com, the company currently has no organized approach to interviewing job candidates. Three people, Jennifer, Mel, and Greg (from the board of directors), interview each candidate, and the three then get together to discuss them. Unfortunately, they usually reach strikingly different conclusions. For example, Greg thought a particular candidate was "stellar" and would be able to not only sell, but eventually assume various administrative responsibilities to take the load off Jennifer and Mel. Mel thought this particular candidate was hopeless: "I've been selling for eight years and have hired many salespeople, and there's no

way this person's going to be a closer" is the way he put it. Jennifer, noting that a friend of her mother had recommended this particular candidate, was willing to take a wait-and-see attitude: "Let's hire her and see how she does" is the way she put it. Mel replied that this was no way to hire a salesperson, and, in any case, hiring another administrator was pretty far down their priority list, so "I wish Greg would stick to the problem at hand, namely hiring a 100% salesperson."

Jennifer was sure that inadequate formal interviewing practices, procedures, and training accounted for at least some of the problems they were having in hiring and keeping good salespeople. They did hire one salesperson whom they thought was going to be terrific, based on her references' recommendations and on what they understood her previous sales experience had been; she stayed for a month and a half, sold hardly anything, cost the company almost $10,000 of its precious cash, and then left for another job.

The problem wasn't just with the salespeople. For one thing, they hired a programmer largely based on his assertion that he was expert in various Web-related programming including HTML, Java script, and Flash. They followed up with one of his references, who was neutral regarding the candidate's programming abilities. But, being desperate, Jennifer and Mel hired him anyway—only to have him leave three weeks later, more or less by mutual consent.

"This is a total disaster," said Jennifer, and Mel could only agree. It was obvious that in some respects their inter-views were worse than not interviewing at all: For example, if they didn't have interviews, perhaps they'd have used more caution in following up with the candidates' references. In any case, they now want you, their management consultants, to tell them what to do. Here's what they want you to do for them.

Questions and Assignments

1. Tell us what we're doing wrong.
2. In general, what can we do to improve our employee interviewing practices? Should we develop interview forms that list questions for our various jobs? If so, what format should these take?
3. What are five questions we should ask salespeople candidates, and five questions we should ask programmer candidates?

7 Chapter

Training and Developing Employees

After studying this chapter, you should be able to:

- Describe the basic training process.
- Effectively train an employee.
- Develop and implement a training program.
- Explain how to distinguish between problems you can fix with training and those you can't.
- Explain how to use five training techniques.
- Describe and illustrate how you would go about identifying training requirements.

STRATEGIC OVERVIEW Channel 4 is one of four land-based TV channels in the United Kingdom, with two mandates—to serve minority interests, and to be on the cutting edge of TV broadcasting. However, changes in TV broadcasting over the last few years have certainly meant it had to work hard to stay on the cutting edge. For one thing, its strategy had to change. Because of a new broadcasting act in the UK, Channel 4 had to begin selling and transmitting its own commercial airtime, rather than having those duties handled by ITV, another large UK television network. In turn, this strategic change meant Channel 4 had to expand its sales force and install a new high-tech control system for activities like program and commercial scheduling.[1] Changes like these confronted Channel 4's management with another problem: how to hire and then train, almost overnight, all the necessary employees—the new salespeople, the information technology people, everyone. Management knew it wouldn't be able to implement its new strategy without a world-class training effort.

The previous chapter focused on the methods managers used to interview and select employees. Once employees are hired, they have to be trained. The purpose of this chapter is to increase your effectiveness as a trainer. The main topics we'll cover include orienting employees, the training process, training methods, training for special purposes, managerial development and training techniques, and eval-

uating the training effort. In the following chapter, Managing Strategic Organizational Renewal, we'll turn to HR techniques for implementing organizationwide changes in a firm's structure and culture required by challenges like those facing Channel 4. ■

ORIENTING EMPLOYEES

Recruiting and selecting high-potential employees doesn't guarantee they'll perform effectively. For one thing, people who don't know what to do or how to do it can't perform effectively even if they want to. Your next step is therefore to ensure that your employees know what to do and how to do it—you have to orient and train them. Let's start with orientation.

Why Orientation Is Important

Employee orientation provides new employees with the basic background information required to perform their jobs satisfactorily, such as information about company rules. Programs may range from brief, informal introductions to lengthy, formal courses.

employee orientation
A procedure for providing new employees with basic background information about the firm.

The HR specialist (or, in smaller firms, the office manager) usually performs the first part of the orientation, by explaining basic matters like working hours and vacations. That person then introduces the new employee to his or her new supervisor. The supervisor continues the orientation by explaining (see Figure 7-1) the exact nature of the job, introducing the person to his or her new colleagues, familiarizing the new employee with the workplace, and helping to reduce first-day jitters. Orientation typically includes information on employee benefits, personnel policies, the daily routine, company organization and operations, and safety measures and regulations, as well as a facilities tour.

At a minimum, new employees usually receive either printed or Internet-based *employee handbooks*. These explain things like working hours, performance reviews, getting on the payroll, and vacations. Under certain conditions, the courts may find that the employee handbook's contents represent legally binding employment commitments. Therefore, companies often include disclaimers to make it clear that statements of company policies, benefits, and regulations do not constitute the terms and conditions of an employment contract either expressed or implied. Also, companies generally do not insert statements such as "no employee will be fired without just cause" or statements that imply or state that employees have tenure. Indeed, it's usually best to emphasize that the employment relationship is strictly "at-will."

Don't underestimate orientation's importance. Without basic information on things like rules and policies, new employees may make time-consuming or even dangerous errors. Their performance—and the firm's—will suffer. Furthermore, orientation is not just about rules. It's also about making the new person feel welcome and at home and part of the team, all potentially important if you want him or her to be productive. At Saturn Corporation, orientation is step 1 in the firm's new-employee socialization process—the ongoing process of instilling in employees the attitudes, standards, values, and patterns of behavior the firm expects of them.[2] At Saturn, for instance, orientation is where new employees are first exposed to the firm's core values of teamwork and quality by receiving their "Saturn Values" card, and by watching presentations by co-workers.

A successful orientation should accomplish four main things: The new employee should feel welcome and at ease; he or she should understand the organization in a broad sense (its past, present, culture, and vision of the future), as well as key facts such as policies and procedures; the employee should be clear

▼ **FIGURE 7-1 New Employee Departmental Orientation Checklist**

UCSD *Healthcare* **NEW EMPLOYEE DEPARTMENTAL ORIENTATION CHECKLIST**
(Return to Human Resources within 10 days of Hire)

NAME:	HIRE DATE:	SSN:	JOB TITLE:
DEPARTMENT:	NEO DATE:	DEPARTMENTAL ORIENTATION COMPLETED BY:	

TOPIC	DATE REVIEWED	N/A
1. HUMAN RESOURCES INFORMATION		
a. Departmental Attendance Procedures and UCSD Healthcare Work Time & Attendance Policy	a. _____	☐
b. Job Description Review	b. _____	☐
c. Annual Performance Evaluation and Peer Feedback Process	c. _____	☐
d. Probationary Period Information	d. _____	☐
e. Appearance/Dress Code Requirements	e. _____	☐
f. Annual TB Screening	f. _____	☐
g. License and/or certification Renewals	g. _____	☐
2. DEPARTMENT INFORMATION		
a. Organizational Structure-Department Core Values Orientation	a. _____	☐
b. Department/Unit Area Specific Policies & Procedures	b. _____	☐
c. Customer Service Practices	c. _____	☐
d. CQI Effort and Projects	d. _____	☐
e. Tour and Floor Plan	e. _____	☐
f. Equipment/Supplies	f. _____	☐
• Keys issued		☐
• Radio Pager issued		☐
• Other _____		☐
g. Mail and Recharge Codes	g. _____	☐
3. SAFETY INFORMATION		
a. Departmental Safety Plan	a. _____	☐
b. Employee Safety/Injury Reporting Procedures	b. _____	☐
c. Hazard Communication	c. _____	☐
d. Infection Control/Sharps Disposal	d. _____	☐
e. Attendance at annual Safety Fair (mandatory)	e. _____	☐
4. FACILITES INFORMATION		
a. Emergency Power	a. _____	☐
b. Mechanical Systems	b. _____	☐
c. Water	c. _____	☐
d. Medical Gases	d. _____	☐
e. Patient Room	e. _____	☐
• Bed		☐
• Headwall		☐
• Bathroom		☐
• Nurse Call System		☐
5. SECURITY INFORMATION		
a. Code Triage Assignment	a. _____	☐
b. Code Blue Assignment	b. _____	☐
c. Code Red – Evacuation Procedure	c. _____	☐
d. Code 10 – Bomb Threat Procedure	d. _____	☐
e. Departmental Security Measures	e. _____	☐
f. UCSD Emergency Number 6111 or 911	f. _____	☐

This generic checklist may not constitute a complete departmental orientation or assessment. Please attach any additional unit specific orientation material for placement in the employee's HR file

I have been oriented on the items listed above_____

Source: *UCSD*Healthcare. Used with permission.

about what is expected in terms of work and behavior; and the person should have begun the process of becoming socialized into the firm's ways of acting and doing things.[3]

Using Orientation to Reduce Stress

Reducing jitters is important. In fact, the ROPES orientation method (for "realistic orientation programs for new employees' stress") emphasizes orientation's stress-reduction role. To reduce entry shock and employee stress, "newcomers should be forewarned about the typical disappointments they can expect . . ." and how to deal with them (such as, "your new boss is tough, so if you don't understand something, make sure to ask"). Supervisors should also provide general support and reassurance.[4]

Not all new hires react to orientation in the same way.[5] Supervisors should therefore be vigilant, and follow up and encourage new employees to engage in those activities that will enable each to "learn the ropes" and become productive quickly.

THE TRAINING PROCESS

Training refers to the methods used to give new or present employees the skills they need to perform their jobs. Training might mean showing a new Web designer the intricacies of your site, a new salesperson how to sell your firm's product, or a new supervisor how to interview and evaluate employees. Training is a hallmark of good management, and a task managers overlook at their peril. Having high-potential employees doesn't guarantee they'll succeed. Instead, they have to know what you want them to do and how you want them to do it. If they don't, they'll do the jobs their way, not yours. Or they will improvise, or, worse, do nothing productive at all. Good training is vital.

training
The process of teaching new employees the basic skills they need to perform their jobs.

Why the Training Business Is Booming

"Training" is more inclusive than it used to be. Training used to focus mostly on teaching technical skills, such as training assemblers to solder wires or teachers to write lesson plans.[6] Today, such technical training is no longer enough. Employers today have to adapt to technological change, improve product and service quality, and boost productivity to stay competitive.[7] Doing so often requires remedial education. For example, quality improvement programs require employees who can produce charts and graphs and analyze data.[8] Similarly, today's employees need skills (and thus training) in team building, decision making, and communication, as well as technological and computer skills (such as desktop publishing and computer-aided design and manufacturing).[9] And as competition demands better service, employees increasingly require customer service training. McDonald's swung into action with a new training program in 2001, for instance, when it found that many of its in-store customers complained of poor service.

As one trainer puts it: "we don't just concentrate on the traditional training objectives anymore . . . We sit down with management and help them identify strategic goals and objectives and the skills and knowledge needed to achieve them. Then we work together to identify whether our staff has the skills and knowledge, and when they don't, that's when we discuss training needs."[10]

Trends like these help explain why training is booming. In one survey, about 84% of employees reportedly received some type of formal training while with their current employers.[11] On average, employees annually received about 45 hours of training, about one-third of which was formal, and two-thirds informal.[12] Larger U.S. firms spent about $54 billion training employees in 2000. Much of that paid the salaries of in-house training specialists, but more than $19 billion went to outside vendors for materials, courses, and services.

The Five-Step Training and Development Process

Training programs consist of five steps. The first, or *needs analysis* step, identifies the specific job performance skills needed, analyzes the skills and needs of the prospective trainees, and develops specific, measurable knowledge and performance objectives. In the second step, *instructional design*, you decide on, compile, and produce the training program content, including workbooks, exercises, and activities; here, you'll probably use techniques like those discussed in this chapter, such as on-the-job training and computer-assisted learning. There may be a third, *validation* step, in which the bugs are worked out of the training program by presenting it to a small representative audience. The fourth step is to *implement* the program, by actually training the targeted employee group. Fifth is an *evaluation and follow-up* step, in which management assesses the program's successes or failures.

Most employers probably do not (and need not) create their own training materials, since many materials are available on- and offline. For example, the professional development site thinq.com offers a wide range of Web-based courses employees can take online. And many firms, including American Media, Inc., of West Des Moines, Iowa, provide turnkey training packages. These include a training leader's guide, self-study book, and video for improving skills in areas such as customer service, documenting discipline, and appraising performance.

Training and Learning

Training is essentially a learning process, and studies show there are several things you can do to improve learning.

Make Learning Meaningful It is usually easier for trainees to understand and remember material that is *meaningful*.[13] Therefore:

1. At the start of training, provide a bird's-eye view of the material to be presented. Knowing the overall picture facilitates learning.
2. Use a variety of familiar examples.
3. Organize the information so you can present it logically, and in meaningful units.
4. Use terms and concepts that are already familiar to trainees.
5. Use as many visual aids as possible.

Make Skills Transfer Easy Make it easy to *transfer* new skills and behaviors from the training site to the job site:[14]

1. Maximize the similarity between the training situation and the work situation.
2. Provide adequate practice.
3. Label or identify each feature of the machine and/or step in the process.
4. Direct the trainees' attention to important aspects of the job. For example, if you're training customer service representatives how to handle incoming calls, first explain the different types of calls they will encounter and how to recognize such calls.[15]
5. Provide "heads-up," preparatory information. For example, trainees learning to become first-line supervisors often face stressful conditions, high workload, and difficult subordinates back on the job. Studies suggest you can reduce the negative impact of such events by letting trainees know they might happen.[16]

Motivate the Learner Here are some ways to motivate the trainee:[17]

1. People learn best by doing. Try to provide as much realistic practice as possible.
2. Trainees learn best when the trainers immediately reinforce correct responses, perhaps with a quick "well done."
3. Trainees learn best at their own pace. If possible, let them pace themselves.
4. Create a perceived training need in the trainees' minds.[18] In one study, pilots who had experienced pretraining accident-related events subsequently learned more from an accident-reduction training program than did those experiencing fewer such events.[19] You could illustrate the need for the training by showing videos of simulated accidents. Similarly, "before the training, managers need to sit down and talk with the trainee about why they are enrolled in the class, what they are expected to learn and how they can use it on the job."[20]
5. The schedule is important too: The learning curve goes down late in the day, so that "full day training is not as effective as half the day or three-fourths of the day."[21]

Legal Aspects of Training

Various laws apply to training program design and implementation.[22] For example, employers may unknowingly violate EEO laws by training relatively few women or minorities. Or perhaps the reading level of the training manuals is too high for some minority trainees, who are thus doing poorly, quite aside from their aptitude for the jobs they're being trained for. You may eventually have to show that your training admissions process is valid—that it predicts performance in the training program or on the job. In one recent ADA case, the former employee said that in addition to terminating him, General Motors had denied him training because of his HIV/AIDS disability. The person received $7,000 in back pay and $28,000 in compensatory damages.

Negligent training is another legal hazard. **Negligent training** occurs when an employer fails to train adequately, and the employee subsequently harms a third party.[23] This is particularly a problem when the business (such as armed security guard) is aimed at serving the public.[24] Precautions to take include these:

negligent training
A situation where an employer fails to train adequately, and the employee subsequently harms a third party.

1. Confirm claims of skill and experience for all applicants.
2. Extensively train employees who work with dangerous equipment, materials, or processes.
3. Ensure that the training includes procedures to protect third parties' health and safety (including those of other employees).
4. Evaluate the training activity to determine its effectiveness in reducing negligence risks.[25]

Analyzing Training Needs

Before training someone, it obviously makes sense to know whether the person really requires training and, if so, what the training should achieve. Training therefore traditionally starts with determining what training is required.

How you analyze training needs depends on whether you're training new or current employees. The main task in analyzing *new* employees' training needs is to determine what the job entails and to break it down into subtasks, each of which you then teach to the new employee. Analyzing *current* employees' training needs can be more complex, since you have the added task of deciding whether training is the solution. For example, performance may be down because the standards aren't clear or because the person is not motivated.

task analysis
A detailed study of a job to identify the specific skills required.

performance analysis
Verifying that there is a performance deficiency and determining whether that deficiency should be corrected through training or through some other means (such as transferring the employee).

Task analysis and performance analysis are two main ways to identify training needs. **Task analysis** is especially suitable for determining the needs of employees who are new to their jobs. **Performance analysis** appraises the performance of current employees to determine whether training could reduce problems like excess scrap or low output. Supplementary methods used to identify training needs include supervisors' reports, personnel records, management requests, observations, tests of job knowledge, and questionnaire surveys.[26]

Some firms, like Capital One Financial, create development plans for each of their employees. Each plan identifies areas in which each employee needs to develop his or her skills, and identifies specific ways to do so. The firm links each person's goals to its desired strategic competencies (such as improved Web-based delivery of services). Employees receive ongoing mentoring and coaching regarding their developmental progress.[27] The employers that comprise *Computerworld's* ten "best places to work in IT for training" tie each employee's training goals to employee appraisals, as well as to factors such as the person's day-to-day work and the companies recruiting goals.[28]

In any case, get employee input. It's often true that no one knows as much about the job as the people actually doing it.[29]

Task Analysis: Assessing New Employees' Training Needs

Particularly with lower-level workers, it's common to hire inexperienced personnel and train them.[30] Your aim here is to give these new employees the skills and knowledge they need to do the job. You use task analysis to determine the new employees' training needs.

Task analysis is a detailed study of the job to determine what specific skills—like Java (in the case of a Web developer) or interviewing (in the case of a supervisor)—the job requires. Job descriptions and job specifications are helpful here. These list the job's specific duties and skills and thus provide the basic reference point in determining the training required. You can also uncover training needs by reviewing performance standards, performing the job, and questioning current job holders and their supervisors.[31]

Some employers supplement the job description and specification with a *task analysis record form*. This consolidates information regarding required tasks and skills in a form that's especially helpful for determining training requirements. As Table 7-1 illustrates, a task analysis record form contains six types of information, such as "Skills Required."

Performance Analysis: Assessing Current Employees' Training Needs

Performance analysis is the process of verifying that there is a performance deficiency and determining if such deficiency should be corrected through training or through some other means (like transferring the employee).

There are several methods you can use to identify a current employee's training needs. These include supervisor, peer, self, and 360-degree performance reviews; job-related performance data (including productivity, absenteeism and tardiness, accidents, short-term sickness, grievances, waste, late deliveries, product quality, downtime, repairs, equipment utilization, and customer complaints); observation by supervisors or other specialists; interviews with the employee or his or her supervisor; tests of things like job knowledge, skills, and attendance; attitude surveys; individual employee daily diaries; and assessment centers.

▲ *After some false starts with a mandatory training program, Julie McHenry, CEO of Wilson McHenry Co., a small strategic business communications company in California, found that one of the reasons employees disliked the program was that all of them were forced to take the same classes regardless of their needs. Under a new training program run by a five-employee committee, staff members sign up for the courses of their choice each semester and learn such skills as how to write a press release or conduct a media tour. None of the courses are mandatory, although managers may suggest those they feel would be helpful to particular employees.*

▼ **TABLE 7-1 Task Analysis Record Form**

Task List	When and How Often Performed	Quantity and Quality of Performance	Conditions Under Which Performed	Skills or Knowledge Required	Where Best Learned
1. Operate paper cutter	4 times per day		Noisy pressroom: distractions		
1.1 Start motor					
1.2 Set cutting distance		±tolerance of 0.007 in.		Read gauge	On the job
1.3 Place paper on cutting table		Must be completely even to prevent uneven cut		Lift paper correctly	On the job
1.4 Push paper up to cutter				Must be even	On the job
1.5 Grasp safety release with left hand		100% of time, for safety		Essential for safety	On the job but practice first with no distractions
1.6 Grasp cutter release with right hand				Must keep both hands on releases	On the job but practice first with no distractions
1.7 Simultaneously pull safety release with left hand and cutter release with right hand					
1.8 Wait for cutter to retract		100% of time, for safety		Must keep both hands on releases	On the job but practice first with no distractions
1.9 Retract paper				Wait till cutter retracts	On the job but practice first with no distractions
1.10 Shut off		100% of time, for safety			On the job but practice first with no distractions
2. Operate printing press					
2.1 Start motor					

Note: Task analysis record form showing some of tasks and subtasks performed by a printing press operator.

The first step is usually to compare the person's performance to what it should be. Examples of specific performance deficiencies include:

I expect each salesperson to make ten new contacts per week, but John averages only six.

Other plants our size average no more than two serious accidents per month; we're averaging five.

Distinguishing between can't do and won't do problems is the heart of performance analysis. First, determine whether it's a *can't do* problem and, if so, its specific causes. For example: The employees don't know what to do or what your standards are; there are obstacles in the system such as lack of tools or supplies; there are no job aids (such as color-coded wires that show assemblers which wire goes where), or no electronic performance support systems that provide on-screen, computerized, step-by-step instructions; you've hired people who haven't the skills to do the job; or inadequate training.

On the other hand, it might be a *won't do* problem. Here employees could do a good job if they wanted to. Perhaps you need to change the reward system. One expert says, "perhaps the biggest trap that trainers fall into is [developing] training for problems that training just won't fix."[32]

If training is the solution, you need to set objectives. These specify what the trainee should be able to accomplish upon completing the training program—repair a copier in 30 minutes, program a simple Web site in half a day, or sell five advertising banners per day, for instance.[33]

TRADITIONAL TRAINING METHODS

Once you've decided to train employees and what they're to learn, you have to design the training program. You can create the content and program sequence yourself, but there is also a vast selection of on- and offline content and packages from which to choose. You'll find turnkey, off-the-shelf programs on virtually any topic—from occupational safety to sexual harassment to Web design—from tens of thousands of providers.

In any case, there are various methods companies use to actually deliver the training. We'll start with what is probably the most popular: on-the-job training.

On-the-Job Training

on-the-job training (OJT)
Training a person to learn a job while working at it.

On-the-job training (OJT) means having a person learn a job by actually doing it. Every employee, from mailroom clerk to company president, gets on-the-job training when he or she joins a firm. In many firms, OJT is the only training available.[34]

The most familiar type of on-the-job training is the *coaching or understudy method*. Here, an experienced worker or the trainee's supervisor trains the employee. At lower levels, trainees may acquire skills by observing the supervisor. But this technique is widely used at top-management levels, too. A potential future CEO might spend a year as assistant to the current CEO, for instance. *Job rotation*, in which an employee (usually a management trainee) moves from job to job at planned intervals, is another OJT technique. Jeffrey Immelt progressed through such a process in becoming GE's new CEO. *Special assignments* similarly give lower-level executives firsthand experience in working on actual problems. The Men's Wearhouse, with 455 stores nationwide, makes extensive use of on-the-job training. It has few full-time trainers. Instead, the Men's Wearhouse has a formal process of "cascading" responsibility for training: Every manager is formally accountable for the development of his or her direct subordinates.[35]

OJT has several advantages. It is relatively inexpensive; trainees learn while producing; and there is no need for expensive off-site facilities like classrooms or programmed learning devices. The method also facilitates learning, since trainees learn by doing and get quick feedback on their performance. But there are several points to note when using OJT.

Most important, don't take the success of an on-the-job training program for granted.[36] Carefully train the trainers themselves, and provide the necessary training materials. Trainers should know, for instance, the principles of learning and perhaps the four-step job instruction technique that follows. Low expectations on the trainer's part may translate into poorer trainee performance (a phenomenon researchers have called "the golem effect"). Those training others should thus emphasize the high expectations they have for their trainees' success.[37]

Here are some steps to help ensure success.

Step 1. Prepare the Learner
1. Put the learner at ease—relieve the tension.
2. Explain why he or she is being taught.
3. Create interest, encourage questions, find out what the learner already knows about this or other jobs.

4. Explain the whole job and relate it to some job the worker already knows.
5. Place the learner as close to the normal working position as possible.
6. Familiarize the worker with equipment, materials, tools, and trade terms.

Step 2. Present the Operation
1. Explain quantity and quality requirements.
2. Go through the job at the normal work pace.
3. Go through the job at a slow pace several times, explaining each step. Between operations, explain the difficult parts, or those in which errors are likely to be made.
4. Again go through the job at a slow pace several times; explain the key points.
5. Have the learner explain the steps as you go through the job at a slow pace.

Step 3. Do a Tryout
1. Have the learner go through the job several times, slowly, explaining each step to you. Correct mistakes and, if necessary, do some of the complicated steps the first few times.
2. Run the job at the normal pace.
3. Have the learner do the job, gradually building up skill and speed.
4. As soon as the learner demonstrates ability to do the job, let the work begin, but don't abandon him or her.

Step 4. Follow Up
1. Designate to whom the learner should go for help.
2. Gradually decrease supervision, checking work from time to time against quality and quantity standards.
3. Correct faulty work patterns before they become a habit. Show why the learned method is superior.
4. Compliment good work; encourage the worker until he or she is able to meet the quality and quantity standards.[38]

Apprenticeship Training

More employers are implementing apprenticeship programs, an approach that began in the Middle Ages. **Apprenticeship training** is a structured process by which people become skilled workers through a combination of classroom instruction and on-the-job training. It is widely used to train individuals for many occupations.[39] It traditionally involves having the learner/apprentice study under the tutelage of a master craftsperson.[40]

Several U.S. facilities currently use this approach. For example, the Siemens Stromberg-Carlson plant in Florida has apprenticeships for adults and high school students for electronics technician jobs:

> *Adults work on the factory floor, receive classroom instruction at Seminole Community College, and also study at the plant's hands-on apprenticeship lab. Graduates receive Associates Degrees in telecommunications and electronics engineering. High school students spend two afternoons per week at the apprenticeship lab.*[41]

The U.S. Department of Labor's Employment and Training Administration offers apprenticeship training, along with a number of other types of training programs (see Webnote).

apprenticeship training
A structured process by which people become skilled workers through a combination of classroom instruction and on-the-job training.

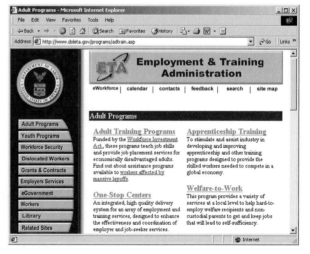

▲ **WEBNOTE**
The federal Employment and Training Administration runs apprenticeship training programs, as well as other types of programs, tailored to specific needs, like "Welfare to Work."
www.doleta.gov

Informal Learning

About two-thirds of industrial training isn't formal at all, but results from day-to-day unplanned interactions between the new worker and his or her colleagues.[42] Informal learning is "any learning that occurs in which the learning process isn't determined or designed by the organization."[43]

Although managers don't arrange informal learning, there's still a lot they can do to ensure it occurs. Most of the steps are simple. For example, Siemens Power Transmission and Distribution in Raleigh, North Carolina, places tools in cafeteria areas to take advantage of the work-related discussions taking place.[44] Even things like installing white boards and keeping them stocked with markers can facilitate informal learning.

Job Instruction Training

job instruction training (JIT)
Listing each job's basic tasks, along with key points, in order to provide step-by-step training for employees.

Many jobs consist of a logical sequence of steps and are best taught step-by-step. This step-by-step process is called **job instruction training (JIT)**. To begin, list all necessary steps in the job, each in its proper sequence. Alongside each step also list a corresponding "key point" (if any). The steps show what is to be done, and the key points show how it's to be done—and why. Here is an example of a job instruction training sheet for teaching a trainee how to operate a large motorized paper cutter:

Steps	**Key Points**
1. Start motor	None
2. Set cutting distance	Carefully read scale—to prevent wrong-sized cut
3. Place paper on cutting table	Make sure paper is even—to prevent uneven cut
4. Push paper up to cutter	Make sure paper is tight—to prevent uneven cut
5. Grasp safety release with left hand	Do not release left hand—to prevent hand from being caught in cutter
6. Grasp cutter release with right hand	Do not release right hand—to prevent hand from being caught in cutter
7. Simultaneously pull cutter and safety releases	Keep both hands on corresponding releases—avoid hands being on cutting table
8. Wait for cutter to retract	Keep both hands on releases—to avoid having hands on cutting table
9. Retract paper	Make sure cutter is retracted; keep both hands away from releases
10. Shut off motor	None

Lectures

Lecturing has several advantages. It is a quick and simple way to provide knowledge to large groups of trainees, as when the sales force needs to learn the special features of a new product. You could use written materials, but they may involve considerably more production expense and don't encourage the give-and-take questioning that lectures do.

Here are some useful guidelines for presenting a lecture:[45]

■   Give your listeners signals to help them follow your ideas. For instance, if you have a list of items, start by saying something like, "There are four reasons why the sales reports are necessary. . . . The first . . . the second . . ."

- ▓ Don't start out on the wrong foot. For instance, don't open with an irrelevant joke or story or by saying something like, "I really don't know why I was asked to speak here today."
- ▓ Keep your conclusions short. Just summarize your main point or points in one or two succinct sentences.
- ▓ Be alert to your audience. Watch body language for negative signals like fidgeting and crossed arms.
- ▓ Maintain eye contact with the trainees. At least look at each section of the audience during your presentation.
- ▓ Make sure everyone in the room can hear. Use a mike if necessary. Repeat questions that you get from trainees before you answer.
- ▓ Control your hands. Get in the habit of leaving them hanging naturally at your sides rather than letting them drift.
- ▓ Talk from notes rather than from a script. Write out clear, legible notes on large index cards or on PowerPoint slides, and use these as an outline, rather than memorizing your presentation.
- ▓ Break a long talk into a series of five-minute talks. Speakers often give a short overview introduction, and then spend the rest of a one-hour presentation going point by point through their material. Unfortunately, most people quickly lose interest in your list. Experts suggest breaking the long talk into a series of five-minute talks, each with its own introduction. Each introduction highlights what you'll discuss, why it's important to the audience, and your credibility—why they should listen to you.[46]
- ▓ Practice. If possible, rehearse under conditions similar to those under which you will actually give your presentation.

Programmed Learning

Whether the medium is a textbook, computer, or the Internet, **programmed learning** (or **programmed instruction**) is a step-by-step self-learning method that consists of three parts:

1. Presenting questions, facts, or problems to the learner
2. Allowing the person to respond
3. Providing feedback on the accuracy of answers

Generally, it presents facts and follow-up questions. The learner can then respond, and subsequent frames provide feedback on the accuracy of his or her answers.

Programmed learning's main advantage is that it reduces training time.[47] It also facilitates learning, because it lets trainees learn at their own pace, provides immediate feedback, and (from the learner's point of view) reduces the risk of error. On the other hand, trainees do not learn much more from programmed learning than they would from a traditional textbook. You therefore need to weigh the cost of developing the manuals and/or software programmed instruction against the potentially accelerated but not improved learning.

Audiovisual Tools

Audiovisual-based training techniques like films, PowerPoints, video conferencing, audiotapes, and videotapes can be very effective and are widely used.[48] The Ford Motor Company uses films in its dealer training sessions to simulate problems and sample reactions to various customer complaints, for example.

Audiovisuals are more expensive than conventional lectures but offer some advantages. Of course, they tend to be more interesting. In addition, consider using them in the following situations:

1. When there is a need to illustrate how to follow a certain sequence over time, such as when teaching fax machine repair. The stop-action, instant replay, and fast- or slow-motion capabilities of audiovisuals can be useful.

programmed learning
A systematic method for teaching job skills involving presenting questions or facts, allowing the person to respond, and giving the learner immediate feedback on the accuracy of his or her answers.

2. When there is a need to expose trainees to events not easily demonstrable in live lectures, such as a visual tour of a factory or open-heart surgery.
3. When you need organizationwide training and it is too costly to move the trainers from place to place.

There is a vast range of training materials available in audiovisual format. For example, the training video *Encouraging the Heart* aims to help managers understand why it's important to recognize employee performance. The video makes its points in part by using footage from actual companies, including a utility firm and software developer.[49] The video *Bad Apples: How to Deal with Difficult Attitudes* shows trainees a five-step procedure for dealing with difficult people, each illustrated with a different vignette.[50]

Simulated Training

simulated training
Training employees on special off-the-job equipment, as in airplane pilot training, so training costs and hazards can be reduced.

Simulated training (occasionally called vestibule training) is a method in which trainees learn on the actual or simulated equipment they will use on the job, but are actually trained off the job. It is a necessity when it is too costly or dangerous to train employees on the job. Putting new assembly-line workers right to work could slow production, for instance, and when safety is a concern—as with pilots—simulated training may be the only practical alternative.

Simulated training may take place in a separate room with the same equipment the trainees will use on the job. However, it often involves the use of equipment simulators. In pilot training, for instance, airlines use flight simulators for safety, learning efficiency, and cost savings, including savings on maintenance, pilot cost, fuel, and the cost of not having an aircraft in regular service.[51]

ELECTRONIC TRAINING

Computerized and Internet-based tools have revolutionized the training process. Specific methods here include computer-based training, electronic performance support systems, and learning portals.

Computer-Based Training

With computer-based training, the trainee uses computer-based and/or CD-ROM systems to interactively increase his or her knowledge or skills.[52] For example, one employer uses computer-based training (CBT) to train interviewers to conduct correct and legally defensible interviews.[53] Trainees start with a computer screen that shows the applicant's completed employment application, as well as information about the nature of the job. The trainee then begins a simulated interview by typing in questions, which a videotaped model acting as the applicant answers, based on responses to a multitude of questions already in the computer. Some items require follow-up questions. As each question is answered, the trainee records his or her evaluation of the applicant's answer and makes a decision about the person's suitability for the position. At the end of the session, the computer tells the trainee where he or she went wrong (perhaps in asking discriminatory questions, for instance) and offers further instruction to correct these mistakes.[54]

Instead of sending new rental sales agents to weeklong classroom-based training courses, Value Rent-a-Car now provides them with interactive, multimedia-based training programs utilizing CD-ROMs. These help them learn the car rental process by walking them through various procedures, such as operating the rental computer system.[55] McDonald's developed about 11 different courses for its franchisees' employees, and put the programs on CD-ROMs. The programs consist of graphics-supported lessons, and require trainees to make choices to show their understanding.[56]

CBT programs have real advantages. Interactive technologies reduce learning time by an average of 50%.[57] They can also be cost effective once designed and produced. Other advantages include instructional consistency (computers, unlike human trainers, don't have good days and bad days), mastery of learning (if the trainee doesn't learn it, he or she generally can't move on to the next step), increased retention, and increased trainee motivation (resulting from responsive feedback). FedEx had success with such a system and now is moving to put more of its training—such as that for customer service reps—online.[58]

Specialist multimedia software houses like Graphic Media of Portland, Oregon, produce much of the content for CBT programs like these. They produce both custom titles and generic programs like a $999 package for teaching workplace safety.

Electronic Performance Support Systems (EPSS)

People don't remember everything they learn. The same applies to training. Dell Computer, for example, introduces about 80 new products per year, so it's unrealistic to expect Dell's technical support people to know everything about every product. Dell's training therefore focuses on the skills they need every day, such as Dell's rules, culture and values, and systems and work processes. Computer-based support systems then deliver the rest of what they need to know, when they need it: When a customer calls about a specific problem, the computerized training aid helps walk the customer rep through the solution, question by question.[59]

Employers have long used job aids of one sort or another. A **job aid** is a set of instructions, diagrams, or similar methods available at the job site to guide the worker.[60] Job aids work particularly well on more complex jobs that require multiple steps, or where it's dangerous to forget a step. Airline pilots use job aids (such as a checklist of things to do prior to takeoff). The General Motors Electromotive Division in Chicago gives workers job aids in the form of diagrams; these show, for example, where the locomotive wiring runs and which color wires go where.

Electronic performance support systems (EPSS) are today's job aids. They are sets of computerized tools and displays that automate training, documentation, and phone support, integrate this automation into applications, and provide support that's faster, cheaper, and more effective than the traditional methods.[61]

When you call a Dell service representative about a problem with your new computer, he or she is probably asking questions that are prompted by an EPSS; it takes you both, step by step, through an analytical sequence. Without the EPSS, Dell would have to train its service reps to memorize an unrealistically large number of solutions.

Similarly, without EPSS, a new travel agent might require months of training, rather than days. At Apollo Travel Services, in Chicago, an EPSS guides travel agents' questions, and makes it harder to make mistakes. For example, when agents start to schedule an option that goes against a customer's established travel policies—such as booking managers to fly first class instead of coach—a dialogue box reminds the agent of the policy. It also asks him or her to choose from a list of appropriate reasons, if overriding the policy.[62]

Distance and Internet-Based Training

Firms today use various forms of distance learning methods for training. Distance learning methods include traditional paper-and-pencil correspondence courses, as well as teletraining, videoconferencing, and Internet-based classes.[63]

job aid
Is a set of instructions, diagrams, or similar methods available at the job site to guide the worker.

electronic performance support systems
Sets of computerized tools and displays that automate training, documentation, and phone support, integrate this automation into applications, and provide support that's faster, cheaper, and more effective than traditional methods.

Teletraining With teletraining, a trainer in a central location teaches groups of employees at remote locations via television hookups.[64] For example, AMP Incorporated used satellites to train its engineers and technicians at 165 sites in the United States and 27 other countries. (The firm makes electrical and electronic connection devices.) To reduce costs for one training program, AMP supplied the program content. PBS affiliate WITF, Channel 33 of Harrisburg, Pennsylvania, supplied the equipment and expertise required to broadcast the program to five AMP facilities in North America.[65] Macy's established the Macy's Satellite Network, in part to provide training for 59,000 employees around the country.[66]

One low-tech twist is to use the telephone. For example, Cadillac has used what it calls the Craftsman's League, which is a training, testing, and motivational program for Cadillac dealers' mechanics. Employees receive Cadillac materials and service manuals for factory-approved service procedures and ongoing technical changes. Then, four times a year, technicians take a phone exam on any one of eight categories including, for instance, paint repair, electrical, and mechanical.[67]

Honda America Corp. began by using satellite technology to train engineers and now uses it for many other types of employee training. For example, its Ohio-based subsidiary purchases seminars from the National Technological University, a provider of satellite education that uses courses from various universities and specialized teaching organizations. The price per course varies, but it averages $200 to $250 per employee per seminar. "It is much more cost effective to keep workers at home and not pay for them to travel," one of the firm's training managers says.[68]

Videoconferencing Firms use videoconferencing to train employees who are geographically separated from each other—or from the trainer.[69] Videoconferencing allows people in one location to communicate live via a combination of audio and visual equipment with people in another city or country or with groups in several cities.[70] Keypads allow audience interactivity. For instance, in a program at Texas Instruments, the keypad system lets instructors call on remote trainees and lets the latter respond.[71] Management Recruiters International (MRI) uses the firm's desktop ConferView system to train hundreds of employees—each in their individual offices—simultaneously.[72]

▲ *Doug Donkin, an instructor for Management Recruiters International (MRI), uses the firm's ConferView system to conduct MRI University training. ConferView is one type of videoconferencing technology that allows companies to train hundreds of employees simultaneously.*

There are several things to keep in mind before lecturing in front of the camera. For example, because the training is remote, it's particularly important to prepare a training guide ahead of time, specifically a manual the learners can use to follow the points the trainer is making, and a script for the trainer to follow. A sampling of other hints would include: Avoid bright, flashy jewelry or heavily patterned clothing; arrive at least 20 minutes early; test all equipment you will be using; have all participants introduce themselves; avoid presenting just to the video camera and not to the in-house participants; remember that excessive physical movement will cause video image distortion with compressed telephone transmission.[73]

Training Via the Internet Many firms use the Internet and/or their proprietary intranets to deliver computer-based training. For example, Silicon Graphics transferred many of its training materials to CD-ROMs. However, since not every desktop computer had a CD-ROM player, many employees couldn't access the programs. Silicon Graphics therefore replaced the CD-ROM system by distributing training materials via its intranet. "Now employees can access the programs whenever they want. Distribution costs are zero, and if the company wants to make a change to the program, it can do so at a central location."[74] The HR.*NET* box shows another example.

GTE's Technology-Based Training

After a major downsizing and merger, telecommunications giant GTE's training managers knew they had to make the firm's training programs more cost effective—but how? The answer was to make at least half their training programs technology based.[75] For one new program, for instance, GTE's training staff had to train thousands of workers in how to use the firm's new order processing system. The staff created an intranet-based program to simulate the order entry system, complete with sample customer names, addresses, and requests for service.

The new training package was a big success. It eliminated the need to have instructors available to answer questions during the training, and let employees learn at their own pace. GTE now uses its intranet to deliver ongoing and constantly updated training programs like this one, and to facilitate interaction between each of the trainees' computers and the firm's central computers.

Delivering training online can be cost effective. For example, Delta Airlines customer service personnel now receive about 70% of their annual required FAA training via the Internet. Employees reportedly like it because it's interactive; Delta likes it because "prior to online training, employees had to travel to one of five training centers, keeping them away from their jobs for at least the day."[76]

Learning Portals Many firms are using business portals today. Also called enterprise information portals (EIPs), they are, like Yahoo!, windows to the Internet, but focused on the needs of a specific business. Through its business portal, categories of a firm's employees—secretaries, engineers, salespeople—are able to access all the corporate applications they need, like industry news and competitive data, or tools to analyze data.[77]

Some business portals are highly specialized. Thus (as we saw in Chapter 1), NCR uses a "benefits portal" to help its HR call center counselors answer benefits questions. Similarly, training is increasingly found and delivered through training-oriented learning portals. Business-to-consumer (B2C) portals such as fat-brain, learn.com, ScheduleEarth.com, and SmartPlanet aggregate training content for "free agent learners"—individuals anywhere who want to upgrade their knowledge and skills on their own. Business-to-business (B2B) portals such as Digitalthink, thinq.com, headlight.com, and Click2learn.com target the business community. They contract with employers to become their learning portals, and deliver training options—often Web based—to the firm's employees.

Many firms are creating their own learning portals for their employees. They let the company contract with specific training content providers, which offer their training content to the firm's employees via the portal.[78] Thus, Prentice Hall might deliver a textbook-based training program to a client firm's employees via the firm's learning portal. By one estimate, Web-based training will soon account for 80% of employee education and development. A 13 member consortium of *Fortune* 500 companies offers more than 500,000 online development courses to its 2.5 million employees worldwide via learning portals like thinq.com and skillsoft.[79]

The technology of the learning portals puts "more and more information into everyone's hands." Instead of limiting training opportunities to teacher-led conventional classes or to periodic training sessions, training becomes available 24/7. Employees learn at their own pace, when they want to.[80]

◆ **HIGH-PERFORMANCE INSIGHT** ADC Telecommunications installed such a system. The fast-growing firm supplies equipment and services for broadband communications, and has 16,000 employees worldwide. The firm's training department concluded that its existing instructor-led training was not meeting its needs. The company decided that the solution was to deliver training programs online; to accomplish this, ADC turned to Click2learn. Click2learn creates learning portals for firms like ADC. It creates and aggregates online courses on a variety of business topics, and has the online infrastructure that enables firms like ADC to manage its online course offerings—such as helping ADC keep track of who is studying what. Click2learn installed a version of its standard portal for ADC.

The program has been successful. As the ADC manager on this project points out, "Our Click2learn e-learning site gives ADC personnel access to the wide variety of online courses available in the learning network . . . and all displayed in a way that makes it easy for users to find what they are looking for. And with the pay-as-you-go model, we're only paying to train those who need it."[81]

STRATEGIC HR

Channel 4 Becomes Competitive

In the UK, Channel 4's strategy has changed dramatically in the last few years. With the UK's new broadcasting act, Channel 4 had to start selling and transmitting its own air time. And that meant quickly instituting training programs to support an expanded sales force and new high-tech control system.

Management accomplished this in part by introducing a series of interactive, intranet-based e-learning training programs. Says the managing director of the company that created the programs for Channel 4, "By working closely with the HR, business affairs and ultimate rights departments at Channel 4, we have produced a series of learning programs that are high on visual impact and fit in with the culture of the channel." Employees access the training modules through Channel 4's intranet. The training programs include animated meetings that demonstrate the different scenarios employees might face on the job.[82]

So far, the new strategy seems to be working. For example, Channel 4 was primarily responsible for the "Big Brother" television phenomenon that became one of the highest rated shows in the UK and many countries around the world.[83]

TRAINING FOR SPECIAL PURPOSES

Today training does more than prepare employees to perform their jobs effectively. Training for special purposes—dealing with AIDS and adjusting to diversity, for instance—is required, too. Here is a sampling of such special-purpose training programs.

Literacy Training Techniques

Functional illiteracy—the inability to handle basic reading, writing, and arithmetic—is a serious problem at work. By one estimate, 50% of the U.S. population reads below the eighth-grade level, and about 90 million adults are functionally illiterate.[84] For example, a survey of 316 employers concluded that about 43% of all new hires required basic skill improvements, as did 37% of current employees.[85]

This reflects, in part, the changing nature of workers' jobs. For example, "the textile worker who once could feel with her hands for irregularities in the yarn as it moves through a loom must now accurately interpret data by reading a bar graph displayed on a video monitor that tracks yarn tangling, cloth breakage or lost threads. She must learn to do so because the U.S. textile industry is collectively spending $2 billion each year to incorporate these new technologies in order to remain competitive with foreign companies that employ cheaper labor."[86]

Employers are responding in two main ways. First, companies are testing job candidates' basic skills. Of the 1,085 companies that responded to an American Management Association (AMA) workplace testing survey, 39% indicated they conduct basic skills testing.[87] About 85% of the responding companies refuse to hire job applicants who are deficient in basic skills. About 3% test (and often reject) candidates for promotion based on their literacy scores.

The second response is to set up basic skills and literacy programs. For example, after using the University of Massachusetts for many years for remedial skills training, Smith and Wesson recently instituted a more comprehensive program. Phase 1 involved assessing each job task and determining its required skill level. (This was important because the firm's jobs were increasingly technology based and performed by teams.) It became apparent that many jobs required higher math skills (for instance, for understanding numerical control equipment), better reading and writing skills, and better oral communication skills for interacting on the factory floor. Yet a literacy audit and testing revealed that many of the 676 factory employees fell below the required eighth-grade level. Formal classes were instituted to help employees raise their math and reading skills, and 70% of class attendees did so.[88] Another approach is to have supervisors give employees writing and speaking exercises, and provide personal feedback.[89]

Employees with weak reading, writing, or arithmetic skills may be reluctant to admit the problem. Supervisors therefore should watch for employees who avoid doing a particular job or using a particular tool; do not follow written directions or instructions; do not take written phone messages; take home forms to complete; or make the same mistakes repeatedly.[90]

AIDS Education

Many of the estimated 1 million Americans infected with the AIDS virus are in the workforce, and this creates anxiety for many noninfected employees and a dilemma for employers. On the one hand, employers generally must allow infected employees to remain on their jobs, for both moral and legal reasons. On the other hand, the infected person's co-workers often require training to reduce anxieties and maximize the chances that the employees will be able to work together as a team.

Many firms therefore establish AIDS education programs. These cover topics like transmission of contagious diseases such as AIDS and tuberculosis, awareness of the precautions necessary to limit any danger related to worker interaction, and removing the social stigma some attach to the disease.[91]

Some say employers are becoming too complacent: "There is a general impression that the crisis is over, that AIDS is declining, so the workplace doesn't have to confront the problem anymore."[92] In fact, many HIV positive workers reportedly still struggle over whether to disclose their situation to employers and co-workers. And many firms and their employees still react to AIDS with fear, prejudice, and discrimination. Seminars about AIDS and how managers and workers should react to it thus remain important.

The program at the Wellesley, Massachusetts, office of Sun Life of Canada, an insurance company, is typical.[93] Groups of 20 to 30 employees attended 90-minute seminars that provided information about AIDS, plus a forum for discussion and questions. Management employees attended three-hour seminars in groups of 10 to 12. These seminars covered additional AIDS-related issues, including the need for confidentiality, the impact of discrimination laws, and the company's AIDS policy.

Training for Global Business

Firms competing in a global marketplace often implement special global training programs. The reasons for doing so include avoiding lost business due to cultural insensitivity, improving job satisfaction and retention of overseas staff, and enabling a newly assigned employee to communicate with colleagues abroad.[94]

Many firms opt for prepackaged training programs. A sampling helps illustrate the wide range of programs available, as well as what global training programs actually involve:

- *Executive Etiquette for Global Transactions*: This program prepares managers for conducting business globally by training them in business etiquette in other cultures.
- *Cross-Cultural Technology Transfer*: This program shows how cultural values affect perceptions of technology and technical learning.
- *International Protocol and Presentation*: This program shows the correct way to handle people with tact and diplomacy in countries around the world.
- *Business Basics for the Foreign Executive*: This program covers negotiating cross-culturally, working with U.S. clients, making presentations, writing for U.S. business, and using the phone in the United States.
- *Language training*: Language training delivered by certified instructors, usually determined by the learner's needs rather than by the requirements of a predetermined curriculum or textbook.[95]

Diversity Training

With an increasingly diverse workforce, more firms are implementing diversity training programs. As an HR officer for one firm put it, "We're trying to create a better sensitivity among our supervisors about the issues and challenges women and minorities face in pursuing their careers."[96] Diversity training aims to create better cross-cultural sensitivity, with the aim of fostering more harmonious working relationships among a firm's employees. According to one survey of HR directors, diversity-based programs included (from most used to least used): improving interpersonal skills; understanding and valuing cultural differences; improving technical skills; socializing employees into the corporate culture; reducing stress; indoctrinating new workers into the U.S. work ethic; mentoring; improving English proficiency; improving basic math skills; and improving bilingual skills for English-speaking employees.[97]

For example, Adams Mark Hotel & Resorts conducted a diversity training seminar for about 11,000 employees. It combined lectures, video, and employee role playing to emphasize sensitivity to race and religion.[98] After settling a huge lawsuit for race discrimination, Coca-Cola implemented an ongoing diversity training program. It includes "leveraging the power of people and ideas," a new two-day diversity training course that all U.S. employees are required to attend annually. (The firm also took other steps, including appointing a diversity director, establishing a diversity advisory council, and tying management compensation to reaching diversity goals.)[99]

A supervisory training program at Kinney Shoe Corp. provides another example.[100] The firm conducts eight-hour "valuing diversity" seminars for store managers. By presenting a number of hypothetical situations, they show, for instance, how people from various cultures react differently to workplace situations. For example, one situation makes the point that public praise from his or her supervisor might embarrass a Native American worker.

Diversity training is no panacea, and a poorly conceived program can backfire. Potential negative outcomes include "the possibility of . . . participant discomfort, reinforcement of group stereotypes, perceived disenfranchisement or backlash by white males, and even lawsuits based on managers' exposure of stereotypical beliefs blurted out during 'awareness raising' sessions."[101]

Customer Service Training

Today, almost two-thirds of U.S. workers are in service jobs, and more firms must compete based on quality of service. It's no longer enough, for instance, to offer a clean room at a decent price when a customer checks into a hotel. The Westin St. Louis hotel spent 13 days training its 160 employees before the hotel opened in March 2001. Most of the training focused on how to deal with and solve problems for unhappy guests.[102] Many firms implement such programs, and they're not necessarily always "service" firms, as the New Workplace box illustrates.

THE NEW WORKPLACE

Training Employees to Please Customers

Québecor World, Inc., is the world's largest printing company, with 160 plants in 14 countries and 43,000 employees. When it heard from customers that "our people in the plants were so different that each plant was like a different company," the firm decided to implement a customer service program for its customer service and account representatives. The program involved three sessions of three days each, and a series of exercises. One exercise involved professionals' presentations of role-play situations between employees and customers, so trainees could evaluate and learn the right way to react to typical situations.[103]

To improve service, Gulf Breeze Hospital, in Gulf Breeze, Florida, gives each employee its health care performance standards. These list specific behaviors employees must engage in at work, such as a positive attitude, and good appearance and communication.[104]

Teamwork Training

Teamwork doesn't just happen; you have to train employees to be good team members. For instance, Toyota spends dozens of hours training new employees to listen to each other and to cooperate. It uses short exercises to illustrate examples of good and bad teamwork and to mold new employees' attitudes toward teamwork.

Some firms use off-premises training like Outward Bound to build teamwork.[105] Sometimes this involves taking a firm's management team into rugged, mountainous terrain. There they learn team spirit and cooperation and the need to rely on each other to overcome physical obstacles. As one participant put it, "Every time I climbed over a rock, I needed someone's help."[106] Eight public relations executives from Shandwick International recently took over the kitchen at a restaurant in Baltimore in a team-building effort called "recipes for success." The executives worked in teams—one preparing pan-seared chicken and another preparing sea scallops—to help hone their skills in areas like handling conflicts and giving orders.[107]

Many team-training programs are technology-based. For example, Essentials of Team Building is a CD-based program with three segments. There is a 70-minute team-building concepts segment, followed by a 55-minute managing-the-process segment and a 45-minute team exercise segment. The first helps participants define a team and describes basic team processes. The second segment—managing the process—covers topics like recognizing and modifying ineffective team behaviors. The final segment presents a scenario trainees use to size up eight possible team candidates and decide which four to use on a four-person team.[108]

Providing Lifelong Learning

lifelong learning
Providing continuing training from basic remedial skills to advanced decision-making techniques throughout the employees' careers.

Firms today depend on their first-line employees—those actually building the cars, or greeting the hotel guests—to recognize new opportunities, identify problems, and react quickly with analyses and recommendations. This requires a continuing upgrade of employees' skills. **Lifelong learning** means providing continuing training from basic remedial skills to advanced decision-making techniques throughout employees' careers.

A Canadian Honeywell manufacturing plant called its lifelong learning program the Honeywell-Scarborough Learning for Life Initiative.[109] It began with adult basic education.[110] Here the company, in partnership with the employees' union, offered courses in English as a second language, basic literacy, arithmetic, and computer literacy.

Next, the factory partnered with a local community college to provide college-level courses for all factory employees—hourly, professional, and managerial. Employees now had the opportunity to earn college diplomas and certificates.[111] This part of the program included a 15-hour "skills for success" program designed to refresh the study habits required to succeed academically. All courses took place at the factory immediately after work.

The firm also provided job-related training for two hours every other week. These sessions focused on skills specifically important to the job, such as "the principles of just-in-time inventory systems, team effectiveness, interpersonal communication skills, conflict resolution, problem solving and dealing with a diverse work force."[112]

MANAGERIAL DEVELOPMENT AND TRAINING

Managers, like other employees, have to be trained, and many of the methods we've discussed to this point apply equally well to them. Yet training for managers is often different, in several ways: It tends to be more future oriented. It also tends to be more complex, just as a CEO's performance tends to be a product of more complex forces—competitors' actions, unions' demands, foreign exchange rates—than does that of a front-line supervisor. We'll therefore look at management development and training as a topic of its own.

What Is Management Development?

management development
Any attempt to improve current or future management performance by imparting knowledge, changing attitudes, or increasing skills.

Management development is any attempt to improve managerial performance by imparting knowledge, changing attitudes, or increasing skills. The ultimate aim is, of course, to enhance the future performance of the company itself. The general management development process consists of (1) assessing the company's strategic needs (for instance, to fill future executive openings, or to boost competitiveness), (2) appraising the managers' performance, and then (3) developing the managers (and future managers).

Some development programs are companywide and involve all or most new (or potential) managers. Thus, new MBAs may join Ford's management development program and rotate through various assignments and educational experiences, with the dual aims of identifying their management potential and giving them breadth of experience (in, say, production and finance). The firm may then slot superior candidates onto a "fast track," a development program that prepares them more quickly for senior-level commands.

Other programs aim to fill specific positions, such as CEO. This usually involves succession planning. **Succession planning** refers to the process through which a company plans for and fills senior-level openings. For example, GE spent several years developing, testing, and watching potential replacements for CEO Jack Welch before finally choosing Jeffrey Immelt.

The typical succession planning process involves several steps: First, *anticipate management needs* based on factors like planned expansion. Next, *review your firm's management skills* inventory (data on things like educational and work experience, career preferences, and performance appraisals) to assess current talent. Then, *create replacement charts* that summarize potential candidates and each person's development needs. (As in the earlier example, in Figure 4-4, page 95, the development needs for a future division vice president might include job rotation, executive development programs—to provide training in strategic planning—and assignment for two weeks to the employer's in-house management development center.[113]) *Management development* can then begin, using methods like managerial on-the-job training, discussed below.

> **succession planning**
> A process through which senior-level openings are planned for and eventually filled.

The New Leadership Development Methods

There's an emphasis today on choosing management development methods that are more organizationally relevant and effective than they have been in the past; this is mostly a byproduct of global competitive pressures. There is, for instance, more emphasis on clarifying the development program's business purpose and desired outcomes; linking the program more clearly to the company's missions; involving the top management team; focusing on specific concrete competencies and knowledge, rather than just attitudes; and supplementing traditional development methods (such as lectures, discussion groups, and simulations) with more realistic methods like action learning projects.[114]

Managerial on-the-Job Training

On-the-job training is not just for nonmanagers. Managerial on-the-job training methods include job rotation, the coaching/understudy approach, and action learning.

Job Rotation Job rotation means moving management trainees from department to department to broaden their understanding of all parts of the business and to test their abilities. The trainee—often a recent college graduate—may spend several months in each department. The person may just be an observer in each department, but more commonly gets fully involved in its operations. The trainee thus learns the department's business by actually doing it, while discovering what jobs he or she prefers.

There are several ways to improve a rotation program's success.[115] It should be tailored to the needs, interests, and capabilities of the individual trainee, and not be a standard sequence that all trainees take. How fast the person is learning should determine the length of time the trainee stays in a job. And the manager to whom the person reports needs training to assess and mentor the person in a competent way.

> **job rotation**
> A management training technique that involves moving a trainee from department to department to broaden his or her experience and identify strong and weak points.

Coaching/Understudy Approach Here the trainee works directly with a senior manager or with the person he or she is to replace; the latter is responsible for the trainee's coaching. Normally, the understudy relieves the executive of certain responsibilities, giving the trainee a chance to learn the job.

action learning
A training technique by which management trainees are allowed to work full time analyzing and solving problems in other departments.

Action Learning Action learning programs give managers and others released time to work full time on projects, analyzing and solving problems in departments other than their own.[116] Trainees meet periodically in four- or five-person project groups to discuss their findings. Several trainees may work together as a project group, or compare notes and discuss each other's projects.[117]

Pacific Gas & Electric Company (PG&E) uses an approach it calls Action-Forum Process.[118] The idea of the Action-Forum Process is to focus on smaller issues that the employees themselves know the most about, and the program has reportedly been a success. In three years, PG&E hosted almost 80 Action-Forums and saved more than $270 million as a result of them.

The Action-Forum Process has three phases: (1) a "framework" phase of 6 to 8 weeks—this is basically an intense planning period during which the team defines an issue to work on; (2) the Action-Forum itself—2 to 3 days at PG&E's learning center discussing the issue and developing recommendations; and (3) accountability sessions, when the teams meet with the leadership group at 30, 60, and 90 days to review the status of their action plans and to make any necessary changes.

◆ **RESEARCH INSIGHT** Do women make better managers? Employees often talk about the need to "shatter the glass ceiling"—the transparent but often impermeable barrier many women still face in trying to move up to top management. The glass ceiling is not a real barrier, of course, but rather the net effect of various prejudices and lack of networking opportunities women face that make it difficult for them to move into the top jobs.

While it certainly makes sense to shatter the glass ceiling for equity's sake, research suggests there may be another reason to do so—the possibility that women may simply make better managers these days than men. The basic point is that with the trend toward high-involvement work teams, consensus decision making, and empowerment, the sorts of leadership styles that women already exhibit may be much more appropriate than men's.

This conclusion is based on the assumption that female managers' leadership styles are different than males', and based on this research, that appears to be the case. Specifically, women scored higher than men on such traditional measures of transformational leadership as encouraging followers to question their old ways of doing things or to break with the past, providing simplified emotional appeals to increase awareness and understanding of mutually desired goals, and providing learning opportunities. On the other hand, male managers were more likely to commend followers if they complied or to discipline them if they failed.

Why male and female managers differed on these leadership measures is not entirely clear. The researchers conclude that the more plausible explanation for the observed differences regarding transformational leadership ratings "may lie in the tendencies of women to be more nurturing, interested in others, and more socially sensitive." In any case, insofar as such transformational leadership behaviors may be increasingly appropriate in organizations today, it could be that female managers have an edge in exhibiting these behaviors.[119]

Off-the-Job Training and Development Techniques

There are also many off-the-job techniques for training and developing managers.

case study method
A development method in which the manager is presented with a written description of an organizational problem to diagnose and solve.

The Case Study Method As most everyone knows, the **case study method** presents a trainee with a written description of an organizational problem. The person then analyzes the case, diagnoses the problem, and presents his or her findings and solutions in a discussion with other trainees.[120]

Integrated case scenarios expand the case analysis concept by creating long-term, comprehensive case situations. For example, the FBI Academy recently created an integrated case scenario. It starts with "a concerned citizen's telephone call and ends 14 weeks later with a simulated trial. In between is the stuff of a genuine investigation, including a healthy sampling of what can go wrong in an actual criminal inquiry." To create such scenarios, scriptwriters (often employees in the firm's training group) write the scripts. The scripts include themes, background stories, detailed personnel histories, and role-playing instructions. In the case of the FBI, the scenarios are aimed at developing specific training skills, such as interviewing witnesses and analyzing crime scenes.[121]

Management Games With computerized or CD-ROM-based **management games**, trainees are divided into five- or six-person groups, each of which competes with the others in a simulated marketplace. Each group typically must decide, for example, (1) how much to spend on advertising, (2) how much to produce, (3) how much inventory to maintain, and (4) how many of which product to produce. Usually the game itself compresses a two- or three-year period into days, weeks, or months. As in the real world, each company team usually can't see what decisions (such as to boost advertising) the other firms have made, although these decisions do affect their own sales.[122]

> **management game**
> A development technique in which teams of managers compete by making computerized decisions regarding realistic but simulated situations.

Management games can be good development tools. People learn best by getting involved, and the games can be useful for gaining such involvement. They help trainees develop their problem-solving skills, as well as to focus attention on planning rather than just putting out fires. The groups also usually elect their own officers and organize themselves; they can thus develop leadership skills and foster cooperation and teamwork.

Outside Seminars Many companies and universities offer Web-based and traditional management development seminars and conferences. For example, the American Management Association provides thousands of courses in areas ranging from accounting and controls to assertiveness training, basic financial skills, information systems, project management, purchasing management, and total quality management.[123]

University-Related Programs Many universities provide executive education and continuing education programs in leadership, supervision, and the like. These can range from 1- to 4-day programs to executive development programs lasting one to four months. An increasing number of these are offered online.

The Advanced Management Program of the Graduate School of Business Administration at Harvard University is one more traditional example. A class in this program consists of experienced managers from around the world. It uses cases and lectures to provide top-level management talent with the latest management skills, and with practice analyzing complex organizational problems.

Video-linked classrooms are another option. For example, a video link between the School of Business and Public Administration at California State University, Sacramento, and a Hewlett-Packard facility in Roseville, California, allows HP employees to take courses at their facility.

Role Playing The aim of **role playing** is to create a realistic situation and then have the trainees assume the parts (or roles) of specific persons in that situation.

> **role playing**
> A training technique in which trainees act out parts in a realistic management situation.

Figure 7-2 presents a role from a famous role-playing exercise called the New Truck Dilemma. When combined with the general instructions and other roles for the exercise, role playing can trigger spirited discussions among the role player/trainees. The aim is to develop trainees' skills in areas like leadership and

▶ **FIGURE 7-2
Typical Role in a
Role-Playing
Exercise**

WALT MARSHALL—SUPERVISOR OF REPAIR CREW

You are the head of a crew of telephone maintenance workers, each of whom drives a small service truck to and from the various jobs. Every so often you get a new truck to exchange for an old one, and you have the problem of deciding which of your crew members you should give the new truck. Often there are hard feelings, since each seems to feel entitled to the new truck, so you have a tough time being fair. As a matter of fact, it usually turns out that whatever you decide is considered wrong by most of the crew. You now have to face the issue again because a new truck, a Chevrolet, has just been allocated to you for assignment.

In order to handle this problem you have decided to put the decision up to the crew. You will tell them about the new truck and will put the problem in terms of what would be the fairest way to assign the truck. Do not take a position yourself, because you want to do what they think is most fair.

Source: Normal R. F. Maier and Gertrude Casselman Verser, *Psychology in Industrial Organizations*, 5th ed., p. 190. Copyright 1982 by Houghton Mifflin Company. Used by permission of the publishers.

delegating. For example, a supervisor could experiment with both a considerate and an autocratic leadership style, whereas in the real world the person might not have the luxury of experimenting. It may also train someone to be more aware of and sensitive to others' feelings.[124]

behavior modeling
A training technique in which trainees are first shown good management techniques in a film, are asked to play roles in a simulated situation, and are then given feedback and praise by their supervisor.

Behavior Modeling **Behavior modeling** involves (1) showing trainees the right (or "model") way of doing something, (2) letting trainees practice that way, and then (3) giving feedback on the trainees' performance.[125] Firms have used it, for instance, to train first-line supervisors to handle common supervisor–employee interactions like giving recognition, disciplining, introducing change, and improving poor performance.

The basic behavior modeling procedure is as follows:

1. *Modeling.* First, trainees watch films or videotapes that show models behaving effectively in a problem situation. The tape might show a supervisor effectively disciplining a subordinate, if teaching how to discipline is the aim of the training program.

2. *Role playing.* Next, the trainees are given roles to play in a simulated situation; here they practice and rehearse the effective behaviors demonstrated by the models.

3. *Social reinforcement.* The trainer provides reinforcement in the form of praise and constructive feedback based on how the trainee performs in the role-playing situation.

4. *Transfer of training.* Finally, trainees are encouraged to apply their new skills when they are back on their jobs.

Behavioral modeling can be effective.[126] Participants in one study were 160 members of a navy construction battalion based in Gulfport, Mississippi, being trained to use new computer work stations. Three training techniques were used: conventional instruction (primarily, a lecture and slide show); computer assisted (students received a manual at the beginning of the session, as well as the diskette needed to work through exercises at their new work stations); and behavior modeling. Measures of learning and skill development were highest for behavior modeling, followed by computer-assisted training, and then conventional instruction.

in-house development center
A company-based method for exposing prospective managers to realistic exercises to develop improved management skills.

Corporate Universities and In-House Development Centers Many firms, particularly larger ones, establish **in-house development centers**. *Fortune* magazine calls General Electric's Crotonville, New York, Management Development Institute the Harvard of corporate America. Its catalog offers a wide array of management development courses. These range from entry-level programs in manufacturing and sales to a course for English majors called "Everything You Always Wanted to Know About Finance," as well as advanced management training.[127]

In-house development centers needn't produce all (or most) of their own training and development programs. In fact, employers are increasingly collaborating with academic institutions, training and development program providers, and Web-based educational portals to create packages of programs and materials appropriate to their employees' needs.[128]

For many firms, learning portals are becoming their virtual corporate universities. While firms such as GE have long had their own bricks-and-mortar corporate universities, learning portals let even smaller firms have corporate universities. Bain & Company, a management consulting firm, has such a Web-based virtual university for its employees. It provides a means not only for conveniently coordinating all the company's training efforts, but also for delivering Web-based modules that cover topics from strategic management to mentoring.[129]

Some firms retain "executive coaches." These are executive development experts who work one on one with managers for 6 to 12 months, helping them develop the skills and knowledge they need to exhibit more appropriate leader behaviors.[130]

Executive Development in Global Companies

Developing managers to run the firm's overseas operations can be a problem. There can be "an alarmingly high failure rate when executives are relocated overseas." Poor selection and preplacement development are often the causes.[131] Yet in a global economy, employers must develop managers for assignments abroad.

Many firms have successful international executive assignment programs. Based on their experiences, effective overseas assignment training programs should include the following:

1. Choose candidates whose educational backgrounds and experiences are appropriate for overseas assignments. The person who has a record of successfully adapting to foreign cultures (perhaps through overseas college studies and summer internships) is more likely to succeed as an international transferee.
2. Choose those whose personalities and family situations can withstand the cultural changes they will encounter in their new environments. When many of these executives fail, it is because their spouses or children were unhappy in their new setting.
3. Brief candidates fully on all relocation policies, including moving expenses, salary differentials, and benefits such as paid schooling for children.
4. Give executives and their families comprehensive training in their new culture and language. At Dow Chemical, for instance, the firm first explains its transfer policy. The relocating executive then gets a briefing package (compiled by the person's new office) containing information about local matters, such as shopping and housing. In addition, an adviser (often the spouse of a recently returned expatriate) visits the transferee and his or her spouse to explain emotional issues they are likely to face in the early stages of the move—such as feeling remote from relatives. The family gets the option of attending a two-week language and cultural orientation program offered by a school like Berlitz.
5. Provide all relocating executives with a mentor to monitor their overseas careers and to help them secure appropriate jobs with the company when they return. At Dow, for instance, this person is usually a high-level supervisor in the expatriate's functional area. The overseas employee keeps the mentor up to date on his or her activities. Similarly, the mentor monitors the expatriate's career while he or she is overseas.
6. Establish a repatriation program that helps returning executives and their families readjust to their professional and personal lives in their home country. At Dow, for instance, the person's mentor arranges the new job up to a year in advance of the expatriate's scheduled return.[132]

EVALUATING THE TRAINING EFFORT

After trainees complete their training (or perhaps at planned intervals during the program), the firm evaluates the program to see how well its goals have been met and whether this is the best method for reaching the goals.

Training and development can be effective.[133] For example, as one study concluded, "firms that establish workplace education programs and reorganize work report noticeable improvements in their workers' abilities and the quality of their products."[134] Another study found that businesses operating below their expected labor productivity levels had significant increases in productivity growth after implementing new employee training programs.[135] A recent evaluation of a total quality leadership program at the Department of the Navy led to the conclusion that training can produce fundamental changes in the way organizations perform.[136]

There are two basic issues to address when evaluating training programs. The first is the design of the evaluation study and, in particular, whether to use controlled experimentation. The second issue is: What should we measure?

controlled experimentation
Formal methods for testing the effectiveness of a training program, preferably with before-and-after tests and a control group.

Designing the Study

Controlled experimentation is the evaluation process of choice. A controlled experiment uses both a training group and a control group that receives no training. Data (for instance, on quantity of sales or quality of Web designs) are obtained both before and after the group is exposed to training and before and after a corresponding work period in the control group. This makes it possible to determine the extent to which any change in performance in the training group resulted from the training rather than from some organizationwide change like a raise in pay that would have affected employees in both groups equally.[137]

In terms of current practices, one survey found that less than half the companies responding attempted to obtain before-and-after measures from trainees; the number of organizations using control groups was negligible.[138] It's advisable to at least use an evaluation form like the one shown in Figure 7-3 to evaluate the training program.[139]

Training Effects to Measure

You can measure four basic categories of training outcomes:

1. *Reaction.* Evaluate trainees' reactions to the program. Did they like the program? Did they think it worthwhile?

2. *Learning.* Test the trainees to determine whether they learned the principles, skills, and facts they were supposed to learn.

3. *Behavior.* Ask whether the trainees' on-the-job behavior changed because of the training program. For example, are employees in the store's complaint department more courteous toward disgruntled customers?

4. *Results.* Probably most important, ask: What final results were achieved in terms of the training objectives previously set? Did the number of customer complaints about employees drop? Did the reject rate improve? Reactions, learning, and behavior are important. But if the program doesn't produce results, then it probably hasn't achieved its goals. If so, the problem may lie in the program. But remember that the results may be poor because the problem could not be solved by training in the first place.

▲ *One of the surest ways to evaluate a company's training programs is to look at the results. At Necco Co., savvy makers of old-fashioned candies, the opportunity to move the company's manufacturing plant to a bigger and more modern location presents a painful dilemma for management because the company's employees are so well trained in the operation of the machinery. As Domenic Antonellis, Necco's CEO, says, "I've got skilled labor here. With the kind of things we do, you can't build those skills into people quickly enough so that a move wouldn't hurt the product."*

▼ **FIGURE 7-3 A Sample Training Evaluation Form**

| OPM | *INSTRUCTOR HANDOUTS* | *United States Office of Personnel Management* |

TRAINING EVALUATION FORM

TITLE OF COURSE: "Work and Family Issues - A Module for Supervisors and Managers"
NAME OF INSTRUCTOR:

DATE OF TRAINING
Started:_____
Ended:_____

NAME (Optional):	**POSITION TITLE/GRADE:**

AGENCY:	**OFFICE PHONE:** (Optional)	**OFFICE ADDRESS:** (Optional)

Rate Your Knowledge and Skill Level (circle your rating)	**Overall, how would you rate this course?**
Before this course Low------------------------------------High 1 2 3 4 5	__ Excellent __Very Good __ Good
After this course Low------------------------------------High 1 2 3 4 5	__ Fair __ Poor

EVALUATION OF COURSE
(Check appropriate box)

ITEMS OF EVALUATION How did the course sharpen your knowledge or skills in:	Excellent	Very Good	Good	Fair	Poor	Not Applicable
1. What Work and Family Programs Are	°	°	°	°	°	°
2. Who Uses Work and Family Programs	°	°	°	°	°	°
3. How to Recognize/Solve Work/Family Issues	°	°	°	°	°	°
4. Helping You Take Practical Steps on the Job	°	°	°	°	°	°

RATING OF INSTRUCTOR

1. Presentation, organization, delivery	°	°	°	°	°	°
2. Knowledge and command of the subject	°	°	°	°	°	°
3. Use of audio-visuals or other training aids	°	°	°	°	°	°
4. Stimulation of an open exchange of ideas, participation & group interaction	°	°	°	°	°	°

STRONG POINTS OF THE COURSE
°
°
°

WEAK POINTS OF THE COURSE
°
°
°

ADDITIONAL DATA YOU WOULD LIKE TO HAVE COVERED IN COURSE
°
°
°

ADDITIONAL COMMENTS/OR RECOMMENDATIONS

Source: www.opm.gov/wrkfam/

While these four basic categories are understandable and widely used, there are several things to keep in mind. Perhaps most important, "reaction" measures (such as "How did you like the program?") generally aren't good substitutes for other training effects like learning, behavior, or results. Getting trainees' reactions—often the measurement of choice when firms evaluate training—may provide some insight into how they liked the program. However, it probably won't provide much insight into what they learned or how they'll behave once they're back on the job.[140]

Computerization is facilitating the evaluation process. For example, Bovis Land Lease in New York City offers its 625 employees numerous courses in construction and other subjects. The firm uses special learning management software to monitor which employees are taking which courses, and the extent to which employees are improving their skills.[141]

We invite you to visit **www.prenhall.com/dessler** on the Prentice Hall Web site for our online study guide, Internet exercises, current events, links to related Web sites, and more.

Summary

1. The training process consists of five steps: needs analysis, instructional design, validation, implementation, and evaluation.
2. Principles of learning that are useful for training include: Make the material meaningful (by providing a bird's-eye view and familiar examples, organizing the material, splitting it into meaningful chunks, and using familiar terms and visual aids); make provision for transfer of training; and try to motivate trainees.
3. Basic training techniques include on-the-job training, apprenticeship training, informal learning, job instruction training, lectures, programmed learning, audiovisual tools, simulated training, computer-based training, electronic performance support systems, and distance and Internet-based training.
4. On-the-job training is a common training technique. It might take the form of the understudy method, job rotation, or special assignments and committees. In any case, it should have four steps: preparing the learner, presenting the operation (or nature of the job), doing performance tryouts, and following up.
5. Special-purpose training techniques include literacy training, AIDS education, diversity training, customer service training, teamwork training, and lifelong learning.
6. Management development prepares employees for future jobs by imparting knowledge, changing attitudes, or increasing skills.
7. Managerial on-the-job training methods include job rotation, coaching, and action learning. Basic off-the-job techniques include case studies, management games, outside seminars, university-related programs, role playing, behavior modeling, and in-house development centers.
8. In gauging the effectiveness of a training program, there are four categories of outcomes companies can measure: reactions, learning, behavior, and results. In some cases where training seems to have failed, it may be because training was not the appropriate solution to the problem.

Tying It All Together

As we saw at the start of this chapter, recruiting, selecting, and hiring high-potential employees doesn't guarantee they'll perform effectively. People who don't know what to do or how to do it can't perform effectively even if they want to. As a result, after hiring employees and staffing the organization, your next job is to ensure that they are effectively oriented and trained. The current chapter therefore focused on training and development, including the training process, basic training methods, management development, and evaluating the training program. As in companies like Channel 4, it frequently happens today that training is only part of a broader organizational change initiative, one aimed at also changing the firm's organizational structure and culture, for instance. We'll therefore turn in the following chapter to HR's role in the important process of managing organizational renewal.

Discussion Questions

1. "A well-thought-out orientation program is essential for all new employees, whether they have experience or not." Explain why you agree or disagree with this statement.
2. You're the supervisor of a group of employees whose task is to assemble disk drives that go into computers. You find that quality is not what it should be and that many of your group's devices have to be brought back and reworked; your boss says that "You'd better start doing a better job of training your workers."
   a. What are some of the "staffing" factors that could be contributing to this problem?
   b. Explain how you would go about assessing whether it is in fact a training problem.
3. Explain how you would apply our principles of learning in developing a lecture, say, on orientation and training.
4. John Santos is an undergraduate business student majoring in accounting. He has just failed the first accounting course, Accounting 101, and is understandably upset. Explain how you would use performance analysis to identify what, if any, are John's training needs.
5. What are some typical on-the-job training techniques? What do you think are some of the main drawbacks of relying on informal on-the-job training for breaking new employees into their jobs?
6. One reason for implementing global training programs is the need to avoid business losses "due to cultural insensitivity." What sort of cultural insensitivity do you think is referred to, and how might that translate into lost business? What sort of training program would you recommend to avoid such cultural insensitivity?
7. Describe the pros and cons of five management development methods.
8. Do you think job rotation is a good method to use for developing management trainees? Why or why not?

Individual and Group Activities

1. Pick out some task with which you are familiar—mowing the lawn, making a salad, or tuning a car—and develop a job instruction training sheet for it.
2. Working individually or in groups, you are to develop a short programmed learning program on the subject "Guidelines for Giving a More Effective Lecture."
3. Working individually or in groups, use the phone or the Web to contact a provider of management development seminars such as the American Management Association. Obtain copies of its recent listings of seminar offerings. At what levels of managers are the seminar offerings aimed? What seem to be the most popular types of development programs? Why do you think that's the case?
4. Working individually or in groups, develop several concrete examples to illustrate how a professor teaching human resource management could use at least four of the techniques described in this chapter in teaching his or her HR course.
5. Working individually or in groups, develop an orientation program for high school graduates entering your university as freshmen.

EXPERIENTIAL EXERCISE

Purpose: The purpose of this exercise is to give you practice in developing a training program for the job of airline reservation clerk for a major airline.

Required Understanding: You should be fully acquainted with the material in this chapter and should read the following description of an airline reservation clerk's duties:

Customers contact our airline reservation clerks to obtain flight schedules, prices, and itineraries. The reservation clerks look up the requested information on our airline's online flight schedule systems, which are updated continuously. The reservation clerk must deal courteously and expeditiously with the customer, and be able to quickly find alternative flight arrangements in order to provide the customer with the itinerary that fits his or her needs. Alternative flights and prices must be found quickly, so that the customer is not kept waiting, and so that our reservations operations group maintains its efficiency standards. It is often necessary to look under various routings, since there may be a dozen or more alternative routes between the customer's starting point and destination.

You may assume that we just hired 30 new clerks, and that you must create a 3-day training program.

How to Set Up the Exercise/Instructions: Divide the class into teams of 5 or 6 students.

Airline reservation clerks obviously need numerous skills to perform their jobs. JetBlue Airline has asked you to quickly develop the outline of a training program for its new reservation clerks. You may want to start by listing the job's main duties. In any case, please produce the requested outline, making sure to be very specific about what you want to teach the new clerks, and what methods and aids you suggest using to train them.

APPLICATION CASE *Reinventing the Wheel at Apex Door Company*

Jim Delaney, president of Apex Door, has a problem. No matter how often he tells his employees how to do their jobs, they invariably "decide to do it their way," as he puts it, and arguments ensue between Jim, the employee, and the employee's supervisor. One example is the door-design department, where the designers are expected to work with the architects to design doors that meet the specifications. While it's not "rocket science," as Jim puts it, the designers invariably make mistakes—such as designing in too much steel, a problem that can cost Apex tens of thousands of wasted dollars, once you consider the number of doors in, say, a 30-story office tower.

The order processing department is another example. Jim has a very specific and detailed way he wants the order written up, but most of the order clerks don't understand how to actually use the multipage order form. They simply improvise when it comes to a detailed question such as whether to classify the customer as "industrial" or "commercial."

The current training process is as follows. None of the jobs has a training manual per se, although several have somewhat out-of-date job descriptions. The training for new people is all on the job. Usually the person leaving the company trains the new person during the one- or two-week overlap period, but if there's no overlap, the new person is trained as well as possible by other employees who have filled in occasionally on the job in the past. The training is basically the same throughout the company—for machinists, secretaries, assemblers, and accounting clerks, for example.

Questions
1. What do you think of Apex's training process? Could it help to explain why employees "do things their way" and if so, how?
2. What role do job descriptions play in training?
3. Explain in detail what you would do to improve the training process at Apex. Make sure to provide specific suggestions, please.

CONTINUING CASE: LearnInMotion.com *The New Training Program*

"I just don't understand it," said Mel. "No one here seems to follow instructions, and no matter how many times I've told them how to do things they seem to do them their own way." At present, LearnInMotion.com has no formal orientation or training policies or procedures. Jennifer believes that is one reason why employees generally ignore the standards that she and Mel would like employees to adhere to.

Several examples illustrate this. One of the jobs of the Web designer (her name is Maureen) is to take customers' copy for banner ads and adapt it for placement on LearnInMotion.com. She has been told several times not to tinker in any way with a customer's logo: Most companies put considerable thought and resources into logo design, and, as Mel has said, "whether or not Maureen thinks the logo is perfect, it's the customer's logo, and she's to leave it as it is." Yet just a week ago, they almost lost a big customer when Maureen, to "clarify" the customer's logo, modified its design before posting it on LearnInMotion.

That is just the tip of the iceberg. As far as Jennifer and Mel are concerned, it is the sales effort that is completely out of control. For one thing, even after several months on the job, it still seems as if the salespeople don't know what they're talking about. For example, LearnInMotion has several co-brand arrangements with Web sites like Yahoo!. This means if they are interested in ordering educational courses or CDs, other sites' users can easily click through to LearnInMotion. Jennifer has noticed that during conversations with customers, the two salespeople often have no idea of which sites co-brand with LearnInMotion, or how to get to the LearnInMotion site from the partner Web site. The salespeople also need to know a lot more about the products themselves. For example, one salesperson was trying to sell someone who produces programs on managing call centers on the idea of listing its products under LearnInMotion's "communications" community. In fact, the "communications" community is for courses on topics like interpersonal communications and how to be a better listener; it has nothing to do with managing the sorts of call centers that, for instance, airlines use for handling customer inquiries. As another example, the Web surfer is supposed to get a specific e-mail address with a specific person's name for the salespeople to use; instead he often just comes back with an "information" e-mail address off a Web site. The list goes on and on.

Jennifer feels the company has had other problems because of the lack of adequate employee training and orientation. For example, a question came up recently when employees found they weren't paid for the July 4 holiday:

They assumed they'd be paid, but they were not. Similarly, when a salesperson left after barely a month on the job, there was considerable debate about whether the person should receive severance pay and accumulated vacation pay. Other matters to cover during an orientation, says Jennifer, include: company policy regarding lateness and absences; health and hospitalization benefits (there are none, other than workers' compensation); and matters like maintaining a safe and healthy workplace, personal appearance and cleanliness, personal telephone calls and e-mail, substance abuse, and eating or smoking on the job.

Jennifer believes that implementing orientation and training programs would help ensure that employees know how to do their jobs. She and Mel further believe that it is only when employees understand the right way to do their jobs that there is any hope those jobs will in fact be carried out in the way the owners want them to be. Now, they want you, their management consultants, to help them. Here's what they want you to do for them.

Questions and Assignments

1. Specifically, what should we cover in our new employee orientation program, and how should we convey this information?

2. In the HR course Jennifer took, the book suggested using a task analysis record form to identify tasks performed by an employee. Should we use a form like this for the salespeople? If so, what, roughly speaking, should the completed, filled-in formal look like?

3. Which specific training techniques should we use to train our salespeople, Web designer, and Web surfer, and why?

Managing Strategic Organizational Renewal

After studying this chapter, you should be able to:

- Explain and illustrate the steps in the change process.
- Reduce employee resistance to change.
- Describe the basic process for managing organizational change and development.
- Give specific examples of HR's role in total quality management programs.
- Show how companies use HR methods to create team-based organizations.
- Discuss the critical role of HR in business process reengineering.
- More effectively implement an organizational change.

STRATEGIC OVERVIEW Wisconsin-based Signicast Corporation had to make a decision. The firm produces metal parts from a casting process: Workers use wax molds to create ceramic molds, which they in turn use to cast the metal parts. To compete strategically, the firm knew it had to reinvent itself, by building a new, highly automated plant about 25 miles away. But it discovered that "in the real world, new automation technology requires a new kind of employee." How should Signicast select, train, and organize the employees so the new plant would be a success?[1]

The previous chapter focused on the training and management development methods managers use to give employees the knowledge and skills they need to do their jobs. However, training and development are often just part of a broader managerial effort to renew or reinvent the firm so it can meet a strategic challenge. We therefore now turn to Managing Strategic Organizational Renewal, and to a broader view of how all the HR functions—including screening, training, appraising, and compensating workers—enable companies to tackle the tough new world of global competition. The main purpose of this chapter is to provide you with the concepts and skills you need to more successfully implement organizational changes. We'll discuss organizational change, and how HR methods support quality, team-building, and reengineering programs. The following chapter, Appraising and Managing Performance, focuses more closely on how managers appraise the performance of their trained and developed employees.

HR'S ROLE IN ORGANIZATIONAL CHANGE

To some, the idea that HR should be a "strategic partner" may seem a little theoretical, but not to firms like Signicast. Signicast has to reinvent itself, and it needs to apply advanced HR methods to do so.

Signicast is not alone. For example, Microsoft recently reorganized the whole company to fit its new ".Net" strategy, and—just after AOL and Time Warner merged—AOL's entire CNN operation was revamped. We'll see in this chapter that as at Signicast, HR plays a crucial role in such efforts.[2]

This chapter focuses on the process and techniques of organizational change and renewal, and on HR's role in that process. We'll start with the overall process of organizational change, and then cover HR's role in four specific renewal efforts: total quality programs; team-based organizations; reengineering; and flexible work schedules.

MANAGING ORGANIZATIONAL CHANGE AND DEVELOPMENT

Change—and helping firms deal with it—is a major issue for HR. Professor Edward Lawler recently conducted an extensive survey of HR practices and concluded that ". . . focusing on strategy, organizational development, and organizational change is a high payoff activity for the HR organization."[3] Another expert says that "as more and more HR professionals are stepping into the role of change leader in organizations, [an understanding of] change dynamics has become increasingly important."[4] Let's look at the organizational change process.

What to Change

You've just taken over as CEO of a troubled company, and you know you have to make changes. What are your options—what is it about the company that you can change? In practice, you can change several things, including *strategy, culture, structure, technologies,* and the *attitudes and skills* of the people. But to do so, as we'll see, you'll need a firm command of HR methods. Some examples follow.

Strategic Change Organizational renewal often starts with a change in the firm's strategy, mission, and vision—with **strategic change**. For example, faced with intense competition from Amazon.com, Barnes & Noble managers knew, several years ago, that they had to expand onto the Internet. This new strategy, in turn, triggered vast changes in the technologies the firm used, and in its organizational structure and culture.

strategic change
A change in a company's strategy, mission, and vision.

Cultural Change For one thing, going from "bricks" to "clicks" means **cultural change**, adopting new corporate values—new notions of what employees view as right and wrong, and what they should or shouldn't do. Moving fast, embracing technology, and keeping lines of communication open were a few of the new values Barnes & Noble management needed employees to adopt.

cultural change
A change in a company's shared values and aims.

But how to get employees to embrace new values and adopt a new culture? One expert advocates five main ways to change a company's culture, each of which requires HR's support and advice:

1. *Make it clear* to your employees what you pay attention to, measure, and control. For example (as in Barnes & Nobles' case), use the appraisal system to direct your employees' attention toward learning more about technology or making faster decisions.
2. *React appropriately* to critical incidents and organizational crises. For example, if you want to emphasize the value that "we have to keep communications lines open," don't react to declining profits by trying to keep that fact a secret.

3. *Deliberately role-model*, teach, and coach the values you want to emphasize. For example, Wal-Mart founder Sam Walton embodied the values of "hard work, honesty, neighborliness, and thrift" that he wanted Wal-Mart employees to have. So although he was one of the richest men in the world, he drove a pickup truck, a preference he explained by saying, "If I drove a Rolls-Royce, what would I do with my dog?"

4. *Communicate your priorities* by the way you allocate rewards and status. Leaders communicate priorities and values by how they award pay raises and promotions. For example, top management at General Foods decided several years ago to reorient its strategy from cost minimization to diversification and sales growth. It then had the HR department revise the pay plan to link bonuses to sales volume (rather than just increased earnings, as in the past).

5. *Make your HR procedures and criteria consistent* with the values you hold. For example, when Ford CEO Jacques Nasser decided to stress competitiveness in 2001, he ordered a change in the firm's management appraisal process: Those in the bottom 10% were henceforth subject to dismissal. (His plan met with accusations of age discrimination, and was scrapped—along with Mr. Nasser.)[5]

MetLife Insurance is a case in point. Before going public several years ago, it hired Lisa Weber, as executive vice president of human resources. As she said, "We needed to shed our low-risk, bureaucratic, hierarchical culture. An entitlement kind of mentality." She and her team took several steps. For instance, after discovering that about 86% of the firm's leadership was traditionally rated as "very effective" or "exceptional," she instituted a new appraisal system that measures how each person compares to others in the company on the same level, on a 1–5 scale. Top performers now get special treatment: The company works with them to plan their development and help them set and meet new goals. High performers now receive about 65% more in bonus than those rated lower. And, the firm is conducting intense training in management skills.[6]

Structural Change   Reorganizing—in other words, redesigning the company's departmental structure, coordination, span of control, reporting relationships, tasks, or decision-making procedures—is a relatively quick and direct way to change an organization. For its new strategy, Barnes & Noble needed a new division for its Internet initiative, complete with new reporting relationships to and from the "bricks" division. And it needed this division almost overnight. It also needed to redesign specific employees' and teams' jobs and authority.

structural change
The reorganizing or redesigning of an organization's departmentalization, coordination, span of control, reporting relationships, or decision-making process.

    Structural changes like these require HR. For example, downsizings require performance reviews to decide who stays and who goes, and an outplacement effort. Reorganizing requires job analysis, personnel planning, and selection. Flattening the organization may mean consolidating pay levels into fewer, broader bands.

Changes in People, Attitudes, and Skills   And all this means that sometimes the employees themselves must change.[7] Here, for example, training and development can provide new or current employees with the skills they need to perform their jobs. Similarly, HR-based **organizational development interventions** (discussed later in this chapter) can modify employees' attitudes, values, and behavior.

organizational development interventions
HR-based techniques aimed at changing employees' attitudes, values, and behavior.

Technological Change   Organizational renewal today often entails embracing or modifying technology. For Barnes & Noble (and many other firms), this means transferring a host of activities to the Internet. For other firms, it means reengineering work processes, or automating production processes. In any case, managers today realize that **technological change** is futile without employee support. After studying a huge new computerized paper production process at Mead Corporation's Escanaba, Michigan, plant, here's how one expert put it:

> *The flexibility of the plant depended much more on people than on any technical factor. Although high levels of computer integration can provide critically needed advantages in quality and cost effectiveness, operational flexibility is determined primarily by a plant's operators and the extent to which managers cultivate, measure, and communicate with them.*[8]

And that means, as we'll see, applying HR methods like building teamwork, drafting new job descriptions, boosting skill and knowledge levels, and installing more flexible work arrangements.

technological change
Modifications to the work methods an organization uses to accomplish its tasks.

Leading Change: Lewin's Process

Actually implementing and leading an organizational change can be tricky, even for CEOs with lots of clout. The change may require the cooperation of dozens or even hundreds of managers and supervisors; resistance may be considerable; and you may have to accomplish the change while the firm continues to serve its customer base.

Resistance can be a problem. Psychologist Kurt Lewin formulated the classic explanation of how to implement a change in the face of resistance. To Lewin, all behavior in organizations was a product of two kinds of forces—those striving to maintain the status quo and those pushing for change. Implementing change thus meant either weakening the status quo forces or building up the forces for change. Lewin's process consisted of these three steps:

1. *Unfreezing.* Unfreezing means reducing the forces that are striving to maintain the status quo, usually by presenting a provocative problem or event to get people to recognize the need for change and to search for new solutions.

2. *Moving.* Moving means developing new behaviors, values, and attitudes, sometimes through structural changes and sometimes through the sorts of HR-based organizational change and development techniques explained later in this chapter. The aim is to alter people's behavior.

3. *Refreezing.* Lewin assumed that organizations tend to revert to their former ways of doing things unless you reinforce the changes. How do you do this? By "refreezing" the organization into its new equilibrium. Specifically, Lewin advocated instituting new systems and procedures (such as compensation plans and appraisal processes) to support and maintain the changes.

A 10-Step Change Process

In practice, accomplishing such a change involves a process like the following:[9]

1. Establish a sense of urgency. Once they become aware of the need to change, most leaders start by creating a sense of urgency. For example, when Charles Schwab found it was running into resistance with its "bricks to clicks" Internet strategy, CEO David Pottruck got about 100 of the firm's senior managers together by San Francisco's Golden Gate Bridge. Each manager got a jacket that said CROSSING THE CHASM, and then together they crossed the bridge. Pottruck calls this the start of reinventing his company.

2. Mobilize commitment through joint diagnosis of problems. Having established a sense of urgency, leaders then create one or more task forces to diagnose the problems facing the company. Such teams can produce a shared understanding of what they can and must improve, and thereby mobilize the commitment of those who must actually implement the change.

3. Create a guiding coalition. Major transformations—such as Steve Case achieved in 2000–2001 by merging his AOL with Time Warner—are sometimes associated with just one or two highly visible leaders. But no one can really implement such changes alone. Most companies create a guiding coalition of influential people, who work together as a team to act as missionaries and implementers.

4. Develop a shared vision. Organizational renewal also requires a new leadership vision, "a general statement of the organization's intended direction that evokes emotional feelings in organization members." For example, when Barry Gibbons became CEO of Spec's Music, its employees, owners, and bankers—all its stakeholders—required a vision of a renewed Spec's around which they could rally. Gibbons's vision of a leaner Spec's offering a diversified blend of concerts and retail music helped provide this sense of direction.

5. Communicate the vision. Change expert John Kotter says, "the real power of a vision is unleashed only when most of those involved in an enterprise or activity have a common understanding of its goals and directions."[10] To do this, you have to communicate the vision. The key elements in doing so include:[11]

- Keep it simple. Eliminate all jargon and wasted words. For example: "We are going to become faster than anyone else in our industry at satisfying customer needs."
- Use multiple forums. Try to use every channel possible—big meetings and small, memos and newspapers, formal and informal interaction—to spread the word.
- Use repetition. Ideas sink in deeply only after employees have heard them many times.
- Lead by example. "Walk your talk"—make sure your behaviors and decisions are consistent with the vision you espouse.

6. Help employees to make the change. It's futile to communicate your vision and to have employees want to make it a reality, if they haven't the wherewithal to do so. Perhaps a lack of skills stands in the way; or policies, procedures, and the organization chart make it difficult to act; or some bosses may actually discourage employees from acting. At Allied Signal, Lawrence Bossidy put every one of his 80,000 people through quality training. He also created geographic "councils" (for instance, for Asia) so Allied employees in those areas could get together, share market intelligence, and compare notes.[12]

7. Generate short-term wins. Changes such as redesigning a firm's control system, or launching a new division, may take time, but the teams working on them need some intermediate reinforcement.[13] For example, one company team set its sights on producing one successful new product about 20 months after the start of the organizational change effort.[14] They selected the product in part because they knew they could meet this goal.

8. Consolidate gains and produce more change. Such short-term wins can generate the credibility to move ahead—to change all the systems, structures, and policies that don't fit well with the company's new vision. Leaders continue to produce more change by hiring and promoting new people; by identifying selected employees to champion the continuing change; and by providing additional opportunities for short-term wins by employees.[15]

9. Anchor the new ways of doing things in the company's culture. We've seen that organizational changes usually require a corresponding change in culture and values. A "team-based, quality-oriented, adaptable organization" is not going to happen if the values employees share still emphasize selfishness, mediocrity, and bureaucratic behavior. Leaders thus take steps to role-model and communicate the new values.

10. Monitor progress and adjust the vision as required. Finally, monitor how you're doing. One firm appointed an oversight team to monitor the progress and challenges faced by its new self-managing team-based organization.

An Example Here's how one firm implemented this process within its HR group. Responding to a change in the parent firm's strategy, the HR department change process at Philadelphia-based PECO Energy began with a *visioning event.* The purpose of this three-day meeting was to develop the vision for HR and to determine the principles that should guide activities over the next five months. It was critical at the outset to make sure all key stakeholders agreed on the direction HR needed to take. After agreeing on the vision, participants chose five "critical" processes (such as employee selection) to be changed to support the group's new vision.

Next, the core HR change team held "town hall" meetings with all HR employees. Team members explained the new vision, mission, and principles, and received feedback they could incorporate into their second session. They held that second session, a *process design/redesign event,* one month later. The five critical HR processes identified at the first session were revised and reinvented. This

▲ *Lawrence Bossidy (on right) succeeded in changing the values and culture at Allied Signal by organizing meetings with employees, instituting new training programs, and changing compensation plans.*

included revising the firm's selection and placement, employee planning, and job pricing processes. Consultants from other companies offered ideas, and PECO's own computer experts provided technological recommendations for implementing the new processes.

Once these five basic processes were redesigned, management had to rethink the distribution of HR's jobs. During a third session, the *organizational design event,* PECO employees focused on deciding who would be responsible for those processes in the future. As a result, much of HR's routine work was transferred to line employees and managers.

At the final event, *implementation,* the HR team reviewed the implementation plan, confirmed the steps required to make the change, and ensured the continued commitment of the firm's managers to the change. This session also introduced PECO's new HR leadership team, and laid plans to sustain the effort over the next four to six months.[16]

Using Organizational Development

There are many ways to identify the need for an organizational change, and to implement the change itself. One of the most widely used is organizational development, or OD for short. **Organizational development (OD)** is a special approach to organizational change in which the employees themselves formulate the change that's required and implement it, often with the assistance of a trained consultant. Particularly in large companies, the OD process (including hiring of facilitators) is almost always handled through HR. As an approach to changing organizations, OD has several distinguishing characteristics:

organizational development (OD)
A method aimed at changing the attitudes, values, and beliefs of employees so that employees can improve the organization.

1. It usually involves *action research,* which means collecting data about a group, department, or organization and then feeding the information back to the employees so they can analyze it and develop hypotheses about what the problems in the unit might be.

2. It applies behavioral science knowledge to improve the organization's effectiveness.

3. It changes the attitudes, values, and beliefs of employees so that the employees themselves can identify and implement the technical, procedural, structural, or other changes needed to improve the company's functioning.

4. It changes the organization in a particular direction—toward improved problem solving, responsiveness, quality of work, and effectiveness.[17]

The number and variety of OD applications (also called OD interventions or techniques) have increased substantially over the past few years. OD got its start with what experts called *human process interventions*. The basic aim of such activities was to help employees develop a better understanding of their own and others' behaviors, and thereby improve that behavior for the benefit of firm.

Today, as you can see in Table 8-1, many more applications are available. OD practitioners have become increasingly involved not just in changing behaviors, but also in directly altering the firm's structure, practices, strategy, and culture.

There are four basic types of OD applications: human process, technostructural, human resource management, and strategic applications. Action research—getting the employees themselves to collect the required data and to design and implement the solutions—is the basis of all four.

▶ **TABLE 8-1**
Examples of OD Interventions and the Organizational Levels They Affect

Interventions	Primary Organizational Level Affected		
	Individual	Group	Organization
Human Process			
T-groups	X	X	
Process consultation		X	
Third-party intervention	X	X	
Team building		X	
Organizational confrontation meeting		X	X
Intergroup relations		X	X
Technostructural			
Formal structural change			X
Differentiation and integration			X
Cooperative union–management projects	X	X	X
Quality circles	X	X	
Total quality management		X	X
Work design	X	X	
Human Resource Management			
Goal setting	X	X	
Performance appraisal	X	X	
Reward systems	X	X	X
Career planning and development	X		
Managing workforce diversity	X		
Employee wellness	X		
Strategic			
Integrated strategic management			X
Culture change			X
Strategic change			X
Self-designing organizations		X	X

Human Process Applications Human process OD techniques generally aim first at improving human relations skills. The goal is to give employees the insight and skills required to analyze their own and others' behavior more effectively, so they can then solve interpersonal and intergroup problems. **Sensitivity training** is perhaps the most widely used technique in this category.

Sensitivity, laboratory, or t-group training (the *t* is for "training") was one of the earliest OD techniques. Its use has diminished a great deal since its heyday 25 years ago, but you'll still find it today. Sensitivity training's basic aim is to increase the participant's insight into his or her own behavior and the behavior of others by encouraging an open expression of feelings in the trainer-guided t-group. Typically, 10 to 15 people meet, usually away from the job, with no specific agenda. Instead, the focus is on the feelings and emotions of the members in the group. The facilitator encourages participants to portray themselves as they are in the group rather than in terms of past behaviors or future problems. The t-group's success depends on the feedback each person gets from the others, and on the participants' willingness to be candid about how they perceive each other's behavior. The process requires a climate of "psychological safety," so participants feel safe enough to reveal themselves, to expose their feelings, to drop their defenses, and to try out new ways of interacting.[18]

It's not surprising that t-group training is a controversial technique. The personal nature of such training suggests that participation should be voluntary. Some view it as unethical because you can't really consider participation "suggested" by one's superior as strictly voluntary.[19] Others argue that it can actually be a dangerous exercise if led by an inadequately prepared trainer.

OD's distinctive emphasis on action research is quite evident in **team building**, which refers to a specific process for improving team effectiveness. This is another example of a human process OD application.

According to experts French and Bell, the typical team-building meeting begins with the consultant interviewing each of the group members and the leader before the meeting.[20] They are all asked what their problems are, how they think the group functions, and what obstacles are keeping the group from performing better. The consultant then categorizes the interview data into themes (such as "inadequate communications") and presents the themes to the group at the start of the meeting. The group ranks the themes in terms of importance, and the most important ones become the agenda for the meeting. The group then explores and discusses the issues, examines the underlying causes of the problems, and begins devising solutions.

Other human process interventions aim to bring about intergroup or organizationwide changes. Organizational **confrontation meetings** can help clarify and bring misconceptions and problems about intergroup relationships into the open so that they can be resolved. The basic approach here is that the participants themselves provide the input (such as "here's how you make me feel") for the meeting. They then meet and thrash out misperceptions in an effort to reduce tensions.

Survey research, another human process OD technique, requires that employees throughout the organization fill out attitude surveys. The facilitator then uses that data as a basis for problem analysis and action planning. In general, such surveys are a convenient way to unfreeze a company's management and employees, by providing a comparative, graphic illustration of the fact that the organization does have problems to solve.[21] Employee attitude surveys' continuing popularity reflects the fact that:

> There is validity in employee reports of their experiences and these reports can be very useful as diagnoses of the degree to which a new strategy is being implemented and the degree to which policies and practices are related to the achievement of strategic goals like customer satisfaction and customer attention.[22]

sensitivity training
A method for increasing employees' insights into their own behavior by candid discussions in groups led by special trainers.

team building
Improving the effectiveness of teams such as corporate officers and division directors through use of consultants, interviews, and team-building meetings.

confrontation meetings
A method for clarifying and bringing into the open intergroup misconceptions and problems so that they can be resolved.

survey research
A method that involves surveying employees' attitudes and providing feedback to the work groups as a basis for problem analysis and action planning.

Technostructural Interventions OD practitioners are also increasingly involved in changing firms' structures, methods, and job designs using an assortment of technostructural interventions. These interventions (as well as the human resource management and strategic interventions described in the following sections) generally focus directly on improving productivity and efficiency.

For example, in a *formal structural change* program, the employees collect data on the company's existing organizational structure; they then jointly redesign and implement a new one.

Human Resource Management Applications OD practitioners increasingly use action research to enable employees to analyze and change their firm's personnel practices. Targets of change here might include the performance appraisal and reward systems, as well as installing diversity programs.

Strategic Applications Strategic interventions are organizationwide OD programs aimed at achieving a fit among a firm's strategy, structure, culture, and external environment.

Integrated strategic management is one example of how to use OD to create or change a strategy. It consists of four steps: Managers and employees analyze current strategy and organizational design, choose a desired strategy and organizational design, and design a strategic change plan—"an action plan for moving the organization from its current strategy and organizational design to the desired future strategy and design."[23] Finally, implement the strategic change plan, and measure and review the results to ensure that they are proceeding as planned.[24]

INSTITUTING TOTAL QUALITY MANAGEMENT PROGRAMS

When you buy a new Ford, call Lands' End, or install your Dell computer, the one thing you expect is high-quality products or service. Thanks to global competition, the days when cars came with multiple defects and stores gave indifferent service are generally gone. Firms have had to boost their quality to survive. Most have instituted quality management programs to do so.

There are several remarkable things about these quality programs. One is that by boosting quality, productivity has risen as well, as firms stripped quality-draining waste from processes. Also remarkable are the changes these programs have meant to employee–management relations: Firms discovered that no quality management program can succeed without the intelligent application of HR methods. Let's look more closely at this.

What Is Quality?

quality
The totality of features and characteristics of a product or service that bear on its ability to satisfy given needs.

Quality is the totality of features and characteristics of a product or service that bears on its ability to satisfy given needs. In other words, "quality measures how well a product or service meets customer needs."[25] The basic consideration is thus always the extent to which the product or service meets the customer's expectations.

ISO 9000
The written standards for quality management and assurance of the International Organization for Standardization.

Quality standards today are international. Doing business in Europe often means complying with **ISO 9000**, the quality standards of the European Community (EC). If required to do so by a customer, the vendor would have to prove that its manuals, procedures, and job instructions all comply with the ISO 9000 standards.

Total Quality Management Programs

Total quality management (TQM) programs are organizationwide programs aimed at maximizing quality and customer satisfaction through continuous improvements.[26] In the United States, this approach often goes by the name *continuous improvement, zero defects*, or *six sigma* (a reference to the statistical unlikelihood of having a defect); in Japan it's known as *Kaizen*.[27] Many of these programs are based on 14 quality principles laid down by W. E. Deming, such as "institute extensive training on the job."

To recognize quality efforts, the U.S. Department of Commerce created the Malcolm Baldrige Award, named after a former secretary of commerce. Most U.S. manufacturing firms, service firms, and small businesses are eligible to apply for the Baldrige. Winners have included Motorola, FedEx, and Xerox.

> **total quality management (TQM)**
> A type of program aimed at maximizing customer satisfaction through continuous improvements.

HR's Role in Quality Management

Quality programs rely so heavily on well-trained, committed employees that it's hard to separate the two. For example, in one study of 66 small to medium-sized manufacturing firms, a total quality management program was most effective when supported by significant training and a group-based incentive plan.[28] The quality program at Lands' End provides another illustration.

◆ **HIGH-PERFORMANCE INSIGHT** A friendly phone staff is a key to customer service at Lands' End, and that friendliness doesn't just happen.[29] It's the end result of extensive screening and training. The number one selection trait for a sales representative is that he or she be friendly—and love to talk. Lands' End explicitly tells its customer sales representatives that they are there not to sell, but to provide service. Director of Customer Service Joan Conlin explains that "our customer sales representatives are there to help customers accomplish what they called for—to meet a customer's need; they are not there to market other products. . . . their job is to listen and respond to customer needs; it's service, not sales."

New hires at Lands' End get 80 hours of training on all the company's basic product lines and core items, even fabrics, so they have a basic understanding of what Lands' End sells. They get training in politeness and how to act when assisting customers. New employees also get training on the computer system and on a simulated phone system that replicates the actual one. As a result of this training, most new representatives feel comfortable when they start taking real orders. Nevertheless, a trainer sits behind them for a few days to answer questions. Even when the formal training ends, reps can use an assist button to summon a supervisor. They can also call on specialty shoppers if a customer needs special assistance. Lands' End evaluates service representatives on a continuing basis. Supervisors listen to at least four calls for each representative each month. They fill out monitoring forms for these calls and provide feedback to the representative. Monitoring is done at random: The representative does not know when it is happening.

The speed with which Lands' End answers is one indicator of customer service quality. The goal is to answer 90% of calls within 20 seconds. The average answering speed is five seconds—maybe two rings—and most callers don't even hear a ring. An automatic call distribution system in each of its phone centers allows Lands' End to monitor each center and shift calls to any of the centers when the need arises. Supervisors also monitor call duration (talk time). The company wants to make sure that operators aren't too chatty—something customers don't like either.

Lands' End takes customer comments seriously. Positive and negative phone comments to sales representatives are logged and, on a monthly basis, looked at by every department in the company. The bottom line is that service quality is the heart of the Lands' End strategy, and the firm's quality reflects its well-conceived and executed HR selection, training, and evaluation program.

HR and Six Sigma Achieving six-sigma quality can be an intense experience. The six-sigma standard aims for only 3.4 defects per million processes, whereas 66,000 defects per million is where most firms operate now. But the rewards of the six-sigma waste identification and process improvement techniques can be enormous. For example, Motorola reportedly saved $15 billion during 11 years of six sigma.

HR methods play a central role in six-sigma programs. For one thing, training is crucial. A common practice is to start with top managers and train them to be "six-sigma black belts." Then the firm trains its other employees. In addition, "performance needs to be measured and reviewed against goals, achievement recognized and celebrated, and rewards and compensation linked to employee participation and progress."[30] These are all HR processes.

HR and Baldrige Awards HR also plays a central role in winning Baldrige Awards. A board of quality experts evaluates all applicants. As Figure 8-1 shows, they examine seven basic areas. These include *senior executive leadership* (top management's symbolic commitment to quality) and *information and analysis* (an adequate system for collecting statistical data on matters such as product or service quality).

Evaluating the applicant's HR systems plays an important role in this process. Examiners focus on the extent to which the firm uses HR and related techniques (such as employee empowerment, training, and career development) to tap each employee's potential. For example, judges expect applicant companies to train employees to use problem-solving and group decision-making skills.

▶ **FIGURE 8-1**
Baldrige Award Criteria Framework

Senior executive leadership is the "driver" of total quality management, with each of the other six elements, or Baldrige Categories, playing a crucial role.

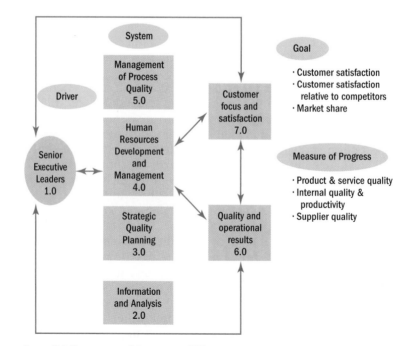

Source: U.S. Department of Commerce, 1992.

HR and ISO 9000 ISO 9000 refers to the International Organization for Standardization's basic written standards for quality management and assurance.[31] Certification usually requires a five-step process: ISO assessment (reviewing the company's quality systems and procedures); quality assurance and policy manual preparation (compiling the specific quality-oriented techniques and policies to be followed); training of employees in ISO 9000; documentation of work instructions (documenting each new work procedure, for instance); and registration audit (having the quality system reviewed by a special "registrar" who audits the company's quality efforts).

Employee training and related HR activities (such as selection) play an important role in gaining ISO 9000 certification. In one instance:

> *Perhaps the most serious problem was that even though a number of people were doing excellent work, they were simply unaware of the physical procedures they were following. Informal on-the-job training that was prevalent in the division was the culprit.*[32]

Training for ISO 9000 would typically cover, for instance, the quality vocabulary associated with ISO 9000, and the requirements regarding record keeping and measurements embedded in each ISO 9000 section.[33]

CREATING TEAM-BASED ORGANIZATIONS

Companies today are also increasingly team based. Here, the units of work—be they cars, textbooks, or mortgage approvals—are organized not around departments or functional areas, but around teams. One study found that 82% of U.S. firms have organized at least some of their work around teams.[34] Saturn, Toyota, Corning, and others are increasingly organizing the work around small self-contained teams, which are variously labeled self-managed teams, high-performance teams, or autonomous work groups.[35]

HR managers help teams in many ways. They work with them in developing new policies and procedures in areas like performance appraisals and disciplining team members, for instance. They also work closely with the teams in helping them instill new values. For example, the HR group at Pharmacia, a St. Louis-based pharmaceuticals firm, works with its teams to encourage them to act based on five "best managed behaviors," such as "shared accountability," "ongoing listening and learning," and "coaching colleagues."[36]

The Nature of Self-Directed Teams and Worker Empowerment

Self-directed teams have several distinguishing characteristics. They generally perform sets of *naturally interdependent tasks* (such as all the steps required to assemble a Saturn door). They all use *consensus decision making* to choose team members, solve job-related problems, design their own jobs, and schedule their own break time. The team's members perform *enriched jobs*, in that they do many of the tasks formerly done by supervisors, such as dealing with vendors and monitoring quality. Self-directed teams are also *highly trained*—to solve problems, to design jobs, to interview candidates, and to understand financial reports. Employers *empower* the teams and their individual members: They give them the training, ability and authority to get the jobs done.

Employee empowerment isn't just for major corporations like Saturn. Many small businesses, like Time Vision, Inc., of Irving, Texas, rely on it too, as the Entrepreneurs + HR feature illustrates.

self-directed team
A work team that uses consensus decision making to choose its own team members, solve job-related problems, design its own jobs, and schedule its own break time.

ENTREPRENEURS HR

Lois Melbourne of Time Vision

Entrepreneur Lois Melbourne founded Time Vision, which offers Web-based services to other firms, in 1994 (see Webnote). Melbourne, a veteran of large corporations, empowered her employees almost from the start. Recently, for instance, the firm had to add several new salespeople to its 20-person staff. The 33-year-old CEO assigned the recruiting and screening to her two salespeople. They drafted the job description and job specification, posted it on an online job bank, reviewed résumés, interviewed candidates, and made the final recommendation. Management didn't get involved until the salary negotiation, and Melbourne never even met the new hire until her first day on the job.

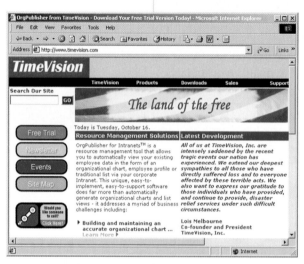

▲ **WEBNOTE**
Time Vision provides many different Web support services to client and partner firms.
www.timevision.com

Melbourne finds empowering employees works especially well for matters directly affecting them, such as benefits. For example, she formed a team to investigate switching from an employee retirement savings plan that relied on individual retirement accounts to a 401(k) plan. The team opted for the more complex and costly plan, and Melbourne agreed to it. "They decided we'd be more competitive in the marketplace with that benefit," she says. Her employees also do their own vacation scheduling, and other administrative tasks. Melbourne applied HR methods to make employee empowerment work. For example, having employees make the decisions means hiring the right people in the first place: "Hire intelligent people if you're going to let them make decisions," is the way she puts it. And, she says, your employees also have to understand the issues, be trained to comprehend financial statements, and know how to use decision-making techniques to make good decisions. Training is thus central to worker empowerment at Time Vision, Inc.

Melbourne found employee empowerment doesn't come without costs. For one thing, it takes resources to train employees and to educate them about the company's financial performance and goals. "You have to spend more time in the early parts of projects and in the early parts of employees' careers teaching [about] the boundaries and [expectations] of the company," she says. It also takes a different managerial mind-set: "You have to let people make the decisions that you formerly made yourself and that you want to make yourself." But Lois Melbourne is convinced that employee empowerment is the way to go.[37]

How HR Helps to Build Productive Teams

Building productive teams requires effective selection, training, and motivation, and thus can't be achieved without HR. Some HR-related guidelines for building effective teams include:[38]

■ Establish urgent, demanding performance standards. All team members should believe the team has urgent and worthwhile purposes, and they need to know what their performance standards are.

■ Select members for attitudes and skills. Careful screening is crucial. For example (not surprisingly), a person's agreeableness and conscientiousness is a significant factor in how teammates rate him or her.[39]

- Train leaders to "coach," not "boss." Self-directed work teams have the authority, tools, and information they need to be self-managing. The firm therefore has to train supervisors and team leaders to understand that their jobs are to support and to coach.
- Exploit the power of positive feedback. There are many HR-based ways to do this. For example, have a senior executive speak directly to the team about the urgency of its mission, and use special awards and team-based incentives to recognize the team's contributions.
- Select people who like teamwork. For example, Toyota recruits and selects employees who have a history of preferring to work in teams and of being good team members. Loners and antisocial types don't usually make good team members.
- Train, train, train. Perhaps HR's main role is to ensure team members have the skills required to do their jobs. Training should cover topics such as the philosophy of doing work through teams, how teams make decisions, interpersonal and communication skills for team members, and the technical and problem-solving skills team members need to analyze problems and perform their jobs.
- Cross-train for flexibility. Team members also require cross-training, to learn the jobs of other team members either informally or through scheduled rotating assignments. This can help reduce disruptions due to absenteeism and boost flexibility, since all team members are always ready to fill in when required.

▲ *People who like teamwork are often more successful at working in groups than others. Thus careful selection of members can directly contribute to the group's success. This creative team at the New York advertising agency of TBWA/Chiat/Day recently completed work on a successful ad campaign for the city's Board of Education's teacher recruitment efforts, working under a contract that specified no profit would be made.*

◆ **HIGH-PERFORMANCE INSIGHT** As an example, the product improvement teams at Kaiser Electronics in San Jose, California, perform several crucial functions. They identify and correct problems affecting performance, costs, schedules, and customer satisfaction, and they improve engineering and manufacturing processes to reduce cycle times and defects per unit. Kaiser forms teams for specific product lines, and each establishes and maintains its own missions, visions, goals, and working style. Several years ago, teams like these did not exist at Kaiser: Production and engineering managers controlled all defect and product improvement activities. The system was reportedly reactive rather than proactive, and its ineffectiveness led to the development of the product improvement teams.

When the plant establishes a new team, it conducts a seven-day team-building event to launch the team and develop its mission and vision. Each team has a sponsor and a trained team leader. The teams meet frequently, normally five times per week. Members develop and apply their own task improvement strategies.

Training plays a big role. Teams are trained to use Pareto charts—special graphs that show defects and their frequencies—to identify the most frequent sources of problems. Kaiser Electronics' Root Cause Problem Solving (RCPS) Roadmap Process is a basic tool for determining root causes and implementing corrective action. The company displays special metrics and progress charts on boards in the plant.

Overall, Kaiser's team process is useful for achieving continuous incremental improvements. The focus is moving error detection upstream, earlier in the process, for less costly, earlier detection. This in turn is boosting the firm's performance.[40]

STRATEGIC HR

Creating Teams at Signicast

To compete strategically, Wisconsin-based Signicast Corp. decided to build a new, highly automated plant. But it discovered that "in the real world, new automation technology requires a new kind of employee." Strategy implementation, it quickly discovered, depended on HR—in this case, building effective teams.[41]

HR's involvement began at the plant design stage. HR people invited employees from the existing facility to participate in planning and design meetings; they solicited suggestions on matters ranging from how to design a new piece of equipment to the work flow in the new plant: "Employees would come up with suggestions; we'd implement them, and bring them back to [employees] for confirmation."[42]

HR's role as a strategic partner in the building of this new plant was apparent in other ways. As the new plant began to take shape, HR had to select and train the new workforce. The new automated plant would produce parts almost five times faster than the old plant, which would leave no time for rework or errors. The new plant's employees would therefore have to have more responsibility, and in many ways be more highly trained and carefully selected than their counterparts at the old facility.

The new plant's selection standards were thus tighter. At the old plant, for example, no specific prior experience was required—the only hiring requirements were a high school diploma and a good work ethic. The 135 employees at the new plant would require the same high school degree and work ethic plus team orientation, good trainability, good communication skills, and a willingness to do varied jobs over a 12-hour shift.[43] HR also had to create a cross-training program, so that employees could do each other's jobs, so as not to become bored or tired during their 12-hour shifts.[44] A new compensation plan paid workers not just for performance, but also for knowledge and for the number of new jobs at which they became competent. HR therefore played a crucial role in implementing Signicast's expansion strategy.

HR and Employee Involvement Programs

employee involvement program
Any formal program that lets employees participate in formulating important work decisions or in supervising all or part of their own work activities.

Teams are examples of employee involvement programs. An **employee involvement program** is any formal program that lets employees participate in formulating important work decisions or in supervising all or part of their own work activities.[45]

Managers rank such programs as their biggest productivity boosters. For example, the editors of *National Productivity Review* found that "increased employee involvement in the generation and implementation of ideas was ranked the highest priority productivity improvement action by the respondents." Employee involvement "was similarly ranked number one as the top cause of improvement over the past two years at these firms." (The other eight causes of improvement, in descending order, were quality programs, improved process methods, top management, equipment, technology, training, computers, and automation.) In another study, self-managing teams were listed as "most valuable" in a survey of CEOs, who were asked how their firms used 39 "high-performance" practices.[46]

Teams are an obvious example of employee involvement, but they're not the only way to get workers involved. The Work in America Institute conducted a research project called PAR (participations, achievement, reward). The study found many concrete actions successful firms took to encourage employee involvement. At Miller Brewing Company's plant in Trenton, Ohio, self-directed work teams were responsible for the day-to-day management of the business units; they coordinated production, conducted routine maintenance and quality checks, and ensured safety. At Ford Motor Company's transmission plant in Sharonville, Ohio, Ford and its union established a joint labor–management steering committee to deal with areas like quality, training, and fair practices. At a plant in New Carlisle, Indiana, 10-person groups analyze and solve technical process problems, and investigate and solve communication flow problems. Eastman Kodak's precision components manufacturing division holds "town meetings" where employees get to hear the company's plans and discuss strategies. There are thus many ways to encourage worker involvement.

Based on examples like these, the Work in America Institute recommends the following HR-related steps for creating a culture of employee involvement and participation:

1. Educate all employees regarding business plans. Explain that their increased participation in these plans will require major changes in the employees' roles and responsibilities.
2. Devote enough time, planning, and resources to the transition and to worker involvement, especially to building the necessary HR systems (training, selection, and so on) to reinforce desired behaviors.
3. If your company has unions, involve them as partners at every stage; develop jointly all key principles and guidelines concerning, for instance, team structure and development, training, and information flow; and give employees access to information on business plans and operational performance.
4. Involve employees in designing and implementing new operating systems, and in selecting suppliers.
5. Provide training in using new technologies.
6. Promote employees' continuous communication with engineers and suppliers.
7. Involve employees in assessing the effects of the new technology on their health and safety.
8. Use telecommunications technology (e-mail and so forth) to support a culture of teamwork and continuous improvement.[47]

Not everyone is enthusiastic about worker empowerment. One manager says that the way most firms do it, empowerment is more talk than action: "Empowerment is just another management sedative dished up by self-serving power mongers to trick hard-working people into thinking they have a brighter future." However, most evidence suggests that most programs are well received and successful.[48]

Bayer Corporation's Myerstown, Pennsylvania, plant is an example. After changing ownership three times in 7 months before its purchase by Bayer, the plant's employees were understandably somewhat shell-shocked. Now, they were to meet Bayer's expectations for a 24-hour per day, 7 day per week production schedule. The HR team worked with the employees to build morale and to win their commitment to the new schedule. They picked 93 employees at random to participate in focus group meetings to get answers to questions like "Why do people work here?" and "Why do people leave here?" A "roadmap for change" team of employee volunteers worked with management to gather data and to recommend and make improvements to plant operations, to prepare the facility for its new operating schedule. HR then instituted a new incentive plan, called "productivity plus," that lets employees earn up to 8% of their base pay for meeting or exceeding performance goals.[49]

While self-directed teams may be effective in the United States, the approach doesn't necessarily work as well abroad, as the New Workplace feature shows.

THE *NEW* WORKPLACE

Extending Participative Decision Making Abroad

There are deep and often irreconcilable cross-cultural differences in values and attitudes from country to country, so that techniques that work in one country may actually backfire in another. The findings of one recent study illustrate this problem.[50] The study examined how one U.S. multinational manufacturing company tried to implement participative decision making in its European subsidiaries, and how managers and employees in three European countries reacted to the company's efforts.

The company was hoping to implement programs similar to ones that had been successful in the United States, but it got unexpected reactions from the European employees. Most Dutch managers felt that the U.S. efforts to improve participation by instituting work teams could actually hurt performance and motivation, because the program failed to take into account individual employee differences. Several Dutch managers stated that "the type of programmatic, formalized efforts favored by the American parent would not allow managers to encourage participation in ways and at a pace that was consistent with their own styles or the needs of their subordinates."[51] In other words, the program forced the Dutch managers to be too participative, too soon.

British managers had similar reservations about the "American approach" to team-based participative management. In their case, they were concerned that the program ignored individual differences in managerial styles and employee abilities. The British managers seemed threatened by the decision-making authority the new work teams would receive.

Interestingly, most of the Spanish managers endorsed the idea of self-directed work teams and said it could work in the Spanish plant. But the Spanish managers' stated beliefs were actually a bit misleading: In fact, Spanish managers reported lower levels of participation among subordinates than did their Dutch and U.S. counterparts. In other words, the actual participation resulting from the program was lower—not higher—in the Spanish plants than elsewhere in Europe, although the managers were relatively enthusiastic about the program.

Results like these show that U.S. managers have different values and perspectives on employee participation than do their counterparts in Britain, Holland, and Spain. Therefore, before exporting HR programs like self-directed work teams, HR managers should try to achieve three basic goals:

1. Build trust by communicating to local managers that previous corporate HR efforts may have reflected culturally specific beliefs that do not always fit local needs, and that the parent company is committed to developing locally sensitive policies.
2. Become more aware of the local cultural traditions that may affect attitudes toward participation in decision making.
3. Develop a working partnership with local HR executives to create blended strategies for employee participation, ones that fit the local culture while offering something of value to the corporation as a whole. This requires joint decision making between U.S. HR executives and their foreign counterparts.[52]

HR AND BUSINESS PROCESS REENGINEERING

Many firms today—from IBM to tiny firms—are reengineering their work processes in order to compete better, faster, and more efficiently in a global marketplace. In this, too, HR methods play a central role.

What Is Business Process Reengineering?

Two experts, Michael Hammer and James Champy, define **business process reengineering** as "the fundamental rethinking and radical redesign of business processes to achieve dramatic improvements in critical, contemporary measures of performance such as cost, quality, service, and speed."[53] One of business process reengineering's basic assumptions is that the traditional way of organizing departments and processes around specialized tasks is inherently wasteful and unresponsive to the firm's customers. In reengineering a firm's processes, the basic questions are "Why do we do what we do?" and "Why do we do it the way we do?" Let's look at an example.

IBM Credit Corporation finances the computers, software, and services sold by IBM. Prior to reengineering, the credit approval process took several weeks. (A *process* is a collection of activities with a clear customer goal. For example, the credit approval process is the sequence of activities that starts with a credit request as its input, and sees that request through a sequence of steps until approval or rejection.) At IBM Credit, a salesperson would call to get credit for a prospective customer. Individual workers then performed a sequence of steps. They logged in the request, carted the request upstairs to the credit department, entered the information into a computer system, checked the credit, and dispatched it to the next link in the chain.

When IBM assessed this process, it made a monumental discovery: If the employee who received the credit request walked it through all the stages personally and at each stage did what had to be done, the whole process took 90 minutes rather than a week or more! Reengineering the process here meant substituting several generalists for all the separate task specialists, and letting one generalist do all the tasks for a request, rather than having the process carried out like a relay race.[54]

This example illustrates the basic characteristics of business process reengineering. First, several jobs are combined into one, so an assembly-line process is replaced by generalists (or teams) who carry out all the tasks themselves. Second, workers make more decisions. For example, each of the new IBM Credit generalists was now solely responsible for deciding on a potential client's creditworthiness. Third, reengineering reduces checks and controls; instead, there's an emphasis on selecting and training competent generalists. And fourth, reengineered processes tend to take a "case manager" approach to dealing with customers: Each customer ends up with a single point of contact when checking on the status of a request.[55]

business process reengineering (BPR) The redesign of business processes to achieve improvements in such measures of performance as cost, quality, service, and speed.

HR's Role in Reengineering Processes

Two years after Hammer and Champy introduced the concepts and techniques of reengineering, it was obvious that something was lacking. With their single-minded focus on reorganizing the work and eliminating duplicate operations, many reengineered companies had failed to set up new HR practices. They hadn't changed their hiring procedures, or compensation policies, or training practices, for instance. As a result, these firms had failed to win the commitment of managers and employees to the new reengineered jobs, and many of their efforts had failed. It was another example of the fact that any technological change that ignores the people who have to make it succeed is doomed to fail.[56] Today, experts understand that HR plays a crucial role in implementing reengineering efforts. Here are some aspects of that role.

Building Commitment As Champy says, "[Reengineering is] about an ongoing, never-ending commitment to doing things better."[57] Therefore, a key to reengineering is winning people's commitment to the organizational changes and to what those changes mean. HR can play a big role here—for instance, by hiring competent employees, by providing the right incentives, and by installing effective two-way communication practices.

Building Teams Business process reengineering generally means switching from functional departments to process-oriented teams (such as the teams of generalists now processing the IBM credit requests). We've seen in this chapter that HR plays a role in making such teams more effective, for instance by hiring carefully selected "team players" and providing the required training.

Redesigning Compensation Reengineering also has significant compensation implications. In one study, raters were asked to rate a position's pre- and postreengineering job description. They rated the job on three important determinants of pay—accountability, know-how, and problem solving. The job's know-how and problem-solving requirements rose significantly after it was reengineered, suggesting that pay would have to rise as well.[58]

Redesigning the Work Itself With reengineering, jobs generally change from specialized tasks to multitask, enriched, generalist work. Each worker becomes responsible for a broader, more enriched job. And the employees now must "share joint responsibility with team members for performing the whole process, not just a small piece of it."[59] Each worker needs to be capable of using a much broader range of skills from day to day. HR drafts the new job descriptions and training programs, and selects high-potential employees.

Moving from Controlled to Empowered Jobs Selecting and training employees for reengineered jobs is a special challenge. As at IBM Credit, "reengineered" employees are empowered to perform a broad set of tasks with relatively little supervision.[60] This means that in selecting employees, values play a bigger role.[61] As two experts put it,

> It is no longer enough merely to look at prospective employees' education, training, and skills; their character becomes an issue as well. Are they self-starting? Do they have self-discipline? Are they motivated to do what it takes to please a customer?[62]

FLEXIBLE WORK ARRANGEMENTS

Organizational renewal doesn't always require a massive transformation. At many companies, a change as (relatively) simple as flexible hours can sometimes provide a good start. Since it's generally HR that designs and institutes such plans, in this last section we'll focus on various flexible work arrangements.

Flextime and Compressed Workweeks

flextime
A plan whereby employees build their workday around a core of midday hours.

Flextime is a plan whereby employees' workdays are built around a core of midday hours, such as 11 A.M. to 2 P.M. Workers determine their own starting and stopping hours. For example, they may opt to work from 7 A.M. to 3 P.M. or from 11 A.M. to 7 P.M. About 28% of full-time wage and salary workers have flexible work schedules, but the proportion varies by occupational group. Around 16% of manual operators, laborers, and precision production, craft, and repair employees have flexible schedules, as do about 23% of administrative support employees, 41% of the salespeople, and 42% of executive, administrative, and managerial employees.[63]

In practice, most employers give employees only limited freedom regarding the hours they work. Most hold fairly close to the traditional 9 A.M. to 5 P.M. workday. For example, in about half the firms, employees can't start work later than 9 A.M., and employees in about 40% of the firms must be in by 10 A.M. Therefore, the effect of flextime for most employees is to give them about one hour of leeway before 9 A.M. or after 5 P.M.

Conditions for Success Several things can make a flextime program more successful.[64] First, management resistance—particularly at the supervisory level and particularly before the program is actually tried—has torpedoed several programs before they became operational, so supervisory indoctrination programs are important. Second, flextime is usually more successful with clerical, professional, and managerial jobs, and less so with factory jobs (the nature of which tends to demand interdependence among workers). Third, the greater the flexibility of a flextime program, the greater the benefits the program can produce (although the disadvantages, of course, multiply as well). Fourth, the way you install the program is important; appoint a flextime project director to oversee the program, and hold frequent meetings with supervisors and employees to allay their fears and clear up misunderstandings. A pilot study, say, in one department, is advisable.[65]

Compressed Workweeks Many employees, like airline pilots, do not work conventional five-day 40-hour workweeks. It would hardly do, for instance, for the pilot on a 12-hour flight to have to clock out midway across the Atlantic. Similarly, hospitals may want doctors and nurses to provide continuing care to a patient, or manufacturers may want to reduce the productivity lost whenever workers change shifts.

▲ *Telecommuting is becoming a more common option as technology makes keeping in touch easier and more reliable. Harriet Donnelly, here enjoying a visit to her office from her son Sean and one of the family dogs, is president of Technovative Marketing, a small public relations firm whose 23 employees all work from home. Employees who take time off during the day for family activities are expected to call in periodically for messages, says Ms. Donnelly, but clients no longer raise questions about the creative work arrangements.*

Nonconventional ("compressed") workweeks come in many flavors. Some firms have four-day workweeks, with four 10-hour days. Others have employees work two days on, two days off, three days on, then two days off, two days on, and so forth. Some workers—in hospitals, for instance—work three 12-hour shifts, and then are off for the next four days. About half of 500 employers in one recent survey said they now use 12-hour shifts for many of their employees.[66]

◆ **RESEARCH INSIGHT** How effective are flextime and compressed workweek programs? One review suggests the following. Flexible work schedules do have positive effects on employee productivity, job satisfaction, satisfaction with work schedule, and employee absenteeism; the positive effect on absenteeism was much greater than on productivity. Compressed workweeks positively affected job satisfaction and satisfaction with work schedule; absenteeism did not increase, and productivity was not positively affected. Highly flexible programs were actually less effective than less flexible ones.[67]

Some experts argue that longer, 12-hour shifts may increase fatigue, and therefore accidents. However, one report suggests 12-hour shifts can actually be safer, in some respects. For example, the "general workplace confusion" that often occurs during shift changes is reduced with 12-hour shifts, since there are fewer shift changes. To further reduce potential detrimental side effects, a Texas DuPont

job sharing
A concept that allows two or more people to share a single full-time job.

work sharing
A temporary reduction in work hours by a group of employees during economic downturns as a way to prevent layoffs.

telecommuting
A work arrangement in which employees work at remote locations, usually at home, using video displays, computers, and other telecommunications equipment to carry out their responsibilities.

plant provides portable treadmills and exercise bikes shift workers can use to get their "blood pumping"; a South Texas power plant installed a special "light box" that mimics daytime sun by providing intense, full-spectrum light.[68]

Other Flexible Work Arrangements

Employers are taking other steps to accommodate employees' scheduling needs. **Job sharing** allows two or more people to share a single full-time job. For example, two people may share a 40-hour-per-week job, with one working mornings and the other working afternoons. About 105 of the firms questioned in one survey indicated that they allow job sharing.[69] These include Gannett newspapers and PepsiCo, which has offered it for more than 20 years.[70] **Work sharing** refers to a temporary reduction in work hours by a group of employees during economic downturns as a way to prevent layoffs. Thus, 400 employees may all agree to work (and get paid for) only 35 hours per week, to avoid having to lay off 30 workers.

Telecommuting is another option. Here employees work at home, usually with computers, and use phones and the Internet to transmit letters, data, and completed work to the home office. For example, Best Western Hotels in Phoenix used the residents of the Arizona Center for Women, a minimum-security prison, as a telecommuting office staff.

HR.NET

Telecommuting

Daniel Briddle, owner of Mesa, Arizona–based PC Information Technology Services, proves you don't have to be a hermit to telecommute. He spends about 80% of his work time interacting continuously with customers from his home office and spends the rest of the time doing on-site tech support for his small Web hosting service.

Like most telecommuters today, Briddle's business depends almost entirely on his being able to communicate in real time via the Internet and personal digital assistants. For one thing, he carries a text-based pager, and has one e-mail account configured to forward messages straight to the device. He also has a toll-free number where clients can leave him both voice and fax messages. When he gets a message on this number, the service e-mails him a message immediately, and he goes online to hear the message over the Internet or listen by phone. "It works perfectly for me. Plus, my clients see that I have a toll-free number."

Digital devices allow Briddle to handle his clients' crises almost as soon as they occur. Many of his clients need to reach him because they can't get their e-mail or make Web site changes since they've forgotten their passwords. At home, of course, Briddle can check his computerized records and get right back to clients. On the road, Briddle opens his notebook PC, finds the nearest available phone jack, taps into his laptop, and then gets right back to the clients. He also carries a personal digital assistant (a Palm), into which he inserted a lot of the technical information about each client's system. That makes it even easier for him to respond quickly when a client has a problem. And of course, it makes it easier to run a business based on telecommuting.[71]

We invite you to visit **www.prenhall.com/dessler** on the Prentice Hall Web site for our online study guide, Internet exercises, current events, links to related Web sites, and more.

Summary

1. Managers in their leadership roles can focus on various change targets. They can change the strategy, culture, structure, tasks, technologies, or attitudes and skills of the people in the organization.

2. A 10-step process for actually leading organizational change consists of establishing a sense of urgency; mobilizing commitment to change through joint diagnosis of business problems; creating a guiding coalition; developing a shared vision; communicating the vision; removing barriers to the change and empowering employees; generating short-term wins; consolidating gains and producing more change; anchoring the new ways of doing things in the company's culture; and monitoring progress and adjusting the vision as required.

3. Organizational development is a special approach to organizational change that basically involves letting the employees themselves formulate and implement the change that's required, often with the assistance of a trained consultant. OD applications include human process applications, technostructural interventions, human resource management applications, and strategic applications.

4. Quality measures how well a product or service meets customer needs. Quality standards today are international, as shown by the introduction of ISO 9000. Improving quality has become necessary to companies all over the world.

5. Total quality management programs are organizationwide programs that aim to integrate all business functions, including design, planning, production, distribution, and service, with the aim of maximizing customer service through continuous improvement.

6. Many firms are organizing work around self-contained teams, which are sometimes called self-managing teams, high-performance teams, autonomous work groups, and even superteams. These teams are trained to solve problems, design jobs, interview and hire candidates, and understand financial reports.

7. Reengineering is the fundamental rethinking and radical redesign of business processes to achieve dramatic improvements in critical, contemporary measures of performance, such as cost, quality, service, and speed. HR contributes to reengineering processes by its effect on building commitment to reengineering, team building, changing the nature of work, and empowering jobs.

8. Flextime and other flexible work arrangements such as job sharing, compressed workweeks, work sharing, and telecommuting can be effective. There's generally a positive impact on employee morale and attendance, and perhaps productivity.

Tying It All Together

This part of the book, Training and Development, focuses on the methods managers use to give employees the knowledge and skills they need to do their jobs, and on how the managers then monitor and appraise employees' performance. The previous chapter focused specifically on training and development methods. Training and development, though, are often merely part of a broader organizational effort by the firm's management to renew or reinvent the firm to meet some strategic challenge. We therefore focused in this chapter on the role of HR methods in transforming organizations—for instance, into team-based, high-quality, reengineered companies. Having provided employees with the knowledge and skills they need to do their jobs, we'll now turn to the methods managers use to appraise performance.

Discussion Questions

1. Outline the steps in the organizational change process.
2. What steps would you take to institute self-directed work teams?
3. List the pros and cons of flextime and the four-day workweek.
4. Give specific examples of HR's role in Total Quality Management programs.

Individual and Group Activities

1. Working individually or in groups, outline the objectives for and steps in an organizational change program for improving service in an area of your university or college that you feel is in need of improvement.
2. Working individually or in groups, develop a brief example of how you would reengineer a familiar process such as class enrollment at the start of a semester.

3. Working individually or in groups, use the Internet to find three organizations that have gone through one of the following types of organizational change within the last three years: strategic change, cultural change, structural change, technological change, or attitudes and skills of people. What organizational process did top management seem to use to achieve the change?

EXPERIENTIAL EXERCISE

Purpose: The purpose of this exercise is to give you practice identifying the sources of resistance to change, and in identifying how you might deal with that resistance.

Required Understanding: You should understand the material in this chapter and particularly the material devoted to organizational change and resistance to change.

How to Set Up the Exercise/Instructions: Set up teams of four to six students for this exercise. The first step in developing planned change is finding and reducing the forces that favor the status quo. Imagine that you are a consultant to a large machine manufacturing business. To boost productivity, the firm wants to install new automated equipment and put all employees on an incentive pay plan. After the first day of meetings, you have met and talked with a number of different stakeholders. Before your next meeting with the client, you want to complete the following table:

Stakeholder	A Why might this group support the status quo rather than change?	B How might we help them recognize the need for change?
1. Factory workers—All manufacturing employees belong to a union.		
2. Clerical workers—Most of the clerical workers have been with your organization for over a decade.		
3. Sales force—The sales force is compensated entirely by salary.		
4. Top management team—The top management team has been in place for 6 years without a major change in membership.		

To Accomplish This: After dividing each class into teams, have each student on the team individually write responses to the questions in column "A." Each team should:

1. Decide which response(s) seem most likely.

2. Have the team identify two possible responses (column B) for every stakeholder issue raised.

3. Repeat the first three steps for each stakeholder group.

Once the teams have completed their work, they should report their suggestions back to the class if time permits.

APPLICATION CASE *We're Getting Nowhere Fast*

Martin Star, president and founder of Star Valve Co. knows his little company has a problem. Star Valve designs and manufactures sophisticated valves used to control the flow of liquids and gases through pollution control systems in chemical plants. While many of Star's products are real innovations, the company hasn't grown appreciably in the five years prior to 2002.

It was not for lack of trying. Star had replaced the head of his accounting, manufacturing, and sales departments in the prior five years, and had recently begun a search for a new sales manager for Europe. And yet by almost any criterion—productivity, sales growth, profit margins, or profits, for instance—the company had either not made headway in the five-year period or was actually somewhat behind.

The company is highly labor intensive. Star Valve is basically an engineering firm. Of its 100 or so employees, about 15 are engineers involved in designing valves in response to customers' requests, about 35 work in the plant in various semiskilled or skilled machining-type jobs, and the rest are managers or office employees.

Of particular concern to Mr. Star, aside from the financial results, is the fact that quality is beginning to diminish, as measured by complaints from several long-term customers. Employees also seem to be increasingly ignoring the administrative structure of the firm, such as the network of policies, procedures, and checklists that the company traditionally uses to ensure, for instance, that when a request for a proposal comes in the engineers ask all the required questions. Mr. Star recently met with several members of his board of directors, seeking their advice. "I don't know what the problem is," he said. "All I know is that we're getting nowhere fast."

Questions

1. Which organizational change and development techniques discussed in Chapter 8 would you recommend Mr. Star use to try to determine what exactly the problems are at the company? Please be specific.

2. Given the admittedly limited information in the case description, would you recommend that Star implement a team-based organization? Why? Why not?

3. Do you think it would be helpful for Star to implement a total quality management program? Be prepared to tell Mr. Star what the pros and cons of implementing such a program in his company might be.

CONTINUING CASE: LearnInMotion.com *Teamwork*

Like most companies with less then 10 employees, LearnInMotion.com doesn't have a formal organization chart. Instead, the company usually has several projects and activities in the works at any one time, each of which is managed by a team; employees typically serve on at least one team.

The projects and activities are typical of companies like these. There is, for instance, the front-page development team, whose task is to see that the overall format of the company's opening page (as well as its various subsidiary pages, and communities) makes sense in terms of what the company is trying to achieve. In addition to Jennifer and Mel, the team includes the Web designer, as well as one of the two salespeople (whose job it is to relay information regarding the customers' needs). The sales team—charged with managing the company's sales effort—consists of the two salespeople, as well as Jennifer, Mel, and Greg (of the board of directors).

LearnInMotion.com is creating a Web-based calendar (technically, a "personal information manager," or PIM); Mel is on the calendar committee, as is the representative of the consulting firm that's developing the calendar, as well as the company's programmer/independent contractor. Many dotcoms have a separate "business development" manager, whose role is to conceive and then implement relationships with other Web sites. For example, LearnInMotion already has several relationships with job finding/career Web sites; the assumption is that job hunters may be looking for business courses, and people interested in business courses may be looking for jobs. LearnInMotion can't afford its own business development manager, so this is a function that Jennifer fulfills, with help from a business development team that also includes Mel, Greg, and one of the salespeople.

This all sounds logical, but the problem is, it isn't working. Sales are stagnant, the calendar is two months behind, and the company has been able to finalize only a handful of business development arrangements. Jennifer and Mel are not sure what to do. There is no way they can afford to go out and hire managers and employees to oversee activities like these. On the other hand, the company is falling behind. Now they want you, their management consultants, to help them figure out what to do. Here's what they want you to do for them.

Questions and Assignments

1. Tell us what you think the problem is: Is our team approach a good idea?

2. Are there any new approaches, such as total quality management programs, that we should consider applying to our situation?

3. What do you think we should do, and why?

9 Chapter

Appraising and Managing Performance

STRATEGIC OVERVIEW When Jacques Nasser took over as CEO of Ford Motor Company a few years ago, he didn't want to just make Ford the world's best car company, he wanted it to be one of the world's best companies of any kind. He pursued that strategy with enormous intensity: He reorganized the firm, eliminated layers of bureaucracy, promoted non-Americans to prominent positions, brought in new executives from outside the industry, and initiated dozens of quality improvement and similar programs throughout the firm. However, he knew that to make the firm world-class he also needed a new, more intense way of evaluating the firm's 18,000 managers. What method should he use?

The last three chapters addressed selecting, training, and developing employees. Once employees have been on the job for some time, you have to evaluate their performance. The purpose of this chapter is to show you how to appraise employees' performance. The main topics we cover include the appraisal process, appraisal methods, appraisal performance problems and solutions, and the appraisal interview. Developing a career plan for the employee is an important part of any appraisal process: We'll turn to career planning in the following chapter.

THE APPRAISAL PROCESS

Performance appraisal means evaluating an employee's current or past performance relative to the person's performance standards. Appraisal involves: (1) setting work standards; (2) assessing the employee's actual performance relative to these standards; and (3) providing feedback to the employee with the aim of motivating that person to eliminate deficiencies or to continue to perform above par.

You've probably had experience with performance appraisals. For example, some colleges ask students to rank instructors on scales like the one in Figure 9-1. Do you think this is an effective scale? Do you see any way to improve it? You'll be able to answer these questions by the end of this chapter.

Why appraise performance?[1] There are four reasons. First, appraisals provide information upon which you make promotion and salary decisions. Second, they provide an opportunity for you and your subordinate to review his or her work-related behavior. This in turn lets both of you develop a plan for correcting any deficiencies the appraisal might have unearthed, and for reinforcing things done right. Third, the appraisal is part of the firm's career-planning process, because it provides an opportunity to review the person's career plans in light of his or her strengths and weaknesses. Finally, appraisals help you better manage and improve your firm's performance.

In reviewing the appraisal tools we discuss below, don't miss the forest for the trees. It doesn't matter which tool you use if you're inclined to be less than candid when your subordinate is not doing well. Not all managers are devotees of such candor, but some firms, like GE, are famous for hardhearted appraisals. GE's former CEO Jack Welch has said, for instance, that there's nothing crueler than telling someone who's doing a mediocre job that he or she is doing well.[2] Someone who might have had the chance to correct bad behavior or find a more appropriate vocation may instead end up spending years in a dead-end situation, only to have to leave when a tough boss comes along.

There are many practical motivations for giving soft appraisals: the fear of having to hire and train someone new; the unpleasant reaction of the appraisee; or a company appraisal process that's not conducive to candor, for instance. Ultimately, though, it's the person doing the appraising who must decide if the potential negative effects of less-than-candid appraisals—on the appraisee's long-term peace of mind, and on the performance of the appraiser and his or her firm—outweigh the assumed benefits.

The Supervisor's Role

Appraising performance is both a difficult and an essential supervisory skill. The supervisor—not HR—usually does the actual appraising, and a supervisor who rates his or her employees too high or too low is doing a disservice to them, to the company, and to him- or herself. Supervisors must be familiar with basic appraisal techniques, understand and avoid problems that can cripple appraisals, and know how to conduct appraisals fairly.

The HR department serves a policy-making and advisory role. In one survey, about 80% of the firms responding said the HR department provides advice and assistance regarding the appraisal tool to use, but leaves final decisions on procedures to operating division heads. In the rest of the firms, HR prepares detailed forms and procedures and insists that all departments use them.[3] HR is also responsible for training supervisors to improve their appraisal skills. Finally, HR is responsible for monitoring the appraisal system and, particularly, for ensuring that the format and criteria being measured comply with EEO laws and aren't

▶ **FIGURE 9-1**
Classroom Teaching
Appraisal by
Students

Evaluating Faculty for Promotion and Tenure
Classroom Teaching Appraisal by Students

Teacher _____ Course _____

Term _____ Academic Year _____

Thoughtful student appraisal can help improve teaching effectiveness. This questionnaire is designed for that purpose, and your assistance is appreciated. Please do not sign your name.

Use the back of this form for any further comments you might want to express; use numbers 10, 11, and 12 for any additional questions that you might like to add.

Directions: Rate your teacher on each item, giving the highest scores for exceptional performances and the lowest scores for very poor performances. Place in the blank space before each statement the rating that most closely expresses your view.

Excep-tional		Moderately Good				Very Poor	Don't Know
7	6	5	4	3	2	1	X

_____ 1. How do you rate the agreement between course objectives and lesson assignments?

_____ 2. How do you rate the planning, organization, and use of class periods?

_____ 3. Are the teaching methods and techniques employed by the teacher appropriate and effective?

_____ 4. How do you rate the competence of the instructor in the subject?

_____ 5. How do you rate the interest of the teacher in the subject?

_____ 6. Does the teacher stimulate and challenge you to think and to question?

_____ 7. Does he or she welcome differing points of view?

_____ 8. Does the teacher have a personal interest in helping you in and out of class?

_____ 9. How would you rate the fairness and effectiveness of the grading policies and procedures of the teacher?

_____ 10. _____

Faculty Evaluation Rating Forms

_____ 11. _____

_____ 12. _____

_____ 13. Considering all the above items, what is your overall rating of this teacher?

_____ 14. How would you rate this teacher in comparison with all others you have had in the college or university?

Source: Richard I. Miller, *Evaluating Faculty for Promotion and Tenure* (San Francisco: Jossey-Bass Publishers, 1987), pp. 164–165. Copyright © 1987 Jossey-Bass, Inc., Publishers. All rights reserved. Reprinted with permission.

outdated. In one survey, half the employers were in the process of revising their appraisal programs, while others were conducting reviews to see how well their programs were working.[4]

Steps in Appraising Performance

The performance appraisal process contains three steps: define the job, appraise performance, and provide feedback. *Defining the job* means making sure that you and your subordinate agree on his or her duties and job standards. *Appraising performance* means comparing your subordinate's actual performance to the standards that have been set; this usually involves some type of rating form. Third, performance appraisal usually requires one or more *feedback sessions*. Here the two of you discuss the subordinate's performance and progress, and make plans for any development required.

When appraisals fail, they do so for reasons that parallel these three steps—defining the job, appraising performance, and providing feedback. Some fail because subordinates don't know ahead of time exactly what you expect in terms of good performance. Others fail because of problems with the forms or procedures used to actually appraise the performance: a lenient supervisor might rate as "high," for instance, subordinates who are actually substandard. Other problems, like arguing and poor communication, undermine the interview-feedback session. Let's look first at defining your expectations. We'll discuss the other problems toward the end of the chapter.

How to Clarify Your Expectations

Clarifying what you expect is trickier than it may appear. Employers usually write job descriptions not for specific jobs, but for groups of jobs, and the descriptions rarely include specific goals. All sales managers in the firm might have the same job description, for instance. Your sales manager's job description may list duties such as "supervise sales force" and "be responsible for all phases of marketing the division's products." However, you may expect your sales manager to personally sell at least $600,000 worth of products per year by handling the division's two largest accounts; to keep the sales force happy; and to keep customers away from the executives (including you).[5] Unfortunately, some supervisors tend to be lax when it comes to setting specific goals for their employees.

▲ *The best performance appraisal systems, as we'll see, are those in which the supervisor or manager makes an ongoing effort to coach and monitor employees, instead of leaving evaluation to the last minute.*

You therefore have to quantify your expectations. The most straightforward way to do this (for the sales manager job above, for example) is to set measurable standards for each expectation. You might measure the "personal selling" activity in terms of how many dollars of sales the manger is to generate personally. Perhaps measure "Keeping the sales force happy" in terms of turnover (on the assumption that less than 10% of the sales force will quit in any given year if morale is high). Measure "Keeping customers away from executives" with "no more than 10 customer complaints per year." The point is this: Employees should always know ahead of time how and on what basis you're going to appraise them. Now let's look at some appraisal methods.

APPRAISAL METHODS

Managers usually conduct the appraisal using a predetermined and formal method like one or more of those described next. It is "predetermined" insofar as most firms do (or should) decide ahead of time what tools and processes they're going to use. (The process would include specific decisions like what time of year appraisals are done, and who will review the completed appraisals.) Some firms create their own appraisal forms and tools; others—especially smaller ones—use off-the-shelf methods from HR suppliers like G. Neil.

Graphic Rating Scale Method

The **graphic rating scale** is the simplest and most popular technique for appraising performance. Figure 9-2 shows part of a typical rating scale. A graphic rating scale lists traits (such as quality and reliability) and a range of performance

graphic rating scale
A scale that lists a number of traits and a range of performance for each. The employee is then rated by identifying the score that best describes his or her level of performance for each trait.

▼ **FIGURE 9-2   One Page of a Two-Page Graphic Rating Scale with Space for Comments**

Performance Appraisal

Employee Name _____   Title _____

Department _____   Employee Payroll Number _____

Reason for Review: ☐ Annual   ☐ Promotion   ☐ Unsatisfactory Performance

                      ☐ Merit   ☐ End Probation Period   ☐ Other _____

Date employee began present position ____/____/____

Date of last appraisal ____/____/____   Scheduled appraisal date ____/____/____

Instructions: Carefully evaluate employee's work performance in relation to current job requirements. Check rating box to indicate the employee's performance. Indicate N/A if not applicable. Assign points for each rating within the scale and indicate in the corresponding points box. Points will be totaled and averaged for an overall performance score.

RATING IDENTIFICATION

O—Outstanding—Performance is exceptional in all areas and is recognizable as being far superior to others.

V—Very Good—Results clearly exceed most position requirements. Performance is of high quality and is achieved on a consistent basis.

G—Good—Competent and dependable level of performance. Meets performance standards of the job.

I—Improvement Needed—Performance is deficient in certain areas. Improvement is necessary.

U—Unsatisfactory—Results are generally unacceptable and require immediate improvement. No merit increase should be granted to individuals with this rating.

N—Not Rated—Not applicable or too soon to rate.

GENERAL FACTORS	RATING SCALE		SUPPORTIVE DETAILS OR COMMENTS
1. **Quality—**The accuracy, thoroughness, and acceptability of work performed.	O ☐ 100–90 V ☐ 90–80 G ☐ 80–70 I ☐ 70–60 U ☐ below 60	Points	
2. **Productivity—**The quantity and efficiency of work produced in a specified period of time.	O ☐ 100–90 V ☐ 90–80 G ☐ 80–70 I ☐ 70–60 U ☐ below 60	Points	
3. **Job Knowledge—**The practical/technical skills and information used on the job.	O ☐ 100–90 V ☐ 90–80 G ☐ 80–70 I ☐ 70–60 U ☐ below 60	Points	
4. **Reliability—**The extent to which an employee can be relied upon regarding task completion and follow-up.	O ☐ 100–90 V ☐ 90–80 G ☐ 80–70 I ☐ 70–60 U ☐ below 60	Points	
5. **Availability—**The extent to which an employee is punctual, observes prescribed work break/meal periods, and the overall attendance record.	O ☐ 100–90 V ☐ 90–80 G ☐ 80–70 I ☐ 70–60 U ☐ below 60	Points	
6. **Independence—**The extent of work performed with little or no supervision.	O ☐ 100–90 V ☐ 90–80 G ☐ 80–70 I ☐ 70–60 U ☐ below 60	Points	

▼ **FIGURE 9-3   Portion of a Sample Performance Appraisal Form for Actual Duties**

Name _____	Rating Scale Key
Position _____	☐1 Fails to meet job requirements
Rating period from _____ to _____	☐2 Essentially meets job requirements
Rater name _____	☐3 Fully meets job requirements
Rater title _____	☐4 Meets job requirements with distinction
Department _____	☐5 Exceeds job requirements

Part II: Rating Scales for Task Areas

Position: Administrative Secretary Duties and Responsibilities		
Reception PCT. (30%)	RATING: 1 ☐ 2 ☐ 3 ☐ 4 ☐ 5 ☐	
Receiving and recording initial contacts in person or on the telephone and courteously assisting callers or visitors: Answers incoming telephone calls, takes message, provides information or routes call to appropriate individual; greets visitors, provides information or directs to appropriate office or individual; acts as hostess and provides incidental services to visitors in waiting status; operates automatic answering service; maintains log of callers and visitors to cooperative.	Comments	

Source: James Buford Jr., Bettye Burkhalter, and Grover Jacobs, "Link Job Description to Performance Appraisals." *Personnel Journal*, June 1988, pp. 135–136.

values (from unsatisfactory to outstanding) for each trait. You rate each subordinate by circling or checking the score that best describes his or her performance for each trait. You then total the assigned values for the traits.

Instead of appraising generic factors (such as quality and quantity) that apply to all or most jobs, you may focus on the job's actual duties. For example, Figure 9-3 shows part of an appraisal form for an administrative secretary.[6] The form uses the job's five main sets of duties, one of which is "Reception." HR took the five duties from the job description and prioritized them. It then assigned an importance rating to each duty, shown as a percentage at the top of each of the five duties (reception is 30%). There is also space on the form for comments and for evaluation of general performance attributes like reporting for work on time and observing work rules. The supervisor rates the person on each job duty. Combining the rating for each duty with the duty's importance weighting produces an overall rating for the job.

Alternation Ranking Method

Ranking employees from best to worst on a trait or traits is another option. Since it is usually easier to distinguish between the worst and best employees, an **alternation ranking method** is most popular. First, list all subordinates to be rated, and then cross out the names of any not known well enough to rank. Then, on a form like that in Figure 9-4, indicate the employee who is the highest on the characteristic being measured and also the one who is the lowest. Then choose the next highest and the next lowest, alternating between highest and lowest until all employees have been ranked.

alternation ranking method Ranking employees from best to worst on a particular trait, choosing highest, then lowest, until all are ranked.

Paired Comparison Method

The **paired comparison method** helps make the ranking method more precise. For every trait (quantity of work, quality of work, and so on), you pair and compare every subordinate with every other subordinate.

paired comparison method Ranking employees by making a chart of all possible pairs of the employees for each trait and indicating which is the better employee of the pair.

► **FIGURE 9-4**
Alternation
Ranking Scale

ALTERNATION RANKING SCALE

For the Trait: _____

For the trait you are measuring, list all the employees you want to rank. Put the highest-ranking employee's name on line 1. Put the lowest-ranking employee's name on line 20. Then list the next highest ranking on line 2, the next lowest ranking on line 19, and so on. Continue until all names are on the scale.

Highest-ranking employee

1. _____   11. _____
2. _____   12. _____
3. _____   13. _____
4. _____   14. _____
5. _____   15. _____
6. _____   16. _____
7. _____   17. _____
8. _____   18. _____
9. _____   19. _____
10. _____   20. _____

Lowest-ranking employee

Suppose you have five employees to rate. In the paired comparison method, you make a chart, as in Figure 9-5, of all possible pairs of employees for each trait. Then, for each trait, indicate (with a + or –) who is the better employee of the pair. Next add up the number of +s for each employee. In Figure 9-5, Maria ranked highest (has the most + marks) for quality of work, whereas Art was ranked highest for creativity.

► **FIGURE 9-5**
Ranking Employees
by the Paired
Comparison Method

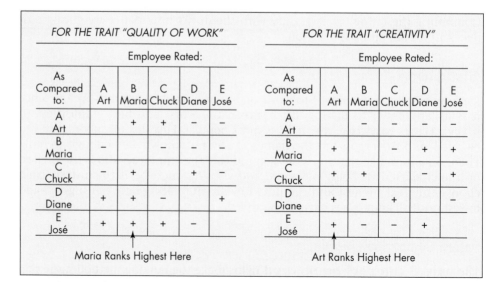

FOR THE TRAIT "QUALITY OF WORK"

Employee Rated:

As Compared to:	A Art	B Maria	C Chuck	D Diane	E José
A Art		+	+	–	–
B Maria	–		–	–	–
C Chuck	–	+		+	–
D Diane	+	+	–		+
E José	+	+	+	–	

Maria Ranks Highest Here

FOR THE TRAIT "CREATIVITY"

Employee Rated:

As Compared to:	A Art	B Maria	C Chuck	D Diane	E José
A Art		–	–	–	–
B Maria	+		–	+	+
C Chuck	+	+		–	+
D Diane	+	–	+		–
E José	+	–	–	+	

Art Ranks Highest Here

Note: + means "better than." – means "worse than." For each chart, add up the number of +'s in each column to get the highest-ranked employee.

Forced Distribution Method

The **forced distribution method** is similar to grading on a curve. With this method, you place predetermined percentages of ratees into performance categories. For example, you may decide to distribute employees as follows:

15% high performers

20% high-average performers

30% average performers

20% low-average performers

15% low performers

(The proportions in each category need not be symmetrical; GE uses top 20%, middle 70%, and bottom 10% for managers.)

As for students at school, forced distribution means two things for employees: Not everyone can get an A; and one's performance is always rated relative to one's peers. One practical, if low-tech, way to do this is to write each employee's name on a separate index card. Then, for each trait (quality of work, creativity, and so on), place the employee's card in the appropriate performance category.

More firms are adopting this practice. Sun Microsystems recently began forced ranking of all its 43,000 employees. Managers appraise employees in groups of about 30, and 10% of each group gets 90 days to improve. If they're still in the bottom 10% in 90 days, they get a chance to resign and take severance pay. Some decide to stay, but "If it doesn't work out," the firm fires them without severance.[7] At (now bankrupt) Texas energy company Enron Corp., managers appraised employees twice a year; those in the bottom 15% had 6 months to improve or leave.[8]

◆ **HIGH-PERFORMANCE INSIGHT** Merck and Company has used this approach for all exempt employees who receive merit pay raises based on their performance ratings.[9] It began doing so when Merck discovered that 80% of its exempt employees were receiving ratings of 4 and above on the 5-point scale.

At Merck, exempt employees receive annual performance appraisals in December. They meet with their supervisors to review their annual accomplishments (relative to their goals) and receive one of five ratings: EX (exceptional), WD (with distinction), HS (high Merck standard), RI (room for improvement), and NA (not acceptable). Five percent of the department's employees can receive EX ratings, 15% WD ratings, and the vast majority—70%—should fall in the "high Merck standard" middle range.

It's not realistic to force managers with only four or five employees to assign them to five classes. Merck therefore uses a roll-up system: The managers of several departments in the same division review their own exempt employees, and then negotiate a divisionwide allocation. The biggest problem was getting employees who viewed themselves as EX to understand that getting an HS (high Merck standard) isn't the equivalent of getting a C. But things are not as easy in a small business; let's look.

forced distribution method
Similar to grading on a curve; predetermined percentages of ratees are placed in various performance categories.

ENTREPRENEURS + HR

Appraisals at Glenroy

Appraising employees is different when you're running your own business. For one thing, "quartiling" your employees—putting the worst 10% or 20% in the bottom group, and threatening them with dismissal—is certainly possible, and many small firms do this. Yet doing so is easier when you're running a 1,000-employee division than when you're running an 8-person store. Managers in large firms can call on their HR support staff for help in conducting the appraisals and handling any repercussions—such as employees threatening to leave or to sue. And of course, they have HR to replace those who leave, and a large staff to pick up the extra work while HR finds the replacements.

This kind of support is rarely available to small firms, and particularly to small retail stores. Staffing the business with world-class employees is no less important here. Yet in practice, the owner-manager is under pressure to keep the business staffed, and to manage varied tasks, from sales to banking, for which larger firms have specialists. Some therefore turn to much more informal appraisal processes. For example, Glenroy, Inc., of Menomonee Falls, Wisconsin, manufactures packaging materials for food and personal care items. It stopped doing formal appraisals years ago. "We are more involved in [constant communication] instead of saving things up once a year and then springing it on them," says the firm's head of finance and administration.[10]

Critical Incident Method

critical incident method
Keeping a record of uncommonly good or undesirable examples of an employee's work-related behavior and reviewing it with the employee at predetermined times.

With the **critical incident method**, the supervisor keeps a log of positive and negative examples (critical incidents) of a subordinate's work-related behavior. Every six months or so, supervisor and subordinate meet to discuss the latter's performance, using the incidents as examples.

This method has several advantages. It provides actual examples of good and poor performance the supervisor can use to explain the person's rating. It ensures that the manager or supervisor thinks about the subordinate's appraisal all during the year. The rating does not just reflect the employee's most recent performance. The list hopefully provides examples of what specifically the subordinate can do to eliminate any deficiencies. However, without some numerical rating, this method is not too useful for comparing employees or making salary decisions.

It's useful to accumulate incidents that are tied to the employee's goals. In Table 9-1, one of the assistant plant manager's continuing duties was to supervise procurement and to minimize inventory costs. The critical incident log shows that the assistant plant manager let inventory storage costs rise 15%; this provides a specific example of what performance must be improved in the future.

Narrative Forms

The final written appraisal is often in narrative form. For example, Figure 9-6 presents part of a Performance Improvement Plan; managers use it to evaluate the progress and development of employees. As you can see, the person's supervisor is

▶ **TABLE 9-1**
Examples of Critical Incidents for an Assistant Plant Manager

Continuing Duties	Targets	Critical Incidents
Schedule production for plant	Full utilization of personnel and machinery in plant; orders delivered on time	Instituted new production scheduling system; decreased late orders by 10% last month; increased machine utilization in plant by 20% last month
Supervise procurement of raw materials and inventory control	Minimize inventory costs while keeping adequate supplies on hand	Let inventory storage costs rise 15% last month; overordered parts "A" and "B" by 20%; underordered part "C" by 30%
Supervise machinery maintenance	No shutdowns due to faulty machinery	Instituted new preventative maintenance system for plant; prevented a machine breakdown by discovering faulty part

◀ **FIGURE 9-6**
Employee
Improvement Plan

PERFORMANCE IMPROVEMENT PLAN

Name _____   Date _____

Position Title _____   Dept./Div. _____

I. Purpose and Objective

This form and process is designed to assist the supervisor in analyzing *how* an employee is performing his or her work, that is, the individual skills and knowledge they use in performing their job responsibilities. The primary objective for you in completing this Performance Analysis and subsequent discussions with the employee is to help the person improve.

II. Steps in the Process

A. Performance Factors and Skills—The individual skills and performance factors represent the major abilities that are required of most employees to perform their jobs. After reading the description of each factor, assign a rating of the employee's skill proficiency using the following guide:

S—Strength
SA—Satisfactory
N—Needs Improvement
NA—Not Applicable

Space is provided at the end of this form to write out performance factors/skills which you may consider to be important and are not found on this form. We suggest, however, that you avoid adding personality traits that do not influence performance.

B. Performance Analysis and Examples—This section is provided for you to support your judgment with specific *performance related* examples of observed behavior. These examples should be stated in terms of what the employee did or said (in completing a task or project) as it relates to the performance factor.

C. Improvement Plan—Specific actions should be listed in this section that will be taken to assist the employee in those areas that require performance improvement. It is suggested that supervisor and subordinate develop this plan jointly in a discussion session. These actions should focus on activities, tasks, training, expanded job duties, etc., that will afford the employee an opportunity to develop the needed skill. The written Improvement Plan should also state *who* is responsible for completing each step, a *timetable* for completion and a *feedback/followup* process that will monitor the progress.

D. Discussion with the Employee—The performance rating and analysis of each factor or skill must be discussed with the employee. The principal focus of this meeting should be on problem solving, i.e., to stimulate the employee to think about the probable causes of the skill or knowledge deficiency and to generate ideas on how to bring about performance improvement in these areas. Working together, supervisor and employee should examine the cause of each deficiency and then jointly develop and agree upon a logical course of action for improvement. The Improvement Plan should be realistic, written down, and followed up in future sessions.

Performance Factors/Skills	Performance Analysis & Examples	Improvement Plan
PLANNING—Forecasting, setting objectives, establishing strategies and courses of action, budgeting, scheduling, programming, and outlining procedures.		
ORGANIZING—Grouping of activities to achieve results, delegating, staffing, and using available resources.		

Source: *Handbook of Personnel Forms, Records, and Reports* (New York: McGraw-Hill, 1982), pp. 216–219.

asked (1) to rate the employee's performance for each performance factor or skill, and (2) to write down examples, and (3) an improvement plan. This aids the employee in understanding where his or her performance was good or bad, and how to improve that performance.

Behaviorally Anchored Rating Scales

behaviorally anchored rating scale (BARS)
An appraisal method that aims at combining the benefits of narrative critical incidents and quantified ratings by anchoring a quantified scale with specific narrative examples of good and poor performance.

A **behaviorally anchored rating scale (BARS)** combines the benefits of narratives, critical incidents, and quantified (graphic rating type) scales, by anchoring a rating scale with specific behavioral examples of good or poor performance. Its proponents say it provides better, more equitable appraisals than do the other tools we discussed.[11]

Developing a BARS typically requires five steps:

1. *Generate critical incidents.* Ask persons who know the job (job holders and/or supervisors) to describe specific illustrations (critical incidents) of effective and ineffective performance.

2. *Develop performance dimensions.* Have these people cluster the incidents into a smaller set of (5 or 10) performance dimensions, and define each dimension, such as "conscientiousness."

3. *Reallocate incidents.* Another group of people who also know the job then reallocate the original critical incidents. They get the cluster definitions and the critical incidents, and must reassign each incident to the cluster they think it fits best. Retain a critical incident if some percentage (usually 50% to 80%) of this second group assigns it to the same cluster as did the first group.

4. *Scale the incidents.* This second group then rates the behavior described by the incident as to how effectively or ineffectively it represents performance on the dimension (7- to 9-point scales are typical).

5. *Develop a final instrument.* Choose about six or seven of the incidents as the dimension's behavioral anchors.[12]

◆ **RESEARCH INSIGHT** Three researchers developed a BARS for grocery checkout clerks.[13] They collected critical incidents, and then clustered these into eight performance dimensions:

> Knowledge and Judgment
> Conscientiousness
> Skill in Human Relations
> Skill in Operation of Register
> Skill in Bagging
> Organizational Ability of Checkstand Work
> Skill in Monetary Transactions
> Observational Ability

They then developed a behaviorally anchored rating scale for one of these dimensions, "knowledge and judgment." It contained a scale (ranging from 1 to 9) for rating performance from "extremely poor" to "extremely good." Then a specific critical incident ("by knowing the price of items, this checker would be expected to look for mismarked and unmarked items") helped anchor or specify what was meant by "extremely good" (9) performance. Similarly, they used several other critical incident anchors along the performance scale from (8) down to (1).

Advantages While more time consuming than other appraisal tools, BARS may also have advantages:[14]

1. *A more accurate gauge.* People who know the job and its requirements better than anyone develop the BARS. This should produce a good gauge of job performance.

2. *Clearer standards.* The critical incidents along the scale make clear what to look for in terms of superior performance, average performance, and so forth.

3. *Feedback.* The critical incidents make it easier to explain the ratings to appraisees.

4. *Independent dimensions.* Systematically clustering the critical incidents into five or six performance dimensions (such as "knowledge and judgment") should help to make the dimensions more independent of one another. For example, a rater should be less likely to rate an employee high on all dimensions simply because he or she was rated high in "conscientiousness."

5. *Consistency.*[15] BARS evaluations also seem to be relatively consistent and reliable, in that different raters' appraisals of the same person tend to be similar.

Management by Objectives (MBO)

Stripped to its basics, **management by objectives (MBO)** requires the manager to set specific measurable goals with each employee and then periodically discuss the latter's progress toward these goals. You could engage in a modest MBO program with subordinates by jointly setting goals and periodically providing feedback. However, the term *MBO* generally refers to a comprehensive, organizationwide goal-setting and appraisal program consisting of six steps:

> **management by objectives (MBO)**
> Involves setting specific measurable goals with each employee and then periodically reviewing the progress made.

1. *Set the organization's goals.* Establish an organizationwide plan for next year and set company goals.

2. *Set departmental goals.* Next, department heads take these company goals (like "boost profits by 20%") and, with their superiors, jointly set goals for their departments.

3. *Discuss departmental goals.* Department heads discuss the department's goals with all subordinates, often at a departmentwide meeting. They ask employees to set their own preliminary individual goals; in other words, how can each employee contribute to the department's goals?

4. *Define expected results* (set individual goals). Department heads and their subordinates set short-term individual performance targets.

5. *Performance reviews.* Department heads compare each employee's actual and targeted performance.

6. *Provide feedback.* Department heads and employees discuss and evaluate the latters' progress.

There are three problems in using MBO. Setting unclear, unmeasurable objectives is the main one. An objective such as "will do a better job of training" is useless. On the other hand, "will have four subordinates promoted during the year" is a measurable objective.

Second, MBO is time consuming. Setting objectives, measuring progress, and giving

▲ *One of the foundations of a good Management by Objectives program is open communication, which fosters employee commitment to the objectives and goals.*

feedback can take several hours per employee per year, over and above the time you already spend doing each person's appraisal.

Third, setting objectives with the subordinate sometimes turns into a tug-of-war, with you pushing for higher quotas and the subordinate pushing for lower ones. Knowing the job and the person's ability is important. To motivate performance, the objectives must be fair and attainable. The more you know about the job and the person's ability, the more confident you can be about the standards you set.

Computerized and Web-Based Performance Appraisal

Several relatively inexpensive performance appraisal software programs are on the market.[16] These generally enable managers to keep notes on subordinates during the year, and then to electronically rate employees on a series of performance traits. The programs then generate written text to support each part of the appraisal.

Employee Appraiser (developed by the Austin-Hayne Corporation, San Mateo, California) presents a menu of more than a dozen evaluation dimensions, including dependability, initiative, communication, decision making, leadership, judgment, and planning and productivity. Within each dimension are various performance factors, again presented in menu form. For example, under "communication" are separate factors for writing, verbal communication, receptivity to feedback and criticism, listening skills, ability to focus on the desired results, keeping others informed, and openness. When the user clicks on a performance factor, the person sees a relatively sophisticated version of a graphic rating scale. Instead of a scale with numbers, however, Employee Appraiser uses behaviorally anchored examples. For example, for verbal communication, there are six choices, ranging from "presents ideas clearly" to "lacks structure." After the manager picks the phrase that most accurately describes the worker, Employee Appraiser generates sample text.

PerformanceReview.com, from KnowledgePoint of Petaluma, California, lets managers evaluate employees online based on their competencies, goals, and development plans. Managers can choose from standard competencies such as "communications," or create their own.

PerformancePro.net from the Exxceed Company of Chicago, Illinois, is another Internet-based performance review system. It helps the manager and his or her subordinates develop performance objectives for the employee and conduct the annual review.[17]

The Web site improvenow.com lets employees fill out a 60-question assessment online with or without their supervisor's approval, and then gives the supervisor the team's feedback with an overall score.[18] Evaluators recently rated two appraisal packages outstanding: PeopleSoft HR management (version 7.5), and SAP r/3 hr (version 7.5).[19]

Electronic performance monitoring (EPM) is in some respects the ultimate in computerized appraising. EPM means having supervisors electronically monitor the amount of computerized data an employee is processing per day, and thereby his or her performance.[20] As two researchers note, "organizations now use computer networks, sophisticated telephone systems, and both wireless audio and video links to monitor and record the work activities of employees." It's estimated

▲ **WEBNOTE**
Exxceed provides a number of HR services that utilize the Internet, including PerformancePro.net, as its home page shows.

www.exxceed.com

that as many as 26 million U.S. workers have their performance monitored electronically. This fact has already triggered congressional legislation aimed at requiring that employees receive precise notification of when they will be monitored.

How do employees react to EPM? Studies suggest two things. First, "participants [employees] with the ability to delay or prevent electronic performance monitoring indicated higher feelings of personal control and demonstrated superior task performance." In other words, let employees have some control over how and when they're monitored.[21] If you can't, then the findings suggest this: Don't let them know when you're actually monitoring them. Participants who knew exactly when the monitoring was taking place actually expressed lower feelings of personal control than did those who did not know when the monitoring was on.

▲ *Technology has updated the appraisal process. New software programs enable employees to check their own performance against prescribed criteria.*

Mixing the Methods

Most firms combine several methods. Figure 9-2 (page 244) presents an example. Basically, this is a graphic rating scale, with descriptive phrases included to define each trait. However, it also has a section for comments below each trait. This lets the rater provide several critical incidents. The quantifiable rating facilitates comparing employees, and is useful for salary, transfer, and promotion decisions. The critical incidents provide specific examples for developmental discussions.[22]

APPRAISING PERFORMANCE: PROBLEMS AND SOLUTIONS

Few of the things a manager does are fraught with more peril than appraising subordinates' performance. Employees in general tend to be overly optimistic about what their ratings will be. You and they know their raises, career progress, and peace of mind may well hinge on how you rate them. This alone should make it difficult to rate performance; even more of a problem, however, are the numerous technical problems that can cast doubt on just how fair the whole process is. Let's turn to some of these more technical appraisal problems and how to solve them, and to several other pertinent appraisal issues.

Dealing with Rating Scale Appraisal Problems

Most employers still depend on graphic-type rating scales to appraise performance, but these scales are especially susceptible to several problems: unclear standards, halo effect, central tendency, leniency or strictness, and bias.

Unclear Standards   Table 9-2 illustrates the **unclear standards** problem. This graphic rating scale seems objective, but would probably result in unfair appraisals because the traits and degrees of merit are ambiguous. For example, different supervisors would probably define "good" performance, "fair" performance, and so on differently. The same is true of traits such as "quality of work" or "creativity."

There are several ways to fix this problem. The best way is to develop and include descriptive phrases that define each trait, as in Figure 9-2. There the form specified what was meant by "outstanding," "superior," and "good" quality of

unclear standards
An appraisal scale that is too open to interpretation.

► **TABLE 9-2**
A Graphic Rating
Scale with Unclear
Standards

	Excellent	Good	Fair	Poor
Quality of work				
Quantity of work				
Creativity				
Integrity				

Note: For example, what exactly is meant by "good," "quantity of work," and so forth?

halo effect
In performance appraisal, the problem that occurs when a supervisor's rating of a subordinate on one trait biases the rating of that person on other traits.

central tendency
A tendency to rate all employees the same way, such as rating them all average.

strictness/leniency
The problem that occurs when a supervisor has a tendency to rate all subordinates either high or low.

work. This specificity results in appraisals that are more consistent and more easily explained.

Halo Effect Experts define **halo effect** as "the influence of a rater's general impression on ratings of specific ratee qualities."[23] For example, supervisors often rate unfriendly employees lower on all traits, rather than just for the trait "gets along well with others." Being aware of this problem is a major step toward avoiding it. Supervisory training can also alleviate the problem.[24]

Central Tendency Some supervisors stick to the middle when filling in rating scales. For example, if the rating scale ranges from 1 to 7, they tend to avoid the highs (6 and 7) and lows (1 and 2) and rate most of their people between 3 and 5. If you use a graphic rating scale, this **central tendency** could mean that you rate all employees "average." That may distort the evaluations, making them less useful for promotion, salary, or counseling purposes. Ranking employees instead of using graphic rating scales can reduce this problem, since ranking means you can't rate them all average.

Leniency or Strictness Other supervisors tend to rate all their subordinates consistently high (or low), just as some instructors are notoriously high or low graders. This **strictness/leniency** problem is especially severe with graphic rating scales, when firms don't tell their supervisors to avoid giving all their employees high (or low) ratings. On the other hand, ranking forces them to distinguish between high and low performers.

Therefore, if a graphic rating scale must be used, it may be a good idea to impose a distribution—that, say, about 10% of the people should be rated "excellent," 20% "good," and so forth. In other words, try to get a spread (unless, of course, you're sure all your people really do fall into just one or two categories).

The appraisal you do may be less objective than you think. One study focused on how personality influenced the evaluations students gave their peers. Raters who scored higher on "conscientiousness" tended to give their peers lower ratings—they were more strict, in other words; those scoring higher on "agreeableness" gave higher ratings—they were more lenient.[25]

It's not just the appraiser's tendencies but the purpose of the appraisal that causes strictness/leniency. Two researchers reviewed 22 studies of performance appraisal leniency.[26] They concluded that "performance appraisal ratings obtained for administrative purposes [such as pay raises or promotions] were nearly one-third of a standard deviation larger than those obtained for research or employee development purposes."[27]

Bias Appraisees' personal characteristics (such as age, race, and sex) can affect their ratings, often quite apart from each ratee's actual performance.[28] In one study researchers found a systematic tendency to evaluate older ratees (over 60 years of age) lower on "performance capacity" and "potential for development" than younger employees.[29]

A study of registered nurses shows how age distorts ratings. For nurses 30 to 39 years old, they and their supervisors each rated the nurses' performance virtually the same. In the 21-to-29 category, supervisors actually rated nurses higher than the nurses rated themselves. However, for the 40-to-61 nurse age category, the supervisors rated nurses' performance lower than the nurses rated their own performance. One interpretation is that supervisors are tougher in appraising older subordinates. They don't give them as much credit for their successes, while attributing any low performance to lack of ability.[30]

Race can also affect the rating a person receives. One study reviewed performance ratings from over 20,000 bosses, 50,000 peers, and 40,000 subordinates.[31] Researchers concluded that black raters rated black ratees higher than white ratees; that white bosses (but not white subordinates) assigned more favorable ratings to white ratees than to black ratees; and that black raters assigned higher ratings than did whites, regardless of the ratee's race.[32] Such results sound a cautionary signal for employers: Since most bosses are white, "black managers who are rated by white bosses may advance at a lower rate than black managers who are rated by black bosses."[33]

However, the **bias** is not necessarily always against the minorities or women. In one study, supervisors rated low-performing blacks higher than low-performing whites, and high-performing females higher than high-performing males.[34] Even how the employee performed in the past can bias his or her current appraisal.[35] The actual error can take several forms: Some raters overestimate improvements by poor workers or declines by good ones. Sometimes—especially when the behavior change is more gradual—raters are simply insensitive to improvement or decline. In any case, the bottom line is to rate performance as objectively as possible. Try to block out the influence of factors such as previous performance, gender, age, or race.

bias
The tendency to allow individual differences such as age, race, and sex to affect the appraisal ratings employees receive.

◆ **RESEARCH INSIGHT** One study illustrates how bias can influence the way one person appraises another. In this study, researchers sought to determine the extent to which pregnancy is a source of bias in performance appraisals.[36] The subjects were 220 undergraduate students between the ages of 17 and 43 attending a midwestern university.

Two videotapes were prepared of a female "employee." Each video showed three 5-minute scenarios in which this "employee" interacted with another woman. For example, she acted as a customer representative to deal with an irate customer, tried to sell a computer system to a potential customer, and dealt with a problem subordinate. In each case, the performance level of the "employee" was designed to be average or slightly above average. The "employee" was the same in both videotapes, and the videotapes were identical—except for one difference. Researchers shot the first videotape in the "employee's" ninth month of pregnancy, the second about 5 months later. The aim of the study was to investigate whether the "employee's" pregnancy influenced the performance appraisal ratings she received in the various situations.

Several groups of student raters watched either the "pregnant" or "not pregnant" tape. They rated the "employee" on a 5-point graphic rating scale for individual characteristics such as "ability to do the job," "dependability," and "physical mannerisms."

The results suggest that pregnant women may face more workplace discrimination than do women in general. Despite seeing otherwise identical behavior by the same woman, the student raters "with a remarkably high degree of consistency" assigned lower performance ratings to a pregnant woman as opposed to a nonpregnant one.[37] And men raters seemed more susceptible to negative influence than did women. Given the fact that most employees still report to male supervisors and that supervisory ratings often determine advancement, the researchers concluded that any bias could make it even harder for women to have both children and careers.

How to Avoid Appraisal Problems

It's probably safe to say that problems like these can make an appraisal worse than no appraisal at all. Would an employee not be better off with no appraisal than with a seemingly objective but actually biased one? Problems like these aren't inevitable, though, and you can minimize them.

First, learn and understand the potential problems, and the solutions (like clarifying standards) for each. Understanding the problem can help you avoid it.

Second, use the right appraisal tool. Each tool has its own pros and cons. For example, the ranking method avoids central tendency but can cause bad feelings when employees' performances are in fact all "high"; and the ranking and forced distribution methods both provide relative—not absolute—ratings.

Third, train supervisors to reduce rating errors such as halo, leniency, and central tendency.[38] In one training program, raters watched a videotape of people at work, and then rated the workers. The trainers then placed the supervisors' ratings of these workers on a flip chart, and explained and illustrated the various errors (such as leniency and halo).[39] Packaged training programs are available. For example, Harvard Business School Publishing offers *Assessing Performance*, for about $150. It lists the steps and things to consider in preparing for and conducting the appraisal interview.[40]

Training isn't always the solution, however. In practice, several factors—including the extent to which employees' pay is tied to performance ratings, union pressure, employee turnover, time constraints, and the need to justify ratings—may be more important than training. This means that improving appraisal accuracy calls not just for training, but also for reducing the effect of outside factors such as union pressure and time constraints.[41]

A fourth solution—diary keeping—is worth the effort.[42] One study involved 112 first-line supervisors from a large electronics firm. Some attended a special training program on diary keeping. The program explained the role of critical incidents, and how the supervisors could compile these incidents into a diary or incident file to use later as a reference for a subordinate's appraisal.[43] Then came a practice session, followed by a feedback and group discussion session aimed at reinforcing the importance of recording both positive and negative incidents.[44]

The conclusion of this and similar studies is that you can reduce the adverse effects of appraisal problems by having raters compile positive and negative critical incidents as they occur during the appraisal period. Maintaining such records instead of relying on memories is definitely the preferred approach.[45]

Diary keeping is preferred but not foolproof. In one study, raters were required to keep a diary, but the diary keeping actually undermined the performance appraisal's objectiveness.[46] What could account for such apparently bizarre findings? One possibility is that managers may develop positive or negative feelings toward ratees. The managers may then seek out and record incidents that are consistent with how they feel about the ratees. In any case, it's apparent that even diary keeping is no guarantee of objectivity, and that as a rater you must always keep the cognitive nature of the appraisal process in mind. Raters bring to the task a bundle of biases, inclinations, and decision-making shortcuts, so that, potentially at least, the appraisal is bound to be a product (or victim, some might argue) of the rater's biases and inclinations.[47]

Legal and Ethical Issues in Performance Appraisal

Appraisals affect promotions, raises, and dismissals. Since passage of Title VII in 1964, courts have therefore addressed the link between appraisals and personnel actions.[48] They have often found that the inadequacies of an employer's appraisal system lay at the root of illegal discriminatory actions,[49] particularly in cases concerning layoffs, promotions, discharges, merit pay, or combinations of these.[50]

An illustrative case involved layoff decisions. The court held that the firm had violated Title VII when it laid off several Hispanic-surnamed employees on the basis of poor performance ratings.[51] The court concluded that the practice was illegal because:

1. They based the appraisals on subjective supervisory observations.
2. They didn't administer and score the appraisals in a standardized fashion.
3. Two of the three supervisory evaluators did not have daily contact with the employees they appraised.

Personal bias, unreasonably rating everyone high (or low), and relying just on recent events are some other reasons courts gave for deciding firms' appraisal processes and subsequent personnel actions were unfair.[52] Furthermore, *legal* doesn't always mean *ethical*, but ethics should be the bedrock of an appraisal. Most managers (and college students) understand that appraisers or professors can "stick to the rules" and do lawful performance reviews but still fail to provide honest assessments. As one commentator puts it:

> The overall objective of high-ethics performance reviews should be to provide an honest assessment of performance and to mutually develop a plan to improve the individual's effectiveness. That requires that we tell people where they stand and that we be straight with them.[53]

Here are some guidelines for developing a legally defensible appraisal process:[54]

1. Make sure you know what you mean by "successful performance." Conduct a job analysis to establish the criteria and standards (such as "timely project completion").
2. Incorporate these criteria and standards into a rating instrument (BARS, graphic rating scale, and so on).
3. Use clearly defined job performance dimensions (like "quantity" or "quality") rather than undefined, global measures of job performance (like "overall performance").
4. Communicate performance standards to employees and to those rating them, in writing.
5. When using graphic rating scales, avoid abstract trait names (such as "loyalty" or "honesty"), unless you can define them in terms of observable behaviors.
6. Use subjective supervisory ratings (essays, for instance) as only one component of the overall appraisal process.
7. Train supervisors to use the rating instrument properly. Give instructions on how to apply performance appraisal standards ("outstanding," and so on) when making judgments. (In 6 of 10 cases decided against the employer, the plaintiffs were able to show that supervisors applied subjective standards unevenly to minority and majority employees.)[55] If formal rater training is not possible, at least provide raters with written instructions for using the rating scale.
8. Allow appraisers substantial daily contact with the employees they're evaluating.
9. Base your appraisals on separate ratings for each of the job's performance dimensions. Using a single overall rating of performance, or ranking of employees on some global standard, is not acceptable to the courts, which often characterize such systems as vague.[56] Courts generally require combining separate ratings for each performance dimension with some formal weighting system to yield a summary score.
10. Whenever possible, have more than one appraiser conduct the appraisal, and conduct all such appraisals independently. This can help to cancel out individual errors and biases.

11. One appraiser should never have absolute authority to determine a personnel action. This is one reason why a multiple-rater procedure is becoming more popular.
12. Include an employee appeal process. Employees should have the opportunity to review and make comments, written or verbal, about their appraisals before they become final, and should have a formal appeals process through which to appeal their ratings.
13. Document all information and reasons bearing on any personnel decision: "Without exception, courts condemn informal performance evaluation practices that eschew documentation."[57]
14. Where appropriate, provide corrective guidance to assist poor performers in improving their performance.

If your case gets to court, which of these 14 guidelines will be most important in influencing the judge's decision? A review of almost 300 U.S. court decisions is informative[58]: Actions reflecting fairness and due process were most important. In particular, performing a job analysis, providing raters with written instructions, permitting employee review of results, and obtaining agreement among raters were the four practices that seemed to have the most consistent impact in most of the judicial decisions. The courts placed little emphasis on whether or not the employers formally validated their performance appraisal tools or processes.[59]

Who Should Do the Appraising?

Traditionally, the person's direct supervisor appraises his or her performance. However, other options are certainly available and are increasingly used. We'll look at the main ones.

The Immediate Supervisor Supervisors' ratings are the heart of most appraisals. This makes sense: The supervisor should be—and usually is—in the best position to observe and evaluate the subordinate's performance, and is responsible for that person's performance.

Peer Appraisals With more firms using self-managing teams, peer or team appraisals—the appraisal of an employee by his or her peers—are becoming more popular.[60] For example, an employee chooses an appraisal chairperson each year. That person then selects one supervisor and three other peers to evaluate the employee's work.

Peer appraisals can predict future management success. In one study of military officers, peer ratings were accurate in predicting which officers would be promoted and which would not.[61] In another study of more than 200 industrial managers, peer ratings were accurate in predicting who the firm would promote.[62] However, *logrolling*—when several peers collude to rate each other highly—can be a problem. Peer ratings have other benefits. One study involved placing undergraduates into self-managing work groups. The researchers found that peer appraisals had "an immediate positive impact on [improving] perception of open communication, task motivation, social loafing, group viability, cohesion, and satisfaction."[63]

Rating Committees Many employers use rating committees. These committees usually contain the employee's immediate supervisor and three or four other supervisors.

Using multiple raters can be beneficial. While there may be a discrepancy in ratings by individual supervisors, the composite ratings tend to be more reliable, fair, and valid.[64] Such ratings have higher inter-rater reliability or consistency than do ratings obtained from several peers.[65] Several raters can also help cancel out problems like bias and halo effects. Furthermore, when there are differences in ratings, they usually stem from the fact that raters at different levels observe different facets of an employee's performance, and the appraisal ought to reflect these differences.[66] Even when a committee is not used, it is customary to have the appraisal reviewed by the manager immediately above the one who makes the appraisal. This was standard practice in 16 of the 18 companies surveyed in one study.[67]

Self-Ratings Should employees appraise themselves? The basic problem, of course, is that employees usually rate themselves higher than they are rated by supervisors or peers. In one study, for instance, it was found that when asked to rate their own job performances, 40% of the employees in jobs of all types placed themselves in the top 10% ("one of the best"), while virtually all remaining employees rated themselves either in the top 25% ("well above average"), or at least in the top 50% ("above average").[68] Usually no more than 1% or 2% will place themselves in a below-average category, and then almost invariably in the top below-average category. One study concludes that individuals do not necessarily always have such positive illusions about their own performances, although in rating the performance of their group, group members did consistently give the group unrealistically high performance ratings.[69]

Supervisors requesting self-appraisals to accompany their own should therefore know that doing so may accentuate differences and rigidify positions, rather than aid the process.[70] Furthermore, even if you don't ask for a self-appraisal, your employee will almost certainly enter the performance review with his or her own self-appraisal in mind, and this will usually be higher than your rating. Therefore, come prepared for a dialogue, with specific critical incidents to make your point.

Appraisal by Subordinates More firms today let subordinates anonymously rate their supervisor's performance, a process some call *upward feedback*.[71] The process helps top managers diagnose management styles, identify potential "people" problems, and take corrective action with individual managers as required. Subordinate ratings are especially valuable when used for developmental rather than evaluative purposes.[72] Managers who receive feedback from subordinates who identify themselves view the upward appraisal process more positively than do managers who receive anonymous feedback; however, subordinates (not surprisingly) are more comfortable giving anonymous responses, and those who have to identify themselves tend to provide inflated ratings.[73]

An Example FedEx uses a three-phase upward feedback system called Survey Feedback Action (SFA). First, HR gives a standard, anonymous survey each year to every employee. It contains items designed to gather information about those things that help and hinder employees in their work environment. Sample items include: I can tell my manager what I think; my manager tells me what is expected; my manager listens to my concerns; upper management listens to ideas from my level; FedEx does a good job for our customers; and I am paid fairly for this kind of work. HR then compiles the results for a work group, and sends them to the manager. (To ensure anonymity, smaller units don't receive their own results; their results are folded in with those of several other similar units until a department of 20 or 25 people obtains the overall group's results.)

Phase 2 is a feedback session between the manager and his or her work group. The goal here is to identify specific concerns or problems, examine specific causes for these problems, and devise action plans to correct them. FedEx trains its managers to ask probing questions. For example, suppose a low-scoring survey item was, "I feel able to tell my manager what I think." Managers ask their groups questions such as, "What do I do that makes you feel I'm not interested?"

The feedback meeting should lead to a third, "action plan" phase. The action plan itself is a list of actions the manager will take to address employees' concerns and boost results. Managers use an action-planning worksheet with four columns: (1) What is the concern? (2) What is your analysis? (3) What is the cause? (4) What should be done?

◆ **RESEARCH INSIGHT** How effective is upward feedback in improving supervisors' behavior? Very, to judge from the evidence. One study involved 92 managers who were rated by one or more subordinates in each of four administrations of an upward feedback survey over two years.[74] The subordinates rated themselves and their managers on 33 behavioral statements. The feedback managers received included results from previous administrations of the survey, so they could track their performance over time.[75]

The results were impressive. According to the researchers, "managers whose initial level of performance (defined as the average rating from subordinates) was 'low' improved between administrations one and two, and sustained this improvement two years later."[76] Interestingly, the results also suggest that it's not necessarily the specific feedback that caused the performance improvement (since low-performing managers seemed to improve over time even if they didn't receive any feedback). Instead, learning what the critical supervisory behaviors were (as a result of themselves filling out the appraisal surveys), plus knowing their subordinates would be appraising them, may have been enough to cause the improved behavior.

360-Degree Feedback Many firms have expanded the idea of upward feedback into "360-degree feedback." Ratings are collected "all around" an employee, from supervisors, subordinates, peers, and internal or external customers.[77] According to one study, 29% of the responding employers already use 360-degree feedback (also called "multi-source assessment"), and another 11% had plans to implement it.[78] The feedback is generally used for development, rather than for pay increases.[79]

Most 360-degree feedback systems contain several common features. Appropriate parties—peers, supervisors, subordinates, and customers, for instance—complete surveys on an individual. The surveys take many forms but often include supervisory skill items such as "returns phone calls promptly," "listens well," or "[my manager] keeps me informed."[80] Computerized systems then compile all this feedback into individualized reports that HR presents to the ratees. The ratees are often the only ones who get these completed reports. They then meet with their own supervisors and sometimes with their subordinates and share the information they feel is pertinent for the purpose of developing a self-improvement plan.[81]

HR.NET

Avoiding 360-Degree Paperwork

With multiple employees to appraise and multiple raters for each employee, 360-degree assessments can be paperwork nightmares. One chemical company president received a book-length 360-degree review, in which reviewers numerically rated the president on 96 categories.[82] Several net-based programs are now available. For example, Visual 360 from MindSolve Technologies of Gainsville, Florida (see Webnote), lets the rater log in, open a screen with a rating scale, and then rate the person along a series of competencies with ratings such as "top five percent."[83]

Another way to avoid 360-degree paperwork problems is to put the whole process on the Net. For example, the Internet-based system used at Farmington, Connecticut based Otis Elevator Company allows peers, customers, teammates, supervisors, direct subordinates, and suppliers to appraise managers. All information is encrypted; passwords ensure that only authorized persons access the actual evaluations.

Otis's worldwide engineering group implemented this system for several reasons. Earlier (non-Internet and non-360) systems consumed too much time and required too much paperwork. Employees viewed evaluations as an unavoidable hassle and, worse, most felt they weren't helpful for either the employees or the company. The parent firm had also just implemented a new competency-based approach to evaluating project teams, so for the first time the firm wanted its engineering managers' leadership skills evaluated.

After reviewing several 360-degree feedback tools, the division decided to go with a system designed by the firm's consultants. The Internet-based system gives managers feedback on team leadership skills, and particularly on behaviors required to manage project teams. A total of 75 items measure desirable behaviors such as "employee uses humor to diffuse tension and create harmony," and undesirable ones like "employee tends to blame people when performance is poor." Appraisers choose those that apply.

The system is now working effectively, but there were several people-related start-up glitches. Appraisers were less computer savvy than they thought they were; they forgot passwords; questions were raised about confidentiality; and some had problems giving, receiving, and reacting to feedback. However, the bottom line seems to be that "an Internet-based 360-degree feedback system can produce the information needed for coaching and individual developmental plans much faster than the typical paper and pencil evaluation."[84]

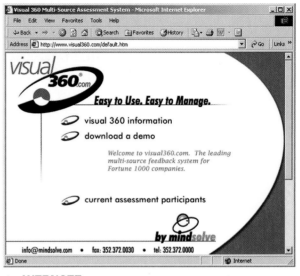

▲ **WEBNOTE**

Visual 360.com is a software program that eliminates the paperwork involved in 360-degree feedback.

www.visual360.com

Some doubt 360-degree's practicality. Employees usually do these reviews anonymously, so those with an ax to grind can misuse the system. A Dilbert cartoon strip, announcing that evaluations by co-workers will help decide raises, has one character asking, "If my co-workers got small raises, won't there be more available in the budget for me?"[85]

Today the procedure's use is diminishing. After much initial fanfare, some firms, like GE, backed off from this approach. Some found the paperwork overwhelming; others found that some employees colluded with peers to give each other high ratings. But others still argue that progressive executives welcome 360-degree feedback, since "by laying themselves open to praise and criticism from all directions and inviting others to do the same, they guide their organizations to new capacities for continuous improvement."[86]

THE APPRAISAL INTERVIEW

An appraisal typically culminates in an **appraisal interview**. Here, supervisor and subordinate review the appraisal and make plans to remedy deficiencies and reinforce strengths. Interviews like these are potentially uncomfortable, since few people like to receive—or give—negative feedback.[87] Adequate preparation and effective implementation are therefore essential.

appraisal interview
An interview in which the supervisor and subordinate review the appraisal and make plans to remedy deficiencies and reinforce strengths.

Types of Interviews

There are three basic types of appraisal interviews, each with its own objectives:

Appraisal Interview Type	Appraisal Interview Objective
1. Performance is satisfactory— Employee is promotable	1. Make development plans
2. Satisfactory—Not promotable	2. Maintain performance
3. Unsatisfactory—Correctable	3. Plan correction

If the employee is unsatisfactory and the situation is uncorrectable, you can usually skip the interview. You either tolerate the person's poor performance for now, or dismiss the person.

Satisfactory—Promotable is the easiest of the three appraisal interviews: The person's performance is satisfactory and there is a promotion ahead. Your objective is to discuss the person's career plans and to develop a specific action plan for the educational and professional development the person needs to move to the next job.

Satisfactory—Not promotable is for employees whose performance is satisfactory but for whom promotion is not possible. Perhaps there is no more room in the company. Some employees are also happy where they are and don't want a promotion.[88] Your objective here is to maintain satisfactory performance. This is not easy. The best option is usually to find incentives that are important to the person and enough to maintain satisfactory performance. These might include extra time off, a small bonus, additional authority to handle a slightly enlarged job, and reinforcement, perhaps in the form of an occasional "well done!"

When the person's performance is unsatisfactory but correctable, the interview objective is to lay out an action plan (as explained below) for correcting the unsatisfactory performance.

How to Conduct the Appraisal Interview

First, prepare for the interview.[89] Assemble the data. Study the person's job description, compare performance to the standards, and review the employee's previous appraisals. Next, prepare the employee. Give the employee at least a week's notice to review his or her work, read over the job description, analyze problems, and gather questions and comments. Finally, choose the time and place.

Find a mutually agreeable time for the interview and allow enough time for the entire interview. Interviews with lower-level personnel like clerical workers and maintenance staff should take no more than an hour. Appraising management employees often takes two or three hours. Be sure the interview is done in a private place where you won't be interrupted by phone calls or visitors.

There are four things to keep in mind in actually conducting the interview:

1. *Be direct and specific.* Talk in terms of objective work data. Use examples such as absences, tardiness, quality records, inspection reports, scrap or waste, orders processed, productivity records, material used or consumed, timeliness of tasks or projects, control or reduction of costs, numbers of errors, costs compared to budgets, customers' comments, product returns, order processing time, inventory level and accuracy, accident reports, and so on.

2. *Don't get personal.* Don't say, "You're too slow in producing those reports." Instead, try to compare the person's performance to a standard ("These reports should normally be done within 10 days"). Similarly, don't compare the person's performance to that of other people ("He's quicker than you are").

3. *Encourage the person to talk.* Stop and listen to what the person is saying; ask open-ended questions such as, "What do you think we can do to improve the situation?" Use a command such as "Go on," or "Tell me more." Restate the person's last point as a question, such as, "You don't think you can get the job done?"

4. *Don't tiptoe around.* Don't get personal, but do make sure the person leaves knowing specifically what he or she is doing right and doing wrong. Give specific examples; make sure the person understands; and get agreement before he or she leaves on how things will be improved, and by when. Develop an action plan showing steps and expected results, as in Figure 9-7.[90]

How to Handle a Defensive Subordinate Defenses are an important and familiar aspect of our lives. When a supervisor tells someone his or her performance is poor, the first reaction is often denial. By denying the fault, the person avoids having to question his or her own competence. Others react to criticism with anger and aggression. This helps them let off steam and postpones confronting the immediate problem until they are able to cope with it. Still others react to criticism by retreating into a shell.

In any event, understanding and dealing with defensiveness is an important appraisal skill. In his book *Effective Psychology for Managers*, psychologist Mortimer Feinberg suggests the following:

1. Recognize that defensive behavior is normal.
2. Never attack a person's defenses. Don't try to "explain someone to themselves" by saying things like, "You know the real reason you're using that excuse is that you can't bear to be blamed for anything." Instead, try to concentrate on the act itself ("sales are down") rather than on the person ("you're not selling enough").
3. Postpone action. Sometimes it is best to do nothing at all. People frequently react to sudden threats by instinctively hiding behind their "masks." But given sufficient time, a more rational reaction takes over.
4. Recognize your own limitations. Don't expect to be able to solve every problem that comes up, especially the human ones. More important, remember that a supervisor should not try to be a psychologist. Offering your people understanding is one thing; trying to deal with deep psychological problems is another matter entirely.

How to Criticize a Subordinate When criticism is required, do it in a manner that lets the person maintain his or her dignity and sense of worth. Criticize in private, and do it constructively. Provide examples of critical incidents and specific suggestions of what could be done and why. Avoid once-a-year "critical broadsides" by giving

◀ **FIGURE 9-7**
Example of an Action Plan

ACTION PLAN

Date: May 18, 2002

For: John, Assistant Plant Manager
Problem: Parts inventory too high
Objective: Reduce plant parts inventory by 10% in June

Action Steps	When	Expected Results
Determine average monthly parts inventory	6/2	Establish a base from which to measure progress
Review ordering quantities and parts usage	6/15	Identify overstock items
Ship excess parts to regional warehouse and scrap obsolete parts	6/20	Clear stock space
Set new ordering quantities for all parts	6/25	Avoid future overstocking
Check records to measure where we are now	7/1	See how close we are to objective

feedback on a daily basis, so that at the formal review there are no surprises. Never say the person is "always" wrong (since no one is ever "always" wrong or right). Finally, criticism should be objective and free of any personal biases on your part.

How to Ensure the Interview Leads to Improved Performance You should clear up job-related problems and set improvement goals and a schedule for achieving them. In one study, the researchers found that whether or not subordinates expressed satisfaction with their appraisal interview depended mostly on three factors: (1) not feeling threatened during the interview; (2) having an opportunity to present their ideas and feelings and to influence the course of the interview; and (3) having a helpful and constructive supervisor conduct the interview.[91]

However, you don't just want subordinates to be satisfied with their appraisal interviews. Your main aim is to get them to improve their subsequent performance. Here, researchers found that clearing up job-related problems with the employee and setting measurable performance targets and a schedule for achieving them—an action plan—were the actions that consistently led to improved performance.

How to Handle a Formal Written Warning There will be times when an employee's performance is so poor that a formal written warning is required. Such written warnings serve two purposes: (1) They may serve to shake your employee out of his or her bad habits, and (2) they can help you defend your rating, both to your own boss and (if needed) to the courts. Written warnings should identify the standards by which the employee is judged, make it clear that the employee was aware of the standard, specify any violation of the standard, and show the employee had an opportunity to correct the behavior.

Current Practice

A study sheds light on current practice in regard to how companies appraise employees.[92] The sample consisted of 250 managers in the midwestern United States, all of whom were members of the Society for Human Resource Management. About 89% reported that performance appraisal was required of all their employees. Many reported using more than one appraisal format. About 32% said they used MBO, 24% used the graphic rating scale, 10% used "other," and, interestingly, about 34% used a narrative essay format; here raters take an open-ended approach to describing their employees' behaviors. None of those responding used behaviorally anchored rating scales. Eighty percent conduct annual evaluations; most of the rest do semiannual appraisals, and 92% require a review and feedback session as part of the appraisal process.

STRATEGIC HR

Ford Gets Tough

Ford CEO Jacques Nasser wanted Ford to be one of the world's top companies, and he knew that to do this, Ford needed a new way to evaluate its 18,000 managers. He wanted the new appraisal process to send the message that performance was paramount, and that those who didn't perform had no place at the new world-class Ford.

He modeled the new management appraisal process on one long used by firms like IBM and GE. Under the program, managers receive grades of A, B, or C. Nasser reportedly initially wanted 10% of managers to be graded C, but quickly reduced that to 5%. Executives rated C risked losing their bonuses or raises. And C grades two years in a row means that Ford may demote or fire the executive.

The new appraisal process immediately kicked up a storm. Executives claimed it was unfair, and several filed lawsuits. Some claimed Ford was trying to target middle-aged male executives as a way of clearing them out. Ford's initial response to the suits was that "the program is going to continue," but that "there is always review going on of all of our processes." One outside expert pointed out that there is always initial resistance to change, and that what Nasser was trying to do ". . . is a no-brainer. No company can be world-class without world-class people."

That may be true, but Ford soon discontinued the program. Some say that what works at a firm like GE may not work at one where one family controls 40% of the votes: They may not like how the program reflects on the family. At the same time, Nick Scheele, chairman of Ford of Europe, was brought in to help Nasser run the firm and execute its strategy.[93] Nasser left the firm within a year.

THE ROLE OF APPRAISALS IN MANAGING PERFORMANCE

Do Appraisals Really Help to Improve Performance?

Many experts feel that traditional appraisals don't improve performance and may actually backfire. They argue that most performance appraisal systems neither motivate employees nor guide their development.[94] Furthermore, "they cause conflict between supervisors and subordinates and lead to dysfunctional behaviors."[95] The traits measured are often personal in nature, and "Who likes the idea of being evaluated on his or her: honesty, integrity, teamwork, compassion, cooperation [objectivity] . . .?"[96]

In fact, traditional appraisals can be useless or counterproductive. Researchers in Korea recently found that, even when employees were allowed to participate in the review discussion and goals were clearly set and career issues discussed, few of the reviews had a positive impact on the employee's subsequent job performance.[97] In a study of almost 300 managers from midwestern U.S. companies, 32% rated their performance appraisals as "very ineffective," while only 4% rated them "effective to a large extent."[98] Another survey of 181 manufacturing and service organizations concluded that 11% had stopped using annual appraisals, while 25% more planned to discontinue them within two years.[99]

Some argue for dumping appraisals entirely. For example, quality management experts like W. Edwards Deming basically argue as follows:[100] They say the organization is a system of interrelated parts, and that an employee's performance is more a function of factors like training, communication, tools, and supervision than of his or her own motivation.[101] Furthermore, performance appraisals can have unanticipated consequences. (For example, employees might make themselves look better in terms of customer service by continually badgering customers to send in letters of support.) Forced distribution appraisal in particular can undermine teamwork.[102] These experts were therefore very skeptical about traditional appraisal methods.

Criticisms like these have merit, but managers still need some way to review subordinates' work-related behavior. And, although Deming reportedly hated performance reviews, "he really didn't offer any concrete solution to the problem or an alternative, other than to just pay everybody the same salary."[103] What are the alternatives?

The Performance Management Approach

Today, there are two philosophies regarding how to appraise employee performance. One is the "get tough" approach pursued by firms like IBM, GE, and (initially, at least) Ford under Jacques Nasser. Employers here view appraisal as an integral part of the firm's performance management efforts: They use the appraisal process as one way to improve the firm's performance. This approach is typified by Andrall Pearson, CEO of Tricon Global Restaurants, who ". . . recommends sorting your population into four groups, ranging from poor to superior, and then asking for a specific plan for the people in each group. Always focus first on the bottom group; rooting out the

performance management
Managing all elements of the organizational process that affect how well employees perform.

poorest performers will foster a climate of continual improvement. If everyone in the bottom quartile is replaced, the third quartile becomes the new bottom group and the focus of subsequent improvement efforts."[104]

Performance management refers to managing all elements of the organizational process that affect how well employees perform.[105] The performance management process may thus encompass goal setting, worker selection and placement, performance appraisal, compensation, training and development, and career management—in other words, all those parts of the HR process that affect how an employee performs.[106] One firm renamed the function responsible for appraisal, compensation, training, and management development to "Performance Management and Rewards." It did so to reflect the firm's new focus on performance management. "We were too nice in our desire not to hurt people's feelings. . . . Our forced turnover was less than 1.5%, and we had too few occurrences of people getting an MP—a marginal performer rating. We were terrific at managing mediocrity. We needed to learn how to manage and reward excellence."[107]

Performance management thinking should produce an integrated performance-management-oriented system. With this system, management designs all the firm's HR functions—from job design to recruiting, selecting, training, compensating, and then appraising employees—with the specific aim of improving employee performance relative to the company's overall goals. Performance management starts, in a sense, at the end and works back to the beginning: Top management says, "What is our strategy and what are our performance goals?" and then, "What does this mean for how we recruit and select and compensate employees, and for the standards and tools and processes we use to appraise them?" Performance management can be especially valuable when the employees are far away, since the company's goals can serve as the glue that keeps far-flung units working in unison.

THE NEW WORKPLACE

Performance Management Abroad

Qualcomm uses the performance management approach with its 400 employees outside the United States. The vice president of international administration and a staff corporate HR person communicate Qualcomm's overall performance goals to the units abroad. The local HR unit ensures that the employee's personal performance standards reflect those of the particular region, which in turn reflect Qualcomm's overall corporate goals. Each Qualcomm employee then has an annual performance review with his or her manager. In this way, little is left to chance: Activities like recruiting, training, and appraising aren't performed in an informal or unfocused way. Instead, local managers design and assess each activity based on the extent to which it contributes to the goals the company is trying to achieve.[108]

TQM-Based Appraisals

Some believe performance-management-type forced distribution methods are inherently unfair. For example, the newly hired HR vice president at Electronic Data Systems abruptly left when the CEO instituted a quartiling plan despite employee resistance. These people recommend a more developmental approach to the appraisal process.

total quality management (TQM)
An organizationwide program that integrates all functions and processes of the business so that design, planning, production, distribution, and field service are focused on maximizing customer satisfaction through continuous improvement.

Some advocate a **total quality management (TQM)** approach, one fashioned on the principles of W. E. Deming. TQM is an organizationwide program that integrates all functions and processes of the business so that design, planning, production, distribution, and field service are focused on maximizing customer satisfaction through continuous improvement.[109] The idea here is to get employees to want to improve operations. Deming, an early proponent, said such programs are built on 14 principles such as "cease dependence on inspection to achieve quality," "drive out fear so that everyone may work effectively for the company," and "eliminate work standards (quotas) on the factory floor."[110]

Some argue that applying principles like these can foster employee support of quality efforts, by producing more developmental, less adversarial appraisals.[111]

The characteristics of such "TQM-oriented appraisals" include:

- An appraisal scale with few performance-level categories that avoids a forced distribution.[112]
- Ways to objectively measure results, avoiding subjective criteria such as teamwork and integrity.[113]
- A way to ascertain whether a performance deficiency is a result of (1) employee motivation, (2) inadequate training, or (3) factors (like poor supervision) that are outside the employee's control.
- 360-degree feedback from several sources, not just supervisors but internal and possibly external "customers" of the employee as well.[114]
- Adequate samples of work behavior—"regular observations of staff members' work behaviors and performance."[115]
- An atmosphere of partnership and constructive advice.[116]
- Basing performance appraisal standards on a thorough analysis of key external and internal customers' needs and expectations. (For example, if "accurately completing the sales receipt" is important for the accounting department, then appraise the retail sales clerk in part on this dimension.)

Figure 9-8 shows a form for implementing a TQM-oriented performance management appraisal. It consists of a performance contract specifying customer expectations and performance goals, as well as an internal customer feedback form.[117]

◀ **FIGURE 9-8**
Performance Contract and Internal Customer Feedback Forms

PERFORMANCE CONTRACT

Within the next year, I understand that our organization's objectives are _____ _____ and that the goals of our department are _____. I also understand that our work unit goals are _____.

My key internal customers are _____ and their work needs and expectations are _____.

To make my contribution toward attaining the goals stated above, I understand that I am expected to do the following:

My individual performance goals are _____.

My goals for improving work methods (process) are _____.

My goals for improving specific interpersonal work behaviors when I interact with the following _____ are _____.

I believe these goals are acceptable and attainable. I also understand that I will be evaluated by multiple appraisal sources (supervisor, peers, internal, and, if appropriate, external customers).

Compensation for my work performance will be based on whether my performance was (1) outstanding, (2) fully competent, or (3) unsatisfactory. I understand that the following forms of compensation will be considered: (1) merit award for my individual performance goal attainment, (2) enhancement and utilization of my skills, (3) my work unit's or team's performance (gainsharing), and (4) our organization's performance (profit sharing).

_____   _____
Your signature   Supervisor's signature

Source: David Antonioni, "Improving the Performance Management Process Before Discontinuing Performance Appraisals," *Compensation and Benefits Review*, May–June 1994, pp. 33, 34.

▶ **FIGURE 9-8**
**Performance
Contract and
Internal Customer
Feedback Forms**
(*continued*)

INTERNAL CUSTOMER FEEDBACK

As an internal customer of (name) _____ , please give him/her feedback regarding his/her work performance and work behaviors. After you have completed this form, send it to _____ . Your responses will be tabulated and then discussed with the individual.

To what extent did this individual meet your expectations of work quality in the areas you indicate as important:

	Exceeds	Meets	Doesn't Meet
1. Accuracy of the work you received			
2. Timeliness of the work you received			
3. Dependability of the work you received			
4. Sharing relevant information to help you do your work more efficiently			

In terms of your interactions with this person, please feel free to comment on any of the following:

1. The type of errors and the amount of rework

2. The nature of any work delays

3. Collaborative efforts to improve work or business processes

4. Interpersonal work behaviors

Please list any *new* expectations that you have regarding the work you receive from this person.

Thank you for completing this feedback form. A follow-up interview with you may be established to discuss the feedback, and if necessary, improvement goals and an action plan will be developed.

Whether the firm pursues a "get tough" GE-type performance management approach or the more congenial TQM-type approach, one thing seems sure: Firms are well advised not to leave their appraisals to chance. "Where in the past the system may have been used merely to tell old Joe how he was doing and justify his annual increase, organizations now see [such] systems as having tremendous power to transform the culture of the Corporation."[118]

We invite you to visit **www.prenhall.com/dessler** on the Prentice Hall Web site for our online study guide, Internet exercises, current events, links to related Web sites, and more.

1. People want and need feedback regarding how they are doing, and appraisal provides an opportunity to give them that feedback.
2. Before the appraisal, make sure to clarify the performance you expect so that the employee knows what he or she should be shooting for. Ask, "What do I really expect this person to do?"
3. Performance appraisal tools include the graphic rating scale, alternation ranking method, forced distribution method, BARS, MBO, critical incident method, and computer and Web-based methods.
4. Appraisal problems to beware of include unclear standards, halo effect, central tendency, leniency or strictness problems, and bias.
5. Most subordinates probably want a specific explanation or examples regarding why they were appraised high or low, and for this, compiling a record of positive and negative critical incidents can be useful. Even if your firm requires that you summarize the appraisal in a form like a graphic rating scale, a list of critical incidents can be useful when the time comes to discuss the appraisal with your subordinate.
6. The subordinate should view the appraisal as a fair one, and in this regard there are four things to do: Evaluate performance frequently; make sure you are familiar with the person's performance; make sure there is an agreement between you and your subordinate concerning job duties; and finally, solicit the person's help when you formulate plans for eliminating performance weaknesses.
7. There are three types of appraisal interviews: unsatisfactory but correctable performance; satisfactory but not promotable; and satisfactory—promotable.
8. To bring about constructive change in a subordinate's behavior, get the person to talk in the interview. Use open-ended questions, state questions in terms of a problem, use a command question, use questions to try to understand the feelings underlying what the person is saying, and restate the person's last point as a question. On the other hand, don't do all the talking, don't use restrictive questions, don't be judgmental, don't give free advice, and don't get involved with name calling, ridicule, or sarcasm.
9. Appraisals should ideally serve a role in managing performance by providing a concrete and nonthreatening basis for an analysis of an employee's work-related performance. Creating more effective appraisals is one way to accomplish this.

Tying It All Together

Once employees have been hired and trained and on the job for some time, you have to appraise their performance. Firms use various methods to accomplish this, ranging from graphic rating scales to ranking methods, to behaviorally anchored rating scales and computer-based methods. However, in some respects, the important thing about appraisal is not so much the method, but the philosophy that underlies the process. Some take a more congenial approach, and emphasize avoiding the sort of "Darwinism" that ranking and forced distribution systems reflect. Others emphasize appraisal's central role in managing employee performance, and the need to do so in order to make the firm truly world-class. Whichever approach you use, the appraisal should contribute in a meaningful way to helping the employee plan his or her career, a topic we turn to in the following chapter.

Discussion Questions

1. What is the purpose of a performance appraisal?
2. Discuss the pros and cons of at least four performance appraisal tools.
3. Explain how you would use the alternation ranking method, the paired comparison method, and the forced distribution method.
4. Explain in your own words how you would go about developing a behaviorally anchored rating scale.
5. Explain the problems to be avoided in appraising performance.
6. Discuss the pros and cons of using different potential raters to appraise a person's performance.

7. Explain the four types of appraisal interview objectives and how they affect the way you manage the interview.

8. Answer the question, "How would you get the interviewee to talk during an appraisal interview?"

Individual and Group Activities

1. Working individually or in groups, develop a graphic rating scale for the following jobs: secretary, engineer, directory assistance operator.

2. Working individually or in groups, describe the advantages and disadvantages of using the forced distribution appraisal method for college professors.

3. Working individually or in groups, develop, over the period of a week, a set of critical incidents covering the classroom performance of one of your instructors.

EXPERIENTIAL EXERCISE

Purpose: The purpose of this exercise is to give you practice in developing and using a performance appraisal form.

Required Understanding: You are going to develop a performance appraisal form for an instructor and should therefore be thoroughly familiar with the discussion of performance appraisals in this chapter.

How to Set Up the Exercise/Instructions: Divide the class into groups of four or five students.

Instructions

1. First, based on what you now know about performance appraisal, do you think Figure 9-1 (see page 242) is an effective scale for appraising instructors? Why? Why not?

2. Next, your group should develop its own tool for appraising the performance of an instructor. Decide which of the appraisal tools (graphic rating scales, alternation ranking, and so on) you are going to use, and then design the instrument itself.

3. Next, have a spokesperson from each group put his or her group's appraisal tool on the board. How similar are the tools? Do they all measure about the same factors? Which factor appears most often? Which do you think is the most effective tool on the board?

4. The class should select the top 10 factors from all of the appraisal tools presented to create what the class perceives to be the most effective tool for appraising the performance of the instructor.

APPLICATION CASE *Appraising the Secretaries at Sweetwater U*

Rob Winchester, newly appointed vice president for administrative affairs at Sweetwater State University, faced a tough problem shortly after his university career began. Three weeks after he came on board in September, Sweetwater's president, Rob's boss, told Rob that one of his first tasks was to improve the appraisal system used to evaluate secretarial and clerical performance at Sweetwater U. Apparently, the main difficulty was that the performance appraisal was traditionally tied directly to salary increases given at the end of the year. So most administrators were less than accurate when they used the graphic rating forms that were the basis of the clerical staff evaluation. In fact, what usually happened was that each administrator simply rated his or her clerk or secretary as "excellent." This cleared the way for all support staff to receive a maximum pay increase every year.

But the current university budget simply did not include enough money to fund another "maximum" annual increase

for every staffer. Furthermore, Sweetwater's president felt that the custom of providing invalid feedback to each secretary on his or her year's performance was not productive, so he had asked the new vice president to revise the system. In October, Rob sent a memo to all administrators telling them that in the future no more than half the secretaries reporting to any particular administrator could be appraised as "excellent." This move, in effect, forced each supervisor to begin ranking his or her secretaries for quality of performance. The vice president's memo met widespread resistance immediately—from administrators, who were afraid that many of their secretaries would begin leaving for more lucrative jobs in private industry, and from secretaries, who felt that the new system was unfair and reduced each secretary's chance of receiving a maximum salary increase. A handful of secretaries had begun quietly picketing outside the president's home on the university campus. The picketing, caustic remarks by disgruntled administrators, and rumors of an impending slowdown by the secretaries (there were about 250 on campus) made Rob Winchester wonder whether he had made the right decision by setting up forced ranking. He knew, however, that there were a few performance appraisal experts in the School of Business, so he decided to set up an appointment with them to discuss the matter.

He met with them the next morning. He explained the situation as he had found it: The present appraisal system had been set up when the university first opened 10 years earlier, and the appraisal form had been developed primarily by a committee of secretaries. Under that system, Sweetwater's administrators filled out forms similar to the one shown in Table 9-2 (page 254). This once-a-year appraisal (in March) had run into problems almost immediately, since it was apparent from the start that administrators varied widely in their interpretations of job standards, as well as in how conscientiously they filled out the forms and supervised their secretaries. Moreover, at the end of the first year it became obvious to everyone that each secretary's salary increase was tied directly to the March appraisal. For example, those rated "excellent" received the maximum increases, those rated "good" received smaller increases, and those given neither rating received only the standard across-the-board cost-of-living increase. Since universities in general—and Sweetwater U in particular—have paid secretaries somewhat lower salaries than those prevailing in private industry, some secretaries left in a huff that first year. From that time on, most administrators simply rated all secretaries excellent in order to reduce staff turnover, thus ensuring each a maximum increase. In the process, they also avoided the hard feelings aroused by the significant performance differences otherwise highlighted by administrators.

Two Sweetwater experts agreed to consider the problem, and in two weeks they came back to the vice president with the following recommendations. First, the form used to rate the secretaries was grossly insufficient. It was unclear what "excellent" or "quality of work" meant, for example. They recommended instead a form like that in Figure 9-2 (page 244). In addition, they recommended that the vice president rescind his earlier memo and no longer attempt to force uni-

versity administrators arbitrarily to rate at least half their secretaries as something less than excellent. The two consultants pointed out that this was, in fact, an unfair procedure since it was quite possible that any particular administrator might have staffers who were all or virtually all excellent—or conceivably, although less likely, all below standard. The experts said that the way to get all the administrators to take the appraisal process more seriously was to stop tying it to salary increases. In other words, they recommended that every administrator fill out a form like that in Figure 9-2 for each secretary at least once a year and then use this form as the basis of a counseling session. Salary increases would have to be made on some basis other than the performance appraisal, so that administrators would no longer hesitate to fill out the rating forms honestly.

Rob thanked the two experts and went back to his office to ponder their recommendations. Some of the recommendations (such as substituting the new rating form for the old) seemed to make sense. Nevertheless, he still had serious doubts as to the efficacy of any graphic rating form, particularly if he were to decide in favor of his original forced ranking approach. The experts' second recommendation—to stop tying the appraisals to automatic salary increases—made sense but raised at least one very practical problem: If salary increases were not to be based on performance appraisals, on what were they to be based? He began wondering whether the experts' recommendations weren't simply based on ivory tower theorizing.

Questions

1. Do you think that the experts' recommendations will be sufficient to get most of the administrators to fill out the rating forms properly? Why? Why not? What additional actions (if any) do you think will be necessary?
2. Do you think that Vice President Winchester would be better off dropping graphic rating forms, substituting instead one of the other techniques we discussed in this chapter, such as a ranking method? Why?
3. What performance appraisal system would you develop for the secretaries if you were Rob Winchester? Defend your answer.

CONTINUING CASE: LearnInMotion.com *The Performance Appraisal*

Jennifer and Mel disagree over the importance of having performance appraisals. Mel says it's quite clear whether any particular LearnInMotion employee is doing his or her job. It's obvious, for instance, if the salespeople are selling, if the Web designer is designing, if the Web surfer is surfing, and if

the content management people are managing to get the customers' content up on the Web site in a timely fashion. Mel's position, like that of many small-business managers, is that "we have 1,000 higher-priority things to attend to" such as boosting sales and creating the calendar. And in any case, he says, the employees already get plenty of day-to-day feedback from him or Jennifer regarding what they're doing right and what they're doing wrong.

This informal feedback notwithstanding, Jennifer believes that a more formal appraisal approach is required. For one thing, they're approaching the end of the 90-day "introductory" period for many of these employees, and the owners need to make decisions about whether they should go or stay. And from a practical point of view, Jennifer just believes that sitting down and providing formal, written feedback is more likely to reinforce what employees are doing right, and to get them to modify what they may be doing wrong. "Maybe

this is one reason we're not getting enough sales," she says. They've been debating this for about an hour. Now, they want you, their management consultants, to advise them on what to do. Here's what they want you to do for them.

Questions and Assignments
1. Is Jennifer right about the need to evaluate the workers formally? Why or why not? If you think she's right, how do you explain away Mel's arguments?
2. Develop a performance appraisal method for the salespeople, or Web designer, or Web surfer. Please make sure to include any form you want the owners to use.

Chapter 10

Managing Careers and Fair Treatment

After studying this chapter, you should be able to:

- Discuss the basics of career management.
- Outline how to manage promotions and transfers.
- Show how career management influences employee commitment.
- Explain the three main considerations in managing fair treatment.
- More effectively manage dismissals.

STRATEGIC OVERVIEW The Crystal Gateway Marriott Hotel's new competitive strategy was to differentiate itself from others by emphasizing customer service. The problem, management knew, is that you can't have world-class customer service without the dedicated efforts of front-line employees—the front desk clerks, the bell persons, waiters, and maids. So, to achieve its strategic goal, Crystal Gateway had to win its employees' commitment to customer service. Management would do so, in part, by vastly expanding the information it shared with employees. How should it do so?

Chapter 9 focused on appraising employees' performance. Once you've appraised their performance, it's usually necessary to address career-related issues and to communicate these issues to your subordinates. The main purpose of this chapter is to help you be more effective at managing your employees' careers and at instituting fair treatment systems for them. We discuss career development (including the employer's and supervisor's role in career management), as well as managing promotions and transfers, and the link between career management activities and employee commitment. We'll discuss managing fair treatment (including disciplining and employee privacy issues), and explain how to more effectively manage dismissals. This chapter completes Part 3, which addressed training and development. Once you've trained and appraised employees, you need to turn to the question of how to pay them, the topic we cover in the next three chapters.

THE BASICS OF CAREER MANAGEMENT

Many people look back on their careers—on the sequence of occupational positions they've had—with satisfaction, knowing that what they might have achieved they did achieve. Others are less fortunate and feel that they didn't achieve their potential.

Careers today are not what they used to be. "Careers were traditionally viewed as an upward, linear progression in one or two firms or as stable employment within a profession."[1] Now, someone's career is more likely to be "driven by the person, not the organization [and] reinvented by the person from time to time, as the person and the environment change."[2] Thus, the sales rep laid off by a publishing firm that's just merged may reinvent her career for the next few years as a security analyst specializing in media companies, or as an account executive at a brokerage firm.[3]

This has several implications. For one thing, the psychological contract between employers and workers has changed. Yesterday, employees "exchanged loyalty for job security."[4] Today, "employees instead exchange performance for the sort of training and learning and development that will allow them to remain marketable."[5] This in turn means you can't just design HR activities (like selection and training) to serve the company's needs; they also have to serve the employee's long-run interests, so the person can realize his or her potential. Table 10-1 illustrates how HR activities like training and appraisal can provide more of such a **career planning and development** focus.

John Madigan, vice president of HR for the Hartford Insurance Company's 3,500-member IT group, discovered how important development activities can be when he conducted a survey. Of the employees who left the organization, "Ninety percent of people who left voluntarily talked about career and professional development and the level of support their managers gave them in this area," he says.[6]

career planning and development
The deliberate process through which a person becomes aware of personal career-related attributes and the lifelong series of stages that contribute to his or her career fulfillment.

Career Development Roles

Ultimately, of course, each person must accept responsibility for his or her own career; assess his or her own interests, skills, and values; and take the steps required to ensure a happy and fulfilling career. It's unwise, to say the least, to

▶ **TABLE 10-1 Traditional Versus Career Development Focus**

HR Activity	Traditional Focus	Career Development Focus
Human resource planning	Analyzes jobs, skills, tasks—present and future. Projects needs. Uses statistical data.	Adds information about individual interests, preferences, and the like to data.
Training and development	Provides opportunities for learning skills, information, and attitudes related to job.	Provides career path information. Adds individual growth orientation.
Performance appraisal	Rating and/or rewards.	Adds development plans and individual goal setting.
Recruiting and placement	Matching organization's needs with qualified individuals.	Matches individual and jobs based on a number of variables including employees' career interests.
Compensation and benefits	Rewards for time, productivity, talent, and so on.	Adds non-job-related activities to be rewarded, such as United Way leadership positions.

Source: Adapted from Fred L. Otte and Peggy G. Hutcheson, *Helping Employees Manage Careers* (Upper Saddle River, NJ: Prentice Hall, 1992), p. 10.

leave these jobs to others. You'll find techniques to help you in the Managing Your Career appendix, on the book's Web site. Many people use the Web today to help analyze and evaluate their careers, as the following feature illustrates.

Career Planning and the Web

Anyone can use the Web to take a career interests inventory from the comfort of their own home. Well-known Web-based career assessment tools include: self-directed-search.com; review.com/birkman; keirsey.com; and careerdiscovery.com. Some firms have created their own internal career development Web sites. For example, Unisys's Web-based career center helps its employees identify their strengths and improve their career understanding and progress.[7]

When job hunting, you can post your résumé on the Web. But while many people do so, Web-based résumés can cause problems. "Once I put my résumé on the Internet, I couldn't do anything to control it," said one technical consultant after his boss had stumbled across the fact that several months before he had been job hunting. If you do post your résumé on the Web, experts suggest taking precautions. At a minimum, date your résumé (in case it lands on your boss's desk two years from now); insert a disclaimer forbidding unauthorized transmission by headhunters; check ahead of time to see who has access to the database on which you're posting your résumé; and try to cloak your identity by listing your capabilities but not your name or employer—just an anonymous e-mail account to receive inquiries.[8]

However, the employee's manager and employer also have roles in the person's career development. The manager should provide timely and constructive performance feedback and developmental assignments and support. The employer can provide career-oriented training and development opportunities, offer career management programs, and establish career-oriented performance appraisal and job posting policies. Let's take a closer look at what employers can do.

The Employer's Role in Career Management

A survey illustrates the range of career management practices employers can engage in. The researchers surveyed 524 organizations in the United Kingdom to determine how often they used 17 career management practices. "Posting job openings" was the most frequently applied career practice. The other top career practices, in descending order, were: formal education; career-oriented performance appraisals; counseling by managers; lateral, developmental moves; counseling by HR; retirement preparation; and succession planning.[9] For example, Sun Microsystems maintains a career development center staffed by seven certified counselors to help employees fill in the gaps in their development and choose internal career opportunities at Sun. The firm believes its program helps explain why its average employee tenure of four years is more than twice what it is estimated to be at other Silicon Valley firms.[10]

Employers can take many steps to help make a new employee's introduction to the job more productive. Before hiring, *realistic job previews* can help prospective employees more accurately gauge whether the job is indeed for them, and particularly whether a job's demands are a good fit with a candidate's skills and interests. Especially for recent college graduates, the first job can be crucial for building confidence and a more realistic picture of what he or she can

▲ *Breaking the glass ceiling: Jenny Ming, president of Gap Inc.'s Old Navy chain since April 1999, and one of* Business Week's *top 25 managers for 1999.*

and cannot do: Providing *challenging first jobs* (rather than relegating new employees to "jobs where they can't do any harm"), as well as an experienced mentor who can help the person learn the ropes, is important. Some refer to this as preventing **reality shock**, a phenomenon that occurs when a new employee's high expectations and enthusiasm confront the reality of a boring, unchallenging job.

After the person has been on the job for a while, an employer can take many steps to contribute in a positive way to the employee's career. *Career-oriented appraisals*—in which the manager is trained not just to appraise the employee but also to match the person's strengths and weaknesses with a feasible career path and required development work—is one important step. Similarly, providing periodic, planned **job rotation** can help the person develop a more realistic picture of what he or she is (and is not) good at, and thus the sort of future career moves that might be best.

Firms can also provide **mentoring** opportunities. Mentoring may be formal or informal. Informally, mid- and senior-level managers may voluntarily help less experienced employees—for instance, giving them career advice and helping them navigate political pitfalls. Other informal means—such as increasing the opportunities for networking and interactions among diverse employees—can also be effective.[11] Other firms also have formal mentoring programs. For instance, the employer may pair protégés with potential mentors. Many provide instructional manuals, to help mentor and protégé better understand their respective responsibilities.

Provide Career Planning Workshops and Software Some employees don't think about their careers until it's too late, or haven't the skills to assess their career options. Firms therefore organize career planning workshops. A career planning workshop is "a planned learning event in which participants are expected to be actively involved, completing career planning exercises and inventories and participating in career skills practice sessions."[12] A typical workshop includes three main activities. There is a self-assessment activity in which individual employees analyze their own career interests, skills, and career aspirations. Then there is an environmental assessment phase in which they receive relevant information about the company and its career options and staffing needs. It concludes with a goal-setting and action-planning segment in which the individual sets career goals and creates a career plan.

Software programs are available for improving the organizational career-planning process (see Webnote). For example, WorkforceVision from Criterion, Inc., in Irving, Texas, helps the company analyze an employee's training needs. Clicking on the employee's name launches his or her work history, competencies, career path, and other information. For each competency (such as leadership and customer focus), a "gap analysis" is shown graphically on a bar chart, highlighting the person's strengths and weaknesses. The firm can then organize developmental activities around the person's needs.[13]

First USA Bank has what it calls the Opportunity Knocks program. Its purpose is to help employees crystallize their career goals and achieve them within the company. In addition to career development training and follow-up support, First USA Bank has also outfitted special career development facilities at its work sites that employees can use on company time.[14]

---

reality shock
Results of a period that may occur at the initial career entry when the new employee's high job expectations confront the reality of a boring, unchallenging job.

job rotation
Moving an employee through a preplanned series of positions in order to prepare the person for an enhanced role with the company.

mentoring
Formal or informal programs in which mid- and senior-level managers help less experienced employees—for instance, by giving them career advice and helping them navigate political pitfalls.

▲ **WEBNOTE**
WorkforceVision is one of many software programs that help companies manage career planning.
www.eeodiversity.peopleclick.com

MANAGING PROMOTIONS AND TRANSFERS

Promotions and transfers are integral parts of most people's careers. **Promotions** traditionally refer to advancements to positions of increased responsibility; **transfers** are reassignments to similar (or higher) positions in other parts of the firm.

Making Promotion Decisions

Most working people look forward to promotions, which usually mean more pay, responsibility, and (often) job satisfaction. For employers, promotions can provide opportunities to reward exceptional performance, and to fill open positions with tested and loyal employees. Yet the promotion process isn't always a positive experience for either employee or employer. Unfairness, arbitrariness, or secrecy can diminish the effectiveness of the process for all concerned. Several decisions therefore loom large in any firm's promotion process.

Decision 1: Is Seniority or Competence the Rule? Probably the most important decision is whether to base promotion on seniority or competence, or some combination of the two.

Today's focus on competitiveness favors competence, as does the fact that promotion based on competence is the superior motivator. However, a company's ability to use competence as the criterion depends on several things, most notably whether or not union agreements or civil service requirements govern promotions. Union agreements sometimes contain clauses that emphasize seniority, such as: "In the advancement of employees to higher paid jobs when ability, merit, and capacity are equal, employees with the highest seniority will be given preference."[15] And civil service regulations that stress seniority rather than competence often govern promotions in many public sector organizations.[16]

Decision 2: How Should We Measure Competence? If the firm opts for competence, how should it define and measure competence? Defining and measuring past performance is relatively straightforward: Define the job, set standards, and use one or more appraisal tools to record the employee's performance. But promotions require something more: You also need a valid procedure for predicting a candidate's potential for future performance.

Most employers use prior performance as a guide, and assume that (based on his or her prior performance) the person will do well on the new job. This is the simplest procedure. Others use tests or assessment centers to evaluate promotable employees and to identify those with executive potential.

An increasing number of employers take a more comprehensive approach. For example (particularly given the public safety issues involved), police departments have traditionally taken a relatively systematic approach when evaluating candidates for promotion to command positions. Traditional promotional reviews include a written knowledge test, an assessment center, credit for seniority, and a score based on recent performance appraisal ratings. Other departments are adding a personnel records review. This includes evaluation of job-related dimensions such as supervisory-related education and experience, ratings from multiple sources, and systematic evaluation of behavioral evidence.[17]

Decision 3: Is the Process Formal or Informal? Many firms have informal promotion processes. They may or may not post open positions, and key managers may use their own "unpublished" criteria to make promotion decisions.[18] Here employees may (reasonably) conclude that noncompetence factors like "who you

promotions
Advancements to positions of increased responsibility.

transfers
Reassignments to similar (or higher) positions in other parts of the firm.

know" are more important than performance, and that working hard to get ahead—at least in this firm—is futile.

Many employers therefore establish formal, published promotion policies and procedures. These have several components. Employees get a *formal promotion policy* describing the criteria by which the firm awards promotions. A *job-posting policy* states the firm will post open positions and their requirements, and circulate these to all employees. As explained in Chapter 4, many employers also maintain *employee qualification briefs*, and use replacement charts and computerized employee information systems. Systems like these may be especially useful for women employees, as explained next.

THE *NEW* WORKPLACE

Promotion and Career Management for Women

Women still don't make it to the top of the career ladder in numbers proportionate to their numbers in U.S. industry. For example, while women constitute 40% of the workforce, they hold less than 2% of top-management positions.[19]

Experts offer many explanations.[20] Blatant or subtle discrimination, including the belief that "women belong at home and are not committed to careers,"[21] inhibits many managers from taking women as seriously as men. The "old-boy network" of informal friendships forged over lunch, at social events, or at club meetings is usually not open to women, although it's often here that promotional decisions are made. And "women aspiring to executive positions have to stay within narrow bands of acceptable behavior. Here they may exhibit only certain traditional masculine and feminine qualities, and walking this fine line represents one of the most difficult tasks for executive women."[22] Unlike many men, women must also make the "career versus family" decision, since the responsibilities of raising the children and managing the household still falls disproportionately on women. A lack of women mentors makes it harder for women to find the role models and protectors they need to help guide their careers.

Women and men also face different challenges as they advance through their careers. Women report greater barriers (such as being excluded from informal networks) than do men, and greater difficulty getting developmental assignments and geographic mobility opportunities. Men are more likely to have been given developmental opportunities, while women had to be more proactive to get such assignments. Because developmental experiences like these are so important, "organizations that are interested in helping female managers advance should focus on breaking down the barriers that interfere with women's access to developmental experiences."[23]

Women and their managers and employers can take steps to enhance promotional and career prospects. Perhaps the most important is to focus on taking the career interests of women employees seriously. In other words, accept that there are problems, and work on eliminating the barriers. Then, ensure that in all aspects of promotion and career management—from HR and succession planning to appraisals to selection for training—the process is objective. Instituting more flexible career tracks so women who must take time off to raise a family can do so and resume their careers is also advisable.

Beyond that, experts suggest several things the employee herself can do:[24]

■ Be able and capable: Learn and understand your business.
■ Be seen as able and capable: Do not let your abilities be discounted or ignored.
■ Find a mentor and engage in networking.
■ Train yourself beyond the job and increase your career assets so you will be available when a good job opportunity arises.
■ Know what you want and prepare to balance and prioritize your life.[25]

People of color also tend to experience relatively less career progress in organizations, and, as with women, bias and more subtle barriers are often the cause. Yet this is not necessarily the result of decision makers' racist sentiments.[26] Instead, secondary factors—such as having few people of color employed in the hiring department—may be the cause. In one study, the people of color applying for promotions actually had more work experience, and were therefore ironically seen as plateaued.[27] In any case, the bottom line seems to be that whether it's bias or some other reason, questionable hurdles like these do exist, and need to be found and eliminated.

Decision 4: Vertical, Horizontal, or Other? Promotions aren't necessarily as simple as they may appear. For example, how do you motivate employees with the prospect of promotion when your firm is downsizing? And how do you provide promotional opportunities for those, like engineers, who may have little or no interest in administrative roles?

Several options are available. Some firms, such as the exploration division of British Petroleum, create two parallel career paths, one for managers, and another for "individual contributors" such as high-performing engineers. At BP, individual contributors can move up to nonsupervisory but senior positions, such as "senior engineer." These jobs have most of the financial rewards attached to management-track positions at that level.[28]

Another option is to move the person horizontally. For instance, move a production employee to HR to develop new skills and to test and challenge aptitudes. And in a sense, "promotions" are possible even when leaving the person in the same job. For example, you can usually enrich the job, and provide training to enhance the opportunity for assuming more responsibility.[29]

Handling Transfers

A *transfer* is a move from one job to another, usually with no change in salary or grade. Employees seek transfers for many reasons, including personal enrichment, more interesting jobs, greater convenience—better hours, location of work, and so on—or to jobs offering greater advancement possibilities.[30] Employers may transfer a worker to vacate a position where he or she is no longer needed, to fill one where he or she is needed, or more generally to find a better fit for the employee within the firm. Many firms today boost productivity by consolidating positions. Transfers are a way to give employees who might have nowhere else to go but out a chance for another assignment and, perhaps, some personal growth.

Many firms have had policies of routinely transferring employees from locale to locale, either to expose them to a wider range of jobs or to fill open positions with trained employees. Such easy-transfer policies have now fallen into disfavor. This is partly because of the cost of relocating employees (paying moving expenses, and buying back the employee's current home,

▲ *When Sophie Bouchard, shown here with her family on moving day, was offered a transfer from Montreal to London, she was thrilled. The top sales rep in Canada for executive recruiting firm TMP Worldwide, Inc., Bouchard did have one major concern about taking the job: her husband Stephane Licari would have to leave his own promising sales career behind. But when Bouchard mentioned the problem to her boss, the manager immediately set up an interview for Licari with TMP's European sales head, and he was offered a job in London shortly after. The whole family moved in the fall of 2000. "I wanted to make sure we retained Sophie," said her boss. And, as a bonus, "her husband was perfect for the job."*

for instance) and partly because firms assumed that frequent transfers had a damaging effect on transferees' family life.

One study suggests that the latter argument, at least, is without merit.[31] The main finding was that there were few differences between mobile and stable families. Few families in the mobile group believed moving is easy. However, they were as satisfied with all aspects of their lives (except social relationships—making friends at work, for instance) as were stable families.

CAREER MANAGEMENT AND COMMITMENT

When Allied Signal and Honeywell merged several years ago, the resulting Honeywell dismissed thousands of employees. Mergers and downsizings may have positive effects on a firm's competitiveness. However, they've also undermined the traditional psychological contract between employer and employee, and thereby complicated the tasks of fostering employee commitment and maintaining a motivated staff. The problem is this: How do you maintain employee commitment—an employee's identification with and agreement to pursue the company's mission—if the employee can't be sure he or she will even have a job there at the end of the year? How do you get employees to keep the company's best interests at heart if the company doesn't seem to care about what's good for the employee?

One answer is to provide them with an opportunity to self-actualize—to develop and reach their potential. Most employees understand that (if the day should come) they'll at least be more marketable. The activities that comprise the firm's career management process can be particularly useful in that regard. We'll look at some examples.

Career Development Programs

Ben & Jerry's (now part of Unilever) illustrates the sorts of career development activities that are possible. For example, the firm encourages employees to attend eight 4-hour career planning seminars, the aim of which is to help employees think about and plan their careers. They can then spend 2 or 3 days interning at another company job, on paid time. The firm offers up to 90% funding for tuition reimbursement for up to three courses per year. It also provides classes, seminars, counseling, and tutoring, both on company premises and off. These include college courses taught by the Community College of Vermont and include one-on-one tutoring; computer classes, in which employees can earn a certificate from Ben & Jerry's information services group; adult basic education tutoring and high school diploma program; professional development classes and seminars; and financial planning seminars and individual counseling.

Saturn provides another example. A career workshop uses vocational guidance tools (including a skills assessment disk and other career gap analysis tools) to help employees identify career-related skills and the development needs they possess. This workshop, according to one employee, "helps you assess yourself, and takes 4 to 6 hours. You use it for developing your own career potential. The career disk identifies your weaknesses and strengths: you assess yourself, and then your team assesses you."[32] Tuition reimbursement and other development aids are also available to help employees develop the skills they need to get ahead. Here is how one Saturn employee put it:

> *I'm an assembler now, and was a team leader for two-and-a-half years. My goal is to move into our people-systems [HR] unit. I know things are tight now, but I know that the philosophy here is that the firm will look out for me—they want people to be all they can be. I know here I'll go as far as I can go; that's one reason I'm so committed to Saturn.*[33]

Career-Oriented Appraisals

Performance appraisals should not just be about telling someone how he or she has done. They also provide an ideal opportunity for the supervisor and employee to discuss and link the latter's performance, career interests, and developmental needs into a coherent career plan.

J. C. Penney does this. Figure 10-1 illustrates this retailer's Management Appraisal form. It requires both a "promotability recommendation" and "projections for associate development." Prior to the annual appraisal, the associate and his or her manager review Penney's Management Career Grid (Figure 10-2). The grid itemizes all supervisory positions at J. C. Penney (grouped by kind of job) and includes specific job titles such as "regional catalog sales manager," "cosmetic market coordinator," "regional training coordinator," and "project manager, public affairs." The firm also provides a "work activities scan sheet." This contains thumbnail job descriptions for all the grid's jobs.

The Management Career Grid instructions identify typical promotional routes, and indicate: "When projecting the next assignment for a management associate, you should consider not only merchandise positions but also operations and personnel positions as well as general management positions." Promotional plans can cross these four groups, as well as up one or two job levels. Thus, a senior merchandising manager might aim for promotion to assistant buyer (a general management job at Penney's) or general merchandise manager. The system motivates Penney's managers to think through their career plan at the firm, and thereby nurtures their commitment to the firm and its goals.

Career Records/Job Posting Systems

The purpose of career records/job posting systems is to ensure that the firm matches company candidates' career goals and skills openly, fairly, and effectively with promotional opportunities. For example, consider Goldman Sachs's Internal Placement Center (IPC):[34]

> Its aim is to offer Goldman Sachs employees interested in pursuing career opportunities in different areas of the firm the resources to locate and apply for job openings. The IPC also makes it simpler for managers to consider qualified internal candidates when filling open positions, and furnishes managers with information about openings that could provide career development opportunities for their employees.[35]

▼ **FIGURE 10-1   Portion of J. C. Penney's Appraisal Form**

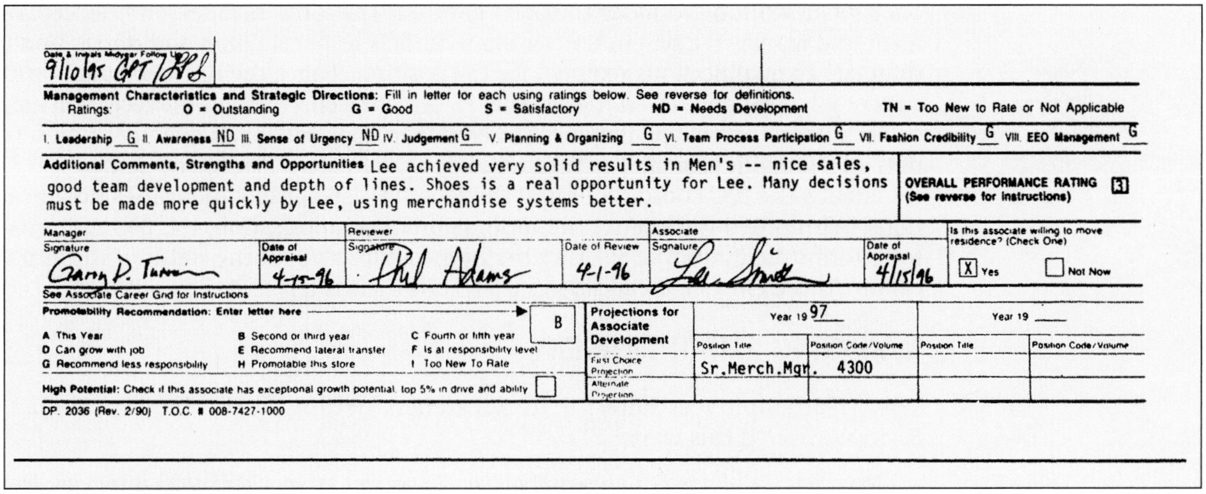

Note: Career-oriented appraisal.

▼ **FIGURE 10-2   Portion of J. C. Penney's Management Career Grid**

Instructions and Use of Grid for Making Associate Projections of Development

1) Promotability—Enter the appropriate Promotability letter in the box provided. If the answer to Promotability is D, F, or I, leave the "High Potential" and "Projections for Associate Development" sections blank.

2) High Potential—The High Potential box should be checked if this associate has exceptional growth potential—is within the top 5 % in drive and ability. Please keep in mind that appraisal ratings and high potential ratings, while related reflect two distinct judgments—performance in current assignment versus exceptional potential for growth. A "1" rated associate is not necessarily high potential or vice versa.

| OPERATIONS | | FIELD MANAGEMENT | |
| | | MERCHANDISE | |
Position Title/Volume	Code	Position Title/Volume	Code
Regional Operations Manager	1002	Manager of Geographic Markets	1017
		Manager of Business Planning	1025
		District Manager	1121
		Store Manager 30+ D.S	0109
		Entity Store Manager	0110
		Store Manager 22–30 D.S.	0108
		Store Manager 15–22 D.S.	0107
		Regional Business Planning Manager	1026
		Store Manager 10–15 D.S.	0106
		Store Manager Under 10 D.S.	0105
Regional Catalog Sales Center Manager	1150	Regional Merchandiser/Geographic Markets	1146
Regional Programs Manager	1100		
Regional Systems Manager	1027		
		Store Manager 5–10 S.L.	0104
Regional Catalog Sales Manager	1139	Business Planning Manager	**40( )0
District Operations Manager	2290	District Special Events & Publicity Manager	2800
District Operations/Personnel Manager	2310	Store Merchandise & Marketing Manager	4260
Regional Loss Prevention Manager	4804		
Operations Manager 30+ D.S.	1329	Store Manager 3–5 S.L.	0103
District Merchandise Systems Coordinator	2330	General Merchandising Manager 30+ D.S.	4299

The IPC process contains five steps. First, the hiring manager can choose to conduct an internal, external, or combined (internal and external) search, but "an internal or combined search is strongly encouraged."[36] Next, the manager and recruiter fill out a job description form for the open position. The form includes job title, department and manager, a description of the position's responsibilities and duties, and a summary of qualifications required for the position. Third, the firm's recruiter posts current job opportunities in the Internal Placement Center and in the reception area on each floor. Fourth, any employee interested in applying for an open position submits an IPC application and current résumé to the Internal Placement Center.

Finally, the IPC coordinator and the recruiter assess each applicant's qualifications. Within two weeks after the submission of an application, the IPC coordinator informs the employee at his or her home address about the status of the application. Those chosen as candidates then start their interviews.

MANAGING FAIR TREATMENT

Why treat employees fairly? Two researchers writing in the *Harvard Business Review* answered this way:

> *Never has the idea of fair process been more important for managers than it is today. Fair process turns out to be a powerful management tool for companies struggling to make the*

transition from a production-based to a knowledge-based company, in which value creation depends increasingly on ideas and innovation. Fair process profoundly influences attitudes and behaviors critical to high performance. It builds trust and unlocks ideas. With it, managers can achieve even the most painful and difficult goals while gaining the voluntary cooperation of the employees affected. Without fair process, even outcomes that employees might favor can be difficult to achieve.[37]

One study found that employees who felt their firms were treating them fairly were more likely to take those discretionary actions their companies need to stay flexible—for instance, to respond quickly to competitors' actions.[38] Treating employees fairly makes sense for other reasons, too. An increasingly litigious workforce makes it important that employers have disciplinary and discharge procedures that will survive arbitrators' and courts' scrutiny.

Creating a Better Environment

Some of the things that motivate managers to be fair may (or may not) be surprising. For one thing, the old saying "the squeaky wheel gets the grease" seems to be true. One study investigated the extent to which assertiveness on the subordinate's part influenced the fairness with which the person's supervisor treated him or her.[39] Did supervisors treat their pushier employees more fairly? Yes, they did: "individuals who communicated assertively were more likely to be treated fairly by the decision maker."[40] Studies also suggest that large organizations have to work particularly hard to set up procedures that make the workplace seem fair to employees.[41]

How do you measure "fair treatment"? In practice, fair treatment reflects underlying elements such as "employees are trusted," "employees are treated with respect," and "employees are treated fairly" (see Table 10-2).[42]

Workplace unfairness can be blatant. For example, some supervisors are "workplace bullies," yelling at or ridiculing subordinates, humiliating them, and sometimes even implying threats. Employers should of course prohibit such extreme behavior, and many firms have general antiharassment policies. For example, at the Oregon Department of Transportation, "it is the policy of the department that all employees, customers, contractors, and visitors to the work site are entitled to a positive, respectful, and productive work environment, free from behavior, actions, or language constituting workplace harassment."[43] Not surprisingly, employees of abusive supervisors are more likely to quit their jobs, and to report lower job and life satisfaction and higher stress if they remain in those jobs.[44]

There are other concrete things employers can do to create a more just environment at work—such as build two-way communications, emphasize fairness in disciplining, and manage employee privacy. Let's discuss these.

Build Two-Way Communications

Whether you're an irate customer, student, or employee, having the other person listen to what you're saying and perhaps explain the situation helps signal that you've been treated fairly. A study illustrates this everyday observation. The researchers concluded that three things contributed to perceived fairness in various business settings. One was *engagement* (involving individuals in the decisions that affect them by asking for their input and allowing them to refute the merits of one another's ideas and assumptions). A second was *explanation* (ensuring that everyone understood why final decisions were made as they were, and of the thinking that underlies the decisions). Third was *expectation clarity* (making sure everyone knows up front by what standards they'll be judged and the penalties for failure).[45]

▶ **TABLE 10-2
Perceptions of Fair
Interpersonal
Treatment Scale**

What is your organization like most of the time? Circle YES if the item describes your organization, NO if it does not describe your organization, and ? if you cannot decide.

In This Organization . . .			
1. Employees are praised for good work	Yes	?	No
2. Supervisors yell at employees (R)*	Yes	?	No
3. Supervisors play favorites (R)*	Yes	?	No
4. Employees are trusted*	Yes	?	No
5. Employee's complaints are dealt with effectively	Yes	?	No
6. Employees are treated like children (R)*	Yes	?	No
7. Employees are treated with respect*	Yes	?	No
8. Employees' questions and problems are responded to quickly*	Yes	?	No
9. Employees are lied to (R)*	Yes	?	No
10. Employees' suggestions are ignored (R)*	Yes	?	No
11. Supervisors swear at employees (R)*	Yes	?	No
12. Employees' hard work is appreciated*	Yes	?	No
13. Supervisors threaten to fire or lay off employees	Yes	?	No
14. Employees are treated fairly*	Yes	?	No
15. Co-workers help each other out	Yes	?	No
16. Co-workers argue with each other (R)	Yes	?	No
17. Co-workers put each other down	Yes	?	No
18. Co-workers treat each other with respect*	Yes	?	No

Note: R = item is reverse scored.
*Item included in the 12-item version of the scale administered to the midwestern university.
Source: Michelle A. Donovan, et al., "The Perceptions of Their Interpersonal Treatment Scale: Development and Validation of a Measure of Interpersonal Treatment in the Workplace," *Journal of Applied Psychology* 83, no. 5 (1998), p. 691. Copyright © (1997) by Michella A. Donovan, Fritz Drasgow, and Liberty J. Munson at the University of Illinois at Urbana-Champaign. All rights reserved.

Many firms have installed fairness programs that provide for engagement, explanation, and expectation clarity. We'll look at programs at FedEx, Toyota, and Saturn.

Speak-Up Programs (Toyota) **Speak-up! programs** encourage upward communications. They enable employees to express concerns ranging from malfunctioning vending machines to unlit parking lots to managers spending too much of the department's money on travel.

Toyota Motor Manufacturing in Lexington, Kentucky, calls its program the Hotline.[46] Its purpose is to provide Toyota employees with an anonymous way to bring questions or problems to the company's attention. The Hotline is available 24 hours a day. Employees can pick up any plant phone, dial the Hotline extension (HR posts the number on plant bulletin boards), and deliver their messages to the recorder. Toyota guarantees that HR will review and investigate all Hotline inquiries.

Opinion Surveys (FedEx) Many firms administer periodic anonymous **opinion surveys**. FedEx's Survey Feedback Action (SFA) program (mentioned in Chapter 9) is an example. It includes an anonymous survey that allows employees to express feelings about the company and their managers. Each manager gets his or her overall results, and discusses these with his or her subordinates. The aim is to design a blueprint for improving work group communications and commitment.

speak-up! programs
Communication programs that allow employees to register questions, concerns, and complaints about work-related matters.

opinion surveys
Communication devices that use questionnaires to regularly ask employees their opinions about the company, management, and work life.

Sample items include:

> I can tell my manager what I think.
>
> FedEx does a good job for the customers.
>
> In my environment we use safe work practices.
>
> I am paid fairly for this kind of work.

Top-Down Programs (Saturn) Many firms use various downward communication programs (**top-down programs**) to get information to all employees. Saturn, for instance, supplies information continuously via its internal television network to TVs in the plant's rest areas. Employees also have "town hall" meetings once a month. The Gateway Marriott program which follows is another example.

top-down programs
Communications activities including in-house television centers, e-mail, intranet postings, round-table discussions, and in-house newsletters that provide continuing opportunities for the firm to keep all employees up to date on company matters.

STRATEGIC HR

To differentiate itself strategically with world-class customer service, Crystal Gateway Marriott needed its front-line employees' commitment. It achieved this in part by distributing financial information to all associates (employees) in an easily understood format during quarterly meetings. Preliminary profit and loss statements for each operating department are given to the respective department heads for review. Critique meetings are held after each reporting period for a Lessons Learned session and for evaluation of the final report results. These sessions focus on improvement and learning, as opposed to "why did something happen and who is at fault." This information-sharing effort enhanced employee awareness and increased the ability of the hotel and its employees to manage financial issues in the business, since all associates now have a shared understanding and purpose.[47]

Communicating Financial Information at Gateway Marriott

Emphasize Fairness in Disciplining

The purpose of **discipline** is to encourage employees to behave sensibly at work (where *sensible* is defined as "adhering to rules and regulations"). In an organization, rules and regulations serve about the same purpose that laws do in society; discipline is called for when one of these rules or regulations is violated.[48] Fairness in this case means three things—rules and regulations, a system of progressive penalties, and an appeals process.

Rules and regulations address issues such as theft, destruction of company property, drinking on the job, and insubordination. Examples of rules include:

discipline
A procedure that corrects or punishes a subordinate because a rule or procedure has been violated.

- Poor performance is not acceptable. We expect each employee to perform his or her work properly and efficiently and to meet established standards of quality.
- Alcohol and drugs do not mix with work. Our company prohibits the use of either during working hours and reporting for work under their influence.
- Our company prohibits gambling in any form as well as the vending of anything in the plant without authorization.

The purpose of these rules is to inform employees ahead of time what is and is not acceptable behavior. You should tell employees, preferably in writing, what the firm does not permit. The employee orientation handbook usually lists these rules and regulations.

A system of progressive penalties is a second foundation of effective discipline. Penalties may range from oral warnings to written warnings to suspension from the job to discharge. The severity of the penalty is usually a function of the type of offense and the number of times the offense has occurred. For example, most

▲ *Electronic monitoring of employees' use of the Internet is on the increase, and one author notes that 70% of all Net surfing is done at work. A survey by Websense, a maker of Internet monitoring systems, found that one of three companies it surveyed reported that it had terminated an employee for improper use of the Internet at work. New monitoring programs allow managers to conduct scans specific enough to screen outgoing e-mails for particular words, such as "résumé."*

companies issue warnings for the first unexcused absence. However, for a third or fourth offense, discharge is the more usual disciplinary action. Finally, an appeals process helps ensure that supervisors dispense discipline fairly and equitably. Some discipline guidelines include:

■ Make sure the evidence supports the charge of employee wrongdoing.
■ Ensure that the employees' due process rights are protected.
■ Warn the employee of the disciplinary consequences.
■ The rule that was allegedly violated should be "reasonably related" to the efficient and safe operation of the particular work environment.
■ Fairly and adequately investigate the matter before administering discipline.
■ The investigation should produce substantial evidence of misconduct.
■ Rules, orders, or penalties should be applied evenhandedly.
■ The penalty should be reasonably related to the misconduct and to the employee's past work history.
■ Maintain the employee's right to counsel.
■ Don't rob your subordinate of his or her dignity.
■ Remember that the burden of proof is on you.
■ Get the facts. Don't base your decision on hearsay or on your general impression.
■ Don't act while angry.

Traditional discipline has two main potential flaws. It makes the employee feel bad, which could leave a residue of resentment and resistance. Second (and related to the first), forcing rules on employees may gain their short-term compliance, but not their cooperation when you're not around to enforce the rules. Discipline without punishment (or nonpunitive discipline) may avoid these problems. Its aim is to gain employee acceptance of company rules by reducing the punitive nature of the discipline. In summary:[49]

1. Issue an oral reminder. Your goal here is to get the employee to agree to solve the problem.
2. Should another incident arise within six weeks, issue the employee a formal written reminder, a copy of which you place in the personnel file. In addition, hold a second private discussion with the employee, again without any threats.
3. Give a paid one-day "decision-making leave." If another incident occurs after the written warning in the next six weeks or so, tell the employee to take a one-day leave with pay to stay home and consider whether or not the job is right for him or her and whether he or she wants to abide by the company's rules. When the employee returns to work, he or she meets with you and gives you a decision regarding whether he or she will follow the rules.
4. If no further incidents occur in the next year or so, purge the one-day paid suspension from the person's file. If the person repeats the behavior, dismissal (see later discussion) is mandatory.[50] On the other hand, exceptional circumstances might require exceptional measures. Criminal behavior or fighting might be grounds for immediate dismissal, for instance. And if several incidents occurred at close intervals, you might skip step 2—the written warning.

◆ **RESEARCH INSIGHT** Do male and female supervisors differ in how they discipline subordinates? A recent study shed some light on this. The researchers interviewed 163 workers. The workers held a range of jobs and their bosses had disciplined them in various ways, from firings to just reminding them to do better. About 40% of the workers changed their behavior after their scoldings, whether the boss was a man or woman. However, the male bosses were much more severe than the women. For example, the men were three times as likely to suspend or sack a subordinate, and only half as likely to just give an oral scolding. That harshness seemed to have a predictable effect: For example, 82% of female subordinates who were disciplined by males felt responsible for their bad behavior, while only 48% of those with female bosses felt responsible.[51]

Manage Employee Privacy

Electronic monitoring and searches of employees are widespread. About 75% of U.S. firms now record and review some type of employee communications and/or activity, such as e-mail, phone calls, computer files, and Internet use; that's about double the figure in 1997.[52] One reason is that companies reportedly lost $5.3 billion as a result of recreational Web surfing in 1999.[53]

Electronic eavesdropping is easier than most people think. One review says, for instance, that today's electronic systems "provide the tools to collect data and monitor the workplace with dazzling efficiency." It goes on to say "at the touch of a button, it's possible to view e-mail messages employees send to one another, listen to voice mail or telephone conversations, and actually see what's on their monitors while they're sitting at their computer terminals."[54] Several years ago, Pillsbury fired a regional manager after intercepting a supposedly private e-mail message making threatening comments about supervisors.[55]

Electronic eavesdropping is legal—at least to a point. For example, federal law and most state laws allow employers to monitor employees' phone calls "in the ordinary course of business," according to one legal expert, but they must stop listening once it becomes clear that a conversation is personal rather than business related.[56] You can also intercept e-mail service to protect the property rights of the e-mail provider.[57] However, to be safe, employers often issue e-mail and online service usage policies. These warn employees that those systems are meant to be used for business purposes only. Employers also have employees sign e-mail and telephone monitoring acknowledgment statements like that in Figure 10-3.

One reason for explicit, signed policy statements is the possibility that employers may be held liable for illegal acts committed by their employees via e-mail. For example, messages sent by supervisors that contain sexual innuendo, or ones defaming an employee can ensnare employers that haven't taken steps to prohibit such e-mail system misuse.[58]

Videotaping in the workplace seems to call for more legal caution. In one case, the U.S. Court of Appeals for the First Circuit ruled that an employer's continuous

◄ **FIGURE 10-3**
Sample Telephone Monitoring Acknowledgment Statement

> I understand that my telephone and e-mail communications will be monitored periodically by my supervisor and other [company] management staff. I understand that the purpose of this monitoring is to improve:
>
> • The quality of customer service provided to policyholders and prospective customers
> • My product knowledge and presentation skills
>
> _____   _____
> Signature   Date
>
> _____   _____
> Print Name   Department

Source: Reprinted with permission from *Bulletin to Management (BNA Policy and Practice Series)* 48, no. 14, Part II, (April 3, 1997) p. 7. Copyright 1997 by The Bureau of National Affairs, Inc.

video surveillance of employees in an office setting did not constitute an unconstitutional invasion of privacy.[59] But a Boston employer recently had to pay over $200,000 to five workers it secretly videotaped in an employee locker room, after they sued in state court.[60]

The four main types of privacy violations upheld by courts are intrusion (locker room and bathroom surveillance), publication of private matters, disclosure of medical records, and appropriation of an employee's name or likeness for commercial purposes.[61] Background checks, awareness of off-duty conduct and lifestyle, drug testing, workplace searches, and monitoring of workplace activities triggered most privacy violations.[62]

MANAGING DISMISSALS

dismissal
Involuntary termination of an employee's employment with the firm.

Dismissal is the most drastic disciplinary step you can take against an employee, and one you should take with deliberate care.[63] There should be sufficient cause for dismissal. And the dismissal should happen only after all reasonable steps to rehabilitate or salvage the employee have failed. However, there are undoubtedly times when speedy dismissal is required; in these instances, you should carry it out at once.[64]

You don't always have the right to dismiss employees. For more than 100 years, the prevailing rule in the United States was that without a contract, either the employer or the employee can **terminate at will** the employment relationship. In other words, the employee could resign for any reason, at will, and the employer could similarly dismiss an employee for any reason, at will. Today, however, dismissed employees are increasingly taking their cases to court, and many employers have found they no longer have a blanket right to fire. Instead, federal EEO and other laws and various state laws and court rulings increasingly limit management's right to dismiss employees at will. For example, firing a "whistle blower" might trigger "public policy" exceptions to firing at will; or a statement in an employee handbook may imply a contractual agreement to keep an employee on.

terminate at will
The idea, based in law, that the employment relationship can be terminated at will by either the employer or the employee for any reason.

Grounds for Dismissal

Companies dismiss employees for four reasons: unsatisfactory performance, misconduct, lack of qualifications for the job, and changed requirements (or elimination) of the job. *Unsatisfactory performance* is a persistent failure to perform assigned duties or to meet prescribed standards on the job.[65] Specific reasons include excessive absenteeism, tardiness, a persistent failure to meet normal job requirements, or an adverse attitude toward the company, supervisor, or fellow employees. *Misconduct* is a deliberate and willful violation of the employer's rules and may include stealing, rowdy behavior, and insubordination.

Lack of qualifications for the job refers to an employee's inability to do the assigned work although he or she is diligent. The employee may be trying to do the job, so it's especially important to make an effort to salvage him or her—perhaps by reassigning or training the person. *Changed job requirements* refers to an employee's inability to do the work after the nature of the job has changed. And of course, firms often dismiss employees when they eliminate their jobs. Again, the employees may be industrious, so firms often make an effort to retrain or transfer such employees.

insubordination
Willful disregard or disobedience of the boss's authority or legitimate orders; criticizing the boss in public.

Insubordination, a form of misconduct, is sometimes the grounds for dismissal, but may be more difficult to prove. Stealing, chronic tardiness, and poor-quality work are obvious grounds for dismissal, but insubordination can be harder to put into words. Remember that some acts are generally insubordinate whenever and wherever they occur. These include, for instance:

1. Direct disregard of the boss's authority. At sea, this is mutiny.
2. Flat-out disobedience of, or refusal to obey, the boss's orders—particularly in front of others.
3. Deliberate defiance of clearly stated company policies, rules, regulations, and procedures.
4. Public criticism of the boss. Contradicting or arguing with him or her is also negative and inappropriate.
5. Blatant disregard of the boss's reasonable instructions.
6. Contemptuous display of disrespect; making insolent comments, for example; and, more important, portraying these feelings in the attitude shown while on the job.
7. Disregard for the chain of command, shown by going around the immediate supervisor or manager with a complaint, suggestion, or political maneuver. Although the employee may be right, that may not be enough to save him or her from the charges of insubordination.
8. Participation in (or leadership of) an effort to undermine and remove the boss from power.[66]

Dismissals are never pleasant, but there are several things you can do to ensure the dismissal is viewed as fair.[67] One recent study found, for instance, that "individuals who reported that they were given full explanations of why and how termination decisions were made were more likely to (1) perceive their layoff as fair, (2) endorse the terminating organization, and (3) indicate that they did not wish to take the past employer to court."[68] Instituting a formal multistep procedure (including warning) and a neutral appeal process also fosters fairness.[69]

Who actually does the dismissing is important. One study focused on an R&D facility.[70] Survivors whose managers informed them of the impending layoff viewed the entire dismissal procedure as much fairer than did those told by, say, HR. The quality of the prelayoff relationship between the employee and the manager did affect whether or not the employee preferred to get the news from the manager. Based on this study, at least, one has to question the wisdom of centralizing responsibility for matters like these in the HR department, particularly where the relationship between the employees and their supervising manager has been good.[71] Amazon.com recently took what some feel was a less diplomatic approach to dismissing some employees in the Seattle area. The firm had an in-person meeting to announce the downsizing, but telecommuter employees who were unable to attend got the news by e-mail, once the meeting was underway.[72]

◆ **HIGH-PERFORMANCE INSIGHT** Security measures are important whenever dismissals take place. Common sense has always dictated using a checklist to ensure dismissed employees returned all keys and company property and (often) were accompanied out of their offices. Widespread Internet access makes security measures even more important today. For example, it's necessary to disable passwords and accounts of former employees, to plug holes that could allow an ex-employee to exploit someone else's user account to gain illegal access, and to have formal rules for return of company laptops and handhelds. "Measures range from simply disabling access and changing passwords to reconfiguring the network and changing IP addresses, remote access procedures and telephone numbers," says one chief technology officer. When a Verizon employee is terminated, it's that person's immediate supervisor who must ensure that all access privileges are cut off and accounts are deleted; the company's security group then checks to make sure all processes have been followed.[73]

Avoiding Wrongful Discharge Suits

wrongful discharge
An employee dismissal that does not comply with the law or does not comply with the contractual arrangement stated or implied by the firm via its employment application forms, employee manuals, or other promises.

Wrongful discharge occurs when an employee's dismissal violates the law or the contractual arrangements stated or implied by the firm via its employment application forms, employee manuals, or other promises. The time to protect against such suits is before you make mistakes and suits are filed.

Avoiding wrongful discharge suits requires a two-pronged approach. First, set up employment policies and dispute-resolution procedures to make employees feel the firm treated them fairly.[74] People who are fired and who walk away feeling they've been embarrassed, stripped of their dignity, or treated unfairly financially (for instance, in terms of severance pay) are more likely to seek retribution in the courts. There is no way to make a termination pleasant, but it helps to at least make sure it's viewed as fair.

Second, do the preparatory work—starting with the employment application—that will help avoid such suits. Pay particular attention to the employee handbook. It should include an acknowledgment form like that in Figure 10-4, which makes clear that the material in the handbook does not constitute a contract. Table 10-3 summarizes some of the steps you can take.

▶ **FIGURE 10-4**
TJP Inc. Employee Handbook Acknowledgment Form

TJP INC. EMPLOYEE HANDBOOK ACKNOWLEDGMENT FORM

This employee handbook has been given to _____

on (date) _____

by _____ (title) _____

Employee's effective starting date _____

Employee's pay period _____

Employee's hours and workweek are _____

Welcome to TJP Inc. Below are a list of your benefits with their effective date:

Benefit	**Effective Date**
Hospitalization _____	_____
Life insurance _____	_____
Retirement _____	_____
Vacation _____	_____
Sick leave _____	_____
Holidays _____	_____
Personal days _____	_____
Bereavement _____	_____
Worker's compensation _____	_____
Social Security _____	_____
Your first performance appraisal will be on _____	_____

I understand that my employee handbook is for informational purposes only and that I am to read and refer to the employee handbook for information on employment work rules and company policies. TJP Inc. may modify, revoke, suspend or terminate any and all policies, rules, procedures and benefits at any time without prior notice to company employees. This handbook and its statements do not create a contract between TJP Inc. and its employees. This handbook and its statements do not affect in any way the employment-at-will relationship between TJP Inc. and its employees.

(Employee's signature) _____

(Date) _____

◄ **TABLE 10-3**
Protecting the
Company Against
Wrongful Discharge
Suits

- Have applicants sign the employment application. Make sure it contains a statement that employment is for no fixed term and that the employer can terminate at any time. It should also inform the job candidate that "nothing on this application can be changed."
- Review your employee manual to delete statements that could prejudice your defense in a wrongful discharge case. For example, delete any reference to the fact that "employees can be terminated only for just cause" (unless you really mean that).
- Consider not outlining performance appraisal or progressive discipline procedures in the manual: You may be obligated to follow the steps exactly or face a suit for not doing so.
- Always include a waiver statement in the front of the handbook that asserts the company hires only at will.[a]
- References to probationary periods or permanent employment may be unwise, since they imply a permanence you may not mean.
- Never limit the right to discharge or list specific reasons for discharge.[b] Always add a sentence or paragraph that reserves for the employer the right to make changes to the handbook in the future. An acknowledgment form can be useful to show that the handbook is not a contract and that employment-at-will remains in force.[c]
- Make sure that no one in a position of authority makes promises you do not intend to keep, such as by saying, "If you do your job here, you can't get fired."
- Have clear written rules listing infractions that may require discipline, and then adhere to the rules. Give employees an opportunity to correct unacceptable behavior, and be careful not to single out anyone.
- If a rule is broken, get the worker's side of the story in front of witnesses, and preferably get it signed. Then make sure to check out the story, getting both sides of the issue.
- Be sure to evaluate employees at least annually. If an employee is showing evidence of incompetence, give that person a warning and provide a chance to improve. Put all evaluations in writing, and have the employee sign them.[d]
- Keep records of all actions such as employee evaluations, warnings, or notices; memos outlining how the person can improve; and so on. Memorialize all efforts at counseling or discipline and keep them confidential to avoid defamation charges.[e]
- Make sure the company's policy about probationary periods is clear and that employees cannot infer that once they are past the probationary period their jobs are "safe."[f]

Notes:
[a]See Teresa Brady, "Employee Handbooks: Contracts or Empty Promises?" *Management Review*, June 1993, pp. 33–35.
[b]Bureau of National Affairs, *The Employment-at-Will Issue* (Washington, DC: BNA, 1982). See also Emily Joiner, "Erosion of the Employment at Will Doctrine," *Personnel* 61, no. 5 (September–October 1984), pp. 12–18; Harvey Steinberg, "Where Law and Personnel Policies Collide: The At Will Employment Crossroad," *Personnel* 62, no. 6 (June 1985), pp. 37–43.
[c]Brady, "Employee Handbooks," p. 35.
[d]Note, however, that under recent court rulings at least one U.S. court of appeals (for the Seventh Circuit) has held that employee handbooks distributed to long-term employees before employers began amending their handbooks to contain "no contract" and "at-will employment" disclaimers may still be viewed by the court as contracts with these employees. The case was *Robinson v. Ada S. McKinley Community Services, Inc.*, 19 F.3d 359 (7th Cir. 1994); see Kenneth Jenero, "Employers Beware: You May Be Bound by the Terms of Your Old Employee Handbooks," *Employee Relations Law Journal* 20, no. 2 (autumn 1994), pp. 299–312.
[e]Robert Paul and James Townsend, "Wrongful Termination: Balancing Employer and Employee Rights—A Summary with Recommendations," *Employee Responsibilities and Rights Journal* 6, no. 1 (1993), pp. 69–82. Wrongful termination is particularly a problem when the employee is a "whistle blower." See, for example, Rosalia Costa-Clarke, "The Cost Implications of Terminating Whistle-Blowers," *Employment Relations Today* 21, no. 4 (winter 1994), pp. 447–454.
[f]Ibid., p. 81.

Before you actually dismiss the person, do a final review. The 12-step checklist reduces wrongful discharge litigation exposure: (1) Is employee covered by any type of written agreement, including a collective bargaining agreement? (2) Have written or oral representations been made to form a contract? (3) Is a defamation claim likely? (4) Is there a possible discrimination or whistle-blower allegation? (5) Is there any workers' compensation involvement? (6) Have reasonable rules and regulations been communicated and enforced? (7) Has the employee been given an opportunity to explain any rule violations or to correct poor performance? (8) Have all monies been paid within 24 hours of separation? (9) Has employee been advised of his or her rights under COBRA? (10) Has employee been advised of what the employer will tell a prospective employer in response to a reference inquiry?[75] (11) Have you reviewed the person's personnel file? For example, long-seniority employees may merit more opportunities to correct their actions than newly hired ones. (12) Have you considered "buying out" a wrongful discharge claim with settlement pay? Don't stand in the way of a terminated employee's future employment, since a person with a new job is less likely to sue the former employer than someone who remains unemployed.[76]

Finally, telling the employee why you are dismissing her or him is important. While some managers try to avoid hurting the person's feelings or triggering an argument, not being frank and honest can backfire. A recent U.S. Supreme Court decision suggests that in certain cases an employee who simply shows that the employer's stated reason for discharging him or her is a lie could have the right to take the case to a jury.[77]

If humanitarianism and wrongful discharge suits aren't enough to encourage you to be fair in carrying out dismissals, consider this. A study found that managers run double the risk of suffering a heart attack during the week after they fire an employee.[78] Between 1989 and 1994, physicians interviewed 791 working people who had just undergone heart attacks, to find out what might have triggered them. The researchers concluded that the stress associated with firing someone doubled the usual risk of a heart attack for the person doing the firing, during the week following the dismissal.

The Termination Interview

termination interview
The interview in which an employee is informed of the fact that he or she has been dismissed.

Dismissing an employee is one of the most difficult tasks you can face at work.[79] The dismissed employee, even if warned many times, may still react with disbelief or even violence. Guidelines for the **termination interview** itself are as follows:

1. Plan the interview carefully. According to experts at Hay Associates, this includes:

   Make sure the employee keeps the appointment time.

   Never inform an employee over the phone.

   Allow 10 minutes as sufficient time for the interview.

   Use a neutral site, never your own office.

   Have employee agreements, the human resource file, and a release announcement (internal and external) prepared in advance.

   Be available at a time after the interview in case questions or problems arise.

   Have phone numbers ready for medical or security emergencies.

2. Get to the point. Do not beat around the bush by talking about the weather or making other small talk. As soon as the employee enters the meeting room, give the person a moment to get comfortable and then inform him or her of your decision.

3. Describe the situation. Briefly, in three or four sentences, explain why the person is being let go. For instance, "Production in your area is down 4%, and we are continuing to have quality problems. We have talked about these problems several times in the past three months. We have to make a change."[80] Remember to describe the situation, rather than attacking the employee personally by saying things like "Your production is just not up to par." Also emphasize that the decision is final and irrevocable.

4. Listen. Continue the interview until the person appears to be talking freely and reasonably calmly about the reasons for his or her termination and the support package (including severance pay).

5. Review all elements of the severance package. Describe severance payments, benefits, access to office support people, and the way you'll handle references. However, under no conditions imply any promises or benefits beyond those already in the support package.
6. Identify the next step. The terminated employee may be disoriented and unsure what to do next. Explain where the employee should go next, upon leaving the interview.

Outplacement Counseling[81]   **Outplacement counseling** is a systematic process by which someone you've terminated is trained and counseled in the techniques of conducting a self-appraisal and securing a new job that is appropriate to his or her needs and talents.[82] As the term is generally used, outplacement does not imply that the employer takes responsibility for placing the person in a new job. Instead, it is a counseling service whose purpose is to provide the person with advice, instructions, and a sounding board to help formulate career goals and successfully execute a job search. Outplacement counseling is part of the terminated employee's support or severance package and is often done by specialized outside firms.

Outplacement firms do more than counsel displaced employees; they also help the employer devise its dismissal plan. For about two months before announcing its downsizing plan, MacLean, Virginia-based Getronics worked with an outplacement firm to develop a plan regarding how to break the news, deal with dismissed employees' emotional reactions, and institute the appropriate severance pay and equal employment plans.[83]

> **outplacement counseling**
> A systematic process by which a terminated person is trained and counseled in the techniques of self-appraisal and securing a new position.

Exit Interviews   Many employers conduct exit interviews with employees who are leaving the firm. The HR department usually conducts them. They aim at eliciting information about the job or related matters that might give the employer a better insight into what is right—or wrong—about the company. The assumption, of course, is that because the employee is leaving, he or she will be candid.

Exit interview questions to ask include: How were you recruited? Why did you join the company? Was the job presented correctly and honestly? Were your expectations met? What was the workplace environment like? What was your supervisor's management style like? What did you like most/least about the company? Were there any special problem areas? Why did you decide to leave, and how was the departure handled?[84]

Based on one survey, the quality of information you can expect from exit interviews is questionable. The researchers found that at the time of separation, 38% of those leaving blamed salary and benefits, and only 4% blamed supervision. Followed up 18 months later, however, 24% blamed supervision and only 12% blamed salary and benefits. Getting to the real problem during the exit interview may thus require some heavy digging.[85] Yet they can be useful. When Blue Cross of Northeastern Pennsylvania laid off employees, many said, in exit interviews, "This is not a stable place to work." The firm took steps to correct that misperception for those who stayed with Blue Cross.

Layoffs and the Plant Closing Law

Nondisciplinary separations are a fact of corporate life. For the employer, reduced sales or profits may require layoffs or downsizing. Employees may terminate their employment to retire or to seek better jobs.

Ironically, today's emphasis on "human capital" notwithstanding, layoffs and downsizings, if anything, are up. For example, annual layoffs recently reached a 10-year high of over 1.5 million. This has prompted experts to suggest considering alternatives to reducing employee head counts. Suggestions include finding volunteers who are interested in reduced hours or part-time work; using attrition; opting for voluntary early-retirement packages; and networking with local employers concerning temporary or permanent redeployments.[86]

The Plant Closing Law   Until 1989, there were no federal laws requiring notification of employees when an employer decided to close its facility. However, in that year the Worker Adjustment and Retraining Notification Act (popularly known as the **plant closing law**) became law. It requires employers of 100 or more employees to give 60 days' notice before closing a facility or starting a layoff of 50 people or more. The law does not prevent the employer from closing down, nor does it require saving jobs. It simply gives employees time to seek other work or retraining by giving them advance notice of the shutdown.

Employers are responsible for giving notice to employees who will (or who reasonably may be expected to) experience a covered "employment loss." *Covered employment losses* include **terminations** (other than discharges for cause, voluntary departures, or retirement), **layoffs** exceeding 6 months, and reductions of more than 50% in employees' work hours during each month of any 6-month period. Generally, the firm needn't notify workers it reassigns or transfers to certain employer-sponsored programs or who get an opportunity to transfer or relocate to another company location within a reasonable commuting distance. While there are exceptions to the law, the penalty for failing to give notice is fairly severe: 1 day's pay and benefits to each employee for each day's notice that should have been given, up to 60 days.

The law is not entirely clear about how to word the notice to employees. However, if you write a letter to individual employees, a paragraph that might suit the purpose would be as follows:

> *Please consider this letter to be your official notice, as required by the federal plant closing law, that your current position with the company will end 60 days from today because of a [layoff or closing] that is now projected to take place on [date]. After that day your employment with the company will be terminated, and you will no longer be carried on our payroll records or be covered by any company benefit programs. Any questions concerning the plant closing law or this notice will be answered in the HR office.*[87]

A layoff, in which workers are sent home for a time, is a situation in which three conditions are present: (1) there is no work available for the employees, (2) management expects the no-work situation to be temporary and probably short term, and (3) management intends to recall the employees when work is again available.[88] A layoff is therefore not a termination, which is a permanent severing of the employment relationship. After the World Trade Center attack, most U.S. airlines laid off ("furloughed") about 20% of their employees, but expected eventually to bring them back. However, some employers use the term *layoff* as a euphemism for discharge or termination.

Bumping/Layoff Procedures   Employers who encounter frequent business slowdowns and layoffs may have procedures that let employees use their seniority to remain on the job. Most such **bumping/layoff procedures** have these features in common:

1. Seniority is usually the ultimate determinant of who will work.
2. Seniority can give way to merit or ability, but usually only when no senior employee is qualified for a particular job.
3. Seniority is usually based on the date the employee joined the organization, not the date he or she took a particular job.

plant closing law
The Worker Adjustment and Retraining Notification Act, which requires notifying employees in the event an employer decides to close its facility.

termination
A permanent severing of the employment relationship.

layoff
A situation in which there is a temporary shortage of work and employees are told there is no work for them but that management intends to recall them when work is again available.

bumping/layoff procedures
Detailed procedures that determine who will be laid off if no work is available; generally allow employees to use their seniority to remain on the job.

4. Because seniority is usually companywide, an employee in one job can usually bump or displace an employee on another job, provided the more senior person can do the job without further training.[89] When the New York Stock Exchange recently eliminated all "reporter" jobs on the exchange, many of these people applied for and "bumped" lower seniority employees, for instance from "messenger" jobs.

Alternatives to Layoffs Given the investments they have in recruiting, screening, and training employees, many employers are hesitant to lay off people at the first signs of business decline.

There are several alternatives. With the **voluntary reduction in pay plan**, all employees agree to reductions in pay to keep everyone working. Other employers arrange for all or most employees to concentrate their vacations during slow periods. They don't have to hire temporary help for vacationing employees during peak periods, and staffing automatically declines when business declines. For example, Sun (as well as many Silicon Valley employers) had all employees stay home for a week when the economy slowed in mid-2001. Other employees agree to take **voluntary time off**, which again has the effect of reducing the employer's payroll and avoiding layoffs. Many firms including IBM reduce layoffs with a **rings of defense** approach. They hire temporary supplemental employees, often as independent contractors, with the understanding their work is temporary. When layoffs come, the first ring of defense is the supplemental workers.[90] Some firms seek volunteers as an alternative to dismissing large numbers of employees. Procter & Gamble offered buyout packages to about 20,000 nonmanufacturing U.S. employees, in its quest to find enough volunteers to avoid dismissing 5,600 people.[91]

Adjusting to Downsizings and Mergers

Downsizing—reducing, usually dramatically, the number of people the firm employs—is increasingly utilized.[92] Yet many firms discover operating earnings don't rise after major cuts.[93] Low morale among those remaining may contribute to the problem.[94]

From a practical point of view, firms can take steps to reduce the remaining employees' uncertainty and to address their concerns.[95] A postdownsizing program at Duracell, Inc. (now part of Dow), illustrates what you can do. The program had postdownsizing-announcement activities, including a full staff meeting at the facility; immediate follow-up in which remaining employees were split into groups with senior managers to express their concerns and have their questions answered; and long-term support, for instance by encouraging supervisors to meet with employees frequently and informally to encourage an open-door atmosphere. Other companies, such as the Diners Club subsidiary of Citigroup, use attitude surveys to help management monitor how postdownsizing efforts are progressing.[96]

Regardless of why you're downsizing, think through the process, both to avoid unnecessary consequences and to ensure the process is fair. Here are some guidelines for implementing a reduction in force:[97]

- Identify objectives and constraints. For example, decide how many positions to eliminate at which locations, and what criteria to use to pinpoint the employees to whom you'll offer voluntary exit incentives.
- Form a downsizing team. This management team should prepare a communication strategy for explaining the downsizing, establish hiring and promotion levels, produce a downsizing schedule, and supervise the displaced employees' benefit programs.

voluntary reduction in pay plan
An alternative to layoffs in which all employees agree to reductions in pay to keep everyone working.

voluntary time off
An alternative to layoffs in which some employees agree to take time off to reduce the employer's payroll and avoid the need for a layoff.

rings of defense
An alternative layoff plan in which temporary supplemental employees are hired with the understanding that they may be laid off at any time.

downsizing
The process of reducing, usually dramatically, the number of people employed by the firm.

■ Address legal issues. You'll want to ensure that others won't view the downsizing as a subterfuge to lay off protected classes of employees. Therefore, review factors such as age, race, and gender before finalizing and communicating any dismissals.

■ Plan postimplementation actions. Activities such as surveys and explanatory meetings can help maintain morale. Similarly, some suggest a hiring freeze of at least 6 months after the layoffs have taken effect.[98]

■ Address security concerns. As with any large layoffs, it may be wise to have security personnel in place in case there's a problem from one or two employees, and to follow the dismissal checklist discussed earlier in this chapter.

In terms of dismissals, mergers and acquisitions are usually one sided: One company essentially acquires the other, and it is often the employees of the latter who find themselves looking for new jobs. In such a situation, employees in the acquired firm will be hypersensitive to mistreatment of their colleagues. It thus behooves you to take care that you treat those let go fairly. Seeing your former colleagues fired is bad enough for morale. Seeing them fired under conditions that look like bullying rubs salt in the wound and poisons the relationship. As a rule, therefore:

Avoid the appearance of power and domination.

Avoid win–lose behavior.

Remain businesslike and professional in all dealings.

Maintain as positive a feeling about the acquired company as possible.

Remember that the degree to which your organization treats the acquired group with care and dignity will affect the confidence, productivity, and commitment of those remaining.[99]

For example, Jack Brown, Chairman of Slater Brothers, knew it was crucial to maintain good relations with the employees of the 33 Albertson's and 10 Lucky Stores his company recently acquired. Slater first created a transition team headed by a top executive, who, among other things, offered jobs to all employees of the 43 stores. His firm also devoted a great deal of time and effort to communicating with the new employees. As he says, "I took a month and talked to all of them. . . . All people got to stay at the same store with the same pay, the same benefits, and the same seniority."[100]

Retirement

retirement
The point at which a person gives up one's work, usually between the ages of 60 to 65, but increasingly earlier today due to firms' early-retirement incentive plans.

Retirement for many employees is bittersweet. The employee may be free of the daily requirements of his or her job, but at the same time be slightly adrift because of not having a job. About 30% of the employers in one survey therefore reported having formal **preretirement counseling** aimed at easing the passage of their employees into retirement. The most common preretirement practices were:

preretirement counseling
Counseling provided to employees who are about to retire, which covers matters such as benefits advice, second careers, and so on.

Explanation of Social Security benefits (reported by 97% of those with preretirement education programs)

Leisure time counseling (86%)

Financial and investment counseling (84%)

Health counseling (82%)

Psychological counseling (35%)

Counseling for second careers outside the company (31%)

Counseling for second careers inside the company (4%)

There's no reason to wait until a person is ready to retire to provide retirement planning assistance. For example, American Express recently introduced an online asset allocation tool for use by its employer-clients' retirement plan participants. The Web-based tool, called Retirement Guidance Planner, lets an employer's retirement plan participants calculate and keep track of progress toward retirement income goals and more easily allocate assets among different investments online.[101]

Another important trend is granting part-time employment to employees as an alternative to outright retirement. Several surveys of blue- and white-collar employees showed that about half of all employees over age 55 would like to continue working part time after they retire.[102]

Retirement procedures must comply with the law. For example, 10 current and former agents of New York Life Insurance Company recently filed a suit alleging that the company defrauded about 10,000 agents of their retirement and health insurance benefits. Among other things, the suit claims that agents were systematically forced out as they got close to the 20 years of service that would qualify them for full retirement benefits. New York Life says most of the terminations were for other reasons, such as compliance problems or the agents' own decisions to move on.[103]

We invite you to visit **www.prenhall.com/dessler** on the Prentice Hall Web site for our online study guide, Internet exercises, current events, links to related Web sites, and more.

Summary

1. Employers play an important role in the career management process. Important guidelines include: Avoid reality shock, be demanding, provide realistic job previews, conduct career-oriented performance appraisals, and encourage job rotation.

2. More firms today engage in career development activities, such as career-oriented appraisals, career records/job posting programs, and training and educational opportunities. Many firms also have comprehensive career management/promotion-from-within programs that help foster employee commitment.

3. Managing fair treatment includes giving employees vehicles through which to express opinions and concerns. For example, Toyota's Hotline provides employees with an anonymous channel through which they can express concerns to top management. Firms such as IBM and FedEx engage in periodic anonymous opinion surveys.

4. One part of fair treatment is a fair and just discipline process based on three prerequisites: rules and regulations, a system of progressive penalties, and an appeals process.

5. Managing dismissals is an important part of any supervisor's job. Among the reasons for dismissal are unsatisfactory performance, misconduct, lack of qualifications, changed job requirements, and insubordination. In dismissing one or more employees, however, remember that great care should be taken to avoid wrongful discharge suits. In the termination interview, plan what you will say, get to the point, describe the situation, listen, review the benefits, and identify the next step.

Tying It All Together

Chapters 3 through 6 explained how to recruit, test, interview, and select employees. Chapters 7 through 10 (Part 3, Training and Development) focused on how to assimilate these new employees, and how to train and develop them, appraise their performance, and create an environment that helps meld their careers and commitment with the company's aims. Next, we turn to the matter of how to compensate employees: This brings us to the next part of this book and to Chapter 11, Establishing Strategic Pay Plans.

<table>
<tr><td>

Discussion Questions

</td><td>

1. Explain career-related factors to keep in mind when making the employee's first assignments.
2. Describe specific techniques you would use to foster top-down communication in an organization.
3. Describe the similarities and differences between discipline without punishment and a typical discipline procedure.
4. Explain how you would ensure fairness in disciplining, discussing particularly the prerequisites to disciplining, disciplining guidelines, and the discipline-without-punishment approach.
5. Give several examples of career development activities that organizations can provide for their employees.

</td></tr>
</table>

<table>
<tr><td>

Individual and Group Activities

</td><td>

1. Working individually or in groups, choose three occupations (such as management consultant, HR manager, or salesperson) and make an assessment of the future demand for this occupation over the next 10 years or so. Does this seem like a good occupation to pursue? Why or why not?
2. Working individually or in groups, choose several occupations, such as programmer, lawyer, and accountant, and identify as many job openings for these occupations on the Internet as you can. Do you think the Internet is a valuable job search source for these occupations? Why or why not?
3. Working individually or in groups, obtain copies of the employee handbook for your college and determine to what extent there are potential problems in it that might reduce the college or university's ability to fire someone at will.
4. Working individually or in groups, review your college's student manual. Does it have a discipline process? How would you improve it?

</td></tr>
</table>

EXPERIENTIAL EXERCISE

Purpose: The purpose of this exercise is to provide you with some experience in analyzing and handling a disciplinary situation.

Required Understanding: Students should be thoroughly familiar with the following case. However, *do not read the "Award" or "Discussion" sections until after the groups have completed their deliberations.*

How to Set Up the Exercise/Instructions: Divide the class into groups of four or five students. The group should take the arbitrator's point of view and assume that they are to analyze the case and make the arbitrator's decision. Review the case again at this point, but please do not read the "Award" section.

Each group should answer the following questions:

1. What would your decision be if you were the arbitrator? Why?

2. Do you think the employer handled the disciplinary situation correctly? Why? What would you have done differently?

Facts: A computer department employee made an entry error that botched an entire run of computer reports. Efforts to rectify the situation produced a second set of improperly run reports. As a result of the series of errors, the employer incurred extra costs of $2,400, plus a weekend of overtime work, by other computer department staffers. Management suspended the employee for 3 days for negligence, and also revoked a promotion for which the employee had previously been approved.

Protesting the discipline, the employee stressed that she had attempted to correct her error in the early stages of the run by notifying the manager of computer operations of her mistake. Maintaining that the resulting string of errors could have been avoided if the manager had followed up on her report and stopped the initial run, the employee argued that she had been treated unfairly because the manager had not been disciplined even though he compounded the problem, whereas she was severely punished. Moreover, citing her "impeccable" work record and management's acknowledgment that she had always been a "model employee," the employee insisted that the denial of her previously approved promotion was "unconscionable."

(*Please do* not *read beyond this point until after you have completed the experiential exercise.*)

Award: The arbitrator upholds the 3-day suspension, but decides that the promotion should be restored.

Discussion: "There is no question," the arbitrator notes, that the employee's negligent act "set in motion the train of events that resulted in running two complete sets of reports reflecting improper information." Stressing that the employer incurred substantial cost because of the error, the arbitrator cites "unchallenged" testimony that management had commonly issued 3-day suspensions for similar infractions in the past. Thus, the arbitrator decides, the employer acted with just cause in meting out an "evenhanded" punishment for the negligence.

Turning to the denial of the already approved promotion, the arbitrator says that this action should be viewed "in the same light as a demotion for disciplinary reasons." In such cases, the arbitrator notes, management's decision normally is based on a pattern of unsatisfactory behavior, an employee's inability to perform, or similar grounds. Observing that management had never before reversed a promotion as part of a disciplinary action, the arbitrator says that by tacking on the denial of the promotion in this case, the employer substantially varied its disciplinary policy from its past practice. Because this action on management's part was not "evenhanded," the arbitrator rules, the promotion should be restored.

APPLICATION CASE *The Mentor Relationship Turns Upside Down*

"I wish I could talk this problem over with Walter," Carol Lee thought. Walter Lemaire had been her mentor for several years at Larchmont Consulting, yet now he was her problem.

Carol thought back to the beginning of her association with Larchmont and with Walter. She had joined the firm as a writer and editor; her job during those early years had been to revise and polish the consultants' business reports. The work brought her into frequent contact with Walter, who was a senior vice president at the time. Carol enjoyed discussing the consultants' work with him, and when she decided to try to join the consulting team she asked for his help. Walter became her mentor as well as her boss and guided her through her successful transition to consultant and eventually partner.

At each promotion along the way to partner, Carol cemented her relationship with her new subordinates and peers by acknowledging the inevitable initial awkwardness and by meeting with each person individually to forge a new working relationship. Her career prospered, and when Walter moved on to run a start-up software publishing venture for Larchmont, Carol was promoted to take his place. However, his new venture faltered, and the partners decided someone else would have to step in. Despite the fact that Carol was much younger than Walter and once had worked for him, she was given the assignment of rescuing the start-up operation.

Carol's discomfort over the assignment only grew as she began to review the history of the new venture. Her rescue mission was going to entail undoing much of what Walter had done, reversing his decisions about everything from product design to marketing and pricing. Carol was so reluctant to second-guess her old mentor and boss that she found herself all but unable to discuss any of her proposed solutions with him directly. She doubted that any of her past experience had prepared her to assume the role of Walter's boss, and in these difficult circumstances her need to turn the operation around would be, she felt, like "pouring salt on his wounds."

Questions

1. What is Carol's role in Walter's career development now? Should Larchmont have any such role? Why or why not?
2. What advice would you offer Carol for approaching Walter?
3. If Carol has to dismiss Walter, how specifically would you suggest she proceed?
4. Assume Carol has heard a rumor that Walter has considered resigning. What should she do about it?

Note: The incident in this case is based on an event at an unidentified firm described in Jennifer Frey, "Pride and Your Promotion," *Working Woman*, October 1996.

CONTINUING CASE: LearnInMotion.com *The Career Planning Program*

Career planning has always been a low priority item for LearnInMotion.com, since "just finding good employees and keeping them is enough of a problem," as Mel likes to say. "And don't forget," he recently said, "this isn't General Motors and our employees haven't got hundreds of possible positions they can make plans to be promoted to."

Yet, Jennifer thought it might not be a bad idea to give some thought to what a career planning program might involve for LearnInMotion.com. For one thing, she knew three employees—the Web surfer, and two content managers—were students at local colleges, and so obviously had higher career aspirations: "Why not at least create the possibility that they could continue their careers with us, if everything works out right?" she said. Jennifer also knew that Maureen, the Web designer—who could now only handle the "front-end" design of the site, wanted to learn more about programming, so she could also handle the "back end"—the actual programming of the site. And, while one of the salespeople seemed to be dedicated to the sales function, the other had several times expressed an interest in getting more involved in the management of the company. Jennifer thinks providing more career-oriented support might build commitment. "Jennifer, that's a great theory, but we've got so many other things to do," replied Mel.

After discussing the issue, they're at least willing to give formalizing a simple career management program a try. Now they want you, their management consultants, to help them actually do it. Here's what they want you to do for them:

Questions and Assignments

1. What would be the advantages to LearnInMotion.com of setting up a career planning program?
2. Who should participate in the program, and why? All employees? Selected employees?
3. Describe the program you would propose for injecting a career planning and development perspective into LearnInMotion.com.

Chapter 11

Establishing Strategic Pay Plans

After studying this chapter, you should be able to:

- List the basic factors in determining pay rates.
- Explain in detail how to establish pay rates.
- Describe how to price managerial and professional jobs.
- Discuss current trends in compensation.
- Establish a pay plan.

STRATEGIC OVERVIEW When he became CEO of IBM, Louis Gerstner Jr. knew he had to spark the firm out of its lethargy. For years, IBM people had worked in a sort of cocoon, insulated from the market, paid not on performance but primarily on seniority. He had to refocus his employees' attention on a new set of values: Winning must be an obsession; execution is built on speed and decisiveness; and teamwork is something IBM must cultivate. One of Gerstner's first steps was to order a dramatic overhaul of IBM's entire compensation plan. The new plan had to make rewards contingent on performance, on the market, and on winning.

The previous chapters explained training, appraising, and developing employees. Once employees have done their jobs and been appraised, they expect to be paid. The main purpose of this chapter is to show you how to establish a pay plan. We explain job evaluation techniques, techniques for finding the relative worth of a job, and how to conduct on- and offline salary surveys. We also show you how to price the jobs in your firm by developing pay grades and ranges. In the following chapter, we'll focus more specifically on pay-for-performance and incentive plans.

DETERMINING PAY RATES

employee compensation
All forms of pay or rewards going to employees and arising from their employment.

Employee compensation refers to all forms of pay or rewards going to employees and arising from their employment,[1] and it has two main components: **direct financial payments** (in the form of wages, salaries, incentives, commissions, and bonuses), and **indirect payments** (in the form of financial benefits like employer-paid insurance and vacations).

direct financial payments
Pay in the form of wages, salaries, incentives, commissions, and bonuses.

In turn, there are basically two ways to make direct financial payments to employees: on increments of time and on performance. Time-based pay is still most popular: Blue-collar workers get hourly or daily wages, for instance, and others, like managers or Web designers, tend to be salaried and paid by the week, month, or year. The second option is to pay for performance. Piecework is an example; it ties compensation to the amount of production (or number of "pieces") the worker produces, and is popular as an incentive plan. For instance, you divide a worker's hourly wage by the standard number of units he or she is to produce in one hour. Then for each unit produced over and above this standard, pay the worker an incentive. Sales commissions are another example of performance-based (in this case, sales-based) compensation. In this chapter, we explain how to formulate plans for paying employees a time-based wage or salary; subsequent chapters cover performance-based financial incentives and bonuses, and employee benefits.

indirect financial payments
Pay in the form of financial benefits such as insurance.

Several basic factors influence the design of any pay plan: legal, union, company policy, and equity. We'll start with legal factors.

Legal Considerations in Compensation

Various laws specify things like minimum wages, overtime rates, and benefits.[2] For example, the **1931 Davis-Bacon Act** allows the secretary of labor to set wage rates for laborers and mechanics employed by contractors working for the federal government. Amendments provide for paid employee benefits. The **1936 Walsh-Healey Public Contract Act** sets basic labor standards for employees working on any government contract that amounts to more than $10,000. It contains minimum wage, maximum hour, and safety and health provisions, and requires time-and-a-half pay for work over 40 hours a week. **Title VII of the 1964 Civil Rights Act** makes it unlawful for employers to discriminate against any individual with respect to hiring, compensation, terms, conditions, or privileges of employment because of race, color, religion, sex, or national origin. Other significant compensation-related laws include the 1938 Fair Labor Standards Act, the 1963 Equal Pay Act, and the 1974 Employer Retirement Income Security Act.

Davis-Bacon Act (1931)
A law that sets wage rates for laborers employed by contractors working for the federal government.

Walsh-Healey Public Contract Act (1936)
A law that requires minimum wage and working conditions for employees working on any government contract amounting to more than $10,000.

Title VII of the 1964 Civil Rights Act
This act makes it unlawful for employers to discriminate against any individual with respect to hiring, compensation, terms, conditions, or privileges of employment because of race, color, religion, sex, or national origin.

1938 Fair Labor Standards Act This law, originally passed in 1938 and since amended many times, contains minimum wage, maximum hours, overtime pay, equal pay, record-keeping, and child labor provisions that are familiar to most working people. It covers the majority of U.S. workers—virtually all those engaged in the production and/or sale of goods for interstate and foreign commerce. In addition, agricultural workers and those employed by certain larger retail and service companies are included.

Fair Labor Standards Act (1938)
This act provides for minimum wages, maximum hours, overtime pay, and child labor protection. The law has been amended many times and covers most employees.

One familiar provision governs overtime pay. It says employers must pay overtime at a rate of at least one and a half times normal pay for any hours worked over 40 in a workweek. Thus, if a worker covered by the act works 44 hours in one week, he or she must be paid for 4 of those hours at a rate equal to one and a half times the hourly or weekly base rate the person would have earned for 40 hours. For example, if the person earns $8 an hour (or $320 for a 40-hour week), he or she would be paid at the rate of $12 per hour (8 times 1.5) for each of the 4 overtime hours worked, or a total of $48 extra. If the employee instead receives time off for the overtime hours, the employer must also compute the number of hours granted off at the one-and-a-half-times rate. So the person would get six hours off for the four hours of overtime, in lieu of overtime pay.

The act also sets a *minimum wage*, which sets a floor for employees covered by the act (and usually bumps up wages for practically all workers when Congress raises the minimum). The minimum wage in 2001 was $5.15 for the majority of those covered by the act. *Child labor provisions* prohibit employing minors between 16 and 18 years old in hazardous occupations, and carefully restrict employment of those under 16.

Specific categories of employees are exempt from the act or certain provisions of the act, and particularly from the act's overtime provisions—they are "exempt employees." A person's exemption depends on his or her responsibilities, duties, and salary. Bona fide executive, administrative (like office managers), and professional employees (like architects) are generally exempt from the minimum wage and overtime requirements of the act.[3] Unfortunately, some regulations haven't been updated for decades. For example, under the 1975 regulations an employee making $250 per week ($13,000 per year) could be considered an executive. The General Accounting Office therefore recently recommended the Department of Labor revise its Fair Labor Standards Act regulations.[4]

Violating provisions of this act can be costly. For example, several years ago a federal judge ordered the owners of a Colorado beef processing plant to pay nearly $2 million in back wages to 5,071 employees. The firm violated the Fair Labor Standards Act by not paying those employees one and a half times their regular pay rate for hours worked in excess of 40 per week, and for not keeping required records.[5] And trying to evade the letter of the law by claiming that the employees are "independent contractors" who are more like consultants than employees is also no solution, as we'll see.[6] Microsoft paid almost $97 million to settle contingent workers' lawsuits related to such a problem.[7]

1963 Equal Pay Act The Equal Pay Act, an amendment to the Fair Labor Standards Act, states that employees of one sex may not be paid wages at a rate lower than that paid to employees of the opposite sex for doing roughly equivalent work. Specifically, if the work requires equal skills, effort, and responsibility and involves similar working conditions, employees of both sexes must receive equal pay, unless the differences in pay stem from a seniority system, a merit system, the quantity or quality of production, or "any factor other than sex."

Equal Pay Act (1963)
An amendment to the Fair Labor Standards Act designed to require equal pay for women doing the same work as men.

1974 Employee Retirement Income Security Act (ERISA) This act provides for the creation of government-run employer-financed corporations to protect employees against the failure of their employer's pension plan. In addition, it sets regulations regarding vesting rights. (*Vesting* refers to the equity or ownership the employees build up in their pension plan should their employment be terminated before retirement.) And it regulates *portability rights* (the transfer of an employee's vested rights from one organization to another), and contains fiduciary standards to prevent dishonesty in pension plan funding.

Employee Retirement Income Security Act (ERISA)
The law that provides government protection of pensions for all employees with company pension plans. It also regulates vesting rights (employees who leave before retirement may claim compensation from the pension plan).

Other Legislation Affecting Compensation Various other laws influence compensation decisions. For example, the Age Discrimination in Employment Act prohibits age discrimination against employees who are 40 years of age and older in all aspects of employment, including compensation.[8] The Americans with Disabilities Act prohibits discrimination against qualified persons with disabilities in all aspects of employment, including compensation. The Family and Medical Leave Act aims to entitle eligible employees, both men and women, to take up to 12 weeks of unpaid, job-protected leave for the birth of a child or for the care of a child, spouse, or parent. And various executive orders require employers that are federal government contractors or subcontractors to not discriminate and to take affirmative action in various employment areas, including compensation.

Each of the 50 states has its own workers' compensation laws, which today cover over 85 million workers. Among other things, these aim to provide prompt, sure, and reasonable income to victims of work-related accidents. The Social Security Act of 1935 (as amended) aims to protect workers from economic destitution in the event of termination of employment beyond their control. Employers and employees contribute equally to the benefits it provides. This act also provided for unemployment compensation—jobless benefits—for workers unemployed through no fault of their own for up to 26 weeks. (We'll discuss Social Security payments—payments to those who are disabled or retired, for instance—in Chapter 12.) The federal wage garnishment law limits the amount of an employee's earnings that employers can withhold (garnish) per week, and protects the worker from discharge due to garnishment.

Union Influences on Compensation Decisions

Unions and labor relations laws also influence pay plan design. The National Labor Relations Act of 1935 (or Wagner Act) and associated legislation and court decisions legitimized the labor movement. It gave unions legal protection and granted employees the right to organize, to bargain collectively, and to engage in concerted activities for the purpose of collective bargaining or other mutual aid or protection. Historically, the wage rate has been the main issue in collective bargaining. However, unions also negotiate other pay-related issues, including time off with pay, income security (for those in industries with periodic layoffs), cost-of-living adjustments, and benefits like health care.[9]

The 1935 Act created the National Labor Relations Board (NLRB) to oversee employer practices and ensure employees receive their rights. Its rulings underscore the need to involve union officials in developing the compensation package. For example, employers must give the union a written explanation of the employer's "wage curves"—the graph that relates job to pay rate. The union is also entitled to know the salary of each employee it is representing.[10]

Corporate Policies and Competitive Strategy

The compensation plan should further the firm's strategic aims—management should produce an *aligned reward strategy*. In other words, management should ask "how can I construct a total portfolio of reward programs that all link to both short and longer-term business success, drive shareholder value, encourage the behaviors that we need, and deliver true value to our employees?"[11] IBM is a good example. Gerstner's aim at IBM was to install a new compensation plan that focused employees' attention on productivity and competitiveness, rather than seniority.

As at IBM, aligning rewards with strategy means asking five questions: What are the organization's key competitive success factors? What are the behaviors or actions necessary to successfully implement this competitive strategy? What compensation program should we use to reinforce those behaviors? What requirements should each pay element meet to fulfill its purpose? And how well do the current reward programs match these requirements? The employer's basic task is always to create a bundle of rewards—a total reward package—specifically aimed at eliciting those employee behaviors the firm needs to support and achieve its competitive strategy. Table 11-1 summarizes this process.

◀   **TABLE 11-1**
Developing an
Aligned Reward
Strategy

1. What are the organization's key success factors? What does the firm need to do to be successful in fulfilling its mission or achieving its desired competitive position?
2. What are the behaviors or actions necessary to successfully implement this competitive strategy?
3. What program should we use to reinforce those behaviors? What should be the purpose of each program in reinforcing each desired behavior?
4. What requirements should each program meet to be successful in fulfilling its purpose? What value should it deliver to employees, and how do we know it is valued?
5. How well do the current reward programs match these requirements?

Source: Jack Dolmat-Connell, "Developing a Reward Strategy That Delivers Shareholder and Employee Value," *Compensation and Benefits Review,* March–April 1999, p. 51.

Exactly how the firm will use its pay plan to further its strategic aims will manifest itself in the firm's pay policies. The HR or compensation manager will write the policies in conjunction with top management, in a manner that's consistent with the firm's strategic aims.[12] For example, will the firm be a leader or a follower regarding pay?[13] A top hospital like Johns Hopkins, for example, might have a policy of starting nurses at a wage of 20% above the prevailing market wage.

Whether to emphasize seniority or performance is another issue. For example, U.S. federal employees get raises based on longevity. The government groups jobs into grades based on things like skill and education, and there are 15 salary steps within each grade. It now takes 18 years for an employee to progress from step 1 to step 9. Seniority-based pay may be advantageous to the extent that employees perceive seniority as an objective standard. One disadvantage, though, is that top performers may get the same raises as poor ones. IBM, on the other hand, like many firms, stresses performance.

Other policies usually cover the pay cycle, as well as how to award salary increases and promotions, overtime pay, probationary pay, and leaves for military service, jury duty, and holidays. For example, pay cycle policies vary from weekly to monthly. In one survey, 24% of respondents issued weekly paychecks, 48% paid biweekly, 22% paid twice a month, and 5% paid monthly.[14]

How to handle salary compression is another policy issue. **Salary compression**, which means longer-term employees' salaries are lower than those of workers entering the firm today, is a creature of inflation. Prices (and starting salaries) go up faster than the company's salaries, and firms need a policy to handle it. Constructing one is tricky. On the one hand, you don't want to treat current employees unfairly or to have them leave with their knowledge and expertise. However, mediocre performance or lack of assertiveness, not salary compression, may explain some low salaries. One policy is to give raises based on longevity (or, preferably, on longevity plus skills). Another is to install a more aggressive merit pay program. Others authorize supervisors to recommend "equity" adjustments for selected employees who are both highly valued and victims of pay compression.

Geography also plays a policy role. Cost-of-living differences between cities can be considerable. For example, a family of four might live in Miami for just over $39,000 per year, while the same family's annual expenditures in Chicago or Los Angeles would be over $56,000. Employers handle cost-of-living differentials in several ways. One is to give the transferred person a nonrecurring payment, usually in a lump sum or perhaps spread over 1 to 3 years. Others pay a differen-

salary compression
A salary inequity problem, generally caused by inflation, resulting in longer term employees in a position earning less than workers entering the firm today.

tial for ongoing costs in addition to a one-time allocation. For example, one employer pays a differential of $6,000 per year to people earning $35,000 to $45,000 whom it transfers from Atlanta to Minneapolis. Others simply raise the employee's base salary. Compensating expatriate employees is still another policy problem, as the New Workplace feature illustrates.

THE NEW WORKPLACE

Compensating Expatriate Employees

The question of cost-of-living differentials has particular significance to multinational firms. The annual cost of keeping a U.S. expatriate in France might average $193,000, while in neighboring Germany the cost would be $246,000.[15]

How should multinationals compensate expatriate employees—those it sends overseas? Two basic international compensation policies are popular: home-based and host-based plans.[16]

With a *home-based salary plan*, an international transferee's base salary reflects his or her home country's salary. The employer then adds allowances for cost-of-living differences—housing and schooling costs, for instance. This is a reasonable approach for short-term assignments, and avoids the problem of having to change the employee's base salary every time he or she moves.

In the *host-based plan*, the firm ties the international transferee's base salary to the host country's salary structure. In other words, the manager from New York who is sent to France would have his or her base salary changed to the prevailing base salary for that position in France, rather than keep the New York base salary. The firm usually tacks on cost-of-living, housing, schooling, and other allowances here as well.

A survey of multinational enterprises suggests most set expatriates' salaries according to their home-country base pay.[17] (Thus, a French manager assigned to Kiev by a U.S. multinational will generally have a base salary that reflects the salary structure in the manager's home country, in this case France.) In addition, the person typically gets allowances including cost-of-living, relocation, housing, education, and hardship allowances (the latter for countries with a relatively hard quality of life, such as China). The employer also usually pays any extra tax burdens resulting from taxes the manager is liable for over and above those he or she would have to pay in the home country. In time, globalization of business may lead to more global standardizing of pay rates for most occupations around the world.[18]

Equity and Its Impact on Pay Rates

Last but not least, no one likes to think they're paid less than they deserve. So equity, both external and internal, is crucial in determining pay. Externally, pay must compare favorably with rates in other organizations, or an employer will find it hard to attract and retain good employees. Pay rates must also be equitable internally: Each employee should view his or her pay as equitable given other pay rates in the organization. Some firms administer surveys to learn employees' perceptions and feelings about their compensation system. Questions typically include "How satisfied are you with your pay?" "What criteria were used for your recent pay increase?" and "What factors do you believe are used when your pay is determined?"[19]

When employees become aware of inequities in the pay system, disappointment and often conflict can result. Some firms therefore maintain strict secrecy over pay matters. But online pay forums on sites like vault.com and easy access to salary data on sites like Salary.com have made it easier for employees to judge if they're being paid equitably.[20]

Salary inequities can trigger a big response. With morale down due to widespread concerns about inequitable salaries, layoffs, and a racial discrimination suit, Coca-Cola Co. undertook a salary review of 500 other companies ranging from competitors like PepsiCo to others like Procter & Gamble and Yahoo!. Coke recently announced raises ranging from about $1,000 to as much as $15,000 for most of its employees.[21]

The process of establishing pay rates while ensuring external and internal equity consists of five steps:

1. Conduct a salary survey of what other employers are paying for comparable jobs (to help ensure external equity).
2. Determine the worth of each job in your organization through job evaluation (to ensure internal equity).
3. Group similar jobs into pay grades.
4. Price each pay grade by using wave curves.
5. Fine-tune pay rates.

The next section focuses on each of these steps.

▲ *When employees become aware of in-equities in the pay system, disappointment and often conflict can result. Some firms maintain strict secrecy over pay matters for this reason.*

ESTABLISHING PAY RATES

Step 1. The Salary Survey

It's difficult to set pay rates if you don't know what others are paying, so salary surveys play a big role in pricing jobs. Virtually every employer conducts at least an informal telephone, newspaper, or Internet **salary survey**.[22]

Employers use these surveys in three ways. First, they use survey data to price **benchmark jobs**, around which the firm then slots its other jobs, based on their relative worth to the firm. (Job evaluation, explained next, helps determine the relative worth of each job.) Second, employers typically price 20% or more of their positions directly in the marketplace (rather than relative to the firm's benchmark jobs), based on a formal or informal survey of what comparable firms are paying for comparable jobs. (A dot-com firm might do this for jobs like Web programmer, whose salaries fluctuate widely and often.) Third, surveys also collect data on benefits like insurance, sick leave, and vacations to provide a basis for decisions regarding employee benefits.

Salary surveys can be formal or informal.[23] Informal telephone or Internet surveys are good for checking on a relatively small number of easily identified and quickly recognized jobs, such as when a bank's HR director wants to confirm the salary at which to advertise a newly open cashier's job. Such informal techniques are also good for checking discrepancies, such as when the HR director wants to find out if some area banks are really paying tellers on some sort of incentive plan.

Perhaps 20% of large employers use their own formal questionnaires to collect compensation information from other employers. Most inquire about things like number of employees, overtime policies, starting salaries, and paid vacations. For a survey to be useful, it must be specific; most respondents in one study claimed the survey's job categories were too broad or imprecise.

salary survey
A survey aimed at determining prevailing wage rates. A good salary survey provides specific wage rates for specific jobs. Formal written questionnaire surveys are the most comprehensive, but telephone surveys and newspaper ads are also sources of information.

benchmark job
A job that is used to anchor the employer's pay scale and around which other jobs are arranged in order of relative worth.

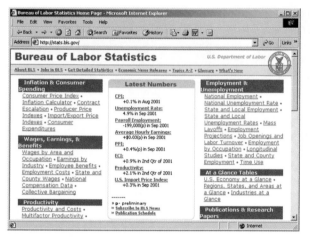

▲ **WEBNOTE**
The Bureau of Labor Statistics makes a vast amount of salary data available online.
http://stats.bls.gov/

Commercial, Professional, and Government Salary Surveys

Many employers use surveys published by consulting firms, professional associations, or government agencies. For example, the Bureau of Labor Statistics (BLS) conducts three annual surveys: (1) area wage surveys; (2) industry wage surveys; and (3) professional, administrative, technical, and clerical (PATC) surveys.

About 200 annual area wage surveys provide data for a variety of clerical and manual occupations ranging from secretary to messenger to office clerk. Area wage surveys also provide data on weekly work schedules, paid holidays and vacation practices, health insurance and pension plans, as well as on shift operations and differentials. Industry wage surveys provide similar data, but by industry. They provide national pay data for workers in selected jobs for industries like building, trucking, and printing. PATC surveys collect pay data on 80 occupations, including accounting, legal services, personnel management, engineering, chemistry, buying, clerical supervisory, drafting, and clerical. They provide information about earnings as well as production bonuses, commissions, and cost-of-living increases. The BLS recently organized its various pay surveys into a new national compensation survey, and began publishing this information on the Web. The Internet site is http://stats.bls.gov (see Webnote).

Private consulting and/or executive recruiting companies like Hay Associates, Heidrick and Struggles, and Hewitt Associates publish data covering compensation for top and middle management and members of boards of directors. Professional organizations like the Society for Human Resource Management and the Financial Executives Institute publish surveys of compensation practices among members of their associations.

Watson Wyatt Data Services of Rochelle Park, New Jersey, publishes several compensation surveys. Its top-management compensation surveys cover dozens of top positions, including chief executive officer, top real estate executive, top financial executive, top sales executive, and top claims executive, all categorized by function and industry. Watson Wyatt also offers middle-management compensation surveys, supervisory management compensation surveys, sales and marketing personnel surveys, professional and scientific personnel surveys, and surveys of technician trades, skilled trades, and office personnel, among others. The surveys generally cost about $500 to $700 each, but can be worth the expense if they help avoid the dual hazards of (1) paying too much, or (2) suffering turnover because of uncompetitive pay.

Using the Internet to Do Compensation Surveys Finding salary data is not as mysterious as it used to be, thanks to the Internet. A rapidly expanding array of Internet-based options makes it easy for anyone today (especially smaller firms) to access published compensation survey information. Table 11-2 shows some popular salary survey Web sites; see also Webnote.

▲ **WEBNOTE**
Wageweb is one of many sites offering online access to specialized salary data.
www.wageweb.com//hr1.htm

▼ **TABLE 11-2 Some Pay Data Web Sites**

Sponsor	Internet Address	What It Provides	Downside
Salary.com	Salary.com	Salary by job and zip code, plus job and description, for hundreds of jobs	Adapts national averages by applying local cost-of-living differences
Wageweb	www.wageweb.com	Average salaries for more than 150 clerical, professional, and managerial jobs	Charges $100 for breakdowns by industry, location, etc.
Exec-U-Net	www.execunet.com	Salary, bonus and options for about 650 management posts	Charges an initial $125 for job details
PinPoint Salary	members.aol.com/ payraises	Individualized pay analyses based on title, experience, desired industry, etc.	First job analysis costs $95
Futurestep*	www.futurestep.com	Pay analyses for people eligible for managerial posts paying $50,000 to $200,000 a year	Participants automatically subject to queries from Korn/Ferry recruiters

*An alliance between recruiters Korn/Ferry International and the *Wall Street Journal*.

Source: Adapted from Joann S. Lublin, "Web Transforms Art of Negotiating Raises," *Wall Street Journal*, September 22, 1998, p. B1. See also Susan Marks, "Can the Internet Help You Hit the Salary Mark?" *Workforce* 80, no. 1 (January 2001), pp. 86–93.

HR.NET

Doing an Internet-Based Salary Survey

You can also access Internet-based government and other salary data. Let's look at an example (this one is based on pricing a job in Miami, Florida, although you could use the same system for any city or state). Assume that your accounting clerk has just resigned. You are interested in advertising for a new employee, but first you need a reasonable pay range. You've already spoken with a representative at your local state unemployment office to get a preliminary picture, and perhaps to managers at one or two local personnel staffing firms. You've also checked a few Internet and newspaper-based classified ads. Now you want to use the Internet to obtain additional information. How do you do it?

In Florida, you might start by accessing the state's Florida Occupational Employment Wage Survey (ftp://lmi.floridajobs.org/library/OWS/msa5000.txt). You scan down the list by Metropolitan Statistical Area (MSA), and choose the listing of jobs for the Miami MSA, starting with Accountants & Auditors. You go down the list to Bookkeeping, Accounting & Auditing Clerks. Here the data would show an hourly pay rate of $8.44 to $12.71 per hour, with a mean of $10.93 and median of $10.61. You can access other similar state of Florida reports by searching for Florida Occupational Wage Survey. The U.S. government's Bureau of Labor Statistics also publishes an Internet-based series you can use for comparison purposes. Find this at http://stats.bls.gov/ocshome.htm.

In practice, the data published by both the U.S. and state governments tend to be somewhat out of date. To get a real-time picture of what employers in your area are paying accounting clerks, it's useful to access the online Internet sites of one or two of your local newspapers. In this case, the *South Florida Sun-Sentinel* has a site called careerbuilder. It lists career opportunities—in other words, just about all the jobs listed in the newspaper by category and, in many instances, wage rates (http://www.careers.sun-sentinel.com/xp/_790005_/index.xml). From this listing, you'll find jobs listed for "Accounts receivable clerks—$10.00 per hour," "Accounting clerk—$25k," "Accounting clerk—credit clerk, to $22k," and "Accounts payable clerk, $22–26k," among many others. Switching to the *Miami Herald's* online Web site (called HeraldLink) classifieds, you similarly find a list of several dozen related job listings. For example, there is a "Payroll clerk, Doral area, $25k," an "Accounting clerk—City of Hialeah starting at $594 biweekly," and "Accounting assistant—Miami Lakes area, to $29k." More Web sites for compensation purposes are available from consulting firms; others are listed in this textbook's Web site page for this chapter, and in Table 11-2.

The Internet also provides numerous fee-based sources of international salary data. For example, William M. Mercer, Inc., an international consulting firm (http://www.mercer.com), publishes an annual global compensation planning report summarizing compensation trends for more than 40 countries plus representative pay data for four common benchmark jobs.[24] Accounting firm KPMG International (http://www.kpmg.com) includes reports from surveys compiled by KPMG's various international offices. Watson Wyatt Worldwide (http://www.watsonwyatt.com) publishes an annual global remuneration planning report on worldwide pay levels.

In most cases, as noted above, salary survey data are used to price benchmark jobs, around which other jobs are then slotted based on the job's relative worth. Determining the relative worth of a job is the purpose of job evaluation, which we'll address next.

Step 2. Job Evaluation

job evaluation
A systematic comparison done in order to determine the worth of one job relative to another.

Job evaluation is aimed at determining a job's relative worth. It is a formal and systematic comparison of jobs to determine the worth of one job relative to another and eventually results in a wage or salary hierarchy. The basic principle is this: Jobs that require greater qualifications, more responsibilities, and more complex job duties should be paid more highly than jobs with lesser requirements.[25] The basic procedure is to compare the jobs in relation to one another—for example, in terms of required effort, responsibility, and skills. Suppose you know (based on your salary survey) how to price key benchmark jobs, and then use job evaluation to determine the relative worth of all the other jobs in your firm relative to these key jobs. You are then well on your way to being able to price all the jobs in your organization equitably.

compensable factor
A fundamental, compensable element of a job, such as skills, effort, responsibility, and working conditions.

Compensable Factors You can use two basic approaches to compare several jobs. First, you can take an intuitive approach. You might decide that one job is more important than another and not dig any deeper into why. As an alternative, you could compare the jobs by focusing on certain basic factors the jobs have in common. Compensation management specialists call these **compensable factors**. They are the factors that establish how the jobs compare to one another, and that set the pay for each job.

Some employers develop their own compensable factors. However, most use factors popularized by packaged job evaluation systems or by federal legislation. For example, the Equal Pay Act focuses on four compensable factors—skills, effort, responsibility, and working conditions. The method popularized by the Hay consulting firm focuses on three factors: know-how, problem solving, and accountability.

Identifying compensable factors plays a central role in job evaluation. You usually compare each job with all comparable jobs using the same compensable factors. The compensable factors you use depend on the job and the job evaluation method. For example, you might choose to include "decision making" for a manager's job, though it might be inappropriate for a cleaner's job.[26]

Preparing for the Job Evaluation Job evaluation is mostly a judgmental process, one demanding close cooperation among supervisors, HR specialists, and employees and union representatives. The main steps include identifying the need for the program, getting cooperation, and then choosing an evaluation committee. The committee then performs the actual evaluation.[27]

Identifying the need for job evaluation should not be difficult. For example, dissatisfaction reflected in high turnover, work stoppages, or arguments may result from paying employees different rates for similar jobs. Managers may express uneasiness with an informal way of assigning pay rates to jobs, accurately sensing that a more systematic assignment would be more equitable.

Next (since employees may fear that a systematic evaluation of their jobs may actually reduce their pay rates), getting employees to cooperate in the evaluation is a second important step. You can tell employees that as a result of the impending job evaluation program, pay rate decisions will no longer be made just by management whim, that job evaluation will provide a mechanism for considering the complaints they have been expressing, and that no present employee's rate will be adversely affected as a result of the job evaluation.[28]

Next, choose a job evaluation committee. There are two reasons for doing so. First, the committee should include several people who are familiar with the jobs in question, each of whom may have a different perspective regarding the nature of the jobs. Second, if the committee is composed at least partly of employees, the committee approach can help ensure greater employee acceptance of the job evaluation results.

So the composition of the committee is important. The group usually consists of about five members, most of whom are employees. Management has the right to serve on such committees, but employees may view this with suspicion. However, an HR specialist can usually be justified on the grounds that he or she has a more impartial outlook than line managers and can provide expert assistance. One option is to have this person serve in a nonvoting capacity. Union representation is possible. In most cases, though, the union's position is that it is accepting job evaluation only as an initial decision technique and is reserving the right to appeal actual job pricing decisions through grievance or bargaining channels.[29] Once appointed, each committee member should receive a manual explaining the job evaluation process, and special instructions that explain how to conduct a job evaluation.

The evaluation committee performs three main functions. First, it usually identifies 10 or 15 key benchmark jobs. These will be the first jobs to be evaluated and will serve as the anchors or benchmarks against which the relative importance or value of all other jobs can be compared. Next, the committee may select compensable factors (although the HR department will usually choose these as part of the process of determining the specific job evaluation technique the firm will use). Finally, the committee performs its most important function— actually evaluating the worth of each job. For this, the committee will probably use one of the following methods: ranking, job classification, point method, or factor comparison.

Job Evaluation Methods: Ranking The simplest job evaluation method ranks each job relative to all other jobs, usually based on some overall factor like "job difficulty." There are several steps in the job **ranking method**.

1. *Obtain job information.* Job analysis is the first step: Job descriptions for each job are prepared and are usually the basis for ranking jobs. (Sometimes job specifications are also prepared, but the job ranking method usually ranks jobs according to the whole job, rather than a number of compensable factors. Therefore, job specifications—which list the job's demands in terms of problem solving, decision

ranking method
The simplest method of job evaluation that involves ranking each job relative to all other jobs, usually based on overall difficulty.

making, and skills, for instance—are not as necessary with this method as they are for other job evaluation methods.)

2. *Select jobs.* It is often not practical to make single ranking for all jobs in an organization. The usual procedure is to rank jobs by department or in clusters (such as factory workers or clerical workers). This eliminates the need for direct comparison of, say, factory jobs and clerical jobs.

3. *Select compensable factors.* In the ranking methods, it is common to use just one factor (such as job difficulty) and to rank jobs based on the whole job. Regardless of the number of factors you choose, it's advisable to explain the definition of the factor(s) to the evaluators carefully so that they evaluate the jobs consistently.

4. *Rank jobs.* The simplest way is to give each rater a set of index cards, each of which contains a brief description of a job. Then they rank these cards from lowest to highest. Some managers use an "alternation ranking method" for making the procedure more accurate. Here you take the cards, first choosing the highest and the lowest, then the next highest and next lowest, and so forth until you've ranked all the cards. Table 11-3 illustrates a job ranking. Jobs in this small health facility are ranked from orderly up to office manager. The corresponding pay scales are on the right. After ranking, it becomes possible to slot additional jobs between those already ranked and to assign an appropriate wage rate.

5. *Combine ratings.* Usually several raters rank the jobs independently. Then the rating committee (or the employer) can simply average the rankings.

This is the simplest job evaluation method, as well as the easiest to explain. And it usually takes less time than other methods.

Some of its drawbacks derive more from how it's used than from the method itself. For example, there's a tendency to rely too heavily on "guesstimates." Similarly, ranking provides no yardstick for quantifying the value of one job relative to another. For example, job number 4 may in fact be five times "more valuable" than job number 5, but with the ranking system all you know is that one job ranks higher than the other. Ranking is usually more appropriate for small organizations that can't afford the time or expense of developing a more elaborate system.

Job Evaluation Methods: Job Classification **Job classification** (or **job grading**) is a simple, widely used method in which raters categorize jobs into groups. The groups are called **classes** if they contain similar jobs, or **grades** if they contain jobs that are similar in difficulty but otherwise different. Thus, in the federal government's pay grade system, a "press secretary" and a "fire chief" might both be graded "GS-10" (*GS* stands for "General Schedule"). On the other hand, in its job class system, the state of Florida might classify all "secretary IIs" in one class, all "maintenance engineers" in another, and so forth.

There are several ways to categorize jobs. One is to draw up class or grade descriptions (similar to job descriptions) and place jobs into classes or grades based on how well they fit these descriptions. Another is to draw up a set of rules

job classification (or grading) method
A method for categorizing jobs into groups.

classes
Grouping jobs based on a set of rules for each group or class, such as amount of independent judgment, skill, physical effort, and so forth, required. Classes usually contain similar jobs.

grades
A job classification system like the class system, although grades often contain dissimilar jobs, such as secretaries, mechanics, and firefighters. Grade descriptions are written based on compensable factors listed in classification systems.

▶ **TABLE 11-3**
Job Ranking by Olympia Health Care

Ranking Order	Annual Pay Scale
1. Office manager	$43,000
2. Chief nurse	42,500
3. Bookkeeper	34,000
4. Nurse	32,500
5. Cook	31,000
6. Nurse's aide	28,500
7. Orderly	25,500

for each class (for instance, how much independent judgment, skill, physical effort, and so on, does the class of jobs require?). Then categorize the jobs according to these rules.

The usual procedure is to choose compensable factors and then develop class or grade descriptions for each class in terms of amount or level of the compensable factor(s) in those jobs. The federal classification system in the United States, for example, employs the following compensable factors: (1) difficulty and variety of work, (2) supervision received and exercised, (3) judgment exercised, (4) originality required, (5) nature and purpose of interpersonal work relationships, (6) responsibility, (7) experience, and (8) knowledge required. Based on these compensable factors, raters write a **grade definition** like that in Figure 11-1. This one shows one grade description (GS-7) for the federal government's pay grade system. Then the evaluation committee reviews all job descriptions and slots each job into its appropriate grade. The federal government system, for instance, classifies the positions automotive mechanic, welder, electrician, and machinist in grade GS-10.

The classification method has several advantages. The main one is that most employers usually end up classifying jobs anyway, regardless of the evaluation method they use. They do this to avoid having to work with and price an unmanageable number of jobs; job classification automatically groups all jobs into classes. The disadvantages are that it is difficult to write the class or grade descriptions, and considerable judgment is required to apply them. Yet many employers (including the U.S. government) use this method with success.

Job Evaluation Methods: Point Method The **point method** is a more quantitative technique. It involves identifying (1) several compensable factors, each having several degrees, as well as (2) the degree to which each of these factors is present in the job. Assume there are five degrees of "responsibility" a job could contain. Further assume you assign a different number of points to each degree of each factor. Once the evaluation committee determines the degree to which each compensable factor (like "responsibility") is present in the job, it can calculate a total point value for the job by adding up the corresponding points for each factor. The result is a quantitative point rating for each job. The point method is apparently the most widely used job evaluation method; the appendix to this chapter (found on the book's Web site) covers it in detail.

Job Evaluation Methods: Factor Comparison The **factor comparison method** entails deciding which jobs have more of the chosen compensable factors. The method is actually a refinement of the ranking method. With the

grade definition
Written descriptions of the level of, say, responsibility and knowledge required by jobs in each grade. Similar jobs can then be combined into grades or classes.

point method
The job evaluation method in which a number of compensable factors are identified and then the degree to which each of these factors is present on the job is determined.

factor comparison method
A widely used method of ranking jobs according to a variety of skill and difficulty factors, then adding up these rankings to arrive at an overall numerical rating for each given job.

▼ **FIGURE 11-1 Example of a Grade Level Definition**
This is a summary chart of the key grade level criteria for the GS-7 level of clerical and assistance work. Do not use this chart alone for classification purposes; additional grade level criteria are in the Web-based chart.

GRADE	NATURE OF ASSIGNMENT	LEVEL OF RESPONSIBILITY
GS-7	Performs specialized duties in a defined functional or program area involving a wide variety of problems or situations; develops information, identifies interrelationships, and takes actions consistent with objectives of the function or program served.	Work is assigned in terms of objectives, priorities, and deadlines; the employee works independently in resolving most conflicts; completed work is evaluated for conformance to policy; guidelines, such as regulations, precedent cases, and policy statements require considerable interpretation and adaptation.

Source: http://www.opm.gov/fedclass.gscler.pdf. August 29, 2001.

ranking method, you generally look at each job as an entity and rank the jobs on some overall factor like job difficulty. With the factor comparison method, you rank each job several times—once for each of several compensable factors. For example, you might first rank jobs in terms of the compensable factor "skill." Then rank them according to their "mental requirements," and so forth. Then combine the rankings for each job into an overall numerical rating for the job. This too is a widely used method, also found in more detail in the appendix to this chapter (found on the book's Web site).

Computerized Job Evaluations Using a quantitative job evaluation method such as the point plan can be time consuming. Accumulating the information about "how much" of each compensable factor the job contains traditionally involves a tedious process in which evaluation committees debate the level of each compensable factor in a job. They then write down their consensus judgments and manually compute each job's point values.

CAJE—computer-aided job evaluation—can streamline this process. Computer-aided job evaluation, says one expert, can simplify job analysis, help keep job descriptions up to date, increase evaluation objectivity, reduce the time spent in committee meetings, and ease the burden of system maintenance. CAJE includes electronic data entry, computerized checking of compensable factor questionnaire responses, and automated output of job evaluations, and of a variety of compensation reports.[30]

Most of these systems have two main components. There is, first, a structured questionnaire. This contains items such as "enter total number of employees who report functionally to this position." Second, all CAJE systems use statistical models. These allow the computer program to price jobs more or less automatically, based on information on things like number of employees reporting to the positions, prices of benchmark jobs, current pay, and current pay grade midpoints.

Step 3. Group Similar Jobs into Pay Grades

Once it's used job evaluation to determine the relative worth of each job, the committee can turn to the task of assigning pay rates to each job; however, it will usually want to first group jobs into **pay grades**. If the committee used the ranking, point, or factor comparison methods, it could of course just assign pay rates to each individual job.[31] But for a large employer, such a plan would be difficult to administer, since there might be different pay rates for hundreds or even thousands of jobs. And even in smaller organizations, there's a tendency to try to simplify wage and salary structures as much as possible. Therefore, the committee will probably group similar jobs (in terms of their ranking or number of points, for instance) into grades for pay purposes. Instead of having to deal with hundreds of pay rates, it might only have to focus on, say, 10 or 12.[32]

A pay grade is comprised of jobs of approximately equal difficulty or importance as established by job evaluation. If the committee used the point method, then the pay grade consists of jobs falling within a range of points. With the ranking method, the grade consists of all jobs that fall within two or three ranks. The classification method automatically categorizes jobs into classes or grades. (With the factor comparison method, the grade consists of a specified range of pay rates, as the appendix to this chapter, found on the book's Web site, explains.) Ten to 16 grades per "job cluster" (a *cluster* is a logical grouping, such as factory jobs, clerical jobs, and so on) are common.

pay grade
A pay grade is comprised of jobs of approximately equal difficulty.

Step 4. Price Each Pay Grade—Wage Curves

The next step is to assign pay rates to your pay grades. (Of course, if you chose not to slot jobs into pay grades, you would have to assign individual pay rates to each individual job.) You'll typically use a **wage curve** to help assign pay rates to each pay grade (or to each job).

The wage curve shows the pay rates currently paid for jobs in each pay grade, relative to the points or rankings assigned to each job or grade by the job evaluation. Figure 11-2 presents an example. Note it shows pay rates on the vertical axis, and pay grades (in terms of points) along the horizontal axis. The purpose of the wage curve is to show the relationships between (1) the value of the job as determined by one of the job evaluation methods and (2) the current average pay rates for your grades.

The pay rates on the wage curve are traditionally those now paid by the employer. However, if there is reason to believe the current pay rates are out of step with the market rates for these jobs, choose benchmark jobs within each pay grade, and price them via a compensation survey. These new market-based pay rates then replace the current rates on the wage curve. Then slot in your other jobs (and their pay rates) around the benchmark jobs.[33]

There are several steps in pricing jobs with a wage curve. First, find the average pay for each pay grade, since each of the pay grades consists of several jobs. Next, plot the pay rates for each pay grade as was done in Figure 11-2. Then fit a line, called a *wage line*, through the points just plotted. You can do this freehand or by using a statistical method. Finally, price the jobs. Wages along the wage line are the target wages or salary rates for the jobs in each pay grade. If the current rates being paid for any of your jobs or grades fall well above or below the wage line, raises or a pay freeze for that job may be in order. Your next step, then, is to fine-tune your pay rates.

Step 5. Fine-Tune Pay Rates

Fine-tuning involves developing pay ranges and correcting out-of-line rates.

Developing Pay Ranges Most employers do not pay just one rate for all jobs in a particular pay grade. Instead, they develop vertical pay (or "rate") ranges for each horizontal pay grade. These **pay ranges** may appear as vertical boxes within

wage curve
Shows the relationship between the value of the job and the average wage paid for this job.

pay ranges
A series of steps or levels within a pay grade, usually based upon years of service.

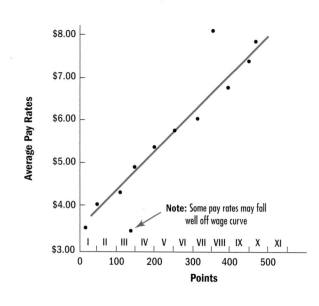

◀ **FIGURE 11-2**
Plotting a Wage Curve

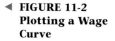

Note: Some pay rates may fall well off wage curve

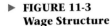

▶ **FIGURE 11-3**
Wage Structure

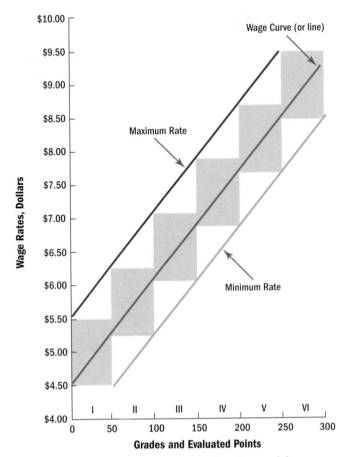

Note: This shows overlapping wage classes and maximum-minimum wage ranges.

each grade, showing minimum, maximum, and midpoint pay rates for that grade, as in Figure 11-3. (Specialists call this graph a *wage structure*. It graphically depicts the range of pay rates—in this case, per hour—paid for each pay grade.) Or you may depict the pay range as steps or levels, with specific corresponding pay rates for each step within each grade. Table 11-4 illustrates this, and shows the pay rates and steps for some federal government grades. As of the time of this pay schedule, for instance, employees in positions classified in grade GS-10 could be paid annual salaries between $39,969 and $51,964, depending on the level or step at which they were hired into the grade, the amount of time they were in the grade, and their merit increases (if any).

▼ **TABLE 11-4   Federal Government Pay Schedule: Grades GS-8–GS-10, New York, Northern New Jersey, Long Island, January 2000**

Grade	Annual Rates for Steps (in dollars)									
	1	**2**	**3**	**4**	**5**	**6**	**7**	**8**	**9**	**10**
GS-8	32,859	33,954	35,049	36,145	37,140	38,335	39,430	40,525	41,620	42,715
GS-9	36,295	37,504	38,714	39,923	41,133	42,342	43,551	44,761	45,970	47,180
GS-10	39,969	41,302	42,635	43,967	45,300	46,633	47,966	42,298	50,631	51,964

Source: info@fedamerica.com.

There are several reasons to use pay ranges for each pay grade. First, it lets the employer take a more flexible stance in the labor market. For example, it makes it easier to attract experienced, higher-paid employees into a pay grade if the starting salary for the lowest step may be too low to attract them. Pay ranges also let companies provide for performance differences between employees within the same grade or between those with different seniorities. As in Figure 11-3, most employers structure their pay ranges to overlap a bit, so an employee with more experience or seniority may earn more than an entry-level position in the next higher pay grade.

The wage line or curve usually anchors each pay range. The firm might then arbitrarily decide on a maximum and minimum rate for each grade, such as 15% above and below the wage line. As an alternative, some employers allow the pay range for each grade to become wider for the higher pay ranges, reflecting the greater demands and performance variability inherent in more complex jobs.

Correcting Out-of-Line Rates The wage rate for a particular job may fall well off the wage line or well outside the rate range for its grade, as shown in Figure 11-2. This means that the average pay for that job is currently too high or too low, relative to other jobs in the firm. You should raise the wages of underpaid employees to the minimum of the rate range for their pay grade.

Points falling above are a different story. These are "red circle," "flagged," or "overrates," and there are several ways to cope with this problem. One is to freeze the rate paid to employees until general salary increases bring the other jobs into line. A second option is to transfer or promote some or all of the employees involved to jobs for which you can legitimately pay them their current pay rates. The third option is to freeze the rate for six months, during which time you try to transfer or promote the overpaid employees. If you cannot, then cut the rate you pay these employees to the maximum in the pay range for their pay grade.

ENTREPRENEURS HR

Developing a Workable Pay Plan

Developing a pay plan is as important in a small firm as a large one. Paying wage rates that are too high may be unnecessarily expensive, and paying less may guarantee inferior help and high turnover. And internally inequitable wage rates will reduce morale and cause endless badgering by employees demanding raises "the same as Joe down the hall." The president who wants to concentrate on major issues like sales would thus do well to institute a rational pay plan promptly.

First, conduct a wage survey. Four sources can be especially useful. The Sunday classified newspaper ads should yield useful information on wages offered for jobs similar to those you are trying to price. Second, local Job Service offices can provide a wealth of information, as they compile extensive information on pay ranges and averages for many of the jobs listed in the *Dictionary of Occupational Titles* or on O*NET. Third, local employment agencies, always anxious to establish ties that could grow into business relationships, should be able to provide good data. Fourth, the Internet and Web sites like Salary.com can yield a wealth of information on area pay rates.

Smaller firms are making use of the Internet in other ways. StockHouse Media Corp. is an international provider of online financial content and community development products with 210 employees from the U.S. to Canada, Japan, and Singapore. Shawnee Love, the firm's global HR director, makes extensive use of the Web for determining salaries for all the firm's personnel. For example, she uses e-mail to request salary data from professional groups like the Human Resource Management Association, and surfs the Internet to monitor rates and trends by periodically checking job boards, company Web sites, and industry associations. "We source information that is both industry related as well as functionally related and of varying geographies, such as state, provincial, countrywide versus marketing, sales, HR, tech, etc.," she says.[34]

If you employ more than 20 employees or so, conduct at least a rudimentary job evaluation. You will need job descriptions, since these will be the source of data regarding the nature and worth of each job. Checking a Web site like JobDescription.com can be useful here.

You may find it easier to split employees into three clusters—managerial/professional, office/clerical, and plant personnel. For each of the three groups, choose compensable factors and then rank or assign points to each job based on the job evaluation. For each job or class of jobs (such as assemblers), you will want to create a pay range. In general, you should choose as the midpoint of that range the target salary required by your job evaluation, and then produce a range of about 30% around this average, broken into a total of five steps. (Thus, assemblers might earn from $6.00 to $9.60 per hour, in five steps.)

Compensation policies are important, too. For example, you need a policy on when and how to compute raises. Many small-business owners make the mistake of appraising employees on their anniversary date, a year after they are hired. The problem here is that the raise for one employee then becomes the standard for the next, as employees have time to compare notes. This produces a never-ending cycle of appraisals and posturing for ever-higher raises.

The better alternative is to have a policy of once-a-year raises during a standard one-week appraisal period, preferably about four weeks before you produce the budget for next year. In this way, the administrative headache of conducting these appraisals and awarding raises is dealt with during a one-week (or two-week) period, and the raises are known before the budget is compiled. Other required compensation policies include amount of holiday and vacation pay (as explained in Chapter 13), overtime pay policy, method of pay (weekly, biweekly, monthly), garnishments, and time card or sign-in sheet procedures. (For sources of sample policies, see the HR systems appendix on this book's Web site.)

Local and state compensation laws often cover employers not covered by the Fair Labor Standards Act, but the latter is actually quite comprehensive. It covers most employees of enterprises engaged in activities affecting interstate or foreign commerce.

Misclassification of exempt employees is probably the biggest mistake smaller firms make. A common mistake is to assume that putting employees on a yearly salary exempts them from the overtime provisions of the FLSA. You cannot make workers exempt simply by paying them a yearly salary, nor can you make them exempt by claiming they are "managers" because they spend some of their time supervising other employees. Strictly speaking, employees have to spend at least 50% of their time actually supervising other employees to be executive, managerial, or supervisory employees.[35] Employees in administrative jobs "directly related to management policies or general business operations" and whom you pay annual salaries of at least $250 a week may be exempt. These might include the executive assistant to the president or executive secretaries, and staff members who act as advisory specialists, such as HR directors, controllers, and credit managers.[36]

Improperly classifying employees as exempt or not paying overtime can lead to a Department of Labor (DOL) investigation. Investigations can produce four possible outcomes: a clean bill of health for the company; a letter of commitment promising to remedy problem areas; a conciliation agreement with mandatory follow-up (such as reports to the agency); and back pay awards.[37]

There are other common wage-hour traps to avoid.[38] With respect to meal and break periods, an employee must generally be paid for meal periods unless the period is at least 20 minutes long, the employee is completely relieved of duties, and the employee can leave his or her work post. Also take care when it comes to paying for time recorded. For example, suppose employees are required to clock in. They consistently clock in 15 minutes early or get into the habit of not clocking out for lunch. A wage and hour inspector may conclude you underpaid the employees, since there is no record they clocked out for the period for which you did not pay them.

And beware of how you use so-called independent contractors. Many small businesses hire management consultants or part-time bookkeepers and classify these people as independent contractors. Independent contractors are not employees of the firm and are thus not eligible for unemployment compensation, workers' compensation, or any other benefits accruing to employees. However, you can't call legitimate employees "independent contractors" just to avoid paying them benefits. Many factors determine whether a person is in fact an independent contractor. For example, a worker who is required to comply with another person's instructions about when, where, and how he or she is to work is probably an employee, not an independent contractor.[39] Other factors include the extent to which the services rendered are an integral part of the employer's business; the permanence of the business relationship between the parties; and the amount of individual investment in facilities and equipment by the worker.[40]

PRICING MANAGERIAL AND PROFESSIONAL JOBS

Developing compensation plans for managers or professionals is similar in many respects to developing plans for any employee.[41] The basic aim is the same: to attract and keep good employees. And job evaluation—classifying jobs, ranking them, or assigning points to them, for instance—is as applicable to managerial and professional jobs as to production and clerical ones.

There are some big differences, though. For one thing, job evaluation provides only a partial answer to the question of how to pay managers and professionals. These jobs tend to stress harder-to-quantify factors like judgment and problem solving more than do production and clerical jobs. There's also more emphasis on paying managers and professionals based on ability—based on their performance or on what they can do—rather than on the basis of static job demands like working conditions. Developing compensation plans for managers and professionals therefore tends to be relatively complex; job evaluation, while still important, usually plays a secondary role to nonsalary issues like bonuses, incentives, and benefits.

Compensating Managers

Compensation for a company's top executives usually consists of four main elements: base pay, short-term incentives, long-term incentives, and executive benefits and perks.[42] *Base pay* includes the person's fixed salary as well as, often, guaranteed bonuses such as "10% of pay at the end of the fourth fiscal quarter, regardless of whether or not the company makes a profit." *Short-term incentives* are usually cash or stock bonuses for achieving short-term goals, such as year-to-year increases in sales revenue. *Long-term incentives* aim to encourage the executive to take actions that drive up the value of the company's stock, and include things like stock options; these generally give the executive the right to purchase stock at a specific price for a specific period. Finally, *executive benefits and perks* might include supplemental executive retirement plans, supplemental life insurance, and health insurance without a deductible or coinsurance. With so many complicated elements, employers must be alert to the tax and securities law implications of their executive compensation decisions.[43]

▲ *Very high base salaries of executives like Hewlett Packard's Carly Fiorina are usually an indication of their worth to the firm's stockholders. However, the salaries of female CEOs still lag far behind that of their male counterparts. In April 2001 total compensation for the 20 highest-paid male executives in the United States averaged $138.5 million, while for females the figure was $11.2 million.*

What Really Determines Executive Pay? Salary is the cornerstone of executive compensation; it's the element on which employers layer benefits, incentives, and perquisites—all normally bestowed in proportion to base pay. Executive compensation emphasizes performance incentives more than do other employees' pay plans, since organizational results are likely to reflect executives' contributions more directly than those of lower-echelon employees. Incentives equal 25% or more of a typical executive's base pay in many countries, including the United States, United Kingdom, France, and Germany.[44] We'll discuss short- and long-term incentives in Chapter 12.

The traditional wisdom is that company size significantly affects top managers' salaries.[45] Yet in studies the usual standards, like company size and company performance, explain only about 30% of the variation in CEO pay. Instead, each firm seemed to take a unique approach: "In reality, CEO pay is set by the board taking into account a variety of factors such as the business strategy, corporate trends, and most importantly where they want to be in a short and long term."[46] Another study concluded that CEOs' pay depends on the complexity and unpredictability of the decisions they make.[47] In this study, complexity was a function of such things as the number of businesses controlled by the CEO's firm, the number of corporate officers in each firm, and the level of R&D and capital investment activity.[48] Regardless of performance, firms paid CEOs based on the complexity of the jobs they filled.

The firm's industry does have an impact on CEO pay, but less than what you'd expect. For example, a recent survey by accountants PricewaterhouseCoopers found that total CEO compensation (salary plus annual incentives plus long-term incentives) averaged $3.6 million in 261 for-profit companies in 17 industry groups. For most industries, total CEO compensation generally fell within plus or minus 15% of this average. The main exceptions were the pharmaceuticals, capital markets and investment management, insurance, and real estate industry firms, where CEO pay averaged over $7 million.[49]

In any event, shareholder activism tightened the restrictions on what top executives are paid.[50] For example, the Securities and Exchange Commission now has rules regarding executive compensation communications. The company must disclose the chief executive officer's pay, as well as other officers' pay if their compensation (salary and bonus) exceeds $100,000. One result is that boards of directors must act responsibly in reviewing and setting executive pay. That, says one expert, includes determining the key performance requirements of the executive's job; assessing the appropriateness of the firm's current compensation practices; conducting a pay-for-performance survey; and testing shareholder acceptance of the board's pay proposals.[51] The government also changed the federal tax code in the early 1990s to make CEO pay above $1 million a year nondeductible as a corporate business expense if the pay was not related to performance.[52]

The trend is therefore toward reducing the relative importance of base salary while boosting the emphasis on incentives.[53] The big issue here is identifying the appropriate performance standards and then determining how to link these to pay. Typical short-term measures of shareholder value include revenue growth and operating profit margin. Long-term shareholder value measures include rate of return above some predetermined base, and what is known as economic value added. (We'll discuss these in Chapter 12.)

Performance-based pay can focus a manager's attention. When heavy truck production recently tumbled, CEO Joseph Magliochetti saw sales of his auto parts maker Dana Corp. drop by 6%, and profits by 44%. At the end of the year, he still got his $850,000 salary. But his board of directors eliminated his bonus and stock grant, which the year before had earned him $1.8 million. The board said he had failed to beat the profit goals it had set for him.[54]

Managerial Job Evaluation Despite questions about the rationality of executive pay, job evaluation is still important in pricing executive and managerial jobs in most large firms. The basic approach is to classify all executive and management positions into a series of grades, to which a series of salary ranges is attached.

As with nonmanagerial jobs, one alternative is to rank the executive and management positions in relation to each other, grouping those of equal value. However, firms also use the job classification and point evaluation methods, with compensable factors like position scope, complexity, difficulty, and creative demands. Job analysis, salary surveys and the fine-tuning of salary levels around wage curves also play central roles.

Compensating Professional Employees

Compensating nonsupervisory professional employees like engineers and scientists presents unique problems.[55] Analytical jobs like these emphasize creativity and problem solving, compensable factors not easily compared or measured. Furthermore, how do you measure performance? The professional's economic impact on the firm often relates only indirectly to his or her actual efforts. For example, the success of an engineer's invention depends on many factors, like how well the firm markets it.

Employers can use job evaluation for professional jobs.[56] Compensable factors here tend to focus on problem solving, creativity, job scope, and technical knowledge and expertise. Firms use the point method and factor comparison methods, although job classification seems most popular. (Here, you slot jobs into grades based on grade descriptions.) Yet in practice, firms rarely use traditional job evaluation methods for professional jobs, since it is so difficult to quantify factors that make a difference in professional work.[57] "Knowledge and the skill of applying it are extremely difficult to quantify and measure."[58]

Most employers use a market-pricing approach. They price professional jobs in the marketplace as best they can, to establish the values for benchmark jobs. Then they slot these benchmark jobs and their other professional jobs into a salary structure. Each professional discipline (like engineering or R&D) usually ends up having four to six grade levels, each with a broad salary range. This helps employers remain competitive when bidding for professionals whose skills and attainments vary widely, and who literally have global employment possibilities.[59]

COMPENSATION TRENDS

Today's new workplace often demands new approaches to paying employees. In team-based organizations, for instance, firms want employees to learn several skills, so skill-based pay becomes important. We'll look at several such trends in this section.

Skill-Based Pay

With what experts call competence-, knowledge-, or skill-based pay, the company pays for the employee's range, depth, and types of skills and knowledge, rather than for the job title he or she holds.[60] One expert defines competencies as "demonstrable characteristics of the person, including knowledge, skills, and behaviors, that enable performance."[61]

Why pay employees based on the skill levels they achieve, rather than on the jobs they're assigned to? For example, why pay an Accounting Clerk II who has achieved a certain mastery of accounting techniques the same (or more than) someone who is an Accounting Clerk IV? For several reasons.

With more companies organizing around teams, employers often expect employees to rotate among jobs (and thus know several skills). Similarly, jobs increasingly overlap as individuals work together on projects or processes. Knowledge- or skill-based pay can also support a firm's strategy. For example, Sony's strategic emphasis on miniaturization and precision manufacturing means Sony should reward some employees based on their skills and knowledge in these two strategically crucial areas, not just the jobs they're assigned to. There are four key differences between skill-based pay (SBP) and job-evaluation-driven job-based pay (JBP):

1. *Competence testing.* With JBP, you receive the pay attached to your job regardless of whether you acquire the competence needed to perform the job. With SBP, your supervisor must certify that you're competent in the skills required by the job before you get a pay increase.

2. *Effect of job change.* With JBP, your pay usually changes when you switch jobs. With SBP, if you move up, you must demonstrate proficiency before getting a raise. Similarly, you can, for instance, fill in for a missing colleague in a lower-paying job, but still receive your (higher-skill) pay.

3. *Seniority and other factors.* JBP systems often tie pay to time in grade or seniority. SBP pays for skills, not seniority.

4. *Advancement opportunities.* There tend to be more opportunities for advancement with SBP plans than with JBP plans because the companywide focus on skill building fosters more development and more opportunities. Similarly, SBP enhances organizational flexibility because workers' skills are applicable to more jobs and thus more portable.[62]

Skill-based programs generally contain four main components: (1) a system that defines specific skills, and a process for tying the person's pay to his or her skill; (2) a training system that lets employees seek and acquire skills; (3) a formal competency testing system; and (4) a work design that lets employees move among jobs to permit work assignment flexibility. A study of one such skill-based pay program concluded that it had resulted in 58% greater productivity, 16% lower labor cost per part, and an 82% reduction in scrap, versus a comparison facility.[63]

◆ **HIGH-PERFORMANCE INSIGHT** A General Mills manufacturing facility implemented one such plan.[64] This facility paid workers based on attained skill levels. There were basically four clusters (or "blocks") of jobs, corresponding to the four production areas: mixing, filling, packaging, and materials. Within each block, workers could attain three levels of skill. Level 1 indicates limited ability, such as knowledge of basic facts and ability to perform simple tasks without direction.[65] Level 2 means the employee attained partial proficiency and could, for instance, apply technical principles on the job. Attaining Level 3 means the employee is fully competent in the area and could, for example, analyze and solve production problems. Each production block had a different average wage rate. There were, therefore, 12 pay levels (four blocks with three pay levels each) in the plant.

General Mills set the wages for the 12 skill levels (four blocks with three levels each) in part by making the pay for the lowest of the three pay levels in each block equal to the average entry-level pay rate for similar jobs in the community. A new employee could start in any block, but always at Level 1. If after several weeks he or she was certified at the next higher skill level, General Mills raised his or her salary. Employees freely rotated from block to block, as long as they could achieve Level 2 performance within their current block. The plan appeared to boost flexibility.

Issues in Skill-Based Pay Whether skill-based pay improves productivity is an open question. When used in conjunction with team-building and worker involvement and empowerment programs, it does appear to lead to higher quality as well as lower absenteeism rates and fewer accidents.[66] However, the findings in one firm, which are not conclusive, suggest that productivity was higher at its non-skill-based-pay facility.[67]

▲ *Construction workers today are often compensated for their work through the method of skill-based pay, which originated with the craft guilds of the Middle Ages.*

Basing pay on skills rather than jobs is easier said than done.[68] However, it's estimated that over 50% of Fortune 1,000 firms use some form of skill-based pay.[69] One aerospace firm uses skill-based pay by having all exempt employees negotiate "learning contracts" with their supervisors. The employees then get raises for meeting learning (skills-improvement) objectives.[70]

Broadbanding

We've seen that many firms develop pay plans that consist of multiple classes or grades, each with its own vertical rate range. For example, the U.S. government's pay plan consists of 18 main grades (GS-1 to GS-18), each with its own rate range. Categorizing jobs into classes or grades makes sense, because if you did not do so you might have to craft rate ranges for hundreds or thousands of jobs. Thus, in Figure 11-3 (p. 316) each grade includes all the jobs falling within 50 job evaluation points. Therefore, *all* the jobs in each specific grade are treated the same for pay purposes—for instance, in answering questions like, "What's the most someone in this job can earn?" and "What must this person's starting salary be?"

The question, though, is "How wide should the salary grades be, in terms of the number of job evaluation points they include?" There is a downside to having narrow grades: For an employee whose job falls in one of these grades, the rate range for that grade dictates his or her minimum and maximum salary. So, for instance, if you want someone whose job is in grade 2 to fill in for a time in a job that happens to be in grade 1, it's difficult to reassign that person without lowering his or her salary. Similarly, if you want the person to learn about a job that happens to be in grade 3, the employee might object to the reassignment without a corresponding raise to grade 3 pay. In other words, traditional multiclass/grade pay plans can breed inflexibility.

That's why some firms are **broadbanding** their pay plans. Broadbanding means combining salary grades and ranges into just a few wide levels or bands, each of which contains a relatively wide range of jobs and salary levels. Figure 11-4

broadbanding
Consolidating salary grades and ranges into just a few wide levels or "bands," each of which contains a relatively wide range of jobs and salary levels.

illustrates this. In Figure 11-4, the six pay grades from Figure 11-3 are consolidated into two broadbands. A company may create broadbands for all its jobs, or for specific groups such as managers or professionals. The rate range of the broadband is relatively large, since it ranges from the minimum pay of the lowest grade the firm merged into the broadband up to the maximum pay of the highest merged grade. For the jobs that fall in this broadband, there is therefore a much wider range of pay rates. You can move employees from job to job within the broadband more easily, without worrying about the employees moving outside the relatively narrow rate range associated with a single pay grade. Broadbanding therefore breeds flexibility.

Companies broadband for several reasons, most often to support strategic initiatives. Broadbanding's basic advantage is that it injects greater flexibility into employee compensation.[71] It is especially sensible where firms flatten their hierarchies and organize into self-managing teams. The new, broad salary bands can include both supervisors and subordinates and also facilitate moving employees slightly up or down along the pay scale, without bumping the person into a new salary range. For example, "the employee who needs to spend time in a lower-level job to develop a certain skill set can receive higher-than-usual pay for the work, a circumstance considered impossible under traditional pay systems."[72]

Broadbanding also makes it easier to have less-specialized "boundaryless" jobs and organizational structures. Less specialization and more participation in cross-departmental processes generally require enlarged duties and more possibilities for alternative career tracks; broader, more inclusive salary bands facilitate this. (One expert argues that traditional quantitative evaluation plans actually reward

▶ **FIGURE 11-4**
Broadbanded
Structure and How
It Relates to
Traditional Pay
Grades and Ranges

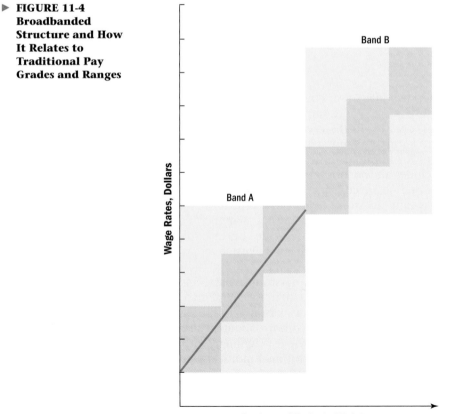

unadaptability.[73] He argues that jobs narrowly defined by compensable factors such as "know-how" are unlikely to encourage job incumbents to be flexible. Instead, the tendency may be for workers to take a "that's not my job" attitude and to concentrate on their specific tasks.)

However, broadbanding can be a little unsettling, particularly for new employees. For example, Home Depot has used broadbanding for about 10 years, and "when employees want to learn something new, they play to the level [on that project] that they're capable of," says the firm's head of information systems. That's motivating once you get used to it. However, it can make a new employee feel a little adrift: "There's a sense of a permanence in the set of job responsibilities often attached to job titles," he says. That sense of permanence isn't nearly as clear when employees can (and are expected to) move frequently from project to project and job to job.[74]

A recent survey of 783 employers found that about 15% were using broadbanding.[75] One British company did so to support a new strategy of cutting costs and flattening and downsizing the organization. The flattening meant fewer jobs, each of which had broader responsibilities, and broadbanding made it easier to get employees to assume their new, broader roles.[76] Home Depot has used broadbanding for about 10 years. One advantage, according to the firm's vice president of information systems, is that it encourages employees to de-emphasize job titles and more willingly consider changing roles and responsibilities.[77] Dow Jones & Company implemented broadbanding for its 1,000 IT professionals in 2001.

Even with trends like skill-based pay and broadbanding, 60% to 70% of U.S. firms still use point and factor comparison plans.[78] Job evaluation's relative ease of use and familiarity are probably the main reasons. And neither skill-based pay nor broadbanding eliminates the need for evaluating the worth of one job relative to others.[79]

Broadbanding involves several steps. First, you need to decide on the number of bands and how many points they will include, and assign each band a salary range. The bands usually have wide salary ranges and overlap substantially. A band may consist of a number of jobs, each with a market wage rate. More often, bands contain several skill levels. Workers must increase their skills and knowledge to get raises.[80] Broadbanding is most often used in conjunction with some strategic initiative; IBM is a good example.

STRATEGIC HR

IBM's Pay Plan Supports Its New Strategy

As most everyone knows by now, IBM is a classic example of an organizational renewal. It dominated its industry through the early 1980s. But by the 1990s, it was failing to exploit new technologies and losing touch with its customers.[81] Its board hired Louis Gerstner. His first strategy was to transform IBM from a sluggish giant to a lean winner.

Accomplishing this meant doing more than downsizing and reorganizing the firm; Gerstner had to transform IBM's culture—the shared values, attitudes, and behavior patterns that guided employees' behavior. He sought to emphasize winning, execution, speed, and decisiveness.

IBM's existing compensation pay plan did the opposite. Everyone in this huge company was in a job whose relative worth was based on a decades-old point-factor-based job evaluation.[82] What were some of the implications? For one thing, maintaining the point system for over 100,000 employees required "a massive and cumbersome" attention to point-factor-manual-based evaluations. This structure also cultivated a preoccupation with internal equity rather than with market, competitive rates of pay. Gerstner knew he had to change the pay plan to drive the new culture he sought to create.

To change this situation, Gerstner's team made four major changes in IBM's compensation plan:

1. *The marketplace rules.* The company switched from its previous single salary structure (for nonsales employees) to different salary structures and merit budgets for different job families. This enabled IBM to take different compensation actions for different job families (for instance, for accountants, engineers, programmers, and so on). In particular, this enabled IBM to concentrate on paying employees in different job families in a more market-oriented way. The new approach sends the strong cultural signal that "a market-driven company must watch the market closely and act accordingly."[83]

2. *Fewer jobs, evaluated differently, in broadbands.* Second, IBM scrapped its point factor job evaluation system and its traditional salary grades. The new system has no points at all. The old system contained 10 different compensable factors; the new one slots jobs into 10 bands based on just 3 (skills, leadership requirements, and scope/impact).

In the United States, the number of separate job titles dropped from over 5,000 to fewer than 1,200[84] and 24 salary grades dropped to 10 broadbands. This communicated a new organizational model: IBM was to be a flatter organization that could "deliver goods and services to market faster."[85]

3. *Managers manage.* The previous compensation plan based raises on a complex comparison that linked performance appraisal scores to salary increases measured in tenths of a percent. The new system is streamlined. Managers get a budget and some coaching, the essence of which is: "Either differentiate the pay you give to stars versus acceptable performers or the stars won't be around too long."[86] The new approach lets managers rank employees on a variety of factors (such as critical skills, and results). The managers decide which factors are used and what weights they're given.

4. *Big stakes for stakeholders.* As IBM was floundering in the early 1990s, every nonexecutive employee's cash compensation (outside the sales division) consisted of base salary (plus overtime, shift premiums, and some other adjustments). Pay for performance was a foreign concept. By 1997, most IBM'rs around the world "had 10% or more of their total cash compensation tied to performance."[87] In the new system, there are only three performance appraisal ratings. "A top-rated employee receives two-and-one-half times the award of an employee with the lowest ranking. (Awards are calibrated as percentages of pensionable earnings.)"[88]

The changes illustrate how one company used its compensation plan to support its strategic aims. The new pay plan refocused IBM employees' attention on the values of winning, execution, and speed, and on being better, faster, and more competitive.

Compensation Plans in Practice

Yet in practice, discussions of compensation's strategic role may now reflect more smoke than fire. In one recent survey, only 40% of the participants reported that they attempted to assess the effectiveness of their new compensation systems. Based on this survey, "There is little evidence that pay is seen as a management tool or that measuring and monitoring program effectiveness is an important priority. Payroll may be the single largest item in the budget, but that apparently has not prompted many companies to determine if they are getting enough bang for their buck."[89] Another survey found that only 34% of organizations had an articulated compensation strategy, and only 27% of employees within these organizations understood the reward program. Only 20% of the employees said the reward program encouraged the desired behaviors.[90] Most employers would therefore do well to study the results Mr. Gerstner got by changing the pay plan at IBM.

Compensation Plans for Dot-Com Companies

Traditional compensation practices haven't been applied across the board to dot-com companies. Traditional firms, for instance, generally slot jobs into grades based on market rates and internal equity. But in the dot-com world, "competitive salaries for these positions gyrate too rapidly for any corporate compensation structure to keep up with the changes." For example, with the pay for Web designers and programmers jumping (often wildly) from month to month, hiring and keeping good employees is futile if the compensation plan isn't flexible. Furthermore, you don't always hire people for specific positions in fast-moving dot-com firms: "That's why the most successful dot-com companies don't hire people to fill positions—they hire the best people possible and find jobs for them."[91]

Dot-com compensation plans therefore tend to be relatively flexible. They "link hiring pay to competitive practice for that position, based on real-time external research (not out of date surveys)"; they make salary adjustments based on the value the employee creates; and "they don't wait until the end of the year to adjust salaries—they reinforce value creation by giving raises when the individual has made himself or herself more valuable."[92]

◆ **RESEARCH INSIGHT** On the other hand, dot-com employees want more than good pay. In addition to competitive compensation and benefits, for instance, dot-com employees expect an entrepreneurial work environment and numerous skill development opportunities.[93]

Research conducted by PricewaterhouseCoopers indicates that dot-com employees have specific expectations of their employers. These expectations fall into three categories: culture, rewards, opportunity.

1. *Cultural expectations*: Entrepreneurial work environment, high visibility within the organization, respect for work–life balance.

2. *Rewards expectations*: Competitive compensation and benefits, recognition for unique contributions, a piece of the action.

3. *Career opportunity expectations*: Skill development opportunities, active career mentoring, flexibility in career pathing.[94]

Other important features of dot-com company rewards include these: Most dot-com firms ignore internal equity and *rely exclusively on market-based pay* (because of fast turnover and the urgent need for advanced skills). Dot-coms traditionally *emphasize stock ownership* over cash in the compensation mix—one expert contends that "dot-com executives received cash compensation packages that were less than half what they might have earned at a traditional employer." Dot-coms also tend to start new hires at market rates of pay, *eliminate regular merit increases*, and keep an employee's salary constant until the person changes his or her role.

Of course, the ups and downs of the dot-com sector are forcing changes. Up to now, base salary and stock options were the traditional compensation elements of choice, but "dot-com organizations have recently developed cash incentive programs."[95]

Comparable Worth

Comparable worth refers to the requirement to pay men and women equal wages for jobs of comparable (rather than strictly equal) value to the employer. In its broadest sense, comparable worth may mean comparing quite dissimilar jobs, such as nurses to fire truck mechanics or secretaries to technicians.[96] The problem is, women often have jobs that are quite dissimilar to those of men. Should you pay women who are performing jobs *equal* to men's or just *comparable* to men's the same as men? This is the basic issue in comparable worth.

For years, "equal" was the standard in the United States, though "comparable" was and is used in Canada and many European countries.[97] As a result of court rulings, some experts[98] now believe that comparable worth may become more impor-

comparable worth
The concept by which women who are usually paid less than men can claim that men in comparable rather than strictly equal jobs are paid more.

tant in the United States.[99] This issue is not going away. For example, representative Eleanor Holmes Norton (D-DC) is advocating a new "fair pay act" under which employers would have to provide equal pay for different but "comparable" jobs.[100]

County of Washington v. Gunther (1981) was a pivotal case for comparable worth. It involved Washington County, Oregon, prison matrons who claimed sex discrimination. The county had evaluated comparable but nonequal men's jobs as having 5% more "job content" (based on a point evaluation system) than the women's jobs, but paid the men 35% more.[101] After seesawing through the courts to the U.S. Supreme Court, Washington County finally agreed to pay 35,000 employees in female-dominated jobs almost $500 million in pay raises over seven years to settle the suit.

Comparable worth has implications for job evaluation. Some experts argue that job evaluation methods (like the point method) are unfair because they ignore or underestimate important skills associated with jobs often held by women.[102] One expert argues that many of the skills associated with jobs like nursing and teaching go unrecognized as compensable factors because they "mirror traditional duties within the home"; they are ignored because it's assumed that they need not be learned on the job or are somehow less important than skills based on on-the-job training.[103] Similarly, while men "typically receive points for dirt and grease that they encounter on the job under a factor designated 'working conditions,' nurses, who deal with [dirt and blood] on a daily basis, receive no such points."[104]

There may also be bias in the job evaluation plan itself. As in the Gunther case, some point plans "tend to result in higher point totals for jobs traditionally held by males than for those traditionally held by females."[105] For example, the factor "supervisory responsibility" might heavily weight chain-of-command factors like number of employees supervised, and downplay the importance of gaining the voluntary cooperation of other employees. One solution is to rewrite the factor rules, to give more weight to the sorts of activities that female-dominated positions often emphasize.[106]

In any event, comparable worth has important implications for employers' job evaluation procedures. Virtually every comparable worth case that reached a court involved the use of the point method of job evaluation. (Here, you'll recall, each job is evaluated in terms of several factors like effort, skill, and responsibility, and then assigned points based on the degree of each factor present in the job.) Point plans facilitate comparability ratings among different jobs. For example, two positions such as Clerk-Typist IV and Junior Engineer might have the same number of points and, therefore, comparable worth. This would suggest the firm should pay both jobs the same, although in practice market wages may be higher for the male-dominated junior engineers than for the female-dominated clerk-typists.[107]

So can firms still use point-type plans? Some argue that "comparable worth" doesn't require avoiding point plans, just using them more wisely.[108] One approach is for employers to price their jobs as they see fit (with or without point plans), but to ensure women have equal access to all jobs. In other words, eliminate the wage discrimination issue by eliminating sex-segregated jobs.[109]

All this notwithstanding, the fact is that women in the United States still earn only about 77% as much as men. Overall, female full-time wage and salary workers earned a weekly median $473, compared with $618 for males.

What accounts for this strange result? One specialist cites four factors: women's starting salaries are traditionally lower, because employers traditionally view them as having less leverage; salary increases for women in professional jobs do not reflect their above-average performance, whereas men with equal performance receive bigger raises; in white-collar jobs, men tend to change jobs more frequently, which enables them to be promoted to higher-level jobs over women with more seniority; and in blue-collar jobs, women tend to be placed in departments with lower-paying jobs.[110] Employers can and should establish procedures to avoid such inequitable practices.

We invite you to visit **www.prenhall.com/dessler** on the Prentice Hall Web site for our online study guide, Internet exercises, current events, links to related Web sites, and more.

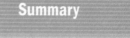

1. There are two bases on which to pay employee compensation—increments of time and volume of production. The former includes hourly or daily wages and salaries. Basing pay on volume of production ties compensation directly to the amount of production (or number of "pieces") the worker produces.
2. Establishing pay rates involves five steps: Conduct salary survey, evaluate jobs, develop pay grades, use wage curves, and fine-tune pay rates.
3. Job evaluation determines the relative worth of a job. It compares jobs to one another based on their content, which is usually defined in terms of compensable factors like skills, effort, responsibility, and working conditions.
4. The five-step ranking method of job evaluation is simple to use, but there is a tendency to rely too heavily on estimates. The classification (or grading) method is a second qualitative approach that categorizes jobs based on a class description or classification rules for each class.
5. Quantitative methods include the point method, which requires identifying a number of compensable factors and then determining the degree to which each of these factors is present in the job. The factor comparison method entails deciding which jobs have more of certain compensable factors than others.
6. Most managers group similar jobs into wage or pay grades for pay purposes. These are comprised of jobs of approximately equal difficulty or importance as determined by job evaluation.
7. Developing a compensation plan for executive, managerial, and professional personnel is complicated by the fact that factors like performance and creativity must take precedence over static factors like working conditions. Market rates, performance, and incentives and benefits thus play a much greater role than does job evaluation for these employees.
8. Trends in compensation include skill-based pay, broadbanding, and adjustments for comparable worth.

The previous chapters explained training, appraising, and developing employees. Once employees have done their jobs and been appraised, they expect to be paid. The purpose of the current chapter, Establishing Pay Plans, is to explain and illustrate the methods managers use to decide how employees are to be paid. The main topics include factors in determining and establishing pay rates, and current trends in compensation. This chapter illustrates the increasing emphasis firms like IBM place on pay for performance. In the following chapter, we'll focus more specifically on pay-for-performance and incentive plans.

1. What is the difference between exempt and nonexempt jobs?
2. Should the job evaluation depend on an appraisal of the job holder's performance? Why? Why not?
3. What is the relationship between compensable factors and job specifications?
4. Compare and contrast the following methods of job evaluation: ranking, classification, factor comparison, and point method.

5. What are the pros and cons of broadbanding, and would you recommend your current employer (or some other firm you're familiar with) use it? Why or why not?

6. It was recently reported in the news that the average pay for most university presidents ranged around $200,000 per year, but that a few earned closer to $500,000 per year. What would account for such a disparity in the pay of universities' chief executive officers?

7. Do small companies need to develop a pay plan? Why or why not?

Individual and Group Activities

1. Working individually or in groups, conduct salary surveys for the following positions: entry-level accountant and entry-level chemical engineer. What sources did you use, and what conclusions did you reach? If you were the HR manager for a local engineering firm, what would you recommend that you pay for each job?

2. Working individually or in groups, develop compensation policies for the teller position at a local bank. Assume that there are four tellers: two were hired in May and the other two were hired in December. The compensation policies should address the following: appraisals, raises, holidays, vacation pay, overtime pay, method of pay, garnishments, and time cards.

3. Working individually or in groups, access relevant online Web sites to determine what equitable pay ranges are for jobs as chemical engineer, marketing manager, and HR manager with a bachelor's degree and five years of experience in the following cities: New York, New York; San Francisco, California; Los Angeles, California; Houston, Texas; Dallas, Texas; Denver, Colorado; Miami, Florida; Atlanta, Georgia; Chicago, Illinois; Birmingham, Alabama; Detroit, Michigan; and Washington, D.C. For each position in each city, what are the pay ranges and the average pay? Does geographical location impact the salaries of the different positions? If so, how?

EXPERIENTIAL EXERCISE

Purpose: The purpose of this exercise is to give you experience in performing a job evaluation using the ranking method.

Required Understanding: You should be thoroughly familiar with the ranking method of job evaluation and obtain job descriptions for your college's dean, department chairperson, director of admissions, library director, registrar, and your professor.

How to Set Up the Exercise/Instructions: Divide the class into groups of four or five students. The groups will perform a job evaluation of the positions of dean, department chairperson, and professor using the ranking method.

1. Perform a job evaluation by ranking the jobs. You may use one or more compensable factors.

2. If time permits, a spokesperson from each group can put his or her group's rankings on the board. Did the groups end up with about the same results? How did they differ? Why do you think they differed?

APPLICATION CASE *Salary Inequities at Acme Manufacturing*

Joe Black was trying to figure out what to do about a problem salary situation he had in his plant. Black recently took over as president of Acme Manufacturing. The founder, Bill George, had been president for 35 years. The company was family owned and located in a small eastern Arkansas town. It had approximately 250 employees and was the largest employer in the community. Black was a member of the family that owned Acme, but he had never worked for the company prior to becoming president. He had an MBA and a law degree, plus 5 years of management experience with a large manufacturing organization, where he was senior vice president for human resources when he made his move to Acme.

A short time after joining Acme, Black started to notice that there was considerable inequity in the pay structure for salaried employees. A discussion with the human resources director led him to believe that salaried employees' pay was very much a matter of individual bargaining with the past president. Hourly paid factory employees were not part of the problem because they were unionized and their wages were set by collective bargaining. An examination of the salaried payroll showed that there were 25 employees, ranging in pay from that of the president to that of the receptionist. A closer examination showed that 14 of the salaried employees were female. Three of these were front-line factory supervisors and one was the human resources director. The other 10 were nonmanagement.

This examination also showed that the human resources director appeared to be underpaid, and that the three female supervisors were paid somewhat less than any of the male supervisors. However, there were no similar supervisory jobs in which there were both male and female job incumbents. When asked, the HR director said she thought the female supervisors may have been paid at a lower rate mainly because they were women, and perhaps George did not think that women needed as much money because they had working husbands. However, she added the thought that they were paid less because they supervised less-skilled employees than did male supervisors. Black was not sure that this was true.

The company from which Black had moved had a good job evaluation system. Although he was thoroughly familiar and capable with this compensation tool, Black did not have time to make a job evaluation study at Acme. Therefore, he decided to hire a compensation consultant from a nearby university to help him. Together, they decided that all 25 salaried jobs should be in the same job evaluation cluster, that a modified ranking method of job evaluation should be used, and that the job descriptions recently completed by the HR director were current, accurate, and usable in the study.

The job evaluation showed that there was no evidence of serious inequities or discrimination in the nonmanagement jobs, but that the HR director and the three female supervisors were being underpaid relative to comparable male salaried employees.

Black was not sure what to do. He knew that if the underpaid female supervisors took the case to the local EEOC office, the company could be found guilty of sex discrimination and then have to pay considerable back wages. He was afraid that if he gave these women an immediate salary increase large enough to bring them up to where they should be, the male supervisors would be upset and the female supervisors might comprehend the total situation and want back pay. The HR director told Black that the female supervisors had never complained about pay differences, and they probably did not know the law to any extent.

The HR director agreed to take a sizable salary increase with no back pay, so this part of the problem was solved. Black believed he had four choices relative to the female supervisors:

1. To do nothing.
2. To gradually increase the female supervisors' salaries.
3. To increase their salaries immediately.
4. To call the three supervisors into his office, discuss the situation with them, and jointly decide what to do.

Questions

1. What would you do if you were Black?
2. How do you think the company got into a situation like this in the first place?
3. Why would you suggest Black pursue the alternative you suggested?

Source: This case was prepared by Professor James C. Hodgetts of the Fogelman College of Business and Economics of the University of Memphis. All names are disguised. Used by permission.

CONTINUING CASE: LearnInMotion.com *The New Pay Plan*

LearnInMotion.com does not have a formal wage structure, nor does it have rate ranges or use compensable factors. Jennifer and Mel base wage rates almost exclusively on those prevailing in the surrounding community, and temper these by trying to maintain some semblance of equity between what workers with different responsibilities are paid. As Jennifer says, "Deciding what to pay dot-com employees is an adventure: Wages for jobs like Web designer and online salesperson are always climbing dramatically, and there's not an awful lot

of loyalty involved when someone else offers you 30% or 40% more than you're currently making." Jennifer and Mel are therefore continuously scanning various sources to see what others are paying for positions like theirs. They peruse the want ads almost every day, and conduct informal surveys among their friends in other dot-coms. Once or twice a week, they also check compensation Web sites like Salary.com.

While the company has taken a somewhat unstructured, informal approach to establishing its compensation plan, the firm's actual salary schedule is guided by several basic pay policies. For one thing, the difficulty they had recruiting and hiring employees caused them to pay salaries 10% to 20% above what the market would seem to indicate. Jennifer and Mel write this off to the need to get and keep good employees. As Jennifer says, "If you've got 10 Web designers working for you, you can afford to go a few extra weeks without hiring another one, but when you need one designer and you have none, you've got to do whatever you can to get that one designer hired." Their somewhat informal approach has also led to some potential inequities: For example, the two salespeople—one a man, the other a woman—are earning different salaries, and the man is making about 30% more.

If everything was going fine—for instance, if sales were up, and the calendar was functional—perhaps they wouldn't be worried. However, the fact is that the two owners are wondering if a more structured pay plan would be a good idea. Now they want you, their management consultants, to help them decide what to do. Here's what they want you to do for them.

Questions and Assignments

1. Is the company at the point where it should be setting up a formal salary structure complete with job evaluations? Why or why not?
2. Is the company's policy of paying more than the prevailing wage rates a sound one? What do you base that on?
3. Is the salesperson's male–female differential wise? If not, why not?
4. What would you suggest we do now?

Chapter 12

Pay for Performance and Financial Incentives

After studying this chapter, you should be able to:

- Discuss the main incentives for operations employees.
- Describe the main incentives for managers and executives.
- Discuss the pros and cons of incentives for salespeople.
- Name and define the most popular organizationwide variable pay plans.
- Outline the steps in developing effective incentive plans.
- Establish an incentive plan.

STRATEGIC OVERVIEW   At Tampa-based AmeriSteel, losses for the third successive year meant it had to be more productive—and fast. The alternative—possible bankruptcy—was unacceptable. To implement the new strategy, one of the first things management turned to was the firm's compensation plan. While the plan offered above-average pay and above-average benefits, it didn't adequately link pay with performance. As a result, "employees had come to expect annual raises in good times and bad."[1] Management needed an incentive plan that would support its new strategic emphasis on productivity and competitiveness.

Chapter 11, Establishing Strategic Pay Plans, focused on developing pay plans and on non-performance-based elements such as salaries and wages. The main purpose of this chapter is to show you how to use incentives to motivate employees. We'll discuss incentives for operating employees, incentives for managers and executives, incentives for salespeople, incentives for professionals, and organizationwide variable pay plans. We'll explain why incentive plans fail, and provide a checklist for creating an effective plan. In the following chapter, Benefits and Services, we'll turn to financial and nonfinancial benefits and services, such as pay for time not worked and insurance benefits, which are also part of the compensation package.

MONEY AND MOTIVATION

There's nothing new about using incentives to motivate workers. Frederick Taylor popularized the use of financial incentives—financial rewards paid to workers whose production exceeds some predetermined standard—in the late 1800s. As a supervisory employee of the Midvale Steel Company, Taylor had become concerned with what he called "systematic soldiering"—the tendency of employees to work at the slowest pace possible and to produce at the minimum acceptable level. What especially intrigued him was the fact that some of these same workers still had the energy to run home and work on their homes, even after a 12-hour day. Taylor knew that if he could find some way to harness this energy during the workday, his firm could achieve huge productivity gains.

Primitive piecework systems were already in use, but were generally ineffective. Workers were paid a piece rate for each piece they produced, based on quotas arrived at informally. However, rate cutting by employers was flagrant, and the workers knew that if they earned too much, employers would cut the piece rate. Most workers therefore produced just enough to earn a decent wage, but not enough to cause the firm to cut the piece rate.

One of Taylor's great insights was in seeing the need for a standardized, acceptable view of a **fair day's work**. As he saw it, this fair day's work should depend not on vague supervisory estimates, but on a careful, formal, scientific process of inspection and observation. This need to evaluate each job scientifically led to the **scientific management** movement. Then, in the depression-plagued 1930s, scientific management gave way to the human relations movement and its focus on satisfying workers' social—not just financial—needs. For many years, incentive plans declined in popularity.

Performance and Pay

Competition, shareholder value, and turbulence characterize business today, and they've produced a renaissance for financial incentive/pay-for-performance plans. Studies show why. One involved 34 stores of a large retailer, 15 of which installed a new sales incentive plan. The researchers found that installing the plan "enables a store to capture more customers from its competitors [especially] when there is more intense competition."[2] The new plan was particularly effective in the stores facing the greatest competition. Another study focused on 20 Fortune 500 companies.[3] The researchers concluded "our data showed that organizations in which turbulence was greater shifted the financial risk to their managers by paying proportionally higher levels of variable pay."[4] (Turbulence included events like reductions in force, sale of assets, acquisition by another company, mergers, joint ventures, and attempted takeovers.) The incentives focused the managers' attention on performance.

The DuPont Company recently put all its 50,000 U.S.-based chemicals and specialties employees on a performance-based pay plan.[5] Why? "This was," said its president, "the first time in DuPont's history that the compensation of all [this division's] employees can be linked directly to their specific business's performance. . . . Our goal is to ensure that we provide shareholders with superior performance and value creation. . . . With employees focused on business performance and their specific role in the success of their business, we believe we will achieve this goal more quickly."[6]

Types of Incentive Plans

As you probably know from your own experience, incentive plans can be classified in several ways. They can, for example, be classified by *level*. *Individual incentive* plans provide income over and above base salary to individual employees

fair day's work
Frederick Taylor's observation that haphazard setting of piecework requirements and wages by supervisors was not sufficient, and that careful study was needed to define acceptable production quotas for each job.

scientific management
The careful, scientific study of the job for the purpose of boosting productivity and job satisfaction.

who meet specific individual performance standards.[7] *Group incentive* programs pay all members when the group or team collectively meets its performance standard.[8] *Profit sharing plans* are generally organization-wide, and provide all or most employees with a share of the company's profits in a specified period.[9] Plans can also be classified by *employee group*—such as plans for operating employees, sales employees, or managers. We'll look more closely at these classifications in a moment.

Managers often use two terms synonymously with incentive plans. **Variable pay** is a group incentive plan that ties pay to some measure of the firm's (or the facility's) overall profitability;[10,11] profit-sharing plans (discussed below) are one example.[12] However, confusing as it may be, some experts do include individual incentive plans within the category of variable pay.[13] Traditionally, all incentive plans are *pay-for-performance* plans: They pay all employees based on the employees' performance.

Incentives certainly don't have to be financial, and are only limited by the manager's creativity. For example, Patagonia, the outdoor clothing maker, rewards employees with time off.[14] *Incentive* magazine recently ran a program to identify the best Web-based incentive sites. (Many firms use these to set up and administer their incentive programs.) It received 214 nominations and selected 41 sites. They included gift certificate sites (such as GiftCertificates.com, see Webnote, and corporategear.com), merchandise sites (plasticpremiums.com, Spiegelrewards.com), services sites (branders.com, marketinginnovators.com), and travel incentive sites (allmeetings.com, corporatecruises.com).[15]

▲ **WEBNOTE**

Sites like giftcertificates.com make it easy for supervisors to provide quick, on-the-spot awards to employees.

www.giftcertificates.com

variable pay
Any plan that ties pay to productivity or profitability, usually as one-time lump payments.

INCENTIVES FOR OPERATIONS EMPLOYEES

All firms have "operations employees"—they are the people who actually do the work. Operations employees include the cleaning staff at your local hotel, the data processing clerks at your local bank, and the assembly-line workers who built your car—to name a few. Several incentive plans are particularly suited for use with operations employees.

Piecework Plans

Piecework is the oldest incentive plan and is still the most widely used: You pay the worker a sum (called a *piece rate*) for each unit he or she produces. Thus, if Tom the Web surfer gets $.40 for each e-mail sales lead he finds for the firm, he would make $40 for bringing in 100 a day and $80 for 200.

In a perfect world, developing a workable piece rate plan requires industrial engineering (that's how Frederick Taylor got his start). The crucial issue is the production standard, and industrial engineers usually set this—for instance, in terms of a standard number of e-mail leads per hour or a standard number of minutes per e-mail lead. In Tom's case, a job evaluation indicated that his Web surfing job was worth $8 an hour. The industrial engineer determined that 20 good leads per hour was the standard production rate. Therefore, the piece rate (for each lead) was $8 divided by 20, or $.40 per sales lead. (Of course, we need to ensure that

piecework
A system of pay based on the number of items processed by each individual worker in a unit of time, such as items per hour or items per day.

Tom makes at least the minimum wage, so we'd probably pay him $5.15 per hour—the minimum wage—whether or not he brought in 13 leads, and then pay him $.40 per lead for each over 13.)

Piecework generally implies **straight piecework**, which entails a strict proportionality between results and rewards regardless of output. However, some piecework plans allow for sharing productivity gains between employer and worker, such that the worker receives extra income for some above-normal production.[16] So if Tom starts bringing in 30 leads per hour instead of the "standard" 20, his piece rate for leads above 25 might bump up to $.45 each.

Piecework plans have pros and cons. They are understandable, appear equitable in principle, and can be powerful incentives, since rewards are proportionate to performance. However, workers may resist attempts to revise production standards, even if the change is justified.[17] Indeed, these plans may promote rigidity: Employees concentrate on output and are less willing to concern themselves with meeting quality standards or switching from job to job (since doing so could reduce their productivity).[18] Attempts to introduce new technology or processes may trigger resistance, for much the same reason. Options in such an event include team-based incentives and gainsharing programs, both discussed below.

The **standard hour plan** is like the piece rate plan, with one difference. Instead of getting a rate per piece, the worker gets a premium equal to the percent by which his or her performance exceeds the standard. So if Tom's standard is 160 leads per day (and thus $64 per day), and he brings in 200 leads, he'd get an extra 25%, or $80 for the day. Some firms find that expressing the incentive in percentages reduces the workers' tendency to link their production standard to pay (thus making the standard easier to change). It also eliminates the need to recompute piece rates whenever hourly wage rates are changed.[19]

In some industries, the term *piecework* has a poor reputation, and not just because managers have a history of changing the production standards. For example, some garment manufacturers had operators assemble items (like shirts) in their homes, and paid them for each piece they completed. Unfortunately, the hourly pay for this work didn't always fulfill the minimum wage requirements of the Wage and Hour Act. The problem continues today, in a more modern form. For example, an electronics firm had a woman who assembled cables for the firm during the day take home parts to assemble at night. Working with her sister, the two reportedly assembled cables in their downtown San Jose, California, apartment, allegedly averaging only $2 to $2.50 an hour for the piecework—about half the minimum wage.[20]

While still widely used, even industries that traditionally stressed piecework incentive plans, such as textiles, are reportedly moving to other plans. "People did work harder under these programs, but they posed problems. For one thing, they created quality problems," says one expert. Firms also tend to be more interested in incentive plans "that focus on profitability and profitability-related accomplishments," rather than just production volume, says another expert. More firms are therefore moving to the team incentive plans, gain sharing plans, and organization-wide incentive pay programs we'll discuss later in this chapter.[21]

Team or Group Variable Pay Incentive Plans

Team or group incentive plans pay incentives to the team based on the team's performance.[22] One way to do this is to set work standards for each team member and then calculate each member's output. Members are then paid based on one of three formulas: (1) All members receive the pay earned by the highest producer, (2) all members receive the pay earned by the lowest producer, or (3) all members receive pay equal to the average pay earned by the group. A second

---

straight piecework
An incentive plan in which a person is paid a sum for each item he or she makes or sells, with a strict proportionality between results and rewards.

standard hour plan
A plan by which a worker is paid a basic hourly rate but is paid an extra percentage of his or her base rate for production exceeding the standard per hour or per day. Similar to piecework payment but based on a percent premium.

team or group incentive plan
A plan in which a production standard is set for a specific work group, and its members are paid incentives if the group exceeds the production standard.

approach is to set an engineered production standard based on the output of the group as a whole: All members then receive the same pay, based on the piece rate for the group's job. This group incentive can use the piece rate or standard hour plan, but the latter is more prevalent.

A third option is to tie rewards to goals based on some overall standard of group performance, such as "total labor hours per final product." Doing so avoids the need for a precisely engineered piecework standard.[23] One company established such an incentive plan for its teams. If the firm reached 100% of its goal, the employees would share in about 5% of the improvement (in labor costs saved). The firm divided the 5% pool by the number of employees to compute the value of a "share." Each work team then received two goals, and if the team achieved both goals, each employee earned one share in addition to his or her base pay. If the teams achieved one goal, they each got half a share. The results of this plan—in terms of changing employee attitudes and focusing teams on strategic goals—were reportedly "extraordinary."[24]

▲ *Shown in the photo are Toyota workers on the assembly line in Japan. Toyota is known for its team- and work-group-based systems, which it uses successfully in its U.S. plants as well. Japanese companies reward the group—to make group members indebted to one another, and to encourage a sense of cooperation.*

Team incentives often make a lot of sense. Much work today is organized around teams—project teams publish books, assembly teams assemble cars, and new-product teams launch new products. Performance here reflects not just individual but team effort, so team incentives make sense. Team-based plans reinforce team planning and problem solving, and help ensure collaboration.[25] In Japan, "the first rule is never reward only one individual." Instead, Japanese companies reward the group—to reduce jealousy, to make group members indebted to one another, and to encourage a sense of cooperation.[26] Team incentives also facilitate training, since each member has an interest in getting new members trained as fast as possible.[27]

The main disadvantage is that a worker's pay may not be proportionate to his or her own efforts, which may demotivate hard workers. In one study (where researchers paid the group based on the best member's performance), group incentives were as effective as individual ones in improving performance.[28] But workers who share in the team's pay but don't put their hearts into the effort can be a problem. Solutions include having team members commit in writing to putting the goals of the team before their own, and basing part of each worker's pay on individual (not just team) performance.[29]

INCENTIVES FOR MANAGERS AND EXECUTIVES

Managers play a central role in influencing divisional and corporate profitability, and most firms therefore put considerable thought into how to reward them. Most managers get short-term bonuses and long-term incentives in addition to salary.[30] For firms offering short-term incentive plans, virtually all—96%—provide those incentives in cash. For those offering long-term incentive plans, about 48% offer stock options, which are intended to motivate and reward management for long-term corporate growth, prosperity, and shareholder value. For mature companies, executives' base salary, short term incentives, long-term incentives, and benefits might be 60%, 15%, 15%, and 10%, respectively. For growth companies, the corresponding figures were 40%, 45%, 25%, and 10%.[31] About 69% of companies in one survey had short-term incentives, although nearly a third of those said they didn't consider them effective in boosting employee performance.[32]

Short-Term Incentives: The Annual Bonus

Most firms have **annual bonus** plans aimed at motivating the short-term performance of managers and executives. Short-term bonuses can easily result in plus or minus adjustments of 25% or more to total pay. There are three basic issues to consider when awarding short-term incentives: eligibility, fund size, and individual awards.

Eligibility Most firms opt for broad eligibility—they include both top- and lower-level managers—and mainly decide who's eligible in one of two ways. Based on one survey, about 25% of companies decide eligibility based on job level or job title. About 54% decide eligibility based on a combination of factors, including job level/title, base salary level, and discretionary considerations (such as identifying key jobs that have a measurable impact on profitability). Base salary level alone is the sole determinant in less than 3% of the companies polled.[33]

The size of the bonus is usually greater for top-level executives. Thus, an executive earning $150,000 in salary may be able to earn another 80% of his or her salary as a bonus, while a manager in the same firm earning $80,000 can earn only another 30%. Similarly, a supervisor might be able to earn up to 15% of his or her base salary in bonuses. Average bonuses range from a low of 10% to a high of 80% or more. A typical company might establish a plan whereby executives could earn 45% of base salary, managers 25%, and supervisory personnel 12%.

Fund Size The firm must also decide the total amount of bonus money to make available—fund size. Some use a *nondeductible formula*. They use a straight percentage (usually of the company's net income) to create the short-term incentive fund. Others use a *deductible formula*, on the assumption that the fund should start to accumulate only after the firm has met a specified level of earnings. Some firms don't use a formula at all, but make that decision on a totally discretionary basis.[34]

There are no hard-and-fast rules about the proportion of profits to pay out. One alternative is to reserve a minimal amount of the profits, say, 10%, for safeguarding stockholders' investments, and then to establish a fund for bonuses equal to, say, 20% of the corporate operating profit before taxes in excess of this base amount. Thus, if the operating profits were $100,000, then the management bonus fund might be 20% of $90,000 or $18,000.[35] Other formulas used for determining the executive bonus fund are as follows:

1. Ten percent of net income after deducting 5% of average capital invested in business.
2. Twelve and one-half percent of the amount by which net income exceeds 6% of stockholders' equity.
3. Twelve percent of net earnings after deducting 6% of net capital.[36]

Individual Awards The third task is deciding the actual individual awards. Typically, a target bonus (as well as maximum amount, perhaps double the target bonus) is set for each eligible position, and the actual award reflects the person's performance. The firm computes performance ratings for each manager, computes preliminary total bonus estimates, and compares the total amount of money required with the bonus fund available. If necessary, it then adjusts the individual bonus estimates.

One question is whether managers will receive bonuses based on individual performance, corporate performance, or both. Here again, there are no hard-and-fast rules. Firms usually tie top-level executive bonuses to overall corporate results (or divisional results if the executive heads a major division). But as one moves farther down the chain of command, corporate profits become a less accurate gauge of a manager's contribution. For, say, supervisors or the heads of functional departments, it often makes more sense to tie the bonus to individual performance.

Many firms tie short-term bonuses to both organizational and individual performance.[37] Perhaps the simplest way is the split-award method, which breaks the bonus into two parts. Here the manager actually gets two separate bonuses, one based on his or her individual effort and one based on the organization's overall performance. Thus, a manager might be eligible for an individual performance bonus of up to $10,000, but receive only $2,000 at the end of the year, based on his or her individual performance evaluation. But the person might also receive a second bonus of $8,000, based on the firm's profits for the year.

One drawback to this approach is that it may give marginal performers too much—for instance, someone could get a company-based bonus, even if his or her own performance is mediocre. One way to get around this is to use the multiplier method. In other words, make the bonus a product of both individual and corporate performance. As Table 12-1 illustrates, multiply the target bonus by 1.00 or .80 or zero (if the firm's performance is excellent, and person's performance is excellent, good, fair, or poor). A manager whose own performance is poor does not even receive the company-based bonus.

Whichever approach you use, the rule is: Don't pay outstanding performers less than their target reward, regardless of organizational performance, and pay them substantially larger awards than you do other managers. The company cannot afford to lose these people. Conversely, marginal or below-average performers should never receive normal or average awards, and poor performers should get nothing. Give the money saved on those people to the above-average performers.[38]

Long-Term Incentives

Employers use long-term incentives to inject a long-term perspective into their executives' decisions. With only short-term criteria to shoot for, a manager could boost profitability by reducing plant maintenance, for instance; this tactic might catch up with the company two or three years later. Long-term incentives also encourage executives to stay with the company by letting them accumulate capital (usually options to buy company stock) that can only be cashed in after a certain number of years—"golden handcuffs," as some call them.

Firms don't just use stock options for this: Other popular long-term incentives (discussed below) include cash, stock, stock appreciation rights, and phantom

◄ **TABLE 12-1**
Multiplier Approach to Determining Annual Bonus

| | | Company Performance (based on sales targets, weight .50) | | | |
		Excellent	Good	Fair	Poor
Individual	Excellent	1.00	.90	.80	.70
Performance	Good	.80	.70	.60	.50
(based on appraisal, weight .50)	Fair	0.00	0.00	0.00	0.00
	Poor	0.00	0.00	0.00	0.00

Note: To determine the dollar amount of a manager's award, multiply the maximum possible (target) bonus by the appropriate factor in the matrix.

stock.[39] The popularity of these plans changes over time due to economic and market conditions and trends, internal company financial pressures, changing attitudes toward long-term incentives, changes in tax law, and other factors.[40] However, the recent emphasis on competitiveness and shareholder value has prompted more boards of directors to emphasize stock options at the expense of alternatives like cash incentives.[41]

Stock Options Stock option awards to company executives have soared. For example, it's estimated that stock options accounted for almost 63% of the compensation paid by America's top companies in 2000 to their CEOs; that is up from 26% in 1994, and 2% in the mid-1980s. In one recent year, firms like Apple Computer, PacifiCare Health Systems, and Lehman Brothers all granted shares and stock options to their employees equal to about 15% of their total shares outstanding.[42] Yet one survey of several industries found that over half the executives responding saw little or no relationship between their performance and the value of their stock options.[43]

stock option
The right to purchase a stated number of shares of a company stock at today's price at some time in the future.

A **stock option** is the right to purchase a specific number of shares of company stock at a specific price during a specific period of time; the executive thus hopes to profit by exercising his or her option to buy the shares in the future but at today's price. The assumption is that the price of the stock will go up. Unfortunately, this depends partly on considerations outside the manager's control, such as general economic and market conditions. When the market for Internet stocks plummeted in 2000, many managers saw their options go "underwater." Many of these firms then had to scramble to sweeten their managers' incentive plans. *Nonqualified stock options* are the most popular. They are options to purchase stock at a stated price, usually the fair market value at the time of the grant.[44]

mega-option grants
Large, upfront grants in lieu of annual grants.

More firms, like Disney, are awarding their CEOs **mega-option grants**. Mega-option grants are large, upfront grants in lieu of annual grants. The number of options the CEO gets as well as their exercise price (the price at which the CEO can purchase shares of company stock) are fixed at the time of the grants, and the total value of the megagrant is generally close to $10 million. Megagrants create the most high-powered incentives for value creation, since the CEO gets this enormous grant up front, rather than over three or four years. If he or she can get the stock price to skyrocket, the proceeds can be enormous: For example, every few years over the last 15 years or so, Disney's Michael Eisner has received a megagrant of several million shares. In 1999, Mr. Eisner exercised 22 million options on Disney stock, netting him more than $500 million.[45]

Different Stock Option Plans Different employees tend to have different stock option plans. Plans for key employees (such as top executives) typically provide for a very significant upside in the value of stock the employee can receive. On the other hand, more companies today are implementing broad-based stock option plans in which the potential appreciation is relatively modest, but in which all or most employees can participate. A recent study by compensation specialist William Mercer Company found that 18% of 350 large U.S. companies offered broad-based employee options grants in 1999, up from 6% in 1993.[46] Several years ago, IBM more than tripled the number of employees who get stock options.[47] Why do this? As two compensation experts put it, "Companies are asking more from employees than ever before. They have cut out layers of management, downsized, outsourced, empowered employees. . . .[48]" "By giving stock options to non-executives, companies make good the promise of letting employees share in the company's success."[49]

The *key employee program* may go to a handful of top executives and provides significant economic incentives to motivate these people and to keep them on board. On the other hand, the non-key program like the one in place at IBM offers a broad list of employees a highly competitive total compensation package to emphasize that the company intends to share its success with its employees.[50]

Too many stock options can be too much of a good thing. Compensation experts use the term "stock market overhang" to refer to stock options granted (plus those remaining to be granted) as a percent of the firm's total shares outstanding. Firms with high overhang suffer significantly higher stock price volatility. The problem may be that "Executives with increasingly large stock option holdings have an added incentive to undertake riskier business strategies. . . ." Their options provide an incentive to go for spectacular results, but since they have not actually bought the stock yet, they don't risk their own money. The solution is to draft the option plan so it forces recipients to convert their options to stock more quickly.[51]

Other Plans There are several other stock-related long-term incentive plans. *Stock appreciation rights* permit the recipient to exercise the stock option (by buying the stock) or to take any appreciation in the stock price in cash, stock, or some combination of these. A *performance achievement plan* awards shares of stock for the achievement of predetermined financial targets, such as profit or growth in earnings per share. With *restricted stock plans*, the firm usually awards shares without cost to the executive: The employee can sell the stock (for which he or she paid nothing), but is restricted from doing so for, say, five years. Under *phantom stock plans*, executives receive not shares but "units" that are similar to shares of company stock. Then at some future time, they receive value (usually in cash) equal to the appreciation of the "phantom" stock they own.[52]

Performance Plans Traditional executive incentives (like stock options) often don't build in any real risk for the executive, so the executives' and the shareholders' interests could diverge.[53] Often, for instance, managers can exercise options with little or no cash outlay, and then quickly sell their stock. So today there is an emphasis on building more executive risk into the long-term incentive formula.[54]

The solution is to design the plan so that executives don't prosper unless the company does. Performance plans are one means for doing so. They are "plans whose payment or value is contingent on financial performance measured against objectives set at the start of a multi-year period."[55] They are essentially bonuses, but the measurement period is longer than a year. For example, the plan may award 0 to 300 "performance units" worth $2,000 per unit, depending on the company's earnings-per-share growth over several years. Thus, at the end of the period, the executive might be eligible to receive, say, a $300,000 cash grant, in proportion to his or her success in meeting his or her financial goals.

Cash Versus Stock Options Should firms award their top executives stock options or cash bonuses? A study by consultants McKinsey & Company suggests that stock options may be the simplest and wisest route. About half the companies surveyed had stock options only, and about half had performance-based plans in which managers were given cash bonuses for long-term performance.

In most cases, the benefit to shareholders of companies with long-term cash performance incentives did not differ significantly from that of companies that had only stock-based incentive plans (like stock options). This was so even though companies that paid cash bonuses had spent more to fund their incentive plans. The most serious problem in awarding cash bonuses lay in identifying the proper performance measures. The survey recommends using measures of performance that correlate with shareholder wealth creation, such as return on equity.[56]

THE NEW WORKPLACE

Long-Term Incentives for Overseas Executives

Developing long-term incentives for a firm's overseas operations presents some tricky problems, particularly with regard to taxation. For example, extending a U.S. stock option plan to local nationals in a firm's overseas operations could subject them to immediate local taxation on the stocks, even though the shares could not be sold because of requirements built into the company's plan.[57]

The problem extends to U.S. executives stationed overseas. For example, it's not unusual for an executive to be taxed $40,000 on $140,000 of stock option income if he or she is based in the United States. However, if that person receives the same stock option income while stationed overseas, he or she may be subject to both the $40,000 U.S. tax *and* a foreign income tax (depending on the country) of perhaps $94,000. Therefore, ignoring the overseas country's tax burden has the effect of virtually eliminating the incentive value of the stock from the executive's point of view or dramatically boosting the cost of the stock to the company (assuming the company pays the foreign income tax). In any case, firms cannot assume that they can simply export their executives' incentive programs. Instead, they must consider various factors, including tax treatment, the regulatory environment, and foreign exchange controls.[58]

Strategy and Executive Compensation

Few HR practices have as profound or obvious an impact on strategic success as the company's long-term incentives. Whether expanding through joint ventures abroad, consolidating operations and downsizing the workforce, or following some other strategy, few firms can fully implement strategies in just one or two years. As a result, the long-term signals you send your managers and executives regarding what you will (or won't) reward can have a big effect on whether your firm's strategy succeeds. A strategy to boost sales by expanding abroad might suggest linking long-term rewards to increased sales abroad. A cost-reduction strategy might require linking them to improved profit margins.

Employers designing long-term incentives thus ignore their firm's strategy at their peril. Compensation experts suggest first defining the strategic context for the executive compensation plan, and then creating the compensation package itself:

1. Define the strategic context for the executive compensation program, including the internal and external issues that face the company, and the firm's business objectives. For example, ask: What are our organization's long-term goals, and how can the compensation structure support them? What defines the organization's work culture—its basic values regarding what people should and should not do—and how will the compensation program mold that culture? What competitive challenges do we face? What are our company's specific business objectives—for example, growth in market share or expansion abroad—and how can the compensation program help push the company in that direction? And how will the executive compensation program fit into the organization's overall pay strategy?[59]

2. Based on your strategic aims, shape each component of the executive compensation package (base salary, short-term incentives, long-term incentives, and benefits and perquisites), and then group the components into a balanced plan that makes sense in terms of these aims.

3. Create a stock option plan that gives the executive compensation package the special character it needs to meet the unique needs of the executives and the company and its strategy.

4. Check the executive compensation plan for compliance with all legal and regulatory requirements and for tax effectiveness.

5. Install a process for reviewing and evaluating the executive compensation plan whenever a major business change occurs.

As part of this process, try to identify the main financial factors that drive the company's business.[60] One expert says, "In many companies, a careful analysis of historical financials shows that well over 90% of economic value change is driven by a few simple items that can be separated out."[61] For example, you may find that about 10 or 15 financial items—pricing, discounts, raw material costs, and net sales, for instance—are the controllable factors that drive the improvements in the value of the company and the value of the shareholders' investment.[62] You should link executives' incentives to these items. More firms today are tying top managers' incentives to *economic value* rather than just to profits. This approach assumes that the managers who play a direct role in managing the firm's major business entities can have a big influence on economic value drivers like expenses, net operating capital, manufacturing costs, and inventories.

Firms are also working to improve supply chain efficiencies. All production and distribution processes are part of a broader supply chain. For example, Dell Computer encourages customers to monitor order status online, since doing so reduces the need for employees answering order status questions. Manufacturers like Ford insist that their suppliers apply six-sigma quality improvement processes, since doing so results in lower supply costs to Ford. Airlines encourage fliers to book their travel online, since this means less need for reservations clerks—and fewer commissions to travel agents.

The problem is, companies often spend millions on supply chain efficiencies, only to find they fail because employees resist the changes. Many firms are therefore using incentives to support these programs. Doing so communicates the importance of the changes to the workforce, and (hopefully) motivates employees to modify how they do things.[63] For example, one incentive program at Sun Microsystems focuses on customer satisfaction metrics. Employees receive incentives based on achieving supply-chain-related improvements in activities like on-time delivery and customer returns. K*Tec electronics established a similar incentive system. Each of the firm's program management teams has a dedicated customer. K*Tec teams are rewarded based on how well they manage supply-chain-related activities such as inventory turnover and capital invested. The programs are mostly for mid- to upper-level managers.

INCENTIVES FOR SALESPEOPLE

Sales compensation plans typically rely heavily on incentives (sales commissions). However, some salespeople get straight salaries, and most receive a combination of salary and commissions.[64]

Salary Plan

Some firms pay some of their salespeople fixed salaries (perhaps with occasional incentives in the form of bonuses, sales contest prizes, and the like).[65] Straight salaries make particular sense when the main job involves prospecting (finding new clients), or when it mostly involves account servicing, such as developing and executing product training programs for a customer's sales force or participating in national and local trade shows.[66] You'll often find jobs like these in industries that sell technical products. This is one reason why the aerospace and transportation equipment industries emphasize sales salary plans.

The straight salary approach has pros and cons. Straight salary makes it simple to switch territories or to reassign salespeople, and it can foster loyalty among the sales staff. Commissions tend to shift the salesperson's emphasis to making the sale rather than to prospecting and cultivating long-term customers. The main disadvantage, of course, is that pay isn't proportionate to results,[67] which can constrict sales and demotivate potentially high-performing salespeople.

Commission Plan

Commission plans pay salespeople for results, and only for results. Under these plans salespeople have the greatest incentive, and there's a tendency to attract high-performing salespeople who see that effort clearly leads to rewards. Sales costs are proportionate to sales rather than fixed, and the company's fixed sales costs are low. It's a plan that's easy to understand and compute.

However, it's not without drawbacks. Salespeople tend to focus on making the sale and on high-volume items, and may neglect nonselling duties like servicing small accounts, cultivating dedicated customers, and pushing hard-to-sell items. Wide variations in income may occur; this can lead to a feeling that the plan is inequitable. In addition, pay is often excessive in boom times and low in recessions. Also keep in mind that sales performance—like any performance—is a product of not just motivation, but of ability too. If the person hasn't the sales skills, then commissions won't produce sales.

◆ **RESEARCH INSIGHT** Research evidence provides further insights into the pros and cons of sales commissions. One study addressed whether commission plans influenced salesperson turnover. One potential drawback of commission-only plans is that working without a financial safety net may induce salespeople to leave. When pay is 100% at risk, as one sales representative put it,

> *If I go on vacation, I lose money. If I'm sick, I lose money. If I'm not willing to drop every-thing on a moment's notice to close with a customer, I lose money. I can't see how anyone could stay in this job for long. It's like a trapeze act and I'm working without a net!*[68]

Participants in this study were 225 field sales representatives from a telecommunications company. About 85% were men, 65% were married; their ages ranged from 22 to 62, and their average age was 39. Twenty-one percent had a bachelor's degree and 3% a master's degree. Median tenure was six months, so about half the employees left by the end of that period.

As it turns out, paying salespersons under maximally contingent reward conditions—in other words, where commissions accounted for 100% of pay—was the situation with by far the highest turnover. Turnover was much lower when salespersons were paid a combination of a base pay plus commissions.[69] These findings suggested that 100% commissions can drive higher sales by focusing strong-willed salespeople on maximizing sales. However, it can also undermine the desire of less strong-willed salespeople to stay. Thus, the effects of a commission plan depend on the salesperson's skills and personality.

A second study further illustrates this. In this study, 154 sales representatives were responsible for contacting and renewing existing members, and identifying and adding new members.[70] Some of the sales reps in this study were more extroverted than others; in other words, they were more sociable, outgoing, talkative, aggressive, energetic, and enthusiastic.[71] One might expect that the extroverted salespeople would generate higher sales than the less extroverted ones, but this was not always the case. In this study, extroversion was positively associated with higher performance (in terms of percentage of existing members renewing their memberships, and the number of new members paying membership fees). But this was only so when the firm explicitly rewarded salespeople for accomplishing these tasks. In other words, being extroverted didn't always lead to higher sales; extroverts only sold more when rewards were contingent on performance. So don't just hire extroverted salespeople; pay them on commission.

Combination Plan

Most companies pay salespeople a combination of salary and commissions, usually with a sizable salary component. Early studies suggested that the most popular salary/commission split was 80% base salary and 20% incentives, with 70/30 and 60/40 splits being the second and third most frequently reported arrangements.[72] These splits have not appeared to change dramatically over the years. For example, one compensation expert recently used a 70% base salary/30% incentive mix as a target; this cushioned the downside risk for the salesperson, while limiting the risk that the upside rewards would get out of hand from the firm's point of view.[73]

Combination plans have pros and cons. They give salespeople a floor to their earnings, let the company specify what services the salary component is for (such as servicing current accounts), and still provide an incentive for superior performance. However, the salary component isn't tied to performance, so the employer is obviously trading away some incentive value. Combination plans also tend to become complicated, and misunderstandings can result.

This might not be a problem with a simple salary plus commission plan, but most plans are not so simple. For example, in a "commission plus drawing account" plan, a salesperson is paid on commissions but can draw on future earnings to get through low sales periods. Similarly, in the "commission plus bonus" plan, the firm pays its salespeople mostly based on commissions. However, they also get a small bonus for directed activities like selling slow-moving items.

An example can help illustrate the complexities of the typical combination plan. In one company, the following three-step formula is applied:

> Step 1: Sales volume up to $18,000 a month. Base salary plus 7% of gross profits plus 0.5% of gross sales.
>
> Step 2: Sales volume from $18,000 to $25,000 a month. Base salary plus 9% of gross profits plus 0.5% of gross sales.
>
> Step 3: Over $25,000 a month. Base salary plus 10% of gross profits plus 0.5% of gross sales.

In all cases, base salary is paid every two weeks, while the earned percentage of gross profits and gross sales is paid monthly.[74]

The sales force also may get various special awards.[75] Oakite Company, for instance, uses several recognition awards to boost sales. A President's Cup is awarded to the top division manager, and there is a VIP Club for the top 105 of the sales force in total dollars sales. Oakite publicizes the VIP Club within the firm, and belonging carries a lot of prestige. Other firms such as Airwick Industries award televisions and Lenox china as special sales awards.

When Metiom, Inc, a New York–based e-commerce infrastructure firm, needed a sales incentive program, it set up one called the "inner circle." After meeting specific sales quotas, the firm's 30 top salespeople and their significant others got a trip to Paradise Island in the Bahamas. The program not only motivated the company's sales force, but had the benefit of encouraging family support for the salesperson's success.[76]

Employers increasingly use the Web to support their sales incentive programs. For example, SalesDriver, in Maynard, Massachusetts, runs Web-based sales-performance-based incentive programs. Firms like these specialize in setting up online sales incentive programs; sales managers just have to make some choices.

For example, SalesDriver can help a company launch a campaign template in a day or less. Using the template, the sales manager can select from a catalog of 1,500 reward items, and award these to sales and marketing reps for meeting quotas for things like lead generation and total sales.[77] The HR.NET feature provides additional Web-based incentives options.

HR.NET

Online Award Programs

Reward programs like Oakite's are increasingly popular, and they're not limited to salespeople. One survey estimates that the corporate incentive market grew from $23 billion in 1996 to about $30 billion in 2000, with offerings ranging from barge trips through Burgundy to Mark Cross pens.

If there's a downside to reward programs, it's that they're expensive to administer. For example, many firms run anniversary awards programs to recognize employees on significant dates like their fifth year with the company. The HR department usually has to choose the merchandise, create the rewards catalog, print and mail the catalog, and monitor everyone's anniversary dates and make sure the employee actually gets his or her award. This can be very time consuming.

▲ **WEBNOTE**
Sales incentive sites like this make it easy for sales managers to establish and deliver sales incentive programs for their salespeople.

www.incentivecity.com

Many firms—including Nortel Networks, Nextel Communications, Levi Strauss & Co., Barnes & Noble, Citibank, and Wal-Mart—now partner with online incentive firms to improve and expedite the whole process. Management consultant Hewitt Associates uses www.bravanta.com to help its managers more easily recognize exceptional employee service with special awards. After just eight days, the number of award requests online exceeded those from both its offline programs, in part because the whole system makes recognizing employees and letting them choose the awards so much easier: "the gifts are good and easy to order from the desktop . . . and we value the ability to update gift choices easily, so the program doesn't become stagnant," says Hewitt's program's administrator.[78] Internet incentive/recognition sites include bravanta.com, premierchoiceaward.com, givenanything.com, incentivecity.com, netcentives.com, salesdriver.com, and kudoz.com. The accompanying Webnote illustrates one of these, incentivecity.com.

There are many reasons to use sites like these to manage your awards program. The sites can offer a much broader range of products than most employers could catalog and offer themselves. And perhaps most important, the whole process is expedited—it's much easier to bestow and deliver the awards. That in turn lets companies like Nortel reinforce superior performance at once, when it will have the biggest impact.[79]

Setting Sales Quotas

Experts traditionally suggested "locking in" sales quotas and incentive plans, on the assumption that frequent changes undermine motivation and morale. But in today's fast-changing business scene, such inflexibility is usually not advisable.

One expert says, "Now that product life cycles are often in the six-month to even six-week range, the traditional approaches to most sales plans cannot accommodate the pace. The sales organization and its emphasis must become more flexible than it has been." Firms therefore tend to review their sales compensation plans and quotas more often.[80]

Setting effective quotas is an art. Questions to ask include: Have we communicated quotas to the sales force within one month of the start of the period? Does the sales force know exactly how its quotas are set? Do you combine bottom-up information (like account forecasts) with top-down requirements (like the company business plan)? Does 60% to 70% of the sales force generally hit their quota? Do high performers hit their targets consistently? Do low performers show improvement over time? Are quotas stable through the performance period? Are returns and debookings reasonably low? And has your firm generally avoided compensation-related lawsuits?[81]

It may seem obvious, but make sure the commission rates let the company pay its bills. There is a tendency to set commission rates informally, without considering how much each sale must contribute to covering expenses. Each salesperson's effort should contribute to covering his or her share of fixed costs and variable costs, and to the company's profit. Fixed costs include the person's salary and benefits, as well as his or her share of office space, utilities, and salaries for support staff and management. Variable costs include telephone charges and travel expenses. In computing the sales commission rates, ensure that what's left over from the sale (after commissions) contributes to profits, too.[82]

An Example: Auto Dealers Commission rates vary by industry, but a look at how auto dealers set their salespersons' commission rates provides some interesting insights into how to set rates to achieve specific aims. Compensation for car salespeople ranges from a high of 100% commission to a small base salary with commission accounting for most of total compensation. Commission is generally based on the net profit on the car when it's delivered to the buyer. This encourages precisely the sorts of behaviors the car dealer wants to encourage. For example, it encourages the salesperson to hold firm on the retail price, and to push "after-sale products" like floor mats, side moldings, undercoating, car alarms, and trunk-mounted CDs. Car dealers also use short-term incentives. For helping sell slow-moving vehicles, the salesperson may be offered a "spiff"—a car dealer term for an extra incentive bonus over commission.[83]

Strategic Sales Incentives

Sales commissions remain popular, but employers increasingly link them to nonvolume-based measures. At Compaq Computer, sales revenue growth accounts for only about half of total sales compensation. Compaq awards the rest of its sales commissions based on what it calls focused sales objectives. These objectives include account profitability as well as nonfinancial measures like finding new applications within existing accounts. Procter & Gamble measures and rewards its salespeople's (which it calls "customer consultants") commissions based on their success in helping customers lower other inventories.[84] At Siebel systems, about 40% of each salesperson's incentive is based on factors like customers' reported satisfaction with service. The firm's vice president of technical services says, "I think our people are better sales reps because of it. There's a lot of value to using this metric as opposed to using only traditional quotas."[85]

INCENTIVES FOR OTHER PROFESSIONALS AND NONMANAGERIAL EMPLOYEES

Professionals—engineers and computer specialists, for instance—and other non-managerial employees also typically receive incentive payments. As mentioned above, these increasingly include stock options. Merit pay is another, more traditional incentive; we'll look at this first.

Merit Pay As an Incentive

merit pay (merit raise)
Any salary increase awarded to an employee based on his or her individual performance.

Merit pay or a **merit raise** is any salary increase the firm awards to an employee based on his or her individual performance. It is different from a bonus in that it usually becomes part of the employee's base salary, whereas a bonus is a one-time payment. Although the term *merit pay* can apply to the incentive raises given to any employee—exempt or nonexempt, office or factory, management or nonmanagement—the term is more often used for white-collar employees and particularly professional, office, and clerical employees. Based on a survey of 341 Fortune 1,000 companies, merit increases for exempt employees averaged about 4.1% for the four years through 2000, and between 3.9% and 4.0% for nonexempt salaried and nonexempt hourly workers.[86]

Merit pay is the subject of much debate.[87] Advocates argue that only pay or other rewards tied directly to performance can motivate improved performance. They contend that the effect of awarding pay raises across the board (without regard to individual merit) may actually detract from performance, by showing employees they'll be rewarded regardless of how they perform. Detractors present good reasons why merit pay can backfire. One is the dubious nature of many firms' appraisal processes: If the appraisals are unfair, so too will be the merit pay you base them on.[88] Similarly, supervisors often tend to minimize differences in employee performance when computing merit raises. They give most employees about the same raise, either because of a reluctance to alienate some employees or because of a desire to give everyone a raise that will at least help them stay even with the cost of living. A third problem is that almost every employee thinks he or she is an above-average performer, so getting a below-average merit increase can be demoralizing.[89]

One study focused on the relationship between performance ratings and merit pay raises for 218 workers in a nuclear waste facility. The researchers found a "very modest relationship between merit pay increase and performance rating."[90] However, while problems like these can undermine a merit pay plan, there seems little doubt that merit pay can improve performance. But you must be sure to conduct the appraisals and allocations fairly and effectively.[91]

Merit Pay Options

Two adaptations of merit pay plans are becoming more popular. One awards merit raises in a lump sum once a year (making them, in effect, short-term bonuses for lower-level workers). The other ties merit awards to both individual and organizational performance.[92] Traditional merit increases are cumulative, but most *lump-sum merit raises* are not. Therefore, the rise in payroll expenses can be significantly slowed. (Traditionally, someone with a salary of $30,000 per year might get a 5% increase. This moves the employee to a new base salary of $31,500. If the employee gets another 5% increase next year, then the new merit increase of 5% is tacked on not just to the $30,000 base salary, but to the extra $1,500 the employee received last year.) Lump-sum merit increases can also be more dramatic motivators than traditional merit pay raises. For example, a 5% lump-sum merit payment to our $30,000 employee is $1,500 cash, as opposed to a traditional weekly merit payout of $29 for 52 weeks.

◀ **TABLE 12-2**
Lump-Sum Award
Determination
Matrix (an example)

The Employee's Performance (Weight = .50)	The Organization's Performance (Weight = 0.50)				
	Outstanding	Excellent	Commendable	Marginal or Acceptable	Unacceptable
Outstanding	1.00	0.90	0.80	0.70	0.00
Excellent	0.90	0.80	0.70	0.60	0.00
Commendable	0.80	0.70	0.60	0.50	0.00
Acceptable	—	—	—	—	—
Unacceptable	—	—	—	—	—

Source: John F. Sullivan, "The Future of Merit Pay Programs." *Compensation and Benefits Review*, May–June 1989, p. 29. *Instructions*. To determine the dollar value of each employee's incentive award. (1) multiply the employee's annual, straight time wage or salary as of June 30 times his or her maximum incentive award and (2) multiply the resultant product times the appropriate percentage figure from this table. For example, if an employee had an annual salary of $20,000 on June 30 and a maximum incentive award of 7% and if her performance and the organization's performance were both "excellent," the employee's award would be $1,120: ($20,000 × 0.07 × 0.80 = $1,120).

Tying lump-sum merit pay to both individual and organizational performance is another option. Table 12-2 presents a sample matrix for doing so. In this example, the company's performance is measured, for instance, by rate of return, or sales divided by payroll costs. Company performance and the employee's performance (using his or her performance appraisal) receive equal weight in computing the merit pay. Here an outstanding performer would receive 70% of his or her maximum lump-sum award even if the organization's performance were marginal. However, employees with unacceptable performance would get no lump-sum awards even in years in which the firm's performance was outstanding. The bonus plan at Discovery Communications is an example. Executive assistants can receive bonuses of up to 10% of their salaries. The boss's evaluation of the assistant's individual performance accounts for 80% of the potential bonus; 10% is based on how the division does, and 10% on how the company as a whole does.[93]

Incentives for Professional Employees

Professional employees are those whose work involves the application of learned knowledge to the solution of the employer's problems. They include lawyers, doctors, economists, and engineers. Professionals reach their positions through prolonged periods of formal study.[94]

Making incentive pay decisions for professional employees can be challenging. For one thing, firms usually pay professionals well anyway; for another, they're already driven—by the desire to produce high-caliber work and receive recognition from colleagues. In some cases, offering financial rewards to people like these may actually diminish their intrinsic motivation—not add to it.[95]

However, that's certainly not to say that professionals don't want financial incentives, particularly those in high-demand jobs like software and systems developers for information technology (IT) firms. A recent survey of 300 IT departments found that 77% were paying bonuses and incentives, including stock options and profit sharing, to IT professionals.[96] Many are also offering benefits that are highly attractive to professionals, including better vacations, more flexible work hours,[97] equipment for home offices,[98] and improved pension plans.[99] Texas Instruments began offering stock option grants to about a third of its engineers when it discovered it was losing about 15% of them to the competition.[100] Several firms, including IBM and Motorola, now award bonuses to employees whose work wins patents for the firms.[101]

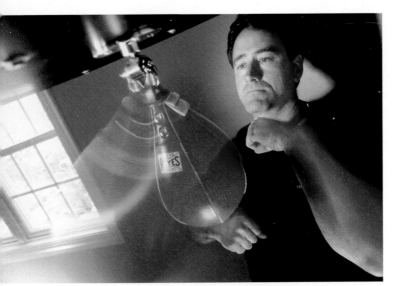

▲ *After a long decline, revenues, net income, and shares all were up recently at software maker PeopleSoft in California. New CEO Craig Conway credits many strategies with making the turnaround possible. But the most important change, according to Conway, was his decision to raise morale and halt employee attrition by raising salaries across the board, repricing stock options, and reducing the employee vesting schedule from four years to two.*

ORGANIZATIONWIDE VARIABLE PAY PLANS

Many employers have incentive plans in which most employees can participate. These variable pay plans include profit sharing, employee stock ownership (ESOP), and Scanlon/gainsharing plans.

Profit-Sharing Plans

Profit-sharing plans (in which all or most employees receive a share of the firm's annual profits) are popular today. American Airlines's employees split $250 million in profit-sharing bonuses,[102] Ford Motor recently introduced a profit-sharing plan for salaried employees,[103] and General Motors increased its profit-sharing payout when profits improved.[104] Yet research on such plans' effectiveness is sketchy. In one early survey, about half the employers believed their profit-sharing plans had been beneficial,[105] but the benefits were not necessarily in terms of increased performance and motivation. Instead, the plans may increase each worker's sense of commitment, participation, and partnership. They may also reduce turnover and encourage

profit-sharing plan
A plan whereby employees share in the company's profits.

employee thrift. One study concludes that there is "ample" evidence that profit-sharing plans boost productivity, but that their effect on profits is insignificant, once you factor in the costs of the plans' payouts.[106]

There are several types of profit-sharing plans. In *cash plans*, the most popular, the firm simply distributes a percentage of profits (usually 15% to 20%) as profit shares to employees at regular intervals. The *Lincoln incentive system*, first instituted at the Lincoln Electric Company of Ohio, is a more complex plan. In one version, employees work on a guaranteed piecework basis, and the firm distributes total annual profits (less taxes, 6% dividends to stockholders, and a reserve for investment) each year among employees based on their merit rating.[107] The Lincoln plan also includes a suggestion system that pays individual workers rewards for savings resulting from their suggestions. The plan has been quite successful.

There are also *deferred profit-sharing plans*: The firm places a predetermined portion of profits in each employee's account under a trustee's supervision. There is a tax advantage here, since income taxes are deferred, often until the employee retires and the money is taxed at a lower rate.

Employee Stock Ownership Plan (ESOP)

employee stock ownership plan (ESOP)
A corporation contributes shares of its own stock to a trust in which additional contributions are made annually. The trust distributes the stock to employees on retirement or separation from service.

Employee stock ownership plans are companywide plans in which a corporation contributes shares of its own stock—or cash to be used to purchase such stock—to a trust established to purchase shares of the firm's stock for employees.[108] The firm generally makes these contributions annually in proportion to total employee compensation, with a limit of 15% of compensation. The trust holds the stock in individual employee accounts, and distributes it to employees upon retirement (or other separation from service), assuming the person has worked long enough to earn ownership of the stock. (Stock options, as discussed earlier in this chapter, go directly to the employees individually to use as they see fit, rather than into a retirement trust.)

ESOPs have several advantages. The company gets a tax deduction equal to the fair market value of the shares that are transferred to the trustee, and can also claim an income tax deduction for dividends paid on ESOP-owned stock.[109] Employees aren't taxed until they receive a distribution from the trust, usually at retirement when their tax rate is lower. The Employee Retirement Income Security Act (ERISA) allows a firm to borrow against employee stock held in trust and then repay the loan in pretax rather than after-tax dollars, another tax incentive for using such plans.[110]

ESOPs can also help the shareholders of closely held corporations (in which, for instance, a family owns virtually all the shares) to diversify their assets by placing some of their own shares of the company's stock into the ESOP trust and purchasing other marketable securities for themselves in their place.[111]

Research suggests that ESOPs do encourage employees to develop a sense of ownership in and commitment to the firm.[112] They do so in part because they provide increased financial incentives, create a new sense of ownership, and help to build teamwork.[113] The following "High-Performance Insight" illustrates how one company "shares the wealth" through companywide bonuses and ESOP plans.

◆ **HIGH-PERFORMANCE INSIGHT** According to management, employees of Thermacore, Inc., of Lancaster, Pennsylvania, are the key to the company's success in transforming itself from a low-volume research and development enterprise to a high-volume production facility and technology leader. Thermacore developed various bonus and employee stock purchase programs, which it feels accounts in part for its success.

The annual employee bonus is one way it lets employees share in the wealth generated by operations during the year. All employees of Thermacore and its parent corporation, DTX, are eligible. The unique aspect of the program is that all employees receive the same amount of bonus regardless of total compensation, seniority, or position in the company.

The bonus pool is based on pre-tax income minus a minimum, threshold guarantee to the stockholders. The guarantee is typically 15% of the firm's equity at the beginning of the year. The income to place in the bonus pool is determined by multiplying company income (less the 15%-of-equity guarantee) by an employee bonus pool rate determined by the board of directors and senior management. Regular employees then receive a full share, and part-time employees receive a share based on the percentage of time worked. One recent year, the bonus pool rate was 12%, and the full bonus share was more than $1,300 per employee.

Thermacore also has a stock ownership plan for all employees. Each year, the stockholders and the board of directors approve a dollar value of stock to offer to employees. For example, the board may decide to make available $100,000 of company stock. No one employee may subscribe for more than $10,000 worth of stock. Thermacore is a private company, so stock trades only within the company. The firm sells shares to the employees at a discount; the company has the right of first refusal should the employee wish to leave the company or sell stock. Employees can pay for the stock in cash at the closing of the subscription period or by payroll deduction.[114]

Scanlon Plan

Few would argue with the fact that the most powerful way of ensuring commitment is to synchronize the organization's goals with those of its employees—to ensure that the two sets of goals overlap, and that by pursuing his or her goals, the worker pursues the employer's goals as well. Experts have proposed many

Scanlon plan
An incentive plan developed in 1937 by Joseph Scanlon and designed to encourage cooperation, involvement, and sharing of benefits.

techniques for attaining this idyllic state, but few are used as widely or successfully as the **Scanlon plan**, an incentive plan developed in 1937 by Joseph Scanlon, a United Steel Workers Union official.[115] It is still popular today.

The Scanlon plan is remarkably progressive, considering that it is now almost 70 years old. As currently implemented, Scanlon plans have the following basic features.[116] The first is Scanlon's *philosophy of cooperation*. This philosophy assumes that managers and workers must rid themselves of the "us" and "them" attitudes that normally inhibit employees from developing a sense of ownership in the company. It substitutes a climate in which everyone cooperates because he or she understands that economic rewards are contingent on cooperation. A pervasive philosophy of cooperation must exist in the firm for the plan to succeed.[117]

A second feature of the plan is what its practitioners call *identity*. This means that to focus employee involvement, the company must clearly articulate its mission or purpose, and employees must understand how the business operates in terms of customers, prices, and costs. *Competence* is a third basic feature. The program today, say three experts, "explicitly recognizes that a Scanlon plan demands a high level of competence from employees at all levels."[118] The plan assumes that hourly employees can perform their jobs competently as well as identify and implement improvements, and that supervisors have leadership skills for the participative management that is crucial to a Scanlon plan.

The fourth feature of the plan is the *involvement system*.[119] This takes the form of two levels of committees—the departmental level and the executive level. Employees present improvement suggestions to the appropriate departmental-level committees, which transmit the valuable ones to the executive-level committee. The latter then decides whether to implement the suggestion.

The fifth element of the plan is the *sharing of benefits formula*. The Scanlon plan assumes that employees should share directly in any extra profits resulting from their cost-cutting suggestions. If a suggestion is implemented and successful, all employees usually share in 75% of the savings. For example, assume that the normal monthly ratio of payroll costs to sales is 50%. (Thus, if sales are $600,000, payroll costs should be $300,000.) Assume the firm implements suggestions that result in payroll costs of $250,000 in a month when sales were $550,000 and payroll costs should have been $275,000 (50% of sales). The savings attributable to these suggestions is $25,000 ($275,000 minus $250,000). Workers would typically share in 75% of this ($18,750), while $6,250 would go to the firm. In practice, the firm sets aside a portion, usually one-quarter of the $18,750, for the months in which labor costs exceed the standard.

The Scanlon plan has been quite successful at reducing costs and fostering a sense of sharing and cooperation among employees. In one study, labor costs dropped by 10% and grievances dropped by half after implementation of such a plan.[120]

There are several conditions required for Scanlon plans' success. They are usually more effective when the number of participants is fewer than 1,000. They are more successful when there are stable product lines and costs, since it is important that the labor costs/sales ratio remain fairly stable. Good supervision and healthy labor relations seem essential. And of course, it is crucial that there be strong commitment to the plan on the part of both workers and management, particularly during the phase-in period.[121]

gainsharing plan
An incentive plan that engages employees in a common effort to achieve productivity objectives and share the gains.

Gainsharing Plans

The Scanlon plan is one early version of what today we call a **gainsharing plan**. Gainsharing is an incentive plan that engages many or all employees in a common effort to achieve a company's productivity objectives, with any resulting cost-savings gains shared among employees and the company.[122] In addition to the Scanlon plan, other types of gainsharing plans include the Rucker and Improshare plans.

The basic difference among these plans is the formula used to determine employee bonuses.[123] For example, the Scanlon formula divides payroll expenses by total sales. The Rucker formula uses sales value minus materials and supplies, all divided into payroll expenses. In a survey of 223 companies with gainsharing plans, 95 had custom-designed plans, and the rest used standardized plans like Scanlon, Rucker, or Improshare.[124]

Implementing a Plan   In general there are eight basic steps in implementing a gainsharing plan:[125]

1. Establish general plan objectives. These might include boosting productivity or lowering costs.
2. Choose specific performance measures. For example, use productivity measures such as labor hours per unit produced, or financial measures like return on net assets to measure employee performance.
3. Decide on a funding formula. What portion of gains will employees receive? In one study, employees received, by formula, an average of 46.7% of incremental gains; the remainder stayed with the company.[126]
4. Decide on a method for dividing and distributing the employees' share of the gains. Standard methods include equal percentage of pay or equal shares; however, some plans also modify awards based on individual performance.
5. Make the disbursement significant enough to get participants' attention and to motivate their behavior. One expert suggests a potential of 4% to 5% of pay and a 70% to 80% chance of achieving the plan's performance objectives as an effective combination.
6. Choose the form of payment. This is usually cash, but occasionally is common stock.
7. Decide how often to pay bonuses. Firms tend to compute financial performance measures for this purpose annually, labor productivity measures quarterly or monthly.
8. Develop the involvement system. The most commonly used systems include steering committees, update meetings, suggestion systems, coordinators, problem-solving teams, department committees, training programs, newsletters, inside auditors, and outside auditors.

As an example, assume a supplier wants to boost quality. Doing so would translate into fewer customer returns, less scrap and rework, and therefore higher profits.[127] Historically, $1 million in output results in $200,000 (2%) scrap, returns, and rework. The company tells its employees that if next month's production results in only 1% scrap, returns, and rework, the 1% saved would be a gain, to be split 50/50 with the workforce, less a small amount for reserve for months in which scrap exceeds 2%. The firm posts awards monthly but allocates them quarterly.[128]

Making the Plan Work   You can do several things to enhance a gainsharing plan's success. Many firms use multiple measures to ensure employees don't ignore important activities. For example, one firm chose seven variables (productivity, cost performance, product damage, customer complaints, shipping errors, safety, and attendance) and set specific goals for each (such as zero lost-time accidents, for safety). It attached specific monthly bonuses to each goal achieved.[129]

Managers must be committed to the plan, since they'll have to set and maintain team goals, foster an atmosphere conducive to team effort and cooperation, and reduce adversarial relationships between management and employees.[130] The financial formula should be simple and should measure and reward performance with a specific set of measurable goals and a clear allocation method. Employee involvement is vital. The partnership between management and employees requires two-way communication, rather than just goal setting and top-down directives.[131]

At-Risk Variable Pay Plans

at-risk variable pay plans
Plans that put some portion of the employee's weekly pay at risk, subject to the firm's meeting its financial goals.

At-risk variable pay plans are essentially plans that put some portion of the employee's weekly pay at risk, subject to the firm's meeting its financial goals. If employees meet or exceed their goals, they earn incentives. If they fail to meet their goals, they forgo some of the pay they would normally have earned.

At one DuPont division, the employee's at-risk pay is a maximum of 6%. This means each employee's base pay will be 94% of his or her counterpart's salary in other (non-at-risk) DuPont divisions.[132] Employees can then match or exceed their counterparts' pay if their department reaches certain predetermined financial goals. Saturn initially designed its at-risk component to be about 20%, but then cut it back to 5%.

The basic idea is to turn employees into committed partners. To the extent that at-risk pay is part of a comprehensive program aimed at turning employees into committed partners—a program stressing trust and respect, extensive communications, and participation and opportunities for advancement—at-risk programs should be successful.

STRATEGIC HR

AmeriSteel's New Incentive Plan

AmeriSteel's top managers knew that designing a new incentive plan for the firm's workforce was central to turning the company around. With four mini steel mills, each with about 250 employees, the firm's whole strategy—to address a three-year trend of losses and declining market share by reorienting the firm to focus on productivity and competitiveness—depended on having an incentive plan that signaled to employees that they had to be productive. They called their new plan Partners in Performance.

But if AmeriSteel employees were to be partners, then all employees from CEO down had to put part of their pay at risk. The new pay plan therefore mandated that base pay was to be reduced 15% across the board immediately. The plan replaced this 15% with a new gainsharing incentive: For every 1% improvement in productivity over 70% of productivity in the plan's initial year, employees would earn .5% of their base pay. Thus, at 100% of that year's productivity, employee compensation would be whole. In addition, employees could earn an additional .5% of their base pay for each 1% improvement over 100%. In effect, this meant that the company was willing to share 33% of the gains from improved productivity with the employees.

To help ensure success, management introduced various support programs. An "open-book management" program let employees continually monitor the firm's performance via computers in the employee lounges. The company trained supervisors to be more communicative. And it set aside 7.5% of the company's stock for nonmanagement employees.

The plan appears to have been a success. The firm began attracting more results-oriented applicants. In the three years following implementation, the firm's production (in millions of tons) rose by about 20%, and profits rose from $22 million to $38 million per year. The HR-based Partners in Performance had helped AmeriSteel achieve its strategic aims.

DEVELOPING MORE EFFECTIVE INCENTIVE PLANS

The idea behind incentive plans is, in some respects, too good to be true. Whether it's Frederick Taylor's or a more modern variety, the basic idea is usually this: Link the employee's rewards with what he or she produces, and so transform the person's thinking from "employee" to "partner." Taylor called this "The great revolution that takes place in the mental attitude of [the management and the workers]" as they both "take their eyes off the division of the surplus—and together turn their attention toward increasing the size of the surplus."[133]

Why Incentive Plans Don't Work

Unfortunately, things often don't work out that way, and experts have proposed many explanations for why they do not. We can summarize their reasoning with the following points:

- *Performance pay can't replace good management.* Performance pay is supposed to motivate workers, but lack of motivation is not always the culprit. Ambiguous instructions, lack of clear goals, inadequate employee selection and training, unavailability of tools, and a hostile workforce (or management) are just a few of the factors that impede performance.
- *You get what you pay for.* Psychologists say that people often put their effort where they know they'll be rewarded. But this also can backfire. An incentive plan that rewards a group based on how many pieces they produce may lead to rushed production and lower quality. A plantwide incentive for reducing accidents may simply reduce the number of reported accidents.
- *"Pay is not a motivator."*[134] Psychologist Frederick Herzberg says that money only buys temporary compliance, and that as soon as you remove the incentive, the motivation disappears. Herzberg says employers should provide adequate financial rewards, and then build other, more effective motivators (like opportunities for achievement and psychological success) into jobs.
- *Rewards punish.* Many view punishment and reward as two sides of the same coin. They say "Do this and you'll get that" is not very different from "Do this or you won't get that."[135]
- *Rewards rupture relationships.* Incentive plans have the potential for encouraging individuals (or individual groups) to pursue financial rewards for themselves. Some performance appraisal systems may then make the situation worse—for instance, by forcing the ranking of employees or groups.
- *Rewards can unduly restrict performance.* One expert says: "Excellence pulls in one direction; rewards pull in another. Tell people that their income will depend on their productivity or performance rating, and they will focus on the numbers. Sometimes they will manipulate the schedule for completing tasks or even engage in patently unethical and illegal behavior."[136]
- *Rewards may undermine responsiveness.* When employees' main focus is on achieving some specific goal like cutting costs, any changes or distractions make achieving that goal harder. Incentive plans can therefore mediate against change and responsiveness.
- *Rewards undermine intrinsic motivation.* There is considerable evidence that contingent financial rewards (incentives) may actually undermine the intrinsic motivation that often results in optimal performance.[137] The argument is that financial incentives undermine the feeling that the person is doing a good job voluntarily.
- *People work for more than money.* As one observer recently put it, "People do work for money, but they work for meaning in their lives. In fact, they work to have fun."

How to Implement Incentive Plans

What can you do to make your incentive plan more effective? Some guidelines follow:

1. *Use common sense.* Sometimes incentive pay doesn't make as much sense. For example: when employees are unable to control quantity or output (such as on machine-paced assembly lines); when delays in the work are frequent and beyond employees' control; or (often) when quality rather than quantity is the main consideration. Therefore, in general, it makes more sense to use an incentive plan when there is a clear relationship between employee effort and quantity or quality of output, the job is standardized, the work flow is regular, delays are few or consistent, and quality is less important than quantity—or, if quality is important, employees can easily measure and control it.[138]

2. *Link the incentive with your strategy.* As at AmeriSteel and IBM, decide how the incentive plan will contribute to implementing the firm's strategy and objectives.

3. *Make sure effort and rewards are directly related.* The incentive plan should reward employees in direct proportion to increased productivity or quality. Employees must also perceive that they can actually do the tasks required. The standard has to be attainable, and you have to provide the necessary tools, equipment, and training.[139]

4. *Make the plan easy for employees to understand.* Employees should be able to calculate their rewards for various levels of effort.

5. *Set effective standards.* Make standards high but reasonable—there should be about a 60% to 70% chance of success. And the goal should be specific—this is much more effective than telling someone to "do your best."

6. *View the standard as a contract with your employees.* Once the plan is working, use caution before decreasing the size of the incentive.[140] Rate cuts have long been the nemesis of incentive plans.[141]

7. *Get employees' support for the plan.* Restrictions by members of the work group can undermine the plan.

8. *Use good measurement systems.* In the case of merit pay, for instance, the process used to appraise performance must be clear and fair if the plan is to be of any use.[142]

9. *Emphasize long-term as well as short-term success.*[143] For example, just paying assembly workers for quantity produced may be shortsighted: Longer-term improvements like those deriving from work-improvement suggestions are often equally important in increasing the firm's value.

10. *Take the corporate culture into consideration.* Compensation experts recommend making the incentive plan consistent with the culture you want to create.[144] For example, a consulting firm had difficulty getting its geographic divisions to share information and refer new business leads to each other. The company instituted a cross-selling commission system. Now employees in one division can earn extra commissions by referring new business to another division better suited for the client. Over time, "this was enough to change the thought process from 'me' to 'we.'"[145]

11. *Adopt a comprehensive, commitment-oriented approach.* From the employees' point of view, incentive plans don't exist in isolation. For example, trying to motivate employees with a new incentive plan when they don't have the skills to do the job, or are demoralized by unfair supervisors or a lack of respect, might well fail. Therefore, it's best to install the program within a framework of HR-related practices that promote employee commitment by making the company a place in which employees want to work and do feel like partners.

HR activities that contribute to building commitment include: clarifying and communicating the goals and mission of the organization; guaranteeing organizational justice—for instance, by having a comprehensive grievance procedure and extensive two-way communications; creating a sense of community by emphasizing teamwork and encouraging employees to interact; supporting employee development, perhaps by emphasizing promotion from within, developmental activities, and career-enhancing activities; and generally committing to "people-first values."[146]

ENTREPRENEURS HR

Incentive Plans in a Small Business

Several other guidelines are especially relevant for entrepreneurs. First, consider the firm's life cycle.[147] Small firms experiencing rapid growth prefer broader-based profit-sharing-type plans to the more complicated individual incentive- or gainsharing-type plans. Profit-sharing plans tend to be simpler and less expensive to implement, and require less planning and administrative paperwork. Small firms' employees also tend to feel more directly tied to the company's profitability than do those in big firms. Similarly, companies in a survival or turn-around situation, or those threatened by takeover, might also opt for less- complicated profit-sharing plans. Managers can then focus on the crisis, rather than on the administrative effort required to design and implement more complicated incentive plans.

The complications are illustrated by a second guideline: remember to include incentive payments in overtime pay calculations.[148] Overtime rates are paid to nonexempt employees based on their previous week's earnings, and unless you structure the incentive bonuses properly, the bonus itself becomes part of the week's wages. It must then be included in base pay when computing any overtime that week.

Certain bonuses are excludable from overtime pay calculations. For example, Christmas and gift bonuses that are not based on hours worked, or are so substantial that employees don't consider them a part of their wages, do not have to be included in overtime pay calculations. Similarly, purely discretionary bonuses in which the employer retains discretion over how much if anything to pay are excludable.

The problem is that many other types of incentive pay must be included. Under the FLSA, bonuses to be included in overtime pay computations include those promised to newly hired employees, those provided in union contracts or other agreements, and those announced to induce employees to work more productively, steadily, rapidly, or efficiently or to induce them to remain with the company. Such bonuses would include individual and group production bonuses, bonuses for quality and accuracy of work, efficiency bonuses, attendance bonuses, length-of-service bonuses, and sales commissions.[149]

Consider the following example: Alison works 45 hours in a particular week at a straight-time rate of $6 an hour. In that week she also earns a production bonus of $18. Her new regular rate for that week becomes $45 \times \$6 = \$270 + \$18 = \$288$, and $288 divided by 45 = $6.40 per hour. Her new hourly rate is therefore $6.40 per hour for that week. Additional half-time pay ($3.20 per hour) is due her for the 5 hours overtime she worked as part of her 45 hours. Her total weekly pay for that week is, therefore, $288 + (5 \times 3.20) = \$304$.

The computation can be even more complicated with gainsharing and other productivity-related bonuses, since the firm usually pays these over intervals longer than a single pay period. Here, you can defer determining the new regular rate for overtime pay calculations until after the bonus is determined. However, at that point you must apportion the bonus over the workweeks in which it was earned. This actually requires employers to go back and recalculate overtime rates for all those weeks retroactively. As you can see, there's an incentive for entrepreneurs to keep their plans simple.

▲ *FedEx's strong emphasis on pay for performance is carried out in a number of programs, including a merit program, Pro Pay, Star/Superstar, profit sharing, Bravo Zulu Vouchers, and Golden Falcon Awards.*

Incentive Plans in Practice

In practice, most companies have several incentive plans, including individual performance awards, team awards, and gainsharing plans. Based on this sample of 1,244 companies, about 41% have individual performance awards, 25% have team awards, and 19% have gainsharing plans. An example of a comprehensive compensation plan containing a variety of incentive awards is presented in the following High-Performance feature.

◆ **HIGH-PERFORMANCE INSIGHT** FedEx's pay plan illustrates how progressive firms use innovative incentive plans to boost quality and productivity.[150] FedEx uses quarterly pay reviews and periodic national and local salary surveys to maintain competitive salary ranges. However, there is also a strong emphasis on pay for performance. As one manager put it, "We are convinced people want to see a relationship between performance and reward. . . . I think people want to know that when they knock themselves out to reach their part of our 100% customer satisfaction goal, their efforts will not go unnoticed."[151] Federal Express pay-for-performance plans include the following:

■ Merit program. All salaried employees receive merit salary increases based on their individual performance. Many hourly employees also now receive merit increases rather than automatic step progression increases to recognize individual performance.[152]

■ Pro Pay. Many hourly FedEx employees can receive lump-sum merit bonuses once they reach the top of their pay range. An employee is only eligible for Pro Pay if he or she has been at the top of his or her pay range for a specified period of time (normally 6 months) and with an above-average performance review.

■ Star/Superstar Program. Supervisors can nominate salaried employees with a specified performance rating for a Star or Superstar lump-sum bonus. Stars represent up to the top 10% of performers in each division, whereas Superstars represent up to the top 1% of performers in each division.

■ Proft sharing. FedEx's profit-sharing plan distributes profits based on the overall profit of the corporation. The board of directors annually sets the amount paid, based on pretax profits. Payments to the plan can be in the form of stock, cash, or both. FedEx designed the plan to integrate with the firm's pension and savings plans to provide a comprehensive retirement program.

■ MBO/MIC and PBO/PIC Programs. The Management Incentive Compensation (MIC) and Professional Incentive Compensation (PIC) Programs generally reward managers and professionals for achievement of divisional and corporate profit goals.[153] The bonuses are tied to individual managers' or professionals' attainment of people-, service-, or profit-related goals. For a regional sales manager, a "people" goal could be an improvement in the person's leadership index score on the firm's annual feedback action survey.[154]

■ Bravo Zulu Voucher Program. The Bravo Zulu Voucher Program allows managers to provide immediate rewards to employees for outstanding performance. (*Bravo Zulu* is a title borrowed from the U.S. Navy's semaphore signal for "well done.") Bravo Zulu vouchers can be in the form of a check or some other reward (such as dinner vouchers or theater tickets). It's estimated that more than 150,000 times a year, a FedEx manager presents an employee with one of these awards, which average about $50.[155]

■ Golden Falcon Award. FedEx gives the Golden Falcon Award to permanent employees who demonstrate service to customers that is above the call of duty.

Unsolicited internal or external customer letters citing the candidate's outstanding performance usually trigger the employee's nomination. The firm's Golden Falcon committee reviews the candidates, and the chief operating officer makes the final selection. They receive a Golden Falcon lapel pin and shares of FedEx common stock.

With the exception of the merit program, all FedEx pay-for-performance programs are lump-sum payments. In other words, FedEx pays Pro Pay, Star/Superstar, profit sharing, MBO/MIC, PBO/PIC, Bravo Zulu, and Golden Falcon Awards as one-time lump-sum awards, separate from base pay. They all let the company reward outstanding performance without permanently increasing its fixed payroll costs. The variability also reflects changes in business conditions and allows FedEx to react to adverse economic conditions while maintaining its full-employment policy.

We invite you to visit **www.prenhall.com/dessler** on the Prentice Hall Web site for our online study guide, Internet exercises, current events, links to related Web sites, and more.

Summary

1. The scientific use of financial incentives can be traced back to Frederick Taylor. Although such incentives became somewhat less popular during the middle of the twentieth century, most writers today agree that they can be quite effective.
2. Piecework, where a worker is paid a piece rate for each unit he or she produces, is the oldest type of incentive plan. With a straight piecework plan, workers are paid on the basis of the number of units produced. With a guaranteed piecework plan, each worker receives his or her base rate (such as the minimum wage) regardless of how many units he or she produces.
3. Other useful incentive plans for operations personnel include the standard hour plan and group incentive plans. The former rewards workers by a percent premium that equals the percent by which their performance is above standard. Group incentive plans are useful where the workers' jobs are highly interrelated.
4. Most sales personnel are paid on some type of salary plus commission (incentive) basis. Management employees are often paid according to a bonus formula that ties the bonus to, for example, increased sales. Stock options are one of the most popular executive incentive plans.
5. Profit sharing and the Scanlon plan are examples of organizationwide incentive plans. Gainsharing and merit plans are two other popular plans. The problem with such plans is that the link between a person's efforts and rewards is sometimes unclear. On the other hand, such plans may contribute to developing a sense of commitment among employees.
6. Incentive plans work best when units of output are easily measured, when employees can control output, when the effort—reward relationship is clear, when work delays are under employees' control, when quality is not paramount, and when the organization must know precise labor costs anyway (to stay competitive).

Tying It All Together

Chapters 11 and 12 focused on two main components of employees' compensation—base salary and performance-based incentives. In Chapter 13 we turn to the third component of most employees' compensation—benefits.

1. Compare and contrast six types of incentive plans.
2. Explain five reasons why incentive plans fail.
3. Describe the nature of some important management incentives.
4. When and why would you pay a salesperson a salary and commission combined?
5. What is merit pay? Do you think it's a good idea to award employees merit raises? Why or why not?
6. In this chapter, we listed a number of reasons experts give for not instituting a pay-for-performance plan (such as "rewards punish"). Do you think these points (or any of them) are valid? Why or why not?
7. What is a Scanlon plan? Based on what you've read in this book so far, what features of a commitment-building program does the Scanlon plan include?
8. Give four examples of when you would suggest using team or group incentive programs rather than individual incentive programs.

1. Working individually or in groups, develop an incentive plan for the following positions: chemical engineer, plant manager, used-car salesperson. What factors did you have to consider in reaching your conclusions?
2. A state university system in the Southeast recently instituted a "Teacher Incentive Program" (TIP) for its faculty. Basically, faculty committees within each university's colleges were told to award $5,000 raises (not bonuses) to about 40% of their faculty members based on how good a job they did teaching undergraduates, and how many they taught per year. What are the potential advantages and pitfalls of such an incentive program? How well do you think it was accepted by the faculty? Do you think it had the desired effect?

EXPERIENTIAL EXERCISE

Purpose: The purpose of this exercise is to give you practice developing an incentive plan.

Required Understanding: Be thoroughly familiar with this chapter, and read the following:

Express Automotive, an automobile megadealership with over 600 employees that represents 22 brands, has just received a very discouraging set of survey results. It seems customer satisfaction scores have fallen for the ninth straight quarter. Customer complaints include:

It was hard to get prompt feedback from mechanics by phone.

Salespeople often did not return phone calls.

The finance people seemed "pushy."

New cars were often not properly cleaned or had minor items that needed immediate repair or adjustment.

Cars often had to be returned to have repair work redone.

The table on page 361 describes Express Automotive's current compensation system.

How to Set Up the Exercise/Instructions: Divide the class into groups of 5–6 students. Assign one or more groups to each of the 5 teams in column one. Each group should analyze the compensation package for its team. Each group should be able to identify the ways in which the current compensation plan (1) helps company performance and/or (2) impedes company performance. Once the groups have completed their analysis, discuss the following questions as a class:

1. In what ways might your team's compensation plan contribute to the customer service problems?
2. Would you recommend a team incentive plan within each of the five teams and an incentive plan based on the overall customer service of Express Automotive? If so, how would you structure the two different incentive plans?
3. What recommendations would you make to improve the compensation system in a way that would likely improve customer satisfaction?

Express Compensation System

Team	Responsibility	Current Compensation Method
1. Sales force	Persuade buyer to purchase a car.	Very small salary (minimum wage) with commissions. Commission rate increases with every 20 cars sold per month.
2. Finance office	Help close the sale; persuade customer to use company finance plan.	Salary, plus bonus for each $10,000 financed with the company.
3. Detailing	Inspect cars delivered from factory, clean, and make minor adjustments.	Piecework paid on the number of cars detailed per day.
4. Mechanics	Provide factory warranty service, maintenance and repair.	Small hourly wage, plus bonus based on (1) number of cars completed per day and (2) finishing each car faster than the standard estimated time to repair.
5. Receptionists/phone service personnel	Primary liaison between customer and sales force, finance, and mechanics.	Minimum wage.

APPLICATION CASE *Bringing the Team Concept into Compensation—or Not*

One of the first things Sandy Caldwell wanted to do in his new position at Hathaway Manufacturing was improve productivity through teamwork at every level of the firm. As the new human resource manager for the suburban plant, Sandy set out to change the culture to accommodate the team-based approach he had become so enthusiastic about in his most recent position.

Sandy started by installing the concept of team management at the highest level, to oversee the operations of the entire plant. The new management team consisted of manufacturing, distribution, planning, technical, and human resource executives. Together they developed a new vision for the 500-employee facility, which they expressed in the simple phrase "Excellence Together." They drafted a new mission statement for the firm that focused on becoming customer driven and team based, and that called upon employees to raise their level of commitment and begin acting as "owners" of the firm.

The next step was to convey the team message to employees throughout the company. The communication process went surprisingly well, and Sandy was happy to see his idea of a "workforce of owners" begin to take shape. Teams trained together, developed production plans together, and embraced the technique of 360-degree feed-back, in which an employee's performance evaluation is obtained from supervisors, subordinates, peers, and internal or external customers. Performance and morale improved, and productivity began to tick upward. The company even sponsored occasional celebrations to reward team achievements, and the team structure seemed firmly in place.

Sandy decided to change one more thing. Hathaway's long-standing policy had been to give all employees the same annual pay increase. But Sandy felt that in the new team environment, outstanding performance should be the criterion for pay raises. After consulting with CEO Regina Cioffi, Sandy sent a memo to all employees announcing the change to team-based pay for performance.

The reaction was immediate and 100% negative. None of the employees was happy with the change, and foremost among their complaints two stood out. First, because the 360-degree feedback system made everyone responsible in part for someone else's performance evaluation, no one was comfortable with the idea that pay raises would be linked to peer input. Second, there was a widespread perception that the way the change was decided upon, and the way it was announced, put the firm's commitment to team effort in doubt. Simply put, employees felt left out of the decision process.

Sandy and Regina arranged a meeting for early the next morning. Sitting in her office over their coffee, they began a painful debate. Should the new policy be retracted as quickly as it was adopted, or should it be allowed to stand?

Questions

1. Does the pay-for-performance plan seem like a good idea? Why or why not?
2. What advice would you give Regina and Sandy as they consider their decision?

3. What mistakes did they make in adopting and communicating the new salary plan? How might Sandy have approached this major compensation change a little differently?
4. Assuming the new pay plan were eventually accepted, how would you address the fact that in the new performance evaluation system, employees' input affects their peers' pay levels?

Note: The incident in this case is based on an actual event at Frito-Lay's Kirkwood, New York, plant, as reported in C. James Novak, "Proceed with Caution When Paying Teams," *HR Magazine*, April 1997, p. 73.

CONTINUING CASE: LearnInMotion.com *The Incentive Plan*

Of all its HR programs, those relating to pay for performance and incentives are LearnInMotion.com's most fully developed. For one thing, the venture capital firm that funded it was very explicit about reserving at least 10% of the company's stock for employee incentives.

The agreement with the venture capital firm also included very explicit terms and conditions regarding LearnInMotion's stock option plan. The venture fund agreement included among its 500 or so pages the specific written agreement that LearnInMotion.com would have to send to each of its employees, laying out the details of the company's stock option plan. While there was some flexibility, the stock option plan details came down, in a nutshell, to this: (1) Employees would get stock options (the right to buy shares of LearnInMotion.com stock) at a price equal to 15% less than the venture capital fund paid for those shares when it funded LearnInMotion.com; (2) the shares will have a vesting schedule of 36 months, with one-third of the shares vesting once the employee has completed 12 full months of employment with the company, and one-third vesting upon successful completion of each of the following two full 12 months of employment; (3) if an employee leaves the company for any reason prior to his or her first full 12 months with the firm, the person is eligible for no stock options; (4) if the person has stock options and leaves the firm for any reason, he or she must exercise the options within 90 days of the date of leaving the firm, or lose the right to exercise them.

The actual number of options an employee gets depends on the person's bargaining power and on how much Jennifer and Mel think the person brings to the company: The options granted generally ranged from options to buy 10,000 shares for some employees up to 50,000 shares for other employees, but this has not raised any questions to date. When a new employee signs on, he or she receives a letter of offer. This provides minimal details regarding the option plan; after the person has completed the 90-day introductory period, he or she receives the five-page document describing the stock option plan, which Jennifer or Mel, as well as the employee, signs.

Beyond that, the only incentive plan is the one for the two salespeople. In addition to their respective salaries, both salespeople receive about 20% of any sales they bring in, whether those sales are from advertising banners or course listing fees. It's not clear to Jennifer and Mel whether this incentive is effective. Each salesperson gets a base salary regardless of what he or she sells (one gets about $50,000, the other about $35,000). However, sales have simply not come up to the levels anticipated. Jennifer and Mel are not sure why. It could be that Internet advertising dried up after March 2000. It could be that their own business model is no good, and there's not enough demand for their company's services. They may be charging too much or too little. It could be that the salespeople can't do the job due to inadequate skills or inadequate training. Or, of course, it could be the incentive plan. ("Or it could be all of the above," as Mel somewhat dejectedly said late one Friday evening.) They want to try to figure out what the problem is. They want you, their management consultants, to help them figure out what to do. Here's what they want you to do for them.

Questions and Assignments

1. Up to this point we've awarded only a tiny fraction of the total stock options available for distribution. Should we give anyone or everyone additional options? Why or why not?
2. Should we put other employees on a pay-for-performance plan that somehow links their monthly or yearly pay to how well the company is doing sales-wise? Why or why not? If so, how should we do it?
3. Is there another incentive plan you think would work better for the salespeople? What is it?
4. On the whole, what do you think the sales problem is?

Chapter 13

Benefits and Services

After studying this chapter, you should be able to:

- Name and define each of the main pay for time not worked benefits.
- Describe each of the main insurance benefits.
- Discuss the main retirement benefits.
- Outline the main employees services benefits.
- Explain the main flexible benefit programs.

STRATEGIC OVERVIEW Ohio-based Patio Enclosures, Inc., is one of America's largest custom manufacturers and installers of quality sunrooms and solariums, and it had a problem. With 41 locations and more than 750 employees, the firm's success depended on its ability to attract and keep skilled trades employees. But in 1998, Patio found itself with 40% turnover and a tightening labor market. As a result, it lost an estimated $5.5 million in sales—about 7% of total sales—because it couldn't hire and keep enough good employees. Management knew such problems "could potentially hurt the Company's image for quality and integrity"—and thus undermine its competitive strategy.[1] Management therefore decided to revamp the compensation and benefits plans. But what exactly should the company do?

The previous chapter, Pay for Performance and Financial Incentives, explained how to use financial incentives to motivate employees. The main purpose of this chapter is to improve your ability to weigh the pros and cons of various employee benefit plans. We discuss four main types of plans: supplemental pay benefits (such as sick leave and vacation pay); insurance benefits (such as workers' compensation); retirement benefits (such as pensions); and employee services (such as child care facilities). We'll see that employees' preferences for various benefit plans differ, and that it's therefore useful to individualize benefits packages. This chapter completes our discussion of employee compensation and benefits. The next chapter, Labor Relations and Collective Bargaining, starts a new part of this book, and focuses on another important HR task, labor and management relations.

THE BENEFITS PICTURE TODAY

benefits
Indirect financial and
nonfinancial payments
employees receive for
continuing their employment
with the company.

"What are your benefits?" is the first question many applicants ask. **Benefits**—indirect financial and nonfinancial payments employees receive for continuing their employment with the company—are an important part of just about every employee's compensation.[2] They include things like health and life insurance, pensions, time off with pay, and child care facilities.

Benefits are a major expense for most employers. After almost a decade of little or no growth, private sector employers' benefit costs jumped 3.5% recently, possibly indicating a return to the days when such costs rose rapidly. Benefits as a percentage of payroll are about 41% today. That translates to around $15,000 in total annual benefits per employee, or close to $7 per payroll hour. Payments for time not worked represent the biggest chunk of benefits payments, followed by legally required payments for unemployment compensation, retirement plan payments, insurance payments, and severance pay.[3]

Most full-time employees in the United States receive benefits.[4] In one survey of about 33 million full-time employees, roughly 89% received paid holidays, 96% got paid vacations, and 77% received employer-provided medical coverage. Similarly, 80% of employees benefit from some type of employer-supported retirement plan, and about 87% receive life insurance benefits.

In developing benefits plans, employers must address a number of policy issues. These include: what benefits to offer; who receives coverage; whether to include retirees in the plan; whether to deny benefits to employees during initial "probationary" periods; how to finance benefits; the degree of employee choice in determining benefits; cost-containment procedures; and how to communicate benefits options to employees.[5]

There are many benefits and various ways to classify them. We will classify them as (1) pay for time not worked, (2) insurance benefits, (3) retirement benefits, and (4) services. We start our discussion with pay for time not worked.

PAY FOR TIME NOT WORKED

supplemental pay benefits
Benefits for time not worked
such as unemployment
insurance, vacation and
holiday pay, and sick pay.

Pay for time not worked—also called **supplemental pay benefits**—is the 1,000-pound gorilla of most benefits plans. It is generally an employer's most costly benefit because of the large amount of time off that many employees receive. According to a new U.S. Chamber of Commerce annual survey, paid time off was the most costly company benefit in 1999, at 30% of total benefits; medical benefits (26%) were the second most expensive benefit.[6] Common time-off-with-pay periods include holidays, vacations, jury duty, funeral leave, military duty, personal days, sick leave, sabbatical leave, maternity leave, and unemployment insurance payments for laid-off or terminated employees.

Unemployment Insurance

unemployment insurance
Provides benefits if a person is
unable to work through some
fault other than his or her own.

All states have **unemployment insurance** or compensation acts. These provide for benefits if a person is unable to work through no fault of his or her own. The benefits derive from a tax on employers that can range from 0.1% to 5% of taxable payroll in most states. An employer's unemployment tax rate reflects its rate of personnel terminations. States have their own unemployment laws, but they all follow federal guidelines.

Firms aren't required to pay everyone they dismiss unemployment benefits—only those released through no fault of their own. Thus, strictly speaking, a worker fired for chronic lateness can't legitimately claim benefits. But many managers take a lackadaisical attitude toward protecting their employers against unwarranted claims. Employers therefore spend thousands of dollars per year on unemployment taxes that would not be necessary if they protected themselves.

Following the procedures listed in Table 13-1 can help protect the employer. Determine whether you could answer yes to questions such as, "Do you tell employees who to call when they're late?" Or "Do you have a rule that three days' absence without calling is reason for automatic discharge?" Establishing and following rules in these areas should enable you to better demonstrate that a dismissal was a result of the person's inadequate performance rather than lack of work or some other cause beyond his or her control.

Vacations and Holidays

The number of paid employee vacation days varies considerably from employer to employer. In the United States, the average is about 10 days per year. However, even for the same employer, long-term employees traditionally get more vacation days. Thus, a typical U.S. company policy might call for:

1. One week after 6 months to 1 year of service;
2. Two weeks after 1 to 5 years of service;
3. Three weeks after 5 to 10 years of service;
4. Four weeks after 15 to 25 years of service; and
5. Five weeks after 25 years of service.[7]

The average number of annual vacation days is generally greater in industrialized countries outside the United States. For example, vacation allowances vary from 6 days in Mexico to 10 days in Japan, 25 in Sweden, 25 in France, and 33 in Denmark. (On the other hand, Denmark, France, and several other European countries also have six-day workweeks.)

In the United States, the number of paid holidays also varies considerably from employer to employer, from a minimum of about 5 days to 13 or more. The most common paid holidays include New Year's Day, Memorial Day, Independence Day, Labor Day, Thanksgiving Day, and Christmas Day. Other common holidays include Martin Luther King Jr. Day, Good Friday, Presidents' Day, Veterans Day, the Friday after Thanksgiving, the day before Christmas Day, and the day before New Year's Day.[8]

Firms have to address several holiday- and vacation-related policy issues. They must decide, of course, how many days off employees will get, and what (if any) the paid holidays will be. Other policy decisions include: Will employees get their regular base pay while on vacation, or vacation pay based on average earnings (which may include overtime)? Will employees get paid for accrued vacation time if they leave before taking their vacations? Will we pay employees for a holiday if they don't come to work the day before and the day after the holiday? And, should we pay some premium—such as time and a half—when employees must work on holidays? Wage surveys and Web sites like hrtools.com (see Webnote) provide sample policies for inclusion in the firm's employee manual.

Vacation/holiday benefits are becoming very competitive, particularly in the high-tech industry. For example, Microsoft recently confirmed that it was granting some executives and software engineers unlimited vacation time, a move that one recruiting firm said could "fundamentally change the landscape of benefits" in the high-tech industry.[9]

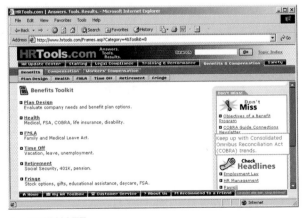

▲ **WEBNOTE**

Sites like hrtools.com make it easy for employers to formulate benefits policies.

www.hrtools.com

▶ **TABLE 13-1**
An Unemployment
Insurance Cost-
Control Checklist

Cause—Do You . . .	Yes	No	Sometimes
Lateness			
1. Tell employees whom to call when late	___	___	___
2. Keep documented history of lateness and warning notices	___	___	___
3. Suspend chronically late employees before discharging them	___	___	___
Absenteeism			
1. Tell employees whom to call when absent	___	___	___
2. Rule that three days' absence without calling in is reason for automatic discharge	___	___	___
3. Keep documented history of absence and warning notices	___	___	___
4. Request doctor's note on return to work	___	___	___
Illness			
1. Keep job open, if possible	___	___	___
2. Offer leave of absence	___	___	___
3. Request doctor's note on return to work	___	___	___
Pregnancy			
1. Follow EEOC ruling, "no discharge"	___	___	___
2. Request doctor's note indicating how long employee may work	___	___	___
3. Change jobs within company when practical	___	___	___
4. Offer maternity leave	___	___	___
Leave of Absence			
1. Make written approval mandatory	___	___	___
2. Stipulate date for return to work	___	___	___
3. Offer position at end of leave	___	___	___
Leave Job Voluntarily			
1. Conduct exit interview	___	___	___
2. Obtain a signed resignation statement	___	___	___
3. Mail job abandonment letter	___	___	___
4. Mail job review questionnaire three to six months after separation	___	___	___
Layoff			
1. Hire employees with established "benefit year" if you anticipate layoffs	___	___	___
2. Keep employees on when the cost to replace them would more than offset paying their salary	___	___	___
3. Transfer employees to different departments	___	___	___
4. Have a flexible workweek that reflects high and low periods of productivity	___	___	___
5. Temporarily lay off employees for one week during slack periods	___	___	___
6. Attempt to find temporary or part-time jobs for laid-off employees	___	___	___

Cause—Do You . . .	Yes	No	Sometimes	◀ **TABLE 13-1** (Continued)

Job Refusal

1. Issue a formal notice to employees collecting benefits to return to work __ __ __
2. Require new employees to stipulate in writing their availability to work overtime, night shifts, etc. __ __ __

Not Qualified

1. Set probationary periods to evaluate new employees __ __ __
2. Conduct follow-up interviews one to two months after hire __ __ __

Deliberate Unsatisfactory Performance

1. Document all instances, recording when and how employees did not meet job requirements __ __ __
2. Require supervisors to document the steps taken to remedy the situation __ __ __
3. Require supervisors to document employee's refusal of advice and direction __ __ __

Violation of Company Rule

1. Make sure all policies and rules of conduct are understood by all employees __ __ __
2. Require all employees to sign a statement acknowledging acceptance of these rules __ __ __
3. Meet with employee and fill out documented warning notice __ __ __
4. Discharge at the time violation occurs, or suspend __ __ __

Wrong Benefit Charges

1. Check state charge statement for
   (a) correct employee __ __ __
   (b) correct benefit amount __ __ __
   (c) correct period of liability __ __ __

Claim Handling

1. Assign a claims supervisor or central office to process all separation information __ __ __
2. File the protest against a former employee's claim on time (usually within 10 days) __ __ __
3. Know your local unemployment insurance official __ __ __
4. Use proper terminology on claim form and attach documented evidence regarding separation __ __ __
5. Attend hearings and appeal unwarranted claims __ __ __
6. Conduct availability checks and rehire employees collecting benefits __ __ __
7. Check every claim against the individual's personnel file __ __ __

Cause—Do You . . .	Yes	No	Sometimes
Administration			
1. Have a staff member who knows unemployment insurance laws and who			
(a) works with the personnel department to establish proper use of policies and procedures	___	___	___
(b) anticipates and reports costly turnover trends	___	___	___
(c) successfully protests unwarranted claims and charges for unemployment benefits	___	___	___
2. Routinely conduct exit interviews to produce information for protesting unemployment claims	___	___	___
3. Audit the annual benefits charges statement to find errors	___	___	___
Communication			
1. Hold periodic workshops with supervisors to review procedures and support effort to reduce turnover costs	___	___	___
2. Immediately investigate who or what is responsible for costly errors and why	___	___	___
Management Reports			
1. Identify turnover problems as they occur by			
(a) location	___	___	___
(b) department	___	___	___
(c) classification of employee	___	___	___
2. Evaluate the effectiveness of current policies and procedures used to			
(a) recruit	___	___	___
(b) select	___	___	___
(c) train	___	___	___
(d) supervise	___	___	___
(e) separate	___	___	___
3. Help create policies and procedures for			
(a) less costly layoffs	___	___	___
(b) increased survival rate	___	___	___
(c) retention of employees	___	___	___

Source: Adapted and updated from the January 1976 issue of *Personnel Administrator*. Copyright 1976, the American Society for Personnel Administration.

Sick Leave

sick leave
Provides pay to an employee when he or she is out of work because of illness.

Sick leave provides pay to employees when they're out of work due to illness. Most sick leave policies grant full pay for a specified number of sick days—usually up to about 12 per year. The sick days usually accumulate at the rate of, say, one day per month of service.

Sick leave pay causes difficulty for many employers. The problem is that while many employees use their sick days only when they are legitimately sick, others use sick leave as extensions to vacations, whether they are sick or not. In one survey, for instance, personal illnesses accounted for only about 45% of unscheduled sick leave absences. Family issues (27%), personal needs (13%), a mentality of "entitlement" (9%), and stress (6%) were other reasons cited.[10] While the figure varies considerably by size of firm, unscheduled absenteeism for all employers averages about 1.6% of all scheduled work hours. Thus a company with 10 employees and a 40-hour workweek might expect to have employees calling in with unscheduled absences at the rate of about .016 × 400 or 6.4 hours per week.[11]

Employers have tried several tactics to reduce the problem. Some now repurchase unused sick leave at the end of the year by paying their employees a daily equivalent sum for each sick leave day not used. The drawback is that the policy can encourage legitimately sick employees to come to work despite their illness.[12] Others have experimented with holding monthly lotteries in which only employees with perfect monthly attendance are eligible for a cash prize. Marriott has a program called BeneTrade through which employees can trade the value of some sick days for other benefits. Others aggressively investigate all absences, for instance, by calling the absent employees at their homes when they are out sick.

A leave bank of paid time off (PTO) is another option; it basically gives employees a total figure for all annual time off.[13] For example, one hospital previously granted new employees 25 days off per year (10 vacation days, 3 personal days, and 12 sick days). Employees used, on average, 5 of those 12 sick days (as well as all vacations and personal days).[14] The new PTO policy allowed new employees to accrue 18 PTO days to use as they saw fit. ("Catastrophic leaves"— defined as short-term illnesses causing absences for more than five consecutive workdays, as well as special absences like jury duty and bereavement leave—were handled with separate accounts.) The new plan reportedly resulted in substantial cash savings, including almost $400,000 over three years in lower overtime, and $350,000 in reduced temporary help.

Parental Leave and the Family and Medical Leave Act

Parental leave is an important benefit. About half of workers today are women, and about 80% will become pregnant during their work lives.[15] Furthermore, many women and men are heads of single-parent households. Partly as a response, former president Clinton signed the Family and Medical Leave Act of 1993 (FMLA). Among its provisions, the law stipulates that:

1. Private employers of 50 or more employees must provide eligible employees up to 12 weeks of unpaid leave for their own serious illness, the birth or adoption of a child, or the care of a seriously ill child, spouse, or parent.
2. Employers may require employees to take any unused paid sick leave or annual leave as part of the 12-week leave provided in the law.
3. Employees taking leave are entitled to receive health benefits while they are on unpaid leave, under the same terms and conditions as when they were on the job.
4. Employers must guarantee employees the right to return to their previous or equivalent position with no loss of benefits at the end of the leave; however, the law provides a limited exception from this provision to certain highly paid employees.

Some employers have found complying with this act somewhat onerous. "We have found that basically any illness is now covered by the law," said one benefits director. Another contends that her company can no longer "impose any discipline—even the downgrading of attendance ratings—for absences due to any cause covered by the law."[16] Employees also seem to be surprisingly aware of their rights under the act, with over half the complaints filed with the Department of Labor's Wage and Hour Division in some recent years stemming from the act.[17] And courts have found supervisors (not just employers) liable under the act for improperly preventing workers from exercising their FMLA rights.[18]

Family and Medical Leave Act leaves are usually unpaid, but they're not cost-less to the employer. One study concluded that the costs associated with recruiting new temporary replacement workers, training them, and compensating for their lower productivity could represent a significant expense over and above what employers would normally pay full-time employees.[19] However, about 77% of employers in a recent survey experienced no significant FMLA-related effects on business productivity, although this was down from 86% in 1995.[20] (Find out more about the FMLA at www.dol.gov/elaws.)

Employers therefore need clear procedures for leaves of absence (including those awarded under the Family and Medical Leave Act); a form (as in Figure 13-1) should be the centerpiece of any such procedure. In general, no employee should be given a leave until it's clear what the leave is for. If the leave is for medical or family reasons, the employer should obtain medical certification from the attending physician or medical practitioner. A form like this also places on record the employee's expected return date, and the fact that without an authorized extension, the firm may terminate his or her employment. One employment lawyer says employers should "kind of bend over backward" when deciding if an employee is eligible for leave based on an FMLA situation, and not be too abrupt in turning the person down.[21] However employers can require independent medical assessments before approving paid FMLA disability leaves.[22]

Severance Pay

severance pay
A one-time payment some employers provide when terminating an employee.

Many employers provide **severance pay**—a one-time payment when terminating an employee. Severance pay makes sense on several grounds. It is a humanitarian gesture, and good public relations. In addition, most managers expect employees to give them at least one or two weeks' notice if they plan to quit; it therefore seems appropriate to provide at least one or two weeks' severance pay if an employee is being dismissed. Avoiding litigation from disgruntled former employees is another reason for severance pay. And the Worker Adjustment and Retraining Notification ("plant closing") Act requires covered employers to give employees 60 days' written notice (but not severance pay) of plant closures or mass layoffs.

For whatever reason, severance pay is increasingly common. In one survey of 3,000 HR managers, 82% of responding organizations (ranging from 66% for very small firms to over 90% for larger firms) reported having a severance policy.[23] The reason for the dismissal affects whether the employee gets severance pay. For example, about 95% of employees dismissed due to downsizings got severance pay, while only about a third of employers offered severance in cases of termination for poor performance. About half the employees receiving severance pay get lump-sum amounts; the other half receive salary continuation for a time. The average maximum severance is 39 weeks for executives and about 30 weeks for other downsized employees.[24] Severance pay at the rate of one week of severance pay for each year of service is the policy at about half the firms responding to another survey.[25]

Supplemental Unemployment Benefits

supplemental unemployment benefits
Provide for a "guaranteed annual income" in certain industries where employers must shut down to change machinery or due to reduced work. These benefits are paid by the company and supplement unemployment benefits.

In some industries, such as automaking, shutdowns to reduce inventories or change machinery are common, and laid-off or furloughed employees must depend on unemployment insurance. Some companies pay **supplemental unemployment benefits**. As the name implies, these supplement the employee's unemployment compensation, and help the person maintain his or her standard of living for the time he or she is out of work. They provide benefits over and above state employment compensation for three contingencies: layoffs, reduced workweeks, and relocations.

▼ **FIGURE 13-1   Leave of Absence Request Form**

P E A R S O N   E D U C A T I O N
LEAVE OF ABSENCE REQUEST FORM

This form is required for any employee eligible for leave under the Family and Medical Leave Act and for all leave of absence requests including employee's own illness (including Short Term Disability and Workers' Compensation), family member illness, Parental or Serious Illness in the Family Leave, and all paid or unpaid leave. All paid and unpaid leave time taken for the above-listed reasons will be counted towards your 12-week FMLA allotment, if you meet the eligibility criteria below. Unpaid personal leaves for circumstances not described above are not counted towards the 12-week FMLA and are subject to your supervisor's approval.

THE FAMILY AND MEDICAL LEAVE ACT
If eligible, you may take up to a total of 12 weeks during a 12-month period for any one or more of the following reasons:
- to care for a child after birth, placement for adoption or foster care;
- to care for a spouse, child or parent who has a serious health condition;
- where a serious health condition makes you unable to perform the functions of your job.

You are eligible for an FMLA leave if you've worked for the Company for one year and have worked at least 1,250 hours over the 12 months preceding the requested leave.

Eligibility Requirements		
Employment Status: ☐ Full-time Regular ☐ Short-hour Regular ☐ Term-of-Project Full-Time ☐ Term-of-Project Short-Hour		
Have you been employed with the Company for at least one year?	☐ Yes	☐ No
Have you worked a minimum of 1250 hours in the last 12 months?	☐ Yes	☐ No
If you leave is for child care, was the birth or placement within the last 12 months?	☐ Yes	☐ No
If you are applying for Parental Leave, was the birth or placement within the last 6 months?	☐ Yes	☐ No
Do you have backup documentation on the child's birth or placement?	☐ Yes	☐ No
If you have answered "NO" to any one of the questions above, you are not eligible for FMLA or Parental/Serious Illness in the Family Leave.		
Have you used any FMLA or Parental/Serious Illness in the Family Leave within the last 12 months?	☐ Yes	☐ No
If yes, please indicate the start and end date of your last leave: _____ Start Date _____ End Date		
If you have used your 12 week FMLA allotment and /or your 2 week Parental/Serious Illness in the Family Leave within the past year, you are not eligible for additional FMLA and/or Parental/Serious Illness in the Family Leave until one year from the start date of your previous leave.		

To determine which forms you need to fill out, please check the appropriate box(es) below:

Type of Leave Requested	Requirements
☐ FMLA Leave for Employee's Own Serious Illness	• Complete Part I of this form • Coordinate Short Term Disability or Workers Comp with your Human Resources Manager
☐ FMLA/Parental Leave	• Complete Part I of this form
☐ FMLA/Serious Illness in the Family Leave	• Complete Parts I and II of this form
☐ FMLA/Unpaid Family & Medical leave	• Complete Parts I and II of this form
☐ Unpaid Personal Leave of Absence	• Complete Part I of this form

---

Source: Pearson Education. Used with permission.

▼ **FIGURE 13-1**   **(Continued)**

Part I

Employee Information

Date Submitted		Social Security Number	
Last Name		First Name	
Date of Hire	Title		
Department	Division		Supervisor
Work Phone		Home Phone	

Leave Specifications

Type of Leave Requested:	☐ Consecutive Time Off	☐ Intermittent Leave	

Total Amount of Time Requested: _____ days and/or _____ weeks

Date Leave Begins:		Expected Return Date:	
Paid Leave Begins:	Paid Leave Ends:	Type of Pay Received: ☐STD ☐ PSIL ☐ Workers' Comp	# of Days:
Paid Leave Begins:	Paid Leave Ends:	Type of Paid Leave: ☐STD ☐ PSIL ☐ Workers' Comp	# of Days:
Paid Leave Begins:	Paid Leave Ends:	Type of Paid Leave: ☐STD ☐ PSIL ☐ Workers' Comp	# of Days:
Unpaid Leave Begins:	Unpaid Leave Ends:	Type of Unpaid Leave: ☐ FMLA ☐ Personal	# of Days:
Unpaid Leave Begins:	Unpaid Leave Ends:	Type of Unpaid Leave: ☐ FMLA ☐ Personal	# of Days:
Number of Paid Vacation Days to be taken:		Number of Paid Personal Days to be taken:	

I understand that all paid leave time (except vacation) must be exhausted and will be counted towards the 12 week FMLA allotment. I understand that I must request a leave of absence as far in advance as reasonably and practically possible with a minimum of 30 days notice when the need is foreseeable. I understand that I will be required to provide medical certification to support my need for leave and I understand that my employer may require additional medical opinions and periodic re-certifications. I also understand that I may be required to provide periodic reports during FMLA leave regarding my status and intent to return to work. I understand that if FMLA leave is for planned medical treatment, I must schedule treatment so that it will not unduly disrupt my employer's operation. I understand that during any unpaid portion of my leave I will be responsible for the payment of my health insurance premiums.

My signature below confirms that I have reviewed and understand the Leave of Absence Request Form and that I acknowledge that the information provided here is accurate. I have been provided copies of this form and the Pearson Education Family and Medical Leave Act Policy.

Employee:_____ _____ Date:_____

Human Resource Manager: _____Date:_____

INSURANCE BENEFITS

Most employers also provide a number of required or voluntary insurance benefits, such as workers' compensation and health insurance.

Workers' Compensation

Workers' compensation laws[26] aim to provide sure, prompt income and medical benefits to work-related accident victims or their dependents, regardless of fault.[27] Every state has its own workers' compensation law and administrative commission, and some run their own insurance programs. However, most require employers to carry workers' compensation insurance with private state-approved insurance companies. Neither the state nor the federal government contributes any funds for workers' compensation.

How Benefits Are Determined Workers' compensation benefits can be monetary or medical. In the event of a worker's death or disablement, the person's dependents are paid a cash benefit based on prior earnings—usually one-half to two-thirds the worker's average weekly wage, per week of employment. In most states, there is a set time limit—such as 500 weeks—for which benefits can be paid. If the injury causes a specific loss (such as an arm), the employee may receive additional benefits based on a statutory list of losses, even though he or she may return to work. In addition to these cash benefits, employers must furnish medical, surgical, and hospital services as required by the employee.

For workers' compensation to cover an injury or work-related illness, one must only prove that it arose while the employee was on the job. It does not matter that the employee may have been at fault; if the person was on the job when the injury occurred, he or she is entitled to workers' compensation. For example, suppose you instruct all employees to wear safety goggles when at their machines. One worker does not and experiences an injury while on the job. The company must still provide workers' compensation benefits. The employment provisions of the Americans with Disabilities Act (ADA) influence most employers' workers' compensation procedures. For one thing, ADA provisions generally prohibit employers from inquiring about an applicant's workers' compensation history, a practice that was widespread before passage of the act. Furthermore, the ADA makes it more important that injured employees get back to work quickly or be accommodated if their injury leads to a disability. Failing to let an employee who is on workers' compensation because of an injury return to work, or failing to accommodate him or her, could lead to lawsuits under ADA.[28]

Controlling Workers' Compensation Costs Minimizing the number of workers' compensation claims (and therefore accidents and lost hours) is an important goal for all employers. While the employer's insurance company usually pays the claims, the costs of the premiums depend on the number and dollar amount of claims.

In practice, there are several ways to reduce such claims. You can screen out accident-prone workers. You can reduce accident-causing conditions in your facilities. And you can reduce the accidents and health problems that trigger these claims—for instance, by instituting effective safety and health programs and complying with government safety standards.

It's also important to get injured employees back on the job as fast as possible, since workers' compensation costs accumulate as long as the person is out of work. Many firms have rehabilitation programs that include physical therapy (including exercise equipment); career counseling to guide injured employees into new, less strenuous jobs; and nursing assistance to help reintegrate recipients back into your workforce.[29] Employers can also affect their premiums by selecting insurers based on their level of service and flexibility in negotiating rates.[30]

Case management is an increasingly popular option. It is "the treatment of injured workers on a case-by-case basis by an assigned manager, usually a registered nurse, who coordinates with the physician and health plan to determine which care settings are the most effective for quality care and cost."[31] Firms can reportedly reduce their workers' compensation costs considerably by assigning a professional to coordinate and oversee the worker's rehabilitation and gradual reassimilation into its workforce. Respondents in one survey found that safety/injury protection and case management were the most common workers' compensation cost-containment measures. Other effective techniques included monitoring health care providers for compliance with their fee schedules, and auditing medical bills.[32] The following "High-Performance Insight" illustrates one company's workers' compensation program.

◆ **HIGH-PERFORMANCE INSIGHT** Weirton Steel Corporation of Weirton, West Virginia, established a workers' compensation program to review, contain, and reduce the costs of workers' compensation. The firm now thoroughly reviews and monitors injury claims, as well as payout periods and employee recovery times.

For example, Weirton modified its reporting process to allow a more thorough review of injuries by including independent medical examiners and third-party administrators. HR must submit accident reports for a ruling within 24 hours of filing, or within three days if questioned. The firm holds weekly management meetings to review each case. Weirton established an aggressive Modified Duty Program to return employees to the workplace in a suitable area. Unique to the program is the Options Rehab Program, in which the injured person agrees to rehabilitation treatment. The program requires that if the employee needs surgery, it will occur as soon as possible, followed by prescribed rehabilitation, and a proper transition back to work. The company is developing a treatment protocol for high-frequency injuries such as back strain, knee injuries, and shoulder injuries. There is also increased follow-up of employees off work through biweekly physician visits and calls from case managers.

Weirton's workers' compensation program, with its aggressive, proactive approach toward case reduction, has reduced the number of cases and produced substantial cost savings. In the mid-1990's, workers' comp cases dropped from 140 monthly to 77; payouts dropped from $153,000 monthly to $101,000. The firm expanded its efforts with a "zero-accidents" program in 2001.[33]

Hospitalization, Health, and Disability Insurance

Health and hospitalization insurance looms large in many people's choice of employer, because such insurance is so expensive. Most employers—about 80% of medium and large firms and 69% of small firms—therefore offer their employees some type of hospitalization, medical, and disability insurance; along with life insurance, these benefits form the cornerstone of most benefits programs.[34]

Hospitalization, health, and disability insurance helps protect against hospitalization costs and the loss of income arising from off-the-job accidents or illness. Many employers purchase the insurance from life insurance companies, casualty insurance companies, or Blue Cross (for hospital expenses) and Blue Shield (for physician expenses) organizations. Others contract with health maintenance organizations or preferred provider organizations, which we discuss below.

Most health insurance plans provide at least basic hospitalization and surgical and medical insurance for all eligible employees at group rates. Insurance is generally available to all employees—including new nonprobationary ones—regardless of health or physical condition. Most basic plans pay for hospital room and board, surgery charges, and medical expenses (such as doctors' visits to the hospital). Some also provide major medical coverage to meet the high medical expenses resulting from long-term or serious illnesses. Employers' health and hospitalization plans must comply with the Americans with Disabilities Act.[35] For example, the plan shouldn't make distinctions based on disability unless those distinctions are justified by recognized differences based on actuarial data or historic costs.[36]

Many employers also sponsor insurance plans that cover health-related expenses like eye care and dental services. In most employer-sponsored dental plans, employees pay a specific amount of deductible dental expenses (typically $25 or $50 each year) before the plan kicks in with benefits. In most cases, the premiums are paid entirely by the employers.[37]

Other plans pay for diagnostic visits to the doctor's office, vision care, hearing aids, and prescription drugs. *Accidental death and dismemberment* coverage provides a lump-sum benefit in addition to life insurance benefits when death is accidental. It also provides benefits in case of accidental loss of limbs or sight. Employers must provide the same health care benefits to employees over the age of 65 that they do to younger workers, even though the older workers are eligible for federally funded Medicare health insurance.[38] *Disability insurance* provides income protection for loss of salary due to illness or accident. Payments usually start when normal sick leave payments end, and may continue till age 65 or beyond.[39] The benefits usually range from 50% to 75% of the employee's base pay if he or she is disabled.

Many employers offer membership in a **health maintenance organization (HMO)** as a hospital/medical option. The HMO itself is a medical organization consisting of specialists (surgeons, psychiatrists, and so on) operating out of a community-based health care center. It provides routine medical services to employees who pay a nominal fee. The HMO also receives a fixed annual fee per employee from the employer (or employer and employee), regardless of whether it provides that person service.[40]

Preferred provider organizations (PPOs) are a cross between HMOs and the traditional doctor–patient arrangement: They are "groups of health care providers that contract with employers, insurance companies, or third-party payers to provide medical care services at a reduced fee."[41] Unlike HMOs (whose relatively limited lists of health care providers are often located in one health care center), PPOs let employees select providers (like doctors) from a relatively wide list, and see them in their offices. The providers agree to provide discounts and submit to certain utilization controls, such as on the number of diagnostic tests they can order.[42] About 62% of employers in one recent survey said they offer coverage under HMOs, while 84% offer coverage under PPOs.[43] Many employers offer both.

Reducing Health Benefits Costs Caught between rising health benefits costs and the belt tightening occurring in firms today, many managers find controlling and reducing health care costs high on their to-do lists.[44] As a result, many employers have been changing their medical plans to do the following:

1. Move away from 100% medical cost payments. Over 70% of plans include a deductible.
2. Increase annual deductibles. Almost 40% of firms use a deductible of $150 or more.
3. Require medical contributions. Most employers require employee contributions to their medical premiums.[45]
4. Use gatekeepers. Using general practitioners as gatekeepers to channel patients to the appropriate specialists and/or hospitals was "very effective" in reducing costs, according to 69% of employers in one survey.[46]

---

health maintenance organization (HMO)
A prepaid health care system that generally provides routine round-the-clock medical services as well as preventive medicine in a clinic-type arrangement for employees, who pay a nominal fee in addition to the fixed annual fee the employer pays.

---

preferred provider organizations (PPOs)
Groups of health care providers that contract with employers, insurance companies, or third-party payers to provide medical care services at a reduced fee.

5. Encourage preventive health care. This is a popular option. One survey found that 56% of the firms were sponsoring drug and alcohol abuse programs; 31% stop-smoking sessions; 45% physical fitness classes; and 18% had exercise facilities on the premises. Seventy percent were training employees in first aid and CPR. Fifty-four percent offered tips about how to use company health benefits wisely.[47] Others offered preventive care programs including mammograms, prostate exams, and well-baby care.[48] Thirty-nine percent of respondents in another survey used financial incentives to encourage good health (such as higher premiums for smokers).[49] Unfortunately, it's not clear whether wellness programs reduce health care costs or boost performance; in one survey, only about 1 in 10 employers even tried to put a dollar figure on savings.[50]

6. Form health care coalitions.[51] In Memphis, Tennessee, 11 self-insured employers including FedEx and Holiday Inn formed a coalition to study health care costs, identify more efficient health care providers, and use their purchasing power to obtain discounts on health and hospital care prices.[52]

7. Manage the cost of AIDS.[53] Several insurance companies have concluded that the best way to manage the cost of AIDS is to treat the AIDS sufferer in his or her home, and to allow that cost to be paid under the medical benefits plan (as is often not allowed now). There is also a growing emphasis on individual case management (ICM). The insurance company assigns a special ICM nurse to the patient and designs an individualized treatment plan. The plan considers the patient's ability to care for him- or herself, the availability of others to help in the person's treatment, and the patient's age and condition.

Mental Health Benefits Employers spend just over 8% of their health plan dollars on mental health treatment.[54] These costs are rising because of widespread drug and alcohol problems, an increase in the number of states that require employers to offer a minimum package of mental health benefits, and the fact that other health care claims are higher for employees with high mental health claims. The Mental Health Parity Act of 1996 sets minimum mental health care benefits at the national level.[55]

Some employers are slowing the rise in mental health benefits by monitoring the benefit's process. One New York financial services firm, faced with a big jump in mental health costs in one recent year, rejected the idea of placing across-the-board limits on coverage. Instead, it redesigned the mental health portion of its health plan. The plan now includes a utilization review to certify treatment, increased outpatient benefits, and a network of cost-efficient providers.[56]

The Pregnancy Discrimination Act As explained in Chapter 2, this act requires employers to treat women affected by pregnancy, childbirth, or related medical conditions the same as any employees not able to work, with respect to all benefits, including sick leave and disability benefits, and health and medical insurance. Thus, it's illegal for most employers to discriminate against women by providing benefits of lower amount or duration for pregnancy, childbirth, or related medical conditions. For example, if an employer provides up to 26 weeks of temporary disability income to employees for all illnesses, it must now provide up to 26 weeks for pregnancy and childbirth, too.

COBRA Requirements The ominously titled COBRA—Comprehensive Omnibus Budget Reconciliation Act—requires most private employers to continue to make health benefits available to terminated or retired employees and their families for a period of time, generally 18 months. The former employee must pay for the coverage, as well as a small fee for administrative costs.

Employers who fail to follow COBRA's regulations do so at their peril. For one thing, you don't want terminated or retired employees to become injured and then claim you never told them their insurance coverage could have been continued. Therefore, when a new employee first becomes eligible for your company's insurance plan, that person must receive (and acknowledge receiving) an explanation of his or her COBRA rights. Similarly, all employees separated from the company for any reason should sign a form acknowledging that they received and understand the information about their COBRA rights.

Long-Term Care Today, the oldest baby boomers are in their 50s, and long-term care insurance—care to support people in their old age—is emerging as the key new employee benefit.[57] The Health Insurance Portability and Accountability Act, enacted in 1996, lets employers and employees deduct the cost of long-term care insurance premiums from their annual income taxes, making this particular benefit even more attractive.[58] Employers can provide insurance benefits for several types of long-term care, such as adult day care, assisted living, and custodial care.

Life Insurance

In addition to hospitalization and medical benefits, most employers provide **group life insurance** plans. As with health insurance, employees can obtain lower rates in a group plan. And group plans usually accept all employees—including new nonprobationary ones—regardless of health or physical condition.

In many cases, the employer pays 100% of the base premium, which usually provides life insurance equal to about two years' salary. The employee then pays for any additional coverage. In some cases, the cost of the base premium is split 50/50 or 80/20 between employer and employee. In general, there are three key personnel policies to address: the benefits-paid schedule (the amount of life insurance benefits is usually tied to the employee's annual earnings), supplemental benefits (continued life insurance coverage after retirement, and so on); and financing (the amount and percent that the employee contributes).[59]

> **group life insurance**
> Provides lower rates for the employer or employee and includes all employees, including new employees, regardless of health or physical condition.

Benefits for Part-Time Workers

Until quite recently, most employers ignored their part-time workers, at least in terms of benefits. That is changing, however. The Bureau of Labor Statistics, which defines part-time work as less than 35 hours a week, says 13.6% of the nation's workforce—about 19 million people—work part-time. An aging workforce, more phased retirement programs, a desire to better balance work and family life issues, and more women in the workforce help explain this phenomenon. In any case, a recent study found that 80% of the firms surveyed provide holiday, sick leave, and vacation benefits, and over 70% offer some form of health care benefits to part-time workers.[60]

RETIREMENT BENEFITS

As the 77 million or so baby boomers born between 1946 and 1964 stampede into retirement, employers are revising and improving their retirement benefits.[61] The first contingent of baby boomers turns 65 in the year 2011, and many reportedly won't wait that long to retire; 38% of boomers aged 45 to 52 want to retire by age

55.[62] Employers are therefore being more aggressive about enhancing their retirement plans.[63] The major retirement benefits are the federal Social Security program and employer pension/retirement plans, like the 401(k).

Social Security

Social Security
Federal program that provides three types of benefits: retirement income at the age of 62 and thereafter; survivor's or death benefits payable to the employee's dependents regardless of age at time of death; and disability benefits payable to disabled employees and their dependents. These benefits are payable only if the employee is insured under the Social Security Act.

Most people assume that **Social Security** provides income only when they are over 62, but it actually provides three types of benefits. The familiar *retirement benefits* provide an income if you retire at age 62 or thereafter and are insured under the Social Security Act. Second are *survivor's* or *death benefits*. These provide monthly payments to your dependents regardless of your age at death, again assuming you are insured under the Social Security Act. Finally, there are *disability payments*. These provide monthly payments to employees who become totally disabled (and their dependents) if they work and meet certain requirements.[64] The Social Security system also administers the Medicare program, which provides a wide range of health services to people 65 or over.

A tax on the employee's wages, shared equally by employees and employers, funds Social Security (technically, it is called "Federal Old Age and Survivor's Insurance"). In 2001, the employer and employee each paid 7.65% of the employee's gross salary, up to $80,400. Self-employed individuals paid 15.3% of their taxable income up to $80,400 (less 2% of their self-employed income). "Full retirement age" according to Social Security is 65—the usual age for retirement. However, full retirement age is rising: It will soon be 67 for those born in 1960 or later. President George Bush and Congress are looking at programs that might allow employees to divert part of what they're now paying into Social Security into private sector investments.[65]

Pension Plans

pension plans
Plans that provide a fixed sum when employees reach a predetermined retirement age or when they can no longer work due to disability.

Pensions provide income to individuals in their retirement, and just over half of full-time workers participate in some type of **pension plan** at work. However, the actual rate of participation depends on several things. For example, older workers tend to have a higher participation rate, and employees of larger firms have participation rates as much as three times as high as those in small firms.[66] Workers earning lower incomes (particularly under $25,000 a year) are more at risk of receiving little or no pension income, because they contribute significantly less to pension plans than do workers earning more.[67]

We can classify pension plans in three basic ways: *contributory versus noncontributory* plans; *qualified versus nonqualified* plans; and *defined contribution versus defined benefit* plans.[68] The employee contributes to the contributory pension plan, while the employer makes all contributions to the noncontributory pension plan. There are certain tax benefits employers derive from contributing to qualified pension plans, such as tax deductions for contributions; nonqualified pension plans get less favorable tax treatment for employees and employers.

defined benefit pension plan
A plan that contains a formula for determining retirement benefits.

With **defined benefit plans**, the employee knows ahead of time the pension benefits he or she will receive. The defined pension benefit itself is usually set by a formula that ties the person's retirement pension to an amount equal to a percentage of the person's preretirement pay (for instance, to an average of his or her last five years of employment), multiplied by the number of years he or she worked for the company.

defined contribution pension plan
A plan in which the employer's contribution to employee's retirement or savings funds is specified.

Defined contribution plans specify what contribution the employee and employer will make to the employee's retirement or savings fund. Here, in other words, the contribution is defined, not the pension. With a defined benefit plan, the employee knows what his or her retirement benefits will be upon retirement. With a defined contribution plan, the person's pension will depend on the amounts contributed to the fund and on the retirement fund's investment earnings. Defined contribution plans are increasingly popular among employers today, because of their relative ease of administration, favorable tax treatment, and other factors.

401(k) Plans Plans based on section 401(k) of the Internal Revenue Code, called **401(k) plans**, are popular defined contribution plans. Here an employee authorizes the employer to deduct a certain amount of money from his or her paycheck before taxes and to invest it in the 401(k) plan. This results in a pretax reduction in pay, so the employee pays no tax on those set-aside dollars until after he or she retires (or removes the money from the 401(k) plan). The employee decides how much the employer will deduct and deposit in the 401(k) plan; the person can deduct up to the legal maximum (the IRS sets an annual dollar limit—$10,500 in 2001). The employer arranges, usually with an investment company such as Fidelity Investments, to actually manage the 401(k) plan and to make various investment options available to the company's 401(k) plan. The options typically include mutual stock funds and bond funds.

Employers should choose their 401(k) providers with the utmost care, not only because of the employer's responsibility to its employees but also because changing 401(k) providers can be a "grueling venture."[69] About 50 million American workers, or about 40% of the U.S. workforce, have 401(k) plans.[70]

▲ *"We never thought we could afford this," says Carmella Owens of Kosola & Associates, speaking about the firm's new 401(k) plan, whose adoption she spearheaded. "Now I'm actually going to have a retirement, and my kids will have money if something happens to me."*

401(k) plan
A defined contribution plan based on section 401(k) of the Internal Revenue Code.

Managing 401(k) Plans Online

In addition to reliability, employers want a 401(k) plan provider that makes it easy for employer and employee to participate in the plan. For example, Ford Motor Company helps employees manage their accounts by offering Fidelity Investment's Internet-based retirement portfolio planning tool to its 145,000 401(k) plan participants.[71] Fidelity can establish online, fully Web-based 401(k) plans even for small firms, with 10 to 50 employees. Employees get various online tools—such as an "asset allocation planner."

Other Types of Defined Contribution Plans There are several types of defined contribution plans.[72] In a **savings and thrift plan** (of which a 401(k) is one example), employees contribute a portion of their earnings to a fund; the employer usually matches this contribution in whole or in part. The employer's contributions can be considerable, particularly where competition for employees is intense. For example, Harleysville Group, Inc., matches up to 100% of an employee's contribution up to 6% of his or her salary, in an effort to attract and retain information technology (IT) workers. However, Radio Shack Corporation in Fort Worth, Texas, probably sets a record: It matches 401(k) contributions at *159%*.[73]

In **deferred profit-sharing plans**, employers typically contribute a portion of their profits to the pension fund, regardless of the level of employee

savings and thrift plan
Plan in which employees contribute a portion of their earnings to a fund; the employer usually matches this contribution in whole or in part.

deferred profit-sharing plan
A plan in which a certain amount of profits is credited to each employee's account, payable at retirement, termination, or death.

employee stock ownership plan (ESOP)
A qualified, tax-deductible stock bonus plan in which employers contribute stock to a trust for eventual use by employees.

contribution. An **employee stock ownership plan (ESOP)** is a qualified, tax-deductible stock bonus plan in which employers contribute stock to a trust for eventual use by employees. Overall, about 91% of employers in one recent survey offer 401(k) salary reduction plans; 67% also offer defined benefit pension plans alongside their 401(k)s, and 18% offer other deferred profit-sharing savings plans.[74]

Pension Planning

Pension planning is complicated, partly because of the many federal laws governing pensions. For example, companies (and employees) usually want to ensure their pension contributions are "qualified," or tax deductible, so they must follow the pertinent income tax codes. The **Employee Retirement Income Security Act (ERISA)** of 1974 restricts what companies can, cannot, and must do in regard to pension plans (more on this in a moment). In unionized companies, the employer must let the union participate in pension plan administration.

Employee Retirement Income Security Act (ERISA)
Signed into law by President Ford in 1974 to require that pension rights be vested and protected by a government agency, the PBGC.

In developing pension plans to meet their unique needs, employers have to consider several key policy issues:[75]

- *Membership requirements.* For example, what is the minimum age or minimum service at which employees become eligible for a pension?
- *Benefit formula.* This usually ties the (defined) pension to the employee's final earnings, or an average of his or her last three or four years' earnings.
- *Plan funding.* How will you fund the plan? Will it be contributory or noncontributory?
- *Vesting.* Vested funds are the money employer and employee have placed in the latter's pension fund that cannot be forfeited for any reason. The employees' contributions are always theirs, of course. However, until the passage of ERISA, many pension plans didn't vest the employer's contribution till the employee retired. So you could have worked for a company for 30 years and been left with no pension if the company went out of business 1 year before you were to retire. That generally can't happen today.[76]

vesting
Provision that money placed in a pension fund cannot be forfeited for any reason.

Pensions and the Law

Passage of ERISA was a pivotal step in protecting the pensions of workers and stimulating the growth of pension plans.[77] Today, under ERISA, participants in pension plans must have a nonforfeitable right to 100% of their accrued benefits after five years of service; as an alternative, the employer may choose to phase in vesting over a period of three to seven years. Under the Tax Reform Act of 1986, an employer can require that an employee complete a period of no more than two years' service to the company before becoming eligible to participate in the plan. However, if you require more than one year of service before eligibility, the plan must grant employees full and immediate vesting rights at the end of that period.[78]

Pension Benefits Guarantee Corporation (PBGC)
Established under ERISA to ensure that pensions meet vesting obligations; also insures pensions should a plan terminate without sufficient funds to meet its vested obligations.

ERISA established the **Pension Benefits Guarantee Corporation (PBGC)** to oversee and insure pensions should a plan terminate without sufficient funds to meet its vested obligations.[79] However, the PBGC guarantees only defined benefit plans, not defined contribution plans. Furthermore, it will only pay an individual a pension of up to about $27,000 per year. This may seem like a lot, but might not be to, say, an airline pilot who retired expecting a pension of $70,000 per year.[80]

Pension Trends

Many firms today, faced with the need to reduce their workforces, are offering early-retirement windows and other voluntary separation arrangements.

Early-Retirement Windows Some plans take the form of **early-retirement window** arrangements in which specific employees (often age 50-plus) are eligible to participate. The "window" means that for a limited time, the company opens up the opportunity for employees to retire earlier than usual. The financial incentive is generally a combination of improved or liberalized pension benefits plus a cash payment. About 13% of 362 employers provided early-retirement windows in one survey.[81] Deteriorating financial conditions for the company often precede early-retirement programs. In turn, announcements of early-retirement programs tend to be followed by positive stock market reactions for up to two years, since investors "likely view declines in long-term head counts as more favorable than the initial short-term costs of funding the early retirement programs."[82]

Employers should use programs like these cautiously. Age discrimination is the fastest-growing type of discrimination claim today, and unless structured properly, early-retirement programs can be challenged as de facto methods for forcing the discharge of older employees against their will.[83] While it is generally legal to use incentives to encourage individuals to choose early retirement, the employee's decision must be voluntary. In fact, in several cases individuals who were eligible for and elected early retirement later challenged their early retirement by claiming their decisions weren't voluntary. In one case *(Paolillo v. Dresser Industries, Inc.)*, the employer told employees on October 12 that they were eligible to retire under a "totally voluntary" early-retirement program, and must inform the company by October 18 of their decision. However, employees didn't get the details of the program until October 15. The employees subsequently sued, claiming coercion. The U.S. Court of Appeals for the Second Circuit (New York) agreed with them, arguing that an employee's decision to retire must be voluntary and made without undue strain.[84]

Employers must also exercise caution in encouraging employees to take early retirement. The waiver of future claims they sign should meet EEOC guidelines. In particular, it must be knowing and voluntary, not provide for the release of prospective rights or claims, and not be an exchange for benefits to which the employee was already entitled. It should give the employee ample opportunity to think over the agreement and to seek advice from legal counsel.[85] The Older Workers' Benefit Protection Act (OWBPA), signed into law in 1990, imposes specific limitations on waivers that purport to release a terminating employee's potential claims against his or her employer based on age discrimination.[86]

Portability Today's needs for flexible staffing and the realities of ongoing corporate restructurings are also prompting employers to make their pension plans more *portable*. For example, Duracel International redesigned its pension plan to make it easier for employees to take their retirement income when they leave, and roll it over into a new employer's savings plan.[87] Employers often do this by switching from defined benefit to defined contribution plans, since the former are more appropriate for employees who plan to stay with the firm until retirement. Another approach is to allow workers who leave the firm before retirement to receive initial benefits at a younger age.[88]

Cash Balance Pension Plans These are defined benefit plans for federal tax purposes, but they work differently. In a typical defined benefit plan, the employer multiplies the employee's average pay over the last few years of his or her employment by a predetermined multiple, and the result represents the person's annual retirement income. This approach tends to favor older employees (whose income is often higher and who have been with the firm for a number of years). Younger employees who may not be planning to stay with the firm their entire careers may prefer **cash balance plans**. Under these plans, the employer contributes a percentage of

early-retirement window
A type of offering by which employees are encouraged to retire early, the incentive being liberal pension benefits plus perhaps a cash payment.

cash balance pension plans
Defined benefit plans under which the employer contributes a percentage of employees' current pay to the employees' pension plans every year, and employees earn interest on this amount.

employees' current pay to the employees' pension plans every year, and employees earn interest on this amount. Cash balance plans therefore provide the portability of defined contribution plans with the employer funding of defined benefit plans.[89]

STRATEGIC HR

Patio's Better Benefits Program

Patio Enclosures, Inc.'s, competitive strategy was based on quality and consistency, and management knew it couldn't maintain quality and consistency if it couldn't hire and retain high-quality employees.

Patio's solution was to install a comprehensive new HR program called the PEI Apprentice Program, with a new benefits package as one major component. Figure 13-2 summarizes PEI's main components. Management focused PEI Apprentice on supporting its effort to attract and retain high-quality employees; that goal in turn supported the firm's quality and consistency competitive strategy.

▼ **FIGURE 13-2   The PEI Apprentice Program at a Glance**

The PEI Apprentice Program at a Glance

Purpose: To help the company attract and retain employees during the current labor shortage

Launched:
  Created   ➤ Early 1999
  5 Beta Test Sites ➤ Mid-1999
  National Rollout ➤ Late 1999

Preprogram:
  Employment statistics ➤ 40% turnover
                          ➤ 85% hiring capacity
                          ➤ $5.5 million estimated in lost sales due to shortage of employees

Postprogram:
  Results   ➤ Reduced turnover by 60%
                ➤ 97% hiring capacity
                ➤ Less than $1 million in lost sales due to shortage of employees

  Program   The PEI Apprentice Program has the following components:

                ➤ A clearly defined and well-documented career path for new employees
                ➤ Comprehensive training at each new level of the apprenticeship to enable employees to develop the skills that will advance them to new levels
                ➤ Financial rewards and title increases at each new level
                ➤ Consistent health care benefits
                ➤ The ability to move through levels quickly
                ➤ An apprentice "chart" that enables employees to track their own progress, giving them ownership of the program and a constant reminder of the rewards ahead
                ➤ An education program at hiring and periodically during the apprenticeship that stresses the benefits to staying long term with the company
                ➤ Emphasis on "career" over "job" to young people and new hires
                ➤ Ownership benefits through ESOP
                ➤ Promotion of the program through schools and trade schools, with the emphasis of using skills to establish a long-term career
                ➤ Program materials such as brochures

Source: Compensation and Benefits Review, September/October 2000, p. 37.

As you can see, the program contained 11 main components. These included providing employees with a clear and well-documented career path and comprehensive training, improved financial rewards, and several new benefits programs. For example, the firm's

ESOP puts shares of company stock into each employee's retirement fund at the close of each year, and bases the amount on the firm's performance. Improved health care benefits are another key component. In the construction industry, employees tend to lose their benefits when they're laid off in the down season. At Patio Enclosures, employees can keep 100% of their benefits, as long as they're willing to be on call during the year.

Other factors may have affected the firm's performance, but management believes the PEI Apprentice Program contributed to a significant improvement in the firm's operating performance. Within about one year, for instance, turnover dropped from 40% to about 16%; the firm was able to hire many more candidates; and lost sales due to shortages of employees dropped from $5.5 million to less than $1 million.[90]

EMPLOYEE SERVICES

While time off, insurance, and retirement benefits account for the lion's share of benefits costs, most employers also provide various services, including personal services (such as legal and personal counseling), job-related services (such as child care facilities), educational subsidies, and executive perquisites (such as company cars and planes for its executives).

Personal Services

Many companies provide personal services that most employees need at one time or another. These include credit unions, legal services, counseling, and social and recreational opportunities.

Credit Unions Credit unions are usually separate businesses established with the employer's assistance to help employees with borrowing and saving needs. Employees usually become members by purchasing a share of the credit union's stock for $5 or $10. Members can then deposit savings that accrue interest at a rate determined by the credit union's board of directors. Perhaps more important to most employees, loan eligibility and the loan's rate of interest are usually more favorable than those of banks and finance companies. Many credit unions are large, multibranch operations. For example, Arrowhead Credit Union has 100,000 members and 17 branches, with ATMs, checking, and a full range of banking services.[91]

Counseling Services Many firms provide a wide range of counseling services. These include financial counseling (for example, how to overcome existing indebtedness); family counseling (for marital problems and so on); career counseling; outplacement counseling (for helping terminated or disenchanted employees find new jobs); preretirement counseling; and legal counseling through legal insurance plans.[92]

Employee Assistance Programs (EAPS) **Employee assistance programs** provide counseling and/or treatment for problems such as substance abuse, gambling, or stress. Fifty to 75 percent of all employers with 3,000 or more employees offer EAPs,[93] and there are several models in use.[94] For example, with the in-house model, the company employs the EAP staff. With the out-of-house model, the company contracts with a vendor to provide EAP staff and services. In the consortium model, several firms pool their resources to develop a collaborative EAP program. The trend today is toward offering one-stop-shopping EAP benefits from large off-site providers. One study found that personal mental health was the most common problem addressed by employee assistance programs, followed by family problems.[95]

employee assistance program (EAP)
A formal employer program for providing employees with counseling and/or treatment programs for problems such as alcoholism, gambling, or stress.

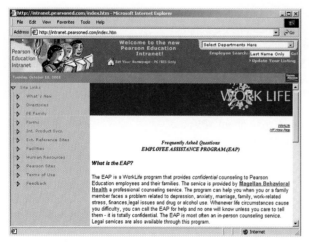

▲ **WEBNOTE**

The employer's Web site often explains the services provided by its Employee Assistance Program (EAP).

Key steps for launching a successful EAP program include:

- *Specify goals and philosophy.* Include the short- and long-term goals you expect the employee and firm to achieve.
- *Develop a policy statement.* Here, define the program's purpose, employee eligibility, the roles and responsibility of various personnel in the organization, and procedures for using the plan.
- *Ensure professional staffing.* Consider the professional and state licensing requirements.
- *Maintain confidential record-keeping systems.* Everyone involved with the EAP, including secretaries and support staff, must understand the importance of confidentiality. Also ensure files are locked, access is limited and monitored, and identifying information is minimized.
- *Train supervisors.* Supervisors should understand the program's policies, procedures, and services, as well as the company's policies regarding confidentiality. Train them to recognize the symptoms of problems like substance abuse, and to encourage employees to use the EAP.
- *Be aware of legal issues.* For example, in most states counselors must disclose suspicions of child abuse to an appropriate state agency. Get legal advice on establishing the EAP, carefully screen the credentials of the EAP staff, and obtain professional liability insurance for the EAP.[96]

Other Personal Services Some employers provide social and recreational personal services—some quite creative. Examples include:[97]

- *Vacation facilities.* One company owns lakeshore property and rents cottages and campsites to employees at low rates.
- *Cultural subsidy.* The company will pay 33% of the cost of tickets to cultural activities such as theater, ballet, museum, and so on up to $100 per year per employee.
- *Lunch-and-learn programs.* Interested employees can attend lunchtime talks on a variety of subjects, including stress management, weight control, computer literacy, fashion, and travel.[98]

Job-Related Services

Job-related services like child care make it easier for employees to perform their jobs.

Subsidized Child Care Today, over 50% of all U.S. women with children under six years old are in the workplace, and a Commerce Department survey reported there were almost 10 million children younger than age five requiring child care.[99] Child care is thus an increasingly desirable benefit.

Most employees still make private provisions to take care of their children; relatives accounted for 48% of all child care providers in one study.[100] Organized day care centers of all types accounted for another 30% of the child care arrangements, and nonrelatives accounted for most of the remaining arrangements.

How do employers help? Many employers simply investigate the day care facilities in their communities and recommend certain ones to interested employees. But more employers are setting up company-sponsored day care facilities, both to attract employees and to reduce absenteeism. Often (as at the Wang Laboratories day care facility in Lowell, Massachusetts), the center is a private tax-exempt venture run separately from but subsidized by the firm. Employees are charged $30 a week for a child's care. Successful day care facilities are usually close to the workplace (often in the same building), and the employer covers at least half of the operating costs.[101]

By establishing subsidized day care centers, employers can gain via improved recruiting results, lower absenteeism, improved morale, favorable publicity, and lower turnover.[102] But to ensure the program is worthwhile and cost-effective, good planning is required. This often starts with a questionnaire to employees to answer questions like, "What would you be willing to pay for care for one child in a child care center near work?" and "Have you missed work during the past six months because you needed to find new care arrangements?"

Elder Care With an aging population, elder care has become more of an issue for many employees.[103]

Elder care benefits are important for much the same reasons as are child care benefits: The responsibility for caring for an aging relative can affect the employee's performance at work.[104] How do employees adjust their schedules when they must care for an elderly family member? One study found that 64% took sick days or vacation time, 33% decreased work hours, 22% took leaves of absence, 20% changed their job status from full to part time, 16% quit their jobs, and 13% retired early. The problem will grow more acute as the segment of the population over age 65 grows from about 35 million today to 82 million in 2050.

How are firms responding? So far, not too well. About 26% of employers offer an elder care service of some sort. One percent offer company-supported elder care centers or subsidized elder care. Flexible work arrangements now seem to be the solution of choice for handling elder care issues.[105] Other efforts include long-term care insurance for elder relatives.

Elder care programs don't have to be complicated or expensive. For example, utilizing a kit from the American Association of Retired Persons (AARP), one company set up a three-part program:

1. A lunchtime elder care fair at which 31 community organizations providing services to older people came to explain the services that were available.
2. Ten lunchtime information sessions for employees explained various aspects of elder care, such as independent versus assisted living and housing, the aging process, and legal concerns of elder care.
3. The company also distributed the AARP "Care Management Guide," which lists potential problems associated with elder care.[106]

Other Job-Related Benefits Some employers provide subsidized *employee transportation*.[107] In one such program, Seattle First National Bank negotiated separate contracts with a transit system to provide free year-round transportation to more than 3,000 of the bank's employees. *Food services* are provided in some form by many employers; they let employees purchase meals, snacks, or coffee, usually at relatively low prices. Most food operations are nonprofit, and, in fact, some firms provide food services below cost.

Educational subsidies such as tuition refunds have long been popular benefits for employees seeking to continue or complete their educations. Payments range from all tuition and expenses to some percentage of expenses to a flat fee of several hundred dollars per year. Many employers provide in-house college programs, where faculty teach on the employer's premises. Other in-house educational programs include remedial work in basic literacy and training for improved supervisory skills.

As far as tuition reimbursement programs are concerned, one survey found that nearly all the 619 companies surveyed pay for courses directly related to an employee's present job. Most companies also reimburse non-job-related courses (such as a Web designer taking an accounting class) that pertain to the company business. Some employers pay for self-improvement classes, such as foreign language study, even though they are unrelated to company business or the employee's job.[108] DaimlerChrysler, Ford, and General Motors provide $1,000 annually to dependents of current or retired UAW members for tuition.[109]

THE *NEW* WORKPLACE

Family-Friendly Benefits

Several trends are changing the landscape of benefits administration: There are more households in which both adults work; more one-parent households; more women in the workforce; more workers over 55. And there's the "time bind"—people working harder and longer, without the time to do all they'd like to do.

The pressures of balancing work and family life have led many employers to bolster what they call their family-friendly benefits. While there is no single list of what does or does not constitute a "family-friendly benefit," they generally include child care, elder care, fitness facilities, and flexible work schedules that enable employees to better meet the demands of their family and work lives. As two experts put it:

> *On-site child care, fitness and medical facilities, flexible work scheduling, telecommuting, occasional sabbaticals, loan programs for home computers, stock options, concierge services, even insurance for the family pet are all part of the compensation package in the new workplace.*[110]

Ninety percent of responding employees in one survey said such work/life benefits were "important" or "very important" to them; important benefits included on-site day care, flexible work schedules (discussed in Chapter 8), referral services for child care and elder care, long-term care insurance, and family leave.[111]

Many more employers have therefore added these kinds of benefits. A survey by Hewitt Associates found that 85% of employers provided at least some type of child care assistance and that elder care benefits jumped to 26% from 12% during the 1990s.[112] The Society for Human Resource Management recently found that, of the firms responding, 58% offer flextime, 31% offer compressed workweeks, and 24% permit employees to bring a child to work in emergencies.[113]

Sample Programs

Rationales for the family-friendly benefits at several firms are typical. Eddie Bauer, Inc., reportedly "believes its associates shouldn't confuse having a career with having a life."[114] It therefore introduced more than 20 new family-friendly type benefits ranging from on-site mammography to emergency child care services. Also included are a casual dress code, subsidies for liberal paid parental leave, alternative transportation options, and a compressed workweek and telecommuting.[115] First Tennessee Bank in Memphis calls its family-friendly benefits program Family Matters. Its main emphasis is on flexibility; for example, the bank's previous policy forced employees to take vacations in two-week blocks and required dismissal for any employee who missed more than eight days per year. With Family Matters, employees can now follow flextime schedules, scale back to working as few as 20 hours a week and still keep benefits, and schedule more hours of work early in the month to take time off late in the month if that's what they need to do.[116]

Family-friendly firms routinely turn up on "best companies to work for" lists. For example, BMC (56th on Fortune's list of the 100 best companies to work for) includes a kitchen on each floor with free fruit, popcorn, soda, and TV. Forty-six of Fortune's 100 best companies offer take-home meals. Twenty-six have concierge services to help with time-consuming details like buying birthday presents.[117] More firms, like snowball.com—which has two people sharing one vice presidency—offer job sharing as a benefit. (The two share not only the VP's job, but also an e-mail address, a phone number, a business card, and common files.)[118]

Software giant SAS Institute offers preschool child care centers, a 36,000-square-foot gym, meditation rooms, a full-time in-house elder care consultant, high chairs in the cafeterias (where employees are allowed to bring their children for lunch), three weeks paid vacation, a flexible work schedule, and a standard 35-hour workweek.[119] Sun Microsystems offers sunrooms with pool tables, and basketball and volleyball courts. Adobe Systems employees get three-week paid sabbaticals every five years.[120]

A main problem in implementing family-friendly benefits seems to be employees' reluctance to use them because of "perceptions that managers frown upon those who take advantage of work/life programs."[121] In one survey, many employees said their supervisors "send mixed signals if employees try to use the benefit," and as a result many simply do not use them.[122] Establishing a management training program to "demonstrate work/life benefits' value in improving business productivity" is therefore not just prudent but probably necessary.[123]

▲ *To say that employee benefits at SAS Institute Inc. are generous is to understate the case. The North Carolina firm keeps turnover at 4% in an industry where 20% is typical, in large part by encouraging employees to go home at 5 P.M. and offering paid maternity leave, day care on site, lunchtime piano concerts, attractive office space that includes outdoor recreation areas and atriums, massages, a free medical clinic, unlimited sick days, yoga classes, free car washes, and even a farmer's market and high school on site.*

Effect on Performance   But do these family-friendly programs improve productivity? There is not a lot of evidence. Many firms that implement these plans do so as part of broader commitment-building programs. These typically also include, for instance, emphasizing employee development, promotion from within, and open communications.[124] Implemented in this manner, studies suggest work/life benefits may in fact contribute to employees' willingness to "go the extra mile" for their employers.[125]

On the other hand, benefits like these don't come cheap. For example, the CEO of one firm that provides concierge services to employees estimates that for a large company, concierge services cost $100,000 per year. Aetna found it saved $400,000 by making employees at its Blue Bell, Pennsylvania, office buy their own coffee and tea. Excite@home saved $165,000 by eliminating free sodas.[126]

◆ **RESEARCH INSIGHT**   Offering family-friendly benefits assumes that work–family conflicts affect the employee's job, and somehow undermine job satisfaction and performance. A study suggests that this is, in fact, the case.[127] Two researchers reviewed all studies focusing on work and family conflict, job satisfaction, and life satisfaction. They found that "the relationship between job satisfaction and various [work–family] conflict measures is strong and negative across all samples; people with high levels of [work–family] conflict tend to be less satisfied with their jobs."[128] There was also a strong negative correlation between work–family conflict and measure of "life satisfaction"—the extent to which the employees were satisfied with their lives in general. Managers should therefore understand that offering employees family-friendly benefits and letting them use them can have positive effects on employees, one of which is making them more satisfied with their work and their jobs.

Executive Perquisites

When you reach the pinnacle of the organizational pyramid—or at least get close to the top—you will find, waiting for you, the Executive Perk. Perquisites (perks, for short) usually only go to a few top executives. Perks can range from substantial to almost insignificant. In addition to a $200,000 annual salary, for instance, the president of the United States has free use of the White House and Camp David (not to mention a fleet of limousines, Air Force One, and various helicopters).[129] On the other hand, perks may entail little more than the right to use the executive washroom.

Many popular perks fall between these extremes. These include management loans (which typically enable senior officers to exercise their stock options); salary guarantees (also known as golden parachutes), to protect executives if their firms become targets of acquisitions or mergers; financial counseling (to handle top executives' investment programs); and relocation benefits, often including subsidized mortgages, purchase of the executive's current house, and payment for the actual move.[130] A selection of other executive perks includes time off with pay (including sabbaticals and severance pay), outplacement assistance, company cars, chauffeured limousines, security systems, company planes and yachts, executive dining rooms, physical fitness programs, legal services, tax assistance, liberal expense accounts, club memberships, season tickets, credit cards, and children's education. As you can see, employers have many ways of making their hardworking executives' lives as pleasant as possible!

Indeed, this tendency continues even in the face of a decade of corporate downsizings, restructurings, and more restrictive tax laws.[131] Some of the most visible status perks such as executive apartments and suites are more rare, as are company planes and full-time chauffeurs. However, over 60% of firms offer supplemental executive retirement plans (the most popular perk) to mid- to top-level managers.[132] Fifty-seven percent offer leased automobiles, and 43% offer change in control agreements (which provide benefits to top management in case of a change in corporate ownership). Fastest-growing executive perks were mobile phones, golden parachutes, and individual financial counseling. What are the most expensive perks firms provide? A private driver costs $23,882 per year per executive. Aircraft usage averages $22,363 a year. The least expensive perk? Forget the aircraft and give your executives an airport club membership, for an average annual cost of $308 per executive. And more than 32% of surveyed firms cover their CEO's spouse's travel expenses.[133]

FLEXIBLE BENEFITS PROGRAMS

"Variety is the spice of life," the saying goes. This applies very well to employee benefits, since the benefits one worker finds attractive may be unattractive to another. As a result there is a trend toward building flexibility into benefits programs by letting employees choose the benefits options they prefer.

◆ **RESEARCH INSIGHT** One classic study illustrates employees' preferences for various benefits.[134] The researcher mailed questionnaires listing seven possible benefit options to 400 employees of a midwestern public utility company. He got back completed questionnaires from 149 employees (about 38% of those surveyed). Overall, two extra weeks of vacation was clearly the most preferred benefit, while a pay increase was second. Overall, a shorter seven-hour, 35-minute workday was the least preferred benefit option.

But this is not the full story; the employee's age, marital status, and sex influenced his or her choice of benefits. For example, younger employees significantly favored the family dental plan. Younger employees also showed a greater preference for the four-day workweek. As might be expected, preference for the pension option increased significantly with employee age. Married workers showed more preference for the pension increase and for the family dental plan than did single workers.

When given the opportunity to choose, employees do prefer flexibility in their benefits plans. In a survey of working couples, for instance, 83% took advantage of flexible hours, 69% took advantage of the sorts of flexible-style benefits options packages we'll discuss next; and 75% said that flexible-style benefits plans are the sorts of plans they would like to see their companies offer.[135]

More recently, the online job listing service jobtrak.com asked college students and recent graduates, "Which benefit do you desire most?" More than 3,000 responded. Thirty-five percent sought flexible hours; 19% stock options; 13% more vacation time; 12% a better health plan; and 9% wanted a signing bonus. Most of the preferred benefits had to do with lifestyle issues rather than financial ones.[136]

The Cafeteria Approach

Because employees do have different preference for benefits, more employers today let employees individualize their benefits plans. The "cafeteria" approach is the main way to do this. (The terms **flexible benefits plan** and **cafeteria benefits plan** are generally used synonymously.) A cafeteria plan is one in which the employer gives each employee a benefits fund budget, and lets the person spend it on the benefits he or she prefers, subject to two constraints. First, the employer must carefully limit total cost for each benefits package. Second, each benefits plan must include certain required items—for example, Social Security, workers' compensation, and unemployment insurance. New IRS regulations should make cafeteria plans more attractive, by making them more flexible. Thus, employees can now make midyear changes to their plans if, for instance, their dependent care costs rise and they want to divert more contributions to this expense.[137]

> **flexible benefits plan/cafeteria benefits plan**
> Individualized plans allowed by employers to accommodate employee preferences for benefits.

Cafeteria plans come in several varieties. *Flexible spending accounts* let employees pay for certain benefits expenses (such as dental care) with pretax dollars. Periodically, employees can elect the amount of salary reduction dollars they wish to allocate to various elements in their plans. *Core plus option plans* establish a core set of benefits (such as medical insurance), which are usually mandatory for all employees. Beyond the core, employees can then choose from various benefits options.[138]

The "Life Plan" at Pitney Bowes provides an example.[139] Pitney Bowes attaches a "price" to every benefit offered and allows employees to "shop" for the benefits they need each year. Each employee gets a certain number of "flex dollars" to spend each year on the benefits he or she prefers. Employees can buy whatever benefits they want up to the limit of their available flex dollars; they can even supplement that amount with their personal funds if they so choose.

The flex dollars themselves are awarded based on an employee's salary, length of service, age, and number of dependents covered by benefits.[140] In establishing the program, Pitney Bowes included numerous traditional benefits such as medical, dental, short-term disability insurance, pension plans, and vacations. In addition, however, it expanded its choices to include things like group legal services, a loan broker to help employees shop for the best college financing, and unlimited personal financial planning (for a special fee of $175 per year).[141]

Flexible Programs: Pros and Cons

Flexible benefits programs have pros and cons.[142] Flexibility is of course the main advantage: Employees can choose the package that suits them best, and the firm can adapt to workers' changing needs. Flexible programs also make it cheaper to introduce new benefits, since the employer doesn't have to lock them in for all employees. However, employees may make bad choices and find themselves not covered for emergencies, and the administrative costs of such plans can be burdensome. Employers have to price and periodically update each employee's package, so even a medium-sized firm should computerize the administration of its plan.[143] Various benefits firms have therefore developed computerized aids, as explained next.

Computers and Benefits Administration

Whether it is flexible benefits or some other plan, computers play an important role in benefits administration. PC-based systems let employees interactively update and manipulate their benefits packages, as do various Web sites like www.401k.com. Inter- and intranet systems enable employees to get medical information about hospitals and doctors and to do interactive financial planning and investment modeling.[144] Firms also use computerized systems to inform employees about their benefits and to answer routine questions that might otherwise go unasked or take up a human resource manager's time.[145] Such questions include: "In which option of the medical plan am I enrolled?" "Who are my designated beneficiaries for the life insurance plan?" "If I retire in two years, what will be my monthly retirement income?" and "What is the current balance in my company savings plan?"

Systems like these are not just for Fortune 500 companies. Administering the benefits for even a small company with 25 or 30 employees can be a chore. For example, consider the paperwork involved when an employee asks, "Can I take my vacation next week?" Answering may require digging through time cards, spreadsheets, and HR folders, and then considering whether the request falls under the Family and Medical Leave Act or COBRA. Even smaller firms thus often use software like HROffice, from Ascentis Software Corporation. HROffice includes over 100 built-in reports on matters ranging from attendance and benefits to performance reviews and bonuses.[146] They may also use employee leasing, to which we now turn.

ENTREPRENEURS + HR

Benefits and Employee Leasing

The 40 employees at First Weigh Manufacturing in Sanford, Florida, may not work for a giant company, but they get employee benefits and HR services as if they do. That's because Tom Strasse, First Weigh's boss, signed up with ADP Total Source, a professional employee organization that now handles all First Weigh's HR processes. "I didn't have the time or the personnel to deal with the human resources, safety and OSHA regulations," Strasse says. "We were always looking for new insurance."[147]

Strasse's experience is typical of small businesses that turn to *employee leasing*. Employee leasing firms (generally called professional employer organizations, or staff leasing firms) arrange to have all the employer's employees transferred to the employee leasing firm's payroll. The leasing firm becomes the employees' legal employer, and usually handles all employee-related activities such as recruiting, hiring (with client firms' supervisors' approvals), and paying taxes (Social Security payments, unemployment insurance, and so on).

However, benefits management is often the big attraction. Getting health and other insurance can be a big problem for smaller firms. Even group rates for life or health insurance can be quite high when only 20 or 30 employees are involved. First Weigh Manufacturing's health insurance carrier dropped the firm after its first two years, and Strasse had to go scrambling to find a new carrier—which he did, with premiums that were 30% higher.

That's where the leasing firm comes in. Remember that the leasing firm is the legal employer of your employees. The employees therefore are absorbed into a much larger insurable group, along with other employers' former employees. As a result, a small-business owner may be able to get insurance for its people that it couldn't otherwise afford. An added benefit: The Alexandria, Virginia–based National Association of Professional Employer Organizations (which represents employee leasing firms) estimates that the average cost of regulations, paperwork, and tax compliance for smaller firms is about $5,000 per employee per year.[148] With expenses like that, it's understandable that many small-business owners figure what they save on managing their own HR activities pretty much pays for the employee leasing firm's fees. Now, for instance, when Strasse has a question about HR legal issues or safety concerns, he can just call his representative at the employee leasing firm.

Employee leasing may sound too good to be true, and it often is. Many employers aren't comfortable letting a third party become the legal employer of their employees (who literally have to be terminated by the employer and rehired by the leasing firm). However, there are other, more concrete risks to consider. Several years ago, for instance, the employee leasing industry tarnished itself when one or two firms manipulated the pension benefits offered to higher-paid employees.[149] The arrangement can also raise liability concerns. For example, in the typical employee leasing arrangement, the professional employer organization and the client employer agree to share the various responsibilities, a concept known as co-employment. So, for instance, in states where courts have not universally upheld workers' compensation as the sole remedy for injuries at work (there are some such states), it's very important to specify whether the client company or the leasing firm is insuring the workers' compensation exposure.[150]

We invite you to visit **www.prenhall.com/dessler** on the Prentice Hall Web site for our online study guide, Internet exercises, current events, links to related Web sites, and more.

Summary

1. Financial incentives are usually paid to specific employees whose work is above standard. Employee benefits, on the other hand, are available to all employees based on their membership in the organization.
2. There are four basic types of benefits plans: pay supplements, insurance, retirement benefits, and services.
3. Supplemental pay benefits provide pay for time not worked. They include unemployment insurance, vacation and holiday pay, severance pay, and supplemental unemployment benefits.
4. Insurance benefits include workers' compensation, group hospitalization, accident and disability insurance, and group life insurance.

5. Retirement benefits include Social Security and pension plans. Social Security does not cover just retirement benefits but survivor's and disability benefits as well. Pension plans include defined benefit plans, defined contribution plans, deferred profit sharing, and savings plans. One of the critical issues in pension planning is vesting. ERISA basically ensures that pension rights become vested and protected after a reasonable amount of time.

6. Most employers also provide benefits in the form of employee services. These include food services, recreational opportunities, legal advice, credit unions, and counseling.

7. Surveys suggest two conclusions regarding employees' preferences for benefits. First, time off seems to be the most preferred benefit. Second, the employee's age, marital status, and sex clearly influence choice of benefits. This suggests the need for individualizing the organization's benefits plans.

8. Flexible benefits plans, also called the cafeteria approach, allow the employee to put together his or her own benefits plan, subject to total cost limits and the inclusion of certain nonoptional items. Many firms have installed cafeteria plans; they require considerable planning and computer assistance.

Tying It All Together

Employee compensation (Part IV of this book) includes establishing pay plans, providing pay for performance and financial incentives, and employee benefits. In the current chapter, we focused on benefits and services, including pay for time not worked, insurance benefits, retirement benefits, employee services benefits, and flexible benefits programs. So far in this book, we discussed the strategic role of human resource management and equal opportunity (Part 1), recruitment and placement (Part 2), training and development (Part 3), and, now, compensation (Part 4). The following chapter, Labor Relations and Collective Bargaining, takes us to a new part of the book and to another major HR topic, the union's role in HR practices.

Discussion Questions

1. You are applying for a job as a manager and are at the point of negotiating salary and benefits. What questions would you ask your prospective employer concerning benefits? Describe the benefits package you would try to negotiate for yourself.

2. What is unemployment insurance? Is an organization required to pay unemployment benefits to all dismissed employees? Explain how you would go about minimizing your organization's unemployment insurance tax.

3. Explain how ERISA protects employees' pension rights.

4. In this chapter, we presented findings concerning the preferences by age, marital status, and sex for various benefits. What are these findings and how would you make use of them if you were a human resource manager?

5. What is "portability"? Why do you think it is (or isn't) important to a recent college graduate?

6. What are the provisions of the FMLA?

Individual and Group Activities

1. Working individually or in groups, find out the unemployment insurance rate and laws of your state. Write a summary detailing your state's unemployment laws. Assuming Company X has a 30% rate of personnel terminations, calculate Company X's unemployment tax rate in your state.

2. Assume you run a small business. Working individually or in groups, visit the Web site www.dol.gov/elaws. Write a two-page summary explaining: (1) the various retirement savings programs available to small-business employers, and (2) which retirement savings program you would choose for your small business and why.

3. You are the HR consultant to a small business with about 40 employees. At the present time the firm offers only five days of vacation, five paid holidays, and legally mandated benefits such as unemployment insurance payments. Develop a list of other benefits you believe it should offer, along with your reasons for suggesting them.

EXPERIENTIAL EXERCISE

Purpose: The purpose of this exercise is to provide practice in developing a benefits package for a small business.

Required Understanding: Be very familiar with the material presented in this chapter. In addition, review chapter 11 to reacquaint yourself with sources of compensation survey information, and come to class prepared to share with your group the benefits package for the small business in which you work or in which someone with whom you're familiar works.

How to Set Up the Exercise/Instructions: Divide the class into groups of four or five students. Your assignment is as follows: Maria Cortes runs a small personnel recruiting office in Miami and has decided to start offering an expanded benefits package to her 25 employees. At the current time, the only benefits are 7 paid holidays per year and 5 sick days per year. In her company, there are 2 other managers, as well as 17 full-time recruiters and 5 secretarial staff members. In the time allotted, your group should create a benefits package in keeping with the size and requirements of this firm.

APPLICATION CASE *"Benefits? Who Needs Benefits?"*

The fast-growing Fastonal Company may be in a league of its own when it comes to benefits. The company's business is about as low tech as you can get: It sells nuts and bolts—almost 50,000 different kinds—through 620 company-owned stores. But while its products may be mundane, its financial performance is anything but: Profits have been rising at over 38% per year for five years, and the total return to shareholders of over 40% annually was higher than Coca-Cola's or GE's. Whatever accounts for that kind of performance, it's certainly not the company's fringe benefits. When Bob Kierlan, the company's founder and president, travels (or, often, his firm's other employees travel), he doesn't fly business class; in fact, he doesn't fly at all. On one recent trip, for instance, he drove 5,000 miles round trip in one of the company's vans. He and the company's chief financial officer dined on that trip at Burger King and Subway. And following company policy, they didn't get reimbursed for their road meals since "you've got to eat anyway." When they travel, employees stay at Days Inn–type establishments. Furthermore, the company provides no stock option, 401(k), or other pension plans. At Fastonal, the "benefits" are more often in terms of the wide range of decisions employees get

to make and the opportunity to quickly move up and manage a company store, often after only six months at the company.

Questions

1. It would be an exaggeration, of course, to imply that the company offers no benefits at all. What sort of benefits must a company like this absolutely provide in order to successfully recruit and retain high-quality employees? Why?
2. What are the advantages and disadvantages to Fastonal of offering a pension plan? Do you think it should implement one? Why or why not?
3. Some critics argue that the labor market is too tight for Fastonal to continue to grow as fast as it has in the past. Critics therefore suggest the company has a dilemma. Minimizing benefits is a good idea because it keeps costs down; however, it may soon become less of a good idea if it makes it more difficult to hire good employees. What do you think the company should do? Why?

Source: Based on Richard Teitelbanm, "Who is Bob Kierlan—and Why Is He So Successful?" *Fortune,* December 8, 1997, pp. 240–248.

CONTINUING CASE: LearnInMotion.com *The New Benefits Plan*

LearnInMotion.com provides only legislatively required benefits for its employees. These include participation in New York's unemployment compensation program, Social Security, and workers' compensation (which is provided through the same insurance carrier that insures the company for such hazards as theft and fire). Jennifer, Mel, and

their families have individual family-supported health and life insurance.

Jennifer can see several things wrong with the company's policies regarding benefits and services. First, she wants to determine whether similar companies' experiences with providing health and life insurance benefits suggest it makes hiring easier and/or reduces employee turnover. Jennifer is also concerned that the company has no policy regarding vacations or for sick leave. Informally, at least, it is understood that employees get a one-week vacation after one year's work. However, the policy regarding pay for days such as New Year's and Thanksgiving has been inconsistent: Sometimes employees on the job only two or three weeks are paid fully for one of these holidays; sometimes employees who have been with the firm for six months or more get paid for only half a day. No one really knows what the company's chosen "paid" holidays are. Jennifer knows these policies must be more consistent.

She also wonders about the wisdom of establishing some type of retirement plan for the firm. While everyone working for the firm is still in their 20s, she believes a plan like a 401(k) (in which employees contribute a portion of their pretax salary, to be matched up to some limit by a contribution by LearnInMotion.com) would contribute to the sense of commitment she and Mel would like to create among the LearnInMotion.com team. However, Mel isn't so

sure: His position is that if they don't get sales up pretty soon, they're going to burn through their cash. Now they want you, their management consultants, to help them decide what to do. Here's what they want you to do for them.

Questions and Assignments

1. Draw up a policy statement regarding vacations, sick leave, and paid days off for LearnInMotion.com, based on sources such as those discussed in this and the previous two chapters.
2. What are the advantages and disadvantages to LearnInMotion.com of providing its employees with health, hospitalization, and health insurance programs?
3. In terms of competitors and any other information that you think is relevant, do you or do you not think it's a good idea for LearnInMotion.com to establish a 401(k) or other retirement plan for its employees? If they were to establish such a plan, briefly summarize the plan as you see it.

Chapter 14

Labor Relations and Collective Bargaining

After studying this chapter, you should be able to:

- Give a brief history of the American labor movement.
- Discuss the main features of at least three major pieces of labor legislation.
- Present examples of what to expect during the union drive and election.
- Describe five ways to lose an NLRB election.
- Illustrate with examples bargaining that is not in good faith.
- Develop a grievance procedure.

STRATEGIC OVERVIEW   After years of losses, Amazon's Jeff Bezos knew his firm needed a new strategy. Amazon.com had begun as an online marketer and seller of books, with independent wholesalers handling distribution. The firm had focused on growth rather than profitability. As Amazon grew and added new product lines, its strategy evolved: It began opening company-owned call centers and distribution centers, staffed with its own employees. By 2001, facing huge losses, it had revised its strategy of growth for growth's sake, and begun focusing on profitability. The firm, however, now faced a dilemma: 50 customer service representatives in its Seattle call center were trying to organize a union. If they were successful, and the union effort spread across Amazon, it might hamper the firm's strategy to cut costs and boost profitability.

The previous chapter focused on employee benefits and services—always important when dealing with unions. This chapter starts a new part of the book. The main purpose of this chapter is to provide you with information you'll need to deal effectively with unions and grievances. After briefly discussing the history of the American labor movement, we describe some basic labor legislation, including the subject of unfair labor practices. We explain labor negotiations, including the union actions you can expect during the union campaign and election. And we explain what you can expect during the actual bargaining sessions, and

how to handle grievances, an activity often called contract administration. In the following chapter, Employee Safety and Health, we'll turn to the techniques managers use to provide employees with a safe and healthy workplace. ■

THE LABOR MOVEMENT

Today, just over 16 million U.S. workers belong to unions—around 14.1% of the total number of men and women working in this country.[1] Many are still traditional blue-collar workers, but unions increasingly appeal to white-collar workers, too. For instance, workers including doctors, psychologists, graduate teaching assistants, and even fashion models are forming or joining unions.[2] Federal, state, and local governments employ almost 7 million union members, who account for almost 38% of total government employees. And in some industries—including transportation and public utilities, where over 26% of employees are union members—it's still relatively hard to get a job without joining a union.[3] Union membership in other countries is declining, but is still very high: 37% of employed workers in Canada, 43% in Mexico, 44% in Brazil, 44% in Italy, and 24% in Japan.[4] Why are unions important? How did they get that way? Why do workers join them? How do employers and unions hammer out agreements? These are questions we'll address in this chapter.

A Brief History of the American Union Movement

To understand what unions are and what they want, it is useful to understand "where they've been." The history of the union movement in the United States has been one of alternate expansion and contraction. As early as 1790, skilled craftsmen (shoemakers, tailors, printers, and so on) organized themselves into trade unions. They posted their minimum wage demands and had "tramping committees" go from shop to shop to ensure that no member accepted a lesser wage. Union membership grew until a major depression around 1837 resulted in a membership decline. Membership then began increasing as the United States entered its industrial revolution. In 1869, a group of tailors met and formed the Knights of Labor. The Knights were interested in political reform. By 1885, they had 100,000 members, which (as a result of winning a major strike against a railroad) exploded to 700,000 the following year. Partly because of their focus on social reform, and partly due to a series of unsuccessful strikes, the Knights' membership dwindled rapidly thereafter, and they dissolved in 1893.

In 1886, Samuel Gompers formed the American Federation of Labor. It consisted mostly of skilled workers and, unlike the Knights, focused on practical bread-and-butter gains for its members. The Knights of Labor had engaged in a class struggle to alter the form of society, and thereby get a bigger

▲ *Making fenders at an early Ford factory in Ypsilanti, Michigan. In addition to heavy physical labor, workers faced health hazards— poor lighting, dust, and dangerous machinery.*

chunk of benefits for its members. Gompers aimed to reach the same goal by raising day-to-day wages and improving working conditions. The AFL grew rapidly until after World War I, at which point its membership exceeded 5.5 million people.

The 1920s was a period of stagnation and decline for the U.S. union movement. This was a result of several events, including a postwar depression, manufacturers' renewed resistance to unions, Samuel Gompers's death, and the apparent prosperity of the 1920s. By late 1929, due to the Great Depression, millions of workers had lost their jobs, and by 1933 union membership was down to under 3 million workers.

Membership began to rise in the mid-1930s. As part of his New Deal programs, President Franklin Delano Roosevelt passed the National Industrial Recovery Act, which made it easier for labor to organize. Other federal laws as well as prosperity and World War II also contributed to the rapid increase in members, which topped out at about 21 million workers in the 1970s. Then membership again began to decline, to about 16 million wage and salary workers today.[5] Now, as we'll see, the labor movement is again undergoing change.[6]

Why Do Workers Organize?

Experts have spent much time and money trying to discover why workers unionize, and they've proposed many theories. Yet there is no simple answer to the question, partly because each worker probably joins for his or her own reasons.

It does seem clear that workers don't unionize just to get more pay or better working conditions, though these are very important. In fact, weekly earnings of union members are much higher than those of nonunion workers: about $50 a week more in service jobs, $60 in manufacturing, $130 in government, and as much as $300 a week more in construction jobs, for instance.[7] Union workers receive significantly more holidays, sick leave, unpaid leave, insurance plan benefits, long-term disability benefits, and various other benefits than do nonunion workers.[8]

Yet the urge to unionize often seems to boil down to the belief on the part of workers that it is only through unity that they can get their fair share of the pie and also protect themselves from management whims. (For example, several years ago angry FedEx pilots for a time rejected a proposed agreement backed by their own union leaders, in part, said one pilot, because "there was a trust relationship that has deteriorated."[9]) In practice, therefore, low morale, fear of job loss, and poor communication help foster unionization. Yet unions can't always protect job security, as evidenced by the huge loss of union jobs in manufacturing industries and airlines over the past few years.[10]

◆ **RESEARCH INSIGHT** Studies demonstrate the complexities driving pro-union voting. In one study, it was dissatisfaction with basic bread-and-butter issues like job security and pay, rather than with noneconomic issues like type of work and supervision, that led to pro-union voting (although noneconomic issues were somewhat important, too).[11]

The author of this study contends that dissatisfaction alone won't automatically lead to unionization. Instead, she says, dissatisfied employees must first believe they are without the ability to influence the conditions causing the dissatisfaction. Then enough employees have to believe they could improve things through collective action. Thus, dissatisfied employees who believe the union can help them achieve their goals present a potent combination.[12] Indeed, union instrumentality—the workers' belief that the union can get them the improvements they seek—

is a powerful predictor of pro-union voting.[13] Here is how one writer describes the motivation behind the early unionization of automobile workers:

> In the years to come, economic issues would make the headlines when union and management met in negotiations. But in the early years the rate of pay was not the major complaint of the autoworkers. . . . Specifically, the principal grievances of the autoworkers were the speed-up of production and the lack of any kind of job security. As production tapered off, the order in which workers were laid off was determined largely by the whim of foremen and other supervisors. . . . The worker had no way of knowing when he would be laid off, and had no assurance when, or whether, he would be recalled. . . . Generally, what the workers revolted against was the lack of human dignity and individuality, and a working relationship that was massively impersonal, cold, and nonhuman. They wanted to be treated like human beings—not like faceless clockcard numbers.[14]

What Do Unions Want?

We can generalize by saying that unions have two sets of aims, one for union security and one for improved wages, hours, working conditions, and benefits for their members.

Union Security   First and probably foremost, unions seek security for themselves. They fight hard for the right to represent a firm's workers and to be the exclusive bargaining agent for all employees in the unit. (As such, they negotiate contracts for all employees, including those not members of the union.) Five types of union security are possible:

1. **Closed shop.**[15] The company can hire only union members. Congress outlawed this in 1947, but it still exists in some industries (such as printing).

2. **Union shop.** The company can hire nonunion people, but they must join the union after a prescribed period of time and pay dues. (If not, they can be fired.)

3. **Agency shop.** Employees who do not belong to the union still must pay union dues on the assumption that the union's efforts benefit all the workers.

4. **Open shop.** It is up to the workers whether or not they join the union—those who do not, do not pay dues.

5. Maintenance of membership arrangement. Employees do not have to belong to the union. However, union members employed by the firm must maintain membership in the union for the contract period.

Improved Wages, Hours, and Benefits for Members   Once their security is assured, unions fight to improve wages, hours, and working conditions. The typical labor agreement also gives the union a role in other HR activities, including recruiting, selecting, compensating, promoting, training, and discharging employees.

The AFL-CIO

The American Federation of Labor and Congress of Industrial Organizations (AFL-CIO) is a voluntary federation of about 100 national and international labor unions in the United States. The AFL and CIO merged in 1955, with the AFL's George Meany as its first president. For many people in the United States, it is synonymous with the word *union*. About 2.5 million workers belong to unions not affiliated with the AFL-CIO. Of these workers, about half belong to the largest independent union, the United Auto Workers (about 1 million members).[16]

There are three layers in the structure of the AFL-CIO (and other U.S. unions). First, there is the local union. This is the union the worker joins, and to which he

---

closed shop
A form of union security in which the company can hire only union members. This was outlawed in 1947 but still exists in some industries (such as printing).

---

union shop
A form of union security in which the company can hire nonunion people, but they must join the union after a prescribed period of time and pay dues. (If they do not, they can be fired.)

---

agency shop
A form of union security in which employees who do not belong to the union must still pay union dues on the assumption that union efforts benefit all workers.

---

open shop
Perhaps the least attractive type of union security from the union's point of view, the workers decide whether or not to join the union; and those who join must pay dues.

or she pays dues. The local union also usually signs the collective bargaining agreement determining the wages and working conditions. The local is in turn a single chapter in the national union. For example, if you were a teacher in Detroit, you would belong to the local union there, which is one of hundreds of local chapters of the American Federation of Teachers. The third layer in the structure is the national federation, in this case, the AFL-CIO. This federation is composed of about 100 national and international unions, which in turn are comprised of over 60,000 local unions.

Most people tend to think of the AFL-CIO as the most important part of the labor movement, but it is not. The AFL-CIO itself really has little power, except what its constituent unions let it exercise. Thus, the president of the teachers' union wields more power in that capacity than in her capacity as a vice president of the AFL-CIO. Yet as a practical matter, the AFL-CIO does act as a spokesperson for labor, and its president, John Sweeney, has political clout far in excess of a figurehead president.

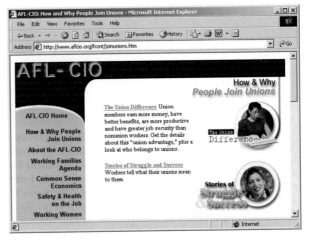

▲ **WEBNOTE**

The AFL-CIO is comprised of and represents more than 60,000 local unions.

www.aflcio.org

UNIONS AND THE LAW

Until about 1930, there were no special labor laws. Employers were not required to engage in collective bargaining with employees and were virtually unrestrained in their behavior toward unions; the use of spies, blacklists, and firing of union agitators were widespread. "Yellow dog" contracts, whereby management could require nonunion membership as a condition for employment, were widely enforced. Most union weapons—even strikes—were illegal.

This one-sided situation lasted until the Great Depression (around 1930). Since then, in response to changing public attitudes, values, and economic conditions, labor law has gone through three clear periods: from "strong encouragement" of unions, to "modified encouragement coupled with regulation," and finally to "detailed regulation of internal union affairs."[17]

Period of Strong Encouragement: The Norris-LaGuardia (1932) and National Labor Relations or Wagner Acts (1935)

The **Norris-LaGuardia Act of 1932** set the stage for a new era in which union activity was encouraged. It guaranteed to each employee the right to bargain collectively "free from interference, restraint, or coercion." It declared yellow dog contracts unenforceable. And it limited the courts' abilities to issue injunctions (stop orders) for activities such as peaceful picketing and payment of strike benefits.[18]

Yet this act did little to restrain employers from fighting labor organizations by whatever means they could find. So in 1935, Congress passed the **National Labor Relations (or Wagner) Act** to add teeth to Norris-LaGuardia. It did this by (1) banning certain unfair labor practices; (2) providing for secret-ballot elections and majority rule for determining whether a firm's employees would unionize; and (3) creating the **National Labor Relations Board (NLRB)** to enforce these two provisions.

As part of its duties, the NLRB periodically issues interpretive rulings. For example, the NLRB recently ruled that temporary employees could join the unions of permanent employees in the companies where their employment agencies assign them to work.[19]

Norris-LaGuardia Act (1932)
This law marked the beginning of the era of strong encouragement of unions and guaranteed to each employee the right to bargain collectively "free from interference, restraint, or coercion."

National Labor Relations (or Wagner) Act
This law banned certain types of unfair practices and provided for secret-ballot elections and majority rule for determining whether or not a firm's employees want to unionize.

National Labor Relations Board (NLRB)
The agency created by the Wagner Act to investigate unfair labor practice charges and to provide for secret-ballot elections and majority rule in determining whether or not a firm's employees want a union.

Unfair Employer Labor Practices The Wagner Act deemed "statutory wrongs" (but not crimes) five unfair labor practices used by employers:

1. It is unfair for employers to "interfere with, restrain, or coerce employees" in exercising their legally sanctioned right of self-organization.
2. It is unfair practice for company representatives to dominate or interfere with either the formation or the administration of labor unions. Among other management actions found to be unfair under practices 1 and 2 are bribing employees, using company spy systems, moving a business to avoid unionization, and blacklisting union sympathizers.
3. Employers are prohibited from discriminating in any way against employees for their legal union activities.
4. Employers are forbidden to discharge or discriminate against employees simply because the latter file unfair practice charges against the company.
5. Finally, it is an unfair labor practice for employers to refuse to bargain collectively with their employees' duly chosen representatives.

Unions file an unfair labor practice charge (see Figure 14-1) with the National Labor Relations Board. The board then investigates the charge and decides if it should take action. Possible actions include dismissal of the complaint, request for an injunction against the employer, or an order that the employer cease and desist.

These complaints are not unusual. When Knight Ridder consolidated the separate online operations of several of its papers into the new Knight Ridder.com, it triggered a labor dispute. Citing possible unfair labor practices, the unions asked the NLRB to investigate whether Knight Ridder.com violated labor law by not negotiating the transfer of workers with the union.[20] The Communications Workers of America recently filed unfair labor practice charges against AT&T. The union said that AT&T had not complied with its commitment to stay neutral on union organizing with the company's cable, wireless, and local service divisions.[21]

From 1935 to 1947 Union membership increased quickly after passage of the Wagner Act in 1935. Other factors such as an improving economy and aggressive union leadership contributed to this rise. But by the mid-1940s, after the end of World War II, the tide had begun to turn. Largely because of a series of massive postwar strikes, public policy began to shift against what many viewed as union excesses. The stage was set for passage of the Taft-Hartley Act.

Period of Modified Encouragement Coupled with Regulation: The Taft-Hartley Act (1947)

Taft-Hartley Act (1947)
Also known as the Labor Management Relations Act, this law prohibited union unfair labor practices and enumerated the rights of employees as union members. It also enumerated the rights of employers.

The **Taft-Hartley (or Labor Management Relations) Act of 1947** reflected the public's less enthusiastic attitude toward unions. It amended the National Labor Relations (Wagner) Act by limiting unions in four ways: (1) prohibiting unfair labor practices, (2) enumerating the rights of employees as union members, (3) enumerating the rights of employers, and (4) allowing the president of the United States to temporarily bar national emergency strikes.

Unfair Union Labor Practices The Taft-Hartley Act enumerated several labor practices that unions were prohibited from engaging in:

1. First, it banned unions from restraining or coercing employees from exercising their guaranteed bargaining rights. Some specific union actions the courts have held illegal under this provision include stating to an anti-union employee that he or she will lose his or her job once the union gains recognition, and issuing patently false statements during union organizing campaigns.
2. It is also an unfair labor practice for a union to cause an employer to discriminate in any way against an employee in order to encourage or discourage his or her membership in a union. In other words, the union cannot try to force an

▼ **FIGURE 14-1   NLRB Form 501: Filing an Unfair Labor Practice Charge**

FORM NLRB-501	UNITED STATES OF AMERICA	DO NOT WRITE IN THIS SPACE	
	NATIONAL LABOR RELATIONS	CASE	DATE FILED
	CHARGE AGAINST EMPLOYER		

EMPLOYER AGAINST WHOM CHARGE IS BROUGHT

a. Name of Employer		b. Number of workers employed
U.S. Postal Service		**800+**

c. Address *(street, city, state, Zip code)*	d. Employer Representative	e. Telephone No.

f. Type of Establishment *(factory, mine, wholesaler, etc.)*	g. Identify principal product or service **U.S. Mail**

h. The above-named employer has engaged in and is engaging in unfair labor practices within the meaning of section 8(a), subsections (1) and *(list subsections)* _____ of the National Labor Relations Act.

and these unfair practices affecting commerce within the meaning of the Act.

2. Basis of the Charge *(set forth a clear and concise statement of the facts constituting the alleged unfair labor practices)*

By the above and other acts, the above-named employer has interfered with, restrained, and coerced employees in the exercise of the rights guaranteed in Section 7 of the ACT

3. Full name of party filing charge *(if labor organization, give full name, including local name and number)*

American Postal Workers Union

4a. Address *(street and number, city, state, and Zip code)*	4b. Telephone No.

5. Full name of national or international labor organization of which it is an affiliate or constituent unit *(to be filled in when charge is filed by a labor organization)* **American Postal Workers Union 1300 L St. NW Washington, DC 20005**

DECLARATION **I declare that I have read the above charge and the statements are true to the best of my knowledge and belief.**

By _____

(signature of representative or person making charge) (title if any)

Address _____

Telephone Date _____

WILLFUL FALSE STATEMENTS ON THIS CHARGE CAN BE PUNISHED BY FINE AND IMPRISONMENT (U.S. CODE, TITLE 18, SECTION 1001)

Source: National Labor Relations Board.

employer to fire a worker because he or she doesn't attend union meetings, opposes union policies, or refuses to join a union. There is one exception: Where a closed or union shop prevails (and union membership is therefore a prerequisite to employment), the union may demand discharge for a worker who fails to pay his or her initiation fees and dues.

3. It is an unfair labor practice for a union to refuse to bargain in good faith with the employer about wages, hours, and other employment conditions. Certain strikes and boycotts are also unfair practices.
4. It is an unfair labor practice for a union to engage in "featherbedding" (requiring an employer to pay an employee for services not performed).

Rights of Employees   The Taft-Hartley Act also protected the rights of employees against their unions. For example, many people felt that compulsory unionism violated the basic right of freedom of association. New right-to-work laws sprang up in 19 states (mainly in the South and Southwest). These outlawed labor contracts that made union membership a condition for keeping one's job. In New York, for example, many printing firms have union shops. You can't work as a press operator unless you belong to a printers' union. In Florida, such union shops—except those covered by the Railway Labor Act—are illegal, and printing shops typically employ both union and nonunion press operators. Even today, union membership varies widely by state, from a high of 26.8% in New York to a low of 3.7% in South Carolina (other representative membership densities are California, 16.5%; Florida, 7.4%; Texas, 6.5%; Michigan, 23.9%; and Ohio, 19.4%).[22] This employee rights provision also allowed an employee to present grievances directly to the employer (without going through the union). And it required the employee's authorization before the union could have dues subtracted from his or her paycheck.

Rights of Employers   The Taft-Hartley Act also explicitly gave employers certain rights. First, it gave them full freedom to express their views concerning union organization. For example, you as a manager can tell your employees that in your opinion unions are worthless, dangerous to the economy, and immoral. You can even, generally speaking, hint that unionization and subsequent high-wage demands might result in the permanent closing of the plant (but not its relocation). Employers can set forth the union's record concerning violence and corruption, if appropriate. In fact, the only major restraint is that employers must avoid threats, promises, coercion, and direct interference with workers who are trying to reach a decision. There can be no threat of reprisal or force or promise of benefit.[23]

The employer (1) cannot meet with employees on company time within 24 hours of an election or (2) suggest to employees that they vote against the union while they are at home or in the employer's office, although he or she can do so while in their work area or where they normally gather.

National Emergency Strikes   The Taft-Hartley Act also allows the U.S. president to intervene in **national emergency strikes**. These are strikes (for example, on the part of steel workers) that might "imperil the national health and safety." The president may appoint a board of inquiry and, based on its report, apply for an injunction restraining the strike for 60 days. If the parties don't reach a settlement during that time, the president can have the injunction extended for another 20 days. During this last period, employees take a secret ballot to ascertain their willingness to accept the employer's last offer.

national emergency strikes
Strikes that might "imperil the national health and safety."

Period of Detailed Regulation of Internal Union Affairs: The Landrum-Griffin Act (1959)

In the 1950s, Senate investigations revealed unsavory practices on the part of some unions, and the result was the **Landrum-Griffin Act** (officially, the **Labor Management Reporting and Disclosure Act) of 1959**. An overriding aim of this act was to protect union members from possible wrongdoing on the part of their unions. Like Taft-Hartley, it also amended the National Labor Relations (Wagner) Act.

Landrum-Griffin Act (1959)
The law aimed at protecting union members from possible wrongdoing on the part of their unions.

First, the law contains a bill of rights for union members. Among other things, it provides for certain rights in the nomination of candidates for union office. It also affirms a member's right to sue his or her union and ensures that no member can be fined or suspended without due process, which includes a list of specific charges, time to prepare a defense, and a fair hearing.

This act also laid out rules regarding union elections. For example, national and international unions must elect officers at least once every five years, using some type of secret-ballot mechanism. And it regulates the kind of person who can serve as a union officer. For example, persons convicted of felonies (bribery, murder, and so on) are barred from holding union officer positions for a period of five years after conviction.

Senate investigators also discovered flagrant examples of employer wrong-doing. Employers and their "labor relations consultants" had bribed union agents and officers, for example. That had been a federal crime starting with the passage of the Taft-Hartley Act. But Landrum-Griffin greatly expanded the list of unlawful employer actions. For example, companies can no longer pay their own employees to entice them not to join the union. The act also requires reports from unions and employers covering such practices as the use of labor relations consultants.

Union laws like these aren't just issues for big companies like FedEx and GE. They're increasingly an issue for high-tech entrepreneurs too, as the following illustrates.

ENTREPRENEURS · HR

Dot-Coms and Unions

Dot-com entrepreneurs ranging from the heads of giant Amazon.com down to tiny LearnInMotion.com are getting a quick and unexpected lesson in labor relations. For most of their short corporate lives, they assumed that "new economy" jobs like Web designer and business development head were immune from union efforts. But with several e-commerce firms, including Amazon.com and Etown.com, facing union organizing efforts, they've had to change those assumptions, and fast.

There are many reasons why dot-coms are not as immune from unions as their entrepreneur founders thought they'd be. For one thing, many employees at "new economy" online retailers such as Amazon.com are doing very "old economy" tasks like loading and unloading trucks and packing shipments—precisely the sorts of jobs that unions successfully organize in traditional bricks-and-mortar companies. Even many of the Web designers, programmers, and other high-tech employees—who traditionally see themselves playing big roles in their dot-com companies—got increasingly frustrated as stock options lost most of their value in 2000–2001 and dot-coms went out of business or shrank drastically.

And when it comes to attracting unions, many of these entrepreneurs have been their own worst enemies. Focusing almost all their resources on building sales and meeting customer demand, many paid little attention to writing personnel policies, developing effective performance appraisal systems, or staying in touch with employees' concerns. As one labor attorney puts it, "they have been lax about overtime, pay scales, and just having an employee handbook with policies and procedures clearly defined. . . . The high-tech industry has always been so confident that none of their own would ever want the union that they've been amazingly ignorant of basic labor law." Even the dot-com entrepreneurs' love affairs with their intranets may work against them: For example, many store all personal information regarding employees in computer files that are easily accessed by employees who want to start union organizing campaigns.

What is a dot-com entrepreneur to do? Revise (or enact) written personnel policies and practices, so union organizers have less reason to view your firm as a loosely run and vulnerable target. Improve the security of employee records files. And (since unionization attempts in dot-coms tend to focus on support services such as call centers, distribution, and help desks)—one labor lawyer says—"don't lose touch with the people taking the calls. And don't think it is just about compensation. It is also the work environment. An hourly call center employee who punches a clock day after day while watching the engineers come and go as they please may get ideas."[24]

THE UNION DRIVE AND ELECTION

It is through the union drive and election that a union tries to be recognized to represent employees.[25] This process has five basic steps.

Step 1. Initial Contact

During the initial contact stage, the union determines the employees' interest in organizing, and establishes an organizing committee.

The initiative for the first contact between the employees and the union may come from the employees, from a union already representing other employees of the firm, or from a union representing workers elsewhere. In any case, there is an initial contact between a union representative and a few employees.

Once an employer becomes a target, a union official usually assigns a representative to assess employee interest. The representative visits the firm to determine whether enough employees are interested to make a union campaign worthwhile. He or she also identifies employees who would make good leaders in the organizing campaign and calls them together to create an organizing committee. The objective here is to "educate the committee about the benefits of forming a union, the law and procedures involved in forming a local union, and the issues management is likely to raise during a campaign."[26]

The union must follow certain rules when it starts contacting employees. The law allows organizers to solicit employees for membership as long as the effort doesn't endanger the performance or safety of the employees. Therefore, much of the contact takes place off the job, for example, at home or at eating places near work. Organizers can also safely contact employees on company grounds during off hours (such as lunch or break time). Yet, in practice, there will be much informal organizing going on at the workplace as employees debate the merits of organizing. In any case, this initial contact stage may be deceptively quiet. Sometimes the first inkling management has of the campaign is the distribution or posting of handbills soliciting union membership.

Technology, in the form of e-mail, is of course affecting the organizing process. However, preventing union employees from sending pro-union e-mail messages on company e-mail is easier said than done. Prohibiting only union e-mail may violate NLRB decisions, for instance. And instituting a rule barring workers from using e-mail for all non-work-related topics may also be futile if the company actually does little to stop e-mail other than pro-union messages.

Labor Relations Consultants Both management and unions now use outside advisers, and these labor relations consultants are increasingly influencing the unionization process. The consultants may be law firms, researchers, psychologists, labor relations specialists, or public relations firms. In any case, their role is to provide advice and related services not just when a vote is expected (although this is when most of them are used), but at other times, too. For the employer, the consultant's services may range from ensuring that the firm properly fills out routine forms to managing the whole union campaign. Unions may use public relations firms to improve their image, or specialists to manage corporate campaigns aimed at pressuring shareholders and creditors to get management to agree to the union's demands.

The widespread use of such consultants—only some of whom are actually lawyers—has raised the question of whether some have advised their clients to engage in activities that are illegal or questionable under labor laws. One tactic, for instance, is to delay the union vote with lengthy hearings at the NLRB. The longer the delay in the vote, they argue, the more time the employer has to drill anti-union propaganda into the employees. During these delays, employers can also try to eliminate employees who are not anti-union, and pack the bargaining unit with promanagement employees.[27] Others accuse consultants of advising employers to lie to the NLRB, for example, by backdating memos in order to convince the board that the wage increase being offered was decided months before the union campaign ever began.[28]

Union Salting Unions are not without creative ways to win elections. **Union salting** is an organizing tactic by which full time undercover union organizers are hired by unwitting employers. A 1995 U.S. Supreme Court decision held the tactic to be legal.[29] For employers, the solution is to make sure you know who you're hiring.[30]

However, employers must proceed with care. Recently, for instance, the National Labor Relations Board concluded that an employer did commit an unfair labor practice by refusing to consider hiring nine members of Plumbers and Pipe Fitters, Local 520. Not hiring the people simply because as members of the local union they might be pro-union or union salts would be discriminatory. On the other hand, if the employer could show that it would not hire the applicants regardless of their union affiliation—perhaps because they didn't have the qualifications for the position, or others were more qualified—then the refusal to hire them is defensible.[31] The NLRB said its local office had to review each case to determine if the employer's decisions were nondiscriminatory.

Step 2. Obtaining Authorization Cards

For the union to petition the NLRB for the right to hold an election, it must show that a sizable number of employees may be interested in organizing. The next step is thus for union organizers to try to get the employees to sign **authorization cards**. Among other things, these usually authorize the union to seek a representation election and state that the employee has applied to join the union. Thirty percent of the eligible employees in an appropriate bargaining unit must sign before the union can petition the NLRB for an election.

During this stage, both union and management use various forms of propaganda. The union claims it can improve working conditions, raise wages, increase benefits, and generally get the workers better deals. Management can attack the union on ethical and moral grounds and cite the cost of union membership. Management can also explain its track record, express facts and opinions, and explain the law applicable to organizing campaigns. However, neither side can threaten, bribe, or coerce employees. And an employer may not make promises of benefit to employees or make unilateral changes in terms and conditions of employment that were not planned to be implemented prior to the onset of union organizing activity.

Management can take several steps with respect to the authorization cards themselves. For example, the NLRB ruled "an employer may lawfully inform employees of their right to revoke their authorization cards, even when employees have not solicited such information." The employer can also distribute pamphlets that explain just how employees can revoke their cards.[32] However, man-

union salting
A union organizing tactic by which workers who are in fact employed full time by a union as undercover organizers are hired by unwitting employers.

authorization cards
In order to petition for a union election, the union must show that at least 30% of employees may be interested in being unionized. Employees indicate this interest by signing authorization cards.

agement can go no farther than explaining to employees the procedure for card revocation and furnishing resignation language. The law prohibits any material assistance such as postage or stationery. The employer also cannot check to determine which employees have actually revoked their authorization cards.

What else can you do to educate employees who have not yet decided whether to sign their cards? It is an unfair labor practice to tell employees they can't sign a card. What you can do is prepare supervisors so they can explain what the card actually authorizes the union to do. For example, the typical authorization card actually does three things. It lets the union seek a representation election (it can be used as evidence that 30% of your employees have an interest in organizing). It designates the union as a bargaining representative in all employment matters. And it states that the employee has applied for membership in the union and will be subject to union rules and bylaws. The latter is especially important; the union, for instance, may force the employee to picket and fine any member who does not comply with union instructions. Explaining the serious legal and practical implications of signing the card can thus be an effective management weapon.

One thing management should *not* do is look through signed authorization cards if confronted with them by union representatives. The NLRB could construe that as an unfair labor practice, as spying on those who signed. It could also later form the basis of a charge alleging discrimination due to union activity, if the firm subsequently disciplines someone who signed a card.

During this stage, unions can picket the company, subject to three constraints: (1) The union must file a petition for an election within 30 days after the start of picketing; (2) the firm cannot already be lawfully recognizing another union; and (3) there cannot have been a valid NLRB election during the past 12 months. Unions today use the Internet to distribute and collect authorization cards.

Step 3. Hold a Hearing

Once the union collects the authorization cards, one of three things can occur. If the employer chooses not to contest *union recognition*, the parties need no hearing, and a special "consent election" is held. If the employer chooses not to contest the union's *right to an election*, and/or the scope of the bargaining unit, and/or which employees are eligible to vote in the election, no hearing is needed and the parties can stipulate an election. If an employer *does* wish to contest the union's right, it can insist on a hearing to determine those issues. An employer's decision about whether to insist on a hearing is a strategic one based on the facts of each case and whether it feels it needs additional time to try to persuade a majority of its employees not to elect a union to represent them.

Most companies do contest the union's right to represent their employees, claiming that a significant number of them don't really want the union. It is at this point that the National Labor Relations Board gets involved. The union usually contacts the NLRB, which requests a hearing. The regional director of the NLRB then sends a hearing officer to investigate. The examiner sends both management and union a notice of representation hearing (NLRB Form 852; see Figure14-2) that states the time and place of the hearing.

The hearing addresses several issues. First, does the record indicate there is enough evidence to hold an election? (For example, did 30% or more of the employees in an appropriate bargaining unit sign the authorization cards?) Second, the examiner must decide what the bargaining unit will be. The latter is a crucial matter for the union, for employees, and for the employer. The **bargaining unit** is the group of employees that the union will be authorized to represent and bargain for collectively. If the entire organization is the bargaining unit, the union will represent all nonsupervisory, nonmanagerial, and nonconfi-

bargaining unit
The group of employees the union will be authorized to represent.

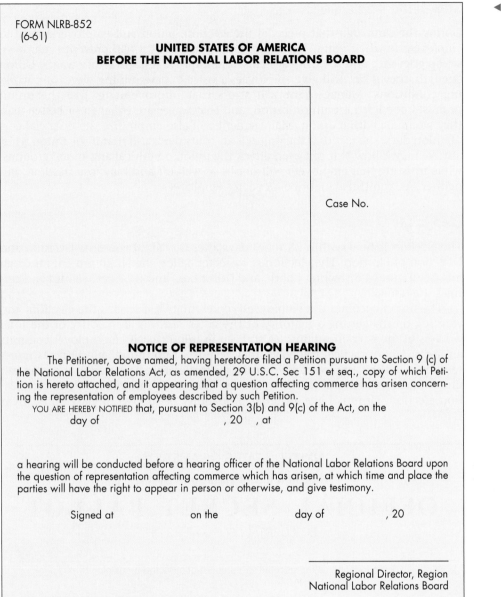

◄ **FIGURE 14-2**
NLRB Form 852;
Notice of
Representation
Hearing

FORM NLRB-852
(6-61)

UNITED STATES OF AMERICA
BEFORE THE NATIONAL LABOR RELATIONS BOARD

Case No.

NOTICE OF REPRESENTATION HEARING

The Petitioner, above named, having heretofore filed a Petition pursuant to Section 9 (c) of the National Labor Relations Act, as amended, 29 U.S.C. Sec 151 et seq., copy of which Petition is hereto attached, and it appearing that a question affecting commerce has arisen concerning the representation of employees described by such Petition.

YOU ARE HEREBY NOTIFIED that, pursuant to Section 3(b) and 9(c) of the Act, on the day of   , 20   , at

a hearing will be conducted before a hearing officer of the National Labor Relations Board upon the question of representation affecting commerce which has arisen, at which time and place the parties will have the right to appear in person or otherwise, and give testimony.

Signed at   on the   day of   , 20

Regional Director, Region
National Labor Relations Board

dential employees, although the union may be oriented mostly toward blue-collar workers. (Professional and nonprofessional employees can be included in the same bargaining unit only if the professionals agree to it.) If your firm disagrees with the examiner's decision regarding the bargaining unit, it can challenge the decision. This will require a separate step and NLRB ruling.

The NLRB hearing addresses other questions. These include: "Does the employer qualify for coverage by the NLRB?" "Is the union a labor organization within the meaning of the National Labor Relations Act?" "Do any existing collective bargaining agreements or prior elections bar the union from holding a representation election?"

If the results of the hearing are favorable for the union, the NLRB will order holding an election. It will issue a Notice of Election (NLRB Form 707) to that effect, for the employer to post.

Step 4. The Campaign

During the campaign that precedes the election, union and employer appeal to employees for their votes. The union emphasizes that it will prevent unfairness, set up grievance and seniority systems, and improve unsatisfactory wages. Union strength, they'll say, will give employees a voice in determining wages and working conditions. Management will stress that improvements like the union promises don't require unionization, and that wages are equal to or better than they would be with a union. Management will also emphasize the financial cost of union dues; the fact that the union is an "outsider"; and that if the union wins, a strike may follow.[33] It can even attack the union on ethical and moral grounds, while insisting that employees will not be as well off and may lose freedom. But neither side can threaten, bribe, or coerce employees.

Step 5. The Election

The election is held within 30 to 60 days after the NLRB issues its Decision and Direction of Election. The election is by secret ballot; the NLRB provides the ballots (see Figure14-3), voting booth, and ballot box, and counts the votes and certifies the results.

The union becomes the employees' representative if it wins the election, and winning means getting a majority of the votes *cast*, not a majority of the total workers in the bargaining unit. (Also keep in mind that if an employer commits an unfair labor practice, the NLRB may reverse a "no union" election. As representatives of their employer, supervisors must therefore be careful not to commit unfair practices.) Several things influence whether the union wins the certification election. Unions have a higher probability of success in geographic areas

► **FIGURE 14-3**
Sample NLRB Ballot

UNITED STATES OF AMERICA

National Labor Relations Board

OFFICIAL SECRET BALLOT

FOR CERTAIN EMPLOYEES OF

_____

Do you wish to be represented for purposes of collective bargaining by —

_____

MARK AN "S" IN THE SQUARE OF YOUR CHOICE

_____

YES

☐

NO

☐

DO NOT SIGN THIS BALLOT. Fold and drop in ballot box.
If you spoil this ballot return it to the Board Agent for a new one.

with a higher percentage of union workers, in part because union employees enjoy higher wages and benefits. High unemployment seems to lead to poorer results for the union, perhaps because employees fear that unionization might result in reduced job security or employer retaliation. Unions usually carefully pick the size of their bargaining unit (all clerical employees in the company, only those at one facility, and so on), because it's clear that the larger the bargaining unit, the smaller the probability of union victory. The more workers vote, the less likely a union victory, probably because more workers who are not strong supporters vote. The union is important, too: The Teamsters union is less likely to win a representation election than other unions.[34]

How to Lose an NLRB Election

Employers lost almost half of the 3,160 collective bargaining elections held in one recent year, but a study suggests many such elections need not be lost.[35] According to expert Mathew Goodfellow, there is no sure way employers can win elections. However, there are five sure ways to lose one:[36]

Reason 1. Asleep at the Switch In one study, in 68% of the companies that lost to the union, executives were caught unaware. In these companies, turnover and absenteeism had increased, productivity was erratic, and safety was poor. Grievance procedures were rare. When the first reports of authorization cards began trickling back to top managers, they usually responded with a barrage of letters describing how the company was "one big family" and calling for a "team effort." As Goodfellow observes,

> Yet the best strategy is to not be caught asleep in the first place: Overall, prudence dictates that management spend time and effort even when the atmosphere is calm testing the temperature of employee sentiments and finding ways to remove irritants. Doing that cuts down on the possibility that an election will ever take place. . . .[37]

Reason 2. Appointing a Committee Of the losing companies, 36% formed a committee to manage the campaign. According to the expert, there are three problems in doing so: (1) Promptness is essential in an election situation, and committees are notorious for moving slowly. (2) Most committee members are NLRB neophytes. Their views therefore are mostly reflections of wishful thinking rather than experience. (3) A committee's decision is usually a compromise decision. The result is often close to the most conservative opinion—but not necessarily the most knowledgeable or most effective one. This expert suggests giving full responsibility to a single decisive executive. A human resource director and a consultant or adviser with broad experience in labor relations should in turn assist this person.

Reason 3. Concentrating on Money and Benefits In 54% of the elections studied, the company lost because top management concentrated on the wrong issues: money and benefits. As this expert puts it:

> Employees may want more money, but quite often if they feel the company treats them fairly, decently, and honestly, they are satisfied with reasonable, competitive rates and benefits. It is only when they feel ignored, uncared for, and disregarded that money becomes a major issue to express their dissatisfaction.[38]

Reason 4. Industry Blind Spots The researcher found that in some industries, employees felt more ignored and disregarded than in others. In highly automated industries (such as paper manufacturing and automobiles), there was some tendency for executives to ignore hourly employees, although this is changing today as firms implement more quality improvement programs. Here (as in reason 3), the solution is to pay more attention to employees' needs and attitudes.

Reason 5. Delegating Too Much to Divisions For companies with plants scattered around the country, organizing several of the plants gives the union a wedge to tempt other plants' workers. Unionizing one or more plants tends to lead to unionizing others. Part of the solution is to keep the first four reasons above in mind, and thus diminish the union's ability to organize those first few plants. Also, don't abdicate all personnel and industrial relations decisions to plant managers.[39] Dealing effectively with unions—monitoring employees' attitudes, reacting properly when the union appears, and so on—generally requires centralized guidance from the main office and its HR staff.

The Supervisor's Role

Supervisors are an employer's first line of defense when it comes to the unionizing effort. They are often in the best position to sense evolving employee attitude problems, for instance, and to discover the first signs of union activity. Unfortunately, there's another side to that coin: They can also inadvertently take actions that hurt their employers' union-related efforts.

Supervisors therefore need special training. Specifically, they must be knowledgeable about what they can and can't do to legally hamper organizing activities. Unfair labor practices could (1) cause the NLRB to hold a new election after your company has won a previous election, or (2) cause your company to forfeit the second election and go directly to contract negotiation.

In one case, a plant superintendent reacted to a union's initial organizing attempt by prohibiting distribution of union literature in the plant's lunchroom. Since solicitation of off-duty workers in nonwork areas is generally legal, the company subsequently allowed the union to post union literature on the company's bulletin board and to distribute union literature in nonworking areas inside the plant. However, the NLRB still ruled that the initial act of prohibiting distribution of the literature was an unfair labor practice, one not "made right" by the company's subsequent efforts. The NLRB used the superintendent's action as one reason for invalidating an election that the company had won.[40]

Rules Regarding Literature and Solicitation

There are steps you can take to legally restrict union organizing activity:[41]

1. Employers can always bar nonemployees from soliciting employees during their work time—that is, when the employee is on duty and not on a break. Thus, if the company cafeteria is open to whoever is on the premises, union organizers can solicit off-duty employees who are in the cafeteria, but not the cafeteria workers (such as cooks) who are not on a break.
2. Employers can usually stop employees from soliciting other employees for any purpose if one or both employees are on paid-duty time and not on a break.
3. Most employers (not including retail stores, shopping centers, and certain other employers) can bar nonemployees from the building's interiors and work areas as a right of private property owners. They can also sometimes bar nonemployees from exterior private areas—such as parking lots—if there is a business reason (such as safety) and the reason is not just to interfere with union organizers.

     Whether or not employers must give union representatives permission to organize on employer-owned property at shopping malls is a matter of legal debate. The U.S. Supreme Court ruled in *Lechmere, Inc. v. National Labor Relations Board* that employers may bar nonemployees from their property if the nonemployees have reasonable alternative means of communicating their message to the intended audience. However, if the employer lets other organizations like the

Salvation Army set up at their workplaces, the NLRB may view discriminating against the union organizers as an unfair labor practice.[42]

4. Employers can deny on- or off-duty employees access to interior or exterior areas only if they can show the rule is required for reasons of production, safety, or discipline.

Such restrictions are valid only if the employer doesn't discriminate against the union. For example, if the employer lets employees collect money for wedding, shower, and baby gifts, to sell Avon products or Tupperware, or to engage in other solicitation during their working time, it may not be able to lawfully prohibit them from union soliciting during work time. To do so would discriminate based on union activity, which is an unfair labor practice. Here are two examples of specific rules aimed at limiting union organizing activity:

"Solicitation of employees on company property during working time interferes with the efficient operation of our business. Nonemployees are not permitted to solicit employees on company property for any purpose. Except in break areas where both employees are on break or off the clock, no employee may solicit another employee during working time for any purpose."

"Distribution of literature on company property not only creates a little problem but also distracts us from our work. Nonemployees are not allowed to distribute literature on company property. Except in the performance of his or her job, an employee may not distribute literature unless both the distributor and the recipient are off the clock or on authorized break in a break area or off company premises. Special exceptions to these rules may be made by the company for especially worthwhile causes such as United Way, but written permission must first be obtained and the solicitation will be permitted only during break periods."[43]

THE *NEW* WORKPLACE

Unions Go Global

Any company that thinks it can avoid unionization by sending manufacturing and jobs abroad is sorely mistaken.[44] Today, as we've seen, most businesses are "going global," and regional trade treaties like the North American Free Trade Agreement (NAFTA) will further boost the business firms do abroad. This fact is not lost on unions, some of which are already expanding their influence abroad.

For example, U.S. unions are helping Mexican unions to organize, especially in U.S.-owned factories. Thus, the United Electrical Workers is subsidizing organizers at Mexican plants of the General Electric Company. And when the Campbell Soup Company threatened to move some operations to Mexico, the Farm Labor Organizing Committee, a midwestern union, discouraged the move by helping its Mexican counterpart win a stronger contract, one that would have cost Campbell Soup higher wages if it made the move.

Reebok's recent experience provides another example of how unions reach across national boundaries. It has been working with the AFL-CIO to make the unions representing its overseas factories' employees more effective in protecting its workers' human rights.[45] Safety and work conditions are thus improving.

U.S. unions gain several things by forming alliances with unions abroad. By helping workers in other countries unionize, they help raise the wages and living standards of local workers. That may in turn discourage corporate flight from the United States in search of low wages. Unions also help their own positions in the U.S. with the added leverage they get from having unions abroad that can help them fight their corporate campaigns.

Decertification Elections: Ousting the Union

decertification
Legal process for employees to terminate a union's right to represent them.

Winning an election and signing an agreement do not necessarily mean that the union is in the company to stay—quite the opposite. The same law that grants employees the right to unionize also gives them a way to legally terminate their union's right to represent them. The process is **decertification**. There are around 450 to 500 decertification elections each year, of which unions usually win around 30%.[46] That's actually a more favorable rate for management than the rate for the original, representation elections. For example, of 1,474 representation elections held in early 2000, unions won 52.4%.[47]

Decertification campaigns don't differ much from certification campaigns.[48] The union organizes membership meetings and house-to-house visits, mails literature into the homes, and uses phone calls, NLRB appeals, and (sometimes) threats and harassment to win the election.[49] For its part, management uses meetings—including one-on-one meetings, small-group meetings, and meetings with entire units—as well as legal or expert assistance, letters, improved working conditions, and subtle or not-so-subtle threats to try to influence the votes.[50]

THE COLLECTIVE BARGAINING PROCESS

What Is Collective Bargaining?

collective bargaining
The process through which representatives of management and the union meet to negotiate a labor agreement.

When and if the union becomes your employees' representative, a day is set for management and labor to meet and negotiate a labor agreement. This agreement will contain specific provisions covering wages, hours, and working conditions.

What exactly is **collective bargaining**? According to the National Labor Relations Act:

For the purpose of [this act,] to bargain collectively is the performance of the mutual obligation of the employer and the representative of the employees to meet at reasonable times and confer in good faith with respect to wages, hours, and terms and conditions of employment, or the negotiation of an agreement, or any question arising thereunder, and the execution of a written contract incorporating any agreement reached if requested by either party, but such obligation does not compel either party to agree to a proposal or require the making of a concession.

In plain language, this means that both management and labor are required by law to negotiate wage, hours, and terms and conditions of employment "in good faith." In a moment, we will see that the specific terms that are negotiable (since "wages, hours, and conditions of employment" are too broad to be useful in practice) have been clarified by a series of court decisions.

What Is Good Faith?

good faith bargaining
Both parties are making every reasonable effort to arrive at agreement; proposals are being matched with counterproposals.

Good faith bargaining is the cornerstone of effective labor–management relations. It means that both parties communicate and negotiate, that they match proposals with counterproposals, and that both make every reasonable effort to arrive at an agreement.[51] It does not mean that one party compels another to agree to a proposal. Nor does it require that either party make any specific concessions (although as a practical matter, some may be necessary).

When is bargaining not in good faith? As interpreted by the NLRB and the courts, a violation of the requirement for good faith bargaining may include the following:

1. *Surface bargaining.* Going through the motions of bargaining without any real intention of completing a formal agreement.

2. *Inadequate concessions.* Unwillingness to compromise, even though no one is required to make a concession.

3. *Inadequate proposals and demands.* The NLRB considers the advancement of proposals to be a positive factor in determining overall good faith.

4. *Dilatory tactics.* The law requires that the parties meet and "confer at reasonable times and intervals." Obviously, refusal to meet with the union does not satisfy the positive duty imposed on the employer.

5. *Imposing conditions.* Attempts to impose conditions that are so onerous or unreasonable as to indicate bad faith.

6. *Making unilateral changes in conditions.* A strong indication that the employer is not bargaining with the required intent of reaching an agreement.

7. *Bypassing the representative.* The duty of management to bargain in good faith involves, at a minimum, recognition that the union representative is the one with whom the employer must deal in conducting negotiations.

8. *Committing unfair labor practices during negotiations.* Such practices may reflect poorly upon the good faith of the guilty party.

9. *Withholding information.* An employer must supply the union with information, upon request, to enable it to understand and intelligently discuss the issues raised in bargaining.

10. *Ignoring bargaining items.* Refusal to bargain on a mandatory item (one must bargain over these) or insistence on a permissive item (one may bargain over these).[52]

Of course, requiring good faith bargaining doesn't mean that negotiations can't grind to a halt. For example, Northwest Airlines wouldn't let its negotiators meet with mechanics' union representatives because, Northwest said, the union didn't respond to company proposals the last three times they met.[53] Claiming that Bryant College negotiators were not sufficiently responsive with respect to wages and benefits, the Service Employees International Union, Local 134, filed an unfair labor practice claiming Bryant failed to negotiate in good faith.[54]

The Negotiating Team

Both union and management send a negotiating team to the bargaining table, and both teams usually go into the bargaining sessions having "done their homework." Union representatives will have sounded out union members on their desires and conferred with representatives of related unions.

Management uses several techniques to prepare for bargaining. First, it prepares the data on which to build its bargaining position.[55] It compiles data on pay and benefits that include comparisons with local pay rates and to rates paid for similar jobs within the industry. Data on the distribution of the workforce (in terms of age, sex, and seniority, for instance) are also important, because these factors determine what the company will actually pay out in benefits. Internal economic data regarding cost of benefits, overall earnings levels, and the amount and cost of overtime are important as well.

▲ *In March 2001, about 3,000 employees of New York City's Metropolitan Transportation Authority demonstrated in midtown Manhattan in a dispute between their employer and their union, the Transit Workers Union, over a health benefits trust that had been negotiated two years earlier.*

Management will also "cost" the current labor contract and determine the increased cost—total, per employee, and per hour—of the union's demands. It will use information from grievances and feedback from supervisors to determine what the union's demands might be, and prepare counteroffers and arguments.[56] Other popular tactics are attitude surveys to test employee reactions to various sections of the contract that management may feel require change, and informal conferences with local union leaders to discuss the operational effectiveness of the contract and to send up trial balloons on management ideas for change.

Bargaining Items

voluntary bargaining items
Items in collective bargaining over which bargaining is neither illegal nor mandatory—neither party can be compelled against its wishes to negotiate over those items.

Labor law sets out categories of items that are subject to bargaining: These are mandatory, voluntary, and illegal items.

Voluntary (or permissible) bargaining items are neither mandatory nor illegal; they become a part of negotiations only through the joint agreement of both management and union. Neither party can compel the other to negotiate over voluntary items. You cannot hold up signing a contract because the other party refuses to bargain on a voluntary item.

illegal bargaining items
Items in collective bargaining that are forbidden by law; for example, a clause agreeing to hire "union members exclusively" would be illegal in a right-to-work state.

Illegal bargaining items are forbidden by law. A clause agreeing to hire union members exclusively would be illegal in a right-to-work state, for example.

Table 14-1 presents some of the 70 or so **mandatory bargaining items**, over which bargaining is mandatory under the law. They include wages, hours, rest periods, layoffs, transfers, benefits, and severance pay. Others, such as drug testing, are added as the law evolves.[57]

mandatory bargaining items
Items in collective bargaining that a party must bargain over if they are introduced by the other party—for example, pay.

Bargaining Stages[58]

The actual bargaining typically goes through several stages.[59] First, each side presents its demands. At this stage, both parties are usually quite far apart on some issues. Second, there is a reduction of demands. At this stage, each side trades off

▶ **TABLE 14-1**
    Bargaining Items

Mandatory	Permissible	Illegal
Rates of pay	Indemnity bonds	Closed shop
Wages	Management rights as to	Separation of employees
Hours of employment	union affairs	based on race
Overtime pay	Pension benefits of retired	Discriminatory treatment
Shift differentials	employees	
Holidays	Scope of the bargaining	
Vacations	unit	
Severance pay	Including supervisors in the	
Pensions	contract	
Insurance benefits	Additional parties to the	
Profit-sharing plans	contract such as the	
Christmas bonuses	international union	
Company housing,	Use of union label	
meals, and discounts	Settlement of unfair	
Employee security	labor changes	
Job performance	Prices in cafeteria	
Union security	Continuance of past	
Management–union	contract	
relationship	Membership of bargaining	
Drug testing	team	
of employees	Employment of strike	
	breakers	

Source: Michael B. Carrell and Christina Heavrin, *Labor Relations and Collective Bargaining* (Upper Saddle River, NJ: Prentice Hall, 2001), p. 177.

some of its demands to gain others. Third come the subcommittee studies; the parties form joint subcommittees to try to work out reasonable alternatives. Fourth, the parties reach an informal settlement, and each group goes back to its sponsor. Union representatives check informally with their superiors and the union members; management representatives check with top management. Finally, once everything is in order, the parties fine-tune and sign a formal agreement.

Bargaining Hints

Expert Reed Richardson has the following advice for bargainers:

1. Be sure to set clear objectives for every bargaining item, and be sure you understand the reason for each.
2. Do not hurry.
3. When in doubt, caucus with your associates.
4. Be well prepared with firm data supporting your position.
5. Always strive to keep some flexibility in your position.
6. Don't concern yourself just with what the other party says and does; find out why.
7. Respect the importance of face saving for the other party.
8. Be alert to the real intentions of the other party—not only for goals, but also for priorities.
9. Be a good listener.
10. Build a reputation for being fair but firm.
11. Learn to control your emotions and use them as a tool.
12. As you make each bargaining move, be sure you know its relationship to all other moves.
13. Measure each move against your objectives.
14. Pay close attention to the wording of every clause negotiated; they are often a source of grievances.
15. Remember that collective bargaining is a compromise process. There is no such thing as having all the pie.
16. Try to understand people and their personalities.
17. Consider the impact of present negotiations on those in future years.[60]

Impasses, Mediation, and Strikes[61]

In collective bargaining, an **impasse** occurs when the parties are not able to move farther toward settlement. An impasse usually occurs because one party is demanding more than the other will offer. Sometimes an impasse can be resolved through a third party—a disinterested person such as a mediator or arbitrator. If the impasse is not resolved in this way, the union may call a work stoppage, or strike, to put pressure on management.[62]

Third-Party Involvement Negotiators use three types of third-party interventions to overcome an impasse: mediation, fact finding, and arbitration. With **mediation**, a neutral third party tries to assist the principals in reaching agreement. The mediator usually holds meetings with each party to determine where each stands regarding its position, and then uses this information to find common ground for further bargaining. The mediator is always a go-between, and does not have the authority to dictate terms or make concessions. He or she communicates assessments of the likelihood of a strike, the possible settlement packages available, and the like.

In certain situations, as in a national emergency dispute, a fact finder may be appointed. A **fact finder** is a neutral party who studies the issues in a dispute and makes a public recommendation for a reasonable settlement.[63] Presidential emergency fact-finding boards have successfully resolved impasses in certain critical transportation disputes.

---

impasse
Collective bargaining situation that occurs when the parties are not able to move farther toward settlement, usually because one party is demanding more than the other will offer.

---

mediation
Intervention in which a neutral third party tries to assist the principals in reaching agreement.

---

fact finder
A neutral party who studies the issues in a dispute and makes a public recommendation for a reasonable settlement.

arbitration
The most definitive type of third-party intervention, in which the arbitrator usually has the power to determine and dictate the settlement terms.

Arbitration is the most definitive type of third-party intervention, because the arbitrator often has the power to determine and dictate the settlement terms. Unlike mediation and fact finding, arbitration can guarantee a solution to an impasse. With *binding arbitration*, both parties are committed to accepting the arbitrator's award. With *nonbinding arbitration*, they are not. Arbitration may also be voluntary or compulsory (in other words, imposed by a government agency). In the United States, voluntary binding arbitration is the most prevalent.

strike
A withdrawal of labor.

Strikes A **strike** is a withdrawal of labor, and there are four main types of strikes. An **economic strike** results from a failure to agree on the terms of a contract. Unions call **unfair labor practice strikes** to protest illegal conduct by the employer. A **wildcat strike** is an unauthorized strike occurring during the term of a contract. A **sympathy strike** occurs when one union strikes in support of the strike of another union.[64]

economic strike
A strike that results from a failure to agree on the terms of a contract that involve wages, benefits, and other conditions of employment.

For example, in sympathy with employees of the *Detroit News, Detroit Free Press*, and *USA Today*, the United Auto Workers enforced a nearly six-year boycott that prevented the papers from being sold at Detroit-area auto plants, cutting sales by about 20,000 to 30,000 copies a day.[65]

unfair labor practice strike
A strike aimed at protesting illegal conduct by the employer.

Picketing, or having employees carry signs announcing their concerns near the employer's place of business, is one of the first activities to occur during a strike. Its purpose is to inform the public about the existence of the labor dispute and often to encourage others to refrain from doing business with the struck employer.

wildcat strike
An unauthorized strike occurring during the term of a contract.

Employers can make several responses when they become the object of a strike. One is to shut down the affected area and halt operations until the strike is over. A second is to contract out work in order to blunt the effects of the strike. A third response is to continue operations, perhaps using supervisors and other nonstriking workers to fill in for the striking workers. A fourth alternative is hiring replacements for the strikers.

sympathy strike
A strike that takes place when one union strikes in support of the strike of another.

In an economic strike, replacements can be permanent and would not have to be let go to make room for strikers who decided to return to work. If the strike were an unfair labor practice strike, the strikers would be entitled to return to their jobs upon making an unconditional offer to do so. Major work stoppages involving 1,000 or more workers have varied dramatically in the last 20 or so years, from about 400 work stoppages per year in the 1970s to 17 in 1999 and 39 in 2000.[66]

picketing
Having employees carry signs announcing their concerns near the employer's place of business.

When a strike is imminent, plans must be made to deal with it. For example, as negotiations between the Hibbing Taconite Steel Plant in Minnesota and the United Steelworkers of America headed toward a deadline, the firm began preparations that included bringing in security workers and trailers to house them.[67]

Two experts say that following these guidelines can minimize confusion:

- Pay all striking employees what you owe them on the first day of the strike.
- Secure the facility. Management should control access to the property. The company should consider hiring guards to protect replacements coming to and from work and to watch and control the picketers, if necessary.
- Notify all customers, and prepare a standard official response to all queries.
- Contact all suppliers and other persons who will have to cross the picket line. Establish alternative methods of obtaining supplies.
- Make arrangements for overnight stays in the facility and for delivered meals in case the occasion warrants such action.
- Notify the local unemployment office of your need for replacement workers.
- Photograph the facility before, during, and after picketing. If necessary, install videotape equipment and devices to monitor picket line misconduct.
- Record all facts concerning strikers' demeanor and activities and such incidents as violence, threats, mass pickets, property damage, or problems. Record the police response to requests for assistance.

■ Gather the following evidence: number of pickets and their names; time, date, and location of picketing; wording on every sign carried by pickets; and descriptions of picket cars and license numbers.[68]

Other Alternatives Management and labor each have other weapons they can use to try to break an impasse and achieve their aims. The union, for example, may resort to a corporate campaign. A **corporate campaign** is an organized effort by the union that exerts pressure on the corporation by pressuring the company's other unions, shareholders, directors, customers, creditors, and government agencies, often directly. Thus, the union might surprise individual members of the board of directors by picketing their homes, and organize a **boycott** of the company's banks.[69]

The Web is another potent union tool. For example, when the Hotel Employees and Restaurant Employees Union, Local 2, wanted to turn up the heat on the San Francisco Marriott, it launched a new Web site. The site explains the union's eight-month boycott and provides a helpful list of union-backed hotels where prospective guests can stay. It also lists organizations that decided to stay elsewhere in response to the boycott.[70]

Inside games are another union tactic, one often used in conjunction with corporate campaigns. **Inside games** are union efforts to convince employees to impede or to disrupt production—for example, by slowing the work pace, refusing to work overtime, filing mass charges with government agencies, refusing to do work without receiving detailed instructions from supervisors, and engaging in other disruptive activities such as sick-outs.[71] Inside games are basically strikes—albeit "strikes" in which the employees are being supported by the company, which continues to pay them. In one inside game at Caterpillar's Aurora, Illinois, plant, United Auto Workers' grievances in the final stage before arbitration rose from 22 to 336. The effect was to clog the grievance procedure and tie up workers and management in unproductive endeavors on company time.[72]

For their part, employers can try to break an impasse with lockouts. A **lockout** is a refusal by the employer to provide opportunities to work. It (sometimes literally) locks out employees and prohibits them from doing their jobs (and getting paid). The NLRB generally doesn't view lockouts as an unfair labor practice. For example, if your product is a perishable one (such as vegetables), then a lockout may be a legitimate tactic to neutralize or decrease union power. The NLRB views lockouts as an unfair labor practice only when the employer acts for a prohibited purpose. It is not a prohibited purpose to try to bring about a settlement on terms favorable to the employer.

Lockouts are not widely used today; employers are usually reluctant to cease operations when employees are willing to continue working (even though there may be an impasse at the bargaining table).[73] However, when the NBA Players Union threatened a strike in 1998, the owners instituted a lockout.

Both employers and unions can seek an injunction from the courts if they believe the other side is taking actions that could cause irreparable harm to the other party. An **injunction** is a court order compelling a party or parties either to resume or to desist from a certain action.[74]

The Contract Agreement

The actual contract agreement may be a 20- or 30-page document; or it may be even longer. It may contain just general declarations of policy or detailed rules and procedures. The tendency today is toward the longer, more detailed contract. This is largely a result of the increased number of items the agreements have been covering.

---

corporate campaign
An organized effort by the union that exerts pressure on the corporation by pressuring the company's other unions, shareholders, directors, customers, creditors, and government agencies, often directly.

boycott
The combined refusal by employees and other interested parties to buy or use the employer's products.

inside games
Union efforts to convince employees to impede or to disrupt production—for example, by slowing the work pace.

lockout
A refusal by the employer to provide opportunities to work.

injunction
A court order compelling a party or parties either to resume or to desist from a certain action.

The main sections of a typical contract cover subjects such as these:

(1) management rights, (2) union security and automatic payroll dues deduction, (3) grievance procedures, (4) arbitration of grievances, (5) disciplinary procedures, (6) compensation rates, (7) hours of work and overtime, (8) benefits: vacations, holidays, insurance, pensions, (9) health and safety provisions, (10) employee security seniority provisions, and (11) contract expiration date.

STRATEGIC HR

Amazon.com and Unionization

As it turned out, Amazon's strategy of expanding its network of company-owned call centers and distribution centers probably helped prompt efforts by the union to organize Amazon's workers. Call centers and distribution centers had the sorts of employees—customer service representatives and package handlers—who typically find unions attractive. But the union's efforts ran headlong into Amazon's new strategy of cutting costs and boosting profitability. Barely three months after the union began its organizing attempt in Seattle, Amazon fired over 300 customer service reps, including many pushing for the union, and closed its Seattle center. Some call center operations now take place in less expensive locales—for instance, at the firm's call center outside New Delhi, India. Jeff Bezos was quoted as saying to Wall Street analysts that closing the Seattle call center "was clearly the right business decision for us as we pursue making this into a profitable company."

The company's position is that the closing had nothing to do with union organizing attempts there. Given Amazon's need to start showing a profit after more than five years of losing money, its argument is more than a little plausible. In any case, Amazon is doing its part to try to keep workers from talking about the events surrounding the closings. For example, it's asking departing workers to sign a general release that basically affirms they won't file any complaints, lawsuits, and so forth against the company. Even one of the union organizers at the Seattle center decided to sign: "They are holding out a pretty large carrot" he says.[75]

GRIEVANCES

Hammering out a labor agreement is not the last step in collective bargaining; in some respects, it is just the beginning. No labor contract can cover all contingencies and answer all questions. For example, suppose the contract says you can only discharge an employee for "just cause." You subsequently discharge someone for speaking back to you in harsh terms. Was it within your rights to discharge this person? Was speaking back to you harshly "just cause"?

grievance
Any factor involving wages, hours, or conditions of employment that is used as a complaint against the employer.

The labor contract's **grievance** procedure usually handles problems like these. This procedure provides an orderly system whereby both employer and union determine whether some action violated the contract.[76] It is the vehicle for administering the contract on a day-to-day basis. The grievance process allows both parties to interpret and give meaning to various clauses, and transforms the contract into a "living organism." Remember, though, that this day-to-day collective bargaining involves interpretation only; it usually doesn't involve negotiating new terms or altering existing ones.

Sources of Grievances

From a practical point of view, it is probably easier to list those items that *don't* precipitate grievances than to list the ones that do. Employees may use just about any factor involving wages, hours, or conditions of employment as the basis of a grievance.

However, certain grievances are more serious, since they're usually more difficult to settle. Discipline cases and seniority problems including promotions, transfers, and layoffs would top this list. Others would include grievances growing out of job evaluations and work assignments, overtime, vacations, incentive plans, and holidays.[77] Here are four examples of grievances:

- *Absenteeism.* An employer fired an employee for excessive absences. The employee filed a grievance stating that there had been no previous warnings or discipline related to excessive absences.
- *Insubordination.* An employee on two occasions refused to obey a supervisor's order to meet with him unless a union representative was present at the meeting. As a result, the employee was discharged and subsequently filed a grievance protesting discharge.
- *Overtime.* The employer discontinued Sunday overtime work after a department was split. Employees affected filed a grievance protesting loss of the overtime work.
- *Plant rules.* The plant had a posted rule barring employees from eating or drinking during unscheduled breaks. The employees filed a grievance claiming the rule was arbitrary.[78]

A grievance is often just a symptom of an underlying problem. Sometimes, bad relationships between supervisors and subordinates are to blame: This is often the cause of grievances over "fair treatment," for instance. Organizational factors such as automated jobs or ambiguous job descriptions that frustrate or aggravate employees also cause grievances. Union activism is another cause; the union may solicit grievances from workers to underscore ineffective supervision. Problem employees are yet another cause of grievances. These are individuals, who, by their nature, are negative, dissatisfied, and prone to complaints.[79] Discipline and dismissal, explained in Chapter 10, are both major sources of grievances.

The Grievance Procedure

Most collective bargaining contracts contain a very specific grievance procedure. It lists the various steps in the procedure, time limits associated with each step, and specific rules such as "all charges of contract violation must be reduced to writing." Virtually every labor agreement signed today contains a grievance procedure clause. (Nonunionized employers need such procedures, too, as explained in Chapter 10.)

Union grievance procedures differ from firm to firm. Some contain simple two-step procedures. Here the grievant, union representative, and company representative meet to discuss the grievance. If they don't find a satisfactory solution, the grievance is brought before an independent third-person arbitrator, who hears the case, writes it up, and makes a decision. Figure 14-4 shows a Grievance Record Form.

At the other extreme, the grievance procedure may contain six or more steps. The first step might be for the grievant and shop steward to meet informally with the grievant's supervisor to try to find a solution. If they don't find one, the employee files a formal grievance, and there's a meeting with the employee, shop steward, and the supervisor's boss. The next steps involve the grievant and union representatives meeting with higher-level managers. Finally, if top management and the union can't reach agreement, the grievance may go to arbitration.

Sometimes the grievance process gets out of hand. For example, in the first half of 2001, members of American Postal Workers Union, Local 482, filed 1,800 grievances at the Postal Service's Roanoke mail processing facility (the usual rate is about 800 grievances per year). The employees apparently were responding to job changes, including transfers triggered by the Postal Service's efforts to further automate its processes.[80]

▶ **FIGURE 14-4**
A Standard Grievance Record Form

GRIEVANCE NUMBER _97-003_   DATE FILED _4/23/00_   UNION _Local 1233_
NAME OF GRIEVANT(S) _Davis, Henry_   CLOCK # _0379_
DATE CAUSE OF GRIEVANCE OCCURRED _4/20/00_
CONTRACTUAL PROVISIONS CITED _Articles III, VII, and others_
STATEMENT OF THE GRIEVANCE

   On April 20, Foreman George Moore asked Henry Davis to go temporarily to the Rolling Mill for the rest of the turn. Davis said he preferred not to, and that he was more senior to others who were available. The foreman never ordered Davis to take the temporary assignment. He only requested that Davis do so.
   Davis was improperly charged with insubordination and suspended for three days. The foreman did not have just cause for the discipline.

RELIEF SOUGHT:

   Reinstatement with full back pay and seniority.

GRIEVANT'S SIGNATURE _____Henry Davis_____   DATE _4/22/00_
STEWARD'S SIGNATURE _____Jim Bob Smith_____   DATE _4/23/00_

STEP 1

DISPOSITION:

   Foreman Moore gave Davis clear instructions to report temporarily to the Rolling Mill for the remainder of the shift. Davis refused to do so and was warned that it could result in discipline. When he again refused the foreman's directive, he was disciplined.
   The discipline was for just cause. The grievance is rejected.

SIGNATURE OF
EMPLOYER REPRESENTATIVE _____Paul Roberts_____   DATE _4/26/00_
_____ Grievance Withdrawn or __✓__ Referred to Step 2
SIGNATURE OF
UNION REPRESENTATIVE _____Jim Bob Smith_____   DATE _4/28/00_

Source: Michael Carrell and Christina Heavrin, *Labor Relations and Collective Bargaining* (Upper Saddle River, NJ: Prentice Hall, 2001), p. 415.

Guidelines for Handling Grievances

The best way to handle a grievance is to develop a work environment in which grievances don't occur in the first place.[81] Hone your ability to recognize, diagnose, and correct the causes of potential employee dissatisfaction (such as unfair appraisals, inequitable wages, or poor communications) before they become grievances.

   As a manager, you are on the firing line and must steer a course between treating employees fairly and maintaining management's rights and prerogatives. One expert has developed a list of do's and don'ts as useful guides in handling grievances.[82] Some critical ones include:

Do

1. Investigate and handle each case as though it may eventually result in arbitration.
2. Talk with the employee about his or her grievance; give the person a full hearing.
3. Require the union to identify specific contractual provisions allegedly violated.
4. Comply with the contractual time limits for handling the grievance.
5. Visit the work area of the grievance.
6. Determine whether there were any witnesses.

7. Examine the grievant's personnel record.
8. Fully examine prior grievance records.
9. Treat the union representative as your equal.
10. Hold your grievance discussions privately.
11. Fully inform your own supervisor of grievance matters.

Don't

12. Discuss the case with the union steward alone—the grievant should be there.
13. Make arrangements with individual employees that are inconsistent with the labor agreement.
14. Hold back the remedy if the company is wrong.
15. Admit to the binding effect of a past practice.
16. Relinquish to the union your rights as a manager.
17. Settle grievances based on what is "fair." Instead, stick to the labor agreement.
18. Bargain over items not covered by the contract.
19. Treat as subject to arbitration claims demanding the discipline or discharge of managers.
20. Give long written grievance answers.
21. Trade a grievance settlement for a grievance withdrawal.
22. Deny grievances because "your hands have been tied by management."
23. Agree to informal amendments in the contract.

THE FUTURE OF UNIONISM

The 1980s and 1990s were hard times for unions. About 22% of the nonfarm U.S. workforce belonged to unions in 1975. By 2000, that figure had dropped to about 14.1%.

Why Union Membership Is Declining

Several factors contributed to the decline. Most easily organized workers in industries like mining, transportation, and manufacturing were unionized years ago. More recently, unions faced a declining proportion of blue-collar jobs, and more service sector, high-tech, and white-collar service jobs. The permanent layoff of hundreds of thousands of union members, the permanent closing of company plants, the relocation of companies to nonunion settings (either in the United States or overseas), and mergers and acquisitions further eliminated union jobs and affected collective bargaining agreements. And, ironically, the EEO, safety, and similar laws described elsewhere in this book now provide the sort of protection that up to a few years ago only unions could provide.

What's Next for Unions?

This doesn't mean unions will disappear. But it does mean they'll change how they operate and see themselves. For one thing, unions are becoming both more aggressive and more sophisticated in how they present themselves to the public. The AFL-CIO has a program to train 1,000 unionists in the fundamentals of how to come across well on television, for instance. It's also taking more targeted steps. For example, the AFL-CIO housing investment trust recently formed a partnership with the Federal National Mortgage Association (Fannie Mae) to help provide affordable lending options to AFL-CIO members in the Milwaukee area who want to purchase homes.[83] Unions are also entering into cooperative pacts with employers, such as working with them in developing team-based employee participation programs. We'll look more closely at this in a moment.

HR.NET

Unions and the Internet

The Internet is also revolutionizing union activity, much as it revolutionized how firms do business. E-mail and the Internet mean unions can mass e-mail announcements to collective bargaining unit members, and use mass e-mail to reach supporters and government officials for their corporate campaigns.

Union-based Web sites are becoming integral parts of many such unionization campaigns; Alliance@IBM provides a good example. Managed by the communications workers of america, Alliance@IBM seeks to encourage IBM employees to join the Communications Workers of America. It does so by providing information on a range of issues, such as why IBM employees need a union, questions and concerns about unions, and how employees can join the union and get involved. For example, one page addresses the issue "Why We Need Alliance@IBM." Another page provides background information and instructions for Alliance organizers at IBM. It contains downloadable, online flyers for distribution; articles on topics like "Renewing a Union in the New Economy" and "Working Hard, Earning Less: The Story of Job Growth in America." The site even includes a downloadable authorization card.[84]

Employee Participation Programs and Unions

Employers and unions are grappling with the issue of how to deal with employee participation programs. For one thing, the proliferation of employee participation programs—quality circles, quality improvement programs, quality of work life teams, and so on—has added urgency to an old question: Are employee participation programs like these "sham unions" and therefore unfair labor practices under the National Labor Relations Act?[85]

A UPS program is typical. Under this program, hourly employees in self-directed teams establish priorities on how to do their jobs. UPS argues that employee involvement and teamwork can produce higher productivity. The Teamsters union (which represents the company's drivers and other hourly workers) is suspicious that the program is merely a tactic for subverting the union's influence on its members.[86]

To understand the problem, it's useful to know that one goal of the National Labor Relations (or Wagner) Act was to outlaw "sham unions." Two years before passage of the NLRA, the National Recovery Act (1933) tried to give employees the right to organize and to bargain collectively. This triggered an enormous increase in unions that were actually company-supported organizations aimed at keeping legitimate unions out. This helped lead to passage of the National Labor Relations Act.

The problem is that, because of how the courts often interpret the NLRA, they might view participative programs such as quality circles and quality improvement teams as sham unions. After all, the NLRA defines a labor organization as

Any organization of any kind, or any agency or employee representation committee or plan, in which employees participate and which exists for the purpose, in whole or in part, of dealing with employers concerning grievances, labor disputes, wages, rates of pay, hours of employment, or conditions of work.[87]

Whether a court views an employer's participation program as impermissible revolves around two main criteria. One is dominance. For example, if the employer formulates the idea for the committees, creates them, controls the development of their constitution or governing rules, or maintains control over the committees' functions, they could be viewed as unfairly dominated by the employer.[88] Second is the program's actual role. If the committees focus just on issues such as quality and productivity improvement, courts are more likely to view them as outside the scope of the National Labor Relations Act. Being involved in union-type matters such as wages, working conditions, and hours of work may be more questionable.

For now, employers can take these steps to avoid having their employee participation programs viewed as sham unions:[89]

- Involve employees in the formation of these programs to the greatest extent practical.
- Continually emphasize to employees that the committees exist for the exclusive purpose of addressing issues such as quality and productivity. They are not intended as vehicles for dealing with management on mandatory bargaining-type items such as pay and working conditions.
- Don't try to establish such committees at the same time union organizing activities are beginning in your facility.
- Fill the committees with volunteers rather than elected employee representatives, and rotate membership to ensure broad employee participation.
- Minimize your participation in the committees' day-to-day activities, to avoid unlawful interference or, worse, the perception of domination.

Some firms are signing new types of labor contracts, called *modern operating agreements* (MOA), to formalize the new, cooperative union management arrangements. Unlike traditional union agreements, MOAs "are designed to give hourly workers a greater say in how their jobs are performed. The agreements establish work teams, decentralize decision making, put union representatives on key plant operating committees, reduce the number of job classifications, and use a pay-for-knowledge system that links employees' pay to the number of operations they can perform."[90] Perhaps these MOAs reflect the future of labor management relations.

We invite you to visit **www.prenhall.com/dessler** on the Prentice Hall Web site for our online study guide, Internet exercises, current events, links to related Web sites, and more.

---

1. Union membership has been alternately growing and shrinking since as early as 1790. A major milestone was the creation in 1886 of the American Federation of Labor (AFL) by Samuel Gompers. Today, the AFL-CIO is a national federation of 100 national and international unions. Most recently the trend in unionization has been toward organizing white-collar workers, particularly since the proportion of blue-collar workers has been declining.

2. In addition to improved wages and working conditions, unions seek security when organizing. We discussed five possible arrangements, including the closed shop, the union shop, the agency shop, the open shop, and maintenance of membership.

3. The Norris-LaGuardia Act and the Wagner Act marked a shift in labor law from repression to strong encouragement of union activity. They did this by banning certain types of unfair labor practices, by providing for secret-ballot elections, and by creating the National Labor Relations Board.

4. The Taft-Hartley Act reflected the period of modified encouragement coupled with regulation. It enumerated the rights of employees with respect to their unions, enumerated the rights of employers, and allowed the U.S. president to temporarily bar national

Summary

emergency strikes. Among other things, it also enumerated certain unfair union labor practices. And employers were explicitly given the right to express their views concerning union organization.

5. The Landrum-Griffin Act reflected the period of detailed regulation of internal union affairs. It grew out of discoveries of wrongdoing on the part of both management and union leadership and contained a bill of rights for union members.

6. There are five steps in a union drive and election: the initial contact, obtaining authorization cards, holding a hearing with the NLRB, the campaign, and the election itself. The union need only win a majority of the votes cast, not a majority of the workers in the bargaining unit eligible to vote.

7. There are five surefire ways to lose an NLRB election: Be caught sleeping at the switch, form a committee, emphasize money and benefits, have an industry blind spot, and delegate too much to divisions.

8. Bargaining collectively in good faith is the next step if and when the union wins the election. Good faith means that both parties communicate and negotiate, and that proposals are matched with counterproposals. Bargaining items are categorized as mandatory, voluntary, or illegal.

9. An impasse occurs when the parties aren't able to move farther toward settlement. Third-party involvement—namely, arbitration, fact finding, or mediation—is one alternative. Sometimes, though, a strike occurs. Boycotts and lockouts are two other anti-impasse weapons sometimes used by labor and management.

10. Grievance handling has been called day-to-day collective bargaining. It involves the continuing interpretation of the collective bargaining agreement but usually not its renegotiation.

11. Most agreements contain a carefully worded grievance procedure ranging from two to six or more steps. The steps usually involve meetings between higher- and higher-echelon managers until (if agreement isn't reached) the grievance goes to arbitration. Grievance handling is as important in nonunion organizations as in those that are unionized.

Tying It All Together

Unions—the subject of this chapter—influence many of the HR policies and practices we've discussed to this point in the book. At many firms—Saturn, for instance—the union agreement allows the employees themselves to choose who comes to work on their teams. Unions increasingly play a role in training and developing employees and in managing organizational renewal and change—for instance, through their roles in quality circles and other participatory programs. And, of course, employee compensation—the topic of the last three chapters—usually plays a central role in labor and management negotiations, as the union presses for better pay and benefits for its members. The following chapter, Employee Safety and Health, focuses on another topic that plays an important role in labor–management discussions, in particular the steps management can and should take to provide a safer and healthier work environment for its employees.

Discussion Questions

1. Why are unions formed? What are the advantages and disadvantages of being a union member?
2. Discuss five sure ways to lose an NLRB election.
3. Describe important tactics you would expect the union to use during the union drive and election.
4. Briefly explain why labor law has gone through a cycle of repression and encouragement.
5. Explain in detail each step in a union drive and election.
6. What is meant by good faith bargaining? When is bargaining not in good faith?
7. Define impasse, mediation, and strike, and explain the techniques that are used to overcome an impasse.

1. You are the manager of a small manufacturing plant. The union contract covering most of your employees is about to expire. Working individually or in groups, discuss how to prepare for union contract negotiations.

2. Working individually or in groups, use Internet resources to find situations where company management and the union reached an impasse at some point during their negotiation process, but eventually resolved the impasse. Describe the issues of both sides that led to the impasse. How did they move past the impasse? What were the final outcomes?

Individual and Group Activities

EXPERIENTIAL EXERCISE

Purpose: The purpose of this exercise is to give you practice in dealing with some of the elements of a union organizing campaign.

Required Understanding: You should be familiar with the material covered in this chapter, as well as the following incident, "An Organizing Question on Campus."

How to Set Up the Exercise/Instructions: Divide the class into groups of 5 or 6 students. Assume that you are labor relations consultants retained by the college to identify the problems and issues involved and to advise Art Tipton on the university's rights and what to do next. Each group will spend about 45 minutes discussing the issues and outlining those issues as well as an action plan for Tipton. What should he do next?

If time permits, a spokesperson from each group should list on the board the issues involved and the group's recommendations.

INCIDENT: An Organizing Question on Campus: Art Tipton is a human resource director of Pierce University, a private university located in a large urban city. Ruth Ann Zimmer, a supervisor in the maintenance and housekeeping services division of the university, has just come into Art's office to discuss her situation. Zimmer's division of the university is responsible for maintaining and cleaning physical facilities of the university. Zimmer is one of the department supervisors who supervises employees who maintain and clean on-campus dormitories.

In the next several minutes, Zimmer proceeds to express her concerns about a union organizing campaign that has begun among her employees. According to Zimmer, a representative of the Service Workers Union has met with a number of the employees, urging them to sign union authorization cards. She has observed several of her employees "cornering" other employees to talk to them about joining the union and to urge them to sign union authorization (or representation) cards. Zimmer even observed this during the working hours as employees were going about their normal duties in the dormitories. Zimmer reports that a number of her employees have come to her asking for her opinions about the union. They reported to her that several other supervisors in the department had told their employees not to sign any union authorization cards and not to talk about the union at any time while they were on campus. Zimmer also reports that one of her fellow supervisors told his employees in a meeting that anyone who was caught talking about the union or signing a union authorization card would be disciplined and perhaps dismissed.

Zimmer says that the employees are very dissatisfied with their wages and many of the conditions that they have endured from students, supervisors, and other staff people. She says that several employees told her that they had signed union cards because they believed that the only way university administration would pay attention to their concerns was if the employees had a union to represent them. Zimmer says that she made a list of employees whom she felt had joined or were interested in the union, and she could share these with Tipton if he wanted to deal with them personally. Zimmer closes her presentation with the comment that she and other department supervisors need to know what they should do in order to stomp out the threat of unionization in their department.

APPLICATION CASE *Disciplinary Action*

The employee, a union shop steward, was on her regularly scheduled day off at home. She was called by her supervisor and told to talk to three union members and instruct them to attend a work function called a "Quest for Quality Interaction Committee" meeting. The Quest for Quality pro-

gram was a high priority with the employer for improving patient care at the facility and was part of a corporate program. The union had objected to the implementation of the Quest for Quality program and had taken the position that employees could attend the program if their jobs were threatened, but they should do so under protest and then file a grievance afterward.

On the day in question, the union shop steward, in a conference call with the three employees, said she would not order them to attend the Quest for Quality meeting, although her supervisor had asked her to. The supervisor who had called the union shop steward had herself refused to order the employees to attend the meeting, but relied on the union shop steward to issue the order to the employees. When the shop steward failed to order the employees to attend the meeting, the employer suspended her for two weeks. She grieved the two-week suspension.

The union position was that the company had no authority to discipline the union shop steward on her day off for failure to give what it termed "a management direction to perform the specific job function of attending a mandatory corporate meeting." The union pointed out that it was unfair that the employer refused to order the employees directly to attend the meeting but then expected the union shop steward to do so. The union argued that while it is not unusual to call a union shop steward for assistance in problem solving, the company had no right to demand that he or she replace supervisors or management in giving orders and then discipline the union official for refusing to do so.

The company position was that the opposition of the union to the Quest for Quality meetings put the employees in a position of being unable to attend the meetings without direction from the union shop steward; that the union shop steward was given a job assignment of directing the employees to attend the meeting; and that failure to follow that job assignment was insubordination and just cause for her suspension.

Nonetheless, the union contended that the arbitrator must examine the nature of the order when deciding whether the insubordination was grounds for discipline. As to the nature of the order in this case, the employer had to demonstrate that the order was directly related to the job classification and work assignment of the employee disciplined. The refusal to obey such an order must be shown to pose a real challenge to supervisory authority. The employee did not dispute the fact that she failed to follow the orders given to her by her supervisor, but pointed out that she was not on duty at the time and that the task being given to her was not because of her job with the company but because of her status as a union shop steward.

Questions

1. As the arbitrator, do you think the employer had just cause to discipline the employee? Why or why not?
2. If the union's opposition to the Quest for Quality program encouraged the employees not to participate, why shouldn't the union be held responsible for directing the employees to attend?

Source: Adapted from Cheltenham Nursing Rehabilitation Center, 89 LA 361 (1987); in Michael Carrell and Christina Heavrin, *Labor Relations and Collective Bargaining* (Upper Saddle River, NJ: Prentice Hall, 1995), pp. 100–101.

CONTINUING CASE: LearnInMotion.com *Keeping a Watchful Eye Out for the Union*

The employees at dot-coms like LearnInMotion.com are young, well paid, and technologically sophisticated, and they're doing interesting, creative work with flexible hours. They are, in other words, exactly the sort of employees you might assume would have no interest in joining a union.

Jennifer, however, was surprised to find that unions are actively attempting to organize several dot-coms. For example, one article she happened to come across said, "union activity at U.S. Internet companies is on the increase and is illustrated by the Washington alliance of technology workers attempting to unionize Amazon.com. [The union] claims to be receiving enquiries on a daily basis regarding union membership, as workers at Amazon complain of low pay and long hours" ("U.S.: Rise in Union Activity at Dot.com Firms," *Guardian*, December 13, 2000, p. 18). "That's all we'd need is to have some disgruntled current or former employee call a union in on us," said Mel.

The facts that LearnInMotion.com is in New York (which has a relatively high proportion of union workers) and that several employees have left under less-than-pleasant circumstances suggest to Jennifer that perhaps she should be vigilant, and take steps now to prevent a problem later. The question is, what should she and Mel do? Now, they want you, their management consultants, to help them decide what to do. Here's what they want you to do for them.

Questions and Assignments

1. Use the Internet to determine if the union mentioned above or any other union organized or tried to organize a dot-com in the New York area in the past two years.
2. Produce a one-page position paper for us on the subject "concrete steps we can take today to avoid being unionized tomorrow."
3. How can we tell we're in the first, early stages of an organizing campaign? How can we find out for sure?

Chapter 15

Employee Safety and Health

After studying this chapter, you should be able to:

■ Provide a safer environment for your employees.

■ Minimize unsafe acts by employees.

■ Explain the basic facts about OSHA.

■ Explain the supervisor's role in safety.

■ Describe and illustrate techniques for reducing accidents.

■ Explain how to deal with important occupational health problems.

STRATEGIC OVERVIEW   For almost 180 years, you could sum up the strategy of Con Edison, New York City's utility company, with the phrase, "Get the lights back on fast." The company delivers electricity as well as gas and steam to more than 3 million homes and businesses in New York City, and reliability has always been the firm's top priority. Con Ed has the best reliability record of any utility in the country. The company and its employees had a "can do" attitude, and safety was sometimes ignored for the sake of getting outages fixed, and fast.

All that changed when an explosion near New York City's Gramercy Park killed two Con Ed employees and a neighborhood resident. To make matters worse, the explosion contaminated an apartment building with asbestos, but Con Ed executives insisted there was no hazard. After several years of litigation, Con Ed accepted the blame, and adopted a new strategy: "Get the lights back on fast—but, first do it safely." Now it had to implement that strategy.[1]

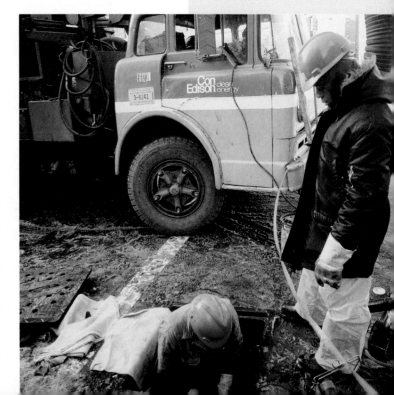

The previous chapter explored union–management relations, and the issues unions typically focus on when negotiating agreements. Employee safety is usually one of these. The main purpose of this chapter is to provide you with the basic knowledge you'll need to deal more effectively with employee safety and health problems at work. Today, every manager needs a working knowledge of OSHA—the Occupational Safety and Health Act—and so we discuss it at some length. Specifically, we review its purpose, standards, and inspection procedures, as well as the rights and responsibilities of employees and employers under OSHA. We also stress the importance of the supervisor and of top-management commitment to organizationwide safety. We'll see that there are three basic causes of accidents: chance occurrences, unsafe conditions, and unsafe acts—and several techniques for preventing accidents. We'll also discuss several important employee health problems, such as substance abuse and workplace violence, and what to do about them. ■

WHY EMPLOYEE SAFETY AND HEALTH ARE IMPORTANT

Safety and accident prevention concern managers for several reasons, one of which is the staggering number of work-related accidents. For example, 6,026 U.S. workers recently died in workplace incidents, and there were over 6.2 million nonfatal injuries and illnesses resulting from accidents at work—roughly 6.3 cases per 100 full-time workers in the United States per year.[2] Many safety experts believe such figures actually underestimate the true numbers. One study, published in the *Journal of the American Medical Association,* said workers actually suffer an estimated 13.2 million nonfatal injuries, and 862,200 illnesses annually, for a total cost of $171 billion each year.[3] Many injuries and accidents, the theory goes, just go unreported.

And injuries aren't just a problem in traditionally "unsafe" industries like mining and construction. For example, every year over 15,000 reportable injuries or illnesses occur among semiconductor workers, another 15,000 among circuit board assemblers, and another 15,000 among manufacturers of computers and computer peripherals.[4] In fact, an increasingly technology-based economy is triggering new health concerns, as more employees spend more time in sealed buildings and mechanically controlled office environments. Even new computers contribute to "sick building syndrome"—symptoms like headaches and sniffles, which some experts blame on poor ventilation and dust and fumes from on-site irritants.[5] Two engineers recently found that new computers emit chemical fumes (which, however, diminish after running constantly for a week[6]). And "safe" office work is actually susceptible to many other health and safety problems, including ". . . Repetitive trauma injuries related to computer use, respiratory illnesses stemming from indoor air quality, and high levels of stress, which are associated with a variety of factors, including task design."[7]

But even facts like these don't tell the whole story. They don't reflect the human suffering incurred by the injured workers and their families or the economic costs incurred by employers—costs that averaged over $23,000 per serious accident.[8] Nor do they reflect the legal implications. When a boiler explosion at Ford's Rouge Power Plant killed 6 workers and injured 14, Ford was slapped with a $1.5-million fine, and also agreed to spend almost $6 million instituting various safety measures. The state of Michigan concluded that Ford hadn't followed safety procedures, and that gas had leaked into the furnace because employees hadn't closed valves properly.[9]

OCCUPATIONAL SAFETY LAW

Occupational Safety and Health Act
The law passed by Congress in 1970 "to assure so far as possible every working man and woman in the nation safe and healthful working conditions and to preserve our human resources."

Congress passed the **Occupational Safety and Health Act** in 1970 "to assure so far as possible every working man and woman in the nation safe and healthful working conditions and to preserve our human resources."[10] The only employers it doesn't cover are self-employed persons, farms in which only immediate members of the employer's family work, and some workplaces already protected by other federal agencies or under other statutes. The act covers federal agencies, though its provisions usually don't apply to state and local governments in their role as employers.

The act created the **Occupational Safety and Health Administration (OSHA)** within the Department of Labor. OSHA's basic purpose is to administer the act and to set and enforce the safety and health standards that apply to almost all workers in the United States. The Department of Labor enforces the standards, and OSHA has inspectors working out of branch offices around the country to ensure compliance.

OSHA Standards and Record Keeping

OSHA operates under the "general" standard that each employer:

shall furnish to each of his [or her] employees employment and a place of employment which are free from recognized hazards that are causing or are likely to cause death or serious physical harm to his [or her] employees.

To carry out this basic mission, OSHA is responsible for promulgating legally enforceable standards. These are contained in five volumes covering general industry standards, maritime standards, construction standards, other regulations and procedures, and a field operations manual.

The standards are very complete and seem to cover just about every conceivable hazard in great detail. (Figure 15-1 presents a small part of the standard governing handrails for scaffolds.) And OSHA regulations don't just list specific standards. For example, OSHA's standard on respiratory protection includes requirements for program administration; work-site-specific procedures; requirements regarding the selection, use, cleaning, maintenance, and repair of respirators; employee training; respirator fit tests; and medical evaluations of the employees who use the respirators.[11]

Under OSHA, employers with 11 or more employees must maintain records of, and report, occupational injuries and occupational illnesses. An **occupational illness** is any abnormal condition or disorder caused by exposure to environmental factors associated with employment. This includes acute and chronic illnesses caused by inhalation, absorption, ingestion, or direct contact with toxic substances or harmful agents. As summarized in Figure 15-2, employers must report all occupational illnesses.[12] They must also report most occupational injuries, specifically those that result in medical treatment (other than first aid), loss of consciousness, restriction of work (one or more lost workdays), restriction of motion, or transfer to another job.[13] If an on-the-job accident results in the death of an employee or in the hospitalization of five or more employees, all employers, regardless of size, must report the accident in detail to the nearest OSHA office. Figure 15-3 shows the OSHA form used to report occupational injuries or illness.

OSHA's record-keeping requirements are broader than you might think, because its definition of occupational injuries and illnesses is so broad.[14] Examples of recordable conditions include: food poisoning suffered by an employee after eating in the employer's cafeteria, colds compounded by drafty work areas, and ankle sprains that occur during voluntary participation in a com-

Occupational Safety and Health Administration (OSHA)
The agency created within the Department of Labor to set safety and health standards for almost all workers in the United States.

occupational illness
Any abnormal condition or disorder caused by exposure to environmental factors associated with employment.

◄ **FIGURE 15-1**
OSHA Standards Example

Guardrails not less than 2" x 4" or the equivalent and not less than 36" or more than 42" high, with a midrail, when required, of a 1" x 4" lumber or equivalent, and toeboards, shall be installed at all open sides on all scaffolds more than 10 feet above the ground or floor. Toeboards shall be a minimum of 4" in height. Wire mesh shall be installed in accordance with paragraph (a) (17) of this section.

Source: General Industry Standards and Interpretations, U.S. Department of Labor, OSHA (Volume 1: Revised 1989, Section 1910.28(b) (15)), p. 67.

▶ **FIGURE 15-2**
What Accidents
Must Be Reported
Under the
Occupational Safety
and Health Act
(OSHA)

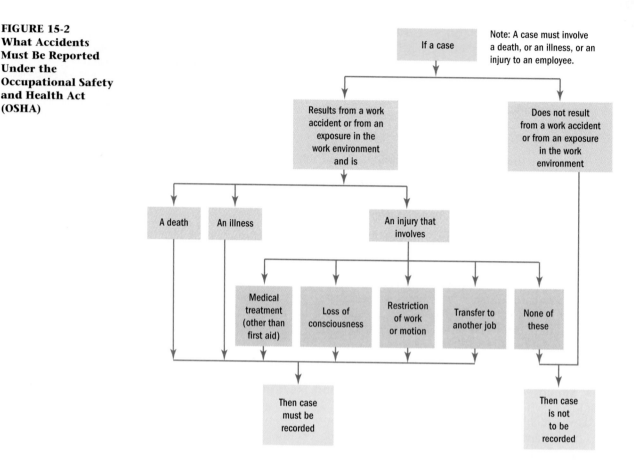

pany softball game at a picnic the employee was required to attend.[15] OSHA pursues record-keeping violations during investigations, so it behooves employers to record injuries or illnesses incurred at work carefully.

Inspections and Citations

OSHA enforces its standards through inspections and (if necessary) citations. Today, OSHA may not conduct warrantless inspections without an employer's consent. However, it may inspect after acquiring an authorized search warrant or its equivalent.[16]

Inspection Priorities Imminent danger situations get top priority. Here, it's likely there is a danger that can immediately cause death or serious physical harm. Second priority is catastrophes, fatalities, and accidents that have already occurred. (Employers must report such situations to OSHA within 48 hours.) Third priority is valid employee complaints of alleged violation standards. Next in priority are periodic special-emphasis inspections aimed at high-hazard industries, occupations, or substances. Random inspections and reinspections generally have last priority. (Most inspections result from employee complaints.)

Under its priority system, OSHA conducts an inspection within 24 hours when a complaint indicates an immediate danger, and within three working days when a serious hazard exists. For a "nonserious" complaint filed in writing by a worker or a union, OSHA will respond within 20 working days. OSHA handles other nonserious complaints by writing to the employer and requesting corrective action.

▼ **FIGURE 15-3   Form Used to Record Occupational Injuries and Illnesses**

Occupational Safety and Health Administration
Supplementary Record of
Occupational Injuries and Illnesses

U.S. Department of Labor

This form is required by Public Law 91-596 and must be kept in the establishment for 5 years.
Failure to maintain can result in the issuance of citations and assessment of penalties.

Case or File No.

Form Approved
O.M.B. No. 1218-0176

See OMB Disclosure
Statement on reverse.

Employer

1. Name

2. Mail address (No. and street, city or town, State, and zip code)

3. Location, if different from mail address

Injured or Ill Employee

4 Name (First, middle, and last)

Social Security No.

5. Home address (No. and street, city or town, State, and zip code)

6. Age

7. Sex (Check one)   Male ☐   Female ☐

8. Occupation (Enter regular job title, not the specific activity he was performing at the time of injury.)

9. Department (Enter name of department or division in which the injured person is regularly employed, even though he may have been temporarily working in another department at the time of injury.)

The Accident or Exposure to Occupational Illness

If accident or exposure occurred on employer's premises, give address of plant or establishment in which it occurred. Do not indicated department or division within the plant or establishment. If accident occurred outside employer's premises at an identifiable address, give that address. If it occurred on a public highway or at any other place which cannot be identified by number and street, please provide place references locating the place of injury as accurately as possible.

10. Place of accident or exposure (No. and street, city or town, State, and zip code)

11. Was place of accident or exposure on employer's premises?   Yes ☐   No ☐

12. What was the employee doing when injured? (Be specific. If he was using tools or equipment or handling material, name them and tell what he was doing with them.)

13. How did the accident occur? (Describe fully the events which resulted in the injury or occupational illness. Tell what happened and how it happened. Name any objects or substances involved and tell how they were involved. Give full details on all factors which led or contributed to the accident. Use separate sheet for additional space.)

Occupational Injury or Occupational Illness

14. Describe the injury or illness in detail and indicate the part of body affected. (E.g., amputation of right index finger at second joint; fracture of ribs; lead poisoning; dermatitis of left hand, etc.)

15. Name the object or substance which directly injured the employee. (For example, the machine or thing he struck against or which struck him; the vapor or poison he inhaled or swallowed; the chemical or radiation which irriatated his skin; or in cases of strains, hernias, etc., the thing he was lifting, pulling, etc.)

16. Date of injury or initial diagnosis of occupational illness

17. Did employee die? (Check one)   Yes ☐   No ☐

Other

18. Name and address of physician

19. If hospitalized, name and address of hospital

Date of report	Prepared by	Official position

OSHA No. 101 (Feb. 1981)

(See Next Page/Reverse)

Source: U.S. Department of Labor.

The Inspection Itself The inspection itself begins when the OSHA officer arrives at the workplace.[17] He or she displays official credentials and asks to meet an employer representative. (You should always insist on seeing the officer's credentials, which include photograph and serial number.) The officer explains the visit's purpose, the scope of the inspection, and the standards that apply. An authorized employee representative accompanies the officer during the inspection. The inspector can also stop and question workers (in private, if necessary) about safety and health conditions. The act protects each employee from discrimination for exercising his or her disclosure rights. In 2000, OSHA beefed up its rules, requiring even greater employee involvement in OSHA's on-site consultations, and that employees be informed of the inspections results.[18]

OSHA inspectors look for violations of all types, but some potential problem areas—such as scaffolding and fall protection—seem to grab more of their attention. The 5 most frequent OSHA inspection violation areas are scaffolding, fall protection, hazard communication, lockout/tagout (electrical repairs), and machine guarding.

Finally, after checking the premises and employer's records, the inspector holds a closing conference with the employer's representative. Here the inspector discusses apparent violations for which OSHA may issue or recommend a **citation** and penalty. At this point, the employer can produce records to show compliance efforts.

citation
Summons informing employers and employees of the regulations and standards that have been violated in the workplace.

Penalties OSHA can also impose penalties. These generally range from $5,000 up to $70,000 for willful or repeat serious violations, although in practice the penalties can be far higher. For example, in a negotiated settlement, Pennzoil Products agreed to pay a $1.5-million penalty to settle citations received after an explosion at its Rouseville, Pennsylvania, refinery killed five employees.[19] The parties settle many OSHA cases before litigation, in "pre-citation settlements": OSHA issues the citation and agreed-on penalties simultaneously, after negotiations with the employer.[20] There is also a maximum of $7,000 a day in penalties for failure to correct a violation.

In general, OSHA calculates penalties based on the gravity of the violation and usually takes into consideration factors like the size of the business, the firm's compliance history, and the employer's good faith.[21] In practice, OSHA must have a final order from the independent Occupational Safety and Health Review Commission (OSHRC) to enforce a penalty.[22] An employer who files a notice of contest can drag out an appeal for years.[23]

Many employers do appeal their citations, at least to the OSHA district office, in part (reportedly) because small-business people in particular feel that OSHA may be "investing too much time and energy looking for little ways to trip up honest, safety-conscious employers."[24]

Inspection Guidelines What should managers do when OSHA inspectors unexpectedly show up? Suggestions include:

Initial Contact

Refer the inspector to your OSHA coordinator.

Check the inspector's credentials.

Ask the inspector why he or she is inspecting your workplace: Complaint? Regular scheduled visit? Fatality or accident follow-up? Imminent danger?

If the inspection is a complaint, you are entitled to know whether the person is a current employee, though not the person's name.

Notify your counsel, who should review all requests for documents and information, as well as documents and information you provide.

Opening Conference

Establish the focus and scope of the planned inspection.

Discuss the procedures for protecting trade secret areas.

Show the inspector you have safety programs in place. He or she may not go to the work floor if paperwork is complete and up to date.

Walk-Around Inspection

Accompany the inspector and take detailed notes.

If the inspector takes a photo or video, you should, too.

Ask for duplicates of all physical samples and copies of all test results.

Be helpful and cooperative, but don't volunteer information.

To the extent possible, immediately correct any violation the inspector identifies.[25]

Responsibilities and Rights of Employers and Employees

Both employers and employees have responsibilities and rights under the Occupational Safety Health Act. Employers, for example, are responsible for meeting their duty to provide "a workplace free from recognized hazards," for being familiar with mandatory OSHA standards, and for examining workplace conditions to make sure they conform to applicable standards. Employers have the right to seek advice and off-site consultation from OSHA, request and receive proper identification of the OSHA compliance officer before inspection, and to be advised by the compliance officer of the reason for an inspection.

Employees also have rights and responsibilities, but OSHA can't cite them for violations of their responsibilities. They are responsible, for example, for complying with all applicable OSHA standards, for following all employer safety and health rules and regulations, and for reporting hazardous conditions to the supervisor. Employees have a right to demand safety and health on the job without fear of punishment. The act forbids employers from punishing or discriminating against workers who complain to OSHA about job safety and health hazards.

Dealing with Employee Resistance While employees have a responsibility to comply with OSHA standards, they often resist, and in most such cases the employer remains liable for any penalties.[26] The refusal of some workers to wear hard hats as mandated by the OSHA requirements typifies this problem. Employers have attempted to defend themselves against penalties for such noncompliance by citing worker intransigence and their own fear of wildcat strikes and walkouts. Yet in most cases, courts have held employers liable for safety violations at the workplace regardless of the fact that the violations were due to employee resistance.[27] The result is that an employer is in a difficult position. On the one hand, the courts and OSHA claim that employers must obtain employee compliance; on the other hand, doing so is often all but impossible.

▲ *Noise pollution in the workplace is not only distracting, it also affects productivity and employee satisfaction. FedEx adheres to OSHA noise guidelines by frequent monitoring, testing employees' hearing annually, conducting hearing protection training programs, and providing earplugs and earmuffs.*

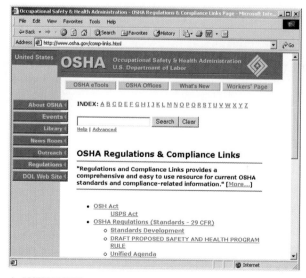

▲ **WEBNOTE**

OSHA's Web site provides information about firms' enforcement histories, among other things.

www.osha.gov

Yet it is possible for employers to reduce their liability, since "courts have recognized that it is impossible to totally eliminate all hazardous conduct by employees."[28] In the event of a problem, the courts may take into consideration facts such as whether the employer's safety procedures were adequate; whether the training really gave employees the understanding, knowledge, and skills required to perform their duties safely; and whether the employer really required employees to follow the procedures.

There are several other ways to address the liability problem.[29] First, the courts have held that an employer can bargain with its union for the right to discharge or discipline any employee who disobeys an OSHA standard. But most unions refuse to bargain over hard hats (and many other OSHA issues) because they oppose having penalties assessed against their members. As a second alternative, the use of a formal arbitration process by aggrieved employers could provide a relatively quick and inexpensive method for resolving an OSHA-related dispute with an employee. Other employers have turned to positive reinforcement and training for gaining employee compliance; more on this shortly. However, the only surefire way to eliminate liability is to ensure that no safety violations occur.

The Changing Nature of OSHA

OSHA seems to be moving toward achieving its aims more through cooperation.[30] One example is its Cooperative Compliance program,[31] implemented in 1998 and aimed at getting employers to voluntarily provide safe workplaces.[32] To the chagrin of some employers, OSHA is also using technology to report its inspection results. For example, OSHA's Web site (www.osha.gov) gives you easy access to your company's (or your competitors') OSHA enforcement history. All the details are there, ranging from the results of the inspections conducted at small firms such as ABC Plumbing Company in North Carolina to those at large firms such as Capital City's ABC (part of Disney), the media giant.[33]

ENTREPRENEURS + HR

Getting Workers to Comply

OSHA isn't just there to take punitive measures. For example, when Jan Anderson, president of her own steel installation company in Colorado, realized her firm's workers' compensation costs were higher than her payroll, she knew she had to do something. Her firm had tried to train employees in proper safety and health techniques, but the industry's "tough man" image made it hard. Anderson joined with similar Colorado firms for help. Together, the group established new safety and health programs, implemented programs for identifying hazards and accidents, and installed systems to record and track employee complaints and to train supervisors and employees. At the group's request, OSHA helped draft new safety systems, created educational materials, and provided inspections that were more cooperative than adversarial. As a result, says Anderson, "Our workers' compensation costs have decreased significantly, we have had no accidents, and there is an awareness that we take safety seriously and if you work for us, you have to take it seriously too."[34]

MANAGEMENT COMMITMENT AND SAFETY

On the next few pages, we'll see that reducing accidents often boils down to reducing accident-causing conditions and accident-causing acts—but do not miss the forest for the trees. Telling supervisors to watch for spills and telling employees to work safely is futile if everyone in the firm believes management isn't serious about safety. Safety starts with top-management commitment.

Historically, for instance, DuPont's accident rate has been much lower than that of the chemical industry as a whole. If DuPont's record had been average, it would have spent an additional $26 million in workers compensation and other costs, or about 3% of its profits.[35] This good safety record is partly due to an organizational commitment to safety, which is evident in the following description:

> One of the best examples I know of in setting the highest possible priority for safety takes place at a DuPont Plant in Germany. Each morning at the DuPont Polyester and Nylon Plant the director and his assistants meet at 8:45 to review the past 24 hours. The first matter they discuss is not production, but safety. Only after they have examined reports of accidents and near misses and satisfied themselves that corrective action has been taken do they move on to look at output, quality, and cost matters.[36]

Everyone should see convincing evidence of top management's commitment. This includes top management's being personally involved in safety activities; giving safety matters high priority in meetings and production scheduling; giving the company safety officer high rank and status; and including safety training in new workers' training. Ideally, "safety is an integral part of the system, woven into each management competency and a part of everyone's day-to-day responsibilities."[37] In addition:

- Institutionalize management's commitment with a safety policy, and publicize it. This should emphasize that the firm will do everything practical to eliminate or reduce accidents and injuries. Emphasize that accident and injury prevention are not just important but of the utmost importance.
- Analyze the number of accidents and safety incidents and then set specific achievable safety goals.[38] Georgia-Pacific reduced its workers compensation costs with a policy that forces managers to halve accidents or forfeit 30% of their bonuses.[39]

Safety programs can be effective. One safety program at a Missouri ABB Business Services plant resulted in OSHA total cases reduced 80% in one year; OSHA lost-time rate reduced 86% in one year; and $560,000 contributed to profit.[40]

STRATEGIC HR

Con Ed and "Safety First"

A main reason companies need strategies is because strategies provide the frameworks within which the firms' employees make their decisions. Until the Gramercy Park explosion, "Get the lights back on fast" summed up Con Ed's strategy.

Safety is particularly a problem in a large, complex utility like Con Ed, many of whose facilities go back 50 years or more. Back then, people didn't understand the risks of using products like asbestos, so today Con Ed employees find themselves working with hazardous materials on a daily basis. The Gramercy Park explosion forced management to redefine Con Ed's strategy. Today, "get the lights back on fast—but, first do it safely" sums up the firm's basic corporate approach, and that new approach has triggered big changes in how the company does things.

Injecting a "safety first" mentality into all the firm's operations involved many HR activities, most of which continue to this day. Con Ed recruited and carefully trained over 80 new people for its environmental health and safety staff. The firm's health and safety staff no longer operates from a centralized, isolated department; instead, the unit's 126 members are spread out throughout Con Ed's local operating units, where they can monitor safety on a real-time basis. Con Ed also created thousands of pages of new policies and procedures that translate federal, state, and local environmental regulations into operating procedures its employees can actually use. The environmental health and safety staff produces a monthly video called *The eXcellence Files*; one of its regular features is "close calls," in which employees describe narrow escapes and lessons they can share with other workers. In one, an electrical worker describes how he heard a telltale clicking or "arcing" sound and fled just before flames shot out the end of the pipe.

The firm's new safety strategy also meant empowering Con Ed's tens of thousands of employees. The new "timeout" program is a good example. Each employee carries a small green laminated card showing a silhouetted referee holding his arms in a "timeout" signal, and reading: "You can always call a timeout if you have a safety question or an environmental concern." The idea is that when an employee calls a timeout, workers and their supervisors discuss the issue and, if necessary call in an expert from the environmental health and safety staff. Steps like these went a long way toward improving Con Ed's safety climate: Now all employees instinctively put safety first. Con Ed's experience shows how top management can translate its strategy into specific HR strategies and practices.

WHAT CAUSES ACCIDENTS?

There are three basic causes of workplace accidents: chance occurrences, unsafe conditions, and unsafe acts on the part of employees. Chance occurrences (such as walking past a plate-glass window just as someone hits a ball through it) contribute to accidents but are more or less beyond management's control. We will therefore focus on unsafe conditions and unsafe acts.

Unsafe Conditions and Other Work-Related Factors

unsafe conditions
The mechanical and physical conditions that cause accidents.

Unsafe conditions are one main cause of accidents. They include such things as:

Improperly guarded equipment

Defective equipment

Hazardous procedures in, on, or around machines or equipment

Unsafe storage—congestion, overloading

Improper illumination—glare, insufficient light

Improper ventilation—insufficient air change, impure air source[41]

The basic remedy is to eliminate or minimize the unsafe conditions. OSHA standards address these mechanical and physical conditions that cause accidents. Furthermore, a checklist of unsafe conditions can be useful for spotting problems. Figure 15-4 presents one such checklist. (Another is in Figure 15-5 at the end of this chapter.)

While accidents can happen anywhere, there are some danger zones. About one-third of industrial accidents occur around forklift trucks, wheelbarrows, and other handling and lifting areas. The most serious accidents usually occur near metal and woodworking machines and saws, or around transmission machinery like gears, pulleys, and flywheels.[42] Falls on stairs, ladders, walkways, and scaffolds are the third most common cause of industrial accidents. Hand tools (like chisels and screwdrivers) and electrical equipment (extension cords, electric drop-lights, and so on) are other major causes of accidents.[43] In addition to unsafe con-

▼ **FIGURE 15-4** **Checklist of Mechanical or Physical Accident-Causing Conditions**

I. GENERAL HOUSEKEEPING

Adequate and wide aisles—no materials protruding into aisles

Parts and tools stored safely after use—not left in hazardous positions that could cause them to fall

Even and solid flooring—no defective floors or ramps that could cause falling or tripping accidents

Waste cans and sand pails—safely located and properly used

Material piled in safe manner—not too high or too close to sprinkler heads

Floors—clean and dry

Firefighting equipment—unobstructed

Work benches orderly

Stockcarts and skids safely located, not left in aisles or passageways

Aisles kept clear and properly marked; no air lines or electric cords across aisles

II. MATERIAL HANDLING EQUIPMENT AND CONVEYANCES

On all conveyances, electric or hand, check to see that the following items are all in sound working conditions:

Brakes—properly adjusted

Not too much play in steering wheel

Warning device—in place and working

Wheels—securely in place; properly inflated

Fuel and oil—enough and right kind

No loose parts

Cables, hooks or chains—not worn or otherwise defective

Suspended chains or hooks conspicuous

Safely loaded

Properly stored

III. LADDERS, SCAFFOLD, BENCHES, STAIRWAYS, ETC.

The following items of major interest to be checked:

Safety feet on straight ladders

Guardrails or handrails

Treads, not slippery

No splinted, cracked, or rickety

Properly stored

Extension ladder ropes in good condition

Toeboards

IV. POWER TOOLS (STATIONARY)

Point of operation guarded

Guards in proper adjustment

Gears, belts, shafting, counterweights guarded

Foot pedals guarded

Brushes provided for cleaning machines

Adequate lighting

Properly grounded

Tool or material rests properly adjusted

Adequate work space around machines

Control switch easily accessible

Safety glasses worn

Gloves worn by persons handling rough or sharp materials

No gloves or loose clothing worn by persons operating machines

V. HAND TOOLS AND MISCELLANEOUS

In good condition—not cracked, worn, or otherwise defective

Properly stored

Correct for job

Goggles, respirators, and other personal protective equipment worn where necessary

VI. WELDING

Arc shielded

Fire hazards controlled

Operator using suitable protective equipment

Adequate ventilation

Cylinder secured

Valves closed when not in use

VII. SPRAY PAINTING

Explosion-proof electrical equipment

Proper storage of paints and thinners in approved metal cabinets

Fire extinguishers adequate and suitable; readily accessible

Minimum storage in work area

VIII. FIRE EXTINGUISHERS

Properly serviced and tagged

Readily accessible

Adequate and suitable for operations involved

Source: Courtesy of the American Insurance Association. From "A Safety Committee Man's Guide," pp. 1–64.

ditions, three other work-related factors contribute to accidents: the job itself, the work schedule, and the psychological climate of the workplace.

Certain jobs are inherently more dangerous. For example, the job of crane operator results in about three times more accident-related hospital visits than does the job of supervisor. Similarly, some departments' work is inherently safer. A bookkeeping department usually has fewer accidents than a shipping department.

Work schedules and fatigue also affect accident rates. Accident rates usually don't increase too noticeably during the first five or six hours of the workday. But after that, the accident rate increases faster than the increase in the number of hours worked. This is due partly to fatigue and partly to the fact that accidents occur more often during night shifts.

Unfortunately, some of the most important working-condition-related causes of accidents are not as obvious, because they involve workplace psychology. One researcher reviewed the official hearings regarding fatal accidents suffered by off-shore oil workers in the British sector of the North Sea.[44] From this and similar studies, it's apparent that several psychological aspects of the work environment set the stage for unsafe acts. A strong pressure within the organization to complete the work as quickly as possible, employees who are under a great deal of stress, and a poor safety climate—for instance, supervisors who never mention safety—are a few of these psychological conditions. Similarly, accidents occur more frequently in plants with a high seasonal layoff rate and where there is hostility among employees, many garnished wages, and blighted living conditions. Temporary stress factors like high workplace temperature, poor illumination, and a congested workplace also correlate with accident rates.[45]

What Causes Unsafe Acts? (A Second Basic Cause of Accidents)

Most safety experts and managers know it's impossible to eliminate accidents just by reducing unsafe conditions. People cause accidents with unsafe acts such as throwing materials, using unsafe procedures in loading, placing, or mixing, or by lifting improperly.

While unsafe acts can undo even the best attempts to minimize unsafe conditions, there are, unfortunately, no easy answers to the question of what causes them. For years psychologists assumed that some employees were simply more accident prone than others, and that accident-prone people generally caused more accidents. However, studies have failed to consistently support this assumption.[46]

Therefore, while some believe that most accident-prone people are impulsive, most experts today doubt that accident proneness is universal—that some people will have more accidents no matter what the situation. Instead, the consensus is that the person who is accident prone on one job may not be so on a different job. They say that accident proneness is situational.

Various human traits do relate to accident proneness in specific situations. For example, accident-prone drivers performed worse on a test of motor skills than did drivers with fewer accidents, and older adults with impaired vision were at a higher risk for falls and motor vehicle crashes. People who were more fatalistic, negative, and cynical were more likely to exhibit violent behavior on the job.[47]

◆ **RESEARCH INSIGHT** As you may deduce from the preceding discussions, there is usually no one single cause—whether acts or conditions—of workplace injuries; instead, accident causes tend to be multifaceted.

A recent study of employed adolescents illustrates this. Participants were 319 adolescents recruited by the researcher through advertisements at three colleges and 37 high schools in New York State. To be eligible, the student had to be between 16 and 19 years old, currently working for pay in a formal organization at least five hours per week, and a full-time student. The researchers asked the students to complete detailed questionnaires. These questionnaires measured both possible predictors of workplace injuries (such as gender) as well as the number and nature of any job injuries actually suffered.

It was clear that several factors or predictors related to the number of workplace injuries these adolescents suffered. For example, gender was important: Adolescent boys reported more work injuries than did adolescent girls (perhaps because they also reported greater exposure to physical hazards on the job). Personality was important: For example, "negative affectivity"—the extent to which individuals experience negative moods and emotional reactivity, as measured by items such as "Often I get irritated at little annoyances"—related positively to work injuries. Other predictors related to work injuries included job tenure (the longer on the job, the more injuries, perhaps because more experienced workers got the jobs involving higher skill levels and greater exposure to risks), exposure to physical hazards, excessive workloads, boredom, poor physical health, and on-the-job substance abuse.

The results of a study focusing on adolescents don't necessarily apply to working adults. However, one likely implication is that employers need comprehensive safety programs—they can't just rely on a single "magic bullet" such as trying to screen out high-risk individuals. Accidents seem to have multiple causes.[48] With that in mind, let's turn to a discussion of how to prevent accidents.

HOW TO PREVENT ACCIDENTS

In practice, accident prevention boils down to two basic activities: (1) reducing unsafe conditions and (2) reducing unsafe acts.

Reducing unsafe conditions is always an employer's first line of defense. Safety engineers should design jobs to remove or reduce physical hazards. In addition, supervisors and managers play a role in reducing unsafe conditions. A checklist like the one in Figure 15-4 (page 437) or the self-inspection checklist in Figure 15-5 (pages 458–461) can help identify and remove potential hazards.

Employers use computerized tools to design safer equipment. For example, Designsafe (from Designsafe Engineering, Ann Arbor, Michigan) facilitates hazard analysis, risk assessment, and the identification of safety control options. Designsafe helps the safety designer identify the task's main processes and subprocesses, and the worker behaviors associated with them. It then helps the designer choose the most appropriate safety control device for keeping the worker safe, from a list of devices such as adjustable enclosures, presence-sensing devices, and personal protective equipment.[49]

Sometimes the solution for eliminating an unsafe condition is obvious, and sometimes it's more subtle. For example, slips and falls at work are often the result of debris or a slippery floor.[50] Relatively obvious remedies for problems like these include slip-reducing floor coatings, floor mats, better lighting, and a system to quickly block off spills. But perhaps less obviously, special safety gear can also reduce the problems associated with otherwise unsafe conditions. For example, slip-resistant footwear with grooved soles can reduce slips and falls. Cut-resistant gloves reduce the hazards of working with sharp objects.

Getting employees to wear personal protective equipment can be a famously difficult chore. Including the employees in planning the program, reinforcing appropriate behaviors, and addressing comfort issues can smooth the way for more widespread use of protective equipment.[51] Wearability is important. In addition to providing reliable barrier protection and durability, protective clothing should fit properly; be easy to care for, maintain, and repair; be flexible and lightweight; provide comfort and reduce heat stress; have rugged construction; be relatively easy to put on and take off; and be easy to clean, dispose of, and recycle.[52]

Again, reducing unsafe conditions—by designing the job properly and having managers watch for hazards—should always be the first choice. Then come administrative controls, such as job rotation to reduce long-term exposure to the hazard. Only then turn to personal protective equipment.[53]

Reducing unsafe acts—through screening, training, or incentive programs, for example—is the second basic way to reduce accidents. Let's look at how to do this.

Reducing Unsafe Acts by Emphasizing Safety

As mentioned above, it is the supervisor's responsibility to set the tone so subordinates want to work safely. This involves more than talking up safety, ensuring that workers wipe up spills, or enforcing safety rules, although such things are important.[54] It's necessary to show by both word and deed that safety is crucial. For example, supervisors should:

Praise employees when they choose safe behaviors;

Listen when employees offer suggestions, concerns, or complaints;

Be a good example, for instance, by following every safety rule and procedure;

Visit plant areas regularly;

Maintain open safety communications—for instance, by telling employees as much as possible about safety activities such as testing alarms and changing safety equipment or procedures;

Link managers' bonuses to safety improvements.[55]

Creating the right safety climate isn't just academic. One study assessed safety climate in terms of items such as "my supervisor says a good word whenever he sees the job done according to the safety rules," and "my supervisor approaches workers during work to discuss safety issues." The study found that (1) employees did develop consistent perceptions concerning supervisory safety practices, and (2) these safety climate perceptions predicted safety records in the months following the survey.[56]

Reducing Unsafe Acts Through Selection and Placement

Screening is another way to reduce unsafe acts. Here, the aim is to isolate the trait (such as visual skill) that might predict accidents on the job in question, then screen candidates for this trait. As noted above, tests have distinguished between those who do and do not have more car accidents, falls, and violent outbursts. Studies suggest that a test like the Employee Reliability Inventory (ERI) can help employers reduce unsafe acts at work. The ERI purportedly measures reliability dimensions such as emotional maturity, conscientiousness, safe job performance, and courteous job performance.[57] While the findings of one study were not definitive, using the ERI in the selection process did seem to be associated with reductions in work-related accidents.[58]

Also, ask at least a few related questions during the selection interview—for instance, "What would you do if you saw another employee working in an unsafe way?" and "What would you do if your supervisor gave you a task, but didn't provide any training on how to perform it safely?"[59]

The Americans with Disabilities Act has particular relevance for safety-related screening. For example, under the ADA it is unlawful to inquire (prior to hiring) about an applicant's workers' compensation injuries and claims. You also cannot ask applicants whether they have a disability, or require them to take tests that tend to screen out those with disabilities. However, you can usually ask whether an applicant has the ability to perform a job. You can even ask, "Do you know of any reason why you would not be able to perform the various functions of the job you are seeking?"[60]

Reducing Unsafe Acts Through Training

Safety training is another way to reduce unsafe acts. This is especially appropriate for new employees. You should instruct them in safe practices and procedures, warn them of potential hazards, and work on developing a safety-conscious attitude. OSHA has published two useful booklets, "Training Requirements Under OSHA" and "Teaching Safety and Health in the Workplace."

You can't just provide training and assume it will be successful. OSHA standards require demonstrated proficiency in numerous areas, and OSHA has been "making it increasingly clear that it is not sufficient merely to ensure that employees be provided with safety related training materials; they must be able to do certain things as a result of the training they receive." For example, OSHA's respiratory protection standard requires that each employee be able to demonstrate how to inspect, put on, remove, use, and check respirator seals.[61]

Bilingual training is important. With increasing numbers of Hispanic workers in the United States, sometimes in hazardous jobs, experts are expressing concern about the level of safety training they're receiving. Employers are already taking steps to remedy the problem. For example, the Greater Houston Environmental and Safety Institute recently met with several construction company safety directors and began offering safety classes in Spanish. All safety training is increasingly Web-based, as the following illustrates.

▲ **WEBNOTE**

Puresafety.com enables employers to use the puresafety template to create their own company safety Web site, and to populate it with safety courses from puresafety.

www.puresafety.com

HR NET

Using the Web to Promote Safety

Health and safety programs use the Web for training employees. For example, Puresafety.com (www.puresafety.com) enables firms to create their own training Web sites, complete with a "message from the safety director." Once an employer arranges to install the Puresafety Web site, it can populate the site with courses from companies that supply health and safety courses via Puresafety.com. The courses themselves are available in various formats, including digital versions of videotape training, and PowerPoint presentations. Puresafety.com also develops or modifies existing courses for employers.

A site like Puresafety.com makes it easy for an employer to quickly organize and launch a health and safety program for its employees, and to deliver individual courses to employees when and where they want them.[62]

Reducing Unsafe Acts Through Motivation: Posters, Incentive Programs, and Positive Reinforcement

Safety posters also help reduce unsafe acts. In one study, their use apparently increased safe behavior by more than 20%. However, posters are no substitute for a comprehensive safety program; instead, employers should combine them with other techniques (like screening and training) to reduce unsafe conditions and acts, and also change them often.[63]

You might not expect people to need incentives to work safely (given that they are the ones who are liable to be hurt). However, incentive programs have also been successful at reducing workplace injuries. For example, UPS has given its drivers safety awards since 1993.[64] Clariant Corporation annually evaluates managers and employees on meeting goals in four key areas, including safety performance; bonuses (up to 8% of gross pay) then depend on their safety records.[65]

Some contend that programs like these are misguided. OSHA has argued, for instance, that they don't cut down on actual injuries or illnesses, but only on injury and illness *reporting*. One option is to emphasize "nontraditional" incentives—for instance, by giving employees recognition awards for attending safety meetings, for identifying hazards, or for demonstrating their safety and health proficiency.[66] Another firm rewards workers with a sweatshirt for 250,000 worker-hours without a lost-time accident, a windbreaker for 500,000, a $500 savings bond and a quartz clock for 750,000 hours, and a commemorative silver coin and a safety jacket for 1 million accident-free hours.[67]

Others use positive reinforcement programs to improve safety at work.[68] Researchers introduced one program in a wholesale bakery that bakes, wraps, and transports pastry products to retail outlets nationwide.[69] An analysis of the safety-related conditions existing in the plant before the study suggested a number of areas that needed improvement. For example, new hires received no formal safety training, and managers rarely mentioned safety on a day-to-day basis. The firm placed commercial safety posters at the entrance to the work area and on a bulletin board in the dining room but often neglected to update them. No single person was responsible for safety. Managers said little or nothing to employees who took the time to act safely. Although the accident rate had been climbing, many employees had yet to experience an injury from unsafe performance, so this "punishment" was also missing.

The new safety program included positive reinforcement and training. The firm set and communicated a reasonable goal (in terms of observed incidents performed safely). It ensured workers knew what the firm expected of them in terms of this goal. A training phase was next. Employees received safety information during a 30-minute training session by viewing pairs of slides depicting scenes that the researchers staged in the plant. One slide, for example, showed the supervisor climbing over a conveyor; the parallel slide showed the supervisor walking around the conveyor. After viewing an unsafe act, employees had to describe what was wrong ("what's unsafe here?"). Then, after airing the problem, the researchers demonstrated the same incident again but performed in a safe manner, and explicitly stated the safe-conduct rule ("go around, not over or under, conveyors.").

At the conclusion of the training phase, supervisors showed employees a graph with their pretraining safety record (in terms of observed incidents performed safely) plotted. They were encouraged to consider increasing their performance to the new safety goal for the following reasons: for their own protection, to decrease costs for the company, and to help the plant get out of last place in the safety ranking of the parent company. Then the researchers posted the graph and a list of safety rules in a conspicuous place in the work area.

The graph helped provide positive reinforcement. Whenever observers walked through the plant collecting safety data, they posted on the graph the percentage of incidents they had seen performed safely by the group as a whole, thus providing the workers with feedback. Workers could compare their current safety performance with both their previous performance and their assigned goal. In addition, supervisors praised workers when they performed selected incidents safely. Safety in the plant subsequently improved markedly.[70]

Behavior-Based Safety

Behavior-based safety involves identifying the worker behaviors that contribute to accidents and then training workers to avoid these behaviors. For example, Tenneco Corporation (which manufactures automobile exhaust systems and Monroe brand suspensions) implemented a behavior-based safety program at its 70 manufacturing sites in 20 countries. The firm selected internal consultants from among its quality managers, training managers, engineers, and production workers. After training, the internal consultants identified five critical behaviors for Tenneco's first safety program, such as: *Eyes on task:* Does the employee watch his or her hands while performing a task? The consultants made observations, collected data regarding the behaviors, and then instituted on-site training programs to get employees to perform these activities properly.[71]

behavior-based safety
Identifying the worker behaviors that contribute to accidents and then training workers to avoid these behaviors.

Conduct Safety and Health Inspections

Again, however, programs for reducing unsafe acts are no substitute for eliminating hazards. Routinely inspect all premises for possible safety and health problems, using checklists as aids. Investigate all accidents and "near misses." Have a system in place for letting employees notify managers about hazards.[72] Use employee safety committees to do the inspecting. Committee activities include evaluating safety adequacy, monitoring safety audit findings, and suggesting strategies for improving health and safety performance.[73]

Table 15-1 summarizes actions for reducing unsafe conditions and acts.

Safety Beyond the Plant Gate

Off-work safety programs are important, too. Experts estimate, for instance, that U.S. businesses pay about $400 per employee yearly to cover the health care costs resulting from off-the-job injuries to employees and their families.[74] In 2000, OSHA tried to extend its health and safety guidelines to workers who work at home, but the resulting complaints forced it to rescind the policy.[75]

A volunteer employee safety team at Rohm & Haas's Deerpark, Texas, facility organized several programs to reduce off-the-job injuries. One month the safety team conducted a seat belt check: "If employees had their seatbelts on when they drove up to the plant, they received a scratch-off lottery ticket and information on seatbelt safety."[76]

Safety management is a high priority for companies around the world, as the following feature illustrates.

◀ **TABLE 15-1**
Reducing Unsafe Conditions and Acts: A Summary

Reduce Unsafe Conditions
Emphasize top-management commitment.
Emphasize safety.
Establish a safety policy.

Reduce Unsafe Acts
Reduce unsafe acts through selection.
Provide safety training.
Use posters and other propaganda.
Use positive reinforcement.
Use behavior-based safety programs.
Conduct safety and health inspections regularly.

Safety at Saudi Petrol Chemical

The industrial safety and security manager for the Saudi Petrol Chemical Co. in Jubail City, Saudi Arabia, says that his company's excellent safety record is a result of the fact that "our employees are champions of safety. . . ."[77] Employees are involved in every part of the safety process. They serve on safety committees, develop and lead daily and monthly safety meetings, and conduct job safety analyses, for instance.

Safety begins with the company's top management. Senior-management representatives serve on the company's Management Health and Safety Committee. This committee meets monthly to review incident reports, establish health and safety goals, review safety statistics, and endorse and sponsor safety programs.

The firm cultivates its "safety first" culture from the day a new employee arrives at work. For example, new employees are encouraged to participate in the safety process during orientation. Then (about six weeks later) they attend a one-day orientation where company officials explain and emphasize the importance of the company's health, safety, and environmental policies and programs. Employees also participate in monthly departmental training sessions to discuss departmental safety issues and safety suggestions. They work with their departmental committees to conduct monthly safety audits, to review and document departmental job safety, and to submit safety suggestions (about 60 suggestions are submitted per month). Employees are required to report every safety incident and near miss, and more than 600 reports are submitted each year.

Controlling Workers' Compensation Costs

Workers' compensation costs have soared.[78] There's therefore both a humanitarian and financial impetus for reducing claims.

Before the Accident The time to start "controlling" workers' compensation claims is before the accident happens, not after. This involves taking all the safety steps described above. The approach doesn't have to be complicated. For example, LKL Associates, Inc., of Orem, Utah, cut its workers' compensation premiums in half by communicating written safety and substance abuse policies to workers and then strictly enforcing those policies.[79]

After the Accident The injury can be traumatic for the employee, and how the employer handles it is important. The employee will have questions, such as where to go for medical help and whether he or she gets paid for time off. It's also usually at this point that the employee decides whether to retain a workers' compensation attorney to plead his or her case. Provide first aid, and make sure the worker gets quick medical attention; make it clear that you are interested in the injured worker and his or her fears and questions; document the accident; file required accident reports; and encourage a speedy return to work.[80]

It doesn't help that half the employees who return after workers' comp face indifference, criticism, or dismissal.[81] Perhaps the most important thing an employer can do is develop an aggressive return-to-work program, including making light-duty work available. The best solution, for both employer and employee, is for the worker to become a productive member of the company again instead of a victim living on benefits.[82]

Analyzing Claims Claims-tracking software can help employers understand what's driving their workers' compensation claims. For example, a health services agency in Bangor, Maine, purchased CompWatch, a workers' compensation claims management and tracking program, from Benefit Software, Inc. As illustrated in the Webnote, CompWatch enables an employer to track and analyze each of its workers' compensation claims. The agency entered all its previous claims, including near-miss incidents, and used CompWatch to analyze trends. For example, CompWatch could divide automobile accidents into those in which its driver was at fault, and those in which another person caused the accident (or the responsibility could not be determined). The agency discovered some of the auto accidents were apparently due to its drivers' need for training, so the agency introduced a driver safety program. Doing so reduced accidents: In one department, this apparently led to a 42% reduction in auto accidents from one year to the next.[83]

EMPLOYEE HEALTH: PROBLEMS AND REMEDIES[84]

A number of health-related substances and problems can undermine employee performance at work. These include alcoholism, stress, asbestos, computer use, AIDS, and workplace violence.

Alcoholism and Substance Abuse

Alcoholism and substance abuse are serious and widespread problems at work.[85] While the percentage of full-time U.S. workers engaging in illegal drug use has reportedly dropped by more than half in the last 15 years or so, about 15% of workers still report having used illicit drugs in the past year, 7.3% report currently using drugs, and 7.4% report continued heavy alcohol use.[86] Fifty percent of alcoholics are women, 25% are white-collar workers, 45% are professional or managerial personnel, 37% are high school graduates, and 50% have completed or attended college. Studies suggest that 70% of illicit drug users age 18 to 49 work full time, and that drug-using employees are over three and a half times more likely to be involved in workplace accidents.[87]

Some experts estimate that as many as 50% of all "problem employees" in industry are actually alcoholics. In one auto assembly plant, 48.6% of the grievances filed over the course of a year were alcohol related.[88] One estimate places the cost of a substance abuser's damage to a company at $7,000 per abuser per year.[89]

The effects of alcoholism on the worker and the work are severe.[90] Both the quality and quantity of the work decline sharply, and a form of "on-the-job absenteeism" occurs as efficiency declines. The alcoholic's on-the-job accidents usually don't increase significantly, apparently because he or she becomes much more cautious (but effectiveness suffers). However, the off-the-job accident rate is three to four times higher than for nonalcoholics. Morale of other workers drops as they have to shoulder the work of their alcoholic peer.

Recognizing the alcoholic on the job is another problem. Early symptoms such as tardiness can be similar to those of other problems and thus hard to classify. The supervisor is not a psychiatrist, and without specialized training, identifying—and dealing with—the alcoholic is difficult.

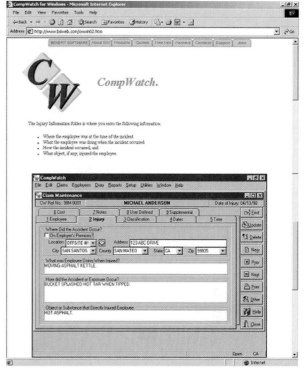

▲ **WEBNOTE**

CompWatch helps employers track and understand the reasons for their workers compensation claims.
www.bsiweb.com

Table 15-2 presents a chart showing observable behavior patterns that indicate alcohol-related problems. As you can see, alcohol-related problems range from tardiness in the earliest stages of alcohol abuse to prolonged unpredictable absences in its later stages.[91]

Dealing with Substance Abuse   For many employers, dealing with alcohol and substance abuse begins with substance abuse testing. More than one-third of businesses reported testing applicants and/or employees for alcohol.[92] Of those administering such tests, about three-fourths test if there's reasonable cause and following an accident. About 48% also have random testing programs, and about 12% do regular, periodic alcohol testing of their employees.[93]

The big question is what to do when an employee tests positive for alcohol or drugs. Disciplining, discharge, in-house counseling, and referral to an outside agency are the four traditional prescriptions. Firms traditionally use discipline short of discharge more often with alcoholics than with drug problems.[94] In practice, each employer tends to develop its own approach to dealing with substance abuse problems. One HR director says: "We present the employee with the option of a mandatory professional assessment (which may result in rehab and/or coun-

▼   **TABLE 15-2   Observable Behavior Patterns Indicating Possible Alcohol-Related Problems**

Stage	Absenteeism	General Behavior	Job Performance
I Early	Tardiness Quits early Absence from work situations ("I drink to relieve tension")	Complaints from fellow employees for not doing his or her share Overreaction Complaints of not "feeling well" Makes untrue statements	Misses deadlines Commits errors (frequently) Lower job efficiency Criticism from the boss
II Middle	Frequent days off for vague or implausible reasons ("I feel guilty about sneaking drinks"; "I have tremors")	Marked changes Undependable statements Avoids fellow employees Borrows money from fellow employees Exaggerates work accomplishments Frequent hospitalization Minor injuries on the job (repeatedly)	General deterioration Cannot concentrate Occasional lapse of memory Warning from boss
III Late Middle	Frequent days off; several days at a time Does not return from lunch ("I don't feel like eating"; "I don't want to talk about it"; "I like to drink alone")	Aggressive and belligerent behavior Domestic problems interfere with work Financial difficulties (garnishments, and so on) More frequent hospitalization Resignation: does not want to discuss problems Problems with the laws in the community	Far below expectation Punitive disciplinary action
IV Approaching Terminal Stage	Prolonged unpredictable absences ("My job interferes with my drinking")	Drinking on the job (probably) Completely undependable Repeated hospitalization Serious financial problems Serious family problems: divorce	Uneven Generally incompetent Faces termination or hospitalization

Note: Based on content analysis of files of recovering alcoholics in five organizations. From *Managing and Employing the Handicapped: The Untapped Potential*, by Gopal C. Pati and John I. Adkins Jr., with Glenn Morrison (Lake Forest, IL: Brace-Park, Human Resource Press, 1981).

Source: Gopal C. Pati and John I. Adkins Jr., "The Employer's Role in Alcoholism Assistance," *Personnel Journal* 62, no. 7 (July 1983), p. 570.

seling depending on the results of the assessment). If the employee refuses the professional assessment, employment is terminated."[95] Another, perhaps summarizing well the current thinking among employers, describes her company's policy this way:

> *Some employers have zero tolerance and terminate immediately. Some employers don't have a choice (pharmaceutical labs, for example). Others are lenient. Our policy is a three-strikes-and-you're-out process. The first step is a warning notification and permission given to us to test the employee at any time we want—for a period of five years. The second step is a mandatory substance abuse rehabilitation program at the employee's own expense . . . the third step is immediate termination for cause.*[96]

Other steps involve supervisory training or company policy.[97] Trice recommends training supervisors to identify alcoholics and the problems they create. Employers should also establish and communicate a company policy. This policy should state management's position on alcohol and drug abuse and on the use and possession of illegal drugs on company premises. It should also list the methods (such as urinalysis) used to determine the causes of poor performance, state the company's views on rehabilitation, including workplace counseling, and specify penalties for policy violations.

Supervisors are in a tricky position: They should be the company's first line of defense in combating workplace drug abuse, but should avoid becoming detectives or medical diagnosticians. Guidelines supervisors should follow include these:

- If an employee appears to be under the influence of drugs or alcohol, ask how the employee feels and look for signs of impairment such as slurred speech. Send an employee judged unfit for duty home. (See Table 15-2.)
- Make a written record of your observations and follow up each incident. In addition to issuing a written reprimand, managers should inform workers of the number of warnings the company will tolerate before requiring termination.
- Refer troubled employees to the company's employee assistance program.

Additional steps employers take to combat substance abuse on the job include conducting workplace inspections (searching employees for illegal substances), and using undercover agents (only as a last resort, according to one expert).[98]

Workplace Substance Abuse and the Law The federal Drug-Free Workplace Act requires employers with federal government contracts or grants to ensure a drug-free workplace by taking (and certifying that they have taken) a number of steps. For example, to be eligible for contract awards or grants, employers must agree to:

- Publish a policy prohibiting the unlawful manufacture, distribution, dispensing, possession, or use of controlled substances in the workplace.
- Establish a drug-free awareness program that informs employees about the dangers of workplace drug abuse.
- Inform employees that they are required, as a condition of employment, not only to abide by the employer's policy but also to report any criminal convictions for drug-related activities in the workplace.[99]

U.S. Department of Transportation rules expanding drug testing in the transportation industry went into effect in 1995.[100] These rules require random breath alcohol tests as well as preemployment, postaccident, reasonable suspicion, and return-to-duty testing for workers in safety-sensitive jobs in transportation industries including aviation, interstate motor carrier, railroad, pipeline, and commercial marine.

Legal Risks Dealing with alcoholism and drugs at work does entail legal risks: Employees have sued for invasion of privacy, wrongful discharge, defamation, and illegal searches. Therefore, before implementing any drug control program, ask:

- How will you inform workers about your substance abuse policy? Use employee handbooks, bulletin board postings, pay inserts, and the like to publicize your substance abuse plans.
- What testing, such as urinalysis, will be required of prospective and current employees? Explain the conditions under which testing may occur and the procedures for handling employees who refuse to be tested.
- What accommodations would you make for employees who voluntarily seek treatment? Substance abuse is a physical handicap under federal and some state laws. You may be required to make reasonable accommodations for employees who enter alcohol or drug treatment programs.

Job Stress and Burnout

Problems such as alcoholism and drug abuse sometimes result from stress, especially job stress. Here, job-related factors such as overwork, relocation, and problems with customers eventually put the person under such stress that a pathological reaction such as drug abuse occurs.

A variety of external, environmental factors can lead to job stress. These include work schedule, pace of work, job security, route to and from work, and the number and nature of customers or clients. Even noise, including people talking and telephones ringing, contributes to stress: 54% of office workers in one recent survey said such noise often bothered them.[101] The effect of the stress depends on its source. For example, one study found a positive relationship between challenge-related stress and job satisfaction, and a negative relationship between challenge stress and searching for a new job. Hindrance-related stress was negatively related to job satisfaction and positively related to job search and turnover.[102]

However, no two people react to the job in the same way, because personal factors also influence stress. For example, Type A personalities—people who are workaholics and who feel driven to always be on time and meet deadlines—normally place themselves under greater stress than do others. Similarly, your tolerance for ambiguity, patience, self-esteem, health and exercise, and work and sleep patterns can also affect how you react to stress. Add to job stress the stress caused by non-job problems like divorce and, as you might imagine, many workers are problems waiting to happen.

Job stress has serious consequences for both employer and employee. The human consequences include anxiety, depression, anger, and various physical consequences, such as cardiovascular disease, headaches, and accidents. For the organization, consequences include reductions in the quantity and quality of job performance, increased absenteeism and turnover, and increased grievances and health care costs.[103] A study of 46,000 employees concluded that stress and depression may cause employees to seek medical care for vague physical and psychological problems and can in fact lead to more serious health conditions. High-stress workers' health care costs were 46% higher than those of their less-stressed coworkers.[104]

Of course, stress is not necessarily dysfunctional. Some people work well only when under a little stress and find they are more productive as a deadline approaches. Others find that stress may result in a search

▲ *Many employers and employees have come up with innovative ways to deal with job stress. Volunteering is one avenue that works for Andy Lerer, a cash analyst for VNU/USA, a New York publishing company. He delivers meals to AIDS patients during his lunch hour. "It's important to switch gears," Lerer says. "I enjoy the clients, and it makes them happy to see me at lunchtime. That makes me feel good and gives me perspective."*

that leads to a better job or to a career that makes more sense, given their aptitudes. A modest level of stress may even lead to more creativity if a competitive situation results in generating new ideas.[105] As a rule, however, for obvious reasons, employers focus on dysfunctional stress and its negative consequences.

Reducing Job Stress There are a number of ways to alleviate stress. These range from commonsense remedies (such as getting more sleep and eating better) to more exotic remedies like biofeedback and meditation. Finding a more suitable job, getting counseling, and planning and organizing each day's activities are other sensible responses.[106] In his book *Stress and the Manager*, Dr. Karl Albrecht suggests the following ways to reduce job stress:

- Build rewarding, pleasant, cooperative relationships with colleagues and employees.
- Don't bite off more than you can chew.
- Build an especially effective and supportive relationship with your boss.
- Negotiate with your boss for realistic deadlines on important projects.
- Learn as much as you can about upcoming events and get as much lead time as you can to prepare for them.
- Find time every day for detachment and relaxation.
- Take a walk around the office to keep your body refreshed and alert.
- Find ways to reduce unnecessary noise.
- Reduce the amount of trivia in your job; delegate routine work whenever possible.
- Limit interruptions.
- Don't put off dealing with distasteful problems.
- Make a constructive "worry list." That includes solutions for each problem.[107]

The employer and its HR specialists and supervisors can also play a role in identifying and reducing job stress. Supportive supervisors and fair treatment are two obvious steps. Based on a survey of 1,299 employers by one insurance company, other steps include:

- Reduce personal conflicts on the job.
- Have open communication between management and employees.
- Support employees' efforts, for instance, by regularly asking how they are doing.
- Ensure effective job–person fit, since a mistake can trigger stress.[108]
- Give employees more control over their jobs.[109]
- Provide employee assistance programs including professional counseling.[110]

Burnout **Burnout** is a phenomenon closely associated with job stress. Experts define burnout as the total depletion of physical and mental resources caused by excessive striving to reach an unrealistic work-related goal.[111] Signs of impending burnout include:

burnout
The total depletion of physical and mental resources caused by excessive striving to reach an unrealistic work-related goal.

- You are unable to relax.
- You identify so closely with your activities that when they fall apart, you do, too.
- The positions you worked so hard to attain often seem meaningless now.
- You would describe yourself as a workaholic and constantly strive to obtain your work-related goals to the exclusion of almost all outside interest.[112]

What can a burnout candidate do? Here are some suggestions:

- Break your patterns. First, survey how you spend your time. Are you doing a variety of things or the same one repeatedly? The more well rounded your life is, the better protected you are against burnout.
- Get away from it all periodically. Schedule occasional periods of introspection during which you can get away from your usual routine, perhaps alone, to seek a perspective on where you are and where you are going.

▓ Reassess your goals in terms of their intrinsic worth. Are the goals you've set for yourself attainable? Are they really worth the sacrifices you'll have to make?

▓ Think about your work. Could you do as good a job without being so intense or by also pursuing outside interests?

◆ **RESEARCH INSIGHT** If you're thinking of taking a vacation to eliminate your burnout, you might as well save your money, according to one study.[113] In this study, 76 clerks in an administrative department in the headquarters of an electronics firm in central Israel completed questionnaires measuring job stress and burnout twice before a vacation, once during the vacation, and twice after the vacation.

The clerks' burnout certainly did decline during the vacation. The problem was the burnout quickly returned to prevacation levels by the time of the second postvacation survey. At least for these 76 clerks, burnout moved partway back toward its prevacation level by three days after the vacation, and all the way by three weeks after they returned to work.[114]

The good news, of course, is that burnout can apparently be reduced by removing the stressors that caused it in the first place. The bad news is that (without other changes) the burnout will quickly return once the vacation is over. One implication, as these researchers point out, is that mini vacations during the workday—"such as time off for physical exercise, meditation, power naps, and reflective thinking"—might help reduce stress and burnout.[115]

Asbestos Exposure at Work

There are four major sources of occupational respiratory diseases: asbestos, silica, lead, and carbon dioxide. Of these, asbestos has become a major concern, in part because of publicity surrounding asbestos in buildings such as schools constructed before the mid-1970s. Major efforts are now under way to rid these buildings of the substance.

OSHA standards require several actions with respect to asbestos. Companies must monitor the air whenever an employer expects the level of asbestos to rise to one-half the allowable limit. (You would therefore have to monitor if you expected asbestos levels of 0.1 fiber per cubic centimeter.) Engineering controls—walls, special filters, and so forth—are required to maintain an asbestos level that complies with OSHA standards. Only then can employers use respirators if additional efforts are still required to achieve compliance.

Computer-Related Health Problems

The fact that many workers today must spend hours each day working with computers is creating health problems at work. Short-term eye problems like burning, itching, and tearing as well as eyestrain and eye soreness are common complaints among video display users. Surveys have found that 47% to 76% of operators complain of such problems, and while no permanent vision problems have surfaced yet, long-term studies are under way.

With respect to radiation, researchers conclude "the [video display] does not present a radiation hazard to the employees working at or near a terminal."[116] Another National Institute for Occupational Safety and Health (NIOSH) study concluded that pregnant women who use computer monitors don't run any greater risk of having miscarriages than do women who are not exposed to video displays.[117]

Backaches and neckaches are widespread among display users. These often occur because employees try to compensate for problems like glare by maneuvering into awkward body positions. Researchers also found that employees who used video displays and had heavy workloads were prone to psychological distress like anxiety, irritability, and fatigue. There may also be a tendency for computer users to suffer from cumulative motion disorders, such as carpal tunnel syndrome, caused by repetitive use of the hands and arms at uncomfortable angles.[118]

NIOSH has therefore provided general recommendations regarding the use of video displays. These include:

1. Give employees rest breaks. The institute recommends a 15-minute rest break after two hours of continuous work for operators under moderate workloads and 15-minute breaks every hour for those with heavy workloads.
2. Design maximum flexibility into the work station so it can be adapted to the individual operator. For example, use adjustable chairs with midback supports, and a video display in which screen height and position are independently adjustable.
3. Reduce glare with devices such as shades over windows, terminal screen hoods properly positioned, and recessed or indirect lighting.
4. Give workers a complete preplacement vision exam to ensure properly corrected vision for reduced visual strain.
5. Place the keyboard in front of the employee, tilted away with the rear portion lower than the front.
6. Place the computer mouse and mouse pad as close to the user as possible, and ensure there are no obstructions on the desk that impede mouse movement.[119]
7. Allow the user to position his or her wrists at the same level as the elbow.
8. Put the monitor at or just below eye level, at a distance of 18 to 30 inches from the eyes.
9. Let the wrists rest lightly on a pad for support.
10. Put the feet flat on the floor, or on a footrest.[120]

AIDS and the Workplace

Some of employers' most important AIDS-related questions concern their legal responsibilities in dealing with AIDS sufferers.[121] While case law is still evolving on this issue, we can draw several conclusions. First, you cannot single out an employee for AIDS testing, because doing so would subject the person to discriminatory treatment under the ADA. Similarly, while you can probably require a physical exam that includes an AIDS test as a condition of employment, refusing to hire the person because of positive test results could put you at risk of a handicap discrimination suit. Mandatory leave cannot be required of a person with AIDS unless work performance has deteriorated. And, preemployment inquiries about AIDS (as with inquiries about any other illnesses or disabilities) would not be advisable, given the prohibitions of the Americans with Disabilities Act.[122]

Keep in mind several practical legal issues. For one thing, all employees (including managers) should be familiar with their obligations under the Americans with Disabilities Act and the Family and Medical Leave Act. For example, make sure supervisors know to provide reasonable accommodations such as refrigerator access for storage of medicines, and periodic daily medical breaks.[123]

Your company's AIDS procedure usually starts with a statement of its AIDS policy.[124] Points to cover (you'll find a sample AIDS policy at http://www.shrm.org/diversity/AIDSGuide) might include:

- The company will not tolerate discrimination or harassment.
- The company will attempt to reasonably accommodate employees.
- Medical information will remain confidential.
- HIV-positive employees can continue working as long as they can safely and effectively perform the essential functions of their jobs.
- Employees have no medical basis to refuse to work with other employees or customers who are HIV positive.
- The company takes seriously concerns of employees who fear HIV-positive co-workers and customers, and will address these with appropriate information and counseling.[125]

Workplace Smoking

Smoking is a serious problem for both employees and employers. As early as the 1980s, the Congressional Office of Technology Assessment estimated that each employee-smoker cost an employer between $2,000 and $5,000 yearly.[126] These costs derive from higher health and fire insurance, as well as increased absenteeism and reduced productivity (which occurs when, for instance, a smoker takes a 10-minute break to finish a cigarette down the hall). Studies even show that for some reason, smokers have a significantly greater risk of occupational accidents than do nonsmokers, as well as much higher absenteeism rates. In a study of Boston postal workers, this was so even controlling for factors such as drug use, age, exercise habits, and race.[127] In general, "smoking employees are less healthy than nonsmokers, are absent more, make more and more expensive claims for health and disability benefits, and endanger co-workers who breathe smoky air."[128]

As if that's not enough, nonsmoking employees who are concerned with inhaling secondhand smoke are suing their employers. The California Environmental Protection Agency estimates that each year in the United States, secondhand smoke causes 3,000 deaths due to lung cancer and 35,000 to 62,000 illnesses due to heart problems (not all work related).[129]

What You Can and Cannot Do   Suppose you want to institute a smoking ban, or a policy against hiring any smokers in the future: What are your legal rights? The answer depends on several things, including the state in which you are located, whether or not your firm is unionized, and the details of the situation. For example, instituting a smoking ban in a unionized facility which formerly allowed employees to smoke means altering conditions of work. It is therefore subject to collective bargaining.[130]

In general, you can deny a job to a smoker as long as you don't use smoking as a surrogate for some other kind of discrimination.[131] A "no-smokers-hired" policy does not, according to one expert, violate the Americans with Disabilities Act (since smoking is not considered a disability), and in general "employers' adoption of a no-smokers-hired policy is not illegal under federal law. . . ."[132] The problem arises, of course, when you try to implement smoking restrictions in a facility where you already have smokers. Here the best advice seems to be to proceed with aid of counsel or one step at a time, starting with restrictions that are not too confining.

Smoking Policies   Policies can range from total prohibitions to "Smokers and nonsmokers should courteously work out a compromise among themselves."

Smoking bans can be effective. Findings in one study showed that bans (which ranged from loose to total prohibition) reduced workplace smoking by 4% to 6% and daily consumption by 10%. Workers who do not smoke preferred workplaces that ban smoking.[133]

Violence at Work

Violence against employees has become an enormous problem at work. Homicide is the second biggest cause of fatal workplace injuries. Based on the national crime victimization survey for 1992–1996, there were an average of 1,000 workplace murders and 1.5 million workplace assaults each year.[134] However, like U.S. crime in general, workplace murders actually fell almost 40% (to 645) between 1995 and 1999, while violence-related injuries fell 27%.[135]

While robbery was the primary motive for homicide at work, a co-worker or personal associate committed roughly one of seven workplace homicides.[136] And these numbers are just the tip of the iceberg. For example, 29 U.S. Postal Service supervisors and colleagues were slain by disgruntled postal workers in one 10-year period, but there were also 350 assaults by postal workers in one year alone.[137] By one estimate, workplace violence costs employers about $4 billion a year.[138]

While men have more fatal occupational injuries than do women, the proportion of women who are victims of assault is much higher. Of all women who die on the job, 39% are the victims of assault, whereas only 18% of males who died at work were murdered.[139] The Gender-Motivated Violence Act, part of the comprehensive Violence Against Women Act passed by Congress in 1994, imposes significant liabilities on employers whose women employees become violence victims.[140] Fatal workplace violence against women has three main sources. Over three-fourths of all women (many working in retail establishments) murdered at work were victims of random criminal violence carried out by an assailant unknown to the victim, as might occur during a robbery. Co-workers, family members, or previous friends or acquaintances carried out the remaining homicides. In a survey of nearly 600 full-time men and women workers nationwide, clients, patients, and other strangers accounted for 68% of all violent attacks.[141] Co-workers accounted for about 20% of the attacks, and an employer or boss about 7%.

One report refers to bullying as the "silent epidemic" of the workplace, "where abusive behavior, threats, and intimidation often go unreported."[142] Workplace violence doesn't just strike people. It can also manifest itself in sabotaging the firm's property, software, or information databases.[143]

Employers need to eliminate such violence on humanitarian grounds, but there are legal reasons for doing so too. For example, the employee-victim may sue the employer, on the theory that the employer negligently hired or retained someone the employer should have known could be violent.[144]

Employers can take several concrete steps to reduce workplace violence. Let's look at them.

Heightened Security Measures Heightened security measures are an employer's first line of defense against workplace violence, whether that violence comes from co-workers, customers, or outsiders. NIOSH suggests these sensible precautions for reducing the risk of workplace violence:[145] Improve external lighting; use drop safes to minimize cash on hand and post signs noting that only a limited amount of cash is on hand; install silent alarms and surveillance cameras; increase the number of staff on duty; provide staff training in conflict resolution and nonviolent response; and close establishments during high-risk hours late at night and early in the morning.[146] Employers can also issue a weapons policy that states, for instance, that employees cannot bring firearms and other dangerous or deadly weapons onto the facility, openly or concealed, regardless of their legality.[147]

Because about half of workplace homicides occur in the retail industry, OSHA issued voluntary recommendations aimed at reducing homicides and injuries in such establishments. Particularly for late-night or early-morning retail workers, the suggestions include: Install mirrors and improved lighting; provide silent and personal alarms; reduce store hours during high-risk periods; install drop safes and signs that indicate little cash is kept on hand; erect bullet-resistance enclosures; and increase staffing during high-risk hours.[148]

Improved Employee Screening Screening out potentially explosive employees and applicants is the employer's next line of defense. At a minimum, this means a rigorous preemployment investigation. Obtain a detailed employment application and solicit an applicant's employment history, educational background, and references.[149] A

▲ *Barbara Marlowe, of the Boston law office of Mintz Levin Cohn Ferris Glovsky and Popeo PC, sees intervention in problems of domestic violence among employees as an exception to the rule that business shouldn't get involved in employees' lives. What makes the difference for her is the enormous impact violence at home can have on a worker's well-being and performance.*

personal interview, personnel testing, and a review and verification of all information provided should also be included. Sample interview questions to ask might include, for instance, "What frustrates you?" and "Who was your worst supervisor and why?"[150]

Certain background circumstances should indicate the need for a more in-depth background investigation of the applicant. Red flags include:[151]

An unexplained gap in employment

Incomplete or false information on the résumé or application

A negative, unfavorable, or false reference

Prior insubordinate or violent behavior on the job

A criminal history involving harassing or violent behavior

A prior termination for cause with a suspicious (or no) explanation

A history of depression or significant psychiatric problems

A history of drug or alcohol abuse

Strong indications of instability in the individual's work or personal life as indicated, for example, by frequent job changes or geographic moves

Lost licenses or accreditations[152]

Workplace Violence Training Employers should supplement enhanced security and screening with workplace training. Several firms offer video training programs that explain what workplace violence is, identify its causes and signs, and offer tips on how to prevent it and what to do when it occurs.[153] Firms should also train supervisors to identify the clues that typically precede violent incidents. These include:[154]

- *Verbal threats.* Individuals often talk about what they may do. An employee might say, "Bad things are going to happen to so-and-so," or "That propane tank in the back could blow up easily."
- *Physical actions.* Troubled employees may try to intimidate others, gain access to places where they do not belong, or flash a concealed weapon in the workplace to test reactions.
- *Frustration.* Most cases do not involve a panicked individual; a more likely scenario would involve an employee who has a frustrated sense of entitlement to a promotion, for example.
- *Obsession.* An employee may hold a grudge against a co-worker or supervisor, and some cases stem from romantic interest.[155]

A related step is to create a workplace culture emphasizing mutual respect and civility. Of course, this is easier said than done. In general, management should emphasize by word and deed that it believes deeply in and demands civility.[156] One of many opportunities to do so occurs during layoffs and downsizings. As one writer puts it, "as difficult as downsizings and layoffs are, they're often made worse because they're handled insensitively—marginalizing everyone in the workplace . . . [many have been] marched into a large hall and fired. The message is that everyone is disposable." The remedy is to treat all with courtesy, civility, and respect—including those who must leave the organization.[157]

Supervisors would do well to remember that unfair treatment precipitates violent acts, particularly where security is lax. One study focused on 136 men employed full-time. For these men, two personal characteristics—history of aggression and amount of alcohol consumed—predicted aggression against co-workers. However, it was two workplace factors—procedural justice (fairness in dealing with subordinates, and so on) and the availability (or absence) of workplace security and surveillance—that predicted aggression against the men's supervisors.[158]

Enhanced Attention to Employee Retention/Dismissal Particularly given the potential liability of retaining employees who subsequently commit violent acts, employers also need effective procedures for deciding which employees should be retained. Circumstances to watch out for in deciding whether or not to retain employees include:

An act of violence on or off the job

Erratic behavior evidencing a loss of awareness of actions

Overly defensive, obsessive, or paranoid tendencies

Overly confrontational or antisocial behavior

Sexually aggressive behavior

Isolationist or loner tendencies

Insubordinate behavior with a suggestion of violence

Tendency to overreact to criticism

Exaggerated interest in war, guns, violence, catastrophes

The commission of a serious breach of security

Possession of weapons, guns, knives at the workplace

Violation of privacy rights of others such as searching desks or stalking

Chronic complaining and frequent, unreasonable grievances

A retribution-oriented or get-even attitude[159]

Dismissing Violent Employees Use caution when firing or disciplining potentially violent employees. Analyze and anticipate, based on the person's history, what kind of aggressive behavior to expect. Have a security guard or a violence expert present when the dismissal takes place. Clear away furniture and things the person might throw. Don't wear loose clothing that the person might grab. Don't make it sound as if you're accusing the employee; instead say that according to company policy, you're required to take action. Maintain the person's dignity and try to emphasize something good about the employee. Providing job counseling for terminated employees may also help get the employee over the traumatic post-dismissal adjustment.[160] Consider the case of an executive recently suspected of sabotaging his former employer's computer system, causing up to $20 million in damage. What made this man, who'd been earning $186,000 a year, do such a thing? A note he wrote anonymously to the president provides some insight: "I have been loyal to the Company in good and bad times for over thirty years. . . . What is most upsetting is the manner in which you chose to end our employment. I was expecting a member of top management to come down from his ivory tower to face us directly with a layoff announcement, rather than sending the kitchen supervisor with guards to escort us off the premises like criminals. . . . We will not wait for God to punish you—we will take measures into our own hands."[161]

Dealing with Angry Employees What do you do when confronted by an angry, potential explosive employee? Here are some suggestions:[162]

Make eye contact.

Stop what you are doing and give your full attention.

Speak in a calm voice and create a relaxed environment.

Be open and honest.

Let the person have his or her say.

Ask for specific examples of what the person is upset about.

Be careful to define the problem.

Ask open-ended questions and explore all sides of the issue.

Listen: As one expert says, "Often, angry people simply want to be listened to. They need a supportive, empathic ear from someone they can trust."[163]

Legal Constraints on Reducing Workplace Violence   As sensible as it is to try to screen out potentially violent employees, doing so incurs the risk of liability and lawsuits. Most states have policies that encourage the employment and rehabilitation of ex-offenders, and some states therefore limit the use of criminal records in hiring decisions.[164] For example, except in certain limited instances, Article 23-A of the New York Corrections Law makes it unlawful to discriminate against job applicants based on their prior criminal convictions. Similarly, courts have interpreted Title VII of the Civil Rights Act of 1964 as restricting employers from making employment decisions based on arrest records, since doing so may unfairly discriminate against minority groups.

Aside from federal law, most states prohibit discrimination under any circumstances based on arrest records, and on prior convictions unless a direct relationship exists between the prior conviction and the job, or the employment of the individual presents an unreasonable risk to people or property.[165] And developing a "violent employee" profile could end up merely describing a mental impairment and thus violate the Americans with Disabilities Act.[166] Eliminating workplace violence while safely navigating the legal shoals is, therefore, a risky business.

We invite you to visit **www.prenhall.com/dessler** on the Prentice Hall Web site for our online study guide, Internet exercises, current events, links to related Web sites, and more.

Summary

1. The area of safety and accident prevention is of concern to managers at least partly because of the staggering number of deaths and accidents occurring at work. There are also legal and economic reasons for safety programs.

2. The purpose of OSHA is to ensure every working person a safe and healthful workplace. OSHA standards are very complete and detailed and are enforced through a system of workplace inspections.

3. Supervisors play a key role in monitoring workers for safety. Workers in turn have a responsibility to act safely. A commitment to safety on the part of top management is an important aspect of any safety program.

4. There are three basic causes of accidents: chance occurrences, unsafe conditions, and unsafe acts on the part of employees. In addition, three other work-related factors (the job itself, the work schedule, and the psychological climate) also contribute to accidents.

5. Most experts doubt that there are accident-prone people who have accidents regardless of the job. Instead, the consensus seems to be that the person who is accident prone in one job may not be on a different job.

6. There are several approaches to preventing accidents. One is to reduce unsafe conditions. The other approach is to reduce unsafe acts—for example, through an emphasis on safety, selection and placement, training, and positive reinforcement.

7. Alcoholism, drug addiction, stress, and emotional illness are four important and growing health problems among employees. Alcoholism is a particularly serious problem and one that can drastically lower the effectiveness of your organization. Disciplining, discharge, in-house counseling, and referrals to an outside agency are techniques used to deal with these problems.

8. Stress and burnout are other potential health problems at work. Asbestos, video display health problems, AIDS, and workplace smoking are other employee health problems discussed in this chapter.
9. Violence against employees is an enormous problem at work. Steps that can reduce workplace violence include improved security arrangements, better employee screening, and violence-reduction training.

Analyzing jobs, training employees, and appraising and paying them are only part of the manager's HR-related tasks. They must also negotiate and manage relations with the employer's union, and we discussed union-management relations in Chapter 14. The employer and its managers must also provide a safe and healthy workplace, and this chapter explained how they do this. Now, in the next and final chapter, we turn to the international context of the firm, and to applying all the HR activities in a multinational firm.

Tying It All Together

1. Explain how to minimize the occurrence of unsafe acts on the part of your employees.
2. Discuss the basic facts about OSHA—its purpose, standards, inspection, and rights and responsibilities.
3. Explain the supervisor's role in safety.
4. Explain what causes unsafe acts.
5. Describe at least five techniques for reducing accidents.
6. Analyze the legal and safety issues concerning AIDS.
7. Explain how you would reduce stress at work.
8. Describe the steps employers can take to reduce workplace violence.

Discussion Questions

1. Working individually or in groups, answer the question, "Is there such a thing as an accident-prone person?" Develop your answer using examples of actual people you know who seemed to be accident-prone on some endeavor.
2. Working individually or in groups, compile a list of the factors at work or in school that create dysfunctional stress for you. What methods do you use for dealing with the stress?

Individual and Group Activities

EXPERIENTIAL EXERCISE

Purpose: The purpose of this exercise is to give you practice in identifying unsafe conditions.

Required Understanding: You should be familiar with material covered in this chapter, particularly that on unsafe conditions and that in Figure 15-4.

How to Set Up the Exercise/Instructions: Divide the class into groups of four.

Assume that each group is a safety committee retained by the school's safety engineer to identify and report on any possible unsafe conditions in and around the school building. Each group will spend about 45 minutes in and around the building you are now in for the purpose of identifying and listing possible unsafe conditions. (Make use of the checklists in Figure 15-5.)

Return to the class in about 45 minutes. A spokesperson for each group should list on the board the unsafe conditions you think you have identified. How many were there? Do you think these also violate OSHA standards? How would you go about checking?

▼ **FIGURE 15-5   Self-Inspection Safety and Health Checklist**

GENERAL

		OK	ACTION NEEDED
1.	Is the required OSHA workplace poster displayed in your place of business as required where all employees are likely to see it?	☐	☐
2.	Are you aware of the requirement to report all workplace fatalities and any serious accidents (where 5 or more are hospitalized) to a federal or state OSHA office within 48 hours?	☐	☐
3.	Are workplace injury and illness records being kept as required by OSHA?	☐	☐
4.	Are you aware that the OSHA annual summary of workplace injuries and illnesses must be posted by February 1 and must remain posted until March 1?	☐	☐
5.	Are you aware that employers with 10 or fewer employees are exempt from the OSHA record-keeping requirements, unless they are part of an official BLS or state survey and have received specific instructions to keep records?	☐	☐
6.	Have you demonstrated an active interest in safety and health matters by defining a policy for your business and communicating it to all employees?	☐	☐
7.	Do you have a safety committee or group that allows participation of employees in safety and health activities?	☐	☐
8.	Does the safety committee or group meet regularly and report, in writing, its activities?	☐	☐
9.	Do you provide safety and health training for all employees requiring such training, and is it documented?	☐	☐
10.	Is one person clearly in charge of safety and health activities?	☐	☐
11.	Do all employees know what to do in emergencies?	☐	☐
12.	Are emergency telephone numbers posted?	☐	☐
13.	Do you have a procedure for handling employee complaints regarding safety and health?	☐	☐

WORKPLACE
ELECTRICAL WIRING, FIXTURES AND CONTROLS

		OK	ACTION NEEDED
1.	Are your workplace electricians familiar with the requirements of the National Electrical Code (NEC)?	☐	☐
2.	Do you specify compliance with the NEC for all contract electrical work?	☐	☐
3.	If you have electrical installations in hazardous dust or vapor areas, do they meet the NEC for hazardous locations?	☐	☐
4.	Are all electrical cords strung so they do not hang on pipes, nails, hooks, etc.?	☐	☐
5.	Is all conduit, BX cable, etc., properly attached to all supports and tightly connected to junction and outlet boxes?	☐	☐
6.	Is there no evidence of fraying on any electrical cords?	☐	☐
7.	Are rubber cords kept free of grease, oil, and chemicals?	☐	☐
8.	Are metallic cable and conduit systems properly grounded?	☐	☐
9.	Are portable electric tools and appliances grounded or double insulated?	☐	☐
10.	Are all ground connections clean and tight?	☐	☐
11.	Are fuses and circuit breakers the right type and size for the load on each circuit?	☐	☐
12.	Are all fuses free of "jumping" with pennies or metal strips?	☐	☐
13.	Do switches show evidence of overheating?	☐	☐
14.	Are switches mounted in clean, tightly closed metal boxes?	☐	☐
15.	Are all electrical switches marked to show their purpose?	☐	☐
16.	Are motors clean and kept free of excessive grease and oil?	☐	☐
17.	Are motors properly maintained and provided with adequate overcurrent protection?	☐	☐
18.	Are bearings in good condition?	☐	☐
19.	Are portable lights equipped with proper guards?	☐	☐
20.	Are all lamps kept free of combustible material?	☐	☐
21.	Is your electrical system checked periodically by someone competent in the NEC?	☐	☐

Develop Your Own Checklist.

These Are Only Sample Questions.

▼ **FIGURE 15-5** (Continued)

	OK	ACTION NEEDED	
EXITS AND ACCESS			**Develop Your Own Checklist.**
1. Are all exits visible and unobstructed?	☐	☐	
2. Are all exits marked with a readily visible sign that is properly illuminated?	☐	☐	**These Are Only Sample Questions.**
3. Are there sufficient exits to ensure prompt escape in case of emergency?	☐	☐	
4. Are areas with limited occupancy posted and is access/egress controlled to persons specifically authorized to be in those areas?	☐	☐	
5. Do you take special precautions to protect employees during construction and repair operations?	☐	☐	

	OK	ACTION NEEDED
FIRE PROTECTION		
1. Are portable fire extinguishers provided in adequate number and type?	☐	☐
2. Are fire extinguishers inspected monthly for general condition and operability and noted on the inspection tag?	☐	☐
3. Are fire extinguishers recharged regularly and properly noted on the inspection tag?	☐	☐
4. Are fire extinguishers mounted in readily accessible locations?	☐	☐
5. If you have interior standpipes and valves, are these inspected regularly?	☐	☐
6. If you have a fire alarm system, is it tested at least annually?	☐	☐
7. Are plant employees periodically instructed in the use of extinguishers and fire protection procedures?	☐	☐
8. If you have outside private fire hydrants, were they flushed within the last year and placed on a regular maintenance schedule?	☐	☐
9. Are fire doors and shutters in good operating condition?	☐	☐
Are they unobstructed and protected against obstruction?	☐	☐
10. Are fusible links in place?	☐	☐
11. Is your local fire department well acquainted with your plant, location and specific hazards?	☐	☐
12. Automatic Sprinklers:		
Are water control valves, air and water pressures checked weekly?	☐	☐
Are control valves locked open?	☐	☐
Is maintenance of the system assigned to responsible persons or a sprinkler contractor?	☐	☐
Are sprinkler heads protected by metal guards where exposed to mechanical damage?	☐	☐
Is proper minimum clearance maintained around sprinkler heads?	☐	☐

	OK	ACTION NEEDED
HOUSEKEEPING AND GENERAL WORK ENVIRONMENT		
1. Is smoking permitted in designated "safe areas" only?	☐	☐
2. Are NO SMOKING signs prominently posted in areas containing combustibles and flammables?	☐	☐
3. Are covered metal waste cans used for oily and paint soaked waste?	☐	☐
Are they emptied at least daily?	☐	☐
4. Are paint spray booths, dip tanks, etc., and their exhaust ducts cleaned regularly?	☐	☐
5. Are stand mats, platforms or similar protection provided to protect employees from wet floors in wet processes?	☐	☐
6. Are waste receptacles provided, and are they emptied regularly?	☐	☐
7. Do your toilet facilities meet the requirements of applicable sanitary codes?	☐	☐
8. Are washing facilities provided?	☐	☐
9. Are all areas of your business adequately illuminated?	☐	☐
10. Are floor load capacities posted in second floors, lofts, storage areas, etc.?	☐	☐
11. Are floor openings provided with toe boards and railings on a floor hole cover?	☐	☐
12. Are stairways in good condition with standard railings provided for every flight having four or more risers?	☐	☐

▼ **FIGURE 15-5**   **(Continued)**

	OK	ACTION NEEDED
13. Are portable wood ladders and metal ladders adequate for their purpose, in good condition and provided with secure footing?	☐	☐
14. If you have fixed ladders, are they adequate, and are they in good condition and equipped with side rails or cages or special safety climbing devices, if required?	☐	☐
15. For Loading Docks:		
Are dockplates kept in serviceable condition and secured to prevent slipping?	☐	☐
Do you have means to prevent car or truck movement when dockplates are in place?	☐	☐

MACHINES AND EQUIPMENT

	OK	ACTION NEEDED
1. Are all machines or operations that expose operators or other employees to rotating parts, pinch points, flying chips, particles or sparks adequately guarded?	☐	☐
2. Are mechanical power transmission belts and pinch points guarded?	☐	☐
3. Is exposed power shafting less than 7 feet from the floor guarded?	☐	☐
4. Are hand tools and other equipment regularly inspected for safe condition?	☐	☐
5. Is compressed air used for cleaning reduced to less than 30 psi?	☐	☐
6. Are power saws and similar equipment provided with safety guards?	☐	☐
7. Are grinding wheel tool rests set to within $1/8$ inch or less of the wheel?	☐	☐
8. Is there any system for inspecting small hand tools for burred ends, cracked handles, etc.?	☐	☐
9. Are compressed gas cylinders examined regularly for obvious signs of defects, deep rusting or leakage?	☐	☐
10. Is care used in handling and storing cylinders and valves to prevent damage?	☐	☐
11. Are all air receivers periodically examined, including the safety valves?	☐	☐
12. Are safety valves tested regularly and frequently?	☐	☐
13. Is there sufficient clearances from stoves, furnaces, etc., for stock, woodwork, or other combustible materials?	☐	☐
14. Is there clearance of at least 4 feet in front of heating equipment involving open flames, such as gas radiant heaters, and fronts of firing doors of stoves, furnaces, etc.?	☐	☐
15. Are all oil and gas fired devices equipped with flame failure controls that will prevent flow of fuel if pilots or main burners are not working?	☐	☐
16. Is there at least a 2-inch clearance between chimney brickwork and all woodwork or other combustible materials?	☐	☐
17. For Welding or Flame Cutting Operations:		
Are only authorized, trained personnel permitted to use such equipment?	☐	☐
Have operators been given a copy of operating instructions and asked to follow them?	☐	☐
Are welding gas cylinders stored so they are not subjected to damage?	☐	☐
Are valve protection caps in place on all cylinders not connected for use?	☐	☐
Are all combustible materials near the operator covered with protective shields or otherwise protected?	☐	☐
Is a fire extinguisher provided at the welding site?	☐	☐
Do operators have the proper protective clothing and equipment?	☐	☐

Develop Your Own Checklist.

These Are Only Sample Questions.

MATERIALS

	OK	ACTION NEEDED
1. Are approved safety cans or other acceptable containers used for handling and dispensing flammable liquids?	☐	☐
2. Are all flammable liquids that are kept inside buildings stored in proper storage containers or cabinets?	☐	☐
3. Do you meet OSHA standards for all spray painting or dip tank operations using combustible liquids?	☐	☐
4. Are oxidizing chemicals stored in areas separate from all organic material except shipping bags?	☐	☐
5. Do you have an enforced NO SMOKING rule in areas for storage and use of hazardous materials?	☐	☐
6. Are NO SMOKING signs posted where needed?	☐	☐

▼ **FIGURE 15-5   (Continued)**

	OK	ACTION NEEDED
7. Is ventilation equipment provided for removal of air contaminants from operations such as production grinding, buffing, spray painting and/or vapor degreasing, and is it operating properly?	☐	☐
8. Are protective measures in effect for operations involved with X-rays or other radiation?	☐	☐
9. For Lift Truck Operations:		
Are only trained personnel allowed to operate forklift trucks?	☐	☐
Is overhead protection provided on high lift rider trucks?	☐	☐
10. For Toxic Materials:		
Are all materials used in your plant checked for toxic qualities?	☐	☐
Have appropriate control procedures such as ventilation systems, enclosed operations, safe handling practices, proper personal protective equipment (e.g., respirators, glasses or goggles, gloves, etc.) been instituted for toxic materials?	☐	☐

EMPLOYEE PROTECTION

	OK	ACTION NEEDED
1. Is there a hospital, clinic or infirmary for medical care near your business?	☐	☐
2. If medical and first-aid facilities are not nearby, do you have one or more employees trained in first aid?	☐	☐
3. Are your first-aid supplies adequate for the type of potential injuries in your workplace?	☐	☐
4. Are there quick water flush facilities available where employees are exposed to corrosive materials?	☐	☐
5. Are hard hats provided and worn where any danger of falling objects exists?	☐	☐
6. Are protective goggles or glasses provided and worn where there is any danger of flying particles or splashing of corrosive materials?	☐	☐
7. Are protective gloves, aprons, shields or other means provided for protection from sharp, hot or corrosive materials?	☐	☐
8. Are approved respirators provided for regular or emergency use where needed?	☐	☐
9. Is all protective equipment maintained in a sanitary condition and readily available for use?	☐	☐
10. Where special equipment is needed for electrical workers, is it available?	☐	☐
11. When lunches are eaten on the premises, are they eaten in areas where there is no exposure to toxic materials, and not in toilet facility areas?	☐	☐
12. Is protection against the effect of occupational noise exposure provided when the sound levels exceed those shown in Table G-16 of the OSHA noise standard?	☐	☐

Develop Your Own Checklist.

These Are Only Sample Questions.

APPLICATION CASE *The New Safety Program*

Employees' safety and health are very important matters in the laundry and cleaning business. Each facility is a small production plant in which machines, powered by high-pressure steam and compressed air, work at high temperatures washing, cleaning, and pressing garments often under very hot, slippery conditions. Chemical vapors are continually produced, and caustic chemicals are used in the cleaning process. High-temperature stills are almost continually "cooking down" cleaning solvents in order to remove impuri-

ties so that the solvents can be reused. If a mistake is made in this process—such as injecting too much steam into the still—a boilover occurs, in which boiling chemical solvent erupts out of the still, onto the floor, and onto anyone who happens to be standing in its way.

As a result of these hazards and the fact that chemically hazardous waste is continually produced in these stores, several government agencies (including OSHA and the Environmental Protection Agency) have instituted strict guidelines regarding the management of these plants. For example, posters have to be placed in each store notifying employees of their right to be told what hazardous chemicals they are dealing with and what is the proper method for handling each chemical. Special waste management firms must be used to pick up and properly dispose of the hazardous waste.

A chronic problem the owners have is the unwillingness on the part of the cleaning-spotting workers to wear safety goggles. Not all the chemicals they use require safety goggles, but some—like the hydrofluorous acid used to remove rust stains from garments—are very dangerous. The latter is kept in special plastic containers because it dissolves glass. Some of the employees feel that wearing safety goggles can be troublesome; they are somewhat uncomfortable, and they

also become smudged easily and thus cut down on visibility. As a result, it is sometimes almost impossible to get employees to wear their goggles.

Questions

1. Using Figure 15-5, list at least five potential hazards in a dry cleaning store.
2. How should a laundry go about identifying hazardous conditions that should be rectified?
3. Would it be advisable for a firm to set up a procedure for screening out accident-prone individuals?
4. How would you suggest that owners get all employees to behave more safely at work? Also, how would you advise them to get those who should be wearing goggles to do so?

CONTINUING CASE: LearnInMotion.com *The New Safety and Health Program*

At first glance, a dot-com is one of the last places you'd expect to find potential safety and health hazards—or so Jennifer and Mel thought. There's no danger of moving machinery, no high-pressure lines, no cutting or heavy lifting, and certainly no forklift trucks. However, there are safety and health problems.

In terms of accident-causing conditions, for instance, the one thing dot-com companies have lots of are cables and wires. There are cables connecting the computers to each other and to the servers, and in many cases separate cables running from some computers to separate printers. There are 10 telephones in the office, all on 15-foot phone lines that always seem to be snaking around chairs and tables. There is, in fact, an astonishing amount of cable considering this is an office with less than 10 employees. When the installation specialists wired the office (for electricity, high-speed DSL, phone lines, burglar alarms, and computers), they estimated they used well over five miles of cables of one sort or another. Most of these are hidden in the walls or ceilings, but many of them snake their way from desk to desk, and under and over doorways. Several employees have tried to reduce the nuisance of having to trip over wires whenever they get up by putting their plastic chair pads over the wires closest to them. However, that still leaves many wires unprotected. In other cases, they brought in their own packing tape, and tried to tape down the wires in those spaces where they're particularly troublesome, such as across doorways.

The cables and wires are only one of the more obvious potential accident-causing conditions. The firm's programmer, before he left the firm, had tried to repair the main

server while the unit was still electrically alive. To this day, they're not sure exactly where he stuck the screwdriver, but the result was that he was "blown across the room," as Mel puts it. He was all right, but it was still a scare. And while they haven't received any claims yet, every employee spends hours at his or her computer, so carpal tunnel syndrome is a risk, as are a variety of other problems such as eyestrain and strained backs.

One recent accident particularly scared them. The firm uses independent contractors to deliver the firm's book- and CD-ROM-based courses in New York and two other cities. A delivery person was riding his bike at the intersection of Second Avenue and East 64th Street in New York when he was struck by a car. Luckily he was not hurt, but the bike's front wheel was wrecked, and the close call got Mel and Jennifer thinking about their lack of a safety program.

It's not just the physical conditions that concern the company's two owners. They also have some concerns about potential health problems such as job stress and burnout. While the business may be (relatively) safe with respect to physical conditions, it is also relatively stressful in terms of the demands it makes in hours and deadlines. It is not at all unusual for employees to get to work by 7:30 or 8 o'clock in the morning and to work through until 11 or 12 o'clock at night, at least five and sometimes six or seven days per week. Just getting the company's new calendar fine-tuned and operational required 70-hour workweeks for three weeks from five of LearnInMotion.com's employees.

The bottom line is that both Jennifer and Mel feel quite strongly that they need to do something about implementing a health and safety plan. Now, they want you, their management consultants, to help them actually do it. Here's what they want you to do for them.

Questions and Assignments

1. Based upon your knowledge of health and safety matters and your actual observations of operations that are similar to ours, make a list of the potential hazardous conditions employees and others face at LearnInMotion.com. What should we do to reduce the potential severity of the top five hazards?

2. Would it be advisable for us to set up a procedure for screening out stress-prone or accident-prone individuals? Why or why not? If so, how should we screen them?

3. Write a short position paper on the subject "what should we do to get all our employees to behave more safely at work?"

4. Based on what you know and on what other dot-coms are doing, write a short position paper on the subject "what can we do to reduce the potential problems of stress and burnout in our company?"

16 Chapter

Managing Global Human Resources

After studying this chapter, you should be able to:

- More effectively manage international HR-related tasks.
- Illustrate how intercountry differences affect HRM.
- Explain five ways to improve international assignments through selection.
- Discuss how to train and maintain international employees.

STRATEGIC OVERVIEW   Siemens is a 150-year-old German company, but it's not the company it was even a few years ago. Until recently, Siemens focused on producing electrical products. As its CEO says, "Only a few years ago, business at Siemens used to be dominated by production. Today, [diversification into] software, engineering, and services are the backbone of our business—and the key to success." Siemens today is also global—"one of the few true global players in this new world," with over 400,000 employees working in 190 countries. In other words, Siemens became a world leader by pursuing a corporate strategy that emphasized diversifying into high-tech products and services, and doing so on a global basis.

With a corporate strategy like that, global HR plays a big role at Siemens: Sophisticated engineering and services require more focus on employee selection, training, and compensation than in the average firm, and globalization requires delivering these services globally.

To this point in the book, we've discussed the basic concepts and techniques of HR management, including job analysis, recruitment, selection, training, appraisal, compensation, and labor relations and safety. The purpose of the current (and final) chapter, Managing Global Human Resources, is to make you more effective at managing the international aspects of your HR duties. The topics we'll focus on include the internationalization of business, intercountry dif-

ferences affecting HR, improving international assignments through selection, and training and maintaining international employees. Looking at how Siemens devised and implemented its HR strategy is a fitting way to end this book, as more companies become technologically and globally based in this new millennium.[1] ■

HR AND THE INTERNATIONALIZATION OF BUSINESS

U.S.-based companies are increasingly doing business abroad. Huge firms like Procter & Gamble, IBM, and Citicorp have long had extensive overseas operations, of course. But with the European market unification, the introduction of the euro currency, the opening of Eastern Europe, and the rapid development of demand in Asia and other parts of the world, even small firms are finding that success depends on their ability to market and manage overseas.

This confronts firms with some interesting management challenges. Market, product, and production plans must be coordinated on a worldwide basis, for instance, and organization structures capable of balancing centralized home-office control with adequate local autonomy must be created. And, of course, the firm must extend its HR policies and systems abroad: For example, "Should we staff the local offices with local or U.S. managers?" "How should we appraise and pay our local employees?" "How should we deal with the unions in our offices abroad?"

At Ford Motor Company, for instance, managers try to make decisions on a global basis. They plan activities such as product development and vehicle design on a worldwide basis, rather than just in regional development centers. They handle manufacturing and purchasing globally.[2] Ford approaches HR the same way, "moving employees from anywhere to anywhere if they're the best ones to do the job."[3] The firm's new head of auto operations, for example, spent most of his career abroad.

The HR Challenges of International Business

When researchers asked senior international HR managers in eight large companies, "What are the key global pressures affecting human resource management practices in your firm currently and for the projected future?" the three that emerged were:[4]

- ■ *Deployment.* Easily getting the right skills to where we need them, regardless of geographic location.
- ■ *Knowledge and innovation dissemination.* Spreading state-of-the-art knowledge and practices throughout the organization regardless of where they originate.
- ■ *Identifying and developing talent on a global basis.* Identifying who can function effectively in a global organization and developing his or her abilities.[5]

Dealing with global staffing pressures like these is quite complex. For example, it involves addressing, on a global basis, activities including candidate selection, assignment terms and documentation, relocation processing and vendor management, immigration processing, cultural and language orientation and training, compensation administration and payroll processing, tax administration, career planning and development, and handling of spouse and dependent matters.[6]

At firms like Ford, having a global HR perspective "requires understanding different cultures, what motivates people from different societies, and how that's reflected in the structure of international assignments."[7] In China, for instance, special insurance should cover emergency evacuations for serious health problems; telephone communication can be a "severe handicap" in Russia; and medical facilities in Russia may not meet international standards.[8] So the challenge of conducting HR activities abroad comes not just from the vast distances involved (though this is important), but also from the cultural, political, legal, and economic differences among countries and their peoples. Let's look at this.

How Intercountry Differences Affect HRM

Companies operating only within the borders of the United States generally have the luxury of dealing with a relatively limited set of economic, cultural, and legal variables. The United States is a capitalist, competitive society. And while the U.S. workforce reflects a multitude of cultural and ethnic backgrounds, shared values (such as an appreciation for democracy) help to blur potentially sharp cultural differences. Although the different states and municipalities certainly have their own laws affecting HR, a basic federal framework helps produce a fairly predictable set of legal guidelines regarding matters such as employment discrimination, labor relations, and safety and health.

A company operating multiple units abroad isn't blessed with such homogeneity. For example, minimum legally mandated holidays range from none in the United Kingdom to 5 weeks per year in Luxembourg. And while Italy has no formal requirements for employee representatives on boards of directors, they're required in Denmark for companies with more than 30 employees. The point is that the need to adapt personnel policies and procedures to the differences among countries complicates HR management in multinational companies. For example, consider the following.[9]

Cultural Factors Countries differ widely in their *cultures*—in other words, in the basic values their citizens adhere to, and in the ways these values manifest themselves in the nation's arts, social programs, politics, and ways of doing things.

Cultural differences from country to country necessitate corresponding differences in management practices among a company's subsidiaries. For example, in a study of about 330 managers from Hong Kong, the People's Republic of China, and the United States, the U.S. managers tended to be most concerned with getting the job done. Chinese managers were most concerned with maintaining a harmonious environment, and Hong Kong managers fell between these extremes.[10] A classic study by Professor Geert Hofstede identified other international cultural differences. For example, Hofstede says societies differ in *power distance*—in other words, the extent to which the less powerful members of institutions accept and expect an unequal distribution of power.[11] He concluded that acceptance of such inequality was higher in some countries (such as Mexico) than in others (such as Sweden).

Studies show how such cultural differences can influence HR policies.[12] For example, compared to U.S. employees, "Mexican workers expect managers to keep their distance rather than to be close, and to be formal rather than informal." Similarly, compared to the United States, in Mexican organizations "formal rules and regulations are not adhered to unless someone of authority is present."[13] In Mexico, individualism is not valued as highly as it is in

▲ *After many years of protectionism, corruption, bureaucratic difficulties, and sudden shifts in policy, Vietnam is at last making it easier for other countries to do business within its borders. A trade agreement with the United States was signed in January 2000, and a fledgling stock market, shown here, has finally opened. But cultural factors may soon make global business difficult.*

the United States. As a result, some workers don't place as much importance on self-sufficiency. They tend to expect to receive a wider range of services and benefits (such as food baskets and medical attention for themselves and their families) from their employers.[14]

In fact, the list of cultural differences is endless. In Germany, you should never arrive even a few minutes late and should always address senior people formally, with their titles.[15] Such cultural differences are a two-way street, and employees from abroad need orientation to avoid the culture shock of coming to work in the United States.[16] For example, in the Intel booklet "Things You Need to Know About Working in the U.S.A.," topics covered include sexual harassment, recognition of gay and lesbian rights, and Intel's expectations about behavior.[17]

Economic systems Differences in economic systems also translate into differences in HR practices. For one thing, some countries are more wedded to the ideals of free enterprise than are others. For instance, France—though a capitalist society—recently imposed tight restrictions on employers' rights to discharge workers, and limited the number of hours an employee could legally work each week.

Differences in labor costs are also substantial. Hourly compensation costs in U.S. dollars for production workers range from $2.46 in Mexico to $5.98 in Taiwan, $15.88 in the United Kingdom, $19.86 in the United States, and $24.01 in Germany, for instance.[18]

There are other labor costs to consider. For example, there are wide gaps in hours worked. Portuguese workers average about 1,980 hours of work annually, while German workers average 1,648 hours. Several European countries, including the United Kingdom and Germany, require substantial severance pay to departing employees, usually equal to at least two years' service in the United Kingdom and one year's in Germany.[19] Compared to the usual two or three weeks of U.S. vacation, workers in France can expect 2½ days of paid holiday per full month of service per year, Italians usually get between four and six weeks off per year, and Germans get 18 working days per year after six months of service.[20]

Legal and Industrial Relations Factors Legal as well as industrial relations (the relationships among the worker, the union, and the employer) factors vary from country to country. For example, the U.S. practice of employment at will does not exist in Europe, where firing and laying off workers is usually time consuming and expensive. And in many European countries, *work councils* replace the informal or union-based worker–management mediations typical in U.S. firms. Works councils are formal, employee-elected groups of worker representatives that meet monthly with managers to discuss topics ranging from no-smoking policies to layoffs.[21]

Codetermination is the rule in Germany and several other countries. Codetermination means employees have the legal right to a voice in setting company policies. Workers elect their own representatives to the supervisory board of the employer, and there is a vice president for labor at the top-management level.[22] In the United States, HR policies on most matters such as wages and benefits are set by the employer, or by the employer in negotiations with its labor unions. The codetermination laws, including the Works Constitution Act, largely determine the nature of HR policies in many German firms.

The European Union[23] In the 1990s, the separate countries of the former European Community (EC) were unified into a common market for goods, services, capital, and even labor called the European Union (EU). Tariffs for goods moving across borders from one EU country to another generally disappeared, and employees (with some exceptions) now find it easy to move freely between jobs in the EU countries. The introduction of a single currency—the euro—has further blurred many of these differences. The euro replaced the local currencies of most member countries in early 2002.

In addition to participative processes (like codetermination) found in some EU countries, European Union law currently requires multinationals to consult workers about certain corporate actions such as mass layoffs. However, a new EU directive will greatly expand this requirement. By 2008, more companies—including all those with 50 or more employees in the EU—must "inform and consult" employees about employee-related actions, even if the firms don't operate outside their own borders. And the consultation will then be "ongoing" rather than just for major, strategic decisions.[24]

However, intra-EU differences remain. Many countries have minimum wages while others don't, and workweek hours permitted vary from no maximum in the United Kingdom to 48 per week in Greece and Italy. Other differences exist in minimum number of annual holidays, and minimum advance notice of termination. Employment contracts are another big difference. For most U.S. positions, written correspondence is normally limited to a short letter listing the date, job title, and initial compensation for the new hire.[25] In most European countries, employers are usually required to provide a detailed statement of the job. The European Union, for instance, has a directive requiring employers to provide such a statement (including details of terms and conditions of work) within two months of the employee's starting work.[26]

Even within the EU, however, requirements vary. In England, a detailed written statement is required, including rate of pay, date employment began, hours of work, vacation entitlement, place of work, disciplinary rules, and grievance procedure. While Germany doesn't require a written contract, it's still customary to have one specifying most particulars about the job and conditions of work. In Italy, as in Germany, written agreements aren't legally required. However, "even more so than in Germany, prudence dictates providing written particulars in the complex, and at times confusing, legal structure in Italy."[27]

The EU's increasing internal coordination will gradually reduce these differences. However, cultural differences will remain, and will translate into differences in management styles and practices. Such differences "may strain relations between headquarters and subsidiary personnel or make a manager less effective when working abroad than at home."[28] Firms therefore risk operational problems abroad unless they take special steps to select, train, and compensate their international employees and assignees. We'll turn to how to do this next.

IMPROVING INTERNATIONAL ASSIGNMENTS THROUGH SELECTION

International assignments are the heart of international HR, and it's therefore disconcerting to see how often such assignments fail. U.S. expatriates' assignments that end early (the failure rate) range from 16% to 50%, and the direct costs of each such failure can reach hundreds of thousands of dollars or more.[29] (In another survey, European and Japanese multinationals reported lower failure rates, with only about one-sixth of Japanese multinationals and 3% of European multinationals reporting more than a 10% expatriate recall rate.)[30]

The exact number of failures is hard to quantify, in part because "failure" means different things to different people. An early return rate is perhaps the most obvious indicator. However, some expatriates may fail less conspicuously, quietly running up the hidden costs of reduced productivity and poisoned customer and staff relations.[31]

Why International Assignments Fail

Discovering why such assignments fail is therefore an important research task, and experts have made considerable progress. Personality is one factor. For example, in a study of 143 expatriate employees, extroverted, agreeable, and emotionally stable individuals were less likely to want to leave early.[32] And the person's intentions are important: For example, people who want expatriate careers try harder to adjust to such a life.[33] Nonwork factors like family pressures usually loom large in expatriate failures: In one study, U.S. managers listed, in descending order of importance for leaving early: inability of spouse to adjust, managers' inability to adjust, other family problems, managers' personal or emotional immaturity, and inability to cope with larger overseas responsibility.[34] Managers of European firms emphasized only the inability of the manager's spouse to adjust as an explanation for the expatriate's failed assignment. Other studies similarly emphasize dissatisfied spouses' effects on the international assignment.[35]

These findings underscore a truism regarding international assignee selection: It's usually not incompetence, but family and personal problems that undermine the international assignee. As one expert puts it:

> The selection process is fundamentally flawed. . . . Expatriate assignments rarely fail because the person cannot accommodate to the technical demands of the job. The expatriate selections are made by line managers based on technical competence. They fail because of family and personal issues and lack of cultural skills that haven't been part of the process.[36]

Yet while nonwork aspects of foreign assignments (like living conditions in general, housing conditions, health care, and the adjustment of the spouse or significant other) can prompt assignees to leave early, that result certainly isn't inevitable. Providing realistic previews of what to expect, careful screening, improved orientation, and improved benefits packages are some obvious solutions. A less obvious solution is to institute procedures that ensure your firm treats its employees fairly—treating them with respect, providing an appeal process, and so on. In one study of international assignees, nonwork problems were "significantly less pronounced when the organization's procedures were judged to be more fair."[37]

One way to reduce assignment problems is simply to shorten the length of the assignment, something employers are doing. A recent survey reports that 23% of the employers' overseas assignments lasted over three years, down from 32% in 1996.[38]

International Staffing: Home or Local?

Multinational companies (MNCs) employ several types of international managers. *Locals* are citizens of the countries where they are working. *Expatriates* are noncitizens of the countries in which they are working.[39] *Home-country nationals* are citizens of the country in which the multinational company has its headquarters.[40] *Third-country nationals* are citizens of a country other than the parent or the host country—for example, a British executive working in the Tokyo branch of a U.S. multinational bank.[41] Expatriates still represent a minority of multinationals' managers. Thus, "most managerial positions are filled by locals rather than expatriates in both headquarters or foreign subsidiary operations."[42]

There are several reasons to rely on local managers to fill your foreign subsidiary's management ranks. Many people don't want to work in a foreign country, and the cost of using expatriates is usually far greater than the cost of using local workers.[43] Locals may view the multinational as a "better citizen" if it uses local management talent, and some governments even press for the "nativization" of local management.[44] There may also be a fear that expatriates, knowing they're posted to the foreign subsidiary for only a few years, may overemphasize short-term projects rather than more necessary long-term tasks.[45]

Yet there are also reasons for using expatriates—either home-country or third-county nationals—for staffing subsidiaries. The major reason is usually technical competence: In other words, employers often can't find local candidates with the required technical qualifications.[46] Multinationals also view a successful stint abroad as a required step in developing top managers. (For instance, after a term abroad, the head of General Electric's Asia-Pacific region was transferred back to a top executive position as vice chairman at GE.) Control is another important reason to use expatriates. The assumption is that home-office managers are readily steeped in the firm's policies and culture, and thus more likely to implement headquarters' instructions and ways of doing things.

One potential pitfall in hiring employees from abroad—bogus credentials—doesn't seem to be a widespread problem. However, prudence suggests taking some precautions. For one thing, a "4-year college degree" from institutions of higher learning abroad doesn't necessarily mean the same as it might, say, from a U.S. school: in some countries those four years include part of what Americans usually call high school. Some suggestions:[47]

- Don't rush into accepting a credential if you have reservations.
- If you have any questions about a document, try to get the original.
- Confirm the existence of the institution through references such as the *International Handbook of Universities*, or the *Commonwealth Universities Handbook*. You can also call the appropriate foreign consulate or embassy in New York or Washington. Also check the Internet.
- Write or fax the institution named and enclose a copy of the document submitted for verification.
- If you must accept documents from countries not diplomatically related to the U.S. (such as Iran), have the applicant sign a form declaring that the document's information is true and have his or her signature notarized.
- Verify the applicant's foreign credentials even if the person is now transferring from a school in your country.
- Beware of telltale signs that may indicate fraudulent credentials: poor copies, stains over key information, type erasures, evidence of substituted names, credentials received too late to make proper verification possible, or typed material that's added on at an angle, for instance.[48]

Values and International Staffing Policy

Experts sometimes classify top executives' values as ethnocentric, polycentric, or geocentric, and these values translate into corresponding corporate behaviors and policies.[49] In an ethnocentrically run corporation, "the prevailing attitude is that home country attitudes, management style, knowledge, evaluation criteria, and managers are superior to anything the host country might have to offer."[50] In the polycentric corporation, "there is a conscious belief that only host country managers can ever really understand the culture and behavior of the host country market; therefore, the foreign subsidiary should be managed by local people."[51] Geocentric executives believe they must scour the firm's whole management staff on a global basis, on the assumption that the best manager of a specific position anywhere may be in any of the countries in which the firm operates.

These values translate into three broad international staffing policies. With an *ethnocentric* staffing policy, the firm fills key management jobs with parent-country nationals.[52] At Royal Dutch Shell, for instance, most financial officers around the world are Dutch nationals. Reasons given for ethnocentric staffing policies include lack of qualified host-country senior-management talent, a desire to maintain a unified corporate culture and tighter control, and the desire to transfer the parent firm's core competencies (for instance, a specialized manufacturing skill) to a foreign subsidiary more expeditiously.[53]

A *polycentric*-oriented firm would staff its foreign subsidiaries with host-country nationals, and its home office with parent-country nationals. This may reduce the local cultural misunderstandings that might occur if it used expatriate managers. It will also almost undoubtedly be less expensive. One expert estimates that an expatriate executive can cost a firm up to three times as much as a domestic executive because of relocation expenses and other expenses such as schooling for children, annual home leave, and the need to pay income taxes in two countries.[54]

A *geocentric* staffing policy "seeks the best people for key jobs throughout the organization, regardless of nationality"—similar to what Ford Motor Company does.[55] This may let the global firm use its human resources more efficiently by transferring the best person to the open job, wherever he or she may be. It can also help build a stronger and more consistent culture and set of values among the entire global management team.

Values like these translate into other behaviors. For example, the ethnocentric ("we're the best") behaviors of host-country employees had a negative effect on workers' abilities to adjust in one study of 250 international assignees.[56]

Selecting International Managers

The processes firms use to select managers for their domestic and foreign operations obviously have many similarities. For either assignment, the candidate should have the technical knowledge and skills to do the job, and the intelligence and people skills to be a successful manager.[57]

However, we've seen that foreign assignments are different. There is the need to cope with colleagues whose culture may be drastically different from one's own, and the stress that being alone in a foreign land can put on the single manager. And if spouse and children will share the assignment, there are the complexities and pressures that the family will have to confront, from learning a new language to finding new friends and attending new schools.

Selecting managers for these assignments therefore sometimes means testing them for traits that predict success in adapting to new environments. One study asked 338 international assignees from various countries and organizations to specify which traits were important for the success of managers on foreign assignment. The researchers identified five factors that contribute to success in such assignments: job knowledge and motivation, relational skills, flexibility/adaptability, extracultural openness, and family situation (spouse's positive opinion, willingness of spouse to live abroad, and so on; Figure 16-1 shows some of the specific items that make up each of the five factors).[58] The five factors were not equally important in the foreign assignee's success, according to the assignees. "Family situation was generally found to be the most important factor, a finding consistent with other research on international assignments and transfers."[59]

With flexibility and adaptability often appearing high on results in studies like these, *adaptability screening* is sometimes part of the expatriate screening process. Often conducted by a psychologist or psychiatrist, adaptability screening aims to assess the assignee's (and spouse's) probable success in handling the foreign transfer, and to alert them to issues (such as the impact on children) the move may involve.[60] Here, experience is often the best predictor of future success. Companies like Colgate-Palmolive therefore look for overseas candidates whose work and nonwork experience, education, and language skills already demonstrate a commitment to and facility for living and working with different cul-

▶ **FIGURE 16-1**
Five Factors
Important in
International
Assignee
Importance Factors'
Components

I) Job Knowledge and Motivation
Managerial ability
Organizational ability
Imagination
Creativity
Administrative skills
Alertness
Responsibility
Industriousness
Initiative and energy
High motivation
Frankness
Belief in mission and job
Perseverance

II) Relational Skills
Respect
Courtesy and tact
Display of respect
Kindness
Empathy
Nonjudgmentalness
Integrity
Confidence

III) Flexibility/Adaptability
Resourcefulness
Ability to deal with stress
Flexibility
Emotional stability
Willingness to change
Tolerance for ambiguity
Adaptability
Independence
Dependability
Political sensitivity
Positive self-image

IV) Extracultural Openness
Variety of outside interests
Interest in foreign cultures
Openness
Knowledge of local language(s)
Outgoingness and extroversion
Overseas experience

V) Family Situation
Adaptability of spouse and family
Spouse's positive opinion
Willingness of spouse to live abroad
Stable marriage

Source: Adapted from Arthur Winfred Jr., and Winston Bennett Jr. "The International Assignee: The Relative Importance of Factors Perceived to Contribute to Success," *Personnel Psychology* 48 (1995), pp. 106–107.

tures.[61] Even several successful summers spent traveling overseas or participating in foreign student programs might provide some basis to believe that the potential transferee can adjust when he or she arrives overseas.

Many firms also use paper-and-pencil tests such as the Overseas Assignment Inventory. Based on 12 years of research with more than 7,000 candidates, the test reportedly identifies the characteristics and attitudes international assignment candidates should have.[62] Realistic previews about the problems to expect in the new job (such as mandatory private schooling for the children) as well as about the cultural benefits, problems, and idiosyncrasies of the country are another important part of the screening process. The rule, say some experts, should always be to "spell it all out" ahead of time, as many multinationals do for their international transferees.[63]

Unfortunately theory doesn't always translate into practice. The importance of adaptability screening notwithstanding, 70% of respondents in one survey listed "skills or competencies" as the most important selection criteria when choosing candidates for international assignments. They ranked "job performance" second. The ability to adapt to new cultural conditions—as measured by items like "prior international living experience or assignment," and "familiarity with assignment country"—were rarely ranked as most important or second most important.[64] One study found that selection for positions abroad is so informal that the researchers called it "the coffee machine system": Two colleagues meet at the office coffee machine, strike up a conversation about the possibility of a position abroad, and based on that and little more a selection decision is made.[65] Perhaps this helps explain the high failure rate of foreign assignees. The "New Workplace" box provides another perspective.

General selection procedures also differ from country to country. One study surveyed 959 organizations in 20 countries. Those using structured interviews ranged from 10.3% in Italy to 12.1% in Sweden, 17.1% in Germany, 22.9% in France, 29.2% in Spain, 33% in the United Kingdom, 34.6% in the United States,

37.5% in Hong Kong, 54.8% in Canada, and 59.1% in Australia. On the other hand, some staffing practices (such as using educational qualifications in screening) exhibited little variability across countries.[66]

THE *NEW* **WORKPLACE**

While the number and proportion of women managers working domestically has climbed in the past few years, the same isn't true of those assigned abroad. Women filled only about 6% of the overseas international management positions at major companies, according to one estimate, compared with about 49% of domestic U.S. management positions. Women comprise only about 13% of the total expatriate population, according to another survey.[67]

Inaccurate stereotypes may account for much of this discrepancy. For example, a new survey ("Passport to Opportunity: U.S. Women in Global Business") found that respondents believed women aren't as internationally mobile as men; yet 80% of female expatriates say they've never turned down a relocation assignment, compared with 71% of men. Another myth is that women might have a tougher time building relationships with businesspeople overseas; yet 77% of U.S. women in this survey said they were effective at building business relationships with men abroad.[68]

Various factors contribute to women expatriates' success. In one study of 38 American female expatriates, married expatriates experienced greater cross-cultural adjustments than single ones, apparently because of the support they got from their spouses. (One would assume the same applies to male expatriates.) The results also suggest it's important that companies "continue to support the cross-cultural adjustments of their female expatriates throughout the entire period of their overseas assignments."[69]

Sending Women Managers Abroad

TRAINING AND MAINTAINING INTERNATIONAL EMPLOYEES

Careful screening is just the first step in ensuring the foreign assignee's success. The employee may then require special training, and the firm will also need special international HR policies for compensating the firm's overseas employees and for maintaining healthy labor relations.

Orienting and Training Employees on International Assignment

When it comes to providing the orientation and training required for success overseas, the practices of most U.S. firms reflect more form than substance. One consultant says that despite many companies' claims, there is generally little or no systematic selection and training for assignments overseas. In one survey, a sample of company executives agreed that international business required that employees be firmly grounded in the economics and practices of foreign countries. However, few of their companies actually provide such training to their employees.[70] A survey of U.S. companies that assign employees abroad found that only 42% have a "formal program for briefing employees regarding conditions in the host country."[71]

What sort of special training do overseas candidates need? One firm specializing in such programs prescribes a four-step approach.[72] Level 1 training focuses on the impact of cultural differences, and on raising trainees' awareness of such differences and their impact on business outcomes. Level 2 aims at getting participants to understand how attitudes (both negative and positive) are formed

▲ *Managers abroad continue to need training and development. INSEAD in France offers classroom programs that provide the kinds of educational opportunities executives need.*

and how they influence behavior. (For example, unfavorable stereotypes may subconsciously influence how a new manager responds to and treats his or her new foreign subordinates.) Level 3 training provides factual knowledge about the target country, while Level 4 provides skill building in areas like language and adjustment and adaptation skills.

Beyond these special training needs, managers abroad continue to need traditional training and development. At IBM, for instance, such development includes rotating assignments that permit overseas managers to grow professionally. IBM and other firms also have management development centers around the world where executives can hone their skills. And classroom programs (such as those at the London Business School, or at INSEAD in France) provide overseas executives the sorts of educational opportunities (to acquire MBAs, for instance) that similar stateside programs do for their U.S.-based colleagues.

Designed correctly, international management development activities can also have a more subtle impact on the managers and their firms. For example, rotating assignments can help managers form bonds with colleagues around the world, and they can use these contacts to get decisions made more expeditiously. And activities such as periodic seminars (in which the firm brings together managers from its far-flung subsidiaries and steeps them for a week or two in the firm's values, strategy, and policies) are also useful. They can improve control by building a unifying set of values, standards, and corporate culture.

There are several trends in expatriate training and development. First, rather than providing only predeparture cross-cultural training, more firms are providing continuing, in-country cross-cultural training during the early stages of an overseas assignment. Second, employers are using returning managers as resources to cultivate the "global mind-sets" of their home-office staff. For example, automotive equipment producer Bosch holds regular seminars in which newly arrived returnees pass on their knowledge and experience to relocating managers and their families.

There's also increased use of software and the Internet for cross-cultural training. For example, *Bridging Cultures* is a self-training multimedia package for people who will be traveling and/or living overseas. It uses short video clips to introduce case study intercultural problems, and then guides users to selecting the strategy to best handle the situation. Cross-cultural training firms' Web sites include: www.bennettinc.com/indexie.htm; www.livingabroad.com; www.worldwise-inc.com; and www.globaldynamics.com.[73]

International Compensation

The whole area of international compensation presents some tricky problems. On the one hand, there is logic in maintaining companywide pay scales and policies so that, for instance, divisional marketing directors throughout the world are paid within the same narrow range. This reduces the risk of perceived inequities, and dramatically simplifies the job of keeping track of disparate country-by-country wage rates.

Yet not adapting pay scales to local markets can produce more problems than it solves. The fact is, it can be enormously more expensive to live in some countries (like Japan) than others (like Greece); if these cost-of-living differences aren't considered, it may be almost impossible to get mangers to take "high-cost" assignments. However, the answer is usually not just to pay, say, marketing directors more in one country than in another. For one thing, you could get resistance when you tell a marketing director in Tokyo who's earning $3,000 per week to move to your division in Spain, where his or her pay for the same job will drop by half (cost of living notwithstanding). One way to handle the problem is to pay a similar base salary companywide, and then add on various allowances according to individual market conditions.[74]

Determining equitable wage rates in many countries is no simple matter. There is a wealth of "packaged" compensation survey data available in the United States, but such data are not so easy to come by overseas. As a result, "one of the greatest difficulties in managing total compensation on a multinational level is establishing a consistent compensation measure between countries that builds credibility both at home and abroad."[75]

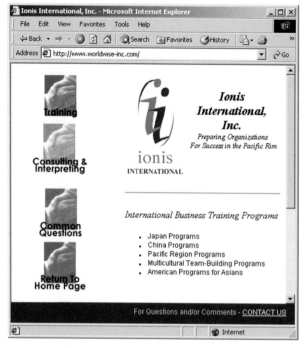

▲ **WEBNOTE**
Sites like this provide cross-cultural training and other services.
www.worldwise-inc.com

Some multinational companies conduct their own local annual compensation surveys. For example, Kraft conducts an annual study of total compensation in Belgium, Germany, Italy, Spain, and the United Kingdom. It focuses on the total compensation paid to each of 10 senior-management positions held by local nationals in these firms. The survey covers all forms of compensation including cash, short- and long-term incentives, retirement plans, medical benefits, and perquisites.[76] This information becomes the basis for annual salary increases and proposed changes in the benefits package.

The Balance Sheet Approach The most common approach to formulating expatriate pay is to equalize purchasing power across countries, a technique known as the balance sheet approach.[77] More than 85% of North American companies reportedly use this approach.

The basic idea is that each expatriate should enjoy the same standard of living he or she would have had at home. With the balance sheet approach, four main home-country groups of expenses—income taxes, housing, goods and services, and discretionary expenses (child support, car payments, and the like)—are the focus of attention. The employer estimates what each of these four expenses is in the expatriate's home country, and what each will be in the host country. The employer then pays any differences—such as additional income taxes or housing expenses.

In practice, this usually boils down to building the expatriate's total compensation around five or six separate components. For example, base salary will normally be in the same range as the manager's home-country salary. In addition, however, there might be an overseas or foreign service premium. The executive receives this as a percentage of his or her base salary, in part to compensate for the cultural and physical adjustments he or she will have to make.[78] There may also be several allowances, including a housing allowance and an education allowance for the expatriate's children. Income taxes represent another area of concern. A

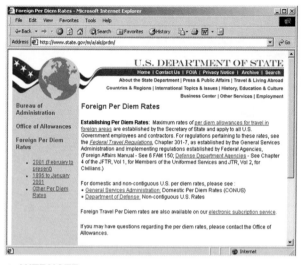

U.S. manager posted abroad must often pay not just U.S. taxes but also income taxes in the host country.

Table 16-1 illustrates the balance sheet approach. In this case, the manager's annual earnings are $80,000, and she faces a U.S. income tax rate of 28%, and a Belgium income tax rate of 70%. The other costs are based on the index of living costs abroad published in the "U.S. Department of State Indexes of Living Costs Abroad, Quarters Allowances, and Hardship Differentials," available at http://www.state.gov. (See Webnote.)

Incentives Performance-based incentives tend to be less prevalent abroad. In Europe, firms traditionally emphasize a guaranteed annual salary and companywide bonus.[79] Based on one survey, European compensation directors do want to see more performance-based pay. However, they first have to overcome several problems—including the public relations aspects of such a move (such as selling the idea of more emphasis on performance-based pay). A survey several years ago suggests that U.S. firms that offer overseas managers long-term incentives (80% in this survey) use overall corporate performance criteria (like worldwide profits) when awarding incentive pay—although, ironically, a manager's local performance may have little or no effect on how the company as a whole performs.[80]

What U.S. companies do offer are various incentives to get expatriates to accept and stay on international assignment. **Foreign service premiums** are financial payments over and above regular base pay, and typically range between 10% and 30% of base pay. Note, though, that since managers tend to get these premiums in small increments with their base pay, it's easy to misconstrue these as regular "pay raises," and then to become disillusioned when the premium stops upon the expatriates' return. **Hardship allowances** compensate expatriates for exceptionally hard living and working conditions at certain foreign locations. Differentials recently ranged from 5% in Mexico and Greece to 15% in Bombay, 20% in Belarus, and 25% in Sierra Leone.[81] Employers also usually pay these incrementally (with each paycheck), so it's important to make it clear that this is not a permanent raise. **Mobility premiums** are typically lump-sum payments to reward employees for moving from one assignment to another.

In general, executive compensation systems around the world are becoming more similar: "The structures have common broadband base salary ranges, flexible annual incentive targets/maximums and internationally established share option guideline awards."[82] And, as in the United States, more multinational employers are granting more stock options to a broader group of their employees overseas, a step that requires even more attention to complying with local tax laws.[83]

---

foreign service premiums
Financial payments over and above regular base pay, typically ranging between 10% and 30% of base pay.

---

hardship allowances
Compensate expatriates for exceptionally hard living and working conditions at certain locations.

---

mobility premiums
Typically, lump-sum payments to reward employees for moving from one assignment to another.

► **TABLE 16-1**
The Balance Sheet Approach (Assumes base salary of $80,000)

Annual Expense	Chicago, USA	Brussels, Belgium (U.S.$ equivalent)	Allowance
Housing & utilities	$35,000	$67,600	$32,600
Goods & services	6,000	9,500	3,500
Taxes	22,400	56,000	33,600
Discretionary income	10,000	10,000	0
Total	$73,400	$143,100	$69,700

Source: Joseph Martocchio, *Strategic Compensation* (Upper Saddle River, NJ: Prentice Hall, 2001), Table 12-15, p. 294.

Beyond Compensation Particularly for employees in less industrialized countries, HR managers also take nonmonetary rewards into account. For example, a Johnson & Johnson HR manager points out that after losing professional talent at a rate of over 25% per year, "I talked to lots of our people and people in other companies and I found that most of them joined a multinational to enhance their careers through training and development. If they didn't get that, they left."[84] Many firms, including ABB, P&G, and Siemens, therefore look beyond financial rewards, and provide local employees with state-of-the-art training and development programs.[85]

Performance Appraisal of International Managers

Several things complicate the task of appraising an expatriate's performance.[86] For one thing, the question of who actually appraises the expatriate is crucial. Obviously, local management must have some input, but cultural differences here may distort the appraisals. Thus, host-country bosses might evaluate a U.S. expatriate manager in India somewhat negatively if they find his or her use of participative decision making culturally inappropriate. On the other hand, home-office managers may be so out of touch that they can't provide valid appraisals, since they're not fully aware of the situation the manager faces locally. Similarly, the procedure may be to measure the expatriate by objective criteria such as profits and market share, but local events (such as political instability) may affect the manager's performance while remaining "invisible" to home-office staff.

Two experts make these suggestions for improving the expatriate appraisal process:[87]

1. Stipulate the assignment's difficulty level. Most would view being an expatriate manager in China more difficult than working in England; the appraisal should take into account such difficulty-level differences.
2. Weigh the evaluation more toward the on-site manager's appraisal than toward the home-site manager's distant perceptions of the employee's performance.
3. If (as is usually the case) the home-office manager does the actual written appraisal, have him or her use a former expatriate from the same overseas location for advice. This helps ensure consideration of unique local issues during the appraisal.
4. Modify the normal performance criteria used for that particular position to fit the overseas position. For example, "maintaining positive labor relations" might be more important in Chile, where labor instability is more common, than in the United States.[88]

International Labor Relations

Firms opening subsidiaries abroad will find substantial differences in labor relations practices among the world's countries and regions. This is important; remember that while union membership as a percentage of wage and salary earners is dropping in the U.S., it is still relatively high in most countries compared with the United States' 14%: for example, Brazil, 44%; Argentina, 39%; Germany, 29%; Denmark, 80%; Japan, 24%; Egypt, 39%; and Israel, 23%.[89]

The following synopsis illustrates some of these labor relations differences by focusing on Europe. However, similarly significant differences would exist as we move, say, to South and Central America, and to Asia.[90]

- *Centralization.* In general, collective bargaining in Western Europe is likely to be industrywide or regionally oriented, whereas in the U.S. it generally occurs at the enterprise or plant level.
- *Union structure.* European collective bargaining is more centralized, and local unions tend to have less autonomy and decision-making power than in the United States.

- *Employer organization.* Due to the prevalence of industrywide bargaining in Europe, employer associations (rather than individual employers) tend to perform the employer's collective bargaining role.
- *Union recognition.* Union recognition for collective bargaining in Western Europe is much less formal than in the United States. For example, in Europe there is no legal mechanism requiring an employer to recognize a particular union; even if a union claims to represent 80% of an employer's workers, another union can try to organize and bargain for the other 20%.
- *Union security.* Union security in the form of formal closed-shop agreements is largely absent in continental Western Europe.
- *Content and scope of bargaining.* U.S. labor–management agreements tend to focus on wages, hours, and working conditions. European agreements tend to be brief and to specify minimum wages and employment conditions, with individual employers free to institute more generous terms. This is because industrywide bargaining makes it difficult to write detailed contracts applicable to individual enterprises. And in Europe, the government is heavily involved in setting terms of employment (such as vacations and working conditions).
- *Grievance handling.* In Western Europe, grievances occur much less often than in the U.S.; when raised, legislated machinery outside the union's formal control usually handles them.
- *Strikes.* With some exceptions, strikes generally occur less frequently in Europe. This is probably due to industrywide bargaining, which generally elicits less management resistance than in the United States, where union demands "cut deeper into the individual enterprise's revenues."[91]
- *Worker participation.* Worker participation has a long history in Western Europe, where it tends to go far beyond matters such as pay and working conditions. The aim is to create a system by which workers can participate directly in the management of the enterprise. Works councils and codetermination are two examples.[92]

Safety and Fair Treatment Abroad

Making provisions to ensure employee safety and fair treatment doesn't stop at a country's borders. While the U.S. has often taken the lead with respect to matters such as occupational safety, other countries are also quickly adopting such laws. In any event, it's hard to make a legitimate case for being less safety conscious or fair with workers abroad than you are with those at home.

High-profile companies including Nike, Inc., have recently received bad publicity for—and taken steps to improve—the working conditions, long hours, and low pay rates for factory workers in countries such as Indonesia.[93] Also under discussion is a plan to create the Fair Labor Association. This would be a private entity controlled by both corporate and human rights or labor representatives. It would take steps such as accrediting auditors to certify whether or not companies comply with their code of conduct.[94]

Having employees abroad does raise some unique safety and fair treatment issues, however. For example, kidnapping has become a way of life in some countries south of the U.S. border, and in many places—"Brazil, Nigeria, the Philippines, Russia, and New Guinea, to name a few—street crime is common, although tourists and business people are rarely kidnapped or assassinated."[95] As one security executive at an oil company put it, "It's crucial for a company to understand the local environment, local conditions and what threat exists."[96] Keeping business travelers out of crime's way is a specialty all its own, but suggestions here include:[97]

- Provide expatriates with general training about traveling, living abroad, and the place they're going to, so they're more oriented when they get there.
- Tell them not to draw attention to the fact they're Americans—by wearing flag emblems or T-shirts with American names, or by using American cars, for instance.

- Have travelers arrive at airports as close to departure time as possible and wait in areas away from the main flow of traffic where they're not as easily observed.
- Equip the expatriate's car and home with adequate security systems.
- Tell employees to vary their departure and arrival times and take different routes to and from work.
- Keep employees current on crime and other problems by regularly checking, for example, the State Department's travel advisory service and consular information sheets (http://travel.state.gov/travel_warnings.html). These provide up-to-date information on possible threats in almost every country of the world.
- Advise employees to remain confident at all times: Body language can attract perpetrators, and those who look like victims often become victimized.[98]

As another matter, firms like Coca-Cola and Exxon increasingly acknowledge that the AIDS epidemic can have devastating effects on the citizens of many of the countries in which they do business—and on their local employees. Thus, Exxon is providing HIV prevention education for employees, and Chevron donated $250,000 in medical supplies for state-of-the-art blood testing.[99]

HR NET

Human Resource Information Systems

As a company grows, relying on manual HR systems to manage activities like worldwide safety, benefits administration, payroll, and succession planning becomes unwieldy. More firms are therefore automating and integrating their HR systems into human resource information systems (HRIS). We can define an HRIS as interrelated components working together to collect, process, store, and disseminate information to support decision making, coordination, control, analysis, and visualization of an organization's human resource management activities.[100]

For global firms, it makes particular sense to expand the firm's human resource information systems abroad. For example, electrical components manufacturer Thomas & Betts once needed 83 faxes to get a head count of its 26,000 employees in 24 countries; it can now do so with the push of a button, thanks to its global HR system.[101] Most global HRIS uses are more sophisticated. Without a database of a firm's worldwide management talent, for instance, selecting employees for assignments abroad, and keeping track of each unit's compensation schemes, benefits, and personnel practices and policies can be overwhelming. However, any HRIS is no better than the accuracy of its data, and "such a database needs to be constantly reviewed and updated. . . ."[102]

Integrating and updating a firm's HR systems, particularly in a global firm, makes using an Internet-based HRIS especially beneficial. For example, when Buildnet, Inc., decided to integrate its separate HR systems, it chose a Web-based software package called MyHRIS, from NuView, Inc. (www.nuviewinc.com). This is an Internet-based system that includes human resource and benefits administration, applicant tracking and résumé scanning, training administration, and succession planning and development.[103] With MyHRIS, managers at any of the firm's locations around the world can access and update more than 200 built-in reports such as "termination summary" or "open positions."[104] And the firm's home-office managers can monitor global HR activities on a real-time basis.

Repatriation: Problems and Solutions

Effectively repatriating returning employees is important. Particularly after companies spend hundreds of thousands of dollars helping the person develop international expertise, it's disconcerting to know that perhaps 50% of returnees leave their companies within two years of coming home. In one survey, 76% of employers said providing returnees with opportunities to use their foreign experiences (advising future expatriates, managing projects that involve the former host country, and so on) is the best way to avoid having them leave the firm prematurely.[105] However, that's only part of the solution.[106]

For one thing, expatriates often fear they're "out of sight, out of mind" during an extended foreign stay, and such fears are often well founded. Many firms hurriedly assign returning expatriates to mediocre or makeshift jobs.[107] Perhaps more exasperating is discovering that the firm has promoted the expatriate's former colleagues while he or she was overseas. Even the expatriate's family may undergo a sort of reverse culture shock, as they face the task of picking up old friendships and starting new schools, and giving up the perks of the overseas job, like a company car and driver. Consider Scott Fedje's experience. As an executive with a Fortune 500 apparel manufacturer, he'd spent five years in Hong Kong, and came home to a promotion and pay raise. But "I felt lost," he says. "Most of us who returned went from a position of high responsibility and a dynamic environment to a cubicle, a project and a whole month to make a single decision." People he had worked with at the home office five years before had moved on, and his new position lacked the intellectual stimulation he got during five years in Hong Kong. He resigned a few months later.[108]

Progressive multinationals anticipate and avoid these problems by taking several sensible steps:[109]

- Have written repatriation agreements. These guarantee in writing that the international assignee will not be kept abroad longer than some period (such as three years), and that on return he or she will be given a mutually acceptable job. Many firms, including Dow Chemical and Union Carbide, use such repatriation agreements.
- Assign a sponsor. The employee should get a sponsor (such as a senior manager at the parent firm's home office) whose role is to look after the expatriate while he or she is away. This includes keeping the person apprised of significant company events and changes back home, monitoring his or her career progress and interests, and nominating the person for key openings when he or she is due to come home.
- Provide career counseling. Formal career counseling sessions can ensure that the returnee's new job assignments meet his or her needs.[110]
- Keep communications open. Keep the expatriate "plugged in" to home-office business affairs by providing management meetings around the world, frequent home leave combined with stays at headquarters for specific projects, and regularly scheduled meetings at headquarters.[111]
- Develop reorientation programs. Provide the repatriate and his or her family with a reorientation program to facilitate their adjustment back into the home culture.

STRATEGIC HR

Siemens Global HR Management

When Siemens celebrated its 150th anniversary recently, it was, according to its CEO, "a perfect occasion to analyze the enduring qualities that helped us survive so long—and identify what we must have to succeed in the future." As part of this review, one of the central questions was: Which human resource strategies will ensure that Siemens's people—and the company—can succeed in tomorrow's challenging global environment? The answers help illustrate why the concepts and techniques we've discussed in this book are important in supporting a firm's strategy. And, they illustrate how managers apply these concepts and techniques in multinational firms. Siemens sums up its basic HR strategy in five points. These show how HR supports Siemens's strategy.

1. *A living company is a learning company.* The technological and competitive markets in which Siemens does business are evolving, and the firm's HR processes therefore have to enable employees to learn on a continuing basis. Siemens, first, uses its system of combined classroom and hands-on apprenticeship training around the world. The firm also knows more jobs in the future will cut across many disciplines. It therefore provides its technical trainees with backgrounds in management, and its management trainees with schooling in technology. It offers its employees extensive continuing education and management development, "so they always keep up with market needs, wherever they work. The concept of employability is the best answer to the end of guaranteed lifetime jobs."

2. *Global teamwork is the key to developing and using all the potential of the firm's human resources.* At Siemens, teamwork "means breaking down all the traditional barriers within the corporate world"—employees must be able to work across divisions, across disciplines, and across regions. This means employees have to understand the whole process, not just bits and pieces. This in turn means Siemens employees have to assume more responsibility, which in turn means the firm must provide extensive training and development so its employees can handle added responsibilities: "In China, for example, we have 17,000 employees—and only 200 Germans to provide technology transfer and training. We have opened a Management Institute in Beijing to help shift responsibility to locals." Optimizing global teamwork also means taking steps to ensure that all employees feel they're part of a strong, unifying corporate identity. Siemens accomplishes this in part by bringing together managers from around the world in various management development activities. And Siemens increasingly emphasizes cross-border, cross-cultural experiences as prerequisites for career advances, even for lower-level employees.

3. *Redefine management to meet the challenges of globalization.* To help it do this, Siemens instituted regular strategic performance assessments that encourage each employee to develop his or her potential. The firm's "management dialogue process" provides regular feedback from the bottom to the top to let Siemens managers know how they are doing—and how they can improve.

4. *Long-term growth and profitability depend on achieving a balance of interests.* Building shareholder value is important, but "we can be profitable only with creative, satisfied, and highly motivated people." Providing challenging growth opportunities and a supportive work environment are therefore cornerstones on which the firm builds its HR practices. This manifests itself, for instance, in the firm's career development and compensation policies.

5. *A climate of mutual respect is the basis of all relationships—within the company and with society.* At Siemens (and at other firms), it's not realistic to believe you can build a skilled, motivated, creative, and contented workforce without a culture of mutual respect. Particularly at a global company, "the wealth of nationalities, cultures, languages, and outlooks represented by our people is one of our most valuable assets. This great diversity demands openness, transparency, and fairness in the way we deal with one another."[112]

A FINAL WORD: STRATEGIC HR

Strategy and Strategic HR

In Chapter 1, we said that when a firm's competitiveness depends on its employees, the business function responsible for acquiring, training, appraising, and compensating those employees takes on an expanded, strategic role. This is the case in today's team-based and empowered companies. *Strategic human resource management* is "the linking of HRM with strategic goals and objectives in order to improve business performance and develop organizational cultures that foster innovation and flexibility." *HR strategies* are the HR courses of action the company uses to achieve its strategic aims.

Siemens illustrates this well. Strategies of diversification and globalization turned Siemens into a global high-tech firm. Its new emphasis on sophisticated engineering and services delivered worldwide meant the firm had to decide—as its CEO put it—which human resource strategies would ensure that Siemens's people could succeed in tomorrow's challenging global environment. In essence, the firm's management stepped back and asked, "What does competing in sophisticated engineering and services worldwide mean for the sorts of employees and skills our company will need?" Their answer: "A living company is a learning company; global teamwork; management must meet the challenges of globalization; there must be a balance of interests; and a climate of mutual respect."

For example, the strategic HR objective "A living company is a learning company" meant an expansion of Siemens's combined classroom and hands-on apprenticeship training around the world. "A balance of interests" meant providing employees with challenging growth opportunities. "A climate of mutual respect" meant emphasizing openness, transparency, and fairness. The firm's corporate strategy produced strategic objectives for HR; and the strategic HR objectives produced specific HR strategies (like the emphasis on apprenticeship training).

Thinking of HR in its strategic context has meant—among other things—professionalizing the field of HR. For example, thousands of HR professionals have already passed one or more of the HR professional certification exams offered by the Human Resource Certificate Institute (hrci@shrm.org). The two levels of exams test professional knowledge in all aspects of HR, including management practices, staffing, HR development, compensation, labor relations, and health and safety. Successful completion merits the title PHR (Professional in Human Resources) or SPHR (Senior Professional in Human Resources).

Management Values and Philosophy

It would be nice to believe that all strategies are products of an entirely objective thought process, but that's not usually the case. People always base their actions in part on the assumptions they make and the values they hold, and that certainly applies to management strategizing. For example, an ethnocentric manager may view an opportunity to expand abroad with some skepticism, while a geocentric manager seizes the same opportunity. The same applies to how managers approach their HR-related responsibilities. Decisions about the people you hire, the training you provide, the procedures you institutionalize, and your leadership style won't just reflect the objective demands of the situation. Instead, they'll be influenced by the basic assumptions you make about people—Can they be trusted? Do they dislike work? Can they be creative? Why do they act as they do? Your decisions will reflect your basic people philosophy.

The question is, what values underlie your people philosophy? What standard should you use? Some managers use *earning employee commitment* as one standard. They institute HR practices that foster employee commitment. **Employee commitment** is an employee's identification with and agreement to pursue the company's mission. Committed employees act more like owners than employees. In today's fast-moving companies, fostering employee commitment makes sense.[113] Today's team-based organizations need employees who exercise self-control. They need employees who exercise what some experts call *organizational citizenship* behavior. These employees willingly make "discretionary contributions." The company needs these to survive, but can't anticipate and require them ahead of time.[114]

In today's organizations, in other words, the idea is to get employees—the Siemens engineer on special assignment abroad, the Hilton front-desk clerk, or

---

employee commitment
An employee's identification with and agreement to pursue the company's or the unit's mission—to act like an owner rather than as an employee.

the Saturn assembler—to use their brains and initiative and creativity as if they owned the company, and not just when their supervisor is around. Several companies, such as FedEx, Toyota, and Saturn, use this commitment-building approach with success. Important commitment-building HR practices in firms like these include:

- *Establish people-first values.* As one Saturn manager said, "you start the process of boosting employee commitment by making sure you know how you and your top managers really feel about people." Managers in firms like these commit to the idea that their employees are their most important assets and must be trusted, treated with respect, and encouraged to grow and reach their full potential. The FedEx's managers' guide states: "I have an inherent right to be treated with respect and dignity and that right should never be violated."
- *Guarantee fair treatment.* As we saw earlier in this book, firms like FedEx have comprehensive grievance procedures that help to ensure fair treatment of all employees. Toyota's in-plant "Hotline" gives team members a 24-hour channel for bringing questions or problems to management attention.
- *Use value-based hiring.* Ben & Jerry's uses tests, interviews, and background checks to screen out managers who don't share the firm's social goals. Toyota screens out nonteam players, and Goldman Sachs emphasizes integrity. At FedEx, prospective supervisors who don't fit with the firm's people-first values get screened out by their subordinates before moving into management.
- *Encourage employees to actualize.* Many of these firms engage in practices that aim to ensure all employees have an opportunity to use all their skills and gifts at work and become all they can be. Here's how one Saturn assembler put it:

I'm committed to Saturn in part for what they did for me; for the 300 plus hours of training and problem solving and leadership that helped me expand my personal horizon; for the firm's "Excel" program that helps me push myself to the limit; and because I know that at Saturn I can go as far as I can go. This company wants its people to be all that they can be.

Auditing the HR Function

Whether it's apprenticeship training at Siemens or guaranteed fair treatment at FedEx, a manager would be lax not to periodically follow up to see how effective his or her HR policies and procedures have been.

You can use several approaches to do this. One expert suggests conducting an HR review aimed at tapping the opinions of HR and line managers regarding the HR function's effectiveness.[115] The review basically involves a series of surveys, followed by analyses, discussions, and (where necessary) decisions about new ways to proceed. The process involves five steps: (1) HR and line managers answer the question "What should HR's functions be?" (2) Participants then rate each of these functions on a 10-point scale to answer the question "How important are each of these functions?" (3) Next, they answer the question "How well are each of the functions performed?" (4) Here, discussions focus on "What needs improvement?" (5) Then, top management needs to answer the question, "How effectively does the HR function use its resources? In other words, are there steps that we can take—such as creating a centralized HR call center, or putting more HR activities on the Web—that can improve how our firm uses its HR resources?"

Sometimes an HR audit requires more of an expert opinion. An HR review like the one above can help pinpoint concerns and suggestions from the firm's managers about things they'd like to see HR change. However, there is often no substitute for having outside HR experts methodically audit each step in the firm's HR process. HR Solutions is one of many companies ranging from big-six consulting firms to small specialty firms that conduct these audits. The usual procedure is to evaluate each of the firm's HR activities, including job descriptions, recruitment and selection practices, wage and salary programs, performance appraisal systems, and safety and health, often using an extensive checklist approach. Audits like these can identify legal compliance issues the firm needs to address. And they can pinpoint areas that could benefit from today's leading-edge HR management practices—such as those discussed in this book.

We invite you to visit **www.prenhall.com/dessler** on the Prentice Hall Web site for our online study guide, Internet exercises, current events, links to related Web sites, and more.

Summary

1. International business is important to almost every business today, and so firms must increasingly be managed globally. This confronts managers with many new challenges, including coordinating production, sales, and financial operations on a worldwide basis. As a result, companies today have pressing international HR needs with respect to selecting, training, paying, and repatriating global employees.

2. Intercountry differences affect a company's HR management processes. Cultural factors such as individualism versus collectivism suggest differences in values, attitudes, and therefore behaviors and reactions of people from country to country. Economic and labor cost factors help determine whether HR's emphasis should be on efficiency, commitment building, or some other approach. Industrial relations and specifically the relationship between the worker, the union, and the employer influence the nature of a company's specific HR policies from country to country.

3. A large percentage of expatriate assignments fail, but the batting average can be improved through careful selection. There are various sources HR can use to staff domestic and foreign subsidiaries. Often managerial positions are filled by locals rather than expatriates, but this is not always the case.

4. Selecting managers for expatriate assignments means screening them for traits that predict success in adapting to dramatically new environments. Such traits include adaptability and flexibility, cultural toughness, self-orientation, job knowledge and motivation, relational skills, extracultural openness, and family situation. Adaptability screening focusing on the family's probable success in handling the foreign assignment can be an especially important step in the selection process.

5. Training for overseas managers typically focuses on cultural differences, on how attitudes influence behavior, and on factual knowledge about the target country. The most common approach to formulating expatriate pay is to equalize purchasing power across countries, a technique known as the balance sheet approach. The employer estimates expenses for income taxes, housing, goods and services, and reserve, and pays supplements to the expatriate in such a way as to maintain the same standard of living he or she would have had at home.

6. The expatriate appraisal process can be complicated by the need to have both local and home-office supervisors provide input into the performance review. Suggestions for improving the process include stipulating difficulty level, weighing the on-site manager's appraisal more heavily, and having the home-site manager get background advice from managers familiar with the location abroad before completing the expatriate's appraisal.

7. Repatriation problems are common but you can minimize them. They include the often well-founded fear that the expatriate is "out of sight, out of mind" and difficul-

ties in reassimilating the expatriate's family back into the home-country culture. Suggestions for avoiding these problems include using repatriation agreements, assigning a sponsor, offering career counseling, keeping the expatriate plugged in to home-office business, providing financial support to maintain the expatriate's home-country residence, and offering reorientation programs to the expatriate and his or her family.

8. *Strategic human resource management* is "the linking of HRM with strategic goals and objectives in order to improve business performance and develop organizational cultures that foster innovation and flexibility." *HR strategies* are the courses of action the company uses to achieve its strategic aims. Siemens illustrates this well. Its corporate strategy produced strategic objectives for HR, and the strategic HR objectives produced specific HR strategies. At Siemens, as at all firms, the HR strategies should be consistent with and support the firm's overall strategies.

Tying It All Together

In Chapters 1 through 15, we discussed the basic concepts and techniques of HR management, including job analysis, recruitment, selection, appraisal, compensation, and labor relations and safety. Applying concepts and techniques like these abroad confronts the manager with a range of challenges. These stem not just from the distances involved, but from a variety of cultural, legal, economic and labor relations differences among countries. This final chapter, Managing Global Human Resources, therefore focused on how managers apply the basic HR concepts and techniques once their firms go global.

Discussion Questions

1. You are the president of a small business. What are some of the ways you expect "going international" will affect your business?
2. What are some of the specific uniquely international activities an international HR manager typically engages in?
3. What intercountry differences affect HRM? Give several examples of how each may specifically affect HRM.
4. You are the HR manager of a firm that is about to send its first employees overseas to staff a new subsidiary. Your boss, the president, asks you why such assignments often fail, and what you plan to do to avoid such failures. How do you respond?
5. What special training do overseas candidates need? In what ways is such training similar to and different from traditional diversity training?
6. How does appraising an expatriate's performance differ from appraising that of a home-office manager? How would you avoid some of the unique problems of appraising the expatriate's performance?
7. As an HR manager, what program would you establish to reduce repatriation problems of returning expatriates and their families?

Individual and Group Activities

1. Working individually or in groups, write an expatriation and repatriation plan for your professor, who your school is sending to Bulgaria to teach HR for the next three years.
2. Give three specific examples of multinational corporations in your area. Check in the library or Internet or with each firm to determine in what countries these firms have operations, and explain the nature of some of their operations, and whatever you can find out about their international HR policies.
3. Choose three traits useful for selecting international assignees, and create a straightforward test to screen candidates for these traits.
4. Use a library or Internet source to determine the relative cost of living in five countries as of this year, and explain the implications of such differences for drafting a pay plan for managers being sent to each country.

EXPERIENTIAL EXERCISE *Compensation Incentives for Expatriate Employees*

Purpose: The purpose of this exercise is to give you practice adjusting expatriate's pay to the rigors of foreign service.

Required Understanding: You should be thoroughly familiar with this chapter and with the following:

It's common for companies to offer financial supplements for executives living abroad. The international operations division has asked your HR department to develop a standard supplementary compensation plan for expatriate employees. The division's managers have provided you with a list of issues that seem to make their typical foreign assignment more difficult than a domestic one. They want you to decide which of these issues are most important and to specify the effect each should have on compensation.

Your Ranking	Issues	Description	Effect on Compensation
	Health care	Physicians and hospital do not meet Western standards.	Make contingency money available to fly expatriate to closest country with Western-style health care. (Example)
	Family life	There are no English language schools for children—children of expatriates will need to attend private boarding schools.	
	Inflation	Target country currency is unstable. Currency may inflate by as much as 20% per month.	
	Infrastructure	The expatriate will not be able to have his or her own phone or TV.	
	Political risk	Assigned country faces the risk of political upheaval.	

How to Set Up the Exercise/Instructions: Divide the class into teams of 5–6 students. Ask each team to perform the following tasks:

1. Rank the issues from 1 to 5 (number 1 being the most important). List their effects.
2. Assume that each employee has a base salary equal to his or her U.S. compensation of $80,000.

You may add from 0 to 50% to that as a supplement for each item on the list.

Answer the following discussion questions as a team:

1. What will be the effect of each on compensation?
2. How much did you need to increase compensation overall to satisfy the expected needs of your expatriate workers?
3. What problems might this level of compensation create?

APPLICATION CASE *"Boss, I Think We Have a Problem"*

Central Steel Door Corporation has been in business for about 20 years, successfully selling a line of steel industrial-grade doors, as well as the hardware and fittings required for them. Focusing mostly in the United States and Canada, the company had gradually increased its presence from the New York City area, first into New England and then down the Atlantic Coast, then through the Midwest and West, and finally into Canada. The company's basic expansion strategy was always the same: Choose an area, open a distribution center, hire a regional sales manager, then let that regional sales manager help staff the distribution center and hire local sales reps.

Unfortunately, the company's traditional success in finding sales help has not extended to its overseas operations. With the introduction of the new European currency, Mel Fisher, president of Central Steel Door, decided to expand his company abroad, into Europe. However, the expansion has not gone smoothly at all. He tried for three weeks to find a sales manager by advertising in the *International Herald Tribune*, which is read by businesspeople in Europe and by American expatriates living and working in Europe. Although the ads placed in the *Tribune* also run for about a month in the *Tribune's* Internet Web site, Mr. Fisher so far has received only five applications. One came from a possibly viable candidate, whereas four came from candidates whom Mr. Fisher refers to as "lost souls"—people who seem to have spent most of their time traveling restlessly from country to country sipping espresso in sidewalk cafés. When asked what he had done for the last three years, one told Mr. Fisher he'd been on a "walkabout."

Other aspects of his international HR activities have been equally problematic. Fisher alienated two of his U.S. sales managers by sending them to Europe to temporarily run the European operations, but neglecting to work out a compensation package that would cover their relatively high living expenses in Germany and Belgium. One ended up staying the better part of the year, and Mr. Fisher was rudely surprised to be informed by the Belgian government that his sales manager owed thousands of dollars in local taxes. The managers had hired about 10 local people to staff each of the two distribution centers. However, without full-time local European sales managers, the level of sales was disappointing, so Fisher decided to fire about half the distribution center employees. That's when he got an emergency phone call from his temporary sales manager in Germany: "I've just been told that all these employees should have had written employment agreements and that in any case we can't fire anyone without at least one year's notice, and the local authorities here are really up in arms. Boss, I think we have a problem."

Questions

1. Based on the chapter and the case incident, compile a list of 10 international HR mistakes Mr. Fisher has made so far.
2. How would you have gone about hiring a European sales manager? Why?
3. What would you do now if you were Mr. Fisher?

CONTINUING CASE: LearnInMotion.com *Going Abroad*

According to its business plan, and in practice, LearnInMotion.com "acquires content globally but delivers it locally." In other words, all the content and courses and other material that it lists on its site come from content providers all over the world. However, the "hard copy" (book and CD-ROM) courses are delivered, with the help of independent contracting delivery firms, locally, in three northeastern cities.

Now the company is considering an expansion. While the most logical strategic expansion would probably entail adding cities in the United States, one of its major content providers—a big training company in England—believes there is a significant market for LearnInMotion services in England, and particularly in London, Oxford, and Manchester (all of which are bustling business centers, and all of which have well-known universities). The training company has offered to finance and co-own a branch of LearnInMotion.com, in London. They want it housed in the training firm's new offices in Mayfair, near Shepherds Market. This is an easily accessible (if somewhat expensive) area, within easy walking distance of Hyde Park and Hyde Park corner, and not far from the London Underground Picadilly line, which runs directly through the city to Heathrow airport.

Everyone concerned wants to make sure the new operation can "hit the ground running." This means either Jennifer or Mel will have to move to London almost at once, and take one salesperson and one of the content management people along. Once there, this small team could hire additional employees locally, and then, once the new operation is running successfully, return to New York, probably within three or four months.

Jennifer and Mel have decided to go ahead and open the London office, but this is not a decision they've taken lightly, since there are many drawbacks to doing so. The original, New York–based site is not generating anywhere near the sales revenue it was supposed to at this point, and being short three key employees is not going to help. Neither the board of directors nor the representatives of the venture capital fund were enthusiastic about the idea of expanding abroad, either. However, they went along with it; and the deciding factor was probably the cash infusion that the London-based training firm was willing to make. It basically provided enough cash to run not just the London operation but the New York one for an additional six months.

Having made the decision to set up operations abroad, Jennifer and Mel now need to turn to the multitude of matters involved in the expansion—obtaining the necessary licenses to open the business in England, and arranging for phone lines, for instance (all carried out with the assistance of the London-based training firm). However, it's also obvious to Jennifer and Mel that there are considerable human resource management implications involved in moving LearnInMotion employees abroad, and in staffing the operation once they're there. Now, they want you, their management consultants, to help them actually do it. Here's what they want you to do for them.

Questions and Assignments

1. What do you see as the main HR-related implications and challenges we face as a result of opening the operation in London?

2. How should we go about choosing the person who will be the permanent manager for the new operation? Should we hire someone locally, or use one of the people from our existing operation? Why?

3. Based upon any sources available to you, including the Internet, tell us what we need to know about the comparative cost of living of London and New York, including housing and transportation, as well as comparative salaries.

4. Write a short position paper on the subject: "a list of the HR-related things we need to do in sending our three people abroad."

Endnotes

Chapter 1

1. "Dell Computer Vows to Persist with Price Strategy," *Knight Ridder/Tribune Business News*, May 18, 2001, item 01138000.
2. Quoted in Fred K. Foulkes, "The Expanding Role of the Personnel Function," *Harvard Business Review* (March–April 1975), pp. 71–84. See also Michael Losey, "HR Comes of Age," *HR Magazine* 9 (1998), pp. 40–53.
3. See Robert Saltonstall, "Who's Who in Personnel Administration," *Harvard Business Review* 33 (July–August 1955), pp. 75–83, reprinted in Paul Pigors, Charles Meyers, and F. P. Maim, *Management of Human Resources* (New York: McGraw-Hill, 1969), pp. 61–73.
4. For a description of this see, for example, "SHRM-BNA Survey No. 63: Human Resource Activities, Budgets, & Staffs, 1997–98," *BNA Bulletin to Management*, June 18, 1998, pp. 10–12.
5. Saltonstall, "Who's Who," p. 65.
6. "Employee Advocacy Remains HR Priority," *BNA Bulletin to Management*, September 26, 1996, p. 312.
7. U.S. Department of Labor, Bureau of Labor Statistics, *Occupational Outlook Handbook*, Bulletin 2250, 1986–1987 edition, pp. 45–47.
8. "SHRM-BNA Survey No. 63: Human Resource Activities, Budgets, & Staffs, 1999–2000," *BNA Bulletin to Management*, June 29, 2000, pp. S6–S10.
9. "Human Resource Activities, Budgets and Staffs, 1999–2000," *BNA Bulletin to Management*, June 29, 2000.
10. Arthur Thompson and A. J. Strickland, *Strategic Management* (Burr Ridge, IL: McGraw-Hill, 2001), pp. 16–18.
11. *The World Almanac and Book of Facts*, 2000; www.census.gov/foreign-trade/press-release/2000pr/final revisions-2001/exh1.pdf.
12. Charles W. Hill, *International Business* (Burr Ridge, IL: McGraw-Hill, 2000), p. 10. See also "The Impact of Globalization on HR," *Workplace Visions*, Society for Human Resource Management 5 (2000), pp. 1–8.
13. Bryan O'Reilly, "Your New Global Workforce," *Fortune*, December 14, 1992, pp. 52–66.
14. Paul Judge, "How I Saved $100 Million on the Web," *Fast Company*, February 2001, pp. 174–181.
15. Richard Crawford, *In the Era of Human Capital* (New York: Harper, 1991), p. 26.
16. O'Reilly, "Your New Global Workforce," p. 63.
17. "Futurework," *Occupational Outlook Quarterly*, summer 2000, pp. 31–37.
18. Rachel Moskowitz and Drew Warwick, "The 1994–2005 Job Outlook in Brief," *Occupational Outlook Quarterly* 40, no. 1 (spring 1996), pp. 2–41. See also Mahlon Apgar, IV, "The Alternative Workplace: Changing Where and How People Work," *Harvard Business Review*, May–June 1998, pp. 121–136; and "The Outlook for College Graduates, 1998–2000," *Occupational Outlook Quarterly*, fall 2000, pp. 3–8.
19. Richard Crawford, *In the Era of Human Capital* (New York: Harper, 1991), p. 10.
20. Peter Drucker, "The Coming of the New Organization," *Harvard Business Review*, January–February 1988, p. 45. See also Richard Cappelli, "Rethinking the Nature of Work: A Look at the Research Evidence," *Compensation & Benefits Review*, July/August 1997, pp. 50–59.
21. "Major Changes Redefine the Modern Workplace," *BNA Bulletin to Management*, July 3, 1997, p. 209.
22. Gerald Ferris, Dwight Frink, and M. Carmen Galang, "Diversity in the Workplace: The Human Resources Management Challenge," *Human Resource Planning* 16, no. 1, p. 42.
23. "Immigrants in the Workforce," *BNA Bulletin to Management Datagraph*, August 15, 1996, pp. 260–261.
24. Howard Fullerton Jr., "Another Look at the Labor Force," *Monthly Labor Review*, November 1993, pp. 31–40; "The American Workforce, 1994–2005," *BNA Bulletin to Management*, January 4, 1996, pp. 4–5.
25. "Immigrants in the Workforce," p. 38.
26. Ibid., p. 37.
27. "Workforce Becoming Older, Better Educated," *BNA Bulletin to Management*, October 17, 1996, pp. 332–333.
28. Ferris et al., "Diversity in the Workplace," p. 43.
29. Ibid.
30. For related discussions see, for example, Felice Schwartz, "Women in American Business: The Demographic Imperative," *Business and the Contemporary World*, summer 1993, pp. 10–19; Karen Stephenson and Valdis Krebs, "A More Accurate Way to Measure Diversity," *Personnel Journal*, October 1993, pp. 66–74.
31. Rosabeth Moss Kanter, "The New Managerial Work," *Harvard Business Review*, November–December 1989, p. 88.
32. Ibid.
33. Thomas A. Steward, "How GE Keeps Those Ideas Coming," *Fortune*, August 12, 1991, p. 42.
34. "Human Capital Critical to Success," *Management Review*, November 1998, p. 9.
35. Charles Greer, *Strategy and Human Resources* (Upper Saddle River, NJ: Prentice Hall, 1995), p. 105.
36. This discussion is based on Losey, "HR Comes of Age."
37. Catherine Truss and Lynda Gratton, "Strategic Human Resource Management: A Conceptual Approach," *International Journal of Human Resource Management* 5, no. 3 (September 1994), p. 663. See also Peter Bamberger and Ilan Meshoulam, *Human Resource Strategy: Formulation, Implementation, and Impact* (Thousand Oaks, CA: Sage, 2000).
38. This is based on Timothy Galpin and Patrick Murray, "Connect Human Resource Strategy to the Business Plan," *HR Magazine*, March 1997, pp. 99–104. See also Kathryn Tyler, "Strategizing for HR," *HR Magazine*, February 2001, pp. 93–98.
39. While still largely nonunionized, FedEx's pilots did vote to join the Airline Pilots Union in 1995.
40. For a discussion, see Peter Boxall, "Placing HR Strategy at the Heart of Business Success," *Personnel Management* 26, no. 7 (July 1994), pp. 32–34.
41. Ibid., p. 32.
42. For a discussion, see Catherine Truss and Lynda Gratton, "Strategic Human Resource Management: A Conceptual Approach," *International Journal of Human Resource Management* 5, no. 3 (September 1994), pp. 670–671.
43. Ibid., p. 670.
44. For a discussion see, for example, Randall Schuler, Peter Dowling, and Helen DeCieri, "An Integrative Framework of Strategic International Human Resource Management," *Journal of Management* 19, no. 2 (1993), pp. 419–459; Vida Scarpello, "New Paradigm Approaches to Strategic Human Resource Management," *Group and Organization Management* 19, no. 2 (June 1994), pp. 160–164; and Sharon Peck, "Exploring the Link Between Organizational Strategy and the Employment Relationships: The Role of Human Resources Policies," *Journal of Management Studies* 31, no. 5 (September 1994), pp. 715–736.
45. Jeremy Hunt and Peter Boxall, "Are Top Human Resource Specialists 'Strategic Partners'? Self-Perceptions of a Corporate Elite," *International Journal of Human Resource Management* 9, no. 5 (October 1998), pp. 767–781.
46. Ibid., p. 778.
47. Ibid., p. 779.
48. "HR Department Gaining Respect," *HR Magazine*, February 1, 1999, p. 30.
49. See also Ramon Valle, et al., "Business Strategy, Work Processes and Human Resource Training: Are They Congruent?" *Journal of Organizational Behavior* 21, no. 3 (May 2000) pp. 283–297.
50. Samuel Greengard, "You're Next! There's No Escaping Merger Mania!" *Workforce*, April 1997, pp. 52–62. See also Bill Leonard, "Will This Marriage Work?" *HR Magazine*, April 1999, pp. 35–40.

51. Arthur Thompson Jr. and A. J. Strickland III, *Strategic Management: Concepts and Cases* (New York: McGraw-Hill, 2001), pp. 129–131.

52. Gillian Glenn, "Out of the Red, Into the Blue," *Workforce*, March 2000, pp. 50–52.

53. "Outsourcing Gains Attention," *BNA Bulletin to Management*, June 5, 1997, pp. 181–182. See also Linda Davidson, "Cut Away Non-Core HR," *Workforce*, January 1998, pp. 41–45.

54. William Henn, "What the Strategist Asks From Human Resources," *Human Resource Planning* 8, no. 4 (1985), p. 195; quoted in Greer, *Strategy and Human Resources*, pp. 117–118.

55. Ibid., p. 105.

56. Ibid., p. 117.

57. "HR Execs Trade Notes on Human Resource Information Systems," *BNA Bulletin to Management*, December 3, 1998, p. 1.

58. Adapted from Kenneth Laudon and Jane Laudon, *Management Information Systems: New Approaches to Organization and Technology* (Upper Saddle River, NJ: Prentice Hall, 1998), p. G-7.

59. Samuel Greengard, "Finding Time to Be Strategic," *Personnel Journal*, October 1996, pp. 84–89.

60. Annette Cardwell, "Cut Through HR Paperwork," *Ziff-Davis Smart Business for the New Economy*, May 1, 2000, p. 60.

61. Chris Pickering, "A Look Through the Portal," *Software Magazine* 21, no. 1 (February 2001), pp. 18–19.

62. Ibid., p. 19.

63. Jill Elswick, "How NCR Corp. Undertook an Intranet Makeover to Improve Access to HR Information," *Employee Benefit News*, January 1, 2001, item 01008001.

64. Sharon McDonnell, "More Out of ERP," *Computerworld*, October 2, 2000, p. 56.

65. "The Employee–Market Value Connection," *Management Review*, February 2000, p. 7.

66. See, for example, Benjamin Schneider and David Bowen, "The Service Organization: Human Resources Management Is Crucial," *Organizational Dynamics* 21, no. 4 (1993), pp. 39–52.

67. Commerce Clearing House, "HR Role: Maximize the Competitive Advantage of People," *Ideas and Trends in Personnel*, August 5, 1992, p. 121.

68. Jennifer Laabs, "HR's Vital Role at Levi Strauss," *Personnel Journal*, December 1992, p. 37.

69. "Inside a Layoff: An Up Close Look at How One Company Handles the Delicate Task of Downsizing," *Time*, April 16, 2001, pp. 38–40; "Dell Computer Vows to Persist with Price Strategy."

70. "Human Resource Goes High-Tech: The 1999 HR Technology Conference and Exposition," *BNA Bulletin to Management*, October 14, 1999, pp. S1–S4.

71. Carla Joinson, "Changing Shapes," *HR Magazine*, March 1999, pp. 41–48.

72. Carla Joinson, "Moving at the Speed of Dell," *HR Magazine*, April 1999, pp. 51–56.

73. John Delery and D. Harold Doty, "Modes of Theorizing in Strategic Human Resource Management: Tests of Universalistic, Contingency, and Configurational Performance Predictions," *Academy of Management Journal* 39, no. 4 (1996), p. 825.

74. Linda Stroh and Paula Caligiuri, "Strategic Human Resources: A New Source for Competitive Advantage in the Global Arena," *International Journal of Human Resource Management* 9, no. 1 (February 1998), pp. 1–17.

75. Brian Becker and Barry Gerhart, "The Impact of Human Resource Management on Organizational Performance: Progress and Prospects," *Academy of Management Journal* 39, no. 4 (1996), p. 797.

76. Delery and Doty, "Modes of Theorizing," pp. 802–835.

77. Ibid., p. 825.

78. Ibid.

79. Mark Youndt, Scott Snell, James Dean, Jr., and David Lepak, "Human Resource Management, Manufacturing Strategy, and Firm Performance," *Academy of Management Journal* 39, no. 4 (1996), pp. 836–866.

Chapter 2

1. Orlando Richard, "Racial Diversity, Business Strategy, and Firm Performance: A Resource Based View," *Academy of Management Journal* 43, no. 2 (April 2000), pp. 164–175.

2. Kevin Wallsten, "Diversity Pays Off in Big Sales for Toyota Dealership," *Workforce* 77, no. 9 (September 1998), pp. 91–93.

3. "Section 1981 Covers Racial Discrimination in Hiring and Promotion, But No Other Situation," Commerce Clearing House, *Human Resources Management*, June 28, 1989, p. 116.

4. Based on or quoted from Principles of Employment Discrimination Law, International Association of Official Human Rights Agencies, Washington, D.C. In addition, see W. Clay Hamner and Frank Schmidt, Contemporary Problems in Personnel, rev. ed. (Chicago: St. Clair Press, 1977), Chapter 3. See also Bruce Feldacker. Labor Guide to Labor Law (Upper Saddle River, NJ: Prentice Hall, 2000); and www.eeoc.gov/. *Employment discrimination law is a changing field, and the appropriateness of the rules, guidelines, and conclusions in this chapter and book may also be affected by factors unique to the employer's operation. They should be reviewed by the employer's attorney before implementation.*

5. James Higgins, "A Manager's Guide to the Equal Employment Opportunity Law," *Personnel Journal* 55, no. 8 (August, 1976), p. 406.

6. The Equal Employment Opportunity Act of 1972. Sub-Committee on Labor or the Committee of Labor and Public Welfare, U.S. Senate, March 1972, p. 3. In general, it is not discrimination but unfair discrimination against a person merely because of that person's race, age, sex, national origin, or religion that federal statues forbid. In the federal government's Uniform Employee Selection Guidelines, "unfair" discrimination is defined as follows: "unfairness is demonstrated through a showing that members of a particular interest group perform better or poorer on the job than their scores on the selection procedure (test, etc.) would indicate through comparison with how members of the other group performed." For a discussion of the meaning of fairness, see James Ledvinka. "The Statistical Definition of Fairness in the Federal Selection Guidelines and Its Implications for Minority Employment." *Personnel Psychology* 32 (August 1979), pp. 551–562. In summary, a selection device (like a test) may discriminate, say, between low and high performers. However, it is unfair discrimination that is illegal—discrimination that is based solely on the person's race, age, sex, national origin, or religion.

7. "OFCCP Lists Egregious Bias Cases," *BNA Fair Employment Practices*, November 28, 1996, p. 139.

8. Bureau of National Affairs, *Fair Employment Practices*, October 8, 1992, p. 117. See also Lawrence Kleiman and David Denton, "Downsizing: Nine Steps to ADA Compliance," *Employment Relations Today* 27, no. 3 (fall 2000), pp. 37–45.

9. Note that under the Rehabilitation Act, the law strictly speaking applied only to a particular "program" of the employer. In March 1988, Congress passed the Civil Rights Restoration Act of 1987, overturning this interpretation. Now, with few exceptions, any institution, organization, corporation, state agency, or municipality using federal funding in any of its programs must abide by the section of the act prohibiting discriminating against handicapped individuals. See Bureau of National Affairs, "Federal Law Mandates Affirmative Action for Handicapped," *Fair Employment Practices*, March 30, 1989, p. 42.

10. *Tanberg v. Weld County Sheriff*, SUDA Colo. No. 91-B-248, 3/18/92.

11. Howard J. Anderson and Michael D. Levin-Epstein, *Primer of Equal Employment Opportunity*, 2nd ed. (Washington, DC: Bureau of National Affairs, 1982), p. 507; and Commerce Clearing House, "Federal Contractors Must File VETS-100 by March 31," *Ideas and Trends*, February 23, 1988, p. 32.

12. Ann Harriman, *Women/Men Management* (New York: Praeger, 1985), pp. 66–68.

13. Commerce Clearing House, "Pregnancy Leave," *Ideas and Trends*, January 23, 1987, p. 10.

14. Bureau of National Affairs, "High Court Upholds Pregnancy Law," *Fair Employment Practices*, January 22, 1987, p. 7; Betty Sonthard Murphy, Wayne E. Barlow, and D. Diane Hatch, "Manager's Newsfront: U.S. Supreme Court Approves Preferential Treatment for Pregnancy," *Personnel Journal* 66, no. 3 (March 1987), p. 18.

15. Bureau of National Affairs, "First Two Chapters of Long-Awaited Manual Released by OFCCP," *Fair Employment Practices*, January 5, 1989, p. 6.

16. Oscar A. Ornati and Margaret J. Eisen, "Are You Complying with EEOC's New Rules on National Origin Discrimination?" *Personnel* 58

(March–April 1981), pp. 12–20; Paul S. Greenlaw and John P. Kohl. "National Origin Discrimination and the New EEOC Guidelines," *Personnel Journal* 60, no. 8 (August 1981), pp. 634–636.

17. Lawrence S. Kleiman and Robert Faley, "The Applications of Professional and Legal Guidelines for Court Decisions Involving Criterion-Related Validity: A Review and Analysis," *Personnel Psychology* 38, no. 4 (winter 1985), pp. 803–833.

18. Patricia Linenberger and Timothy Keaveny, "Sexual Harassment: The Employer's Legal Obligations," *Personnel* 58 (November–December 1981), pp. 60–68.

19. Milton Zall, "What to Expect from the Civil Rights Act," *Personnel Journal* 71 (March 1992), p. 50.

20. Mary Rowe, "Dealing with Sexual Harassment," *Harvard Business Review* 61 (May–June 1981), pp. 42–46.

21. Edward Felsenthal. "Justices' Ruling Further Defines Sex Harassment," *Wall Street Journal*, March 5, 1998, pp. B1, B5.

22. Robert H. Faley, "Sexual Harassment: Critical Review of Legal Cases with General Principles and Preventive Measures," *Personnel Psychology* 35, no. 3 (autumn 1982), pp. 590–591; Bureau of National Affairs, "In Terms of Sexual Harassment, What Makes an Environment 'Hostile'?" *Fair Employment Practices*, June 1988, p. 78. See also Annette Davies and Robyn Thomas, "Gender and Human Resource Management: A Critical Review," *International Journal of Human Resource Management* 11, no. 6 (December 2000), pp. 1125–1136.

23. Michael W. Sculnick, "The Supreme Court 1985–86 EEO Decisions: A Review," *Employment Relations Today* 13, no. 3 (fall 1986), pp. 197–206; *Brown v. City of Guthrie*, 22FEP Cases 1627, 1980. See also Donald Petersen and Douglas Massengill, "Sexual Harassment Cases Five Years After *Meritor Savings Bank v. Vinson*," *Employee Relations Law Journal* 18, no. 3 (winter 1992–1993), pp. 489–515.

24. See the discussion in "Examining Unwelcome Conduct in a Sexual Harassment Claim," *BNA Fair Employment Practices*, October 19, 1995, p. 124. See also Molly Bowers, et al., "Just Cause in the Arbitration of Sexual Harassment Cases," *Dispute Resolution Journal* 55, no. 4 (November 2000), pp. 40–55.

25. Commerce Clearing House, *Sexual Harassment Manual for Managers and Supervisors* (Chicago: Commerce Clearing House, 1991), pp. 28–29.

26. Ibid., p. 8.

27. Louise Fitzgerald, et al., "Antecedents and Consequences of Sexual Harassment in Organizations: A Test of an Integrated Model," *Journal of Applied Psychology* 82, no. 4 (1997), pp. 577–589.

28. "Adequate Response Bars Liability," *BNA Fair Employment Practices*, June 26, 1997, p. 74.

29. Frederick L. Sullivan, "Sexual Harassment: The Supreme Court Ruling," *Personnel* 65, no. 12 (December 1986), pp. 42–44. Also see the following for additional information on sexual harassment; Jonathan S. Monat and Angel Gomez, "Decisional Standards Used by Arbitrators in Sexual Harassment Cases," *Labor Law Journal* 37, no. 10 (October 1985), pp. 712–718.

30. See the discussion in "Examining Unwelcome Conduct."

31. Ibid.

32. Rowe, "Dealing with Sexual Harassment."

33. *Griggs v. Duke Power Company*, 3FEP Cases 175.

34. This is applicable only to Title VII and CRA 91; other statutes require intent.

35. James Ledvinka, *Federal Regulation of Personnel and Human Resources Management* (Boston: Kent, 1982), p. 41.

36. James Ledvinka and Lyle Schoenfeldt, "Legal Development in Employment Testing: *Albemarle* and Beyond," *Personnel Psychology* 31, no. 1 (spring 1978), pp. 1–13. Note that the Court, in its *Albemarle* opinion, made one important modification regarding the EEOC guidelines. Up through the *Griggs* decision, it was not enough to just validate the test; instead, the employer also had to show that some other tests or screening tools were not available that were (1) also valid but that (2) did not screen out a disproportionate number of minorities or women. In the *Albemarle* case, the Court held that the burden of proof was no longer on the employer to show that there was no suitable alternative screening device available. Instead, the burden for that was now on the charging party (the person allegedly discriminated against) to show that a suitable alternative is available. Ledvinka and Schoenfeldt, "Legal Development," p. 4; Gary Lubben, Dwayne

Thompson, and Charles Klasson, "Performance Appraisal: The Legal Implications of Title VII," *Personnel* (May–June 1980).

37. This was quoted from Commerce Clearing House, "Supreme Court Releases First 'Mixed Motives' Decision Under Title VII," *Ideas and Trends*, May 17, 1989, p. 82.

38. Ibid., p. 82.

39. "High Court Makes Race, Sex Bias in Work Place Tougher to Prove," *Miami Herald*, June 6, 1989, p. 4A.

40. Commerce Clearing House, "The Supreme Court Explains How Statistics Are to Be Used in Fair Employment Suits," *Ideas and Trends*, June 14, 1989, p. 109.

41. Based on ibid.

42. Commerce Clearing House, "House and Senate Pass Civil Rights Compromise by Wide Margin," *Ideas and Trends in Personnel*, November 13, 1991, p. 179.

43. Mark Kobata. "The Civil Rights Act of 1991," *Personnel Journal*, March 1992, p. 48.

44. Commerce Clearing House, "House and Senate Pass Civil Rights Compromise," p. 182.

45. For a discussion, see Commerce Clearing House, *Ideas and Trends in Personnel*, November 13, 1991, p. 182. See also Glen Nager and Edward Bilich, "The Civil Rights Act of 1991 Going Forward," *Employee Relations Law Journal* 21, no. 2 (autumn 1994), pp. 237–251.

46. Patricia Feltes, Robert Robinson, and Ross Fink, "American Female Expatriates and the Civil Rights Act of 1991; Balancing Legal and Business Interests," *Business Horizons*, March–April 1993, pp. 82–85.

47. Ibid., p. 84.

48. Title VII does not apply to foreign operations not owned or controlled by a U.S. employer, however.

49. This is based on Gregory Baxter, "Over There: Enforcing the 1991 Civil Rights Act Abroad," *Employee Relations Law Journal* 19, no. 2 (autumn 1993), pp. 257–266.

50. Ibid., p. 265.

51. Ibid. See also Gerald Maatman Jr., "Legal Trends: A Global View of Sexual Harassment," *HR Magazine* 45, no. 7 (July 2000), pp. 151–158.

52. Elliot H. Shaller and Dean Rosen, "A Guide to the EEOC's Final Regulations on the Americans with Disabilities Act," *Employee Relations* 17, no. 3 (winter 1991–1992), pp. 405–430. See also Brenda Sunoo, "Accommodating Workers with Disabilities," *Workforce* 80, no. 2 (February 2001), pp. 86–93.

53. Bureau of National Affairs, "ADA: Simple Common Sense Principles," *Fair Employment Practices*, June 4, 1992, p. 63.

54. Shaller and Rosen, "A Guide to the EEOC's Final Regulations," p. 408. See also James McDonald Jr., "The Rise of Psychological Issues in Employment Law," *Employee Relations Law Journal* 25, no. 3 (winter 1999), pp. 85–97.

55. Ibid., p. 409.

56. Bureau of National Affairs. "Guidelines on AIDS," *Fair Employment Practices*, March 30, 1989, p. 39.

57. David B. Ritter and Ronald Turner, "AIDS: Employer Concerns and Options," *Labor Law Journal* 38, no. 2 (February 1987), pp. 67–83.

58. "No Sitting for Store Greeter," *BNA Fair Employment Practices*, December 14, 1995, p. 150.

59. "Reasonable Accommodation Issues in the Workplace," *BNA Fair Employment Practices*, June 12, 1997, p. 69.

60. *Palmer v. Circuit Court of Cook County, Illinois*, c7#95-3659-6/26/97; reviewed in "No Accommodation for Violent Employee," *BNA Fair Employment Practices*, July 10, 1997, p. 79. Also see *Miller v. Illinois Department of Corrections*, CA7, 1997, 6ad cases 678; reviewed in "Courts Define Parameters of the Americans with Disabilities Act," *BNA Fair Employment Practices*, March 20, 1997, p. 34.

61. "Blind Bartender Not Qualified for Job, Court Says in Dismissing Americans with Disabilities Act Claim," *BNA Fair Employment Practices*, February 4, 1999, p. 17.

62. "Differing Views: Punctuality as Essential Job Function," *BNA Fair Employment Practices*, April 27, 2000, p. 56.

63. James McDonald Jr., "The Americans with Difficult Personalities Act," *Employee Relations Law Journal* 25, no. 4 (spring 2000), pp. 93–107.

64. These are adapted from Wayne Barlow and Edward Hane, "A Practical Guide to the Americans with Disabilities Act," *Personnel Journal* 72 (June 1992), p. 59.

65. "Tips for Employers with Asymptomatic HIV-Positive Employees," *BNA Fair Employment Practices*, November 27, 1997, p. 141.

66. "EEOC Explains Legal Boundaries of Job Questions Under ADA," *BNA Fair Employment Practices*, June 2, 1994, p. 63.

67. *Krocka v. Bransfield*, DC N111, #95C627, 6/24/97; reviewed in "Test for Prozac Violates ADA," *BNA Fair Employment Practices*, August 7, 1997, p. 91.

68. Elliot Shaller, "Reasonable Accommodation Under the Americans with Disabilities Act: What Does It Mean," *Employee Relations Law Journal* 16, no. 4 (spring 1991), pp. 445–446.

69. Ibid., p. 446. See also Michael Esposito. "Are You 100 Percent ADA-Compliant?" *Management Review*, February 1993, pp. 27–29; and William R. Tracey, "Auditing ADA Compliance," *HR Magazine*, October 1994, pp. 88–90.

70. "Odds Against Getting Even Are Long in ADA Cases," *BNA Bulletin to Management*, August 20, 2000, p. 229.

71. "Determining Employers' Responsibilities Under ADA," *BNA Fair Employment Practices*, May 16, 1996, p. 57.

72. www.eeoc.gov/press/6-14-01.html.

73. James Ledvinka and Robert Gatewood. "EEO Issues with Preemployment Inquiries," *Personnel Administrator* 22, no. 2 (February 1997), pp. 22–26.

74. These are based on Bureau of National Affairs, "A Wrap-Up of State Legislation: 1988 Anti-Bias Laws Focus on AIDS," *Fair Employment Practices*, January 5, 1989, pp. 3–4.

75. "1996 State Anti-Bias Laws Focus on Harassment, Genetic Testing," *BNA Fair Employment Practices*, January 9, 1997, pp. 1–3.

76. Bruce Feldacker, *Labor Guide to Labor Law* (Upper Saddle River, NJ: Prentice Hall, 2000), p. 513.

77. "The Eleventh Circuit Explains Disparate Impact, Disparate Treatment," *BNA Fair Employment Practices*, August 17, 2000, p. 102.

78. John Klinfelter and James Thompkins, "Adverse Impact in Employment Selection," *Public Personnel Management*, May–June 1976, pp. 199–204.

79. H. John Bernardin, Richard Beatty, and Walter Jensin. "The New Uniform Guidelines on Employee Selection Procedures in the Context of University Personnel Decisions," *Personnel Psychology* 33 (summer 1980), pp. 301–316.

80. International Association of Official Human Rights Agencies, Principles of Employment Discrimination Law; James M. Higgins. "A Manager's Guide to the Equal Opportunity Laws," *Personnel* 55 (August 1976); James Ledvinka, *Federal Regulation*.

81. *Professional Pilots Federation v. Federal Aviation Administration*, U.S. SUP CT #97-1267, cert. denied 5/18/98.

82. "Congress Legislates to Increase Commercial Pilot Age," *Airline Industry Information*, March 15, 2001.

83. *Usery v. Tamiami Trail Tours*, 12FEP cases 1233; see also Anderson and Levin-Epstein, *Primer of Equal Employment Opportunity*, p. 57.

84. Ledvinka, *Federal Regulation*, p. 82. For a further discussion of religious and other types of accommodation and what they involve see, for example, Bureau of National Affairs, *Fair Employment Practices*, January 21, 1988, pp. 9–10; Bureau of National Affairs, *Fair Employment Practices*, April 14, 1988, pp. 45–46; and James G. Frierson. "Religion in the Work Place," *Personnel Journal* 67, no. 7 (July 1988), pp. 60–67.

85. Ledvinka, *Federal Regulation*.

86. Anderson and Levin-Epstein. *Primer of Equal Employment Opportunity*, pp. 13–14.

87. *U.S. v. Bethlehem Steel Company*, 3FEP cases 589.

88. *Robinson v. Lorillard Corporation*, 3FEP cases 653.

89. *Spurlock v. United Airlines*, 5FEP cases 17.

90. Anderson and Levin-Epstein, *Primer of Equal Employment Opportunity*, p. 14.

91. Quoted in Wayne Cascio, *Applied Psychology in Personnel Management* (Reston, VA; Reston, 1978), p. 25.

92. This isn't ironclad, however. For example the U.S. Supreme Court, in *Stots*, held that a court cannot require retention of black employees hired under a court's consent decree in preference to higher-seniority white employees who were protected by a bona fide seniority system. It's unclear whether this decision also extends to personnel decisions not governed by seniority systems. *Firefighters Local 1784 v. Stotts* (BNA, April 14, 1985).

93. Ledvinka and Gatewood, "EEO Issues with Preemployment Inquiries," pp. 22–26.

94. John Wymer III and Deborah Sudbury, "Employment Discrimination 'Testers'—Will Your Hiring Practices 'Pass'?" *Employee Relations Law Journal* 17, no. 4 (spring 1992), pp. 623–633.

95. Levinka and Gatewood, "EEO Issues with Preemployment Inquiries," pp. 22–26.

96. Anderson and Levin-Epstein, *Primer of Equal Opportunity*, p. 27.

97. Richard Connors, "Law at Work," lawatwork.com/news/applicat.html.

98. This is based on Anderson and Levin-Epstein, *Primer of Equal Opportunity*, p. 93–97.

99. This is based on Bureau of National Affairs, *Fair Employment Practices*, April 13, 1989, pp. 45–47.

100. Eric Matusewitch, "Tailor Your Dress Codes," *Personnel Journal* 68, no. 2 (February 1989), pp. 86–91; Matthew Miklaue, "Sorting Out a Claim of Bias," *Workforce* 80, no. 6 (June 2001), pp. 102–103.

101. http://eeoc.gov/stgats/changes.html.

102. If the charge was filed initially with a state or local agency within 180 days after the alleged unlawful practice occurred, the charge may then be filed with the EEOC within 30 days after the practice occurred or within 30 days after the person received notice that the state or local agency has ended its proceedings.

103. Bureau of National Affairs, *Fair Employment Practices*, May 21, 1992, p. 59.

104. "Backing of Pending EEOC Cases," *BNA Fair Employment Practices*, June 16, 1994, p. 67.

105. "EEOC Reached Record Monetary Benefits, Continued Cutting Inventory of Last Year," *BNA Fair Employment Practices*, February 3, 2000, p. 15.

106. "EEOC Reaps Record Benefits," *BNA Fair Employment Practices*, April 2, 1998, p. 37. The proliferation of employment class-action suits (Coca-Cola recently paid $192.5 million to settle one such suit) has understandably increased the need for concern. Deborah Sudberry, et al., "Keeping the Monster in the Closet: Avoiding Employment Class-Action," *Employee Relations Law Journal* 26, no. 2 (fall 2000), pp. 5–33: "Coca-Cola Agrees to Pay $192.5 Million, Make HR Policy Changes to Settle Lawsuit," *BNA Fair Employment Practices*, 36, no. 911 (November 23, 2000), pp. 141–142.

107. Robert H. Sheahan, "Responding to Employment Discrimination Charges," *Personnel Journal* 60, no. 3 (March 1981), pp. 217–220; Wayne Baham, "Learn to Deal with Agency Investigations," *Personnel Journal* 67, no. 9 (September 1988), pp. 104–107.

108. "Conducting Effective Investigations of Employee Bias Complaints," *BNA Fair Employment Practices*, July 13, 1995, p. 81.

109. Note, however, that there are certain general guidelines regarding the archival data your firm must periodically compile. See E. Bryan Kennedy, "Archival Data Must Be Accurate," *Personnel Journal* 6, no. 11 (November 1988), pp. 108–111.

110. Based on Commerce Clearing House, *Ideas and Trends*, January 23, 1987, pp. 14–15.

111. "Tips for Employers on Dealing with EEOC Investigations," *BNA Fair Employment Practices*, October 31, 1996, p. 130.

112. Ibid., p. 219.

113. Ibid., p. 220.

114. "EEOC's New Nationwide Mediation Plan Offers Option of Informal Settlements," *BNA Fair Employment Practices*, February 18, 1999, p. 21.

115. "Independent Report Shows High Satisfaction for Participants," *BNA Fair Employment Practices*, October 12, 2000, p. 127.

116. Timothy Bland, "Sealed Without a Kiss," *HR Magazine*, October 2000, pp. 85–92.

117. Stuart Bonpey and Michael Pappas, "Is There a Better Way? Compulsory Arbitration of Employment Discrimination Claims After Gilmer," *Employee Relations Law Journal* 19, no. 3 (winter 1993–1994), pp. 197–216.

118. These are based on ibid., pp. 210–211.

119. Ibid., p. 210.

120. Ibid.

121. David Nye, "When the Fired Fight Back," *Across-the-Board*, June 1995, pp. 31–34.

122. "EEOC Opposes Mandatory Arbitration," *BNA Fair Employment Practices*, July 24, 1997, p. 85.

123. Adapted from Copyright 1998, Best Manufacturing Practices Center of Excellence.

124. James Coil III and Charles Rice, "Managing Work-Force Diversity in the 90s: The Impact of the Civil Rights Act of 1991," *Employee Relations Law Journal* 18, no. 4 (spring 1993), pp. 547–565.

125. Richard Orlando, "Racial Diversity, Business Strategy, and Firm Performance: A Resource Based View," *Academy of Management Journal* 43, no. 2 (2000), pp. 164–177.

126. Michael Carrell and Everett Mann, "Defining Work Force Diversity in Public Sector Organizations," *Public Personnel Management* 24, no. 1 (spring 1995), pp. 99–111.

127. Martin Peters, "New AOL Executive Will Seek to Improve Workplace Diversity," *Wall Street Journal*, June 28, 2001, p. B10.

128. Patricia Digh, "Creating a New Balance Sheet: The Need for Better Diversity Metrics," *Mosaics*, Society for Human Resource Management, September–October 1999, p. 1.

129. Taylor Cox Jr., *Cultural Diversity in Organizations: Theory, Research and Practice* (San Francisco: Berrett-Koehler, 1993), p. 236.

130. Orlando, "Racial Diversity."

131. Ibid.

132. Coil and Rice, "Managing Work-Force Diversity in the 90s," p. 548.

133. Ibid., p. 562–563.

134. Madeline Heilman, Winston McCullough, and David Gilbert, "The Other Side of Affirmative Action: Reactions of Nonbeneficiaries to Sex-Based Preferential Selection," *Journal of Applied Psychology* 81, no. 4 (1996), pp. 346–357.

135. Ibid., p. 346.

136. This discussion is based on Kenneth Marino, "Conducting an Internal Compliance Review of Affirmative Action," *Personnel* 59 (March–April 1980), pp. 24–34.

137. See Michael W. Sculnick, "The Supreme Court 1985–86 EEO Decisions: A Review," *Employment Relations Today* 13, no. 3 (fall 1986).

138. Ibid.

139. Ibid.

140. Aric Press and Ann McDaniel, "A Woman's Day in Court," *Newsweek*, April 6, 1987, pp. 58–59.

141. Marino, "Conducting an Internal Compliance Review"; Lawrence Kleiman and Robert Faley, "Voluntary Affirmative Action and Preferential Treatment: Legal and Research Implications," *Personnel Psychology* 42, no. 3 (autumn 1988), pp. 481–496.

142. Lisa Vaas, "Minorities Are Crossing the Digital Divide—Industry, Government Work to Close the Gap," *PC Week*, January 31, 2000, pp. 65–66.

Chapter 3

1. "Customer Retention: If You're Angry at the Bank, They Have Specialists on Your Case," *Financial Services Marketing* (January–February 2000), pp. 1, 2, 35.

2. For a good discussion of job analysis, see James Clifford, "Job Analysis: Why Do It, and How Should It Be Done?" *Public Personnel Management* 23, no. 2 (summer 1994), pp. 321–340.

3. Ernest J. McCormick, "Job and Task Analysis," in Marvin D. Dunnette, ed., *Handbook of Industrial and Organizational Psychology* (Chicago: Rand McNally, 1976), pp. 651–696.

4. James Clifford, "Manage Work Better to Better Manage Human Resources: A Comparative Study of Two Approaches to Job Analysis," *Public Personnel Management* (spring 1996), pp. 89–102.

5. Richard Henderson, *Compensation Management: Rewarding Performance* (Upper Saddle River, NJ: Prentice Hall, 1994), pp. 139–150. See also Patrick W. Wright and Kenneth Wesley, "How to Choose the Kind of Job Analysis You Really Need," *Personnel* 62, no. 5 (May 1985), pp. 51–55; C. J. Cranny and Michael E. Doherty, "Importance Ratings in Job Analysis: Note on the Misinterpretation of Factor Analyses," *Journal of Applied Psychology* (May 1988), pp. 320–322.

6. Wayne Cascio, *Applied Psychology in Human Resource Management* (Upper Saddle River, NJ: Prentice Hall, 1998), p. 142. See also Michael Lundell, et al., "Relationships Between Organizational Content and Job Analysis Task Ratings," *Journal of Applied Psychology* 83, no. 5 (1998), pp. 769–776.

7. See Henderson, *Compensation Management*, pp. 148–152.

8. Note that the PAQ (and other quantitative techniques) can also be used for job evaluation, which is explained in Chapter 11.

9. Again, we will see that job evaluation is the process through which jobs are compared to one another and their values determined. Although usually viewed as a job analysis technique, the PAQ is, in practice, actually as much or more of a job evaluation technique and could therefore be discussed in either this chapter or in Chapter 11. For a discussion of how to use PAQ for classifying jobs, see Edwin Cornelius III, Theodore Carron, and Marianne Collins, "Job Analysis Models and Job Classifications," *Personnel Psychology* 32 (winter 1979), pp. 693–708. See also Edwin Cornelius III, Frank Schmidt, and Theodore Carron, "Job Classification Approaches and the Implementation of Validity Generalization Results," *Personnel Psychology* 37, no. 2 (summer 1984), pp. 247–260.

10. Jack Smith and Milton Hakel, "Comparisons Among Data Sources, Response Bias, and Reliability and Validity of a Structured Job Analysis Questionnaire," *Personnel Psychology* 32 (winter 1979), pp. 677–692. See also Edwin Cornelius III, Angelo DeNisi, and Allyn Blencoe, "Expert and Naive Raters Using the PAQ: Does It Matter?" *Personnel Psychology* 37, no. 3 (autumn 1984), pp. 453–464; Lee Friedman and Robert Harvey, "Can Raters with Reduced Job Description Information Provide Accurate Position Analysis Questionnaires (PAQ) Ratings?" *Personnel Psychology* 34 (winter 1986), pp. 779–789; Robert J. Harvey, et al., "Dimensionality of the Job Element Inventory, A Simplified Worker-Oriented Job Analysis Questionnaire," *Journal of Applied Psychology* (November 1988), pp. 639–646; and Stephanie Butler and Robert Harvey, "A Comparison of Holistic Versus Decomposed Rating of Position Analysis Questionnaire Work Dimensions," *Personnel Psychology* (winter 1988), pp. 761–772.

11. This discussion is based on Howard Olson, et al., "The Use of Functional Job Analysis in Establishing Performance Standards for Heavy Equipment Operators," *Personnel Psychology* 34 (summer 1981), pp. 351–364.

12. Frederick P. Morgeson and Michael A. Campion, "Social and Cognitive Sources of Potential Inaccuracy in Job Analysis," *Journal of Applied Psychology* 82, no. 5 (1997), pp. 627–655.

13. Ibid., p. 648.

14. Regarding this discussion, see Henderson, *Compensation Management*, pp. 175–184. See also Louisa Wah, "The Alphabet Soup of Job Titles," *Management Review* 87, no. 6, pp. 40–43.

15. James Evered, "How to Write a Good Job Description," *Supervisory Management* (April 1981), pp. 14–19; Roger J. Plachy, "Writing Job Descriptions That Get Results," *Personnel* (October 1987), pp. 56–58. See also Matthew Mariani, "Replace with a Database," *Occupational Outlook Quarterly* 43, no. 1 (spring 1999), pp. 2–9.

16. Ibid., p. 16.

17. This discussion is based on Ibid.

18. Ibid., p. 16.

19. Ibid., p. 17.

20. Deborah Kearney, *Reasonable Accommodations: Job Descriptions in the Age of ADA, OSHA, and Workers Comp* (New York: Van Nostrand Reinhold, 1994), p. 9. See also Paul Starkman, "The ADA's Essential Job Function Requirements: Just How Essential Does an Essential Job Function Have to Be?" *Employee Relations Law Journal* 26, no. 4 (spring 2001), pp. 43–102.

21. Ibid. Unless otherwise noted, questions are based on or quoted from Kearney.

22. Michael Esposito, "There's More to Writing Job Descriptions Than Complying with the ADA," *Employment Relations Today* (autumn 1992), p. 279. See also Richard Morfopoulos and William Roth, "Job Analysis and the Americans with Disabilities Act," *Business Horizons* 39, no. 6 (November 1996), pp. 68–72; and Kristin Mitchell, George Alliger, and Richard Morfopoulos, "Toward an ADA-Appropriate Job Analysis," *Human Resource Management Review* 7, no. 1 (spring 1997), pp. 5–16.

23. James Evered, "How to Write a Good Job Description," p. 18.

24. Matthew Mariani, "Replaced with a Database: O*NET Replaces the *Dictionary of Occupational Titles*," *Occupational Outlook Quarterly* 43 (spring 1999), pp. 2–9.

25. Based on Ernest J. McCormick and Joseph Tiffin, *Industrial Psychology* (Upper Saddle River, NJ: Prentice Hall, 1974), pp. 56–61.

26. Steven Hunt, "Generic Work Behavior: An Investigation into the Dimensions of Entry-Level, Hourly Job Performance," *Personnel Psychology* 49 (1996), pp. 51–83.

27. Jorgen Sandberg, "Understanding Competence at Work," *Harvard Business Review* (March 2001), p. 28.

28. David Shair, "Wizardry Makes Charts Relevant," *HR Magazine* (April 2000), p. 127.

29. William Bridges, "The End of the Job," *Fortune*, September 19, 1994, p. 64.

30. For example, Charles Babbage listed six reasons for making jobs as specialized as possible: There is less time required for learning; there is less waste of material during the training period; there is less time lost in switching from task to task; proficiency increases with practice; hiring is made more efficient; and parts become uniform and interchangeable. Charles Babbage, *On the Economy of Machinery and Manufacturers* (London: Charles Knight, 1832), pp. 169–172; reprinted in Joseph Litterer, *Organizations* (New York: John Wiley & Sons, 1969), pp. 73–75.

31. J. Richard Hackman and Greg Oldham, "Motivation Through the Design of Work: Test of a Theory," *Organizational Behavior and Human Performance* 16, no. 2 (August 1976), pp. 250–279.

32. William H. Miller, "Chesebrough-Ponds at a Glance," *Industry Week*, October 19, 1992, pp. 14–15. For an interesting discussion of the need to move from an "it's-not-my-job" mentality from the point of view of an employee, see Kathy Shaw, "It's Not in My Job Description," *CMA Magazine* (June 1994), p. 42.

33. Larry Hirschhorn and Thomas Gilmore, "The New Boundaries of the Boundaryless Company," *Harvard Business Review* (May–June 1992), pp. 104–108. For another point of view, see George Stack Jr. and Jill Black, "The Myth of the Horizontal Organization," *Canadian Business Review* (Winter 1994), pp. 28–31.

34. Michael Hammer and James Champy, *Reengineering the Corporation* (New York: Harper Business, 1993), p. 32.

35. Ibid., p. 51.

36. Ibid., p. 68.

37. William Bridges, "The End of the Job," p. 68.

38. Sharon Leonard, "The Demise of Job Descriptions," *HR Magazine*, August 2000, p. 184.

39. Carla Joinson, "Refocusing Job Descriptions," *HR Magazine*, January 2001, pp. 65–72.

40. William Bridges, "The End of the Job," p. 68. See also Gilbert Siegel, "Job Analysis in the TQM Environment," *Public Personnel Management* 25, no. 4 (winter 1997), pp. 485–494.

41. Hammer and Champy, *Reengineering the Corporation*, p. 72.

42. Ibid.

43. Milan Moravec and Robert Tucker, "Job Descriptions for the 21st Century," *Personnel Journal* (June 1992), pp. 37–44.

44. "Customer Retention," pp. 1, 2, 35.

Chapter 4

1. Maria Seminerio, "E-Recruiting Takes Next Step—Tools Help High-Techs Spot the Best IT People," *The Week*, April 23, 2001, pp. 49–51.

2. Herbert G. Heneman Jr., and George Seitzer, "Manpower Planning and Forecasting in the Firm: An Exploratory Probe," in Elmer H. Burack and James Walker, *Manpower Planning and Programming* (Boston: Allyn & Bacon, 1972), pp. 102–120; Sheldon Zedeck and Milton Blood, "Selection and Placement," from *Foundations of Behavioral Science Research in Organizations* (Monterey, CA: Brooks/Cole, 1974), in J. Richard Hackman, Edward Lawler III, and Lyman Porter, *Perspectives on Behavior in Organizations* (New York: McGraw-Hill, 1977), pp. 103–119. For a discussion of equal employment implications of workforce planning, see James Ledvinka, "Technical Implications of Equal Employment Law for Manpower Planning," *Personnel Psychology* 28 (autumn 1975). See also Roger Hawk, *The Recruitment Function* (New York: American Management Association, 1967); "Spreadsheets Just Don't Cut It," *Management Accounting* 79 (January 1998), pp. 56–57.

3. Based on an idea in Elmer H. Burack and Robert D. Smith, *Personnel Management: A Human Resource Systems Approach* (St. Paul, MN: West, 1997), pp. 134–135. Reprinted by permission. Copyright 1997 by West Publishing Co. All rights reserved.

4. Glenn Bassett, "Elements of Manpower Forecasting and Scheduling," *Human Resource Management* 12, no. 3 (fall 1973), pp. 35–43; Pat Sweet, "Model Future: Business Intelligence Software Is Giving Finance Directors the Time and Space to Think about the Future," *Accounting* 123 (March 1999), pp. 4–6.

5. For an example of a computerized supply-chain-based personnel planning system, see Dan Kara, "Automating the Service Chain," *Software Magazine* 20 (June 2000), pp. 3, 42.

6. Shunyin Lam, et al., "Retail Sales Force Scheduling Based on Store Traffic Forecasting," *Journal of Retailing* 74, no. 1 (spring 1998), pp. 61–89.

7. Laura Mandaro, "B of A Hiring, Training to Boost Investment Unit," *American Banker* 166, no. 139 (February 17, 2001), p. 3.

8. "America Trade Plans a Second Round of Layoffs," *Web Finance*, April 16, 2001, item 0110700e.

9. John Markoff, "Bill Gates's Brain Cells, Dressed Down for Action," *New York Times*, March 25, 2001, pp. B1, B12.

10. For discussions of skill inventories, see, for example, John Lawrie, "Skill Inventories: Pack for the Future," *Personnel Journal* (March 1987), pp. 127–130; John Lawrie, "Skill Inventories: A Developmental Process," *Personnel Journal* (October 1987), pp. 108–110.

11. See, for example, Erin Callaway, "Taking Stock of IT's Most Precious Resource," *PC Week* 14, November 10, 1997, pp. 91–93.

12. Amiel Sharon, "Skills Bank Tracks Talent, Not Training," *Personnel Journal*, (June 1988), pp. 44–49.

13. Donald Harris, "A Matter of Privacy: Managing Personnel Data in Computers," *Personnel*, February 1987, pp. 334–339.

14. This section is based on ibid.

15. Lyn Berry, "Hiring May Slow in Spring," *Denver Business Journal* 51, no. 30 (March 10, 2000), p. 12a.

16. Ara Trembly, "Dot-Bomb Castoffs Swell IT Candidate Ranks, But Recruiting Is Still Difficult," *National Underwriter Life and Health, Financial Services Edition* 105, no. 18 (April 30, 2001), p. 16.

17. Scott Bailey, "Nurses Shortage Here Reaching Crisis Stage," *San Antonio Business Journal* 15, no. 6 (March 2, 2001), p. 1.

18. Carole Ann King, "Frustration Mounts as Recruiting Gets Harder," *National Underwriter Life and Health, Financial Services Edition* 105, no. 12 (March 19, 2001), p. 6.

19. Shari Caudron, "Low Unemployment Is Causing a Staffing Draught," *Personnel Journal* (November 1996), pp. 59–67.

20. "High-Stakes Recruiting in High-Tech," *BNA Bulletin to Management*, February 12, 1998, p. 48.

21. See, for example, Nina Munk, "Organization Man," *Fortune*, March 16, 1998, pp. 63–82.

22. Ibid., p. 65.

23. Ibid.

24. "High Stakes Recruiting in High-Tech," p. 48.

25. See also "Are Your Recruitment Methods Discriminatory?" *Workforce* 79, no. 5 (May 2000), pp. 105–106.

26. Sara Rynes, Robert Breta Jr., and Barry Gerhart, "The Importance of Recruitment in Job Choice: A Different Way of Looking," *Personnel Psychology* 44, no. 3 (autumn 1991), pp. 487–521.

27. David Dahl and Patrick Pinto, "Job Posting, an Industry Survey," *Personnel Journal* 56, no. 1 (January 1977), pp. 40–41. See also "Standardized Job Posting Formats Needed for Web Sites," *Internet Health Care* 2 (March 2001), p. 39.

28. Jeffrey Daum, "Internal Promotion—Psychological Asset or Debit? A Study of the Effects of Leader Origin," *Organizational Behavior and Human Performance* 13 (1975), pp. 404–413.

29. Arthur R. Pell, *Recruiting and Selecting Personnel* (New York: Regents, 1969), pp. 10–12.

30. Ibid., p. 11.

31. See "Hiring Workers the Second Time Around," *BNA Bulletin to Management*, January 30, 1997, p. 40.

32. Carol Vinzant, "They Want You Back," *Fortune*, October 2, 2000, pp. 271–272.

33. "Hiring Works the Second Time Around," p. 40.

34. Andy Cohen, "Back to the Future," *Sales and Marketing Management*, 153, no. 2 (February 2001), p. 13.

35. "Hiring Works the Second Time Around," p. 40.

36. Ibid.

37. Peter Wallum, "A Broader View of Succession Planning," *Personnel Management*, September 1993, p. 45.

38. Pell, *Recruiting and Selecting Personnel*, pp. 16–34. See also Barbara Hunger, "How to Choose a Recruitment Advertising Agency," *Personnel Journal* 64, no. 2 (December 1985), pp. 60–62. For an excellent review

of ads, see Margaret Magnus, *Personnel Journal* 64 and 65, no. 8 (August 1985 and 1986); and Bob Martin, "Recruitment Ad Ventures," *Personnel Journal* 66 (August 1987), pp. 46–63. For a discussion of how behavior can influence the initial attraction to an advertisement, see Tom Redman and Brian Matthews, "Advertising for Effective Managerial Recruitment," *Journal of General Management* 18, no. 2 (winter 1992), pp. 29–42.

39. John Kohl, David Stephens, and Jen-Chieh Chang, "Illegal Recruitment Advertising: A Ten Year Retrospect," *Employee Responsibilities and Rights* 10, no. 3 (September 1977), pp. 213–224.

40. Michelle Martinez, "Winning Ways to Recruit," *HR Magazine*, June 2000, pp. 57–64.

41. Pell, *Recruiting and Selecting Personnel*, pp. 34–42.

42. Susan Saulney, "New Jobless Centers Offer More Than a Benefit Check," *New York Times*, September 5, 2001, p. A1.

43. Lynn Doherty and E. Norman Sims, "Quick, Easy Recruitment Help—From a State?" *Workforce*, May 1998, p. 36.

44. Ibid.

45. Doherty and Sims, "Quick, Easy Recruitment Help," p. 40.

46. Allison Thompson, "The Contingent Work Force," *Occupational Outlook Quarterly* (spring 1995). p. 45.

47. Ibid., p. 47.

48. Brenda Palk Sunoo, "From Santa to CEO—Temps Play All Roles," *Personnel Journal* (April 1996), pp. 34–44.

49. "Part-Time and Other Alternative Staffing Practices," *BNA Bulletin to Management*, June 23, 1988, pp. 1–10.

50. "Temps Get a Boss of Their Own," *BNA Bulletin to Management*, November 7, 1996, p. 30.

51. "The Newest Shop in the Mall: An Employment Center," *BNA Bulletin to Management*, May 14, 1998, p. 145.

52. One Bureau of Labor Statistics study suggests that temporary employees produce the equivalent of two or more hours of work per day more than their permanent counterparts. For a discussion, see Shari Caudron, "Contingent Workforce Spurs HR Planning," *Personnel Journal* (July 1994), p. 54.

53. Thompson, "The Contingent Work Force," p. 47.

54. Amy Kover, "Manufacturing's Hidden Asset: Temp Workers," *Fortune*, November 10, 1997, pp. 28–29.

55. "How Three Companies Make Seasonal Hires," *Workforce* (July 2001), pp. 62–67.

56. Caudron, "Contingent Workforce Spurs HR Planning," p. 60.

57. Ibid., p. 56.

58. Linda Davidson, "The Temp Pool Is Shrinking," *Personnel Journal* (April 1997), pp. 72–79.

59. Daniel Feldman, Helen Doerpinghaus, and William Turnley, "Managing Temporary Workers: A Permanent HRM Challenge," *Organizational Dynamics* 23, no. 2 (fall 1994), p. 49.

60. Except as noted, the following are based on or quoted from ibid., pp. 58–60.

61. Barbara Ettorre, "The Contingency Work Force Moves Mainstream," *Management Review*, p. 15.

62. This is based on or quoted from Nancy Howe, "Match Temp Services to Your Needs," *Personnel Journal* (March 1989), pp. 45–51.

63. Thomas Greble, "A Leading Role for HR in Alternative Staffing," *HR Magazine*, February 1997, p. 100.

64. "Search and Destroy," *Economist*, June 27, 1998, p. 63. See also Geoffrey Colvin and Patrice Sellers, "How Many Heads Can a Headhunter Hunt?" *Fortune*, May 29, 2000, pp. 118–128.

65. "Search and Destroy."

66. Ibid.

67. Ibid.

68. John Wareham, *Secrets of a Corporate Headhunter* (New York: Playboy Press, 1981), pp. 213–225; Chip McCreary, "Get the Most out of Search Firms," *Workforce* 76 (August 1997), pp. S28–S30.

69. Michelle Martinez, "Working with an Outside Recruiter? Get It in Writing," *HR Magazine* 46, no. 1 (January 2001), pp. 98–105.

70. Pell, *Recruiting and Selecting Personnel*, pp. 56–63; David L. Chicci and Carl Knapp, "College Recruitment from Start to Finish," *Personnel Journal* 50, no. 8 (August 1980), pp. 653–657.

71. Paul Falcone, "Reaching Out," *HR Magazine*, August 2001, pp. 119–124.

72. Bill Leonard, "Recruiting from the Competition," *HR Magazine*, February 2001, pp. 78–86.

73. Sara Rynes, Marc Orlitzky, and Robert Bretz Jr., "Experienced Hiring Versus College Recruiting: Practices and Emerging Trends," *Personnel Psychology* 50 (1997), pp. 309–339.

74. Robert Dipboye, Howard Fronkin, and Ken Wiback, "Relative Importance of Applicant Sex, Attractiveness, and Scholastic Standing in Evaluation of Job Applicant Resumes," *Journal of Applied Psychology* 61 (1975), pp. 39–48. See also Laura M. Graves, "College Recruitment: Removing the Personal Bias from Selection Decisions," *Personnel*, March 1989, pp. 48–52; "A Measure of the HR Recruitment Function: The 1994 College Relations and Recruitment Survey," *Journal of Career Planning and Employment* 55, no. 3 (spring 1995), pp. 37–49; "College Recruiting," *Personnel*, May–June 1980. For a study of how applicant sex can impact recruiters' evaluations, see, for example, Laura Graves and Gary Powell, "The Effect of Sex Similarity on Recruiters' Evaluations of Actual Applicants: A Test of the Similarity-Attraction Paradigm," *Personnel Psychology* 48, no. 1 (spring 1995), pp. 85–98.

75. Helena Miller, "Fewer Firms on Campus Recruiting," *Business Journal* 16, no. 3 (April 20, 2001), p. 16.

76. See, for example, Richard Becker, "Ten Common Mistakes in College Recruiting—or How to Try Without Really Succeeding," *Personnel* 52, no. 2 (March–April 1975), pp. 19–28. See also Sara Rynes and John Boudreau, "College Recruiting in Large Organizations: Practice, Evaluation, and Research Implications," *Personnel Psychology* 39 (winter 1986), pp. 729–757.

77. *Personnel Administrator*, March 1987. Copyright 1987, The American Society for Personnel Administration, 606 North Washington Street, Alexandria, VA 22314.

78. Pell, *Recruiting and Selecting Personnel*, pp. 62–63.

79. "Internships Provide Workplace Snapshot," *BNA Bulletin to Management*, May 22, 1997, p. 168.

80. Michelle Martinez, "The Headhunter Within," *HR Magazine*, August 2001, pp. 48–56.

81. "Employee Referrals Improve Hiring," *BNA Bulletin to Management*, March 13, 1997, p. 88.

82. Ibid., p. 13.

83. The study on employment referrals was published by Bernard Hodes Advertising, Dept. 100, 555 Madison Avenue, New York, NY 10022. See also Allan Halcrow, "Employees Are Your Best Recruiters," *Personnel Journal* (November 1988), pp. 41–49; Andy Hargerstock and Hank Engel, "Six Ways to Boost Employee Referral Programs," *HR Magazine* (December 1994), pp. 72ff.

84. Erica Brown, "Have Friends, Will Hire," *Forbes*, October 30, 2000, p. 62.

85. "High-Stakes Recruiting in High-Tech," *BNA Bulletin to Management*, February 12, 1998, p. 48.

86. Charlene Solomon, "The Creative Approach to Staffing," *Workforce*, p. 76.

87. Ruth Thaler Carter, "Your Recruitment Advertising," *HR Magazine*, June 2001, pp. 93–100.

88. Michael A. Zottoli and John Wanous, "Recruitment Source Research: Current Status and Future Directions," *Human Resource Management Review* 10 (November 4, 2000), pp. 353–382.

89. Michelle Neely Martinez, "Get Job Seekers to Come to You," *HR Magazine*, August 2000, 45–52.

90. "Snail Mail Still Rules the Resume Race, But HR Predicts More Electronic Delivery," *BNA Bulletin to Management*, May 25, 2000, p. 161.

91. Elaine Appleton, "Recruiting on the Internet," *Datamation*, August 1995, p. 39.

92. Julia King, "Job Networking," *Enterprise Networking*, January 26, 1995.

93. Gillian Flynn, "Cisco Turns the Internet Inside (and) Out," *Personnel Journal*, (October 1996), pp. 28–34.

94. "Does Your Company's Website Click with Job Seekers?" *Workforce* (August 2000), p. 26.

95. "Study Says Career Web Sites Could Snare More Job Seekers," *BNA Bulletin to Management*, February 1, 2001, p. 36.

96. "Internet Recruiting Holds Promise," *BNA Bulletin to Management*, July 17, 1997, p. 232.

97. "Internet Recruiting Takes Off," *BNA Bulletin to Management*, February 20, 1997, p. 64.

98. Tyler Maroney, "Web Recruiting Is Fine, But We Like a Job Fair," *Fortune*, March 20, 2000, p. 236.

99. "Internet Recruiting Takes Off," *BNA Bulletin to Management*, February 20, 1997, p. 64.

100. Laura Romei, "Human Resource Management Systems Keep Computers Humming," *Managing Office Technology*, November 1994, p. 45.

101. William Dickmeyer, "Applicant Tracking Reports Make Data Meaningful," *Workforce* 80, no. 2 (February 2001), pp. 65–67.

102. Paul Gilster, "Channel the Resume Flood with Applicant Tracking Systems," *Workforce* (January 2001), pp. 3–34; Dickmeyer, "Applicant Tracking Reports," pp. 65–67.

103. Seminerio, "E-Recruiting Takes Next Step," pp. 49–51.

104. Thomas Stewart, "In Search of Elusive Tech Workers," *Fortune*, February 16, 1998, pp. 171–172.

105. Ibid., p. 171.

106. Ibid.

107. Unless otherwise noted, this section is based on Judith Casey and Marcie Pitt-Catsouphes, "Employed Single Mothers: Balancing Job and Home Life," *Employee Assistance Quarterly* 9, no. 3–4 (1994), pp. 37–53.

108. Ibid., p. 42.

109. Ibid., p. 44.

110. Ibid., p. 45.

111. Ibid., p. 43.

112. Ibid., p. 48.

113. Ibid., p. 48.

114. "Retirees Increasingly Reentering the Workforce," *BNA Bulletin to Management*, January 16, 1997, p. 17.

115. Diane Cyr, "Lost and Found—Retired Employees," *Personnel Journal* (November 1996), p. 41.

116. Harold E. Johnson, "Older Workers Help Meet Employment Needs," *Personnel Journal* (May 1988), pp. 100–105; "Labor Force Diversity Grows," at (http://www.infoplease.com/ipa/A0104513.html), accessed September 9, 2001.

117. Robert W. Goddard, "How to Harness America's Gray Power," *Personnel Journal* (May 1987), p. 33.

118. "Older Workers Valued but Hard to Find, Employers Say," *BNA Bulletin to Management*, April 30, 1998, pp. 129–134.

119. For this and other examples here, see Goddard, "How to Harness America's Gray Power."

120. Abby Ellin, "Supervising the Graybeards," *New York Times*, January 16, 2000, p. B16.

121. Elizabeth Blackarczyk, "Recruiters Challenged by Economy, Shortages," *HR News*, February 1990, p. 84. Diversity management programs may also make a firm more attractive to job candidates. See, for example, Margaret Williams and Talya Bauer, "The Effect of Managing Diversity Policy on Organizational Attractiveness," *Group & Organization Management* 19, no. 3 (September 1994), pp. 295–308.

122. Jennifer Koch, "Finding Qualified Hispanic Candidates," *Recruitment Today* 3, no. 2 (spring 1990), p. 35.

123. This compares with 21.5% for black job seekers and 23.9% for white job seekers. Michelle Harrison Ports, "Trends in Job Search Methods, 1990–92." *Monthly Labor Review*, October 1993, p. 64.

124. Bill Leonard, "Welfare Reform: A New Deal for HR," *HR Magazine*, March 1997, pp. 78–86; Jennifer Laabs, "Welfare Law: HR's Role in Employment," *Workforce* (January 1998), pp. 30–39.

125. Isabel Sawhill, "From Welfare to Work," Brookings Review, (summer 2001), p. 34.

126. "Welfare-to-Work: No Easy Chore," *BNA Bulletin to Management*, February 13, 1997, p. 56.

127. Herbert Greenberg, "A Hidden Source of Talent," *HR Magazine*, March 1997, pp. 88–91.

128. "Welfare to Work: No Easy Chore," p. 56.

129. Jennifer Laabs, "Recruiting in the Global Village," *Workforce* (spring 1998), pp. 30–33.

130. Scott Graham, "Hospitals Recruiting Overseas," *Baltimore Business Journal*, June 1, 2001, p. 1.

131. Victor Infante, "Small World Keeps Getting Smaller," *Workforce* (February 2001), p. 80.

132. "Recruiting in the Global Village," pp. 30–33.

133. This is based on Jennifer Laabs, "The Global Talent Search," *Personnel Journal* (August 1991), pp. 38–42.

134. Shannon Peters Talbott, "Building a Global Workforce Starts with Recruitment," *Personnel Journal* (March 1996), pp. 9–11.

135. Ibid.

136. Ibid.

137. Circuit City Stores, Inc., Employment Packet, January 1997.

138. De'Ann Weimer and Stephanie Anderson Forest, "Forced Into Arbitration? Not Anymore," *Business Week*, March 16, 1998, pp. 66, 68.

139. *Ryan's Family Steakhouse Inc. v. Floss*; "Supreme Court Let Stand Decision Finding Prehire Arbitration Agreements Unenforceable," *BNA Bulletin to Management*, January 11, 2001, p. 11.

140. Ibid.

141. Fred Mael, Mary Connerley, and Ray Morath, "None of Your Business: Parameters of Biodata Invasiveness," *Personnel Psychology* 49 (1996), pp. 613–650.

Chapter 5

1. Gilbert Nicholson, "Automated Assessments for Better Hires," *Workforce* 29, no. 12 (December 2000), pp. 102–104.

2. For brief overviews of this process, see, for example, Philip Schofield, "Improving the Candidate Job-Match," *Personnel Management* 25, no. 2 (February 1993), p. 69, and Clive Fletcher, "Testing Times for the World of Psychometrics," *Personnel Management*, December 1993, pp. 46–50.

3. See, for example, Ann Marie Ryan and Marja Lasek, "Negligent Hiring and Defamation: Areas of Liability Related to Pre-employment Inquiries," *Personnel Psychology* 44, no. 2 (summer 1991), pp. 293–319.

4. Ibid.

5. Ibid.

6. Steven Mitchell Sack, "Fifteen Steps to Protecting Against the Risk of Negligent Hiring Claims," *Employment Relations Today*, August 1993, pp. 313–320.

7. Leona Tyler, *Tests and Measurements* (Upper Saddle River, NJ: Prentice Hall, 1971), p. 25. More technically, "validity refers to the degree of confidence one can have in inferences drawn from scores, considering the whole process by which the scores are obtained. Stated differently, validity refers to the confidence one has in the meaning attached to scores." See Robert Guion, "Changing Views for Personnel Selection Research," *Personnel Psychology* 40, no. 2 (summer 1987), p. 208.

8. As indicated, a third way to demonstrate a test's validity is construct validity. A construct is a trait such as intelligence. Therefore, to take a simple example, if intelligence is important to the position of engineer, a test that measures intelligence would have construct validity for that position. To prove construct validity, an employer has to prove that the test actually measures the construct and that the construct is in turn required for the job. Federal agency guidelines make it difficult to prove construct validity, however, and as a result few employers use this approach as a means of satisfying the federal guidelines. See James Ledvinka, *Federal Regulation of Personnel and Human Resource Management* (Boston: Kent, 1982), p. 113.

9. Bureau of National Affairs, *Primer of Equal Employment Opportunity* (Washington, DC: BNA, 1978), p. 18.

10. Ledvinka, *Federal Regulation*, p. 111.

11. Anne Anastasi, *Psychological Patterns* (New York: Macmillan, 1968), reprinted in W. Clay Hamner and Frank Schmidt, *Contemporary Problems in Personnel* (Chicago: St. Claire Press, 1974), pp. 102–109. Discussion of reliability is based on Marvin Dunnette, *Personnel Selection and Placement* (Belmont, CA: Wadsworth Publishing Company, 1966), pp. 29–30.

12. Calvin Hoffman, Barry Nathan, and Lisa Holden, "A Comparison of Validation Criteria: Objective versus Subjective Performance Measures and Self- versus Supervisory Ratings," *Personnel Psychology* 44 (1991), pp. 601–619. For a recent discussion of some of the issues to be taken into consideration when choosing criteria, see Wilfried de Corte, "A Note on the Success Ratio and the Utility of Fixed Hiring Rate Personnel Selection Decisions," *Journal of Applied Psychology* 84, no. 6 (1999), pp. 952–958.

13. Based on J. Tiffin and E. J. McCormick, *Industrial Psychology* (Upper Saddle River, NJ: Prentice Hall, 1965), pp. 104–105; C. H. Lawshe and M. J. Balma, *Principles of Personnel Testing*, 2nd ed. (New York: McGraw-Hill, 1966); Duane Schultz and Sydney Ellen Schultz, *Psychology and Work Today* (Upper Saddle River, NJ: Prentice Hall, 1998), p. 102.

14. Experts sometimes have to develop separate expectancy charts and cutting points for minorities and nonminorities if the validation studies indicate that high performers from either group (minority or nonminority) score lower (or higher) on the test. See our discussion of differential validity in the Web appendix to this chapter. For a good discussion of how to evaluate a selection test, see Raymond Berger and Donna Tucker, "How to Evaluate a Selection Test," *Personnel Journal* 66, no. 6 (February 1987), pp. 88–91.

15. James Ledvinka and Lyle Schoenfeldt, "Legal Developments in Employment Testing: Albemarle," *Personnel Psychology* 31, no. 1 (spring 1978), p. 9. See also Robert Wood and Helen Bearon, "Psychological Testing Free from Prejudice," *Personnel Management*, December 1992, pp. 34–37; and Travis Gibbs and Matt Riggs, "Reducing Bias in Personnel Selection Decisions: Positive Effects of Attention to Irrelevant Information," *Psychological Reports* 74 (1994), pp. 19–26.

16. Ledvinka, *Federal Regulation*, p. 109.

17. Douglas Baker and David Terpstra, "Employee Selection: Must Every Job Be Validated?" *Personnel Journal* 61 (August 1982), pp. 602–605.

18. This is based on Marilyn Quaintance, "Test Security: Foundations of Public Merit Systems," *Personnel Psychology* 33, no. 1 (spring 1980), pp. 25–32.

19. William Roskind, "DECO Versus NLRB, and the Consequences of Open Testing in Industry," *Personnel Psychology* 33, no. 1 (spring 1980), pp. 3–9; and James Ledvinka, Val Markos, and Robert Ladd, "Long-Range Impact of 'Fair Selection' Standards on Minority Employment," *Journal of Applied Psychology* 67, no. 1 (February 1982), pp. 18–36.

20. Mark Schmit and Ann Marie Ryan, "Applicant Withdrawal: The Role of Test-Taking Attitudes and Racial Differences," *Personnel Psychology* 50 (1997), pp. 855–876.

21. Robert Ployhart and Ann Marie Ryan, "Applicants' Reactions to the Fairness of Selection Procedures: The Effects of Positive Rule Violations and Time of Measurement," *Journal of Applied Psychology* 83, no. 1 (1998), pp. 3–16.

22. Dirk Steiner and Stephen Gilliland, "Fairness Reactions to Personnel Selection Techniques in France and the United States," *Journal of Applied Psychology* 81, no. 2 (1996), pp. 134–141.

23. Ibid., p. 134.

24. Susan Mendelsohn and Katheryn Morrison, "The Right to Privacy at the Work Place, Part I: Employee Searchers," *Personnel*, July 1988, p. 20. See also Talya Bauer, et al., "Applicant Reactions to Selection: Development of the Selection Procedural Justice Scale," *Personnel Psychology* 54 (2001), pp. 387–419.

25. Wayne Outten and Noah A. Kinigstein, *The Rights of Employees* (New York: Bantam Books, 1984), pp. 53–54.

26. Mendelson and Morrison, "The Right to Privacy in the Work Place," p. 22.

27. Outten and Kinigstein, *The Rights of Employees*, pp. 54–55.

28. Ibid., p. 55.

29. *Kehr v. Consolidated Freightways of Delaware*, Docket No. 86–2126, July 15, 1987, U.S. Seventh Circuit Court of Appeals. Discussed in Commerce Clearing House, *Ideas and Trends*, October 16, 1987, p. 165.

30. For a discussion of these see Commerce Clearing House, *Ideas and Trends*, October 16, 1987, pp. 165–166.

31. "Workplace Testing and Monitoring," *Management Review*, October 1998, pp. 31–42.

32. "Workers Find Employment Less of a Test as the Use of Medical, Psych Exams Subsides," *BNA Bulletin to Management*, August 24, 2000: 265–266.

33. Rachel Emma Silverman, "Sharpen Your Pencil," *The Wall Street Journal*, December 5, 2000.

34. See Rebecca Bennett and Sandra Robinson, "Development of a Measure of Workplace Deviance," *Journal of Applied Psychology* 85, no. 3 (2000), p. 349.

35. "Employees' Dirty Deeds Caused Companies 6 Percent of Annual Revenue, Report Says," *BNA Bulletin to Management*, August 17, 2000, p. 257.

36. Neal Schmitt, et al., "Computer-Based Testing Applied to Selection of Secretarial Candidates," *Personnel Psychology* 46 (1991), pp. 149–165.

37. Randall Overton, et al., "The Pen-Based Computer as an Alternative Platform for Test Administration," *Personnel Psychology* 49 (1996), pp. 455–464.

38. Scott Hayes, "Kinko's Dials into Automated Applicants Screening," *Workforce* 78, no. 11 (November 1999), pp. 71–73; Gilbert Nicholson, "Automated Assessments for Better Hires," *Workforce* 79, no. 12 (December 2000), pp. 102–107.

39. Except as noted, this is based largely on Laurence Siegel and Irving Lane, *Personnel and Organizational Psychology* (Burr Ridge, IL: McGraw-Hill, 1982), pp. 170–185. See also Tyler, *Tests and Measurements*, pp. 38–79; Lawshe and Balma, *Principles of Personnel Testing*, pp. 83–160; Cabot Jaffee, "Measurement of Human Potential," *Employment Relations Today* 17, no. 2 (summer 2000), pp. 15–27; Maureen Patterson, "Overcoming the Hiring Crunch; Tests Deliver Informed Choices," *Employment Relations Today* 27, no. 3 (fall 2000), pp. 77–88; Kathryn Tyler, "Put Applicants' Skills to the Test," *HR Magazine* 45, no. 1 (January 2000), p. 74; Schultz and Schultz, *Psychology and Work Today*, pp. 109–124.

40. See, for example, Richard Reilly, Sheldon Zedeck, and Mary Tenopyr, "Validity and Fairness of Physical Ability Tests for Predicting Performance in Craft Jobs," *Journal of Applied Psychology* 64, no. 3 (June 1970), pp. 262–274. See also Barten Daniel, "Strength and Endurance Testing," *Personnel Journal*, June 1987, pp. 112–122.

41. Results of meta-analyses in one study indicated that isometric strength tests were valid predictors of both supervisory ratings of physical performance, and performance on work simulations. See Barry R. Blakley, Miguel Quinones, Marnie Swerdlin Crawford, and I. Ann Jago, "The Validity of Isometric Strength Tests," *Personnel Psychology* 47 (1994), pp. 247–274.

42. William Wagner, "All Skill, No Finesse," *Workforce*, (June 2000), pp. 108–116.

43. Cora Daniels, "Does This Man Need a Shrink?" *Fortune*, 143, no. 3 (February 5, 2001), pp. 205–206.

44. Reach Assessment Systems Corporation at 2233 University Avenue, Suite 440, St. Paul, MN 55114; 612-647-9220.

45. Mark Schmit, Jennifer Kihm, and Chet Robie, "Development of a Global Measure of Personality," *Personnel Psychology* 53 (2000), pp. 153–193.

46. If you read note 8, you will see that this approach calls for construct validation which, as was pointed out, is extremely difficult to demonstrate.

47. Brad Bushman and Gary Wells, "Trait Aggressiveness and Hockey Penalties: Predicting Hot Tempers on the Ice," *Journal of Applied Psychology* 83, no. 6 (1998), pp. 969–974.

48. Charles Sarchione, et al., "Prediction of Dysfunctional Job Behaviors Among Law-Enforcement Officers," *Journal of Applied Psychology* 83, no. 6 (1998), pp. 904–912.

49. Paula Caligiuri, "The Big Five Personality Characteristics as Predictors of Expatriate's Desire to Terminate the Assignment and Supervisor Rated Performance," *Personnel Psychology* 53 (2000), pp. 67–68.

50. Brian Niehoff and Robert Paula, "Causes of Employee Theft and Strategies That HR Managers Can Use for Prevention," *Human Resource Management* 39, no. 1 (spring 2000), pp. 51–64. See also Andrew Vinchur, et al., "A Meta Analytic Review of Predictors of Job Performance for Salespeople," *Journal of Applied Psychology* 83, no. 4 (1998), pp. 586–596. For a sample of the employment tests available, see, for example, "Introduction to 1999 Testing and the Employee Survey Matrix," *HR Magazine*, February 1999, pp. 153–167.

51. See, for example, Douglas Cellar, et al., "Comparison of Factor Structures and Criterion-Related Validity Coefficients for Two Measures of Personality Based on the Five Factor Model," *Journal of Applied Psychology* 81, no. 6 (1996), pp. 694–704; and Jesus Salgado, "The Five Factor Model of Personality and Job Performance in the European Community," *Journal of Applied Psychology* 82, no. 1 (1997), pp. 30–43.

52. Murray Barrick and Michael Mount, "The Big Five Personality Dimensions and Job Performance: A Meta-Analysis," *Personnel Psychology* 44, no. 1 (spring 1991), pp. 1–26.

53. Timothy Judge, Joseph Martocchio, and Carl Thoresen, "Five-Factor Model of Personality and Employee Absence," *Journal of Applied Psychology* 82, no. 5 (1997), pp. 745–755.

54. Timothy Judge, et al., "The Big Five Personality Traits, General Mental Ability, and Career Success Across the Lifespan," *Personnel Psychology* 52 (1999), pp. 621–652.

55. See "Can Testing Prevent Violence?" *BNA Bulletin to Management*, November 28, 1996, p. 384.

56. For a study describing how matching (1) task and working condition preferences of applicants with (2) actual job and working conditions

can be achieved, see Ronald Ash, Edward Levine, and Steven Edgell, "Study of a Matching Approach: The Impact of Ethnicity," *Journal of Applied Psychology* 64, no. 1 (February 1979), pp. 35–41. For a discussion of how a standard clerical test can be used to screen applicants who will have to use video displays, see Edward Silver and Corwin Bennett, "Modification of the Minnesota Clerical Test to Predict Performance on Video Display Terminals," *Journal of Applied Psychology* 72, no. 1 (February 1987), pp. 153–155.

57. Gilbert Nicholson, "Automated Assessments for Better Hires," *Workforce* (December 2000), pp. 102–107.

58. Jeff Weekley and Casey Jones, "Video-Based Situational Testing," *Personnel Psychology* 50 (1997), p. 25.

59. Paul Wernamont and John T. Campbell, "Signs, Samples, and Criteria," *Journal of Applied Psychology* 52 (1968), pp. 372–376; James Campion, "Work Sampling for Personnel Selection," *Journal of Applied Psychology* 56 (1972), pp. 40–44, reprinted in Hamner and Schmidt, *Contemporary Problems in Personnel*, pp. 168–180; Sidney Gael, Donald Grant, and Richard Ritchie, "Employment Test Validation for Minority and Nonminority Clerks with Work Sample Criteria," *Journal of Applied Psychology* 60, no. 4 (August 1974); Frank Schmidt, et al., "Job Sample vs. Paper and Pencil Trades and Technical Test: Adverse Impact and Examinee Attitudes," *Personnel Psychology* 30, no. 7 (summer 1977), pp. 187–198.

60. See, for example, George Burgnoli, James Campion, and Jeffrey Bisen, "Racial Bias in the Use of Work Samples for Personnel Selection," *Journal of Applied Psychology* 64, no. 2 (April 1979), pp. 119–123.

61. Siegel and Lane, *Personnel and Organizational Psychology*, pp. 182–183.

62. Annette Spychalski, Miguel Quinones, Barbara Gaugler, and Katja Pohley, "A Survey of Assessment Center Practices in Organizations in the United States," *Personnel Psychology* 50, no. 1 (spring 1997), pp. 71–90.

63. Steven Norton, "The Empirical and Content Validity of Assessment Centers Versus Traditional Methods of Predicting Management Success," *Academy of Management Review* 20 (July 1977), pp. 442–453. Interestingly, one review concludes that assessment centers do predict managerial success, but after an extensive review, "we also assert that we do not know why they work." Richard Klimoski and Mary Brickner, "Why Do Assessment Centers Work? The Puzzle of Assessment Center Validity," *Personnel Psychology* 40, no. 2 (summer 1987), pp. 243–260.

64. David Groce, "A Behavioral Consistency Approach to Decision Making in Employment Selection," *Personnel Psychology* 34, no. 1 (spring 1981), pp. 55–64.

65. For an alternative to assessment centers, see Donald Brush and Lyle Schoenfeldt, "Identifying Managerial Potential: An Alternative Assessment Center," *Personnel* 57 (May–June 1980), pp. 72–73.

66. Weekley and Jones, "Video-Based Situational Testing," p. 26.

67. Ibid., p. 30.

68. Ibid., p. 46.

69. Arthur Cosiegel, "The Miniature Job Training and Evaluation Approach: Traditional Findings," *Personnel Psychology* 36, no. 1 (spring 1983), pp. 41–56.

70. Edward Robinson, "Beware—Job Seekers Have No Secrets," *Fortune*, December 29, 1997, p. 285.

71. Ibid.

72. Seymour Adler, "Verifying a Job Candidate's Background: The State of Practice in a Vital Human Resources Activity," *Review of Business* 15, no. 2 (winter 1993), p. 6.

73. Ibid., pp. 3–8.

74. Robinson, "Beware," p. 285.

75. Floyd Norris, "An Executive's Missing Years: Papering Over Past Problems," *New York Times*, July 16, 2001, pp. A1–A12.

76. This is based on Samuel Greengard, "Have Gangs Invaded Your Workplace?" *Personnel Journal*, February 1996, pp. 47–48.

77. For additional information, see Lawrence E. Dube Jr., "Employment References and the Law," *Personnel Journal* 65, no. 2 (February 1986), pp. 87–91. See also Mickey Veich, "Uncover the Resume Ruse," *Security Management*, October 1994, pp. 75–76.

78. Thomas von der Embse and Rodney Wyse, "Those Reference Letters: How Useful Are They?" *Personnel* 62, no. 1 (January 1985), pp. 42–46.

79. "Undercover Callers Tipoff Job Seekers to Former Employers' Negative References," *BNA Bulletin to Management*, May 27, 1999, p. 161.

80. James Bell, James Castagnera, and Jane Patterson Yong, "Employment References: Do You Know the Law?" *Personnel Journal* 63, no. 2 (February 1984), pp. 32–36. In order to demonstrate defamation, several elements must be present: (a) the defamatory statement must have been communicated to another party; (b) the statement must be a false statement of fact; (c) injury to reputation must have occurred; and (d) the employer must not be protected under qualified or absolute privilege. For a discussion, see Ryan and Lasek, "Negligent Hiring and Defamation," p. 307. See also James Burns Jr., "Employment References: Is There a Better Way?" *Employee Relations Law Journal* 23, no. 2 (fall 1997), pp. 157–168.

81. "Jury Awards Manager Accused of Theft $1.25 Million," *BNA Bulletin to Management*, March 27, 1997, p. 97.

82. "Reference Checks Hit Wall of Silence," *BNA Bulletin to Management*, July 6, 1995, p. 216.

83. "Getting Applicant Information Difficult but Still Necessary," *BNA Bulletin to Management*, February 5, 1999, p. 63.

84. Jeffrey M. Hahn, "Pre-Employment Information Services: Employers Beware?" *Employee Relations Law Journal* 17, no. 1 (summer 1991), pp. 45–69.

85. "State-by-State Review: Laws and Regulations on Access to and Use of Criminal Records," *BNA Bulletin to Management*, June 20, 1996, p. 13.

86. Ibid., p. 51.

87. "Database Helps Employers Screen Applicants for Theft," *BNA Bulletin to Management*, June 12, 1997, p. 186.

88. Ibid., p. 191.

89. Ibid.

90. James Frierson, "New Polygraph Tests Limits," *Personnel Journal*, December 1988, pp. 84–89.

91. This is based on "When Can Workers Refuse Lie Detector Tests?" *BNA Bulletin to Management*, March 9, 1995, p. 73, and is based on the case Lyle Z. Mercy Hospital Anderson, DCS Ohio, 1995, 10 IER cases 401.

92. John Jones and William Terris, "Post-Polygraph Selection Techniques," *Recruitment Today*, May–June 1989, pp. 25–31.

93. Norma Fritz, "In Focus: Honest Answers—Post Polygraph," *Personnel*, April 1989, p. 8.

94. For a discussion of the earlier caveats see, for example, Kevin Murphy, "Detecting Infrequent Deception," *Journal of Applied Psychology* 72, no. 4 (November 1987), pp. 611–614.

95. John Bernardin and Donna Cooke, "Validity of an Honesty Test in Predicting Theft Among Convenience Store Employees," *Academy of Management Journal* 36, no. 5 (1993), pp. 1097–1108.

96. Paul Sackett and James Wanek, "New Developments in the Use of Measures of Honesty, Integrity, Conscientiousness, Dependability, Trustworthiness, and Reliability for Personnel Selection," *Personnel Psychology* 49 (1996), p. 821.

97. The following is based on Judith Collins and Frank Schmidt, "Personality, Integrity, and White Collar Crime: A Construct Validity Study," *Personnel Psychology* 46 (1993), pp. 295–311.

98. Ibid. For a description of another approach see, for example, Peter Bullard, "Pre-Employment Screening to Weed Out 'Bad Apples,'" *Nursing Homes*, June 1994, pp. 29–31.

99. These are based on Commerce Clearing House, *Ideas and Trends*, December 29, 1998, pp. 222–223. See also "Divining Integrity Through Interviews," *BNA Bulletin to Management*, June 4, 1987, p. 184.

100. This example is based on *BNA Bulletin to Management*, February 26, 1987, p. 65.

101. See, for example, "Corporate Lie Detectors Under Fire," *Business Week*, January 13, 1973. For a discussion of how to improve the validity of the polygraph test, see Robert Forman and Clark McCauley, "Validity of a Positive Control Polygraph Test Using the Field to Practice Model," *Journal of Applied Psychology* 71, no. 4 (November 1986), pp. 691–698.

102. Bill Leonard, "Reading Employees," *HR Magazine* 44, no. 4 (April 1999), pp. 67–73.

103. Ibid.

104. Mick Haus, "Pre-Employment Physicals and the ADA," *Safety and Health*, February 1992, pp. 64–65.

105. Scott MacDonald, Samantha Wells, and Richard Fry, "The Limitations of Drug Screening in the Workplace," *International Labor Review* 132,

no. 1 (1993), p. 98. Not all agree that drug testing is worthwhile. See, for example, Mark Karper, Clifford Donn, and Marie Lyndaker, "Drug Testing in the Transportation Industry: The Maritime Case," *Employee Responsibilities and Rights* 71, no. 3 (September 1994), pp. 219–233.

106. Eric Rolfe Greenberg, "Workplace Testing: Who's Testing Whom?" *Personnel*, May 1989, pp. 39–45.

107. "Drug Testing: The Things People Will Do," *American Salesman* 46, no. 3 (March 2001), p. 20.

108. Chris Berka and Courtney Poignand, "Hair Follicle Testing—An Alternative to Urinalysis for Drug Abuse Screening," *Employee Relations Today* (winter 1991–1992), pp. 405–409.

109. MacDonald, et al., "The Limitations of Drug Screening," pp. 102–104.

110. R. J. McCunney, "Drug Testing: Technical Complications of a Complex Social Issue," in *American Journal of Industrial Medicine* 15, no. 5 (1989), pp. 589–600; discussed in MacDonald, et al., "The Limitations of Drug Screening," p. 102.

111. MacDonald, et al., "The Limitations of Drug Screening," p. 103.

112. For a discussion of this, see Ibid, pp. 105–106.

113. This is based on Ann M. O'Neill, "Legal Issues Presented by Hair Follicle Testing," *Employee Relations Today* (winter 1991–1992), pp. 411–415.

114. Ibid., p. 411.

115. Ibid., p. 413.

116. Richard Lisko, "A Manager's Guide to Drug Testing," *Security Management* 38, no. 8 (August 1994), p. 92.

117. For an additional perspective on drug testing as it applies to public agencies and unions, see, for example, Nancy C. O'Neill, "Drug Testing in Public Agencies: Are Personnel Directors Doing Things Right?" *Public Personnel Management* 19, no. 4 (winter 1990), pp. 391–397; Michael H. LeRoy, "The Presence of Drug Testing in the Workplace and Union Member Attitudes," *Labor Studies Journal* (fall 1991), pp. 33–42. For another approach, see, for example, Darold Barnum and John Gleason, "The Credibility of Drug Tests: A Multi-Stage Bayesian Analysis," *Industrial and Labor Relations Review* 47, no. 4 (July 1994), pp. 610–621.

118. Eric Rolfe Greenberg, "Workplace Testing: Results of a New AMA Survey," *Personnel*, April 1988, p. 40.

119. Michael A. McDaniel, "Does Pre-Employment Drug Use Predict on the Job Suitability?" *Personnel Psychology* 41, no. 4 (winter 1988), pp. 717–729.

120. *Exxon Corp. v. Esso Workers Union, Inc.*, CA1#96–2241, 7/8/97; discussed in *BNA Bulletin to Management*, August 7, 1997, p. 249.

121. This is based on Mark Thomas and Harry Brull, "Tests Improve Hiring Decisions at Franciscan," *Personnel Journal*, (November 1993), pp. 89–92.

122. For another view, see, for example, Raymond Berger and Donna Tucker, "Recruitment: How to Evaluate a Selection Test," *Personnel Journal New Product News*, March 1994, pp. 2, 3.

123. David E. Terpstra and Elizabeth Rozell, "The Relationship of Staffing Practices to Organizational Level Measures of Performance," *Personnel Psychology* 46 (1993), pp. 27–48.

124. Nicholson, "Automated Assessments for Better Hires," pp. 102–104.

125. These are quoted from Commerce Clearing House, *Ideas and Trends*, May 1, 1987, pp. 70–71.

126. Rusell Gerbman, "License to Work," *HR Magazine*, June 2000, pp. 151–160.

127. "Worker Verification Changes Come Slowly," *BNA Bulletin to Management*, May 29, 1997, p. 176.

128. "I-9 Form and Document Revisions Still Up in the Air," *BNA Bulletin to Management*, October 9, 1997, p. 322.

Chapter 6

1. Dawn Shand, "Talent Scouts: They Excel at Spotting, Hiring, and Keeping Key Players," *Computerworld*, April 10, 2000, pp. 52–53.

2. Michael McDaniel, et al., "The Validity of Employment Interviews: A Comprehensive Review and Meta-analysis," *Journal of Applied Psychology* 79, no. 4 (1994), p. 599. See also Laura Graves and Ronald Karren, "The Employee Selection Interview: A Fresh Look at an Old Problem," *Human Resource Management* 35, no. 2 (summer 1996), pp. 163–180.

3. L. Ulrich and D. Trumbo, "The Selection Interview Since 1949," *Psychological Bulletin* 63 (1965), pp. 100–116, quoted in Michael McDaniel, et al., "The Validity of Employment Interviews," p. 599.

4. Laura Gollub Williamson, et al., "Employment Interview on Trial: Linking Interview Structure with Litigation Outcomes," *Journal of Applied Psychology* 82, no. 6 (1996), p. 900.

5. Alan Huffcutt, et al., "A Meta-Analytic Investigation of Cognitive Ability in Employment Interview Evaluations: Moderating Characteristics and Implications for Incremental Validity," *Journal of Applied Psychology* 81, no. 5 (1996), p. 459.

6. Duane Schultz and Sydney Schultz, *Psychology and Work Today* (Upper Saddle River, NJ: Prentice Hall, 1998), p. 830.

7. McDaniel, et al., "The Validity of Employment Interviews," p. 602.

8. Williamson, et al., "Employment Interview on Trial," p. 908.

9. Ibid., p. 601.

10. McDaniel, et al., "The Validity of Employment Interviews," p. 602.

11. Bill Stoneman, "Matching Personalities with Jobs Made Easier with Behavioral Interviews," *American Banker* 165, no. 229 (November 30, 2000), p. 8a.

12. "Job Hunt as Head Trip? More Companies Use Behavioral Interviews to Screen Candidates," *Los Angeles Times*, May 20, 2001, p. W. 1.

13. Martha Frase-Blunt, "Games Interviewers Play," *HR Magazine*, January 2001, pp. 104–114.

14. Shand, "Talent Scouts," pp. 52–53.

15. Arthur Pell, *Recruiting and Selecting Personnel* (New York: Regents, 1969), p. 119.

16. "Phone Interviews Might Be the Most Telling, Study Finds," *BNA Bulletin to Management*, September 1998, p. 273.

17. Douglas Rodgers, "Computer-Aided Interviewing Overcomes First Impressions," *Personnel Journal*, April 1987, pp. 148–152; see also Linda Thornburg, "Computer-Assisted Interviewing Shortens Hiring Cycle," *HR Magazine* 43, no. 2 (February 1998), p. 73ff.

18. Ibid.

19. Gary Robins, "Dial-an-Interview," *Stores*, June 1994, pp. 34–35.

20. William Bulkeley, "Replaced by Technology: Job Interviews," *Wall Street Journal*, August 22, 1994, pp. B1, B7.

21. Ibid.

22. For additional information on computer-aided interviewing's benefits, see, for example, Christopher Martin and Denise Nagao, "Some Effects of Computerized Interviewing on Job Applicant Responses," *Journal of Applied Psychology* 74, no. 1 (February 1989), pp. 72–80.

23. This is quoted from or paraphrased from Bulkeley, "Replaced by Technology," pp. B1, B7.

24. Jeff Moad, "Smile! You're Alive on the Air," *PC Week*, January 22, 2001, p. 54.

25. Timothy Judge, et al., "The Employment Interview: A Review of Recent Research and Recommendations for Future Research," *Human Resource Management* 10, no. 4 (2000), p. 392.

26. Huffcutt, et al., "A Meta-Analytic Investigation of Cognitive Ability in Employment Interview Evaluations," p. 459.

27. Williamson, "Employment Interview on Trial," p. 900.

28. Ibid.

29. This validity discussion and these findings are based on McDaniel, et al., "The Validity of Employment Interviews," pp. 607–610; the validities for situational, job-related, and psychological interviews were (.50), (.39), and (.29), respectively.

30. Mean validities were structured (.44) and unstructured (.33). The researchers note that in this case even the unstructured interviews were relatively structured, suggesting that "the validity of most unstructured interviews used in practice may be lower than the validity found in this study." Ibid., p. 609.

31. Murray Barrick, et al., "Accuracy of Interviewer Judgments of Job Applicant Personality Traits," *Personnel Psychology* 53 (2000), pp. 925–951.

32. McDaniel, et al., "The Validity of Employment Interviews," p. 608.

33. Anthony Dalessio and Todd Silverhart, "Combining Biodata Test and Interview Information: Predicting Decisions and Performance Criteria," *Personnel Psychology* 47 (1994), p. 313.

34. S. W. Constantin, "An Investigation of Information Favorability in the Employment Interview," *Journal of Applied Psychology* 61 (1976),

pp. 743–749. It should be noted that a number of the studies discussed in this chapter involve having interviewers evaluate interviews based on written transcripts (rather than face to face) and that a study suggests that this procedure may not be equivalent to having interviewers interview applicants directly. See Charles Gorman, William Grover, and Michael Doherty, "Can We Learn Anything About Interviewing Real People from 'Interviews' of Paper People? A Study of the External Validity Paradigm," *Organizational Behavior and Human Performance* 22, no. 2 (October 1978), pp. 165–192. See also John Binning, et al., "Effects of Pre-interview Impressions on Questioning Strategies in Same and Opposite Sex Employment Interviews," *Journal of Applied Psychology* 73, no. 1 (February 1988), pp. 30–37; and Sebastiana Fisicaro, "A Reexamination of the Relation Between Halo Error and Accuracy," *Journal of Applied Psychology* 73, no. 2 (May 1988), pp. 239–246.

35. David Tucker and Patricia Rowe, "Relationship Between Expectancy, Causal Attribution, and Final Hiring Decisions in the Employment Interview," *Journal of Applied Psychology* 64, no. 1 (February 1979), pp. 27–34. See also Robert Dipboye, Gail Fontenelle, and Kathleen Garner, "Effect of Previewing the Application on Interview Process and Outcomes," *Journal of Applied Psychology* 69, no. 1 (February 1984), pp. 118–128.

36. Anita Chaudhuri, "Beat the Clock: Applying for Job? A New Study Shows That Interviewers Will Make Up Their Minds about You Within a Minute," *The Guardian*, June 14, 2000, pp. 2–6.

37. Don Langdale and Joseph Weitz, "Estimating the Influence of Job Information on Interviewer Agreement," *Journal of Applied Psychology* 57 (1973), pp. 23–27; for a review of how to determine the human requirements of a job, see Anthony W. Simmons, "Selection Interviewing," *Employment Relations Today*, winter 1991, pp. 305–309.

38. R. E. Carlson, "Effects of Applicant Sample on Ratings of Valid Information in an Employment Setting," *Journal of Applied Psychology* 20 (1967), pp. 259–280.

39. R. E. Carlson, "Selection Interview Decisions: The Effects of Interviewer Experience, Relative Quota Situation, and Applicant Sample on Interview Decisions," *Personnel Psychology* 20 (1967), pp. 259–280.

40. T. V. McGovern and H. E. Tinsley, "Interviewer Evaluations of Interviewees' Nonverbal Behavior," *Journal of Vocational Behavior* 13 (1978), pp. 163–171. See also Keith Rasmussen Jr., "Nonverbal Behavior, Verbal Behavior, Resume Credentials, and Selection Interview Outcomes," *Journal of Applied Psychology* 60, no. 4 (1984), pp. 551–556; Robert Gifford, Cheuk Fan Ng, and Margaret Wilkinson, "Nonverbal Cues in the Employment Interview: Links Between Applicant Qualities and Interviewer Judgments," *Journal of Applied Psychology* 70, no. 4 (1984), pp. 729–736; Scott T. Fleishmann, "The Messages of Body Language in Job Interviews," *Employee Relations* 18, no. 2 (summer 1991), pp. 161–166.

41. Tim DeGroot and Stephen Motowidlo, "Why Visual and Vocal Interview Cues Can Affect Interviewers' Judgments and Predicted Job Performance," *Journal of Applied Psychology*, December 1999, pp. 968–984.

42. David Caldwell and Jerry Burger, "Personality Characteristics of Job Applicants and Success in Screening Interviews," *Personnel Psychology* 51 (1998), pp. 119–136.

43. Ibid., p. 130.

44. C. K. Stevens and A. L. Kristof, "Making the Right Impression: A Field Study of Applicant Impression Management During Interviews," *Journal of Applied Psychology* 80, pp. 587–606; Schultz and Schultz, *Psychology and Work Today*, p. 82.

45. See, for example, Madelaine Heilmann and Lewis Saruwatari, "When Beauty Is Beastly: The Effects of Appearance and Sex on Evaluation of Job Applicants for Managerial and Nonmanagerial Jobs," *Organizational Behavior and Human Performance* 23 (June 1979), pp. 360–372; and Cynthia Marlowe, Sondra Schneider, and Carnot Nelson, "Gender and Attractiveness Biases in Hiring Decisions: Are More Experienced Managers Less Biased?" *Journal of Applied Psychology* 81, no. 1 (1996), pp. 11–21.

46. Marlowe, et al., "Gender and Attractiveness Biases," p. 11.

47. Ibid., p. 18.

48. Ibid., p. 11.

49. Amelia J. Prewett-Livingston, et al., "Effects of Race on Interview Ratings in a Situational Panel Interview," *Journal of Applied Psychology* 81, no. 2 (1996), pp. 178–186.

50. Alan Huffcutt and Philip Roth, "Racial Group Differences in Employment Interview Evaluations," *Journal of Applied Psychology* 83, no. 2 (1998), pp. 179–189.

51. This is based on John F. Wymer III and Deborah A. Sudbury, "Employment Discrimination: 'Testers'—Will Your Hiring Practices 'Pass'?" *Employee Relations Law Journal* 17, no. 4 (spring 1992), pp. 623–633.

52. See, for example, *Lea v. Cone Mills Corp.*, 438 F2d 86 (1971).

53. Bureau of National Affairs, *Daily Labor Report*, December 5, 1990, p. D1.

54. Wymer and Sudbury, "Employment Discrimination," p. 629.

55. Urban Institute, *Opportunities Denied, Opportunities Diminished: Discrimination in Hiring*.

56. Adapted from Wymer and Sudbury, "Employment Discrimination," pp. 631–632.

57. Arthur Pell, "Nine Interviewing Pitfalls," *Managers Magazine*, January 1994, p. 20.

58. Thomas Dougherty, Daniel Turban, and John Callender, "Confirming First Impressions in the Employment Interview: A Field Study of Interviewer Behavior," *Journal of Applied Psychology* 79, no. 5 (1994), p. 663.

59. See Pell, "Nine Interviewing Pitfalls," p. 29; Parth Sarathi, "Making Selection Interviews Effective," *Management and Labor Studies* 18, no. 1 (1993), pp. 5–7.

60. Pell, "Nine Interviewing Pitfalls," p. 30.

61. This section is based on Elliot Pursell, et al., "Structured Interviewing," *Personnel Journal* 59, (November 1980), pp. 907–912 and G. Latham, et al., "The Situational Interview" *Journal of Applied Psychology* 65, (1980), pp. 422–427. See also Michael A. Campion, Elliott Pursell, and Barbara Brown, "Structured Interviewing," pp. 25–42; and Weekley and Gier, "Reliability and Validity of the Situational Interview," pp. 484–487.

62. See also Phillip Lowry, "The Structured Interview: An Alternative to the Assessment Center?" *Public Personnel Management* 23, no. 2 (summer 1994), pp. 201–215. See also Steven Maurer, "The Potential of the Situational Interview: Existing Research and Unresolved Issues," *Human Resource Management Review* 7, no. 2 (summer 1997), pp. 185–201.

63. Pursell, et al., "Structured Interviewing," p. 910.

64. From a speech by industrial psychologist Paul Green and contained in *BNA Bulletin to Management*, June 20, 1985, pp. 2–3.

65. Williamson, et al., "Employment Interview on Trial," p. 901; Michael Campion, David Palmer, and James Campion, "A Review of Structure in the Selection Interview," *Personnel Psychology* 50 (1997), pp. 655–702.

66. Unless otherwise specified, the following are based on Williamson, et al., "Employment Interview on Trial," pp. 901–902.

67. Campion, Palmer, and Campion, "A Review of Structure," p. 668.

68. Carlson, "Selection Interview Decisions," pp. 259–280.

69. Campion, Palmer, and Campion, "A Review of Structure," pp. 655–702.

70. "The Tables Have Turned," *American Management Association International*, September 1998, p. 6.

71. William Tullar, Terry Mullins, and Sharon Caldwell, "Effects of Interview Length and Applicant Quality on Interview Decision, Time," *Journal of Applied Psychology* 64 (December 1979), pp. 669–674. See also Tracy McDonald and Milton Hakel, "Effects of Applicants' Race, Sex, Suitability, and Answers on Interviewers' Questioning Strategy and Ratings," *Personnel Psychology* 38, no. 2 (summer 1985), pp. 321–334; David Caldwell and Jerry Burger, "Personality Characteristics of Job Applicants and Success in Screening Interviews," *Personnel Psychology* 51, no. 1 (spring 1998), pp. 119–136.

72. Edwin Walley, "Successful Interviewing Techniques," *CPA Journal*, September 1993, p. 70.

73. Pamela Kaul, "Interviewing Is Your Business," *Association Management*, November 1992, p. 29.

74. Walley, "Successful Interviewing Techniques," p. 70.

75. Jennifer Burnett, Chenche Fan, Stephen Motowidlo, and Tim DeGroot, "Interview Notes and Validity," *Personnel Psychology* 51 (1998), pp. 375–396.

76. Ibid., p. 395.

77. Robin Rimmer Hurst, "Video Interviewing. Take One!" *HR Magazine* November 1996, pp. 100–104.

78. This is based on John Drake, *Interviewing for Managers: A Complete Guide to Employment Interviewing* (New York, AMACOM, 1982).

79. Ibid.

80. Based on Gary Dessler, *Winning Commitment* (New York; McGraw-Hill Book Company, 1993). Similarly, see Glenn Bassett, "From Job Fit to

Cultural Compatibility: Evaluating Worker Skills and Temperament in the 90s," *Optimum, The Journal of Public Sector Management* 25, no. 2 (summer 1994), pp. 11–17.

81. Matthew Brelis, "Simple Strategy Makes Southwest a Model for Success," *Boston Globe*, November 5, 2000, p. F-1.

82. Chris Maynard, "New High-Tech Recruiting Tools: Unicycles, Yahtzee and Silly Putty," *Wall Street Journal*, June 6, 2000, p. B.14; see also Paul McNamara, "Extreme Interview," *Network World*, June 25, 2001, p. 65

Chapter 7

1. Cathy Cooper, "Connect Four," *People Management* 7, no. 3 (February 8, 2001), pp. 42–45.

2. For a recent discussion of socialization, see, for example, Georgia Chao, et al., "Organizational Socialization: Its Content and Consequences," *Journal of Applied Psychology* 79, no. 5 (1994), pp. 730–743.

3. Sabrina Hicks, "Successful Orientation Programs," *Training & Development*, April 2000, p. 59. See also Howard Klein and Natasha Weaver, "The Effectiveness of an Organizational Level Orientation Program in the Socialization of New Hires," *Personnel Psychology* 53 (2000), pp. 47–66.

4. John Wanous and Arnon Reichers, "New Employee Orientation Programs," *Human Resource Management Review* 10, no. 4 (2000), p. 442.

5. Susan Ashford and Jay Stewart Black, "Proactivity During Organizational Entry: The Role of Desire for Control," *Journal of Applied Psychology* 81, no. 2 (1996), pp. 199–214.

6. See, for example, Carolyn Wiley, "Training for the 90s: How Leading Companies Focus on Quality Improvement, Technological Change, and Customer Service," *Employee Relations Today*, spring 1993, p. 80.

7. See, for example, our discussion in Chapter 1. Also see ibid., p. 80.

8. The following is based on ibid., pp. 81–82.

9. Harley Frazis, Diane Herz, and Michael Horrigan, "Employer-Provided Training: Results from a New Survey," *Monthly Labor Review*, May 1995, pp. 3–17.

10. Christine Ellis and Sarah Gale, "A Seat at the Table," *Training*, March 2001, pp. 90–96.

11. "Training Receives Renewed Emphasis," *BNA Bulletin to Management*, October 31, 1996, p. 352.

12. Ibid.

13. Based on Kenneth Wexley and Gary Yukl, *Organizational Behavior and Personnel Psychology* (Burr Ridge, IL: McGraw-Hill, 1977), pp. 289–295; E. J. McCormick and J. Tiffin, *Industrial Psychology* (Upper Saddle River, NJ: Prentice Hall, 1974), pp. 232–240.

14. Wexley and Yukl, *Organizational Behavior*, pp. 289–295.

15. Janice A. Cannon-Bowers, et al., "Framework for Understanding Pre-Practice Conditions and Their Impact on Learning," *Personnel Psychology* 51 (1998), pp. 291–320.

16. Ibid., p. 305.

17. R. E. Silverman, *Learning Theory Applied to Training* (Reading, MA: Addison-Wesley, 1970), Chapter 8; McCormick and Tiffin, *Industrial Psychology*, pp. 239–240.

18. Kimberly A. Smith-Jentsch, et al., "Can Pre-Training Experiences Explain Individual Differences in Learning?" *Journal of Applied Psychology* 81, no. 1 (1996), pp. 110–116.

19. Ibid.

20. Kathryn Tyler, "Focus on Training," *HR Magazine*, May 2000, pp. 94–102.

21. Ibid.

22. This is based on Kenneth Wexley and Gary Latham, *Developing and Training Human Resources in Organizations* (Glenview, IL: Scott, Foresman, 1981), pp. 22–27. Note that these legal aspects apply equally to technical training and management development. See also Ron Zemke, "What is Technical Training, Anyway?" *Training* 23, no. 7 (July 1986), pp. 18–22. See also Bureau of National Affairs, "Sexual Harassment: Training Tips," *Fair Employment Practices*, June 25, 1987, p. 84.

23. Kenneth Sovereign, *Personnel Law* (Upper Saddle River, NJ: Prentice Hall, 1994), pp. 165–166.

24. Ibid., pp. 165–166; J. Fenton, William Ruud, and J. Kimbell, "Negligent Training Suits: A Recent Entry into the Corporate Employment Negligence Arena," *Labor Law Journal* 42, June 1991, p. 351.

25. These are based on Sovereign, *Personnel Law*, pp. 165–166.

26. B. A. Bass and J. A. Vaughan, "Assessing Training Needs," in Craig Schneier and Richard Beatty, *Personnel Administration Today* (Reading, MA: Addison-Wesley, 1978), p. 311. See also Ronald Ash and Edward Leving, "Job Applicant Training and Work Experience Evaluation: An Empirical Comparison of Four Methods," *Journal of Applied Psychology* 70, no. 3 (1985), pp. 572–576; John Lawrie, "Break the Training Ritual," *Personnel Journal* 67, no. 4 (April 1988), pp. 95–97; Theodore Lewis and David Bjorkquist, "Needs Assessment—A Critical Reappraisal," *Performance Improvement Quarterly* 5, no. 4 (1992), pp. 33–54; Sasha Cohen, "EPSS to Go," *Training and Development* 52, no. 3 (March 1998), pp. 54–57.

27. Tammy Galvin, "Birds of a Feather," *Training*, March 2001, pp. 58–68.

28. Leslie Goff, *Computerworld*, June 25, 2001, pp. 38–39.

29. See, for example, Gean Freeman, "Human Resources Planning—Training Needs Analysis," *Human Resources Planning* 39, no. 3 (fall 1993), pp. 32–34.

30. McCormick and Tiffin, *Industrial Psychology*, p. 245. See also James C. Georges, "The Hard Realities of Soft Skills Training," *Personnel Journal* 68, no. 4 (April 1989), pp. 40–45; Robert H. Buckham, "Applying Role Analysis in the Workplace," *Personnel* 64, no. 2 (February 1987), pp. 63–65; and J. Kevin Ford and Raymond Noe, "Self-Assessed Training Needs: The Effects of Attitudes Towards Training, Management Level, and Function," *Personnel Psychology* 40, no. 1 (spring 1987), pp. 39–54.

31. Nick Blanchard and James Thacker, *Training Systems, Strategies and Practices* (Upper Saddle River, NJ: Prentice Hall, 1999), pp. 138–139.

32. Tom Barron, "When Things Go Haywire," *Training and Development*, February 1999, pp. 25–27.

33. For an additional perspective, see Danny Langdon, "Objectives: Get Over Them," *Training and Development*, February 1999, pp. 54–58. See also Joan Brett and Don VandeWalle, "Goal Orientation and Goal Content As Predictors of Performance in a Training Program," *Journal of Applied Psychology* 84, no. 6 (1999), pp. 863–873.

34. Wexley and Latham, *Developing and Training*, p. 107.

35. Donna Goldwasser, "Me a Trainer?" *Training*, April 2001, pp. 60–66.

36. Ibid., pp. 107–112.

37. Oranit Davidson and Dov Eden, "Remedial Self-Fulfilling Prophecy: Two Field Experiments to Prevent Golem Effects Among Disadvantaged Women," *Journal of Applied Psychology* 85, no. 3 (2000), pp. 386–396.

38. Four steps in on-the-job training based on William Berliner and William McLarney, *Management Practice and Training* (Burr Ridge, IL: McGraw-Hill, 1974), pp. 442–443. See also Robert Sullivan and Donald Miklas, "On-the-Job Training That Works," *Training and Development Journal* 39, no. 5 (May 1985), pp. 118–120; Stephen B. Wehrenberg, "Supervisors as Trainees: The Long-Term Gains of OJT," *Personnel Journal* 66, no. 4 (April 1987), pp. 48–51.

39. Harley Frazis, Diane Herz, and Michael Horrigan, "Employer-Provided Training: Results from a New Survey," *Monthly Labor Review*, May 1995, p. 4.

40. "German Training Model Imported," *BNA Bulletin to Management*, December 19, 1996, p. 408.

41. Ibid.

42. Nancy Day, "Informal Learning Gets Results," *Workforce*, June 1998, p. 31.

43. Ibid.

44. Ibid.

45. Donald Michalak and Edwin G. Yager, *Making the Training Process Work* (New York: Harper & Row, 1979), pp. 108–111. See also Richard Wiegand, "Can All Your Trainees Hear You?" *Training and Development Journal* 41, no. 8 (August 1987), pp. 38–43.

46. Jacqueline Schmidt and Joseph Miller, "The Five-Minute Rule for Presentations," *Training and Development*, March 2000, pp. 16–17.

47. G. N. Nash, J. P. Muczyk, and F. L. Vettori, "The Role and Practical Effectiveness of Programmed Instruction," *Personnel Psychology* 24 (1971), pp. 397–418; Duane Schultz and Sydney Ellen Shultz, *Psychology and Work Today* (Upper Saddle River, NJ: Prentice Hall, 1998), pp. 181–183.

48. Wexley and Latham, *Developing and Training*, pp. 131–133. See also Teri O. Grady and Mike Matthews, "Video . . . Through the Eyes of the Trainee," *Training* 24, no. 7 (July 1987), pp. 57–62. For a description of the use of computer-based multimedia training, see Erica Schroeder, "Training Takes Off, Using Multimedia," *PC Week*, August 29, 1994, pp. 33–34.

49. Bill Ellett, "Encouraging the Heart," *Training and Development* 55, no. 4 (April 2001), p. 69.

50. Ibid.

51. Wexley and Latham, *Developing and Training*, p. 141. See also Raymond Wlozkowski, "Simulation," *Training and Development Journal* 39, no. 6 (June 1985), pp. 38–43.

52. See, for example, Tim Falconer, "No More Pencils, No More Books!" *Canadian Banker*, March–April 1994, pp. 21–25.

53. Ralph E. Ganger, "Training: Computer-Based Training Works," *Personnel Journal* 73, no. 11 (November 1994), pp. 51–52. See also Anat Arkin, "Computing: The Future Means of Training?" *Personnel Management* 26, no. 86 (August 1994), pp. 36–40.

54. For another example, see Mickey Williamson, "High-Tech Training," *byte*, December 1994, pp. 74–89.

55. Shari Caudron, "Your Learning Technology Primer," *Personnel Journal*, June 1996, p. 130.

56. Dina Berta, "Computer-Based Training Clicks with both Franchisees and Their Employees," *Nation's Restaurant News*, July 9, 2001, pp. 1, 18; see also Daniel Cable and Charles Parsons, "Socialization Tactics and Person-Organization Fit," *Personnel Psychology*, 54, 2001, pp. 1–23.

57. These are summarized in Rockley Miller, "New Training Looms," *Hotel and Motel Management*, April 4, 1994, pp. 26, 30.

58. Ibid., p. 26. Theresa Bechard, "IXL to Help FedEx with Online Training Program," *Memphis Business Journal* 21, no. 32 (December 10, 1999), p. 6.

59. Tyler, "Focus on Training," p. 96.

60. Blanchard and Thacker, *Effective Training*, p. 163.

61. Craig Marion, "What Is the EPSS Movement and What Does It Mean to Information Designers?" http://www.chesco.com/~cmarion/pcd/epssimplications.html.

62. http://www.epss.com/lb/casestud/casestud.htm.

63. Michael Blotzer, "Distance Learning," *Occupational Hazards*, March 2000, pp. 53–54.

64. Mary Boone and Susan Schulman, "Teletraining: A High-Tech Alternative," *Personnel* 62, no. 5 (May 1985), pp. 4–9. See also Ron Zemke, "The Rediscovery of Video Teleconferencing," *Training* 23, no. 9 (September 1986), pp. 28–36; and Carol Haig, "Clinics Fill Training Niche," *Personnel Journal* 66, no. 9 (September 1987), pp. 134–140.

65. Joseph Giusti, David Baker, and Peter Braybash, "Satellites Dish Out Global Training," *Personnel Journal*, June 1991, pp. 80–84.

66. "Macy's Goes 'On Air' to Inform Employees," *BNA Bulletin to Management*, May 15, 1997, p. 160.

67. "Cadillac Offers a Top-of-the-Line Training Program," *Personnel Journal*, February 1996, p. 25.

68. "Personnel Shop Talk," *BNA Bulletin to Management*, February 12, 1998, p. 46.

69. Michael Emery and Margaret Schubert, "A Trainer's Guide to Videoconferencing," *Training*, June 1993, p. 60.

70. Ibid.

71. "Employer to Learn the Benefits of Distance Learning," *BNA Bulletin to Management*, April 25, 1996, p. 130.

72. Caudron, "Your Learning Technology Primer," pp. 120–136.

73. These are based on or quoted from Emery and Schubert, "A Trainer's Guide to Videoconferencing," p. 61.

74. Larry Stevens, "The Internet: Your Newest Training Tool?" *Personnel Journal*, July 1996, pp. 27–31.

75. Karl Rayl, "GTE's Training Goes High-Tech," *Workforce*, April 1998, pp. 36–40.

76. Ellen Zimmerman, "Better Training Is Just a Click Away," *Workforce*, January 2001, pp. 36–42.

77. David Kirkpatrick, "The Portal of the Future? Your Boss Will Run It," *Fortune*, August 2, 1999, pp. 222–227.

78. Tom Barron, "A Portrait of Learning Portals," http://www.learningcircuits.com/may2000/barron.html.

79. Dana Baynton, "Cyber Learning Fortunes," *Training*, April 2001, p. 22.

80. Eileen Garger, "Goodbye Training, Hello Learning," *Workforce*, November 1999, pp. 35–42.

81. "Creating Portals to Effective Learning," *Training* 538, no. 1, January 2001, pp. 41–42.

82. Cathy Cooper, "Connect Four," *People Management* 7, no. 3 (February 8, 2001), pp. 42–45.

83. Ibid.

84. Dannah Baynton, "America's $60 Billion Problem," *Training* 38, no. 5 (May 2001), p. 51.

85. "Skill Deficiencies Pose Increasing Problems," *BNA Bulletin to Management*, October 26, 1995, pp. 337–338.

86. John Comings, et al., "Today's Economy Demands New Level of Literacy," *Boston Business Journal* 21, no. 11 (April 20, 2001), p. 63.

87. This is based on Ellen Sherman, "Back to Basics to Improve Skills," *Personnel*, July 1989, pp. 22–26.

88. Baynton, "America's $60 Billion Problem," p. 51.

89. Nancy Lynn Bernardon, "Let's Erase Illiteracy from the Workplace," *Personnel*, January 1989, p. 92.

90. Kathryn Tyler, "Brushing Up on the Three Rs," *HR Magazine*, October 1999, p. 88.

91. Tracy Tuten, et al., "The Impact of an Education and Training Program on Attitudes of Employees Toward Coworkers with AIDS," *SAM Advanced Management Journal* 65, no. 2 (spring 2000), p. 30.

92. Susan Vaughn, "Companies Work Not Over on HIV and AIDS Education," *Los Angeles Times*, July 8, 2001, p. W1.

93. Jeffrey Mello, "AIDS Education in the Work Place," *Training and Development Journal*, December 1990, pp. 65–70.

94. This is based on Sylvia Odenwald, "A Guide for Global Training," *Training and Development*, July 1993, pp. 22–31.

95. For a full description of these programs as well as the names of the vendors, see ibid., pp. 24–27.

96. See Joyce Santora, "Kinney Shoes Steps into Diversity," *Personnel Journal*, September 1991, p. 74.

97. Willie Hopkins, Karen Sterkel-Powell, and Shirley Hopkins, "Training Priorities for a Diverse Workforce," *Public Personnel Management* 23, no. 3 (fall 1994), p. 433.

98. "Adams Mark Hotel & Resorts Launches Diversity Training Program," *Hotel and Motel Management* 216, no. 6 (April 2001), p. 15.

99. Henry Unger, "Coca-Cola Employees to Attend Diversity Training Annually," *Knight Ridder/Tribune Business News*, October 10, 2000, item 0028501d.

100. Santora, "Kinney Shoes Steps into Diversity," pp. 72–77.

101. Sara Rynes and Benson Rosen, "What Makes Diversity Programs Work?" *HR Magazine*, October 1994, p. 64. See also Thomas Diamante and Leo Giglio, "Managing a Diverse Workforce: Training as a Cultural Intervention Strategy," *Leadership and Organization Development Journal* 15, no. 2 (1994), pp. 13–17.

102. Tom Anderson, "Hotels Training Employees in Handling Customer Upsets," *St. Louis Business Journal* 21, no. 30 (March 30, 2001), p. 38.

103. Jennifer Laabs, "Serving Up a New Level of Customer Service at Québecor," *Workforce* 80, no. 3 (March 2001), pp. 40–42.

104. Brenda Sunoo, "Results-Oriented Customer Service Training," *Workforce* 80, no. 5 (May 2001), p. 84.

105. This is based on Jennifer Laabs, "Team Training Goes Outdoors," *Personnel Journal*, June 1991, pp. 56–63.

106. Ibid., p. 56. See also Shari Caudron, "Teamwork Takes Work," *Personnel Journal* 73, no. 2 (February 1994), pp. 41–49.

107. Jeff Barbian, "Now Work Cooking," *Training*, February 2001, p. 26.

108. Jan Hayes, "Good Start on Team Success," *Training Media Review* 9, no. 1 (January 2001), p. 13.

109. This is based on Norman Nopper, "Reinventing the Factory with Lifelong Learning," *Training*, May 1993, pp. 55–57.

110. Ibid., p. 56.

111. Ibid.

112. Ibid., p. 57. For another example, see also Kelly Dunn, "Rutgers University Creates Culture of Lifelong Learning," *Workforce* 79, no. 5 (May 2000), pp. 108–109.

113. For discussions of the steps in succession planning, see, for example, Kenneth Nowack, "The Secrets of Succession," *Training and Development*, November 1994, pp. 49–55; Donald Brookes, "In Management Succession: Who Moves Up?" *Human Resources*, January–February 1995, pp. 11–13.

114. Jack Zenger, Dave Ulrich, and Norm Smallwood, "The New Leadership Development," *Training and Development*, March 2000, pp. 22–27.

115. Wexley and Latham, *Developing and Training*, p. 118.

116. This is based on Nancy Fox, "Action Learning Comes to Industry," *Harvard Business Review* 56 (September–October 1977), pp. 158–168. See

also Nancy Dixon, "Action Learning," *Performance Improvement Quarterly* 11, no. 1 (1998), pp. 44–58.

117. Gillian Flynn, "Thinktanks Power Up Employees," *Personnel Journal,* June 1996, pp. 100–108.

118. Ibid., p. 101.

119. Bernard Bass and Bruce Avolio, "Shatter the Glass Ceiling: Women May Make Better Managers," *Human Resource Management* 33, no. 4 (winter 1994), pp. 549–560.

120. Chris Argyris, "Some Limitations of the Case Method: Experiences in a Management Development Program," *Academy of Management Review* 5, no. 2 (1980), pp. 291–298.

121. Chris Whitcomb, "Scenario-Based Training at the FBI," *Training and Development,* June 1999, pp. 42–46.

122. For a discussion of management games and also other noncomputerized training and development simulations, see Charlene Marner Solomon, "Simulation Training Builds Teams Through Experience," *Personnel Journal,* June 1993, pp. 100–109; Kim Slack, "Training for the Real Thing," *Training and Development,* May 1993, pp. 79–89; Bruce Lierman, "How to Develop a Training Simulation," *Training and Development,* February 1994, pp. 50–52.

123. American Management Association, *Catalog of Seminars: April–December, 1998.*

124. Norman Maier, Allen Solem, and Ayesha Maier, *The Role Play Technique* (San Diego: University Associates, 1975), pp. 2–3. See also David Swink, "Role-Play Your Way to Learning," *Training and Development,* May 1993, pp. 91–97; Alan Test, "Why I Do Not Like to Role Play," *American Salesman,* August 1994, pp. 7–20.

125. This section is based on Allen Kraut, "Developing Managerial Skill via Modeling Techniques: Some Positive Research Findings—A Symposium," *Personnel Psychology* 29, no. 3 (autumn 1976), pp. 325–361.

126. Steve Simon and Jon Werner, "Computer Training Through Behavioral Modeling, Self-Paced, and Instructional Approaches: A Field Experiment," *Journal of Applied Psychology* 81, no. 6 (1996), pp. 648–659.

127. Thomas Stewart, "How GE Keeps Those Ideas Coming," *Fortune,* August 12, 1991, p. 43.

128. Martha Peak, "Go Corporate U!" *Management Review* 86, no. 2 (February 1997), pp. 33–37.

129. Russell Gerbman, "Corporate Universities 101," *HR Magazine,* February 2000, pp. 101–106.

130. Liz Thach and Tom Heinselman, "Executive Coaching Defined," *Training and Development,* March 1999, pp. 35–39.

131. Paul Blocklyn, "Developing the International Executive," *Personnel,* March 1989, pp. 44–47. See also T. S. Chan, "Developing International Managers: A Partnership Approach," *Journal of Management Development* 13, no. 3 (1994), pp. 38–46.

132. This section is based on ibid. See also "Developing Global Executives," *BNA Bulletin to Management* 44, no. 10 (March 11, 1993), pp. 73–74.

133. Carolyn Wiley, "Training for the 90s," p. 79.

134. Laurie Bassi, "Upgrading the U.S. Workplace: Do Reorganization & Education Help?" *Monthly Labor Review,* May 1995, pp. 37–47.

135. Ann Bartol, "Productivity Gains from the Implementation of Employee Training Programs," *Industrial Relations* 33, no. 4 (October 1994), pp. 411–425.

136. Pamela Kidder and Janice Rouiller, "Evaluating the Success of a Large-Scale Training Effort," *National Productivity Review* 16, no. 2 (1997), pp. 79–89.

137. See, for example, Charlie Morrow, M. Quintin Jarrett, and Melvin Rupinski, "An Investigation of the Effect and Economic Utility of Corporate-Wide Training," *Personnel Psychology* 50 (1997), pp. 91–119.

138. R. E. Catalano and D. L. Kirkpatrick, "Evaluating Training Programs—The State of the Art," *Training and Development Journal* 22, no. 5 (May 1968), pp. 2–9. See also J. Kevin Ford and Steven Wroten, "Introducing New Methods for Conducting Training Evaluation and for Linking Training Evaluation to Program Redesign," *Personnel Psychology* 37, no. 4 (winter 1984), pp. 651–666; Basil Paquet, et al., "The Bottom Line," *Training and Development Journal* 41, no. 5 (May 1987), pp. 27–33; Harold E. Fisher and Ronald Weinberg, "Make Training Accountable: Assess Its Impact," *Personnel Journal* 67, no. 1 (January 1988), pp.

73–75; Timothy Baldwin and J. Kevin Ford, "Transfer of Training: A Review and Directions of Future Research," *Personnel Psychology* 41, no. 1 (spring 1988), pp. 63–105; Anthony Montebello and Maurine Haga, "To Justify Training, Test, Test Again," *Personnel Journal* 73, no. 1 (January 1994), pp. 83–87; John Barron, et al., "How Well Do We Measure Training?" *Journal of Labor Economics* 15, no. 3 (July 1997), pp. 507–528.

139. Donald Kirkpatrick, "Effective Supervisory Training and Development, Part 3: Outside Programs," *Personnel* 62, no. 2 (February 1985), pp. 39–42. See also James Bell and Deborah Kerr, "Measuring Training Results: Key to Managerial Commitment," *Training and Development Journal* 41, no. 1 (January 1987), pp. 70–73. Among the reasons training might not pay off on the job are a mismatching of courses and trainee's needs, supervisory slipups (with supervisors signing up trainees and then forgetting to have them attend the sessions when the training session is actually given), and no help applying skills on the job. For a discussion, see Ruth Colvin Clark, "Nine Ways to Make Training Pay Off on the Job," *Training* 23, no. 11 (November 1986), pp. 83–87. See also Herman Birnbrauer, "Troubleshooting Your Training Program," *Training and Development Journal* 41, no. 9 (September 1987), pp. 18–20; George Bickerstaffe, "Measuring the Gains from Training," *Personnel Management,* November 1993, pp. 48–51; Jim Spoor, "You Can Quantify Training Dollars and Program Value," *HR Focus,* May 1993, p. 3; Jack Trynor, "Is Training a Good Investment?" *Financial Analyst Journal,* September–October 1994, pp. 6–8; Sarah Dolliver, "The Missing Link: Evaluating Training Programs," *Supervision,* November 1994, pp. 10–12.

140. This is based on George Alliger, Scott Tannenbaum, Winston Bennett Jr., Holly Traver, and Allison Shotland, "A Meta-Analysis of the Relations Among Training Criteria," *Personnel Psychology* 50 (1997), pp. 341–358. See also Robert Rowden, "A Practical Guide to Assessing the Value of Training in Your Company," *Employee Relations Today* 25, no. 2 (summer 1998), pp. 65–73.

141. Todd Raphel, "What Learning Management Reports Do for You," *Workforce* 80, no. 6 (June 2001), pp. 56–58.

Chapter 8

1. Ben Nagler, "Recasting Employees into Teams," *Workforce,* January 1998, pp. 101–106.

2. Roberta Russell and Bernard Taylor III, *Operations Management* (Upper Saddle River, NJ: Prentice Hall, 1998), pp. 324–336.

3. Edward Lawler III and Susan Mohrman, "Beyond the Vision: What Makes HR Effective?" *Human Resource Planning* 23, no. 4 (December 2000), p. 10.

4. Karen Jansen, "The Emerging Dynamics of Change: Resistance, Readiness, and Momentum," *Human Resource Planning* 23, no. 2 (June 2000), p. 53.

5. Edgar Schein, *Organizational Culture and Leadership* (San Francisco: Jossey-Bass, 1985), pp. 224–237; Peter Wright, Mark Kroll, and John Parnell, *Strategic Management Concepts* (Upper Saddle River, NJ: Prentice Hall, 1996), pp. 233–236. See also Thomas Begley and David Boyd, "Articulating Corporate Values Through Human Resource Policies," *Business Horizons* 43, no. 4 (July 2000), pp. 8–12.

6. Jennifer Laabs, "MetLife Shifts Culture Quickly," *Workforce* 80, no. 7, p. 18.

7. Roger Harrison, "Choosing the Depth of Organization Intervention," *Journal of Applied Behavioral Science* 2 (April–May–June, 1970), pp. 181–202. See also Aslaug Mikkelsen and Per Oystein, "Learning from Parallel Organizational Development Efforts in Two Public Sector Settings: Findings from Research in Norway," *Public Personnel Administration* 18, no. 1 (spring 1998) p. 5–22.

8. David Upton, "What Really Makes Factories Flexible?" *Harvard Business Review,* July–August 1995, p. 75.

9. The 10 steps are based on Michael Beer, Russell Eisenstat, and Burt Spector, "Why Change Programs Don't Produce Change," *Harvard Business Review,* November–December 1990, pp. 158–166; Thomas Cummings and Christopher Worley, *Organization Development and Change* (Minneapolis: West Publishing Company, 1993); John P. Kotter, "Leading Change: Why Transformation Efforts Fail," *Harvard Business Review,* March–April 1995, pp. 59–66; and John P. Kotter, *Leading*

Change (Boston: Harvard Business School Press, 1996). Change doesn't necessarily have to be painful. See, for example, Eric Abrahamson, "Change Without Pain," *Harvard Business Review,* July–August 2000, pp. 75–79. And some people are just more open to change than are others. As just one example, self-esteem and optimism were related to higher levels of change acceptance in one recent study: Connie Wanberg, "Predictors and Outcomes of Openness to Changes in a Reorganizing Workplace," *Journal of Applied Psychology* 85, no. 1 (2000), pp. 132–42. See also Michael Beer and Nitin Nohria, "Cracking the Code of Change," *Harvard Business Review,* June 2000, pp. 133–141.

10. Kotter, "Leading Change," p. 85.

11. Ibid., pp. 90–91.

12. Noel Tichy and Ram Charan, "The CEO as Coach: An Interview with Allied Signal's Lawrence A. Bossidy," *Harvard Business Review,* March–April 1995, p. 77. See also Nicholas DiFonzo and Prashant Borgia, "A Tale of Two Corporations: Managing Uncertainty During Organizational Change," *Human Resource Management* 37, nos. 3 & 4 (winter 1998), pp. 95–304.

13. This is based on Kotter, "Leading Change," pp. 60–61.

14. Ibid., p. 65.

15. Beer, Eisenstat, and Spector, "Why Change Programs Don't Produce Change," p. 164.

16. *Workforce,* September 1997, p. 99.

17. Cummings and Worley, *Organization Development,* p. 3.

18. Based on J. T. Campbell and M. D. Dunnette, "Effectiveness of T-Group Experiences in Managerial Training and Development," *Psychological Bulletin* 7 (1968), pp. 73–104; reprinted in W. E. Scott and L. L. Cummings, *Readings in Organizational Behavior and Human Performance* (Burr Ridge, IL: McGraw-Hill, 1973), p. 571.

19. Robert J. House, *Management Development* (Ann Arbor, MI: Bureau of Industrial Relations, University of Michigan, 1967), p. 71; Louis White and Kevin Wooten, "Ethical Dilemmas in Various Stages of Organizational Development," *Academy of Management Review* 8, no. 4 (1983), pp. 690–697.

20. Wendell French and Cecil Bell Jr., *Organization Development* (Upper Saddle River, NJ: Prentice Hall, 1995), pp. 171–193.

21. Benjamin Schneider, Steven Ashworth, A. Catherine Higgs, and Linda Carr, "Design Validity, and Use of Strategically Focused Employee Attitude Surveys," *Personnel Psychology* 49 (1996), pp. 695–705.

22. Ibid., p. 74.

23. Cummings and Worley, *Organization Development,* p. 501.

24. For a description of how to make OD a part of organizational strategy, see Aubrey Mendelow and S. Jay Liebowitz, "Difficulties in Making OD a Part of Organizational Strategy," *Human Resource Planning* 12, no. 4 (1995), pp. 317–329.

25. James Evans, et al., *Applied Production and Operations Management* (St. Paul, MN: West Publishing Company, 1984), p. 39.

26. Based in part on Joel E. Ross, *Total Quality Management: Text, Cases and Readings* (Delray Beach, FL: St. Lucie Press, 1993), p. 1.

27. Barry Render and Jay Heizer, *Principles of Operations Management* (Upper Saddle River, NJ: Prentice Hall, 1997), p. 96. Manufacturing establishments were more likely to use total quality management and team approaches, according to one study. See Larry Hunter, "The Adoption of Innovative Work Practices in Service Establishments," *International Journal of Human Resource Management* 11, no. 3 (June 2000), pp. 477–496.

28. Gaylen Chandler and Glenn McEvoy, "Human Resource Management, TQM, and Firm Performance in Small and Medium-Sized Enterprises," *Entrepreneurship: Theory and Practice* 25, no. 1 (fall 2000), p. 43.

29. Russell and Taylor, *Operations Management,* p. 81.

30. Joseph DeFeo, "An ROI Story: The Black Belts of Six Sigma," *Training and Development,* July 2000, pp. 25–33; Joseph DeFeo, "Six Sigma: New Opportunities for HR, New Career Growth for Employees," *Employee Relations Today* 27, no. 2 (summer 2000), pp. 1–6.

31. Rob Murakami, "How to Implement ISO 9000," *CMA Magazine,* March 1994, p. 18.

32. Sidney Emmons, "ISO 9000 on a Shoestring," *Quality Progress,* May 1994, p. 50; see also Darren McCabe and Adrian Wilkinson, "The Rise and Fall of TQM: The Vision, Meaning, and Operation of Change," *Industrial Relations Journal* 29, no. 1 (March 1998) pp. 18–29.

33. Rob Murakami, "How to Implement ISO 9000," p. 19.

34. See, for example, Cheryl Dahle, "Extreme Teams," *Fast Company,* November 1999, pp. 311–326.

35. See, for example, Brian Dumaine, "Who Needs a Boss?" *Fortune,* May 7, 1990, p. 52; David Hames, "Productivity-Enhancing Work Innovations: Remedies for What Ails Hospitals?" *Hospital and Health Services Administration* 36, no. 4 (winter 1991), pp. 551–552. See also Shari Caudron, "Are Self-Directed Teams Right for Your Company?" *Personnel Journal,* December 1993, pp. 76–84; Kenneth Hultman, "It's a Team Effort," *Training and Development Journal* 52, no. 2 (February 1998), pp. 12–13.

36. Rudy Yandrick, "A Team Effort," *HR Magazine,* June 2001, p. 1141.

37. Mark Henricks: "Give It Away," *Entrepreneur* 28, no. 5 (May 2000), p. 117.

38. Gary Dessler, *Management: Leading People and Organizations in the 21st Century* (Upper Saddle River, NJ: Prentice Hall, 1998), pp. 476–478.

39. George Neuman and Julia Wright, "Team Effectiveness: Beyond Skills and Cognitive Ability," *Journal of Applied Psychology* 84, no. 3 (1999), pp. 376–389.

40. Adapted from Best Manufacturing Practices Center of Excellence, copyright 1998.

41. Nagler, "Recasting Employees into Teams," pp. 101–106.

42. Ibid., p. 102.

43. Ibid., p. 103.

44. Ibid.

45. For employee involvement survey data, see Lee Towe, "Survey Finds Employee Involvement a Priority for Necessary Innovation," *National Productivity Review* 9, no. 1 (winter 1989–90), pp. 3–15.

46. "Despite Effectiveness, Empowerment Efforts Far from Universal," *BNA Bulletin to Management,* June 11, 1998, p. 181.

47. John Hickey and Jill Casner-Lott, "How to Get True Employee Participation," *Training and Development* 52, no. 2 (February 1998), pp. 58–62.

48. Tom Brown, "The Empowerment Myth," *Across the Board, New York* 38, no. 2 (March/April 2001), pp. 71–72.

49. Jennifer Laabs, "Paving the Way to Profitability," *Workforce* at www.workforce.com/ar. . .topicnane=workforce_oppimas_award_winners, accessed August 6, 2001.

50. This is based on Dean McFarlin, Paul Sweeney, and John Cotton, "Attitudes Toward Employee Participation in Decision-Making: A Comparison of European and American Managers in a United States Multinational Company," *Human Resource Management* 31, no. 4 (winter 1992), pp. 363–383.

51. Ibid., p. 371.

52. These are quoted from ibid., p. 379.

53. Michael Hammer and James Champy, *Reengineering the Corporation* (New York: Harper Business, 1994), p. 32.

54. Ibid., pp. 36–38.

55. For other examples, see David Allen and Robert Nafius, "Dreaming and Doing: Reengineering GTE Telephone Operations," *Planning Review* (March–April 1993), pp. 28–31; D. Brian Harrison and Maurice Pratt, "A Methodology for Reengineering Businesses," *Planning Review* (March–April 1993), pp. 6–11.

56. Hugh Willmott, "Business Process Reengineering and Human Resource Management," *Personnel Review* 3, no. 3 (May 1994), p. 34. See also Bob Kane, "Downsizing, TQM, Reengineering, Learning Organizations, and HRM Strategy," *Asia-Pacific Journal of HRM* 38, no. 1 (2000), pp. 26–49.

57. James Champy, *Reengineering Management* (New York: Harper Business, 1995), p. 104.

58. William Tullar, "Compensation Consequences of Re-engineering," *Journal of Applied Psychology* 83, no. 6 (1998), pp. 975–980.

59. Hammer and Champy, *Reengineering the Corporation,* p. 68.

60. Ibid., p. 70.

61. Ibid., p. 71.

62. Ibid.

63. "Percent of Full-Time Wage and Salary Workers Who Had Flexible Work Schedules, by Occupational Group, May 1997," *Occupational Outlook Quarterly* (fall 1998), p. 60.

64. Donald Peterson, "Flextime in the United States: The Lessons of Experience," *Personnel* 57 (January–February 1980), pp. 29–31.

65. See J. C. Swart, "Flextime's Debit and Credit Option," *Personnel Journal* 58 (January–February 1979), pp. 10–12; and Sarah Gale, "Formalized

Flextime: The Perk that Brings Productivity," *Workforce* 80, no. 2 (February 2001), p. 38.

66. "Improving Well-Being and Morale 24 Hours a Day," *BNA Bulletin to Management,* August 19, 1999.

67. Boris Baltes, et al., "Flexible and Compressed Workweek Schedules: A Meta-Analysis of Their Effects on Work-Related Criteria," *Journal of Applied Psychology* 84, no. 4 (1999), pp. 496–513.

68. "Improving Well-Being and Morale 24 Hours a Day."

69. Commerce Clearing House, *Ideas and Trends,* February 26, 1982, p. 61; Charlene Marmer Solomon, "Job Sharing: One Job, Double Headache?" *Personnel Journal,* September 1994, pp. 88–96.

70. Judith Letterman, "Two People, One Job," *New York Times,* January 14, 2001, p. 8.

71. William VanWinkle, "Your Away-from-Home Office," *Home Office Computing* 19, no. 1 (January 2001), p. 54.

Chapter 9

1. Kenneth Teel, "Performance Appraisal: Current Trends, Persistent Process," *Personnel Journal,* April 1980, pp. 296–301. See also Christina Banks and Kevin Murphy, "Toward Narrowing the Research-Practice Gap in Performance Appraisals," *Personnel Psychology* 38, no. 2 (summer 1985), pp. 335–346. For a description of how to implement an improved performance appraisal system, see, for example, Ted Cocheu, "Performance Appraisal: A Case in Point," *Personnel Journal* 65, no. 9 (September 1986), pp. 48–53; William H. Wagel, "Performance Appraisal with a Difference," *Personnel* 64, no. 2 (February 1987), pp. 4–6; Jeanette Cleveland, et al., "Multiple Uses of Performance Appraisal: Prevalence and Correlates," *Journal of Applied Psychology* 74, no. 1 (February 1989), pp. 130–135; Ian Carlton and Martyn Sloman, "Performance Appraisal in Practice," *Human Resource Management Journal* 2, no. 3 (spring 1992), pp. 80–94. See also "Performance Evaluations: Is It Time for a Makeover?" *HR Focus,* November 2000, p. 11; "Performance Appraisal Reappraised," *Harvard Business Review* 78, no. 1 (January 2000), p. 21.

2. John (Jack) Welch, broadcast interview at Fairfield University, C-Span, May 5, 2001.

3. Teel, "Performance Appraisal," p. 301. For a good explanation of why sole reliance on appraisal by supervisors may not be a good idea, see Keki Bhote, "Boss Performance Appraisal: A Metric Whose Time Has Gone," *Employment Relations Today* 21, no. 1 (spring 1994), pp. 1–9.

4. Ibid. See also Martin Friedman, "Ten Steps to Objective Appraisals," *Personnel Journal* 65, no. 6 (June 1986).

5. For a recent discussion, see Gary English, "Tuning Up for Performance Management," *Training and Development Journal,* April 1991, pp. 56–60.

6. This is based on James Buford Jr., Bettye Burkhalter, and Grover Jacobs, "Link Job Descriptions to Performance Appraisals," *Personnel Journal,* June 1988, pp. 132–140.

7. Del Jones, "More Firms Cut Workers Ranked at Bottom to Make Way for Talent," *USA Today,* May 30, 2001, p. B.01.

8. John Greenwald, "Rank and Fire," *Time* 157, no. 24, June 18, 2001, pp. 38–40.

9. This is based on Commerce Clearing House, "Merck's New Performance Appraisal/Merit Pay System Is Based on Bell-Shaped Distribution," *Ideas and Trends,* May 17, 1989, pp. 88–90.

10. Ellen Paris, "Banished Inquisition," *Entrepreneur* 29, no. 5 (May 2001), p. 32.

11. See, for example, Timothy Keaveny and Anthony McGann, "A Comparison of Behavioral Expectation Scales and Graphic Rating Scales," *Journal of Applied Psychology* 60 (1975), pp. 695–703. See also John Ivancevich, "A Longitudinal Study of Behavioral Expectation Scales: Attitudes and Performance," *Journal of Applied Psychology* 30, no. 3 (autumn 1986), pp. 619–628.

12. Based on Donald Schwab, Herbert Heneman III, and Thomas DeCotiis, "Behaviorally Anchored Scales: A Review of the Literature," *Personnel Psychology* 28 (1975), pp. 549–562. For a discussion, see also Uco Wiersma and Gary Latham, "The Practicality of Behavioral Observation Scales, Behavioral Expectations Scales, and Trait Scales," *Personnel Psychology* 30, no. 3 (autumn 1986), pp. 619–628.

13. Lawrence Fogli, Charles Hulin, and Milton Blood, "Development of First Level Behavioral Job Criteria," *Journal of Applied Psychology* 55 (1971), pp. 3–8. See also Terry Dickenson and Peter Fellinger, "A Comparison of the Behaviorally Anchored Rating and Fixed Standard Scale Formats," *Journal of Applied Psychology,* April 1980, pp. 147–154. See also Joseph Maiorca, "How to Construct Behaviorally Anchored Rating Scales (BARS) for Employee Evaluations," *Supervision,* August 1997, pp. 15–19.

14. Keaveny and McGann, "A Comparison of Behavioral Expectation Scales," pp. 695–703; Schwab, Heneman, and DeCotiis, "Behaviorally Anchored Rating Scales"; and James Goodale and Ronald Burke, "Behaviorally Based Rating Scales Need Not Be Job Specific," *Journal of Applied Psychology* 60 (June 1975).

15. Kevin R. Murphy and Joseph Constans, "Behavioral Anchors as a Source of Bias in Rating," *Journal of Applied Psychology* 72, no. 4 (November 1987), pp. 573–577; Aharon Tziner, "A Comparison of Three Methods of Performance Appraisal with Regard to Goal Properties, Goal Perception, and Ratee Satisfaction," *Group & Organization Management* 25, no. 2, June 2000, pp. 175–191.

16. See, for example, Edward Baig, "So You Hate Rating Your Workers?" *Business Week,* August 22, 1994, p. 14.

17. Gary Meyer, "Performance Reviews Made Easy, Paperless," *HR Magazine,* October 2000, pp. 181–184.

18. Ann Harrington, "Workers of the World, Rate Your Boss!" *Fortune* 16 (2000), pp. 340–342.

19. "Appraisal Puts 15 Leading HRIS's to the Test," *BNA Bulletin to Management,* October 26, 2000, p. 340.

20. Jeffrey Stanton and Janet Barnes-Farrell, "Effects of Electronic Performance Monitoring on Personal Control, Task Satisfaction, and Task Performance," *Journal of Applied Psychology* 81, no. 6 (1996), p. 738.

21. Ibid., p. 738.

22. See Martin Levy, "Almost-Perfect Performance Appraisals," *Personnel Journal* 68, no. 4 (April 1989), pp. 76–83, for a good example of how one company fine-tuned its form for individual performance.

23. Andrew Solomonson and Charles Lance, "Examination of the Relationship Between True Halo and Halo Effort in Performance Ratings," *Journal of Applied Psychology* 82, no. 5 (1997), pp. 665–674.

24. Teel, "Performance Appraisal," p. 298.

25. Ted Turnasella, "Dagwood Bumstead, Will You Ever Get That Raise?" *Compensation and Benefits Review,* September–October 1995, pp. 25–27. See also Solomonson and Lance, "Examination of the Relationship Between True Halo and Halo Effort," pp. 665–674.

26. I. M. Jawahar and Charles Williams, "Where All the Children Are Above Average: The Performance Appraisal Purpose Affect," *Personnel Psychology* 50 (1997), p. 905.

27. Ibid., p. 921.

28. For a discussion of this see, for example, Wayne Cascio, *Applied Psychology in Personnel Management* (Reston, VA: Reston Publishing, 1978), pp. 337–341.

29. B. Rosen and T. H. Gerdee, "The Nature of Job Related Age Stereotypes," *Journal of Applied Psychology* 61 (1976), pp. 180–183.

30. Gerald Ferris, Valerie Yates, David Gilmour, and Kendrith Rowland, "The Influence of Subordinate Age on Performance Ratings and Casual Attributions," *Personnel Psychology* 38, no. 3 (autumn 1985), pp. 545–557. As another example, see Gregory Dobbins and Jeanne Russell, "The Biasing Effects of Subordinate Likeableness on Leader's Responses to Poor Performers: A Laboratory and Field Study," *Personnel Psychology* 39, no. 4 (winter 1986), pp. 759–778. See also Michael E. Benedict and Edward Levine, "Delay and Distortion: Passive Influences on Performance Appraisal Effectiveness," *Journal of Applied Psychology* 73, no. 3 (August 1988), pp. 507–514; James Smither, et al., "Effect of Prior Performance Information on Ratings of Present Performance: Contrast Versus Assimilation Revisited," *Journal of Applied Psychology* 73, no. 3 (August 1988), pp. 487–496.

31. Michael Mount, et al., "Rater-Ratee Race Effects in Developmental Performance Ratings of Managers," *Personnel Psychology* 50 (1997), pp. 51–69.

32. Ibid.; see in particular page 62.

33. Ibid., p. 63. The researchers note, however, that since the true performance of the black managers was unknown, "it is not possible to deter-

mine whether ratings made by black bosses overstate performance, whether ratings made by white bosses understate performance, or both."

34. William Bigoness, "Effect of Applicant's Sex, Race, and Performance on Employer's Performance Ratings: Some Additional Findings," *Journal of Applied Psychology* 61 (February 1976); Duane Thompson and Toni Thompson, "Task-Based Performance Appraisal for Blue-Collar Jobs: Evaluation of Race and Sex Effects," *Journal of Applied Psychology* 70, no. 4 (1985), pp. 747–753.

35. Kevin Murphy, William Balzer, Maura Lockhart, and Elaine Eisenman, "Effects of Previous Performance on Evaluations of Present Performance," *Journal of Applied Psychology* 70, no. 1 (1985), pp. 72–84. See also Kevin Williams, Angelo DeNisi, Bruce Meglino, and Thomas Cafferty, "Initial Decisions and Subsequent Performance Ratings," *Journal of Applied Psychology* 71, no. 2 (May 1986), pp. 189–195.

36. Jane Halpert, Midge Wilson, and Julia Hickman, "Pregnancy as a Source of Bias in Performance Appraisals," *Journal of Organizational Behavior* 14 (1993), pp. 649–663.

37. Ibid., p. 655.

38. W. C. Borman, "Effects of Instruction to Avoid Halo Error in Reliability and Validity of Performance Evaluation Ratings," *Journal of Applied Psychology* 65 (1975), pp. 556–560. Borman points out that since no control group (a group of managers who did not undergo training) was available, it is possible that the observed effects were not due to the short five-minute training experience. G. P. Latham, K. N. Wexley, and E. D. Pursell, "Training Managers to Minimize Rating Errors in the Observation of Behavior," *Journal of Applied Psychology* 60 (1975), pp. 550–555; John Ivancevich, "Longitudinal Study of the Effects of Rater Training on Psychometric Error in Ratings," *Journal of Applied Psychology* 64 (1979), pp. 502–508. For a related discussion, see, for example, Bryan Davis and Michael Mount, "Effectiveness of Performance Appraisal Training Using Computer Assistance Instruction and Behavior Modeling," *Personnel Psychology* 37 (fall 1984), pp. 439–452.

39. Walter Borman, "Format and Training Effects on Rating Accuracy and Rater Errors," *Journal of Applied Psychology* 64 (August 1979), pp. 410–412; Jerry Hedge and Michael Cavanaugh, "Improving the Accuracy of Performance Evaluations: Comparison of Three Methods of Performance Appraiser Training," *Journal of Applied Psychology* 73, no. 1 (February 1988), pp. 68–73.

40. "Assessing Performance," *Training and Development* 55, no. 5 (May 2001), p. 133.

41. Dennis Warnke and Robert Billings, "Comparison of Training Methods for Improving the Psychometric Quality of Experimental and Administrative Performance Ratings," *Journal of Applied Psychology* 64 (April 1979), pp. 124–131. See also Timothy Athey and Robert McIntyre, "Effect of Rater Training on Rater Accuracy: Levels of Processing Theory and Social Facilitation Theory Perspectives," *Journal of Applied Psychology* 72, no. 4 (November 1987), pp. 567–572.

42. Angelo DeNisi and Lawrence Peters, "Organization of Information in Memory and the Performance Appraisal Process: Evidence from the Field," *Journal of Applied Psychology* 81, no. 6 (1996), pp. 717–737.

43. Ibid., p. 722.

44. Ibid., p. 722.

45. Juan Sanchez and Philip DeLaTorre, "A Second Look at the Relationship Between Rating and Behavioral Accuracy in Performance Appraisal," *Journal of Applied Psychology* 81, no. 1 (1996), p. 7.

46. Arup Varna, et al., "Interpersonal Affect and Performance Appraisal: A Field Study," *Personnel Psychology* 49 (1996), pp. 341–360.

47. DeNisi and Peters, "Organization of Information in Memory and the Performance Appraisal Process," pp. 733–734.

48. This is based on Gary Lubben, Duane Tompason, and Charles Klasson, "Performance Appraisal: The Legal Implications of Title VII," *Personnel*, May–June 1980, pp. 11–21. See also Larry Axline, "Ethical Considerations of Performance Appraisals," *Management Review* 83, no. 3 (March 1994), p. 62.

49. Shelley Burchett and Kenneth DeMeuse, "Performance Appraisal and the Law," *Personnel* 62, no. 7 (July 1985), pp. 34–35. See also "The Legal Ramifications of Performance Appraisal: The Growing Significance," *Public Personnel Management* 29, no. 3 (fall 2000), p. 381.

50. David Martin, et al., "The Legal Ramifications of Performance Appraisal: The Growing Significance," *Public Personnel Management* 29, no. 3 (fall 2000), pp. 381–383.

51. See also Ian Carlson and Martyn Sloman, "Performance Appraisal in Practice," *Human Resource Management* 2, no. 3 (spring 1992), pp. 80–94.

52. This is based on Kenneth L. Sovereign, *Personnel Law* (Upper Saddle River, NJ: Prentice Hall, 1994), pp. 113–114; and David Rosen, "Appraisals Can Make—or Break—Your Court Case," *Personnel Journal*, November 1992, pp. 113–118. See also "Avoiding HR Lawsuits," *Credit Union Executive*, November–December 1999, p. 6.

53. Larry Axline, "Ethical Considerations of Performance Appraisals," *Management Review*, March 1994, p. 62.

54. Wayne Cascio and H. John Bernardin, "Implications of Performance Appraisal Litigation for Personnel Decisions," *Personnel Psychology*, summer 1981, pp. 211–212; Gerald Barrett and Mary Kernan, "Performance Appraisal and Terminations: A Review of Court Decisions since *Brito v. Zia* with Implications for Personnel Practices," *Personnel Psychology* 40, no. 3 (autumn 1987), pp. 489–504.

55. Barrett and Kernan, "Performance Appraisal and Terminations," p. 501.

56. James Austin, Peter Villanova, and Hugh Hindman, "Legal Requirements and Technical Guidelines Involved in Implementing Performance Appraisal Systems," in Gerald Ferris and M. Ronald Buckley, *Human Resources Management*, 3rd edition (Upper Saddle River, NJ: Prentice Hall, 1996), pp. 271–288.

57. Ibid., p. 282.

58. Jon Werner and Mark Bolino, "Explaining U.S. Courts of Appeals' Decisions Involving Performance Appraisal: Accuracy, Fairness, and Validation," *Personnel Psychology* 50 (1997), pp. 1–24.

59. Ibid., p. 19.

60. Carol Norman and Robert Zawacki, "Team Appraisals—Team Approach," *Personnel Journal*, September 1991, pp. 101–103.

61. R. G. Downey, F. F. Medland, and L. G. Yates, "Evaluation of a Peer Rating System for Predicting Subsequent Promotion of Senior Military Officers," *Journal of Applied Psychology* 61 (April 1976); Glenn McEvoy and Paul Buller, "User Acceptance of Peer Appraisals in an Industrial Setting," *Personnel Psychology* 40, no. 4 (winter 1987), pp. 785–798. See also Julie Barclay and Lynn Harland, "Peer Performance Appraisals: The Impact of Rater Competence, Rater Location, and Rating Correctability on Fairness Perceptions," *Group and Organization Management* 20, no. 1 (March 1995), pp. 39–60.

62. Allan Kraut, "Prediction of Managerial Success by Peer and Training Staff Ratings," *Journal of Applied Psychology* 60 (February 1975). See also Michael Mount, "Psychometric Properties of Subordinate Ratings of Managerial Performance," *Personnel Psychology* 37, no. 4 (winter 1984), pp. 687–702.

63. Vanessa Druskat and Steven Wolf, "Effects and Timing of Developmental Peer Appraisals in Self-Managing Workgroups," *Journal of Applied Psychology* 84, no. 1 (1999), pp. 58–74.

64. Robert Libby and Robert Blashfield, "Performance of a Composite as a Function of the Number of Judges," *Organizational Behavior and Human Performance* 21 (April 1978), pp. 121–129; Walter Borman, "Exploring Upper Limits of Reliability and Validity in Job Performance Ratings," *Journal of Applied Psychology* 63 (April 1978), pp. 135–144; M. M. Harris and J. Schaubroeck, "A Meta-Analysis of Self-Supervisor, Self-Peer, and Peer-Supervisor Ratings," *Personnel Psychology* 41 (1988), pp. 43–62.

65. Chockalingam Viswesvaran, Denize Ones, and Frank Schmidt, "Comparative Analysis of the Reliability of Job Performance Ratings," *Journal of Applied Psychology* 81, no. 5 (1996), pp. 557–574.

66. Walter C. Borman, "The Rating of Individuals in Organizations: An Alternate Approach," *Organizational Behavior and Human Performance* 12 (1974), pp. 105–124.

67. Teel, "Performance Appraisal," p. 301.

68. George Thornton, III, "Psychometric Properties of Self-Appraisal of Job Performance," *Personnel Psychology* 33 (summer 1980), p. 265. See also Cathy Anderson, Jack Warner, and Cassie Spencer, "Inflation Bias in Self-Assessment Evaluations: Implications for Valid Employee Selection," *Journal of Applied Psychology* 69, no. 4 (November 1984), pp. 574–580. See also Shaul Fox and Vossi Dinur, "Validity of Self-Assessment: A Field Evaluation," *Personnel Psychology* 41, no. 3 (autumn 1988), pp. 581–592; and John W. Lawrie, "Your Performance: Appraise It Yourself!" *Personnel* 66, no. 1 (January 1989), pp. 21–33, a good explanation of how self-appraisals can be used at work.

69. Forest Jourden and Chip Heath, "The Evaluation Gap in Performance Perceptions: Illusory Perceptions of Groups and Individuals," *Journal of Applied Psychology* 81, no. 4 (August 1996), pp. 369–379.

70. Herbert Myer, "Self-Appraisal of Job Performance," *Personnel Psychology* 33 (summer 1980), pp. 291–293. See also Robert Steel and Nestor Ovalle II, "Self-Appraisal Based Upon Supervisory Feedback," *Personnel Psychology* 37, no. 4 (winter 1984), pp. 667–685; Gloria Shapiro and Gary Dessler, "Are Self-Appraisals More Realistic Among Professionals or Non-professionals in Health Care?" *Public Personnel Management* 14 (fall 1985), pp. 285–291; James Russell and Dorothy Goode, "An Analysis of Managers' Reactions to Their Own Performance Appraisal Feedback," *Journal of Applied Psychology* 73, no. 1 (February 1988), pp. 63–67; Harris and Schaubroeck, "A Meta-Analysis of Self-Supervisor, Self-Peer, and Peer-Supervisor Ratings," pp. 42–62.

71. Manuel London and Arthur Wohlers, "Agreement Between Sub-ordinates and Self-Ratings in Upward Feedback," *Personnel Psychology* 47 (1994), pp. 349–355.

72. Ibid., p. 376.

73. David Antonioni, "The Effects of Feedback Accountability on Upward Appraisal Ratings," *Personnel Psychology* 47 (1994), pp. 349–355.

74. Richard Reilly, James Smither, and Nicholas Vasilopoulos, "A Longitudinal Study of Upward Feedback," *Personnel Psychology* 49 (1996), pp. 599–612.

75. Ibid., p. 602.

76. Ibid., p. 599.

77. Kenneth Nowack, "360-Degree Feedback: The Whole Story," *Training and Development*, January 1993, p. 69. For a description of some of the problems involved in implementing 360-degree feedback, see Matthew Budman, "The Rating Game," *Across the Board* 31, no. 2 (February 1994), pp. 35–38.

78. "360-Degree Feedback on the Rise, Survey Finds," *BNA Bulletin to Management*, January 23, 1997, p. 31.

79. Katherine Romano, "Fear of Feedback," *Management Review*, December 1993, p. 39.

80. Ibid.

81. See, for instance, Gerry Rich, "Group Reviews—Are You Up to It?" *CMA Magazine*, March 1993, p. 5. See also Christopher Mabey, "Closing the Circle: Participant Views of a 360-Degree Feedback Programme," *Human Resource Management Journal* 11, no. 1 (2001), pp. 41–53.

82. Carol Hymowitz, "Do 360-Degree Job Reviews by Colleagues Promote Honesty or Insults?" *Wall Street Journal*, December 12, 2000, p. B-1.

83. Jim Meade, "Visual 360: A Performance Appraisal System That's 'Fun,'" *HR Magazine*, July 1999, pp. 118–119.

84. G. Douglas Huet-Cox, et al., "Get the Most from 360-Degree Feedback: Put It on the Internet," *HR Magazine*, May 1999, pp. 92–102.

85. Carol Hymowitz, "Do 360-Degree Job Reviews by Colleagues Promote Honesty or Insults?" *Wall Street Journal*, December 12, 2000, p. B-1.

86. Maury Pieperl, "Getting 360-Degree Feedback Right," *Harvard Business Review*, January 2001, p. 147.

87. Donald Fedor and Charles Parsons, "What Is Effective Performance Feedback?" in Ferris and Buckley, *Human Resources Management*, pp. 265–270.

88. Robert Johnson, *The Appraisal Interview Guide* (New York: Amacom, 1979) Chapter 9. See also John Kikoski, "Effective Communication in the Performance Appraisal Interview: Face to Face Communication for Public Managers in the Culturally Diverse Workplace," *Public Personnel Management*, (winter 1998) p. 491 (1), and Gerard McMahon, "A Lovely Audience," *People Management*, March 25, 1999, pp. 60–62.

89. Judy Block, *Performance Appraisal on the Job: Making It Work* (New York: Executive Enterprises Publications, 1981), pp. 58–62. See also Terry Lowe, "Eight Ways to Ruin a Performance Review," *Personnel Journal* 65, no. 1 (January 1986); Donald Feder, et al., "Performance Improvement Efforts in Response to Negative Feedback: The Roles of Source Power and Recipient Self-Esteem," *Journal of Management* 27, no. 1 (January 2001), pp. 79–80.

90. Block, *Performance Appraisal on the Job.*

91. Ronald Burke, William Weitzel, and Tamara Weis, "Characteristics of Effective Employee Performance Review and Development Interviews: Replication and Extension," *Personnel Psychology* 31 (winter 1978), pp. 903–919. See also Joane Pearce and Lyman Porter, "Employee Response to Formal Performance Appraisal Feedback," *Journal of Applied Psychology* 71, no. 2 (May 1986), pp. 211–218.

92. Brian Smith, et al., "Current Trends in Performance Appraisal: An Examination of Managerial Practice," *SAM Advanced Management Journal* 61, no. 3 (summer 1996), p. 16.

93. Alex Taylor III, "Crunch Time for Jac: Can CEO Jacques Nasser Fix Ford's Quality and Sales Woes—and Save His Job?" *Fortune* 143, no. 13 (June 25, 2001), pp. 34–37; "Basking in the Sunshine: Nasser and the Press," *Automotive News* 75, no. 5934 (June 11, 2001), p. 8; Diana Kurylko, "Ford Defends Reviews of Managers," *Automotive News* 75, no. 5937 (July 2, 2001), p. 8.

94. Edward E. Lawler III, "Performance Management: The Next Generation," *Compensation and Benefits Review*, May–June 1994, p. 16. See also Dick Grote, "Performance Appraisals: Solving Tough Challenges," *HR Magazine* 45, no. 7 (July 2000), pp. 145–150.

95. Ibid., p. 16. See also "Making Reviews More Efficient and Fair," *Workforce* 80, no. 4 (April 2001), p. 76.

96. Dr. M. Michael Markowich, "Response: We Can Make Performance Appraisals Work," *Compensation and Benefits Review*, May–June 1995, p. 25. See also "Are Performance Appraisals Obsolete?" *Compensation and Benefits Review*, May–June 2000, p. 3.

97. Mushin Lee and Byoungho Son, "The Effects of Appraisal Review Content on Employees' Reactions and Performance," *International Journal of Human Resource Management* 1 (February 1998), p. 283.

98. David Antonioni, "Improve the Management Process Before Discontinuing Performance Appraisals," *Compensation and Benefits Review*, May–June 1994, p. 29.

99. Ibid. See also Jonathan Siegel, "86 Your Appraisal Process?" *HR Magazine* 45, no. 10 (October 2000), pp. 199–206.

100. See, for example, Greg Boudreaux, "Response: What TQM Says About Performance Appraisal," *Compensation and Benefits Review*, May–June 1994, pp. 20–24.

101. Ibid., p. 21. See also "Improving Employee Acceptance Toward Performance Appraisal and Merit Pay Systems," *Review of Public Personnel Administration*, winter 2000, p. 1.

102. See, for example, Lawler, "Performance Management: The Next Generation," p. 17.

103. Boudreaux, "Response: What TQM Says About Performance Appraisal," p. 23.

104. Dick Grote, "The Secrets of Performance Appraisal," *Across the Board* 37, no. 5 (May 2000), pp. 14–16.

105. Allan Mohrman Jr. and Susan Albers-Mormon, "Performance Management Is Running the Business," *Compensation and Benefits Review*, July–August 1995, p. 69.

106. Ibid.

107. Grote, "The Secrets of Performance Appraisal," pp. 14–16.

108. Rich Wellins and Sheila Rioux, "The Growing Pains of Globalizing," *Training and Development* 54, no. 5 (May 2000), pp. 79–80.

109. Based in part on Joel E. Ross, *Total Quality Management: Text, Cases and Readings* (Delray Beach, FL: Saint Lucie Press, 1993), p. 1. See also Josephine Yong and Adrienne Wilkinson, "Rethinking Total Quality Management," *Total Quality Management* 12, no. 2 (March 2001), pp. 247–248.

110. Ibid., pp. 2–3, 35–36.

111. Boudreaux, "Response: What TQM Says About Performance Appraisal," p. 23.

112. Lawler, "Performance Management: The Next Generation," p. 17.

113. Markowich, "Response: We Can Make Performance Appraisals Work," p. 26.

114. Antonioni, "Improve the Management Process Before Discontinuing Performance Appraisals," p. 30.

115. Ibid.

116. Ibid.

117. See also Clive Fletcher, "Appraisal: An Idea Whose Time Has Gone?" *Personnel Management*, September 1993, pp. 34–37.

118. Grote, "The Secrets of Performance Appraisal," pp. 14–16.

Chapter 10

1. Sherry Sullivan, William Carden, and David Martin, "Careers in the Next Millennium: Directions for Future Research," *Human Resource Management Review* 8, no. 2 (1998), p. 165.

2. Douglas Hall, "Protean Careers of the 21st Century," *Academy of Management Executive* 10, no. 4 (1996), p. 8.

3. Kenneth Brousseau, Michael Driver, Kristina Eneroth, and Rikerd Larsson, "Career Pandemonium: Realigning Organizations and Individuals," *Academy of Management Executive* 10, no. 4 (1996), pp. 52–66; Brent Allred, Charles Snow, and Raymond Miles, "Characteristics of Managerial Careers in the 21st Century," *Academy of Management Executive* 10, no. 4 (1996), pp. 17–27.

4. Sullivan, Carden, and Martin, "Careers in the Next Millennium," p. 165; see also Richard Koonce, "Plan on a Career That Bobs and Weaves," *Training and Development Journal* 52, no. 4 (April 1998), pp. 14–16.

5. Ibid., p. 165.

6. Carla Joinson, "Career Management and Commitment," *HR Magazine* 46, no. 5, (May 2001), pp. 60–64.

7. Gina Imperato, "Get Your Career in Site," *Fast Company*, March 2000, pp. 318–334.

8. "Read This Before You Put a Resume Online," *Fortune*, May 24, 1999, pp. 290–291.

9. Yehuda Baruch and Maury Pieperl, "Career Management Practices: An Empirical Survey and Implications," *Human Resource Management* 39, no. 4 (winter 2000), pp. 347–366.

10. "Career Guidance Steers Workers Away from Early Exits," *BNA Bulletin to Management*, September 7, 2000, p. 287.

11. Belle Rose Ragins, "Diversified Mentoring Relationships in Organizations: A Power Perspective," *Academy of Management Review* 22, no. 2 (1997), p. 513.

12. Fred Otte and Peggy Hutcheson, *Helping Employees Manage Careers* (Upper Saddle River, NJ: Prentice Hall, 1992), p. 143.

13. Jim Meade, "Boost Careers and Succession Planning," *HR Magazine*, October 2000, pp. 175–178.

14. Patrick Kiger, "First USA Bank, Promotions and Job Satisfaction," *Workforce* 80, no. 3, (March 2001), pp. 54–56.

15. See, for example, Daniel Quinn Mills, *Labor-Management Relations* (New York: McGraw-Hill, 1986), pp. 387–396.

16. Charles Halaby, "Bureaucratic Promotion Criteria," *Administrative Science Quarterly* 23 (September 1978), pp. 466–484.

17. George Thornton III and David Morris, "The Application of Assessment Center Technology to the Evaluation of Personnel Records," *Public Personnel Management* 30, no. 1 (spring 2001), p. 55.

18. Joseph Famularo, *Handbook of Modern Personnel Administration* (New York: McGraw-Hill, 1972), p. 17.

19. Robert Marrujo and Brian Kleiner, "Why Women Fail to Get to the Top," *Equal Opportunities International* 11, no. 4 (1992), pp. 1–5.

20. Unless otherwise noted, this is based on ibid.

21. Ibid.

22. P. Watts, "Lending a Helping Hand," *Executive Female* 12 (1989), pp. 38–40; quoted in ibid., p. 1.

23. Karen Lyness and Donna Thompson, "Climbing the Corporate Ladder: Do Female and Male Executives Follow the Same Route?" *Journal of Applied Psychology* 85, no. 1 (2000), pp. 86–101.

24. These are based on Marrujo and Kleiner, "Why Women Fail to Get to the Top," p. 3; and Ann Morrison, P. Whiate, and Ellen Van Velsor, *Breaking the Glass Ceiling* (Reading, MA: Addison-Wesley, 1987).

25. See also Ronald Burke and Carol McKeen, "Supporting the Career Aspirations of Managerial and Professional Women," *Business and the Contemporary World*, summer 1993, pp. 69–80.

26. See, for example, Gary Powell and D. Anthony Butterfield, "Effect of Race on Promotions to Top Management in a Federal Department," *Academy of Management Journal* 40, no. 1 (1997), pp. 112–128.

27. Ibid., p. 124.

28. R. Tucker, M. Moravee, and K. Ideus, "Designing a Dual Career-Track System," *Training and Development* 6 (1992), pp. 55–58; Susan Schmidt, "The New Focus for Career Development," *Journal of Employment Counseling* 31 (March 1994), p. 26.

29. Schmidt, "The New Focus for Career Development," pp. 25–26.

30. See, for example, Richard Chanick, "Career Growth for Baby Boomers," *Personnel Journal* 71, no. 1 (January 1992), pp. 40–46.

31. Ibid.

32. Personal interview, March 1992.

33. Personal interview, March 1992.

34. Goldman Sachs, "Internal Placement Center: Guidelines for Managers."

35. Ibid., p. 1.

36. Ibid.

37. W. Chan Kim and Rene Maugorgne, "Fair Process: Managing in the Knowledge Economy," *Harvard Business Review*, July/August 1997, pp. 65–66.

38. Daniel Skarlicki and Gary Latham, "Increasing Citizenship Behavior Within a Labor Union: A Test of Organizational Justice Theory," *Journal of Applied Psychology* 81, no. 2 (1996), pp. 161–169.

39. M. Audrey Korsgaard, Loriann Roberson, and R. Douglas Rymph, "What Motivates Fairness? The Role of Subordinate Assertive Behavior on Managers' Interactional Fairness," *Journal of Applied Psychology* 83, no. 5 (1998), pp. 731–744.

40. Ibid., p. 735.

41. Marshall Schminke, et al., "The Effect of Organizational Structure on Perceptions of Procedural Fairness," *Journal of Applied Psychology* 85, no. 2 (2000), pp. 294–304.

42. Michelle Donovan, et al., "The Perceptions of Fair Interpersonal Treatment Scale: Development and Validation of a Measure of Interpersonal Treatment in the Workplace," *Journal of Applied Psychology* 83, no. 5 (1998), pp. 683–692.

43. Rudy Yandrick, "Lurking in the Shadows," *HR Magazine*, October 1999, pp. 61–68.

44. Bennett Tepper, "Consequences of Abusive Supervision," *Academy of Management Journal* 43, no. 2 (2000), pp. 178–190.

45. Kim and Maugorgne, "Fair Process: Managing in the Knowledge Economy," pp. 65–75.

46. Toyota Motor Manufacturing, USA, Inc., *Team Member Handbook*, February 1988, pp. 52–53.

47. Best Manufacturing Practices Center of Excellence, copyright 1998.

48. Lester Bittel, *What Every Supervisor Should Know* (New York: McGraw-Hill, 1974), p. 308; see also Paul Falcone, "The Fundamentals of Progressive Discipline," *HR Magazine*, February 1997, pp. 90–92.

49. Based on George Odiorne, *How Managers Make Things Happen* (Upper Saddle River, NJ: Prentice Hall, 1961), pp. 132–143; see also Bittel, *What Every Supervisor Should Know*, pp. 285–298. See also Cynthia Fukami and David Hopkins, "The Role of Situational Factors in Disciplinary Judgments," *Journal of Organizational Behavior* 14, no. 7 (December 1993), pp. 665–676.

50. Nonpunitive discipline discussions are based on David Campbell, et al., "Discipline Without Punishment—At Last," *Harvard Business Review*, July–August 1995, pp. 162–178; Gene Milbourne Jr., "The Case Against Employee Punishment," *Management Solutions*, November 1986, pp. 40–45; Mark Sherman and Al Lucia, "Positive Discipline and Labor Arbitration," *Arbitration Journal* 47, no. 2 (June 1992), pp. 56–58; Michael Moore, Victor Nichol, and Patrick McHugh, "No-Fault Programs: A Way to Cut Absenteeism," *Employment Relations Today*, winter 1992–1993, pp. 425–432; and "'Positive Discipline' Replaces Punishment," *BNA Bulletin to Management*, April 27, 1995, p. 136.

51. "A Woman's Place," *Economist* 356, no. 8184 (August 19, 2000), p. 56.

52. "Study Says Employers Monitor One-Third of Employee E-mail, Internet Use," *Knight Ridder/Tribune Business News*, July 10, 2001, item 01191038.

53. Sasha Cohen, "Thought Cop," *InfoWorld* 23, no. 9 (February 26, 2001), pp. 3–40.

54. Samuel Greengard, "Privacy: Entitlement or Illusion?" *Personnel Journal*, May 1996, p. 74.

55. Eryn Brown, "The Myth of E-mail Privacy," *Fortune*, February 3, 1997, p. 66.

56. "Surveillance of Employees," *BNA Bulletin to Management*, April 25, 1996, p. 136.

57. "Telephone and Electronic Monitoring: A Special Report on the Issues and the Law," p. 2.

58. "Curbing the Risks of E-mail Use," *BNA Bulletin to Management*, April 10, 1997, p. 120. See also Samuel Greengard, "Privacy: An Increasingly Public Matter," *Workforce* 78, no. 10 (October 1999), pp. 120–122.

59. *Vega-Rodriguez v. Puerto Rico Telephone Company* CA1,#.962061,4/8/97, discussed in "Video Surveillance Withstands Privacy Challenge," *BNA Bulletin to Management*, April 17, 1997, p. 121.

60. "Secret Videotaping Leads to $200,000 Settlement," *BNA Bulletin to Management*, January 22, 1998, p. 17.

61. Milton Zall, "Employee Privacy," *Journal of Property Management* 66, no. 3 (May 2001), p. 16.

62. Morris Attaway, "Privacy in the Workplace on the Web," *Internal Auditor* 58, no. 1 (February 2001), p. 30.

63. Joseph Famularo, *Handbook of Modern Personnel Administration* (New York: McGraw-Hill, 1982), pp. 65.3–65.5.

64. Ibid., p. 65.3.

65. Ibid., p. 65.4.

66. Ibid., pp. 65.4–65.5.

67. Brian Klaas and Gregory Dell'omo, "Managerial Use of Dismissal: Organizational-Level Determinants," *Personnel Psychology* 50 (1997), pp. 927–953.

68. Connie Wanberg, et al., "Perceived Fairness of Layoffs Among Individuals Who Have Been Laid Off: A Longitudinal Study," *Personnel Psychology* 2 (1999), pp. 59–84.

69. Klaas and Dell'omo, "Managerial Use of Dismissal," p. 946.

70. Dina Mansour-Cole and Susanne Scott, "Hearing It Through the Grapevine: The Influence of Source, Leader-Relations, and Legitimacy on Survivors' Fairness Perceptions," *Personnel Psychology* 51 (1998), pp. 25–54.

71. Ibid., p. 47.

72. Stephanie Armour, "E-mail Lets Companies Deliver Bad News from Afar," *USA Today*, February 20, 2001, p. B-1.

73. Jaikumar Vijayan, "Downsizings Leave Firms Vulnerable to Digital Attacks," *Computerworld* 25 (2001), pp. 6–7.

74. "Fairness to Employees Can Stave Off Litigation," *BNA Bulletin to Management*, November 27, 1997, p. 377.

75. Kenneth Sovereign, *Personnel Law* (Upper Saddle River, NJ: Prentice Hall, 1999), p. 185.

76. Paul and Townsend, "Wrongful Termination," p. 74.

77. Gillian Flynn, "Grounds for Dismissal," *Workforce* 79, (August 2000), no. 8, pp. 86–90.

78. "One More Heart Risk: Firing Employees," *Miami Herald*, March 20, 1998, pp. C1, C7.

79. Based on James Coil III and Charles Rise, "Three Steps to Creating Effective Employee Releases," *Employment Relations Today*, spring 1994, pp. 91–94. See also Jeffrey Conner, "Disarming Terminated Employees," *HR Magazine* X, no. 1 (January 2000), pp. 113–116; Richard Bayer, "Termination with Dignity," *Business Horizons* 43, no. 5 (September 2000), pp. 4–10.

80. William J. Morin and Lyle York, *Outplacement Techniques* (New York: AMACOM, 1982), pp. 101–131; F. Leigh Branham, "How to Evaluate Executive Outplacement Services," *Personnel Journal* 62 (April 1983), pp. 323–326; Sylvia Milne, "The Termination Interview," *Canadian Manager*, spring 1994, pp. 15–16.

81. Morin and York, *Outplacement Techniques*, p. 117. See also Sonny Weide, "When You Terminate an Employee," *Employment Relations Today*, August 1994, pp. 287–293.

82. Commerce Clearing House, *Ideas and Trends in Personnel*, July 9, 1982, pp. 132–146.

83. Kemba Dunham, "The Kinder Gentler Way to Lay Off Employees—More Humane Approach Helps," *Wall Street Journal*, March 13, 2001, p. B-1.

84. Paul Brada, "Before You Go . . . ," *HR Magazine*, December 1998, pp. 89–102.

85. Joseph Zarandona and Michael Camuso, "A Study of Exit Interviews: Does the Last Word Count?" *Personnel* 62, no. 3 (March 1981), pp. 47–48. For another point of view see "Firms Can Profit from Data Obtained from Exit Interviews," *Knight-Ridder/Tribune Business News*, February 13, 2001, Item 0104 4446.

86. Marlene Piturro, "Alternatives to Downsizing," *Management Review*, October 1999, pp. 37–42; "How Safe Is Your Job?," *Money* 30, no. 13, December 1, 2001, p. 130

87. Commerce Clearing House, *Ideas and Trends*, August 9, 1988, p. 133; see also Bureau of National Affairs, "Plant Closing Notification Rules: A Compliance Guide," *Bulletin to Management*, May 18, 1989. See also Nancy Ryan, "Complying with the Worker Adjustment and Retraining Notification Act (WARNACT)," *Employee Relations Law Journal* 18, no. 1 (summer 1993), pp. 169–176.

88. See, for example, "Mass Layoffs, Third Quarter, 1996," *BNA Bulletin to Management*, April 17, 1997, pp. 124–125.

89. Commerce Clearing House, *Personnel Practices/Communications* (Chicago: CCH, 1992), p. 1402.

90. Ibid., p. 1410.

91. Emily Nelson, "The Job Cut Buyouts Favored by P&G Pose Problems," *Wall Street Journal*, June 12, 2001, p. B-1.

92. See, for example, "Mass Layoffs, Third Quarter, 1996," pp. 124–125.

93. Ibid. See also Lawrence Kleiman and David Denton, "Downsizing: Nine Steps to ADA Compliance," *Employment Relations Today* 27, no. 3 (fall 2000), pp. 37–45.

94. See, for example, "Downsizing: Working Through the Pain," *BNA Bulletin to Management*, June 6, 1996, p. 184; and Jennifer Laabs, "Create Job Orders, Not Pink Slips," *Personnel Journal*, June 1996, pp. 97–99.

95. See, for example, "Cushioning the Blow of Layoffs," *BNA Bulletin to Management*, July 3, 1997, p. 216; and "Levi Strauss Cushions Blow of Plant Closings," *BNA Bulletin to Management*, November 20, 1997, p. 370.

96. Les Feldman, "Duracell's First Aid for Downsizing Survivors," *Personnel Journal*, August 1987, p. 94; James Emshoff, "How to Increase Employee Loyalty While You Downsize," *Business Horizons*, March–April 1994, pp. 49–57. See also Shari Caudron, "Teach Downsizing Survivors How to Thrive," *Personnel Journal*, January 1996, pp. 38–48.

97. These are suggested by attorney Ethan Lipsig and discussed in "The Lowdown on Downsizing," *BNA Bulletin to Management*, January 9, 1997, p. 16.

98. See also "Firms Need Layoff Strategies, Not Hasty Evacuation Plans," *BNA Bulletin to Management*, December 3, 1998, p. 383.

99. James Emshoff, "How to Increase Employee Loyalty While You Downsize." See also Robert Ford and Pamela Perrew, "After the Layoff: Closing the Barn Door Before All the Horses Are Gone," *Business Horizons*, July–August 1993, pp. 34–40.

100. Steve Weinstein, "The People Side of Mergers," *Progressive Grocer* 80, no. 1, January 2001, pp. 29–33.

101. "American Express Adds Tool to Retirement Section," *Financial Net News* 6, no. 17 (April 30, 2001), p. 3.

102. "Preretirement Education Programs," *Personnel* 59 (May–June 1982), p. 47. For a discussion of why it is important for retiring employees to promote aspects of their lives aside from their careers, see Daniel Halloran, "The Retirement Identity Crisis—and How to Beat It," *Personnel Journal* 64 (May 1985), pp. 38–40. For an example of a program aimed at training preretirees to prepare for the financial aspects of their retirement, see, for example, Silvia Odenwald, "Pre-Retirement Training Gathers Steam," *Training and Development Journal* 40, no. 2 (February 1986), pp. 62–63; "Pay Policies," *BNA Bulletin to Management*, March 29, 1990, p. 103.

103. Carroll and Kenya, "Agents Sue New York Life Over Retirement Benefits," *National Underwriter Life and Health Financial Services Edition* 105, no. 10 (March 5, 2001), pp. 49–50.

Chapter 11

1. Thomas Patten Jr., *Pay: Employee Compensation and Incentive Plans* (New York: Free Press, 1977), p. 1. See also Jerry McAdams, "Why Reward Systems Fail," *Personnel Journal* 67, no. 6 (June 1988), pp. 103–113; James Whitney, "Pay Concepts for the 1990s," Part I, *Compensation and Benefits Review* 20, no. 2 (March–April 1988), pp. 33–34; and James Whitney, "Pay Concepts for the 1990s," Part II, *Compensation and Benefits Review* 20, no. 3 (May–June 1988), pp. 45–50. See also "Aligning Work and Rewards: A Round Table Discussion," *Compensation and Benefits Review* 26, no. 4 (July–August 1994), pp. 47–63; Marlene Morganstern, "Compensation and the New Employment Relationship," *Compensation and Benefits Review* 27, no. 2 (March 1995), pp. 37–44; Joseph Martocchio, *Strategic Compensation* (Upper Saddle River, NJ: Prentice Hall, 2001); Richard Henderson, *Compensation Management in a Knowledge-Based World* (Upper Saddle River, NJ: Prentice Hall, 2000).

2. Richard Henderson, *Compensation Management* (Reston, VA: Reston, 1980); Martocchio, *Strategic Compensation*, pp. 44–60.

3. A complete description of exemption requirements is found in U.S. Department of Labor, *Executive, Administrative, Professional & Outside Salesmen Exempted from the Fair Labor Standards Act* (Washington, DC: U.S. Government Printing Office, 1973).

4. "The GAO Report Suggests That Labor Department Revise White-Collar Tests in FLSA Regulations," *BNA Bulletin to Management*, October 21, 1999, p. 329.

5. "Employer Ordered to Pay $2 Million in Overtime," *BNA Bulletin to Management*, September 26, 1996, pp. 308–309.

6. Michael Wolfe, "That's Not an Employee, That's an Independent Contractor," *Compensation and Benefits Review*, July–August 1996, p. 61. See also Ron Lieber, "The Permatemps Contretemps," *Fast Company*, August 2000, pp. 198–214.

7. "Microsoft Agrees to Pay $96.9 Million to Settle Contingent Workers' Lawsuits," *BNA Bulletin to Management*, December 14, 2000, p. 395.

8. Robert Nobile, "How Discrimination Laws Affect Compensation," *Compensation and Benefits Review*, July–August 1996, pp. 38–42.

9. Henderson, *Compensation Management*, pp. 101–127; see also Barry Hirsch and Edward Schumacher, "Unions, Wages, and Skills," *Journal of Human Resources* 33, no. 1 (winter 1998), pp. 201–219.

10. Ibid., p. 115.

11. Jack Dolmat-Connell, "Developing a Reward Strategy That Delivers Shareholder and Employee Value," *Compensation and Benefits Review*, March–April 1999, pp. 46–53.

12. Joseph Famularo, *Handbook of Modern Personnel Administration* (New York: McGraw-Hill, 1972), pp. 27–29. See also Bruce Ellig, "Strategic Pay Planning," *Compensation and Benefits Review* 19, no. 4 (July–August 1987), pp. 28–43; Thomas Robertson, "Fundamental Strategies for Wage and Salary Administration," *Personnel Journal* 65, no. 11 (November 1986), pp. 120–132.

13. Note that the assumption that low wage rates make a firm more competitive may be a "dangerous myth." It's a firm's overall labor costs that determine how competitive it will be, and such costs are driven not just by pay rates but by productivity. As one expert points out, "managers should remember that the issue is not just what you pay people, but also what they produce." Jeffrey Pfeffer, "Six Dangerous Myths About Pay," *Harvard Business Review*, May–June 1998, pp. 109–119.

14. Carla Joinson, "Pay Attention to Pay Cycles," *HR Magazine*, November 1998, pp. 71–78.

15. Jack Anderson, "Compensating Your Overseas Executives, Part II: Europe in 1992," *Compensation and Benefits Review*, July–August 1990, p. 28.

16. This is based on ibid., pp. 29–31.

17. Richard Hodgetts and Fred Luthans, "U.S. Multinationals' Expatriates' Compensation Strategies," *Compensation and Benefits Review*, January–February 1993, pp. 57–62.

18. George Milkovich and Matt Bloom, "Rethinking International Compensation," *Compensation and Benefits Review* 30, no. 1 (January–February 1998), pp. 15–24.

19. Vicki Kaman and Jodie Barr, "Employee Attitude Surveys for Strategic Compensation Management," *Compensation and Benefits Review*, January–February 1991, pp. 52–65.

20. See, for example, "Who Needs Midpoints? On-line Pay Forums Are Convincing Workers of Their Net Worth," *BNA Bulletin to Management*, March 9, 2000, p. 73.

21. Greg Winter, "Coke Issuing Widespread Pay Increases," *New York Times*, October 20, 2000, p. C1.

22. Henderson, *Compensation Management*, pp. 260–269.

23. For more information on these surveys, see the company's brochure, "Domestic Survey References," Watson Wyatt Data Services, 218 Route 17 North, Rochelle Park, NJ 07662, 1998.

24. "International Sources of Salary Data," *Compensation and Benefits Review*, May–June 1998, p. 23.

25. Martocchio, *Strategic Compensation*, p. 138.

26. You may have noticed that job analysis as discussed in Chapter 3 can be a useful source of information on compensable factors, as well as on job descriptions and job specifications. For example, a quantitative job analysis technique like the position analysis questionnaire generates quantitative information on the degree to which the following five basic factors are present in each job: having decision-making/communication/social responsibilities, performing skilled activities, being physically active, operating vehicles or equipment, and processing information. As a result, a job analysis technique like the PAQ is actually as (or some say, more) appropriate as a job evaluation technique in that jobs can be quantitatively compared to one another on those five dimensions and their relative worth thus ascertained. Another point worth noting is that you may find that a single set of compensable factors is not adequate for describing all your jobs. Many managers, therefore, divide their jobs into job clusters. For example, you might have a separate job cluster for factory workers, for clerical workers, and for managerial personnel. Similarly, you would then probably have a somewhat different set of compensable factors for each job cluster.

27. A. N. Nash and F. J. Carroll Jr., "Installation of a Job Evaluation Program," from *Management of Compensation* (Monterey, CA: Brooks/Cole, 1975), reprinted in Craig Schneier and Richard Beatty, *Personnel Administration Today: Readings and Commentary* (Reading, MA: Addison-Wesley, 1978), pp. 417–425; and Henderson, *Compensation Management*, pp. 231–239. According to one survey, about equal percentages of employers use individual interviews, employee questionnaires, or observations by personnel representatives to obtain the actual job evaluation information. See Mary Ellen Lo Bosco, "Job Analysis, Job Evaluation, and Job Classification," *Personnel* 62, no. 5 (May 1985), pp. 70–75. See also Howard Risher, "Job Evaluation: Validity and Reliability," *Compensation and Benefits Review* 21, no. 1 (January–February 1989), pp. 22–36; and David Hahn and Robert Dipboye, "Effects of Training and Information on the Accuracy and Reliability of Job Evaluations," *Journal of Applied Psychology* 73, no. 2 (May 1988), pp. 146–153.

28. As explained later, the practice of red circling is used to delay downward adjustments in pay rates that are presently too high given the newly evaluated jobs. See also E. James Brennan, "Everything You Need to Know About Salary Ranges," *Personnel Journal* 63, no. 3 (March 1984), pp. 10–17.

29. Nash and Carroll, "Installation of a Job Evaluation," p. 419.

30. Sondra O'Neal, "CAJE: Computer-Aided Job Evaluation for the 1990s," *Compensation and Benefits Review*, November–December 1990, pp. 14–19.

31. If you used the job classification method, then of course the jobs are already classified.

32. David Belcher, *Compensation Administration* (Upper Saddle River, NJ: Prentice Hall, 1973), pp. 257–276.

33. In other words, on the graph, plot the benchmark jobs' points (as determined by job evaluation) and their corresponding market pay rates (as determined by the salary survey). Then slot in the other jobs based on their evaluations, to determine what their target pay rates should be.

34. Susan Marks, "Can the Internet Help You Hit the Salary Mark?" *Workforce* 80, January 2001, no. 1, pp. 86–93.

35. Commerce Clearing House, "How to Avoid the Ten Most Common Wage-Hour Traps," *Ideas and Trends*, March 10, 1989, p. 43. See also "20 Facts to Determine Workers Status," supplement to the November 1999 *Workforce*, pp. 1–2.

36. Arthur Silbergeld and Mark Tuvim, "Recent Cases Narrowly Construe Exemption from Overtime Provisions of Fair Labor Standards Act," *Employment Relations Today*, summer 1994, pp. 241–250; see also Charles Fine, "Exempt or Not? Classification Can Mean Big Dollars," *Management Review*, July 1993, pp. 58–60; Matthew Smith and Steven Winterbauer, "Overtime Compensation Under the FLSA: Pay Them Now or Pay Them Later," *Employee Relations Labor Journal* 19, no. 1 (summer 1993), pp. 23–51; Noreen McDermott, "Independent Contractors and Employees: Do You Know One When You See One?" Society for Human Resource Management, legal report, November–December 1999, pp. 1–8.

37. Donald McDermott, "Whither the Glass Ceiling? Conducting a Statistical Pay Audit," *Compensation and Benefits Review*, September–October 2000, pp. 17–22.

38. Silbergeld and Tuvim, "Recent Cases Narrowly Construe Exemption."

39. For a full discussion, see Peter Gold and Michael Esposito, "The Right to Control: Are Your Workers Independent Contractors or Employees?" *Compensation and Benefits Review*, July–August 1992, pp. 30–37.

40. "Employee Versus Independent Contractor," *BNA Bulletin to Management*, March 28, 1996, p. 104.

41. Dale Yoder, *Personnel Management and Industrial Relations* (Upper Saddle River, NJ: Prentice Hall, 1970), pp. 643–645; Famularo, *Handbook of Modern Personnel Administration*, pp. 32.1–32.6, 30.1–30.8.

42. Mark Meltzer and Howard Goldsmith, "Executive Compensation for Growth Companies," *Compensation and Benefits Review*, November–December 1997, pp. 41–50.

43. Douglas Tormey, "Executive Compensation: Creating 'Legal' Checklist," *Compensation and Benefits Review*, July–August 1996, pp. 12–36.

44. "Executive Pay," *Wall Street Journal*, April 11, 1996, pp. R16, R170.

45. Nardash Agarwal, "Determinants of Executive Compensation," *Industrial Relations* 20, no. 1 (winter 1981), pp. 36–45. See also John A. Fossum and Mary Fitch, "The Effects of Individual and Contextual Attributes on the Sizes of Recommended Salary Increases," *Personnel Psychology* 38, no. 3 (autumn 1985), pp. 587–602.

46. James Reda, "Executive Pay Today and Tomorrow," *Corporate Board* 22, no. 126 (January 2001), p. 18.

47. Andrew Henderson and James Frederickson, "Information-Processing Demands as a Determinant of CEO Compensation," *Academy of Management Journal* 39, no. 3 (1996), pp. 576–606.

48. Ibid., pp. 585–586.

49. Jack Lederer and Carl Weinberg, "Setting Executive Compensation: Does the Industry You're in Really Matter?" *Compensation and Benefits Review*, January–February 1999, pp. 13–24.

50. This is based on William White, "Managing the Board Review of Executive Pay," *Compensation and Benefits Review*, November–December 1992, pp. 35–41.

51. Ibid., pp. 38–40; see also H. Anthony Hampson, "Tying CEO Pay to Performance: Compensation Committees Must Do Better," *Business Quarterly* 55, no. 4 (spring 1991), pp. 18–22.

52. Geoffrey Colvin, "It's a Banner Year for CEO Pay," *Fortune*, April 26, 1999, p. 422.

53. William White and Raymond Fife, "New Challenges for Executive Compensation in the 1990s," *Compensation and Benefits Review*, January–February 1993, pp. 27–35. See also W. G. Jurgensen, "Crafting an Executive Stock Purchase Program," *Directors and Boards* 24, no. 1 (fall 1999), pp. 39–41; Allison Wellner, "Golden Handcuffs," *HR Magazine* 45, no. 10 (October 2000), pp. 129–136.

54. Louis Lavelle, "While the CEO Gravy Train May Be Slowing Down, It Hasn't Jumped the Rails," *Business Week*, April 16, 2001, pp. 76–80.

55. Famularo, *Handbook of Modern Personnel Administration*, pp. 30.1–30.1.5.

56. Ibid., pp. 30.1–30.5. See also Patric Moran, "Equitable Salary Administration in High-Tech Companies," *Compensation and Benefits Review* 18, no. 5 (September–October 1986), pp. 31–40.

57. Robert Sibson, *Compensation* (New York: AMACOM, 1981), p. 194.

58. Helen Remick, "The Comparable Worth Controversy," *Public Personnel Management Journal*, winter 1981, pp. 371–383.

59. See also Bernisha Bridges, "The Role of Rewards in Motivating Scientific and Technical Personnel: Experience at Egland AFB," *National Productivity Review*, summer 1993, pp. 337–348.

60. Gerald Ledford Jr., "Three Case Studies on Skill-Based Pay: An Overview," *Compensation and Benefits Review*, March–April 1991, pp. 11–23.

61. Gerald Ledford Jr., "Paying for the Skills, Knowledge, and Competencies of Knowledge Workers," *Compensation and Benefits Review*, July–August 1995, p. 56; see also Richard Sperling and Larry Hicks, "Trends in Compensation and Benefits Strategies," *Employment Relations Today* 25, no. 2 (summer 1998), pp. 85–99.

62. Ledford, "Three Case Studies on Skill-Based Pay," p. 12. See also Kathryn Cofsky, "Critical Keys to Competency-Based Pay," *Compensation and Benefits Review*, November–December 1993, pp. 46–52; Brian Murray and Barry Gerhart, "Skill-Based Pay and Skills Seeking," *Human Resource Management Review* 10, no. 3 (2000), pp. 271–287.

63. Brian Murray and Barry Gerhard, "An Empirical Analysis of a Skill-Based Pay Program and Plant Performance and Outcomes," *Academy of Management Journal* 41, no. 1 (1998), pp. 68–78.

64. Gerald Ledford Jr. and Gary Bergel, "Skill-Based Pay Case Number 1: General Mills," *Compensation and Benefits Review,* March–April 1991, pp. 24–38; see also Gerald Barrett, "Comparison of Skill-Based Pay with Traditional Job Evaluation Techniques," *Human Resource Management Review* 1, no. 2 (summer 1991), pp. 97–105; Barbara Dewey, "Changing to Skill-Based Pay: Disarming the Transition Land Mines," *Compensation and Benefits Review* 26, no. 1 (January–February 1994), pp. 38–43.

65. This is based on Ledford and Bergel, "Skill-Based Pay Case Number 1," pp. 28–29.

66. Kevin Parent and Carline Weber, "Case Study: Does Paying for Knowledge Pay Off?" *Compensation and Benefits Review*, September–October 1994, pp. 44–50; and Edward Lawler III, Gerald Ledford Jr., and Lei Chang, "Who Uses Skill-Based Pay, and Why?" *Compensation and Benefits Review*, March–April 1993, pp. 22–26.

67. Parent and Weber, "Case Study." For a good discussion of the conditions under which competency-based pay is more effective, see Edward Lawler III, "Competencies; A Poor Foundation for the New Pay," *Compensation and Benefits Review*, November–December 1996, pp. 20–26.

68. Lawler, "Competencies: A Poor Foundation for the New Pay," pp. 20–22.

69. Ledford, "Paying for Skills, Knowledge, and Competencies of Knowledge Workers," p. 55.

70. Ibid., p. 58. See also Melvyn Stark, Warren Luther, and Steve Balvano, "Jaguar Cars Drives Toward Competency-Based Pay," *Compensation and Benefits Review*, November–December 1996, pp. 34–40.

71. David Hofrichter, "Broadbanding: A 'Second Generation' Approach," *Compensation and Benefits Review*, September–October 1993, pp. 53–58. See also Gary Bergel, "Choosing the Right Pay Delivery System to Fit Banding," *Compensation and Benefits Review* 26, no. 4 (July–August 1994), pp. 34–38.

72. Ibid., p. 55.

73. For example, see Sondra Emerson, "Job Evaluation: A Barrier to Excellence?" *Compensation and Benefits Review*, January–February 1991, pp. 39–51; Nan Weiner, "Job Evaluation Systems: A Critique," *Human Resource Management Review* 1, no. 2 (summer 1991), pp. 119–132.

74. Dawne Shand, "Broadbanding the IT Worker," *Computerworld* 34, October 9, 2000, no. 41.

75. "Broadbanding Pay Structures Do Not Receive Flat-Out Support from Employers, Survey Finds," *BNA Bulletin to Management*, January 13, 2000, p. 11.

76. Duncan Brown, "Broadbanding: A Study of Company Practices in the United Kingdom," *Compensation and Benefits Review*, November–December 1996, p. 43.

77. Dawne Shand, "Broadbanding the IT Worker," *Computerworld*, October 9, 2000, p. 58.

78. "101 Hot Web Sites for Compensation & Benefits Professionals," American Management Association International, New York, NY, 1998, pp. 53, 57.

79. Emerson, "Job Evaluation," p. 39.

80. This is based on Laurent Dufetel, "Job Evaluation: Still at the Frontier," *Compensation and Benefits Review*, July–August 1991, pp. 53–67.

81. Andrew Richter, "Paying the People in Black at Big Blue," *Compensation and Benefits Review*, May–June 1998, p. 51. See also Robert McNabb and Keith Whitfield, "Job Evaluation and High-Performance Work Practices: Compatible or Conflictful?" *Journal of Management Studies* 38 (March 2001), pp. 293–313.

82. Ibid., pp. 53–54.

83. Ibid., p. 54.

84. Ibid.

85. Ibid.

86. See ibid., p. 55.

87. Ibid., p. 56.

88. Ibid., p. 56.

89. Howard Risher, "Exclusive CBR Survey: Pay Program Effectiveness," *Compensation and Benefits Review*, November–December 1999, pp. 20–26.

90. Jack Dolmat-Connell, "Developing a Reward Strategy That Delivers Shareholder and Employee Value," *Compensation and Benefits Review*, March–April 1999, p. 50.

91. Paul Platten and Carl Weinberg, "Shattering the Myths About Dot.Com Employee Pay," *Compensation and Benefits Review*, January–February 2000, pp. 21–27.

92. Ibid.

93. Ibid.

94. Ibid., p. 26.

95. Carl Weinberg, "Reward Strategies for Dot.Corp Organizations: Lessons from the Front," *Compensation and Benefits*, January–February 2001, pp. 6–14.

96. Helen Remick, "The Comparable Worth Controversy," *Public Personnel Management Journal*, winter 1981, p. 38; U.S. Department of Labor, *Perspectives on Working Women: A Data Book*, October 1980.

97. Remick, "The Comparable Worth Controversy," p. 377.

98. Ibid.

99. Martocchio, *Strategic Compensation*, p. 191.

100. "Comparable Worth Wages: Lawmakers Rethink Equal Pay," *Foodservice Director* 14, no. 6 (June 15, 2001), p. 18.

101. *County of Washington v. Gunther*, U.S. Supreme Court No. 80–429, June 8, 1981.

102. Jennifer Quinn, "Visibility and Value: The Role of Job Evaluation in Assuring Equal Pay for Women," *Law and Policy in International Business* 25, no. 4 (summer 1994), pp. 1403–1444.

103. Ibid., p. 1411.

104. Ibid., p. 1411.

105. Mary Gray, "Pay Equity Through Job Evaluation: A Case Study," *Compensation and Benefits Review*, July–August 1992, p. 46.

106. Ibid., pp. 46–51; see also Teresa Brady, "How Equal is Equal Pay?" *Management Review* 87, no. 3 (March 1998), pp. 59–61.

107. See David Thomsen, "Compensation and Benefits—More on Comparable Worth," *Personnel Journal* 60 (May 1981) pp. 348–349; Marvin Levine, "Comparable Worth in the 1980s: Will Collective Bargaining Supplant Legislative and Judicial Interpretations?" *Labor Law Journal* 38, no. 6 (June 1987), pp. 323–335; Peter Olney Jr., "Meeting the Challenge of Comparable Worth," Part II, *Compensation and Benefits Review* 19, no. 3 (May–June 1987), pp. 45–53; Jennifer Quinn, "Visibility and Value: The Role of Job Evaluation in Assuring Equal Pay for Women," *Law and Public Policy in International Business* 25, no. 4 (summer 1994), pp. 1403–1444. See also Deborah Figart, "Equal Pay for Equal Work: The Role of Job Evaluation in Any Evolving Social Norm," *Journal of Economic Issues* 35, no. 1 (March 2000), p. 1.

108. Brinks, "The Comparable Worth Issue: A Salary Administration Bombshell," *Personnel Administration* 26, no. 11 (November 1981), p. 40.

109. Michael Carter, "Comparable Worth: An Idea Whose Time Has Come?" *Personnel Journal* 60 (October 1981), p. 794; Peter Olney Jr., "Meeting the Challenge of Comparable Worth," Part I, *Compensation and Benefits Review* 19, no. 2 (March–April 1987), pp. 34–44. See also Mary Virginia Moore and Yohannan Abraham, "Comparable Worth: Is It A Moot Issue? Part II: The Legal and Juridical Posture," *Public Personnel Management* 23, no. 2 (summer 1994), pp. 263–286.

110. "Women Still Earned Less Than Men, BLS Data Show," *BNA Bulletin to Management*, June 8, 2000, p. 72. However, there is some indication that there is little or no gender-based pay gap among full-time workers ages 21 to 35 living alone. Kent Hoover, "Study Finds No Pay Gap for Young, Single Workers," *Tampa Bay Business Journal* 20, no. 19 (May 12, 2000), p. 10.

Chapter 12

1. Stephen Gross and Dan Duncan, "Gainsharing Plan Spurs Record Productivity and Payouts at AmeriSteel," *Compensation and Benefits Review*, November–December 1998, pp. 46–50.

2. Rajiv Banker, Seok-Young Lee, Gordon Potter, and Dhinu Srinivasan, "Contextual Analysis of Performance Impacts of Outcome-Based Incentive Competition," *Academy of Management Journal* 39, no. 4 (1996), pp. 940–941.

3. Linda Stroh, Jeanne Brett, Joseph Baumann, and Anne Reilly, "Agency Theory and Variable Pay Compensation Strategies," *Academy of Management Journal* 39, no. 3 (1996), pp. 751–767.

4. Ibid., p. 762.

5. "DuPont to Implement Performance-Based Pay," *BNA Bulletin to Management*, June 11, 1998, pp. 177, 182.

6. Ibid., p. 177.

7. "Non-Traditional Incentive Pay Programs," *Personnel Policies Forum Survey* 148 (May 1991), The Bureau of National Affairs, Inc., Washington, D.C., p. 3.

8. Ibid., p. 13.

9. Ibid., p. 19.

10. "Designing a Variable Pay Plan," *BNA Bulletin to Management*, June 20, 1996, p. 200.

11. Ibid., p. 200.

12. "Employers Use Pay to Lever Performance," *BNA Bulletin to Management*, August 21, 1997, p. 272.

13. See, for example, Kenan Abosch, "Variable Pay: Do We Have the Basics in Place?" *Compensation and Benefits Review*, July–August 1998, pp. 2–22.

14. Bob Nelson, "Give Stressed-Out Employees the Gift of Time to Boost Morale, Increase Workplace Creativity," *San Francisco Business Times* 15, no. 27 (February 9, 2001), p. 49.

15. "The Second Annual Incentive Web Site Awards," *Incentive* 175, no. 3 (March 2001), p. 17.

16. Richard Henderson, *Compensation Management* (Upper Saddle River, NJ: Prentice Hall, 2000), p. 463. For a discussion of the increasing use of incentives for blue-collar employees, see, for example, Richard Henderson, "Contract Concessions: Is the Past Prologue?" *Compensation and Benefits Review* 18, no. 5 (September–October 1986), pp. 17–30. See also A. J. Vogl, "Carrots, Sticks and Self-Deception," *Across-the-Board* 3–1, no. 1 (January 1994), p. 314; Philip Lewis, "Managing Performance-Related Pay Based on Evidence from the Financial Services Sector," *Human Resource Management Journal* 8, no. 2 (1998), pp. 66–77.

17. David Belcher, *Compensation Administration* (Upper Saddle River, NJ: Prentice Hall, 1973), p. 314.

18. For a discussion of these, see Thomas Wilson, "Is It Time to Eliminate the Piece Rate Incentive System?" *Compensation and Benefits Review*, March–April 1992, pp. 43–49.

19. Measured day work is a third type of individual incentive plan for production workers. See, for example, Mitchell Fein, "Let's Return to MDW for Incentives," *Industrial Engineering*, January 1979, pp. 34–37.

20. Oanh Ha, "California Workers Named in Articles Not Asked to Help in Piecework Probe," *Knight Ridder/Tribune News*, March 23, 2000, item 0008408e.

21. William Atkinson, "Incentive Pay Programs That Work in Textile," *Textile World* 151, (February 2001), no. 2, pp. 55–57.

22. Henderson, *Compensation Management*, pp. 367–368. See also David Swinehart, "A Guide for More Productive Team Incentive Programs," *Personnel Journal* 65, no. 7 (July 1986); Anne Saunier and Elizabeth Hawk, "Realizing the Potential of Teams Through Team-Based Rewards," *Compensation and Benefits Review*, July–August 1994, pp. 24–33; and Shari Caudron, "Tie Individual Pay to Team Success," *Personnel Journal* 73, no. 10 (October 1994), pp. 40–46.

23. Other suggestions are as follows: equal payments to all members on the team; differential payments to team members based on their contributions to the team's performance; and differential payments determined by a ratio of each group member's base pay to the total base pay of the group. See Kathryn Bartol and Laura Hagmann, "Team-Based Pay Plans: A Key to Effective Teamwork," *Compensation and Benefits Review*, November–December 1992, pp. 24–29.

24. Richard Seaman, "The Case Study: Rejuvenating an Organization with Team Pay," *Compensation and Benefits Review*, September–October 1997, pp. 25–30.

25. James Nickel and Sandra O'Neal, "Small Group Incentives: Gainsharing in the Microcosm," *Compensation and Benefits Review*, March–April 1990, p. 24. See also Jane Pickard, "How Incentives Can Drive Teamworking," *Personnel Management*, September 1993, pp. 26–32; and Shari Caudron, "Tie Individual Pay to Team Success," *Personnel Journal*, October 1994, pp. 40–46.

26. Jon P. Alston, "Awarding Bonuses the Japanese Way," *Business Horizons* 25 (September–October 1982), pp. 6–8.

27. See, for example, Peter Daly, "Selecting and Assigning a Group Incentive Plan," *Management Review* (December 1975), pp. 33–45. For an explanation of how to develop a successful group incentive program, see K. Dow Scott and Timothy Cotter, "The Team That Works Together Earns Together," *Personnel Journal* 63 (March 1984), pp. 59–67.

28. Manuel London and Greg Oldham, "A Comparison of Group and Individual Incentive Plans," *Academy of Management Journal* 20, no. 1 (1977), pp. 34–41. Note that the study was carried out under controlled conditions in a laboratory setting. See also Thomas Rollins, "Productivity-Based Group Incentive Plans: Powerful, But Use with Caution," *Compensation and Benefits Review* 21, no. 3 (May–June 1989), pp. 39–50, which discusses several popular group incentive

plans, including gainsharing, and lists do's and don'ts for using them.

29. Robert Heneman and Courtney Von Hippel, "Balancing Group and Individual Rewards: Rewarding Individual Contributions to the Team," *Compensation and Benefits Review*, July–August 1995, pp. 63–68.

30. Mark Meltzer and Howard Goldsmith, "Executive Compensation for Growth Companies," *Compensation and Benefits Review*, November–December 1997, pp. 41–50.

31. Ibid.

32. "Short-Term Incentives Considered Ineffective, Survey Reveals," *Society for Human Resource Management*, January 2000, p. 5.

33. Mark Meltzer and Howard Goldsmith, "Executive Compensation for Growth Companies," *Compensation and Benefits Review*, November/December 1997, pp. 44–45. See also Robert E. Wood, et al. "Bonuses, Goals, and Instrumentality Effects," *Journal of Applied Psychology* 84, no. 5 (1999), pp. 703–720.

34. Ibid., p. 188. Meltzer and Goldsmith, "Executive Compensation for Growth Companies," p. 44.

35. See, for example, Ralph Bavier, "Managerial Bonuses," *Industrial Management*, March–April 1978, pp. 1–5. See also Charles Tharp, "Linking Annual Incentive Awards to Individual Performance," *Compensation and Benefits Review* 17 (November–December 1985), pp. 18–43.

36. Ellig, *Executive Compensation*, p. 189.

37. F. Dean Hildebrand Jr., "Individual Performance Incentives," *Compensation Review* 10 (third quarter, 1978), p. 32.

38. Ibid., pp. 28–33.

39. The following is based on Edward Redling, "The 1981 Tax Act: Boom to Managerial Compensation," *Personnel* 57 (March–April 1982), pp. 26–35, and on Meltzer and Goldsmith, "Executive Compensation for Growth Companies," pp. 45–47.

40. See both William M. Mercer Meidinger, Inc., "How Will Reform Tax Your Benefits?" *Personnel Journal* 65, no. 12 (December 1986), pp. 49–63; and Jack H. Schechter, "The Tax Reform Act of 1986: Its Impact on Compensation and Benefits," *Compensation and Benefits Review* 18, no. 6 (November–December 1986), pp. 11–24. See also Paul Bradley, "Justify Executive Bonuses to the Board," *Personnel Journal*, September 1988, pp. 116–125, and his "Long-Term Incentives: International Executives Need Them Too," *Personnel*, August 1988, pp. 40–42.

41. Christopher Young, "Trends in Executive Compensation," *Journal of Business Strategy* 19, no. 2 (March–April 1998), pp. 21–25.

42. "Share and Share Alike," *Economist*, August 7, 1999, pp. 18–20; "CEO Pay Continues to Climb, Driven by Equity Ownership," *Corporate Board* 21 (July 2000), no. 123, p. 26.

43. Belcher, *Compensation Administration*, p. 548; Schechter, "The Tax Reform Act of 1986," p. 23. See also Rein Linney and Charles Marshall, "ISOs vs. NSOs: The Choice Still Exists," *Compensation and Benefits Review* 19, no. 1 (January–February 1987), pp. 13–25; and Leslie Winograd and Beverly Aisenbrey, "Designing State-of-the-Art Executive Stock Ownership Guidelines," *Compensation and Benefits Review*, January–February 2001, pp. 32–38.

44. Meltzer and Goldsmith, "Executive Compensation," pp. 47–48.

45. Brian Hall, "What You Need to Know About Stock Options," *Harvard Business Review*, March–April 2000, pp. 121–129.

46. Ann Harrington, "Saying 'We Love You' with Stock Options," *Fortune*, October 11, 1999, p. 360.

47. Ira Sager, "Stock Options: Lou Takes a Cue from Silicon Valley," *Business Week*, March 30, 1998, p. 34.

48. Jeff Staiman and Cary Thompson, "Designing and Implementing a Broad-Based Stock Option Plan," *Compensation and Benefits Review*, July–August 1998, p. 23.

49. Ibid., p. 23.

50. Ibid., p. 25

51. "Study Finds That Directly Owning Stock Shares Leads to Better Results," *Compensation and Benefits Review*, March–April 2001, p. 7.

52. Ray Stata and Modesto Maidique, "Bonus System for Balanced Strategy," *Harvard Business Review* 59 (November–December 1980), pp. 156–163; Alfred Rappaport, "Executive Incentives Versus Corporate Growth," *Harvard Business Review* 57 (July–August 1978), pp. 81–88. See also Crystal Graef, "Rendering Long-Term Incentives Less Risky for Executives," *Personnel* 65, no. 9 (September 1988), pp. 80–84.

53. Ira Kay, "Beyond Stock Options: Emerging Practices in Executive Incentive Programs," *Compensation and Benefits Review*, November–December 1991, p. 19.

54. For a discussion, see ibid., pp. 18–29.

55. Jeffrey Kanter and Matthew Ward, "Long-Term Incentives for Management, Part 4: Performance Plans," *Compensation and Benefits Review*, January–February 1990, p. 36; Meltzer and Goldsmith, "Executive Compensation for Growth Companies," pp. 46–47.

56. Jude Rich and John Larson, "Why Some Long-Term Incentives Fail," *Compensation Review* 16 (first quarter 1984), pp. 26–37. See also Eric Marquardt, "Stock Option Grants: Is Timing Everything?" *Compensation and Benefits Review* 20, no. 5 (September–October 1988), pp. 18–22.

57. Robert Klein, "Compensating Your Overseas Executives, Part 3: Exporting U.S. Stock Option Plans to Expatriates," *Compensation and Benefits Review*, January–February 1991, pp. 27–38.

58. For a discussion, see ibid.

59. This section is based on Meltzer and Goldsmith, "Executive Compensation for Growth Companies," pp. 41–50. See also James Nelson, "Linking Compensation to Business Strategy," *Journal of Business Strategy* 19, no. 2 (March–April 1998), pp. 25–28.

60. Richard Semler, "Developing Management Incentives That Drive Results," *Compensation and Benefits Review*, July–August 1998, pp. 41–48.

61. Ibid., p. 44.

62. Ibid., p. 47.

63. Jennifer Schott, "Companies Tie Incentives to SCM," *ebusiness*, March 12, 2001, p. 4.

64. John Steinbrink, "How to Pay Your Sales Force," *Harvard Business Review* 57 (July–August 1978), pp. 111–122. See also John Tallitsch and John Moynahan, "Fine-Tuning Sales Compensation Programs," *Compensation and Benefits Review* 26, no. 2 (March–April 1994), pp. 34–37.

65. Straight salary by itself is not, of course, an incentive compensation plan as we use the term in this chapter.

66. Steinbrink, "How to Pay," p. 112.

67. T. H. Patten, "Trends in Pay Practices for Salesmen," *Personnel* 43 (January–February 1968), pp. 54–63. See also Catherine Romano, "Death of a Salesman," *Management Review* 83, no. 9 (September 1994), pp. 10–16.; "Coping with Split Commissions," *Agency Sales Magazine* 3, no. 2, February 2001, p. 53.

68. David Harrison, Meghna Virick, and Sonja William, "Working Without a Net: Time, Performance, and Turnover Under Maximally Contingent Rewards," *Journal of Applied Psychology* 81, no. 4 (1996), p. 332.

69. Ibid., pp. 331–345.

70. Greg Stewart, "Reward Structure as a Moderator of the Relationship Between Extroversion and Sales Performance," *Journal of Applied Psychology* 81, no. 6 (1996), pp. 619–627.

71. Ibid., p. 619.

72. Steinbrink, "How to Pay," p. 115.

73. Bill O'Connell, "Dead Solid Perfect: Achieving Sales Compensation Alignment," *Compensation and Benefits Review*, March–April 1996, pp. 46–47.

74. In the salary plus bonus plan, salespeople are paid a basic salary and are then paid a bonus for carrying out specified activities. For a discussion of how to develop a customer-focused sales compensation plan, see, for example, Mark Blessington, "Designing a Sales Strategy with the Customer in Mind," *Compensation and Benefits Review*, March–April 1992, pp. 30–41. See also Bill O'Connell, "Dead Solid Perfect: Achieving Sales Compensation Alignment," *Compensation and Benefits Review*, March–April 1996, pp. 41–48.

75. This is based on "Sales Incentives Get the Job Done," *Sales and Marketing Management*, September 14, 1981, pp. 67–120.

76. Jeanie Casisom, "Jumpstart Motivation," *Incentive* 175, no. 5 (May 2001), p. 77.

77. Kathleen Cholewka, "Tech Tools," *Sales and Marketing Management* 153, no. 7 (July 2001), p. 24.

78. Paul Gilster, "Online Incentives Sizzle—and You Shine," *Workforce*, January 2001, p. 46.

79. Mark Stiffler, "Incentive Compensation and the Web," *Compensation and Benefits Review*, January–February 2001, pp. 15–19.

80. Bill Weeks, "Setting Sales Force Compensation in the Internet Age," *Compensation and Benefits Review*, March–April 2000, pp. 25–34.

81. S. Scott Sands, "Ineffective Quotes: The Hidden Threat to Sales Compensation Plans," *Compensation and Benefits Review*, March–April 2000, pp. 35–42.

82. David Cocks and Dennis Gould, "Sales Compensation: A New Technology—The Enabled Strategy," *Compensation and Benefits Review*, January–February 2001, pp. 27–31.

83. Peter Glendinning, "Kicking the Tires of Automotive Sales Compensation," *Compensation and Benefits Review*, September–October 2000, pp. 47–53.

84. William Keenan Jr., "More Than Volume," *Industry Week* 249, September 4, 2000, no. 14, p. 21.

85. Eileen Zimmerman, "*Sales and Marketing Management*" 153 (January 2001), no. 1, pp. 58–63.

86. "Buck Survey Finds Pay Raises Will Remain Stable in 2000," *Corporate Board* 21, no. 120 (January 2000), p. 26.

87. See, for example, Herbert Meyer, "The Pay for Performance Dilemma," *Organizational Dynamics*, winter 1975, pp. 39–50; Thomas Patten Jr., "Pay for Performance or Placation?" *Personnel Administrator* 24 (September 1977), pp. 26–29; William Kearney, "Pay for Performance? Not Always," *MSU Business Topics*, spring 1979, pp. 5–16. See also Hoyt Doyel and Janet Johnson, "Pay Increase Guidelines with Merit," *Personnel Journal* 64 (June 1985), pp. 46–50.

88. Nathan Winstanley, "Are Merit Increases Really Effective?" *Personnel Administrator* 27 (April 1982), pp. 37–41. See also William Seithel and Jeff Emans, "Calculating Merit Increases: A Structured Approach," *Personnel* 60, no. 5 (June 1985), pp. 56–68; Donald Campbell, et al., "Merit Pay, Performance Appraisal, and Individual Motivation: An Analysis and Alternative," *Human Resource Management* 37, no. 2 (summer 1998), pp. 131–146.

89. James T. Brinks, "Is There Merit in Merit Increases?" *Personnel Administrator* 25 (May 1980), p. 60. See also Dan Gilbert and Glenn Bassett, "Merit Pay Increases Are a Mistake," *Compensation and Benefits Review* 26, no. 2 (March–April 1994), pp. 20–25.

90. The average uncorrected cross-sectional correlation was .17. Michael Harris, et al., "A Longitudinal Examination of a Merit Pay System: Relationships Among Performance Ratings, Merit Increases, and Total Pay Increases," *Journal of Applied Psychology* 83, no. 5 (1998), pp. 825–831.

91. *Merit Pay: Fitting the Pieces Together* (Chicago: Commerce Clearing House, 1982).

92. Suzanne Minken, "Does Lump Sum Pay Merit Attention?" *Personnel Journal*, June 1988, pp. 77–83. See also Jerry Newman and Daniel Fisher, "Strategic Impact Merit Pay," *Compensation and Benefits Review*, July–August 1992, pp. 38–45.

93. Jonathan Glater, "Varying the Recipe Helps TV Operations Solve Morale Problem," *New York Times*, March 7, 2001, p. C.1.

94. This section is based primarily on Robert Gibson, *Compensation* (New York: AMACOM, 1981), pp. 189–207. See also Rekha Balu, "Bonuses Aren't Just for the Bosses," *Fast Company*, December 2000, pp. 74–76.

95. Edward Deci and Richard Ryan, *Intrinsic Motivation and Self-Determination in Human Behavior* (New York: Plenum Press, 1985).

96. Esther Shein, "Team Spirit: IT Is Getting Creative with Compensation to Foster Collaboration," *PC Week*, May 11, 1998, pp. 69–72.

97. Rose-Robin Pedone, "Engineering the Job Market," *LI Business News*, July 27, 1998, p. 1B.

98. Julia King, "Name Your Price, As Talent Plays Hardball with Software Firms," *Computerworld*, September 16, 1996, p. 32.

99. Richard Arnold, "Catching a Star," *CA Magazine*, October 1998, pp. S30–33.

100. Harrington, "Saying 'We Love You' with Stock Options," p. 316.

101. Betty Sosnin, "A Patent on the Back," *HR Magazine*, March 2000, pp. 107–112.

102. "American Airlines' Profit Sharing Tops $250 Million," *Knight-Ridder/Tribune Business News*, February 27, 1998, p. 227.

103. "Ford Motor Co. Profit-Sharing Plan," *Wall Street Journal*, October 13, 1998, p. B5.

104. "Sharing the Wealth—GM," *Ward's Auto World*, March 1998, p. 7.

105. Bert Metzger and Jerome Colletti, "Does Profit Sharing Pay?" (Evanston, IL: Profit Sharing Research Foundation, 1971), quoted in

Belcher, *Compensation Administration*, p. 353. See also D. Keith Denton, "An Employee Ownership Program That Rebuilt Success," *Personnel Journal* 66, no. 3 (March 1987), pp. 114–118; and Edward Shepart, "Profit Sharing and Productivity: Further Evidence from the Chemicals Industry," *Industrial Relations* 33, no. 4 (October 1994), pp. 452–466.

106. Seongsu Kim, "Does Profit Sharing Increase Firms' Profits?" *Journal of Labor Research*, spring 1998, pp. 351–371.

107. Belcher, *Compensation Administration*, p. 351.

108. Based on Randy Swad, "Stock Ownership Plans: A New Employee Benefit," *Personnel Journal* 60 (June 1982), pp. 453–455.

109. See James Brockardt and Robert Reilly, "Employee Stock Ownership Plans After the 1989 Tax Law: Valuation Issues," *Compensation and Benefits Review*, September–October 1990, pp. 29–36.

110. Donald Sullivan, "ESOPs," *California Management Review* 20, no. 1 (fall 1977), pp. 55–56. For a discussion of the effects of employee stock ownership on employee attitudes, see Katherine Klein, "Employee-Stock Ownership and Employee Attitudes: A Test of Three Models," *Journal of Applied Psychology* 72, no. 2 (May 1987), pp. 319–331; and John Gamble, "ESOPs: Financial Performance and Federal Tax Incentives," *Journal of Labor Research* 19, no. 3 (summer 1998), pp. 529–542.

111. Steven Etkind, "ESOPs Create Liquidity for Shareholders and Help Diversify Their Assets," *Estate Planning* 24, no. 4 (May 1998), pp. 158–165.

112. Everett Allen Jr., Joseph Melone, and Jerry Rosenbloom, *Pension Planning* (Burr Ridge, IL: McGraw-Hill, 1981), p. 316. Note that the Tax Reduction Act of 1975 has also led to the creation of the so-called TRAFOP. This is a regular employee stock ownership plan except that a portion of the investment tax credit that employers receive for investing in capital equipment can be invested in the employee stock ownership plan.

113. William Smith, Harold Lazarus, and Harold Murray Kalkstein, "Employee Stock Ownership Plans: Motivation and Morale Issues," *Compensation and Benefits Review*, September–October 1990, pp. 37–46.

114. Best Manufacturing Practices Center of Excellence, copyright 1998.

115. Brian Moore and Timothy Ross, *The Scanlon Way to Improved Productivity: A Practical Guide* (New York: Wiley, 1978), p. 2.

116. These are based in part on Steven Markham, K. Dow Scott, and Walter Cox Jr., "The Evolutionary Development of a Scanlon Plan," *Compensation and Benefits Review*, March–April 1992, pp. 50–56.

117. J. Kenneth White, "The Scanlon Plan: Causes and Correlates of Success," *Academy of Management Journal* 22 (June 1979), pp. 50–56.

118. Markham, et al., "The Evolutionary Development of a Scanlon Plan," p. 51.

119. Moore and Ross, *The Scanlon Way*, pp. 1–2.

120. George Sherman, "The Scanlon Plan: Its Capabilities for Productive Improvement," *Personnel Administrator*, July 1976.

121. "The Effects of Improshare on Productivity," *Industrial and Labor Relations Review* 45, no. 2 (1991), pp. 311–322.

122. Barry W. Thomas and Madeline Hess Olson, "Gainsharing: The Design Guarantees Success," *Personnel Journal*, May 1988, pp. 73–79. See also "Aligning Compensation with Quality," *Bulletin to Management, BNA Policy and Practice Series*, April 1, 1993, p. 97.

123. See Theresa A. Welbourne and Luis Gomez Mejia, "Gainsharing Revisited," *Compensation and Benefits Review*, July–August 1988, pp. 19–28.

124. Carla O'Dell and Jerry McAdams, *People, Performance, and Pay* (American Productivity Center and Carla O'Dell, 1987), p. 34.

125. Thomas and Olson, "Gainsharing," pp. 75–76. See also Thomas McGrath, "Gainsharing: Engineering the Human Factor of Productivity," *Industrial Engineering*, September 1993, pp. 61–63; Paul Rossler and C. Patrick Koelling, "The Effect of Gainsharing on Business Performance at a Paper Mill," *National Productivity Review*, summer 1993, pp. 365–382.

126. O'Dell and McAdams, *People, Performance, and Pay*, p. 42.

127. This is paraphrased from Woodruff Imberman, "Boosting Plant Performance with Gainsharing," *Business Horizons*, November–December 1992, p. 77.

128. For other examples, see Timothy Ross and Larry Hatcher, "Gainsharing Drives Quality Improvement," *Personnel Journal*, November 1992, pp.

81–89. See also Jerry McAdams, "Employee Involvement and Performance Reward Plans: Design, Implementation, and Results," *Compensation and Benefits Review* 27, no. 2 (March 1995), pp. 45–55.

129. John Belcher Jr., "Gainsharing and Variable Pay: The State of the Art," *Compensation and Benefits Review*, May–June 1994, pp. 50–60. See also Kevin Patton and Dennis Daley, "Gainsharing in Zebulon: What Do Workers Want?" *Public Personnel Management*, 27, no. 1 (spring 1998), pp. 117–132.

130. This is based on Thomas McGrath, "How Three Screw Machine Companies Are Tapping Human Productivity Through Gainsharing," *Employment Relations Today*, winter 1993–94, pp. 437–446.

131. See, for example, Moore and Ross, *The Scanlon Way to Improved Productivity*, pp. 157–164; Jeffrey Ewing, "Gainsharing Plans: Two Key Factors," *Compensation and Benefits Review* 21, no. 1, (January–February 1989), pp. 51–52. For a description of the implementation of a gainsharing plan in health care institutions, see Steven Markham, et al., "Gainsharing Experiments in Health Care," *Compensation and Benefits Review*, March–April 1992, pp. 57–64. See also Dwight Willett, "Promoting Quality Through Compensation," *Business Quarterly*, autumn 1993, pp. 107–111; Robert Masternak, "Gainsharing: Overcoming Common Myths and Problems to Achieve Dramatic Results," *Employment Relations Today*, winter 1993–94, pp. 425–436.

132. Robert McNutt, "Sharing Across the Board: DuPont's Achievement Sharing Program," *Compensation and Benefits Review*, July–August 1990, pp. 17–24.

133. Frederick Taylor, "What Is Scientific Management?" reprinted in Michael Matteson and John Ivancevich, *Management Classics* (Santa Monica, CA: Goodyear, 1977), pp. 5–8.

134. The following five points are based on Alfie Kohn, "Why Incentive Plans Cannot Work," *Harvard Business Review*, September–October 1993, pp. 54–63.

135. Ibid., p. 58.

136. Ibid., p. 62.

137. Ibid; see also Bruce Tulgan, "Real Pay for Performance," *Journal of Business Strategy* 22, May/June 2001, no. 3, pp. 19–22.

138. Belcher, *Compensation Administration*, pp. 309–310.

139. See, for example, James Gutherie and Edward Cunningham, "Pay for Performance: The Quaker Oats Alternative," *Compensation and Benefits Review* 24, no. 2 (March–April 1992), pp. 18–23.

140. Gary Yukl and Gary Latham, "Consequences of Reinforcement Schedules and Incentives Magnitudes for Employee Performance: Problems Encountered in an Industrial Setting," *Journal of Applied Psychology* 60 (June 1975).

141. J. Keith Louden and J. Wayne Deegan, *Wage Incentives* (New York: Wiley, 1959), p. 26.

142. Alfie Kohn, "Challenging Behaviorist Dogma: Myths About Money and Motivation," *Compensation and Benefits Review*, March–April 1998, pp. 27–32.

143. Ibid., pp. 30–31.

144. Francine McKenzie and Matthew Shilling, "Avoiding Performance Measurement Traps: Ensuring Effective Incentive Design and Implementation," *Compensation and Benefits Review*, July–August 1998, p. 64.

145. Ibid., p. 64.

146. Gary Dessler, "How to Earn Your Employees' Commitment," *Academy of Management Executive* 13, no. 2 (1999), pp. 58–67; Steven Gross and Jeffrey Bacher, "The New Variable Pay Programs: How Some Succeed, Why Some Don't," *Compensation and Benefits Review*, January–February 1993, pp. 55–56. See also George Milkovich and Carolyn Milkovich, "Strengthening the Pay-Performance Relationship: The Research," *Compensation and Benefits Review*, November–December 1992, pp. 53–62; Jay Schuster and Patricia Zingheim, "The New Variable Pay: Key Design Issues," *Compensation and Benefits Review*, March–April 1993, pp. 27–34; Nina Gupta and Jason Shaw, "Financial Incentives Are Effective!" *Compensation and Benefits Review*, March–April 1998, pp. 28–32.

147. The following are based on Michael J. Cissell, "Designing Effective Reward Systems," *Compensation and Benefits Review*, November–December 1987, pp. 49–56.

148. This is based on William E. Buhl, "Keeping Incentives Simple for Nonexempt Employees," *Compensation and Benefits Review*, March–April 1989, pp. 14–19.

149. Ibid., pp. 15–16.

150. The following is based on Gary Dessler, *Winning Commitment* (New York: McGraw-Hill Book Company, 1993), Chapter 9.

151. *Blueprints for Service Quality: The Federal Express Approach* (New York: AMA Membership Publication Division, 1991), pp. 31–32.

152. "Compensation at Federal Express," company document, p. 8.

153. Unless otherwise indicated, the section on pay-for-performance is based on "Compensation at Federal Express," pp. 8–9.

154. *Blueprints for Service Quality*, p. 32.

155. Ibid., pp. 34–35.

Chapter 13

1. Floyd Griffin and Jerry Fox, "Facing Up to the Labor Shortage," *Compensation and Benefits Review*, September–October 2000, pp. 34–46.

2. Based on Frederick Hills, Thomas Bergmann, and Vida Scarpello, *Compensation Decision Making* (Fort Worth: The Dryden Press, 1994), p. 424. See also L. Kate Beatty, "Pay and Benefits Break Away from Tradition," *HR Magazine* 39, no. 11 (November 1994), pp. 63–68.

3. "Employee Benefit Costs Declined in 1996, Survey Reveals," *BNA Bulletin to Management*, January 29, 1998, p. 29.

4. This is based on "Employee Benefits in Medium and Large Firms," *BNA Bulletin to Management*, September 4, 1997, pp. 284–285.

5. Joseph Martocchio, *Strategic Compensation* (Upper Saddle River, NJ: Prentice Hall, 2001), p. 262.

6. "Benefit Costs Averaged 36.8 Percent of Payroll in 1999," *Employee Benefit Plan Review* 55, no. 10 (April 2001), pp. 14–16.

7. K. Matthes, "In Pursuit of Leisure: Employees Want More Time Off," *HR Focus* 7 (1992).

8. Richard Henderson, *Compensation Management* (Upper Saddle River, NJ: Prentice Hall, 1994), p. 555.

9. Julekha Dash, "Microsoft Boosts Worker Benefits; Unlimited Vacation Time Could Spark IT Trend," *Computerworld* 28, no. 1 (April 24, 2000).

10. Henderson, *Compensation Management*, p. 116.

11. "BNA's Quarterly Report on Job Absence and Turnover, Third Quarter 1997," *BNA Bulletin to Management*, December 11, 1997, pp. 1–4.

12. Miriam Rothman, "Can Alternatives to Sick Pay Plans Reduce Absenteeism?" *Personnel Journal* 60 (October 1981), pp. 788–791; Richard Bunning, "A Prescription for Sick Leave," *Personnel Journal* 67, no. 8 (August 1988), pp. 44–49.

13. This is based on M. Michael Markowich and Steve Eckberg, "Get Control of the Absentee-Minded," *Personnel Journal*, March 1996, pp. 115–120.

14. Ibid., p. 119.

15. This is based on Margaret Meiers, "Parental Leave and the Bottom Line," *Personnel Journal*, September 1988, pp. 108–115.

16. "Employers Complain About Leave Law and Absences," *BNA Bulletin to Management*, June 19, 1997, p. 193.

17. "Military Duty, Family Leave Laws Produce Complaints," *BNA Bulletin to Management*, June 13, 1996, p. 186.

18. "Individual Liability Under FMLA," *BNA Fair Employment Practices*, November 30, 1995, p. 139.

19. Dawn Gunch, "The Family Leave Act: A Financial Burden?" *Personnel Journal*, September 1993, p. 49.

20. "Employers Describe the FMLA as More Burdensome, But Having Little Effect on Productivity, Profits," *BNA Bulletin to Management*, January 18, 2001, p. 17.

21. Gillian Flynn, "Employers Need an FMLA Brush-Up," *Workforce*, (April 1997), pp. 101–104. See also "Worker Who Was Employee for Less than One Year Can Pursue FMLA Claim, Federal Court Determines," *BNA Fair Employment Practices*, April 26, 2001, p. 51.

22. "Workers Who Come and Go Under FMLA Complicate Attendance Policies, Lawyer Says," *BNA Bulletin to Management*, March 16, 2000, p. 81.

23. "Severance Practices," *BNA Bulletin to Management*, January 11, 1996, pp. 12, 13.

24. Ibid.

25. "Severance Pay Common for Workers Who Lose Jobs," *BNA Bulletin to Management*, August 31, 1995, p. 273.

26. Joseph Famularo, *Handbook of Modern Personnel Administration* (New York: McGraw-Hill, 1972), pp. 51–62. See also Glenn Whittington, "Workers' Compensation Legislation Enacted in 1997," *Monthly Labor Review* 21, no. 1, pp. 23–28; William Atkinson, "Is Workers' Compensation Changing?" *HR Magazine* 45, no. 7 (July 2000) pp. 50–61.

27. Henderson, *Compensation Management*, p. 250. For an explanation of how to reduce workers' compensation costs, see Betty Strigel Bialk, "Cutting Workers' Compensation Costs," *Personnel Journal* 66, no. 7 (July 1987), pp. 95–97.

28. "Workers' Compensation and ADA," *BNA Bulletin to Management*, August 6, 1992, p. 248.

29. See, for example, Bialk, "Cutting Workers' Compensation Costs," pp. 95–97.

30. Steve Lattanzio, "What Can Employers Do to Influence the Cost of Its Workers' Compensation Program?" *Compensation and Benefits Review*, 1997, pp. 20–30.

31. "Using Case Management in Workers' Compensation," *BNA Bulletin to Management*, June 6, 1996, p. 181.

32. "Firms Cite Own Efforts as Key to Controlling Costs," *BNA Bulletin to Management*, March 21, 1996, p. 89. See also "Workers' Compensation Outlook: Cost Control Persists," *BNA Bulletin to Management*, January 30, 1997, pp. 33–44.

33. Best Manufacturing Practices Center of Excellence, copyright 1998. John Matysiak, "The Pursuit of Zero Accidents at Weirton," *New Steel* 17, no. 5, May 2001, p. 34.

34. "Employee Benefits in Small Firms," *BNA Bulletin to Management*, June 27, 1991, pp. 196–197.

35. Richard Gisonny and Michael Langan, "EEOC Provides Guidance on Application of ADA on Health Plans," *Benefits Law Journal* 6, no. 3 (autumn 1993), pp. 461–467.

36. Johnathan Mook, "The ADA and Employee Benefits: A Regulatory and Litigation Update," *Benefits Law Journal* 7, no. 4 (winter 1994–95), pp. 407–429.

37. Rita Jain, "Employer-Sponsored Dental Insurance Eases the Pain," *Monthly Labor Review*, October 1988, p. 23.

38. Bureau of National Affairs, *Bulletin to Management*, December 23, 1982, p. 1; "TEFRA—The Tax Equity and Fiscal Responsibility Act of 1982," *Personnel* 59 (November–December 1982), p. 43.

39. A. N. Nash and S. J. Carroll Jr., "Supplemental Compensation," in *Perspectives on Personnel: Human Resource Management*, Herbert Heneman III and Donald Schwab, eds. (Burr Ridge, IL: McGraw-Hill, 1978), p. 223.

40. Thomas Snodeker and Michael Kuhns, "HMOs: Regulations, Problems, and Outlook," *Personnel Journal* 60 (August 1981), pp. 629–631.

41. Hills, Bergmann, and Scarpello, *Compensation Decision Making*, p. 137.

42. George Milkovich and Jerry Newman, *Compensation* (Burr Ridge, IL: McGraw-Hill, 1993), p. 445.

43. "Employers Continue to Heed Workers' Call for Flexibility and Benefit Plans, Survey Says," *BNA Bulletin to Management*, April 26, 2001, p. 129.

44. "Employee Benefits Costs," *BNA Bulletin to Management*, January 2, 1997, pp. 4–5.

45. Hewitt Associates, "Health Care Costs Becoming Shared Responsibility," *News and Information*, June 21, 1984. See also *Health Care Cost Containment* (New York: William Mercer-Meidinger, 1984), as discussed in *Compensation Review*, fourth quarter 1984, pp. 8–9; Thomas Paine, "Outlook for Compensation and Benefits: 1986 and Beyond," Hewitt Associates, October 30, 1985; Hewitt Associates, *News and Information*, February 6, 1990; "Health Care Cost Sharing: Coating the Pill," *BNA Bulletin to Management*, March 10, 1994, p. 73; "Requiring Employers to Share Health Care Costs Results in Lower Use of All Health Care Services," *BNA Bulletin to Management*, March 10, 1994, p. 79.

46. "Managing Health Care Costs," *BNA Bulletin to Management*, August 27, 1992, p. 272. See also Jennifer Hutchins, "Labor and Management Build a Prescription for Health," *Workforce*, March 2001, pp. 50–52.

47. Hewitt Associates, "Employers Trim Future Health Care Costs by Keeping Employees Well," *News and Information*, June 7, 1984; Morton Grossman and Margaret Magnus, "The Boom in Benefits," *Personnel Journal*, November 1988, pp. 51–55; "Employer Initiatives Help Cycle Health Care Costs," *BNA Bulletin to Management*, July 31, 1997, pp. 241–242.

48. Don Bohl, "Company Bets That Wellness Incentives Plus Preventive Care Will Contain Health Care Costs," *Compensation and Benefits Review*, July–August 1993, pp. 20–23.

49. "Employer Initiatives Help Curb Health Care Costs," *BNA Bulletin to Management*, July 31, 1997, pp. 241–242.

50. "Measuring Success of Wellness Programs Turns Murky on the Bottom Line, Study Says," *BNA Bulletin to Management*, March 8, 1999, p. 81.

51. Shari Caudron, "Teaming up to Cut Health-Care Costs," *Personnel Journal*, September 1993, p. 194. See also "Fraudulent Health Plans Targeted," *BNA Bulletin to Management*, April 14, 1994, p. 120.

52. Ibid., p. 107. See also Ann Knoll, "Top Ten Mistakes Made in Employee Health Benefit Plans," *Compensation and Benefits Review*, January–February 1994, pp. 54–58.

53. The following is based on Michael Gomez, "Managing Health Care Costs, Part I, The Dilemma of AIDS," *Compensation and Benefits Review*, September–October 1988, pp. 23–31; Nancy Breuer, "AIDS Issues Haven't Gone Away," *Personnel Journal* 71, no. 1 (January 1992), pp. 47–49. See also Kato Keeton, "AIDS Related Attitudes Among Government Employees: Implications for Training Programs," *Review of Public Personnel Administration*, spring 1993, pp. 65–90.

54. This is based on Thomas C. Billet, "Managing Health Care Costs, Part II, Coping with Mental Health," *Compensation and Benefits Review*, September–October 1988, pp. 32–36; see also Nancy Jackson, "Health Care on the Home Front," *Workforce* 77, no. 3 (March 1998), pp. 30ff.

55. Ronald Bachman, "Time for Another Look," *HR Magazine*, March 1997, pp. 93–96.

56. Ibid., pp. 35–36.

57. James Weil, "Baby Boomer Needs Will Spur Growth of Long-Term Care Plans," *Compensation and Benefits Review*, March–April 1996, p. 49.

58. Carolyn Hirschman, "Will Employers Take the Lead in Long-Term Care?" *HR Magazine*, March 1997, pp. 59–66.

59. Robert E. Sibson, *Wages and Salaries: A Handbook for Line Managers* (New York: American Management Association, 1967), p. 235.

60. Bill Leonard, "Recipes for Part-Time Benefits," *HR Magazine*, April 2000, pp. 56–62.

61. Geoffrey Coldin, "How to Beat the Boomer Rush," *Fortune*, August 18, 1997, pp. 59–63.

62. Brenda Paik Sunoo, "Millions May Retire," *Workforce*, December 1997, p. 48.

63. "Retirement Plans Getting a Boost, Surveys Find," *BNA Bulletin to Management*, November 7, 1996, p. 353.

64. Jerome B. Cohen and Arthur Hanson, *Personnel Finance* (Burr Ridge, IL: McGraw-Hill, 1964), pp. 312–320. See also *BNA*, January 14, 1988, pp. 12–13. This article explains changes in the Social Security law and presents an exhibit showing how to estimate your Social Security benefits.

65. Harry Plack, "ABCs of Social Security," *Baltimore Business Journal* 19, no. 3 (June 8, 2001), p. 33.

66. "Pension Plan Coverage," *BNA Bulletin to Management*, April 4, 1996, pp. 108–109.

67. "Lower Income Workers' Pensions at Risk, Report Finds," *BNA Bulletin to Management*, August 22, 1996, p. 271.

68. Martocchio, *Strategic Compensation*, pp. 245–248.

69. Lindsay Wyatt, "401(k) Conversion: It's as Easy as Riding a Bike," *Workforce*, (April 1997), p. 66.

70. "401(k) Is Now a Mainstay for Retirement Benefits," *HR Magazine*, April 2000, p. 31.

71. Arlene Jacobius, "Ford Offers Fidelity Planning Tool to Its Participants: The 401(k) Feature Includes Customized Model Portfolios," *Pension and Investments*, May 3, 1999, p. 36.

72. Wyatt, "401(k) Conversion," p. 20.

73. Matt Hamblin, "Benefit Bone and Then Some: When It Comes to Basic Job Perks, IT Pros Want Them All—Plus a Fat Paycheck" *Computerworld* 54, no. 1 (June 19, 2000).

74. Victor Infante, "Retirement Plan Trends," *Workforce*, November 2000, pp. 69–76.

75. Sibson, *Wages and Salaries*, p. 234. For an explanation of how to minimize employee benefits litigation related to pension and health bene-

fits claims, see Thomas Piskorski, "Minimizing Employee Benefits Litigation Through Effective Claims Administration Procedures," *Employee Relations Law Journal* 20, no. 3 (winter 1994–95), pp. 421–431.

76. See Irwin Tepper, "Risk vs. Return in Pension Fund Investment," *Harvard Business Review* 56 (March–April 1977), pp. 100–107; William Rupert, "ERISA: Compliance May Be Easier than You Expect and Pay Unexpected Dividends," *Personnel Journal* 55 (April 1976). For a discussion of a survey regarding retirement planning and the challenges that employees face in planning retirement policy in the new millennium, see Diane Filipowski, "Retirement Planning in the Year 2000," *Personnel Journal*, July 1993, p. 34.

77. Robert Paul, "The Impact of Pension Reform on American Business," *Sloan Management Review* 18 (fall 1976), pp. 59–71. See also John M. Walbridge Jr., "The Next Hurdle for Benefits Manager: Section 89," *Compensation and Benefits Review* 20, no. 6 (November–December 1988), pp. 22–35.

78. Bureau of National Affairs, "Tax Reform Act: Major Changes in Store for Compensation Programs," *Bulletin to Management*, October 9, 1986, p. 1.

79. In fact, unfunded pension liabilities of American firms have continued to grow. "Pension Survey: Unfunded Liabilities Continue to Grow," *Business Week*, August 25, 1980, pp. 94–97. See also James Benson and Barbara Suzaki, "After Tax Reform, Part III, Planning Executive Benefits," *Compensation and Benefits Review* 20, no. 2 (March–April 1988), pp. 45–57; and BNA, "Post-Retirement Benefits Impact of FASB New Accounting Rule," February 23, 1989, p. 57.

80. For a discussion, see Milton Zall, "Understanding the Risks to Pension Benefits," *Personnel Journal*, January 1992, pp. 62–69.

81. "Trends," *BNA Bulletin to Management*, May 7, 1992, p. 143.

82. Wallace Davidson III, Dan Worrell, and Jeremy Fox, "Early Retirement Programs and Firm Performance," *Academy of Management Journal* 39, no. 4 (1996), p. 980.

83. Marco Colosi, Philip Rosen, and Sara Herrin, "Is Your Early Retirement Package Courting Disaster?" *Personnel Journal*, August 1988, pp. 59–67; see also Jenny McCune, "The Future of Retirement," *Management Review* 87, no. 4 (April 1998), pp. 10–16.

84. *Paolillo v. Dresser Industries*, 821F.2d81 (2d cir., 1987).

85. See also Eugene Seibert and Jo Anne Seibert, "Look into Window Alternatives," *Personnel Journal*, May 1989, pp. 80–87.

86. Arthur Silbergeld, "Release Agreements Must Comply with the Older Workers' Benefit Protection Act," *Employment Relations Today*, winter 1992–93, pp. 457–460.

87. Kathleen Murray, "How HR Is Making Pensions Portable," *Personnel Journal*, July 1993, pp. 36–46.

88. Ibid., p. 43.

89. Harold Burlingame and Michael Gulotta, "Cash Balance Pension Plan Facilitates Restructuring the Workforce at AT&T," *Compensation and Benefits Review*, November–December 1998, pp. 25–31; Eric Lekus, "When Are Cash Balance Pension Plans the Right Choice?" *BNA Bulletin to Management*, January 28, 1999, p. 7.

90. Floyd Griffin and Jerry Fox, "Facing Up to the Labor Shortage," *Compensation and Benefits Review*, September–October 2000, pp. 34–46.

91. Tina Carlson, "Arrowhead C.U. to Open Branch on Used Car Lot," *Credit Union Journal* 5, no. 4 (January 22, 2001), p. 6.

92. See Henderson, *Compensation Management*, pp. 336–339. See also Lewis Burger, "Group Legal Service Plans: A Benefit Whose Time Has Come," *Compensation and Benefits Review* 18, no. 4 (July–August 1986), pp. 28–34; Gillian Flynn, "Legal Assistance Offers Prepaid Peace of Mind," *Personnel Journal*, October 1996, pp. 48–56.

93. Richard T. Hellan, "Employee Assistance: An EAP Update: A Perspective for the '80s," *Personnel Journal* 65, no. 6 (1986), p. 51. See also Shelly Cohen, "When Employees' Crises Become HR's Problem," *Workforce* 80, no. 1 (January 2001), pp. 64–69.

94. See Dale Masi and Seymour Friedland, "EAP Actions & Options," *Personnel Journal*, June 1988, pp. 61–67.

95. See Scott MacDonald, et al., "Absenteeism and Other Workplace Indicators of Employee Assistant Program Clients and Matched Controls," *Employee Assistance Quarterly* 15, no. 3 (2000), pp. 51–58.

96. Based on Masi and Friedland, "EAP Actions." See also Harry Turk, "Questions and Answers: Avoiding Liability for EAP Services," *Employment Relations Today*, spring 1992, pp. 111–114.

97. "Employee Benefit Costs," *BNA Bulletin to Management*, January 16, 1992, pp. 12–14.

98. The Research Staff of Hewitt Associations, *Innovative Benefits*, Hewitt Associates.

99. "Child Care Options," *BNA Bulletin to Management*, July 4, 1996, p. 212.

100. Ibid.

101. This is based on ibid., pp. 212–214.

102. "Employers and Child Care: Establishing Services Through the Workplace," Women's Bureau, U.S. Department of Labor, Washington, DC, 1982. See also BNA, "Special Survey on Child Care Assistance Programs," *Bulletin to Management*, March 26, 1987; Donald J. Peterson and Douglas Massengill, "Child Care Programs Benefit Employers, Too," *Personnel* 65, no. 5 (May 1988), pp. 58–62; Toni A. Campbell and David E. Campbell, "Employers and Child Care," *Personnel Journal* 67, no. 4 (April 1988), pp. 84–87; C. David Woodford, "Child Care: The McDonald's Model," *Fortune*, September 18, 2000, pp. 333–338.

103. Commerce Clearing House, "As the Population Ages, There Is Growing Interest in Adding Elder Care to the Benefits Package," *Ideas and Trends*, August 21, 1987, pp. 129–131.

104. Kelli Earhart, R. Dennis Middlemist, and Willie Hopkins, "Elder Care: An Emerging Assistance Issue," *Employee Assistance Quarterly* 8, no. 3 (1993), pp. 1–10.

105. Susan Wells, "The Elder Care Gap," *HR Magazine*, May 2000, pp. 39–46.

106. For another example, see "Elder Care: A Maturing Benefit," *BNA Bulletin to Management*, February 20, 1992, pp. 50–55.

107. Mary Zippo, "Subsidized Employee Transportation: A Three Way Benefit," *Personnel* 57 (May–June 1980), pp. 40–41.

108. Hewitt Associates, *Survey of Educational Reimbursement Programs*, 1984.

109. "Chrysler Benefit to Cover Tuition, Dependent Care," *BNA Bulletin to Management*, October 2, 1997, p. 313.

110. Maureen Hannay and Melissa Northam, "Low-Cost Strategies for Employee Retention," *Compensation and Benefits Review*, July–August 2000, pp. 65–72.

111. "Work/Life Perks Often Avoided by Workers, Poll Finds," *BNA Bulletin to Management*, March 19, 1998, p. 81.

112. "Family-Friendly Benefits Have Spread Greatly," *BNA Bulletin to Management*, March 7, 1996, p. 73.

113. "Employers Continue to Heed Workers' Call for Flexibility and Benefit Plans, Survey Says," *BNA Bulletin to Management*, April 26, 2001, p. 129.

114. Leslie Fraught, "At Eddie Bauer You Can Have Work and Have a Life," *Workforce*, April 1997, p. 84; "Companies' Progressive Work/Life Policies Earned Industry Recognition, Employee Loyalty," *BNA Bulletin to Management*, September 21, 2000, p. 297.

115. Fraught, "At Eddie Bauer, You Can Have Work and Have a Life," p. 84.

116. Gillian Flynn, "Making a Business Case for Balance," *Workforce*, March 1997, pp. 68–74.

117. Jerry Useem, "Welcome to the New Company Town," *Fortune*, January 10, 2000, pp. 62–70.

118. Patricia Nakache, "One VP, Two Brains," *Fortune*, December 20, 1999, pp. 327–328.

119. Charles Fishman, "Moving Toward a Balanced Work Life," *Workforce*, March 2000, pp. 38–42.

120. Quentin Hardy, "Aloft Without Fetters," *Wall Street Journal*, September 29, 1998, p. B1.

121. "Work/Life Perks Often Avoided by Workers, Poll Finds," *BNA Bulletin to Management*, March 19, 1998, p. 81.

122. Ibid., p. 81.

123. Ibid., p. 81. For another point of view, see Michael Schrage, "Family Friendly Firms Will Find That No Good Deeds Go Unpunished," *Fortune*, May 24, 1999, p. 294.

124. P. Osterman, "Work/Family Programs and the Employment Relationship," *Administrative Science Quarterly* 40, no. 1995, pp. 681–700.

125. Susan Lambert, "Added Benefits: The Link Between Work Life Benefits and Organizational Citizenship Behavior," *Academy of Management Journal* 43, no. 5 (2000), pp. 801–815.

126. Matthew Boyle, "How to Cut Perks Without Killing Morale," *Fortune*, February 19, 2001, pp. 241–244.

127. Ellen Ernst Kossek and Cynthia Ozeki, "Work-Family Conflict, Policies, and the Job-Life Satisfaction Relationship: A Review and Direction for

Organizational Behavior-Human Resources Research," *Journal of Applied Psychology* 83, no. 2 (1998), pp. 139–149.

128. Ibid., pp. 143–144.

129. Bruce Ellig, *Executive Compensation: A Total Pay Perspective* (New York: McGraw-Hill, 1982), p. 141.

130. Martocchio, *Strategic Compensation*, pp. 308–309.

131. Matthew Budman, "The Persistence of Perks," *Across the Board* (February 1994), pp. 44–46.

132. "Executive Perks," *Compensation and Benefits Review* 10 (January 1999).

133. Budman, "The Persistence of Perks," p. 45.

134. J. Brad Chapman and Robert Ottermann, "Employee Preference for Various Compensation and Fringe Benefit Options" (Berea, OH: ASPA Foundation, 1975). See also William White and James Becker, "Increasing the Motivational Impact of Employee Benefits," *Personnel*, January–February 1980, pp. 32–37; Barney Olmsted and Suzanne Smith, "Flex for Success!" *Personnel* 66, no. 6 (June 1989), pp. 50–55.

135. "Couples Want Flexible Leave, Benefits," *BNA Bulletin to Management*, February 19, 1998, p. 53.

136. "Money Isn't Everything," *Journal of Business Strategy* 21, no. 2 (March 2000), p. 4.

137. Carolyn Hirschman, "Kinder, Simpler Cafeteria Rules," *HR Magazine*, January 2001, pp. 74–79.

138. Martocchio, *Strategic Compensation*, p. 263.

139. David Hom, "How Pitney Bowes Broadens Benefit Choices with Value-Added Services," *Compensation and Benefits Review*, March–April 1996, pp. 60–66.

140. Ibid., p. 60.

141. Ibid., p. 62.

142. George Milkovich and Jerry Newman, *Compensation* (Burr Ridge, IL: McGraw-Hill, 1993), p. 405.

143. See Caroline A. Baker, "Flex Your Benefits," *Personnel Journal* 67, no. 5 (May 1988), pp. 54–58, for a discussion of the pros and cons of three basic approaches to flexible benefits; and Carol Woodley, "The Benefits of Flexibility," *Personnel Management*, May 1993, pp. 36–39.

144. "Technology Revolutionizes Administration," *BNA Bulletin to Management*, November 9, 1995; "Benefits Merge onto Information Superhighway," *BNA Bulletin to Management*, February 29, 1996, p. 66; Miriam Scott, "Interactive Benefits Systems Save Time and Dollars for Employers, Employees," *Employee Benefit Plan Review*, February 1995, pp. 16–18. See also Neil Schelberg, et al., "Paperless Benefit Plan Administration," *Compensation and Benefits Review*, July/August 2000, pp. 58–64.

145. This is based on Anthony Barra, "Employees Keep Informed with Interactive KIOSKs," *Personnel Journal*, October 1988, pp. 43–51; Schelberg, et al., "Paperless Benefit Plan Administration," pp. 58–64.

146. Jim Meade, "Affordable HRIS Strong on Benefits," *HR Magazine*, April 2000, pp. 132–135.

147. Jane Applegate, "Employee Leasing Can Be Savior for Small Firms," *Business Courier Serving Cincinnati–Northern Kentucky* 16, no. 42 (January 28, 2000), p. 23.

148. Harriet Tramer, "Employee Leasing Agreement Can Ease Personnel Concerns," *Cranes Cleveland Business* 21, no. 31 (July 24, 2000), p. 24.

149. Applegate, "Employee Leasing Can Be Savior for Small Firms," p. 23.

150. Diana Reitz, "Employee Leasing Breeds Liability Questions," *National Underwriter Property and Casualty Risk and Benefits Management* 104, no. 18 (May 2000), p. 12.

Chapter 14

1. "Union Ranks in U.S. Workforce Lessen in 2000," *BNA Bulletin to Management*, March 1, 2001, p. 69.

2. Stephen Greenhouse, "Labor, Revitalized with New Recruiting, Has Regained Power and Prestige," *New York Times*, October 9, 1999, p. A10. One high-profile effort to unionize professionals recently sputtered. Over the past few years, the American Medical Association's Physicians for Responsible Negotiation spent about $3 million to begin organizing physicians. While other physicians' unions—such as the Committee of Interns and Residents, which represents about 11,000 residents at more than 60 hospitals—continue to organize, the AMA is reducing its

efforts, in part because a U.S. Supreme Court decision may make it more difficult for physicians at private hospitals to join labor unions if their duties include supervising other employees. Michael Romano, "Backpedaling: AMA Rethinks Unionizing Efforts, Cites Recent Ruling," *Modern Health Care* 31, no. 14 (June 11, 2001).

3. "Union Ranks in U.S. Workforce Lessen in 2000."

4. "Union Membership Around the World," *BNA Bulletin to Management*, November 13, 1997, pp. 364–365.

5. "Union Membership Fell Again in 1997," *BNA Bulletin to Management*, February 26, 1998, p. 60.

6. "Beyond Unions: A Revolution in Employee Rights Is in the Making," *Business Week*, July 8, 1985, p. 72; Bureau of National Affairs, "Union Membership in 1988," *Bulletin to Management*, April 13, 1989. See also Timothy Koeller, "Union Activity and the Decline in American Trade Union Membership," *Journal of Labor Research* 15, no. 1 (winter 1994), pp. 19–32.

7. "Union Membership and Earnings," *BNA Bulletin to Management*, February 13, 1997, pp. 52–53; "Union Membership Fell Again in 1997," *BNA Bulletin to Management*, February 26, 1998, p. 60.

8. William Wiatrowski, "Employee Benefits for Union and Nonunion Workers," *Monthly Labor Review*, February 1994, p. 35.

9. Nicole Harris, "Flying into a Rage?" *Business Week*, April 27, 1998, p. 119.

10. W. Clay Hammer and Frank Schmidt, "Work Attitude as Predictors of Unionization Activity," *Journal of Applied Psychology* 63, no. 4 (1978), pp. 415–421. See also Amos Okafor, "White Collar Unionization: Why and What to Do," *Personnel* 62, no. 8 (August 1985), pp. 17–20; Michael E. Gordon and Angelo DiNisi, "A Re-Examination of the Relationship Between Union Membership and Job Satisfaction," *Industrial and Labor Relations Review* 48, no. 2 (January 1995), pp. 222–236. Ninety-two percent of labor agreements recently contained provisions designed to enhance workers' employment security. "2001 Employer Bargaining Objectives," *BNA Bulletin to Management*, January 4, 2001, p. 3.

11. Jeanne Brett, "Why Employees Want Unions," *Organizational Dynamics* (spring 1980); John Fossum, *Labor Relations* (Dallas: Business Publications, 1982), p. 4.

12. Clive Fullager and Julian Barling, "A Longitudinal Test of a Model of the Antecedents and Consequences of Union Loyalty," *Journal of Applied Psychology* 74, no. 2 (April 1989), pp. 213–227; Adrienne Eaton, Michael Gordon and Jeffrey Keefe, "The Impact of Quality of Work Life Programs and Grievance Systems Effectiveness on Union Commitment," *Industrial and Labor Relations Review* 45, no. 3 (April 1992), pp. 591–604.

13. See, for example, Satish Deshpande, "A Meta-Analysis of Some Determinants of Union Voting Intent," *Relations Industrielles* 47, no. 2 (1992), pp. 334–341; Hugh Hindman and Charles Smith, "Correlates of Union Membership and Joining Intentions in a Unit of Federal Employees," *Journal of Labor Research* 14, no. 4 (fall 1993), pp. 439–454. See also Lee Graf, et al., "Profiles of Those Who Support Collective Bargaining in Institutions of Higher Learning and Why: An Empirical Examination," *Journal of Collective Negotiations* 23, no. 2 (1994), pp. 151–162.

14. Warner Pflug, *The UAW in Pictures* (Detroit: Wayne State University Press, 1971), pp. 11–12.

15. These are based on Richard Hodgetts, *Introduction to Business* (Reading, MA: Addison-Wesley, 1977), pp. 213–214.

16. "Boardroom Reports," The Conference Board, New York, December 15, 1976, p. 6. See also "Perspectives on Employment," *Research Bulletin* 194 (1986), The Conference Board, 845 Third Avenue, New York, NY 10020.

17. The following material is based on Arthur Sloane and Fred Witney, *Labor Relations* (Upper Saddle River, NJ: Prentice Hall, 2001), pp. 46–124.

18. Ibid., p. 120.

19. Karen Robinson, "Temp Workers Gain Union Access," *HR News*, Society for Human Resource Management 19, no. 10 (October 2000), p. 1.

20. Elizabeth Bennett, "Online Staffers in Dispute with Papers," *Philadelphia Business Journal* 19, no. 48 (January 12, 2001), p. 6.

21. Jeff May, "Union Charges AT&T with Unfair Labor Practices," *Knight Ridder/Tribune Business News*, June 27, 2000, item 00180090.

22. "Union Membership by State and Industry," *BNA Bulletin to Management*, May 29, 1997, pp. 172–173; "Regional Trends: Union

Membership by State and Multiple Jobholding by State," *Monthly Labor Review* 123, no. 9 (September 2000), pp. 40–41.

23. Sloane and Witney, *Labor Relations*, p. 121.

24. Ben Foster, "Tech Firms a New Target for Union Organizers," *Baltimore Business Journal* 18, no. 40 (February 16, 2001), p. 14; Mark Leon, "A Union of Their Own," *InfoWorld* 23, no. 11 (March 12, 2001), pp. 41–42; Loretta Prencipe, "E-mail and the Internet Are Changing the Labor/Management Powerplay," *InfoWorld* 23, no. 11 (March 12, 2001), p. 46; Scott Tillett, "Dot-com Workers Take New Path to Unions," *Internet Week*, January 15, 2001, p. 9.

25. See William J. Glueck, "Labor Relations and the Supervisor," in M. Jean Newport, *Supervisory Management: Tools and Techniques* (St. Paul, MN: West, 1976), pp. 207–234. See also "Big Labor Tries the Soft Sell," *Business Week*, October 13, 1986, p. 126.

26. William Fulmer, "Step by Step Through a Union Election," *Harvard Business Review* 60 (July–August 1981), pp. 94–102. For an interesting description of contract negotiations, see Peter Dramton and Joseph Tracy, "The Determinants of U.S. Labor Disputes," *Journal of Labor Economics* 12, no. 2 (April 1994), pp. 180–209.

27. *Labor Relations Consultants: Issues, Trends, Controversies* (Rockville, MD: Bureau of National Affairs, 1985), p. 71.

28. Ibid., p. 72.

29. For a discussion, see Cory Fine, "Beware the Trojan Horse," *Workforce*, May 1998, pp. 45–51.

30. Ibid., p. 46.

31. Diane Hatch and James Hall, "Salting Cases Clarified by NLRB," *Workforce* 79, no. 8 (August 2000), p. 92.

32. Commerce Clearing House, "More on Management's Pre-election Campaign Strategy," *Ideas and Trends in Personnel*, August 20, 1982, pp. 158–159.

33. Fulmer, "Step by Step," p. 94. See also "An Employer May Rebut Union Misrepresentations," *BNA Bulletin to Management*, January 16, 1986, p. 17.

34. Edwin Arnold, et al., "Determinants of Certification Election Outcomes in the Service Sector," *Labor Studies Journal* 25, no. 3 (fall 2000), p. 51.

35. "Unions Won More Representation Elections Than They Lost in 1997," *BNA Bulletin to Management*, June 4, 1998, p. 173.

36. This section is based on Matthew Goodfellow, "How to Lose an NLRB Election," *Personnel Administrator* 23 (September 1976), pp. 40–44. See also Mark Spagnardi, "Conducting a Successful Union-Free Campaign: A Primer (Part I)," *Employee Relations Law Journal* 24, no. 2, fall 1998, pp. 35–51; Gillian Flynn, "When the Unions Come Calling," *Workforce*, November 2000, pp. 82–87.

37. Ibid.

38. Ibid.

39. Harry Katz, "The Decentralization of Collective Bargaining: A Literature Review and Comparative Analysis," *Industrial and Labor Relations Review* 47, no. 1 (October 1993), p. 11.

40. Frederick Sullivan, "Limiting Union Organizing Activity Through Supervisors," *Personnel* 55 (July–August 1978), pp. 55–65; Richard Peterson, Thomas Lee, and Barbara Finnegan, "Strategies and Tactics in Union Organizing Campaigns," *Industrial Relations* 31, no. 2 (spring 1992), pp. 370–381. See also Alan Story, "Employer Speech, Union Representation Elections, and the First Amendment," *Berkeley Journal of Employment and Labor Law* 16, no. 2 (1995), pp. 356–457.

41. Sullivan, "Limiting Union Organizing Activity," p. 60. See also Jonathon Segal, "Unshackle Your Supervisors to Stay Union Free," *HR Magazine* 43, no. 7 (June 1998), pp. 62–65.

42. "Union Access to Employer's Customers Restricted," *BNA Bulletin to Management*, February 15, 1996, p. 49; "Workplace Access for Unions Hinges on Legal Issues," *BNA Bulletin to Management*, April 11, 1996, p. 113.

43. Ibid., pp. 4–65. The appropriateness of these sample rules may be affected by factors unique to an employer's operation, and they should therefore be reviewed by the employer's attorney before implementation.

44. This is based on David Moberg, "Like Business, Unions Must Go Global," *New York Times*, December 19, 1993, p. 13.

45. Doug Cahn, "Reebok Takes the Sweat Out of Sweatshops," *Business Ethics* 14, no. 1 (January 2000), p. 9.

46. "Union Decertifications Up in First Half of 1998," *BNA Bulletin to Management*, December 24, 1998, p. 406.

47. "More Elections Went the Unions' Way in Early 2000," *BNA Bulletin to Management*, December 21, 2000, p. 405.

48. Michael Carrell and Christina Heavrin, *Labor Relations and Collective Bargaining* (Upper Saddle River, NJ: Prentice Hall, 2001), pp. 120–121; Coleman, "Once a Union, Not Always a Union," pp. 42–45. See also "Decertification: Fulfilling Unions' Destiny?" pp. 144–148.

49. Fulmer, "When Employees Want to Oust Their Union," p. 167. See also David Meyer and Trevor Bain, "Union Decertification Election Outcomes: Bargaining Unit Characteristics and Union Resources," *Journal of Labor Research* 15, no. 2 (spring 1994), pp. 117–136.

50. See also William Fulmer and Tamara Gilman, "Why Do Workers Vote for Union Decertification?" *Personnel* 58 (March–April 1981), pp. 28–35, and Shane Premeaux, et al., "Managing Tomorrow's Unionized Workers," *Personnel* (July 1989), pp. 61–64, for a discussion of some important differences (in preferred management styles) between unionized and nonunionized employees.

51. Michael Ballot, *Labor-Management Relations in a Changing Environment* (New York: John Wiley and Sons, 1992), pp. 169–425; Carrell and Heavrin, *Labor Relations and Collective Bargaining*, pp. 158–161.

52. Carrell and Heavrin, *Labor Relations and Collective Bargaining*, pp. 176–177.

53. "No Talks Until Mechanics Union Softens Demand, Northwest Airlines Says," *Knight Ridder/Tribune Business News*, March 28, 2001, item 01087165.

54. "Bryant Union Says Colleges Bargaining in Good Faith," *Providence Business News* 15, no. 47 (March 12, 2001), p. 19.

55. John Fossum, *Labor Relations*, pp. 246–250.

56. *Boulwareism* is the name given to a strategy, now generally held in disfavor, by which the company, based on an exhaustive study of what it thought its employees wanted, made but one offer at the bargaining table and then refused to bargain any further unless convinced by the union on the basis of new facts that its original position was wrong. The NLRB subsequently found that the practice of offering the same settlement to all units, insisting that certain parts of the package could not differ among agreements, and communicating to the employees about how negotiations were going amounted to an illegal pattern. Fossum, *Labor Relations*, p. 267. See also William Cooke, Aneil Mishra, Gretchen Spreitzer, and Mary Tschirhart, "The Determinants of NLRB Decision-Making Revisited," *Industrial and Labor Relations Review* 48, no. 2 (January 1995), pp. 237–257.

57. Commerce Clearing House, "Drug Testing/Court Rulings," *Ideas and Trends*, January 25, 1988, p. 16.

58. Bargaining items based on Carrell and Heavrin, *Labor Relations and Collective Bargaining*, pp. 176–179.

59. See also Yoder, *Personnel Management*, pp. 517–518.

60. Richardson, *Collective Bargaining*, p. 150.

61. Fossum, *Labor Relations*, pp. 298–322. See also Eilene Zimmerman, "HR Lessons from a Strike," *Workforce*, November 2000, pp. 37–41.

62. Although considerable research has been done on the subject, it's not clear what sorts of situations precipitate impasses. At times, however, it seems that the prospect of having the impasse taken to an arbitrator actually "chills" the negotiation process. Specifically, if neither the union nor the management negotiators want to make the tough political decision to make the tough choices, they might consciously or unconsciously opt to declare an impasse, knowing that the arbitrator will then have to take the heat. See Linda Babcock and Craig Olson, "The Causes of Impasses in Labor Disputes," *Industrial Relations* 31, no. 2 (spring 1992), pp. 348–360.

63. Fossum, *Labor Relations*, p. 312. See also Thomas Watkins, "Assessing Arbitrator Competence," *Arbitration Journal* 47, no. 2 (June 1992), pp. 43–48.

64. Ibid., p. 317.

65. Mark Fitzgerald, "UAW Lifts Boycott," *Editor and Publisher*, February 26, 2001, p. 9.

66. "Major Work Stoppages Stay Near Record Lows in 1998," *BNA Bulletin to Management*, March 4, 1999, p. 69; "More Work Stoppages," *Monthly Labor Review* 124, no. 3 (March 2001), p. 2.

67. Jane Brissett, "Minnesota-Based Taconite Companies Begin Strike Preparations," *Knight/Ridder/Tribune Business News*, July 27, 1999, item 99208075.

68. Stephen Cabot and Gerald Cuerton, "Labor Disputes and Strikes: Be Prepared," *Personnel Journal* 60 (February 1981), pp. 121–126. See also Brenda Sunoo, "Managing Strikes, Minimizing Loss," *Personnel Journal* 74, no. 1 (January 1995), pp. 50ff.

69. For a discussion, see Herbert Northrup, "Union Corporate Campaigns and Inside Games as a Strike Form," *Employee Relations Law Journal* 19, no. 4 (spring 1994), pp. 507–549.

70. Jessica Materna, "Union Launches Web Site to Air Grievances Against San Francisco Marriott" *San Francisco Business Times* 15, no. 39 (May 4, 2001), p. 15.

71. Northrup, "Union Corporate Campaigns and Inside Games," p. 513.

72. Ibid., p. 518.

73. For a discussion of the cost of a strike, see Woodruff Inberman, "Strikes Cost More Than You Think," *Harvard Business Review* 57 (May–June 1979), pp. 133–138. The NLRB held in 1986 in Harter Equipment, Inc., 280 NLRB No. 71, that an employer could lawfully hire temporary replacements during the course of a lockout, in the absence of proof of specific anti-union motivation, in order to bring economic pressure to bear upon a union to support a legitimate bargaining position.

74. Cliffod Koen Jr., Sondra Hartmen, and Dinah Payne, "The NLRB Wields a Rejuvenated Weapon," *Personnel Journal*, December 1996, pp. 85–87.

75. Mark Leon, "A Union of Their Own," *InfoWorld* 23 (March 12, 2001), pp. 41–42. See also Tim Race, "The Updated Context Notwithstanding, the Issues Behind Unionization Drives at Dot-Coms Have a Familiar Ring," *New York Times*, January 22, 2001, p. C4.

76. Arthur A. Sloane and Fred Witney, *Labor Relations*, 10th edition (Upper Saddle River, NJ: Prentice Hall, 2001), pp. 221–227.

77. Carrell and Heavrin, *Labor Relations and Collective Bargaining*, pp. 417–418.

78. Richardson, *Collective Bargaining*.

79. J. Brad Chapman, "Constructive Grievance Handling," in M. Gene Newport, *Supervisory Management* (St. Paul, MN: West Publishing Co., 1976), pp. 253–274. For a discussion of the impact of supervisory behavior on grievance initiation, see Brian Bemmels, "The Determinants of Grievance Initiation," *Industrial and Labor Relations Review* 47, no. 2 (January 1994), pp. 285–301.

80. Duncan, Adams, "Worker Grievances Consume Roanoke, VA Mail Distribution Center," *Knight-Ridder/Tribune Business News*, March 27, 2001, Item 01086009.

81. See, for example, Clyde Summers, "Protecting All Employees Against Unjust Dismissal," *Harvard Business Review* 58 (January–February 1980), pp. 132–139; George Bohlander and Harold White, "Building Bridges: Non-Union Employee Grievance Systems," *Personnel*, July 1988, pp. 62–66. See also Richard Peterson and David Lewin, "Research on Unionized Grievance Procedures: Management Issues and Recommendations," *Human Resource Management* 39, no. 4 (winter 2000), pp. 395–406.

82. See Newport, *Supervisory Management*, p. 273, for an excellent checklist. See also Mark Lurie, "The Eight Essential Steps in Grievance Processing," *Dispute Resolution Journal* 54, no. 4 (November 1999), pp. 61–65.

83. Rich Rovito, "AFL-CIO Launches Housing Program for Union Members," *Business Journal—Milwaukee* 18, no. 29 (April 6, 2001), p. 6.

84. Prencipe, "E-mail and the Internet Are Changing the Labor/Management Powerplay," p. 46.

85. This is based on Kenneth Jenero and Christopher Lyons, "Employee Participation Programs: Prudent or Prohibited?" *Employee Relations Law Journal* 17, no. 4 (spring 1992), pp. 535–566. See also Edward Cohen-Rosenthal and Cynthia Burton, "Improving Organizational Quality by Forging the Best Union-Management Relationship," *National Productivity Review* 13, no. 2 (spring 1994), pp. 215–231.

86. "Union Fights Team Program at UPS," *BNA Bulletin to Management*, March 14, 1996, p. 88.

87. Jenero and Lyons, "Employee Participation Programs," p. 539. One historian recently argued, however, that company unions were, on the whole, a positive development in employee relations, and that it was a mistake to insert language into the Wagner Act banning company unions. Bruce Kaufman, "The Case for the Company Union," *Labor History* 41, no. 3 (August 2000), pp. 321–350.

88. See ibid., p. 551; Mary Pivec and Howard Robbins, "Employee Involvement Remains Controversial," *HR Magazine* 41, no. 11

(November 1996), pp. 145–150; Darren McCabe, "Total Quality Management: Anti-Union Trojan Horse or Management Albatross," *Work Employment and Society* 13, no. 4 (December 1999), pp. 665–691.

89. These are based on ibid., pp. 564–565. See also "Fallout from Electromation," *BNA Bulletin to Management*, March 4, 1993, p. 65; and Bob Smith, "Employee Committee or Labor Union," *Management Review*.

90. "New Agreements Improve Labor Relations," *BNA Bulletin to Management*, September 5, 1991, p. 279; and Joseph D. Reid, "Future Unions," *Industrial Relations* 31, no. 1 (winter 1992), pp. 122–136. For another view, see George Bohlander and Marshall Campbell, "Forging a Labor-Management Partnership: The Magna Copper Experience," *Labor Studies Journal* 18, no. 4 (winter 1994), pp. 3–20.

Chapter 15

1. Minda Zetlin, "Clean Slate: Here's How Con Edison, New York City's Utility Company, Transformed Itself from Environmental Wrongdoer to Environmental Leader," *Management Review*, February 2000, pp. 26–27.

2. "Occupational Injuries and Illnesses," *BNA Bulletin to Management*, January 15, 1998, p. 13; "Workplace Deaths Unchanged: Homicides at Six Year Low," *BNA Bulletin to Management*, August 27, 1998, p. 269; "Workplace Injury, Illness Rates Fall," *Occupational Hazards*, February 2001, p. 33.

3. "Workplace Injuries Cost $171 Billion, Cause 66,500 Deaths, Study Says," *BNAC Communicator*, winter 1998, p. 9.

4. Greg Hom, "Protecting Eyes from High-Tech Hazards," *Occupational Hazards*, March 1999, pp. 53–55.

5. "Blame New Computers for Sick Buildings," *USA Today* 129, no. 2672 (May 2001), p. 8.

6. Michael Pinto, "Why Are Indoor Air Quality Problems So Prevalent Today?" *Occupational Hazards*, January 2001, pp. 37–39.

7. Sandy Moretz, "Safe Havens?" *Occupational Hazards*, November 2000, pp. 45–46.

8. *Workers' Compensation Manual for Managers and Supervisors* (Chicago: Commerce Clearing House, Inc., 1992), p. 12. See also Guy Toxcano and Janice Windau, "The Changing Character of Fatal Work Injuries," *Monthly Labor Review* 117, no. 10 (October 1994), pp. 17–28.

9. Todd Nighswonger, "Rouge Settlement Sparks Safety Initiative at Ford," *Occupational Hazards*, October 1999, pp. 101–102.

10. Much of this is based on "All about OSHA," (revised), U.S. Department of Labor, Occupational Safety and Health Administration (Washington, DC).

11. "Safety Rule on Respiratory Protection Issues," *BNA Bulletin to Management*, January 8, 1998, p. 1.

12. "OSHA Hazard Communication Standard Enforcement," *BNA Bulletin to Management*, February 23, 1989, p. 13.

13. "What Every Employer Needs to Know About OSHA Record Keeping," U.S. Department of Labor, Bureau of Labor Statistics (Washington, DC), report 412–3, p. 3.

14. Brian Jackson and Jeffrey Myers, "Just When You Thought You Were Safe: OSHA Record-Keeping Violations," *Management Review*, May 1994, pp. 62–63.

15. Ibid., p. 62.

16. "Supreme Court Says OSHA Inspectors Need Warrants," *Engineering News Record*, June 1, 1978, pp. 9–10; W. Scott Railton, "OSHA Gets Tough on Business," *Management Review* 80, no. 12 (December 1991), pp. 28–29.

17. This section is based on "All About OSHA," pp. 23–25. See also Robert Sand, "OSHA Access to Privileged Materials: Criminal Prosecutions; Damages for Fear of Cancer," *Employee Relations Law Journal* 19, no. 1 (summer 1993), pp. 151–157; "OSHA Final Rule Expands Employees' Role in Consultations, Protects Employer Records," *BNA Bulletin to Management*, November 2, 2000, p. 345.

18. Diane Hatch and James Hall, "A Flurry of New Federal Regulations," *Workforce* 80, no. 2 (February 2001), p. 98.

19. "Employers Hit with Megafines for OSHA Violations," *BNA Bulletin to Management*, May 9, 1996, p. 146.

20. "Settling Safety Violations Has Benefits," *BNA Bulletin to Management*, July 31, 1997, p. 248.

21. "Enforcement Activity Increased in 1997," *BNA Bulletin to Management*, January 29, 1998, p. 28.

22. Ibid., p. 28.

23. "OSHA Instruction on Penalties," *BNA Bulletin to Management*, February 7, 1991, p. 33; Commerce Clearing House, "OSHA Will Begin Higher Fines March 1st," *Ideas and Trends in Personnel*, January 23, 1991, p. 14; John Bruening, "OSHRC on the Comeback Trail," *Occupational Hazards*, January 1991, pp. 33–36. OSHA is also stressing record-keeping violations. See, for example, Brian Jackson and Jeffrey Myers, "Just When You Thought You Were Safe: OSHA Record-Keeping Violations," *Management Review* 83, no. 5 (May 1994), pp. 62–63.

24. Steve Bates, "When OSHA Calls," *Nation's Business* 86, no. 9 (September 1998), pp. 14–22.

25. Robert Grossman, "Handling Inspections: Tips from Insiders," *HR Magazine*, October 1999, pp. 41–50.

26. Roger Jacobs, "Employee Resistance to OSHA Standards: Toward a More Reasonable Approach," *Labor Law Journal*, (April 1979), pp. 219–230. See also Charles Chadd, "Managing OSHA Compliance: The Human Resources Issues," *Employee Relations Law Journal* 20, no. 1 (summer 1994), pp. 101–113.

27. Ibid., p. 220.

28. Chadd, "Managing OSHA Compliance," p. 106.

29. These are based on Jacobs, "Employee Resistance to OSHA Standards," pp. 227–230.

30. "Initial OSHA Reform Bills Become Law," *BNA Bulletin to Management*, July 30, 1998, p. 236.

31. "OSHA Seeks 'Cooperative Compliance,'" *BNA Bulletin to Management*, September 4, 1997, p. 288; "OSHA's Cooperative Program Shoves Off," *BNA Bulletin to Management*, December 25, 1997, p. 416.

32. Lisa Finnegan, "Is 1999 OSHA's Year?" *Occupational Hazards*, December 1998, p. 28.

33. Gregg LaBar, "Your OSHA Compliance Record: Online," *Occupational Hazards* 59, no. 8 (August 1997), p. 10.

34. Lisa Finnegan, "Industry Partners with OSHA," *Occupational Hazards*, February 1999, pp. 43–45.

35. David S. Thelan, Donna Ledgerwood, and Charles F. Walters, "Health and Safety in the Workplace: A New Challenge for Business Schools," *Personnel Administrator* 30, no. 10 (October 1985), p. 44.

36. Hammer, Occupational Safety Management and Engineering.

37. F. David Pierce, "Safety in the Emerging Leadership Paradigm," *Occupational Hazards*, June 2000, pp. 63–66.

38. *Workers' Compensation Manual for Managers and Supervisors*, p. 24; James Frierson, "An Analysis of ADA Provisions on Denying Employment Because of a Risk of Future Injury," *Employee Relations Law Journal* 13, no. 2 (1993), pp. 3–14.

39. "With Pay on the Line, Managers Improve Safety," *BNA Bulletin to Management*, March 20, 1997, p. 89.

40. "Safety Program Results at ABB Business Services Missouri Plant," *Occupational Hazards*, July 2000, p. 23.

41. "A Safety Committee Man's Guide," Aetna Life and Casualty Insurance Company, Catalog 872684. See also Dan Petersen, "The Barriers to Safety Excellence," *Occupational Hazards*, December 2000, pp. 37–39.

42. "Workplace Fatalities," *BNA Bulletin to Management*, August 28, 1997, pp. 276–277.

43. "A Safety Committee Man's Guide," pp. 17–21. OSHA has identified 10 major causes of accidents: inadequate training, inability to do the job, lack of job understanding, improper tools and equipment, poor-quality materials, poor maintenance, poor work environment, incorrect shop maintenance, tight work schedules, and overly tight schedules. See Myron Peskin and Frances McGrath, "Industrial Safety: Who Is Responsible and Who Benefits?" *Business Horizons* 35, no. 3 (May–June 1992), pp. 66–70. See also Daniel Webb, "Why Safety Programs Fail," *People Management* 1, no. 2 (January 1995), pp. 38–39.

44. For a discussion of this, see David Hofmann and Adam Stetzer, "A Cross-Level Investigation of Factors Influencing Unsafe Behaviors and Accidents," *Personnel Psychology* 49 (1996), pp. 307–308.

45. Willard Kerr, "Complementary Theories of Safety Psychology," in Edwin Fleishman and Alan Bass, *Industrial Psychology* (Burr Ridge, IL: McGraw-Hill, 1974), pp. 493–500. See also Alan Fowler, "How to Make the Workplace Safer," *People Management* 1, no. 2 (January 1995), pp. 38–39.

46. Duane Schultz and Sydney Schultz, *Psychology and Work Today* (Upper Saddle River, NJ: Prentice Hall, 1998), p. 351.

47. Cynthia Owsley, et al., "Visual Processing Impairment and Risk of Motor Vehicle Crash Among Older Adults," *Journal of the American Medical Association* 279, no. 14 (April 8, 1998), pp. 1083–1089; Hosam Kamel, et al., "The Activities of Daily Vision Scale: A Useful Tool to Assess for Risk in Older Adults with Vision Impairment," *Journal of the American Geriatrics Society* 48, no. 11 (November 2000), pp. 1474–1478; Hiroshi Matsuoka, "Development of a Short Test for Accident Proneness," *Perceptual and Motor Skills* 85, no. 3 (December 1997), pp. 903–907; Janice Marra, "Profiling Employees and Assessing the Potential for Violence," *Public Management* 82, no. 2 (February 2000), pp. 25–26.

48. Michael Frone, "Predictors of Work Injuries Among Employed Adolescents," *Journal of Applied Psychology* 83, no. 4 (1998), pp. 565–576.

49. Michael Blotzer, "Safety by Design," *Occupational Hazards*, May 1999, pp. 39–40.

50. Susannah Figura, "Don't Slip Up on Safety," *Occupational Hazards* 58, no. 11 (November 1996), pp. 29–31. See also Russ Wood, "Defining the Boundaries of Safety," *Occupational Hazards*, January 2001, pp. 41–43.

51. Tom Andrews, "Getting Employees Comfortable with PPE," *Occupational Hazards*, January 2000, pp. 35–38.

52. James Zeigler, "Protective Clothing: Exploring the Wearability Issue," *Occupational Hazards*, September 2000, pp. 81–82.

53. "The Complete Guide to Personal Protective Equipment," *Occupational Hazards*, January 1999, pp. 49–60.

54. Michael Pennacchia, "Interactive Training Sets the Pace," *Safety and Health* 135, no. 1 (January 1987), pp. 24–27; and Philip Poynter and David Stevens, "How to Secure an Effective Health and Safety Program at Work," *Professional Safety* 32, no. 1 (January 1987), pp. 32–41. See also Zack Mansdorf, "Organizational Culture and Safety Performance," *Occupational Hazards*, May 1999, pp. 109–112.

55. William Kincaid, "10 Habits of Effective Safety Managers," *Occupational Hazards* 58, no. 11 (November 1996), pp. 41–43.

56. Dov Zohar, "A Group Level Model of Safety Climate: Testing the Effect of a Group Climate on Microaccidents in Manufacturing Jobs," *Journal of Applied Psychology* 85, no. 4 (2000), pp. 587–596. See also Judith Erickson, "Corporate Culture: The Key to Safety Performance," *Occupational Hazards* 62, no. 4 (April 2000), p. 45.

57. Gerald Borofsky, Michelle Bielema, and James Hoffman, "Accidents, Turnover, and Use of a Pre-employment Screening Interview," *Psychological Reports*, 1993, pp. 1067–1076.

58. Ibid., p. 1072.

59. Dan Hartshorn, "The Safety Interview," *Occupational Hazards*, October 1999, pp. 107–111.

60. *Workers' Compensation Manual for Managers and Supervisors*, pp. 22–23.

61. John Rekus, "Is Your Safety Training Program Effective?" *Occupational Hazards*, August 1999, pp. 37–39.

62. Michael Blotzer, "A Look at Two Companies at the Vanguard of Putting Safety and Health Training into Cyberspace," *Occupational Hazards*, September 2, 2000; see also Andrew Sorine, et al., "Safety Training Gets Wired Through Web-Based E-Learning," *Occupational Hazards*, February 2001, pp. 35–37.

63. McCormick and Tiffin, *Industrial Psychology*, p. 537. A group of international experts met in Belgium in 1986 and concluded that a successful safety poster must be simple and specific and reinforce safe behavior rather than negative behavior. See "What Makes an Effective Safety Poster," *National Safety and Health News* 134, no. 6 (December 1986), pp. 32–34.

64. Jennifer Laabs, "Cashing in on Safety," *Workforce*, August 1997, p. 57.

65. Gregg LaBar, "Awards and Incentives in Action," *Occupational Hazards* 59, no. 1 (January 1997), pp. 91–92.

66. James Nash, "Rewarding the Safety Process," *Occupational Hazards*, March 2000, pp. 29–34.

67. Todd Nighswonger, "Wanted: Safe Workers," *Occupational Hazards*, November 1999, p. 106.

68. OSHA has published two useful training manuals: *Training Requirements of OSHA Standards*, February 1976, and *Teaching Safety and Health in the Work Place*, U.S. Department of Labor, Occupational Safety and Health Administration, 1976; J. Surry, "Industrial Accident Research: Human

Engineering Approach" (Toronto: University of Toronto, Department of Industrial Engineering), June 1968, Chapter 4, quoted in McCormick and Tiffin, *Industrial Psychology*, p. 534. For an example of a very successful incentive program aimed at boosting safety at Campbell Soup Company, see Frederick Wahl Jr., "Soups on for Safety," *National Safety and Health News* 134, no. 6 (December 1986), pp. 49–53. For a discussion of how employee involvement can impact job redesign and employee safety, see Douglas May and Catherine Schwoerer, "Employee Health by Design: Using Employee Involvement Teams in Ergonomics Job Redesign," *Personnel Psychology* 47, no. 4 (winter 1994), pp. 861–876.

69. Judi Komaki, Kenneth Barwick, and Lawrence Scott, "A Behavioral Approach to Occupational Safety: Pinpointing and Reinforcing Safe Performance in a Food Manufacturing Plant," *Journal of Applied Psychology* 63 (August 1978), pp. 434–445. See also Robert Reber, Jerry Wallin, and David Duhon, "Preventing Occupational Injuries Through Performance Management," *Public Personnel Management* 22, no. 2 (summer 1993), pp. 301–311; Anat Arkin, "Incentives to Work Safely," *Personnel Management* 26, no. 9 (September 1994), pp. 48–52; Peter Making and Valerie Sutherland, "Reducing Accidents Using a Behavioral Approach," *Leadership and Organizational Development Journal* 15, no. 5 (1994), pp. 5–10.

70. Judi Komaki, Arlene Heinzmann, and Lorealie Lawson, "Effect of Training and Feedback: Component Analysis of a Behavioral Safety Program," *Journal of Applied Psychology* 65 (June 1980), pp. 261–270. See also Jorma Sari, "When Does Behavior Modification Prevent Accidents?" *Leadership and Organizational Development Journal* 15, no. 5 (1994), pp. 11–15.

71. Stan Hudson and Tim Gordon, "Tenneco's Drive to Become Injury Free," *Occupational Hazards*, May 2000, pp. 85–87. See also William Atkinson, "Behavior-Based Safety," *Management Review* 89, no. 2 (February 2000), pp. 41–45.

72. "Workplace Safety: Improving Management Practices," *BNA Bulletin to Management*, February 9, 1989, pp. 42, 47. See also Marlene Morgenstern, "Workers' Compensation: Managing Costs," *Compensation and Benefits Review*, September–October 1992, pp. 30–38; Linda Johnson, "Preventing Injuries: The Big Payoff," *Personnel Journal*, April 1994, pp. 61–64; David Webb, "The Bathtub Effect: Why Safety Programs Fail," *Management Review*, February 1994, pp. 51–54.

73. Lisa Cullen, "Safety Committees: A Smart Business Decision," *Occupational Hazards*, May 1999, pp. 99–104.

74. Virginia Sutcliffe, "Employee Safety: Beyond the Plant Gate," *Occupational Hazards*, December 1998, pp. 41–42.

75. "OSHA Backs Off on Home Rules," *Occupational Hazards*, February 2000, p. 8.

76. Sutcliffe, "Employee Safety," p. 42.

77. S. L. Smith, "Sadaf Drives for Safety Excellence," *Occupational Hazards*, November 1998, p. 41. For further discussion, see also Kathy Seabrook, "10 Strategies for Global Safety Management," *Occupational Hazards*, June 1999, pp. 41–43.

78. *Workers' Compensation Manual for Managers and Supervisors*, p. 10.

79. "Strict Policies Mean Big Cuts in Premiums," *Occupational Hazards*, May 2000, p. 51.

80. See, for example, *Workers' Compensation Manual for Managers and Supervisors*, pp. 36–39.

81. "Study: No Warm Welcome After Comp Leave," *Occupational Hazards*, February 2001, p. 57.

82. Ibid., p. 51.

83. Donna Clendenning, "Taking a Bite Out of Workers' Comp Cause," *Occupational Hazards*, September 2000, pp. 85–86.

84. This section is based largely on John Miner and J. Frank Brewer, "Management of Ineffective Performance," in Marvin Dunnette, ed., *Handbook of Industrial and Organizational Psychology* (Chicago: Rand McNally, 1976), pp. 1005–1023.

85. James Schreir, "Survey Supports Perceptions: Work-Site Drug Use Is on the Rise," *Personnel Journal*, October 1987, pp. 114–118; Pallassana Balgopal, "Combating Alcoholism in Industries: Implications for Occupational Social Work," *Management and Labor Studies* 17, no. 1 (January 1992), pp. 33–42. For a review of the background factors possibly leading to drug abuse, see, for example, Richard Clayton, et al.,

"Risk and Protective Factors: A Brief Review," *Drugs and Society, A Journal of Contemporary Issues* 8, no. 3–4 (1995), pp. 7–14.

86. "Drug Use Among Workers," *BNA Bulletin to Management*, May 2, 1996, pp. 140–141.

87. Todd Nighswonger, "Just Say Yes to Preventing Substance Abuse," *Occupational Hazards*, April 2000, pp. 39–41.

88. Gopal Pati and John Adkins Jr., "The Employer's Role in Alcoholism Assistance," *Personnel Journal* 62, no. 7 (July 1983), pp. 568–572. For a discussion of how the work environment can encourage drug dealing, see Richard Lyles, "Should the Next Drug Bust Be in Your Company?" *Personnel Journal* 63 (October 1994), pp. 46–49.

89. "Facing Facts About Workplace Substance Abuse," *Rough Notes* 144, no. 5 (May 2001), pp. 114–118.

90. Harrison Trice, "Alcoholism and the Work World," *Sloan Management Review* 2 (fall 1970), pp. 67–75, reprinted in W. Clay Hamner and Frank Schmidt, *Contemporary Problems in Personnel*, rev. ed. (Chicago: St. Clair Press, 1977), pp. 496–502. Note also that dependence on ordinary substances can be as devastating as hard drug problems. See, for example, Peter Minetos, "Are You Addicted to Legal Drugs?" *Safety and Health* 136, no. 2 (August 1987), pp. 46–49. For a discussion of substance abuse in the small business, see, for example, Harry Lasher and John Grashof, "Substance Abuse in Small Business: Business Owner Perceptions and Reactions," *Journal of Small Business Management*, January 1993, pp. 63–72.

91. Pati and Adkins, "Employer's Role in Alcoholism Assistance." See also Commerce Clearing House, "How Should Employers Respond to Indications an Employee May Have an Alcohol or Drug Problem?" *Ideas and Trends*, April 6, 1989, pp. 53–57.

92. "Employee Alcohol Testing on the Rise," *BNA Bulletin to Management*, August 20, 1998, p. 261.

93. Ibid., p. 261.

94. Based on Miner and Brewer, "Management of Ineffective Performance." The survey was conducted jointly by the American Society for Personnel Administration and the Bureau of National Affairs. The results were based on an analysis of the questionnaire data made by Professors Miner and Brewer, who acknowledge the assistance of John B. Schappi, associate editor of the Bureau of National Affairs, and Mary Green Miner, director of BNA Surveys, in making this information available.

95. Brenda Sunoo, "Positive Drug Test Results: Terminate or Rehabilitate?" *Personnel Journal*, December 1996, p. 94.

96. Ibid., p. 94.

97. Trice, "Alcoholism and the Work World." See also Larry A. Pace and Stanley J. Smits, "Substance Abuse: A Proactive Approach," *Personnel Journal* 68, no. 4 (April 1989), pp. 84–90; and Commerce Clearing House, "Typical Behavior Changes in an Employee with a Drinking Problem," *Ideas and Trends*, April 6, 1989, p. 56.

98. From Henry Alevic, "Drug Abuse in the Workplace," (Personnel Services, Inc., 2303 W. Meadowview Road, Greensboro, NC 27407), reprinted in *BNA Bulletin to Management*, August 29, 1985, p. 72. Stanley Smits and Larry Pace, "Workplace Substance Abuse: Establish Policies," *Personnel Journal*, May 1989, pp. 88–93.

99. This is quoted from "Drug-Free Workplace: New Federal Requirements," *BNA Bulletin to Management*, February 9, 1989, pp. 1–4. Note that the Drug-Free Workplace Act does not mandate or mention testing employees for illegal drug use.

100. "Alcohol Misuse Prevention Programs: Department of Transportation Final Rules," *BNA Bulletin to Management*, March 24, 1994, pp. 1–8.

101. Eric Sundstrom, et al., "Office Noise, Satisfaction, and Performance," *Environment and Behavior* 26, no. 2 (March 1994), pp. 195–222.

102. This is based on Terry Beehr and John Newman, "Organizational Stress, Employer Health, and Organizational Effectiveness: A Factor Analysis, Model, and Literature Review," *Personnel Psychology* 31 (winter 1978), pp. 665–699. See also Shailendra Singh, "Managing Stress Through Empowerment: A Brief Literature Survey," *Management and Labor Studies* 22, no. 1 (January 1997), pp. 26–32.

103. Michael Manning, Conrad Jackson, and Marceline Fusilier, "Occupational Stress, Social Support, and the Costs of Health Care," *Academy of Management Journal* 39, no. 3 (1996), pp. 738–750.

104. "Stress, Depression Cost Employers," *Occupational Hazards*, December 1998, p. 24. See also Charlene Solomon, "Stressed to the Limit," *Workforce*, September 1999, pp. 48–54.

105. Andre DuBrin, *Human Relations: A Job Oriented Approach* (Reston, VA: Reston, 1978), pp. 66–67.

106. John Newman and Terry Beehr, "Personnel and Organizational Strategies for Handling Job Stress: A Review of Research and Opinion," *Personnel Psychology*, spring 1979, pp. 1–43. See also "Work Place Stress: How to Curb Claims," *BNA Bulletin to Management*, April 14, 1988, p. 120.

107. Karl Albrecht, *Stress and the Manager* (Englewood Cliffs, NJ: Spectrum, 1979). For a discussion of the related symptoms of depression, see James Krohe Jr., "An Epidemic of Depression?" *Across-the-Board*, September 1994, pp. 23–27. See also Todd Nighswonger, "Stress Management," *Occupational Hazards*, September 1999, p. 100.

108. "Solutions to Workplace Stress," *BNA Bulletin to Management*, February 11, 1993, p. 48. See also Christopher Bachler, "Workers Take Leave of Job Stress," *Personnel Journal* 74, no. 1 (January 1995), p. 38.

109. Pascale Carayon, "Stressful Jobs and Non-Stressful Jobs: A Cluster Analysis of Office Jobs," *Ergonomics* 37, no. 2 (1994), pp. 311–323.

110. "Managing Stress in the Workplace," *BNA Bulletin to Management*, January 18, 1996, p. 24.

111. Herbert Freudenberger, *Burn-Out* (Toronto: Bantam Books, 1980). See also Susan Jackson, Richard Schwab, and Randall Schuler, "Toward an Understanding of the Burnout Phenomenon," *Journal of Applied Psychology* 71, no. 4 (November 1986), pp. 630–640; Cary Cherniss, "Long Term Consequences of Burnout: An Exploratory Study," *Journal of Organizational Behavior* 13, no. 1 (January 1992), pp. 1–11; Raymond Lee and Blake Ashforth, "A Further Examination of Managerial Burnout: Toward an Integrated Model," *Journal of Organizational Behavior* 14 (1993), pp. 3–20.

112. Freudenberger, *Burn-Out*. See also "Avoiding Job Burnout: How to Cope When Your Job Feels Like a Life Sentence," *American Salesman* 44, no. 6 (June 1990), pp. 29–31; Pamela Ammondson, "Job Burnout: How to Refocus and Revitalize Without Quitting Your Job," *CMA* 74, no. 2 (April 2000), pp. 11–12.

113. Mina Westman and Dov Eden, "Effects of a Respite from Workout on Burnout: Vacation Relief and Fade-Out," *Journal of Applied Psychology* 82, no. 4 (1997), pp. 516–527.

114. Ibid., p. 516.

115. Ibid., p. 526.

116. See, for example, Michael Smith, et al., "An Investigation of Health Complaints and Job Stress in Video Display Operations," *Human Factors*, August 1981, pp. 387–400. See also "How to Protect Workers from Reproductive Hazards," *BNA Fair Employment Practices*, July 23, 1987, pp. 89–90; Commerce Clearing House, "Suffolk County New York Passes Law Covering Employers with Twenty Terminals or More Regarding VDT Regulation," *Ideas and Trends*, 1988, p. 48.

117. "Fear of Birth Risks from VDTs Dispelled," *BNA Bulletin to Management*, January 22, 1998, p. 20.

118. J. A. Savage, "Are Computer Terminals Zapping Workers' Health?" *Business and Society Review*, 1994; "Carpal Tunnel Claims Up, But Cost Per Claim Down," *BNA Bulletin to Management*, July 25, 1996, p. 233.

119. These are based on "Inexpensive Ergonomic Innovations," *BNA Bulletin to Management*, February 1, 1996, p. 40.

120. Sondra Lotz Fisher, "Are Your Employees Working Ergosmart?" *Personnel Journal* (December 1996), pp. 91–92.

121. Maureen Mineham, "New AIDS Survival Rates Mean Patients Returning to Work," *HR Magazine* 42, no. 10 (October 1997), p. 208.

122. See, for example "AIDS/HIV in the Workplace: A Fact Sheet for Employees," *BNA Bulletin to Management*, October 6, 1994.

123. Ibid., p. 208.

124. Commerce Clearing House, "The Wells Fargo AIDS Policy," *Ideas and Trends*, April 5, 1988, pp. 52–53.

125. Quoted or paraphrased from Michael Esposito and Jeffrey Myers, "Managing AIDS in the Workplace," *Employee Relations Law Journal* 19, no. 1 (summer 1993), p. 68.

126. Marco Colossi, "Do Employees Have the Right to Smoke?" *Personnel Journal*, April 1988, pp. 72–79.

127. "Where There's Smoke There's Risk," *BNA Bulletin to Management*, January 30, 1992, pp. 26, 31.

128. Daniel Warner, "We Do Not Hire Smokers: May Employers Discriminate Against Smokers?" *Employee Responsibilities and Rights Journal* 7, no. 2 (1994), p. 129.

129. Ronald Davis, "Exposure to Environmental Tobacco Smoke: Identifying and Protecting Those at Risk," *Journal of the American Medical Association* 280, no. 22 (December 9, 1998), pp. 147–148; see also Al Karr, "Lighting Up," *Safety and Health* 162, no. 3 (September 2000), pp. 62–66.

130. Kenneth Sovereign, *Personnel Law* (Upper Saddle River, NJ: Prentice Hall, 1999), pp. 76–79.

131. Jim Collison, "Workplace Smoking Policies: Sixteen Questions and Answers," *Personnel Journal*, April 1988, p. 81. See also Daniel Warner, "We Do Not Hire Smokers," pp. 129–140.

132. Warner, "We Do Not Hire Smokers," p. 138.

133. William Evans, et al., "Do Workplace Smoking Bans Reduce Smoking?" *American Economic Review* 89, no. 4 (September 1999), pp. 728–729.

134. Dean Boerger, "Rigorous Workplace Policies Help in Preventing Violence," *Business First—Columbus* 17, no. 41 (June 1, 2001), p. 25; Jane McDonald, "Murder at Work," *Risk Management* 48, no. 3 (March 2001), p. 7.

135. Carlos Tejada, "Danger on the Job: A Special News Report About Life on the Job—and Trends Taking Shape There," *Wall Street Journal*, June 26, 2001, p. A1.

136. Gus Toscano and Janaice Windau, "The Changing Character of Fatal Work Injuries," *Monthly Labor Review*, October 1994, p. 17.

137. Based on Louis DiLorenzo and Darren Carroll, "The Growing Menace: Violence in the Workplace," *New York State Bar Journal*, January 1995, p. 24.

138. "Violence in Workplace Soaring, New Study Says," *Baltimore Business Journal* 18, no. 34 (January 5, 2001), p. 24.

139. This is based on Beverly Younger, "Violence Against Women in the Workplace," *Employee Assistance Quarterly* 9, no. 3–4 (1994), pp. 113–133.

140. Kenneth Diamond, "The Gender-Motivated Violence Act: What Employers Should Know," *Employee Relations Law Journal* 25, no. 4 (spring 2000), pp. 29–41.

141. "Workplace Violence: Sources and Solutions," *BNA Bulletin to Management*, November 4, 1993, p. 345. See also Danny Fogelman, "Minimizing the Risk of Violence in the Workplace," *Employee Relations Today* 27, no. 1 (spring 2000), pp. 83–99.

142. "Bullies Trigger 'Silent Epidemic' at Work, but Legal Cures Remain Hard to Come By," *BNA Bulletin to Management*, February 24, 2000, p. 57.

143. Jennifer Laabs, "Employee Sabotage," *Workforce*, July 1999, pp. 33–42.

144. Alfred Feliu, "Workplace Violence and the Duty of Care: The Scope of an Employer's Obligation to Protect Against the Violent Employee," *Employee Relations Law Journal* 20, no. 3 (winter 1994–95), pp. 381–406.

145. "Workplace Violence: Sources and Solutions," *BNA Bulletin to Management*, November 4, 1993, p. 345.

146. Ibid.

147. "Weapons in the Workplace: A Review of Employer Policies," *BNA Bulletin to Management*, June 5, 1996, pp. 1–7; Lloyd Nigro and William Waugh Jr., "Violence in the American Workplace: Challenges to the Public Employer," *Public Administration Review*, July–August 1996, pp. 326–333.

148. "OSHA Addresses Top Homicide Risk," *BNA Bulletin to Management*, May 14, 1998, p. 148.

149. Feliu, "Workplace Violence and the Duty of Care," p. 395.

150. Dawn Anfuso, "Workplace Violence," *Personnel Journal* (October 1994), pp. 66–77.

151. Feliu, "Workplace Violence and the Duty of Care," p. 395.

152. Quoted from ibid., p. 395.

153. Anfuso, "Workplace Violence," p. 71.

154. "Preventing Workplace Violence," *BNA Bulletin to Management*, June 10, 1993, p. 177. See also Jenny McCune, "Companies Grapple with Workplace Violence," *Management Review* 83, no. 3 (March 1994), pp. 52–57.

155. Quoted or paraphrased from Younger, "Violence Against Women in the Workplace," p. 177, and based on recommendations from Chris Hatcher.

156. Shari Caudron, "Target: HR," *Workforce*, August 1998, p. 48.

157. Helen Frank Bensimon, "What to Do About Anger in the Workplace," *Training and Development* 51, no. 9 (September 1997), pp. 28–32.

158. Liane Greenberg and Julian Barling, "Predicting Employee Aggression Against Co-workers, Subordinates and Supervisors: The Roles of Personal Behaviors and Perceived Workplace Factors," *Journal of Organizational Behavior* 20, no. 6 (November 1999), pp. 897–913.

159. Feliu, "Workplace Violence," pp. 401–402.
160. Shari Caudron, "Target HR," *Workforce*, August 1998, pp. 44–52.
161. Eve Tahmincioglu, "Vigilance in the Face of Layoff Rage," *New York Times*, August 1, 2001, pp. C1, C6.
162. Donna Rosato, "New Industry Helps Managers Fight Violence," *USA Today*, August 8, 1995, p. 1.
163. Helen Frank Bensimon, "What to Do About Anger in the Workplace," *Training and Development* 51, no. 9 (September 1997), pp. 28–32.
164. Louis DiLorenzo and Darren Carroll, "The Growing Menace: Violence in the Workplace," *New York State Bar Journal*, January 1995, p. 25.
165. Quoted from Feliu, "Workplace Violence," p. 393.
166. DiLorenzo and Carroll, "The Growing Menace," p. 27.

Chapter 16

1. Heinrich Pierer, "Managing a Global Player in the Age of Information," *Management International Review*, October 15, 1999, pp. 9–12.
2. Charlene Solomon, "Today's Global Mobility," *Global Workforce*, July 1998, p. 16.
3. Ibid., p. 16.
4. Karen Roberts, Ellen Kossek, and Cynthia Ozeki, "Managing the Global Workforce: Challenges and Strategies," *Academy of Management Executive* 12, no. 4 (1998), pp. 93–106.
5. Ibid., p. 94.
6. Nancy Wong, "Mark Your Calendar! Important Task for International HR," *Workforce*, April 2000, pp. 72–74.
7. Solomon, "Today's Global Mobility," p. 16.
8. "Fifteen Top Emerging Markets," *Global Workforce*, January 1998, pp. 18–21.
9. These are based on Eduard Gaugler, "HR Management: An International Comparison," *Personnel*, August 1988, pp. 24–30. See also Yasuol Kuwahara, "New Developments in Human Resources Management in Japan," *Asia Pacific Journal of Human Resources* 31, no. 2 (1993), pp. 3–11; Charlene Marmer Solomon, "How Does Your Global Talent Measure Up?" *Personnel Journal*, October 1994, pp. 96–108.
10. David Ralston, Priscilla Elsass, David Gustafson, Fannie Cheung, and Robert Terpstra, "Eastern Values: A Comparison of Managers in the United States, Hong Kong, and the People's Republic of China," *Journal of Applied Psychology* 71, no. 5 (1992), pp. 664–671.
11. Geert Hofstede, "Cultural Dimensions in People Management," in Vladimir Pucik, Noel Tishy, and Carole Barnett (eds.), *Globalizing Management* (New York: John Wiley & Sons, 1992), p. 143.
12. Randall Schuler, Susan Jackson, Ellen Jackofsky, and John Slocum Jr., "Managing Human Resources in Mexico: A Cultural Understanding," *Business Horizons*, May–June 1996, pp. 55–61.
13. Ibid.
14. Ibid.
15. Valerie Frazee, "Establishing Relations in Germany," *Global Workforce*, April 1997, p. 17.
16. Charlene Solomon, "Destination U.S.A.," *Global Workforce*, April 1997, pp. 19–23.
17. Ibid., p. 21.
18. Annual 2000 figures.www.bls.gov/news.release/ichcc.hr0.htm
19. "Comparing Employment Practice," *BNA Bulletin to Management*, April 22, 1993, p. 1.
20. "Vacation Policies Around the Globe," *Global Workforce*, October 1996, p. 9.
21. Carolyn Hirschman, "When Operating Abroad, Companies Must Adopt European Style HR Plan," *HR News* 20, no. 3 (March 2001), pp. 1, 6.
22. This is discussed in Gaugler, "HR Management," p. 28. See also Carlos Castillo, "Collective Labor Rights in Latin America and Mexico," *Relations Industrielles/Industrial Relations* 55, no. 1 (winter 2000), p. 59.
23. See Rae Sedel, "Europe 1992: HR Implications of the European Unification," *Personnel*, October 1989, pp. 19–24; Chris Brewster and Ariane Hegewish, "A Continent of Diversity," *Personnel Management*, January 1993, pp. 36–39; and http://europa.eu.int/index_en.htm.
24. "Inform, Consult, Impose: Workers' Rights in the EU," *Economist*, June 16, 2001, p. 3.
25. Alan Chesters, "Employment Contracts—In Writing or Not?" *Global Workforce*, April 1997, p. 12.
26. Ibid., p. 12.
27. Chesters, "Employment Contracts—In Writing or Not?" p. 13.
28. Daniels and Radebaugh, *International Business*, p. 764.
29. For a discussion, see Margaret Shaffer and David Harrison, "Expatriates' Psychological Withdrawal from International Assignments: Work, Nonwork, and Family Influences," *Personnel Psychology* 51 (1998), pp. 87–118.
30. R. L. Tung, "Selection and Training Procedures of U.S., European, and Japanese Multinationals," *California Management Review* 25 (1982), pp. 51–71; see also Jennifer Laabs, "Like Finding a Needle in a Haystack: Recruiting in the Global Village," *Workforce* 77, no. 4 (April 1998), pp. 30–33.
31. Ibid., p. 88.
32. Paula Caliguri, "The Big Five Personality Characteristics as Predictors of Expatriates' Desire to Terminate the Assignment and Supervisor-Rated Performance," *Personnel Psychology* 53, no. 1 (spring 2000), pp. 67–88.
33. Jan Selmer, "Expatriation: Corporate Policy, Personal Intentions and International Adjustment," *International Journal of Human Resource Management* 9, no. 6 (December 1998), p. 997–1007.
34. Discussed in Charles Hill, *International Business*, pp. 511–515.
35. Charlene Solomon, "One Assignment, Two Lives," *Personnel Journal*, May 1996, pp. 36–47; Michael Harvey, "Dual-Career Couples During International Relocation: The Trailing Spouse," *International Journal of Human Resource Management* 9, no. 2 (April 1998), pp. 309–330.
36. Michael Schell, quoted in Charlene Marmer Solomon, "Success Abroad Depends on More Than Job Skills," p. 52.
37. Ron Garonzik, Joel Brockner, and Phyllis Siegel, "Identifying International Assignees at Risk for Premature Departure: The Interactive Effect of Outcome Favorability and Procedural Fairness," *Journal of Applied Psychology* 85, no. 1 (2000), pp. 13–20.
38. Carla Joinson, "Cutting Down the Days," *HR Magazine*, April 2000, pp. 90–97; "Employers Shortened Assignments of Workers Abroad," *BNA Bulletin to Management*, January 4, 2001, p. 7.
39. Daniels and Radebaugh, *International Business*, p. 767. See also Carlos Castillo, "Collective Labor Rights in Latin America and Mexico," *Relations Industrielles/Industrial Relations* 55, no. 1 (winter 2000), p. 59.
40. Arvind Phatak, *International Dimensions of Management* (Boston: PWS Kent, 1989), pp. 106–107.
41. Ibid., p. 106.
42. Daniels and Radebaugh, *International Business*, p. 767.
43. Ibid., p. 769; Phatak, *International Dimensions of Management*, p. 106.
44. Phatak, *International Dimensions of Management*, p. 108.
45. Daniels and Radebaugh, *International Business*, p. 769.
46. Ibid., p. 769; Phatak, *International Dimensions of Management*, p. 106.
47. Christopher Bachler, "Global Impacts—Don't Let Them Surprise You," *Personnel Journal*, June 1996, p. 60.
48. Ibid., p. 60.
49. Howard Perlmutter, "The Torturous Evolution of the Multinational Corporation," *Columbia Journal of World Business* 3, no. 1 (January–February 1969), pp. 11–14, discussed in Phatak, *International Dimensions of Management*, p. 129; Carol Leininger and Rue Yuan, "Aligning International Editing Efforts with Global Business Strategies," *IEEE Transactions on Professional Communication* 41, no. 1, March 1998, pp. 16–24.
50. Phatak, *International Dimensions of Management*, p. 129.
51. Ibid.
52. Hill, *International Business*, p. 507.
53. Ibid., pp. 507–510.
54. Ibid., p. 509.
55. Ibid. See also Michael Harvey, et al., "An Innovative Global Management Staffing System: A Competency-Based Perspective," *Human Resource Management* 39, no. 4 (winter 2000), pp. 381–394.
56. Gary Florkowski and Daniel Fogel, "Expatriate Adjustments and Commitment: The Role of Host Unit Treatment," *International Journal of Human Resource Management* 10, no. 5 (October 1999), pp. 783–807.
57. Phatak, *International Dimensions of Management*, p. 113; Charlene Marmer Solomon, "Staff Selection Impacts Global Success," *Personnel Journal*, January 1994, pp. 88–101. For another view, see Anne Harzing, "The Persistent Myth of High Expatriate Failure Rates," *International*

Journal of Human Resource Management 6, no. 2 (May 1995), pp. 457–474; Mason Carpenter, et al., "International Assignment Experience at the Top Can Make a Bottom-Line Difference," *Human Resource Management* 30, no. 2–3 (summer–fall 2000), pp. 277–285.

58. Winfred Arthur Jr. and Winston Bennett Jr., "The International Assignee: The Relative Importance of Factors Perceived to Contribute to Success," *Personnel Psychology* 48 (1995), pp. 99–114; table on pp. 106–107. See also Edwin Davison and Betty Punnett, "International Assignments: Is There a Role for Gender and Race in Decisions?" *International Journal of Human Resource Management* 6, no. 2 (May 1995), pp. 411–441.

59. Arthur and Bennett, "The International Assignee," p. 110; Gretchen Spreitzer, Morgan McCall Jr., and Joan Mahoney, "Early Identification of International Executive Potential," *Journal of Applied Psychology* 82, no. 1 (1997), pp. 6–29.

60. Phatak, *International Dimensions of Management*, p. 119.

61. See, for example, Blocklyn, "Developing the International Executive," p. 45.

62. Discussed in Madelyn Callahan, "Preparing the New Global Manager," *Training and Development Journal*, March 1989, p. 30. The publisher of the inventory is the New York consulting firm Moran, Stahl & Boyer. See also Jennifer Laabs, "The Global Talent Search," *Personnel Journal*, August 1991, pp. 38–44, for a discussion of how firms such as Coca-Cola recruit and develop international managers; and T. S. Cahn, "Developing International Managers: A Partnership Approach," *Journal of Management Development* 13, no. 3 (1994), pp. 38–46.

63. Blocklyn, "Developing the International Executive," p. 45.

64. "International Assignment Policies and Practices," *BNA Bulletin to Management*, May 1, 1997, pp. 140–141, based on a survey by Organization Resources Counselors, Inc., New York City.

65. Hilary Harris and Chris Brewster, "The Coffee Machine System: How International Selection Really Works," *International Journal of Human Resource Management* 10, no. 3 (June 1999), pp. 488–500.

66. Anne Marie Ryan, et al., "An International Look at Selection Practices: Nation and Culture as Explanations for Variability in Practice," *Personnel Psychology* 52 (1999), pp. 359–391.

67. Nancy Adler, "Women Managers in a Global Economy," *Training and Development*, April 1994, p. 31; Charlene Solomon, "Women Expats: Shattering the Myths," *Global Workforce*, May 1998, p. 12.

68. Erin Strout, "Confronting the Glass Border," *Sales and Marketing Management* 153, no. 1 (January 2001), p. 19. See also Linda Stroh, et al., "Why Are Women Left at Home: Are They Unwilling to Go on International Assignment?" *Journal of World Business* 35, no. 3 (fall 2000), p. 241; "Glass Borders May Impede a Businesswoman Before She Hits a Ceiling," *Wall Street Journal*, October 26, 2000, p. A1.

69. Paula Caligiuri, et al., "Factors Influencing the Adjustments of Women on Global Assignments," *International Journal of Human Resource Management* 10, no. 2 (April 1999), pp. 163–179.

70. Callahan, "Preparing the New Global Manager," p. 29–30. See also Charlene Marmer Solomon, "Global Operations Demand That HR Rethink Diversity," *Personnel Journal*, July 1994, pp. 40–50.

71. Valerie Frazee, "Expats Are Expected to Dive Right In," *Personnel Journal*, December 1996, p. 31.

72. This is based on ibid., p. 30. See also Rita Bennett, et al., "Cross-Cultural Training: A Critical Step in Ensuring the Success of National Assignments," *Human Resource Management* 39, no. 2–3 (summer–fall 2000), pp. 239–250.

73. Mark Mendenhall and Gunther Stahl, "Expatriate Training and Development: Where Do We Go from Here?" *Human Resource Management* 39, no. 2–3 (summer–fall 2000), pp. 251–265.

74. James Stoner and R. Edward Freeman, *Management*, 4th ed. (Upper Saddle River, NJ: Prentice Hall, 1989), p. 783. See also John Cartland, "Reward Policies in a Global Corporation," *Business Quarterly*, autumn 1993, pp. 93–96; Laura Mazur, "Europay," *Across-the-Board*, January 1995, pp. 40–43; Joseph Martocchio, *Strategic Compensation* (Upper Saddle River, NJ: Prentice Hall, 2001).

75. Hewitt Associates, "On Compensation," May 1989, p. 1 (Hewitt Associates, 86–87 East Via De Ventura, Scottsdale, AZ 85258). See also Carolyn Gould, "Expat Pay Plans to Suffer Cutback," *Workforce*, September 1999, pp. 40–46.

76. Hewitt Associates, "On Compensation," p. 2. See also Stephenie Overman, "Check the Vitality of Health-Care Abroad," *HR Magazine*, March 2000, pp. 77–84.

77. Hill, *International Business*, pp. 519–520; Valerie Frazee, "Is the Balance Sheet Right for Your Expats?" *Global Workforce*, September 1998, pp. 19–26; Stephenie Overman, "Focus on International HR," *HR Magazine*, March 2000, pp. 87–92.

78. Phatak, *International Dimensions of Management*, p. 134.

79. Except as noted, this section is based on Martocchio, *Strategic Compensation*, pp. 280–283.

80. This is based on Brian Brooks, "Long-Term Incentives: International Executives Need Them, Too," *Personnel*, August 1988, pp. 40–42. See also James Ward and Mark Blumenthal, "Localization: A Study in Cost Containment," *Innovations in International Compensation* 17, no. 4 (November 1991), pp. 3–4; Mazur, "Europay," pp. 40–43.

81. U.S. Department of State, "U.S. Department of State Indexes of Living Costs Abroad, Quarters Allowances, and Hardship Differentials" (Washington, DC: U.S. Government Printing Office, October 1999). Available online at http://www.state.gov.

82. J. E. Richard, "Global Executive Compensation: A Look at the Future," *Compensation and Benefits Review*, May–June 2000, pp. 35–38.

83. Stan Veliotis, "Offshore Equity Compensation Plans," *Compensation and Benefits Review*, July–August 2000, pp. 39–45.

84. Mike Johnson, "Beyond Pay: What Rewards Work Best When Doing Business in China," *Compensation and Benefits Review*, November–December 1998, p. 53.

85. Ibid., p. 53.

86. Except as noted, this is based on Gary Addou and Mark Mendenhall, "Expatriate Performance Appraisal: Problems and Solutions," in Mark Mendenhall and Gary Addou, *International Human Resource Management* (Boston: PWS Kent Publishing Co., 1991), pp. 364–374.

87. Ibid., p. 366. See also Maddy Janssens, "Evaluating International Managers' Performance: Parent Company Standards as Control Mechanism," *International Journal of Human Resource Management* 5, no. 4 (December 1994), pp. 853–873.

88. Addou and Mendenhall, "Expatriate Appraisal."

89. "Union Membership Around the World," *BNA Bulletin to Management*, November 13, 1997, pp. 364–365.

90. Robert Sauer and Keith Voelker, *Labor Relations: Structure and Process* (New York: Macmillan, 1993), pp. 510–525.

91. Ibid., p. 516. See also Marino Regini, "Human Resource Management and Industrial Relations in European Companies," *International Journal of Human Resource Management* 4, no. 3 (September 1993), pp. 555–568.

92. Quoted from ibid., p. 519.

93. Aaron Bernstein, "A Floor Under Foreign Factories?" *Business Week*, November 2, 1998, p. 126–128.

94. Ibid., p. 126.

95. Samuel Greengard, "Mission Possible: Protecting Employees Abroad," *Workforce*, August 1997, pp. 30–32.

96. Ibid., p. 32.

97. These are based on or quoted from ibid., p. 32.

98. Ibid., p. 32

99. Nancy Breuer, "AIDS Threatens Global Business," *Workforce*, February 2000, pp. 52–55.

100. Adapted from Kenneth Laudon and Jane Laudon, *Management Information Systems: New Approaches to Organization and Technology* (Upper Saddle River, NJ: Prentice Hall, 1998), p. G7.

101. Bill Roberts, "Going Global," *HR Magazine*, August 2000, pp. 123–128.

102. Linda Stroh, et al., "Integrated HR Systems Help Develop Global Leaders," *HR Magazine* 43, no. 5 (April 1998), pp. 14–18.

103. Diane Turner, "NuView Brings Web-Based HRIS to Buildnet," *Workforce* 79, no. 12 (December 2000), p. 90.

104. Jim Meade, "Web-Based HRIS Meets Multiple Needs," *HR Magazine*, August 2000, pp. 129–133.

105. Andrea Poe, "Welcome Back," *HR Magazine*, March 2000, pp. 94–105.

106. See also Linda Stroh, "Predicting Turnover Among Repatriates: Can Organizations Affect Retention Rates?" *International Journal of Human Resource Management* 6, no. 2 (May 1995), pp. 443–456; J. Stewart Black and Hal Gregerson, "The Right Way to Manage Expats," *Harvard Business Review*, March–April 1999, pp. 52–62.

107. Phatak, *International Dimensions of Management*, p. 124. See also Reyer Swaak, "Today's Expatriate Families: Dual Careers and Other Obstacles," *Compensation and Benefits Review* 27, no. 3 (May 1995), pp. 21–26; Michael Harvey, et al., "Strategic Global Human Resource Management: The Role of Inpatriate Managers," *Human Resource Management Review* 10, no. 2 (2000), pp. 153–175; Marja Tahvanainen, "Expatriate Performance Management: The Case of Nokia Telecommunications," *Human Resource Management* 39, no. 2–3 (summer–fall 2000), pp. 267–275.

108. Jobert Abueva, "Many Repatriations Fail, at Huge Cost to Companies," *New York Times*, May 17, 2000, p. E1.

109. These are based on Briscoe, *International Human Resource Management*, p. 66; Phatak, *International Dimensions of Management*, p. 124; Daniels and Radebaugh, *International Business*, p. 772; and Valerie Frazee, "Welcome Your Repatriates Home," *Global Workforce*, April 1997, pp. 24–28.

110. Briscoe, *International Human Resource Management*, p. 66.

111. Phatak, *International Dimensions of Management*, p. 126; Hal Gregersen and Linda Stroh, "Coming Home to the Arctic Cold: Antecedents to Finnish Expatriate and Spouse Repatriation Adjustment," *Personnel Psychology* 50 (1997), p. 651.

112. Heinrich Pierer, "Managing a Global Player in the Age of Information," *Management International Review*, October 15, 1999, pp. 9–12.

113. Except as noted, this is based on Gary Dessler, "How to Earn Your Employees' Commitment," *Academy of Management Executive* 13, no. 2 (1999), pp. 58–67.

114. J. P. Meyer and J. J. Allen, *Commitment in the Workplace: Theory, Research and Application* (Thousand Oaks, CA: Sage Publications, 1997), pp. 11, 12.

115. This is based on Bruce R. Ellig, "Improving Effectiveness Through an HR Review," *Personnel*, June 1989, pp. 56–64.

Glossary

action learning A training technique by which management trainees are allowed to work full time analyzing and solving problems in other departments.

adverse impact The overall impact of employer practices that result in significantly higher percentages of members of minorities and other protected groups being rejected for employment, placement, or promotion.

affirmative action Steps that are taken for the purpose of eliminating the present effects of past discrimination.

Age Discrimination in Employment Act of 1967 (ADEA) The act prohibiting arbitrary age discrimination and specifically protecting individuals over 40 years old.

agency shop A form of union security in which employees who do not belong to the union must still pay union dues on the assumption that union efforts benefit all workers.

Albemarie Paper Company v. Moody The Supreme Court case in which it was ruled that the validity of job tests must be documented and that employee performance standards must be unambiguous.

alternation ranking method Ranking employees from best to worst on a particular trait, choosing highest, then lowest, until all are ranked.

alternative dispute resolution or ADR program Grievance procedure that provides for binding arbitration as the last step.

alternative staffing The use of nontraditional recruitment sources.

Americans with Disabilities Act (ADA) The act requiring employers to make reasonable accommodations for disabled employees; it prohibits discrimination against disabled persons.

annual bonus Plans that are designed to motivate short-term performance of managers and are tied to company profit-ability.

application form The form that provides information on education, prior work record, and skills.

appraisal interview An interview in which the supervisor and subordinate review the appraisal and make plans to remedy deficiencies and reinforce strengths.

apprenticeship training A structured process by which people become skilled workers through a combination of classroom instruction and on-the-job training.

arbitration The most definitive type of third-party intervention, in which the arbitrator usually has the power to determine and dictate the settlement terms.

at-risk variable pay plans Plans that put some portion of the employee's weekly pay at risk, subject to the firm's meeting its financial goals.

authority The right to make decisions, direct others' work, and give orders.

authorization cards In order to petition for a union election, the union must show that at least 30% of employees may be interested in being unionized. Employees indicate interest by signing authorization cards.

bargaining unit The group of employees the union will be authorized to represent.

behavior modeling A training technique in which trainees are first shown good management techniques in a film, are asked to play roles in a simulated situation, and are then given feedback and praise by their supervisor.

behavioral interviews A series of job-related questions that focus on how they reacted to actual situations in the past.

behaviorally anchored rating scale (BARS) An appraisal method that aims at combining the benefits of narrative critical incidents and quantified ratings by anchoring a quantified scale with specific narrative examples of good and poor performance.

behavior-based safety Identifying the worker behaviors that contribute to accidents and then training workers to avoid these behaviors.

benchmark job A job that is used to anchor the employer's pay scale and around which other jobs are arranged in order of relative worth.

benefits Indirect financial and nonfinancial payments employees receive for continuing their employment with the company.

bias The tendency to allow individual differences such as age, race, and sex to affect the appraisal ratings employees receive.

bona fide occupational qualification (BFOQ) Requirement that an employee be of a certain religion, sex, or national origin where that is reasonably necessary to the organization's normal operation. Specified by the 1964 Civil Rights Act.

boundaryless organization Organization marked by the widespread use of teams and similar structural mechanisms that reduce and make more permeable the boundaries that typically separate departments.

boycott The combined refusal by employees and other interested parties to buy or use the employer's products.

broadbanding Consolidating salary grades and ranges into just a few wide levels or "bands," each of which contains a relatively wide range of jobs and salary levels.

bumping/layoff procedures Detailed procedures that determine who will be laid off if no work is available; generally allow employees to use their seniority to remain on the job.

burnout The total depletion of physical and mental resources caused by excessive striving to reach an unrealistic work-related goal.

business necessity Justification for an otherwise discriminatory employment practice, provided there is an overriding legitimate business purpose.

business process reengineering (BPR) The redesign of business processes to achieve improvements in such measures as performance as cost, quality, service, and speed.

candidate-order error An error of judgment on the part of the interviewer due to interviewing one or more very good or very bad candidates just before the interview in question.

career planning and development The deliberate process through which a person becomes aware of personal career-related attributes and the lifelong series of stages that contribute to his or her career fulfillment.

case study method A development method in which the manager is presented with a written description of an organizational problem to diagnose and solve.

cash balance pension plans Defined benefit plans under which the employer contributes a percentage of the employees' current pay to the employees' pension plans every year, and employees earn interest on this amount.

central tendency A tendency to rate all employees the same way, such as rating them all average.

citation Summons informing employers and employees of the regulations and standards that have been violated in the workplace.

Civil Rights Act of 1991 (CRA 1991) It places burden of proof back on employers and permits compensatory and punitive damages.

classes (in compensation) Grouping jobs based on a set of rules for each group or class, such as amount of independent judgment, skill, physical effort, and so forth, required. Classes usually contain similar jobs.

closed shop A form of union security in which the company can hire only union members. This was outlawed in 1947 but still exists in some industries (such as printing).

collective bargaining The process through which representatives of management and the union meet to negotiate a labor agreement.

commitment An employee's identification with and agreement to pursue the company's or the unit's mission.

comparable worth The concept by which women who are usually paid less than men can claim that men in comparable rather than strictly equal jobs are paid more.

compensable factor A fundamental, compensable element of a job, such as skills, effort, responsibility, and working conditions.

computerized forecast Determination of future staff needs by projecting sales, volume of production, and personnel required to maintain this volume of output, using software packages.

confrontation meetings A method for clarifying and bringing into the open intergroup misconceptions and problems so that they can be resolved.

content validity A test that is content valid is one that contains a fair sample of the tasks and skills actually needed for the job in question.

controlled experimentation Formal methods for testing the effectiveness of a training program, preferably with before-and-after tests and a control group.

corporate campaign An organized effort by the union that exerts pressure on the corporation by pressuring the company's other unions, shareholders, directors, customers, creditors, and government agencies, often directly.

criterion validity A type of validity based on showing that scores on the test (predictors) are related to job performance (criterion).

critical incident method Keeping a record of uncommonly good or undesirable examples of an employee's work-related behavior and reviewing it with the employee at predetermined times.

cultural change A change in the company's shared values and aims.

Davis-Bacon Act (1931) A law that sets wages rates for laborers employed by contractors working for the federal government.

decertification Legal process for employees to terminate a union's right to represent them.

deferred profit-sharing plan A plan in which a certain amount of profits is credited to each employee's account, payable at retirement, termination, or death.

defined benefit pension plan A plan that contains a formula for determining specified retirement benefits.

defined contribution pension plan A plan in which the employers' contribution to employees' retirement or savings funds is specified.

dejobbing Broadening the responsibilities of the company's jobs, and encouraging employees not to limit themselves to what's on the their job descriptions.

Department of Labor job analysis procedure Standardized method for rating, classifying, and comparing virtually every kind of job based on data, people, and things.

diary/logs Daily listings made by workers of every activity in which they engage along with the time each activity takes.

direct financial payments Pay in the form of wages, salaries, incentives, commissions, and bonuses.

discipline A procedure that corrects or punishes a subordinate because a rule or procedure has been violated.

dismissal Involuntary termination of an employee's employment with the firm.

disparate rejection rates A test for adverse impact in which it can be demonstrated that there is a discrepancy between rates of rejection of members of a protected group and of others.

downsizing The process of reducing, usually dramatically, the number of people employed by a firm.

early-retirement window A type of offering by which employees are encouraged to retire early, the incentive being liberal pension benefits plus perhaps a cash payment.

economic strike A strike that results from a failure to agree on the terms of a contract that involve wages, benefits, and other conditions of employment.

electronic performance support systems Sets of computerized tools and displays that automate training, documentation, and phone support, integrate this automation into applications, and provide support that's faster, cheaper, and more effective than traditional methods.

employee advocacy HR must take responsibility for clearly defining how management should be treating employees, make sure employees have the mechanisms required to contest unfair practices, and represent the interests of employees within the framework of its primary obligation to senior management.

employee assistance program (EAP) A formal employer program for providing employees with counseling and/or treatment programs for problems such as alcoholism, gambling, or stress.

employee commitment An employee's identification with and agreement to pursue the company's or the unit's missions—to act like an owner rather than as an employee.

employee compensation All forms of pay or rewards going to employees and arising from their employment.

employee involvement program Any formal program that lets employees participate in formulating important work decisions or in supervising all or part of their own work activities.

employee orientation A procedure for providing new employees with basic background information about the firm.

Employee Retirement Income Security Act (ERISA) Signed into law by President Ford in 1974 to require that pension rights be vested and protected by a government agency, the PBGC. The law provides government protection of pensions for all employees with company pension plans. It also regulates vesting rights (employees who leave before retirement may claim compensation from the pension plan).

employee stock ownership plan (ESOP) A corporation contributes shares of its own stock to a trust in which additional contributions are made annually. The trust distributes the stock to employees on retirement or separation from service.

employment or personnel planning The process of deciding what positions the firm will have to fill, and how to fill them.

Equal Employment Opportunity Commission (EEOC) The commission, created by Title VII, is empowered to investigate job discrimination complaints and sue on behalf of complainants.

Equal Pay Act (1963) An amendment to the Fair Labor Standards Act that requires equal pay for equal work, regardless of sex.

expectancy chart A graph showing the relationship between test scores and job performance for a group of people.

fact finder A neutral party who studies the issues in a dispute and makes a public recommendation for a reasonable settlement.

factor comparison method A widely used method of ranking jobs according to a variety of skill and difficulty factors, then adding up these rankings to arrive at an overall numerical rating for each given job.

fair day's work Frederick Taylor's observation that haphazard setting of piecework requirements and wages by supervisors was not sufficient, and that careful study was needed to define acceptable production quotas for each job.

Fair Labor Standards Act (1938) This act provides for minimum wages, maximum hours, overtime pay, and child labor protection. The law has been amended many times and covers most employees.

Federal Violence Against Women Act of 1994 Provides that a person who commits a crime of violence motivated by gender shall be liable to the party injured.

flexible benefits plan/cafeteria benefits plan Individualized plans allowed by employers to accommodate employee preferences for benefits.

flextime A plan whereby employees build their workday around a core of midday hours.

forced distribution method Similar to grading on a curve; predetermined percentages of ratees are placed in various performance categories.

foreign service premiums Financial payments over and above regular base pay, typically ranging between 10% and 30% of base pay.

401(k) plan A defined contribution plan based on section 401(k) of the Internal Revenue Code.

functional control The authority exerted by an HR manager as coordinator of personnel activities.

functional job analysis A method for classifying jobs similar to the DOL method, but additionally taking into account the extent to which instructions, reasoning, judgment, and mathematical and verbal ability are necessary for performing job tasks.

gainsharing plan An incentive plan that engages employees in a common effort to achieve productivity objectives and share the gains.

globalization The tendency of firms to extend their sales, ownership, and/or manufacturing to new markets abroad.

good faith bargaining Both parties are making every reasonable effort to arrive at agreement; proposals are being matched with counterproposals.

good faith effort strategy Employment strategy aimed at changing practices that have contributed in the past to excluding or underutilizing protected groups.

grade definition Written descriptions of the level of, say, responsibility and knowledge required by jobs in each grade. Similar jobs can then be combined into grades or classes.

grades A job classification system like the class system, although grades often contain dissimilar jobs, such as secretaries, mechanics, and firefighters. Grade descriptions are written based on compensable factors listed in classification systems.

graphic rating scale A scale that lists a number of traits and a range of performance for each. The employee is then rated by identifying the score that best describes his or her level of performance for each trait.

grievance Any factor involving wages, hours, or conditions of employment that is used as a complaint against the employer.

Griggs v. Duke Power Company A case heard by the Supreme Court in which the plaintiff argued that his employer's requirement that coal handlers be high school graduates was unfairly discriminatory. In finding for the plaintiff, the Court ruled that discrimination need not be overt to be illegal, that employment practices must be related to job performance, and that the burden of proof is on the employer to show that hiring standards are job related.

group life insurance Provides lower rates for the employer or employee and includes all employees, including new employees, regardless of health or physical condition.

halo effect In performance appraisal, the problem that occurs when a supervisor's rating of a subordinate on one trait biases the rating of that person on other traits.

hardship allowances Compensate expatriates for exceptionally hard living and working conditions at certain locations.

health maintenance organization (HMO) A prepaid health care system that generally provides routine round-the-clock medical services as well as preventive medicine in a clinic-type arrangement for employees, who pay a nominal fee in addition to the fixed annual fee the employer pays.

human capital The knowledge, education, training, skills, and expertise of a firm's workers.

human resource management (HRM) The policies and practices involved in carrying out the "people" or human resource aspects of a management position, including recruiting, screening, training, rewarding, and appraising.

illegal bargaining items Items in collective bargaining that are forbidden by law; for example, a clause agreeing to hire "union members exclusively" would be illegal in a right-to-work state.

impasse Collective bargaining situation that occurs when the parties are not able to move farther toward settlement, usually because one party is demanding more than the other will offer.

implied authority The authority exerted by an HR manager by virtue of others' knowledge that he or she has access to top management (in areas like testing and affirmative action).

indirect financial payments Pay in the form of financial benefits such as insurances.

in-house development center A company-based method for exposing prospective managers to realistic exercises to develop improved management skills.

injunction A court order compelling a party or parties either to resume or to desist from a certain action.

inside games Union efforts to convince employees to impede or to disrupt production—for example, by slowing the work pace.

insubordination Willful disregard or disobedience of the boss's authority or legitimate orders; criticizing the boss in public.

interest inventory A personal development and selection device that compares the person's current interest with those of others now in various occupations so as to determine the preferred occupation for the individual.

ISO 9000 The written standards for quality management and assurance of the International Organization for Standardization.

job aid Is a set of instructions, diagrams, or similar methods available at the job site to guide the worker.

job analysis The procedure for determining the duties and skill requirements of a job and the kind of person who should be hired for it.

job classification (or grading) method A method for categorizing jobs into groups.

job description A list of a job's duties, responsibilities, reporting relationships, working conditions, and supervisory responsibilities—one product of a job analysis.

job enlargement Assigning workers additional same-level activities, thus increasing the number of activities they perform.

job enrichment Redesigning jobs in a way that increases the opportunities for the worker to experience feelings of responsibility, achievement, growth, and recognition.

job evaluation A systematic comparison done in order to determine the worth of one job relative to another.

job instruction training (JIT) Listing each job's basic tasks, along with key points, in order to provide step-by-step training for employees.

job posting Publicizing an open job to employees (often by literally posting it on bulletin boards) and listing its attributes, like qualifications, supervisor, working schedule, and pay rate.

job-related interview A series of job-related questions that focus on relevant past job-related behaviors.

job rotation A management training technique that involves moving a trainee from department to department to broaden his or her experience and identify strong and weak points to prepare the person for an enhanced role with the company; also, systematically moving workers from one job to another to enhance work team performance.

job sharing A concept that allows two or more people to share a single full-time job.

job specification A list of a job's "human requirements," that is, the requisite education, skills, personality, and so on—another product of a job analysis.

Landrum-Griffin Act (1959) The law aimed at protecting union members from possible wrongdoing on the part of their unions.

layoff A situation in which there is a temporary shortage of work and employees are told there is no work for them but that management intends to recall them when work is again available.

lifelong learning Providing continuing training from basic remedial skills to advanced decision-making techniques throughout the employees' careers.

line authority The authority exerted by an HR manager by directing the activities of the people in his or her own department and in service areas (like the plant cafeteria).

line manager A manager who is authorized to direct the work of subordinates and responsible for accomplishing the organization's goals.

lockout A refusal by the employer to provide opportunities to work.

management assessment center A simulation in which management candidates are asked to perform realistic tasks in hypothetical situations and are scored on their performance. It usually also involves testing and the use of management games.

management by objectives (MBO) Involves setting specific measurable goals with each employee and then periodically reviewing the progress made.

management development Any attempt to improve current or future management performance by imparting knowledge, changing attitudes, or increasing skills.

management game A development technique in which teams of managers compete by making computerized decisions regarding realistic but simulated situations.

management process The five basic functions of planning, organizing, staffing, leading, and controlling.

mandatory bargaining items Items in collective bargaining that a party must bargain over if they are introduced by the other party—for example, pay.

mass interview A panel interviews several candidates simultaneously.

mediation Intervention in which a neutral third party tries to assist the principals in reaching agreement.

mega-option grants Large, upfront grants in lieu of annual grants.

mentoring Formal or informal programs in which mid- or senior-level managers help less experienced employees—for instance, by giving them career advice and helping them navigate political pitfalls.

merit pay (merit raise) Any salary increase awarded to an employee based on his or her individual performance.

mobility premiums Typically, lump-sum payments to reward employees for moving from one assignment to another.

national emergency strikes Strikes that might "imperil the national health and safety."

National Labor Relations (or Wagner) Act This law banned certain types of unfair practices and provided for secret-ballot elections and majority rule for determining whether or not a firm's employees want to unionize.

National Labor Relations Board (NLRB) The agency created by the Wagner Act to investigate unfair labor practice charges and to provide for secret-ballot elections and majority rule in determining whether or not a firm's employees want a union.

negligent hiring Hiring workers with questionable backgrounds without proper safeguards.

negligent training A situation where an employer fails to train adequately, and the employee subsequently harms a third party.

Norris-LaGuardia Act (1932) This law marked the beginning of the era of strong encouragement of unions and guaranteed to each employee the right to bargain collectively "free from interference, restraint, or coercion."

occupational illness Any abnormal condition or disorder caused by exposure to environmental factors associated with employment.

Occupational Safety and Health Act The law passed by Congress in 1970 "to assure so far as possible every working man and woman in the nation safe and healthful working conditions and to preserve our human resources."

Occupational Safety and Health Administration (OSHA) The agency created within the Department of Labor to set safety and health standards for almost all workers in the United States.

Office of Federal Contract Compliance Programs (OFCCP) This office is responsible for implementing the executive orders and ensuring compliance of federal contractors.

on-the-job training (OJT) Training a person to learn a job while working at it.

open shop Perhaps the least attractive type of union security from the union's point of view, the workers decide whether or not to join the union; and those who join must pay dues.

opinion surveys Communication devices that use questionnaires to regularly ask employees their opinions about the company, management, and work life.

organization chart A chart that shows the organizationwide distribution of work, with titles of each position and interconnecting lines that show who reports to and communicates with whom.

organizational development (OD) A method aimed at changing the attitudes, values, and beliefs of employees so that employees can improve the organization.

organizational development intervention HR-based techniques aimed at changing employees' attitudes, values, and behavior.

outplacement counseling A systematic process by which a terminated person is trained and counseled in the techniques of self-appraisal and securing a new position.

outsourcing Letting outside vendors provide services.

paired comparison method Ranking employees by making a chart of all possible pairs of the employees for each trait and indicating which is the better employee for that pair.

panel interview An interview in which a group of interviewers questions the applicant.

pay grade A pay grade is comprised of jobs of approximately equal difficulty.

pay ranges A series of steps or levels within a pay grade, usually based upon years of service.

Pension Benefits Guarantee Corporation (PBGC) Established under ERISA to ensure that pensions meet vesting obligations; also insures pensions should a plan terminate without sufficient funds to meet its vested obligations.

pension plans Plans that provide a fixed sum when employees reach a predetermined retirement age or when they can no longer work due to disability.

performance analysis Verifying that there is a performance deficiency and determining whether that deficiency should be corrected through training or through some other means (such as transferring the employee).

performance management Managing all elements of the organizational process that affect how well employees perform.

personnel replacement charts Company records showing present performance and promotability of inside candidates for the most important positions.

picketing Having employees carry signs announcing their concerns near the employer's place of business.

piecework A system of pay based on the number of items processed by each individual worker in a unit of time, such as items per hour or items per day.

plant closing law The Worker Adjustment and Retraining Notification Act, which requires notifying employees in the event an employer decides to close its facility.

point method The job evaluation method in which a number of compensable factors are identified and then the degree to which each of these factors is present on the job is determined.

position analysis questionnaire (PAQ) A questionnaire used to collect quantifiable data concerning the duties and responsibilities of various jobs.

position replacement card A card prepared for each position in a company to show possible replacement candidates and their qualifications.

preferred provider organizations (PPOs) Groups of health care providers that contract with employers, insurance companies, or third-party payers to provide medical care services at a reduced fee.

Pregnancy Discrimination Act (PDA) An amendment to Title VII of the Civil Rights Act that prohibits sex discrimination based on "pregnancy, childbirth, or related medical conditions."

preretirement counseling Counseling provided to employees who are about to retire, which covers matters such as benefits advice, second careers, and so on.

process chart A work flow chart that shows the flow of inputs to and outputs from a particular job.

profit-sharing plan A plan whereby employees share in the company's profits.

programmed learning A systematic method for teaching job skills involving presenting questions or facts, allowing the person to respond, and giving the learner immediate feedback on the accuracy of his or her answers.

promotions Advancements to positions of increased responsibility.

protected class Persons such as minorities and women protected by equal opportunity laws, including Title VII.

qualification inventories Manual or computerized records listing employees' education, career and development interests, languages, social skills, and so on, to be used in selecting inside candidates for promotion.

qualified individuals Under the ADA, those who can carry out the essential functions of the job.

quality The totality of features and characteristics of a product or service that bear on its ability to satisfy given needs.

quota strategy Employment strategy aimed at mandating the same results as the good faith effort strategy through specific hiring and promotion restrictions.

ranking method The simplest method of job evaluation that involves ranking each job relative to all other jobs, usually based on overall difficulty.

ratio analysis A forecasting technique for determining future staff needs by using ratios between, for example, sales volume and number of employees needed.

reality shock Results of a period that may occur at the initial career entry when the new employee's high job expectations confront the reality of a boring, unchallenging job.

recruiting yield pyramid The historical arithmetic relationships between recruitment leads and invitees, invitees and interviews, interviews and offers made, and offers made and offers accepted.

reengineering The fundamental rethinking and radical redesign of business processes to achieve dramatic improvements in critical, contemporary measures of performance, such as cost, quality, service, and speed.

reliability The consistency of scores obtained by the same person when retested with the identical or equivalent tests.

restricted policy Another test for adverse impact, involving demonstration that an employer's hiring practices exclude a protected group, whether intentionally or not.

retirement The point at which a person gives up one's work, usually between the ages of 60 to 65, but increasingly earlier today due to firms' early-retirement incentive plans.

reverse discrimination Claim that due to affirmative action quota system, white males are discriminated against.

rings of defense An alternative layoff plan in which temporary supplemental employees are hired with the understanding that they may be laid off at any time.

role playing A training technique in which trainees act out parts in a realistic management situation.

salary compression A salary inequity problem, generally caused by inflation, resulting in longer term employees in a position earning less than workers entering the firm today.

salary survey A survey aimed at determining prevailing wage rates. A good salary survey provides specific wages rates for specific jobs. Formal written questionnaire surveys are the most comprehensive, but telephone surveys, the Internet, and newspaper ads are also sources of information.

savings and thrift plan Plan in which employees contribute a portion of their earnings to a fund; the employer usually matches this contribution in whole or part.

Scanlon plan An incentive plan developed in 1937 by Joseph Scanlon and designed to encourage cooperation, involvement, and sharing of benefits.

scatter plot A graphical method used to help identify the relationship between two variables.

scientific management The careful, scientific study of the job for the purpose of boosting productivity and job satisfaction.

self-directed team A work team that uses consensus decision making to choose its own team members, solve job-related problems, design its own jobs, and schedule its own break time.

sensitivity training A method for increasing employees' insights into their own behavior by candid discussions in groups led by special trainers.

severance pay A one-time payment some employers provide when terminating an employee.

sexual harassment Harassment on the basis of sex that has the purpose or effect of substantially interfering with a person's work performance or creating an intimidating, hostile, or offensive work environment.

sick leave Provides pay to an employee when he or she is out of work because of illness.

simulated training Training employees on special off-the-job equipment, as in airplane pilot training, so training costs and hazards can be reduced.

situational interview A series of job-related questions that focus on how the candidate would behave in a given situation.

Social Security Federal program that provides three types of benefits: retirement income at the age of 62 and thereafter; survivor's or death benefits payable to the employee's dependents regardless of age at time of death; and disability benefits payable to disabled employees and their dependents. These benefits are payable only if the employee is insured under the Social Security Act.

speak up! programs Communication programs that allow employees to register questions, concerns, and complaints about work-related matters.

staff manager A manager who assists and advises line managers.

standard hour plan A plan by which a worker is paid a basic hourly rate but is paid an extra percentage of his or her base rate for production exceeding the standard per hour or per day. Similar to piecework payment but based on a percent premium.

stock option The right to purchase a stated number of shares of a company stock at today's price at some time in the future.

straight piecework An incentive plan in which a person is paid a sum for each item he or she makes or sells, with a strict proportionality between results and rewards.

strategic change A change in the company's strategy, mission, and vision.

strategic human resource management The linking of HRM with strategic goals and objectives in order to improve business performance and develop organizational cultures that foster innovation and flexibility.

strategy The company's long-term plan for how it will balance its internal strengths and weaknesses with its external opportunities and threats to maintain a competitive advantage.

stress interview An interview in which the applicant is made uncomfortable by a series of often rude questions. This technique helps identify hypersensitive applicants and those with low or high stress tolerance.

strictness/leniency The problem that occurs when a supervisor has a tendency to rate all subordinates either high or low.

strike A withdrawal of labor.

structural change The reorganizing or redesigning of an organization's departmentalization, coordination, span of control, reporting relationships, or decision-making process.

structured or directive interview An interview following a set sequence of questions.

structured sequential interview An interview in which the applicant is interviewed sequentially by several persons; each rates the applicant on a standard form.

succession planning The process of ensuring a suitable supply of successors for current and future senior or key jobs.

supplemental pay benefits Benefits for time not worked such as unemployment insurance, vacation and holiday pay, and sick pay.

supplemental unemployment benefits Provide for a "guaranteed annual income" in certain industries where employees must shut down to change machinery or due to reduced work. These benefits are paid by the company and supplemental unemployment benefits.

survey research A method that involves surveying employees' attitudes and providing feedback to the work groups as a basis for problem analysis and action planning.

sympathy strike A strike that takes place when one union strikes in support of the strike of another.

Taft-Hartley Act (1947) Also known as the Labor Management Relations Act, this law prohibited union unfair labor practices and enumerated the rights of employees as union members. It also enumerated the rights of employers.

task analysis A detailed study of a job to identify the specific skills required.

team building Improving the effectiveness of teams such as corporate officers and division directors through use of consultants, interviews, and team-building meetings.

team or group incentive plan A plan in which a production standard is set for a specific work group, and its members are paid incentives if the group exceeds the production standard.

technological change Modifications to the work methods an organization uses to accomplish its tasks.

telecommuting A work arrangement in which employees work at remote locations, usually at home, using video displays, computers, and other telecommunications equipment to carry out their responsibilities.

terminate at will The idea, based in law, that the employment relationship can be terminated at will by either the employer or the employee for any reason.

termination A permanent severing of the employment relationship.

termination interview The interview in which an employee is informed of the fact that he or she has been dismissed.

test validity The accuracy with which a test, interview, and so on measures what it purports to measure or fulfills the function it was designed to fill.

Title VII of the 1964 Civil Rights Act Section of the act that makes it unlawful for employers to discriminate against any individual with respect to hiring, compensation, terms, condition, or privileges of employment because of race, color, religion, sex, or national origin.

top-down programs Communications activities including in-house television centers, e-mail, intranet postings, round-table discussions, and in-house newsletters that provide continuing opportunities for the firm to keep all employees up to date on company matters.

total quality management (TQM) An organization-wide program that integrates all functions and processes of the business so that design, planning, production, distribution, and field service are focused on maximizing customer satisfaction through continuous improvement.

training The process of teaching new employees the basic skills they need to perform their jobs.

transfers Reassignments to similar (or higher) positions in other parts of the firm.

trend analysis Study of a firm's past employment needs over a period of years to predict future needs.

unclear standards An appraisal scale that is too open to interpretation.

unemployment insurance Provides benefits if a person is unable to work through some fault other than his or her own.

unfair labor practice strike A strike aimed at protesting illegal conduct by the employer.

uniform guidelines Guidelines issued by federal agencies charged with ensuring compliance with equal employment federal legislation explaining recommended employer procedures in detail.

union salting A union organizing tactic by which workers who are in fact employed full time by a union as undercover organizers are hired by unwitting employers.

union shop A form of union security in which the company can hire nonunion people, but they must join the union after a prescribed period of time and pay dues (if they do not, they can be fired).

unsafe conditions The mechanical and physical conditions that cause accidents.

unstructured or nondirective interview An unstructured conversational-style interview in which the interviewer pursues points of interest as they come up in response to questions.

unstructured sequential interview An interview in which each interviewer forms an independent opinion after asking different questions.

value chain analysis Identifying the primary activities that create value for customers and the related support activities.

variable pay Any plan that ties pay to productivity or profitability, usually as one-time lump payments.

vesting Provision that money placed in a pension fund cannot be forfeited for any reason.

Vietnam Era Veterans' Readjustment Assistance Act of 1974 An act requiring that employers with government contracts take affirmative action to hire disabled veterans.

Vocational Rehabilitation Act of 1973 The act requiring certain federal contractors to take affirmative action for disabled persons.

voluntary bargaining items Items in collective bargaining over which bargaining is neither illegal nor mandatory—neither party can be compelled against its wishes to negotiate over those items.

voluntary reduction in pay plan An alternative to layoffs in which all employees agree to reductions in pay to keep everyone working.

voluntary time off An alternative to layoffs in which some employees agree to take time off to reduce the employer's payroll and avoid the need for a layoff.

wage curve Shows the relationship between the value of the job and the average wage paid for this job.

Walsh-Healey Public Contract Act (1936) A law that requires minimum wage and working conditions for employees working on any government contract amounting to more than $10,000.

Wards Cove v. Atonio The U.S. Supreme Court decision involving an Alaska fishery that makes it difficult to prove a case of unlawful discrimination against an employer.

wildcat strike An unauthorized strike occurring during the term of a contract.

work samples Actual job tasks used in testing applicants' performance.

work sampling technique A testing method based on measuring performance on actual basic job tasks.

work sharing A temporary reduction in work hours by a group of employees during economic downturns as a way to prevent layoffs.

workers' compensation Provides income and medical benefits to work-related accident victims or their dependents regardless of fault.

wrongful discharge An employee dismissal that does not comply with the law or does not comply with the contractual arrangement stated or implied by the firm via its employment application forms, employee manuals, or other promises.

Photo Credits

Name and Organization Index

Subject Index